Twentieth-Century Literary Criticism

Guide to Gale Literary Criticism Series

When you need to review criticism of literary works, these are the Gale series to use:

If the author's death date is: **You should turn to:**

After Dec. 31, 1959
(or author is still living)

CONTEMPORARY LITERARY CRITICISM

for example: Jorge Luis Borges, Anthony Burgess,
William Faulkner, Mary Gordon,
Ernest Hemingway, Iris Murdoch

1900 through 1959

TWENTIETH-CENTURY LITERARY CRITICISM

for example: Willa Cather, F. Scott Fitzgerald,
Henry James, Mark Twain, Virginia Woolf

1800 through 1899

NINETEENTH-CENTURY LITERATURE CRITICISM

for example: Fedor Dostoevski, George Sand,
Gerard Manley Hopkins, Emily Dickinson

1400 through 1799

LITERATURE CRITICISM FROM 1400 TO 1800
(excluding Shakespeare)

for example: Anne Bradstreet, Pierre Corneille,
Daniel Defoe, Alexander Pope,
Jonathan Swift, Phillis Wheatley

SHAKESPEAREAN CRITICISM

Shakespeare's plays and poetry

Gale also publishes related criticism series:

CONTEMPORARY ISSUES CRITICISM

Presents criticism on contemporary authors writing
on current issues. Topics covered include the social
sciences, philosophy, economics, natural science, law,
and related areas.

CHILDREN'S LITERATURE REVIEW

Covers authors of all eras. Presents criticism on
authors and author/illustrators who write for the
preschool to junior-high audience.

ISSN 0276-8178

Volume 15

Twentieth-Century Literary Criticism

**Excerpts from Criticism of the
Works of Novelists, Poets, Playwrights,
Short Story Writers, and Other Creative Writers
Who Died between 1900 and 1960,
from the First Published Critical Appraisals
to Current Evaluations**

**Dennis Poupard
James E. Person, Jr.
Editors**

**Thomas Ligotti
Associate Editor**

**Gale Research Company
Book Tower
Detroit, Michigan 48226**

STAFF

Dennis Poupard, James E. Person, Jr., *Editors*

Thomas Ligotti, *Associate Editor*

Lee Fournier, Denise B. Grove, Marie Lazzari, Serita Lanette Lockard, *Senior Assistant Editors*

Earlene M. Alber, Sandra Giraud, Paula Kepos,
Sandra Liddell, Claudia Loomis, Jay P. Pederson, *Assistant Editors*

Lizbeth A. Purdy, *Production Supervisor*
Denise M. Broderick, *Production Coordinator*
Eric Berger, *Assistant Production Coordinator*
Robin Du Blanc, Kelly King Howes, Amy Marcaccio, *Editorial Assistants*

Karen Rae Forsyth, *Research Coordinator*
Jeannine Schiffman Davidson, *Assistant Research Coordinator*
Kevin John Campbell, Victoria B. Cariappa, Rebecca Nicholaides,
Leslie Kyle Schell, Valerie J. Webster, *Research Assistants*

Linda M. Pugliese, *Manuscript Coordinator*
Donna Craft, *Assistant Manuscript Coordinator*
Colleen M. Crane, Maureen A. Puhl, Rosetta Irene Simms, *Manuscript Assistants*

L. Elizabeth Hardin, *Permissions Supervisor*
Janice M. Mach, *Permissions Coordinator*
Filomena Sgambati, *Permissions Associate*
Patricia A. Seefelt, *Assistant Permissions Coordinator, Illustrations*
Margaret A. Chamberlain, Mary M. Matuz, Susan D. Nobles, *Senior Permissions Assistants*
Sandra C. Davis, Kathy Grell, Josephine M. Keene, *Permissions Assistants*
H. Diane Cooper, Dorothy J. Fowler, Yolanda Parker, Mabel C. Schoening, *Permissions Clerks*
Margaret Mary Missar, *Photo Research*

Frederick G. Ruffner, *Publisher*
James M. Ethridge, *Executive Vice-President—Editorial*
Dedria Bryfonski, *Editorial Director*
Christine Nasso, *Director, Literature Division*
Laurie Lanzen Harris, *Senior Editor, Literary Criticism Series*

Library of Congress Catalog Card Number 76-46132
ISBN 0-8103-0229-2
ISSN 0276-8178

Computerized photocomposition by
Typographics, Incorporated
Kansas City, Missouri

Printed in the United States

Contents

Preface

It is impossible to overvalue the importance of literature in the intellectual, emotional, and spiritual evolution of humanity. Literature is that which both lifts us out of everyday life and helps us to better understand it. Through the fictive lives of such characters as Anna Karenin, Jay Gatsby, or Leopold Bloom, our perceptions of the human condition are enlarged, and we are enriched.

Literary criticism can also give us insight into the human condition, as well as into the specific moral and intellectual atmosphere of an era, for the criteria by which a work of art is judged reflects contemporary philosophical and social attitudes. Literary criticism takes many forms: the traditional essay, the book or play review, even the parodic poem. Criticism can also be of several types: normative, descriptive, interpretive, textual, appreciative, generic. Collectively, the range of critical response helps us to understand a work of art, an author, an era.

Scope of the Series

Twentieth-Century Literary Criticism (TCLC) is designed to serve as an introduction for the student of twentieth-century literature to the authors of the period 1900 to 1960 and to the most significant commentators on these authors. The great poets, novelists, short story writers, playwrights, and philosophers of this period are by far the most popular writers for study in high school and college literature courses. Since a vast amount of relevant critical material confronts the student, *TCLC* presents significant passages from the most important published criticism to aid students in their location and selection of criticism on authors who died between 1900 and 1960.

The need for *TCLC* was suggested by the usefulness of the Gale series *Contemporary Literary Criticism (CLC)*, which excerpts criticism on current writing. Because of the difference in time span under consideration *(CLC* considers authors who were still living after 1959), there is no duplication of material between *CLC* and *TCLC*. For further information about *CLC* and Gale's other criticism series, users should consult the Guide to Gale Literary Criticism Series preceding the title page in this volume.

Each volume of *TCLC* is carefully compiled to include authors who represent a variety of genres and nationalities and who are currently regarded as the most important writers of this era. In addition to major authors, *TCLC* also presents criticism on lesser-known writers whose significant contributions to literary history are important to the study of twentieth-century literature.

Each author entry in *TCLC* is intended to provide an overview of major criticism on an author. Therefore, the editors include approximately twenty authors in each 600-page volume (compared with approximately sixty authors in a *CLC* volume of similar size) so that more attention may be given to an author. Each author entry represents a historical survey of the critical response to that author's work: some early criticism is presented to indicate initial reactions, later criticism is selected to represent any rise or decline in the author's reputation, and current retrospective analyses provide students with a modern view. The length of an author entry is intended to reflect the amount of critical attention the author has received from critics writing in English, and from foreign criticism in translation. Critical articles and books that have not been translated into English are excluded. Every attempt has been made to identify and include excerpts from the seminal essays on each author's work. Additionally, as space permits, especially insightful essays of a more limited scope are included.

An author may appear more than once in the series because of the great quantity of critical material available, or because of a resurgence of criticism generated by events such as an author's centennial or anniversary celebration, the republication of an author's works, or publication of a newly translated work or volume of letters. A few author entries in each volume of *TCLC* feature criticism on single works by major authors who have appeared previously in the series. Only those individual works that have been the subjects of vast amounts of criticism and are widely studied in literature classes are selected for this in-depth treatment. George Orwell's *Nineteen Eighty-Four* is the subject of such an entry in *TCLC,* Volume 15.

Organization of the Book

An author entry consists of the following elements: author heading, biographical and critical introduction, principal works, excerpts of criticism (each followed by a bibliographical citation), and an additional bibliography for further reading.

- The *author heading* consists of the author's full name, followed by birth and death dates. The unbracketed portion of the name denotes the form under which the author most commonly wrote. If an author wrote consistently under a pseudonym, the pseudonym will be listed in the author heading and the real name given in parentheses on the first line of the biographical and critical introduction. Also located at the beginning of the introduction to the author entry are any name variations under which an author wrote, including transliterated forms for authors whose languages use nonroman alphabets. Uncertainty as to a birth or death date is indicated by a question mark.

- The *biographical and critical introduction* contains background information designed to introduce the reader to an author and to the critical debate surrounding his or her work. Parenthetical material following many of the introductions provides references to biographical and critical reference series published by Gale. These include *Children's Literature Review, Contemporary Authors, Dictionary of Literary Biography, Something about the Author,* and past volumes of *TCLC.*

- Most *TCLC* entries include *portraits* of the author. Many entries also contain illustrations of materials pertinent to an author's career, including holographs of manuscript pages, title pages, dust jackets, letters, or representations of important people, places, and events in an author's life.

- The *list of principal works* is chronological by date of first book publication and identifies the genre of each work. In the case of foreign authors where there are both foreign language publications and English translations, the title and date of the first English-language edition are given in brackets. Unless otherwise indicated, dramas are dated by first performance, not first publication.

- *Criticism* is arranged chronologically in each author entry to provide a useful perspective on changes in critical evaluation over the years. All titles by the author featured in the critical entry are printed in boldface type to enable the user to ascertain without difficulty the works being discussed. Also for purposes of easier identification, the critic's name and the publication date of the essay are given at the beginning of each piece of criticism. Unsigned criticism is preceded by the title of the journal in which it appeared. When an anonymous essay is later attributed to a critic, the critic's name appears in brackets at the beginning of the excerpt and in the bibliographical citation.

- Important critical essays are prefaced by *explanatory notes* as an additional aid to students using *TCLC.* The explanatory notes provide several types of useful information, including: the reputation of a critic; the importance of a work of criticism; the specific type of criticism (biographical, psychoanalytic, structuralist, etc.); a synopsis of the criticism; and the growth of critical controversy or changes in critical trends regarding an author's work. In many cases, these notes cross-reference the work of critics who agree or disagree with each other. Dates in parentheses within the explanatory notes refer to a book publication date when they follow a book title and to an essay date when they follow a critic's name.

- A complete *bibliographical citation* designed to facilitate location of the original essay or book by the interested reader follows each piece of criticism. An asterisk (*) at the end of a citation indicates that the essay is on more than one author.

- The *additional bibliography* appearing at the end of each author entry suggests further reading on the author. In some cases it includes essays for which the editors could not obtain reprint rights. An asterisk (*) at the end of a citation indicates that the essay is on more than one author.

An appendix lists the sources from which material in each volume has been reprinted. It does not, however, list every book or periodical consulted in the preparation of the volume.

Cumulative Indexes

Each volume of *TCLC* includes a cumulative index to authors listing all the authors who have appeared in *Contemporary Literary Criticism, Twentieth-Century Literary Criticism, Nineteenth-Century Literature Criticism,* and *Literature Criticism from 1400 to 1800,* along with cross-references to the Gale series *Children's Literature Review, Authors in the News, Contemporary Authors, Contemporary Authors Autobiography Series, Dictionary of Literary Biography, Something about the Author,* and *Yesterday's Authors of Books for Children.* Users will welcome this cumulated author index as a useful tool for locating an author within the various series. The index, which lists birth and death dates when available, will be particularly valuable for those authors who are identified with a certain period but whose death date causes them to be placed in another, or for those authors whose careers span two periods. For example, F. Scott Fitzgerald is found in *TCLC,* yet a writer often associated with him, Ernest Hemingway, is found in *CLC.*

Each volume of *TCLC* also includes a cumulative nationality index. Author names are arranged alphabetically under their respective nationalities and followed by the volume numbers in which they appear.

A cumulative index to critics is another useful feature in *TCLC*. Under each critic's name are listed the authors on whom the critic has written and the volume and page where the criticism may be found.

Acknowledgments

No work of this scope can be accomplished without the cooperation of many people. The editors especially wish to thank the copyright holders of the excerpted criticism included in this volume, the permissions managers of many book and magazine publishing companies for assisting us in securing reprint rights, and Jeri Yaryan for assistance with copyright research. We are also grateful to the staffs of the Detroit Public Library, the Library of Congress, University of Detroit Library, University of Michigan Library, and Wayne State University Library for making their resources available to us.

Suggestions Are Welcome

In response to various suggestions, several features have been added to *TCLC* since the series began. Recently introduced features include explanatory notes to excerpted criticism that provide important information regarding critics and their work, a cumulative author index listing authors in all Gale literary criticism series, entries devoted to criticism on a single work by a major author, and more extensive illustrations.

Readers who wish to suggest authors to appear in future volumes, or who have other suggestions, are cordially invited to write the editors.

Authors to Be Featured in *TCLC*, Volumes 16 and 17

James Agee (American novelist and journalist)—Agee's *Let Us Now Praise Famous Men* and *A Death in the Family* are harshly realistic treatments of the moral crises and moral triumphs of mid-twentieth-century America. In addition, Agee's film criticism is recognized as the first serious consideration in English of film as a modern art form.

Ryūnosoke Akutagawa (Japanese short story writer)—Author of the classic novella "Rashomon," Akutagawa is celebrated for his Poe-like tales of the horrific and the bizarre, which critics often view as a literary reflection of his brief and traumatic life.

Hilaire Belloc (English poet and essayist)—One of turn-of-the-century England's premier men of letters, Belloc has been the subject of renewed critical and biographical interest in recent years.

Randolph S. Bourne (American essayist)—A champion of progressive education and pacifism, as well as a fierce opponent of sentimentality in American literature, Bourne is recognized as one of the most astute critics of American life and letters during the era of World War I.

Christopher John Brennan (Australian poet)—Considered one of Australia's greatest poets, he introduced many of the techniques and themes of twentieth-century European literature to the literature of his homeland.

Mikhail Bulgakov (Russian novelist, short story writer, and dramatist)—Bulgakov's works are grotesque and satiric mockeries of Soviet society in particular and communist utopias in general. First translated into English in the late 1960s, Bulgakov's fiction and dramas have since received increasing critical attention in the West.

Colette (French novelist)—Colette's fiction is noted for its depictions of passionate and independent female protagonists. *TCLC* will devote an entire entry to criticism of recently translated collections of Colette's short stories and letters.

Stephen Crane (American novelist)—Author of *The Red Badge of Courage*, Crane was one of America's foremost Realist writers and is credited with establishing American literary Naturalism.

Anne Frank (Dutch diarist)—Composed while its author was in hiding from the Nazis in Amsterdam, *The Diary of Anne Frank* is one of the most enduring and widely read documents of the Holocaust, as well as a testament to the suffering and creative talent of its young author.

Rémy de Gourmont (French critic, novelist, and dramatist)—Gourmont was one of the most prominent French men of letters of the modern era. Displaying an encyclopedic range of learning, his critical writings were extremely influential among early twentieth-century English and American critics.

Thomas Hardy (English novelist)—Hardy's novel *Tess of the D'Urbervilles* was controversial in the late nineteenth century for its sympathetic depiction of an independent female protagonist. *TCLC* will devote an entire entry to the critical reception of this classic work of English fiction.

O. Henry (American short story writer)—O. Henry (William Sydney Porter) was one of America's most popular short story writers. His stories, known for their inventiveness and characteristic surprise endings, are widely anthologized and often compared to the works of Guy de Maupassant.

William Dean Howells (American novelist and critic)—Howells was the chief progenitor of American Realism and the most influential American literary critic of the late nineteenth century. Several of his early novels have been recently reissued, and discussion of his work is growing.

Henrik Ibsen (Norwegian dramatist)—Ibsen's *The Wild Duck* is one of the major works of the twentieth-century stage. *TCLC* will devote an entire entry to critical discussions of this important drama.

James Joyce (Irish novelist)—Joyce's *A Portrait of the Artist as a Young Man* examines the nature of youthful idealism and the role of the artist in modern society. In an entry devoted solely to that work, *TCLC* will present the major critical essays on the novel.

Rudyard Kipling (English short story writer and poet)—Best known for such works as *Kim*, *Captains Courageous*, and *The Jungle Book*, Kipling is one of the most popular authors of this century and one of the finest short story writers in world literature.

Andrew Lang (Scottish historian and editor)—A Scottish man of letters, Lang distinguished himself in a number of genres. Perhaps best known as the author and editor of several renowned anthologies of fairy tales, he was also a key figure in the late nineteenth-century revival of romance literature, a field dominated by his friends H. Rider Haggard and Robert Louis Stevenson.

D. H. Lawrence (English novelist)—Once known primarily as the controversial author of such banned works as *Lady Chatterly's Lover*, Lawrence is one of modern literature's major delineators of the romantic quest for personal freedom, as well as one of the first twentieth-century authors to employ theories of modern psychology in his writing. *TCLC* will devote an entire entry to *Sons and Lovers*, which is among Lawrence's most popular novels.

T. E. Lawrence (English autobiographer)—Lawrence is more popularly known as Lawrence of Arabia, a sobriquet received for his campaign against the Turks during World War I. His chronicle of this period in what has been described as "perhaps the strangest, most adventurous life of modern times" is contained in *The Seven Pillars of*

Wisdom. TCLC will present excerpts from the entire range of criticism on this classic modern work, along with commentary on Lawrence's diary, his letters, and *The Mint*, an account of his experiences following his enlistment as a private in the Royal Air Force.

Isaac Leib Peretz (Polish-born Yiddish short story writer)—Best remembered for his short stories based on Hasidic folklore, Peretz is known as the father of modern Yiddish letters. Along with Sholem Aleichem, he helped create worldwide interest in Yiddish literature.

Detlev von Liliencron (German poet)—The author of works in several genres, Liliencron is most renowned for his lyric poetry, which is praised for its forcefulness and vivid detail.

George Meredith (English novelist and poet)—A prolific author and an associate of England's most famous Victorian literary figures, Meredith ranks among the outstanding writers of his era.

J. Middleton Murry (English critic)—A noted magazine editor and influential literary critic, Murry has contributed important studies on the works of his wife Katherine Mansfield, and his intimate friend D. H. Lawrence.

Rainer Maria Rilke (German poet and novelist)—Rilke's *The Notebooks of Malte Laurids Brigge*, a loosely autobiographical novel that explores the angst-ridden life of a hypersensitive man in Paris, is considered the author's most accomplished prose work. To mark a new translation of this novel, *TCLC* will devote an entire entry to critical discussion of this important work.

Ole Edvart Rølvaag (Norwegian-American novelist)—Born in Norway, Rølvaag emigrated to the United States in his twentieth year, and subsequently depicted in his seven novels the experience of Norwegian immigrants in America. Both as a novelist and as a teacher at Saint Olaf College in Northfield, Minnesota, Rølvaag attempted to preserve among Norwegian-Americans the European values that had become obsolete in their new homeland.

Montague Summers (English critic and historian)—A scholar of Restoration and Gothic literature and a historian of occult subjects such as vampirism and witchcraft, Summers was renowned as one of the most remarkable figures of his time, both for his erudition and his eccentricity.

Leo Tolstoy (Russian novelist)—His *Anna Karenin* is considered one of the greatest novels in world literature. *TCLC* will devote an entire entry to the critical history of this work.

Robert Walser (Swiss novelist and short story writer)—Considered among the most important Swiss authors writing in German, Walser was praised by such major figures of German literature as Franz Kafka and Robert Musil. His fiction is distinguished by a grotesque imagination and black humor suggestive of the Expressionist and Surrealist movements.

Beatrice and Sydney James Webb (English social writers)—Prominent members of the progressive Fabian society, the Webbs wrote sociological works significant to the advent of socialist reform in England and influenced the work of several major authors, including H. G. Wells and Bernard Shaw.

Israel Zangwill (English novelist, short story writer, and essayist)—Zangwill is noted for his detailed fictional depictions of life in the Jewish ghettos of London. His work was responsible for an increased awareness of the effects of anti-Semitism and the plight of the urban poor.

Andrei Zhdanov (Soviet censor)—As Secretary of the Central Committee of the Soviet Communist Party from 1928 until 1948, Zhdanov formulated the official guidelines for all writing published in the Soviet Union. He was instrumental in establishing the precepts of Socialist Realism, which for decades severely circumscribed the subjects deemed suitable for Soviet literature.

Stefan Zweig (Austrian biographer and fiction writer)—Through extensive translation of his works, Zweig's biographical studies of such important figures as Leo Tolstoy, Marie Antoinette, and Sigmund Freud, as well as his dramas and stories, are well known to English-language readers. Zweig stated that his works, both fiction and nonfiction, have as their focus "the psychological representation of personalities and their lives," which was his "main interest in writing."

Additional Authors to Appear
in Future Volumes

Abbey, Henry 1842-1911
Abercrombie, Lascelles 1881-1938
Adamic, Louis 1898-1951
Ade, George 1866-1944
Agustini, Delmira 1886-1914
Akers, Elizabeth Chase 1832-1911
Akiko, Yosano 1878-1942
Aldanov, Mark 1886-1957
Aldrich, Thomas Bailey 1836-1907
Aliyu, Dan Sidi 1902-1920
Allen, Hervey 1889-1949
Archer, William 1856-1924
Arlen, Michael 1895-1956
Austin, Alfred 1835-1913
Austin, Mary 1868-1934
Bahr, Hermann 1863-1934
Bailey, Philip James 1816-1902
Barbour, Ralph Henry 1870-1944
Benét, William Rose 1886-1950
Benjamin, Walter 1892-1940
Bennett, James Gordon, Jr. 1841-1918
Benson, E(dward) F(rederic) 1867-1940
Benson, Stella 1892-1933
Berdyaev, Nikolai Aleksandrovich
  1874-1948
Beresford, J(ohn) D(avys) 1873-1947
Bergson, Henri 1859-1941
Binyon, Laurence 1869-1943
Bishop, John Peale 1892-1944
Blackmore, R(ichard) D(oddridge)
  1825-1900
Blake, Lillie Devereux 1835-1913
Blum, Leon 1872-1950
Bodenheim, Maxwell 1892-1954
Bosschere, Jean de 1878-1953
Bowen, Marjorie 1886-1952
Broch, Hermann 1886-1951
Byrne, Donn 1889-1928
Caine, Hall 1853-1931
Campana, Dina 1885-1932
Cannan, Gilbert 1884-1955
Chand, Prem 1880-1936
Churchill, Winston 1871-1947
Coppée, Francois 1842-1908
Corelli, Marie 1855-1924
Croce, Benedetto 1866-1952
Crofts, Freeman Wills 1879-1957
Crothers, Rachel 1878-1958
Cruze, James (Jens Cruz Bosen) 1884-
  1942
Curros, Enriquez Manuel 1851-1908
Dagerman, Stig 1923-1954
Dall, Caroline Wells (Healy) 1822-1912
Daudet, Leon 1867-1942
Davidson, John 1857-1909

Day, Clarence 1874-1935
Delafield, E.M. (Edme Elizabeth Monica
  de la Pasture) 1890-1943
Deneson, Jacob 1836-1919
DeVoto, Bernard 1897-1955
Douglas, (George) Norman 1868-1952
Douglas, Lloyd C(assel) 1877-1951
Dovzhenko, Alexander 1894-1956
Drinkwater, John 1882-1937
Drummond, W.H. 1854-1907
Durkheim, Emile 1858-1917
Duun, Olav 1876-1939
Eaton, Walter Prichard 1878-1957
Eggleston, Edward 1837-1902
Erskine, John 1879-1951
Fadeyev, Alexander 1901-1956
Ferland, Albert 1872-1943
Feydeau, Georges 1862-1921
Field, Rachel 1894-1924
Flecker, James Elroy 1884-1915
Fletcher, John Gould 1886-1950
Fogazzaro, Antonio 1842-1911
Francos, Karl Emil 1848-1904
Frank, Bruno 1886-1945
Frazer, (Sir) George 1854-1941
Freud, Sigmund 1853-1939
Froding, Gustaf 1860-1911
Fuller, Henry Blake 1857-1929
Futabatei, Shimei 1864-1909
Futrelle, Jacques 1875-1912
Gladkov, Fydor Vasilyevich 1883-1958
Glaspell, Susan 1876-1948
Glyn, Elinor 1864-1943
Golding, Louis 1895-1958
Gosse, Edmund 1849-1928
Gould, Gerald 1885-1936
Gray, John 1866-1934
Grimke, Charlotte L. 1837-1914
Guest, Edgar 1881-1959
Gumilyov, Nikolay 1886-1921
Gyulai, Pal 1826-1909
Hale, Edward Everett 1822-1909
Hall, James 1887-1951
Harris, Frank 1856-1931
Hawthorne, Julian 1846-1934
Hernandez, Miguel 1910-1942
Hewlett, Maurice 1861-1923
Heyward, DuBose 1885-1940
Hilton, James 1900-1954
Hope, Anthony 1863-1933
Howe, Julia Ward 1819-1910
Hudson, W(illiam) H(enry) 1841-1922
Huidobro, Vincente 1893-1948
Hulme, T(homas) E(rnest) 1883-1917
Hviezdoslav (Pavol Orszagh) 1849-1921

Ilyas, Abu Shabaka 1903-1947
Imbs, Bravig 1904-1946
Ivanov, Vyacheslav Ivanovich 1866-
  1949
Jacobs, W(illiam) W(ymark) 1863-1943
James, Will 1892-1942
Jammes, Francis 1868-1938
Jerome, Jerome K(lapka) 1859-1927
Johnson, Fenton 1888-1958
Johnson, Lionel 1869-1902
Johnston, Mary 1870-1936
Jorgensen, Johannes 1866-1956
Kaye-Smith, Sheila 1887-1956
King, Grace 1851-1932
Kirby, William 1817-1906
Kline, Otis Albert 1891-1946
Kohut, Adolph 1848-1916
Korolenko, Vladimir 1853-1921
Kuzmin, Mikhail Alexseyevich 1875-
  1936
Lamm, Martin 1880-1950
Lawson, Henry 1867-1922
Ledwidge, Francis 1887-1917
Leipoldt, C. Louis 1880-1947
Lemonnier, Camille 1844-1913
Leverson, Ada 1862-1933
Lewisohn, Ludwig 1883-1955
Lima, Jorge De 1895-1953
Lindsay, (Nicholas) Vachel 1879-1931
Locke, Alain 1886-1954
Long, Frank Belknap 1903-1959
Louÿs, Pierre 1870-1925
Lucas, E(dward) V(errall) 1868-1938
Lyall, Edna 1857-1903
Maghar, Josef Suatopluk 1864-1945
Manning, Frederic 1887-1935
Maragall, Joan 1860-1911
Marais, Eugene 1871-1936
Martin du Gard, Roger 1881-1958
Masaoka Shiki 1867-1902
Masaryk, Tomas 1850-1939
McClellan, George Marion 1860-1934
McCoy, Horace 1897-1955
Mirbeau, Octave 1850-1917
Mistral, Frederic 1830-1914
Molnar, Ferenc 1878-1952
Monro, Harold 1879-1932
Moore, Thomas Sturge 1870-1944
Morley, Christopher 1890-1957
Morley, S. Griswold 1883-1948
Mqhayi, S.E.K. 1875-1945
Murray, (George) Gilbert 1866-1957
Nansen, Peter 1861-1918
Nathan, George Jean 1882-1958
Nobre, Antonio 1867-1900

Nordhoff, Charles 1887-1947
Norris, Frank 1870-1902
Obstfelder, Sigborn 1866-1900
O'Dowd, Bernard 1866-1959
Ophuls, Max 1902-1957
Orczy, Baroness 1865-1947
Owen, Seaman 1861-1936
Page, Thomas Nelson 1853-1922
Papini, Giovanni 1881-1956
Parrington, Vernon L. 1871-1929
Peck, George W. 1840-1916
Pereda, Jose Maria de 1833-1906
Peret, Benjamin 1899-1959
Phillips, Ulrich B. 1877-1934
Pickthall, Marjorie 1883-1922
Pinero, Arthur Wing 1855-1934
Pontoppidan, Henrik 1857-1943
Porter, Gene(va) Stratton 1886-1924
Prévost, Marcel 1862-1941
Quiller-Couch, Arthur 1863-1944
Quiroga, Horacio 1878-1937
Radnoti, Miklos 1909-1944
Randall, James G. 1881-1953
Rappoport, Solomon 1863-1944
Read, Opie 1852-1939
Reisen (Reizen), Abraham 1875-1953
Remington, Frederic 1861-1909
Renard, Jules 1864-1910
Riley, James Whitcomb 1849-1916
Rinehart, Mary Roberts 1876-1958
Ring, Max 1817-1901

Rohmer, Sax 1883-1959
Rolland, Romain 1866-1944
Roumain, Jacques 1907-1944
Roussel, Raymond 1877-1933
Rozanov, Vasily Vasilyevich 1856-1919
Ruskin, John 1819-1900
Saar, Ferdinand von 1833-1906
Sabatini, Rafael 1875-1950
Saintsbury, George 1845-1933
Sakutarō, Hagiwara 1886-1942
Salinas Pedro 1891-1951
Sanborn, Franklin Benjamin 1831-1917
Santayana, George 1863-1952
Sardou, Victorien 1831-1908
Schickele, Rene 1885-1940
Seabrook, William 1886-1945
Seton, Ernest Thompson 1860-1946
Shestov, Lev 1866-1938
Shiels, George 1886-1949
Skram, Bertha Amalie 1847-1905
Sodergran, Edith Irene 1892-1923
Solovyov, Vladimir 1853-1900
Sorel, Georges 1847-1922
Spector, Mordechai 1859-1922
Spengler, Oswald 1880-1936
Squire, J(ohn) C(ollings) 1884-1958
Stavenhagen, Fritz 1876-1906
Stockton, Frank R. 1834-1902
Subrahmanya Bharati, C. 1882-1921
Sully-Prudhomme, René 1839-1907

Talev, Dimituv 1898-1966
Thoma, Ludwig 1867-1927
Tolstoy, Alexei 1882-1945
Trotsky, Leon 1870-1940
Tuchmann, Jules 1830-1901
Turner, W(alter) J(ames) R(edfern) 1889-1946
Vachell, Horace Annesley 1861-1955
Van Dine, S.S. (William H. Wright) 1888-1939
Van Doren, Carl 1885-1950
Van Dyke, Henry 1852-1933
Vazov, Ivan Minchov 1850-1921
Veblen, Thorstein 1857-1929
Villaespesa, Francisco 1877-1936
Wallace, Edgar 1874-1932
Wallace, Lewis 1827-1905
Walsh, Ernest 1895-1926
Webb, Mary 1881-1927
Webster, Jean 1876-1916
Whitlock, Brand 1869-1927
Wilson, Harry Leon 1867-1939
Wister, Owen 1860-1938
Wolf, Emma 1865-1932
Wood, Clement 1888-1950
Wren, P(ercival) C(hristopher) 1885-1941
Yonge, Charlotte Mary 1823-1901
Zecca, Ferdinand 1864-1947
Zeromski, Stefan 1864-1925

Readers are cordially invited to suggest additional authors to the editors.

Charles A(ustin) Beard

1874-1948

American historian, political scientist, essayist, and journalist.

Beard was one of America's most influential historians. Through his numerous works he directed the course of historiography from the scientific formalism of his predecessors, who believed that natural law governs the course of history, toward the liberal reformism of the progressives, who viewed history as a record of social, economic, and intellectual choices made by individuals and groups, advocated political and social change based on their studies of the past, and thus sought to improve the future. Beard applied his reformist ideology to several areas of study, becoming widely recognized for his expertise in municipal government, educational development, and domestic and foreign policy. In his most famous and controversial work, *An Economic Interpretation of the Constitution of the United States,* he proposed the thesis that underlies most of his works: that America's past can be best interpreted through an examination of its economic forces. Although Beard's studies have been severely criticized for their economic bias, they have nevertheless exerted a profound influence on modern historical thought.

Born on a farm near Knightstown, Indiana, Beard was the son of prosperous parents who consistently encouraged his intellectual development. After Beard's high school graduation in 1891, his father purchased the *Knightstown Sun,* a small weekly newspaper which came to be operated by Beard and his brother Clarence. For four years the two brothers were the newspaper's major contributors, exhibiting both their inherited Republicanism and skeptical worldview in nearly all that they wrote. In 1895 Beard set aside his journalistic ambitions to study for the Methodist ministry at DePauw University. There, however, he came under the influence of two dynamic professors of history, Andrew Stephenson and James R. Weaver, whose sociological approach to history appealed to Beard. He abandoned his religious study and, under the tutelage of Stephenson and Weaver, turned his attention to history and political science. As part of his studies, Beard traveled to Chicago where he witnessed the miserable conditions of workers and the indignities suffered by the poor, a stark contrast to the comfortable small-town community where he had spent his early life. Returning to DePauw, Beard aggressively debated for the levy of income taxes and the organization of labor unions—radical reforms that he believed would help the lot of the underprivileged. Most commentators remark that the scenes of poverty and hopelessness he witnessed in Chicago, coupled with the anti-imperilism advocated by the nationally renowned orator William Jennings Bryan, did much to sway Beard from his staunch conservatism and led him to accept the reformist views that eventually informed his work. While at DePauw, he also met his future wife, the historian Mary Ritter, who became an inspirational force in his career. Together, they coauthored several major works, including *The Rise of American Civilization* and *A Basic History of the United States.*

Graduating in 1898, Beard left for Oxford to study constitutional history. During this time he became increasingly interested in the economic and political problems of English workers, which were giving rise to an English labor movement. The

Culver Pictures

cause appealed to Beard and, with the guidance of historian Frederick York Powell, the American student Walter Vrooman, and the financial backing of Vrooman's wife, Beard founded Ruskin College, an Oxford-affiliated labor school devoted to "training leaders for the unions and cooperative societies." For three years Beard served as the college's extension secretary, lecturing throughout England and Wales on behalf of workers' education. In 1901 he published *The Industrial Revolution,* which is based on his travels through the English mill district and his study of English history. The work is praised as a tribute to the working-class struggle to overcome the injustices of capitalism. Returning to the United States in the early 1900s, Beard earned a doctoral degree at Columbia University, where he was invited to remain as a lecturer. Known for his brilliant discussions and general affability, he became one of the most popular instructors at the university and quickly climbed the ranks of academia. In addition to his teaching, he wrote numerous articles for various journals and published some of his most important studies. By 1917, however, Beard had become deeply disturbed by the conformist attitude of university life. When two of his colleagues were dismissed for their antiwar sentiments, Beard boldly resigned in protest. For a short time thereafter, he worked at the Bureau of Municipal Research in New York City. Beard's knowledge of city management brought him invitations from public officials throughout the United States and around the world to lecture and advise on the problems of urban living. The remainder of his career was spent on research, writing, lecturing, traveling, and actively participating in the political and historical controversies of his day.

With *An Economic Interpretation of the Constitution of the United States,* published in 1913, Beard jarred the idealism of those Americans who revered the Constitution as the united effort of a democratic plurality. The work asserts that the Constitution was "an economic document drawn with superb skill" by a small, undemocratic group of landowners in order to serve their vested interests. Beard further contended that the framers of the Constitution placed their property rights beyond the control of government and "morally beyond the reach of popular majorities." As confirmation of the document's economic basis, the study details the property holdings of those who attended the 1787 Constitutional Convention and recalls that the Constitution was ratified by less than one-sixth of adult male voters, most of whom represented the propertied class. Beard's iconoclastic interpretation naturally drew a diversity of criticism. Some commentators argued that the work was an over-simplification based on unsound research methods, and many faulted Beard for emphasizing only the economic motives of the Founding Fathers. Shortly after the work's publication, ex-President William Howard Taft, in a speech given before numerous governmant officials, harshly attacked *An Economic Interpretation of the Constitution* as a "muckraking investigation." Despite the attacks upon Beard's study, there were those critics who hailed it as "a pioneer work in a new field," and others who believed that it represented a balanced assessment of the Constitution founded on sound historical scholarship. In addition, progressive historians maintained that Beard's work supported their interpretation of American history as a "class and sectional conflict." In *Economic Origins of Jeffersonian Democracy,* Beard continued his economic interpretation of early American government, emphasizing, along the progressive line, what he referred to as "a clear case of a collision of economic interest: fluid capital versus agrarianism." The work is similar in scope to *An Economic Interpretation of the Constitution,* and together they are considered responsible for influencing the economic determinism of later historians, who consider economics to be the primary factor in interpreting history.

Beard's influence on American historiography continued with *The Rise of American Civilization,* published in 1927. In this work Charles and Mary Beard attempted to chronicle the unparalleled growth of American civilization from the time of colonization to the 1920s by decisively applying an economic interpretation to the nation's development. However, in this work the Beards turned their attention beyond politics to encompass every aspect of American civilization, including religion, education, art, and literature. Unencumbered by the footnotes and documentation found in most historical works, the Beards' study was praised for its fluid style and thorough coverage of the expansive subject matter. As a result, *The Rise of American Civilization* had both a popular and scholarly appeal. John Braeman explained the work's popularity when he wrote that "what underlay the book's tremendous popular appeal was how it subsumed the totality of the national experience," and that the work's "portrayal of the clash of rival economic interests as the dominant shaping factor in American history . . . exercised a pervasive influence upon the generation coming to maturity in the 1930s." Similar in its mass appeal to *The Rise of American Civilization,* the Beards' A

Basic History of the United States, a broad overview of American history, increased their reputation as historians writing for the general reader.

The last two works published during Beard's career, *American Foreign Policy in the Making, 1932-1940: A Study in Responsibilities* and *President Roosevelt and the Coming of the War, 1941: A Study in Appearances and Realities,* kept Beard at the center of political controversy until his death in 1948. Joining revisionist historians who believed that Franklin D. Roosevelt deliberately maneuvered the United States into World War II, Beard vigorously attacked Roosevelt's New Deal diplomacy and foreign policy. In both works he insisted that Roosevelt cunningly led the American people to believe that the United States would not be involved in a global war, while surreptitiously charting just such an American military involvement. Both *American Foreign Policy in the Making* and *President Roosevelt and the Coming of War* have been severely criticized. Many commentators have maintained that the studies were highly subjective and based on the emotionalism of Beard's isolationist views. However, less caustic critics believed that any distortions in these two works were due to the unavailability of pertinent government records.

As a result of his aggressive campaign against Roosevelt, Beard's reputation had greatly declined by the time of his death. In the years since, his stimulating historical studies have continued to elicit comment from some of the most prominent historians in America. Although many critics adamantly disagree with Beard's interpretation of the influence of economics on history, they generally regard Beard as an insightful historiographer who has vastly influenced not only their own historical thinking, but that of all Americans. One of Beard's most formidable detractors, historian Lewis Mumford, echoed the consensus of opinion when he conceded that Beard was "the most powerful single figure in the teaching of American history."

(See also *Dictionary of Literary Biography,* Vol. 17: *Twentieth-Century American Historians* and *Something about the Author,* Vol. 18.)

PRINCIPAL WORKS

The Industrial Revolution   (history)   1901
An Introduction to the English Historians   (history)   1906
The Development of Modern Europe: An Introduction to the Study of Current History [with James Harvey Robinson] 2 vols.   (history)   1907-08
The Supreme Court and the Constitution   (history)   1912
An Economic Interpretation of the Constitution of the United States   (history)   1913
Economic Origins of Jeffersonian Democracy   (history) 1915
Cross Currents in Europe To-day   (history)   1922
The Economic Basis of Politics   (history)   1922
The Rise of American Civilization [with Mary R. Beard] 2 vols.   (history)   1927
The Open Door at Home: A Trial Philosophy of National Interest [with George H. E. Smith]   (history)   1934
The Devil Theory of War: An Inquiry into the Nature of History and the Possibility of Keeping Out of War (history)   1936
The Republic: Conversations on Fundamentals   (history) 1943
A Basic History of the United States [with Mary R. Beard] (history)   1944

*American Foreign Policy in the Making 1932-1940: A Study
in Responsibilities* (history) 1946
*President Roosevelt and the Coming of the War, 1941: A
Study in Appearances and Realities* (history) 1948

F. YORK POWELL (essay date 1901)

[*Powell was a distinguished English historian and educator with
whom Beard studied while at Oxford. In the following excerpt
from his introduction to the first edition of* The Industrial Revolution, *he praises the work as a valuable and provocative guide
to understanding the development of modern society.*]

Mr. Beard's book [*The Industrial Revolution*] should make his
readers think; that is what he wants them to do. The good
teacher does not teach things, he tries to make his pupils teach
themselves by honest thinking. No one really knows a thing
that he has not mastered for himself. Here in this little volume
is matter for thought, for further inquiry, for bringing a man
into touch with big and important branches of knowledge. Such
primers are useful; they help one through the hard beginnings
of the subjects; they show one how to go on and master the
thing by one's self. They give one admitted results, and show
one the consequences suspected or ascertained. They work the
mind. (pp. xi-xii)

This little book seems to me to have in its plain pages and its
straightforward substance a good deal of food for thought, a
good deal that is worth remembering, a good deal that is of
the nature of guidance and warning. For instance, we learn
from it how the civilised world has been changed, and our
duties, morals, habits, habitations, and connections all altered
by the discoveries of a few dozen able men. The world is "full
of a number of things," as R. L. Stevenson says, and we have
only learnt to make use of a few of these. There seem almost
endless possibilities open, but they are only open to those who
mean to take advantage of them, who mean to make themselves
and do make themselves able to see the things that the ignorant
and the lazy miss and always will miss. Our trade rivals have
learnt all they knew till a few years ago from us, we can surely
afford to take a lesson from our own ancestors, but we must
be prepared to strip off prejudice and renounce hollow for-
mulae. Even if such a sacred institution as a trades-union stands
in the way of real progress, it must change or go. (pp. xiii-xiv)

> *F. York Powell, in a prefatory note to* The Industrial
> Revolution *by Charles Beard, 1901. Reprint by
> Greenwood Press, Publishers, 1969, pp. vii-xv.*

WILLIAM MacDONALD (essay date 1907)

[*In the following excerpt MacDonald, an American educator and
author, praises* An Introduction to the English Historians *as a
useful tool for students of history.*]

Dr. Beard's addition [*An Introduction to the English Historians*]
to existing helps for elementary historical study has at least the
merit of novelty. Of collections of documents and similar matter there is already a considerable array; indeed, hardly any
field of history, ancient or modern, commonly dealt with in
American schools or colleges now lacks at least one usable
collection of so-called "source material." It can not have escaped notice, however, that the "source method" has unfor-

tunately come to exercise for many teachers, especially for
teachers in secondary schools, a sort of tyranny, and that the
works of secondary authorities, even the best of them, have
not seldom been referred to with somewhat of depreciation.
(p. 101)

Dr. Beard's scholarly and attractive volume will have for many
teachers a peculiar interest, in that it will point the way to a
larger and more systematic use of secondary works. Dr. Beard
has undertaken to extract, from narrative works of acknowledged authority, representative passages relating to typical moments or movements in English history from the earliest times
to the latter part of the nineteenth century. There is a catholic
range of authors—Hallam, Macaulay, Stubbs, Green, Freeman, Bagehot, Cunningham, Bryce, Maitland, Pollock, Froude,
and others. The selections are of varying lengths, an entire
chapter from an author being occasionally included; but save
for abridgment by judicious omissions, the passages are unaltered. There are brief introductory notes and a few references.
The editor of a book of selections ought not, in general, to be
called to account for his choice of topics, and we venture no
adverse criticism of Dr. Beard in this respect, unless it be
adverse criticism to wish that he had dealt more liberally with
Part IX, "The empire in the thirteenth centry."

The usefulness of the volume should be considerable. The
extracts are all well within the grasp of college students, and
the larger number can be profitably used in secondary schools. . . .
Chiefly, however, the book will serve as a well-contrived key
with which the student may unlock the storehouse of English
narrative history; and for all but a small fraction of the community, acquaintance with narrative history must be the beginning and the end of historical knowledge. (pp. 101-02)

> *William MacDonald, in a review of "An Introduction
> to the English Historians," in* Educational Review,
> *Vol. 34, June, 1907, pp. 101-02.*

JOHN H. LATANÉ (essay date 1913)

[*In the following excerpt, Latané strongly disagrees with the unconventional findings of Beard's* An Economic Interpretation of
the Constitution of the United States. *For further discussion of
this work, see the excerpts by Alfred Kazin (1942) and Richard
Hofstadter (1968).*]

Dr. Beard's volume [*An Economic Interpretation of the Constitution of the United States*] . . . is a deliberate attempt to
upset all our traditional ideas as to the motives and purposes
of the men who framed our national government. His work,
it is interesting to note, is based on sources not used by Farrand,
McLaughlin, Fiske, Bancroft, Curtis, and other writers on this
period. These new sources are manuscript records of the treasury department containing records of the transactions in government securities at the time that Hamilton's funding system
went into effect. (pp. 697-98)

The most interesting chapter in the volume is that dealing with
"the economic interests of the members of the convention."
This chapter contains a large amount of new material in regard
to the private financial history of the public men of that day.
Dr. Beard shows that a large number of the members of the
convention were holders of government securities the value of
which was greatly enhanced by the adoption of the new constitution. This fact is not necessarily sinister in its bearing, for
it is evident that any improvement in the government under
the Articles of Confederation would have enhanced the value

of government bonds. It is also true that the condition of people who owned no government securities was greatly improved by the adoption of the Constitution. Dr. Beard signally fails to prove his main theses, namely, that the leaders in the movement for a stronger government were influenced by their financial interests rather than by the public welfare. The mere fact that large amounts of securities were held by members of the convention needs no further explanation than the reminder that the suffrage was strictly limited at that time, that as a general result only men of means were elected to public assemblies, and that in an age when investments were very limited most men of means not actively engaged in industry or commerce put their money in government securities or western lands. The main defect in Dr. Beard's book is that he does not undertake to test his theory by analyzing the votes taken in the convention on specific questions. If his interpretation of history is correct, we should naturally expect to find the larger bondholders voting for a strong central government and the non-bondholders voting against it; but when his theory is applied in detail, we find that such is not the case. Many of the largest bondholders in the convention were opposed to a strong Federal government, and on the contrary some of the staunchest supporters of the new system held no public securities at all. (pp. 698-99)

The economic interpretation of history in the broader sense is being accepted generally by the historians of today, certainly by the younger set. For instance, sectionalism in this country was primarily economic, secondarily political. Members of congress and of other political bodies have always been influenced, sometimes consciously, sometimes un-consciously, by the economic interests of their constituents, and in a country of such diversified interests as ours we have come to regard it as the duty of a representative to look out for the economic interests of his section; but the tendency of Dr. Beard's economic interpretation is to reduce everything to a sordid basis of personal interest. Gustavus Myers has undertaken to apply the same theory in his *History of the Supreme Court of the United States*. Are we not in danger of reading into the past conceptions which are especially characteristic of the present? The problems of political organization, while the problems that we have to face today are essentially problems of industrial organization. At any rate it will require more convincing evidence than Dr. Beard has so far presented to upset the traditional view that the members of the Federal convention were patriotic men earnestly striving to arrive at the best political solution of the dangers that threatened the republic which was still in the experimental stage. (pp. 699-700)

> *John H. Latané, in a review of "An Economic Interpretation of the Constitution of the United States," in* The American Political Science Review, *Vol. VII, No. 4, November, 1913, pp. 697-700.*

E. L. BOGART   (essay date 1916)

[*In the following excerpt, Bogart discusses* Economic Origins of Jeffersonian Democracy, *a work in which Beard examined the development of political parties in America, most notably the Federalists and the Republicans.*]

In his earlier book, ***Economic Interpretation of the Constitution***, Professor Beard essayed to prove that "the Constitution was a product of a struggle between capitalistic and agrarian interests." In [***Economic Origins of Jeffersonian Democracy***] he shows that the same interests which had supported and opposed the adoption of the Constitution divided again after its adoption

into the two parties of Federalists and Republicans. The alignment of the two parties was primarily economic: the Federalists were made up of "security-holding capitalists, who were quite generally merchants, traders, shippers, and manufacturers," while the Republicans were "the debt-burdened agrarians who had fought the Constitution to the bitter end." In the contest between capitalism and agrarianism is to be found the explanation of the formation and policies of the political parties during the first decade of our national existence. (pp. 298-99)

In his treatment of this period, Professor Beard has given us a refreshing discussion of factors which have never been altogether lost sight of, but which have certainly been under-emphasized. In his insistence upon the domination of economic interests in determining many of the political issue of an earlier period, he is introducing a true sense of proportion into historical writing. By the use of unprinted sources and of printed material used in a fresh way the author has thoroughly illuminated his subject, and made it impossible for any one to doubt the truth of his thesis.

There is no intimation in the book that the use of the powers of government by the dominant party to enact measures favorable to the property interests involved any personal corruption on the part of those advocating these measures; indeed, they probably correctly represented the interests of their constituencies, just as the opposing Republicans represented the interests of agrarian communities. On the other hand, the author makes no claim that agrarianism was the embodiment of political virtue—"Jeffersonian Democracy simply meant the possession of the federal government by the agrarian masses led by an aristocracy of slave-owning planters." Professor Beard is interested only in showing that the economic conflict between capitalism and agrarianism is the explanation of the growth of parties and their policies. This task he has performed with ability, learning, and poise. It must be said, however, that when this is proved only half the work of rewriting the history of this period has been performed. Even more important is the reconstruction of the economic life and activities of the people. We must know wherein capitalism consisted, what forms it took, and how it functioned, before we can finally determine the influence which it exerted upon politics. Among those lines scarcely a beginning has as yet been made. (p. 299)

> *E. L. Bogart, in a review of "Economic Origins of Jeffersonian Democracy," in* The Annals of the American Academy of Political and Social Science, *Vol. LXIII, January, 1916, pp. 298-99.*

WALTER LIPPMANN   (essay date 1922)

[*Throughout much of the twentieth-century, Lippmann was considered the dean of American political journalists. He began his career as an investigative reporter for Lincoln Steffens's* Everybody's Magazine *and later helped found the liberal* New Republic *in 1914, serving for several years as associate editor and literary critic. During the 1920s, the focus of his interests swung from literature to politics, and he worked as editor and political writer for various major American periodicals for the rest of his life. In the following review of* The Economic Basis of Politics, *Lippmann asserts that Beard's political theory is vague and not thoroughly developed. This review prompted a reply from Beard (1922), who took Lippmann's comments as a challenge to define his theory.*]

As a polemic against vacant political theorizing, this little book [**"The Economic Basis of Politics"**] is invaluable. But as a scientific concept, Mr. Beard's generalization seems to me to call for rather more thoroughgoing criticism than I can find in this book. For once you grant, as I certainly should, that an intimate connection exists between politics and property, you cannot stop until you have made up your mind what that connection is. And I at least, as an ardent admirer of Mr. Beard's work, have never been able to discover in it a clear conception of how he thinks economics determines politics.

I am in doubt as to what he means by **"The Economic Basis of Politics."** Does he mean that economics is one of the bases of politics, or that economics is the one basis of politics? The very word basis strikes me as confusing. For it is a concealed metaphor with a flavor of eulogy about it. Suppose he were talking about the "basis" of some other human activity, say automobiling. What would he call the basis of automobiling? Would he say it was the combustion engine, the art of metallurgy, the capitalistic organization of the mining industry, the technical schools for engineers, the class of potential automobile buyers, the psychological equipment required to drive an automobile, the good roads movement? Nobody would, I imagine, think of picking out one of these elements to say that was *the* basis of automobiling. He might say that one element was more indispensable than another, the combustion engine more necessary than macadam roads. But if he were eschewing rhetoric, he would probably not speak of *the basis* of automobiling at all.

Now I am in real doubt about the sense in which Mr. Beard uses the word "basis." I think he is in doubt. I think his energy is so much occupied in pounding home a realization that there is a deep connection between economics and politics, and in the joy of depicting unsuspected connections, especially where there are sacred cows, that he has not stayed to make it clear what kind of connection this deep connection is.

Let me illustrate from his text. He is discussing the French Estates General of 1789. He points out the presence of three classes, the clergy, the nobility and the bourgeoisie. He notes that this grouping of classes was converted by a show of force into the National Assembly. And then he says: "Had the clergy and the nobility been willing earlier to surrender some of their privileges, and concede to the third estate a fair portion of political power, the history of the desperate years that followed the peaceful revolution of 1789 might have been far different."

Mr. Beard makes this remark and passes on. But if you pause over the remark you are bound to ask yourself questions that Mr. Beard does not seem to have asked himself. The French clergy and nobility had privileges, economic privileges if you choose to make the word as inclusive as Freud makes the word sex. Theoretically their politics should have turned on defending those privileges. The best way to defend them, says Mr. Beard, was to yield some of them. Here was the true line of self-interest. But, instead, the upper classes "defended" their privileges by a political policy that led to the destruction of those privileges.

There is then no necessary connection between property and the possession of political ideas which lead to political acts that serve the best interests of the property. And because there is no necessary connection, the economic interpretation of politics seems to me a misleading half-truth whenever the man who uses it fails to make clear that the connection between economics and politics is not one of total cause to total effect. Property is a very significant element, but it is an element that acts causally in a highly complicated mixture of tradition, of stereotypes and of special circumstance. And therefore, no historian after the fact and no statesman dealing with the future,

can be inspecting the distribution of property deduce from these data alone the political behavior of men.

He cannot do it because he does not know how men will conceive their property. He cannot tell by analyzing the objective interests of property how those interests will be subjectively regarded. He does not know, for example, from the organization of property alone whether the owners will commit suicide as did the French nobility of 1789 or save themselves by wise concessions as did the British nobility of 1832.

That property interests play an immense part in politics remains true. If you define property widely enough to include anything which men wish to possess that is limited in quantity and that is affected by someone else's desire for possession, then economic considerations take in a very large part of the whole field of political controversy. Thus the use of the air has until recently entered very little into political discussion. For the needs of our breathing air is unlimited. But for flying and radio the air is limited, and with flying and radio, therefore, the rule of the air becomes a political matter.

But how an economic interest appears in politics is the really difficult question for anyone who needs no more converting to the notion that there is a connection. Mr. Beard should, I think, work on the nature of that connection. And when he works on it he will surely have to abandon the assumption—which I think he has taken over largely uncriticized from the early nineteenth century intellectualists—the assumption that men instinctively pursue their own interests knowing what are their interests. To accept that premise is to deny the most obvious everyday experience: that having economic interests, yet we are perpetually puzzled how to preserve or to enhance them. For nothing is easier than to be mistaken about our interests. Nothing is commoner than to own property, misunderstand it and so mismanage it. (pp. 282-83)

Walter Lippmann, "Mr. Beard on Property and Politics," in The New Republic, *Vol. XXVI, No. 400, August 2, 1922, pp. 282-83.*

CHARLES A. BEARD   (essay date 1922)

[*In the following excerpt, Beard rebuts the criticism of Walter Lippmann (1922), who found* The Economic Basis of Politics *unclear and underdeveloped.*]

Mr. Lippmann's essay on my little book about Politics and Economics [*The Economic Basis of Politics;* see excerpt by Lippmann dated 1922] is a challenge rather than a review and, as it is written in good temper and with evident interest in the truth of the matter, I cannot escape making some kind of an answer. . . .

Mr. Lippmann thinks that I have "taken over, largely uncriticized from the early nineteenth century intellectualists the assumption that men instinctively pursue their own interests knowing what are their interests." That is really an unkind cut. I had expected to be called mid-Victorian soon, but here I am already a pre-Victorian! Mr. Lippmann is of the opinion that I believe in the doctrine of the economic man: "Everyone knows his interests and pursues them." Now, that doctrine was exploded long before I was born. I never believed in it. I do not hink I ever knew any person who did believe in it. Certainly, that is a gospel of inerrancy and omnipotence which I never preached. If, in some lapse previous to the Volstead act, I wrote anything that gives Mr. Lippmann reason for thinking that I believe in the dogma of the economic man, I beg of him to point out the passage or passages so that I may quickly expunge them. The dogma is so fallacious and preposterous that I have never thought it necessary to put my readers on their guard against it. When I was teaching I was always careful to warn freshmen against it, but I never thought anybody higher in the educational scale needed any precautionary information on the point. Economic classes contending for what they feel to be their interests are more likely to destroy civilization than to realize anything approaching their "interests"—whatever that may mean.

Mr. Lippmann is quite right when he says that I have nowhere gone into what may be called the metaphysics of the relations between economics and politics. A great deal has been written on the theory of the matter. On that point there is nothing better than Professor Seligman's very clear and interesting Economic Interpretation of History. On the other hand, I have been more busily engaged in the analysis of concrete historical and economic situations than in the metaphysics of the subject. Not that I have been indifferent to the problem mentioned by Mr. Lippmann. I long ago planned to write a book tracing the social implications of economic forces, but in searching for materials I found much speculation and very few facts. Some day when I know more than I do now, I may attack that problem.

Still, in a limited sense, I have at least tried to show what I mean by the economic basis of politics. . . . In every great society, as James Madison said long ago, there are to be found various degrees and kinds of property; there are landed, mercantile, manufacturing and other groups; there are merchants great and small, farmers prosperous and in debt; and so on. From the influence of the different degrees and kinds of property on the sentiments and views of their proprietors there ensues a division of society into different interests and parties. Here is the basis of politics. Mr. Lippmann thinks I am in doubt as to the sense in which I use the word "basis." I may be wrong but I am not in doubt. The dictionary defines "basis" as a fundamental ingredient in a compound. Mr. Lippmann thinks that is rhetorical. It is, because we are dealing with human conduct, not with mass, energy and weight. Still I think there is a great deal of intelligible substance in it. It is not a closed system of infinite wisdom, but it seems to throw some light on politics—more light, in my opinion, than anything else, so much light that those who neglect it are as safe guides as ship captains without a compass. (p. 128)

Mr. Lippmann asks me to explain "how" economics "determines" politics. The word "how" is a vague word, it is rhetorical when applied to human relationships. I have personally tried to avoid the use of the word "determine" as too mechanistic. I sometimes quote other authors who use it. Daniel Webster and Karl Marx used it, but I think wrongly. As to "how" economics even influences politics, I cannot make answer, any more than the physicist can explain "how" a dynamo makes electricity.

The truth is, as William James said, anyone who tries to think his way all through any subject runs into metaphysics. Metaphysically speaking, so-called economic interpretation is as bankrupt as the output of any other school of thought. It cannot answer any of the important questions about "how" and "why". I do not think that economics determines or even explains politics in the philosophic sense. Neither does anything else that I have yet stumbled across in this vale of tears. I venture the opinion that Mr. Lippmann is too impatient with imperfection, inconclusiveness, fractions—with the vague and elusive clouds that float between our understanding and infinity.

It is to his credit that he should be. Impatience produces new work. Still, he must not be too hard on the old fellows who tried to find total cause and total effect and broke their lances on moonshine.

There is only one point in Mr. Lippmann's fine essay that gave me pain. He thinks of my little book as a "polemic." I hope that all concerned will read my book before accepting his sentence of death. I do not traverse that opinion. I appeal the case. (p. 129)

Charles A. Beard, " 'The Economic Basis of Politics'," in The New Republic, *Vol. XXXII, No. 408, September 27, 1922, pp. 128-29.*

CARL BECKER   (essay date 1922)

[*Becker was a distinguished American historian, educator, and member of the Progressive school whose historical writings are as esteemed for their literary merit as they are for their theoretical content. Writing in a clear, concise, often epigrammatic style, Becker's works challenged the way historians studied their subject. Among his important works are:* The History of Political Parties in the Province of New York, 1760-1776 *(1909), which proposed what has come to be known as the "dual revolution" thesis of the American Revolutionary War—that is, that the 1776 revolution was not only a revolt against England's rule, but also a rebellion of the American lower class against the upper class in order to gain a share of political power;* The Declaration of Independence: A Study in the History of Political Ideas *(1922), which utilized a sociological approach to examine Thomas Jefferson's philosophy of government and its historical roots; and* The Heavenly City of the Eighteenth Century Philosophers *(1932). The last work, one of Becker's most popular books, offered an innovative perspective on Englightenment philosophers, maintaining that their "rationalist" thought was based as much on religious faith as on reason. In the following excerpt, Becker discusses* Cross Currents in Europe To-day, *Beard's economic analysis of Europe following World War I.*]

This admirable book, [*Cross Currents in Europe To-day*] "the substance of eight lectures . . . delivered at Dartmouth College on the Guernsey Center Moore Foundation," should be read by every one who desires to know how the war came and what came out of it in the way of economic collapse, political reorganization, and reorientation in radical political and social thinking.

In the first three chapters Mr. Beard has given us, on the basis of the recent diplomatic revelations, a clear and succinct account of the complicated web of diplomatic negotiation and intrigue: of the alliances made, of the "understandings" that could be misunderstood, of the "conversations" that obligated statesmen under certain circumstances to make war but under no circumstances obligated them to inform their parliaments until it was too late to prevent it. Mr. Beard understands that there were other and deeper causes of the war; but he thinks it worth while to point out once more, (1) that "all the diplomats . . . were convinced that a general war was in the highest degree possible and devoted themselves to special alliances and agreements in preparation for the terrible eventuality"; and (2) that "neither the members of parliaments nor the mass of the people knew what was going on behind their backs." And he asks the inevitable question: "Had all the records been open what would have been the result?" Mr. Beard is too wise to answer that question. No one can. But this much seems certain: all the preparations for war from 1904 to 1914 were preparations for war and not for peace. . . .

The economic consequences of the war (and of the peace) Mr. Beard gives us straight; and it is a bitter dose. Many people have consoled themselves, and still do so, with the thought that while the war was destructive and disorganizing, these effects would cease with the cause. They are the people who are still looking for something called normalcy. But it seems that the economic disorganization caused by the war has been getting worse during the last four years. In some countries the debt has doubled since 1918; agricultural production is on the whole less now than four years ago; the profound industrial depression does not lift (are the tariffs not high enough perhaps?); financial systems are a chaos. Most alarming of all, perhaps, such signs of recovery as appear in the industrial world point to an accentuation of those conditions that formerly created the class struggle within, and bitter trade rivalry among, the nations: Stinnes governs and exploits Germany; Great Britain is rapidly grabbing the chief sources of the world's oil supply; the United States is peacefully penetrating every country in the world with its loans. Mr. Beard speaks of the "First World War," and invites us to consider how the survivors of the "Tenth World War" will look back on our relatively simple problems. (p. 552)

And what is the remedy? Mr. Beard hasn't any. In these times that is a great merit. There are plenty of people with remedies—mostly born of their prejudices, their fears, their yearnings, or their hopes, including the hope of royalties. Mr. Beard is too intelligent to be taken in by ready-made formulas—radical, liberal, conservative; too sophisticated not to delight in dispelling illusions; yet too humanely sympathetic to fall back into the easy cynicism of one who is content merely to observe the tragic comedy of existence. He is an exasperated cynic and a warm-hearted friend of suffering humanity. He is a hard-headed idealist, the sworn foe at once of all that is stupid and selfish and disingenuous, and of all that is soft and comforting and merely well intentioned. He is as little tender of the people who are wrong-headed in the right direction as he is of the people who are right-headed in the wrong direction. Perfectly aware of human folly, he never quite loses faith in human nature. In short, he is a penetrating and informed critic of politics and government. That is what makes this book, and all of Mr. Beard's writings, so eminently stimulating and valuable. (p. 553)

> *Carl Becker, "The Shaking World," in* The Nation, *Vol. CXV, No. 2994, November 22, 1922, pp. 552-53.*

CARL VAN DOREN (essay date 1927)

[Van Doren is considered one of the most perceptive critics of the first half of the twentieth century. He worked for many years as a professor of English at Columbia University and served as literary editor and critic of The Nation *and* The Century *during the 1920s. A founder of the Literary Guild and author or editor of several American literary histories, Van Doren was also a critically acclaimed historian and biographer. Howard Moss wrote of him: "His virtues, honesty, clarity and tolerance are rare. His vices, occasional dullness and a somewhat monotonous rhetoric, are merely, in most places, the reverse coin of his excellence." In the following excerpt, Van Doren acknowledges several weaknesses in* The Rise of American Civilization, *but praises the work as "appallingly learned, stirringly enlightened, and movingly human." For other discussions of this work, see the excerpts by Edmund Wilson (1932) and Hugo L. Black (1954).]*

How true can any general history be? In the best work of the sort the specialist reading with his accurate, cynical eye, can find errors of detail. For example, within a dozen pages or so of the Beards' magnificent **"Rise of American Civilization"** the historian of literature will note that Walter F. White is called Stuart White, that Charles Klein's "Lion and the Mouse" is ascribed to Henry Arthur Jones, that the name of Edward MacDowell is given as McDowell. These, with others in the same department of American culture, are of course mere trivial slips, but they remind the skeptical that where enough facts are cited a certain proportion of them are fairly sure to be wrong.

And if this is the case with surface details so easy to correct, how about the more trying details upon which surmises and interpretations are based? No one has ever known enough about a single man to explain his conduct with unchallenged adequacy. No one has ever known enough to analyse all the personal and political motives of a village election. Yet the general historian must deal with millions of men and their doings over, possibly, hundreds of years, must try to understand upon what instincts these men and generations have acted, and must reduce the account to a brevity which will enable it to be read and to a pattern which will enable it to be comprehended by an age which may find the record mystifying if there is no familiar pattern in it. (pp. 1-2)

Speaking strictly, no general history can satisfy an exacting critic. And yet **"The Rise of American Civilization,"** unless impossible and abstract demands are made upon it, is a work which satisfies till it excites. It is appallingly learned, stirringly enlightened, and movingly humane.

The learning of the book is not exhibited in footnotes to every page (indeed, to any page) or in lists of authorities cited. Everything is in the text, which rushes forward with an easy power which must delight the general reader. The special reader, however, will perceive that no position has been taken without reference to all that has been done by minute students to make difficult points clear. The Beards have ransacked a wilderness of monographs and have brought back all the pertinent spoils. In addition, they have done so much investigation at first hand that many of the chapters are themselves monographs, without the drowsy and formidable look of the monographic breed.

At the same time, the work as a whole rises above its authorities and its fresh information. It has that superior kind of learning, generally alien to the specialist, which commands, not follows. It at no point suggests a piecemeal compilation, because it has the unity, every part bearing upon every other part, which proves that its materials have been held without strain in a spacious mind, not spelled out page by page with the past pages forgotten and the future pages not yet planned.

It is as enlightened as it is informed. This quality the Beards have given to their work by telling the story of America as if their motto were "No fables!" Their method is, that is to say, the method which in fiction is called realism. They know that romantic historians tell of deeds as men wish their deeds might have been done: the actions are enlarged with touches of creative memory, and the motives are brought forward rather for the glory of the actors than for the explanations of events. As realistic historians, the Beards are presumably of the opinion that in three hundred years they have built their civilization, whatever its faults, where an almost empty continent stood, without having to have it also said that they have done many things which they have not done, and for motives which men allege ten times as often as they practice them. . . .

Their book sums up in a single narrative the work which many historians have been doing, little by little, during a generation devoted to the scrutiny of these national fables which have been called American history. The Beards, however, spend little of their strength in wrangling with the makers and perpetuators of these fables. Instead, they have preferred to let their story speak as far as possible for itself. And it does it so well that by comparison most of the familiar fables seem dull and tame. This is the bone and meat of history, the blood and native color. All it lacks is the cosmetics. (p. 2)

> *Carl Van Doren, "History without Fables," in* New York Herald Tribune Books, *April 24, 1927, pp. 1-2.*

EDMUND WILSON   (essay date 1932)

[*Wilson, considered America's foremost man of letters in the twentieth century, wrote widely on cultural, historical, and literary matters, authoring several seminal critical studies. He is often credited with bringing an international perspective to American letters through his widely read discussions of European literature. Perhaps Wilson's greatest contributions to American literature were his tireless promotion of writers of the 1920s, 1930s, and 1940s, and his essays introducing the best of modern literature to the general reader. In the following excerpt, Wilson offers a succinct assessment of* The Rise of American Civilization. *For other discussions of this work, see the excerpts by Carl Van Doren (1927) and Hugo L. Black (1954).*]

Mr. Charles A. Beard is one of the best American writers of his generation and **"The Rise of American Civilization"** is a masterpiece of economy and organization. Never perhaps has an immense historical subject been more beautifully and completely articulated in so small a compass. And never have the proportions of popular legend been altered with a bolder and firmer hand. With the Beards, every sentence, every clause, carries its cool facts as the sentences in other books carry nouns and verbs—and the fighting of the Civil War shrinks to three pages while the origins of the forces that produced it take up a couple of hundred. When the Beards got to the end of their story, however, they could only write a brilliant essay on the present—no doubt the best of all the essays because it was the work of wider-ranging as well as more concrete minds than the woolly generalizations that used to come out in the magazines in such quantities. . . . (p. 345)

> *Edmund Wilson, "What Do the Liberals Hope For?" in* The New Republic, *Vol. LXIX, No. 897, February 10, 1932, pp. 345-48.**

HENRY A. WALLACE   (essay date 1935)

[*Wallace was United States Secretary of Agriculture in Franklin Roosevelt's administration during the 1930s, and served as Roosevelt's Vice President from 1940 to 1944. Noted for shaping New Deal policies favorable to the American farmer, Wallace later led the Marxist-dominated Progressive Party, running for President on that party's ticket in 1948. In the following excerpt, Wallace praises* The Open Door at Home, *but finds sections of the book to be more facile than substantial, and deems Beard a better historian than economist.*]

Rarely has a historian come down from his Olympian height with such precise plans for a single nation as has Charles Beard in his book, **"The Open Door at Home."** I approached it with some uneasiness because several of my friends the first week in December said, "Have you read Beard's new book? He has gone isolationist."

Opening the book to page 120, I found him making fun of Raymond L. Buell of the Foreign Policy Association, for saying that the future of capitalism depends on increased foreign purchasing for our exports brought about by lowering the tariff. Beard's sharp pen has long delighted me, but it didn't seem so funny now that he was pricking one of my own pet hobbies. Reading on, I found that Beard, in spite of his rather "smarty" phrase-making, is decidedly bigger than such simple classification as "isolationist" or "internationalist." He has almost as much contempt for agrarians as he has for industrialists. His supreme interest is the national interest. He writes with more intelligent patriotism than any other American I have ever read.

The one thing he hates above everything else is imperialism. . . . This whole sickening round, which involves colonial possessions, spheres of influence, a large navy, and the policy of applying pressure and coercion in order to force outlets for the surpluses of American industry and agriculture, has been described and denounced more vividly by Beard than by anyone else. . . .

In his discussion of agrarian statecraft, Beard assumes that the central policy is "low tariffs." Frankly I question whether this chapter, which is somewhat of an argument for a continuation of high tariffs in the United States at the present time, does much credit to Beard as an economist. But his testimony as a historian is quite impressive. And, of course, he may be right that the economists of the United States today have been seriously infected by the rationalizing of the British free-trade economists of a century ago. Unfortunately Beard has not lived as close to the leaders of agrarian statecraft during the past quarter of a century as is necessary for a really authoritative pronouncement. (p. 225)

On the subject of farm policy, Beard quotes me as follows:

> If we continue toward nationalism we must be prepared to make permanent the withdrawal from cultivation of over fifty million acres of good farmland, and face the consequences of all the social and economic dislocations which are bound to ensue.

And then referring to the middle course which I presented as an alternative to this, he says:

> His program of protection and realization for agriculture is to force dislocations and readjustments in industry, by reducing the tariff, by destroying rights vested under previous tariff policy, and by importing an additional $500,000,000 worth of industrial commodities, in the hope of saving 25,000,000 acres of farmland for their possessors. Likewise, on their side, industrialists have shown themselves willing, and are still willing, to dislocate historic agriculture and force readjustments there. In other words, policy is to be special interest. There is no ambiguity about that. Politics is to continue as an open struggle among special interests, with what long-term outcome for the nation no one knows, although the present impasse in which such a struggle has eventuated is well known.

I must confess it is a little disturbing to find Beard looking on my middle-course proposal as special pleading. It had seemed to me that the dislocations caused to agriculture and to industry were about even under this proposal. Furthermore, I have from time to time, in the advocacy of a great increase in imports to restore agricultural markets, suggested that the shock of such increased imports to vested interests might be broken by special governmental action. Also I have pointed out from time to time that the increased purchasing power coming to export agriculture and export industry, as a result of increased imports into this country, would result in greatly increased activity among those industries which sell products to farmers, and that the status of labor generally might be greatly improved even though it might be necessary for the government to take care of the labor displaced in certain specialized and inefficient industries.

I fear that my review, like Beard's book, does not get down to the really interesting part until the last. He realizes that, since the World War, we have had a long drawn-out stalemate between conflicting interests which has proved terribly disastrous. A decision must be reached. The method of the decision, according to the American tradition, consists of three parts, as follows: (1) Formulate the new policy; (2) take it to the country, debate it and get it adopted; (3) after you get the mandate, carry it into execution.

The Beard policy that is taken to the country for debate by his book, has for its essential background the terrible fear that the United States may get into war. He was deeply disturbed by the careless way in which we loaned money abroad during the 1920's. With the United States such a dominant commercial factor in world affairs, he questions our ability to stay neutral in case war breaks out somewhere else in the world and quotes Charles Warren's article in the April, 1934, Foreign Affairs as to the type of legislation we must have in order to enable us to remain neutral for any great length of time in case there is another serious war overseas. Beard doesn't like the idea of sending great quantities of either commodities or American capital abroad. He thinks American capital, American labor and American farmers have enough to do to make the United States the right kind of a place in which to live. He believes that unless the financial people cannot become as excited about opportunities at home as they have been excited about opportunities abroad, it may be necessary for the government to take increasing quantities of their money away from them by taxation. And he recognizes that, if our labor and capital are devoted more exclusively toward supplying domestic needs, it may be necessary to lay more emphasis on the intellectual, esthetic and scientific forces of the nation to the end that we have more people employed to enable us to enjoy art, recreation and the pleasures of nature and science.

Charles Beard, at heart, is an esthetic, a believer in the Good Life according to academic standards. I am inclined to think that most of his objectives are sound and that they will appear so as soon as the American people are really hungry for them. But on questions of tactics and methods, his judgment is less certain. I have the uneasy feeling that Beard in his approach skates too easily over the economic surface of the American situation. (pp. 225-26)

Beard quite rightly states that the national objectives in their final analysis are ideal in nature, assertions of values which cannot be proved by any system of reasoning. But in discussing possible objectives, it would seem to be exceedingly wise for the American people to use mechanistic economics in weighing the respective advantages and disadvantages of the alternative courses. Beard, in his approach, quite definitely rejects a further continuance of the experimental approach of President

Roosevelt and wants to get down to careful planning both externally and internally at the earliest possible moment. Unfortunately, he has not considered in any detail the very real dislocations that would be brought about by his plan to the farmers of the Middle West and South, and the various types of industries dependent on them. Neither has he presented with sufficient vigor the problem of political resistance to the very real degree of so-called regimentation, external and internal, that would be necessary to carry out his program.

In discussing the various issues with the people of the United States there is nothing to be gained by covering up the economic and spiritual costs of the different possible alternative approaches; neither the path of nationalism nor of internationalism, nor a planned middle course, should be made to appear too rosy. The essential thing is that sooner or later there must be a decision. Beard is quite right in likening this period to that just before the adoption of the Constitution of the United States, when the Federalists, appalled by the anarchy of the day, appealed to the people to support a social document designed to bring order out of chaos. It would seem that the time has arrived for launching a New Federalist to discuss the issues of our present day as significantly as did the Federalist papers of 1787. I should suggest Charles A. Beard himself as its ideal editor. (p. 226)

Yes, I fear Beard has been rationalizing his fundamental prejudices in much the same way as any of the rest of us. Nevertheless, I must admit the man has a better historic sweep than most of us, even though as an economic technician he may be a little misinformed as to the nature of certain difficulties in his nationalistic approach. . . .

In the last two or three pages of his book, Beard dreams a great dream of a beautiful and peaceful future of our great land, remote from the predatory course of foreign nations, "fighting like cats and dogs over crumbs of trade." We would stay at home and provide an adequate army, navy, aviation force and coast defenses to take care of the United States proper, setting an example to other nations of a land at peace and a happy race of people engaged in promoting high living standards and an appreciation of all that is finest and best. The heart thrills to all of this, but I fear that even Beard has not seen the whole problem. He is not quite so good an economic technician as he is a historian. I wish he were, because his contribution would then be even more significant. In the meantime, I trust his book will be debated up and down the breadth of the land this winter. (p. 227)

> *Henry A. Wallace, "Beard: The Planner," in* The New Republic, *Vol. LXXXI, No. 1048, January 2, 1935, pp. 225-27.*

HUBERT HERRING   (essay date 1939)

[*In the following excerpt, Herring closely examines the isolationist policies Beard advocated in his* The Idea of National Interest *and* The Open Door at Home.]

Two volumes which evoked wide dissent are *The Idea of National Interest* and *The Open Door at Home.* . . . These volumes represent Beard's advice to the United States in days when the world seems intent upon suicide. They are variously dismissed as "isolationist," "fantastic," and "craven," while to others they are a sober reading of the times by an astute and devoted lover of America.

Beard quotes Admiral Mahan: ''Self-interest is not only a legitimate, but a fundamental cause for national policy: one which needs no cloak of hypocrisy . . . it is vain to expect governments to act continuously on any other ground than national interest.'' Beard works from that premise. The critics protest. Beard, they say, repudiates all the aspirations of internationalism. But Beard insists that the appeal to ''moral obligation'' by spokesmen for America, far from being a disinterested motive, is chiefly useful for domestic consumption, while foreign offices regard it as dubious, if not hypocritical. Beard finds adequate instance in American history in the arguments for the annexation of Samoa, Hawaii, and the Philippines. America, in a moralizing mood, finds justification for whatever course is deemed to serve its national interest.

Beard troubles the internationalists. He demands that you pick your internationalism with eyes open to motives and ends. If it is a trader's internationalism, then we have the internationalism of Cobden and Bright, the perfect tool of the British manufacturing classes of the middle of the 19th century. If it is industrial or agrarian internationalism intent upon markets— then look at India and Africa. But internationalism without ''economic content . . . is pure sentiment and can furnish no realistic guidance for national policy.'' Such internationalism, insists Beard, ''has failed and must fail to provide measures for bringing great technology into full use, assuring a high and continuous standard of life, and guaranteeing national security.'' Its failure is inevitable ''because it does not correspond to the realities and practices of nations.''

Come to, then, says Beard in effect; let us face the cold realities of international life. The traditional laissez-faire economics have broken down; imperialism as a way to either security or peace is bankrupt; communism offers little promise for, like imperialism, it takes inadequate account of ethical and aesthetic values. Let us search out a system of values rooted in our own American tradition. Let us till our own rich vineyard, for the sake of our own security and stability, and, if you will, for the sake of the example set the world.

Whither then? ''The supreme interest of the United States,'' says Beard, ''is the creation and maintenance of a high standard of life for all its people and ways of industry conducive to the promotion of individual and social virtues within the frame of national security.'' To get it ''there must be the utmost emancipation from dependence upon the course of international exchange.'' ''No prudent family,'' Beard suggests, ''deliberately places any large part of its property and economic concerns in the hands of distant and quarrelsome strangers who periodically set their houses on fire.'' Shall we trade? Yes, with cool caution. We will buy what we need, sell what we can spare. But we will use trade simply for the filling of the gaps in our own larder, not for national profit. The use of trade as a creator of profit inevitably ''thrusts American private interests into the heart of other nations . . . spreads . . . provokes rivalries and conflicts . . . which cannot be defended.'' ''Let us limit our trade in order to increase our security . . . the less trade, the less navy we require . . . the less risks we take.'' ''The security and opulence of the United States can best be attained by the most efficient use of the material endowment of the nation and its technical arts; and, as a corollary, the least possible dependence on foreign imports.''

If we will take this course, then the problem of national defense will be immensely simplified. No longer shall we create an Army and a Navy as ''huckstering and drumming agencies for profitseekers, promoters, and speculators, in the name of 'trade.' '' We shall have a defense machine sufficient to assure ''security of life for the American people in their present geographical home.'' We shall forswear ''aggressive economic and diplomatic actions in distant regions.'' We shall thus make war unlikely. We shall know that the advantages of such war are chimerical; the risks and losses, certain.

Beard hopes for a reordered American economic situation in which there will be ''the greatest possible insulation of internal economy from the disruption of uncontrolled international transactions,'' in which ''national resources shall be used in the development of a high standard of life for the American people.'' Beard, in his *Open Door at Home,* proposes machinery for achieving his ends. He proposes a Foreign Trade Corporation, within the State Department, equipped with ''competent specialists in the physics and chemistry of commodities, in the distribution of the world's resources and industries, and in the present commodity movements of foreign exchange.'' This Corporation, or Authority, will have full power to control exports and imports directly and through license, with suitable checks upon performance. It will decide how much of each commodity we need. It will pick markets in which reciprocal advantages can be obtained. It will decide what and how much we can ship. It may achieve these ends through trade agreements and quotas, or it might conceivably manage the whole affair through readjusted tariff machinery.

''This is nationalism and isolation,'' is the charge most commonly leveled against Charles Beard. But Beard is not afraid of words. He points out that there is nationalism and nationalism. There is a predatory nationalism which devours in the name of its own myths and racial bigotries. There is another nationalism which would file the claws of such predatory forces. This nationalism Beard espouses, a nationalism which merges domestic and foreign policy, and exerts ''positive control over the domestic forces responsible for outward thrusts of power.'' Isolation? Only so far ''as may be necessary to make the most effective use of its own natural resources and technical talents, and offer to the outside world honest goods at a just price in exchange for commodities not efficiently produced at home.''

This policy, Beard contends, does not run counter to ''prudent and generous international collaboration. . . . It attacks the problem at the point where it may be attacked effectively with some prospect of success, namely, within the United States.''

So Beard builds his doctrine. He is not afraid of prophecy, of the projection of faith. He simply sees an America in which opportunity might be realized and hopes redeemed. (pp. 648-50)

> *Hubert Herring, ''Charles A. Beard: Free Lance among the Historians,'' in* Harper's, *Vol. 178, No. 1548, May, 1939, pp. 641-52.*

ALFRED KAZIN (essay date 1942)

[*A highly respected American literary critic, Kazin is best known for his essay collections* The Inmost Leaf *(1955) and* Contemporaries *(1962), and particularly for* On Native Grounds *(1942), a study of American prose writing since the era of William Dean Howells. Having studied the works of ''the critics who were the best writers—from Saint-Beuve and Matthew Arnold to Edmund Wilson and Van Wyck Brooks'' as an aid to his own critical understanding, Kazin has found that ''criticism focussed many— if by no means all—of my own urges as a writer: to show literature as a deed in human history, and to find in each writer the uniqueness of the gift, of the essential vision, through which I hoped to penetrate into the mystery and sacredness of the individual soul.''*

In the following excerpt, Kazin assesses An Economic Interpretation of the Constitution of the United States *as an iconoclastic work which influenced the historical thought of Americans.*]

Like many another contemporary work of realism, ***An Economic Interpretation of the Constitution*** was a "shock" book, an attempt to make up for the naïveté and illusions of the past by dispelling them in a body. Beard had been forced by his reading to admit that the conventional interpretation of the Constitution was a mythological one; and when he discovered that economic motives had been written into the document, he inevitably made too much of them. In Beard's own mind there was no desire to advance the theory of economic determinism as a cause; it was simply an appreciation of one factor in history among other factors, a factor that had never been included by presumably objective historians. Yet it was perhaps only because he was employing economic determinism so empirically that critics were to think him narrow and partisan. As Max Lerner pointed out, Beard seemed to suggest that the Founding Fathers "had stood to gain in immediate and personal economic advantage by the outcome of their work," and the suggestion was certainly unfortunate. Yet though Socialist critics have pointed out that Beard had neglected the *class* and group interests, the general attitude toward property as a contemporary force, Beard had advanced their own theory of the state in so early a work as his 1908 pamphlet on ***Politics***. For it was there that he first, if ever so cautiously, framed the theory that the state is the product of conquest: "It would seem that the real state is not the juristic state but is that group of persons able to work together effectively for the accomplishment of their joint aims, and overcome all opposition to the particular point at issue at a particular time." To say, in 1908, that a nation was an abstraction, that it was only the groups within the state that gave it character, was a prodigious victory of realism— and for its time in America, an extraordinarily audacious one.

It is not strange that Beard's economic interpretation, narrow as it was, had so great an appeal. For the economic interpretation, which at its best gives the historian a new insight and at its worst is mere bigotry and an impediment to thinking, was the highest expression of the Progressive mind. Into it went all the leavings of their nineteenth-century innocence, their brisk dissatisfaction with their own time, their yearning for a simple emancipation, and their fundamental goodness of spirit. Expose evil, the heavens commanded, and it shall vanish; prove the good, and it shall be enacted; we who have stood at Armageddon with T. R., fought the bitter fight with Robert La Follette, and left only Utah and Vermont in the election of 1912 to Big Business, may yet deliver America to virtue. (pp. 153-54)

> Alfred Kazin, *"Progressivism: Some Insurgent Scholars,"* in his On Native Grounds: An Interpretation of Modern American Prose Literature, *Reynal & Hitchcock, 1942, pp. 127-64.*

SIDNEY HOOK (essay date 1943)

[*A distinguished educator and author, Hook has long been one of America's leading philosophers. While studying for his doctorate at Columbia University, he came under the tutorship of the renowned philosopher John Dewey. Influenced by Dewey's philosophy of pragmatism, which conceives of an idea as a preliminary step to the satisfactory resolution or clarification of a problem, Hook applied logical analysis to the social, cultural, and political concerns of modern America. Several of his most important works analyze and define Marxian doctrines that Hook*

subscribed to early in his career. In Towards an Understanding of Karl Marx: A Revolutionary Interpretation *(1933) and* From Hegel to Marx: Studies in the Intellectual Development of Karl Marx *(1936), Hook explained the Marxian views that he believed were essential for Americans to understand. Of these works he states: "The challenge of Marx's ideas to our contemporary social order is so fundamental and pervasive that every intelligent person must now define his attitude towards them." A controversial though respected figure throughout his career, Hook has been described as follows by biographer Paul Kurtz: "Like Jean-Paul Sartre in France and Bertrand Russell in Britain, as heir to John Dewey's mantle in the United States, Hook speaks to the actual conditions of contemporary life; and he has persistently attempted to apply pragmatic intelligence to concrete issues of practical concern. Like Socrates, Hook has been a controversial figure because he has frequently taken unpopular positions, and he has attacked many of the sacred cows of contemporary life. Moreover his brilliant pragmatic intelligence has often devastated the views of some of the leading intellectual figures of our time. . . . Hook has few rivals in his ability to engage in continuing dialogue." In the following excerpt, Hook offers a favorable assessment of Beard's* The Republic: Conversations on Fundamentals. *Much of his discussion focuses on the distinction between a constitutional government and a democratic government, concepts which are addressed in Beard's work.*]

It is not often that a book appears bearing unmistakable signs that it is destined to become a classic in its field. These imaginary dialogues which Charles Beard conducts with lively and intelligent interlocutors constitute such a book. [**"The Republic: Conversations on Fundamentals"**] is a political testament, full of wisdom, set down with patience, buoyed up with a spirit of cheerful skepticism, and marred only by a caution which betrays it into ambiguity on a key point. Above all, it is an inspiring course in the fundamental issues of government and democracy. No intelligent person will find political science dull after reading it, whether he agrees with Beard or not. It should revolutionize the teaching of American government both on the college and the adult-education level.

These conversations are given in twenty-one chapters which begin with an analysis of the opening words of the Preamble to the Constitution, "We, the People," and conclude with "the Fate and Fortunes of Our Republic." As Beard goes from phrase to phrase, from provision to provision in the Constitution, he brings into play a dry humor and common-sense realism which dissolve the mists of rhetoric that usually attend discussions of the Constitution. As exercises in popular semantics these dialogues are excellent.

But let no one who knows the early Beard imagine that he has translated everything into the language of economic determinism. Although he has a sure grip on the economic facts of our day and never loses sight of them, he has traveled a long way from the standpoint of **"An Economic Interpretation of the Constitution,"** whose remarkable and unanswerable findings were forced into too narrow a framework of motivation. Beard recognizes more explicitly than ever before that we cannot simply construe economic motives from economic conditions. Indeed, if anything, he goes to the other extreme and makes of the *Federalist* a kind of philosophical manual of perennial issues in political science without sufficient reference to the economic conditions of the period. He does not deny, of course, that political ideas were originally creatures or servants of interests. But he insists, and rightly, that by molding the outlook, hopes, and language habits of several generations of Americans, ideas enter into the *making* of history and to some extent influence the form and direction taken by present-day interests. History, for Beard, is not a blind working out of economic interests in conflict with each other but "the interplay of *ideas* and *interests* in the time-stream."

Of more topical interest than Beard's ideas on man, history, and causality, which receive only peripheral treatment, are his views on the social and political issues of our time. True to his own theory of why we continually reinterpret the past, Beard's reconstruction of the spirit and meaning of the Constitution is pointed toward a program of action for our own troubled era. On some of these issues, particularly the important problem of the economic underwriting of constitutional democracy, Beard is curiously reticent. He contents himself with exposing inadequacies in the proposals of spokesmen of capital, management, and labor to assure full employment and a rising standard of living for the community. His healthy reminder, here as elsewhere, that we don't know as much as we think we do is a corrective to dogmatism, but it is coupled with an over-caution that suggests that we do not even know enough to make a beginning. (p. 474)

On the home front Beard appears to be an untamed advocate of the New Deal and makes short shrift of those who urge constitutional objections to the policy of government intervention. Very impressive is the way he wrests the Constitution out of the hands of standpatters and reactionaries. He asserts that without altering a line in the document it can become the instrument of the most far-reaching social reforms. But for all his trust in the New Deal, Beard distrusts New Dealers, partly because they lack constitutional understanding and partly because they are subject to the same frailties as other human beings. This reflects not cynicism about human beings but wisdom in the ways of the political world, and awareness that the unintended consequences of what we do are often more fateful than our immediate successes.

An emphasis so marked as to border on a change in political outlook is now apparent in Beard's thought. Constitutional piety is called in as midwife of social reform, and unhistorical reason with its bold logical plans is turned out of doors. Abetted by a little intelligence, constitutional piety guarantees a new birth of freedom and welfare without Caesarean operations. In a sense, Beard has turned Savigny and the historical school inside out. Historical-mindedness is now become an indispensable aid to progressive legislation: arguments and proposals may be "historically true, if utterly unreasonable."

This accent on constitutionalism reaches its climax in Beard's defense of the power of the Supreme Court to declare void any acts of Congress which curtail personal liberties. The abrogation of the veto power of the courts, which ironically enough was a historical usurpation, he deems "undesirable and dangerous." I am in hearty accord with Beard's desire to protect minorities from discriminatory legislation. But to intrust that protection to the Supreme Court seems to me to be demonstrably unreasonable, whether reason is taken as a historical or a logical category. It is a misreading of American history, as Beard's own writings testify, to regard the Supreme Court as a reliable or consistent defender of minority rights and civil liberties. (pp. 474-75)

Charles Beard's position on this and related matters seems to me to grow out of his cloudy distinction between a constitutional government and a democratic one. The latter is defined simply in terms of majority rule; the former is one which limits the power both of officials and majorities by guaranteeing the human rights of individuals. Since rule by majority may be oppressive and degenerate into an elective despotism, democ-

racy is distinguished from constitutional government. In the light of these definitions Beard considers the United States a constitutional rather than democratic republic. A second glance at these definitions will show that they are inadequate for the case in hand. Beard himself admits that in the United States rights of persons and property may be—and have been—destroyed by amendment. True, this requires, as he points out, an "extraordinary" majority. But what is sacred about 75 per cent or 99 per cent? (p. 475)

Morally, rule by majority, ordinary or extraordinary, a minority, a Supreme Court, a despot may be benevolent or malevolent. Our choice between them is based upon the quality of their fruits, of which welfare is only one. All that Beard seems to me to want to say is this: fruits that are forced or plucked too hastily are likely to be bitter; a wise democracy is one in which the majority lays down rules for itself to proceed cautiously. As a rule caution is a good rule. But sometimes a democracy must act quickly and boldly, as none knows better than Beard, the historian. To repent at leisure one must at least survive!

Granted, then, that on a particular occasion democracy may trench upon certain claims and desires that are precious to us. We cannot therefore impugn the validity of the democratic process unless we are prepared to defend the doctrine of absolute natural rights or the principle of aristocratic rule. Beard, happily, is prepared to do neither one nor the other. "If for decency, progress, order, and liberty in the community and the nation, we cannot rely upon the character, sentiments, allegiances, and moral habits of the people, upon what, in heaven's name, can we rely?" Well said! But here speaks the democrat, not the pious constitutionalist who in the course of history has answered: the king, the church, the nobility, the party, the Supreme Court. The majority may be foolish and wicked, but if a democracy be defined and practiced in terms of *freely given consent*, the wise and virtuous minority has at least a talking chance before it decides to yield out of prudence or fight out of principle.

Charles Beard is a great American democrat. It would be a pity if his words were twisted to make him appear a Hamiltonian *pur sang*. (pp. 475-76)

> Sidney Hook, "Charles Beard's Political Testament," in The Nation, *Vol. 157, No. 17, October 23, 1943, pp. 474-76.*

ARTHUR M. SCHLESINGER, JR. (essay date 1946)

[*Schlesinger is a prominent American historian and leading intellectual figure whose historical and political studies have won him both critical and popular acclaim. An influential figure in liberal politics, he served as a special assistant to Presidents John F. Kennedy and Lyndon Johnson. During this time he was instrumental in formulating the "New Frontier" and the "Great Society," the two major social reform movements of the 1960s, which promoted Medicare, the war on poverty, and extensive civil rights legislation. The author of numerous articles, essays, and books, Schlesinger has twice been the recipient of the Pulitzer Prize: the first for* The Age of Jackson *(1945), a provocative examination of Jacksonian democracy as the genesis of American liberalism, and the second for* A Thousand Days: John F. Kennedy in the White House *(1965), a revealing overview of the Kennedy administration. In addition, Schlesinger is considered one of the foremost scholars of Franklin D. Roosevelt's New Deal policies. In his three volume study* The Age of Roosevelt, *which consists of* The Crisis of the Old Order, 1919-1933 *(1957),* The Coming of the New Deal *(1959), and* The Politics of Upheaval *(1960),*

The title of Dr. Beard's new book [*American Foreign Policy in the Making, 1932-1940: A Study in Responsibilities*] is misleading if it makes anyone expect an account of the forces shaping United States foreign policy between 1932 and 1940. The preface tries to put it more precisely: "This volume deals with public statements of foreign policy (1932-1940), not with pronouncements on international morality, or with secret negotiations, offers, and promises in foreign affairs." But this is misleading, too. Broad sections of United States foreign policy, such as the Good Neighbor policy, are hardly mentioned.

The book really is an examination of "the thesis that locates in the United States the responsibility for the policy that eventuated in World War II"—a thesis whose sources are never very systematically investigated but which, Beard implies, was invented and disseminated by persons favoring an internationalist policy. The first two chapters, appraising this hypothesis with respect to the League of Nations, question whether either a small bloc of Senators or the American people as a whole brought about a second world war by refusing to follow through on Wilson's plan for world peace. Beard then sets out to "test the validity of the thesis of popular responsibility" as it has been applied to the period from 1933 to 1940.

The internationalist thesis, he writes, has created the picture of public opinion during the Roosevelt administration insisting on a policy of isolationism, of Roosevelt and Hull endeavoring to put over an internationalist policy, and of public opinion, misled by the isolationists, sabotaging that effort. The isolationists, according to the thesis, lulled the country into a false sense of security and so "must bear the responsibility for the progress of aggressors in Europe and Asia which finally and inevitably 'drew' the United States into the war in spite of President Roosevelt's warnings and his efforts to maintain peace."

This general problem is set forth in the third chapter, "Problems Posed by Charges of War Guilt," which is billed in the preface as describing the "nature and limitations of this work." The remaining seven chapters consist of a straightforward compilation of public statements by Roosevelt bearing upon the large general issues of internationalism and isolationism. The last chapter recites the peace promises made by Roosevelt and Willkie in the 1940 campaign and, without further philosophy or morals, the book comes to an abrupt end.

In terms of its ostensible historical purpose, the book is surely weak. What does Beard mean by foreign policy? He says in his most explicit statement, "Policy is a definite design which has meaning in the concrete terms of the actions necessarily signified and conveys to common understanding the practical purport of the language used in expressing it." If this means what, after due meditation, I think it means, Beard tends to regard foreign policy as essentially a matter of words and not of operations. Now any serious historian, or experienced politician, knows that public statements bear the same relation to

foreign policy that the visible part of an iceberg bears to its concealed bulk. This is not the result of the special iniquity of the Roosevelt administration; it is true of all governments anywhere. The thing that matters in foreign relations is what governments do, not what they say. An examination of "foreign policy in the making" which confines itself to citations of public record is drastically inadequate. The thesis Beard sets up for attack simply cannot be tested by such a limited range of materials.

A second point—equally familiar to the serious historian and the experienced politician—is that foreign policy is not made in a vacuum, and that the policy maker in his public pronouncements does not have quite the same freedom as the scholar in the library. This condition also existed before Roosevelt became president or Willkie became candidate and, though disappointing to idealists, it can hardly be ascribed to any specific internationalist depravity.

These defects in method impair the value of Dr. Beard's book as historical inquiry. They are points, moreover, on which no one can presume the need of instructing Dr. Beard; and the question inevitably arises whether the book should be considered as historical inquiry. What, after all, is Beard arguing? That Roosevelt's foreign policy was often confused, impulsive, disingenuous? That official rhetoric in a democracy often turns out to be "campaign oratory"? What serious student would dispute these things? (p. 244)

Since no one in the trade has argued more eloquently than Dr. Beard that objective history is impossible, we may assume that the factual manner of this work is not to be taken too seriously. Indeed, Beard, the philosopher of history, would require us to search skeptically for the premises and conclusions of Beard, the historian. Occasionally in this book the deadpan slips, and we catch a glimpse of the author's own convictions, as when he points out that in 1934 "I came to the conclusion that the Roosevelt administration would eventually involve the United States in a war with Japan" (which is, I suppose, one way of describing Pearl Harbor). But throughout most of the book the air of objectivity is bravely sustained. (pp. 244-45)

Beard's subtitle for his new book is "A Study in Responsibilities." Among other responsibilities he might have considered are those about which he has written powerfully elsewhere—the responsibilities of the historian to acknowledge his basic presuppositions. (This is not to speak of the responsibility of a great and deservedly influential scholar to the many persons, particularly college students, who were affected by his pre-war isolationism.) Are we to infer from "American Foreign Policy in the Making" that Beard sticks by his isolationism? That he seriously believes in 1946 that the maintenance of strict neutrality in 1940 "would favor, not hinder, the coming of peace"? That he still regrets the passage of the lend-lease bill? On this type of question, which Beard has elsewhere taught us is the fundamental type of question to ask when reading historians, his new book is silent and evasive. An obligation attached to his isolationist activity in 1941, one would think, would be to cast the balance of the competing policies today, instead of writing a book which hides Beard the publicist's own beliefs and seeks instead to discredit his opponent by convicting him of sins which Beard the historian knows to be largely irrelevant. (p. 245)

Arthur M. Schlesinger, Jr., "A Historian's Politics," in The Nation, *Vol. 163, No. 9, August 31, 1946, pp. 244-45.*

LEWIS MUMFORD   (letter date 1947)

[*Mumford is an American sociologist, historian, philosopher, and author whose primary interest is the relationship between the modern individual and his or her environment. Influenced by the works of Patrick Geddes, a Scottish sociologist and pioneer in the field of city planning, Mumford has worked extensively in the area of city and regional planning, and has contributed several important studies of cities, including* The Culture of Cities *(1938),* City Development *(1945), and* The City in History *(1961). All of these works examine the interrelationship between cities and civilization over the centuries. Also indicative of much of his work is Mumford's concern with firm moral values to assure the growth of civilization. Writing for* The Saturday Evening Post, *Mumford noted that: "The test of maturity, for nations as well as for individuals is not the increase of power, but the increase of self-understanding, self-control, self-direction, and self-transcendence. For in a mature society, man himself, not his machines or his organizations, is the chief work of art." In the following excerpt, Mumford bitterly relates to Van Wyck Brooks his disapproval of Beard's selection to receive the National Institute of Arts and Letters's medal of distinction; as chairman of the Institute, Brooks had approved of Beard's selection and thus enraged his longtime friend. Robert E. Spiller, editor of* The Van Wyck Brooks/Lewis Mumford Letters: The Record of a Literary Friendship 1921-63, *explains Mumford's reaction this way: "Mumford protested the award on the grounds that Beard's isolationist position was 'poisonous' and that he was an unethical scholar in that he was willing to warp historical evidence to support it. Brooks's defense that he was acting for the committee rather than for himself and that he had not read Beard's recent work did not deter Mumford's resignation from the Institute."*]

I have indeed said that [Beard] was lacking in scholarly integrity, for in *America in Mid-Passage* and in the Basic History he pretends to describe objectively America's relation to the fascist attack without for a moment describing fascism's aims or suggesting that the civilized world was placed in jeopardy by those aims: it is the democratic governments upon which Beard vents his spleen, and in the Basic History he goes so far as to impute our participation in the war mainly to Roosevelt. His sins in these books are very easy to annotate from the standpoint of common judgment and exact scholarship: but they are mostly sins of supression and omission, and it would be difficult, except under the cover of a book review, to point out the dishonesty of Beard's practices here without opening oneself to a suit for libel it might be impossible, on purely legal grounds, to win. Beard's errors are not of the gross and flagrant kind; but the tendency of his writing during the last seventeen years is unmistakable. Without being either a traitor or a fascist himself, Beard has served the purposes of traitors and fascists, by his manner of presenting and warping the evidence, in supposedly objective works on American history. More outright enemies of the anti-fascist cause, people like Ezra Pound or Knut Hamsun, are much less dangerous than Beard; for they openly believed in fascism, while Beard's method was to give it the utmost benefit of the doubt whilst he insidiously attacked from the rear all who were prepared—and they were and *still are* a pitiful few—to resist fascism. In this Beard was not alone: he had the company of still another old friend of mine, equally venerable, equally identified with the democratic cause, Frank Lloyd Wright; and both of them had the sympathy and support of millions of complacent and unawakened people who never took the trouble to examine what they were doing. Did not the Basic History go into the list of books that went overseas to our soldiers? Grotesquely enough, it did; and so, too, in the midst of the war the Institute welcomed to its membership with equal blandness and affability, Frank Lloyd Wright. (pp. 323-24)

Beard's isolationism is not a trivial matter in times like these, when everything man holds dear depends on our overcoming tribalism and isolation and creating an actively cooperative world society: at this moment in world history his attitude should be something more meaningful to you than merely "unsympathetic," as if it were a taste for a curious native dish. A man of Beard's intellectual stature should not announce himself an isolationist without making every other decent man who hears him denounce him as a betrayer of humanity. Instead, you help to give him further honor and acclaim. (p. 326)

> *Lewis Mumford, in a letter to Van Wyck Brooks on December 3, 1947, in* The Van Wyck Brooks-Lewis Mumford Letters: The Record of a Literary Friendship, 1921-1963, *edited by Robert E. Spiller, E. P. Dutton & Co., Inc., 1970, pp. 323-27.*

MAX LERNER   (essay date 1948)

[*Lerner is a political scientist, educator, author, and nationally syndicated columnist. His career as a social commentator began in 1927 as an editor for the* Encyclopedia of Social Sciences; *from 1936 to 1939 he served as editor of* The Nation; *and since 1949 he has worked as a columnist for the* New York Post. *Throughout his career, Lerner has also interspersed academic work with his writing. Of his political philosophy, he states: "My political convictions are on the left, although I belong to no party. I feel that my energies must lie with the movement toward a democratic socialism." Lerner's numerous works include the popular* It Is Later Than You Think *(1938), a study of contemporary politics, and what he considers his most ambitious work,* America As a Civilization: Life and Thought in the United States Today *(1957). In the following excerpt Lerner surveys Beard's political thinking, maintaining that "his real stature as historian came from his being a satirist."*]

Charles A. Beard died, as he lived, in the thick of an intellectual storm occasioned by his books. His last two works were rather weird affairs, which accused President Roosevelt of starting World War II and being responsible for Pearl Harbor, and they have brought the liberal brickbats down on him. His early books, some thirty-five years ago, portrayed the Founding Fathers as framing the Constitution in the image of their own economic advantage, and for years Beard was an antichrist to the tories. Here obviously was a man of violent contrasts and explosive energies.

I think Beard tussled with demons most of his life—demons within himself but also within the twisted coils of American doctrine and passion. It is hard to be a good novelist, or a good critic, or a good social commentator and theorist when you are torn in every direction by the storm of American life. It is just as hard to be a good historian, for the supposedly dead past refuses to bury its dead, and the historian finds the choice between ghosts as turbulent as that between the living. (p. 20)

He regarded most of the winds of doctrine as merely windy, yet he was himself swept by more of them than he recognized. Indiana-born and Indiana-educated, he never came wholly to accept the intellectuals of the Eastern seaboard and they never wholly accepted him. Like that of his fellow Indianian, Theodore Dreiser, much of his career became a rebellion against the smugly held idealisms and pretensions of the American tradition. He applied to history a good deal of the savage naturalistic scrutiny that Dreiser applied to business and love and morals.

He was a great historian—one of the greatest we have had in the field of American history—mainly because he was more than a historian. He was a political theorist, and a dabbler in philosophy. But his real stature as historian came from his being a satirist; that is what gives strength, bite and pungency to his work. I had suspected this from my memory of individual books, but in reviewing his work as a whole the impression becomes cumulative and overwhelming. The satirist, from Juvenal to Thorstein Veblen, is a stripper. He strips away the veneer to show the grain, strips off the garments to show the body, tears off the mask to show the face. Beard was dedicated to stripping away the moralizing and the rhetoric in the history of ideas and of American social and political movements, and laying bare the operative realities however unlovely they might seem to moralistic eyes and rhetorical ears. This it was which gave his writing that combination of ironic detachment and impassioned caring that only a satirist achieves.

He wrote in the field of American history, but in any area Beard's great themes would have dealt with this gap between rhetoric and logic, and the problem of appearance and reality. He was always on the watch for whatever had not been stipulated in the bond, or "in the premises," as he used to say in a mocking imitation of legal language. Since American history had been viewed by most writers as the achievement of noble-minded patriots, he delighted to show that it had actually been shaped largely by the clash of economic interests, and that the noble-minded patriots cared as much about their pocketbooks as any others. In the field where the clashes seemed mainly between rival statesmen, parties and sections, he delighted to show that the real struggles were between economic groups and classes; and that out of these struggles came parties, platforms and wars. Even wars, Beard showed (witness not only the War of Independence, but also that of 1812 and the Civil War), were not in essence wars: one was the thrust of an agricultural imperialism, the other a revolution.

Thus things were never what they seemed, and the skimmed milk of struggle and greed often masqueraded as the cream of moral unction. And thus also the famous Beardian "economic interpretation," which for a while caused so great a pother, is seen as only a sub-category of Beard's much broader categories of appearance and reality. This was true, of course, of the much greater satirical mind with whom Beard did not like to be associated—Karl Marx. The Marxian method of stripping "ideologies" bare to reveal class interest and class struggle, was also part of an effort to turn appearances topsy-turvy.

But where Marx was anchored to a revolutionary strategy, Beard had no anchorage, and in the stormy voyage of his writing life there are bewildering twists and turns—even on the crucial question of economic interpretation. (pp. 20-1)

For most American radicals Beard's great phase was his first. It included *An Economic Interpretation of the Constitution* . . . and its companion volume, *Economic Origins of Jeffersonian Democracy.* . . . In this phase, Beard roared like a young lion in his Columbia classroom; in it his Jeffersonian and Populist convictions emerged most clearly in writing and teaching; in it he was belabored by the New York *Times* editorialists as a menace to American institutions, and himself carried on an epic feud with President Butler of Columbia; in it he was attacked with concentrated fury by bar and bench, by the rich laity and its servile clergy; in it he wrote ardent interventionist articles against the German tyranny, yet when several anti-war professors were fired by Columbia, Beard resigned in scathing protest. In this period Beard fought for teachers' tenure, argued for a teachers' union. (p. 21)

Beard later claimed he was misunderstood by both Right and Left. No doubt he was: every thinker is. His actual thesis in the two books was stated with great concreteness—that the men who framed the Constitution and led the fight for its ratification were the men of property, who had not only a group interest but direct personal financial motives in getting a strong government which would protect their "personality" holdings against economic collapse and democratic assault; that roughly the same group of men formed the Federalist Party, ran the new government, put through the funding measures, redeemed the (often speculatively acquired) government securities at face value, and protected the shipping and manufacturing interests. He held that the land-and-farmer interests and the propertyless men, who had fought ratification, were the men who formed the core of Jeffersonian democracy and its party. This was the thesis, and Beard drove it home with spikes of documentation.

I have had . . . a minor quarrel with the way he handled his thesis [see Additional Bibliography]. I think he proved more than he had to. A more subtle economic theory of history would stress not the personal economic motives (where do you ever get them that naked?) but the class and group interests which create the powerful psychological stereotypes that are the real compulsion. Writing about a single historical episode, the framing and ratification of the Constitution, Beard found himself using a theory of human action which would have to be modified when he came to deal with the longer sweep of history and the dynamic of social change. In *Jeffersonian Democracy,* he handled this broader theme more flexibly, and his studies of the political ideas of John Adams and of John Taylor are as integral to the analysis as his chapter on "Security-Holding and Politics."

Thus in what is in effect a single two-volume work, using as an instrument of analysis a "theory of economic determinism" which, as he put it, "has not been tried out in American history" and therefore "until it is tried out . . . cannot be found wanting," Beard drove a hard economic logic through the flabby traditional rhetoric on the founding of the American Republic, and through the economic and diplomatic policies and the party battles of the first generation of the Republic. This work gave a clear intellectual clue to the forces at work in American history, and did it so well that it stayed done. No one has been able to undo it.

Not even Beard himself. For it was a sad fact that instead of leaving his early work to speak for itself, Beard kept whittling its meaning down, and explaining and reëxplaining it until he all but explained it away. He was, of course, right in saying he had borrowed far more from Madison, and even from conservatives like Marshall and Webster, than from Marxism. I am talking not of what he said about his intellectual sources, but what he said about his main intent. He insisted he had only meant to "redress the balance" as against the pietistic historians; that his economic determinism was not a considered and rounded view, not "the" interpretation but "an" interpretation—a highly necessary scholarly finger-exercise; and finally that he had meant only to bring the economic emphasis back, and prove how impossible it was to leave economic pressures out of history. It is difficult to take seriously Beard's protestations that he had not meant his books seriously. Despite his efforts to purge himself, and extirpate the Old Bolshevik in himself, the early books and their thesis stand out as part of the great heritage of American realistic thought.

Yet one cannot help feeling that Beard was never wholly at home in the field of economic determinism. As a historian-craftsman, using the economic emphasis as one of the tools of his craft (as he did in the *Rise*), he was superb. As a philosopher of history, seeking to give explicitly the theoretical meaning of the tool, he was often fuzzy. This is true even of his best theoretical book, *The Economic Basis of Politics*. . . . In it he restates Madison's thesis (in the famous No. 10 "Federalist Paper") that parties and party struggles are based on "the various and unequal distribution of property." He makes this, now a theory of economic status underlying political representation (as in the French Estates), now a theory of economic pressure groups, as in the American Congress; at one point he flirts with the then current "pluralistic" theory that the economic associations are as important as the state, and even with the idea of group representation in Parliament.

Obviously Beard was groping. Starting with a theory of direct economic motives he reconsidered it and formulated a looser theory of economic property interests as the basis of politics. He then reconsidered it again, and broadened it into a still looser theory of industrial skills and technology as the basis of political conflict. Grappling with the problems of the continued political cleavage in Russia after the Revolution, he tried to explain it by saying that "a great society, whether capitalistic or communist, must possess different kinds and grades of skill and talent"; that even a revolutionary government "must assume all the complex and staggering burdens of management and exchange"; and that "as efficient production depends to a great extent upon skill, skill itself is a form of property even if property in capital is abolished." But this effort to assimilate the commissar to the capitalist, and crowd the Leninist factional struggles into Madison's formula of unequal property distribution as the basis for faction, was scarcely successful. Beard had moved over from property to technology, from wealth to state-trust management, from the cash dividend to the social dividend. Only in a chapter added to the book in 1945 did he show signs of understanding that new explanations had to be found for power struggles under dictatorship.

I have traced these successive shifts not in a carping spirit, but to show that—with all his wide reading, his academic training, his sharp mind—Beard floundered about as a theorist. I suspect it was because he depended too much on Madison's core insight, which had been undeveloped; and on his own vague sense that the key for unlocking history and politics must be found somehow in economics, but that you must avoid Marx's error and flee a "system" like the very Devil. In his efforts to avoid a system he also avoided a theory. The result was not hard to predict. In 1936 Beard wrote a book, *The Discussion of Human Affairs,* to prove that history was all terribly complex, and no factor could be omitted. It took him almost a quarter-century, but he managed to move from a theory of economic determinism all the way over to the easy and amorphous theory of "multiple causation."

To turn from this into the pages of *The Rise of American Civilization* is to move from murkiness into the clear light of a crisp day. A writer, if he is lucky, will manage to tackle his biggest theme when he is at the fullness of his creative powers. Beard's big theme was the whole history of American civilization, from the first colonial settlements to the flush times of the 1920's. (pp. 21-2)

Freed from academic ties, he wrote with sweep, with a bold, superb structure, without heavy documentation, without a footnote or a bibliographical item. His earlier books had been attacked but not read; these volumes were bought, read, and acclaimed widely. And no wonder. People sensed that this was no dry-as-dust historian who retailed only what Ph.D.'s thought about history, but a man of craggy purposes who was attempting a history of grand proportions in an age of piddling writers and complacent thinkers. But they also sensed that he was not just a "popular" or "literary" historian as Bancroft or John Fiske had been. He wrote well, to be sure; there were flashing phrases, and the sentences—even the cumbersome and majestic ones—had a cutting edge. But they assumed that the reader was a mature person, that he could be trusted not to flinch from the realities of economic power struggles, that he did not have to be shielded from the facts of life. The *Rise* clinched Beard's position as the leader of the "new history" school of economic emphasis and cultural sweep.

I think it is fair to say that Beard's *Rise* permeated downward and outward; it affected professional historians, students, laymen; it left its imprint on a whole generation. The orthodox might rage that this heathen had been permitted to penetrate into the arcana of the historical temple, but the fact was that Beard was no longer an outsider, and some of his former heresies (diluted, of course) were close to establishing new orthodoxies. (pp. 22-3)

> Max Lerner, "*Charles Beard's Stormy Voyage,*" in
> The New Republic, *Vol. 119, No. 17, October 25,
> 1948, pp. 20-3.*

HENRY STEELE COMMAGER   (essay date 1950)

[*An American historian and educator, Commager is the author of several popular historical works which, according to Lawrence Wells Cobb, have allowed "scholars and lay readers both to 'get at' the sources of the American historical record and to understand their heritage more fully." Among his important works are* The Growth of the American Republic *(1930), which he coauthored with Samuel Eliot Morison and which long served as a college history textbook, and* Our Nation *(1941), a popular and instructive textbook used in high-school history classes throughout the United States. In addition, Commager's* Documents of American History *(1934) is regarded as one of the most valuable reference books of its kind. The work, which has had several editions, contains over six hundred documents illustrating the course of American history from the age of discovery to the present. In the following excerpt, Commager discusses Beard's contribution to and influence on the study of history.*]

The fame and influence of Charles A. Beard rest, in no inconsiderable part, upon the very volume of his writings. His industry was prodigious, his curiosity insatiable, and the range of his interests was wider than that of any other major American historian except Henry Adams. Textbooks, from the most elementary to the most sophisticated, popular and semipopular histories, collections of readings and editorial surveys of society and culture, monographs on politics, administration, economics, and foreign policy, studies in English and European as well as in American history, a steady stream of articles, letters, communications, documents, and committee reports flowed from his facile pen. He was ubiquitous and he seemed omniscient; he ranged, almost blithely, from dry investigations of municipal administration to ventures in philosophy. He was not only historian but commentator and critic, an objective— if he would let us use the word—recorder of the past, a vigorous participant in the present, a pamphleteer and polemicist, a veritable Voltaire let loose in the complex world of the twentieth century, with something of Voltaire's wit, irony, and philosophy, and something, too, of his passion.

The most philosophical of modern American historians, Beard never formulated a philosophy of history unless it was—in the end—the negative conclusion that no philosophy of history could be formulated. Probing mercilessly beneath the surface appearance to underlying realities, searching tirelessly for the meaning to be found in apparently casual manifestations, he repudiated the possibility of ascertaining true reality or ultimate meaning. Zealous to fix the role of economics in history and largely responsible for the widespread acceptance of economic determinism by younger scholars, he was himself the foe of any form of determinism. Rejecting contemptuously the "devil theory" of history and persistently warning against the application of the moral standards of the present to the events of the past, his findings provided ammunition for those who saw conspiracy and even deviltry in the making of the Constitution, the fabrication of the Fourteenth Amendment, and American participation in World War II. The most cosmopolitan of scholars, versed in European as in American history, at home in philosophy, law, economics, sociology, and literature, he became the intellectual leader of the isolationists and consorted with those whose views were bound by the Atlantic and the Pacific and whose sympathies were narrow and provincial.

"Any selection and arrangement of facts," said Beard, in his presidential address to the American Historical Association, "pertaining to any large area of history, either local or world, race or class, is controlled inexorably by the frame of reference in the mind of the selector and arranger." His own frame of reference changed, but originally it would seem to have been the Progressive movement, with its insistence upon the economic bases of politics, its attack upon privilege, its passion for reform. (pp. 303-04)

That he was by no means the first in the field is irrelevant; he was assuredly the most influential. Over a decade before the appearance of *An Economic Interpretation of the Constitution,* Beard's colleague, E. R. A. Seligman, had announced that "to economic causes . . . must be traced in last instance those transformations in the structure of society which themselves condition the relation of the social classes and the various manifestations of social life," and six years later Parrington's friend, J. Allen Smith, had described the Constitution as a mechanism calculated to frustrate democracy. Beard's carefully documented analysis had two signal advantages over previous economic interpretations: its method and its timing. It was not so much a polemic as a case study, and a generation more susceptible to scientific evidence than to argument found it all but irresistible. It appeared just as the Progressive movement reached its climax, suggested that the technique of the Pujo Committee was as relevant to the eighteenth as to the twentieth century, and seemed to give historical perspective to the assaults of Roosevelt and Wilson upon privilege and exploitation. As Justice Holmes said of John Marshall, it was "a strategic point in the campaign of history," and part of its greatness consisted "in being there."

It is irrelevant to inquire here into the validity of the *Economic Interpretation of the Constitution* or the *Economic Origins of Jeffersonian Democracy,* Beard's earliest important books and, in many ways, his best. If these interpretations were open to criticism, it was not so much because they assigned to economics a decisive place in history as because they excluded history from a controlling place in economics. They were more concerned with cause than consequence. They might be accepted as definitive but could not be regarded as conclusive, for economic motivation was not a conclusion but a point of departure. What was primarily important was not, after all, the motivation of the men who made the Constitution and formulated the policies of Jeffersonian democracy but the consequences of their work. The search for the recondite led, as it so often does, to the neglect of the obvious, and a generation familiar with the economic influences at work in the Federal Convention was inclined to ignore the fact that the Convention had created a Federal Constitution.

Beard himself was subsequently to moderate his historical materialism and to emphasize pluralism in historical causation, and his advance to moderation and qualification can be read even in the magisterial *Rise of American Civilization.* Meantime the doctrines which he had preached were accepted as gospel by enthusiastic disciples, and for a time almost every student who hoped to share the spoils of history enlisted under his banner. There was nothing disloyal about this: the new loyalty did not require any betrayal of older faiths. (pp. 305-07)

Beard's animus was, to be sure, patriotic and devout rather than censorious: it was because he believed the United States to be the best of all countries and the Americans the most virtuous of peoples that he was so impatient with imperfections. He was, in fact, dissembling his love, even as he kicked his historical characters down the stairs. But this was not always clear. Many readers came from his books with the impression that at last the veil of illusion had been torn aside and they were privileged to look at history divested of its heroics, and heroes of their halos. An age which itself made no great plans found malign satisfaction in the invariable miscarriage of the great plans of the past; an age eager to tear the stuffing out of all shirts was delighted to find that the emperors of the past had no clothes. To his students and disciples, Beard communicated something of his own passionate concern for such truth as could be recovered from the ruins of history. But in those who knew him only through his writings, he encouraged an attitude of iconoclasm and, often, of cynicism.

As Beard grew older, he became fascinated by the metaphysics and epistemology of history. Although no other historian of his time had submitted more facts to an avid public or done more to fix in its mind a pattern of the past, he became, in the thirties, weighed down with the consciousness of the illusiveness of all facts and the subjectivity of all patterns. If he did not, like Henry Adams, repudiate his own handiwork, he did repudiate its controlling formula and, indeed, the propriety of all formulas. Written history, he concluded, was not a science but an "act of faith"; the historian could not know the past; he could only reconstruct such fragments of it as were fortuitously available to him according to some incoherent plan which reflected the inescapable limitations of his own mind. (pp. 307-08)

The real objection to Beard's historism was not that it repudiated certainty but that it was sterile and, in a literal sense, inconsequential. The doctrine of subjectivity and uncertainty, like the doctrine of economic motivation, was not a conclusion but a point of departure, and everything depended on the route and the destination. That history was subjective, fragmentary, and inconclusive—like lamost everything in life—would be readily acknowledged, but if history were to be written at all it was necessary to go on from there. And no more than Henry Adams did Beard appear able to go on and make his philosophy a constructive instrument. Most of those who conned Beard's own writings in the decade of the forties were inclined to feel that the demonstration of the subjectivity of history could be carried too far and that Beard had in fact carried it too far. (p. 309)

Henry Steele Commager, "Innovators in Historical Interpretation: Turner, Parrington, Beard," in his The American Mind: An Interpretation of American Thought and Character since the 1880's, Yale University Press, 1950, pp. 293-309.*

HUGO L. BLACK   (essay date 1954)

[*Black was a justice of the United States Supreme Court from the time of his appointment by Franklin D. Roosevelt in 1937 until his retirement in 1971. A firm supporter of Roosevelt's New Deal policies, he was an influential member of the court's "liberal bloc" who later became known for his unwavering defense of the Bill of Rights. Black believed that the Bill of Rights unequivocally guaranteed the personal rights of individuals over government interests and that this document was to be interpreted literally. With this judicial philosophy, he was instrumental in convincing the Supreme Court that the amendments to the Constitution applied to state as well as federal government and thus insured greater civil liberties to all Americans. In the following excerpt, Black praises* The Rise of American Civilization. *For other discussions of this work, see the excerpts by Carl Van Doren (1927) and Edmund Wilson (1932).*]

Many years ago I read *The Rise of American Civilization,* written by Dr. Beard and his wife. The experience was exhilarating. Here the early history of our country became a moving and fascinating story, as easy to read as a fine novel. Instead of repeating popular myths about early Americans, Dr. Beard brought them down to earth and made them walk and act like men, giving new greatness to their achievements. He showed how our institutions grew out of the ideals and everyday experiences of the people, thus providing stronger support for our national faith in liberty and justice for all. That passionate faith was a constant theme in all the books and articles Dr. Beard wrote.

Hugo L. Black, in a foreword to Charles A. Beard: An Appraisal," edited by Howard K. Beale, University of Kentucky Press, 1954, p. xi.

HAROLD J. LASKI   (essay date 1954)

[*A controversial figure with strongly held Marxian views, Laski was a noted English political scientist and author who, as a popular lecturer and teacher, maintained a large following of students throughout his career. In addition, he was an outspoken and active participant in the British Labour Party, advocating labor reforms that were in line with his socialist thought. While lecturing at several universities in the United States, he became an astute observer of the American social and political scene, as reflected in his works* The American Presidency *(1940),* American Democracy *(1948), and* Reflections on the Constitution *(1951). In an assessment of Laski, Edmund Wilson stated that he was "not only a well-equipped scholar and an able political thinker but a fighter for unpopular ideals whose career as a whole is an example of singularly disinterested devotion." In the following excerpt, Laski provides an overview of Beard's thinking from an English perspective.*]

Beard's *An Economic Interpretation of the Constitution of the United States* . . . and its sequel, the *Economic Origins of Jeffersonian Democracy* . . . , were, from the standpoint of research, books that laid the foundation of a new and creative approach to the subjects with which they dealt. But even more important than the brilliant use of the material that went into

their making was the value of the solid foundation they offered to the criticism of those who sought to see American history in realistic terms. Apart from the maintenance of order, Beard pointed out, "the making of the rules which determine the property relations of members of society" is always the central objective of government. A ruling class, therefore, "whose rights are thus to be determined must perforce obtain from the government such rules as are consonant with the larger interests necessary to the continuance of their economic processes, or they must themselves control the organs of government." Beard showed that the Constitution of 1787 owed its character to those who, with money or public securities in their hands, as manufacturers and traders, or as the shipping interest, were gravely threatened by the chaotic insecurity that developed under the Articles of Confederation. He argued that the men of Philadelphia produced "an economic document based upon the concept that the fundamental private rights of property are anterior to government, and morally beyond the reach of popular majorities." He showed that Jeffersonian democracy was not the outcome of a reasoned debate for and against certain abstract principles of freedom, but "a conflict . . . chiefly between the capitalistic and agrarian classes." "Jeffersonian democracy simply meant the possession of the federal government by the agrarian masses led by an aristocracy of slave-owning planters, and the theoretical repudiation of the right to use the Government for the benefit of any capitalistic groups, fiscal, banking or manufacturing."

These two remarkable works are, as it were, the prelude to the great *Rise of American Civilization,* in which Charles Beard, with his wife, wrote what is certainly one of the half dozen most effective general narratives of a people's history that any nation possesses—a narrative the more valuable in that it was not merely abreast of modern scholarship, but contained, as in its treatment, for example, of the Civil War, new conceptions and ideas as valuable in their suggestiveness to the specialist as to the general reader. What is significant in this historical work is Beard's power to penetrate behind the rationalisations by which men seek to defend their interests, and to make plain the inner essence of the purpose they sought to serve. It is quite unjust to regard this analysis as "materialistic" or to insist that it is intended as a neosocialist attack on American institutions, still less to argue that it seeks to dethrone the great heroes and the great legends of American history. Its value lies, first, in its realism, and, second, in its power to show that behind the mask the great statesman, the great judge, the great business pioneer, is forced to wear in public, there operate the same impulses as in the men and women he influences. More than that. It rescues American history for scientific exploration. It permits us to see how men have to co-operate with their environment in order to master it; it enables us to recognise what it is in their character and experience that makes them willing to effect this co-operation or to refuse to seize their moment when it arrives. The American Constitution, as Charles Beard has analysed it, may be stripped of the false gilt with which men like James M. Beck, in the field of legal rhetoric, or Calvin Coolidge in the political, sought to disguise it. Yet, under Beard's handling, it had the merit of becoming an actual constitution the dynamics of which, at least, emerge intelligible. (pp. 12-14)

The value of Beard's method is the important fact that we see how the play was written as well as what was involved in putting it upon the stage. So, also, with his work in the field of government. It is less an attempt to grapple with the fundamental problems of political philosophy than it is an effort, first, to show how American institutions really work, and, second, so to criticise their working that an indication is given of ways of suitable change. *American Government and Politics*—still, it may be suggested, the best descriptive account of American government and politics in operation—and the *American Leviathan* (written in conjunction with his son, William Beard), with *The Republic,* that interesting combination of major insight with minor, though significant, blindness, together represent an impressive attempt to explain the dynamic of American institutions. Their quality comes from two things: (1) They are written by a man who has tried to see from within the interrelation between men and institutions. (2) They are also the outcome of a mind that is almost restlessly seeking the ways and means whereby government can aid the ordinary man to overcome his servitude to his past and break the fetters of tradition without repeating the tragedy, sordid as well as magnificent, of violent civil war.

For it is important to emphasise that, although Beard, as his well-known pamphlet *The Economic Basis of Politics* makes clear, has always given primacy to the economic factor as that which shapes our social life, still he has never drawn conclusions of a Marxist, or, in any decisive way, even a socialist character. He has never seen in the class war the central instrument of advance to freedom. He has never admitted the necessity of catastrophic change. He has deeply disliked the arrogant certainty of those who are convinced that, with the key of dialectical materialism, the doors of the future can be unlocked in the confidence that we know what lies beyond them. He has never even been a good party man in the sense of being willing to accept the directives of Republican or Democrat or Socialist as more than a rather better choice than the alternative of a given moment in time. Profoundly democratic in temper, strongly progressive in ideas, in the field of political action, Beard has for the most part sought temporary alliances only. There is, indeed, an important sense in which he has been sceptical of those who give thier permanent allegiance to a general corpus of doctrine. Political doctrine must, in its day to day application, be left to the stewardship of men to whom politics mean whatever definition of issues will bring them a majority of votes, and with it, office and power, on election day. Politicians Beard distrusted. He has preferred to give his energy, outside of writing and teaching, to the effort to make the institutions by which we live more fully known, their results more precisely capable of measurement, our power to improve them, as a consequence, more ample. He has sought to make the case for change one sufficiently capable of proof that we argue, not about concepts of a tight and logical system of politics, but of experiences so examined that a repetition of the examination only gives new emphasis to the original results. No one who knows of the time and thought that Beard has given to bodies like the New York Bureau of Municipal Research can fail to see how much of his outlook has been shaped by breaking up general principles into a series of separable problems, and inquiring, without the search for a general metaphysic, how each of them can be answered. (pp. 15-16)

> *Harold J. Laski, "Charles Beard: An English View," in* Charles A. Beard: An Appraisal, *edited by Howard K. Beale, University of Kentucky Press, 1954, pp. 9-24.*

WILLIAM BEARD (essay date 1956)

[*In the following excerpt (written in 1956) Beard's son William, a professor of political science and coauthor of* The American

Leviathan, *discusses the origins of his father's historical and political theories.*]

It is comparatively safe and easy to describe the past in terms of the surface manifestations of politics—such as the provisions of the Constitution of the United States as presented to the states for adoption in 1787, or the official wording of papers traded among diplomats during major disputes over foreign policy. Charles A. Beard was much too outspoken, however, and far too inquisitive to be satisfied with a limited program of this nature. In the course of a long, active, and often stormy career as a writer and university professor, he probed deeply behind the scenes in quest of basic economic explanations for major political developments. (p. vii)

Publicized not only by a host of friends but by foes as well—who felt his work was much too challenging to be ignored—Beard's labors exerted tremendous influence. (p. viii)

From whence came Beard's deep and abiding interest, up to the very end, in economic factors underlying past political events? As he has indicated, it was derived in part from the study of the printed works of others who had engaged in such explorations long ago.

Included in the great mine of ideas on economics and politics from which he drew were the thoughts of Aristotle (384-322 B.C.) who: "When he approaches . . . causes of variations in the forms of the state . . . immediately relates economics and politics." . . . Of a later contributor, Beard remarks that: "In advising the prince, once established, how best to maintain his power, Machiavelli [1469-1527] warns him to take account of the conflict of classes out of which political power springs. . . ." . . . Beard also notes that: "Both the origin and end of the state Locke [1632-1704] finds in the roots of property." . . . Discussing a more recent period, Beard declares that Barnave, in writing about the French Revolution: "displayed a remarkable insight into the economic causes of the struggle. Long before Marx, Barnave had written 'as soon as industry and commerce have entered into the life of a nation and have created a new source of wealth for the support of the working class, a revolution in political institutions begins. A new distribution of wealth produces a new distribution of power. . . .'" Of the Marxians Beard wrote: "In the field of history Marx and his followers undoubtedly helped to turn the attention of historians from purely political and diplomatic affairs to the more permanent and fundamental forces in the development and conflict of nations. . . ." A careful study of numerous other citations given by Beard would permit lengthy expansion of the above list.

Less well-known, perhaps, than his debt to his literary predecessors is the fact that Beard, unlike many historians whose activities have been more largely confined to academic circles, was in unusually close and stimulating contact with the everyday economic life about him, and with its varied political ramifications. These personal experiences supplemented the impetus for economic analysis provided by quiet reading. (pp. x-xi)

Being deeply aware of the vitality and importance of the economic drive in politics, by reading and by direct personal contact, Beard undertook to describe the linkage fearlessly and at length, in print. (p. xiv)

> *William Beard, in an introduction to* The Economic Basis of Politics and Related Writings *by Charles A. Beard, edited by William Beard, Vintage Books, 1957, pp. vii-xiv.*

BERNARD C. BORNING (essay date 1962)

[*In the following excerpt Borning, author of* The Political and Social Thought of Charles A. Beard, *a comprehensive work that discusses the development of Beard's political and social theories, summarizes Beard's thought from the turn-of-the-century until the historian's death.*]

A postulate basic to Beard's thinking on politics was his initial assumption concerning the significance and intrinsic worth of human beings. (p. 7)

Beard's lifetime of thinking and writing about human affairs not only exemplifies the evolution of one man's ideas, but also represents something of a commentary on the wider currents of American social thought since the 1890's. In the early years he had sought to correct the previous underemphasis on economic factors in politics by implying that economics was virtually the only element worth mentioning. Ever after, his thinking had continued to be affected by the problem of how heavily personal responsibility weighs against the determinism of impersonal forces.

During the middle period of his life, Beard had moved from a decided economic interpretation of politics and history to a broader and more indefinite conception of the dynamism in human affairs. Ideas and ethics had received successively greater stress. From an earlier inclination to shun theoretical formulations as meaningless abstractions, he had developed the habit of portraying idea patterns as rationalizing instruments of defense or attack. At length he had come full circle to insist on occasion that thought was the prime determinant in human existence. Yet he had given little evidence of accepting the possibility of "theory" in politics except as found in the classics devoted to "what ought to be." When he had mentally associated politics with causal theory as found in the physical sciences, his thinking had tended to leave the world of empirical science and to soar to an imaginary realm of fate and predetermination. To his mind the "grand drama of history" had come to embrace human values associated with moral choices, as well as deterministic elements.

Now, in the final decade and a half of a long life, Beard's former implicit theory of politics had become vaguer, having developed into a considerably attenuated "realistic dialectics" apparently designed to gather in all relevancies and to omit nothing. He himself had continued strongly cherishing democracy and constitutionalism, or the "civilian way of living together in a republic." In his mind, "majority rule in a time span" had become the most desirable practicable system of politics. But increasingly his thought had been dominated by intense preoccupation with one area of politics—foreign policy. Yet all the arguments he had been able to marshal in defense of his ideal of an insulated American garden had not stemmed the tide. War had come.

Now the republic had entered a "new and dangerous age," its future threatened by internal changes and by developments in the world at large. The old multipower world had given way to a world becoming dangerously polarized between two superstates. Almost unbelievable technological and scientific changes had sprung from those beginnings which Beard as a young man in England had described in his little book, *The Industrial Revolution*. . . . Now he wondered fearfully whether these changes were leading to a nobler civilization or to inevitable catastrophe. As he reminded readers of the final edition of his *American Government and Politics* . . . , we had come to a "revolutionary time in the history of our nation." With

our country now in the thick of world affairs, and laboring under crushing postwar burdens, "the American system of government and liberty" faced its greatest test.

Although Beard was mistaken in his prewar prediction that World War II would spell the end of democratic institutions in America, who knows *what* would survive an atomic missile conflict in the space age? If insulation from impending storms could be seriously advocated as recently as Beard's last decades, who now doubts that, internationally speaking, the era of hermits is irretrievably past? And if the new dark ages arrives tomorrow, can human civilization—in a thousand years, or in ten thousand—once more crawl out of the caves to try again?

Beard's political thought would seem to demonstrate the proposition that a vast fund of knowledge is not by itself a sure guide to policy. His lifetime of thinking indicates that operative philosophies rest ultimately on a few simple principles accepted largely on faith. This appears to be as true of a learned historian charting man's journey through time as it is of an illiterate fisherman sailing by the stars. Yet, regardless of our agreement or disagreement with particular aspects of Beard's thinking, we are in his debt for his stimulating influence on a half century of social thought. (pp. 254-55)

> *Bernard C. Borning, in his* The Political and Social Thought of Charles A. Beard, *University of Washington Press, 1962, 315 p.*

RICHARD HOFSTADTER (essay date 1968)

[*A distinguished American historian and social critic, Hofstadter was one of the first to challenge and reinterpret the works of the Progressive historians, whose so-called liberal reformist ideology he found to be narrow-minded and undemocratic. In his studies, Hofstadter applied a pluralistic, inquisitive, and skeptical approach to historical investigation, never accepting the pat causal explanations of other historians. During his lifetime, he was the recipient of two Pulitzer Prizes: in 1956 for* The Age of Reform: From Bryan to F.D.R. *(1956), a dynamic work that chronicles the political and social climate from the 1890s through Franklin D. Roosevelt's New Deal; and in 1964 for his* Anti-Intellectualism in American Life *(1963), which examines this phenomenon in America's political, cultural, and educational system through the 1950s. In the following excerpt from his* The Progressive Historians: Turner, Beard, Parrington, *Hofstadter discusses the influence upon modern historical thought of Beard's* An Economic Interpretation of the Constitution of the United States. *For other discussions of this work, see the excerpts by John H. Latané (1913) and Alfred Kazin (1942).*]

An Economic Interpretation of the Constitution begins with a brief chapter which tells us what the book is against. It does not question the morals of the Founding Fathers or the merits of the Constitution as a framework of government; rather it attacks certain types of historical interpretation. When one considers this chapter against the intellectual background of the era, it suddenly becomes clear what Beard believed he was doing: he was trying to write a kind of history that the adult mind could respect. The critical intelligentsia had arrived on the scene, too secular to take seriously the old providential explanations of events, too worldly and too free of chauvinism to believe in past notions about special racial aptitudes for self-government, too demanding to think that the claims of science could be met by the "impartial" presentation of naked facts, too realistic to be content with such abstractions as the juristic theory of the state. The word "abstract" keeps recurring when Beard is telling us what he dislikes; and when he tells what he stands for, we read of "explanation" and "significance" . . . but above all of "the critical spirit," "critical interpretation," and "critical analysis." If we are to try to catch in a phrase or two the enduring essence of Beard's contribution to the study of American history—that which remains when all the valid criticisms of his work have been taken into account—it is that, along with [Frederick Jackson] Turner, he did most to put his fellow historians not merely to the retelling of stories but to the study of problems; and that, even more than Turner, he tried to insure that the problems would be studied in an eminently critical way.

Having stated his rejection of the naïve providential interpretations of a [George] Bancroft, the racism of the Teutonic school, and the narrow empiricism of the anti-interpretative historians, Beard goes on to acknowledge his affiliations with the Turner school, especially its receptivity to economic interpretation, and with the intellectual realism of sociological jurisprudence. But above all he reaches back to one of the Founding Fathers to establish a traditional base for his argument: "The inquiry which follows," he writes, "is based upon the political science of James Madison"; and, quoting Madison's formulation of his views in Number 10 of *The Federalist,* he endorses it as "a masterly statement of the theory of economic determinism in politics." Beard's own version then follows: "Different degrees and kinds of property inevitably exist in modern society; party doctrines and 'principles' originate in the sentiments and views which the possession of various kinds of property creates in the minds of the possessors; class and group divisions based on property lie at the basis of modern government; and politics and constitutional law are inevitably a reflex of these contending interests."

With the argument thus posed, Beard surveys economic and social interests as they stood in 1787, traces the movement for the Constitution to those interests most adversely affected under the Articles of Confederation, and gives a short account of limitations on the right to vote. The movement for the Constitution he attributes to those interests concerned to see the government control a revenue sufficient to pay the interest and principal of the public debt, to those seeking commercial regulations advantageous to shippers, manufacturers, and speculators in public lands, and to those seeking to prohibit the state legislatures from resorting to paper money or to acts interfering with the obligations of contracts. Then comes a long chapter, taking up more than a fourth of the whole, tracing the economic interests and holdings of each member of the Federal Convention and giving special attention to their public securities about which Beard had uncovered much new evidence in dusty old Treasury Department records, hitherto unused. We learn that a majority of the framers were lawyers and most came from towns on or near the coast, that not one was drawn from the small farming or mechanic class, and that the overwhelming majority, "at least five-sixths," were directly and personally interested in the outcome of their labors, being economic beneficiaries of the adoption of the Constitution. We learn that forty of the fifty-five who attended had public securities, twenty-four of them in amounts over $5,000, and that fourteen had personalty invested in lands for speculation, twenty-four had money loaned at interest, eleven were investors in mercantile, manufacturing, or shipping businesses, and fifteen were owners of slaves.

After Beard explains the economic implications of the Constitution, he briefly surveys the political doctrines of the framers, stressing their suspicions of majority rule and their "frank recognition of class rights." In the four closing chapters he reviews the fight over ratification in the several states, attempting to establish an economic demarcation between the friends and foes of the Constitution—a "deep-seated conflict" between "a conservative party centered in the towns and resting on financial, mercantile, and personal property interests generally" and "a popular party based on paper money and agrarian interests."

The basic findings of Beard's book, to adapt his own summary of his conclusions, were as follows: the movement for the Constitution was organized by the upper classes whose investments had been unfavorably affected under the Articles of Confederation—namely, those with money on loan, owners of public securities, and those interested in trade, shipping, or the development of manufactures. Men with a direct personal stake in the outcome of the event initiated the move for a new Constitution, and the members of the Philadelphia Convention that framed it were, with few exceptions, directly and personally interested in economic advantages anticipated from the new system. Similar interests pushed the new Constitution through the state ratifying conventions. The Constitution, as shown both by its provisions and by the explicit statements of its advocates in the Philadelphia Convention in defense of property, "was essentially an economic document based upon the concept that the fundamental private rights of property are anterior to government and morally beyond the reach of popular majorities." Moreover, the process by which the Constitution was adopted was far from democratic: no popular vote was taken on the proposal to hold a Constitutional Convention in 1787; a "large propertyless mass," being altogether unrepresented under prevailing suffrage restrictions, was excluded from a voice in framing the Constitution; and in its ratification by the states about three-fourths of the adult males failed to vote either because of their ignorance or indifference to the issue or their disfranchisement by property qualifications. The Constitution was ratified by a vote of probably not more than one sixth of the adult males, and even then it is doubtful that a majority of the voters who did participate in five of the thirteen states actually approved ratification of the Constitution. The ratification contest aligned on one side substantial personalty interests—i.e., holders of liquid capital—against realty interests, the small farmers and debtors, on the other. The Constitution was thus not created by the "whole people," which was a fiction of the jurists; nor by the states, which was a fiction of Southern nullifiers; but was "the work of a consolidated group whose interests knew no state boundaries and were truly national in their scope."

So much has been said about the substance of the argument in Beard's book that we may be in danger of forgetting that it was an innovation in form, in American experience a new historical genre. It was not a narrative history; the narrative detail was stripped to the bare minimum necessary to remind the reader of the essential facts. It was not tricked out with any of the side effects used by popular historians to provide color or "human interest." It was a scholarly monograph, austere and astringent in form. The monograph, of course, was by now a familiar product of professional scholarship. But Beard's book, probably the first truly exciting monograph in the history of American historiography, achieved its excitement solely through the force and provocation of its argument.

It represented a significant departure too because of its systematic procedure, though here it probably owed much to the efforts of the Turner school to answer general questions by the systematic ordering of historical materials. This side of the book is best illustrated by its long central chapter surveying the holdings and interests of the members of the Philadelphia Convention and thus placing them in the tissue of their economic society. This technique of collective biography—the idea of taking the entire personnel associated with an event or grouped in a parliamentary body at a given moment and of examining their relevant characteristics as a way of shedding light on the social situation they refract—was a method of great potentialities. Even when one admits that Beard's particular execution of it was far from sound, one can see that he anticipated by a full generation both the career-line studies of modern sociologists and the basic idea of "structural history" that has come to be associated with the name of Sir Lewis Namier. This technique is both promising and dangerous: promising because it offers a way of disciplining impressionistic insights by the orderly marshaling of evidence; dangerous because its results, being susceptible to statistical statement, and having a delusive appearance of definiteness and finality, can cause the historian who makes a single important interpretative oversight to build his error firmly into the structure of a whole system of interpretation. It is also of some consequence here that a kind of anti-intellectualism—a disposition to downgrade or ignore the significance of ideas—has been charged against both Namier and Beard. (pp. 207-12)

What shocked or irritated many readers was the most novel of Beard's findings: his emphasis on the holdings of the Founding Fathers in public securities, and the insinuation that their interest in the new frame of government arose in good part out of their expectation that these securities would be worth more under a stronger national system. Was Beard simply trying to say that the Founding Fathers were trying to line their own pockets? Or only that they saw public issues as they did because they had certain kinds of interests? Was he casting a crude muckraker's imputation on their motives, or was he trying to offer an economic and sociological account of their ideas?

The book can be read either way, though in the long run it was only the latter interpretation that Beard himself was willing to defend. In the 1935 edition he denied that he had accused the members of the Federal Convention of "working merely for their own pockets." He pointed to a passage in which he said: "The purpose of such an inquiry is not, of course, to show that the Constitution was made for the personal benefit of the members of the Convention. Far from it. . . . The only point considered here is: 'Did they represent distinct groups whose economic interests they understood and felt in concrete, definite form through their own personal experience with identical property rights, or were they working merely under the guidance of abstract principles of political science?'" This is rather cagily put: one might imagine that the alternatives need not be so drastic and that there were additional issues. But it does *seem* to disavow the crudest interpretation of Beard's data. There was another passage of the original text which Beard might also have cited, had he chosen, but which he may have thought embarrassingly equivocal. In closing his long chapter on the economic interests of members of the Convention, he remarks: "It cannot be said, therefore, that the members of the Convention were 'disinterested.' On the contrary, we are forced to accept the profoundly significant conclusion that they knew through their personal experiences in economic affairs the precise results which the new oovernment that they were setting up was designed to attain. As a group of doctrinaires, like the Frankfort assembly of 1848, they would have failed miserably; but as practical men they were able to build the new

government upon the only foundations which could be stable: fundamental economic interests." Thus, while the Fathers cannot be praised for their disinterestedness, they can be praised for their practicality, which is seen, unless Beard was writing with tongue in cheek, as being not merely a private but a civic virtue. (pp. 213-14)

My own conclusion is that we . . . should recognize that the ambiguity in Beard's book was, whatever his conscious strategy, a product of an ambivalence in his mind and temperament. On one side there was Beard the reformer, the moralist, the rebel against authority, the young Beard of Oxford, the Beard who all his days loved the gadfly's role, who was influenced not only by the Progressive hunger for "reality" but also by the iconoclasm, even to a degree the cynicism, of the muck-raking milieu, and who in his eagerness to puncture older ways of historical thought could easily stray into a rather crude economic reductionism. On the other side was the Beard of Knightstown, reared in solid Republicanism, himself strongly driven to achievement, a man who admired mastery and control, a scholar disciplined and inhibited by the ideal of scientific history, an American patriot who did indeed revere the practical genius of the Founding Fathers and who, in the light of all they accomplished, did not feel that the self-serving side of their work was an unforgivable flaw or that it should be taken to discredit their statecraft.

This ambivalence is in itself not startling, nor was it singular in Beard. Among Beard's contemporaries it can be seen, for example, in the naturalistic writers who condemned the dog-eat-dog morality of the competitive world and yet succumbed to admiration for the mastery of the survivors. (pp. 216-17)

Even in his capacity as a reformer, Beard might well have felt the pull of contrary impulses. True, to persuade men to look at the Constitution with less reverence might release social criticism and lower the barriers to reform. Yet many Progressive thinkers . . . were becoming increasingly convinced of the need of a strong, active national state to further their own ends, and accordingly were becoming more critical of the Jeffersonian heritage of weak government and decentralization, more amenable to the Hamiltonian regard for power. One could thus look back on the making of a strong national state, even if somewhat tainted by the immediate personal interests of its founders, as a valuable historical legacy; and in this light the performance of the Fathers was not a thing to be quarreled with. The only thing, in fact, to be quarreled with was just what Beard had attacked in his opening chapter: historical interpretations too remote from the real world to take account of the impact of economic events. What Beard left, then, was a book ambiguous enough to be read, to his great advantage, in different ways by different readers. Scholars interested in the problems of historiographical and juridical interpretation could read it one way, ardent Progressives or Marxists another; and, as Beard later took a certain ironic relish in pointing out, it could even be cited, and indeed was, by a conservative judge of the Supreme Court to justify opposition to a new piece of social legislation. Like many central works of its kind, it was a plastic object, susceptible to a certain manipulation in the minds of its audience. (pp. 217-18)

Richard Hofstadter, "The Constitution As an Economic Document," in his The Progressive Historians: Turner, Beard, Parrington, *Alfred A. Knopf, 1968, pp. 207-45.*

JOHN BRAEMAN   (essay date 1980)

[*In the following excerpt, Braeman discusses Beard's initial enthusiasm and eventual disillusionment with Franklin Roosevelt's*

New Deal, and provides an informative overview of Beard's political thinking.]

Charles A. Beard was probably the most influential and widely read American historian of the twentieth century. Lewis Mumford acknowledged him in 1945 as ''the most powerful single figure in the teaching of American history.'' His influence extended far beyond the historical profession. Over five-and-a-half million copies of his books on American history were sold. But he did more than shape his generation's perception of the American past. His aim—and his achievement—was to mold his fellow Americans' thinking about the nation's present and its future. His *American Government and Politics* was, from its publication in 1910, a standard text for introductory courses in American colleges throughout the country. Through his service on the American Historical Association's Commission on the Social Studies and his involvement with the National Education Association, he played a major role in revamping the teaching of social studies in the schools. His articles in the leading journals of opinion brought his views on current issues before the public.

The message that Beard presented to his readers in the optimistic years after the turn of the century was a message of hope—that the world was moving forward to a new and higher plane of life. ''The central theme of history,'' he wrote in his first book, *The Industrial Revolution* . . . , was man's ''progressive'' realization of his ''right and power . . . corporately to control every form of his material environment.'' Nowhere was this truer than in the United States. The present age, he and his wife exulted at the conclusion of their best-selling *The Rise of American Civilization* . . . , ''is the dawn, not the dusk, of the gods.'' The inexorable forces set loose by the industrial revolution—the triumph of the machine and the rise of modern science—guaranteed a future of ''unlimited progress.'' . . . The machine age had its own inner logic: its hallmarks were co-operation, order, and control. Widening government regulation, even increasing government ownership and operation, he explained in 1928 in a symposium on the future of modern civilization, ''will come about gradually as a necessity of the machine system.'' ''By inherent necessity,'' he prophesied in a follow-up symposium by a group of engineers, the machine process ''forces upon society an ever larger planned area of conduct.''

Yet by the time these words were published, the country had begun its slide into the depths of the Great Depression. The depression confirmed for Beard the inadequacy, indeed, the impossibility, of laissez faire. ''The cold truth,'' he exclaimed, ''is that the individualistic creed of everybody for himself and the devil take the hindmost is principally responsible for the distress in which Western civilization finds itself.'' But he had no sympathy for the totalitarian ideologies offering their own panaceas for the collapse of capitalism. Although he was fleetingly attracted by Mussolini's corporation, his democratic instincts boggled at fascism's ''iron régime of despotism.'' He hever had any illusions about Hitler. Nazi Germany, he told an audience at the New School for Social Research in April, 1934, was ''government by irresponsible brute force, by unquestioning and unchallenged berserker rage.'' Nor did he find the extreme left any more to his way of thinking. His rereading of Marx and Engels reinforced his hostility to Marxism as contrary to all the values and ideals that Americans held dear. He anathematized the Soviet Union as a land ''of political and economic despotism'' ruled ''by tyranny and terror,'' scornfully dismissed the American Communists as puppets and agents

of the Soviet tyranny, and warned his fellow liberals against collaboration with the party.

The depression coupled with the totalitarian threats shattered beyond repair Beard's faith in inevitable, even automatic, progress. Yet he did not abandon his hopes for the future. Progress was still possible; but its achievement would require ''immense efforts of will and intelligence.'' Men must consciously act to shape a future still in the making. (pp. 364-66)

At the same time, Beard limited his hopes for the future to the American nation within its continental bounds. In his younger days, he had shared the internationalist faith that the growing economic unity and interdependence of the world was bringing forth ''a common consciousness'' among all mankind. But his trips abroad after the First World War made him aware of the intractability of long-rooted national ways and traditions, showed him the continuing strength of the Old World's time-encrusted feuds and hatreds, and stimulated a new appreciation of America's distinctiveness and uniqueness. Even before the depression, he had warned that the pursuit of ''trade and profits'' in the Far East would lead to war with Japan. The trade rivalries spurred by the depression heightened his fears that America's continued quest for markets abroad for its surpluses would bring ''a futile and idiotic war in the Far Pacific.'' The worsening threat of war in Europe further reinforced his conviction that the American people should avoid all foreign entanglements and devote their energies and resources to ''tilling our own garden.'' And he underlined that doing so ''involves many drastic changes in capitalism as historically practised.''

Beard shied away from nationalization of industry, even of the railroads and public utilities. Instead, he called for ''national planning''—the application by democratic government of ''engineering rationality'' to the economy. His own ''Five-Year Plan'' for America—as set forth in 1931—envisaged the establishment of a National Economic Council, made up of representatives from ''all the great industries which have reached a high degree of concentration,'' from ''the several organizations in agriculture, wholesaling, and retailing,'' and from ''labor, organized and unorganized,'' to coordinate ''these divisions of the economy.'' (pp. 366-67)

Beard was hazy, even indifferent, about the detailed implementation of this plan. Commentators noted the basic similarity between his plan and the proposal put forth by Gerard Swope, the president of General Electric, for government-sanctioned but business-dominated, cartelization of industry; Beard himself praised the Swope and Chamber of Commerce plans and called for cooperation—''a reasonable meeting of minds''—between business and government. And he too readily assumed that his plan—or any scheme of national planning—would be compatible with the American traditions of democracy, liberty, and enterprise. But he was not so much concerned with drafting a detailed blueprint for the future as with conveying a new message of hope—that ''America has the intelligence, the organizing capacity, the engineering skill, the material endowment, and above all, men and women . . . [with] faith in the mission of their country'' to attain new heights ''far beyond our dim, chill imaginations.''

After his dismay at the paralysis afflicting the last days of the Hoover administration, Beard hailed the New Deal as ''The Future Comes.'' He applauded Roosevelt's action in torpedoing the London Economic Conference as establishing ''the supremacy of the 'national' or domestic point of view in American policy.'' He had praise for nearly every achievement of the First Hundred Days. But he waxed most enthusiastic about the National Industrial Recovery Act for recognizing the historical trend toward consolidation and cooperation in industry, for accelerating that process, and for providing for business "self-regulation" under federal government "supervision" and "control." "Implicit" in the "Recovery Program," he concluded, was "a changed conception of economy and life": abandonment of the "speculative" ideal "of getting rich as quickly as possible" in favor of "reasonable security for all." The New Deal was thus new, even "revolutionary"—"a break with the historic past and the coming of a future collectivist in character." (pp. 367-68)

Yet even at the height of his enthusiasm for the New Deal, Beard felt misgivings. He was disturbed by Roosevelt's big-navy enthusiasm. He was even more worried lest the administration seek by foreign trade expansion to evade the fundamental problem of keeping the American economy "running at a high tempo supplying the intra-national market" through "domestic planning and control." Thus, he viewed with alarm the growing ascendancy of "the sentimental internationalists." . . . (p. 368)

These anxieties were reinforced by his growing doubts about the administration's domestic policies. By the beginning of 1935, he was lamenting that the New Deal had failed to bring about economic recovery, that business, rather than the "little fellow," had benefited most from the existing New Deal programs, and that "not a single instrumentality of economic power had been wrested" from the "party of wealth and talents." He even predicted that at the end of the depression— "if it ever ends"—the concentration of wealth would have reached "a new high point in the evolution of American economy." "If I were President of the United States," he replied when asked what he would do, "I'd summon leaders of big business and ask them if they could put to work our potential industrial machine. I'd say, 'I'll give you three months—then I'll use my powers and the help of Congress to take over these businesses and put this plan into operation.'"

But Roosevelt was failing to provide the leadership required in the crisis. The chief executive, Beard bluntly charged, appeared "at the end of his resources so far as domestic policy is concerned." American history, he added gloomily, was full of examples of statesmen attempting "the adjustment of domestic dissensions by resort to diplomatic fulminations, war scares, and war itself." Would Roosevelt, "confronted by the difficulties of a creeping domestic crisis and by the comparative ease of a foreign war," do otherwise? Beard had his doubts. Not that Roosevelt would "deliberately plunge the country into a Pacific war in his efforts to escape the economic crisis." Rather, he would "stumble into" the conflict. (p. 369)

When Beard reviewed the record of the New Deal as of mid-1938, the pluses still outweighed the minuses. He praised Roosevelt for facing up to, and publicizing, "the basic human and economic problems of American society with a courage and range displayed by no predecessor in his office." He found that "the major measure of the Roosevelt regime, however open to criticism in details or in execution, looked in the direction of strengthening the economic foundations of democracy—salvaging agriculture, fortifying the bargaining powers of industrial workers, minimum wages, social insurance, old age pensions, employment for the idle, security of livelihood and home; protection against the hazards of economic defeat." (pp. 371-72)

But these lingering hopes proved illusory. On the eve of the 1940 elections, Beard penned a damning indictment of the New

Deal's failures. Roosevelt had not followed through with a "cooperative, concerted plan for industrial order and progress" that would put the nation's productive capacity fully to work and restore prosperity. Nor had the New Deal solved "the major problem of concentration in private ownership of the greater part of the country's resources and productive plant, with its consequent private control over production and prices." Thurman Arnold's trust-busting campaign—though "the most vigorous attempt ever to meet the concentration problem"— merely "skirted around the periphery of the problem." With national planning abandoned, and with "direct government ownership of industrial properties along socialistic lines" never even contemplated, the Roosevelt administration had come, in the aftermath of the recession of 1937, to rely upon a continuing high level of government spending to keep the economy "running at even a moderate tempo." Such government spending, Beard warned, could supply no more than a temporary and artificial fillip to the economy, while the growing national debt portended a new and graver "explosion."

At the same time, Roosevelt's Quarantine Speech of October 5, 1937—followed by his call for a major build-up of the navy—convinced Beard that "the central drive of the Roosevelt administration was in the direction of intervention." He accused F.D.R. of seeking to divert the American people from his failure to restore prosperity by taking up "world lecturing and interventionism." Even worse, Roosevelt, like Wilson, had become infatuated with the delusion that he was "commissioned to set the world aright." And the rationale of national defense silenced the "constant and savage nagging" threatening the spending program the administration had come to rely upon to keep the economy afloat. Long before Pearl Harbor, Beard prophesied that F.D.R. was determined to bring this country into the war against Hitler—and that if he could not do so directly, then he would do so by the "roundabout way" of provoking a war with Japan.

Beard's last years were filled with bitterness over hopes gone sour—and with pessimism for the future. He was convinced that the Roosevelt years had done grave, perhaps irreparable, damage to the country's institutions. Even before the war, he had lamented the growing concentration of power in the executive, bemoaned Congress's surrender to the president of "huge discretionary authority," and assailed Roosevelt's building up "a great political 'machine,' composed of government employees . . . millions of the unemployed on work relief, and state and local officials dependent on grants from the federal Treasury. The war had accelerated this trend to an ever more powerful and threatening Leviathan. "The economic man," he concluded in 1945, had been eclipsed by "the political man." (pp. 372-73)

He was convinced that Roosevelt had deceived and misled the American people by plotting war while talking peace—and he was further convinced that in doing so, Roosevelt had brought the country to the verge of Caesarism. The war had diverted and dissipated reform, had left the country saddled with a "stupendous" national debt and "grinding taxes," and had resulted in the emergence of Russia—"another totalitarian regime no less despotic and ruthless" than Nazi Germany and "equally inimical to the democracy, liberties, and institutions of the United States"—as the "dominant power" astride Europe and Asia. To bring Roosevelt to judgment before the bar of history became the consuming passion—and the animating spirit—of his last years. (pp. 373-74)

Beard's growing disillusionment with the shortcomings of the New Deal roughly paralleled the experiences of many of the liberal intellectuals of the time. Nor was his commitment to American isolationism—though stronger and more lasting than for most—atypical of those on the left. What distinguished Beard was the depth and intensity of his bitterness. Such bitterness reflected not simply a dispute over policies, but a more profound sense of personal loss. The historian, he wrote in 1919, "endures only in so far as he succeeds in casting through the warp of the past the weft of the future—the future which he can behold only by prophetic discernment." "It is given to but a few to walk with the gods in the dusk of ages"—and his life-long ambition was to be among that select number who divined where history was moving. During the 1930's, he threw himself into the battle to vindicate his vision of the future that was in the making. Yet events betrayed those hopes—and mocked their prophet. (p. 374)

> *John Braeman, "The Historian As Activist: Charles A. Beard and the New Deal," in* South Atlantic Quarterly, *Vol. 79, No. 4, Autumn, 1980, pp. 364-74.*

ADDITIONAL BIBLIOGRAPHY

Beard, Mary Ritter. *The Making of Charles A. Beard: An Interpretation.* New York: Exposition Press, 1955, 104 p.
  Offers some biographical information on Beard's early life and career, and chronicles his travels in Japan and Yugoslavia.

Benson, Lee. "A Critique of Beard and His Critics." In his *Turner and Beard: American Historical Writing Reconsidered,* pp. 95-214. Glencoe, Ill.: Free Press, 1960.
  Detailed analysis proposes that Beard's economic interpretation of the United States Constitution was "ambiguous and confusing." In this lengthy section devoted to Beard, Benson examines the dualism of Beard's thought by contrasting the ideas of "economic interpretation" and "economic determinism," terms which Beard used interchangeably in his work. Benson also reviews criticism of Beard's work by various commentators, including Robert E. Brown and Forrest McDonald (see Additional Bibliography).

Braeman, John. "Charles A. Beard: The English Experience." *Journal of American Studies* 15, No. 2 (August 1951): 165-89.
  Chronicles Beard's three years in England, where he attended Oxford University and assisted in founding Ruskin College, a school devoted to the labor movement.

Brown, Robert E. *Charles Beard and the Constitution: A Critical Analysis of "An Economic Interpretation of the Constitution."* New York: W. W. Norton & Co., 1956, 219 p.
  Chapter-by-chapter analysis of Beard's *An Economic Interpretation of the Constitution.*

Canby, Henry Seidel. "History by Innuendo." *The Saturday Review of Literature* XXVII, No. 46 (11 November 1944): 12.
  Scathing review of *A Basic History of the United States.* The work, which implies that President Franklin D. Roosevelt willfully maneuvered the United States into World War II, is denounced by Canby as "violently biased in opinion," and "unfair and untrue in implication." As one of Beard's most controversial works, *A Basic History of the United States* drew a diversity of criticism at the time it was published in 1944. For additional commentary on the work, see the entries by Alfred A. Knopf and Freeman Lewis in the Additional Bibliography, and the excerpt by Lewis Mumford (1944).

Commager, Henry Steele. "From Coolidge's America to Roosevelt's: A Magisterial Interpretation of Our Contemporary Evolution." *New York Herald Tribune Books* (21 May 1939): 1-2.*

Favorable review of the Beards' *America in Mid-Passage.*

Deininger, Whitaker T. "The Skepticism and Historical Faith of Charles A. Beard." *Journal of the History of Ideas* XV, No. 4 (October 1954): 573-88.
  Concludes that Beard's views of history were often inadequate in analyzing the various problems and aspects of historical theory, such as epistemology, sociology, and methodology.

Kennedy, Thomas C. *Charles A. Beard and American Foreign Policy.* Gainesville: University Presses of Florida, 1975, 199 p.
  Examines Beard's views of American foreign policy throughout his career, concentrating on the revisionist historical interpretations which he strongly adhered to at the end of his career. Kennedy believes that Beard's views of isolationism, or "continentalism," can also be detected in his early works.

Knopf, Alfred A. "Mr. Knopf Raises Some Questions." *The Saturday Review of Literature* XXVII, No. 51 (16 December 1944): 15.
  Letter to the editor of *The Saturday Review of Literature* directed chiefly at the journal's associate editor, Henry Seidel Canby, for what Knopf believed was his two-faced attitude toward Beard's *A Basic History of the United States.* It seems that at the same time that Canby attacked the work in a review (see Additional Bibliography), the history was also offered by the Book-of-the-Month Club—of which Canby was editor—as the club's monthly book dividend. Of Canby, Knopf questioned: "On which side does he stand?"

Lerner, Max. "Charles Beard Confronts Himself." *The Nation* CXLII, No. 3692 (8 April 1936): 452-54.
  Retrospective commentary on Beard's *An Economic Interpretation of the Constitution of the United States.*

———. "Beard's *Economic Interpretation.*" *The New Republic* LXXXXIX, No. 1275 (10 May 1939): 7-11.
  Discusses the overall influence effected by Beard's *An Economic Interpretation of the Constitution of the United States* after its publication in 1913.

Lewis, Freeman. "The Beard's *Basic History.*" *The Saturday Review of Literature* XXVII, No. 52 (23 December 1944): 13.
  Editor of *A Basic History of the United States* provides background information on its publication and initial distribution in order "to rectify the errors" perpetuated by the work's detractors.

Marcell, David W. "Charles Beard: Civilization in America." In his *Progress and Pragmatism: James, Dewey, Beard, and the American Idea of Progress,* pp. 258-321. Westport, Conn.: Greenwood Press, 1974.
  Offers a biographical introduction and an in-depth discussion of Beard's historical method, which Marcell believes was based on a philosophy of pragmatism.

McDonald, Forrest. *We the People: The Economic Origins of the Constitution.* Chicago: University of Chicago Press, 1958, 436 p.
  Important study refutes, point-by-point, Beard's thesis that the Constitution of the United States was an economic document prepared by its framers to benefit a small group of property owners. Instead, McDonald, a prominent historian and scholar, asserts that a much more diverse group of individuals was responsible for the Constitution's ratification, and that economics did not serve as the entire base of the document. Throughout his work, McDonald discusses the political theorizing and "presentist frame of reference" that resulted in Beard's explanation of the Constitution.

Miller, Perry. "Charles A. Beard." *The Nation* 167, No. 13 (25 September 1948): 344-46.
  Examines Beard's disillusionment with American capitalism and his consequent isolationist views.

Morison, Samuel Eliot. "History through a Beard." In his *By Land and by Sea: Essays and Addresses,* pp. 328-45. New York: Alfred A. Knopf, 1953.
  Posits that Beard selected his historical facts to fit a "'frame of reference' consistent with the sort of America that he wanted." In this negative critique of Beard's historical studies, Morison

attacks Beard for employing innuendo, discounting the importance of the "great man" in history, ignoring the effects of war on history, and for inconsistencies throughout his work.

Mumford, Lewis. "Mr. Beard and His *Basic History*." *The Saturday Review of Literature* XXVII, No. 49 (2 December 1944): 27.
    Vituperative review of Beard's *A Basic History of the United States*.

Nore, Ellen. "Charles A. Beard's Act of Faith: Context and Content." *The Journal of American History* 66, No. 4 (March 1980): 850-66.
    Argues that Beard's idea of historical relativism was evident throughout his career.

Pringle, Henry F. "Was the War Necessary?" *The Saturday Review of Literature* XXXI, No. 17 (24 April 1948): 15.
    Review of *President Roosevelt and the Coming of War, 1941* in which Pringle states that Beard "seems to have slanted his conclusions heavily." For a differing point of view on this work see the entry in the Additional Bibliography by Charles Callan Tansill.

Strout, Cushing. *The Pragmatic Revolt in American History: Carl Becker and Charles Beard*. New Haven, Conn.: Yale University Press, 1958, 182 p.*
    Study of the profound influence Carl Becker and Beard had on American thought during the first half of the twentieth century. Strout maintains that these two historians were often misinterpreted because of the roles they played as "skeptical gadflies to the orthodoxies of their profession."

Tansill, Charles Callan. Review of *President Roosevelt and the Coming of the War, 1941: A Study in Appearances and Realities*, by Charles A. Beard. *The Mississippi Valley Historical Review* XXXV, No. 3 (December 1948): 532-34.
    Favorable review. Tansill was a revisionist historian who wrote the anti-Roosevelt work, *Back Door to War* (1952). For a differing point of view on Beard's work, see the entry in the Additional Bibliography by Henry F. Pringle.

Thomas, Robert E. "A Reappraisal of Beard's *An Economic Interpretation of the Constitution of the United States*." *The American Historical Review* LVII, No. 2 (January 1952): 370-75.
    Defends Beard's *An Economic Interpretation of the Constitution of the United States* against those critics who believed that the work was written "as an attack upon the Supreme Court and a defense of Populist-New Freedom policies." Thomas maintains that there is evidence throughout Beard's work to support the fact that Beard was "an admirer and defender of the Supreme Court."

Louis (Marie Anne) Couperus

1863-1923

Dutch novelist, short story writer, poet, nonfiction writer, and essayist.

Couperus was a popular and critically respected Dutch novelist who, together with other young writers of the Sensitivist school, helped restore the critical prestige of the Dutch novel through the use of contemporary literary techniques and themes. Much of the literature of the Netherlands in Couperus's time had become didactic and cliché-ridden, as Dutch writers had fallen out of touch with the major intellectual trends in Europe and modern developments in the novel. The Sensitivists, and Couperus in particular, were responsible for drawing Dutch writers back into the literary mainstream by introducing them to new literary techniques derived from the Naturalist methods of Émile Zola, and to such controversial contemporary ideas as the philosophy of scientific determinism, which figures importantly in Couperus's novels *Eline Vere* and *Noodlot (Footsteps of Fate)*.

Couperus was born in The Hague. His father, an employee of the Dutch government, was assigned to an important colonial post in Java in the Dutch East Indies when Couperus was nine years old. The family remained in Java for the next five years, during which time Couperus had the opportunity to observe at first hand the exotic settings and culture of Indonesia, and to hear the legends of supernatural powers and mysterious forces that he later incorporated into such fictional works as *De stille kracht (The Hidden Force)* and *Van oude menschen, de dingen de voorbijgaan (Old People and the Things That Pass)*. When Couperus was fifteen, his father died and his family returned to Holland. There Couperus enrolled at the University of The Hague in order to prepare for a career as a teacher. However, though he completed the university's requirements for certification, he never went on to teach, but instead turned his attention to writing. Couperus's early works include *Een lent van vaerzen* and *Orchideeën*, two collections of poems inspired by the contemporary French Symbolist movement. Neither one of these works was received with much enthusiasm by critics, and Couperus soon abandoned poetry.

Couperus's first novel, *Eline Vere* appeared in 1889. Although critically controversial, *Eline Vere* was an immediate success, and at once established Couperus's literary reputation. The story, which traces the mental and emotional disintegration of a young woman who believes herself doomed by her heredity, was attacked by Dutch critics as morbid, decadent, and offensive in its realistic treatment of sexual subjects. However, even those critics who disliked the subject matter of *Eline Vere* often concluded by praising Couperus for his highly polished prose style, refined perceptions, and acute psychological insights. Both the realism and the refinement of Couperus's style were characteristic of the Sensitivist writers who sought to combine the realism of Zola with the perverse sensuality and the sense of nervous exhaustion found in French Decadent literature. The publication of *Eline Vere*, and the advent of Dutch Sensitivism, thus marked an important turning point in the literature of the Netherlands away from the strict puritanism of nineteenth century Dutch culture and toward a more modern conception of literary art.

The theme of disintegration that Couperus explored in *Eline Vere* is of central importance to the understanding of his other works as well. *The Hidden Force* and *Old People and the Things That Pass*, are both, like *Eline Vere*, concerned with disintegration on a personal level, while *De boeken der kleine zielen (The Books of the Small Souls)* examine the gradual decay of a society. The quartet of novels that comprise *The Books of the Small Souls* are still regarded by critics as Couperus's finest works. In writing these novels, Couperus drew on his own experiences as a returned colonial living in The Hague among other well-to-do former colonials for his portrait of an elite, closed society on the brink of ruin. The novels' subject matter and the skillful manner in which the characters are analyzed to expose the internal as well as the external forces of fate that are slowly destroying them and their society has led critics to compare *Small Souls* to both John Galsworthy's *The Forsyte Saga* and Marcel Proust's *Remembrance of Things Past*. Critics agree that the chief flaw of *Small Souls*, as in all but a few of Couperus's works, is excessive length. However, in spite of this shortcoming, several of Couperus's books retain interest today. *The Books of the Small Souls, Old People and the Things That Pass*, and *The Hidden Force* are all held in high esteem by many critics of Dutch literature. *The Hidden Force*, in particular, has been favorably compared with E. M. Forster's *A Passage to India* for the insight it affords into the profound psychological differences that seem to perpetually separate Eastern and Western cultures.

Later in his career, Couperus began to lose interest in contemporary Realism, and devoted more of his time to the writing of works set in a classical antiquity of both myth and historical fact. These include such mythologically-based novels as *Psyche, Dionysos,* and *Heracles,* as well as several historical novels, including *De berg van licht, Xerxes of de hoogmoed (Arrogance; The Conquest of Xerxes),* and *Iskander.* While most critics agree that Couperus's realistic works represent his most important contribution to twentieth-century literature, many have also praised these more imaginative works for their colorful and graceful prose, and the uncanny realism of their ancient settings.

Despite the occasional critical controversies that surrounded them, Couperus's novels were extremely popular. Most of them were available in English translation, and by the time that Couperus died in 1923 at the age of sixty, he was well-known throughout Europe and the United States. His literary stature in his native Holland was such that his sixtieth birthday was the occasion of a national celebration. Couperus's work in the realm of realistic fiction exercised a strong influence on his countrymen, helping to eliminate many of their out-moded ideas about literature as well as awakening their interest in modern artistic developments.

PRINCIPAL WORKS

Een lent van vaerzen   (poetry)   1884
Orchideeën   (poetry)   1886
Eline Vere   (novel)   1889
  [*Eline Vere,* 1892]
Noodlot   (novel)   1890
  [*Footsteps of Fate,* 1891]
Extase   (novel)   1892
  [*Ecstasy,* 1919]
Majesteit   (novel)   1893
  [*Majesty,* 1894]
Wereldvrede   (novel)   1895
Hooge troeven   (novel)   1896
Psyche   (novel)   1898
  [*Psyche,* 1908]
Fidessa   (novel)   1899
Langs lijnen van geleidelijkheid   (novel)   1900
  [*The Law Inevitable,* 1920]
De stille kracht   (novel)   1900
  [*The Hidden Force,* 1921]
Babel   (novel)   1901
De kleine zielen   (novel)   1901
  [*Small Souls,* 1914]
Het late leven   (novel)   1902
  [*The Later Life,* 1915]
Zielenschemering   (novel)   1903
  [*The Twilight of the Souls,* 1917]
Het heilege weten   (novel)   1903
  [*Dr. Adriaan,* 1918]
Dionysos   (novel)   1904
De berg van licht. 3 vols.   (novel)   1905-06
Van oude menschen, de dingen de voorbijgaan   (novel)   1906
  [*Old People and the Things That Pass,* 1919]
Van en over mijzelf en anderen. 4 vols.   (essays)   1910-17
Antiek toerisme   (novel)   1911
  [*The Tour: A Story of Ancient Egypt,* 1920]

Korte Arabesken   (short stories)   1911
Heracles   (novel)   1913
De komedianten   (novel)   1917
  [*The Comedians,* 1926]
Xerxes of de hoogmoed   (novel)   1919
  [*Arrogance: The Conquest of Xerxes,* 1930]
Iskander   (novel)   1920
Het zwevende schaakbord   (novel)   1922
Eighteen Tales   (short stories)   1924
Oostwaarts   (nonfiction)   1924
  [*Eastward,* 1924]
Nippon   (nonfiction)   1925
  [*Nippon,* 1926]
Verzamelde werken. 12 vols.   (novels, short stories, and essays)   1952-57

*These works are collectively referred to as *De boeken der kleine zielen* [*The Books of the Small Souls*].

THE ATHENAEUM   (essay date 1891)

[*In the following excerpt, the critic discusses the literary movement called Sensitivism, with which Couperus was affiliated, and expresses his dislike of Couperus's determinist philosophy.*]

Mr. Couperus is (we may say, of course) a young man, and his writings are emphatically of "the latest seed of time." He belongs to a new and active band of Dutch novelists who have thought it worth their while to take a fresh name—the Sensitives—the better to define their place in literature, and to distinguish their slightly new departure. Their nearest equivalent is to be found in the French Symbolists, perhaps; but the little knot of Dutchmen reject obscurity of language, and aim at a perfectly clear and logical expression—an excessive delicacy of sensation and perception is supposed to be a superadded quality of their own. '**Footsteps of Fate**' is probably a sufficiently good example of the firstfruits of the school, and the only one yet brought within range of English readers. If we may resume a well-known French novelist's opinion (and agree to it) that the mission of the artist is to reproduce truthfully and make his own illusion felt by others, we must allow that Mr. Couperus has achieved a certain measure of success, whatever we may think of his "particular illusion." His fancy and imagination are of a gruesome and gloomy cast; the story is of a thoroughly morbid, even distorted type—a nightmare, but a nightmare with a troubling sense of reality, perturbing, yet in a sense alluring, and marked by keenly described sensations and a suggestion of real temperament. His material is beyond the range of common sense and probability, but is, if one looks closer, not so unwholesome or "perverted" in tone as one might expect, and almost throughout reveals a careful, restrained sobriety of manner and an exceeding clearness of touch, which are not the least curious traits. This sobriety we must insist on, in spite of the two suicides and the brutal murder with, practically speaking, only three persons to bear the brunt of them! The writer compels us to follow him into a distorted world, where abnormal forces bring with them extraordinary issues, as though they were everyday factors and occurrences. Event succeeds event inevitably and naturally. The book reminds one of 'Crime and Punishment,' though of the grim tenacity and concentration of the Russian writer '**Footsteps of Fate**' has but little. It seems the work of a subtle rather than a powerful intelligence, and its originality consists in finding and reproducing a new and hitherto unnoted aspect of familiar objects and situations. Mr. Couperus is evidently more or less a *doctrinaire*, holding theories that now dominate foreign fiction and are in the very air, but he is too good an artist to make them aggressive. The power of heredity and the hypnotic will may very easily be pushed to absurdity; if they escape it here, it is because they are held, as it were, in solution, and only brood over the fortunes of the story. The workings of Van Maeren's mind, his self-insight yet blindness, are tellingly given. Feeble and pitiable as he is, one is oppressed by the sense of a something in his personality that passes beyond his own keeping. The touches of landscape accentuate the character and situations of the three actors, and over all hangs an overmastering sense of man's powerlessness in the hands of destiny, in spite of his appearance of controlling it.

A review of ''Footsteps of Fate,'' in The Athenaeum, *No. 3325, July 18, 1891, p. 93.*

THE ATHENAEUM (essay date 1892)

[*In the following excerpt from an early favorable review of* Eline Vere, *the critic comments on the extreme sensitivity of Couperus's ''quick and nervous'' perceptions that recreate ''the atmosphere of real life, its incompletenesses, fallings away, and vanishings'' in such a way that one becomes completely enveloped in the protagonist's temperament and surroundings.*]

Independently of his particular school—known or unknown as the Sensitives—Mr. Couperus seems to hold a very personal outlook of his own on life and manners. He appears to have sought for himself, and found, what he believes to be the truest expression of what he sees. He is less likely, therefore, than others to become the victim of fixed and arbitrary canons. 'Eline Vere' cannot be said to have charm, but it arrests the attention; it is not what may be called a ''powerful'' novel, but it is impossible not to look on it as clever and interesting. With regard to matter and workmanship (not, we think, with regard to the translation) it appears to be an advance on '**Footsteps of Fate.**' It takes a stronger hold on the reader; it is less charged with vague impalpable forces and strange magnetic influences than the other. There is not so much diseased mental portraiture either—always excepting the principal study; it is more normal, and there are even healthy touches scattered about here and there. Still, when that is said, it must be confessed that the book adds one more brick to the lengthy tale of modern fiction of the dismal sort. Life itself, or the author's conception of it, seems to unfold, and we are for the time enveloped in the atmosphere of real existence, its incompletenesses, fallings away, and vanishings. We believe we recognize the very way in which circumstances treated us or others, though till now it may not have been possible to put it into words, even into thoughts. 'Anna Karenina' is on larger, more epic lines; in its smaller and less robust way, '**Eline Vere**' recalls it. It is the story of a temperament and its surroundings, human and natural, told not with the flat and servile insistence of the naturalist, but with a quick and nervous perception of the real look and essence of things. There is hardly a line of ''presentation'' or description, yet that temperament and those surroundings live, breathe, and reveal themselves for us as our own or our neighbours' might—but rarely do. The introspective process is barely employed; all is conveyed by word, gesture, and action of the utmost flexibility and delicacy. Eline Vere, in all her apparent inconsequence and the lack of apparent *suite* in her ideas and conduct, seems to be from first to last logically,

consistently, and even soberly drawn. One phase follows another with a sense of inevitableness; there are pauses, it is true, in her career that look like saving factors, but the progress, mental and physical, is, in truth, always downwards, till the point is reached where an inexorable Nemesis awaits the little victim cursed with the disease of modern life—*mala vitæ*. Eline is the outcome of a pleasure-seeking, do-nothing epoch grafted on the old Dutch stock. Batavian society and scenery, as depicted here, are not without an interest of their own. At first sight there seem to be too many people in the story; by some process they gradually emerge, however, and each holds his or her identity till the end. Mr. Couperus gives some pleasing types of age and youth—Mrs. Erlevoort and old Mrs. van Raat, for instance, and a whole bevy of young folk.

A review of ''Eline Vere,'' in The Athenaeum, *No. 3359, March 12, 1892, p. 339.*

THE ATHENAEUM (essay date 1895)

[*In the following excerpt from a review of* Majesty, *the critic comments favorably on Couperus's artistic use of contrasts, power of analysis, sense of humor, and ability to portray human relationships realistically.*]

There have been many workers among novelists in the field of royal portraiture, but it may be safely stated that few of those who have essayed this dubious path have achieved more striking results than M. Couperus. 'Majesty' is an extraordinarily vivid romance of autocratic imperialism, and the main aim of the book is so legitimate, and its treatment so sympathetic and artistic, that it is to be regretted that the author should have adopted the portrait form at all. The striking but superficial resemblance between the leading characters of the story and those of more than one reigning imperial house will, no doubt, prove a bait to readers hungry for personalities; but the real merits of the book—its dramatic intensity and powerful characterization—are entirely independent of this factitious interest. Foremost amongst the *dramatis personae* is the Crown Prince Othomar, a truly tragic figure, with noble instincts hampered by a delicate constitution, a Hamlet-like irresoluteness of purpose, and hedged round on every side by Procrustean etiquette. The contrast between him and his bluff sailor cousin, Prince Herman of Gothland, and his devotion for his mother, the empress (a woman whose natural warmth of heart has been numbed and paralyzed by the atmosphere of terror and melancholy which girds the throne), are drawn with great skill, and in the latter case with exquisite tenderness. M. Couperus does not merely turn the search-light of his analysis on the domestic life of the Caesars of to-day: he paints them also in their relations with courtiers and advisers; in their rare moments of contact with the masses; hurrying feverishly from function to function; strange, frozen, lonely figures, oppressed, in the words of the empress, with ''the immeasurable melancholy of being rulers.'' The effect of the whole book is greatly heightened by M. Couperus's artistic use of contrast and his sense of humour. The letter of the little ten-year-old Prince Berengar, describing to his brother the ceremony of his appointment as a Knight of St. Ladislas, is not only charming in itself, but it forms a most admirable anticlimax to the passionate love scene which has gone before.

A review of ''Majesty,'' in The Athenaeum, *No. 3507, January 12, 1895, p. 46.*

THE SPECTATOR   (essay date 1914)

[*In the following excerpt from a favorable review of* Small Souls, *the critic calls this novel a work of the highest creative imagination, depicting Dutch family life and Dutch society in transition.*]

M. Louis Couperus is no stranger to English readers. It is a good many years since an English version of his novel *Majesty* [appeared]. . . . In that powerful romance M. Couperus gave a wonderful picture of the conflict between human emotions and the traditions of State in the mind of a modern autocrat of amiable instincts but wavering purpose. But while impressive in its portrayal of the miseries of greatness, *Majesty* suffered from the inherent drawbacks of portrait fiction. The originals, though skilfully disguised, were easily recognizable, and to that extent the novel could not be regarded as a work of the highest creative imagination. In *Small Souls,* which is now given to us in the admirable translation of Mr. Teixeira de Mattos, the Dutch novelist reveals himself in an entirely different light. The atmosphere of *Majesty* was primarily that of a foreign Court; *Small Souls* could only have been written by a Dutchman, and is exclusively concerned with Dutch types. One might describe it as a study of Dutch society in transition; in which the connexion of Holland with the East Indies, and the influence of contact with France and Belgium and England, new views on the education of the young and their emancipation from the old-fashioned chaperonage, all combine to modify the old patriarchal family ideal. In regard to the first influence, it is extremely interesting to trace the analogy between what we may call the Indo-Dutch and the Anglo-Indian element. In their relations with the natives the severance of the races is less sharp than with us, and the translator reminds us in his introduction that Dutch not only sometimes marry native wives, but that these *nihilo obstante* are "received" by the "family" at home. This fact receives pointed illustration in the story before us, which is primarily concerned with the solidarity of Dutch family life—a solidarity which, though impaired by self-criticism and discontent and intestine jealousies, is still a fine as well as a formidable factor in Dutch social life. M. Couperus treats his subject on a grand scale, since his *dramatis personae* include representatives of four generations, though the time occupied by the events described in the narrative only covers a few months. . . . [Whatever] their age or generation, the measure of [the characters'] souls is in every case to be taken by their attitude to Constance Van der Welcke. Constance's story is easily told. As a young, handsome, and socially ambitious girl she had made a brilliant *mariage de convenance* with a distinguished diplomatist, a contemporary of her father's, nearly forty years her senior, and while at Rome, where her husband was Minister, had fallen in love with a young Secretary of Legation. For a brief hour of passion she had paid with fifteen years of exile and ill-assorted union with her lover, who had married her after the divorce at the bidding of his parents, old-fashioned, upright people of ultra-orthodox views. The scandal had broken his career, and, on the other hand, his wife, though she was glad at the time to regularize her position, could never forgive Van der Welcke for marrying her under compulsion. For thirteen or fourteen years they had lived at Brussels, pensioners on the bounty of their parents, and at the opening of the story, impelled by an irresistible desire to revisit her old home and renew the family associations, Constance had persuaded her husband to return to the Hague. The story sets forth with a minute particularity that is never wearisome how she was received and treated by her mother, brothers, and sisters; how, in spite of external friendliness and individual

cases of generosity, they contrived to make her feel her outcast condition, refused to aid her social rehabilitation, envied her for her grace and elegance, and put the worst construction on her innocent hospitalities. Constance is far from being a true heroine. She is herself terribly irritable and jealous. Yet she clings with a pathetic loyalty to her belief in her family until her eyes are opened to their small-souled, self-protective natures. In the hour of her deepest humiliation she shows a dignity, a self-composure, and a strength of character for which her endless bickerings with her husband had hardly prepared us. At her worst she never forfeits the sympathy of the reader. But if there is no heroine in *Small Souls,* there is a hero, and what is more, a hero of a new, original, and altogether delightful type in the Van der Welckes' little boy Adriaan, the only bond of union between his parents, and at all points worthy of their passionate affection. . . .

The spectacle of this wise little fellow, holding the balance between his parents, granting them favours not as a spoilt child but as a man, dividing his precious time systematically between his work and his father and mother, and conscientiously allotting what was due to each, is extraordinarily moving and beautiful. *Small Souls* is only the first of four novels which describe the fortunes of the Van Lowe family, and no one who has read the opening instalment can fail to look forward with keen expectancy to the sequel.

A review of "Small Souls," in The Spectator, *Vol. 112, No. 4468, February 14, 1914, p. 272.*

STEPHEN McKENNA   (essay date 1923)

[*In the following excerpt from an obituary tribute to Couperus, McKenna, an English novelist who wrote about life among the English upper classes and who translated Couperus's fiction, discusses Couperus's almost uncanny gift for projecting himself into every one of his characters, stating that Couperus knew intuitively what no one could know by experience. McKenna believes that this was Couperus's greatest strength as a novelist and justification for calling him one of "the most eminent figures in the literature of the world."*]

Short though his reign had been in England, the notices of his death agreed that, with Couperus, died the most eminent figure in contemporary Dutch literature and one of the most eminent figures in the contemporary literature of the world. The annals of criticism abound in premature predictions of immortality; and the critic who would strike out that word "contemporary" exposes himself to a more than ordinary risk. He should know something of all other Dutch men of letters before asserting that Couperus is the greatest. He must define "greatness" before claiming a place for any one with the greatest writers of all countries in all ages. Was Couperus a fashion? Or had his genius a quality that transcends all fashions?

He himself let fall in conversation that, when first visiting the north coast of Africa, he found among the Roman remains certain places which he was sure he had visited before. Round such-and-such a corner he knew that he would come upon such-and-such a temple. He put this premonition to the test and discovered that such-and-such a temple contained such-and-such an inscription, of which indeed he had been subconsciously aware before seeing it. He did not imagine imperial Rome, because he had lived in imperial Rome: the heat and cold, the sounds and smells, the "atmosphere" which permeates all his books are less a conscious artistic triumph than a triumph of unconscious memory. In *Majesty* he had been a king (and a diffident crown-prince and a truculent nihilist); in *Ecstasy* a young lover and the woman he loved.

This conviction of metempsychosis is the secret of Couperus' inspiration. The Hague under Queen Wilhelmina was not more familiar to him than Rome under Domitian. He could turn at will from Alexander the Great [in *Iskander*], to an east indian governor of the present day [in *The Hidden Force*], from a young man's emotional discords in *The Tour* to the emotional discords of a young woman in *The Inevitable*. In *Old People* he ranges from infants to nonagenarians.

Couperus would give a conventional explanation of this versatility by confessing that something of himself went into each of his characters. He might have said that everything in his characters came out of himself. He knew intuitively, like Shakespeare and Browning, what no man could know by experience. This power of projecting himself is the key to such a book as *Old People;* it is the only answer to the recurrent criticism: "Couperus is too young to know this, too old to remember that"; it is also one reason, of many, to justify even the critics of his own day in deleting that "contemporary" qualification and in saluting him as the greatest figure among Dutch men of letters and as one of the greatest figures among men of letters in all ages. (p. 260)

Stephen McKenna, "Couperus," in The Bookman, *London, Vol. LXIV, No. 384, September, 1923, pp. 259-60.*

DAVID HALLETT   (essay date 1923)

[*In the following survey of Couperus's works, Hallett argues that, for all the realism of his early works, Couperus was at heart a romantic who became less and less interested in writing realistically as he grew older. Thus, the critic divides Couperus's novels into two categories for discussion: the works in the realist tradition such as* Eline Vere, Footsteps of Fate, *and* The Books of the Small Souls; *and the romantic works. The latter he subdivides into: the imperial novels, such as* Majesty, Wereldvrede *and* Hooge troeven; *simple fairy tales and mythological stories such as* Psyche, Fidessa, *and* Babel; *and novels of historical reconstruction, which include* De berg van licht, Iskander, *and* The Comedians.]

Orchideëon (Orchids) and *Een Lent van Vaerzen (A Spring of Verse)* are interesting rather as psychological documents than as literary productions. The titles alone are clues to some of . . . [Couperus's] characteristics: the latter in its archaic form points to a certain preciosity, a natural affectation which he was never able entirely to throw off; while a predilection for orchids (and one might say that he never ceased to cultivate them) argues a taste for the exotic, the rare and the flamboyant, a tendency to decadence in so far as the word implies a certain "strangeness in the proportion," a quality of super-refinement, an interest in deviations from the strictly normal, and a concentration on detail, sometimes to the detriment of the whole. These poems are only youthful exercises in delicate word-painting, cameos in a rich and too elaborate setting. They are reminiscent of Leconte de Lisle and Hérédia, who, it is interesting to note, also had tropical associations. But Couperus, as he soon discovered for himself, was not a poet, and having found his bearings and a new range of inspiration, he turned to a larger field of action.

The day he began to read Zola was probably the turning point in his career. For *Aylva*, at any rate, "Zola was the immense revelation of a great and healthy insight into life, of life to be visualised such as it was." This, with the added influence of

Balzac, Flaubert and Goncourt, succeeded in counteracting the former purely æsthetic tendencies which, left to themselves, might easily have degenerated into effeteness and artificiality.

Eline Vere, written when the author was twenty-four, was acclaimed as the first really modern Dutch novel. Here at last the public found what it wanted; a faithful picture of contemporary life, the upper class life of The Hague; people with their little joys and sorrows, tea parties and flirtations, rivalries and reconciliations; innumerable silhouettes in ermine and frock coats, gaily flitting in and out of the limelight; and, in the centre of them all, one solitary figure, fairer than the rest, with deeper sorrows, a frailer and more languorous charm, a hothouse plant, a fading orchid. The success of the book was instantaneous and sensational; several fashionable young girls passed as the original of Eline, and Couperus became the accredited painter of Dutch aristocratic life.

For Couperus was a painter, not a philosopher; he observed and refrained from comment; sometimes he appears to be deprived of even the useful prejudices. "Que m'importe que tu sois sage" ["What does it matter to me that you be wise"], he seems to say with Baudelaire, "sois belle et sois triste" ["be beautiful and be sad"]. Free will is an uncertain quantity; men are puppets rushing headlong to their doom. Why pause to inquire into the rights and wrongs of things when we are being perpetually pursued by the rumblings of an ancestral fate? This Greek conception of an omnipotent destiny dogging the footsteps of helpless mankind runs like a purple thread through his whole work. Of Christianity he seems to have borrowed little beyond the ideal of compassion, which humanises what might otherwise be too harsh and relentless in his outlook. Psychologically, *Eline Vere* remains the best of his novels; never again did he think it worth while to search so deeply into the struggling soul, where the issue is in any case a foregone conclusion. His astonishing insight, aided by a completely open mind, continued to reveal itself throughout, but he tended to paint with a bigger brush, to discard the imponderable and to concentrate more on externals, manners, mannerisms, *milieu*. He was another for whom essentially the visible world exists.

It is impossible in a short space to deal adequately with the work of one of the most prolific of writers. His achievement in this respect—as has been pointed out before—was much more remarkable than that of Balzac or Zola who worked according to a plan mapped out from the beginning. Couperus was continually treading new paths; abandoning contemporary life for the realms of fantasy, then dropping into the Greek mythological world, only to find himself the next moment a citizen of the declining Roman Empire. Novels, sketches, and essays followed in breathless succession. For purposes of classification let us briefly consider first of all that portion of his work which continues the realist tradition so brilliantly initiated by *Eline Vere*.

Noodlot, [*(Footsteps of Fate)*] which immediately followed, is written in a more sombre vein and falls short of his very best work. The hand of Fate has ceased to grope blindly in the background; it has become almost a living person. The book was greatly discussed in view of its obviously determinist tendencies and generally condemned by the pious. *Extaze (Ecstasy)* strikes an entirely new note. A simple story of platonic affection with a delicate tinge of theosophy, it stands midway between his realist and his romantic manner. After a rather brief excursion into Utopia, he plunged violently into realism again with *Het Boek der Kleine Zielen,* [*(Small Souls)*] in which the story of a family in all its ramifications is chronicled with extraordinary ability. These four volumes represent Couperus's most comprehensive survey of contemporary Dutch life and constitute a fitting prelude to **Van Oude Menschen, de Dingen die voorbij gaan,** [(**Old People and the Things That Pass**)] the writer's masterpiece in this *genre*.

In a more concentrated and accomplished form, **Van Oude Menschen** has all the characteristics of its predecessor. It is a novel without a hero; the characters are interesting primarily as members of the same family. But here we have a quite exceptional group of human beings; all suffering from some form or other of neurosis, living in isolation, oppressed in varying degrees by the shadow of a crime perpetrated sixty years ago in the backwoods of Java. What an absorbingly interesting group! The very old mother and her lover, waiting erect, majestic and with apparent calm for death to deliver them from intolerable remorse and the fear of discovery; her daughter irresponsible, fickle and charming even at sixty, married three times and as often unhappy; the grandson Lot, already approaching middle age, artistic, a little *fin de siècle*, and living in horror of growing old; and his innumerable aunts and uncles and cousins, each with his or her morbid trend, inherited from the old mother's overwhelmingly passionate nature. It is incomparable portraiture. The characters, however, are static: there is no development; they never do anything unexpected; as they were sketched in the beginning, so they remain to the end. Perhaps for this very reason they strike one as being portraits extraordinarily true to life, rather than actually living beings. And this impression of immobility is increased by verbal repetition, which with Couperus became a trick, generally effective, sometimes a little exasperating. In **Van Oude Menschen,** more than in any other novel of this group, he revealed an almost unique capacity for creating atmospheres; the crime of sixty years ago rustles through every page like a live thing. Conrad alone among the moderns could possibly compare with him in the power of subtle suggestion.

There are reminiscences of India in **De Kleine Zielen,** and Java constitutes the sombre background of **Van Oude Menschen.** Prior to both, and after his marriage, Couperus had travelled to the East, and this trip became the starting point of his one purely Dutch-Indian novel, **De Stille Kracht (The Silent Power),** an interesting, though not wholly convincing, presentment of Dutch life in India during a crisis, where the white man's superior abilities and brute force are pitted against the mysterious resources of native witchcraft. But neither Holland nor even the more opulent Indies could retain Couperus from further intellectual adventures, and after **Van Oude Menschen** he definitely abandoned realism for romance.

In Couperus, then, as in Flaubert, there are two tendencies struggling for mastery, the realist, and the romantic. It is an unequal conflict; his realism was the result of external circumstance, the outcome of the age in which he lived; at bottom he remained a romantic throughout. It stands clearly revealed by his Corinthian style, by that "addition of strangeness to beauty," which, says Pater, constitutes the romantic character in art. Its spirit informs his most realist work, and whereas in his first period he continually abandoned realism and the study of contemporary life in pursuit of the unreal or of the past, one observes that, after 1907, he did not once recur to the former manner.

The romantic portion of his work can be roughly sub-divided into three main groups: the so-called Imperial novels (whose nearest English equivalent is to be found in Anthony Hope's

Prisoner of Zenda), the purely fantastic, and his historical reconstructions. The Imperial cycle, which is first in date, constitutes the only signal failure in a variegated career. It is a series of three novels, **Majesteit** [(**Majesty**)], **Wereldvrede** (**World Peace**), **Hooge Troeven** (**High Trumps**), in which the author introduces us to the Court of the imaginary kingdom of Liparia, in a semi-Slav, semi-Italian atmosphere. They deal mainly with the conflict of two personalities, two conceptions of Government; the old idea of monarchy by divine right incarnated by Oscar, the absolutist sovereign, *versus* the modern ideal of constitutionalism represented by Othomar, the Hamlet Prince, who reads Marx and Bakunin, is sceptical of his rights and fails in all his projects of reform. It is difficult to attribute the success of these books to anything but their topical interest. In **Wereldvrede,** for instance, which appeared in 1899, the year of The Hague Convention, Peace Congress celebrations, mundane frivolities and a revolution breathlessly follow upon one another, constituting an incoherent medley which defies all analysis. One observes even a falling off in the style, a certain cheapness and tawdriness, due perhaps to the author's lack of conviction. Political thought and theory obviously did not interest Couperus. . . . (pp. 520-23)

Liparia was fortunately soon abandoned for the more congenial regions of phantasmagoria. We have seen that with **Eline Vere** Couperus established his reputation as an incomparable painter of Dutch interiors. **Psyche** . . . opened the series of works by which he became the best modern writer of simple fairy tales and mythological stories. In **Psyche, Fidessa, Babel, Dyonysos,** the story is nothing in itself, the manner of telling everything; untrammelled by philosophy, politics, or realities, he transports us where beauty alone resides. It is a world inhabited by satyrs, fauns and nymphs, gambolling in mystic woodland; by knights and languorous princesses leaning over ancestral towers. . . . They are pure creations of joy, outlets for a luxuriant imagination, pretexts for delicate and subtle word painting. The dialogue is not so good, and in its vague and somnambulist meanderings often reminds one of Maeterlinck. **Herakles** is among the best of the series; the loves and labours of the hero, pursued by the wrath of Hera, take two volumes to describe and do not cloy for one moment. (p. 524)

The period Couperus liked best to dwell in is that which witnessed the decline of the Roman Empire, an empire saturated long since by Hellenism and heavily perfumed by the East. His two masterpieces of historical reconstruction are cast in this epoch. **De Berg van Licht (The Mountain of Light)** is the more ambitious of the two, and is quite his most astonishing achievement. We have here the life story of Elagabalus (and, incidentally, a study in intermediate sex), his first years as priest of the Sun among the Syrian splendours of Emesa, then the military rising, organised by the wealthy Mamoea, which set him on the Imperial throne, his triumphal entry into Rome, and the incredible story of his reign and death. If one compares this novel with its sources, Lampridius, Herodian, and Dion Cassius, or even with the equally censorious summary of Gibbon (whose sources are the same), one comes almost inevitably to the conclusion that the writer has deliberately assumed the *rôle* of devil's advocate—or is it the result of a wager? Couperus' Elagabalus is a charming, wayward, almost sympathetic youth, striving hard to maintain an awkward balance as priest of the hermaphroditic cult of the Sun. But alas! the balance always tilts on the wrong side. As a picture of the last days of pagan Rome, it is unrivalled; Herodian and the other sources have been ransacked with a discerning hand and the booty has turned to pure gold. All the old characters reappear to a man:

Mamoea, Alexander, the fatal Hierocles; and, as a counter-poise, Hydaspes, the grand Priest, and Gordian, the elegant and cultured Roman, who was once to become emperor and who mourns the death of Elagabalus as heralding the end of pagan beauty. In *De Berg van Licht* Couperus attempted for the first time to render mass-psychology; it is done in the manner of Zola, less forcefully perhaps, but with greater penetration and a much greater capacity for blurring innumerable shades and *nuances* into one harmonious entity. The characters are ably analysed, but as is usual with Couperus, the analysis does not go deep enough. They turn to caricature by sheer concentration on one or two aspects or attitudes which recur again and again.

De Komedianten (*The Mummers*) brings us back to the reign of the sombre Domitian and reveals, like the previous novel, a considerable understanding and a generally accurate knowledge of Roman life. It relates the adventurous story of two youthful actors in a travelling company and introduces us into the society of Suetonius, Pliny the younger, Tacitus, Quintilian and Martial. One regrets that the historic figures are little more than silhouettes. It is altogether written in a lighter vein, but very well done. The choice of period and subject is characteristic: Rome under the terror of Domitian; a constellation of greatness on the one hand, the common folk on the other, and all perpetually oppressed by the threat of an impending doom. The subject is, besides, very happily chosen; Couperus, who was an accomplished scholar, had a special knowledge of ancient dramatic art and his translation of Plautus' *Menoechmi* has been staged with some success.

An interval of eleven years separates *De Komedianten* from *De Berg van Licht* . . . , during which period Couperus published several minor works in the same line. *Antiek Toerisme* (*Ancient Touring*) is based on a study of the Latin and Greek geographers, and describes the trip of a Roman patrician during the reign of Tiberis across the land of the Pharaohs, in search of a favourite slave. Two collections of short stories, *Schimmen van Schoonheid* (*Shadows of Beauty*) and *Antieke Verhalen van Goden en Keizers, van Dichters en Hetaeren* (*Ancient Tales of Gods and Emperors, Poets and Courtesans*) are delightful in patches, as where the last hours of Hadrian at Tibur are described. But, as a rule, Couperus fails in the short story. His exuberant and discursive genius was at its best where not confined to a "scanty plot of ground." Mention must also be made of his one Moorish novel, *De Ongelukkige* (*The Unfortunate One*), written after a journey to Spain and dealing with the last days of Mohammedan rule in the Peninsula. It falls far short of his good work. The writer was ill at ease in the more sombre and fanatical atmosphere of Spain.

For several years Couperus contributed a collection of articles, travel sketches, and autobiographical essays to *Het Vaderland*, a leading Dutch daily, and they were subsequently published in book form under the title: *Van en over myzelf en anderen* (*About Myself and Others*). The writer, now in the full intoxication of literary success, surrounded by a host of admirers and followers, *arrivé*, as he puts it himself, set out to amuse and instruct by a weekly flow of self-revelation. It makes very diverting reading, and is generally clever, humorous, and full of delicate irony. But absolute sincerity was not among his virtues and he hastens to warn us in a very characteristic and "Wildian" passage not to take him at his face value: "Never trust me when I am telling you anything, for I have chosen the *métier* of liar, I mean of novelist. . . . The lie is my Satanism, I devoutly kneel down before her and worship her as the mistress of the world." (pp. 525-27)

David Hallett, "Louis Couperus," in The London Mercury, *Vol. VIII, No. 47, September, 1923, pp. 519-27.*

ROB NIEUWENHUYS (essay date 1982)

[*In the following excerpt, Nieuwenhuys reveals many of the original sources for people and events described in Couperus's novel* The Hidden Force. *He also discusses the classical form of the tragedy in the novel—that of the European resident in Indonesia—and Couperus's role as an Indies writer who captured the essence of the unusual society of colonials.*]

As [Couperus] said in his *Collected Works* (*Verzameld Werk* . . .): "I was a child born in Holland but within the Indies tradition in mind and spirit." That tradition was that of the class of higher officials in the Indies. The family belonged to the top layer of Indies society for whom it was customary to go and live in Holland after a career in the Indies, and Holland meant invariably The Hague. There, the members of this extensive family would come together again and be united. They lived not as a typical family of The Hague but as an Indies coterie, keeping the Indies constantly in the background because their interests continued to lie there. They lived Indonesian style, as one big happy family, partly because they felt themselves to be different, partly because they were estranged, as they say, but also because Dutch society excluded them. Literature is full of the often repeated complaint of Indies people on furlough and pensioners in Holland that they bore some mark, some Indonesian *tjap* or brand, that made them stand out. As Creusesol put it: "Join us, Indies man . . . come live *with* us, *among* us if you like, but *part* of us you'll never be." . . . [Books] such as Couperus's *The Books of the Small Souls* (*De boeken der kleine zielen* . . .) and *Of Old People and the Things that Pass* (*Van oude menschen, de dingen die voorbijgaan* . . .) show us to what extent family life of the higher Indies officials in The Hague retained the patrimonial characteristics so typical of an Indies way of life. The belief in fate as the great compelling force in life Couperus no doubt derived from the "philosophy" of the period. However, this belief also ties in very well with a culture that tried either to invoke or ward off the constant machinations of fate through prayers, charms, and sacrifices.

It has been said, and for good reason, that Couperus dissociated himself from his family in writing his great novels set in The Hague. This is only partially true. In the first place, it is questionable whether Couperus used just his own family as a model, and we have to consider further Couperus's personal ambivalence as an artistic spectator. Despite having taken some distance from them, he remained one of the family who never severed his ties. He was even an exemplary member of his clan, and behaved "like a dear," to use a typical Indies expression, according to his family. The author Beb Vuyk considered the families described in Couperus's novels set in The Hague "to have more in common with the Indies than with The Hague." "Despite the different background of Hague houses and gray skies," she wrote, "his family portraits retain the pattern of the Indies." And rightly so, we should add, for Couperus himself stresses the relationship of the non-Dutch aspects of his personality with his Indies descent and tradition: "I consider myself to be warmer, sunnier, and more Eastern than my compatriots in Holland are . . . the real Dutch part of me, I'm afraid, is a little taken aback by this." (pp. 123-24)

The Hidden Force (*De stille kracht*) contains much to remind us of Couperus's stay in Tegal and Pasuruan. Even so, we do have to be careful in identifying anyone or anything in Couperus's work. Someone who knew him quite well wrote, following his death in 1923, "Louis would literally put the nose of one person above the mouth of another." He did the same with events and circumstances.

How Couperus came by his theme of the secret, hidden force (which is not, by the way, the basic theme of his novel), is not known. He probably did not have to go out of his way looking for it, but it must have suggested itself in the form of stories of supernatural events which were to remain inexplicable. The Indies have always been buzzing with that sort of tale. The familiar occult manifestations of stones raining down or of objects or things spitting betel juice are fairly well documented. Those occurring in **The Hidden Force** are based on authentic information, which Couperus obtained, according to the paper *Batavian News* (*Bataviaasch Nieuwsblad* of October 8, 1921), from the secret dossiers of the secretary general at Buitenzorg. It so happens that a similar case of stones raining down had occurred in Sumedang some ten years earlier. One Dr. Baudisch wrote a little book about such phenomena and he described that particular incident extensively. At the time, the government had ordered an investigation. The report, which also mentions an overnight stay in a haunted house similar to that in **The Hidden Force**, had since been kept in the archives in Buitenzorg. This Couperus consulted. In **The Hidden Force**, reference is made to the fact that the report, including the resident's findings, "had since been kept in the government's secret archives." (pp. 126-27)

The Hidden Force is an excellent, intelligent, and clever book. Its composition is clever, and its intelligence shows in its understanding of Indies situations, especially those in government circles. Couperus owed this understanding, which exceeds merely being informed, to his brother-in-law De la Valette. Without his inside information, Couperus could never have written a book such as **The Hidden Force**, as he indeed openly admits. Because of all the things De la Valette told him, Couperus could imagine how a resident as head of a district government would act and feel if he had Van Oudijck's character. Van Oudijck is central to the novel, let there be no mistake about that, and "the hidden force" is not. One would certainly be wrong to consider the subject of the occult as its central theme. The mystical and mysterious properties with which Couperus foreshadows and shrouds everything time and again are primarily literary props. They serve mostly to conjure up the atmosphere of dread and fatality which is characteristic of Couperus. He experienced the world of the Indies in a way that was a projection of his own sensibilities. The powers of mystery were a means to focus this projection. Mood and atmosphere permeate the book, as in the description of the pompous residential house at dusk, inhospitable to family life ("always waiting for the next reception"), of the dark yard with the holy banyan trees, of the avenue along the Patjaram estate lined with the pinlike tjemara trees, the crescent moon above and the foliage "like tattered plush and unraveled velvet lumped against the clouds like cotton puffs." Couperus evokes, and the verb is most apt in his case, a scene such as that of a quietly breathing and fragrant courtyard at evening, with deep black shadows and flecks of light on the road or out on the yard. These evocations are charged with an atmosphere which Couperus time and again tries to describe with words such as "dark," "mysterious," "mystical," "incomprehensible." He does so either because he was ignorant of the word *angker*, or because he was reluctant to use it. However, the Javanese word *angker*, which is untranslatable but means something approx-

imating "being magically possessed," is really the very word that describes the qualities Couperus is attempting to suggest. He certainly senses as much, even though he was an outsider and a European. The hidden force also serves to propel the action and to dramatically bring about intrigue and reversal. Still, the depiction of the characters is central, especially that of the main character, Resident van Oudijck. **The Hidden Force** is definitely not a "story about spiritualism and magic" or one about "shivers and ghosts," and even less "a third-rate serial," as Van Deyssel claimed it was in his *Bimonthly Magazine* (*Tweemaandelijksch tijdschrift*). He certainly does not understand anything about the book. A critic of the Semarang daily newspaper *De Locomotief* was quick to point out the error of his ways in no uncertain terms: "Your criticism is an embarrassment to you, a disgrace to your magazine, and a disgrace to literature." That same critic also put his finger on the novel's essence when he added: "**The Hidden Force** is about the tragedy of the resident."

Quite so. Couperus added another dimension to the story, however, that of the resident as the colonial ruler in an alien land. Couperus had no need to portray the colonial as a brute or a usurper. He had no part in the ethical movement but was an artist who refused to take sides because to do otherwise would have meant to diminish "the fullness of life" itself. His portrayal of Van Oudijck is that of an upright ruler, a man who lives for his work and works only to further the welfare of his district, who looks after the interests of its people and protects them from the depradations of "private interest." Van Oudijck acts this way because he wants to do the right thing by his own convictions and not because he is following a particular set of instructions. He personifies the conscientious and upright Dutch government official in being honest, just, and patient, a man who knows his job and whose need for power and authority are entirely satisfied by the office he holds. "No other outfit can hold a candle to the civil service," Couperus has him think. He is the typical civil servant from the glorious days of the Indies civil service, which reigned autocratically with nearly absolute powers based on the principles of strictness and justice. Van Oudijck is a competent official of integrity, of the type who, ever mindful of the interests of the population, brooks no meddling with Dutch authority, which he regards as unassailable. Notions about self-government or democracy are alien to him. He is demanding of those working under him, but he can be jovial, and he lacks the arrogance of the high officials in the capital. He has a great deal of tact as well. He quells a revolt, for example, not through a show of force but through talking, through persuading and convincing people. This satisfied him deeply. He does, however, remain true to type in that he is an imported Hollander, a level-headed man who remains deaf and dumb in many ways. (pp. 128-30)

A discussion of Couperus's final book dealing with the Indies must inevitably be anticlimactic. **Eastward (Oostwaarts . . .)** is little more than a serialized travel journal. It is the account of a tourist asked by the Hague Post (Haagsche Post) to make another jaunt through the Indies with an occasional nod to his hosts and sponsor. The journal also corroborates the traditional European view of the Indies in describing them as prosperous and bursting with energy and, as a matter of course, closely and firmly tied to the Netherlands. Even though he prophesied somewhere that "the autonomy of Indonesia is only a question of time" (and such a prophesy came easily enough), this journal considers, or rather talks about Indonesian nationalism in the same disapproving terms as were then current among Europeans. (pp. 132-33)

Rob Nieuwenhuys, "The Indies World of Couperus," in his Mirror of the Indies: A History of Dutch Colonial Literature, *edited by E. M. Beekman, translated by Frans van Rosevelt, The University of Massachusetts Press, 1982, pp. 123-33.*

ADDITIONAL BIBLIOGRAPHY

"Contrasts." *The Bookman*, London LXII, No. 372 (September 1922): 255.
    Review of *The Hidden Force*. The reviewer calls Couperus's novel, "a splendid story, wonderfully told."

Collins, J. P. "Life Laid Bare." *The Bookman*, London LVII, No. 340 (January 1920): 149-50.
    Favorable review. The critic praises *Old People and the Things That Pass* for its power and its "stark, ironic intensity."

Review of *Majesty*, by Louis Couperus. *The Dial* XIX, No. 217. (1 July 1895): 21.
    Brief, favorable review of Couperus's novel about a degenerate modern dynasty.

Gosse, Edmund. "Louis Couperus." In his *Silhouettes*, pp. 259-68. London: William Heineman, 1925.
    Personal reminiscence of a visit with Couperus by a noted English critic.

Plomer, William. "Louis Couperus." In his *Electric Delights*, pp. 58-65. London: Jonathan Cape, 1978.
    Insightful analysis and discussion of Couperus's novel *The Hidden Force*.

Russell, James Anderson. "Realism and Psychology (Holland)." In his *Romance and Realism: Trends in Belgo-Dutch Prose Literature*, pp. 103-34. Amsterdam: H. J. Paris N.V., 1959.*
    Discusses the conflict between realism and romanticism in Couperus's works and concludes that, for all the merit of his romantic works, Couperus's reputation will endure on the basis of such realistic novels as *The Books of the Small Souls* and *Old People and the Things that Pass*.

Review of *The Later Life*, by Louis Couperus. *The Spectator* 115, No. 4565 (25 December 1915): 923-24.
    Discusses the unfolding of the drama of degeneracy in the second volume of Couperus's tetralogy *The Small Souls*.

Van Riel, Leo. "A Letter from the Low Countries." *The London Mercury* V, No. 25 (November 1921): 82-4.
    Discusses Couperus's novels, stating that "the publication of *Eline Vere* was an event in our literature."

Review of *Footsteps of Fate*, by Louis Couperus. *The Westminister Review* 136, No. 3 (September 1891): 349.
    Brief, unfavorable review discussing the "hideousness" of the story and the improbability of the plot of Couperus's novel *Footsteps of Fate*.

E(ric) R(ucker) Eddison

1882-1945

English novelist, translator, and editor.

Eddison is best known for *The Worm Ouroboros,* a fantasy novel in which his talents as a romantic storyteller are most fully displayed. Radically departing from modern literary trends toward realistic, ironic, or psychoanalytic novels, this work conveys Eddison's admiration for the people and literature of past eras, and has been highly praised by such authors of fantastic fiction as H. P. Lovecraft and C. S. Lewis. Despite this recognition, however, Eddison's works have never had more than a small, but devoted audience.

Eddison was born in Adel, Yorkshire. Both of his parents were interested in literature, and Eddison wrote his first stories at about the age of ten. These childhood efforts distantly foreshadow *The Worm Ouroboros* and introduce the character Horius Parry, who becomes a memorable villain many years later in Eddison's Zimiamvian trilogy. While he was a student at Eton, Eddison began teaching himself the Icelandic language so that he could read the sagas in their original forms. Later, at Oxford, he studied the works of Homer and the poetry of Sappho, which, together with the Icelandic sagas, became enduring influences on his works. Sometime later, Elizabethan prose and the romances of Joseph Conrad also made significant impressions on him. In 1906 Eddison entered the Board of Trade, where he served in a number of increasingly important capacities and was honored for the distinction of his work. During his successful career in civil service, Eddison wrote *The Worm Ouroboros* and three other works, including *Mistress of Mistresses,* the first volume of his Zimiamvian trilogy. He retired in 1938 as Deputy Comptroller of the Overseas Board of Trade, in order to devote his time to writing. He and his family then moved from London to Marlborough, where he lived until his death.

While Eddison had privately printed a small book called *Poems, Letters, and Memories of Philip Sidney Nairn* in 1916, it was the publication of *The Worm Ouroboros* several years later that brought him to the attention of critics and a small circle of fantasy connoisseurs. This heroic romance, described by Orville Prescott as a modern *Iliad,* chronicles an epic war in an imaginary world much like Europe of the Viking Age. The warriors, including the villains, are portrayed as heroic, and war is graphically depicted as a glorious, though gory adventure. At the novel's close, after the victors find the prospect of enduring peace intolerable, a prayer for further adventure is granted; the slain enemy is magically given new life, and the war begins anew. The regal symbol of Ouroboros, illustrated as a serpent swallowing its tail, is an image of eternity and suggests the philosophical concept of the end as the beginning. *The Worm Ouroboros* is a panorama of noble characters, exotic beasts, gorgeous scenery, and material splendor which portrays life as joyful and full of wonder and displays Eddison's extraordinary imagination. The prose in this and his subsequent novels exhibits the influence of both Elizabethan works and Icelandic sagas, forming an archaic style which has proven difficult to some readers and highly compelling to others. Similarly, the complex narrative structure of this work is considered both imaginative and, at times, uncontrolled.

Throughout the novel, character incarnations, digressive adventures, assorted styles of dialogue, time lapses, and incongruities contribute to the intrigue and confusion. Nevertheless, most critics agree that despite the difficulties and eccentricities, there is much to praise and enjoy in the elaborate fantasy and prose of what has been termed Eddison's "flawed masterpiece."

In his next two works, Eddison turned from fantasy to focus on Icelandic history. *Styrbiorn the Strong,* based on a few brief allusions from a history of Norway, recounts the prowess and trials on land and sea of Styrbiorn, Prince of Sweden, during the Viking Age. Eddison followed *Styrbiorn* with *Egil's Saga,* a translation of an Icelandic prose work which is comparable to a modern historical novel. Set in a grim atmosphere of murder and vengeance, the saga tells of the feuds among ancient Icelandic landowning families, and is one of many similar works about eminent Icelanders who lived in the tenth and eleventh centuries. Neither *Styrbiorn* nor *Egil's Saga* have received much critical attention, though in a recent appraisal L. Sprague de Camp has found that while *Styrbiorn* is still highly readable, modern readers might be bogged down by the monotony and endless squabbles in *Egil's Saga.*

Published in 1935, *Mistress of Mistresses* marked Eddison's return to fantasy writing and the beginning of his Zimiamvian trilogy. Zimiamvia, a land briefly mentioned in *The Worm Ouroboros,* bears a resemblance to Renaissance Europe and exists as a kind of Valhalla for the heroes of Eddison's first novel. Character incarnations, including the separate and simultaneous incarnations of the same character, occur amidst Machiavellian intricacies of plot and counterplot. While most critics agree that the many characters and complicated plots of *Mistress of Mistresses* are confusing, a number have found that it is a highly imaginative prose work with memorable characters and events. *A Fish Dinner in Memison* is the next novel of the trilogy. The title refers to a dinner described in the book, at which ten diners discuss worlds they would create if they were gods. Transformed into deities, the diners create these worlds, live in them as gods incarnate, depart from their creations, and eventually bring them to an end. James Stephens, who wrote the introduction, called *A Fish Dinner in Memison* "the most magnificent book of our time," praising Eddison's prose and his aristocratic attitude, which gave his works the grace and charm that Stephens found lacking in modern fiction. He also praised Eddison's portrayal of women who are at once quaint, lovely, and disturbing, and who can be mistresses or empresses as it suits their self-interest. The unfinished last novel of the trilogy, *The Mezentian Gate,* was Eddison's last work. In his introduction, Eddison said that he had a "searching curiosity" about Zimiamvia and that he wrote *The Mezentian Gate* to explore some unanswered questions about King Mezentius's death and about the poor conditions of his kingdoms at the time of his death.

In comparing his major works, critics note that *The Worm Ouroboros* is more purely a heroic adventure, whereas the trilogy is concerned as well with the presentation of Eddison's complex philosophy. According to Lin Carter, it is the thematic simplicity and the epic adventure that makes Eddison's first novel more interesting and appealing than the trilogy. Eddison's primary philosophical belief, present throughout his major works, was that beauty is the one ultimate value, the only thing desirable for itself alone. He reasoned that the value of truth and goodness was contingent upon circumstances, whereas beauty was always valuable. G. Rostrevor Hamilton, though a great admirer of Eddison and his works, takes issue with his philosophy, citing Eddison's failure to include beauty of character in his value system as the chief defect of Eddison's imaginary world, and as a source for the unadmirable qualities of Eddison's heroes and heroines. Eddison also contended that evil was transient and illusory, and that present reality was partial and not final. He suggested looking beyond mundane reality to see the lasting and guiding realities. Thus, nothing is ultimately at risk in his works. Some critics find this conception disturbing in light of the complex and threatening problems of this century. Eddison's philosophy, combined with the virtual absence of modern affairs and concerns in his works, have contributed to a common opinion among critics that Eddison's works are escapist and have little relevance to our world. In a recent critical perspective, however, Sharon Wilson argues that from the beginning Eddison's works have been judged by standards inappropriate to romance. She contends that the virtues of organic unity and simplicity, established by Aristotle as essential qualities of works of art, are unfair criteria for an evaluation of Eddison's work. The romantic tradition, on the other hand, views openendedness, variety, and ornamentation as virtues, and Wilson concludes that Eddison's works, when judged by the standards of romance, can be more fairly appraised, better understood, and more fully appreciated.

De Camp suggests that a reason for Eddison's small readership is that fantasy literature in general had a limited audience for many years. Although Eddison remains an obscure author, the quality of his work can be confirmed by the high praise it has received from the twentieth century's major fantasy writers. J.R.R. Tolkien referred to Eddison as "the greatest and most convincing writer of 'invented worlds' that I have ever read," while C. S. Lewis wrote of Eddison's works that "nowhere else shall we meet this precise blend of hardness and luxury, of lawless speculation and sharply realized detail, of the cynical and the magnanimous. No author can be said to remind us of Eddison."

(See also *Contemporary Authors,* Vol. 109.)

PRINCIPAL WORKS

Poems, Letters, and Memories of Philip Sidney Nairn [editor]   (poetry, letters, and memoirs)   1916
The Worm Ouroboros   (novel)   1922
Styrbiorn the Strong   (novel)   1926
Egil's Saga [editor and translator; from the prose work *Egil's saga Skallagrímsonnor*]   (novel)   1930
*Mistress of Mistresses   (novel)   1935
*A Fish Dinner in Memison   (novel)   1941
*The Mezentian Gate   (unfinished novel)   1958

*These novels comprise the Zimiamvian trilogy.

EDWIN MARKHAM   (essay date 1926)

[*Distinguished for his popular poems "The Man with the Hoe" (1899) and "Lincoln, the Man of the People" (1901), Markham was known as the "dean" of American poetry during the early 1900s. He belonged to a declamatory, moralistic, and hortatory age in American verse, an era that was ending during the time of his most noted achievement. In the following excerpt Markham favorably reviews* The Worm Ouroboros, *praising it as a work written for a select, style-conscious audience. For further favorable discussion of* The Worm Ouroboros, *see the excerpts by H. P. Lovecraft (1933) and Sharon Wilson (1984). For a generally adverse discussion of Eddison's novel, see the excerpt by L. Sprague de Camp (1976).*]

"The Worm Ouroboros," on the title-page of the strange new romance by E. R. Eddison, signifies our old enemy the serpent. This symbol, the serpent with its tail in its mouth, is carved on the thumb-ring of the haughty kings of Witchland, proclaiming that this royal line is to reign eternally, "the end forever at the beginning and the beginning at the end forevermore." The volume runs nearly to five hundred pages—pages damasked, incensed, musicked, embellished with every loveliness that touches sense and spirit. It is written with leisure and spaciousness, in an antique English of poetic flavor and delicate or majestic cadence.

The scene swings from Earth to Mercury, from a quiet English bed-chamber to a palace in another planet. "Time is!" calls out a little martlet at midnight. A chariot, drawn by a winged horse, is at the casement, and Lessingham, through whose eyes we witness the whole story, is off as if convoyed by winds, the first of the sons of men to visit Mercury. Here, with the martlet beside him as guide, he walks impalpable and invisible in the midst of charms and portents, pomps and pleasures, spells and battles and triumphs of the Demonlords and Witchlords of this amazing story.

So suavely runs the narrative, and with so little occasion for disbelief, and so far from to-day is it all, that a Chatterton or a MacPherson might well have passed it on to willing readers as an authentic romance of old, found in some hidden vault or chest, a thing left over from antiquity. From the first, our attention is captivated by the scenery, the architecture, the sculpture and the other decorations, as well as by the stately personages continually disclosed—galaxies of characters of every degree. Indeed, the author, in the appendix, takes four pages to give a table of the characters and the chronology, and a skeleton scenario of the closely interwoven tale. . . .

[The] book reverberates with [a] four-year war, its plots and counterplots, its stratagems and spells, all full of high hazard, and once or twice reaching a pitch of sheer horror seldom matched in any book. One tires, perhaps, of the incessant battling and blood-letting; but there are enticing episodes and interludes, and always a gorgeous panoramic background of places and persons. We behold countless changes of gems and garments—wonderful costumes worn in these weird lands.

The story is told with a gallant seriousness, with no trace of humorous byplay. Wonders happen in every chapter. . . . (p. 697)

The author says there is no allegory lurking behind his pages—nothing but sheer romance. Nevertheless, we sense in it all the meaningless futility of wars, save only that they break the ennui of our sated rulers of peoples and rulers of finance.

This story is a rare and—I believe—a lasting piece of work. It glows with fantasy, poetry, imagination. It is not a book for the hurried commuter or for the book-a-day gourmand. It needs a detached mood, an abundance of time; but it will commend itself to those who care not only for the story but also for the way it is told. It certainly will get any reader out of his little mental rat-run and off the dull, disenchanted earth. (p. 698)

Edwin Markham, "Who's Who on the Planet Mercury," in The Literary Digest International Book Review, *Vol. IV, No. 11, October, 1926, pp. 697-98.*

L. P. HARTLEY   (essay date 1926)

[*Author of the acclaimed novel trilogy* Eustace and Hilda *(1944-47), Hartley was an English novelist and short story writer whose fiction is unified by the theme of the search for individuality and meaning in the post-Christian era. In his examination of moral dilemmas he is often compared to Nathaniel Hawthorne, while his effective use of symbolism and close attention to craft and plot unity evoke frequent comparisons to the works of Henry James. A literary critic as well, Hartley contributed reviews for many years to* The Saturday Review, Time and Tide, The Spectator, *and other periodicals. In the following excerpt from a review of* Styrbiorn the Strong, *Hartley praises Eddison's novel as a work of heroic, lyrical fantasy, finding it marred only occasionally by traces of mundane reality.*]

'Styrbiorn the Strong' takes us back to tenth-century Scandinavia. Gone are the amenities of modern life, but dignity is restored to human nature. Though the ground slip from under their feet (a landslide is needed to kill Styrbiorn) the characters always manage to stand on their dignity. Mr. Eddison has expanded a few pages of history into a full-length novel, recalling the manner of the Icelandic sagas. Faced with the difficulty of inventing a language fit for heroes to talk in, he has evolved a jargon which, in spite of Hibernianisms, preciosities like "easlier" and Americanisms like "eats" (meaning food) is eminently satisfactory. True to its prototypes the story wades knee-deep in gore. . . .

But the book is not all battles. Crude as the relations between the characters are, they have an inflexibility and an emotional integrity that are extremely moving, and the last scene is finely worked up to and described with economy of detail and great dramatic effect. Mr. Eddison's one weakness is the introduction, here and there, of realistic touches which are foreign to the lyrical, unself-conscious mood in which the work as a whole is conceived.

L. P. Hartley, in a review of "Styrbiorn the Strong," in The Saturday Review, *London, Vol. 142, No. 3701, October 2, 1926, p. 388.*

H. P. LOVECRAFT   (letter date 1933)

[*Lovecraft is considered one of the foremost modern authors of supernatural horror fiction. Strongly influenced by Edgar Allan Poe, Lord Dunsany, and early science fiction writers, he developed a type of horror tale that combined occult motifs, modern science, and the regional folklore of his native New England to produce the personal mythology on which he based much of his work. In the following excerpt from a letter to E. Hoffmann Price, Lovecraft highly praises* The Worm Ouroboros. *For further favorable discussion of Eddison's first novel, see the excerpts by Edwin Markham (1926) and Sharon Wilson (1984). For a generally adverse discussion of* The Worm Ouroboros, *see the excerpt by L. Sprague de Camp (1976).*]

Glad you're succumbing to the unique and haunting charm of **Ouroboros**. There is nothing else quite like it—even by the same author. It weaves its own atmosphere, and lays down its own laws of reality. At first one tends to rebel at the laying of the scene in *Mercury* without any attempt to depict conditions peculiar to that planet and alien to the earth (if we except the rather whimsical *horus* of the population), but gradually we come to accept or forget the gesture—taking the whole thing in the spirit of an enthralling fireside tale about it—its naiveté, absence of Cabellian snickers, and subordination of the obtrusive social satire which spoils the charm of so many kindred phantasies. (pp. 156-57)

H. P. Lovecraft, in a letter to E. Hoffman Price on March 2, 1933, in his Selected Letters: 1932-1934, *edited by August Derleth and James Turner, Arkham House Publishers, Inc., 1976, pp. 156-57.*

PERCY HUTCHISON   (essay date 1935)

[*In the following excerpt Hutchison favorably reviews* Mistress of Mistresses, *the first novel in Eddison's Zimiamvian trilogy.*]

Probably in every generation there will be an author moving in an orbit so individually his own as to defy all the measuring instruments of watchers of the literary skies. Such a one is E. R. Eddison, who will be remembered for his strange romance, **"The Worm Ouroborus,"** and who now presents us with **"Mistress of Mistresses,"** so extraordinary and eerie a romance that ordinary and realistic terms are quite inadequate to its description.

As those in Eastern countries who must take off their shoes before they may enter the mysterious depth of the temple, so the reader who would enter into the mysterious life of Mr. Eddison's Valhalla of Zimiamvia must first put from him all preconceived literary likes and dislikes, reverse every conviction of what constitutes the ingredients of fiction, nay, abolish for the moment times and space themselves. If there be such a thing as "pure" romance, then is this fabrication precisely that. . . . If the reader be one who would gaze from

> . . . magic casements, opening on the foam
> Of perilous seas, in faery lands forlorn,

then "**Mistress of Mistresses**" is for him. . . .

[While Eddison] has given something approaching an old Icelandic background to his main scenes, there is no more a strict following of Norse mythology and romance than there is of the romance of the south, Greece and Provence. It might be said, as an attempt to draw a distinction, that in the masculine ingredients Mr. Eddison's romance is northern; in its emotional constituents, southern.

And the observation brings us to the title. Why "**Mistress of Mistresses**"?

This explanation may be no explanation. At least, it is likely to be less clear. For light the reader must turn to his copies of Sappho, of Baudelaire and Swinburne. He must steep his mind in the lore of the Cyprian goddess, of Pentheseleia, Astarte, Semiramis:

> Sparkling-throned heavenly Aphrodite,
> Child of God, beguiler of guiles—Beseech You,
> Not with sating neither with ache and anguish,
> Lady, my heart quell.

This ode of Sappho, in the Wharton rendition, which Mr. Eddison uses at the end of his tale, furnishes the key to one aspect of the romance, or, and perhaps more exactly, the key to the underlying motivation. Lessingham had tenaciously in life clung to a belief in personal immortality. The reader, therefore, may take his choice of explanations of what follows after the old man's death in the introductory pages. . . .

The Sappho ode, when Lord Lessingham is dying (all the translated souls are lords in Valhalla), is recited by Fiorinda. But who is Fiorinda? She is each of the great mistresses of history; she is the earthly Lessingham's lost wife, Mary; she is the Cyprian goddess, Aphrodite, herself. If the reader wishes to follow the tale and not go absolutely mad, he will need the help of all his metaphysical researches and all his reading of mythologies, especially the Norse. . . .

"**Mistress of Mistresses**" demands a heavy cast, but mostly of supernumeraries. But the two antagonists, Lord Lessingham and Lord Horius Parry, are drawn with effective distinction, albeit the author, who has bent all history, as he has bent all mythology, to his service, derives them variously. Lessingham is in every respect an Elizabethan leader and noble. He might easily be Essex. Horius Parry, on the other hand, comes straight out of the sagas. Huge, slow-witted, hairy and with muscles of steel, he feeds his great hunting dogs on raw meat and trains them to pull down his human enemies when the sword or the dagger fails of its purpose. . . .

And just as the author has called on every philosophy, every mythology and most of history, the great tales of ancient times, Homer and the Song of Roland, the Sagas of the Norsemen, to furnish him material for his fiction, so also has he called on a hundred tongues to build him a language and provide him with a syntax. . . . The language of "**Mistress of Mistresses**," while precisely like none other on earth, either among the dead or the living tongues, is singularly effective, melodious, at the same time vigorous and pleasing. One grants that Mr. Eddison has a singular linguistic flair. Now one detects the soft note

of the Greek, now clangs the anvil-smash of the Teutonic, now sound the tempering liquids of old Provence.

What is one to say in summation of so strange a work? This much may safely be said, that the realists, though they have ridden the romanticists hard, have not driven them from the field when they have still so doughty a champion as E. R. Eddison to tilt for them. . . .

[In] the last analysis Mr. Eddison's fabrication is, as romance must ever be, a high exploit in virtuosity. Baudelaire, Swinburne, Sappho herself, were but virtuosos—in the art of love. And all three lacked wit. The saving grace of such landmarks in tour de force as, let us say, the works of James Branch Cabell . . . was seething, irrepressible wit. Our complaint against "**Mistress of Mistresses**" is that there is too much Swinburne and Baudelaire, and too little Cabell.

> *Percy Hutchison, "A Fantasy of Mythological Times,"*
> *in* The New York Times Book Review, *August 11,*
> *1935, p. 2.*

E. R. EDDISON   (essay date 1945)

[*In the following excerpt from his introduction to* The Mezentian Gate, *written during his final year, Eddison discusses the characters, overall plan, and various elements and features of his Zimiamvian trilogy, with particular critical attention paid to* The Mezentian Gate. *For further discussion of the Zimiamvian trilogy, see the excerpts by G. Rostrevor Hamilton (1949), Lin Carter (1969), and L. Sprague de Camp (1976).*]

Dear brother: Not by design, but because it so developed, my Zimiamvian trilogy has been written backwards. *Mistress of Mistresses,* the first of these books, deals with the two years beginning 'ten months after the death, in the fifty-fourth year of his age, in his island fortress of Sestola in Meszria, of the great King Mezentius, tyrant of Fingiswold, Meszria, and Rerek'. *A Fish Dinner in Memison,* the second book, belongs in its Zimiamvian parts to a period of five weeks ending nearly a year before the King's death. This third book, *The Mezentian Gate,* begins twenty years before the King was born, and ends with his death. Each of the three is a drama complete in itself; but, read together (beginning with *The Mezentian Gate,* and ending with *Mistress of Mistresses*), they give a consecutive history, covering more than seventy years in a special world devised for Her Lover by Aphrodite, for whom (as the reader must suspend unbelief and suppose) all worlds are made. (p. xi)

In this world of Zimiamvia, Aphrodite puts on, as though they were dresses, separate and simultaneous incarnations, with a different personality, a different *soul,* for each dress. As the Duchess of Memison, for example, She walks as it were in Her sleep, humble, innocent, forgetful of Her Olympian home; and in that dress She can (little guessing the extraordinary truth), see and speak with her own Self that, awake and aware and well able to enjoy and use Her divine prerogatives, stands beside her in the person of her lady of the bedchamber.

A very unearthly character of Zimiamvia lies in the fact that nobody wants to change it. Nobody, that is to say, apart from a few weak natures who fail on their probation and (as, in your belief and mine, all ultimate evil must) put off at last even their illusory semblance of being, and fall away to the limbo of nothingness. Zimiamvia is, in this, like the sagatime: there is no malaise of the soul. In that world, well fitted to their faculties and dispositions, men and women of all estates enjoy beatitude in the Aristotelian sense of ἐνεργεία κατ᾽ ἀρετην αριστην (activity according to their highest virtue). Gabriel Flores, for instance, has no ambition to be Vicar of Rerek: it suffices his lust for power that he serves a master who commands his dog-like devotion.

It may be thought that such dark and predatory personages as the Vicar, or his uncle Lord Emmius Parry, or Emmius's daughter Rosma, are strangely accommodated in these meads of asphodel where Beauty's self, in warm actuality of flesh and blood, reigns as Mistress. But the answer surely is (and it is an old answer) that 'God's adversaries are some way his owne'. This ownness is easier to accept and credit in an ideal world like Zimiamvia than in our training-ground or testing-place where womanish and fearful mankind, individually so often gallant and lovable, in the mass so foolish and unremarkable, mysteriously inhabit, labouring through bog that takes us to the knees, yet sometimes momentarily giving an eye to the lone splendour of the stars. (pp. xi-xii)

The Mezentian Gate, last in order of composition, is by that very fact first in order of ripeness. It in no respect supersedes or amends the earlier books, but does I think illuminate them. *Mistress of Mistresses*, leaving unexplored the relations between that other world and our present here and now, led to the writing of the *Fish Dinner;* which book in turn, at its climax, raised the question whether what took place at that singular supper party may not have had yet vaster and more cosmic reactions, quite overshadowing those affecting the fate of this planet. I was besides, by then, fallen in love with Zimiamvia and my persons; and love has a searching curiosity which can never be wholly satisfied (and well that it cannot, or mankind might die of boredom). Also I wanted to find out how it came that the great King, while still at the height of his powers, met his death in Sestola; and why, so leaving the Three Kingdoms, he left them in a mess. These riddles begot *The Mezentian Gate.*

With our current distractions, political, social and economic, this story (in common with its predecessors) is as utterly unconcerned as it is with Stock Exchange procedure, the technicalities of aerodynamics, or the Theory of Vectors. Nor is it an allegory. Allegory, if its persons have life, is a prostitution of their personalities, forcing them for an end other than their own. If they have not life, it is but a dressing up of argument in a puppetry of frigid make-believe. To me, the persons *are* the argument. And for the argument I am not fool enough to claim responsibility; for, stripped to its essentials, it is a great eternal commonplace, beside which, I am sometimes apt to think, nothing else really matters.

The book, then, is a serious book: not a fairy-story, and not a book for babes and sucklings; but (it needs not to tell you, who know my temper) not solemn. For is not Aphrodite φιλομμειδης—'laughter-loving'? But She is also αιδοιη—'an awful' Goddess. And She is ξλικοβλξφαρος—'with flickering eyelids', and γλυκυμειλιχος—'honey-sweet'; and She is Goddess of Love, which itself is γλυκυπικρον αμαχανον ορπετον—'Bitter-sweet, an unmanageable Laidly Worm': as Barganax knows. These attributes are no modern inventions of mine: they stand on evidence of Homer and of Sappho, great poets. And in what great poets tell us about the Gods there is always a vein of truth. (pp. xiii-xiv)

So here is my book: call it novel if you like: poem if you prefer. Under whatever label—

> I limb'd this night-peece and it was my best.

(p. xiv)

E. R. Eddison, "Letter of Introduction: To My Brother Colin," in his *The Mezentian Gate, The Curwen Press,* 1958, pp. xi-xiv.

C. S. LEWIS   (essay date 1947)

[Lewis is considered one of the foremost Christian and mythopoeic authors of the twentieth century. Indebted principally to George MacDonald, G. K. Chesterton, Charles Williams, and the writers of ancient Norse myths, he is regarded as a formidable logician and Christian polemicist, a perceptive literary critic, and—most highly—as a writer of fantasy literature. Lewis also held instructoral posts at Oxford and Cambridge, where he was an acknowledged authority on medieval and Renaissance literature. A traditionalist in his approach to life and art, he opposed the modern movement in literary criticism toward biographical and psychological interpretation. In place of this, Lewis practiced and propounded a theory of criticism that stresses the importance of the author's intent, rather than the reader's presuppositions and prejudices. Lewis and Eddison were friends who wrote many letters to each other discussing their works and works-in-progress. In the following excerpt from his essay "On Stories," which states his theory of the well-crafted work of fiction, Lewis praises Eddison as an author who successfully blended theme, style, and plot to create distinguished fantasy novels.]

It must be admitted that the art of Story as I see it is a very difficult one. What its central difficulty is I have already hinted when I complained that in the *War of the Worlds* the idea that really matters becomes lost or blunted as the story gets under way. I must now add that there is a perpetual danger of this happening in all stories. To be stories at all they must be series of events: but it must be understood that this series—the *plot,* as we call it—is only really a net whereby to catch something else. The real theme may be, and perhaps usually is, something that has no sequence in it, something other than a process and much more like a state or quality. Giantship, otherness, the desolation of space, are examples that have crossed our path. The titles of some stories illustrate the point very well. *The Well at the World's End*—can a man write a story to that title? Can he find a series of events following one another in time which will really catch and fix and bring home to us all that we grasp at on merely hearing the six words? Can a man write a story on Atlantis—or is it better to leave the word to work on its own? And I must confess that the net very seldom does succeed in catching the bird. (pp. 103-04)

But it does sometimes succeed. In the works of the late E. R. Eddison it succeeds completely. You may like or dislike his invented worlds (I myself like that of *The Worm Ouroboros* and strongly dislike that of *Mistress of Mistresses*) but there is here no quarrel between the theme and the articulation of the story. Every episode, every speech, helps to incarnate what the author is imagining. You could spare none of them. It takes the whole story to build up that strange blend of renaissance luxury and northern hardness. The secret here is largely the style, and especially the style of the dialogue. These proud, reckless, amorous people create themselves and the whole atmosphere of their world chiefly by talking. (p. 104)

C. S. Lewis, "On Stories," in Essays Presented to Charles Williams, *Oxford University Press, London,* 1947, pp. 90-105.

G. ROSTREVOR HAMILTON   (essay date 1949)

[Hamilton was an English poet and a close friend of Eddison. In the following excerpt he discusses the Zimiamvian trilogy, focus-

Lords Juss, Goldry Bluszco, Spitfire, and Brandoch Daha. From The Worm Ouroboros, *by E. R. Eddison. Illustrated by Keith Henderson. Copyright 1926, 1952 by E. P. Dutton, Inc. Reproduced by permission of the publisher, E. P. Dutton, Inc.*

ing on Eddison's characters, particularly Lessingham's nemesis Lord Horius Parry, Vicar of Rerek. For further discussion of the Zimiamvian trilogy, see the excerpts by E. R. Eddison (1945), Lin Carter (1969), and L. Sprague de Camp (1976).]

Eric Rucker Eddison died in August, 1945. Despite what James Stephens has well called the "heroical magnificence" of his prose [see excerpt dated 1940], he is not known to many readers. The object of this essay is to call attention to the challenge of his work, and at the same time to testify, as I must, to my own admiration. Eddison has obvious faults—incongruities, lapses of taste, mannerisms which are now and then irritating: on the other hand, in his towering fantasy, the sweep of his invention and the grandeur of his style, I find something more than high talent—a vein of genius, setting him apart as one of the most remarkable writers of our age. (p. 43)

Zimiamvia, the country where Eddison's genius is consistently at home, is a mountainous land, rich in woods and streams, with white farmsteads dotted in the valleys. . . . It is a world made for great individuals, lording it, with their retainers, in sumptuous palaces or frowning rock-fortresses: with their scheming and violence, their chivalry and culture, they recall, though with marks of an earlier age, the civilization of fifteenth-century Italy.

The characters speak in a clipped and forcible language, more archaic than the narrative. Here, and in the robust economy of the battlepieces, the influence of the sagas is strong. The abrupt dialogue and the hard, clear light of the action come as a relief to the prevailing luxury and splendour, scenes where the great men feast by torchlight or exercise their wits in the company of beautiful women. . . . Eddison has a gusto for material splendour, for gorgeous banquets and jewels, for physical beauty and physical strength. He gives full rein to fantasy and ex-

travagance. Presence-chambers and dining-halls are built out of huge blocks of precious material, gold and ivory, bronze and stone, elaborately carved and figured. Not seldom the descriptions run to excess and defy all sense of proportion. Yet the saving grace is there, for Eddison has an intoxicating sense of light: it is as though he had learnt from the declining sun, among the mountains which he studied and loved, the power to transfigure solid substance to a thing of no weight or grossness. This same remarkable gift enables him to enchant us with the magic gardens conjured into being by Doctor Vandermast; gardens where time stands still, and dream-like realities of experience are concentrated in an ecstatic moment.

The reader with a taste for romance may easily accept Zimiamvia, with its assemblage of powerful lords and alluring ladies. But now I come to what are, I conceive, real difficulties. Who are the gods of this eclectic world, this highly coloured and barbaric heaven? They are none other than Zeus and Aphrodite: and these deities do not appear as transcendent beings, separate and distinct from the men and women who dwell there. On the contrary, they are identified, in differing degrees of clearness, with the human protagonists. Thus Amalie, Duchess of Memison, Queen Antiope and the Lady Fiorinda are all of them "dresses", or incarnations, chosen for herself by Aphrodite. Amalie and Antiope are at first unaware, or dimly aware, of their essential divinity—being dresses wherein Aphrodite "walked as it were asleep, humble, innocent, forgetful of Her Olympian home"—and they never attain to the full self-consciousness of Fiorinda, in whom the identification with the goddess is complete.

It comes as a shock to find the gods of Greece in a world that delights us with the very un-Greek quality of excess. But we can survive the shock when we realize that they are not, in any purity, the classical Gods of Olympus. I have no doubt that Eddison, who recklessly brings together all that he admires, intended them to be so in greater degree than they are. But his imagination—as is fortunately wont to happen with the creative artist—overrode his intention. The harmony of his whole bizarre conception demanded that Aphrodite should assume many features from the Orient. Often she is less akin to the goddess of Homer or Sappho or Praxiteles than to the terrible Syrian Astarte. (pp. 45-6)

I give all my admiration to Fiorinda's beauty of person, exquisitely robed or in voluptuous naked splendour. I admire her as a lofty, dangerous and unscrupulous woman, or as a goddess of like character, and, as such, she has her just pre-eminence in a country the nobility of which would be nothing without its savage and even brutal aspect. But I rebel when I am asked to recognize her as "*omnium rerum causa immanens*: the sufficient explanation of the world"; one, the service of whom is the only wisdom. And her boundless self-preoccupation is a travesty of that infinite intellectual love with which, in the phrase of Spinoza, God loves His own Self. **Mistress of Mistresses,** and the **Fish Dinner** present high matter for the imagination, and the moral or religious censor would deserve to be prosecuted, should he break in and trespass on this ground. But when, as here and there, the high moral or religious claim is expressed or clearly implied, the censor cannot refuse the invitation to protest.

The truth is that Eddison fell deeply in love with his imagined world, from Fiorinda to the least blade of grass and, like a lover, he could see nothing amiss. He is completely serious and takes his stand on philosophy, reducing Truth, Beauty and Goodness to one ultimate value, Beauty: a thing you may only do, if in Beauty you include not only sensuous beauty of form and beauty of action but also—and not dependent on these—beauty of character, according to the highest conception of the Good. It is his failure to recognize this which I regard as the chief defect in Eddison's Utopia. And yet to bring it into the open is to risk a loss of perspective: for this fault has the same root as his virtue, so that one may almost say—*felix culpa*. It was just because he saw with the eyes of a lover that he was able to present his world with so amazing a vitality.

His philosophical reflections throw light on a point which I have mentioned, viz. that Zeus and Aphrodite are identified, in differing degrees of awareness, with the human protagonists of the drama. "Personality," writes Eddison, "is a mystery: a mystery that darkens as we suffer our imagination to speculate upon the penetration of human personality by Divine, and *vice versa*. Perhaps my three pairs of lovers are, ultimately, but one pair. Perhaps you could as truly say that Lessingham, Barganax, and the King (on the one hand) Mary, the Duchess, and Fiorinda (on the other) are but two persons, each at three several stages of 'awakeness', as call them six separate persons." The result of so fluid a conception of personality is sometimes confusing, but if the reader holds firmly to this clue, it will guide him through the maze. The most perplexing relationship is that between Lessingham and Barganax. In his earthly career Lessingham wins renown in the most diverse spheres, being pre-eminent alike as military leader, artist and mountaineer. In Zimiamvia—where he at length finds Mary again in the person of Queen Antiope—he is first and foremost the man of action, and his previous role as artist and dreamer falls, in a narrower intensity, to Barganax. Between these two, who are cast as chivalrous enemies, there is a close bond of brotherhood, so much so that there are moments of climax when the personality of one passes into that of the other, and each of them, looking into a mirror, sees not his own, but the other's likeness. (pp. 47-8)

If I have shown a certain antipathy to the great Lady Fiorinda, and cannot worship at a shrine of hers, I can at least pay my homage to Mary, Amalie and Antiope, in whom the divinity is veiled by a queenly but human and feminine charm. Among a whole galaxy of fair women on whom Eddison has lavished his art, the young Queen Antiope is supreme. She has a captivating innocence and candour, a fresh delight in existence, a natural warmth and pity and laughter. My eyes follow her with equal admiration as she dismounts from her horse—"a motion to convince the sea-swallow of too dull a grace"—and as, with unselfconscious assurance, she baffles her unwelcome suitor Derxis. And when she comes, through bewilderment, to realize her oneness with Aphrodite, she does so with a sweet seriousness, which has in it nothing of Fiorinda's supercilious amusement or pride. (p. 49)

I have said something of Lessingham and Barganax. Against these men, both of a pagan nobility, stands out in solid relief the Lord Horius Parry, Vicar of Rerek. Here in my judgment is Eddison's masterpiece, a villain of grand Elizabethan stature, and I propose to conclude by presenting him in a closer study. His face has "a singularity of brutish violence joined with some nobler element in a marriage wherein neither was ever all subdued to other, nor yet ever all distinct; so that divorce must needs have crippled a little both, as well the good as the bad". (p. 50)

Befitting his person, he is a man of enormous physical energy, with equal gusto for the pleasures of the table and the life of action. While he governs by fear, he is a capable ruler with a quick instinct for men and situations. He has his moments of cordial and friendly impulse, but round the corner suspicion and craft are always laired in ambush. He cannot endure to be quiet for long, and is too restless in intrigue ever to let well alone. As for crime, he will stop at nothing. Sometimes his treachery is long and carefully planned; sometimes, at a moment of crisis, it will break out suddenly against his own associates, as it does finally against his most faithful servant and shadow, Gabriel Flores. He thinks light of murder, sometimes doing it ferociously by his own hand, and sometimes employing four deaf mutes in his "hidden slaying-place in Laimak".

This formidable being has an irresistible attraction for his noble cousin Lessingham, while he on his side, even when plotting Lessingham's death, is constrained to admit "a kind of love for the man". Part of the attraction is simple enough, for the Vicar supplies that constant element of danger which the adventurer demands. Moreover, he can be excellent company, with a boisterous humour and homely directness of speech. (pp. 50-1)

The bond is too deep, however, to have its root in externals. And it is equally strong between the Vicar and an even more exalted person, King Mezentius, who is the central figure in the *Fish Dinner*. After the Vicar has conspired against the king and then, to save himself, has helped in the slaying of his fellow-conspirators, the king is able to say, "there's something so glues me and you together as neither life nor death shall unglue us." The key to this strange declaration lies in the words with which Mezentius dismisses the dead conspirators, "Such men, alive or dead, lack substantial being: are a kind of nothing." In them evil is a mere negative thing, a defect, while in the Vicar it is much more terrible. It is positive and vital, as evil can only be when interlaced with good. Good and evil, "two twins cleaving together," in Milton's phrase: there lies the secret of the Vicar's power, and there lies the birthbond that "glues" him to his noble antagonists.

The Vicar is certainly no ruined archangel, for there is no gleam of the divine about him. But further, there is very little that is distinctively human, apart from a full self-consciousness that hardly operates above the sensual level. Nobility is there, but it is the nobility of the animal, the ferocity of the lion and the cunning of the snake, and these can still be noble because they retain so much animal purity. There is something bestial even in "his great stubbed finger", and he is frequently described by his animal likeness—he sits "bull-like and erect in an inscrutability as of hewn granite", or his neck swells "like a puff-adder's". The tension within the Vicar is that between the human at its lowest level and the animal in its full development: much of what is evil in him as man is natural and good in him as animal. The wider tension between the Vicar and now Lessingham, now Mezentius, is essentially that between the savage and man in his proper stature. (p. 51)

Zimiamvia is a world that suits the Vicar, as it suits the other principal characters. But while for them it is a world rich in diverse layers, moving upwards from voluptuous pleasure and fierce action to ideal beauty and high speculation, for the Vicar it is sufficient in a one-level simplicity. "Why, as for worlds, this world fits: I ask no other. A world where the best man beareth away the victory. Wine, women, war: nay, I rate it fit enough." The rarer world which the others see and to which he is blind is itself limited, for it is essentially human even in its visitings from the divine. Lessingham is no more than the "high-souled" man of Aristotelian ethics and, in spite of his grandeur, has a certain coldness and lack of reach native to that ideal. This limitation is of high value for Lessingham's relation to the Vicar; for the latter, massive though he be, is not of such stuff as to bear conflict with the divine, and to him even the borderland of divinity can have no meaning.

No conflict with the divine, and yet a value of contrast, as a figure may have at the base of a pyramid. The Vicar is one of the participants in the great symposium of the *Fish Dinner* where, over a board laden with sumptuous fare, the nature of time and creation, of ideal worlds and divine omnipotence, is discussed and in some manner put to demonstration, in chapters of a curious and sustained magnificence. What is the Vicar to make of divine philosophy? (pp. 52-3)

The Vicar is red with furious feasting, he guzzles down his wine: he, for whom one world is enough, will be the sport of no Olympian. When the talk in one of its highest moments pierces beyond Olympus, and suggests that God in his all-experience might choose to know suffering in his own person, he is scandalized and holds it "plain blasphemy". The prospect of other worlds is unfolded: he sits an outsider at the feast, admirably faithful to the only reality that he knows:

> There fell a silence: in the midst of it, the Vicar
> with his teeth cracking of a lobster's claw.
>
> (p. 53)

> *G. Rostrevor Hamilton, "The Prose of E. R. Eddison," in* English Studies, *n.s. Vol. 2, 1949, pp. 43-53.*

J. R. R. TOLKIEN   (letter date 1957)

[*Tolkien is famous as the author of the mythopoeic* Lord of the Rings *trilogy (1954-56) and of its much simpler prequel,* The Hobbit *(1938). With his friend C. S. Lewis and with Charles Williams, Tolkien was also a central member of the Oxford Christians, or "Inklings," a group of like-minded writers and friends who met weekly to discuss literature and read works-in-progress to each other. A longtime professor of medieval English literature and philology at Oxford's Merton College, Tolkien was of quite conservative literary tastes; for years he campaigned to keep "modern" (nineteenth and twentieth-century) English literature off the curriculum at Merton. Like Lewis, he disliked nearly all the formal developments in twentieth-century writing, and his reading tended toward the traditional and the epic, his favorite literature being the ancient Norse sagas. In 1957 Tolkien received a letter from one Caroline Everett, requesting biographical information as background for a thesis she was writing. In the following excerpt from his reply, Tolkien answers the question of Eddison's influence on* The Lord of the Rings.]

I read the works of [E. R.] Eddison, long after they appeared; and I once met him. I heard him in Mr. Lewis's room in Magdalen College read aloud some parts of his own works—from the *Mistress of Mistresses,* as far as I remember. He did it extremely well. I read his works with great enjoyment for their sheer literary merit. My opinion of them is almost the same as that expressed by Mr. Lewis on p. 104 of the *Essays presented to Charles Williams* [see excerpt dated 1947]. Except that I disliked his characters (always excepting the Lord Gro) and despised what he appeared to admire more intensely than Mr. Lewis at any rate saw fit to say of himself. Eddison thought what I admire 'soft' (his word: one of complete condemnation, I gathered); I thought that, corrupted by an evil and indeed silly 'philosophy', he was coming to admire, more and more, arrogance and cruelty. Incidentally, I thought his nomenclature slipshod and often inept. In spite of all of which, I still think of him as the greatest and most convincing writer of 'invented worlds' that I have read. But he was certainly not an 'influence'. (p. 258)

> *J.R.R. Tolkien, in a letter to Caroline Everett on June 24, 1957, in his* The Letters of J.R.R. Tolkien, *edited by Humphrey Carpenter with Christopher Tolkien, Houghton Mifflin Company, 1981, pp. 257-59.*

C. S. LEWIS   (essay date 1958?)

[*In the following excerpt from a brief notice written for the dust-jacket of* The Mezentian Gate, *Lewis praises Eddison's works as stirring tales of fantasy.*]

It is very rarely that a middle-aged man finds an author who gives him, what he knew so often in his teens and twenties, the sense of having opened a new door. One had thought those days were past. Eddison's heroic romances disproved it. Here was a new literary species, a new rhetoric, a new climate of the imagination. Its effect is not evanescent, for the whole life and strength of a singularly massive and consistent personality lies behind it. Still less, however, is it mere self-expression, appealing only to those whose subjectivity resembles the author's: admirers of Eddison differ in age and sex and include some (like myself) to whom his world is alien and even sinister. In a word, these books are works, first and foremost, of *art*. And they are irreplaceable. Nowhere else shall we meet this precise blend of hardness and luxury, of lawless speculation and sharply realised detail, of the cynical and the magnanimous. No author can be said to remind us of Eddison.

> *C. S. Lewis, "A Tribute to E. R. Eddison," in his* On Stories and Other Essays on Literature, *edited by Walter Hooper, Harcourt Brace Jovanovich, Publishers, 1982, p. 29.*

LIN CARTER   (essay date 1969)

[*Carter is a prolific American fantasy writer and essayist whose works reflect his many and diverse interests, which range from L. Frank Baum's Oz books to archaeology and ancient literatures, and include fairy tales, occult philosophy, oriental mythology, and children's books. In the following excerpt he surveys the Zimiamvian trilogy, comparing it unfavorably to* The Worm Ouroboros *but noting its many admirable elements and features. For further discussion of the Zimiamvian trilogy, see the excerpts by E. R. Eddison (1945), G. Rostrevor Hamilton (1949), and L. Sprague de Camp (1976).*]

[After *The Worm Ouroboros*] Eddison went on to write his Zimiamvian trilogy, comprised of [*Mistress of Mistresses, A Fish Dinner in Memison,* and *The Mezentian Gate*]. . . . *Gate* was left unfinished at Eddison's death in 1945, but those portions of it which he had completed, together with his drafts and rather extensive notes, were assembled into a volume which was issued under that title thirteen years after his death.

The Zimiamvian books are less successful than the mighty *Worm* or, at least, they are less interesting to read. *The Worm* has a swift, direct appeal to the primary emotions: it is concerned with nothing but glorious, stirring adventure. But the Zimiamvian books have a dull theme: they are about adventure but are equally involved in the symbolic presentation of a complex and abstruse philosophy. The *Worm* is a richly colored, thundering tale of battle and quest and heroic derring-do. The trilogy is about political intrigue and politics, plot and counterplot. *The Worm* is Homeric; the trilogy is Machiavellian: and most people enjoy reading Homer more than Machiavelli.

The major character in the trilogy is the goddess Aphrodite, who appears throughout in a number of more or less simultaneous avatars: first as Fiorinda, mistress of the ambitious Duke Barganax; then as Queen Antiope; then as the Duchess of Memison, Barganax' mother; and also as the long-dead wife of the adventurer Lessingham, whom we met briefly in the opening pages of *The Worm*. Another major character is King Mezentius, who plays a leading role in one book and is either off-stage or long-since dead in the others. [In a footnote Carter states that ''Eddison, by the way, borrowed the name of this character from a minor figure in the eighth book of the *Aeneid* of Virgil: the deposed tyrant Mezentius, former king of the Tuscans, who appears leagued with the foes of Aeneas and who is slain in battle against the Trojans in a later book.] He, it turns out, is an avatar of the god Zeus.

Despite these faults, the Zimiamvian trilogy has its admirers. There are many good aspects about it, and some superb fantasy elements. The ambiguous figure of the magician, Dr. Vandermast, provides some beautiful fantasy effects, and the trilogy presents some superb original concepts. For example, the locale is the land of Zimiamvia, which the three lords of Demonland glimpsed dimly from afar when they scaled the heights of Kostra Pivrarcha in *The Worm*. They briefly discuss Zimiamvia in that passage, and it seems that to the Witches and Demons of Mercury, Zimiamvia is an enchanted or paradisiacal realm.

Gorice XII. From The Worm Ouroboros, *by E. R. Eddison. Illustrated by Keith Henderson. Copyright 1926, 1952 by E. P. Dutton, Inc. Reproduced by permission of the publisher, E. P. Dutton, Inc.*

In the trilogy the reader discovers that Zimiamvia is actually the heaven or Valhalla of the world of *The Worm*. Curiously, Eddison seems to have done very little with this perfectly lovely concept, although early in the trilogy we learn that the goddess Aphrodite permits the dead adventurer, Lessingham, to be reincarnated (or something like that) in this heavenly realm after his death, where he becomes her lover in one of her incarnations. The development is not very easy to make clear and it is less easy to read. Besides, the structure of the trilogy and the relationship of the three novels to one another is confusing; the books are not really sequential. The first two books more or less run parallel to each other, and the unfinished third takes place before the other two.

However, E. R. Eddison was a master of English prose the like of whom has not been seen in our time. After a few pages, I find that my mind simply refuses to try to follow the Machiavellian intricacies of plot and counterplot, stops attempting to figure out which character is which other character's avatar, and simply gets lost in the rich, fine-textured, luxuriant prose, studded with scraps of splendid verse, curious lore of the Middle Ages, odd-sounding names and all manner of oddities, curiosities, and conceits. (pp. 145-47)

Lin Carter, ''The Men Who Invented Fantasy,'' in his Tolkien: A Look Behind ''The Lord of the Rings,'' Ballantine Books, 1969, pp. 134-51.*

L. SPRAGUE DE CAMP (essay date 1976)

[*De Camp is a highly respected American science fiction writer who is perhaps best known for popularizing Robert E. Howard's character Conan the Cimmerian through his recovery and completion of many of the sword and sorcery manuscripts left unfinished at Howard's death. In the following excerpt, de Camp surveys Eddison's career, offering the most extensive critical commentary to-date on Eddison's works. Although he finds Eddison's four major novels enjoyable, de Camp believes the works are marred in that they glorify violence, war, and a feudal social hierarchy of masters and underlings. For further discussion of* The Worm Ouroboros *and the Zimiamvian trilogy, see the excerpts by Edwin Markham (1926), H. P. Lovecraft (1933), E. R. Eddison (1945), G. Rostrevor Hamilton (1949), Lin Carter (1969), and Sharon Wilson (1984).*]

There is good reason to class [*The Worm Ouroboros*]—nearly 200,000 words long—as the greatest single novel of heroic fantasy. It is told in a marvelous, rolling, blazingly colorful, archaized English, reminiscent of William Morris but more skillfully done.

As more than one critic has said, however, the work is a ''flawed masterpiece.'' If the beginning, with its clumsy device of Lessingham and his hippogriff-chariot, is unsatisfactory, the ending is equally so. When the Witches have been beaten, Juss and his fellows find peace an intolerable bore. So, in answer to Juss's prayer, the gods allow him to turn back time to the beginning and fight the same war over and over again *ad infinitum*. The thought of many readers at this point is: What a fate!

Evidently, the Demon lords—the Good Guys of this novel—fight more for the fun of whacking off arms, legs, and heads than for any humanly rational objective. As for the countless casualties of this ever-recurrent war, nobody gives them a thought.

To Eddison, apparently, war was a romantic adventure. This view was widespread in Western culture in Eddison's generation. People born before 1900 still visualized war as fought with bands and banners, and cavalry charging with sword and lance. Not until realistic accounts of the grim butchery of the Kaiserian War became current in the 1920s was there a reaction against this attitude.

The four Demon lords are not much developed as characters, save that Brandoch Daha has (if I may mix my allusions) a touch of Celtic *chutzpah*. On the other hand, the lords of Witchland are a fine, well-drawn set of mighty, indomitable, fearless scoundrels. So is Lord Gro of Goblinland, the intellectual *manqué*, whose weakness for lost causes makes him a perennial traitor to whichever side he espouses when that side begins to win. (pp. 116-17)

In 1916, Eddison had privately printed a small book called *Poems, Letters, and Memories of Philip Sidney Nairn.* Following *The Worm Ouroboros,* he issued two more books. the first was a historical novel of the Viking Age, *Styrbiorn the Strong.* . . . After that came his translation of *Egil's Saga.* . . .

Strong is an excellent historical novel. Based on a few brief allusions in Snorri's *Heimskringla* (a history of Norway to 1176), it follows the adventures of its mighty and valiant hero and his pet musk ox in the Scandinavian kingdoms and among the Jomsvikings of the Baltic, whose headquarters were on an island off the coast of Pomerania.

Egil's Saga is one of a large body of similar writings, made in Iceland in the twelfth and thirteenth centuries. They tell the stories of eminent Icelanders who lived in the tenth and eleventh centuries. (p. 119)

While *Styrbiorn the Strong* is highly readable, a modern reader may bog down in *Egil's Saga* or in many of the other sagas. After the umpteenth episode in which an Icelandic woman nags a male kinsman or a servant into going out to ambush a member of a rival clan, in revenge for a previous killing, the reader may decide that enough is enough. (p. 120)

Mistress of Mistresses begins with an "Overture," in the form of a monologue by a younger (but still elderly) friend of Edward Lessingham, whom we met at the beginning of *The Worm Ouroboros.* The date is about 1973—our recent past, but several decades in the author's future. (pp. 120-21)

As the unnamed narrator muses, we learn more about Lessingham, and still more in later books of the series. He is the sword-and-sorcery hero *par excellence,* making most of the heroes of the genre look like oafs and simpletons. He is the man of the Renaissance squared. Like Lovecraft's Randolph Carter and Howard's Conan, he is (we may suppose) an idealization of his creator—the man the author would like to have been.

Six and a half feet tall, with a great black beard, Lessingham combines the qualities of Harald Hardraade, Leonardo da Vinci, and James Bond all in one. A rich, well-born English country gentleman, he is a great soldier, administrator, scholar, sportsman, painter, sculptor, writer, poet, and lover all at once. He rides to the hounds, climbs mountains, and collects art treasures. He beat the Germans in East Africa in the Kaiserian War; he overthrew Bela Kun's Communist rule in Hungary after that war; he once made himself dictator of Paraguay. He has written the definitive biography, in ten volumes, of his ancestor, the Emperor Frederick II.

Nobody has ever approached such omnicompetence in the real world, although a few, like Richard F. Burton, Theodore Roo-

sevelt, and Lord Dunsany have done pretty well. When Eddison set himself to imagine a supermannish *alter ego,* there was nothing petty about his phantasm.

This gargantuan character has studied at Eton, Oxford, and Heidelberg. He has served in the French Foreign Legion. At twenty-five, he marries the beautiful and brilliant Lady Mary Scarnside, daughter of Lord Anmering. (pp. 121-22)

After fifteen blissful years, Mary and their only child, a daughter, are killed in a train wreck. Mary had been Lessingham's favorite model for painting; now he destroys all his portraits of her but one. He burns down his stately home, with all its heirlooms and art treasures. He likewise leaves orders with his narrator-friend to burn the Norwegian castle, with its Ming vases, its rugs from Samarkand, and his last portrait of Mary. (A selfish fellow indeed, one thinks, to deprive the world of pleasant things in order to indulge his own solipsistic *hypris*.)

Recovering from his beloved wife's death, Lessingham goes back to his arts, his mistresses, and his adventuring. The reader of *Mistress of Mistresses,* however, drops this Lessingham at the end of the "Overture" and enters another world: Zimiamvia.

This place is described in *The Worm Ouroboros* as a kind of heaven or Valhalla for the souls of dead heroes from the Eddisonian Mercury. The milieu presented in *Mistress of Mistresses* is, however, quite different. Its folk are as mortal as any other, and they include a goodly quota of "dastards and oppressors."

Like Eddison's Mercury, this is a pre-gunpowder, pre-industrial world, but European Renaissance rather than Viking Age. It is like the world of Richard III and Henry VIII of England, Louis XI and François I of France, Emperor Charles V, Nicolò Machiavelli, and Cesare Borgia.

The scene is a group of lands, cut up by mountain chains and arms of the sea: Fingiswold in the North, Meszria in the South, and Rerek in between. Mezentius, king of these three lands, has recently died. (pp. 122-23)

The common speech of Zimiamvia, we learn, is English of a Shakespearean sort. The characters, however, drop into French, Italian, Latin, or Greek. They often quote from earthly Classical and Renaissance literature.

King Mezentius has left two legitimate children by his late Queen Rosma: a son, Styllis, who has become an arrogant youth; and a daughter, Antiope. By his mistress Amalie, Duchess of Memison, Mezentius has a bastard son, Barganax, Duke of Zayana. Mezentius' vicar in Rerek is the mighty, bull-necked, red-bearded Horius Parry. This man represents the powerful Parry family, noted for vitality, ability, brutality, and unscrupulous perfidy.

Horius Parry has a cousin and ally named Lessingham. To distinguish this Lessingham from the earthly Edward Lessingham—he of the Norwegian castle—I shall call the mundane one Lessingham[1] and the Zimiamvian one Lessingham[2].

Lessingham[2] looks much like Lessingham[1] but is more purely a soldier and politician. He has much in common with Duke Barganax, as if both partook of the qualities of Lessingham[1]. But whereas Lessingham[2] got more than his share of Lessingham's[1] military virtues, Barganax received the larger portion of his artistic qualities. Barganax is an artist, esthete, and hedonist, albeit he can also buckle a swash or lead a charge when the occasion demands. Although on opposite sides of the conflict, he and Lessingham[2] are drawn to each other.

Barganax has a secretary and ex-tutor, Doctor Vandermast, a wizard who wears a long white beard and quotes Spinoza. (p. 123)

The story deals with the efforts of Horius Parry to enlarge his power, and of Barganax and other supporters of the late king to thwart him. . . .

It is a splendid story, quite different from *The Worm Ouroboros* but almost on a level with it. The reader, however, is liable to confusion among the many characters and the labyrinthine plots and intrigues. The tale reminds me of a remark by an Italian character in one of John Dickson Carr's detective stories: "Italian history, she's-a hot stuff. Everybody stab everybody!" There is no essential connection between this story and *The Worm Ouroboros*, save that they have different characters bearing the common name of Lessingham. (p. 124)

[*A Fish Dinner in Memison*] is a prequel to *Mistress of Mistresses*, (that is, a story of which the previous tale is a sequel) with many of the same characters. Besides making clear many things obscure in *Mistress of Mistresses, A Fish Dinner* tells the story of Lessingham[1]. (p. 125)

The fish dinner of the title occupies the last quarter of the book. The diners are Mezentius, Amalie, Barganax, Fiorinda, Horius Parry, and five others. In the course of conversation, Amalie says: "If we were Gods, able to make worlds and unmake 'em as we list, what world would we have?"

Among the various suggestions, Fiorinda proposes a world that works in strict accord with the laws of cause and effect, without magic or supernatural intervention. Mezentius cups his hands, and an opalescent sphere forms between them. While the diners sit for half an hour, talking and admiring the king's creation, the world he has made—ours—goes through its history of billions of years, from the Archaeozoic seas with their amebalike organisms to the present. Fiorinda suggests that she and Mezentius enter that world and lead the lives of a couple of the natives thereof.

And so it transpires: Mezentius is an incarnation of Zeus—God—and Fiorinda of his created mate, Aphrodite. Since a god can incarnate in more than one mortal body at a time, there is some Zeus in Barganax and in Lessingham[2], and of Aphrodite in Amalie and in the king's daughter Antiope. In our own world, Zeus and Aphrodite incarnate themselves in Lessingham[1] and Mary Scarnside. When dinner in Memison is over and all have had their fun, Fiorinda pricks the shimmering sphere with a hairpin, and it vanishes like a soap bubble.

When this God takes on a mortal incarnation, it is no gentle-Jesus-meek-and-mild. It is a swaggering, swashbuckling Renaissance bravo, who would as lief hew the head off an ill-wisher as swat a fly. The latent divinity of Lessingham[1] at least makes his godlike achievements more plausible than they would otherwise be, although it seems a little unfair that the rest of us mortals should have to compete with such a demigod. The Goddess, while irresistible by any male on whom she casts an amative glance, is given to caprice, mischief, and cruelty, as shown by her treatment of Morville.

Although Eddison's idea is tremendous, *A Fish Dinner*, while very interesting to the critic, is much less successful as fiction than the two previous novels. The story drowns in talk. Moreover, as if the relationships among the many characters were

not hard enough to keep track of, the frequent shifts between our own world and that of Zimiamvia further confuse the reader. (pp. 127-28)

After *A Fish Dinner in Memison*, Eddison began another Zimiamvian novel, *The Mezentian Gate*. A meticulous outliner, he had planned the whole work and had written about two fifths of it—the beginning, the end, and a few chapters in between—when he died. (p. 128)

The story begins before *A Fish Dinner in Memison* and ends after it, inclosing the other novel as in a frame. The events of *A Fish Dinner*, however, are briefly summarized or alluded to obliquely, since they comprise but a small fraction of the tale. (p. 129)

In its present form, *The Mezentian Gate* suggests the possibility of completion by another hand, as has been done with the unfinished works of other writers. I cannot, however, think of anybody competent for such a task. (I could certainly not do it.) Such a writer should have, not only an exuberant imagination, great technical skill, plenty of time, and a strong drive, but also an old-fashioned Eton-and-Oxford Classical British upper-class education.

Linear-minded persons like myself may wish to read the story through in chronological order of the events, instead of skipping back and forth in time as the author does. This can be approximated by reading in the following order:

1. *The Mezentian Gate*, without the "Praeludium," Books I to VI.
2. *A Fish Dinner in Memison*, Chapters I to VIII, inclusive.
3. *The Worm Ouroboros*, considered a dream of Lessingham[1].
4. The rest of *A Fish Dinner in Memison*.
5. The "Praeludium" to *The Mezentian Gate*.
6. The "Overture" to *Mistress of Mistresses*.
7. The rest of *The Mezentian Gate*.
8. *Mistress of Mistresses*, without the "Overture."

Even this scheme will not straighten things out entirely. Perhaps the reader would do as well to read a whole book at a time in any convenient order.

In judging Eddison's work, one must separate one's literary opinions from those of the author's philosophical and political ideas. Simply as literature, the tetralogy is a monument, although an egregiously imperfect one. *The Worm Ouroboros* is only tenuously connected with the rest. The other three novels are poorly integrated into a whole, and one of them is less than half finished.

Trying to make Eddison's imaginary worlds into a coherent whole merely leaves one more confused than ever. On the theme of worlds-within-worlds, one can see that the world we know is an artifact of the quasi-divine inhabitants of the world of Zimiamvia. Then the world of *The Worm Ouroboros*, being a dream of Lessingham[1] (an incarnation of Mezentius who is an incarnation of Zeus) must be an artifact of this world. But we are told that Zimiamvia is located in the world of *The Worm Ouroboros*. One need not be up on the theory of sets to realize that if A is inside B, and B inside C, C cannot be inside A. Nor is any plausible reason adduced why natives of another world should quote the Elder Edda, Keats, Sappho, and Shakespeare.

As for Eddison's outlook, there are sketches of upper-class English country life, which he evidently knew at first hand, in *A Fish Dinner*. The people express the attitudes of their time and place. Since, at the start of this century, Britain ruled not only the seas but a goodly part of the lands as well, this attitude is firmly ethnocentric. There are allusions to "that unsavoury Jew musician" with whom Lessingham[1] had a fight. Another obnoxious character is a "hulking great rascal, sort of half-nigger."

True, there are signs that the extreme British upper-class social exclusiveness is beginning to break down. Before a dinner party, Mary's father says:

"'My dear girl, you can't have that dancer woman sit down with us.'

"'Why not? She's very nice. Perfectly respectable. I think it would be unkind not to. Anybody else would do it.'

"'It's monstrous, and you're old enough to know better.'

"'Well, I've asked her, and I've asked him. You can order them both out if you want to make a scene.'" (pp. 129-31)

Eddison's characters, especially Lessingham[1], are free with their view of the mass of mankind: "The vast majority of civilized mankind are, politically, a mongrel breed of sheep and monkey: the timidity, the herded idiocy, of the sheep: the cunning, the dissimulation, the ferocity, of the great ape." "Human affairs conducted on the basis of megalopolitan civilization are simply not susceptible of good government. You have two choices: tyranny and mob-rule."

The way to handle the masses is that of Zimiamvia, where the strong, the "great," run things as they should be run and take no back talk. . . . (p. 131)

When a lieutenant of Lessingham[2] comes to Barganax to try to make peace between them, the Duke orders his men to pitch the intruder off the cliff and is barely dissuaded. When a messenger tells Lessingham[2] of Antiope's murder, Lessingham[2] tries to stab the man to death and just fails to do so. When Doctor Vandermast warns Lessingham[2] that his recklessness will cause his early death, Lessingham[2] nearly throttles the old man before being talked out of it.

In short, Eddison's "great men," even the best of them, are cruel, arrogant bullies. One may admire, in the abstract, the indomitable courage, energy, and ability of such rampant egotists. In the concrete, however, they are like the larger carnivora, best admired with a set of stout bars between them and the viewer.

There is some historical basis for such portrayal of the "great" of earlier times, who serve as models for Eddison's characters. Before the rise of bourgeois democracy, some members of ruling classes were much less careful of the feelings of those below them in the scale than is now considered meet. But to ask a modern reader to admire the feudal "insolence of office" is the next thing to asking him to admire heretic-burning, the Roman arena, or cannibalism, all of which have been defended by upright, virtuous men with cogent arguments.

Eddison was not insensible of the worm's eye view:

> When lions, eagles, and she-wolves are let loose among such weak sheep as for the most part we be, we rightly, for sake of our continuance, attend rather to their claws, maws, and talons than stay to contemplate their magnificences. We forget, in our necessity lest our flesh become their meat, that they too, ideally and *sub*

specie aeternitatis, have their places . . . in the hierarchy of true values.

Still, we have here essentially the ancient idea of the benevolent despot: let the "strong" or "great" man have his way, and he will make the right decisions for all of us. This theory was most recently revived by the European Fascist movements of the 1920s and 30s. It was even superimposed, by Lenin and Stalin, on the nominally egalitarian and democratic Communist movement.

This idea is mere sentimental romanticism. If, under such a regime, people occasionally get a Marcus Aurelius or a Duke Federigo of Urbino, they are much more likely to be saddled with a Caracalla or a Cesare Borgia. While popular rule, forsooth, has often bred follies and outrages, these are petty compared to the enormities of despots. Moreover, says Eddison:

> A very unearthly character of Zimiamvia lies in the fact that nobody wants to change it. Nobody, that is to say, apart from a few weak natures who fail on their probation. . . . Gabriel Flores, for instance, has no ambition to be Vicar of Rerek: it satisfies his lust for power that he serves a master who commands his doglike devotion.

In other words, wouldn't it be splendid to be a member of the ruling class (whether called counts, capitalists, or commissars) in a country where the lower orders loyally served and obeyed their betters, without thought of changing either the system or their own status?

The nearest that this ideal has come to realization on this earth is India, with its caste system. The history of India, technologically stagnant and hence perennially conquered by outsiders, gives little cause for enthusiasm. If all mankind were so minded, we should probably still be cowering in caves.

One should not, of course, assume that the author believes everything he makes his characters say. Even when the author's prejudices are patent, . . . that is no reason for not enjoying [his] tales, provided that the stories are enjoyable: absorbing, colorful, exciting, and stimulating. And all these things, despite their faults, Eddison's four fantasy novels are. (pp. 132-34)

> *L. Sprague de Camp, "Superman in a Bowler: E. R. Eddison," in his* Literary Swordsmen and Sorcerers: The Makers of Heroic Fantasy, *Arkham House, 1976, pp. 114-34.*

SHARON WILSON (essay date 1984)

[*In the following excerpt Wilson offers evidence that the few adverse critical comments on* The Worm Ouroboros *are invalid: that Eddison's masterwork must be judged according to the standards of romance literature, "which views embellishment, variety, and open-endedness as virtues." For other favorable discussions of* The Worm Ouroboros, *see the excerpts by Edwin Markham (1926) and H. P. Lovecraft (1933). For an opposing view of Eddison's novel, see the excerpt by L. Sprague de Camp (1976).*]

Moderns hardly know what to do with *The Lord of the Rings, The Charwoman's Daughter,* or, if they have heard of it at all, **The Worm Ouroboros**. If such romances are liked, and the first two are, it is with a guilty appreciation of their "escapism," their "lightness and whimsy," their "fun." In view of the popularity of this kind of literature with students, professors may feel that it is beyond the province of their professional concern. More importantly, because of its radical departure from "the great tradition" of the English novel following Jane Austen, the romance form is all too often relegated to the status of a lovely Christmas gift. (p. 12)

It is not, therefore, surprising that E. R. Eddison, whose deliberately archaic style and complex structure make his work even less palatable to modern tastes than are many other romances, is almost totally unknown in the eighties. For a writer who believes in Beauty as "not a means but the end and mistress of all action, the sole thing desirable for Herself alone, the *causa immanens* of the world and of very Being and Becoming," it is ironic that even his enthusiasts pay so little attention to his art. James Stephens, for example, feels that Eddison writes "a terrific book!" [see Additional Bibliography] but these books do not get the serious attention they deserve, from Stephens or others.

Probably the major charge leveled against *The Worm Ouroboros* . . . by those who do read the book is that Eddison is not in control of his materials. Apparently he forgets about Lessingham, his earthborn observer; engages in storytelling for its own sake; wastes verbal magic on overdecorated palaces [see excerpt dated 1952]; is guilty of incongruities and lapses of taste; and 'recklessly brings together everything he admires" [see excerpt dated 1949]. *The Worm* is said to have a "perilously tenuous plot and diffuse vision" and to present the "utopia of a decadent who wills to escape our present century." As Rosemond Tuve says of Spenser, however, "It is astonishing to observe how like virtues some of [his] presumed lacks or inattentions look if we see how such traits are regarded in theories of romance design. Clearly, the Aristotelian expectation of organic unity and simplicity is as inappropriate a criterion for judging *The Worm* as the medieval historian Lot found it for understanding the prose *Lancelot. The Worm Ouroboros* must be appreciated in a romance tradition which views embellishment, variety, and open-endedness as virtues.

Eugène Vinaver's *Form and Meaning in Medieval Romance* questions "the doctrine of literary absolutism which assumes that the essential forms of literary expression remain static and can be judged by the same standards throughout the ages." . . . [Vinaver] doubts the adequacy of the customary critical norms for pre-seventeenth-century literature, "a period not usually frequented by those concerned with the theory of criticism" and the period which included the great cyclic romances: "Are we not entitled to say that the change from medieval to the so-called modern pattern is a change not from primitiveness to maturity or from maturity to decadence, but from one valid structure to another?" When critics assail the diffuse vision, the ornamentation, and the "tenuous plot" of *The Worm Ouroboros,* they are indeed refusing to recognize as valid a form which not only continues to exist from Chrétien de Troyes to Spenser to Eddison but also one whose very existence affected the novel form to a much greater degree than has usually been realized, as the interlaced technique in *Joseph Andrews, Ulysses,* and *The Power and the Glory* illustrate. (pp. 13-14)

Central to our understanding of this romance, and of the three related volumes [*Mistress of Mistresses, A Fish Dinner in Memison,* and *The Mezentian Gate* . . .]—is the Worm Ouroboros itself, the snake with its tail in its mouth. As Juss of Demonland tells us, it is "an ensample of eternity, whereof the end is ever at the beginning and the beginning at the end for ever more." In *Fish Dinner,* Lessingham, the "He" who is soldier, artist, and dreamer of Earth, Mercury, Zimiamvia, and all possible worlds, wears an Ouroboros ring which contains a master key

to the east wing of the Wastdale house, the location of the Lotus Room. In *The Worm Ouroboros* Lessingham leaves the Lotus Room, "the House of Heart's Desire," for Mercury, where it is Gorice, perpetually reincarnated, who wears the ring of Ouroboros. (p. 14)

As we investigate further, however, we see that the Ouroboros describes not only Gorice's mode of being but also romance form. . . . Or, as James Stephens puts it, "The ideal story is not one in which a person strives and conquers eternal enemies, but that in which a human being is both the battlefield and the battle." The Demons, like the Red Cross Knight or Lancelot, complete one quest, which is often a digression from their main quest, only to begin another in what thus becomes an open-ended, infinitely extendible form. In terms of action, character, and symbol, *The Worm Ouroboros* is really a series of interlaced, richly decorated, concentric circles, very like the painted initials found in the second half of the twelfth century, which often featured lines terminating in the head of an animal with its mouth open, ready to bite through another line. . . . (p. 15)

Even though any attempt to enumerate the woven threads must result in a résumé of the whole work, some exploration of the Ouroboros should demonstrate that Eddison does not "recklessly bring together everything he admires," that, when judged by standards appropriate to romance, many of the apparent faults are in fact merits.

One of the main charges against Eddison has been that Lessingham's appearance is "a distracting and clumsy notion [which] no prospective reader should allow himself to be troubled by" [see excerpt dated 1952]—i.e., that after the first few chapters Eddison forgets about his earth-creature, feebly refers to him a final time . . . , and then drops any pretense of concern for him. Such an interpretation overlooks Lessingham's psychological identification with the figures in his dream, each of which is a projection of Lessingham, Eddison, and Everyman existing eternally as both battlefield and battle. In an important sense Lessingham is continually present in the romance, for it is he who wills into being Juss, Gorice, and Gro, and he who is realized through them. . . . [Since] Lessingham is imaginatively (and in Eddison's cosmology actually) experiencing Juss's slaying of the Beast Mantichora, Gorice's "final" summoning of the powers of the deep, and Gro's continual changing of sides, it is certainly unfair to say Eddison forgets about one strand in his narrative, even though some readers may consider the technique of the later volumes more sophisticated by modern standards.

Another closely related charge is that *The Worm Ouroboros* is diffuse, too varied, and disunified, the kind of criticism with which romance has been plagued since the seventeenth century. To some extent Lessingham functions like Arthur in *The Faerie Queene* in providing a matrix for the quests (though of course Lessingham does not, like Arthur, represent the commonwealth), but there are far fewer characters and adventures, fewer interlaced spirals, than in Spenser or medieval romances. Readers will miss much of the richness of this work, however, if they skip such digressions as those concerning Mivarsh, Corsus, Sriva, and Zeldornius, Helteranius, and Jalcanaius Fostus, or overlook the lush detail of these episodes. We should not expect romance to be economical, and clearly *The Worm Ouroboros* is not; but in terms of its own logic and pattern, what *is* important is the embroidery. So that Juss and Daha may rescue Goldry, in what some would consider the main action, it is not necessary that Mivarsh strive and fail to ride the hippogriff; but his doing so forces the Demons to return home for another hippogriff egg (one of the many instances of circular action within the Ouroboros form), and also foils Juss's later successful attempt. The "changeless round" pursued by Zeldornius, Helteranius, and Jalcanaius Fostus for nine years, "each fleeing one that would fain encounter him, and still seeking another that flies before him" . . . , would be completely superfluous to a single-issued plot. In this case, however, it is a microcosm of the unending struggle which is life, another variation of the worm with its tale in its mouth. . . . (pp. 15-17)

The lush detail of descriptive passages has a similar rationale; it is the journey, and not its completion, that is important. Readers of romance should find no less pleasure than the Foliots in delightful dancing, and they must not rush through the lofty presence chamber of Demonland. . . . (p. 17)

As for Eddison's use of the supernatural, it is, like Spenser's and unlike Ariosto's, always of spiritual significance: the egg of the hippogriff is hatched by the fire of great longing; and in order to receive Goldry, Juss must ride the hippogriff in utter loneliness, pass through the "Ultimate Nothing" . . . , shun illusion, and give to Goldry the kiss he receives from Sophonisba. In these terms it makes little sense to label Eddison, and by implication all contemporary romancers, decadent and escapist. It may be true, as Auerbach and Frye suggest, that human beings always write as a means of understanding the world, of representing some kind of reality; and Frye's low mimetic and ironic modes seem to prevail in twentieth-century literature. But it would be ridiculous to suppose that there is but a single way of viewing the world at any one time or that any tradition in literature is barred to succeeding generations. Malory, of course, drew from interlaced as well as straightforward narrative, and James Joyce draws on numerous literary traditions. Eddison is not setting romance against "real life." Lessingham's dreams are not just diverting excursions of the imagination. Eddison's world is of noble proportions, and it fosters the old values of courage, strength of will, love, friendship, imagination, and beauty; but it is, magnificently, a world everyman knows, of unattainable, not-to-be-wished-for peace, of mutability, and of unending internal combat. The frequent topical references to World War I and the general sociopolitical environment in Eddison's later work suggest an attempt, for the sake of uninformed critics, to demonstrate explicitly the relevance of his romantic vision.

Thus, when viewed in the romance tradition, which involves a great deal more than whimsy, fairies, and fun, Eddison's *The Worm Ouroboros,* although it is widely misrepresented as escapist and inartistic, appears to excel for the very reasons it has been criticized. This is not to say that it is faultless or that it ranks beside *The Faerie Queene* as a work of art. Without exception, however, when *The Worm Ouroboros* has been criticized, it has been with standards inappropriate to romance. What Henry James and Percy Lubbock have done for criticism of the novel must be done for criticism of romance. Vinaver, Tuve, and C. S. Lewis have already made great contributions in this area; but since romance criteria must be formulated through investigation of all the great romances, and since those likely to review modern romances are rarely well-equipped to deal with a medieval romance, the prospect is not hopeful. It seems unlikely that an Eddison, or a Stephens will receive generally fair reviews until, at the very least, the doctrine of literary absolutism has disappeared. (pp. 17-18)

> Sharon Wilson, "The Doctrine of Organic Unity: E. R. Eddison and the Romance Tradition," in Extrapolation, *Vol. 25, No. 1, Spring, 1984, pp. 12-19.*

ADDITIONAL BIBLIOGRAPHY

Burke, Kenneth. "Romance in Vacuo." *New York Herald Tribune Books* (4 July 1926): 3-4.
A review of *The Worm Ouroboros* that discusses fantasy as an outlet for Eddison's primary interest in beauty. Burke finds that the profusion of excitement within *The Worm Ouroboros* produces emotional experiences ranging from temporary insensitivity to rare and purified sentiment, and concludes that the work is difficult to evaluate because some of its qualities are at once irritating and justifiable.

Carter, Lin. "The World's Edge, and Beyond: The Fiction of Dunsany, Eddison and Cabell." In his *Imaginary Worlds: The Art of Fantasy,* pp. 27-48. New York: Ballantine Books, 1973.*
Surveys Eddison's career, offering high praise for *The Worm Ouroboros.* Carter states: "For all its undeniable flaws and eccentricities, E. R. Eddison's *The Worm Ouroboros* is still the best, the most durable, the richest, the most exciting, the most splendidly ringing work of heroic fantasy I have ever read."

Cournos, John. "Out of Time." *The New York Times Book Review* (25 May 1941): 7, 20.
Favorable review of *A Fish Dinner in Memison,* synopsizing the plot and focusing on the quality of the prose and on the characters. Comparing Eddison to Henry James, Cournos considers Eddison superior at creating delicate impressions and at conceiving and utilizing robust and sensuous material.

Fadiman, Clifton P. "A True Epic." *The Nation* CXXIII, No. 3186 (28 July 1926): 87.
Generally favorable review of *The Worm Ouroboros.* Fadiman praises Eddison's storytelling ability and his boldness in departing from the modern literary trend of analytical subtlety.

Glover, Donald E. *C. S. Lewis: The Art of Enchantment.* Athens: Ohio University Press, 1981, 27ff.
Scattered references to Eddison, *The Worm Ouroboros,* and *Mistress of Mistresses* based largely on unpublished correspondence between Lewis and Eddison, which is excerpted and reprinted in Glover's book. Glover discusses the writers' mutual admiration and responses to each other's works. Although Lewis was drawn to the imagination and inventiveness displayed in *The Worm Ouroboros,* he found that *Mistress of Mistresses,* though an exciting narrative, offered no deeper meaning and lacked the quality of warmth he had found in the earlier novel.

Hedonicus [pseudonym]. "A Writer of Prose." *Book Handbook* (1947): 50-3.
Expresses unreserved praise for the formal beauty, elegance, and artistic deliberation of Eddison's prose style in *Mistress of Mistresses.* This brief essay is also a personal reminiscence recounting "Hedonicus's" discovery and initial enjoyment of Eddison's work.

Hamilton, G. Rostrevor. "E. R. Eddison." *Book Handbook* (1947): 53-7.
A brief biographical essay by a friend of Eddison. Hamilton cites Eddison's early literary interest and influences, traces the general development of his career, touches on his family life and nonliterary interests, and describes him as "a man with a zest for passing life, but a mind always set on the ideal."

Johnson, Edgar. Review of *Mistress of Mistresses,* by E. R. Eddison. *New York Herald Tribune Books* (1 September 1935): 8.
A laudatory review of *Mistress of Mistresses* in which Johnson states that the "entire surrender of rationalism and boundaries of everyday" is necessary for a reader to experience and appreciate this extravagant romantic fantasy. He sees Eddison's romanticism not as evasion, but as a "heroic and mystic vision."

Manlove, C. N. "Anaemic Fantasy: Morris, Dunsany, Eddison, Beagle." In his *The Impulse of Fantasy Literature,* pp. 127-54. Kent: Kent State University Press, 1983.*

Examines what the critic considers a crucial flaw in *The Worm Ouroboros:* the fact that evil, in Eddison's imaginative world, is curiously nonthreatening and hollow, existing only to serve as a contrast to goodness. The critic also takes issue with Eddison's preoccupation with detail, which occasionally overwhelms the narrative.

Nelson, Juana. "Frontward Are His Wounds." *New York Herald Tribune Books* (10 October 1926): 7.
Synopsizes and favorably reviews *Styrbiorn the Strong,* stating that it differs from Eddison's first novel in both spirit and content, and noting earthly details which distinguish it from *The Worm Ouroboros.* The momentum of the drama, the rich, colorful descriptions, and Eddison's use of language are among the qualities Nelson praises.

Prescott, Orville. Introduction to *The Worm Ouroboros:* A Romance, by E. R. Eddison, pp. vii-xi. New York: E. P. Dutton, 1952.

Discusses the elements of *The Worm Ouroboros* that make it a great work of fantasy literature.

"Mr. Eddison: Civil Servant and Author." *The Times,* London No. 50,229 (24 August 1945): 6.
Obituary, followed by a brief, informative survey of Eddison's works.

Stephens, James. Introduction to *The Worm Ouroboros: A Romance,* by E. R. Eddison, pp. a-d. New York: E. P. Dutton & Co., 1952.
A favorable appraisal of *The Worm Ouroboros.* Stephen's introduction originally appeared in the 1926 edition of Eddison's novel.

———. Introduction to *A Fish Dinner in Memison,* by E. R. Eddison, pp. xi-xv. New York: Ballantine Books, 1968.
Originally written in 1940. Stephens highly praises *A Fish Dinner in Memison,* discussing Eddison's adept treatment of time and transdimensional travel, and the nobility of his characters.

Ford Madox Ford

1873-1939

(Born Ford Hermann Hueffer; also wrote under pseudonyms Fenil Haig, Daniel Chaucer, and Baron Ignatz von Aschendrof) English novelist, editor, poet, critic, biographer, historian, essayist, and autobiographer.

Regarded as both a major novelist and a highly influential, innovative force behind modern trends in prose and poetry, Ford was an expert craftsman whose close attention to style and technique are most skillfully evidenced in his two masterpieces, *The Good Soldier* and *Parade's End*. These works are recognized for their intricate structure, vividly impressionistic rendering of characters and events, and superb treatment of the author's most recurrent theme: social decay and alienation in the Edwardian age. Although his reputation is based on his fiction, Ford was also a poet, and his belief that poetry should read like prose led him to a free verse style which had a significant impact on such Imagist writers as T. E. Hulme and Ezra Pound. No less significant in establishing Ford's reputation as a literary influence was his creation and editorship of *The English Review* and *The Transatlantic Review*. In these journals Ford provided the reading public with its first exposure to works by D. H. Lawrence, James Joyce, Ernest Hemingway, and other important figures in twentieth-century English and American literature.

Ford was born in Merton, Surrey, to Dr. Francis Hueffer, a scholar of Richard Wagner's works and music critic for *The Times* of London, and Catherine Brown, daughter of the Pre-Raphaelite painter Ford Madox Brown. After Dr. Hueffer died of a heart attack in 1889, Catherine and the children moved in with her father, whose circle of friends included the Rossettis (who were related to Brown by marriage), Algernon Swinburne, William Morris, Lord Tennyson, and Thomas Carlyle. Surrounded by writers of such stature, Ford was drawn to an artistic life. After attending Praetoria House boarding school, Ford was sent to University College School, which he attended for less than a year, leaving by the end of 1890. His first poem was printed the following year in the anarchist journal *The Torch*, produced by his Rossetti cousins. Soon after, Ford saw his first book—*The Brown Owl*, a fairy tale he had conceived for the entertainment of his younger sister—ushered into publication through the aid of his grandfather. Ford published several other books during the 1890s, but it was not until 1898, when he met and began working closely with Joseph Conrad, that he began to develop into a serious writer. Critics generally agree that their collaborative novels *The Inheritors* and *Romance* are not in themselves as important as the influence the two authors had upon each other, with Ford learning greater structural control and the Polish-born Conrad developing his facility with the English language. Both authors shared a devotion to the impeccable style of the French writers Gustave Flaubert and Guy de Maupassant, and to selecting the exact word or phrase (*le mot juste*) in their own works. Through their collaborations, Ford and Conrad were able to concentrate on developing the narrative techniques and the impressionistic style that later characterized their best prose. Although contact between the two waned after Ford suffered a prolonged nervous breakdown in 1903, Ford continued to offer Conrad advice and

Culver Pictures

assistance on such works as *Nostromo* and *The Secret Agent*. The popular success of Ford's nonfictional *The Soul of London* in 1905 helped alleviate his depressed state, which had been brought on in part by the commercial failure of his previous books. His next work, *The Fifth Queen*, a novel set in Tudor England, also helped improve Ford's mental health, as well as his financial situation. This novel and its sequels, *Privy Seal* and *The Fifth Queen Crowned*, succeeded in introducing Ford as a prose craftsman and author of considerable promise. Conrad, in admiration of Ford's display of talent, called the trilogy "the swan song of historical romance."

Ford's next major achievement was the founding of *The English Review* with businessman Arthur Marwood in 1908. The journal was formed, in part, for the purpose of publishing Thomas Hardy's poem "A Sunday Morning Tragedy," a work which was rumored to have been rejected by every review in London. Even though this rumor was untrue, it provided the impetus for a literary periodical that many critics believe has yet to be surpassed in twentieth-century English letters. The first issue of *The English Review* immediately established a high standard of literary excellence, containing contributions from Henry James, John Galsworthy, W. H. Hudson, H. G. Wells, and Conrad. Moreover, Ford's subsequent discovery of Wyndham Lewis and Lawrence brought lasting renown to Ford's editorial perceptiveness. But despite his success as an editor, Ford was an inept business manager, and it is estimated that by the time of his resignation in 1910, the publication was in debt for several thousand pounds.

The period from 1910 to the outbreak of World War I was Ford's most prolific period as a writer; he produced several volumes of poetry, essays, memoirs, and fiction, including his most famous novel, *The Good Soldier*. In 1915 Ford enlisted in the British Army and was severely gassed while on active service. After the war he seemed content to retire from letters and lead an agrarian life with his companion Stella Bowen. At this time Ford rid himself of the surname Hueffer for several reasons, among them an attempt to evade anti-Prussian sentiment and the desire to avoid legal entanglement with his estranged wife Elsie, should Bowen decide to call herself Mrs. Hueffer, as a former lover had already done. However, in 1924 he once again established himself as a prominent literary figure by founding *The Transatlantic Review* with the encouragement of his friend Pound. Although the journal existed for only one year and did not attain the stature of *The English Review*, it attracted a number of authors, including Gertrude Stein, Joyce, and Hemingway, who were to dominate English and American literature in the years to come. The year 1924 also saw the publication of *Some Do Not*, the first novel in the *Parade's End*, or Tietjens, tetralogy, a saga which was to bring Ford considerable financial success and recognition, especially in America. During the last decade of his life Ford lived with artist Janice Biala, residing alternately in the United States and southern France. While his own fame dwindled, Ford continued to aid and exert his influence over another generation of writers, which included Allen Tate, Caroline Gordon, Robert Penn Warren, and Eudora Welty. Although Ford was involved in numerous literary projects near the end of his life, including a plan to revive *The Transatlantic Review*, he continued to experience overwhelming financial difficulties. With the help of a loan from his English publisher, the author sailed from the United States to France in 1939. While en route, he was taken ill with uraemia, and he died in Deauville shortly thereafter.

Although most of Ford's works have been neglected by both readers and critics since the author's death, the past few decades have witnessed a significant resurgence of interest in his fiction. The majority of criticism restricts itself to analyses of *The Good Soldier* and *Parade's End*, generally considered Ford's best works, and virtually ignores such other accomplished novels as *Ladies Whose Bright Eyes*, *A Call*, *The Young Lovell*, and the Fifth Queen trilogy. In *The Good Soldier*, Ford presented an effective rendering of contemporary life, probing his lifelong theme of the psychological dilemmas faced by the person who holds to traditional attitudes and ideals in a world of shifting values. Originally thought by some to be a confusing, disjointed novel because of its frequent disruptions of chronological time, as well as the narrator's continually wavering point of view, *The Good Soldier* has since been regarded as a brilliantly constructed psychological drama similar in manner to the fiction of James. With a Jamesian allusiveness and preeminent interest in the psychology of the individual, *The Good Soldier* reveals the destructive effects of various contradictory religious and sexual values upon four upper middle-class characters, one of whom is driven to suicide. The work is a tightly written, impressionistic rendering of life that managed, according to some critics, to probe human psychology in greater depth than had any work of James. Ford was in fact among a well-known group of writers, including Stephen Crane and Joseph Conrad, who hailed James as "the Master"; he devoted himself to emulating James's controlled style and wrote a critical study of his work.

In *Parade's End*, written after his return from World War I, Ford addressed in greater detail the moral uncertainties of his times; like such authors as Thomas Mann, André Gide, and Eliot, he documented the sense of disorder and degeneration brought on by the war. *Parade's End* is an allegory of social decay in which the protagonist, Christopher Tietjens, frees himself from his harpy-like wife, Sylvia, through a descent into the nightmarish setting of war, and afterwards undergoes a spiritual and psychological rebirth due to the curative power of his mistress Valentine. As its title indicates, the third novel in the tetralogy, *A Man Could Stand Up*, represents an affirmation of an older, chivalric order and of the chivalric man's ability to exist in a seemingly valueless world. Whereas Edward Ashburnham, the protagonist of *The Good Soldier*, eventually commits suicide, Tietjens adapts himself to his environment while maintaining his Victorian code of honor. The differing conclusions of these two works signifies Ford's gradual shift in emphasis from that of a detached observer of life to that of a remedial sociologist concerned with repairing the Western world's war-ravaged civilization. The latter role, which dominates his last works, is most evident in *Provence* and *Great Trade Route*, in which Ford proposes a worldwide system of small ownership and agrarianism as an alternative to the present system of mass production and industry.

Although not as accomplished as his novels, Ford's poetry was influential during his lifetime. Because Ford thought poetry a less suitable medium than prose for conveying human experience, he endeavored to bring the language of his poetry closer to that of prose, gravitating from fairly traditional poetic forms to the free verse style that characterized his best work. This prosaic style was extremely influential among a group of poets that included Pound and H.D. Although not a great poet, Ford has garnered the acclaim of several renowned poets and writers, among them T. S. Eliot, who called Ford's "Antwerp" "the only good poem I have met with on the subject of war."

In addition to his many novels and volumes of poetry, Ford also wrote a wide variety of other works, including fairy tales, historical romances, histories, biographies, reminiscences, essays, a mystery, and several books of criticism. The mixed quality of his literary canon (which comprises some eighty-one books), coupled with his unconventional lifestyle and his tendency to distort the truth in his autobiographies, have long deferred his recognition as a major writer. Yet his comparison to such great novelists of form as James and Conrad continues, as critics increasingly recognize his comparable novelistic skills. In addition, Ford's reputation as an editor of remarkable intuition and foresight is firmly established, and Ford has been recommended as a model for all future editors of literary periodicals. He wielded an incalculable influence over a younger generation of writers that included many of the most important figures in twentieth-century literature. Today, critics consider his importance to the development of the novel, and to twentieth-century letters in general, to be immense.

(See also *TCLC*, Vol. 1 and *Contemporary Authors*, Vol. 104.)

PRINCIPAL WORKS

The Brown Owl (fairy tale) 1892
The Shifting of the Fire (novel) 1892
The Questions at the Well [as Fenil Haig] (poetry) 1893

The Inheritors: An Extravagant Story [with Joseph Conrad]
     (novel) 1901
Romance [with Joseph Conrad] (novel) 1901
The Soul of London (essays) 1905
The Fifth Queen: And How She Came to Court (novel)
     1906
Privy Seal: His Last Venture (novel) 1907
The Fifth Queen Crowned (novel) 1908
A Call (novel) 1910
Ladies Whose Bright Eyes (novel) 1911
Henry James: A Critical Study (criticism) 1913
The Young Lovell (novel) 1913
Antwerp (poetry) 1915
The Good Soldier: A Tale of Passion (novel) 1915
On Heaven, and Poems Written on Active Service (poetry)
     1918
Thus to Revisit (reminiscences) 1921
Joseph Conrad: A Personal Remembrance (reminiscences)
     1924
*Some Do Not (novel) 1924
*No More Parades (novel) 1925
*A Man Could Stand Up (novel) 1926
*The Last Post (novel) 1928
Henry for Hugh (novel) 1934
Provence (nonfiction) 1935
Collected Poems (poetry) 1936
Great Trade Route (nonfiction) 1937
Portraits from Life (criticism) 1937; also published as
     Mightier Than the Sword, 1938
The March of Literature from Confucius' Day to Our Own
     (criticism) 1938
The Critical Writings of Ford Madox Ford (criticism)
     1964
The Letters of Ford Madox Ford (letters) 1965
Buckshee (poetry) 1966

*These works were published as *Parade's End* in 1950.

THE ATHENAEUM   (essay date 1892)

[*In the following excerpt from a review of* The Shifting of the
Fire, *the critic attacks Ford's choice of subject matter and his
employment of distasteful language.*]

[In **"The Shifting of the Fire"**] Mr. Hueffer has chosen for
his motive a singularly repellent situation—the marriage of a
beautiful girl to an entirely loathsome satyr of nearly four-
score—and he has certainly spared no pains to elaborate its
hideous incongruity. Pity is inspired in the reader; but it is
never unaccompanied with disgust, amounting in several passages to positive nausea. Mr. Hueffer's pages bristle with in-
felicitous audacity and cynicism, which he will regret when
he is older. . . . Mr. Hueffer has yet to learn that strong language does not make a strong book. And he has also to learn
the sovereign lesson of self-effacement, instead of obtruding
his own dogmatic generalizations at every turn. Such blunders
as "lusi naturae" are venial trifles in comparison with the errors
in taste and temper which colour the whole story. Mr. Hueffer
has talent and imagination; but his method is headstrong and
gratuitously aggressive. Happily he is young enough to learn
better manners and more legitimate means of attracting readers.

A review of "The Shifting of the Fire," in The Athenaeum, *No. 3395, November 19, 1892, p. 700.*

THE NEW YORK TIMES BOOK REVIEW   (essay date 1901)

[*In the following excerpt from a review of* The Inheritors, *the
critic calls the novel a satire of English manners and traditions
and identifies Joseph Conrad as the principal author of this collaborative novel. For Conrad's views on this critic's appraisal,
in which he reveals how much the novel owes to Ford and corrects
the critic's interpretation of the work, see the excerpt dated 1901.*]

Not long ago Mr. Conrad was catalogued as "a writer of sea
tales." Whoever takes up **"The Inheritors"** under the impression that he has in store one of those masterly studies of the
sea and sailors which delighted us in "The Nigger of the Narcissus" will lay it down half, or, more probably, a fourth,
read, and with the sense of being cheated, unless he is carried
forward by the authors' power to visualize and realize what
they frankly admit on the title page is "An Extravagant Story."
The final verdict pronounced by this unwilling reader will depend upon his capacity to enjoy satire of a subtle and highly
finished order—directed, if he is an Englishman, against some
of the most cherished traditions and achievements of his country—and upon whether he is more interested in event for event's
sake or for its potential and psychological relation to man.

The plot of the story, which has to do with colonization and
development, the fortunes of an unsuccessful novelist, and the
intrigues of an unscrupulous young woman, is, on the face of
it, neither original nor pleasant. But the treatment is fresh and
unconventional, and Mr. Conrad's power of characterization,
a poetic realism not unlike that of Turgeniev, and his sensitive
appreciation of the conflicting subtleties of human motive and
conduct, make the story actual and effective.

The tale moves swiftly and conclusively to a dramatic and
wholly dissatisfying climax, but it is not the plot or the skill
with which it is worked out that interests us, but the people
who develop it and through whom it is developed. They are
drawn "from the life." . . .

"The Inheritors" is more than a clever study of contemporary
manners, morals, and ideals. Mr. Conrad sees the significant
facts of life and character. If he sometimes flashes before us
what we have fondly hoped was a private view, he does it
without malice or coarseness. The book lacks the emotional
power of "Lord Jim," but it is clean, vigorous, and not machine made.

A review of "The Inheritors," in The New York
Times Book Review, *July 13, 1901, p. 499.*

JOSEPH CONRAD   (letter date 1901)

[*Conrad is considered an innovator of novel structure as well as
one of the finest stylists of modern English literature. His novels
are complex moral and psychological examinations of the ambiguities of good and evil. In each work, through the use of such
literary devices as time shifts, flashbacks, and the varying perspectives of several characters, Conrad portrays the unreliability
of human perception and forces the reader to constantly interpret
the information provided. In his preface to* The Nigger of the
"Narcissus" *(1897), an essay that has been called his artistic
credo, Conrad explained that "art itself may be defined as a
single-minded attempt to render the highest kind of justice to the
visible universe, by bringing to light the truth, manifold and one,
underlying its every aspect. It is an attempt to find in its forms,*

in its colours, in its light, in its shadows, in the aspects of matter, and in the facts of life what of each is fundamental, what is enduring and essential—their one illuminating and convincing quality—the very truth of their existence. . . . My task which I am trying to achieve is, by the power of the written work, to make you feel—it is, before all, to make you see. *That—and no more, and it is everything.'' In the following excerpt from a letter to* The New York Times Book Review, *Conrad explains the purpose of* The Inheritors, *in response to what he believes was a misguided interpretation of the novel by a* Times *critic (see excerpt dated 1901). Dismayed by the critic's negligence in failing to mention Ford as coauthor, Conrad emphasizes the substantial role Ford played in the collaboration.]*

Referring to *The New York Times Saturday Review* of July 13 [see excerpt dated 1901], it is impossible not to recognize in the review of one "extravagant story" ["**The Inheritors**"] the high impartiality exercised in estimating a work which, I fear, remains not wholly sympathetic to the critic.

A feeling of regret mingles with gratitude on that account. It is a great good fortune for a writer to be understood; and greater still to feel that he has made his aim perfectly clear. It might have been wished, too, that the fact of collaboration had been made more evident on the face of the notice. The book is emphatically an experiment in collaboration; but only the first paragraph of the review mentions "the authors" in the plural—afterward it seems as if Mr. Conrad alone were credited with the qualities of style and conception detected by the friendly glance of the critic.

The elder of the authors is well aware how much of these generously estimated qualities the book owes to the younger collaborator. Without disclaiming his own share of the praise or evading the blame, the older man is conscious that his scruples in the matter of treatment, however sincere in themselves, may have stood in the way of a very individual talent deferring to him more out of friendship, perhaps, than from conviction; that they may have robbed the book of much freshness and of many flashes of that "private vision" (as our critic calls them) which would have made the story more actual and more convincing.

It is this feeling that gives him the courage to speak about the book—already written, printed, delivered, and cast to the four winds of publicity. Doubtless a novel that wants explaining is a bad novel; but this is only an extravagant story—and it is an experiment. An experiment may bear a certain amount of explanation without confessing itself a failure.

Therefore it may perhaps be permissible to point out that the story is not directed against "some of the most cherished traditions and achievements of Englishmen." It is rather directed at the self-seeking, at the falsehood that had been (to quote the book) "hiding under the words that for ages had spurred men to noble deeds, to self-sacrifice, and to heroism." And, apart from this view, to direct one's little satire at the tradition and the achievements of a race would have been an imbecile futility—something like making a face at the great pyramid. Judge them as we may, the spirit of tradition and the body of achievement are the very spirit and the very body not only of any single race, but of the entire mankind, which, without the vast breadth and colossal form of the past would be resolved into a handful of the dying, struggling feebly in the darkness under an overwhelming multitude of the dead. Thus our Etchingham Granger, when in the solitude that falls upon his soul, he sees the form of the approaching Nemesis, is made to understand that no man is permitted "to throw away with impunity the treasure of his past—the past of his kind—whence springs the promise of his future."

This is the note struck—we hoped with sufficient emphasis—among the other emotions of the hero. And, besides, we may appeal to the general tone of the book. It is not directed against tradition; still less does it attack personalities. The extravagance of its form is meant to point out forcibly the materialistic exaggeration of individualism, whose unscrupulous efficiency it is the temper of the time to worship.

It points it out simply—and no more; because the business of a work striving to be art is not to teach or to prophecy, (as we have been charged, on this side, with attempting,) nor yet to pronounce a definite conclusion.

This, the teaching, the conclusions, even to the prophesying, may be safely left to science, which, whatever authority it may claim, is not concerned with truth at all, but with the exact order of such phenomena as fall under the perception of the senses.

> *Joseph Conrad, in a letter to* The New York Times Saturday Review *on August 2, 1901, in* The New York Times Book Review, *August 24, 1901, p. 603.*

JACOB TONSON [PSEUDONYM OF ARNOLD BENNETT] (essay date 1910)

[Bennett was an Edwardian novelist who is credited with bringing techniques of European Naturalism to the English novel. His reputation rests almost exclusively on The Old Wives' Tale *and the Clayhanger trilogy, novels which are set in the manufacturing district of Bennett's native Staffordshire and which tell of the thwarted ambitions of those who endure a dull, provincial existence. In the following excerpt, Bennett approvingly notes certain Jamesian qualities present in passages of* A Call *but, on the whole, finds the novel undistinguished in style and lacking in verisimilitude.]*

"**A Call**" is a very pretty thing. You can see in it throughout a preoccupation with questions of form, of technique—in short, a preoccupation with the art of literature. A rare quality, and one which must give pleasure to anybody whose reading in fiction has been wide enough, and his judgment sound enough, to enable him to perceive that, for want of that preoccupation, English fiction as a whole is badly second-rate, even the best of it. The style is as a rule distinguished; but in some places it is not, and here and there, in the weak spots, one catches Mr. Hueffer at the craftsman's trick of sticking a word in an unusual situation in a sentence in the hope (vain) of producing distinction by artificial means. In the mere writing, Mr. Hueffer owes something to Mr. Henry James, and perhaps also he has learnt from Mr. James some of the charming grace which is displayed in the construction of the book. It is a mild novel. It deals with tragic matters, but deals with them mildly. It does not engross, and probably is not meant to engross. It induces reverie and reflection. I have seen it upbraided for "coldness." It is not cold. But then, fortunately, it is not sentimental; and most reviewers are unable to differentiate between sentimentality and warmth.

I may say that I consider "**A Call**" to be profoundly and hopelessly untrue to life. It treats of the lazy rich. The characters, with one exception, never do anything except give orders to excellent servants and discuss the states of their bodies and their souls. So far as the novel shows, they have no real interest in any of the arts. They are heroically egotistic. They contribute nothing to the welfare of the Society from which they draw everything. They are, first and last, utterly and in every way idle. The sole thing that can be said in their favour is that they have carried daily manners to a high point of perfection. They are extremely "class-conscious"; constantly talking to each other of "our class." Mr. Hueffer endows these persons with a comprehensive fineness of perception, and a skill in verbal expression, which it is absolutely impossible that they, living the life they do live, could possess. I have never met these persons in their homes, but I have observed them for months at a time on their travels, and I am prepared to defend the proposition that their mental existence resembles much more closely that of the beasts of the field than that credited to them by the amiable idealism of Mr. Hueffer. Such qualities as Mr. Hueffer illustrates are the fruit only of long and often painful activity in the domains of intellect and of artistic emotion. In this fundamental matter **"A Call"** is inferior to Mrs. Wharton's enormously over-praised, slabby, and mediocre novel, "The House of Mirth." But regard **"A Call"** as an original kind of fairy-tale, and it is about perfect.

> Jacob Tonson [*pseudonym of Arnold Bennett*], *in a review of "A Call," in* The New Age, *n.s. Vol. VI, No. 20, March 17, 1910, p. 471.*

EZRA POUND (essay date 1914)

[*Pound is regarded as one of the most innovative and influential figures in twentieth-century Anglo-American poetry. He was instrumental in editorially and financially aiding T. S. Eliot, Wyndham Lewis, James Joyce, and William Carlos Williams, among other poets. His own* Cantos *is among the most ambitious poetic cycles of the century, and his series of satirical poems* Hugh Selwyn Mauberley *is ranked with Eliot's* The Waste Land *as a significant attack upon the decadence of modern culture. An American, Pound considered the United States a cultural wasteland, and therefore spent most of his life in Europe, where he and Ford became friends. Pound's influential involvement with the Imagist movement derived in part from Ford's own belief in revivifying poetry through a* vers libre *style. In the following excerpt, originally published in 1914, Pound applauds Ford for demonstrating both critical and creative foresight by anticipating modernist trends in literature. Pound describes Ford's verse and prose as efficient and precise, and calls "On Heaven" the best long poem yet written in "twentieth-century fashion."*]

Mr. Yeats wrote years ago that the highest poetry is so precious that one should be willing to search many a dull tome to find and gather the fragments. As touching poetry this was, perhaps, no new feeling. Yet where nearly everyone else is still dominated by an eighteenth-century verbalism, Mr. Hueffer has had this instinct for prose. It is he who has insisted, in the face of a still-Victorian press, upon the importance of good writing as opposed to the opalescent word, the rhetorical tradition. Stendhal had said, and Flaubert, De Maupassant and Turgenev had proved, that "prose was the higher art"—at least their prose.

It is impossible to talk about perfection without getting yourself very much disliked. It is even more difficult in a capital where everybody's Aunt Lucy or Uncle George has written something or other, and where the victory of any standard save that of mediocrity would at once banish so many nice people from the temple of immortality. So it comes about that Mr. Hueffer is the best critic in England, one might say the only critic of any importance. What he says today the press, the reviewers, who hate him and who disparage his books, will say in about nine years' time, or possibly sooner. . . . Mr. Hueffer has possessed

the peculiar faculty of "foresight," or of constructive criticism, in a pre-eminent degree. (pp. 129-30)

Mr. Hueffer is still underestimated for another reason: namely, that we have not yet learned that prose is, perhaps, as precious and as much to be sought after as verse, even its shreds and patches. So that, if one of the finest chapters in English is hidden in a claptrap novel, we cannot weigh the vision which made it against the weariness or the confusion which dragged down the rest of the work. Yet we would do this readily with a poem. If a novel have a form as distinct as that of a sonnet, and if its workmanship be as fine as that of some Pleiade rondel, we complain of the slightness of the motive. Yet we would not deny praise to the rondel. So it remains for a prose craftsman like Mr. Arnold Bennett to speak well of Mr. Hueffer's prose, and for a verse-craftsman like myself to speak well of his verses. And the general public will have little or none of him because he does not put on pontifical robes, because he does not take up the megaphone of some known and accepted pose, and because he makes enemies among the stupid by his rather engaging frankness.

We may as well begin with the knowledge that Mr. Hueffer is a keen critic and a skilled writer of prose, and we may add that he is not wholly unsuccessful as a composer, and that he has given us, in **On Heaven,** the best longish poem yet written in the "twentieth-century fashion."

Coleridge has spoken of "the miracle that might be wrought simply by one man's feeling a thing more clearly or more poignantly than anyone had felt it before." The last century showed us a fair example when Swinburne awoke to the fact

Ford and Ezra Pound in Rapallo, Italy, around 1927. Courtesy of Janice Biala.

that poetry was an art, not merely a vehicle for the propagation of doctrine. England and Germany are still showing the effects of his perception. I can not belittle my belief that Mr. Hueffer's realization that poetry should be written at least as well as prose will have as wide a result. He himself will tell you that it is "all Christina Rossetti," and that "it was not Wordsworth, for Wordsworth was so busied about the ordinary word that he never found time to think about *le mot juste.*"

As for Christina, Mr. Hueffer is a better critic than I am, and I would be the last to deny that a certain limpidity and precision are the ultimate qualities of style; yet I can not accept his opinion. Christina had these qualities, it is true—in places, but they are to be found also in Browning and even in Swinburne at rare moments. Christina very often sets my teeth on edge,— and so for that matter does Mr. Hueffer. But it is the function of criticism to find what a given work is, not what it is not. It is also the faculty of a capital or of high civilization to value a man for some rare ability, to make use of him and not hinder him or itself by asking of him faculties which he does not possess. (pp. 130-32)

Mr. Hueffer brings to his work a prose training such as Christina never had, and it is absolutely the devil to try to quote snippets from a man whose poems are gracious impressions, leisurely, low-toned. One would quote *The Starling,* but one would have to give the whole three pages of it. And one would like to quote patches out of the curious medley, *To All the Dead,*—save that the picturesque patches aren't the whole or the feel of it; or Süssmund's capricious *Address,* a sort of *Inferno* to the *Heaven.* (p. 133)

There is in his work . . . [a] phase that depends somewhat upon his knowledge of instrumental music. Dante has defined a poem as a composition of words set to music, and the intelligent critic will demand that either the composition of words or the music shall possess a certain interest, or that there be some aptitude in their jointure together. It is true that since Dante's day—and indeed his day and Cassella's saw a re-beginning of it—"music" and "poetry" have drifted apart, and we have had a third thing which is called "word music." I mean we have poems which are read or even, in a fashion, intoned, and are "musical" in some sort of complete or inclusive sense that makes it impossible or inadvisable to "set them to music." I mean obviously such poems as the First Chorus of *Atalanta* or many of Mr. Yeats' lyrics. The words have a music of their own, and a second "musician's" music is an impertinence or an intrusion.

There still remains the song to sing: to be "set to music," and of this sort of poem Mr. Hueffer has given us notable examples in his rendering of Von der Vogelweide's *Tandaradei* and, in lighter measure, in his own *The Three-Ten.* . . . (pp. 135-36)

Oh well, there are very few song writers in England, and it's a simple old-fashioned song with a note of futurism in its very lyric refrain; and I dare say you will pay as little attention to it as I did five years ago. And if you sing it aloud, once over, to yourself, I dare say you'll be just as incapable of getting it out of your head, which is perhaps one test of a lyric.

It is not, however, for Mr. Hueffer's gift of songwriting that I have considered him at such length; this gift is rare but not novel. I find him significant and revolutionary because of his insistence upon clarity and precision, upon the prose tradition; in brief, upon efficient writing—even in verse. (p. 137)

Ezra Pound, "Ford Madox Hueffer and the Prose Tradition in Verse," in his Pavannes and Divisions, Alfred A. Knopf, 1918, pp. 129-37.

THEODORE DREISER   (essay date 1915)

[*Considered among America's foremost novelists, Dreiser was one of the principal American exponents of literary Naturalism. He is known primarily for his novels* Sister Carrie *(1901),* An American Tragedy *(1926), and the Frank Cowperwood trilogy (1912-47), in each of which the author combined his vision of life as a meaningless series of chemical reactions and animal impulses with a sense of sentimentality and pity for humanity's lot. Deeply concerned with the human condition but contemptuous of traditional social, political, and religious remedies, Dreiser associated for many years with the American socialist and communist movements, an interest reflected in much of his writing after 1925. In the following excerpt from a review of* The Good Soldier, *Dreiser acknowledges the psychological depth and skillful handling of the tragic theme of the novel, but laments that Ford chose to extensively use the device of time-shifts—which the critic believes spoil the story—and argues that the character Dowell is merely a derisive caricature of an American.*]

["**The Good Soldier**"] is a sad story, and a splendid one from a psychological point of view; but Mr. Hueffer, in spite of the care he has bestowed upon it, has not made it splendid in the telling. In the main he has only suggested its splendor. . . . One half suspects that since Mr. Hueffer shared with Mr. Conrad in the writing of "**Romance,**" the intricate weavings to and fro of that literary colorist have, to a certain extent, influenced him in the spoiling of this story. For it is spoiled to the extent that you are compelled to say, "Well, this is too bad. This is quite a wonderful thing, but it is not well done." Personally I would have suggested to Mr. Hueffer, if I might have, that he begin at the beginning, which is where Colonel Powys wishes to marry off his daughters—not at the beginning as some tertiary or quadrutiary character in the book sees it, since it really concerns Ashburnham and his wife. This is neither here nor there, however, a mere suggestion. A story may begin in many ways.

Of far more importance is it that, once begun, it should go forward in a more or less direct line, or at least that it should retain one's uninterrupted interest. This is not the case in this book. The interlacings, the cross references, the re-re-references to all sorts of things which subsequently are told somewhere in full, irritate one to the point of one's laying down the book. As a matter of fact, except for the perception that will come to any man, that here is a real statement of fact picked up from somewhere and related by the author as best he could, I doubt whether even the lover of naturalism—entirely free of conventional prejudice—would go on.

As for those dreary minds who find life morally ordered and the universe murmurous of divine law—they would run from it as from the plague. For, with all its faults of telling, it is an honest story, and there is no blinking of the commonplaces of our existence which so many find immoral and make such a valiant effort to conceal. One of the most irritating difficulties of the tale is that Dowell, the American husband who tells the story, is described as, first, that amazingly tame thing, an Englishman's conception of an American husband; second, as a profound psychologist able to follow out to the last detail the morbid minutiae of this tragedy, and to philosophize on them as only a deeply thinking and observing man could; and lastly as one who is as blind as a bat, as dull as a mallet, and as weak as any sentimentalist ever. The combination proves a little trying before one is done with it.

This story has been called immoral. One can predict such a charge to-day in the case of any book, play, or picture which refuses to concern itself with the high-school ideal of what life should be. It is immoral apparently to do anything except dress well and talk platitudes. But it is interesting to find this English author (German by extraction, I believe) and presumably, from all accounts, in revolt against these sickening strictures, dotting his book with apologies for this, that, and another condition not in line with this high-school standard (albeit it is the wretched American who speaks) and actually smacking his lips over the stated order that damns his book. And worse yet, Dowell is no American. He is that literary packhorse or scapegoat on whom the native Englishman loads all his contempt for Americans. And Captain and Mrs. Ashburnham, whom he so soulfully lauds for their love of English pretence and order, are two who would have promptly pitched his book out of doors, I can tell him. Yet he babbles of the fineness of their point of view. As a matter of fact their point of view is that same accursed thing which has been handed on to America as "good form," and which we are now asked to sustain by force of arms as representing civilization. (p. 155)

But you may well suspect that there is a good story here and that it is well worth your reading. Both suppositions are true. In the hands of a better writer this jointure of events might well have articulated into one of the finest pictures in any language. Its facts are true, in the main. Its theme beautiful. It is tragic in the best sense that the Greeks knew tragedy, that tragedy for which there is no solution. But to achieve a high result in any book its component characters must of necessity stand forth unmistakeable in their moods and characteristics. In this one they do not. Every scene of any importance has been blinked or passed over with a few words or cross references. I am not now referring to any moral fact. Every conversation which should have appeared, every storm which should have contained revealing flashes, making clear the minds, the hearts, and the agonies of those concerned, has been avoided. There are no paragraphs or pages of which you can say "This is a truly moving description," or "This is a brilliant vital interpretation." You are never really stirred. You are never hurt. You are merely told and referred. It is all cold narrative, never truly poignant.

This is a pity. This book had the making of a fine story. I half suspect that its failure is due to the author's formal British leanings, whatever his birth—that leaning which Mr. Dowell seems to think so important, which will not let him loosen up and sing. The whole book is indeed fairly representative of that encrusting formalism which, barnacle-wise, is apparently overtaking and destroying all that is best in English life. The arts will surely die unless formalism is destroyed. And when you find a great theme marred by a sniffy reverence for conventionalism and the glories of a fixed condition it is a thing for tears. I would almost commend Mr. Hueffer to the futurists, or to anyone that has the strength to scorn the moldy past, in the hope that he might develop a method entirely different from that which is here employed, if I did not know that at bottom the great artist is never to be commended. Rather from his brain, as Athena from that of Zeus, spring flawless and shining all those art forms which the world adores and preserves. (p. 156)

Theodore Dreiser, ''The Saddest Story','' in The New Republic, Vol. III, No. 32, June 12, 1915, pp. 155-56.

CONRAD AIKEN   (essay date 1918)

[*An American man of letters best known for his poetry, Aiken was deeply influenced by the psychological and literary theories of Sigmund Freud, Havelock Ellis, Edgar Allan Poe, and Henri Bergson, among others, and is considered a master of literary stream of consciousness. In reviews noted for their perceptiveness and barbed wit, Aiken exercised his theory that "criticism is really a branch of psychology." His critical position, according to Rufus A. Blanshard, "insists that the traditional notions of 'beauty' stand corrected by what we now know about the psychology of creation and consumption. Since a work of art is rooted in the personality, conscious and unconscious, of its creator, criticism should deal as much with those roots as with the finished flower." In the following excerpt from a review of* On Heaven, and Poems Written on Active Service, *Aiken discusses the similarities and differences between the poetic theories of Ford and William Wordsworth and notes the presence of a distinctive rhythm in Ford's free verse that evidences experimental artistry. While Aiken complains of Ford's tendency toward discursiveness, he nevertheless favorably appraises the collection.*]

In the preface to his new book of poems, **On Heaven** . . . , Mr. Ford Madox Hueffer remarks:

> The greater part of the book is, I notice on putting it together, in either vers libre or rhymed vers libre. I am not going to apologize for this or to defend vers libre as such. It is because I simply can't help it. Vers libre is the only medium in which I can convey any more intimate moods. Vers libre is a very jolly medium in which to write and to read, if it be read conversationally and quietly. And anyhow, symmetrical or rhymed verse is for me a cramped and difficult medium—or an easy and uninteresting one.

One recollects, further, that Mr. Hueffer has in the past been also insistent, in theory and in practice, on the point that poetry should be at least as well written as prose—that, in other words, it must be good prose before it can be good poetry. Taken together, these ideas singularly echo a preface written one hundred and twenty odd years ago—Wordsworth's preface to the *Lyrical Ballads*. In the appendix to that volume Wordsworth, it will be recalled, remarked that in works of imagination the ideas, in proportion as they are valuable, whether in prose or verse, "require and exact one and the same language." And throughout he insisted on doing away with all merely decorative language and on using the speech of daily life.

On the matter of meter or rhythm, however, the two poets are not so entirely in agreement as they might appear to be. They are in agreement, it might be said, just in so far as they both seem inclined to regard the question of rhythm as only of minor or incidental importance. "Metre," said Wordsworth, "is only adventitious to composition." Mr. Hueffer, as is seen above, candidly admits that he avoids the strictest symmetrical forms because to use them well is too difficult. Do both poets perhaps underestimate the value of rhythm? In the light of the widespread vogue of free verse at present, it is a question interesting to speculate upon. And Mr. Hueffer's poems, which are excellent, afford us a pleasant opportunity. (p. 417)

Mr. Hueffer confesses in advance that he prefers a less to a more complex form of art. As a matter of fact Mr. Hueffer is too modest. When he speaks of free verse he does not mean, to the extent in which it is usually meant, verse without rhythm. At his freest he is not far from a genuinely rhythmic method; and in many respects his sense of rhythm is both acute and individual. Three poems in his book would alone make it worth printing: **"Antwerp,"** which is one of the three or four brilliant poems inspired by the war; **"Footsloggers,"** which though not so good, is none the less very readable; and **"On Heaven,"** the poem which gives the volume its name. It is true that in all three of these poems Mr. Hueffer very often employs a rhythm which is almost as dispersed as that of prose; but the point to be emphatically remarked is that he does so only by way of variation on the given norm of movement, which is essentially and predominantly rhythmic. Variation of this sort is no more or less than good artistry; and Mr. Hueffer is a very competent artist, in whose hands even the most captious reader feels instinctively and at once secure. Does he at times overdo the dispersal of rhythm? Perhaps. There are moments, in **"Antwerp"** and in **"On Heaven,"** when the relief of the reader on coming to a forcefully rhythmic passage is so marked as to make him suspect that the rhythm of the passage just left was not forceful enough. Mr. Hueffer is of a discursive temperament, viewed from whatever angle, and this leads him inevitably to over-inclusiveness and moments of let-down. One feels that a certain amount of cutting would improve both **"Antwerp"** and **"On Heaven."**

Yet one would hesitate to set about it oneself. Both poems are delightful. Mr. Hueffer writes with gusto and imagination, and—what is perhaps rarer among contemporary poets—with tenderness. **"On Heaven"** may not be the very highest type of poetry—it is clearly of the more colloquial sort, delightfully expatiative, skilful in its use of the more subdued tones of prose—but it takes hold of one, and that is enough. One accepts it for what it is, not demanding of it what the author never intended to give it—that higher degree of perfection in intricacy, that more intense and all-fusing synthesis, which would have bestowed on it the sort of beauty that more permanently endures. (p. 418)

> *Conrad Aiken, "The Function of Rhythm," in* The Dial, *Vol. LXV, No. 777, November 16, 1918, pp. 417-18.*

H. G. WELLS   (letter date 1920)

[Wells is best known today, along with Jules Verne, as a father of modern science fiction and as a utopian idealist who correctly foretold an era of chemical warfare, atomic weaponry, and world wars. His writing was shaped by the influence of Arnold Bennett, Frank Harris, Joseph Conrad, and other contemporaries with whom he exchanged criticism and opinions on the art of writing. Throughout much of his career, Wells wrote and lectured on the betterment of society through education and the advance of scientific innovation. A Fabian socialist and student of zoologist T. H. Huxley, Wells was, until his last bitter years, a believer in the gradual, inevitable moral and intellectual ascent of humanity. Much of his literary criticism was written during the 1890s for The Saturday Review, *under the direction of Harris. Wells was the first person Ford approached with regard to the joint owner-editorship of* The English Review, *but Wells repeatedly delayed committing himself to the venture. The two later fell into an imbroglio over the financial aspects of serializing Wells's Tono-Bungay in the journal. In the following excerpt from a letter to the editor of* The English Review, *Wells reacts unfavorably to a portion of Ford's autobiographical* Thus to Revisit, *which appeared serially in that magazine before its publication in book form. Wells rejects as a "childish falsehood" Ford's claim that he lectured Ford and others on literary technique.]*

Sir,—I have long had an uneasy feeling about my old neighbour in Kent, Mr. Ford Madox Hueffer. I knew that he was capable

of imaginative reminiscences, and that in a small way he had been busy with my name. Fantastic biographical details have drifted round to me. I have heard how Mr. Hueffer gainsaid and withstood me about things I never did and answered neatly things I never said. He is now breaking into print with this stuff. It is a great pity. Mr. Hueffer has written some delightful romances, and he is a very great poet. Why does he make capital of the friendliness and hospitalities of the past to tell stupid and belittling stories of another man who is, by his own showing, a very inferior and insignificant person? This childish falsehood about my lecturing him, or anyone, on how to write a novel, is particularly incredible. "How to do it" was the one topic upon which I never offered a contribution to my Kentish and Sussex neighbours. Only once did I lecture this drawling, blonde young man, as he was then, upon any literary matter. At our first meeting, he informed me that he had persuaded Mr. Joseph Conrad to collaborate with him. I tried to convey to him, as considerately as possible, what a very peculiar and untouchable thing was the Conrad prose fabric, and what a very mischievous enterprise he contemplated. That dead, witless book, **"The Inheritors,"** justifies my warnings. That and a second book, of which I forget the title—it was an entirely stagnant "adventure" story, festering with fine language— were an abominable waste of Conrad's time and energy. For the rest, my conversations upon things literary with Mr. Hueffer were defensive. These endless chatterings about "how it is done," about the New Form of the Novel, about who was "greater" than who, about the possibilities of forming a "Group" or starting a "Movement" are things to be avoided at any cost. There is a subtle mischief in this fussing about literary comment, this preoccupation with phrases and artificial balances in composition and the details of work, these campaigns to establish standard catch-words in criticism and to manipulate reputations, which affects nearly everyone who indulges in these practices. . . . Sedulously I kept myself out of that talk— and it is no good for Mr. Hueffer to pretend that I ever came in. (pp. 178-79)

> *H. G. Wells, in a letter to the editor of* The English Review, *in* The English Review, *Vol. XXXI, August, 1920, pp. 178-79.*

H. L. MENCKEN   (essay date 1925)

[From the era of World War I until the early years of the Great Depression, Mencken was one of the most influential figures in American letters. His strongly individualistic, irreverent outlook on life and his vigorous, invective-charged writing style helped establish the iconoclastic spirit of the Jazz Age and significantly shaped the direction of American literature. As a social and literary critic—the roles for which he is best known—Mencken was the scourge of evangelical Christianity, public service organizations, literary censorship, boosterism, provincialism, democracy, all advocates of personal or social improvement, and every other facet of American life that he perceived as humbug. In his literary criticism, Mencken encouraged American writers to shun the anglophilic, moralistic bent of the nineteenth century and to practice realism, an artistic call-to-arms that is most fully developed in his essay "Puritanism As a Literary Force," one of the seminal essays in modern literary criticism. A man who was widely renowned or feared during his lifetime as a would-be destroyer of established American values, Mencken once wrote: "All of my work, barring a few obvious burlesques, is based upon three fundamental ideas. 1. That knowledge is better than ignorance; 2. That it is better to tell the truth than to lie; and 3. That it is better to be free than to be a slave." In the following excerpt from a review of Ford's Joseph Conrad: A Personal Remembrance, *Mencken predicts that Ford's only lasting fame will stem*

from his collaborations with Conrad, one of the few authors Mencken deeply admired. Despite its mocking tone, Mencken's review is generally favorable, praising Ford for a book "full of valuable information."]

Now that Joseph Conrad is safely entombed in Canterbury, hard by the palace and golf links of the Most Rev. the Archbishop, we may look for a great gush of books about him, some of them judicious. The first to appear, so far as I know, is **"Joseph Conrad: a Personal Remembrance,"** by Ford Madox Ford, *geb.* Hueffer, a friend of early days and collaborator on two of the Conrad books, **"Romance"** and **"The Inheritors."** This Ford, or Hueffer, has been a promising young man in England for thirty years. . . . Once, with Douglas Goldring, he started the *English Review.* Another time he took to writing history and biography. Yet another time he consecrated himself to novels. Lately, apparently despairing of making a permanent go of it in London, he moved to Paris and started a *Tendenz* magazine called the *Transatlantic Review*—the sort of thing that Ezra Pound and his friends were doing ten or fifteen years ago, and that Young Aesthetes out of St. Louis, East Broadway and Rahway, N.J., still play with in the suburbs of Greenwich Village. Luck, I fear, is not with him; even his change of name has not got him anywhere. Half German and half English, he is a sort of walking civil war—too much engrossed by the bombs going off in his own ego to make much of an impression upon the rest of the human race. The high, purple spot of his life came when he collaborated with Conrad, and upon the fact, I daresay, his footnote in the literature books will depend.

In the present volume he makes as much of the episode as he can, and not unnaturally. Every drop of juice in it is squeezed out. The transactions between him and Conrad do not appear as exchanges between a young, pushing and extremely bad storyteller and one of the greatest masters of fiction of all time, but as friendly parleys between full equals, in which Ford, or Hueffer, usually gets rather the better of it, whether as artist, as literary business man or as English country gentleman. The fact seems to distress the English Conradistas, especially those who had places within the dead maestro's circle of intimates. The Widow Conrad herself, in an indignant manifesto in far from impeccable English, roundly denounces Ford-Hueffer as a cuckoo, shamelessly laying eggs in her late husband's nest. "During the years," she says, "that Mr. Hueffer was most intimate with Joseph Conrad, between 1898 and 1909, Ford Madox Hueffer"—she seems to be unaware of his yet worse cuckooing of the patronymic of the Detroit thinker—"never spent more than three consecutive weeks under our roof, and when we returned the visit we always, with few exceptions, had rooms in a cottage close at hand. After 1909 the meetings between the two were very rare and not *once* of my husband's seeking." Have your way, Madame! I am too old and full of scars and bitterness to quarrel with widows, or even to question them. But the fact remains as plain as day that Conrad took in Ford, or Hueffer, as a collaborator on **"Romance"** quite voluntarily, that Ford, or Hueffer, provided the main outline of the story, and that the same Ford, or Hueffer, did his fair share of the writing. (pp. 505-06)

At all events, Ford ben-Hueffer's account of those early years is surely not improbable on its face. What he says, even when he is most impudent, always has a well-greased reasonableness. He depicts a Conrad who is always plausible, and sometimes overwhelmingly convincing. The man emerges from behind his smoky monocle, and begins to take on the color and heat of life. . . . There was always something remote and occult about him. He held himself aloof, and was a bit disdainful,

even while he accepted patronage. Ford, I think, gets at the man within the cloak—perhaps not completely, perhaps not always accurately, but certainly more nearly completely and accurately than the rest of the Conradian exegetes. Himself in youth a blatant and hollow fellow, blown up by the gases of a preposterous egoism, he was yet sufficiently in the possession of sense to know that he stood in the presence of an extraordinary man, and sufficiently skillful to observe that man with sharp care. His book is affected and irritating, but full of valuable information. No matter how violently the Widow Conrad protests in her eccentric English it will be read with joy and profit by all parties at interest. It is packed with little shrewdnesses, and it is immensely amusing. (p. 506)

H. L. Mencken, "The Conrad Wake," in American Mercury, *Vol. IV, No. 16, April, 1925, pp. 505-07.* *

ISABEL PATERSON (essay date 1926)

[*Paterson was a critic with* The New York Herald Tribune, *where she wrote a regular column entitled "Turns with a Bookworm." In the following excerpt Paterson, the first critic to recognize that* Some Do Not, No More Parades, *and* A Man Could Stand Up *together form a single unit, ranks these three novels with John Galsworthy's* Forsyte Saga *and considers Ford's character Christopher Tietjens "the most vital and fully realized character in post-war fiction." Pleased by the perceptiveness of this review, Ford dedicated the final volume of the Tietjens tetralogy,* The Last Post, *to Paterson.*]

[Although **"Some Do Not," "No More Parades,"** and **" A Man Could Stand Up"**] have been published separately, and the first two were reviewed on their publication dates, in 1924 and 1925, they are an organic unit; and the third volume cannot be appreciated at its full value without its predecessors. It resolves the psychological suspense of the situation which was elaborately and compellingly developed in the first two, a solution skillfully postponed by the author, without avoidance of the issue, by the intimation that a man at the front might find the Gordian knot cut for him at any moment.

Indeed, life is always an unfinished story; and even this third installment of the story of Christopher Tietjens makes no factitious pretense of finality. It does, however, come to a definite point, not only with the armistice, but in regard to Christopher's private concerns. It is the end of one phase and, therefore, the beginning of another. There may be a fourth volume, but for the present that is immaterial. These three have a satisfying completeness; they are an astonishing achievement in both form and substance. They rank with Galsworthy's "Forsyte Saga" as a record of the passing of a whole social order and period, the changes being shown by the actions and reactions of two or three significant individuals. Even more cleverly than Galsworthy, Ford avoids the longwinded explanations and sociological footnotes of H. G. Wells; he is dramatically specific. To paraphrase Whistler, he isn't telling you, he's showing you; and seeing is believing.

The result is that Christopher Tietjens emerges as the most vital and fully realized character in post-war fiction. One might go back further still, probably; but there is really no need of comparisons. Christopher is simply himself; and a character can be neither more nor less than that. He is entirely human and quite unlike anybody else; which is the peculiarity of all human beings and the touchstone of character creation.

This is also a genuine novel; that is to say, a manageable portion of life seen through an artists eyes and a rule of thumb test of that is the fact that knowing the plot in advance will not detract from the intelligent reader's enjoyment of the book. It may rather, for the non-professional reader, be helpful. Mr. Ford has employed very brilliantly the modern structure of the novel, in which the events are linked together, not chronologically, but by their realization or recurrence in the consciousness and memory of the various principal persons involved. The period of elapsed time is unimportant; the intensity and lasting consequences of the events determine their artistic value, and their incidence their interrelation, whether as cause and effect or as counter-checks, fixes their place in the narrative. This, to readers accustomed only to the chronological march of the old-fashioned novel is naturally a trifle confusing. Methods of reading are also a matter of habit. But departures from habit are often a source of the keenest pleasure. In this case it is well worth making the effort to follow a new path. . . .

For this is one of those rare novels which becomes a part of the reader's personal experience.

> *Isabel Paterson, "Don Quixote in the Trenches," in*
> New York Herald Tribune Books, *October 17, 1926,*
> *p. 5.*

CONSTANT READER [PSEUDONYM OF DOROTHY PARKER] (essay date 1928)

[*An American critic, short story writer, poet, and dramatist, Parker is noted for the liveliness and caustic humor of her literary works and of her often-quoted epigrams. A woman whose writings reveal an alternately tender and sardonic personality (described by her friend Alexander Woollcott as "so odd a blend of Little Nell and Lady Macbeth"), Parker achieved her greatest fame as the author of the frequently anthologized short story "Big Blonde" (1929) and as the literary and drama critic for* Vanity Fair, Esquire, *and* The New Yorker. *Central to her criticism is a withering contempt for pretentiousness, for predictability, and for unoriginality, as well as high praise for innovation and sophistication. In the following excerpt, Parker places* The Last Post—*the concluding novel in the Tietjens tetralogy—last in terms of literary quality as well. Still, she discerns in it many of the same qualities that make* The Good Soldier *Ford's best novel.*]

In order that my public—my boy and girl, I call them—may have the inestimable benefit of my report, I am supposed to have read "**The Last Post**," by Ford Madox Ford (*né* Hueffer). I have been faithful to my duty, in my fashion. I have read the book. But I did not behave like a regular little soldier about it. I did not sit me down in a hard, straight chair, and read it sternly through at one stretch. I kept putting it down, and sneaking off to the dear, strange things I truly ached to read and to ponder.

It is not that "**The Last Post**" is not a good book. It is not that I do not think Ford Madox Ford is a fine novelist. (There was a time, there, when I thought I was never going to get out of those negatives, but the crisis is passed, now, and I am expected to pull through.) It is that there are certain things set down in black on white beside which even distinguished, searching, passionate novels pale to mediocrity.

There is, for example, a brief story lately printed in a morning paper. . . . It concerns a man who shall here be called William Doe, because he has enough trouble already. He was charged with writing what are journalistically called poison-pen letters to various city officials; the charge was dismissed when handwriting experts declared that the letters were written not by him but by a woman. That, I think, is a fairly good start, but wait. If it were any possible affair of mine, I should quote the cool, exact words of that newspaper story. "Look at this, will you?" I should say, and then I should write down these lines:

"Mr. Doe from the first stoutly denied that he had anything to do with the letters or knew anything about them. He was at a loss to explain them and the use of his name in the signatures. Yesterday he said that the only explanation he could think of was the fact that his mother had kept him and his brother in long dresses until they were nine years old and that he had since then frequently been a victim of practical jokes perpetrated by his childhood acquaintances."

"**The Last Post**" is a tale of human anguish, but it rings flat and thin compared with this short piece. "The Life of William Doe"—there would be a book. (p. 74)

Well, about this latest novel of Ford Madox Ford's. It is the last of his series of four books—what do you call a series of four books, anyway? I can only count up to "trilogy"—beginning with "**Some Do Not . . .**" and going on through "**No More Parades**" and "**A Man Could Stand Up.**" To me, "**The Last Post**" ranks fourth not only in sequence. Ford's style has here become so tortuous that he writes almost as if he were parodying himself. There are grave hardships for the reader in the long interior monologues which make up much of the book. It is a novel to be read with a furrow in the brow. You must constantly turn back pages, to ascertain from inside which character's head the author is writing. (pp. 74-5)

Yet "**The Last Post**" is a novel worth all its difficulties. There is always, for me, a vastly stirring quality in Ford's work. His pages are quick and true. I know of few other novelists who can so surely capture human bewilderment and suffering, for his is a great pity. To me, his best book, and far and away his best, is "**The Good Soldier**"—the novel separate from the books about Christopher Tietjens. Yet all the books of the Tietjens saga have in them some of the same power, the same depth, the same rackingly moving honesty that makes "**The Good Soldier**" so high and fine a work. They are sad books, filled with sad and skinless people. There are some who do not like such books. The world, too, is crowded with the sorrowful and the sensitive. There are many who do not like such a world. (p. 75)

It has always been a thorn to me that the man should have so difficult a name as Christopher Tietjens; and as for the woman he loved, fine and brave though Ford has made her, I could never let her near my heart because her name was Valentine Wannop. That is quibbling, I know, and of the silliest sort. But that's the way I am. Take me or leave me; or, as is the usual order of things, both. . . .

Through "**The Last Post**," as through all his books, there run the long fibres of Ford's hatreds. That is all very well for a writer, that, in fact, is fine for a writer; but it may get him into messes. And it gets Ford into a nasty jam, when he comes to one of his characters, his Amurrican lady, Mrs. De Bray Pape. I am as ready as the next to take a joke on my native sex and my own countrywomen, but here is as clumsy a caricature as you can find. I suggest that Mr. Ford go some place and get good and ashamed of himself for smearing this blemish of heavy buffoonery across the honest pages of his book. (p. 76)

> *Constant Reader [pseudonym of Dorothy Parker],*
> *"A Good Novel, and a Great Story," in* The New
> Yorker, *Vol. III, No. 51, February 4, 1928, pp. 74-7.*

GRAHAM GREENE (essay date 1937)

[Greene, an English man of letters, is generally considered the most important contemporary Catholic novelist. In his major works, he explores the problems of spiritually and socially alienated individuals living in the corrupt and corrupting societies of the twentieth century. Formerly a book reviewer at The Spectator, *Greene is also deemed an excellent film critic, a respected biographer, and a shrewd literary critic with a taste for the works of undeservedly neglected authors. Greene, one of the earliest and most unflagging admirers of Ford, wrote the introduction to and edited* The Bodley Head Ford Madox Ford, *which contains* The Good Soldier, *the* Fifth Queen *trilogy, and the first three volumes of the Tietjens tetralogy. Greene, like Ford, believes that* The Last Post *did not rightfully belong with the rest. In the following excerpt from a lukewarm review of* Great Trade Route, *Greene calls Ford England's finest living novelist.]*

Great Trade Route—that is Mr. Ford's personal dream of a past golden age, a huge oval belt extending from Cathay east and west of the fortieth parallel north through Europe up to the southern coast of England, a place of perfect peace and culture. . . . It is never clear at what period this dream existed in fact; but that doesn't really matter, for to Mr. Ford [as explained in his *Great Trade Route: A Sentimental Journey*] the Great Trade Route means "a frame of mind to which, unless we return, our Occidental civilization is doomed."

Mr. Ford's genius has always been aristocratic. His flirtation with the Fabians was of the briefest; his real heroes were Tories and landowners, Tietjens and the Good Soldier. Perhaps that is why Mr. Ford, so incontestably our finest living novelist and perhaps the only novelist since Henry James to contribute much technically to his art, is not very widely read. The world,

Ford in uniform, around 1915. Courtesy of Janice Biala.

absorbed in the Communist-Fascist dog-fight, is ill prepared to listen to this Tory philosopher who finds the Conservative politician as little to his taste as any other. And yet men of Mr. Ford's character have much to offer: there is something disagreeably easy in the notion that only two political philosophies can exist and that we must choose between them. Mr. Ford is a Catholic, though he has seldom been in sympathy with his Church, and it is no coincidence that the subject of *Great Trade Route* is similar to that of the recent Pastoral Letter issued by the Catholic Bishops in this country. (pp. 422-23)

Mr. Ford's solution, like that of the Catholic Bishops, is the Small Producer, as against the big individual capitalist and the small communist cog. He would have every man a part-time agriculturalist, because such a man is free in a sense unrecognized by either Fascist or Communist, free from the State ideal. (p. 423)

Mr. Ford defines the Small Producer: "He is a man who with a certain knowledge of various crafts can set his hand to most kinds of work that go to the maintenance of humble existences. He can mend or make a rough chest of drawers; he will make shift to sole a shoe or make a passable pair of sandals; he will contrive or repair hurdles, platters, scythe-handles, styes, shingle roofs, harrows. But, above all, he can produce and teach his family to produce good food according to the seasons." It is not a low ideal; it is the ideal of a country gentleman who knows his job; it is in the tradition behind Tietjens, and during this long and rambling journey, while Mr. Ford spots the villain Mass Production (little cellophane packets of corn sold at a high price on land where it had once been cheap as air), some readers will find their chief reward in vivid and dramatic asides which recall the novelist of the Tietjens series: Bismarck "whom I remember to have seen walking along the Poppelsdorfer Allee after his fall, his head dejected and his great hound dejected also, following him, his immense dewlaps almost touching his master's heel;" the bourgeoisie of Flemington: "extraordinarily silent men with harsh, hanging hands and Abraham-Lincoln-like faces who sat for hours without moving or speaking in rooms all shining linoleum, bentwood furniture, and tombstone-like sewing-machine cases."

Their chief reward, because not unexpectedly the landowner with his appeal for "a change of heart" is less practical than the ecclesiastic, who has the technique at hand for "changing hearts." He is a romantic. The enemy of the Great Trade Route was the barbarous North, and Mr. Ford still questionably stages his conflict in the terms of North and South, Yankee against Southerner, Lancashire against Kent. . . . There may be truth in [his] picture of the barbarian North, but to its threat Mr. Ford presents only an unequivocal pacifism: he won't fight even for his small holdings, and he never answers satisfactorily the thoughts in all our minds, that Hitler is a southern Teuton and that it was Italy who first broke the peace in Europe. (pp. 423-24)

Graham Greene, "The Landowner in Revolt," in The London Mercury, *Vol. XXXV, No. 208, February, 1937, pp. 422-24.*

CHARLES WILLIAMS (essay date 1938)

[Williams was a writer of supernatural fiction, a poet whose best works treat the legends of Logres (Arthurian Britain), and one of the central figures of the literary group known as the Oxford Christians or "Inklings." The religious, the magical, and the mythical are recurrent concerns in his works, reflecting his devout

Anglicanism and lifelong interest in all aspects of the preternatural. Although his works are not today as well known as those of his fellow-Inklings C. S. Lewis and J.R.R. Tolkien, Williams was an important source of encouragement and influence among the group. In the following excerpt from a favorable review of Mightier than the Sword, *Williams hails Ford as the most stylistically adept writer of his time.*]

There is no other living writer whose work is more generally effective than Mr. Ford Madox Ford's. I have been aching for years, I now realize, to write that sentence. The method of his effectiveness is, to some extent, defined in a sentence in the present book. He says, of a certain period, that he was trying "to evolve for myself a vernacular of an extreme quietness that would suggest someone of some refinement talking in a low voice to someone else he liked a good deal." One recognizes there the development of a style, from (say) *Ladies Whose Bright Eyes*—and I cannot help it if Mr. Ford now despises that book, but I hope he does not—up to *Great Trade Route* and the present. The clauses of the sentence vary in application. In the Tietjens books the quietness and the accuracy were so extreme that the voice seemed to come from under one's own skin; if the experiences of those books were not one's own, yet the nightmare of them was. The reader was split; it was part of the nightmare. As Mr. Ford's description here of the Tsar reading Turgenev shows. In *Great Trade Route* and in this, the voice is raised by a little, by as much as, coming from one's brain, it would be more audible than coming from one's nerves. And as for "of some refinement," which might be evilly taken, there is no other word which suggests a certain clarity, an apprehension of history, an appreciation of proportion.

All these qualities are in *Mightier than the Sword,* which is a series of "sketches of strong men who lived before today's Agamemnons." They are Henry James, Stephen Crane, Hudson, Conrad, D. H. Lawrence, Hardy, Wells, Galsworthy, Turgenev, Dreiser, Swinburne, with a final note under the heading "There were strong men." It will be safe for any one to assume that Mr. Ford admires the owners of those names, but unsafe, without reading the book, to assume the particular quality of his admiration for each. He has known and been actively concerned with all. But here he has made them more than actual. "I want them," he says, "to be seen pretty much as you see the characters in a novel." *Tam antiqua, tam nova;* they are novel indeed. Mr. Ford has "presented" them in such a way that the quality of his love is part of each figure, and since (as one would expect of the "vernacular . . . of some refinement") he is aware that this must always alter and characterize the figure, he has in every sentence at once pressed and withdrawn that quality, now less and now more personal in his talk, at once conversational and classic, to the many, to the few, to the one, even to the one only imaginary reader whom he "likes a good deal."

Mr. Ford has never been without what, in any one else, would have been a touch of malice. There is a suggestion of malice without tears here, a faint flicker of something that might, elsewhere, be malice, and is no more than the extra sharpness of the pencil, the new ribbon on the typewriter. By love and by brilliant intelligence the book is full of the most thrilling things. . . . It is no less full of comments on our civilization which, also, come to one in a voice of some friendliness, some refinement, some quietness, some sense of danger and fate. This may be because, now, Mr. Ford is one of the very few writers who are not ignorant of our past. . . .

Mr. Ford may or may not remain as a part of English letters. But at least he has been steadily, admiringly, and pleasurably, read by some for a generation. The immortality of a generation for a generation. The immortality of a generation is perhaps the best working substitute for the absolute thing—if he will excuse the temporary offer.

Charles Williams, "Mightier than Most Pens," in Time & Tide, *Vol. XIX, No. 11, March 12, 1938, p. 350.*

EZRA POUND (essay date 1939)

[*In the following excerpt from a posthumous tribute to Ford, Pound emphasizes Ford's importance as a critic, theorist, poet, and novelist.*]

There passed from us this June a very gallant combatant for those things of the mind and of letters which have been in our time too little prized. There passed a man who took in his time more punishment of one sort and another than I have seen meted to anyone else. For the ten years before I got to England there would seem to have been no one but Ford who held that French clarity and simplicity in the writing of English verse and prose were of immense importance as in contrast to the use of a stilted traditional dialect, a 'language of verse' unused in the actual talk of the people, even of 'the best people,' for the expression of reality and emotion. . . .

The justification or programme of such writing was finally (about 1913) set down in one of the best essays (preface) that Ford ever wrote.

It advocated the prose value of verse-writing, and it, along with his verse, had more in it for my generation than all the retchings (most worthily) after 'quantity' (*i.e.,* quantitative metric) of the late Laureate Robert Bridges or the useful, but monotonous, in their day unduly neglected, as more recently unduly touted, metrical labours of G. Manley Hopkins. (p. 178)

That Ford was almost an *halluciné* few of his intimates can doubt. He felt until it paralysed his efficient action, he saw quite distinctly the Venus immortal crossing the tram tracks. He inveighed against Yeats' lack of emotion as, for him, proved by Yeats' so great competence in making literary use of emotion.

And he felt the errors of contemporary style to the point of rolling (physically, and if you look at it as mere superficial snob, ridiculously) on the floor of his temporary quarters in Giessen when my third volume displayed me trapped, flypapered, gummed and strapped down in a jejune provincial effort to learn, *mehercule,* the stilted language that then passed for 'good English' in the arthritic milieu that held control of the respected British critical circles, Newbolt, the backwash of Lionel Johnson, Fred Manning, the Quarterlies and the rest of 'em.

And that roll saved me at least two years, perhaps more. It sent me back to my own proper effort, namely, toward using the living tongue (with younger men after me), though none of us has found a more natural language than Ford did.

This is a dimension of poetry. It is, *magari,* an Homeric dimension, for of Homer there are at least two dimensions apart from the surge and thunder. Apart from narrative sense and the main constructive, there is this to be said of Homer, that never can you read half a page without finding melodic in-

Handwritten note by Ford, dated 11 December 1926, that accompanied the manuscript of New Poems *when it was donated to the Princeton University Library. Courtesy of Princeton University Library.*

vention, still fresh, and that you can hear the actual voices, as of the old men speaking in the course of the phrases.

It is for this latter quality that Ford's poetry is of high importance, both in itself and for its effect on all the best subsequent work of his time. Let no young snob forget this.

I propose to bury him in the order of merits as I think he himself understood them, first for an actual example in the writing of poetry; secondly, for those same merits more fully shown in his prose, and thirdly, for the critical acumen which was implicit in his finding these merits.

As to his prose, you can apply to it a good deal that he wrote in praise of Hudson (rightly) and of Conrad, I think with a bias toward generoisity that in parts defeats its critical applicability. It lay so natural on the page that one didn't notice it. I read an historical novel at sea in 1906 without noting the name of the author. A scene at Henry VIIIth's court stayed depicted in my memory and I found years later that Ford had written it. (pp. 179-80)

As critic he was perhaps wrecked by his wholly unpolitic generosity. In fact, if he merits an epithet above all others, it would be 'The Unpolitic.' Despite all his own interests, despite

all the hard-boiled and half-baked vanities of all the various lots of us, he kept on discovering merit with monotonous regularity.

His own best prose was probably lost, as isolated chapters in unachieved and too-quickly-issued novels. (pp. 180-81)

And of all the durable pages he wrote (for despite the fluff, despite the apparently aimless meander of many of 'em, he did write durable pages) there is nothing that more registers the fact of our day than the two portraits in the, alas, never-finished *Women and Men*. . . . (p. 181)

> Ezra Pound, "Ford Madox (Hueffer) Ford: Obit," in The Nineteenth Century and After, Vol. CXXVI, No. 750, August, 1939, pp. 178-81.

R. P. BLACKMUR (essay date 1948)

[*Blackmur was a highly imaginative and influential critic within the New Criticism movement. Although the New Critics—including Cleanth Brooks, John Crowe Ransom, Robert Penn Warren, and Allen Tate—did not subscribe to a single set of critical principles, all agreed that a work of literature had to be examined as an object in itself through a process of close analysis of symbol, image, and metaphor. For the New Critics, a literary work was not a manifestation of ethics, sociology, or psychology, and could not be evaluated in the general terms of any nonliterary discipline. In the following excerpt, Blackmur discusses Ford's novels, contrasting them thematically with the novels of Henry James and Joseph Conrad, and noting Ford's recurrent concern with such "lost causes" as English Catholicism and Toryism.*]

[Between] 1920 and 1928 I read as many [of Hueffer's novels] as I could lay hands on, without ever a twinge of reaction which might lead to judgment until it was asked for in the present circumstance. (p. 123)

Hueffer at the time seemed to belong to a group: he belonged to Conrad, W. H. Hudson, Stephen Crane; but that was only part of it, for he belonged also to Henry James, Ezra Pound, and T. S. Eliot; he belonged to two generations and to the bridge that over-arched them. He occupied, mysteriously but evidently, all the interstices between all the members of both groups, and somehow contributed an atmosphere in which all of them were able to breathe. He had something to do with the *life*, the genuineness, of the literature written between *Lord Jim* and *The Waste Land*, between *The Dynasts* and *Ulysses*. All this was actual enough at the time; *The English Review*, dug up and read in old numbers, and *the transatlantic review*, both of which Hueffer edited, make the history stand. Yet to think of Hueffer in this way involved a view of him which has little of the truth in it that goes beyond history, the kind of truth which must somehow be our subject here. Atmospheres do not last, and can be re-created only in the living memory. Ford Madox Hueffer bore no real relation to Conrad and Hudson except the editorial relation; he had in his own writing, what corresponds there to the editorial, he had the relation of the chameleon-response to them. When his work was in the felt presence of their work, the skin of his writing changed color accordingly. What he responded with was partly the stock baggage of English literature and partly his own sensibility. I do not see how anybody who had not read Conrad and James could see what Hueffer was up to by way of form and style in their separable senses, or for that matter how anybody not knowing Conrad and James could feel the impact of Hueffer's sensibility attempting to articulate itself in terms of what it had absorbed of theirs. Without that knowledge, Hueffer's novels seem stock and even hack on the formal side and freakish or eccentric on the side of sensibility.

All this is summary description of the sensibility articulated in *The Good Soldier,* and in the four novels of which Christopher Tietjens is the central character, *Some Do Not, No More Parades, A Man Could Stand Up,* and *Last Post.* . . . Aside from *Romance,* written in collaboration with Conrad, I take it that these novels are what we mean when we speak of Hueffer as a novelist. If they stand, we have to put beside them at least one Utopian fantasy, *Ladies Whose Bright Eyes* . . . and perhaps the late Napoleonic romance, *A Little Less than Gods* . . . because his serious novels lie always between fantasy and romance. *Ladies Whose Bright Eyes* is gay, light, tender: the fantasy of a commercially-minded London publisher (himself a fantasy rather than a caricature of the type) transported in a traumatic dream to the England of 1326; in terms of which, when he wakes, he undergoes a kind of backwards conversion, and unearths a corner of fourteenth-century Utopia in modern England. *A Little Less than Gods* is the historical romance of an Englishman who finds himself, a kind of chivalrous traitor, in the service of Napoleon between Elba and Waterloo; it is pompous, stuffy, and sloppy both as romance and as history; but is written, so the dedicatory letter says, in the belief that it is—or means to be—a true sight of history. Each of these books has something to do with the glory of an arbitrary prestige resting on values asserted but not found in the actual world: values which when felt critically deform rather than enlighten action in that world, so that the action ends in the destruction of the values themselves. . . . In writing light novels—more or less unconscious pot-boilers . . . , Hueffer was certainly on the track of what people want in a light and preoccupied way.

In his serious novels, *The Good Soldier* and the novels about Tietjens listed above, what makes them serious is that these same ideas are treated seriously, with all the fanaticism that goes with fresh conversion or the sore point of fixed prejudice. Edward Ashburnham, the hero of *The Good Soldier,* is an extravagant princely sensualist, a wrecker of lives in the pursuit of life; he is also a soldier and he is seen by the narrator as a model of glory—a glory which is brought to a climax when, because his manners make it impossible to accept the body of a young girl brought up in his house, he cuts his throat and drives the young girl mad. Edward is feudal and Protestant; what modern Protestant feudalism cannot do to ruin him through his sensuality is done for him by his wife's Roman Catholicism. Feudalism, sensuality, Roman Catholicism, are, all three, forces which prevent the people in this book from coping with the real world and which exacerbate their relations to it.

In the Tietjens novels Toryism replaces feudalism, as it is the modern form of it, and as Tietjens is a Tory public servant in a world of 1914, or Lloyd George, liberalism; the sensuality is given to the wife rather than to the husband; the wife, being both Roman Catholic and sensualist, is thus more exacerbated than the wife in *The Good Soldier.* Otherwise the ideas are much the same. The virtues of the deprived Tory and the deprived Catholic are seen as the living forms of damnation. The Tory becomes the object of undeserved scandal, leading to disinheritance and his father's suicide, and thus, as a result *only* of his held beliefs as to the proper relations between father, son, and brother in a Tory family, to his own ruin. For her part, the Catholic sensualist becomes a bitch *manquée,* that is to say, an unmotivated destroyer of her own goods. There is not a person of account in the four volumes who is not animated by principle so high as to be a vocation from his or her point of view; but there is not a decent, frank, or satisfying relation between any two of them till the very end; principles get in the way by determining rather than formulating or judging values in conflict. Yet these principles are shown as admirable and exemplary in Christopher Tietjens, and exemplary if not wholly admirable in his wife Sylvia. Indeed the world is shown as in conspiracy against these principles—with the war of 1914-1918 as a particularly foul part of the conspiracy. The war, in presented fact, is only a kind of international Whiggery and interested scandal-mongering—all but those aspects of it which permit Christopher Tietjens to follow the Lord and behave like a princely Yorkshire Tory gentleman. Surely, if we want an easy name for this sort of thing, it is romanticism in reverse; it is the Faustian spirit of mastery turned suicidal on contact with classical clichés; it is also to say that these serious novels are only an intensified form of whatever happens when you put together the ideas of the medieval fantasy and the Napoleonic romance.

What intensifies them is, what we began by saying, the relation they bear to the work of his two immediate masters. And this is to say that Hueffer is a minor novelist in the sense that his novels would have little existence without the direct aid and the indirect momentum of the major writers upon whom he depended. He dealt with loyalty and the conflict of loyalties like Conrad, he dealt with fine consciences and hideously brooded sensualities like James. But all the loyalty he did not find heightened by Conrad was obstinacy, and all the conscience and sensuality he did not find created by James were priggery and moral suicide. Adding this to what has already been said of the chief novels, makes a terrible simplification: it says that Hueffer supplied only the excesses of his characters' vices and virtues, and only the excesses of their situations; and it suggests that his sensibility was unmoored, or was moored only in the sense that a sensibility may be moored to lost causes known to be lost.

Known to be lost. If there is an image upon which Hueffer's sensibility can be seen to declare its own force it is in an image of devotion to lost causes known to be lost; that is what his more serious novels dramatize, that is what his characters bring to their conflicts and situations, otherwise viable, to make them irremediable—for the law is already gone that could provide a remedy. In politics and philosophy we call this the cultivation of ancestral Utopias; in literature, since we can recognize these cultivations with the pang of actuality, they make a legitimate, though necessarily always subordinate, subject matter. They are real, these causes known to be lost—as real as the King over the Water—but they depend for their reality on their relation to causes not lost, much as history depends on the present which it disturbs, not for its truth but for its validity. So it is with Hueffer's novels; the validity of his dramatizations of men and women devoted to causes known to be lost depends on our sense of these same causes in the forms in which they are still to be struggled for. To the purposes of his obsession he chose the right masters in Conrad and James. His lost English Catholic women, his lost English Tories, his lost medievalists and his strange inventions of lost Americans, depend on Conrad's sailors and James's ladies and gentlemen (since they are not men and women) of the world—in whom only the milieu, the ambience of positive sensibility, is strange or lost. The difference is that where the people in Conrad and James are beaten by the life to which they are committed and by the great society of which they believe themselves to be at the heart, in Hueffer the people are beaten because they believe themselves animated by loyalties and consciences utterly alien to the life and the society in which they find themselves. Not only their fate, but also their ideals are intolerable to them. They make of their *noblesse oblige* the substance as well as the instrument of their damnation. They are ourselves beside ourselves the wrong way; and they are so because the sensibility of the novels is identical with that of the characters; there is no foil or relief, whether of aspiration or of form; only that terrible facility with the medium which goes with causes known to be lost.

That is the twinge of reaction that comes in re-reading Hueffer's novels; that as an artist as well as a man he knew his causes to be lost: which is why he had to be facile, and why he could not supply his novels with the materials for judgment. You cannot judge the King over the Water, however you may feel a twinge at the toast proposed. (pp. 123-27)

> R. P. Blackmur, "The King Over the Water: Notes on the Novels of F. M. Hueffer," in The Princeton University Library Chronicle, *Vol. IX, No. 3, April, 1948, pp. 123-27.*

ROBIE MACAULEY (essay date 1949)

[*Macauley was a student of Ford's at Olivet College in Michigan (where Ford taught during the late 1930s), and has written several studies of Ford's work. In the following excerpt from a discussion of* The Good Soldier *and the Tietjens tetralogy, he examines the thematic and structural similarities of the works, focusing in particular on Ford's use of time shifts and interior monologue, and on his portrayal of contemporary social disorder.*]

On some imaginary library shelf there are seventy-five books that carry [Ford's] name; and three-fourths of them do it harm. For here is a case of literary dementia praecox if there ever was one. We can rearrange those books symbolically and the two enemies will become clear. On one side will be Ford the slipshod literary journalist, the smooth potboiler novelist, the peddler of suspect anecdotes, the author of *Thus to Revisit, The Rash Act,* and *Ring for Nancy.* He is a bad writer and a good riddance.

On the other side of the shelf there are a dozen or fifteen books in an unpopular eccentric style. They are superbly written, profoundly serious, and built with enormous skill. One of them is unlike any other novel in the English language. If they stand on the shelf with Henry James, Joseph Conrad, the Brontës and Jane Austen, they do not suffer for it. Some of them are: the four Tietjens novels, *The Good Soldier, Women and Men.* But not all of them are novels.

When the reminiscent sentimentalist, the amateur verse-writer dropped into oblivion, he pulled with him the sturdy author; but now that Ford is dead nine years we can trouble ourselves to divide them and, disentangling the good Ford, we shall have found something.

Beginning the process, I offer two examples. His most perfect miniature performance was *The Good Soldier,* a splendid novel written just before the first World War and published in 1915. It might be the lucky try of a gifted and fortunate minor novelist. It isn't.

It isn't, because of the evidence of the second example, which is the Tietjens series. This is Ford's achievement in size and scope. Here are four novels that are generally thought to be about the 1914-1918 World War and, superficially, they are. They are about it in the same way that *Madame Bovary* is about life in a small provincial French town and the way that *War and Peace* is about the Napoleonic invasion. (pp. 269-70)

He considered . . . [*The Good Soldier*] his "Great Auk's egg," and he might as well die after finishing it. . . . Then he went on to make the tremendous attempt of the Tietjens series. But never again did he try for anything so elaborately simple or so simply elaborate as *The Good Soldier.*

In a general sense it is like his other novels; in an explicit sense it is very different. It is a novel that defies critical weighing and measuring. It will not fall without protest into any type, category, school or genre.

There is only one literary parallel suggested by Ford himself. "I had in those days an ambition: that was to do for the English novel what in *Fort comme la Mort* Maupassant had done for the French." This is misleading. The result was quite different. Very broadly and generally, Ford took a style of language like that of W. H. Hudson, whose naturalness and ease he much admired. The expression is so closely allied to the matter of the plot and so consistently a language of understatement that there are no spots of fine writing, no metaphors that attach themselves to the memory, no *pastiches,* not even any parts that are really quotable in themselves.

His narrator device recalls his apprenticeship with Conrad when the two "wanted the reader to forget that he was reading . . . to be hypnotized into thinking . . . that he was listening to a simple and in no way brilliant narrator who was telling—not writing—a true story." Ford's narrator, John Dowell, in many ways fits this ideal better than Conrad's Marlow, being even less of an idiosyncratic observer. He is an ordinary American from Philadelphia; and that is all we find necessary to know of him.

Finally, like most of Henry James's novels, *The Good Soldier* is an intense story of interacting personal relationships. It is the story of five people and two unhappy marriages unsystematically told.

The phrase, "unsystematically told," of course applies only in a very special sense to either James or Ford. It is more than "unchronologically told," because that does not suggest the extreme artfulness of narration, the superb management of the story. The time-shift is, actually, a structural device that is almost "poetic." As the poet fits together images taken from widely-different areas of knowledge and feeling to make a poem, the novelist ranges over the whole field of memory, selecting events or sequences of events from all the tenses of memory—the past, the perfect, the pluperfect and the "novelistic present"—and fits them together so that they will supplement and comment on each other as images in a poem do. Although step-by-step chronology will be violated, gradually the events will fit into place and the reader will not be lost. (pp. 270-72)

Stripped to its bare essentials, the story is about two good people. Leonora and Edward Ashburnham are condemned by a chance marriage to a war that brings out the worst in each. In the course of that long combat each manages unknowingly to disintegrate the good character of the other and to make the other capable only of acts of hatred and violence. (p. 274)

Into the war between the two are drawn Florence Dowell, Mrs. Maidan and Nancy Rufford and each one is broken by it in turn. To reduce the sides, as they cannot satisfactorily be reduced, to certain terms: it is the struggle between an honest, generous, open, strong, animal and sentimental man with a precise, virtuous, vigorous, intellectual woman. Ford's strange powers of persuasion make us sympathize with both; both seem equally right and wrong, equally good and evil. The final tragedy of Edward Ashburnham's suicide is no more terrible than the sudden slackening of his wife's mind.

Like the Tietjens story, the superficial tragedy of *The Good Soldier* lies in this sexual tangle. More than that, it is a discussion of the natures of men and women, their eternal attraction and their eternal incompatibility. Edward Ashburnham loved only his wife. He loved her with an unconscious admiration for everything about her, but he could never reach her, touch her, or "see with the same eyes." For the woman he loves he takes one substitute after another. But they are not real and none can last. . . . Leonora senses the gulf and even encourages the substitution with the hope that repeated failure will eventually bring her husband to her. The tragic paradox comes when Edward arrives at the last substitution and finds it impossible. (The girl is Nancy Rufford, their ward, and even his sense of honor revolts.) Then they know that the laws of their own natures divide them so inevitably that there never can be a question of either coming to the other. They can love each other only through a third person and finally no third person is possible.

The unhappy story has grown and reached out; with each attempt to use another woman as a temporary Leonora, Ashburnham has complicated and destroyed the lives of others. The narrator sees it involve his own wife and at last kill her. (At first it seems like a natural death.) It kills Mrs. Maidan when she is tossed aside as insufficient and it has the effect of insupportable tension in the mind of Nancy Rufford, who goes mad. Thus the major tragedy becomes surrounded by ancillary minor ones. At the end only the narrator is left. There is a sense that his preservation comes from having understood more of the story than any of the other people in it. When the book closes he is inhabiting the Ashburnham's house in Southhampton.

I have spoken of the nearly perfect union of language, style and narrative, the natural quality Ford worked for. It begins with his choice of words; "literary" words or sentences are rare and unobtrusive. He deliberately puts down the worn-out, the hackneyed, the simple turns of speech. But under his hand they come out new and strong. It is an amazing thing. There is one description of Nancy Rufford in which only the most common coin of language is used and yet in which she comes to life with clarity, with a sense of discovery: "She was very pretty, she was very young; in spite of her heart, she was very gay and light on her feet. . . ."

This note on language suggests the whole peculiar success of *The Good Soldier.* Ford has taken the most common materials and used them artistically: he has employed the wandering style of narration of an ordinary teller and used it for a series of brilliant *progressions d'effet;* he has used a commonplace vocabulary sensitively and precisely, making it sound fresh; he has taken the threadbare plot of unhappy marriage—even the "triangle"—and given it such new life and meaning that it becomes a passionate and universal story. (pp. 275-77)

The physical framework of the story was to be about love. Not love in the ordinary sense. Ford was incapable of simplicities and there is no literature more simple than the love story. Tietjens' relationship with two women throughout the books is the revealing clue for a critique of the whole moral-psychological shift in the relationships between men and women. It implies, symptomatically, a larger conflict.

Ford sensed that the world was deranged. England, specifically, seemed to be emerging from her Pyrrhic victory into social and intellectual chaos, a disorganization of personal lives and concepts. Something disastrous had happened to the whole cultural complex of the nation that had so confidently covered the world with her manners, morals and industrial goods during the last century. Even if it had been preparing for a long time, it seemed to have happened quickly.

Tietjens, who synthesizes in himself the bounded and settled past, undergoes the destructive experience of the present. That, essentially, is Ford's story. Tietjens is Christian, humane, educated in the classics, a Tory. His outlook is feudal and his temperament is chivalric. He represents the culture which the Middle Ages had prepared and the 17th and 18th Century mind regularized. Imaginary as this may have been in fact, it was real as a belief and Tietjens stands for the balanced mind that knew its relation to other men, to nature and to God. (p. 278)

Though hardly "war books," *No More Parades* and *A Man Could Stand Up* occur in wartime France. Ford differs in every respect from those competent realists, Barbusse, Zweig, Remarque, Hemingway, Aldington and Sassoon who went to war and wrote about it. Their books are lessons and the moral is familiar: war is a terrible thing. It is dull and deadly, exhausting and crippling; it destroys minds, bodies and character. It must be treated cynically, seriously, realistically. Ford's war is an effect or a symptom, not a cause. While Sergeant Grischa or Winterbourne sees villages smashed up, Tietjens sees a civilization wrecked.

Now the need for the careful establishment of the hero in *Some Do Not* . . . becomes clear. We need no persuasion to believe that Aldington's protagonist is a young man from the British lower middle classes or that Sassoon's is a type from the upper. But Tietjens, if he is to see more widely and profoundly than they, must be of a philosophical order. Ford has tried to create a modern hero, not simply a protagonist. If the Greek or Romance heroes were of more than human strength or courage, Tietjens, the modern hero, must be taller intellectually. In this 20th Century Trojan War, Tietjens can detect and understand the broad designs of Hera, Zeus, or Aphrodite, but his gift of understanding is finally of no more use than was Hector's gift of strength. (p. 281)

[The Tietjens story] might be defined as a kind of "inductive" psychological novel. The writer explores the motives and feelings of a certain group of characters with immense care and sensitivity. Simultaneously he examines the interaction and interpenetration of each with the other. Since all society is a result of the way human beings act in their relationships, the novel becomes an astute deductive inquiry into the human world at that particular moment. Proust's examination of ennui and the decadence in a character will suggest the symptoms of a common and contagious disease.

As a result, these novels become a type of allegory, penetrating, as they do, further into the human complex than the superficial Balzacian "man-as-a-product-of-his-environment" theory. They are distinct from the novels in which characters play an assigned role in a plot, become actors.

It was this kind of "Jamesian" novel that Ford attempted in the Tietjens series. He tried to enlarge its scope by concerning it with war. James (I quote a common objection) may have falsely refined away too much of the incidental and non-contributory phenomena of ordinary life, purifying his stories to the essential emotion conflicts of their people, thereby losing "reality." Ford felt this danger. He meant to give a broad view (but in the background only) that would suggest the non-significant details of a real world; yet in the foreground he would always keep the intense emotional-psychological-moral study of characters and the interrelation of characters. The war was his excuse for the "intensification." In addition it served as a great outward symbol of the combat going on within the center of the story.

The general "meaning" of the Tietjens books is a meaning common to most of the important writers of the 20th Century. It is a projection of disorder and breakup. Mann, Joyce, Eliot and Gide have perhaps dramatized it in different or larger ways, but no more skillfully than Ford.

After an initial interest, Ford has been neglected by readers and ignored by the critics. The Tietjens series has been wrongly and accidentally classed with that type of ephemeral semi-journalistic "war novel" whose sudden popularity during the 'twenties soon passed. A later generation will perhaps be able to make the separation and to recognize Ford's story as a concentrated examination of human beings during a "time of troubles," an important psychological allegory that is more about a human era than an episode labelled in history books as "World War I." (pp. 287-88)

> Robie Macauley, "The Good Ford," in The Kenyon
> Review, Vol. XI, No. 2, Spring, 1949, pp. 269-88.

WILLIAM CARLOS WILLIAMS (essay date 1951)

[*Williams was one of America's most renowned poets of the twentieth century. Rejecting as overly academic the Modernist poetic style established by T. S. Eliot, he sought a more natural poetic expression, endeavoring to replicate the idiomatic cadences of American speech. Perhaps Williams's greatest accomplishment is* Paterson, *a collection of poems depicting urban America. He is best known, however, for such individual poems as* "The Red Wheelbarrow," "To Waken an Old Lady," *and* "Danse Russe." *Williams developed a long-lasting friendship with Ford, who helped launch Williams's poetic career by publishing his verse in* The Transatlantic Review. *Later, Ford organized the Friends of William Carlos Williams society because he felt the poet wasn't receiving the recognition he deserved. Williams, who shared an equal respect for Ford the writer, composed what is perhaps the most famous memorial to Ford, the poem* "To Ford Madox Ford in Heaven." *In the following excerpt, originally published in 1951, Williams discusses* Parade's End, *finding it an allegorical dramatization of the new replacing the old—not only in socio-political systems, but in the realm of literature as well.*]

Every time we approach a period of transition someone cries out: This is the last! the last of Christianity, of the publishing business, freedom for the author, the individual! Thus we have been assured that in this novel, *Parade's End,* we have a portrait of the last Tory. But what in God's name would Ford Madox Ford be doing writing the tale of the last Tory? He'd far rather have tied it into black knots. (p. 315)

[The Tietjens tetralogy is] as intimate, full, and complex a tale as you will find under the official veneer of our day.

Four books, *Some Do Not, No More Parades, A Man Could Stand Up,* and *The Last Post,* have been for the first time offered in one volume as Ford had wished it. The title, *Parade's End,* is his own choosing. Together they constitute the English prose masterpiece of their time. But Ford's writings have never been popular, as popular, let's say, as the writings of Proust have

been popular. Yet they are written in a style that must be the envy of every thinking man. The pleasure in them is infinite.

When I first read the books I began, by chance, with *No More Parades;* as the story ran the First WorldWar was in full swing, the dirt, the deafening clatter, the killing. So it was a little hard for me to retreat to *Some Do Not,* which deals with the social approaches to that holocaust. At once, in the first scenes of this first book the conviction is overwhelming that we are dealing with a major talent. We are plunged into the high ritual of a breakfast in the Duchemin drawing room—all the fine manners of an established culture. There's very little in English to surpass that, leading as it does to the appearance of the mad cleric himself, who for the most part lies secretly closeted in his own home. Beside this we have the relationship of the man's tortured wife with Tietjens' friend MacMasters; the first full look at Valentine Wannop and of Tietjens himself before he appears in khaki—the whole rotten elegance of the business; Sylvia, at her best, and the old lady's "You are so beautiful, my dear, you must be good." (p. 316)

Sylvia, through all the books, in her determination to destroy her husband, does everything a woman can, short of shooting him, to accomplish her wish. From start to finish she does not falter.

This is where an analysis should begin; for some, who have written critically of *Parade's End,* find Sylvia's extreme hatred of her husband, her inexorable, even doctrinaire hatred, unreal. I think they are wrong. All love between these two or the possibility for it was spent before the story began when Christopher lay with his wife-to-be, unknowing, in another railway carriage, immediately after her seduction by another man. It made an impossible situation. From that moment all that was left for them was love's autopsy, an autopsy and an awakening—an awakening to a new *form* of love, the first liberation from his accepted Toryism. Sylvia was done. Valentine up! A new love had already begun to shimmer above the fog before his intelligence, a new love with which the past was perhaps identical, or had been identical, but in other terms. Sylvia suffers also, while a leisurely torment drives her to desperation. It is the very slowness of her torment, reflected in the minutiae, the passionate dedication, the last agonized twist of Ford's style, that makes the story move.

In his very perception and love for the well-observed detail lies Ford's narrative strength, the down-upon-it affection for the thing itself in which he is identical with Tietjens, his prototype. In spite of all changes, in that, at least, the Tory carries over: concern for the care of the fields, the horses, whatever it may be; the landed proprietor must be able to advise his subordinates who depend on him, he is responsible for them also. That at least was Tietjens, that too was Ford.

When you take those qualities of a man over into the new conditions, that Tietjens paradoxically loved, the whole picture must be altered—and a confusion, a tragic confusion, results, needing to be righted; it is an imperative that becomes a moral duty as well as a duty to letters.

Ford, like Tietjens, paid attention to these things. (pp. 317-18)

His British are British in a way the American, Henry James, never grasped. They fairly smell of it. The true test is his affection for them, top to bottom, a moral, not a literary attribute, his love of them, his wanting to be their Moses to lead them out of captivity to their rigid aristocratic ideals—to the ideals of a new aristocracy. (pp. 319-20)

Sylvia's bitter and unrelenting hatred for Tietjens, her husband, is the dun mountain under the sunrise, the earth itself of the old diabolism. We sense, again and again, more than is stated, two opposing forces. Not who but *what* is Sylvia? (I wonder if Ford with his love of the Elizabethan lyric didn't have that in mind when he named her.)

At the start her husband has, just too late for him, found out her secret; and feeling a responsibility, almost a pity for her, has assumed a superior moral position which she cannot surmount or remove. She had been rudely seduced, and on the immediate rebound, you might almost say with the same gesture, married Tietjens in self-defense. She cannot even assure her husband that the child is his own. She cannot be humble without denying all her class prerogatives. Christopher's mere existence is an insult to her. But to have him pity her is hellish torment. She is forced by everything that is holy to make him a cuckold, again and again. For England itself in her has been attacked. But Valentine can pick up her young heels, as she did at the golf course, and leap a ditch, a thing impossible for Sylvia unless she change her clothes, retrain her muscles and unbend.

But there is a deeper reason than that—and a still more paradoxical—in that Tietjens forced her to do good: that as his wife she serves best when she most hates him. The more she lies the better she serves. This is truly comic. And here a further complexity enters. Let me put it this way: If there is one thing I cannot accede to in a commonality of aspiration, it is the loss of the personal and the magnificent . . . the mind that cannot contain itself short of that which makes for great shows. Not wealth alone but a wealth that enriches the imagination. Such a woman is Sylvia, representing the contemporary emblazonments of medieval and princely retinue. How can we take over our *Kultur,* a trait of aristocracy, without a Sylvia, in short as Tietjens desired her? What is our drabness beside the magnificence of a Sistine Chapel, a gold salt cellar by Cellini, a Taj, a great wall of China, a Chartres? The mind is the thing not the cut stone but the stone itself. The words of a Lear. The sentences of *Some Do Not* themselves that are not likely for this to be banished from our thoughts.

Ford gave the woman, Sylvia, life; let her exercise her full range of feeling, vicious as it might be, her full aramament of woman. Let her be what she is. Would Tietjens divorce her? When there is reason yes, but so long as she is truthfully what she is and is fulfilling what she is manifestly *made* to be, he has nothing but respect for her. Ford uses her to make a meaning. She will not wobble or fail. It is not his business. This is a way of looking at the word.

Ford's philosophy in these novels is all of a piece, character and writing. The word keeps the same form as the characters' deeds or the writer's concept of them. Sylvia is the dead past in all its affecting glamor. Tietjens is in love the while with a woman of a different order, of no landed distinction, really a displaced person seeking replacement. Valentine Wannop is the reattachment of the word to the object—it is obligatory that the protagonist (Tietjens) should fall in love with her, she is Persephone, the rebirth, the reassertion—from which we today are at a nadir, the lowest ebb.

Sylvia is the lie, bold-faced, the big crude lie, the denial . . . that is now having its moment. The opponent not of *le mot juste* against which the French have today been rebelling, but something of much broader implications; so it must be added that if our position in the world, the democratic position, is

difficult, and we must acknowledge that it is difficult, the Russian position, the negative position, the lying position, that is, the Communist position is still more difficult. All that is implied in Ford's writing.

To use the enormous weapon of the written word, to speak accurately that is (in contradiction to the big crude lie) is what Ford is building here. For Ford's novels are written with a convinced idea of respect for the meaning of the words—and what a magnificent use they are put to in his hands! whereas the other position is not conceivable except as disrespect for the word's meaning. He speaks of this specifically in *No More Parades*—that no British officer can read and understand a simple statement unless it be stereotype . . . disrespect for the word and that, succinctly put, spells disaster.

Parenthetically, we shall have to go through some disastrous passages, make no mistake about that, but sooner or later we shall start uphill to our salvation. There is no other way. For in the end we must stand upon one thing and that only, respect for the word, and that is the one thing our enemies do not have. Therefore rejoice, says Ford, we have won our position and will hold it. But not yet—except in microcosm (a mere novel you might say). For we are sadly at a loss except in the reaches of our best minds to which Ford's mind is a prototype.

At the end Tietjens sees everything upon which his past has been built tossed aside. His brother has died, the inheritance is vanished, scattered, in one sense wasted. He sees all this with perfect equanimity—Great Groby Tree is down, the old curse achieved through his first wife's beneficent malevolence, a malevolence which he perfectly excuses. He is stripped to the rock of belief. But he is not really humiliated since he has kept his moral integrity through it all. In fact it is that which has brought him to destruction. All that by his upbringing and conviction he has believed is the best of England, save for Valentine, is done. But those who think that that is the end of him miss the whole point of the story, they forget the Phoenix symbol, the destruction by fire to immediate rebirth. Mark dead, Christopher, his younger brother, has got Valentine with child.

This is not the "last Tory" but the first in the new enlightenment of the Englishman—at his best, or the most typical Englishman. The sort of English that fought for and won Magna Carta, having undergone successive mutations through the ages, has reappeared in another form. And this we may say, I think, is the story of these changes, this decline and the beginning of the next phase. Thus it is not the facile legend, "the last Tory," can describe that of which Ford is speaking, except in a secondary sense, but the tragic emergence of the first Tory of the new dispensation—as Christopher Tietjens and not without international implications. *Transition* was the biggest word of the quarter-century with which the story deals, though its roots, like those of Groby Great Tree, lie in a soil untouched by the modern era. *Parade's End* then is for me a tremendous and favorable study of the transition of England's most worthy type, in Ford's view and affections, to the new man and what happens to him. The sheer writing can take care of itself. (pp. 320-23)

William Carlos Williams, " 'Parade's End'," in his Selected Essays of William Carlos Williams, *Random House, 1954, pp. 315-23.*

REED WHITTEMORE (essay date 1960)

[*In the following excerpt, originally published in 1960, Whittemore compares and contrasts Ford's literary philosophy and style with those of Bernard Shaw, H. G. Wells, and Joseph Conrad.*]

Ford in Toulon, France in 1932, painted by his companion Janice Biala. Courtesy of Janice Biala.

Shaw, Wells, Conrad and F. M. Ford don't constitute a period all by themselves, but enough has been written about them so that they seem to. All of them reached literary maturity well before the First World War; all of them survived the war; and the literary character of only one of them, Ford, seems to have been changed by works written after the war. Wells said of Ford, "the pre-war F.M.H. was torturous but understandable, the post-war F.M.H. was incurably crazy." But it was the incurably crazy Ford who wrote *Parade's End* which is, of all the books by these four authors, probably the one most readily describable as modern—meaning, I suppose, real according to postwar notions of the real. That the post-war Ford didn't fit into Wells's scheme of things suggests to me that Wells's scheme of things remained a prewar scheme. So did Shaw's, I think. I am not sure about Conrad. Anyway, since the creative impulses of the four of them had been thoroughly channeled before the war, I think it is fair to regard *Parade's End* as an impressive freak, and to think of all four authors as prewar figures in what sociologists would call their Life Orientation.

So regarded, many of their vociferous protestations favoring Reality in Art have an air of quaintness for postwar generations which has been much commented on. All of them professed to be great realists in their own ways, and yet their literary equivalents for reality have all been found, by someone, want-

ing. Furthermore they disagreed mightily among themselves about what constituted the real in literature. (pp. 131-32)

[Ford's *Between St. Dennis and St. George*] purported to be a "sketch of three civilizations." It stands up better, though, as simply an attack on Shaw. Shaw is the representative villain in the book, the horror most commonly referred to; and Shaw's wartime essay, "Common Sense About War," is exploded line by line and fact by fact in a dense and lengthy appendix. All the heat that a year of war had engendered went into the book, which was written *for* the British government and which Ford acknowledged to be an elongated polemic. In aim and tone it is perhaps comparable to the MacLeish-Van Wyck Brooks attacks upon the "irresponsibles" before and during World War II.

Ford was most anxious to acknowledge Shaw's artfulness, and indeed used it as a weapon against him. Briefly, his case was as follows:

> My quarrel with Shaw . . . is not that he has written brilliantly about facts, but that he has invented facts and has then written brilliantly about them. Without giving us any *Quellen* at all—any documents by which we may check his utterances—he has written many brilliant sentences with the object of inducing the reader to believe that the German national psychology is exactly the same as the British national psychology.

I note that the word "brilliant" is used three times. I think it is fair to say the premises here are premises Shaw himself might have used, though hardly against Shaw: Shaw's brilliance produces a fine illusion that is simply not backed up by fact. No *Quellen*. As simple as that. It was Ford's thesis that the time (1915) was "at hand when the historian and the historian's methods" should "come into their own again." Nobody respected facts any more; people lived "in an immense cavern, in an immense Hall of the Winds, in a vast Whispering Gallery—of rumour." And though there were as many rumorists as there were journalists and old wives, one rumorist was preeminent among them: Shaw. Shaw had taken the position that the English and French were as responsible as the Germans for the war, and though his position was of course not a popular one his way of arriving at it seemed, to Ford, characteristic of the age. Ford couldn't keep his temper about it at all. He so disliked, he said, to call it imbecility, that he had to "style it sheer intellectual dishonesty." (pp. 143-44)

Shaw was described as a fictionist, *not* dealing with "real history" but concocting fantastic illusions for his own presumably dark ends. Ford then proceeded to try to counter the Shavian melodrama with as much "real history" as he could grub up on the spur of the moment, thus, it is to be noted, setting himself up as the real hard-facts man in the case. . . . I find it interesting that Ford should be trying to beat Shaw at his own game. One may very readily question Ford's facts as well as Shaw's (especially since Ford has been reported to have been a colossal liar), but the fact that he found it important to *be* a hard-facts man, not a master of illusion, not just one of those arty chaps, is instructive. Furthermore, I think it can be shown that Ford liked to think of himself as a hard-facts man in his novels as well as his propaganda pieces for the government. The trouble is that he, like the others, had his own view of what a hard fact is. Just as Shaw's and Wells's hard facts got mixed in with ideas and art, so did Ford's get mixed in with art, ''rendering,'' form.

Robie Macauley has described Ford's book on the English novel as ''crotchety,'' and this is an understatement. It is dense, contradictory and immensely annoying. It plumps for art and reality with equal vigor, and just when it should be working up a fine alliance it abandons the project. This is well illustrated by Ford's discussion of the difference between a nuvvle and a novel. An artist, he said, had to manage the realities; otherwise he was an escapist who wrote a nuvvle. A nuvvle was a ''commercial product that Mama selected for your reading'' and that avoided the ''problems of the day'' and that set up a ''Manor House, inhabited by the Best People.'' A novel on the other hand, well, that was not so easy. It faced up to things all right, as Wells or Shaw would have approved its doing; and it was the sort of thing one couldn't help writing. But its emergence as a novel rather than a nuvvle didn't, oddly, seem to depend upon these urgencies. Instead a novel depended, for its novelness, upon three admirable formal properties: it was rendered rather than told; its characters were treated with aloofness; and its author kept his comments and prejudices out of it.

Such a switch—from the novel's materials to its procedures for rendering the material—suggests something of the same sort of dialectical confusion to me as that propounded by Wells whenever with eloquence he decried eloquence, or by Shaw whenever he brought forth an idea and called it a fact. It is perhaps a more modern confusion, however, since Ford prefers to talk about the reality of a novel in the novel's own terms rather than pretending, as Shaw and Wells did, that raw life would establish the terms. This made it possible for Ford to insist on the realities and at the same time to say, ''the story is the thing, and the story and then the story, and . . . there is nothing else that matters in the world,'' a statement wholly alien to Wells, who professed to think of story as ornamental. The modern world for the Ford position is, I believe, ''autotelic,'' but while there is a good bit of fuss in our classrooms about treating poems and stories on their own terms (letting them establish the reality), I don't think Ford or James or Conrad or any of the later apostles of rendering were either capable or desirous of positively divorcing an artistic reality from its worldly counterpart. What writer, after all, is? To put it differently, they were as conscious of their obligations to something outside their art as Shaw and Wells were to something outside the unmanageable realities, but the focus in each case was different: Wells and Shaw didn't like to admit to artifice; Ford talked of reality in terms of artifice. Furthermore Ford was committed to a quite different kind of artifice from those of Shaw or Wells. I suppose that we now call it impressionism. This was a novelty, at least to Wells, and so he was struck by its artificiality. Such matters are hard to generalize about but, to put it crudely, the argument between the two camps seems to resolve itself at least partly into a disagreement about the validity of different artistic techniques—though there is a deeper disagreement that I will get to presently.

The case of Tietjens is appropriate to illustrate the technical difference, but it also carries on Ford's contempt for Shaw's kind of realism. Tietjens is Ford's version of a realist; he is a kind of antidote to the Shaw realists who have no *Quellen*. He knows everything he has ever read by heart; he can tell a genuine Chippendale from a fake at fifty paces; he knows horses and birds better than any man in England. Furthermore he is anti-Shavian politically. He does not move ahead in a Machiavellian manner, but over and over again rejects that

kind of leadership, turning down high posts, insulting those who might help him on, hating ''any occupation of a competitive nature.'' Nor is he, like Shaw's heroes, contemptuous of the past, of tradition, of conventions: he refuses to get a divorce because one does not *do* that; he is the first to ask for the removal of two city slickers from a highbrow golf course because they are unmannerly; he is ''so formal he can't do without all the conventions there are and so truthful he can't use them.'' Nor is he, like Shaw's heroes, a man of common sense: he is always getting into ''obscure rows'' about principle that only do him harm, and he goes off into the thick of the war though any man in his position, as several examples in the book indicate, could readily have stayed at home in a bank. So his realism, which is insisted upon, makes him a figure wholly unlike Shaw's Caesar, St. Joan or Undershaft. Equally alien to Shaw (or Wells) is the manner by which his actions are presented:

> An immense tea-tray, august, its voice filling
> the black circle of the horizon, thundered to
> the ground. Numerous pieces of sheet-iron said,
> ''Pack. Pack. Pack.'' In a minute the clay floor
> of the hut shook, the drums of ears were pressed
> inwards, solid noise showered about the uni-
> verse, enormous echoes pushed these men. . . .

This, if you will, is rendering. The sights, sounds, sensations received by Tietjens and others in the hut are ''recorded'' (the word is deceptive) rather more directly than would be the case in a conventional narrative, where it first would be announced that a bombing *was* taking place, that the scene was a battlefield, and so on. Ford, as any reader of *Parade's End* knows, worried incessantly about the pace of his novel; he didn't want the action to stop while the exposition went on, and so he, like so many of his successors, devoted a good deal of his artifice to the tricky problem of getting in the exposition and the action simultaneously. This left him, like Conrad, to numberless struggles with Point of View; he shifts us, sometimes with almost no transition, from the events as received by one mind to the events as received by another; but almost always the minds are the minds of the people there, on the scene, in the action, rather than the mind of the author—hence Ford's comment that an author should keep his comments and prejudices out of his novel, a comment with which Wells could not agree. Wells kept insisting that the artist should talk *about* his experience through his novel. Now when one talks about something one has the primary obligation to set everybody straight, to organize the material, provide background for it, and so on. When on the other hand one renders, in the Ford sense, experience, one has an obligation to the experienc*er* which takes precedence over the obligations to exposition, clarity, order. Accordingly Wells and Shaw, with their clarities, could protest about the mysteries of Ford and Conrad; but Ford and Conrad could turn around and complain that Wells and Shaw did not deal with the immediacies. All in the name of reality. (pp. 145-49)

Reed Whittemore, ''The Fascination of the Abomination—Wells, Shaw, Ford, Conrad,'' in his The Fascination of the Abomination: Poems, Stories, and Essays, *The Macmillan Company, 1963, pp. 129-66.*

V. S. PRITCHETT (essay date 1962)

[*Pritchett is a highly esteemed English novelist, short story writer, and critic. Considered one of the modern masters of the short story, he is also one of the world's most respected and well-read literary critics. Pritchett writes in the conversational tone of the familiar essay, a method by which he approaches literature from the viewpoint of a lettered but not overly scholarly reader. A twentieth-century successor to such early nineteenth-century essayist-critics as William Hazlitt and Charles Lamb, Pritchett employs much the same critical method: his own experience, judgment, and sense of literary art are emphasized, rather than a codified critical doctrine derived from a school of psychological or philosophical speculation. His criticism is often described as fair, reliable, and insightful. In the following excerpt, originally published in 1962, Pritchett offers a general discussion of Ford's career, finding Ford to have been artistically successful in only three works:* The Good Soldier, the Fifth Queen trilogy, *and* Parade's End.*].*

"I once told Fordie that if he were placed naked and alone in a room without furniture, I would come back in an hour and find total confusion." Ezra Pound's joke about Ford Madox Ford hits the mark. Confusion was the mainspring of his art as a novelist. He confused to make clear. As an editor, as a source of literary reminiscence, he attracts because he is always sketching his way from inaccuracy to inaccuracy in order to arrive at some personal, translucent truth. His unreliability may have annoyed, but it is inspired.

As a novelist—and he wrote some thirty novels, nearly all forgotten—he is one of those whose main obstacle is his own talent. A Conrad cannot invent; a Lawrence cannot narrate; such deficiencies are fortunate. They force a novelist to compensate, with all his resources, so that we shall hardly be aware of what is lacking and shall, in any case, think it unimportant. Ford is obstructed less by his defects than by the effusiveness of total ability. He has been called brilliant, garrulous and trivial, but what really happened was that, with the exception of *The Good Soldier,* parts of the Tietjens trilogy and most of *The Fifth Queen,* he never sank into the determined stupor out of which greater novelists may eventually have their stroke of luck: *The Good Soldier* is a small masterpiece. (p. 1)

The dilemma of "the gentleman" preoccupied Shaw, James, Conrad, Galsworthy, and has even been revived in the latest novels of Evelyn Waugh. It was once a burning topic—one that Forster, with his marvellous aversion to burning topics, ignored. But there are overtones in Ford's writing on the subject which recall his own criticism of what the Pre-Raphaelites felt about love—they swooned. Swooning about love was a way of not knowing the facts. Ford swooned about the country gentry, and nothing dates so much as fashion in love.

Still, *The Good Soldier* survives the swooning over the character of Colonel Ashburnham and does so because, for once, Ford had his excessive gifts under control. For once he remembered that if he was to be an Impressionist writer, he had better not confuse writing with painting. The confusion of memory need not be coloured; indeed, in writing, if the parts are too prismatically brilliant, the whole will become grey instead of luminous. As this novel shows, Ford was equipped by intelligence and by grief to be a moralist once he could be freed from the paint-box and, above all, from High Art. Conrad must have been a very bad influence on a man who had already too much vagueness in him; Henry James can have only been harmful to one with already so much consciousness. To them Art did nothing but good; the idea is excellent in itself; but it is dangerous to a man of talent who only very seldom in a laborious literary life hits upon a subject that draws out all his experience.

The Good Soldier and *The Fifth Queen* succeed. The former has the compact and singeing quality of a French novel; it is

a ruthless and yet compassionate study in the wretchedness of conventional assumptions and society's war upon the heart. The latter is a historical romance and tells the story of Henry VIII and Katharine Howard; it suffers a little from Ford's chronic allusiveness, but a great issue is at stake and the ambiguities in it awaken all his interest in intrigue. His mind was one that hated conclusions, not because it was a sceptical mind but because it wanted to be put to one more test. From this spring his ingenuity as a story-teller—a gift so rare that it is often scorned—and his constant concern with technique. Critics have usually praised this technical capacity, but have said that this was all he had; yet it is—and one ought not to have to say so—a capacity of enormous importance. (Imagine that Jane Austen had left *Sense and Sensibility* in its epistolary draft!) One can see that to a mind as given to confusion and to posture as Ford's was, technical capacity was his one reality. He asks nothing better than to be seen making difficulties work for him. The famous device of the "time-shift", which was a mania with him, enabled him to begin his scene in the middle and yet arrive with a whole tale of suspense that was thick with suggestion and memories caught on the way ashore.

In *The Good Soldier* the time-shift enabled him to effect those dramatic revaluations of people which give his novels their point. We had supposed, for example, that Leonora was vulgarly jealous when she slapped Mrs Maidan's face; but in a page or two we dart back in time to discover that there was another and stronger motive, one that exposes a hidden part of Leonora's nature: her shocked frigidity, her greed for money. When that is threatened, her passion for appearances collapses. In choosing for the narrator a dull and unemotional man who fumbles his way through a tale of passion which leads to death and madness, Ford has found someone who will perfectly put together the case of the heart versus conventional society, for he is a mild American Quaker perpetually astonished by Catholic puritanism. Meanwhile his own do-gooding wife is, unknown to him, a destroyer and nymphomaniac. Ford is often accused, by the hospital nurses of criticism, of triviality, but in this book the trivia are sharp and enhance the awful dull force of the tragedy.

Re-write *The Good Soldier* in straightforward narrative and Ford's vision of life as a minutely operating process of corrosion vanishes, and with that, of course, his particular Catholic outlook. Corrosion, as it is presented in this novel, means that we have more parts to our lives than one and that they work fatally upon each other. One has a quite extraordinary sense in the book of the minds of people perpetually thinking away their heartbeats.

Ford's preoccupation with technique—point of view, time-shift, *progression d'effet,* rendering and so on—was both a godsend and a curse, for he was constitutionally distracted, impatient and shy of coming to terms. By concentrating on the *means* of creating an impression he seems to have hoped, in some of his novels, to find that the means would suggest an End darker, more inscrutable and mysterious, than anything in the author's mind at the outset. Life was an intrigue that was never resolved, a meaningless experiment. This approach might lead, as it does in the works of Conrad, to fogginess; in Ford it could lead only to an excessive high-lighting of detail and to staginess. The secret, Romantic Ford leans too much on the ominous and sardonic outsider, the shadow figure breathing heavily down the neck of the reader, Art pretending to be Destiny. But when Ford is at one with his subject, as he is in *The Fifth Queen,* he stages well. His delight in playing fast and loose with time, in beginning a scene in the middle of a broken sentence, dropping it and picking it up again until the crisis is built up, his whole patterning and puzzling, are vividly justified.

He succeeds, more often than not, in his ingenious system of getting at the inside of things by looking intensely at the surface alone. This, of course, he inherited from the painters. He may see more than we can in the way people's hands lie in their laps, or how their legs look when they are kneeling, or how much of Henry VIII appeared as he went upstairs; but in the larger pictorial actions—Tom Culpepper rushing up drunk from Greenwich to Smithfield eager to see some martyrs at the stake because he'd never seen a burning before—the sense of daily life dancing by in a man's mind is wonderfully conveyed. Ford was a master of episode. If he is stagey, he does not ham. We notice, for example, that Tom Culpepper doesn't in fact see the actual burning because he gets into an absurd brawl. As a story-teller Ford recognised life when he saw complication and chance. His brutal scenes are benevolently comic; his women are originals; wherever there's human naivety and deviousness he is as happy as Kipling was, but with compassion. And throughout there is no detail that fails to bear on the religious quarrel which is his central subject. He responded very much in all his work to the margin men and women leave in their minds, to their long-headedness; and one can see that he found a parallel between the corruption of the Reformation and that of the Edwardian world which had killed the heart, he would have said, by reducing virtue and honour to the condition of masks.

No doubt *The Fifth Queen* is too close to the eye in a cinematic way to have the spacious historical sense of a great historical novel like *Old Mortality;* it hasn't the coolness of Mérimée's superb short novel, the *Chronicle of Charles IX;* but it makes most of our historical fiction up to 1914 look like the work of interior decorators. Literature for Ford was a passion; its rituals were sacred. But there is no doubt about his moral seriousness or the cumulative effect of the main story. How, by what stages, will Katharine bring the King to the point of making his submission to Rome? How will the King procrastinate? What lies will trap the Queen? Will the King, for once, be able to escape from his changeable and fatally political nature? What belongs to Caesar, what to God—and what to Good Learning? There is nothing allusive in the handling of this massive central conflict and it is brought to its climax without melodrama. One thing Impressionism could do was to catch the day as it passed through the minds of the actors in it. It could record confusion by a scrupulous and ingenious use of the means of art. Allowing for Ford's pleasant vanity in the imposture, this bravura piece—as Graham Greene calls it in his introduction to the Bodley Head collection of Ford's stories—is rather fine. (pp. 2-6)

[Ford] succeeded in only three remarkable stories—*The Good Soldier,* the *Fifth Queen* trilogy and *Parade's End.* They vindicate his happy yet tortured incapacity to go straight from a starting-point, for he had none. They put his lack of self-confidence, his shortness of spiritual breath, his indolence, to use. They brought out and exploited with full resource the price he had to pay for his extraordinary cleverness: the emotion of anguish. One is tempted to say "passion" also—but one has to hesitate here. The writers who convey passion also convey the terrible calm of its purgation and aftermath and Ford is too full of his own skill and ironical humour to allow that. But he does leave us with an indignant sense of unforgettable pain. One always finds that at the bottom of the baggage Ford left about the world.

Some pain is self-sought—the pain, for example, of our choice of impossible incarnations. It is hard, here, to separate the factitious from the inevitable. When he became incarnate as Tietjens in *Parade's End,* Ford could not obliterate Ford. One does not want him to do so, for Tietjens is Ford's anguished hallucination. No novelist can completely become another character; in Tietjens Ford constructed an English gentleman as only something like German romanticism or idealism could see him. Ford was no gentleman; he was a fine artist. He seems minutely to have observed the type, and at the same time to have loaded him with history and an inhuman willingness to suffer everything for the sake of suffering. So often one has seen expatriates find their home in a past that has not existed: Ford's plain feudal Yorkshire squire, with his love of the pre-industrial way of life, his scorn of the vulgar modern world, his dislike of ambition, his irritable abstention, his martyred sense of decency, looks today like a romancing not about a man but a code.

When Ford created Tietjens the dilemma of the gentleman was very much the fashion, as I have said. These talented agrarians existed. The coarse businessmen, speculators and careerists were breaking in on them, the press had turned yellow, the conventions were shocking when they worked and even more shocking when they did not. If Tietjens and his scruples about sex and society seem odd now, they did not fifty years ago. Rock-like before the unanswered slanders of his bankers, his military friends, his father, his cold, promiscuous wife who tricked him over the paternity of his child, Tietjens was exactly the figure to expose by his silence and his suffering the rottenness of Edwardian society. Further, he was not a Roman Catholic but his wife was, and the curse on the Tietjens family is thought to go back to the Reformation and the thieving of Roman Catholic lands. This adds to Tietjens's martyrdom, a touch of destiny which is pretty gamey stuff. That old row has been hung too long to be digestible. One is rather exasperated by Tietjens's stubborn determination to collect all the slings and arrows going; after all, where does the family get its millions from? From the sacred soil of a great estate? Hardly. Towards the end of the novel there is a hint that the family controls a lot of industry in Middlesbrough. Tietjens is just as much a child of the industrial revolution as anybody else. He may not like the men of the new order who were coming in just before 1914: not being gentlemen they were certain to cheat. But isn't he simply an idealiser of convention? One has a sneaking sympathy for his wife, who at one moment complains that her husband is trying to be Jesus Christ as well as the misunderstood son of a great landowner. Her cruelties are an attempt to turn a martyr into a man.

In creating Tietjens, Ford chose a character utterly unlike himself and did the detail admirably. He caught the obtuse pride of the social masochist. He caught the spleen of the gentleman because this accorded well with the ironic spleen that Ford himself felt as an artist, even when it was a pose. The gregarious, voluble, intelligent nature of Ford could not be prevented from mingling with the Yorkshire squire; what one does not accept in Tietjens is the romantic German aura. Any German can do a better job of being an English gentleman and Tietjens is just a Germanised squire. He is even a classical scholar. (pp. 6-8)

The general picture of a whole society floundering is done with a wonderful precision and not in the form of easy diatribe. Tietjens is just the right kind of numbed Homeric figure to record the sudden killing of a man in the staff dugout, a man to whom he had refused leave; or the explosion of a mine and the rescuing of the buried. As a character Tietjens escapes from the cliché of almost all the war novels of that time in which the hero conveys that the whole war has been declared against him personally. Tietjens knows that a civilisation, or at any rate a class, is sinking. Responsible and capable, Ford-Tietjens has an unselfed and almost classical sub-Olympian view of the experience. Although he was self-consciously an impressionist, Ford has some inner sense of a moral order. Or, if not that, a moral indignation at the lack of it. Or, if not that, a taste for the moral consolations of defeat. He brings not only an eye but a judgment to what he sees.

There is something odd but also—from a novelist's point of view—tolerant about this judgment. A craftsman, through and through, in everything, Ford is interested in the way things are done. Even corruption has its curious status. What are gunners like, what are their interests, their follies, what is the *virtu* of the trade? He is deeply interested in the idle detail of human nature and his own lazy aloofness enabled him to catch the detail perfectly. A variety of scenes comes to mind: the death of O Nine Morgan or the astonishing scene where a gunner chases a solitary German with shells.

> His antics had afforded these gunners infinite amusement. It afforded them almost more when all the German artillery on that front, imagining that God knew what was the matter, had awakened and plastered heaven and earth and everything between them for a quarter of an hour with every imaginable kind of missile. And had then abruptly shut up.

And it had all happened merely because Tietjens had lightly told a gunner that any Italian peasant with a steam-plough could pulverise a field at a cost of thirty shillings, which was cheaper than the cost of high explosives. As a craftsman the gunner was put on his mettle.

That incident is anecdotal, but Ford could create the people who lived the anecdotes. His art—particularly the theory of the time-shift—was in part based on an analysis of talk, the way it plunges and works back and forth. The method was perfected in *The Good Soldier;* in the later, Tietjens novel, it does not succeed so well. It often becomes a device for refusing to face a major scene. One has only a confused notion of what went on in the hotel bedroom when the drunken General broke in on Tietjens and his wife at a crucial point in their sado-masochistic relationship, when it is important that we should know all. Ford's view seems to have been that no one ever quite knows what goes on at the crucial moments of life. His craftsmanship becomes obscurely crafty at such moments, as though, with tiresome cleverness, he had decided that it was the business of art to impose chaos on order. At his worst, he turns never saying Yes and never saying No into an aesthetic neurosis. (pp. 9-11)

Like a first-class teacher Ford gives his ideas the force of his personal life. But, except in his two best books, he had so many ideas that he was exhausted by the time he got to the page. He had not the breath. He creates the spell of someone always on the move; the pen itself was expatriate. His theories, in the end, become devices for postponing the novelist's task: which is to settle and confront. Impressionism—and with it a desire to impress—becomes an unconscious journalism. One sees him, and his characters also, wearing themselves out by continually changing trains. (p. 12)

V. S. Pritchett, "Fordie," in his The Working Novelist, *Chatto & Windus, 1965, pp. 1-12.*

PAUL L. WILEY (essay date 1962)

[*In the following excerpt, Wiley discusses the last decade of Ford's career, positing that Ford—like W. B. Yeats, T. S. Eliot, D. H. Lawrence, and Aldous Huxley—was attempting in his own way to portray the disintegration of a predominantly Christian culture.*]

The physical tribulations of gas and shellshock notwithstanding, Ford survived the Great War hardened, like Christopher Tietjens, in character and purpose; and much can be said to favor the opinion of Douglas Goldring [see Additional Bibliography] that Ford's real literary strength came with the war and found best expression in the continued productivity of his later years with its varied output of fiction, memoirs, and critical and discursive writing in such works as [**Great Trade Route, Provence,** and **The March of Literature**]. Whether or not due to active soldiering or the rout of the late Victorian world against which he had chafed in his youth, Ford gained maturity in release from the fidgeting over the dilemma of art and action which had earlier distracted him; and for all of its eccentricities, his writing during the 1930's and up to his death in 1939—an event which occurred with his work on a novel still in progress—has the assurance of a man exploring conviction and settled in the acceptance of his literary calling. (p. 248)

[By] enlisting with the postwar literary forces, and through his own immersion in the process of Victorian breakdown, Ford moved inevitably from his earlier stand of detached historian to that of proponent of remedies for the illness of contemporary civilization, an impulse that became overmastering as he neared the age of sixty and lived in apprehension of general cultural collapse, though its rise towards fuller statement may be seen clearly enough in **No Enemy.** This enterprise led to no abandonment of the historian's function which was still essential to social and cultural diagnosis. Nor did it mean discarding Impressionist method, since Ford held faithful to his adopted theories despite sociological trends in literature of the 1930's, though he did relinquish much of the Jamesian urbanity that he had cultivated in his Edwardian phase and introduced notes of the violent and sinister that recall Dostoevski or the Conrad of *Under Western Eyes* and that better accord with the darkening era of world depression and fascism reflected in the novels of such near adherents to his literary creed as Graham Greene and Faulkner. But Ford's preoccupation with the shaping of personal belief into something more tangible than the hints contained in early books like **Mr. Apollo** and **Ladies Whose Bright Eyes,** or even the temporary expedient suggested by the pastoralism of **No Enemy,** and with the formulating of schemes for the repair of Western civilization grows steadily into its central place in such semididactic works of his later years as **Provence** and **Great Trade Route.** In a purely fictional context this concern takes creative form in the related novels, [**The Rash Act, Henry for Hugh,** and **Vive LeRoy**], books in which the historian yields largely to the maker of a myth with features unique in the body of contemporary literature. By the 1930's, therefore, Ford had joined in the quest of that notable band of desert travelers, dismayed by the toppling of Christian culture and seeking roothold, that included Yeats, Eliot, Lawrence, Huxley, and had taken his own path among divergent roads.

While, then, essentially Impressionistic in manner, Ford's late novels display his customary adaptability to change in literary

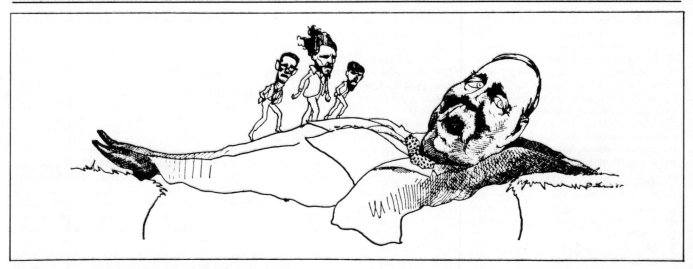

Caricature by David Levine of Ford serving as a "bridge" between nineteenth-century and modern literature. Here, Ford aids in the advance of James Joyce, Ezra Pound, and D. H. Lawrence. Copyright © 1965 Nyrev, Inc. Reprinted with permission from The New York Review of Books.

circumstance and fashion, most particularly in their employ-ment of mythical elements as well as in their effort to incor-porate the substance and tone of contemporary language and speech. But they are also notable for their broadened focus upon American scene and character, a more tolerant attitude of understanding towards such materials than Ford had shown in early novels like *An English Girl* or *The Good Soldier* and a fairer presentation of American types than he had offered in his war period books with such disagreeable caricatures as Senator Pappenheim in *The Marsden Case* and Mrs. de Bray Pape in *The Last Post.* (pp. 249-50)

Quite clearly, in fact, he undertakes in the 1930's to turn from his previous commitment as analyst and critic of the English people to a similar task with respect to America; and in doing so he reveals in an illuminating way both the limitations and resources of his Impressionism as a tool for the novelist-his-torian.

In accordance with the assumptions of this doctrine, Ford is often at fault in matters of specific detail, in which department he betrays the restricted knowledge of the outsider or of the writer dependent for general information on books of social summary like Dorothy Dudley's *Dreiser and the Land of the Free.* His attempt, for example, to portray American adoles-cents in *When the Wicked Man* is plainly weak, even though he had never at any time been much attracted to child char-acters. Yet with respect to what he regarded as the principal aim of the Impressionist novel, not documentation but the shap-ing of a single and imaginative vision of a selected milieu, Ford often wins assent for his impression of America sheerly by the strength of his literary intelligence and intuition, his customary sensitiveness to atmosphere and to the signs of his-torical disturbance or crisis, an ability by which he was able to hold his ground against many of those better provided with a store of facts. In the end, furthermore, his concern is not with local events but with the placement of America within the large scale cultural map that to the end of his life he was striving to design, for which reason in the late novels American scene and character tend increasingly to occupy an orbit which includes that part of the continent of Europe which Ford thought worth salvaging from the waste land. The rescue of an "ersatz-

civilization'' from further ruin makes necessary the creation of a bond between America, as the new leader of Anglo-Sax-ondom, and the remaining vestiges of a Provençal-Mediter-ranean tradition.

Although incentives to this plan for a reconstructed and unified culture certainly at times were present in Ford early in his career and now and again affected the themes of his novels, they did not become urgent until he had seen and grasped the consequences of the war; and the clearest proof of his personal understanding of the modern sexual-religious dilemma lies in the Tietjens tetralogy with its persistent emphasis upon the tortured relationship between Sylvia and Christopher.... At the close of the tetralogy the faith adopted by Tietjens has no relevance to existing society, and the pastoralism of *No Enemy* supposes an independent communal association apart from any church, so that Ford appears to have been as firmly persuaded as Shaw or Wilfred Owen of the failure of institutional religion:

> And so the whole Western world once the war was finished plunged into a sort of Albigens-ism.... What else could it do, the parallel being so very exact? . . . For the appalled sol-diery saw all the churches of the world plunge into that hellish struggle with the enthusiasm of school boys at a rat hunt. Not a pulpit thun-dered that if you slay your fellow man your forehead will bear the brand of Cain. Great lights of the churches plunged into the whirl-pool itself—and not armed only with maces, either. . . .

The Albigensian reference, though it had sometimes occurred in statements by Ford when young and had perhaps been made familiar to him through his father's study of the troubadours, develops in his last years into a fixed analogy between the modern world depressed by war and the old culture of Provence disrupted by the massacre which had rooted out the gentle heretics. By the same measure he comes to assert the need for a recovery of original Provençal virtues, these being associated in his mind with qualities of art and a spirit of graceful conduct somewhat like Gringoire's individual standard in *No Enemy,* this opinion having evolved seemingly from his prewar idea of a basic antagonism in civilization due to the incompatibility of barbaric ''Nordic'' habits and the amenities of the Mediterranean South. Although this antithesis hovers in the background of *The Good Soldier*, it acquires solid dimensions with Ford after the war, which he regarded as a culminating riot of Nordic savagery, motivated by a Prussian temper that he by no means charged to the Germans alone or as a people and leaving for its aftermath a world doomed to the Nordic tyranny of business power and scientific weapons. (pp. 251-53)

[If in *No Enemy* Ford] merely presents his own description of the waste land state, his chart for reclamation of the dismembered territory follows original lines and is typically cultural rather than political. As set forth in *Great Trade Route*, published in the same year as Ford's last novel, the proposal is to restore a lost circuit of civilized commerce over a road steering away from the Nordic area of swamps and marshes and in this way to outlaw the tradition of the sword by reviving the free movement of peaceful traders or merchants carrying along the latitude of Washington, Constantinople, Samarkand, and Peking wares beneficial to culture, the products of graceful leisure and the arts. Such a retracing of the buried thoroughfares of a world civilization might conduce to the unburdening of the mind that stands for one of the features of Provence. . . . In itself a figure of considerable charm, the Great Road likewise belongs to the time when literary visions of a return to cultural unity could produce symbolic forms as different as the Byzantium of Yeats and the dark god community of Lawrence. To Yeats, perhaps, Ford stands closer than to Lawrence, since Ford's desire is for an urbane and harmonious culture grounded in civilized tradition and allowing for commerce between West and East. Nothing in his outlook suggests a yearning after premental sources of vitality, although he shares with both Yeats and Lawrence the hope for a change and freshening of the rhythm of existence, a revival of the dance as image of joy. . . . (pp. 254-55)

Ford's Trader, therefore, as purveyor of the means of enjoyment and art, displaces the soldier and the priest—participants in the Nordic massacre of the War—in assuming the leadership of a cult of pleasure connected with the forgotten basis of civilized life. Such a role, possibly, Tietjens approaches, since at the end of the tetralogy he is in his own way a trader free of national ties and prejudice. In its recognition of the merchant and of the place of Christianity within the tradition Ford's myth, too, has something in common with Eliot's in *The Waste Land*, both writers employing an inclusive symbol recalling sources of order prior to the Christian synthesis and Ford designating the Trader as precursor on the great route to Christ as well as Arthur. Through the myth Ford may well have resolved at last the religious perplexities that enter into early novels like *Mr. Apollo* and *Ladies Whose Bright Eyes*, where already he seeks to embody in some way the image of joy that he proclaims frankly in his work of the 1930's. (pp. 255-56)

Through the final phase of his work, consequently, Ford has in view a double purpose: from the historical side a demonstration of the Albigensian ills of contemporary life including the suicidal impulse so prominent in the late novels; from the remedial a piloting of the way towards the Great Road—these aims coalescing in his main accomplishment of the 1930's, the related books of *The Rash Act* and *Henry for Hugh*. The resulting effects are often bizarre, one of the more eccentric devices employed in all of the novels being that of double or mistaken identity frequently associated with a *doppelgänger* motif. Although Ford had experimented with the theme of

mutation of personality in early books like *Ladies Whose Bright Eyes* and had made the confusion of identity between Ney and Fréjus a central feature of *A Little Less Than Gods* in 1928, the pattern becomes so insistent in the fiction of the 1930's as to surround the latter with an aura of fantasy. The theme is, nevertheless, germane to the context of the novels and its two aspects complementary—the doubling or *doppelgänger* incidents expressing dramatically, and after the manner of Dostoevski or Conrad, the ailment of modern self-division; the exchange or fusion of identities representing a conception of the self transformed or unified through awareness of tradition, the latter state probably being connected with the myth of the cycle of kingship and so affording an answer to the problem of disrupted inheritance involved in works like *The Good Soldier* and the Tietjens sequence. Whereas this emphasis upon doubling seems a natural outgrowth of Ford's handling of self-recognition in such early novels as *A Call*, it is notable in the later work not only for its elaborated reference but also for the presentation of the issue not in terms of current psychology but instead in those of the legendary or occult. If the choice doubtless exhibits Ford's preference for the magical, as approximating the religious, rather than the scientific, of which, according to Goldring, Ford refused to believe a word, it also conduced to technical advantage in the way of narrative interest and suspense.

Although *When the Wicked Man* . . . is the first of the late novels to display a blend of the modern and the legendary, it alludes to the Provençal ideal, if at all, only by inference, the action being directly concerned with big business as a version of the Inferno. In comparison with Ford's depiction of anxiety and guilt a work like *Babbitt* appears comparatively genial; for if *When the Wicked Man* deals ostensibly with a world of Manhattan company directors, the latter reveal traits originating in the Nordic swamps and forests to the north of the Great Trade Route. (pp. 256-57)

In great part . . . the novel offers a satire on the plight of Notterdam as a Faustian man with Henrietta Felise for his Gretchen and Lola Porter for his sensual Helen, a creature of romantic guilt and uncertain origins who can describe himself in affirming that ''. . . Nostradamus and Notre Dame and Notterdam were all the same.'' . . . Devoid of religious clarity but superstitious, he displays the irresolution and painful conscience of the sinner by default who achieves neither heroism nor villainy because embroiled in the confusion of Christian and pagan motives that lies behind his psychic illness. Although different in kind from Dowell's Victorian hypocrisy in *The Good Soldier*, much of Notterdam's thinking is a process of evasion or forced compromise which Ford skilfully illuminates by a language made up of tentative or disguised assertions: ''If one were maudlin one might well say that one had slain one's brother.'' . . . In a similar light the *doppelgänger*, likewise the product of romantic tradition and so again characteristic of Notterdam, remains ironically ambiguous like the ghosts in *The Turn of the Screw* in having no concrete status as a positive force of evil outside Notterdam but being potent enough as a product of superstition to torture his mind and to invest his world with an almost Gothic atmosphere of nightmare. Because of this basic absence of conviction, in society as well as in the individual, the environment becomes dark and death becomes, as in *The Secret Agent*, an inexplicable horror. Like the suicide of Gilda Leroy in *Mr. Fleight* the death of Porter, an instance of metropolitan indifference to the disappearance of the individual, is too small a matter to disturb public apathy; yet as a personal experience affecting the unsteady mind, it may acquire an exaggerated power to terrify, as Notterdam finds on confronting Porter's body. . . . (pp. 268-69)

Because of the rapid pace of **When the Wicked Man** the manner in which the themes interlock is not at once evident; and the prominence of the *doppelgänger* motif tends to overshadow the equally significant theme of the absence of communal relationship between Notterdam and Porter, an aspect of the story that Ford stressed rather awkwardly by the ironical transfer to Notterdam of Porter's identity and the late shift of scene to England for the purpose of enlarging upon the idea of homelessness. Since Ford's immediate aim was, however, to reveal a state of waste-land neurosis, the balance of the novel leans understandably towards individual disintegration rather than towards the prospect of cultural recovery and hence of renewed personal ties which becomes a main issue in the richer mythical setting of the two-part novel . . . **The Rash Act** and **Henry for Hugh.** In this work, the most elaborate attempt by Ford to deal in fictional terms with a symbolic resolution of the passional-religious dilemma, the art differs not only from the satirical effect of **When the Wicked Man** but also from the more openly didactic handling of matters of contemporary faith in such an early novel as **Mr. Apollo.**

By incorporating the death-rebirth cycle, **The Rash Act** and **Henry for Hugh** stand as a refined example of the funerary art peculiar to the modernism which followed the Great War. (p. 269)

To the end Ford's art remains labyrinthine and allusive in defiance of the growing mechanization of the world, and in this respect **Vive Le Roy** is as rich in funerary symbolism and mythical overtone as the two novels preceding it. In an obvious rebirth pattern, colored by both Egyptian and classical associations, Cassie under the protection of the strong and omniscient Penkethman seeks her lover in the underworld of contemporary evil; and, having endured the terror of death, she and Walter emerge at last from the "circular grave" . . . in the maze of history, leaving a passageway excavated in the war year of 1914, . . . and return to a new life together in America. (p. 288)

[The] Provençal myth of restored harmony continues to manifest itself in **Vive Le Roy,** which, like **The Rash Act** and **Henry for Hugh,** is a novel featuring the reconciliation of characters of varying nationality and religious background. . . . (p. 289)

In his later work Ford did not enlarge measurably the catalogue of afflictions that he had begun to recognize in even his earliest novels, but he did advance in resolving them within the scheme of his Nordic contra Provençal myth with its supplementary images like that of the Great Road.

Whereas this accretion of personal myth in the later fiction is a feature peculiar to Ford's postwar phase, it is not of sudden origin, having emerged out of his early preoccupation with matters of faith, nor incompatible with his Impressionism and its use of representative figures and situations. But in taking a mythical direction from a contemporary base, Ford indicated ways in which the novel might occupy new areas of form and sensibility. (pp. 291-92)

> *Paul L. Wiley, in his* Novelist of Three Worlds: Ford Madox Ford, *Syracuse University Press, 1962, 321 p.*

FRANK MacSHANE (essay date 1965)

[*In the following excerpt, MacShane discusses* The Inheritors *and* Romance *as effective collaborations that improved the novelistic technique of both Ford and Joseph Conrad, with Ford learning greater structural control and Conrad developing his facility with the English language.*]

When Conrad first read the book that was to become **The Inheritors,** he found it attractive—'trés chic,' as he put it. Its subject was political, and therefore was bound to be of interest to the man who was to write *The Secret Agent* and *Under Western Eyes.* Today, the novel seems somewhat trivial; to begin with, it is dated and, since it is a *roman à clef,* much of its interest depends on the identity of the politicians and public figures on whom the characters were based. . . .

What is important, however, is not the novel itself, but what it did for the two writers who created it. In later years neither men liked the book, which is understandable, but each was willing to comment on it. From the inscriptions Conrad wrote on its fly-leaves it would appear that Ford was responsible for the idea and for most of the actual writing. (p. 45)

He and Conrad had both tried in their dialogues to represent the indefiniteness that characterizes almost all English conversations. Ford himself had noticed that ordinary conversation in England consists of little more than allusive reference to things understood but never uttered: 'A. says: "What sort of a fellow is . . . *you* know!" B. replies: "Oh, he's a sort of a . . ." and A. exclaims: "Ah, I always thought so . . .".' In his own writing, Ford had tried to reproduce as exactly as possible this style of 'communicating by means of words.' The result, as far as **The Inheritors** was concerned was that its first draft 'consisted of a series of vague scenes in which nothing definite was ever said.' . . .

Thus Conrad's function 'was to give to each scene a final tap; these in a great many cases, brought the whole meaning of the scene to the reader's mind.' Rereading the book in later years, Ford said he found innumerable passages which he remembered as having been completed and made definite by Conrad. (p. 46)

Doubtless the exercise of working over a work of no great intellectual importance helped Conrad become more flexible and fluent, but Ford learned the difference between a loose first draft and a publishable book.

More important to both men, however, was the many months' work they devoted to **Romance.** After preliminary readings of Ford's *Seraphina,* they drew up a synopsis for the new book; then in practice they changed whatever was necessary in order to produce a finished novel.

The synopsis opens:

> The story begins in a farmhouse in Kent, goes on in Jamaica, then on the Cuban coast and ends in England.
>
> The narrator, John Kemp, driven out of his house by his mother's severity, walks down to Hythe; falls in with some smugglers; joins them recklessly in a 'tub-raising' expedition during which the boat sinks, and is rescued by an outward bound ship.

This straightforward plan underwent many changes under collaboration. As it stood, it relied heavily on chance: it was accidental that Kemp fell in with the smugglers, accidental that he was rescued by a passing ship. What Conrad and Ford did to this section then was to 'thicken' it—to provide in the first place more credible reasons than his mother's tyranny for Kemp's desire to leave the house, to provide connexions in Jamaica to whom Kemp could go, to fill in the background of smuggling on the Kentish coast and to have Kemp mistakenly revealed to the British police as a smuggler himself so that he is required to leave England as a refugee rather than as an adventurer. Such changes were also required in order that every action in the early sections would have a tangible result towards the end. (pp. 47-8)

Further changes were made in the synopsis that tidied up the plot and enlivened interest in the story. In the first version, Kemp's relations with the Jamaicans failed to carry the story ahead: they were, in fact, digressions, for in the synopsis these people never reappear. Thus as the two men worked together on this section, they came to realize 'that every word set on paper—*every* word set on paper—must carry the story forward and, that as the story progressed, the story must be carried forward faster and faster and with more and more intensity. That is called *progression d'effet,* words for which there is no English equivalent.

It therefore followed that one of Conrad's principal concerns in the third and fourth sections, for which he was largely responsible, was to increase the pace of the work. (p. 48)

In general what Conrad did was to simplify the somewhat tangled narrative of this portion of the novel. The published version is more straightforward and clear than the original, as are both the characters and their relationships with one another. As Ford had written it, the novel contained ambiguities, and the characters were not so clear and blunt as they emerged from under Conrad's pen. What is lost, then, is a certain subtlety, but the lucidity and suspense that is gained is certainly more important in this sort of novel.

The final section has been described by Conrad as being 'certainly three quarters MS. F.M.H. with here and there a par. by me.' (p. 49)

In later years Ford wrote an analysis of this final passage which shows how Conrad's paragraphs summarize and bring together the events of the tale as a whole: they are like the formal conclusion of an essay. In other words, Conrad was repeating his function in *The Inheritors:* with his definite statement, he was giving the book as a whole 'a final tap'. Thus the collaboration was, as Ford later said, 'a continual attempt on the part of the one collaborator to key up and of the other to key down.' Conrad's concept of the novel as a dramatic rendering of life was the real occasion for most of the changes and simplifications made in *Romance,* and since this novel is primarily an adventure story, his instincts were certainly right.

Yet that Conrad was sensitive to Ford's attempt at artistic rendering is borne out by his recognition that a passage by Ford contained 'the only immortal line in *Romance.*'

This line occurs in a section where the judge of the Spanish court in Havana is questioning a witness from a small village:

> 'Where do you come from?'
>
> 'The town of Rio Medio, Excellency.'
>
> 'Of what occupation?'
>
> 'Excellency—a few goats . . .'
>
> 'Why are you here?'
>
> 'My daughter, Excellency, married Pepe of the posada in the Calle . . .'

The 'famous sentence', as Conrad characterized it, 'at which we both exclaimed: "This is Genius!"' is, as anyone with an eye for literary effects will see, 'Excellency—a few goats. . . .' These four words of dialogue succeed in summarizing the whole character of the villager, so that neither his physical appearance nor his manner of speaking need be described.

Except for a slight piece, *The Nature of a Crime, Romance* was the last real collaboration between the two men. This is not a cause for surprise, since the experience had taught them both what it could, and neither had much to gain from further joint work. (pp. 50-1)

In his memorial book on Conrad, Ford himself tried to assess the collaboration as a whole. He denied the claim that he had taught Conrad English, and said instead: 'When I am disposed to rate my interferences with his work at a minimum I think that I merely acted for him as a sort of Thesaurus—a handy dictionary of synonyms.' (p. 52)

Conrad's attitude towards the result of the collaboration seems to have varied. While still at work with Ford he wrote to Edward Garnett that 'strangely enough it is yet my share of *Romance* (collab'on stuff with Ford) that fills me with least dismay.' In later years, however, he tended to disparage the book, considering it of no real importance and claiming that it had been written merely in order to make money. On the other hand, he always defended the writing itself. . . . Thus the experimental nature of the enterprise seems to have proved successful for . . . Conrad had originally proposed the collaboration in order to gain fluency and that he believed he could accomplish this end only while working on a book about which he would care relatively little. In the end, he became more involved than he probably assumed he would, but this did not lessen the effectiveness of the experiment.

For his part, Ford acknowledged that Conrad had helped him in his own work by advising him to pay attention to cadences, and in general he believed the writing of *Romance* to have been worth the labour expended upon it. 'I at least,' he said, 'learned the greater part of what I know of the technical side of writing during the process . . .' In a letter which must be taken *cum grano salis* he also wrote: 'I learned all I know of Literature from Conrad—and England has learned all it knows of Literature from me—I do not mean to say that Conrad did not learn a great deal from me when we got going; I dare say he learned more actual stuff of me than I of him. . . . But, but for him, I should have been a continuation of DANTE GABRIEL ROSSETTI—and think of the loss that would have been for you young things . . . and think what English Literature would be without Conrad and James. . . . There would be nothing.' (p. 53)

> *Frank MacShane, in his* The Life and Work of Ford Madox Ford, *Routledge & Kegan Paul, 1965, 298 p.*

ARTHUR MIZENER (essay date 1971)

[*Mizener, who wrote the first major biography of F. Scott Fitzgerald, has also written the most exhaustive biography of Ford,* The Saddest Story. *In the following excerpt from that work, he discusses the relationship of Ford's life to his writings, positing that the protagonist of* The Good Soldier *is modelled closely on Ford.*]

The Saddest Story was the title Ford Madox Ford himself chose for his most brilliant novel; it was only when his publisher protested that it was an unfortunate choice for a novel issued during a war that, half ironically, he suggested *The Good Soldier. The Good Soldier* is not a bad title, either for Edward Ashburnham's life or for Ford's. Edward was a fine officer and an honorable man: the Ashburnhams were "good people." He was also a simple man with the simple man's sense of duties and responsibilities. He was a good soldier, both literally and figuratively. There was a part of Ford that was like that too; much of the time he acted the role of the good soldier, fulfilling his responsibilities, sacrificing himself for literature as the editor of *The English Review* or for his country as a soldier in the First World War.

But *The Good Soldier* contains more than Edward Ashburnham; it includes a judgment of the world in which Edward Ashburnham has to exist and an ironic awareness of the impossibility of Edward's conduct in that world. John Dowell, the novel's narrator, would not have had Edward different; he loved and admired what Edward was. But he could see—if Edward could not—that Edward's conception of how he ought to live, however admirable, was impossible to realize; neither the world nor strong elements in Edward's own very human nature would permit it. Dowell's judgment of Edward's defeat is not that Edward was a tragic hero; you do not have tragedy in a comedy-of-manners world or with a nature like Edward's that is fulfilled by the good soldier's wholehearted performance of his role. The lives of such simple souls are only sad. But they can be very sad, as Edward was. There are no cheerful resolutions for dilemmas like this. Edward's innocent conception of his life as a Tory landlord redeemed by the love of a good woman so that he could devote himself to the care of his tenants, especially the women and children, was—perhaps always has been and always will be—impossible; it was, in a key word of John Dowell's, "sentimental." It was nonetheless the finest idea of a life Ford could conceive, sentimental not simply in the sense that it was impossibly idealistic but also in the sense that it was based on the finest sentiments.

Ford saw the sad impracticality of the life Edward innocently imagined he could live; he was as much John Dowell as he was Edward Ashburnham. His own dream of a life was the life of Edward Ashburnham, and he dreamed—both his good dreams and his bad dreams—with an intensity that it is difficult for ordinary people to comprehend. (pp. xiii-xiv)

Just as *The Good Soldier* has its Dowell to look at Edward Ashburnham with irony for his simplicity as well as with admiration for his idealism, so *No Enemy* has its Compiler, with his limited patience for Gringoire's easy assumption that he can live the life his romantic poet's imagination has conceived. When Ford talked directly about the Gringoire in himself, he usually did so half jokingly, as when he said toward the end of his life,

> I have written at least fifty-two books, of which a couple might stand; I have dug, hoed, pruned, and sometimes even harvested twenty-six kitchen gardens that I can remember . . . and thirteen times I have travelled the round that goes from London to New York, New Orleans, the Azores, Gibraltar, Marseilles, Paris, London. . . . If I had not so constantly travelled, I should have reaped better harvests and written more and better books; if I weren't, when travelling, constantly impeded by the desire to settle down somewhere and start something growing and write something, I should have travelled more happily and farther. And if suddenly, when

dunging or irrigating in . . . Provence . . . I hadn't been filled with the itch to be walking across Sheridan Square . . . and if I hadn't incontinently gone and done it all—I should have eaten many more cabbages, oranges, and ears of corn of my own growing.

Attractive as this is in its frank recognition of a tendency to go in too many directions at once, it still leaves the impression that this fault has hardly been serious: the fifty-two books and the twenty-six kitchen gardens were still achieved. This was the best Ford could do when he spoke in his own character about this aspect of himself (most of the time he did much worse), and it seems scarcely to recognize how serious the consequences of his own divided nature were.

But his best fiction does recognize those consequences. As early as the *Fifth Queen* trilogy he produced what is in some ways his subtlest dramatization of this fundamental division in his nature. Here he not only doubled his hero, as he did in *The Good Soldier, No Enemy,* and a number of other novels, but, in Henry VIII, produced a believable character who is almost as radically mixed in his impulses as Ford himself was. He faced the complexity of his own nature this way in all his best novels; it is what gives them the insight and the passion that raises them above his other work, however skillful. (pp. xiv-xv)

There is . . . a sense in which Ford's life was the saddest of stories in the way the paired lives of Edward Ashburnham and John Dowell were. Part of him believed in the honorable and simple life of the Tory gentleman and gifted poet of his dream and believed in it so intensely that he could not imagine it was unachievable, and part of him was the skeptical observer who was reduced to hopeless inaction by his common-sense recognition that it was. It was only in the best and most creative moments of his life that he could endure to face steadily the conflict between these two sides of his nature and to admit that for such natures life is, as Dowell says, "all a darkness." It is impossible not to believe that, most of the time, the vision of the Ashburnham in him dominated his consciousness and made him, as Ezra Pound said, a *halluciné*. But it is not easy to suppose either that he could permanently suppress the voice of Dowell; in some hidden and mostly neglected corner of his mind he must always have heard Dowell commenting on his conduct, pointing out how much of a fool, practically speaking, he was making of himself.

The effect of this division in his nature on his work is even sadder. Pound was always irritated by what seemed to him Ford's refusal to write the book Pound was sure he had it in him to write, and everyone who studies Ford's career has to face the problem of why Ford's achievement was not what his gifts would lead us to expect. Taken in one way—at the level of judgment that looks for talent and skill—Ford's career was brilliant. But when, like Pound, one applies to this career the standard that is set by Ford's own best work and asks why he wrote so many merely promising or clever books—not to mention that formidable mass of journalism—one is confronted by a further consequence of his divided nature. He had a romantic need, far more developed—or at least far more indulged—than in most men, to see himself as admirable and his defeats as undeserved, to revise in his imagination his actual conduct in such a way as to make himself the virtuous victim of a malicious world. Stella Bowen, who loved him, called this "weakness of character" quite simply "vanity."

This irrepressible need to invent and to impose on others an improved account of his own life and character did him very great harm. (pp. xv-xvi)

[Ford] was not the greatest writer of his time, and despite the unfortunate things he occasionally said about himself, he never believed he was. (p. xxi)

But if he neither was nor thought himself the greatest writer of his time, he was nonetheless a superbly talented man. It is almost literally true that he could, in the words Conrad ascribed to their agent, J. B. Pinker, write anything and write it well. He wrote poetry that anticipates—in style if not feeling—some of the essential qualities of twentieth-century poetry. He was, at moments, a fine novelist and produced at least five distinguished novels [*The Good Soldier* and the Tietjens tetralogy]; even more frequently he was a very good novelist who wrote half-a-dozen period books [the Katherine Howard trilogy, *A Call, Ladies Whose Bright Eyes,* and *The Young Lovell*] that will stand comparison with the work of contemporaries such as Galsworthy and Bennett and Wells and several clever experimental novels [*The Inheritors, Romance, Mr. Apollo, The Simple Life Limited, The New Humpty Dumpty, Mr. Fleight, The Marsden Case,* and *No Enemy*]. He practically invented a form of fictional reminiscence; it may be a dubious genre, but in it he wrote two fascinating books [*Return to Yesterday* and *It Was the Nightingale*]. He wrote half-a-dozen books of intelligent literary criticism, at least one of which, his much-abused book about Conrad, is a remarkable achievement. Despite his scorn for facts, he wrote half-a-dozen books of a scholarly nature on literature and painting, one of which—his life of Ford Madox Brown—is still, after more than sixty years, the standard work on the subject.

Ford also had a remarkable eye for talent in other men and he loved good writing with a devotion that made him able to bear almost anything for it, so that he was a great editor, especially during the period of *The English Review*. He was also for more than thirty years one of the most effective literary journalists in the English-speaking world, able to write interestingly on anything from Amenemhet I's advice to his son to Joyce's *Ulysses*. We ought to remind ourselves that this last achievement is not so insignificant as we are sometimes asked to believe. (pp. xxi-xxii)

Most of Ford's astonishing quantity of work was produced by the writer of talent in him, the skillful craftsman with his irrepressible delight in his métier. But somewhere inside him, apparently beyond the control of his conscious will, there was another self in Ford, what he called in his novels "the under self." This under self is the source of his best work. Its voice can be heard from time to time in his early books, but it is clearest in *The Good Soldier* and *Parade's End*. It fades out in his later work, for much as he longed to be a part of the new literary world that he, as an Edwardian rebel, had helped to make possible, his under self remained an old Bolshevik. It is a false ascription of motive but a fair judgment of the fiction Ford wrote in his last years to say, as Ambrose Gordon, Jr., does, that "for his last ten years [Ford] subsided into the novelistic equivalent of anagrams or acrostics, the elaborate amusements of 'an old man mad about writing' [see Additional Bibliography]. These late novels are skillful exercises in the special form Ford had gradually developed over the great years of his career, but they have no significant subject. Only the final poems, the expression of his feelings for Janice Biala, speak with the voice of his under self.

Ford saw before any other writer of his age the peculiar conflict between the possible and the actual that has been the subject of twentieth-century literature, and at his best, he made images of it that are very moving. But they are all more or less limited by his inclination to make his heroes—like himself—"too like thee, tameless and swift and proud," so that they are subject only to romantic irony; and romantic irony, even when it is carried to the point where it actually deceives some readers—as the irony about Edward Ashburnham of *The Good Soldier* does—is never a measure of the hero's complicating defects: he has no defects. The irony is only a measure of the world's inadequacy to his fineness. "[Ford's limitations] deprive him of co-status with Pound, Eliot, and Joyce," Hugh Kenner has said. "[He is] a little anachronistic, writing from a basis a little closer to the time in which the novels are set than to that in which they were conceived."

Nevertheless, young and old, over a span of nearly fifty years, from the publication of *The Brown Owl* in 1891 to the publication of *The March of Literature* in 1938, Ford's love of literature and his productive energy were unflagging. David Harvey's fine bibliography of his work lists eighty-one books, 419 contributions to periodicals, and fifty-seven miscellaneous contributions to other men's books. This formidable achievement has never really been given its due, partly because the enemies Ford so effectively created and provided with such powerful ammunition have made good use of their opportunities and partly because the very quantity of Ford's work has tended to obscure the best of it. (pp. xxii-xxiii)

Arthur Mizener, in his The Saddest Story: A Biography of Ford Madox Ford, *The World Publishing Company, 1971, 616 p.*

WILLIAM GASS   (essay date 1981)

[*Gass is an American fiction writer and critic. Widely praised for the virtuosity of his prose style, he is among the most conspicuous modern proponents of the view that literature's sole meaning lies in the aesthetic forms an author creates with language. This position is developed in two collections of critical essays,* Fiction and the Figures of Life *(1971) and* The World within the Word *(1978), and forms the creative principle behind the stories of* In the Heart of the Heart of the Country *(1968), the novel* Omensetter's Luck *(1966), and the long essay* On Being Blue *(1976). As opposed to the representational theory of art, which holds that literature should be a rendering of human experience more or less in the manner of history or journalism, such essays as "The Medium of Fiction" and "Philosophy and the Form of Fiction" disclaim the injunction that fiction should, or indeed is able to present anything to the reader except an aesthetic pattern composed of rhetorical devices and the poetic qualities of words themselves. This is exemplified by Gass's demonstration in "The Concept of Character in Fiction" that a character may be defined as a series of verbal strategies focusing on a proper noun which in turn serves as one element among many in a larger aesthetic design. Applied to a given work of literature, this critical approach dispenses with psychological, social, moral, or any other consideration which would attempt to offer the meaning of that work in nonliterary terms. While such an abstract account of Gass's work might suggest that his is a purely decorative form of literature, one exclusive of human emotion, he has in fact criticized such writers as Samuel Beckett and Jorge Luis Borges for just such a lack of feeling, and he has made it clear in many of his works that for him the rhetorical substance of literature is perfectly capable of embodying, in aesthetic form, all the passions of life. In the following excerpt, Gass decries the longstanding critical neglect of* The Fifth Queen. *Citing Ford as the pivotal force behind the development of modernism in English literature, he praises*

The Fifth Queen *as the "final and most complete expression" of the nineteenth-century historical novel.*]

The style [of *The Fifth Queen*] is stagy, melodramatic, artificial, even quaint; themes are packed into paragraphs like fish in tins; individuals are addressed as though they were crowds; terms are dragged from their graves and put once more in the line of fire like ghosts given rifles; qualifying phrases are repeated like Homeric epithets; scenes are set the slow deliberate way posts are sunk in concrete; there is such a high tone taken you really might believe you were at court . . . but are these merely history's playing cards—these characters? Do they stand precariously in their designs like figures in *Alice*? (p. 25)

Will the value of these characters simply vary with the course of play, though their stiffly posed and tinted images remain vividly the same? There will be a critical fuss about this. Why, in a world of change, don't these people alter something other than their loyalties? And we might answer by asking how the stream of time might run but between unyielding banks, or how we might measure its motion except in the eddies it makes about rocks. Or do we prefer illusions, and like to fancy people grow new characters like their beards and bellies, whereas, in fact, by the time the bosom has budded and the first blood run, even the sweetest maid is beyond shaping. (pp. 25-6)

The Fifth Queen resembles the maze at Hampton Court. Meanings multiply among the corridors its sentences suggest. When a torch flares, they return like luminous echoes from concealed corners, cul-de-sacs, and distant doors. In fact, the work is so intensely visual, so alternately light and dark, you might think the words were being laid on the page like Holbein's paint. . . .

The style of this novel cannot be escaped, and readers who prefer their literature to be invisibly literary should shun it. There are no merely workmanlike words here, anxious to get the job done so they can suds themselves up at some pub on the way back to the dictionary. (p. 26)

The Fifth Queen, then, is like Eisenstein's *Ivan:* slow, intense, pictorial, and operatic. Plot is both its subject and its method. Execution is its upshot and its art. *The Fifth Queen* is like Verdi's *Otello:* made of miscalculation, mismaneuver, and mistake. Motive is a metaphor with its meaning sheathed like a dagger. It is one of Shakespeare's doubtful mystery plays. Even though it includes clowns who berate one another, they make no successful jokes, and *The Fifth Queen* remains relentlessly tragic. It must be read with the whole mouth—lips, tongue, teeth—like a long slow bite of wine. For prose, it is the recovery of poetry itself. (p. 27)

The struggle which *The Fifth Queen* represents—between the Old Faith and the New Learning—occurs at the stage of style and literary theory, as well as within the local practice of the genre, and not merely at the level of political, religious ideology or historical event. And the loss to later English life which Katharine Howard's fall signifies to Ford is regained by the writing itself. Rather than butt helplessly against the conventions of that coal-stove Realism which stands for the triumph of the Puritan business spirit, *The Fifth Queen* seeks a language which springs from the traditions of the land and can be cultivated like another crop; so that Ford's return to the historical romance, despite its dubious popularity and retinue of pleasing scribblers, is intended to recover and release the word. (p. 28)

Ford knew, and knew he knew, and what's more (unfortunately combining the correctness of his conceit with an unmannerly candor), *said* he knew more about the strategies of the traditional novel than anyone writing in English. *The Fifth Queen* is a textbook of technique, a catalogue of resources, an art of the English fugue. The struggle it depicts is both historical and literary. But Ford is not an innovator in the same sense that Joyce is, or Gertrude Stein, or Faulkner, or even Virginia Woolf. He is essentially a nineteenth-century novelist—the last of his line—with twentieth-century theories and a sixteenth-century taste on his tongue. His themes concern the conflict between periods, the dependence of principles (alas!) on times, our changing attitudes toward vice and virtue. Katharine Howard's sweet waist is grasped by the *Geist*. There is no future forward, yet there is no going back. Where rib confronts rib, Ford has none of the hope the lung has for its next breath. He has Hardy heavy on his one hand, Joyce will soon weigh down the other, Lawrence is standing on his chest. Ford will soon hail with regret that "finely sculptured surface of sheer words," as Wyndham Lewis wrote, which will protect the novel's center from the world, and constitute the main concern of much of the work to come.

So if, as Conrad declared, *The Fifth Queen* is the swan song of the historical romance, then *The Good Soldier* brings the Jamesian tradition to a close, just as *Parade's End* concludes the lifetime of its kind. (p. 34)

The Tudor trilogy is a muscle show, all right, a strut, a flex of force, but it is not a simple deceptive flourish like General Beauregard's marching the same small squad round and round his camp to simulate the nick-of-time arrival of a rescuing army. Its surface is more accessible than that of *Pale Fire;* it plays no games with its readers and is never facetious like *Lolita.* There is no parody like that which sends the humorless reader away from *At Swim-two-birds.* It is not as exotic and apparently "worked up" out of history as *Salammbô,* nor is it as narrowly focused as *The Awkward Age,* although equally and severely scenic. It is tragic, but not as fanatically gloomy as the writing of Samuel Beckett. Unlike John Barth's *Letters,* it wears its learning lightly, and even lets its Latin sound like Oscar Wilde. The linguistic difficulties are minor, and its length does not exceed that of *Ulysses* or many of Thomas Mann's novels, or George Eliot's *Romola,* for that matter. It is a virtuoso performance—the first of Ford's great shows—and closes out the historical novel like an emptied account. Later he will try for a similar triumph over the realistic novel by inventing Christopher Tietjens, a truly good "good soldier." In an arrogant display of literary genius, Ford Madox Ford brought the nineteenth-century novel, in each of its principal areas of excellence, to its final and most complete expression. For this he has not been forgiven. (p. 35)

The neglect of this novel, the critical obtuseness which the Tudor trilogy has had to endure, the indifference of readers to an accomplished art, and a major talent, the failure of scholarship even to disclose the real clay feet of the real Ford, even the esteem in which *The Good Soldier* is held, as if that book were being used to hide the others, but, above all, the unwillingness of writers to respond to a master, constitute a continuing scandal which hushing up will only prolong; yet one does wonder what is to be done. Certainly no adequate history of the recent English novel can be composed that does not recognize the door through which that novel passed to become modern. (p. 42)

William Gass, "The Neglect of 'The Fifth Queen'," in The Presence of Ford Madox Ford: A Memorial Volume of Essays, Poems, and Memoirs, *edited by Sondra J. Stang, University of Pennsylvania Press, 1981, pp. 25-43.*

C. H. SISSON (essay date 1981)

[*In the following excerpt, Sisson explores Ford's critical thought as espoused in* The Critical Attitude.]

It is very hard to gauge the weight of Ford's contribution to the critical mind of the twentieth century. There is a sense in which this cannot be done by looking at his critical books; it can certainly not be done by looking at those alone. For readers who, over the years, have browsed over any considerable number of his seventy or eighty volumes—novels, reminiscences, even the verse, read in the light of the prose—there remains an atmosphere, an uncertainty in the air, which is really the critical benefit received. An uncertainty, because about Ford's most swashbuckling assertions there is something tentative. He claims no more than that unprovable verity, "absolute truth as to the impression." And to hell with the facts! It is the stance of a man who knows he cannot rely on his memory and yet is aware of a level of apprehension which takes account of past experience as it were tacitly and gives him an assurance among his uncertainties. The surface of Ford's writing is wavering, offering sometimes sharp, definite sketches and assertions which are inconsistent with one another; yet one carries away from his work the impression of a truthfulness hidden somewhere in this unstable mass. At the center, wherever it is, there is a passionate and painful care for good writing. In a sense the seriousness of Ford is in his technical interests, which a few times in his life met a subject worthy of them, but often did not. The absorption in technical matters gives even his lesser work a solid point of reference against which the uncertainties show up. To his explicitly critical writing it gives an interest which might easily be missed by anyone who does not suspect the recesses behind his casual and often throw-away tone. (p. 109)

If there is one book in which, more directly than in another, Ford attempted to indicate his radical concerns, it is *The Critical Attitude* . . . , which consists of articles contributed originally to the *English Review*. Even here it would be wrong to look for anything like an unimpugnable statement, for it is of the very nature of Ford's method that what is offered is provisional—"suggestions not dictates," as he says in *The English Novel*. Ford does not want to be taken too literally, but he does want to be taken seriously; "in perusing this sort of book the reader must be prepared to do a great deal of the work himself— within his own mind." There is no place for the goggle-eyed student with a notebook, who expects to be told all. The most that can happen, Ford knows, is that the reader is put on the way to seeing for himself—much or little according to the acuteness of his vision. In *The Critical Attitude* the chapters, the pages within a single chapter, are of very unequal value, but they all help to cajole the reader to take up the desiderated attitude and, with his mind thus primed, to go into the world of literature and look for himself.

The object of the *English Review*, Ford says in his introductory chapter, was "to make the Englishman think"—a state of affairs so unusual, he thought, that the very name of the magazine was "a contradiction in terms." "No sane man would set out to make the ass play a musical instrument, the respectable journal take broad views, or the hyena distil eau-de-cologne." No less hopeless was it "to enjoin upon the Englishman a critical attitude." With these characteristic flourishes Ford set out to do just that, and it may be said that in England at least—let us not venture any opinions about *elsewhere*—the task always remains to be done afresh, for no sooner has a critical mind persuaded a number of people that some widely diffused view does not contain the whole truth about a problem than most of the number settle down to be as smugly convinced that the new aspect of the subject just brought to light is all there is to be said about it—lethargy being the condition to which most of us long most of the time to return. Ford pursues his subject with characteristic enthusiasm, for the moment looking neither to right nor to left. "But for his own particular islands, where Luther and Darwin like consecutive steam-rollers extinguished by force of criticism all possibility of simple faith, the Englishman has founded three hundred and forty-seven religions. And each of these religions is founded upon a compromise. That is what the Englishman does to, that is how he floors"—the critical attitude." The point is that, rather than make a clean break, the Englishman will move to an intermediate position. To arrive at this conclusion, which is itself merely a stage in the formulation on which Ford is bent in the introductory chapter, "The Objection to the Critical Attitude," he flounders through several assertions more or less approximate and misleading, so that the reader who is unwary may imbibe as he goes half-suggestions that Luther was particularly influential in England—which is not true—and that in the rest of the western world "revealed religion" survived with less damage—which is hardly true either.

The next stage of the formulation is to maintain that "logic is inhuman and that criticism, though it need not be actively inhumane, must, as far as possible, put aside sympathy with human weaknesses." The illustration Ford gives is again one-eyed, boisterous and could not for a moment withstand the force of the sort of criticism he himself proposes. He takes his stand on logic but uses it sparingly himself. "If it be granted . . . that a Poor Law system based on kindness will be a drag upon a State whose necessity is economic strength, it would become the duty of the critic of that state to put forward some such theories" as, for example, that "the consumptive or the sufferer from any permanent infectious disease, or the man or woman who is temperamentally unlucky" should "be either executed or relegated to pest colonies." The reader of Ford will never for a moment suspect Ford of recommending such measures—what he says is part of the pattern of hyperbole and other misrepresentation which will leave the reader convinced at least of the instability of opinion. It is boisterous—and tender-hearted rather than otherwise, even sentimental. Ford is too lazy to work out the practical complications of any social action; it is not his function. He is—again misleadingly—merely using his half-baked illustrations to make the point that the critic who acts as devil's advocate, and explains "remorselessly" the logical consequences of current muddles, in the face of widespread sentiment and prejudice, is performing a valuable function "in the republic." There is little enough that is remorseless, logical, or even tolerably coherent about the process by which he gets there.

What Ford is recommending is not so much criticism as a lack of dogmatism, and not so much lack of dogmatism as a humane recognition of variety, the endless qualification of one view by another. And beyond that, what he is contending for is the variety of impressions, and the validity of such variety in the arts. Of a critical statement of his own he will say: "That is perhaps an exaggerated statement of the case, but it is for a moment worth setting down." That is his provisional way of proceeding, setting things down not as a final truth, but as an interpretation that may help in the formation of a final picture, which however never quite becomes clear. It is with the lighting up of the *reader's* picture that he is concerned, so that he always hangs back a little doubtfully from the final effect of what he has said. It can be argued that such reticence is pusillanimous, that the "serious" critic stakes his reputation on the truth of what he propounds. There is, however, a good deal of civilized wisdom in Ford's hesitations. The justification is in the closeness of the method to that of the artist himself: "the province of the imaginative writer is by exaggeration due to his particular character—by characteristic exaggeration, in fact—precisely to awaken thought." The sort of "thought" Ford stands for is the recognition of differences, and there is a humane basis for this inasmuch as the differences rest on differences of impression, which turn on the variety of character in the observers. Ford adopts without question the romantic and post-romantic language of art as "self-expression." One may regard that phrase with scepticism, but one can hardly dissent from the critical distinction he thus introduces: the artist's "expression of himself exactly as he is, not as he would like other people to think him, the expression of his view of life as it is, not as he would like it to be."

The theme is developed, as always with Ford, in a manner which does not win our assent as being entirely true—which is evidently untrue, at some points—but which assists our discrimination if we understand it with reservations. He is speaking of the value "to the Republic"—by which he means the *res publica* of wherever it may be—of "a really fine renderer of the life of his day." He has in mind the writer in general and the novelist in particular. "Whatever his private views may be," he says, "we have no means of knowing them. He himself will never appear, he will never button-hole us, he will never moralize. He may be a Republican, he may be an Anglican; he may be a believer in autocracy. But he will never, by the fifth of an inch, drag round his pictures of life so as to make it appear that, if the social state were what he desires it to be, all would be well with the world." We do in fact gather a good deal of Ford's "private views" from the manner in which he presents his fictions, as we do with other writers. The point nonetheless is critically valid. It must be taken to mean that the writer's impressions, however superficially disjointed, must be presented as they are, and that this material, which has not been rounded into a theory, is the fundamental matter of art, to which all considered opinions are secondary if not irrelevant. So much for what is sometimes referred to as "commitment" in the artist. "In England, the country of Accepted Ideas, the novelist who is intent merely to register—to *constater*—is almost unknown. Yet it is England probably that most needs him, for England, less than any of the nations, knows where it stands, or to what it tends." Looking back seventy years to the time when those words were written, and in the light of the intervening history, they can hardly be faulted. It is moreover still true that England is a place of Accepted Ideas. What is accepted has changed, but the sloth is the same. It is for other countries to determine whether they enjoy a great superiority in these matters.

Ford believed that the artist who recorded the life of his day was adding to knowledge, and if he denounced the accumulation of facts it was merely because the knowledge he was interested in was—he thought—of a refinement which made it dependent on the observer who could set down his own impressions as only the artist can. Truthfulness to the impression was overridden by a "flaccid and self-satisfied commercialism"—and if that was true in 1908-11 it is overwhelmingly so now. Against this Goliath he saw as the only defense a possible "sober, sincere, conscientious and scientific body of artists, crystallizing, as it were, modern life in its several aspects." (pp. 110-13)

C. H. Sisson, "'The Critical Attidude'," in The Presence of Ford Madox Ford: A Memorial Volume of Essays, Poems, and Memoirs, *edited by Sondra J. Stang, University of Pennsylvania Press, 1981, pp. 109-14.*

ADDITIONAL BIBLIOGRAPHY

Andreach, Robert J. *The Slain and Resurrected God: Conrad, Ford, and the Christian Myth.* New York: New York University Press, 1970, 245 p.*
 Examines Ford's works in light of the author's preoccupation with the mythic pattern of separation, initiation, and return.

Bergonzi, Bernard. "Retrospect II: Fiction." In his *Heroes' Twilight: A Study of the Literature of the Great War,* pp. 171-97. London: Constable and Company, 1965.
 Recognizes *Parade's End* as the best synthesis of the major literary themes of World War I.

Bishop, John Peale. "The Poems of Ford Madox Ford." In his *The Collected Essays of John Peale Bishop,* edited by Edmund Wilson, pp. 283-86. New York: Charles Scribner's Sons, 1948.
 Holds that Ford's contribution to poetry lies in his bringing it closer to the flow of prose. Bishop quotes from "Antwerp," which he calls "one of the distinguished poems of our time."

Cassell, Richard A. *Ford Madox Ford: A Study of His Novels.* Baltimore: Johns Hopkins Press, 1961, 307 p.
 A sympathetic examination of each of Ford's novels.

——, ed. *Ford Madox Ford: Modern Judgements.* London: Macmillan, 1972, 191 p.
 Includes several essays of both general and focused content by prominent critics. The study closes with William Carlos Williams's poem "To Ford Madox Ford in Heaven."

Eliot, T. S. Letter to the editor. *The Transatlantic Review* I, No. 1 (January 1924): 95-6.
 Welcomes the appearance of *The Transatlantic Review.* Eliot advises Ford to seek out the very best young writers, whether they be aligned with or in opposition to those of Eliot's own literary periodical, *The Criterion.*

Gordon, Ambrose, Jr. *The Invisible Tent: The War Novels of Ford Madox Ford.* Austin: University of Texas Press, 1964, 153 p.
 Contends that World War I became Ford's most perfect subject and inspired his best work.

Harvey, David Dow. *Ford Madox Ford: A Bibliography of Works and Criticism.* Princeton: Princeton University Press, 1962, 633 p.
 The most extensive annotated bibliography of criticism on Ford's work.

Heldman, James M. "The Last Victorian Novel: Technique and Theme in *Parade's End.*" *Twentieth Century Literature* 18, No. 4 (October 1972): 271-84.
 Analyzes the significant change in narrative technique in *Parade's End.* Heldman believes that as Ford moves from an omniscient point of view to interior narrative, he symbolically effects the replacement of Victorian society with Edwardian society and the characteristics of the nineteenth-century novel with those of the twentieth century novel.

Huntley, H. Robert. *The Alien Protagonist of Ford Madox Ford.* Chapel Hill: University of North Carolina Press, 1970, 194 p.
 Studies the protagonist's alienation from his environment in Ford's fiction. Huntley discerns the consummation of this character type in *The Good Soldier,* in which Edward Ashburnham best embodies the idealist of an earlier age and his wife Leonora best typifies the new "Time Spirit," the force of modernism that is the antithesis of Ashburnham.

Leer, Norman. *The Limited Hero in the Novels of Ford Madox Ford.* East Lansing: Michigan State University Press, 1966, 235 p.
>   Traces the development of the hero in Ford's fiction, discovering that all the works preceding *The Good Soldier* demonstrate the hero's ineffectiveness. Although Leer sees in *The Good Soldier* a greater sense of the hero's development, it is not until *Parade's End* that he finds the hero learning to adapt himself to the complexities of the modern world.

Lewis, Wyndham. "First Published Work." In his *Rude Assignment: A Narrative of My Career Up-to-Date,* pp. 121-30. London: Hutchinson & Co., 1950.*
>   Exposes Ford's eccentricities, yet praises him as one of the best editors of any English literary review.

Lid, R. W. *Ford Madox: The Essence of His Art.* Berkeley and Los Angeles: University of California Press, 1964, 201 p.
>   Study of Ford's principal novels that focuses on their narrative style.

MacShane, Frank, ed. *Ford Madox Ford: The Critical Heritage.* London: Routledge & Kegan Paul, 1972, 271 p.
>   Contains representative criticism spanning the years 1892-1966. Excerpts from several of these essays are included in this volume.

Meixner, John A. *Ford Madox Ford's Novels: A Critical Study.* Minneapolis: University of Minnesota Press, 1962, 303 p.
>   A highly respected study of Ford's fiction.

Monroe, Harriet. "Great Poetry." *Poetry* XIII, No. 4 (January 1919): 219-24.
>   Praises Ford for his attainment of beauty and intimacy through the *vers libre* style in *On Heaven, and Poems Written on Active Service.*

Ohmann, Carol. *Ford Madox Ford: From Apprentice to Craftsman.* Middletown, Connecticut: Wesleyan University Press, 1964, 185 p.
>   Traces Ford's fictional development to its climax in *The Good Soldier* and *Parade's End.* Unlike many critics, Ohmann finds the Tudor trilogy, on the whole, undeserving of the praise it has received due to its simple prose and failure to properly develop its characters or fully explore its subject.

Rexroth, Kenneth. Introduction to *Buckshee,* by Ford Madox Ford, pp. xviii-xxii. Cambridge, Mass.: Pym-Randall Press, 1966.
>   Discusses *Buckshee* as "the finest ignored poem sequence in modern English."

Smith, Grover. *Ford Madox Ford.* New York: Columbia University Press, 1972, 43 p.
>   A general survey of Ford's work that considers *Parade's End* the primary reason for his enduring interest.

Stang, Sondra J. *Ford Madox Ford.* New York: Frederick Ungar Publishing Co., 1977, 157 p.
>   A survey of Ford's *oeuvre* in which Stang brings to light several overlooked works, such as the introspective *No Enemy,* in which she discovers some of Ford's best writing. Stang considers all the works of Ford's canon to be commonly concerned with bringing the modern world into focus.

————, ed. *The Presence of Ford Madox Ford: A Memorial Volume of Essays, Poems, and Memoirs.* Philadelphia: University of Pennsylvania Press, 1981, 245 p.
>   Includes essays by Graham Greene and Allen Tate (portions of which have already been excerpted in *TCLC,* Vol. 1 and in this volume, respectively), a previously unpublished short story by Ford entitled "The Other," an interview with Janice Biala (painter and companion of Ford), some personal letters of Ford, and an afterword by Edward Crankshaw.

Thornton, Lawrence. "'Deux Bonshommmes Distincts': Conrad, Ford, and the Visual Arts." *Conradiana: A Journal of Joseph Conrad* VIII, No. 1 (1976): 3-12.*
>   Declares Ford to have had the greater impact on modern fiction, following a comparative analysis of the image constructions of his work and that of Conrad.

Wells, H. G. "Edifying Encounters: Some Types of *Persona* and Temperamental Attitude." In his *Experiment in Autobiography: Discoveries and Conclusions of a Very Ordinary Brain (Since 1866),* pp. 509-44. New York: Macmillan Co., 1934.*
>   Claims Ford has been overly neglected while Conrad has received too much attention. Wells believes that Conrad, in addition, owes a great deal to Ford.

Young, Kenneth. *Ford Madox Ford.* Writers and Their Work, edited by Bonamy Dobrée. London: British Council, 1956, 43 p.
>   Short biography followed by criticism of the Tudor trilogy, *The Good Soldier,* and the Tietjens tetralogy.

Oliver St. John Gogarty

1878-1957

(Also wrote under pseudonyms of Gideon Ouseley, Oliver Gay, Alpha and Omega, and J.R.S.) Irish memoirist, poet, novelist, essayist, autobiographer, and dramatist.

Gogarty was an accomplished poet and memoirist whose literary achievements have long been overshadowed by his flamboyant personality and reputation as "the wildest wit in Ireland." Gogarty's brilliant conversation and notorious, often unprintable parodies and limericks were the talk of Dublin in his day, and made him one of the most colorful figures of the Irish Literary Renaissance. Gogarty's wit is commemorated in the memoirs of George Moore and of W. B. Yeats, who avowed that he found inspiration in Gogarty's "swift, indifferent" personality and created a controversy by including seventeen of Gogarty's lyrics in the 1936 *Oxford Book of Modern Verse,* which he edited and from which he excluded the poems of such writers as T. S. Eliot and Wilfred Owen. However, Gogarty is most famous, and will likely remain so, as the prototype of the character Buck Mulligan in James Joyce's novel *Ulysses.* Although Gogarty carried on a long feud with Joyce, and regarded as a scurrilous affront Joyce's portrayal of him as the "gay betrayer" of Stephen Dedalus and of Ireland, Joyce nonetheless preserved in *Ulysses* what Gogarty himself failed to capture in his own memoirs: the brilliance of Gogarty's speech and the excitement of his personality. Critics agree that Gogarty's memoirs, though amusingly written, ingeniously constructed, and valuable for their many anecdotes about Dublin and the writers of the Irish Renaissance, generally do not quite succeed in portraying or explaining the dynamic force of the personality that became a Dublin legend.

Gogarty was born in Dublin. His father was a successful physician, just as his grandfather had been, and Gogarty also elected to study medicine. He received his medical training at Trinity College, Dublin, and at Oxford University. While attending Trinity College in 1901, Gogarty became acquainted with Joyce. The two quickly became friends, and were nearly inseparable companions until shortly before Joyce left Ireland in 1904 for lifelong exile in Europe. During that time they wrote poetry together, undertook drunken expeditions to Dublin's Nighttown slum district, and shared rooms in a Martello Tower, as do Stephen Dedalus and Buck Mulligan in *Ulysses.* The exact reasons for their eventual bitter quarrel are unclear, but it seems likely that, as Ulick O'Connor has recorded, irreconcilable differences of temperament and background were responsible. Joyce, who recorded in his notebook that his companion's "coarseness of speech is the mask of his cowardice of spirit," took his revenge on Gogarty for what he perceived as a betrayal of their friendship by portraying him as Buck Mulligan in *Ulysses,* published in 1922. Mulligan was instantly recognized in Dublin circles as Gogarty, who was by then a respected surgeon as well as a senator for the Irish Free State. Although there was much that was true in Joyce's portrait, Gogarty deeply resented Joyce's exposure of their youthful excesses and never forgave his former friend for his indiscretion. In later years, Gogarty's anger at Joyce often led him to write deprecatingly about the novelist in such ill-considered works as his essay "They Think They Know Joyce," and certain acid-etched sec-

tions of *It Isn't This Time of Year at All!* These accounts tended to damage Gogarty's own credibility, though critics admit that Gogarty's memoirs of Joyce and of other contemporary Irish writers are fascinating. Critics and readers alike still find it difficult to judge Gogarty's works on their own merits without reference to his dispute with Joyce, or to his role in Joyce's legendary novel.

Gogarty was active politically throughout most of his life. As a young man he supported Arthur Griffith and the Sinn Fein movement, but the growing radicalism and violence of the Irish Home Rule Party eventually led him to oppose those whom he had previously supported. In consequence, after the Irish Civil War began in 1921, he was kidnapped from his home and would have been murdered had he not escaped by jumping into the freezing water of the Liffey River and swimming to safety, vowing, in the midst of his desparate escape, to present the Liffey with a pair of swans if his life were spared. His first substantial volume of poems, *An Offering of Swans,* commemorates both this escape and the fulfillment of his vow. In 1922 Gogarty was appointed to the Irish Senate, in which he served until it was abolished fourteen years later. Disgusted by the repressiveness and provincialism that pervaded his country during the 1930s, he left Ireland and settled in the United States, where he lived until his death.

Shortly after the attempt on his life in 1921, Gogarty left Ireland for a year to practice medicine in London. There, he became familiar with the works of Ben Jonson and the Cavalier poets, as well as with Elizabethan balladry. These two influences, together with the classical training he received at Trinity College and his association with Yeats, were instrumental in the development of Gogarty's verse style. Most critics recognize this and readily acknowledge his affinities with both the Classical and Romantic traditions. His poetic vision is frequently characterized as combining a classically mock-heroic sense of the ordinary with what James Carens has described as a Romantic's sensitivity to "beauties beyond the commonplace." Gogarty's *Collected Poems* contain numerous illustrations of this duality of vision. For example, many of his best-known poems, including "Leda and the Swan," the poem credited with inspiring Yeat's famous sonnet of the same name, are written in the mock-heroic manner, while the skepticism and stoicism displayed in such poems as "Non Dolet" and "To Death" are also derived from the classical tradition, most notably from the Latin poet Horace, with whom Gogarty is frequently compared. The influence of the Cavalier poets and the Elizabethan balladeers is equally evident in Gogarty's work. Such lyrics as "Begone O Ghost," "To Maids Not to Walk in the Wind," and "Golden Stockings" echo themes and rhythms found in the verses of Jonson, Robert Herrick, and Richard Lovelace. Yeats, a close friend of Gogarty, also exercised an important influence on his development as a poet. He often edited Gogarty's verse, and persuaded him against the use of poetic diction, inversions, and other archaic devices in his poems. Occasionally, Yeats also contributed whole lines and stanzas to Gogarty's lyrics. Although Gogarty was a competent poet and capable of producing a perfect lyric, he seldom took the time to polish his verses and was often careless about their structure. In consequence, critics agree that although Gogarty wrote many good poems, he wrote few great ones.

Gogarty's earliest nonpoetic works were the dramas that he wrote for the Abbey Theatre between 1917 and 1919 under the pseudonyms "Alpha and Omega" and "Gideon Ouseley." These three essentially satiric productions entitled *Blight, The Enchanted Trousers,* and *A Serious Thing* address social and political issues about which Gogarty felt strongly. *Blight,* the first of the three to be performed, was also the most critically successful. In this play, Gogarty attacked living conditions in the Dublin slums, considered by many the worst in Europe. Through his memorable recreation of the colorful descriptive speech of the Dublin lower classes, Gogarty was able to create comic characters of a wry type never seen on the Dublin stage before. Gogarty's depictions of original characters like Stanislaus Tully and Lily Foley not only demonstrated his adeptness as a playwright, they also deeply impressed young Sean O'Casey, who saw a performance of *Blight* in 1917 and six years later repeated the use of such devices as a tenement setting, naturalistic dialogue, and sardonically funny characters in his own famous trilogy of slum plays. In *The Enchanted Trousers* and *A Serious Thing,* Gogarty attacked the British bureaucracy and the British military forces in Ireland. Although these works retain much of their comic energy today, all are seriously flawed as works of art. Gogarty was as careless about structure in his dramas as he was in his poetry, and of *Blight,* in particular, critics complain that central characters disappear in the late acts without explanation as Gogarty twists plot and logic to make his point.

Gogarty's other prose writings include both conventional novels and works that defy all standard classifications because of the manner in which fictional and autobiographical elements are combined in them. Critics generally agree that Gogarty's novels *Mad Grandeur, Mr. Petunia,* and *Going Native,* though occasionally interesting for the quality of their characterizations, are works of uneven quality, written in a form that was not really suited to Gogarty's unique talents. Gogarty's literary abilities are shown to much better advantage in his more autobiographical works. *As I Was Going Down Sackville Street, Tumbling in the Hay, Rolling Down the Lea* and *I Follow St. Patrick,* all of which are loosely structured, episodic works in which gossip and extemporaneous digression play an important part, have been widely praised by critics for their vitality, romantic outlook, and humorous view of life. *Tumbling in the Hay,* in particular, is today regarded by some critics as a comic masterpiece. This thinly disguised account of Gogarty's years as a medical student has suffered critical neglect over the years and is seldom read today. However, some critics contend that it, and not the better known *Sackville Street,* is Gogarty's best book. Moreover, *Tumbling in the Hay* holds historical interest for students of literature because it contains characters and episodes that are the light-hearted parallels of many found in Joyce's more serious novel, *A Portrait of the Artist as a Young Man,* with Joyce himself portrayed in the character Kinch.

As I Was Going Down Sackville Street is Gogarty's best known, most controversial and most frequently misunderstood book. In it, Gogarty not only related many colorful incidents, both factual and factitious, about life among the guiding geniuses of the Irish Literary Revival and the political leaders of his day, he also bitterly satirized his enemies, giving vent to his frustration over the hopelessness of the political situation in Ireland through attacks on Irish Prime Minister Eamon De Valera. These latter features of the book, together with its unusual structure, are what have created the controversy and misunderstanding over *Sackville Street.* Critics have objected to the book's angry, occasionally ranting tone, and been puzzled by the lack of chronological sequence in its episodes, with some postulating that Gogarty alternated past events with present in order to illustrate how little life in Dublin has changed since the eighteenth century. James Carens, however, taking heed of Gogarty's warning that the names in *Sackville Street* are real, but the characters fictitious, contends that Gogarty structured his book in this peculiar manner as a way of commenting on the relation between illusion and reality. Carens notes: "Determined to control reality by the power of imagination, Gogarty reverses the passage of time and moves backward from the present—Ireland under De Valera—which he satirizes, and into the past, which offers an ideal of freedom and spontaneity. Like other Gogarty quests, this one involves a search for heroic values, and a number of heroic figures are depicted in it. Yet the heroic is also identified with the imaginative process and thus with the method of the book itself." *Sackville Street* is a more complex work than its autobiographical tone suggests, and one that poses some interesting problems for critics.

Despite Gogarty's long literary career, and the generally favorable responses of critics to his work, until recently neither his poetry nor his prose writings have received much serious scrutiny by critics using standard methods of exegesis and interpretation. Doubtless two of the reasons for this critical oversight have been Gogarty's reputation as a wit and public figure and the pyrotechnics of his feud with Joyce, which diverted attention from his literary achievements. Today, however, critics have begun to study Gogarty's work and to analyze its literary merit without reference to the flamboyant personality of its author. Through such studies and through the dissociation of Gogarty from Buck Mulligan, his proper place in twentieth century literature may in the future become clearer.

(See also *Contemporary Authors*, Vol. 109; *Dictionary of Literary Biography*, Vol. 15: *British Novelists, 1930-1959*; and *Dictionary of Literary Biography*, Vol. 19: *British Poets, 1880-1914*.)

PRINCIPAL WORKS

Blight: The Tragedy of Dublin [as Alpha and Omega] (drama) 1917
The Enchanted Trousers [as Gideon Ouseley] (drama) 1919
A Serious Thing [as Gideon Ouseley] (drama) 1919
An Offering of Swans, and Other Poems (poetry) 1923
Wild Apples (poetry) 1928
Selected Poems (poetry) 1933
As I Was Going Down Sackville Street (memoir) 1937
I Follow St. Patrick (memoir) 1938
Tumbling in the Hay (novel) 1939
Going Native (novel) 1940
Mad Grandeur (novel) 1941
Perennial (poetry) 1944
Mr. Petunia (novel) 1945
Mourning Becomes Mrs. Spendlove, and Other Portraits, Grave and Gay (essays) 1948
Rolling Down the Lea (memoir) 1949
Collected Poems (poetry) 1951
It Isn't This Time of Year at All! (An Unpremeditated Autobiography) (autobiography) 1954
A Weekend in the Middle of the Week and Other Essays on the Bias (essays) 1958
William Butler Yeats (memoir) 1963

*These works were published as *The Plays of Oliver St. John Gogarty* in 1972.

W. B. YEATS (essay date 1923)

[*The leading figure of the Irish Renaissance and a major poet of the twentieth century, Yeats was also an active critic of his contemporaries' works. As a critic he judged the works of others according to his own poetic values of sincerity, passion, and vital imagination. In the following excerpt from his introduction to* An Offering of Swans, *Yeats observes and approves the influence upon Gogarty of the Cavalier poets and the Elizabethan balladeers.*]

I wonder if it was the excitement of escape, or the new surroundings, his occasional visits to old English country houses, that brought a new sense of English lyric tradition and changed a wit [Oliver Gogarty] into a poet. The witty sayings that we all repeated, the Rabelaisian verse that we all copied rose out of so great a confused exuberance that I, at any rate, might have foreseen the miracle. Yet no, for a miracle is self-begotten and, though afterwards we may offer swans to Helicon, by its very nature something we cannot foresee or premeditate. Its only rule is that it follows, more often than otherwise, the discovery of a region or a rhythm where a man may escape out of himself. [In *An Offering of Swans*] Oliver Gogarty has discovered the rhythm of Herrick and of Fletcher, something

different from himself and yet akin to himself; and I have been murmuring his "**Non Dolet**," his "**Begone, Sweet Ghost**," and his "**Good Luck**." Here are but a few pages, that a few months have made, and there are careless lines now and again, traces of the old confused exuberance. He never stops long at his best, but how beautiful that best is, how noble, how joyous! (pp. 3-4)

> W. B. Yeats, in a preface to An Offering of Swans, and Other Poems by Oliver St. John Gogarty, 1923. Reprint by Eyre & Spottiswoode, Ltd., 1924, pp. 3-4.

W. B. YEATS (essay date 1930)

[*In the following excerpt from his preface to* Wild Apples, *Yeats notes the unevenness of Gogarty's poetry, but praises the Romantic sense of "hardship borne and chosen out of pride and joy" that informs his best poems.*]

Oliver Gogarty is a careless writer, often writing first drafts of poems rather than poems but often with animation & beauty. He is much like that in his conversation; except that his conversation is wittier & profounder when public events excite him, whereas public events—some incursion of Augustus John, perhaps, benumb his poetry. Why am I content to search through so many careless verses for what is excellent? I do not think that it is merely because they are excellent, I think I am not so disinterested; but because he gives me something that I need and at this moment of time. The other day I was reading Lawrence's description in his 'Revolt of the Desert' of his bodyguard of young Arabs: 'men proud of themselves, and without families. . . . dressed like a bed of tulips;' and because brought up in that soft twilight—'magic casements'; 'syren there'—come down from the great Liberal Romantics, I recognised my opposite, and was startled and excited. The great Romantics had a sense of duty and could hymn duty upon occasion, but little sense of a hardship borne and chosen out of pride and joy. Some Elizabethans had that indeed, though Chapman alone constantly, and after that nobody—until Landor; and after that nobody except when some great Romantic forgot, perhaps under the influence of the Classics, his self-forgetting emotion, and wrote out of character. But certainly nobody craved for it as we do, who sometimes feel as if no other theme touched us. I find it in every poem of Oliver Gogarty that delights me, in the whole poem, or in some astringent adjective. (pp. i-ii)

I recommend Irish Anthologists to select '**Aphorism**' [from *Wild Apples*], which being clear and inexplicable, will be most misjudged. I would be certain of its immortality had it a more learned rhythm and, as it is I have not been able to forget these two years, that Ringsend whore's drunken complaint, that little red lamp before some holy picture, that music at the end. . . . (pp. iii-iv)

> W. B. Yeats, in a preface to Wild Apples by Oliver Gogarty, The Cuala Press, 1930, pp. i-iv.

BABETTE DEUTSCH (essay date 1930)

[*A respected American poet, critic, and translator, Deutsch offers a generally favorable review of* Wild Apples, *but notes a lack of skill that renders Gogarty's poems "engaging" rather than "unforgettable."*]

In his introduction to his old friend's book [*Wild Apples*] AE observes that "a prodigal wit rarely appears the chrysalis out of which we expect the winged lovely creature Poetry to be born'' [see Additional Bibliography]. Oliver Gogarty's verse is one of the instances of such nativity. His tart intellect has for years delighted that wittiest of races to which he belongs, and now he surprises us with the charm of his verse. The alert quality of the poet's mind flashes clearly upon these pages. . . . The lusty injunction, **"To the Maids, Not to Walk in the Wind,"** the gay lines addressed **"To a Friend,"** as, indeed, the general tone of the book, convey the impression of a quick and essentially male intelligence playing in a luminous and open place.

The virility of Gogarty's verse is perhaps more remarkable than its beauty. His metres not seldom limp or move with undue stiffness. His rhymes could be more felicitous, and the strength of his work would gain considerably were his lines more compact. Such a poem as **"The Emperor's Dream"** could be unforgettable. As Gogarty has written it the piece is engaging, but nothing more. It is, nevertheless, plain enough that he responds heartily to all that's lovely, and at moments he snares the bright thing in a net of words.

One fancies that these verses would please the ear, and it is not hard to imagine them recited in that enchanting sing-song Irish poets use. When Mr. Gogarty has learned to please that member at its most critical and fastidious he will doubtless present us with a volume which we can not merely enjoy but also honor.

> *Babette Deutsch, "Tart Fruit," in* New York Herald Tribune Books, *February 9, 1930, p. 10.*

M.D.Z. [MORTON DAUWEN ZABEL] (essay date 1931)

[*Zabel was an American poet, critic, and prominent scholar. From 1928 to 1937 he was associate editor, then editor, of Harriet Monroe's magazine* Poetry, *which was the only journal at that time devoted solely to contemporary poetry. Throughout this period he wrote extensively on English and American poetry. Later in his career, Zabel was influential in increasing the study of North American literature in South America. During the mid-1940s he held the only official professorship on North American literature in Latin America, and wrote two widely used studies of American literature in Portuguese and Spanish. In the following excerpt from his review of* Wild Apples, *Zabel concludes that Gogarty's poetic talent is "authentic within narrow dimensions," and that when Gogarty manages to avoid trite concepts his poems, supported as they are by his knowledge of the classics, are often very good.*]

[*An Offering of Swans* and *Wild Apples*] reveal a talent authentic within narrow dimensions. The poems, turned to a cadence of easy conversational loquacity, are sharpened by a shrewd ability to deduce those lessons in practical values which find normal expression in the aphorism. Gogarty's verse surmounts its limitations of easy frivolity by the candor and succinctness of its judgment. This judgment, moreover, though defined in terms of immediate ordeal and struggle, is supported by the tough fiber of an intelligence schooled in the realism of the Roman lyrists. Something of their lucid vigor blends here with the formal decorum of the English Caroline tradition and the obviously Celtic appeal of direct lyricism. One may mention the sonnet *Non Blandula Illa*, modest stanzas in the cavalier tradition like *Gaze on Me* and *Tell Me Now*, and the pungent quatrains of *Amor*.

This affection for epigram continues in [*Wild Apples*]. However, from among less worthy efforts and occasionally very trite concepts, may be found compositions of freer lyric design,

as in *The Waveless Bay;* or of an austere didactic classicism, as in *Marcus Curtius*. . . . (pp. 350-51)

Apart from its association with the Irish literary tradition, this work is arresting for its capture of an intimate clarity and warmth. Without approximating in any sense the precision of the best formal lyric poets in America, or of Yeats, Gogarty nevertheless overrides the threat of banality and achieves a distinctive tone. The savor of his personal convictions quite invariably supports the taste and temper of his style. (p. 351)

> *M.D.Z. [Morton Dauwen Zabel], "Oliver Gogarty," in* Poetry, *Vol. XXXVII, No. VI, March, 1931, pp. 349-51.*

A. E. (essay date 1933)

[*A key figure in the Irish Literary Renaissance, A. E. (George William Russell) contributed more to the movement through his personality than through his artistry. He was a gifted conversationalist, a popular lecturer, and a generous man who brought many of the members of the Renaissance together. Although his interests were varied, A. E. earned a modest literary reputation based on his mystical poems and his drama* Deirdre. *He was central to the rise of the Irish National Theatre, and, with W. B. Yeats, J. M. Synge, and Lady Gregory, was one of the founders of the Abbey Theatre. Through his work and his charismatic personality, A. E. was an important influence on the writers of the Irish Renaissance, a generation which sought to reduce the influence of English culture and create an Irish national literature. One of Gogarty's closest friends, A. E. called Gogarty "the wildest wit in Ireland," perhaps the most-quoted description of the latter. In the following excerpt from his introduction to* Selected Poems, *A. E. praises Gogarty's poetic artistry, briefly comparing it to his own.*]

I found myself liking Oliver Gogarty when I knew him only as having the wildest wit in Ireland from which nothing in heaven or earth was immune, though often I had reverence for the things he assailed. I never suspected in that rich nature a poet lay hidden, though my intuition should have told me that at the root of all friendships and desires are hidden identities. For all his rich vitality the elements obvious in it seemed incongruous with delicate poetry. An athlete in his youth, an airman in later life, his mind thronged with the knowledge and technique of a specialist, his imagination brimful of Rabelaisian fantasy and that wild wit which in every poet but Heine has made timid the sensitive psyche.

All this was not congruous with poetry. But, among the multitudes he contained, there was a poet, a genie in the innermost who gradually emerged in spite of all the dragons in its path. I was astonished when he began to show us verses so finely carved that his genie seemed to have wrought with words as the Image-maker in his own verse treated the hard jade, making a transient beauty into adamant. (pp. ix-x)

[The] ideal of Oliver's genie was beauty and mystery achieved by precision. His beauty must shine in the sun not in a shade, and its mystery must be its own perfection. That I think is his genie's true intent in its art; but, when it consorts with the crowd of lusty incompatibles in the house of the soul, it is often deflected and becomes witty with the rest, or it listens to scandal and forgets for a time its own ideal. But I always assume that what is best is most real and I find what is best in lovely poems like *The Plum Tree by the House* in which the genie reveals to the poet the manner of its own artistry, to hold fast to the image, to brood on its beauty until it becomes what it contemplates and is itself a blossoming tree. It is not the secret of such art as I have myself, for my genie would melt all form into bodiless spirit. It looks with wonder on its opposite whose art is to project defined and shapely images and which gets its life from this art. That precise carving in words is in the first poem in [*Selected Poems*], where the crab tree grows in the imagination with its stiff, twisted beauty, and, as we read, it becomes as sturdy a dweller in memory as its prototype in earth. Again in the *Coin from Syracuse* how determined the genie is to miss nothing of the hard drawing of the beauty it sees. . . . (pp. x-xi)

Oliver Gogarty has eyes which can see what is most enchanting and alluring in women. He casts a glamour over them, the art which Gainsborough had in painting and which Reynolds, for all his mastery of his craft, had not. How few poets convey to us the enchantment of the women they adored. Their love blurs their art. I doubt if Oliver was in love with any of the women he praises, but, as we read, we feel that we could easily fall in love with the woman he depicts. His cool eye has noticed that second of illumination where the light on limb and dress becomes one with the light in the heart, and he can have no peace until he can give that transience permanence. . . . I some-times think of Herrick after I have read one of Oliver Gogarty's lyrics. The Julia of the English poet is a lovely piece of girl-hood. That is much, but she will never be more to our imag-ination. There is some aristocracy of vision in the Irish poet. He sees the lovely girl, but he suggests, however remotely, the psyche within the flesh. In an instant, she might be trans-figured in the imagination and become the dream stuff out of which goddesses, naiads and nymphs were fashioned. (pp. xii-xiii)

I take so much pleasure in my friend's poetry because it is the opposite to my own. It gives to me some gay and gallant life which was not in my own birthright. He is never the profes-sional poet made dull by the dignity of recognised genius. He has never made a business of beauty: and, because he is dis-interested in his dealings with it, the Muse has gone with him on his walks and revealed to him some airs and graces she kept secret from other lovers who were too shy or too awed by her to laugh and be natural in her presence. (p. xiv)

> A. E., "The Poetry of My Friend," in Selected Poems by Oliver St. John Gogarty, The Macmillan Com-pany, 1933, pp. ix-xiv.

CONRAD AIKEN   (essay date 1937)

[*An American man of letters best known for his poetry, Aiken was deeply influenced by the psychological and literary theories of Sigmund Freud, Havelock Ellis, Edgar Allan Poe, and Henri Bergson, among others, and is considered a master of literary stream of consciousness. In reviews noted for their perceptiveness and barbed wit, Aiken exercised his theory that "criticism is really a branch of psychology." His critical position, according to Rufus A. Blanshard, "insists that the traditional notions of 'beauty' stand corrected by what we now know about the psychology of creation and consumption. Since a work of art is rooted in the personality, conscious and unconscious, of its creator, criticism should deal as much with those roots as with the finished flower." In the following excerpt, Aiken praises Gogarty's accomplishment in* As I Was Going Down Sackville Street.]

If one has been reputed to be a wit, how is one to go about proving it? Wit reported in print is wit bruised, it is like a glass of champagne forgotten overnight and found in the morning; and Gogarty's witticisms are no exception to the sad rule. They are a trifle obtrusively "worked in," in the pattern of [*As I*

Was Going Down Sackville Street], and the threads which in swift talk may have flashed gold or silver now look, alas, a trifle tarnished and thin. Similarly, a brave man, or a gallant lover, or a brilliant surgeon, may not brag of his prowess in these arts, George Moore to the contrary, and here again the legendary hero who turns autobiographer must evaporate a good deal of himself in his own alembic. If he boasts, even by implication, it is almost certain to take a cubit from his—reputedly—heroic statue.

But if Gogarty hasn't always steered the perfect course between these dangers, and now and again makes his reader uncom-fortable for him, especially when he tries too hard to serve the legend, he is also a poet, with a poet's eye, and his book of memoirs is full of good things, and wise and kind ones too. How sound and sensible and, above all, how generous he always is when he talks about poetry—and if not profound (but who is?) at any rate searching. The whole Dublin scene, too, he does really admirably, making it sharp and small again, like the finder of a camera, exactly where Joyce made it phantas-magorically huge—and with Joyce himself sitting in it, more-over, and looking very vivid and tiny precisely because he has been reduced to life-size. And if the portraits of people are uniformly good, and sometimes very moving—notably those of Collins and Griffith—they are also in some instances down-right brilliant. Turgenev would have envied the deer-stalking

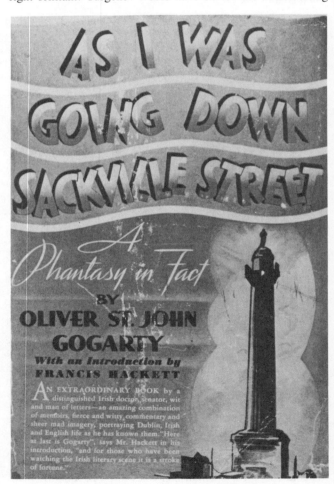

The dust jacket of As I Was Going Down Sackville Street *(American Edition).*

scenes, and Talbot Clifton—infuriating, superbly arrogant as only the English can be, and unforgettable in his simple and fine assumption of so much that nowadays is so hard to assume. Almost as good is the portrait of AE, vatically self-hypnotizing in a monologue as remarkable for its meaninglessness as for its iridescence, or the naughty story of Moore and the naked old lady who burst into the dinner-party in a passion for "a little intelligent conversation." . . . In fact, a delightful book, and if one has a complaint it is only that the moments of quieter and soberer self-revelation are too few, and that Gogarty didn't perhaps stick a little more to his poetry and his medicine, and a little less to his rage against De Valera and the present state of Ireland. Like Ireland itself, a *few* too many circuses, and a *little* too little bread.

> Conrad Aiken, "The Dubliner," *in* The New Republic, *Vol. XCI, No. 1173, May 26, 1937, p. 79.*

CORNELIUS WEYGANDT (essay date 1937)

[*A historian and critic, Weygandt was one of the first American scholars to examine contemporary Irish drama, introducing its major practitioners to American readers in his* Irish Plays and Playwrights *(1913). In the following excerpt, he agrees with W. B. Yeats's judgment (1923) that Gogarty, in spite of the flawed nature of most of his poems, was occasionally capable of producing perfect lyrics in the manner of the Cavalier poets or the Elizabethan balladeers. Weygandt notes certain similarities in attitude between Gogarty and Yeats, and almost apologetically discusses Gogarty as one of his favorite poets.*]

One who should know tells me that Dr. Oliver Gogarty . . . is the third poet of Ireland. "We have Yeats and 'A. E.,'" he said, "and Gogarty." I should rather say that Gogarty is the man who wrote **"Golden Stockings."** That is as winning a poem about a child as we have in all English literature. One thinks of "Noble Lovely Little Peggy" of Prior, and of "Lines to a Lady upon Her Third Birthday" of Lionel Johnson as of its company, but one cannot say that either is a better poem. **"Golden Stockings"** is about a child racing around in a meadow of buttercups. There is sunlight in it, and breeze, and the spring. . . . (p. 238)

The picture of the child in the meadow is good enough in itself. It is made better than good by the simile of little knees bobbing up out of the buttercups like golden pippins tossed out of their leaves by the wind. That is a figure as fresh and fetching as an air of Mozart. It contents us as do all discoveries of beauty. It does not dissipate its effect by carrying us away to other things. It keeps us concerned with what it images, with the child in the meadow of buttercups. The poet makes us, reading, feel as he felt in the seeing, that this is a sight would last through years of blindness.

An Offering of Swans . . . takes its name from the last set of the twenty-three sets of verses that make up the thin volume. **"To the Liffey with the Swans"** is hardly worthy of the circumstances that begot it. Kidnapped by gunmen, and imprisoned in a warehouse by Liffey's side, just above Dublin, Gogarty escaped by the river, and made his way to England. When it was safe for him to come back to Dublin to live he gave two swans to the river that aided and abetted his escape. Yeats tells us this version of the story in his preface to *An Offering of Swans* [see excerpt dated 1923]. There are other versions. What is surer than the correctness of his version is his judgment of the poems in the book. Though he has children of his own, you would not expect Yeats to care greatly for **"Golden Stock-**

ings." That is outside the sorts of poetry that he admires most. Of those sorts are the three all but perfect lyrics he lists as his favorites, **"Non Dolet,"** **"Begone Sweet Ghost,"** and **"Good Luck."** Where his sympathies are enlisted, Yeats's judgment of poetry is unerring. (pp. 238-39)

In the very vein of the Cavalier lyrists is **"Good Luck."** The first stanza is the best stanza of the three, as the first stanza of songs, from the days of the Elizabethan songbooks, is so apt to be the best of all. Stanzas two and three of **"Good Luck"** are, however, only less good than stanza one because that is perfect. The couplet that ends **"Perfection"**:

> Yet, for all the faults of her
> Than Perfection perfecter

is an echo of Francis Thompson's

> Then for her faults you'll fall in love with her.

There is very little, though, in Gogarty, save his fellow-feeling with the Cavalier lyrists, that suggests any other poet. It is only the poetasters, as Dunsany says, that are like each other. The poets are each of his own kind. It is all his own, this style of Gogarty, these clarities, this fall of words. No one else has, to use his own phrase, so "bland" an air, so cool a sunniness about his poetry. . . . [The following couplet] confesses a sentiment that perhaps explains why most of these verses of Gogarty are not so good as their best moments:

> Teach us to save the Spirit's expense
> And win to Fame through indolence.

In the second little gathering of Gogarty's verse, *Wild Apples* . . . , you come upon fresh things with that delighted surprise that is so rare an experience in the reading of minor poetry. His imagination leads him all over the world. At one moment he is in "a sweet air of Persia." At another he is in some "safe Roman croft." At the next he is in "Old days of glory" in Erin. The kinds of beauty Gogarty loves are often aristocratic, "the limestone lordly houses" of yesterday so many of which have been burned since 1916; ladies whose portraits he presents with startling clarity. It isn't often a whole poem of Gogarty is as good as its best parts. It is a bit here and a bit there that you enjoy on turning his pages. You savor the lines that catch and imprison yearning and beauty. "There's hope in the masts at the end of the street" haunts you, and every time you look at poplars after you have read **"Sandymount"** you recall his "votive poplar trees." There are correspondences between thoughts and moods of his and thoughts and moods of Yeats, but the accent of the writing and the fall of words in Gogarty are always his own. He echoes the code that has been growing stronger and stronger in Yeats of admiration for austere and kingly days of old time, and he does not balk at a certain substratum of savagery in them. In **"Castle Corrib"** Gogarty tells us, "The men around me regret the sword." (pp. 239-41)

When it so happens that a poet cares greatly for many of the things for which you, reading, care greatly, you are perhaps prone to set his value higher than less prejudiced sympathy would. Gogarty cares greatly for a damson plum in blossom. . . . His care is my care. His experience is my experience. Every time I pick him up I find some image that has always been a delight to me. So when I read him I am always expecting old adventures of this sort. That makes reading him a gentle sort of excitement and perhaps unsettles the critical judgment. I put this down because I am not quite sure my enthusiasm for his verse is justified.

Had Gogarty lived with these verses of his longer, redreamed and redreamed them; spent his spirit, and his art as a craftsman, upon them, we might have a sheaf of verse from him as memorable in its way as *A Shropshire Lad* in its way. As things are it is remarkable that the busy doctor, the light-hearted wit and the honored statesman should have found time to be the poet he is. (pp. 241-42)

Cornelius Weygandt, *"William Butler Yeats and the Irish Literary Renaissance," in his* The Time of Yeats: English Poetry of To-Day against an American Background, *1937. Reprint by Russell & Russell, 1969, pp. 167-251.**

GERALD GRIFFIN (essay date 1938)

[*In the following excerpt, Griffin discusses the Classical quality of Gogarty's verse, and compares him to the Roman poet Horace for the poignancy and the stoicism of his lyrics. For further discussion of Gogarty's affinities with the Classical poets, see the excerpt by Vivian Mercier (1958).*]

Oliver Gogarty is primarily a poet. It is true that he is frequently 'a rather careless poet,' as Yeats said of him, 'often writing first drafts of poems rather than poems.'

Typical of this carelessness are the lines addressed 'to James Stephens,' which end on a note of banality after opening very exquisitely with the wistful injunction:

> Where are you, spirit, who could pass into our
> hearts and all Hearts of little children, hearts
> of trees and hills and elves?

In his *"Selected Poems"* . . . there are gems like **'The Plum Tree by the House'** and **'The Coin from Syracuse'** which thrill us as they thrilled 'A. E.' But it is especially as a singer of the charms of women that 'A. E.' sees Gogarty's poetic artistry at its best. 'I doubt if Oliver was in love with any of the women he praises,' he says, 'but as we read we feel that we could easily fall in love with the women he depicts. His cool eye has noticed that second of illumination when the light on limb and dress becomes one with the light in the heart, and he can have no peace until he gives that transience permanence.' (pp. 197-98)

But Gogarty's poetic range is not confined to singing the charms of beautiful women. He can be alternately as poignant as Horace and as stoical as Horace too when he broods on the evanescence of beauty and the tragedy of death. And then he can capture another mood of Horace—that of frivolous dalliance with wanton women. (p. 198)

The brevity, ease, simplicity, and melodious beat of true lyrical poetry permeate that most exquisite of his poems—**'Leda and the Swan.'** For deft and delicate delineation of a perfect picture in words the stanza beginning with these four lines is superb:

> Apple Blossoms under
> Hills of Lacedaemon
> With the snow beyond them
> In the still blue air—

In *The Oxford Book of Modern Verse* Yeats gives a vivid account of Gogarty's dramatic escape from his captors, and continues:

> His poetry fits the incident, a gay, stoical—no,
> I will not withhold the word—heroic song. Irish
> by tradition and many ancestors, I love, though
> I have nothing to offer but the philosophy they

deride, swashbucklers, horsemen, swift indifferent men; yet I do not think that this is the sole reason, good reason though it is, why I give him considerable space and think him one of the great lyric poets of the age.

It is true that, to quote 'A. E.' again, Gogarty 'is never the professional poet made dull by the dignity of recognized genius. He has never made a business of beauty; and because he is disinterested in his dealings with it, the muse has gone with him on his walks and revealed to him some airs and graces she kept secret from other lovers who were too shy or too awed by her to be natural in her presence.'

My impression about Gogarty is that his laughter in the presence of the muse is often assumed through fear of appearing too tender or emotional and that he frequently strikes a note of ribaldry or cynicism in the mood of certain lines of Horace's 'Iter ad Brundusium' in order to hide from us his pent-up poetic depth of feeling.

There is even a deep vein of poetic emotion running through many passages of his famous volume of reminiscences—*As I Was Going Down Sackville Street*. The pictures he conjures up of the lovely environment of Dublin, with its crescent bay and its mountains, and his delicate limning of the background of Kylemore House and Renvyle House in Connemara are on a par with L.A.G. Strong's pen-portrait of Dun Laoghaire (ci-devant Kingstown) in *The Sea Wall*.

But to pass from the poetic vein to the facts recorded in *As I Was Going Down Sackville Street*—an autobiographical document of intense interest. What a feast of wit and what a wealth of authentic detail about all grades of society in Dublin for over a quarter of a century! Saints and scholars, poets and artists, pure-souled patriots and time-serving politicians, cranks and fanatics, lunatics and demi-lunatics—an endless throng of the noble, the ignoble, the feckless and the foolish—they are all immortalized in this book.

Himself the 'Buck Mulligan' of the world-famous *Ulysses*, Gogarty now tells in this book with a reminiscent chuckle of the rollicking days when he and Joyce were fellow-students and composed limericks and swilled pints of porter in dens in which the 'underworld' and the 'half-world' of Dublin foregathered. (pp. 199-200)

And then we have his quaint sketch of Endymion, Dublin's village idiot, with his bizarre garb and his sabre, gravely obsessed with his chimerical problems as he strides to and fro through Dublin, and steers his way around with the aid of a compass, although every street and lane of the city are familiar to him. Endymion has stalked through the pages of many books about Dublin, but in none is he so life-like as in Gogarty's work. A man of whimsical humour himself, Gogarty fell in with Endymion's odd whims.

Oliver Gogarty is one of the dramatis personæ of Moore's *Hail and Farewell*, but Moore figures far more vividly in Oliver Gogarty's *As I Was Going Down Sackville Street*. And what a comical figure he cuts too—almost as comical as Endymion!

Another figure of a Dublin that has passed away is embalmed for us in Gogarty's book—Philip Frances Little, the religious maniac and poet who wore a hair-shirt and a huge pectoral cross—the self-appointed censor of morals who suffered from a frustration of sex—the Dublin Savonarola whose appearance in a tram was the signal for all the young women aboard to make a dash for the pavement with screaming precipitation—

in order to flee from the wrath to come—to flee from the holy hooligan's fulminations against short skirts, glad necks, powder and lipstick.

Nothing is immune—nobody is immune from the shafts of Oliver Gogarty's impish sense of humour and from his devastating wit. He even turns his shafts against himself occasionally. Nay, he even pokes fun at the man whom he, I believe, reveres and loves most in Dublin—William Butler Yeats. (pp. 200-01)

Oliver Gogarty is at present busily engaged on a book entitled *In the Footsteps of Saint Patrick.* In a letter which I received from him some time back he stated that it was very difficult to follow the trail of the Saint all over Ireland, as he seemed 'Like Boyle Roche's bird to have been in two places at once.' (p. 205)

> Gerald Griffin, "Doctor Oliver St. John Gogarty," in his The Wild Geese: Pen Portraits of Famous Irish Exiles, 1938. Reprint by Norwood Editions, 1978, pp. 196-205.

CLIFTON FADIMAN (essay date 1940)

[*Fadiman became one of the most prominent American literary critics during the 1930s with his insightful and often caustic book reviews for* The Nation *and* The New Yorker *magazines. He also reached a sizable audience through his work as a radio talk-show host from 1938 to 1948. In the following excerpt, Fadiman praises* Going Native, *noting that Gogarty's lively personality pervades the book, overshadowing its weaknesses.*]

Oliver St. John Gogarty reminds one somehow of Laurence Sterne. The Reverend Mr. Sterne and the irreverent Gogarty have much in common: a liking for unconventional company; a glancing, bizarre, allusive style; egotism; a mind aflutter with whimsies, birdlike in its sudden darts and sallies; and the same delight in the literary strip tease, for neither Sterne nor Gogarty (who calls himself Gideon Ouseley in his new book, "**Going Native**") ever quite climaxes his delicious Cytherean adventures. (As was said of his compatriot George Moore, Gogarty seems to be among those who do not kiss—and tell.) Though Francis Hackett has dubbed Gogarty a Panurge, I deem him more nearly cousin to Sterne than to Rabelais; his wild wit is not really robustious, being indecorous more often than ribald. Withal, remember that this Dublin bhoyo is the one of whom it has been said that you have to ply him with whiskey to sober him up.

"**Going Native**"—suppose we finish this Sterne parallel—might have been entitled "The Sentimental Journey Through Country-House England." The Cavalier Gogarty, ill at ease in De Valera's Roundhead democracy, escaped to England, where they order things better. There he fell half in love with the English damme-monde, a world in which Restoration vicars, no less than lords and ladies, live, love, and talk as they please, making an art of rudeness and an aesthetic way of life out of materialism—all most un-Irish indeed.

I do not propose to summarize this wayward Gogartian travelogue. When not too eccentric to be readable, it is diverting, glittering with neat literary phrases, and pied with conversation that, were not Meredith his own best parody, would sound like a parody of Meredith. . . .

Like many willful but genuine personalities, Gogarty is often irritating and puzzling, but when you get the hang of him (he gives no helpful hints) he exudes a special flavor all his own.

He doesn't try to be everyone's dish. As he might say himself in one of his feebler moments, Oliver is an acquired taste. (p. 66)

> Clifton Fadiman, "Gogarty Invades England—Three Novels," in The New Yorker, Vol. XVI, No. 2, February 24, 1940, pp. 66-8.*

ROBERT GREACEN (essay date 1946)

[*In the following excerpt Greacen, an Irish poet, reviews Gogarty's poetry collection* Perennial. *Greacen dismisses Gogarty as a mere "entertainer" encumbered by the "unfortunate" legacy of W. B. Yeats and applauded only by the "spurious and effete" writers of the Irish Renaissance, whose works, Greacen believes, have long since been superseded by the more significant contributions of the younger generation of Irish writers. However, the critic does approve of those poems in* Perennial *in which Gogarty employs the ballad meter.*]

Dr. Oliver St. John Gogarty's publishers state, by way of blurb, that his poetry—

> has received the unstinted praise of William Butler Yeats, George Moore, James Stephens, AE, and John Masefield.

But the opinions of the big guns of yesterday—and especially that of the 'archpoet'—all very good fellows at giving a testimonial to entertaining friends, can hardly awe any longer even the reader who has only a cursory acquaintance with modern Irish literature. Dr. Gogarty is primarily an entertainer—a wit, a controversialist, a specialist in Dublin conversational sparkle.

Perennial suggests that some of his poems may be hardy annuals. In his ballads, Dr. Gogarty is at his best, for the ballad is nearest to direct speech, to the talk of everyman in the pub. He writes briskly of Bill Baveler who 'kept the Brown Stone Inn'. But perhaps it is in the racing swagger of 'Farrell O'Reilly' that he most felicitously sings the hard-riding Irish gentleman. . . .

Dr. Gogarty achieves a delicate sensuality in '**Leda and the Swan**'. In the shorter poems there is little fire: they are not so much damp squibs as shrivelled faggots. Wit has skipped off and leaves us the residue of sentiments that were better-handled by more original minds thirty years ago. Fortunately there is a good sprinkling of ballad metre. (p. 189)

> Robert Greacen "Two Irish Poets," in Poetry Quarterly, Vol. 8, No. 3, Autumn, 1946, pp. 188-91.*

MAX EASTMAN (essay date 1954)

[*An American essayist, poet, and editor, Eastman was a leftist commentator on American life and literature who greatly influenced American criticism after the first World War. In 1911 and 1917, respectively, he helped found two notable Marxist periodicals,* The Masses *and* The Liberator, *which he edited and which were subjected to government censorship on charges of sedition. At one time a member of the Communist Party, Eastman eventually rejected communism after witnessing firsthand the realities of Stalinist Russia, becoming an outspoken opponent of Marxist-Leninism. As a literary scholar, he is best known for his critical text* The Enjoyment of Poetry *(1913). In the following excerpt from a review of* It Isn't This Time of Year at All!, *Eastman commends Gogarty for his charm and outspokenness in this "un-premeditated autobiography," which contains anecdotes about all of the major figures of the Irish Renaissance.*]

All of the literary vanguard will have to read this charming book [*It Isn't This Time of Year at All!*]. Not because Gogarty has anything pleasant to say about them. On the contrary, he dismisses their way of producing literature as "the outdoor lunatic asylum method." But he has so many and such intimate things to say about their gods—particularly about James Joyce, with whom he lived for a time in an abandoned coast-guard tower outside Dublin. (p. 4)

In times of confusion there is so much pussyfooting among intellectuals, so many of them trying harder to guess right than say what they think, that Gogarty's outspokenness is vitally refreshing. Others about whom he makes pungent and personal remarks (not always unfavorable) are: George Moore, George Russell, Yeats, Dunsany, James Stephens—"the lightest lyrist of them all"—Augustus John, Horace Plunkett, Arthur Griffith, Lady Gregory, Tallulah Bankhead, Winston Churchill—"a blub-faced fellow"—Lord Birkenhead, De Valera. What between literature and revolution, little Ireland has played a big role in the life of our times. And Gogarty, besides having a role of his own as athlete, physician, poet, politician—Senator Gogarty, if you can believe it—has been good friends, or enemies, with all the players.

He sees them with a witty zest that is hard in a brief review to illustrate. Yeats, he tells us, once remarked that George Moore's face looked like a face carved out of a turnip. "But don't get the impression," he adds, "that Yeats was vindictive. He would never have made that remark had not Moore first described him as looking like an umbrella left at a picnic."

The book rises to a dramatic climax in Gogarty's account of an attempt to kidnap and murder him, his feelings and remarks, his ingenious escape from four men guarding him with guns in a dark cellar. Then it subsides into a dreamily philosophic conclusion. They may be unpremeditated, these memoirs, but they are mighty well arranged.

I would omit the first two or three pages, where the author puts on a show of being more haphazard-minded than he is—perhaps as a result of "trying to live a dactylic life when you are born a spondee." For Gogarty is that much out of tune with his name. At any rate, the reader must not be deterred by these first few pages, which ought to be witty but aren't. There is wit inside the book. There is poetry. There are gorgeous prejudices. There are lots of delightful little stories about people you know or wish you did. You like the author and you read his book with a smile. (pp. 4, 31)

> Max Eastman, "With Wit and Gorgeous Prejudices," in The New York Times Book Review, February 7, 1954, pp. 4, 31.

GEORGE DILLON   (essay date 1955)

[*Dillon was a Pulitzer Prize-winning American poet and, at one time, an editor of* Poetry *magazine. In the following excerpt he discusses Gogarty's* Collected Poems, *stating that the poems reveal Gogarty's excellent sense of proportion and his Classical attitude. Dillon also discusses Gogarty's relationship to W. B. Yeats, and their influence upon one another. For further discussion of the role Yeats played in Gogarty's poetic career, see the excerpts by A. Norman Jeffares (1960) and James F. Carens (1972).*]

For Dr. Gogarty, who once described the peasants of a certain region as looking "not only Pre-Celtic but Pre-Anything," the problem [in his *Collected Poems*] has not been to resist popular

sentiment but rather to keep his own virtuosity in hand. There is no denying that his powers of improvisation, strongly encouraged by the group of brilliant friends who were his immediate audience, have sometimes led to diffuseness: Few poems are more entertaining than *Europa and the Bull;* its effect is in the combination of bucolic simplicity and the mock-heroic, but this is somewhat strained by passages of fine-drawn lyricism in the manner of Hodgson's *Eve* or his own *Leda,* and by philosophic asides in an earnest tone: Gogarty wants to have it four or five ways, and nearly succeeds. Yet he is capable of succinctness and measure; indeed he is one of those writers who, in periods of extreme attitudes, help to restore a sense of proportion. His poetry influenced by the externals of romanticism, has nevertheless borne witness to the spirit of classicism; it has been his role to be objective, lucid, undogmatic, equable yet sanguine—not in an aloof, exemplary way, but with appreciation of the contemporary ferment and as one partly involved in it. He acknowledges a primary debt to Yeats for "anything I owe / In the art of making songs," and at times the influence of the "bone-bare" later Yeats combines oddly but effectively with his own expansive rhythms. But no doubt the older poet received much in return on those occasions "When we sat by the household hearth / And, as the autumn glow went out, / Bandied the whole bright world about." Celebrating chiefly courage, imagination, the rigors of love ("a throe / That throws us all") and the laughter that defeats hypocrisy, he is content to "walk for a few paces," and approaches the mystery without flattery or defiance. . . . He is especially good in the poems written to individual friends, such as the sonnet *To A. E. Going to America.* . . . For readers who know something of its background, this *Collected Poems* . . . has the interest of a journal or an autobiography. It makes clear his real importance among the fabulous group of Dubliners whom he, almost alone, survives. (pp. 288-89)

> George Dillon, "Style and the Many-Headed Beast," in Poetry, Vol. LXXXVI, No. 5, August, 1955, pp. 287-95.*

VIVIAN MERCIER   (essay date 1958)

[*Mercier, an advisory editor of* The James Joyce Quarterly, *has written extensively on Irish and French literature—most notably, on the work of Samuel Beckett and Joyce. In the following excerpt he discusses the influence of the Classical poets, especially Horace, upon Gogarty's poetry. For further discussion of Gogarty's affinities with the Classical poets, see the excerpt by Gerald Griffin (1938).*]

"I remember," writes Gogarty in [*A Weekend in the Middle of the Week*] "trying to persuade the poet Yeats to recognize Macaulay. . . . In vain. . . . I went away disconsolate, for if Lord Macaulay was not a poet all my fine frenzies were foolish vanities." Gogarty meant by "my fine frenzies" his enthusiasm for Macaulay and not his own poetry, but he undoubtedly shared many of Macaulay's poetic faults. . . . Like many another good Latinist besides Macaulay, Gogarty was prone to write a poetry of statement rather than suggestion, of rhetoric rather than sensibility, leaning too heavily on ready-made symbols and facile literary or mythological allusions. Yeats, who was unable to master Latin, Greek, or any other language except English, acquired from his father a respect for Classical learning which clearly influenced his unduly high estimate of Gogarty's work. He called it "a gay, stoical—no, I will not withhold the word—heroic song". The first two adjectives, I think, are justified, but in using the third Yeats seems unaware just how much Gogarty traded in Greek and Roman cliché.

Latin scholarship has held danger for English-speaking poets in every generation. They may be led to overwork the Romance vocabulary like Milton, for instance, though that was one error Macaulay avoided. A more insidious peril is the writing of Latin verse as an exercise, for by the schoolmaster's definition good Latin verse cannot be original—it must be Virgilian, Ovidian, Horatian. Hence many modern Latinists—especially those of Irish stock—have excelled only in pastiche and parody. One aspect of Gogarty's talent links him with parodists like "Father Prout," William Maginn, and his Trinity College, Dublin, Latin professor, R. Y. Tyrrell.

Then again, a great deal of chilly rhetoric and mechanical versification by Latinists writing English is chargeable to two simple facts: the first, that the normal word-order of both Greek and Latin is radically different from that of English; the second, that Classical poets were free to depart entirely from normal word-order for the sake of meter or rhetorical effect. Hence we find Gogarty multiplying inversions thus:

> Empyrean is the source
> of indomitable will.
> God the runner to his course
> Holds, and urges on until
> Lips and face of blood are drained. . . .

Admittedly, this quotation comes from a highly official ode written "at the request of the Irish Government." The practice of Pindar—"the prize wind-bag of all ages," Pound has called him—doubtless offers precedents for all this and more.

Yet there are certain qualities, very highly prized by contemporary British and American criticism—"tone", irony (one facet of tone) and wit—which no poet who has read and imitated Classical authors, especially Horace, with insight can ever wholly lack. (pp. 35-6)

[It] was Horace, both as man and as poet, for whom Gogarty showed the deepest affinity, by far. He had enough Latin scholarship for Horace to be "of use" to him; however, that was only the beginning. One doesn't think of Gogarty as being excessively urbane, but was Horace? Cyril Connolly describes him as "irritable", and certainly both Horace and Gogarty could be meanly cruel to their enemies, male or female. Gogarty's prose works bristle with spite against De Valera, Lady Gregory, George Moore, and many another, though, again like Horace, he could express himself nobly when writing about men he admired: A. E., Arthur Griffith, Yeats, and, in his new book, Dr. William Spickers.

It has often been said that Horace represents a state of mind which comes with urbanization and imperialism; how, then, could Gogarty develop the Horatian outlook in a provincial city like Dublin and in such a notoriously non-urbanized country as Ireland? If we stop and think for a moment, we shall realize that Gogarty's Dublin was probably about the same size as Horace's Rome, Pope's London, or the Alexandria of Theocritus. The London or New York of today is far too big and too specialized for Horatianism; is there any living British or American poet who is genuinely intimate with political and commercial big shots among his fellow-citizens in the way Horace or Gogarty was? Or if there is such a poet, does he dare to write poetry belittling the ambitions and the global anxieties of his friends? Gogarty himself found New York too big for him, though he tried to cut the problem down to size by reducing the city to Park Avenue and Third Avenue; even so, he couldn't make poetry out of it, because he could not establish *personal* contact with enough of its myriad aspects.

In the seventh poem of the second book of *Satires*, Horace has painted a mocking word-picture of himself through the mouth of a slave which shows what a bundle of contradictions he was and every true Horatian must be. An urban sophisticate who yearns for his farm; a man who professes to rate personal affection far higher than wealth or power, yet draws his closest friends from the ranks of the wealthy and the powerful; one who prides himself on his frugality and economy, yet succumbs to luxury and extravagance; in short, a divided mind, neither a complete moralist nor a complete hedonist, capable of writing poetry from either point of view—and in the long run readier to mock than to praise, to analyze than to act. Just such a personality was Gogarty, in whom Yeats professed to see a man of action. Though Gogarty was swimming from a firing squad and Horace running from a battle, the most famous military exploit of each was a strategic retreat.

Such a talent may well be at its best in mock-heroic writing. Pope's masterpiece is *The Rape of the Lock,* and Gogarty's may yet prove to be **Leda and the Swan.** A masterpiece of sustained tone it certainly is, running a razor's edge between irony and farce. . . . Why do the critics who like to talk about wit, irony, and ambiguity never take up this poem, though they love to study Yeats's companion piece? If you think Gogarty's poem was easier to write than the Yeats sonnet, just try to produce a similar *tour de force.* A man who can write like that need not be considered too boastful when he claims to have learned something of the art of poetry from Yeats. (pp. 38-40)

> *Vivian Mercier, "Oliver St. John Gogarty," in Poetry, Vol. XCIII, No. 1, October, 1958, pp. 35-40.*

A. NORMAN JEFFARES   (lecture date 1960)

> [*Jeffares is an Irish educator and essayist whose scholarship ranges in interest from the poetry of Geoffrey Chaucer to twentieth-century literature. His major scholarly concern, though, is the life and work of W. B. Yeats, about whom he has written several important critical works. Jeffares is also one of the few critics who have given serious attention to Gogarty's poetry. In the following excerpt from a lecture delivered in 1960, he divides Gogarty's poems into three groups: descriptions of place, descriptions of Irish scenery as seen through an Irish temperament, and poems written out of simple knowledge of self. Jeffares also discusses Gogarty's relationship with Yeats and, like James F. Carens (1972), concludes that Gogarty's verses represent a unique blending of objectivity and emotion.*]

[Gogarty's] poetry records exuberantly the emotional fullness of this life, records the moments of intense perception that charged his batteries for facing the solemnities of life and death as cavalierly as possible. (p. 157)

His **Collected Poems** appeared in 1951, the volume containing 184 poems. Gogarty's revisions, though not on the scale of those of George Moore or Yeats, do present bibliographical problems and so he is best read in this volume containing groupings which differ from the divisions made in earlier books—*Odes and Addresses, Earth and Sea, Satires and Facetiae, Love and Beauty, Life and Death,* and *Elegies.*

This would be considered a dangerous spread of subject by some of our contemporary critics, who confuse solemnity with seriousness, and yet memorable poetry does emerge from these apparently disparate **Collected Poems**. It is, perhaps, best not

A letter from Gogarty to James Joyce, signed "Caddie Rou-selle." Reprinted by permission of Cornell University Library.

But he came into his major strength once he began to combine both sides of his poetic character into the poetry written after 1917 up to his death in 1939. Gogarty, on the contrary, began from a position of balance: he wrote of places he loved, he wrote out of sensitivity or coarseness as he pleased: but like Yeats he wrote in part out of gesture, and, like Yeats, his truth came into focus when he achieved simplicity and knew rather than explored or poetically exploited himself.

Poetry written thus forms the third division of Gogarty's poetry and ultimately it is the most important. It weds a tension in its author. It has the direct speech and economy of classicism, yet it captures romantic awareness of the immediacy of life. Its basis is the realisation that 'Man is in love and loves what vanishes'. It says this, but does not add 'What more is there to say?': its romantic vocabulary, sometimes carried easily, sometimes very uneasily indeed by its classical syntax, served both the poet's objective mind as well as the emotional impulses and instincts of his human heart.

Poems of the first kind, then, are basic, and they depend, as does so much Irish poetry, upon visualisation. Gogarty recounted an early experience in school which relates to this:

> There was an essay to be written about a country fair during the writing of which I had a vision of sorts: I could see a plain with banners and many coloured pennons waving over white tents; some dim association perhaps with the sign of the Brian Boru [Inn]. I saw, although I did not realize it then, that all writing depends on seeing and then projecting the scene graphically.

This power of visualising informs all his poems of place. Many of them deal with water, they reflect their subject succinctly, they are deceptively easy. Many of them people their places with the Danish invaders who were finally defeated by Brian Boru at Clontarf in 1014. Gogarty had gone to school with Tom Kettle, who regarded himself as a descendant of those Danes, but as one who had come in and stayed. As a boy Gogarty himself imagined the arrival of these invaders along the banks of the Liffey and the Tolka near his home Fairfield, originally Daneswell, at Glasnevin: later in his poetry they become symbolically part of the general corruption of the land which comes with city-dwelling. **'Liffey Bridge'** catches this mood graphically. . . . Dublin, the town of the Ford of the Hurdles, is well sited for such a poem, for as you look down along the Liffey—away from the city set neatly and colourfully along its grey quays—to the east you see Howth, Ben Edair, the headland stretching away out into the clear distance of the unsullied sea. The connection between Howth and Dublin is stressed again in **'Fog Horns'**, a poem which moved between contemporary steamers working slowly from the bay into the Liffey mouth and those historic Danes who 'Took a very great prey / Of women from Howth'. In **'High Tide at Malahide'** he again casts before his imagination (fed with his reading for his book on St. Patrick) the dramatic problem of the identity of the ships entering this estuary north of Howth. . . . (pp. 160-63)

His poems of place are often historically peopled, and **'Glenasmole'**, the Irish name of this valley of the thrushes outside Dublin, moves from description of the mild bends of the river in the valley to an ancient battle ambush. Again, **'New Bridge'** describes a Liffey bridge at Droichead Nua but moves into imaginings of 'The long grey lines of steel' which crossed there long ago, all colours and caparison. This poem links up with

to discuss it here under his different headings, or even chronologically, but to consider it under three other divisions. First of all, there are the poems which we look for in any Irish writer: descriptions of actual places in Ireland. From Goldsmith to Allingham, from Yeats to Patrick Kavanagh this vein runs deeply through Irish poetry. Gogarty knew that this, however, though it be an elemental, innate part of an Irish writer's personal emotional equipment, is but one face of the coin:

> Truth to tell, there are two Irelands. One is a geographical land of beauty, the other is a state of mind. And what is so annoying is that they are for the native inextricably that.

In the second category of his poetry he captures a good deal of that elusive state of mind. It is probably because he writes much of his poetry in order to portray Irish scenery and his own delight in it, and much of it to represent Irish temperament through his own ebullient *persona* that he is, to English eyes, a minor poet of the kind Yeats would have been had he ceased writing in 1899. Up till then Yeats wrote upon Irish scenery and upon beauty as seen through mists of symbolism by a sensitive but self-defeated idealistic lover. Then after 1900 he turned to the opposite extreme: political hatred, the coarse cynicism and bare negativity of a bitterly disappointed lover.

'Portrait with Background' describing Dermot, who brought Strongbow and Henry to Ireland.... This poetry in part is an exercise of digging into his inherited past: each image of the past has gone to his making, and peopling these places is part of a continuous process which probably owed much to Yeats's rediscovery of his own ancestors and Anglo-Irish history. Gogarty, 'the wild man' in him cut off from a fully Anglo-Irish ascendancy background or a fully native tradition, seeks kinship with Norse as well as Norman images of the past.

Within the general category of descriptive poetry Gogarty has range and flexibility. **'Sub Ilice'** catches echoes of Browning's talking aloud; **'Fresh Fields'** ... gives us the excitement and clarity of Marvell's 'green Thought in a green Shade' while the mind is equally withdrawn into its happiness. **'The Phoenix'** carries exuberantly lyrical Elizabethan echoes: **'The Waveless Bay'** has the sure simplicity of Browning's 'Parting at Morning'.... **'Between Brielle and Manasquan'**, a romantic picture of old sea-dogs, is paralleled by the Australian poet Kenneth Slessor's poems on retired sailors by the shores of Sydney Harbour, by Dylan Thomas's Captain Cat in *Under Milk Wood*. (pp. 163-65)

Two poems of place bridge the gap between his descriptive poems and poems of attitude, of the Irish state of mind. **'To the Liffey with Swans'** commemorates a famous incident in Gogarty's life as a Senator of the Irish Free State during the civil war which followed the signing of the 1922 Treaty between those who accepted the treaty's creation of the twenty-six country Free State and the extreme Republicans. Gogarty was kidnapped from his home at gunpoint in January 1923 and taken to a house by the Liffey near Chapelizod to be shot. He threw his coat over two of his captors in the darkness and hurled himself into the river, emerging lower down on the same side and, thus escaping, dedicated to the Liffey a brace of swans which he afterwards released upon the river. He did his best in the creation of the new state.... But there were moments, no doubt accelarated by the burning of Renvyle [Gogarty's seventeenth century country house in Connemara] (and with it his books and papers and a portrait of his mother) in the civil war, when he wondered how much had been lost in the change. But the nearest he allows himself this reflection is **'The Dublin-Galway Train'** where the towns come sharply into focus across the central plain, and the train's dignity is contrasted favourably with the change brought by the closer community enforced by a joltingly democratic bus which symbolises levelling change at work in Irish life.

It is time to leave these two descriptive categories and watch Gogarty in his classico-romantic poetry, in particular in his relations to man—and woman. (pp. 166-67)

His love poems (he said 'the best poets are they who praised women best') have the ease of Horace and the same amount, perhaps, of sincerity. His Ninde, Lydia, Hermione, and the rest have Horatian identity: but some poems, such as **'Back from the Country'**, please with an affectionate note of genuine domesticity, others, like **'Golden Stockings'**, retain the Wordsworthianly pleasure-filled poignancy of a moment's visual experience; and others again catch a deeper note from Yeats; **'Thinking Long'**, for instance, echoes 'When You are Old and Grey'.

These two Irish poets offer many interesting parallels. Yeats's superb 'Lullaby', a poem of three stanzas of six lines each, deals with Paris, Tristram, and the Swan: Gogarty's **'Good Luck'** deals in its three similar stanzas with Atalanta, Iseult,

and the poet himself. The first stanzas of each poem use images of gold and red, the second both deal with the effect of the magic potion, though the third part company.

Such minor resemblances are more than fortuitous: Gogarty and Yeats were, after all, close friends.... Gogarty's vitality and gay outrageous speech struck a responsive chord from the older poet, who saw him a swashbuckling cavalier, learned in the classics yet a man of action: gay, stoical, and heroic. And from Yeats Gogarty said he had learned something of poetry.

Small wonder, then, that phrases constantly echo between their work in the twenties and thirties. Dublin literary gossip has long held that Yeats rewrote many of Gogarty's poems (Johnson's reputation towered over Goldsmith's in a similar way and it was not at first thought that Goldsmith's poetry was his own), but Professor Giorgio Melchiori is writing a book on Yeats which argues that Gogarty supplied ideas which Yeats developed in several poems. (pp. 167-68)

'Limestone and Water' achieves the dignity of Yeats's simple yet majestic descriptions of his own tower; and there are many other verbal echoes, and images shared. Because the men were friends; because, too, Dublin had the essential requirement for a literary renaissance. It was a society small enough for knowledge and skill to be shared among the elect, where literary personality could prevail within its own right: an appreciative yet critical audience which knew and was known by its writers. It appreciated rhetoric used as gesture, and this, ultimately, was what Gogarty shared with Yeats. (p. 170)

After Yeats's death in January 1939 Gogarty began his **'Elegy on the Death of the Archpoet'** which sums up the worst of death as the loss of friends, places Yeats with his other lost friends and muses on his own coming death....

Gogarty has probably eluded serious critical attention because of this habit of being gay about matters in which he felt deeply. (He was once called 'a lazy body' in the Senate by a Minister, but the Minister wisely did not take up Gogarty's newspaper challenge to a competition in running, swimming and flying an aeroplane.) This paradoxical side of him, perhaps based on a mixture of energy and contemplation, emerged in his epigram **'To Petronius Arbiter'**: ...

> Teach us to save the Spirit's expense,
> And win to Fame through indolence.

Gogarty was not solemn: he hated to run the risk of boring by portentousness. The solution lay for him in a quicksilver mind, in a cavalier attitude: it naturally demanded that he write with ease.... (p. 171)

This attitude may sometimes have concealed only too successfully the very real generosity in the man who writes with Elizabethan ease and appreciation **'To A.E. Going to America'**.... It is an attitude which permits much flexibility, which allows him to write with metaphysical casualness **'To the Fixed Stars'**.... (p. 172)

It is an attitude, too, which encouraged him to construct strong lines:

> Then do not shudder at the knife
> That Death's indifferent hand drives home,
> But with the Strivers leave the Strife,
>   Nor, after Caesar, skulk in Rome.

He had learned to write English in classical metres, sapphics and anapaests particularly; his classical training had taught him to watch his endings; his cadences are often superb; his architectonic skill can be forced into giving scope for discursive playing with his subject in longer poems like **'Leda and the Swan', 'Europa and the Bull',** and **'The Mill at Naul'.** This wit can successfully adopt the tone of earlier poets, as in the seventeenth-century wit of 'Begone, sweet Ghost, O get you gone! / Or haunt me with your body on.' And all because he saw his poetry as a gesture. Count Mirabel in Disraeli's *Sybil* was equally careless of the dullards with his gay *Vive la Bagatelle,* his advice to take care of the circulation. Mr Ulick O'Connor's [see excerpt dated 1963] sympathetic biography has shown Gogarty walking the wards as well as Sackville Street and in this admirable book his serious outlook on life emerges. This is the real justification for taking his poetry equally seriously, with all the virtues which can emerge when this kind of versatile renaissance man speaks directly out of sentiment, not sentimentality. The proper parallel is with Goldsmith's realisation in *The Deserted Village* that he would never achieve his desire of returning home to Ireland; for this poem allows the essential Goldsmith to speak out of heartfelt sentiment. Yeats achieved this kind of clarity in the last few poems he wrote in which he simply saw the actions and ideas of his life clearly and finally before him, asked himself the point of it all, and said he knew no answer to what lay beyond his approaching death. What is interesting in Gogarty is that this, the testing kind of clarity, has an innate gentleness. This is what he would have wished as epitaph, to be considered as his intimates described him: 'A gentle man on Earth / And gentle 'mid the Shades.' This quality emerges very clearly in the poem **'Death May be Very Gentle'.** . . . It is not altogether unexpected, if we concede that ultimately, beneath the persiflage, and permitting its airy heights, there was, and had to be, as basis, a bedrock of belief. This is what causes Gogarty to rise above mere cliché when he advances the equable acceptance of death; it encourages him to applaud and appreciate, and in so doing to seem (even in an angry age) a very memorable minor poet indeed. . . . (pp. 172-74)

> *A. Norman Jeffares, "Oliver St. John Gogarty, Irishman," in his* The Circus Animals: Essays on W. B. Yeats, *Macmillan, 1970, pp. 147-74.*

ULICK O'CONNOR (essay date 1963)

[*In the following excerpt Gogarty's biographer discusses Gogarty's play* Blight, *observing that in spite of its propagandistic intent, the play demonstrates that Gogarty possessed a genuine flair for comic dialogue and the creation of comic characters. O'Connor also notes that there is strong evidence that* Blight *was an important source of inspiration for Sean O'Casey's slum plays. For further discussion of Gogarty's skill as a dramatist, see the excerpt by James F. Carens (1972).*]

Gogarty's medical duties brought him into direct contact with the conditions in the slums. As a student and intern, he had come across houses with one lavatory for seventy people. He knew the frightful incidences of tuberculosis and venereal disease among the tenement dwellers. The fate of little children growing up in these living hells tortured the side of his nature that was compassionate and kind. . . To try and arouse some sense of the reality of slum life among his fellow townsmen, Gogarty decided to write a play about tenement life.

Blight opened at the Abbey Theatre on the 11th of December, 1917. The production caused a sensation. There had been rumours during the week that the play might be suppressed because of its hard-hitting dialogue.

"Such an audience," stated the *Irish Independent* next day, "has not been at the Abbey since the night Shaw's *Blanco Posnet* was first produced." (pp. 166-67)

The *Independent* critic went on to say,

> **'Blight'** is the Tragedy of Dublin—the horrible, terrible, creeping crawling spectre that haunts the slumdom of the capital of Ireland. It is not horror for horror's sake. That charge may not be levelled against the authors with any hope that it can be maintained, for if I understand aright the meaning of the painters of this lurid picture it is this: Slumdom is the nest of vice; charity as a palliative is no cure. The Charity in fact that endows hospitals and helps those institutions to extend their premises and cater for increased cases is misdirected Charity. Away with the seat of the disease!

The *Irish Times* thought the play "revealed the horrors of slumdom in the naked light of Truth." (p. 167)

The play deals with the life of a Dublin labourer Stanislaus Tully who is awaiting a court award as a result of injuries he incurred when a bag of cement fell on his back. He is living on credit, in expectation of the damages he will receive and carefully nursing his injuries in the meantime so as to extort the maximum of compensation when the time comes. . . . When he wins his case, and receives his award, he becomes a slum landlord himself. In the last act he is shown as a member of the Corporation, and has become a delegate on a Hospital Board to whom he dishonestly attempts to sell tenement property without disclosing that he is the landlord.

It was within the framework of this plot that Gogarty attacked the complacency of the middle classes who refused to face up to the reality of the sickness and poverty in their midst.

An incident in the first act underlines the hypocrisy that surrounded the treatment of venereal disease in Dublin at that time. Lily Foley, the landlady's daughter, a prostitute, is reproved for her way of life by the District Visitor,

> The wages of sin is death.

Lily's reply is:

> The wages of sin is a month in the Lock.

When inevitably she collects her "wages," Gogarty uses the occasion to initiate a discussion between those two survivals from the ballads of his student days "Medical Dick" and "Medical Davy" and inserts a neat propaganda piece in favour of prophylactive treatment for the disease. . . . In the Third Act one of the main points of the play is introduced by Mr. Tumulty, a common sense member of the Hospital Board, who makes a proposal for the demolition of tenement dwellings. But the Hospital Board are intent on building a new mortuary chapel, and the proposal is ignored. This mortuary is a symbol of the ineffectuality of the governing classes. They will build a place to house the dead, but won't take steps to see that the death-rate is diminished. In fact, *three* mortuary chapels require to be built as even in death Catholic and Protestant cannot lie together, and the Non-conformist member of the Board demands "muffled glass" for his chapel so that Quaker corpses won't be compromised by stained glass windows. Tumulty departs in disgust. "I leave you," he says, "to erect your tripartite edifice over the children of the city of blight." He has a final fling at the government for their refusal to alleviate the conditions that have produced the slums:

> Until this Moloch of a Government realises that they must spend more money on education than on police, this city will continue to be the breeding ground of disease, vice, hypocrisy and discontent.

Earlier he states, referring to Mrs. Foley's husband who had returned from the front and found his little boy dying of T.B.:

> He went out to fight for you, and the continuance of the system that betrayed him, did his son to death, and sent his daughter to hell.

Such criticism of the government and the war effort was hot stuff in 1917, with the Allied Forces in retreat, and the resurgence of revolutionary activity in Ireland. In fact, the play was strong meat even for Lady Gregory; and, perhaps reacting to external pressure (for the Abbey was in a precarious position), she took *Blight* off after only ten days' run. But it had played to packed houses, and taken in £160, a record for the Abbey.

A week later Sir John Russell, speaking at a public meeting of a charitable organization, said that when he had gone to see *Blight,* he had seen the truth about the Dublin poor as it had never been told in Dublin.

Blight's importance in dramatic literature is that it marked the first appearance on the Abbey stage of the "slum play," which was to have a vogue six years later, when [Sean] O'Casey produced his three masterpieces. It was the first play to reveal the poetic undertones in Dublin proletarian dialogue. Synge had discovered that the Western peasants spoke language as "fully flavoured as a nut or an apple." Gogarty knew of the striking language current among the Dublin poor and in *Blight,* spotted its possibilities for the stage.

The Charwoman's summing up of the weaknesses of the hospitals:

> What's the good of feeding the little creatures for a few days, and then throwing them back where they caught the diseases. It's like spittin' on a herrin' when the sea's dried up. . . .

are examples of the type of vocabulary that O'Casey later employed to give his dialogue its distinctive quality.

The weakness of *Blight* lies in its construction. Primarily concerned with getting his propaganda across, Gogarty allowed his characters to become victims to the exigencies of the plot. Stanislaus Tully, a well-observed and vital character in the first two acts, virtually fades out in the last. His place is taken by Mr. Tumulty whom we have not met before, and who strictly speaking is merely an indignant voice, and not a character at all.

Despite these serious weaknesses of plot, *Blight* shows that Gogarty possessed a flair for dramatic dialogue and comedy. He also had a gift for character creation as his treatment of Tully shows before it tails off in the last act. Tully's character, too, has a special significance in that it is a forerunner of the personality that was to form the basis of O'Casey's three famous characters: Joxer Daly, Fluther Good, and Captain Boyle. He has the same curious mixture of sardonic sarcasm, combined with a natural courtesy and dignity that endears O'Casey's principal characters to us. Tully affects imaginary pains in his

back as Captain Boyle does in *Juno and the Paycock,* and for the same reason a disinclination to do any hard work.

In both *Juno and the Paycock* and *Blight* the plot turns on the reaction of a tenement family to the prospect of a large sum of money coming to them. The opening scenes of *Blight* and O'Casey's *Shadow of a Gunman* are similar. In both these plays the curtain goes up on a silent stage: there is a bed in the middle of a tenement room and a man asleep on it. O'Casey must have been struck by the marvelous possibilities for comedy inherent in this device when he saw it in *Blight.* In fact, before he wrote his first tenement play, O'Casey, according to Horace Reynolds who asked him about the matter, had only seen two plays, *Blight* and *Androcles and the Lion.* O'Casey's flashing dialogue later captivated critics like Agate and Nathan (Agate thought O'Casey was the greatest master of tragi-comedy since Shakespeare). But it was Gogarty who first saw the possibilities for stage purposes of what Joyce had called the "sacred eloquence of Dublin." (pp. 167-72)

> *Ulick O'Connor, in his* The Times I've Seen: Oliver St. John Gogarty, a Biography, *Ivan Obolensky, Inc., 1963, 365 p.*

DAVID RIDGLEY CLARK (essay date 1972)

[*In the following excerpt Clark provides glosses of several of Gogarty's poems, including* "Non Dolet" *and* "The Crab Tree," *noting the successes and the weaknesses in Gogarty's word choice and imagery.*]

The course of modern Irish verse as Yeats saw it, or at least one course of modern Irish verse, was, first, a return to the folk tradition, but with perhaps too strong a reaction against rhetoric occasionally forcing on such writers as Joseph Campbell, Padraic Colum, and the early Yeats "a facile charm, a too soft simplicity." Then "Synge brought back masculinity . . . with his harsh disillusionment, and later, when the folk movement seemed to support vague political mass excitement, certain poets began to create passionate masterful personality." Oliver St. John Gogarty's poetry, "a gay, stoical . . . heroic song" is instanced as an expression of such personality, and Gogarty is one of the "great lyric poets of our age." . . .

Not all the poems of Gogarty which Yeats anthologizes, still less those chosen by Donagh MacDonagh and Lennox Robinson for the *Oxford Book of Irish Verse,* support either this claim to greatness or the claim of having created passionate masterful personality. **"Non Dolet"** appears in both anthologies. (p. 66)

In this poem a powerful image, the assassination of Caesar, stands for the death of friends which makes life no longer worth bothering with. The poem is certainly written in a dated manner with its personified Beauty, Triumph, Age, Time, and Death and its tired rhymes: fame, name; life, strife. Perhaps these words are typical of what Yeats called the dull, numb words of "an active man speaking." Yeats says that he changed exotic phrases like "the curd-pale moon" to the "brilliant moon" in revising his own early poems in order to get this effect of genuine speech. . . . The sort of personality which Yeats felt to be behind Gogarty's poems would perhaps use succinct terms like Beauty, Triumph, Age, without elaboration.

But I do not feel that the reality of the personality speaking this poem has really been created. The friends, too, are left completely unrealized. We must accept them on faith. One needs only mention Yeats's "The Municipal Gallery Revisited,'' in which he recalls Synge, Lady Gregory, and others, and ends ''And say my glory was I had such friends,'' . . . to realize that Gogarty has left the faces and personalities of the speaker and his friends quite blank.

The handling of the verse too is unexceptional. Look at line three where occurs the same ''so'' rhyme which we [can find] in Wilde's ''Requiescat'': ''so / sweetly she grew.'' The effect here is colloquial, and it intensifies and speeds up the last line, but that is all it does. The poem is saved only by its great last line, which *does* have the energy of personality, being very lordly and scornful about death and making a magnificent gesture:

> Nor, after Caesar, skulk in Rome.

The classical reference is a key to what Gogarty tries to do, echoing Latin poetry of the classical period, echoing also Walter Savage Landor, the foremost practitioner of this sort of thing in recent times, and in past times some of the Cavalier poets, the shorter poems of Ben Jonson, even some of Dryden. But except for the last line the poem seems merely competent verse with nothing memorable about it either in conception or technique.

The classical echoes persist in **''Per Iter Tenebricosum.''** . . . The idea of the poem is certainly a fine one: Why should a man fear to face death since little maidens and Lesbia's sparrow have done the same. And the contrast between men, gladiators, heroes, on the one hand, and sparrows on the other, is effective. The simplicity of the last two lines is very tender and beautiful. The idea is universal and thus moves one. Yet I cannot believe in Gogarty's gladiators. I have never seen a gladiator. The poem doesn't come close to home until ''little maidens''; I do know some of *them.* ''Little maidens'' prepares us to accept the reality of Lesbia (even though she was no maiden), who died nearly 2,000 years ago, and thus to accept the reality of Lesbia's sparrow, who died a little while before that. ''All alone'' is a poignant twist—after all, gladiators die amidst a great deal of company—and the off-rhyme, though a familiar enough one, is effective in the context because it contains the idea: ''gone . . . all alone.''

''Golden Stockings'' is a lovely poem, successful because of its remarkable fineness of observation and of sentiment and the discovery of an apt comparison. . . . The ''dimples of delight'', [in the first stanza], something of an embarrassing phrase, does not refer to the knees, but to the apples which are like the knees. As the poet's daughter . . . runs through the grass, the light hits her moving knees, in the same way that the light hits apples when the wind is blowing the branches so that one keeps mistaking leaf for fruit. The apples regularly bob back into the light just as the knees do. Those ''dimples of delight'' that dance are the apples. Thus the knees are like apples which are dimpled like knees and dance like knees! The tree image associated with childhood all the movement and warmth of summer.

Beginning with **''Golden Stockings,''** the poem ends with a linking image:

> And the gold-dust coming up
> From the trampled butter-cup.

The observation here is fine, almost a symbol—golden stockings trampling the gold dust out of buttercups. It catches the static picture, but it also conveys the rapid, destructive movement of running—careless, joyous, thoughtless of passing time and trampled buttercups. In addition it catches the ephemeral

dust of beauty which arises for a moment from this trampling process and then dissipates. The fact that the picture is seen from the distance of many years, as stanza two tells us, gives especial emphasis to this theme of the passing of time, this running in the sun.

In **''The Crab Tree''** there is an attempt to explore the meaning of another symbol. . . . The poem is full of qualities which the writer associates with Ireland, with a certain spirit that may be found there, with glories that have been and gone. The tree stands ''Firm and erect, / In spite of the thin soil, / In spite of neglect.'' It is a great tree of Erin. The lone tree is a relic of the great forests once found in the North near Lough Neagh. As is Ireland in some ways, it is a unique survival of an earlier time, and thus representative of earlier values and customs. . . . The tree is thus a link between the past and the present, the formed, forming and formless, the substantial and the turbulent, sea, sky and plain. . . . ''What clay enacted'' is I suppose what earth, and man who was formed of clay, have achieved or perpetrated in the past. One perpetration would be the clearing of those forests. ''Living alarm'' would be all the moving elements of the present, not only winds but also I suppose all the human tempests. The tree is a ''vitalised symbol . . . Of Chaos contracted / To intricate form.'' Earth and sky and sea, past and present and future, all tossed about together. With its roots in the ground, and its branches in the air, and in another sense, its roots in the past, its branches in the present, and its leaves exploring towards the future, it seems an epitome of the principle of survival and of creating intricate form out of life's chaotic forces.

It wrestles and has always wrestled with these forces. Its core is sweet, its fruit bitter. There is great sweetness there, deep down, at the core. But a grim life has made its fruit bitter. You taste it at your peril. The fruit is that through which a tree communicates with the nontree world of birds and humans, and the crab tree's message is a bitter one. . . . Is it the sweet virtues, mercy, pity, love, which make for survival, or is it bitter stubbornness, one's unregenerate ''bitchiness,'' which enables one to hang on? That tree would know. It is sweet in the core, bitter in the fruit. The sap which keeps its life flowering may be either.

The verse form is very appropriate to the content of most of the stanzas; the idea of lean strength is conveyed by the short lines with two stresses, the irregular meter, iambic, trochaic, and anapestic by turns, the ten-line stanza, and an intricate rhyme scheme which nevertheless contains a number of non-rhymes and off rhymes. Look for a moment at the rhyme scheme. In stanza one ''Erect'' rhymes with ''neglect,'' ''rock'' (believe it or not) rhymes with ''top'' and ''up'' (as one can tell from the other stanzas—''grown,'' ''alone'' and ''gone,'' for instance, in stanza two), and ''grapples,'' line five, rhymes with ''apples,'' line nine. This odd pattern is maintained throughout. I think it is meant to express, in its odd combination of irregularity and uniformity, the ideas of ''Chaos contracted / To intricate form'' of stanza four. I think it is a clever and successful technical device. The play of feminine versus masculine endings in the poem is also worth looking at. There is no regularity among the unrhymed lines in this regard, but all the rhyme words have masculine endings except the rhyme words of lines five and nine in each stanza: grapples-apples, steading-spreading, dingles-mingles, enacted-contracted, transmitter-bitter. So the form really is fairly ''intricate,'' though there's also plenty of ''thrust'' and ''storm'' in the rhythm and sound of the poem.

On first reading the poem, however, I fear one gets the idea of a tall thin tree, not a "great tree of Erin," a "forest tree spreading," and I think that this is because the meter expresses tallness and thinness. If one wants to suggest spreading limbs one has to use a wider line . . . The content of stanza two then wars a bit with the meter, but the meter is perfect for the content of stanza one where

> The twisted root grapples
> For sap with the rock.

None of the poems I have treated above is particularly effective in conveying the sense of a powerful personality speaking. But in **"Ringsend,"** the poem of Gogarty's which I like best, that personality is in and behind the poem. By including this poem among those from Gogarty in *The Oxford Book of Modern Verse* Yeats ensured that his selection would be superior to any, like that in *The Oxford Book of Irish Verse*, which excluded it. . . . This is a very beautiful poem indeed and, for once, worthy of "one of the great lyric poets of our age." (pp. 68-75)

> *David Ridgley Clark, "Oliver Gogarty: 'The Crab Tree'," in his* Lyric Resonance: Glosses on Some Poems of Yeats, Frost, Crane, Cummings & Others, *edited by Robert G. Tucker and David R. Clark, The University of Massachusetts Press, 1972, pp. 66-75.*

JAMES F. CARENS (essay date 1972)

[*In the following excerpt, Carens discusses the relationship between W. B. Yeats and Gogarty and attempts to define the nature of Gogarty's poetic vision. Carens believes that Gogarty's was primarily a mock-heroic vision, filtered through a consciousness "permeated with the language of Yeats." He then goes on to characterize Gogarty's verse as balanced between the poet's "mordant" and amused sense of the ordinary, and his sensitivity to "beauties beyond the commonplace." For further discussion of Gogarty's professional relationship with Yeats, see the excerpts by George Dillon (1955) and A. Norman Jeffares (1960).*]

It was not really until 1923, relatively late in his career, that Gogarty published other than in a private or limited edition. As early as 1905, he was lamenting the fact that, given his need to establish a medical practice, he was not free to pursue poetry as he would wish and he was berating himself for the things he had produced. "I magnify the importance of wretched, scrannel things, and for wilfulness impute to them intentional & deliberate parodies that they may never have held." He need not have criticized himself so severely. Those parodies were real and they nurtured his talent; they suited his gaily mocking sensibility; they fed his mock-heroic view of things.

Gogarty's nature had its antinomies, too, as AE's description of him suggested: the "wildest wit," "the rich nature of a poet." A mordant sense of the reality of things, a refreshing and often delicate sense of beauty were both his. A scarcely known poem from **Hyperthuleana**, . . . **"Spring in Dublin,"** manifests something of these qualities and evokes Swift. Gogarty's Spring is a bawd, but a delightful one. His Dublin is dirty and dear. Sawdust and laurels, decay and growth, exist in close proximity to one another. . . . (pp. 74-5)

Both **"Europa and the Bull"** and **"Leda and the Swan,"** Gogarty's finest mature poems in the mock-heroic vein, represent the same balance of forces: a keen and amused sense of the ordinary, a delighted sense of beauties beyond the commonplace. His Leda is seen in terms of the latter sense. . . . Masterly in its command of feminine cadence and poised in

tone, the poem tactfully avoids the rape, and, in the mock-heroics of its climax, lightly mingles the miraculous and the mundane:

> Of the tales that daughters
>   Tell their poor old mothers,
> Which by all accounts are
>   Often very odd;
> Leda's was a story
>   Stranger than all others.
> What was there to say but:
>   Glory be to God?

When Vivien Mercier reviewed *The Collected Poems of Oliver St. John Gogarty,* in 1954, he spoke of him as "one of the greatest of living poets," took as his text two lines from a 1923 poem which, he said, "could just as easily—far more easily—have been written in the sixteenth or seventeenth centuries as in the twentieth." "Begone, sweet Ghost, O get you gone! / Or haunt me with your body on. . . ." Professor Mercier went on to assert:

> T. S. Eliot and others have written much on the traditions of wit that was abandoned by English poets about the middle of the eighteenth century, but they show greater skill in writing *about* it than *in* it. For Gogarty, as the two lines above suggest, that tradition never died; he grew up steeped in the first transmitters of it—the Roman poets, with Horace at their head, who first imitated Greek lyric and epigrammatic verse. Much as Gogarty admires Virgil, it is Horace or Catullus that he follows in his most successful poems—or else Greek poets that they imitated.

Surely Professor Mercier, in that review, made the essential point about Gogarty. Among the poets of the first half of the century, Gogarty was *the* master in the classical tradition. He had, among other traits, a command of epigram: . . .

> I give more praise to Troy's redoubt
> For Love kept in, than War kept out.
>   —**"On Troy,"** 1938

Even among his discarded notes, I have come across epigrams so devastating, Gogarty did not consider publication:

> Don't pass Connolly, Death!
> That putrescence is his breath.

Clearly, such classical modes of expression were in no way remote from his daily experience, nor was classical allusion. Probably only an Irish poet and a man who did not separate his verse from the innumerable other activities of his life would have been free enough from the dominant literary fashions of the time to have entered imaginatively the classical world. . . . (pp. 76-8)

Though Gogarty's friendship with Dermot Freyer and F. M. Tancred, members of T. E. Hulme's first poetry club, put him in touch with certain of the notions about language that developed into Imagism, he was, for the most part, insulated from literary dogma and from the experimentalist tendencies that dominated the poetic scene in England and America. We rightly think of Yeats as the greatest of the moderns, and yet the *Oxford Book of Modern Verse* amply reveals Yeats's sense of his own difference from Eliot and Pound. His influence on Gogarty confirmed the latter's disposition to express himself in traditional forms—and to succeed. Like his friend, the painter, Augustus John, Gogarty has paid a penalty for finding his freedom within a set of conventions: his genuine accomplishment has been largely ignored by literary critics. (p. 78)

During the course of his poetic career, Gogarty had little to say about his aims and intentions; but line after line of his poetry carries us back to the Cavaliers, to Herrick, and to the Romans. At his best his classical muse is without cliché, affectation, or fatigue, and his lines are graceful, economic, and lucid. . . . None of the qualities that New Critics sought in the 'thirties and 'forties—tension, ambiguity, levels of meaning—are found in his poetry. Instead there is simplicity, tenderness, delight. . . . The intense ironies that we regard as expressions of our cultural *angst* are nowhere found in his work, but there is the most refreshing and joyous humor. . . . (pp. 78-9)

Setting himself against the complexity and obliquity that was characteristic of modernist verse in his time, Gogarty sought to sing with the greatest simplicity and directness possible. . . . [Contrasting the poem **"Fresh Fields"**] with, say, T. S. Eliot's "Whispers of Immortality," in fairness I think one would have to say that if Eliot gives us something like the tormenting metaphysical shudder of Donne, Gogarty gives us something like the graceful metaphysical ecstasy of Andrew Marvell.

Where, you may ask, was Yeats in all this? The classical not only is not his tradition, but tension, ambiguity, and levels of meaning are surely characteristic of him. It is a long way from "Among School Children" to **"Back from the Country."** The fact is, Yeats had a very clear view of the bent of Gogarty's talent, as he had of his limitations and strengths. In his Preface [see excerpt dated 1923] to *An Offering of Swans* (which he selected), he wrote:

> Oliver Gogarty has discovered the rhythm of Herrick and of Fletcher, something different from himself and yet akin to himself. . . . Here are but a few pages, that a few months have made, and there are careless lines now and again, traces of the old confused exuberance. He never stops long at his best but how beautiful that best is, how noble, how joyous!

Still, searching Gogarty's mature poetry for echoes of Yeats, it is almost startling to discover how few verbal resemblances there are. Passages like "Every solicitor's clerk / Would break out and go mad; / And all the dogs would bark!" or ". . . blood, that tamed and mild, / Can suddenly go wild," may evoke lines in Yeats. A phrase like "Tall unpopular men" or "Imagined, outrageous, preposterous wrongs" may seem reminiscent of him. Yet none of these is a borrowing; none, a very close parallel. Even when, as in the 'thirties, Gogarty increasingly shares Yeats's haughty, aristocratic ideals, his rhythms, structures and images are entirely his own.

It can nonetheless be said that Yeats exercised an influence on Gogarty's poetry, an influence that began on the evening in 1904, when Gogarty heard Yeats recite at [George] Moore's and noticed the use of a commonplace word in a heroic context. More than a year later, he called on Yeats again and has left a letter describing his meeting:

> I received a long lecture on modern literary language. He forgave William Morris for his archaism for it was both original and scholarly. An archaism was . . . only admissable when one had discovered it for oneself: there was no

defence for the continuation of mere metrical conventions: 'Hast', 'shalt', 'thou', 'thee', 'wert', 'art' etc. They were part of a language highly artificial & conscious, a language that would pass for poetry if one found it at a future date in a single instance where the rest of the literature of the period was lost.

Reflecting on this, Gogarty wrote, "I was beginning to see what Yeats wants. . . ." When he turned to the subject of syntax, Yeats called "all inversions in verse & 'thee' & 'thou' convention labour-saving devices. . . ." And he assured Gogarty "that he could improvise verse by the hour if he permitted himself the use of inversions and the conventional language of poetry." . . . Yeats had made his point: Gogarty accepted the criticisms Yeats made . . . and concluded: "I have retreated and am now studying Yeats' work with interest and respect."

Given his fascination with classical forms and metres, Gogarty was often tempted to form matter to manner, to mould the grammar of his subject to the scheme or structure of the verse; and when his syntax seems contrived or forced, I think it is due to his imitation of classical modes or formal ideals. Probably Yeats's greatest contribution to the development of Gogarty's talent, his greatest critical service, was in pointing out the inappropriateness of merely conventional language and of syntactical inversions, the need for naturalness and intensity of expression. His influence on Gogarty in this respect reveals itself in the latter's best poetry, the volumes produced during the 'twenties and 'thirties, when the two men were closest to one another. "When he was reading my book of verse before recommending it to his sister's press, the Cuala," Gogarty has written, "he would offer suggestions which I invariably accepted gratefully." (pp. 79-82)

Georgio Melchiori, in his brilliant book *The Whole Mystery of Art* [see Additional Bibliography], has suggested that Gogarty's **"To the Liffey with the Swans"** and his **"Tell me now"** were among the complex of forces, themes, and associations working upon Yeats when he wrote his great sonnet "Leda and the Swan." He also argues that after Gogarty's *An Offering of Swans* operated as "catalyst for the images that went into Yeats's 'Leda and the Swan,' the debt was amply repaid for the myth of Leda recurs with obsessive insistence in Gogarty's later poetry. . . ." Doubtless he is right in arguing that Gogarty's allusions in the poems he cites were involved in Yeats's imaginative process. But I do think it should be noted that the myth of Leda was well established in Gogarty's poetry long before the time of Yeats's "Leda." It appears not only in . . . [a] stanza of **"To Augustus John,"** which . . . Yeats himself revised but also in **"To a Cock,"** a poem that Gogarty dedicated to John in *Hyperthuliana*. Inasmuch as Yeats selected **"The Feast"** from this volume for inclusion in *An Offering of Swans*, it seems probable that he noticed allusions to Troy, desire, destruction, and "burning" in **"To a Cock."** These allusions . . . should probably be included among the catalysts for Yeats's "Leda" imagery. . . . (pp. 85-6)

"Gay adventurer," Yeats called Oliver Gogarty in his BBC Broadcast on Modern Poetry, adding, his "poems have restored the emotion of heroism to lyric poetry." By the 'thirties, the evidence suggests, Gogarty had become for Yeats something like his "wise and simple" fisherman "in grey Connemara clothes," a mask that is, and an opposite of the dreariness he then observed in Irish political life, in European affairs, and in English poetry. Contributing a Preface for *Wild Apples*, which he selected, he asked, "Why am I content to search through

Gogarty releasing two swans at Island Bridge in April 1924, fulfilling his vow to the Liffey. Present are (from left): W. T. Cosgrave; Gogarty; his wife, Martha Gogarty; W. B. Yeats; and J. O'Reilly. Photograph by J. Cashman.

so many careless verses for what is excellent? I do not think that it is merely because they are excellent, I think I am not so disinterested; but because he gives me something I need at this moment of time "[see excerpt dated 1930]. In Gogarty, he saw passion, a "sense of hardship borne and chosen out of pride and joy." The publication of *As I Was Going Down Sackville Street* was an important literary event in Dublin: Yeats noted in a letter that "Here everybody is reading it." To him it seemed "not all wit," but, he added, "one can say of much of it, as somebody said I think of Raleigh, it is 'high, insolent and passionate.' None of its attacks on things I approve vex me and that is because they are passionate. His only attacks are on modern Ireland. He is passionate not self-complacent and so we forgive him." Better than anyone else, Yeats knew how little there was of calculation in Gogarty, how much of impulse. (pp. 88-9)

"I recommend Irish Anthologists to select '**Aphorism**' which being clear and inexplicable, will be most misjudged," Yeats wrote of Gogarty's finest single poem. It was later titled "**Ringsend (After reading Tolstoi)**".... [It] belongs in all the anthologies of modern poetry in English. Modulating beautifully from its gusty opening, to its tender acceptance of sordid humanity, and on to the cleansing music of the final lines, where sibilants and vowels govern our voices and our emotions, the poem is unforgettable. Clear *and* inexplicable, as Yeats said, its images and cadences reach below the level of consciousness, juxtaposing for us—and without moral censoriousness—the "stew" that is life and the purification of the eternal, archetypal ocean. When he wrote Gogarty, asking permission to use his poems for the *Oxford Book*, Yeats added a personal postscript: "I think you are perhaps the greatest master of the pure lyric now writing in English." His careless, rhyming medical friend had earned those words. (pp. 90-1)

James F. Carens, "Gogarty and Yeats," in Modern Irish Literature: Essays in Honor of William Tindall, edited by Raymond J. Porter and James D. Brophy, Iona College Press, 1972, pp. 67-93.*

JAMES F. CARENS (essay date 1972)

[*In the following excerpt, Carens briefly discusses Gogarty's three dramas. In Carens's opinion,* Blight *and* The Enchanted Trousers *retain interest for readers today, while* A Serious Thing, *the most carelessly written of the three, has become quite dated. For further discussion of Gogarty's skill as a dramatist, see the excerpt by Ulick O'Connor (1963).*]

Blight has survived the passage of time surprisingly well—possibly because the slum itself, like the slum landlord and the political exploiter of slum misery, has also survived. Yet something has to be said too for the vitality of Gogarty's comedy and for the elements of originality in the play. It is, of course, a drama with a thesis; and the directness with which the "purpose" is advanced, in Act III, by Tumulty (Gogarty's *persona*) creates a structural and aesthetic flaw. (The one-dimensional Tumulty overshadows the three-dimensional Stanislaus Tully, who is the strongest link between the first two acts and the third.) Moreover, **Blight** was to some extent influenced by earlier Abbey plays, as Lady Gregory implied in a letter, November 22, 1917, to Dr. Gogarty: "Donovan was rather upset at the thought of another speech from the window as he has one in Lord Mayor, & Eloquent Dempsy." Nevertheless, what distinguishes Gogarty's work from a play like Edward McNulty's *The Lord Mayor* . . . and what marks its importance in the history of the Abbey Theatre is that it not only treats the problems of the slum and political corruption in broadly comic and satiric terms but actually depicts the very conditions of the slum itself. Andrew Malone in his early history of the modern Irish theatre wrote of *Blight,* "It is a play which would bear revival, as it is a play which anticipated Sean O'Casey in its portrayal of the typical Dublin wastrel." And, he should have added, of the Dublin slum. Moreover, *Blight* is at its best in such moments as that when the impudent and fallen Lily turns her mockery upon the fatuously virtuous District Visitor, or when Stanislaus Tully indulges in an outrageously witty flight of rhetoric concerning the social advantages of liquor: "What put a roof on Christ Church Cathedral? Drink. What renovated St. Patrick's and cleared Bull Alley? Drink!" *Blight* was, we are not surprised to learn from O'Casey's autobiography, one of the very few Abbey plays he saw before he began his dramatic career. Somewhat more surprising are the general resemblances between O'Casey's Boyles and the Tully circle in *Blight.* Both Jimmy Foley and Johnny Boyle are crippled; Lily Foley struggles gamely and foolishly against her environment, yet is sexually exploited, as is O'Casey's Mary Boyle; Tully's bogus backaches are a striking precedent for the Paycock's "pains in me legs," as is his boasting for the verbal fantasies of the latter; and Mary Foley's roots in reality go not so deep as Juno's, but they do go deep.

Gogarty's two subsequent plays for the Abbey, both one-actors, were written under the pseudonym of Gideon Ouseley. . . .

Like *Blight* these two works address themselves to particular contemporary issues. *A Serious Thing,* the less successful of the two, resembles Lady Gregory's *The Deliverer* . . . in employing a Biblical theme (the summoning of Lazarus from the tomb) to explore an Irish political situation (the mindless repression of the nationalist movement by the Black and Tans); and, in its turn, probably influenced the handling of the Biblical parallel in Lady Gregory's *The Story Brought by Brigit.* . . . A review that appeared in one Dublin newspaper (preserved in [Joseph] Holloway's *Diary*) noted that the play "kept the house in shrieks of laughter"; and even Holloway, who found it "something of a damp rocket," reported that "the moment that the dead Lazarus awoke from his tomb to join those who wished their country free was the cream of a very brutal joke!" One of a large group of modern Irish literary works—from *Kathleen Ni Houlihan* to *Ulysses*—that explores the myth of rebirth. *A Serious Thing* has its amusing moments but has dated more than *Blight* or, surprisingly, the farcical *Enchanted Trousers.* The play gives signs of hasty composition too, for the Jewish accent of the Second Roman, intended to associate him, through a favorite Irish historical parallel, with the native Irishman under British rule, is not consistently developed, even within single speeches. Yet, as an occasional satiric comment on the total failure of the English to comprehend Ireland's national rising, one cannot doubt its effect on the audience.

The Enchanted Trousers deals with a far slighter subject, but it better survives the years. According to Holloway and one of the reviews that he pasted into his *Diary,* the satire in this play was directed at Plunkett House—Sir Horace Plunkett's agency for agricultural reform. Both the review that appeared in the *Irish Times* and in the *Freeman* (also found in Holloway) indicated some concern that the play satirized not only British rule but also Irish. Doubtless it is this very aspect of the satire that accounts for the play's effectiveness: the "Time" of the play is "Any day in Ireland" and its subject is really the sheer ineptitude of bureaucracy, at any time, in any place. In addition, the *dénouement* in which Humphrey Heavey begins to live the role he has played and turns the situation to his own advantage, rather than to that of his mother and brother, manages both to make a satiric point and to induce the psychological satisfaction we always derive when duper is duped. (pp. 10-12)

[The] dialogue in *The Enchanted Trousers,* if not purest (or impurest) Gogarty, is pretty funny, from the opening passage, which offended Lady Gregory by the number of its references to spitting, on to the climactic imitation Humphrey Heavey gives of the characteristic speech of an upperclass Englishman—"Oh-eh-ah. . . . With a few barbarisms such as 'beastly' and 'awfully,' frequent 'quites,' a few 'damns,' and the ten platitudes added." (p. 13)

James F. Carens, in an introduction to The Plays of Oliver St. John Gogarty *by Oliver St. John Gogarty, edited by James F. Carens, Proscenium Press, 1972, pp. 9-13.*

J. B. LYONS (essay date 1976)

[*In the following excerpt from his biography of Gogarty, Lyons surveys Gogarty's writings and addresses one of the principal problems that confronts critics attempting to evaluate Gogarty's contribution to twentieth century literature: his feud with James Joyce.*]

[Gogarty] was much more than a licensed jester and the crust of wit concealed a compassionate interior. His malicious wit was not in evidence when he delivered an address entitled "The Need of Medical Inspection of School Children in Ireland" to inaugurate the Winter Session of the Meath Hospital in 1911, for the occasion was formal and serious. (p. 29)

And when his first play *Blight* was staged in the Abbey Theatre in 1917 his motif was the insanitary populous tenements of the Dublin slums, gaunt decayed mansions each housing a score of large families, blighting the lives of its inhabitants, seedbeds of vice and disease. His characters are recognizable types, and as Sean O'Casey was a member of his audience it is not unlikely that drunken Stan Tully lent something to the creation of Joxer Daly and Fluther Good, equally shifty, less comic but more calculating, more authentic.

Tully, the "hero" of *Blight,* is a malingerer who takes advantage of an industrial accident and is compensated by some hundred pounds. His celebratory words are well received. "There was a head on that speech like a pint of stale stout," said the Cabman. A laborer found it "One of them fine reassuring speeches that kept its meaning to itself." And Mrs. Larrissey was overcome: 'Wouldn't it put a bull's heart in ye to hear him? The spits of him itself was like a shower iv rain." (pp. 30-1)

Gogarty used his knowledge of the sanctimonious do-gooders who serve on hospital boards to create the members of the board of the Townsend Thanatorium, two of which, Norris Galbraith and Tisdall-Townsley, also resemble in some degree George Moore and Sir Thornley Stoker. Mr. Tumulty voices Gogarty's own thoughts about the futility of private charity in the management of public health and knew that prevention is better than cure. "The less you spend on prevention the more you will pay for cure. Until the citizens realize that their children should be brought up in the most beautiful and favourable surroundings the city can afford, and not in the most squalid, until this floundering Moloch of a Government realize that they must spend more money on education than on police, this city will continue to be the breeding-ground of disease, vice, hypocrisy and discontent."

Medical Dick and Medical Davy (also featured in one of Gogarty's bawdiest poems) provide comic relief. Lily Foley with her streetwalker's cynicism—''The wages of sin is a month in the Lock''—outfaces the cold morality of Miss Maxwell-Knox, a district visitor, but as she herself predicted, she is sent to the Lock Hospital with syphilis.

The theme of *A Serious Thing,* Gogarty's one-act play which was staged at the Abbey Theatre on August 19, 1919, during the Black-and-Tan repression, was ostensibly the threat to Roman rule posed by the early Christians in Galilee but its deeper reference was the conflict against British rule in Ireland. Gogarty poked fun at army regulations; his Centurion's ''Lookey-here now'' was a favorite phrase of Talbot Clifton, a wealthy Englishman who was the author's neighbor in Connemara. It gave him sardonic amusement to see British officers in his audience laughing at the words of the Second Roman: ''I'm thinking it's an extraordinary thing that every country we occupy seems to be inhabited exclusively by rebels.''

His third play, *The Enchanted Trousers,* was an amusing one-act satire on bureaucracy and jobbery in rural Ireland. Humphrey Heavey, a hack actor, is persuaded by his brother Andy, a Clare-Galway schoolteacher, that all he needs to do to be appointed to a well-paid sinecure is to play the part and wear the costume of an Englishman. The clothes—a Norfolk jacket and knickerbockers—are borrowed by Mrs. Heavey from the local sergeant who had been promoted when he wore them for the King's visit. Mrs. Heavey holds up the trousers for inspection and Andy exclaims, ''There you are, Humphrey, when you enter that you enter England.'' When Humphrey is dressed and stands with a monocle in his eye he looks for all the world a Sassenach, so much so that his brother remarks how he resembles ''the auld fellow that blew the tail off the red setter at the Shoot at Moore Hall.''

The officials are taken in, Humphrey gets the job with £2,000 a year but behaves hypocritically when it comes to helping his family. (pp. 31-3)

By his early twenties Oliver Gogarty was already a competent poet and well-read in poetry, taking as his models the Greek and Latin classics and the English Elizabethans. James Stephens has singled him out as Ireland's only classical poet; F. R. Higgins wrote in a personal letter: ''Poetry has many table-lands; yours are peaks scarred with gold—rhythm's mountain ranges illuminated by fastidious craft.'' Austin Clarke, a dissident voice, has said that he ''took every care to avoid the difficult, scarcely-known ways of Irish tradition,'' and faulted him, perhaps unfairly, for ignorance of Gaelic literature, which makes one feel that Clarke was really complaining because Gogarty's Muse did not link arms with his own. But Gogarty, despite his classical leanings, is very much a national poet though in no narrow sense; and more than any other, he has succeeded in marrying the ancient Mediterranean myths with those of ancient Ireland; his eclecticism reestablishes old links between Irish and European cultures.

Scattered through his prose and verse and in his private letters are informative passages on his views of the functions of poetry and poets. ''Verse, if it is to be any good should be as easily called to mind as a wild cherry tree in Spring. It needs no recording.'' And in a letter to John Drinkwater: ''Your poems arrived and I am reading them now and then, when the chance comes, aloud. I think that is the only way poetry should be treated: otherwise it is scriptive and unworthy of the sweet air.'' (pp. 39-40)

Curiously, the inclusion of seventeen of his poems in the *Oxford Book of Modern Verse . . .* has often been cited to Gogarty's discredit. It needs only a swing of fashion, restoring parity to melody and allowing bright images to penetrate the gloom, to vindicate the editor. Meanwhile, can one do other than ascribe a lot of the ill-feeling caused by Yeats's selection to spite, a by-product of envy? But in any case, if poetry is written for anyone except the author it certainly is not primarily intended for other poets and academics; and while their more stringent opinions seem to rank unduly, what really matters is the usually unheard voice of the general reader.

An appreciative Scotsman probably spoke for many when expressing his feelings in a letter to Gogarty.

> It is a good many years since I first came across a selection of your poems in the *Oxford Book of Modern Verse* and finding you in the dry and thirsty Wasteland of most of the moderns was like coming upon a well of water. It was with the greatest eagerness that I ordered a copy of your *Collected Poems* as soon as I saw them advertised and it is with the utmost pride that I now possess one. They seem to me to have wit, gaiety, wisdom and courage as well as formal beauty and clarity of language—and heart. I have found enormous comfort as well as pleasure in them; and not a few of them (as for example, ''*Per Iter Tenebricosum*'') are of that perfection which sends a shiver down the spine, like great music, and seem to me as fine as anything I have come across in English literature.

Another admirer of his verse, a soldier's wife, wrote to say that she was taking his *Collected Poems* with her to Malaya: ''I do not know whether you will find the necessity of taking it to a wooden house in a jungle clearing in Pahang a tribute to the poems or an insult to the binding . . . but I promise that it will be valued very much. They are poems to read and re-read until they are kept in the heart not locked in a dustproof bookshelf as a collector's edition.''

Such untutored testimonies have an important validity but for those fresh from the lecture rooms and for axe-grinding Dubliners unwilling to bestow the accolade on a local the judgment of W. B. Yeats may be reiterated: Yeats in his introduction to the *Oxford Book of Modern Verse* proclaimed Gogarty as ''one of the great lyric poets of our age.'' Why then should lesser men cavil? (pp. 55-7)

''Quaintly he came raiking out of Molesworth Street into Kildare Street, an odd figure moidered by memories . . .'' Thus from the passing show Gogarty picked out ''Endymion,'' a Dublin character who among other peculiarities of dress wore his cuffs on his ankles to indicate that he was standing on his hands. In the National Library register Endymion signs himself James Boyle Tisdell Burke Stewart Fitzsimons Farrell (a name familiar to readers of *Ulysses*) and Gogarty realized that the harmless lunatic was engaged in presenting a cavalcade of Dublin life backwards for thirty years and decided to emulate him. *As I Was Going Down Sackville Street,* Gogarty's first prose work, winds backwards leisurely from the mid-thirties, meandering just as willfully through the decades as the River Liffey does in its course from Kippure and Poulaphouca to the Strawberry Beds until enmities are forgotten and shadows dissolve in bright recollections of a time before the First World War when a picnic could be the most important thing in life.

The title derives from a ballad composed when Sackville Street (now O'Connell Street) was the principal avenue of the city which is the hero of his book, a hero which he defends from autochthonous despoilers who have replaced its former masters. The latter are admired and chided in turn: Gogarty had a largeness of mind that could admire British civilization at its best but contained sufficient of the national disillusion to remember to fear three things, the hoofs of a horse, the horns of a bull, and the smile of a Saxon. (pp. 60-1)

Sackville Street is an uncompromising book. Few other than Irish readers will appreciate to what degree it must have incensed those who differed politically from its author. Sacred cows and national heroes are treated with a candor astonishing for the thirties, however commonplace today. The "hard political women" and the Irregulars who took the Republican side in the Civil War, according to temperament, should have withered under his scorn or perished from rage on reading his pages. . . . And not until recently when Conor Cruise-O'Brien spoke out against the National cult of necrophilia has any Irishman so forcefully condemned the unhealthy adulation of political martyrs. "Damn the vampire dead who have left us nothing but a heritage of hatred . . ."

Fearing that the liberated Kathleen Ni Houlihan was becoming a soured harridan, Gogarty expressed his alarm with accustomed vehemence. He viewed the new political leaders with a suspicion that time has justified. What was their idea of a nation likely to be? "Would it give leave to live to all its Nationals? Would its idea of freedom be universal or restricted to a gang?" . . . *Sackville Street,* however controversial in the thirties, expressed views which are perfectly acceptable today to anyone untouched by political hagiology.

Reminded of [George Moore's] *Hail and Farewell,* Terence de Vere White said it was Moore again, with less malice and less art. But there is enough malice to pepper the pages, and some to spare. Literary "friends" fared hardly better than political enemies. Any dereliction of friendship is forgotten, however, as one marvels over sentences that peg out Edward Martyn like a specimen on a laboratory bench. "But suddenly a fat shout from the plain oaken chair." "His gills cardinalised into crimson."

Sackville Street is thronged with Gogarty's contemporaries under their own names and as thinly disguised fictional characters such as Thwackhurst the graffiti-collector, in reality "Sodomy" Cox, a barrister who earned his sobriquet by expressing sympathy for Oscar Wilde. Senator Fanning was amused to be made the vehicle of Gogarty's own indignation, ex-President Cosgrave took in good part the comment that his piety had embarrassed the Pope. . . . (pp. 61-3)

In *I Follow Saint Patrick* we are taken by a companionable guide to places hallowed by association with "a Columbus of the Faith to the Gael." He approaches his theme in a roundabout way: "As I stood by the wall of Mycenae under the Lion Gate, I thought of Ard Macha and of Niall of the Nine Hostages"; in Bristol he went to the docks "—that is where the coastwise men are to be found"; in Dublin he consulted a metallurgist who took him to a workshop in Harcourt Street basement and showed him the inutility of bronze swords; he obtained new insights in the verses of Claudian.

Having studied the biographies and personally surveyed the terrains in question he is prepared to back his own conclusion that *Bannavem Taburniae,* Patrick's father's village, was near St. David's in South Wales and puts forward the suggestion that "it was a fleet of Niall of the Nine Hostages which captured Patrick in the year of that King's death at sea. . . ."

Martello Tower in Sandycove, where Gogarty and James Joyce lived for a time.

The main facts concerning Patrick's apostolate are well known: sold into slavery in Ireland, he was commanded in a dream to escape; eventually he returned to convert the country of his captivity to Christianity. Gogarty pictures no meek saint but a "fiery and zealous man." (p. 67)

His advantage over the conventional historians is his ability to create vignettes. He brings Totus Calvus, the Saint's bald charioteer, before us with striking clarity: "I could see Totus swinging the natty cobs into the plain of Murrisk with the pole rattling as he trotted them in." With an ingenuity born of his knowledge of literature, he links Saint Patrick's Purgatory with Provence through the translations of Marie de France, the Queen of Troubadours.

He followed the Saint to the penitential mountain in Connaught, which at the time of Patrick's fast was called Mount Aigli but is now named for him, and to Caher Island, the most westerly point of his journey. . . . Caher Island "which lies like a wedge with its raised base oceanwards" is a formidable distance offshore from Murrisk, Patrick's embarkation point, but more easily reached from Renvyle Point. Thus it appears that Gogarty's interest in Saint Patrick (for he was not an instinctive hagiographer) was determined by the circumstances which attached him to Renvyle. (pp. 68-9)

[*Tumbling in the Hay*] is buoyant with youthful memories; it is a joyous, exuberant book, free of the animadversions and disillusion of *Sackville Street,* a worthwhile contribution to literature. Narrated by Gideon Ousley, a transparent disguise for Gogarty himself, it introduces a host of splendid characters limned from life but touched up with artistic skill.

Commencing with a cab journey that takes young Ousley from Cecilia Street medical school (so convenient to Mr. Golly's tavern) to deposit him instead in Trinity College, it finishes six years later with another cab drive (in the Smallpox Cab this time) on a night when Doctor Ousley and his newly qualified friends stand at the end of the irresponsible days that have brought them to the threshold of their professional careers.

In more serious moments of the intervening years a teacher in the Richmond Hospital has warned them that for them the future lies

> with the dying and the diseased. The sunny days will not be yours any longer but days in the crowded dispensaries where you must render service.

Perhaps this confrontation of youth with the harshness of Nature's decrees explains the levity of the medicals, traditionally the wildest of all students. Ousley's friends, Weary Mac, the Citizen, and Silly Barney are typical of the ilk; the four Halogens ("Dolan, Hegarty, McCluskey and Roowan, never found free in Nature, always combined!") are more studious.

Sooner or later they all had to burn the midnight oil, for an immense body of knowledge has to be assimilated by aspirants to a medical degree. Verse was a convenient aide-memoire for Gogarty/Ousley in anatomy:

> "I'm going to swerve,"
> Said the lingual nerve.
> "Well be sure you avoid,"
> Said the pterygoid,
> "Myself and the ramus
> When passing between us." . . .

It assisted too in therapeutics: "Hydrarg. perchlor. and Pot. Iod. / For those who don't believe in God." . . . (pp. 70-2)

Gogarty was no ordinary medico. He could walk with kings as represented by Mahaffy, Tyrrell, and Macran (Dons admirable! Dons of Might! to mix not metaphors but poets) nor lose the common touch that made him at home in Golly's and in Nighttown. . . .

His ability to discern the hilarity concealed by an unprepossessing exterior enabled him to invest a dubious Dublin hostelry, The Hay Hotel, with virtues that constituted a Hegelian dialectic with its vices. (p. 72)

Tumbling in the Hay was an immediate success. Reviewing it, Harold Nicolson referred to the difficulty of re-creating with words an illusion of life's dynamic fantasy. This had been achieved by Smollett and Fielding and now by Gogarty in a book which had immense humanity, and, however much it might cause readers to laugh, was a work of very competent art. (p. 73)

Gideon Ousley makes a reappearance in *Going Native,* in which the author describes his surrogate's fictional experiences in English country houses. The humor in this book borders on burlesque; it satirizes English moods and manners and compares English and Irish attitudes. "There is no Kingdom of Heaven over here; the British Empire has replaced it."

The very names of the people we encounter—Snaith, Snape and Treblecock are of the servants' hall, Sir Chalfont St. Gules very upper-crust—are parodies of social polarization. The characterization is unconvincing; readers may find if difficult to become involved and especially those who cut their teeth on *Couples* or *Last Exit to Brooklyn.* Ousley's comic bedroom encounters—"I to be jilted by a Vicar's niece. It took fifty women to cool Cuchulian from his battle fury."—would have made Fresh Nelly despair of him.

The English have always made "victory out of defeat. The Conquest is a feather in their caps. They have everything both ways." Ousley loses patience with them and recalls the thrushes singing in Glenasmole. Finally he asks himself ". . . how long can I abide this civilization, the greatest civilization on earth? How long can I live with the pirates who put on dinner jackets?"

The best in *Going Native,* and as usual Gogarty excels in descriptive writing, is the art of the essayist and not that of a novelist. . . . But versatile to a fault Gogarty was not deterred from a still more ambitious undertaking, historical fiction.

Mad Grandeur is a romance set in 1798, a year of rebellion. This is a long book and Gogarty's tale of the fortunes of Hyacinth Martyn-Lynch and his bride is set against a detailed background of eighteenth-century Irish life when the existence of gaming, dueling landlords was in dramatic contrast to the plight of an oppressed peasantry. Highwaymen, pugilists, racing touts, including an engaging rascal. Toucher Plant, and the Bucks of the Hell Fire Club, provide additional color.

"Yeats has begun to evict imaginary tenants!" Gogarty joked about his friend's tendency to identify himself with the landed gentry but made no secret of the fact that he, too, loved a lord. The Big Houses in *Mad Grandeur* are composites of Lady Gregory's Coole Park, Edward Martyn's Tulira, Moore Hall, and the Gore-Booth's Lissadell. (pp. 77-9)

During his own years in America Gogarty contributed to a number of magazines, and like others obliged to live by their pens he discovered that what has been sold once can be sold twice, or, indeed, many times. _Mourning Became Mrs. Spendlove_ contains stories (the title is taken from a tall tale about a courtesan) and essays. Unfortunately the former show the short story as an art form in which Gogarty did not excel; the best essay was **"Reminiscences of Yeats." "Dublin Revisited" I and II** describe a visit to his native city—"Back to my unfriendly, friendly, bitter Ithaca"—after six years' absence. These essays of a returned exile were expanded, after a second visit to Ireland, in _Rolling Down the Lea_ . . . , which is a eulogy of Dublin with reservations, and a Connemara rhapsody.

It is springtime in Dublin—"one of the most beautiful cities in Europe, with its five squares, its domes and the Palladian architecture of its public edifices"—and its people are smiling. We meet some of them: MacGlornan, a small-time politician; Richard Best, the scholar; Jack Nugent, mine host of the famous Dolphin Hotel; and Dulcie, "a lady pink and white" who despite her wayward youth had one thing in common with the saints, _fragrance_. "Dulcie diffuses fragrance. She is the only one I ever met who did."

Behind the splendor of the spring our guide discerns human failings; "Meanness, chicanery and self-interest all were there"—just as in Athens. But Gogarty's saving grace is to remember that he himself is "part of the show"; to preserve his sense of the ridiculous, "a precious and salutary gift"; and to be aware of his own astringency in a town where friendliness may veil malevolence.

He rails against the slums as he did in _Blight_. "Those born in slums have a slum outlook. They have been deprived of beauty." (pp. 80-1)

For the city's shortcomings he hurls scorn upon the politicians. (p. 81)

Dublin is surrounded by race courses and Gogarty takes us to one of them passing through tinkers, pedlars and fortune-tellers into the enclosure to join "pink Englishmen, brown foreigners; fat women who were not homebred, and the usual lank hunting-women whom we all knew, and the hurried, busy long-nosed men," and to watch the bookies on their stands "shouting like muezzins." And then surprisingly—or perhaps not, for Gogarty's melancholy has already been noted—watching the bobbing sea of heads, he reflects: "A few years, and they all shall have disappeared like clouds that cross a hill." (pp. 81-2)

The autobiographical _It Isn't this Time of Year at All!_ is a discursive anecdotal account of life in Dublin and elsewhere somewhat carelessly written—the story of Sir Thornley Stoker and Lord Dunsany's butler is repeated within a few pages—in conversational style. This is a defect of Gogarty's later books: the eye of the reader scanning lines of prose has to imagine the quizzical smile that accompanied the telling, but when the hesitations and shifting tones of a matchless raconteur are missing it sometimes falls flat. And if individually published essays are not delicately pruned when collected the recurrence of certain expressions and phrases robs them of freshness.

Horace Reynolds, a generous eulogist of Gogarty, knew his shortcomings: "Gogarty wrote as a tiger hunts: if he missed his spring he would not try again, and this refusal to recognise the work in writing meant that some of what he wrote was mechanical and disconnected. But there were always days when he did not miss his target."

The egoism of advancing years, pardonable and easy to circumvent in conversation but ineradicable on the printed page, was an added defect especially when superimposed on a natural assertiveness. . . . The growing interest and perceptive analysis in America of the works of James Joyce irritated him increasingly. (pp. 83-4)

Gogarty's ill-advised **"They Think They Know Joyce"** had a boomerang effect, shattering his own credibility. It is urged that those who wish to come to an objective appraisal of Gogarty should set aside the dialogue of disparagement in which he and Joyce engaged and also his dehumanizing characterization as Buck Mulligan in _Ulysses_. (p. 84)

Literary judgments use for measurement the variable scale of human affect and are often reversed on appeal. Literary assessments stand on the quicksands of fashion, open to the pull of subconscious prejudice. Besides, the present-day trend to let the books make the tally, scoring nothing for their creators' apparently unrelated virtues, subtracting nothing for their gaucheries and limitations, is a trend that favors the colorless and the single-minded but improverishes literary history.

Let us, then, before we see him off the stage, spare a moment to look once more at Gogarty in the round: it is not enough to credit him, at the minimum, with some consummate lyrics and that comic masterpiece _Tumbling in the Hay;_ we must remember and proclaim those qualities which made him equally at ease with the dons in the common room and with the hearties on the playing fields, that allowed him to walk with assurance into an operating room, a tavern, or a drawing room. He moved in a group where wit was the common currency, the tokens minted as often as not in fires of malice; the recollection of his verbal incontinence must be balanced by the indubitable fact of his gift for friendship. And what friends he had! (pp. 84-5)

> _J. B. Lyons, in his_ Oliver St. John Gogarty, _Bucknell University Press, 1976, 89 p._

ADDITIONAL BIBLIOGRAPHY

A. E. [pseudonym of George William Russell]. Introduction to _Wild Apples_, by Oliver Gogarty, pp. vii-viii. New York: Jonathan Cape and Harrison Smith, 1929.
  A laudatory introduction to Gogarty's poetry. A. E. especially praises the poem "The Plum Tree by the House."

British Broadcasting Corporation. "Oliver St. John Gogarty." In _Irish Literary Portraits: W. B. Yeats, James Joyce, George Moore, George Bernard Shaw, Oliver St. John Gogarty, F. R. Higgins, AE: W. R. Rodgers's Broadcast Conversations with Those Who Knew Them_, pp. 142-68. London: BBC, 1972.
  A collection of intimate biographical vignettes related by Austin Clarke, Padraic Colum, Sir Compton Mackenzie, and others.

Carens, James F. "Four Letters: Sean O'Casey to Oliver St. John Gogarty." _James Joyce Quarterly_ 8, No. 1 (Fall 1970): 111-18.
  Letters that reveal a friendly relationship between the two men, while at the same time making it plain why O'Casey eventually quarreled with everyone involved in the Irish Literary Renaissance.

——. _Surpassing Wit: Oliver St John Gogarty, His Poetry and His Prose_. New York: Columbia University Press, 1979, 266 p.
  A valuable, close reading of Gogarty's works.

Gwynn, Stephen. _Irish Literature and Drama in the English Language: A Short History_, pp. 24ff. London: Thomas Nelson and Sons, 1936, 243 p.

Brief survey. Gwynn's book provides an excellent picture of the time in which Gogarty lived, the intellectual climate in which he worked, and the interplay of personalities that made the era interesting.

Henn, T. R. "The Rhetoric of Yeats." In *In Excited Reverie: A Centenary Tribute to William Butler Yeats, 1865-1939,* edited by A. Norman Jeffares and K.G.W. Cross, pp. 102-122. New York: St. Martin's Press, 1965.*
  Compares Gogarty's use of rhetoric in "Non Dolet" to Yeats's rhetorical technique in "The New Faces."

Huxley, D. J. "Yeats and Dr. Gogarty." *Ariel* 3, No. 3 (July 1972): 31-47.*
  Critical study which discusses the influence of Gogarty's Classicism on Yeats's verse.

Kain, Richard M. *Dublin in the Age of William Butler Yeats and James Joyce,* pp. 20ff. Norman: University of Oklahoma Press, 1962.
  Discussion of Dublin, the literary figures who inhabited it, and the major works of the Irish Renaissance.

Melchiori, Giorgio. "The Birth of Leda." In his *The Whole Mystery of Art: Patterns into Poetry in the Work of W. B. Yeats,* pp. 73-98. New York: Macmillan Co., 1961.*
  Credits Gogarty's poems "Tell Me Now" and "To the Liffey with the Swans" with providing the "catalyst" for W. B. Yeats's sonnet "Leda and the Swan."

Mercier, Vivian. "Ars Poetica." *The Commonweal* LX, No. 19 (13 August 1954): 466-68.
  Review of *The Collected Poems of Oliver St. John Gogarty.* Mercier observes that Gogarty's wit and fondness for traditional meter have alienated some of the New Critics, and prevented the excellence of Gogarty's poetry from being recognized.

————. "Irish Wit and Word-Play." In his *The Irish Comic Tradition,* pp. 78-104. Oxford: Clarendon Press, 1962.
  Survey of Irish humor. Mercier explains the difference between wit and word-play, and the sense in which Gogarty was a master of both.

Moore, George. *Hail and Farewell: Ave, Salve, Vale.* Toronto: Macmillan of Canada, Macklan-Hunter Press, 1976, 774 p.*
  Contains scattered references to Gogarty: "the arch-mocker, the author of all the jokes that enable us to live in Dublin. . . ."

O'Connor, Ulick. "A Famous Friendship." *The Texas Quarterly* 333, No. 2 (Summer 1960): 189-210.*
  Account of Oliver Gogarty's friendship and ultimate enmity with Joyce.

Smith, Grover. "Yeats, Gogarty and the Leap Castle Ghost." In *Modern Irish Literature: Essays in Honor of William York Tindall,* edited by Raymond J. Porter and James D. Brophy, pp. 129-42. New York: Iona College Press, Twayne Publishers, 1972.*
  Comparative study that examines the different manner in which Gogarty and Yeats handled the same folklore materials.

Ishikawa Takuboku

1885-1912

(Born Ishikawa Hajime; also wrote under pseudonym of Ishikawa Hakuhin) Japanese poet, novelist, short story writer, essayist, diarist, and critic.

Takuboku is acknowledged to be one of the most significant poets in modern Japanese literature. His most famous works fuse tanka form, a classic Japanese verse structure consisting of thirty-one syllables, with intellectual and autobiographical subject matter that was not previously considered acceptable for such a traditional poetic form. For this innovation, Takuboku is credited with revitalizing Japanese poetry and strongly influencing the work of many twentieth-century Japanese poets.

Takuboku was born in rural northern Japan, the only son of a Zen priest who broke his vows and secretly married. Although his parents were quite poor, they were committed to providing Takuboku with the finest education they could afford. As a young student, Takuboku showed intellectual and literary ability. His aspirations to become a poet grew particularly strong in his adolescence and never subsided. As an apprentice poet, Takuboku greatly admired the works of Tekkan Yosano and the romantic school to which Yosano belonged. He persistently submitted poems to Yosano's literary journal, *Myojo*, but met with no success. Finally in 1902, *Myojo* accepted one of Takuboku's poems for publication. With renewed confidence and conviction in his future as a poet, Takuboku quit school and moved to Tokyo where he could study under Yosano. In 1905 he published his first volume of poetry, *Akogare*, which was primarily composed of longer lyrical poems written in the "shintai-shi" ("new style"), a form derived from the well-established Western models of poetry found in an 1882 anthology that had considerable impact on Japanese writers of the day. Unimpressed with Takuboku's tanka, Yosano had encouraged him to write poetry in the shintai-shi form, because it was in this mode that he thought Takuboku's poetic gifts would be best displayed. *Akogare* received warm, enthusiastic praise, but it contained little of the fierce individual voice Takuboku would develop a few years later. After the publication of *Akogare*, Takuboku married a woman he had known since childhood. These few months in 1905 marked the happiest and most fulfilling time in his life.

In 1906, Takuboku's father disappeared after being dismissed from the Hōtoko Temple for misuse of temple funds, and upon his son devolved the responsibility of supporting the family. Takuboku left Tokyo and accepted a teaching position in a small village, but his meager income could not adequately provide for a family of five, which included his wife and child, his mother, and an ailing older sister. They all lived close to starvation and steadily declined in health. Unable to cope with these pressures, Takuboku left his teaching post after one year and traveled around Japan, during which time he worked at a variety of jobs, mostly with newspapers and print shops, and continued to send money back to his family. At this time, he suffered from strong internal conflicts regarding his previous romantic perceptions of poetry and an emerging inclination toward Naturalism, a movement which then exerted a strong influence on Japanese fiction writers. Takuboku recorded his perceptions of his gravitation toward Naturalism, as well as

many painful discoveries regarding his own character, in a notebook which is known as *Rōmaji nikki (The Rōmaji Diary)* because it was written in a westernized system of transliteration. Some critics consider *The Rōmaji Diary* an autobiographical Naturalistic novel, in which Takuboku depicts himself heroically struggling with ambition, self-doubt, and the stifling responsibilities life has thrust upon him. For the next five years, Takuboku attempted to write fiction, at which he was largely unsuccessful, and experimented with a new type of poetry which he believed more earnest and vital than the shintai-shi verse he had previously written. In this new poetry he used the verbally spare and precise tanka form to describe the everyday events and impressions that he now believed were essential subjects for poetry. This new verse was published in a volume entitled *Ichiaku no suna (A Handful of Sand)*. During the last two years of his life, Takuboku continued to work when circumstances and his health permitted. Over a span of approximately eighteen months his newborn child died, his wife contracted tuberculosis, and he was operated on for a severe case of peritonitis. Takuboku's aged and ailing mother nursed the family until she too collapsed and died of tuberculosis. Close to death, Takuboku entrusted his last collection of poems, *Kanashiki gangu (Sad Toys)*, to his friend Toki Zemmaro, a poet and scholar who promised to find a publisher for it. A publisher accepted the manuscript and gave Zemmaro a small advance. Takuboku died one week later of tuberculosis and was cremated in a pauper's funeral.

Although Takuboku's poetic career lasted only nine years, it developed rapidly and passed through three distinctive phases: romanticism, naturalism, and a period in which he produced politically conscious poetry. His first volume of poems, *Akogare*, contains the best examples of Takuboku's writing during his romantic period. The poems in *Akogare*, which have a restrained but musical language and a romantic belief in heightened individualism and spiritual awareness, were highly praised by the Tokyo literati. As his life became increasingly filled with poverty and hardship, Takuboku came to believe that poetry, if it was to have lasting meaning and truth, must confront and include these less sublime facts of life. This marks the beginning of the naturalistic phase of his career, the period in which he would introduce new thematic possibilities of form and content to Japanese poetry. During this time, Takuboku gained confidence in his use of the tanka form, which became the exclusive mode of his second volume, *A Handful of Sand*, a highly original work that combines the formal simplicity of classic Japanese poetry with the pathos of life in the modern world. As Shio Sakanishi remarked of Takuboku in his introduction to this work: "Lifting it from anarchy and stiltedness, [he] again restored poetry to the human heart, extended its scope, and made language his willing servant." The following tanka, one of the most famous in *A Handful of Sand*, may serve to illustrate the unconventional nature of poetic expression achieved by Takuboku in this volume: "My sister pitied / my eyes that burned / with insatiable / craving for knowledge / she thought I must be in love." The ironic and intellectual nature of such verse revolutionized tanka, which heretofore was largely devoted to pastoral subject matter. *Sad Toys*, Takuboku's last volume, exhibits his growing social and political awareness. In 1909 he had written a serialized essay, entitled "Poems to Eat," that summarized his emerging conceptions of the highest intentions of poetry. In Takuboku's own words true poetry means "poems written without putting any distance from actual life. They are not delicacies or dainty dishes, but food indispensible for us in our daily meals." The tanka in *Sad Toys* mix colloquial language with classical form, and it is in this volume that most critics feel that Takuboku achieves the artistic and socialistic goals he had sought to attain: the removal of Japanese poetry from its elitist pedestal and its distribution to the masses.

Although Takuboku wrote fiction and produced highly regarded and influential criticism, it is through his poetry that his literary reputation was established and endures. Considered one of the first modern voices in Japanese poetry, he brought to it unprecedented personalism and passion that has had a lasting impact on the poets who have succeeded him. His direct vision and spare but evocative language has also made his work extremely appealing to Western readers.

PRINCIPAL WORKS

Akogare   (poetry)   1905
Chōei   (novel)   1908
Rōmaji nikki   (diary)   1909
   [*Rōmaji Diary* published in anthology *Modern Japanese Literature* (partial translation), 1956]
Ichiaku no suna   (poetry)   1910
   [*A Handful of Sand*, 1934]
Kanashiki gangu   (poetry)   1912
   [*Sad Toys*, 1962; also published as *A Sad Toy*, 1962]

Yosuko to fue   (poetry)   1912
The Poetry of Ishikawa Takuboku   (poetry)   1959
Poems to Eat   (essays)   1966
Takuboku zenshu. 8 vols.   (poetry, novels, short stories, criticism, and essays)   1967-68

SHIO SAKANISHI   (essay date 1934)

[*In the following excerpt, Sakanishi discusses Takuboku's prominence in modern Japanese poetry, praising the dramatic quality of Takuboku's verse and his success in restoring simplicity and fluidity to Japanese poetry.*]

In the development of modern Japanese poetry, Takuboku Ishikawa occupies a place apart. Born in the transitional period when the stilted diction and theme of poetry were no longer sufficient to express a new spirit and the new experiences of men, and acknowledging Tekkan Yosano as his literary master, Takuboku, nevertheless, remained outside the straight line of development that had its starting point in Tekkan. In a brief space of nine years, he lived through the three stages—romantic, naturalistic, and socialistic—which the remaining literary world took the next twenty-five years to experience. Therefore, though a product of his age, he was not of his age, and it was only after his death that the full significance of his work came to be fully appreciated. (p. 1)

The volume entitled *Ichiaku no suna* (*A Handful of Sand*) contained 551 poems. . . . The volume caused a stir in the literary world because of its extreme simplicity of diction and unconventional subject matter. Therefore those who had been nourished on the set notion of what poetry should be raised their hands in horror and denounced it most emphatically. On the other hand, among those who had been frightened away from Japanese poetry because of its classical formalism or who had never had any particular interest in it, his work was welcomed with joy. Takuboku's direct expression as well as the freshness of his verse delighted them. Indeed, with the publication of the *Handful of Sand*, Takuboku humanized Japanese poetry; he took it out of the hands of a select few and gave it to the masses. (pp. 9-10)

In the minds of those who loved Takuboku's poetry the thought of what his genius actually achieved and the pathos of the unfulfilled promise of his life are ever present. Even with no advance of artistic power, but merely with the wider experience and greater independence which are the gifts of time rather than of genius, he might have attained his high ideal. At the age of twenty-five in spite of an uninspiring environment, hostile criticism, and the haunting presence of starvation and illness, he had produced work mature in thought and execution and full of human significance. His subsequent works are further marked by great objective power and dramatic skill.

There is no doubt that Takuboku is one of the great poets of the modern period, but the significance of his poetry in the history of Japanese literature is even greater than its intrinsic value. He recreated Japanese prosody, giving it back the simplicity and the fluidity that it had lost centuries ago. In the early part of the tenth century Ki no Tsurayuki, distinguished courtier and poet, wrote: "The heart of men is the seed whence springs our native poetry and the countless leaves of language." In the course of its development, however, Japanese poetry departed from its original spirit, and fostering tricks and phrases of its own, became in itself a seed. Lifting it from anarchy and stiltedness, Takuboku again restored poetry to the human heart, extended its scope, and made language his willing servant. He saw no reason why the language of poetry had to be different from that of every day life.

Simplicity of expression is complemented in his poetry by simplicity of content. We may call Takuboku a poet of the simpler human experiences. He does not complicate or subtilise the world of the senses by those higher activities of the human spirit which go to create the landscape of Priest Saigyo or of Shelley. In the maturing process which intervenes before the birth of a poem, he does not analyse deeply or reconstruct what he has seen or felt. As he once wrote to a friend, his poems are often no more than entries in a diary, unpremeditated outgrowths of the moment and the event. Only through his genius these spontaneous records of the passing moment acquired glowing intensity and lasting human significance. This achievement of freedom and simplicity within the framework of traditional form was his contribution to Japanese poetry.

The most outstanding characteristic of his poetry, however, is its dramatic quality. Japanese poetry has been known for its brevity and suggestiveness, but Takuboku was able to present a five-act play in the brief space of thirty-one syllables. . . . Indeed, perhaps his greatest ambition was to write a drama. Early in 1905 he had in fact started a play, **Death's Victory,** and advance notice of it was printed in his first volume of poems. How far he might have realized his ambition it is difficult to conjecture. Genius for dramatic writing is seldom developed early, but judging from his poems, Takuboku seems to have possessed it to an eminent degree. (pp. 14-16)

To Takuboku the world of reality was profoundly dissatisfying, and he sought an escape in poetry in which to express his yearning for a fuller life and the good things his spirit and senses lacked. Yet his poems are fully charged with reality. The charm of his native village, the bleak shores of the northern island, the poverty, the disease, the birth and the dying, the friends he made, the women he loved, the ambition that fretted like a hair shirt—all find their place in the simple structure of his poems. Indeed, of all his writings, his poetry is the most autobiographical. Yet he protested at being called a poet, and it is an irony of fate that to-day Takuboku is considered one of the most significant poets of the Meiji period which closed with his death in 1912. (p. 17)

Shio Sakanishi, in an introduction to A Handful of Sand *by Takuboku Ishikawa, translated by Shio Sakanishi, Marshall Jones Company, 1934, pp. 1-17.*

DONALD KEENE (essay date 1967)

[*Keene is one of the foremost translators and critics of Japanese literature. In the following excerpt, originally published in 1967, he discusses Takuboku's mastery of the tanka form and his weaknesses as a fiction writer. Keene also compares Takuboku's career with that of the modern Japanese poet Masaoka Shiki.*]

The life of Ishikawa Takuboku . . . , on the surface at least, much resembles Shiki's. Both were young men from the country who made their way to Tokyo and established themselves as outstanding poets in the four or five years before their deaths. In character, however, they differed entirely. Takuboku utterly lacked the Confucian discipline of Shiki. It is precisely because of this difference that we may say that if Shiki is modern,

Takuboku is contemporary. But it is hard, when one examines the childish features of Takuboku's photographs, to realize that this was the author of the stinging, unsentimental judgments that lace his diaries and letters. Shiki wrote unkindly about Ki no Tsurayuki, a poet of a thousand years before, and occasionally expressed disappointment in his contemporaries, but he was more interested in ideas than in personalities. Takuboku is intensely personal. His poetry is almost entirely about himself or people he knew, rarely about nature. Living a decade after Shiki he finds himself in a world as different as the Japan after the Sino-Japanese War was from the Japan after the Russo-Japanese War of 1904-5, which marked the emergence of Japan as a world power. Takuboku lived in a world of incomparably greater sophistication, and the European books he read were not the *Autobiography* of Benjamin Franklin or Samuel Smiles but Ibsen and Gorki. In literary tastes a century, not ten years, separates the two men.

Takuboku's *tanka* are superior to Shiki's because they made no concessions to being poetic. They are colloquial in manner and sharply responsive to Takuboku's passing moods. Shiki's *tanka* on the wisteria hints at his suffering, but Takuboku's *tanka* strike us with both fists. Sometimes he drops into sentimentality, repeating such words as *kanashiki* (''sad'') or *namida* (''tears'') in a manner incongruous in so tough-minded a poet, but his successful *tanka* make a powerful assault on the reader's mind. Takuboku was familiar with the traditions of the *tanka,* but unlike Shiki, he disregarded them. Shiki once stated that a poem about the wind blowing over streetcar tracks lacked elegance, but Takuboku never concerned himself about elegance. Takuboku was certainly less profound than Shiki. None of his *tanka* would stand up to the detailed and extended treatment that has been given to Shiki's best *haiku.* But the impact of his poetry is overpowering, especially his *tanka,* where his sudden perceptions and emotional reactions are captured in molten state. Nothing in earlier Japanese poetry really prepares us for such a tanka as:

> My sister pitied
> My eyes that were burning with
> Immeasurable
> Craving for knowledge:
> She thought I must be in love.

The words ''craving for knowledge'' especially suggest an area of experience never treated in the *tanka* before Takuboku. (pp. 164-65)

Takuboku's stories are failures because they lack novelistic skill. They are either thinly disguised recountings of his experiences in his village or in Tokyo, or else almost plotless conversations irrelevantly tied to hastily sketched characters. Takuboku was constantly starting new stories, often taking the trouble to invent names for all the characters only to abandon the piece after a page or two. His long serialized novel **Chōei (Shadow of a Bird)** is at once conventional and badly organized, though it has brilliant flashes. The short stories are interesting mainly as records of what Takuboku was thinking at a particular time, not for their characterizations, insights or style. The best of Takuboku's prose is in his diaries and letters, suggesting that he was most effective at impromptu expression. When he revised his old diaries for publication he invariably lessened their literary value by larding them with conventional emotions, rather like a painter who turns his watercolor sketch into a large oil painting by inflating or diluting his original inspiration. Takuboku is starkly direct in his diaries and letters, but his more polished prose is often vitiated by preconceptions of what made for fine writing. (p. 168)

If Takuboku had lived longer he might have developed into a first-class novelist or poet of the modern-style verse (*shin-taishi*), but I doubt that he would have written better *tanka*. The traditional form proved a perfect medium for Takuboku's flashes of irritation, nostalgia or affection, but it was obviously incapable of sustained expression. Takuboku's *tanka* today enjoy greater popularity than any written in the thousand year history of the form. (pp. 169-70)

> Donald Keene, "The Creation of Modern Japanese Poetry: Shiki and Takuboku," *in his* Landscapes and Portraits: Appreciations of Japanese Culture, *Kodansha International Ltd., 1971, pp. 157-70.**

SANFORD GOLDSTEIN and SEISHI SHINODA (essay date 1977)

[*In the following excerpt, Goldstein and Shinoda examine the tanka poems in Takuboku's collection* Sad Toys. *They also discuss Takuboku's conception of tanka both as a poetic form and as a mode of autobiography.*]

In **"Various Kinds of Tanka,"** an article Takuboku Ishikawa serialized in the Tokyo *Asahi* newspaper from December 10 to December 20, 1910, he pointed out that tanka poets ought to be free to use more than the traditional thirty-one-syllable rhythm of 5-7-5-7-7. Even the content of tanka need not be limited, Takuboku insisted, and he urged poets to disregard "the arbitrary restrictions which dictate that some subjects are not fit for tanka and will not make one." Modern readers may be surprised when Takuboku, in this context of defining tanka, suddenly lapsed into the nihilistic frame of mind so deeply rooted in him: "What can I do with those many things which really inconvenience me and pain me? Nothing. No, I cannot continue my existence unless I live a miserable double life, submitting with resignation and servility to these inconveniences. Though I try to justify myself, I cannot help but admit I have become a victim of the present family, class, and capitalist systems and the system of trading in knowledge." (p. 1)

An examination of Takuboku's life provides a kind of synecdoche on the eternal struggle of the artist in society, and while *Sad Toys* contains penetrating moments into that sad life, these poems go beyond it to provide tanka with a much greater range than it had in its twelve-hundred-year history. Along with the famous Akiko Yosano (1878-1942), Takuboku became a supreme tanka-reformer. The words *sad* and *toy*, contradictory and clever and yet edged with pathos—that of a child who cries over his toys—contain on closer scrutiny a much deeper significance when viewed in the light of Takuboku's diaries, letters, and articles.

We ought to keep in mind the fact that Takuboku did not give his second and last tanka collection the title *Sad Toys (Kanashiki Gangu . . .*). His friend Aika Toki had wanted to call the posthumous volume *After "A Handful of Sand": From the End of November 1910,* but the publisher wisely refused because readers might have easily confused it with Takuboku's earlier collection. Toki finally selected the title from the memorable last line in the *Asahi* article. (pp. 1-2)

Poverty, illness, and tanka permeate many of the twenty-six years of Takuboku's life, and like the contradictory manifestations moderns are bombarded with, this triumvirate represents Takuboku's fall and greatness. His own definition of tanka in

"Poems to Eat," an article serialized in the Tokyo *Mainichi* newspaper from November 30 to December 7, 1909, was that "Poetry must not be what is usually called poetry. It must be an exact report, an honest diary, of the changes in a man's emotional life." Takuboku loaded his poems with events from his own personal history. The detailed biographical aspects of that life, like the I-novel which forms so much a part of Japanese literature, cannot be ignored. In an I-novel, the author-hero exploits with a fair degree of accuracy the details of his own life. Takuboku's life is tanka, his tanka his life. (p. 2)

In letters, diary entries, and articles, Takuboku probed his attitude toward tanka. What was this poetic form and who were the people who composed it? In his early days he had difficulty in deciding what the content and the mood of the poem ought to be. "Once," he tells us in his article **"Poems to Eat"** as he continues along this line,

> I used to write "poems." It was for a few years from the age of seventeen or eighteen. At that time there was nothing for me but poetry. My mind, which was yearning after some indescribable thing from morning to night, could find an outlet to some extent only by making poems. And I had absolutely nothing except that mind.— As everyone knows, poetry in those days contained only conventional feelings besides fantasy, crude music, and a feeble religious element or something equivalent to it. Reflecting on my attitude toward poetry at that time, I want to say this: a very complicated process was needed to turn actual feelings into poetry. Suppose, for instance, one derived a certain sentiment from looking at a sapling about three meters tall growing on a small plot lit up by the sun: he had to make the vacant plot a wilderness, the sapling a towering tree, the sun the rising or setting sun, and he had to make himself a poet, a traveler, or a young man in sorrow. Otherwise, the sentiment was not suited to the poetry of those days, and he himself was not satisfied.

With this early attitude that poems ought to emerge from the "inspiration" of the "poet," Takuboku discovered he could not write poems when he felt "inspired," but only "when I was in a mood in which I despised myself or when I was driven by some practical circumstance, such as nearing a deadline. I wrote many poems at the end of every month, for then I found myself in circumstances which made me despise myself." He came, he continues in **"Poems to Eat,"** to reject such words as *poet* and *genius*, and when he recalled those youthful days in which he had written "poems," the regret at no longer being able to turned to sorrow and then to self-scorn. Forced to make a living, Takuboku became a stranger to poetry:

> From my home to Hakodate, from there to Sapporo, then farther on to Kushiro—in that way I wandered from place to place in search of a livelihood. Before I knew it, I had become a stranger to poetry. When I met someone who said he had read my old poems and who talked about the bygone days, I had the same kind of unpleasant feeling one has when a friend who had once indulged in dissipation with him talks about an old flame. The actual experience of life caused a change in me. When a kind old

politician who took me to the office of a newspaper in Kushiro introduced me to someone by saying, ''He is a poet of the new school,'' I felt in his goodwill the greatest contempt I had experienced till then.

What revived Takuboku's interest in poetry and other forms of literature was the naturalist movement in addition to his own boredom in thinking of literature as fantasy (that is, removed from reality). His own tormented grasp of the reality of his own life caused him to further accept the spirit of the new naturalism at work in Meiji Japan. He did not object to the attempt to bring into poetry words from everyday life, yet he drew a line—and this is extremely important in the evolution of his own tanka: ''Naturally poetry is subject to a certain formal restriction. When poetry is completely liberated, it must become prose.''

For this reason Takuboku's later tanka, especially those in *Sad Toys,* are more often than not a mixture of colloquial and formal diction, though even in this last volume many are formal in tone. When he came to Tokyo after living in Hakodate, ''that colonial town in the north, where the crude realities of life were left unveiled,'' he often said he too would write colloquial poems in the new style, but his words were simply for those hard-liners who regarded the form of tanka as fixed, cemented in the techniques of history and tradition. In Tokyo, where the difficult life he lived is so movingly described in his *Romaji Diary,* he apparently wrote four or five hundred tanka during that year, the pleasure from them ''somewhat like that which a husband beaten in a marital quarrel derives from scolding or teasing his child without reason.'' His boardinghouse life, which sometimes hurled him toward the pit of suicide, made him appreciate more fully the spirit behind the new naturalism and the new poetry, the name he gave to the latter being ''poems to eat'': ''The name means poems made with both feet upon the ground. It means poems written without putting any distance from actual life. They are not delicacies or dainty dishes, but food indispensable for us in our daily meal. To define poetry in this way may be to pull it down from its established position, but to me it means to make poetry, which has added nothing to or detracted nothing from actual life, into something that cannot be dispensed with.''

Poetry had become for Takuboku as indispensable as food. In this context, of course, his tanka had to be much more than mere toys. He hacked off the outer protective shell that had made the genre into something curious and rare for the elite few, and he turned it into something to be seized by the very teeth, all moments of life available to it. And this meant that the rarefied name ''poet'' had to be eliminated: ''. . . I deny the existence of a special kind of man called poet. It is quite right that others should call a man who writes poems a poet, but the man should not think himself a poet. My way of putting this may be improper, but if he thinks himself a poet, his poems will degenerate; that is, they will become something needless to us. First of all, a poet must be a man. Second, he must be a man. Third, he must be a man. Moreover, he must possess all that the common man possesses.'' Nor must the content of poetry be ''poetic'' in the refined connotation of its earlier meanings:

> . . . to say that poetry is the purest of arts is tantamount to saying that distilled water is the purest water. It may serve as an explanation of quality, but it cannot be a criterion in deciding its value or necessity. Future poets should not

say such a thing. At the same time they should firmly decline preferential treatment given to poetry and the poet. Like everything else, all literature is in a sense a means or a method to us and to our life. To regard poetry as something high and noble is a kind of idolatry.

> Poetry must not be what is usually called poetry. It must be an exact report, an honest diary, of the changes in a man's emotional life. Accordingly, it must be fragmentary; it must not have organization.

(pp. 31-3)

[Takuboku] felt the gap between the Philistines and the literati or the gap between the actual world and the life in literature itself. He notes in [the 1910 article ''**The Glass Window**''] the rise of naturalism as a movement to bring literature closer to actual life, yet Takuboku concludes that naturalism could not fully bridge the gap between the two. Perhaps Takuboku meant that inevitably naturalism could not remain a literary movement, for the gap that must remain between the created form and life as it is actually lived is one ''which even an operation by the most ingenious surgeon could not suture.'' Takuboku claims that it is only by this gap that literature can preserve its territorial integrity forever (should that line be crossed literature could not call itself such). Nevertheless, Takuboku could not help pointing to the deep sorrow men who create literature must feel because of this gap. (p. 36)

Despite these contradictions Takuboku could not after all abandon tanka. His article ''**A Dialogue between an Egoist and His Friend**'' further explores this ambivalence toward tanka. As the egoist Takuboku had said, tanka would die out, but this event would not occur for many years because the form would continue to exist in the same way a man is said to have lived long when he becomes an octogenarian. Only when the Japanese language was unified would it become possible for tanka to die, and the Japanese language would unify itself only when the confusion existing in its mixture of colloquial and formal in its written forms was eliminated. As for other aspects of tanka structure, Takuboku repeated his belief that tanka itself might contain more than the traditional thirty-one syllables and need not be patterned in the traditional one or two lines. In fact, he claimed that because each tanka is different in tone, each might have different line divisions. (pp. 37-8)

In Takuboku's first collection of tanka, *A Handful of Sand,* 551 poems had been included; yet in *Sad Toys,* posthumously published from the notebook in which the poet kept his tanka (the first two in the volume added by his friend Toki from a slip of paper found later), there were only 194. Illness, poverty, the demands of his job as proofreader, his attempt at writing stories, and the pursuit of socialism provide some explanation for the smaller number of tanka; yet these very conditions, painful as they were, lent themselves to the creation of ''sad toys.'' Is it not possible to speculate that Takuboku made greater demands than ever on tanka that pared life down to the essentials of a ''self'' he was perpetually trying to find? We have seen how Takuboku spent a triumphant three days in his earlier career in which he had set down at least 246 tanka during that short interval. In the slightly less than seventeen months remaining in his life after the publication of *Handful,* he probably demanded more from each tanka so that he was much more critical of each effort. He saw the moments slipping by, each moment in itself containing infinite possibilities for the creation of tanka. . . . (p. 40)

Takuboku felt the necessity of preserving the most ephemeral element in man's life, the individual moment, whether that moment was high or low, bright or dark, inspiring or frustrating, and he set for himself a task no other tanka poet before him had undertaken—that of extending tanka's range, of revising its form and content, of blending the unique mixture of colloquial and formal which adds so much to the complexity of the Japanese language. He carried his tanka to a point where the poem was almost destroyed because it came so close to breaking down into prose. At times he wished tanka might collapse, and he felt that it would at some future day, but he refused to allow himself to be the one to make that disastrous move. He called his tanka "sad toys," but even toys so easily broken can become precious and indispensable, for his tanka were also "poems to eat." Takuboku gave to the Everyman in each of us moments we can immediately recognize and value as commonplace, real, honest, compassionate, unflinching, and human. (pp. 41-2)

> *Sanford Goldstein and Seishi Shinoda, in an introduction to* Sad Toys *by Takuboku Ishikawa, translated by Sanford Goldstein and Seishi Shinoda, Purdue University Press, 1977, pp. 1-42.*

YUKIHITO HIJIYA (essay date 1979)

[*Hijiya is a Japanese professor of English literature and the author of* Ishikawa Takuboku, *the most comprehensive study in English of Takuboku's life and works. In the following excerpt from that work, Hijika discusses the* Rōmaji Diary *and appraises Takuboku's literary importance.*]

Takuboku's diary, which he kept from April 7 to June 1, 1909, is today commonly known as *The Rōmaji Diary* because he wrote it in *rōmaji*, a system of transliteration of the Japanese syllabary which was still relatively new. It presents a candid account of the inner struggle that hastened his maturity as a writer and a thinker. The painful experiences recorded in the diary helped him to develop insight into the value of human life and his individual existence, the insight revealed in various writings produced between late 1909 and the end of 1910. This period of maturation must have included those months during and immediately following *The Rōmaji Diary*. Takuboku's experimentation with *rōmaji* not only helped him in his personal development but also offered a possibility for a new literary genre. For this reason *The Rōmaji Diary* holds a significant place in the bulk of modern Japanese literature as well as in Takuboku's complete works.

The Rōmaji Diary reveals a young man vacillating between hope and despair, between the desire for individual achievement and crippling self-doubt. Moreover, he is further frustrated by family obligations, which impose a strict limit on the extent to which he can devote himself to the pursuit of his ideals. The double burden of financial need and failure as a novelist weighs heavily upon him, sharpening his senses now operating on the extreme edge of despair. It is Takuboku's honest recording of his inner life, however, that gives power and artistic unity to the diary. *The Rōmaji Diary* is more than a diary. Takuboku has unwittingly made it a kind of Naturalistic novel, the hero of which is himself.

Takuboku's dejection is rooted in his feeling of guilt at neglecting his family.... Takuboku complains incessantly of being short of money, but when he obtains any, he spends it recklessly. Thanks to the generosity of the editor of the *Asahi* newspaper he had secured a job as a proofreader in March, the income from which was sufficient to support his family; but instead of sending for them immediately he keeps spending the money on books, expensive meals, and, most of all, on prostitutes. Takuboku worries not so much about how soon he should call his family as about his own reluctance even to correspond with them: "Right now I should be writing to Mother and the others, but I dread it, too. I'm always wanting to write about anything that might please them in order to comfort them. I haven't forgotten my mother or my wife. No, I've been thinking of them every day. Yet I've mailed only one letter and one postcard since the beginning of the year." ... It is clear that in this entry Takuboku is evading the real issue. Whether through choice or from necessity, the young man still searching for his own path in life has been weighed down with too many responsibilities. He is now enjoying a welcome respite from the burden. Looking back at the year before, he remarks: "The summer at Seki-shin-kan [his lodging house]! It was the summer when, in spite of financial difficulties, I was happy to be free from family obligations even for half a year. Right! It was the time when I enjoyed being a semi-bachelor, paying little attention to my family." ... Having once put off the heavy load, Takuboku cannot summon the self-discipline to pick it up again: "I've put on now the heavy, heavy clothes, / The clothes of responsibility. / If I could take them off—Ah! / How enrapturing! / My body would be as light as hydrogen, / Flying high up into the vast sky. / The crowd below would cry out: / 'A skylark!' Ah!'' ... (pp. 50-2)

Takuboku at one point attempts to solve his dilemma by imaginatively sketching the character he wishes to be. Speaking of himself in the third person, he says: "Stripping himself of all the armor of restrictions and conventions, he, 'the mighty one', fought bravely singlehandedly. With an iron heart, with no tears or smiles on his face, he advanced straight toward the objective of his desires, taking no notice of things around him. Abandoning everything called virtue as if it were dust, the brave one performed without regret what no other human would dare." ... Yet these courageous acts are performed only in the mind of the writer. Takuboku recognizes the vanity of what he has written, which in turn increases his anguish: "One hundred days have passed by [since the New Year began] while my body in armor trembled in great anticipation. Whom did I conquer? How strong did I become?" ... Takuboku is too gentlehearted to be an aggressive, egoistic fighter; furthermore, he is too sensitive to sacrifice his family completely for a personal goal. His anxiety for his family is magnified in proportion to his increasing desire to be free from his obligations to them.... The struggle to resolve the conflicting feelings toward his family has quickened Takuboku's imagination.

Takuboku's melancholy develops also from his failure to achieve recognition as a novelist. Despite publishers' constant rejections of his work, Takuboku is too proud to give up his desire to be accepted as a novelist. He frequently excuses himself from work at the newspaper office in order to spend the day writing a story, but he seldom gets beyond the first two pages. His attempt to write is always met with frustration: "I was determined to write something today and I didn't go to work. No, since I didn't want to work, I decided to write. At any rate, I tried to write a story, 'Red Ink,' which I had thought out last night. It's a story about my suicide. I wrote about three pages or so, but I couldn't go any further.

Why can't I write? I can't look at myself objectively. No, I just can't write. I can't think clearly." ... Repeated failures at last lead him to admit defeat: "I had to seriously consider the fact that I simply can't write a novel. I had to concede that there's no hope for my future." . . . (pp. 52-3)

The sense of failure as a writer added to his sense of failure as a son, husband and father leaves Takuboku with the feeling of complete failure as a man. In *The Rōmaji Diary* one comes across entry after entry expressing existential fear:

> I said to myself, "I will give up my literary career." "If I give up literature, what shall I do?" Death! . . . Really, what should I do? Is there anything left for me?
>
> My heart was like a sick bird flapping its wings in an attempt to keep itself from plunging into the pit of darkness.
>
> A useless key! That's it! No matter where I carry it, I can't find a hole the key fits. . . .

Finding no satisfactory answer to the question of his place in life, Takuboku finds a temporary escape in wishful thinking. He fantasizes finding an empty house, where he can sleep as long as he wants; he dreams of riding a train just to be riding; he imagines going either to an isolated place where no other human being can be seen or else to a place jammed with people, such as a movie house, to be lost among the crowd; or, naively believing that illness will liberate him from the burdens of life, he dreams of escape through sickness: "For one year, or even one month, / Or a week, or three days, / God, if you exist, O God, / My wish is only one: Batter my body! / Painful though it may be, I don't care. / Grant me illness!" . . . The irony is that two years later this wish comes true, and a fatal sickness emancipates him from all the burdens of the world. But at the present time, as Takuboku knows well, all these fantasies serve merely to increase his frustration over his confinement by family obligations as well as to intensify the awareness that the freedom he yearns for is only an illusion: "I can neither go to a place where no other humans exist nor discover satisfaction with them. Unable to endure the pain of life, I know no way to cope with life itself. All human relations are shackles and responsibility creeps in. Hamlet said: 'To be, or, not to be'; but today the question of death has become more complicated than in Hamlet's day." . . . (pp. 53-4)

Takuboku cannot conquer despair, but one can observe that his agony has done him a favor. The struggle with despondency has led him to formulate his own view of the writer's responsibility to society: "The writer must be a critic, or at least a reformer, of life, not a mere observer of it." . . . Takuboku has developed also the capacity to empathize with the suffering of others. In one dark account of his hardship, a single incident recorded stands out as a glimmer of light. He writes about an unexpected encounter with two youths from the country: one is from Takuboku's home village, Shibutami, the other from Tokushima Prefecture. Takuboku feels immediate empathy with them; from his own tormenting experience in Tokyo he knows very well what awaits them: "Lured by the flame, summer insects burn themselves to death. These youths, deluded by the apparent glory of city life, drove themselves to it without realizing what the consequences would be. Only one alternative is left for them, either to be burned to death or to fly away." . . . Takuboku helps them find a lodging place, treats them to meals and even offers financial help, all the while neglecting his own family suffering greater hardships. Takuboku seems to be showing off his kindness in order to impress the boys from the country. Yet his generosity to the young men should not be interpreted mainly as a display of vanity. His kindness is gen-

uine, and this act of compassion helps him regain a sense of his own worth. His taking pity on the youths functions as a vicarious expiation of the guilt he feels toward his family.

The Rōmaji Diary closes with a record of Takuboku's reunion with his family and their moving into the upstairs of a barber shop. Miyazaki has taken pity on them and paid their way to Tokyo. This compulsory reunion, however, works favorably for Takuboku, for he is now bound to think of his family first, making it necessary for him to abandon his excessive introspection. This release from self-interrogation brings him to a higher level of objectivity which eventually enables him to mature in his perception of the function of literature in life and, more important, in his understanding of his own place as a man of letters.

But why was the diary a "*rōmaji*" diary? Takuboku's reason for writing the diary in *rōmaji* calls for clarification. At the beginning of the diary he explains: "Why, then, have I decided to write this diary in *rōmaji*? Why? I love my wife and because I love her, I don't want her to read this diary. This is a lie! While it's true that I love her and I don't want her to read this, these two facts are not necessarily related." . . . Takuboku's rationale is odd indeed, for his wife had studied English and could undoubtedly read *rōmaji*. It seems that we should look for the true motive in another direction. As we have seen, whenever Takuboku tries to write a story, he cannot get beyond the first two or three pages. Preoccupied with his problems, he is unable to objectify his experience. Takuboku, then, has used *rōmaji* as a means of looking at himself from a distance, of objectifying his intense emotional experience. Putting his experience down on paper has released his tension and using *rōmaji* has helped him to achieve greater detachment.

Further, using *rōmaji* freed Takuboku from the conventional literary forms associated with both Japanese and Chinese characters, which helped him develop the self-discipline manifested in his simple refined style. That Takuboku enjoyed this stylistic freedom is most apparent in his vivid descriptions of various individuals sketched in the diary. Takuboku's realistic portrayals, nurtured during his apprenticeship to Naturalism, give us the living human beings: his friend Kindaichi, the housemaids at his lodging house, the two youths from the country, various prostitutes who provide him with brief moments of physical gratification; the list goes on. As a result Takuboku's diary resembles a novel. In fact, though the form is that of a diary, it is more like an autobiographical-confessional novel, the genre started by Tayama Katai, the champion of the Japanese Naturalistic movement. The protagonist of *The Rōmaji Diary* is a man struggling alone against the wretchedness of life about which he tells the reader with honesty. The protagonist is real because in him Takuboku has presented himself without speciousness, exactly as he felt and thought. Takuboku's friends and acquaintances function as minor characters who serve to shed light on the character of the protagonist and on the intensity of his inner struggle. His daily factual entry then is the development of plot in which the whole history of the protagonist's inner life is told with realism and exactness of feeling. Revitalizing the old genre of diary with a new approach of writing in *rōmaji* and with a new emphasis on dramatizing his inner life, Takuboku has made *The Rōmaji Diary* a unique literary record of his personal development both as a writer and as a thinker. (pp. 54-6)

Of all the literary figures Meiji Japan produced, few writers, with the possible exception of Natsume Sōseki, have among the general public enjoyed such lasting popularity as Takuboku.

The inner strength with which he confronted a life of privation, the determined will to keep his youthful creative energy active in the face of poverty, and the independent spirit with which he fearlessly spoke up for the value of individualism have won for him the admiration of his readers and have made him an almost legendary figure. Idolized by old and young, rich and poor, Takuboku continues to live as the symbol of eternal youth in the minds and hearts of those who enjoy literature.

Takuboku's popularity, however, is due almost entirely to his tanka, in which his influence on subsequent generations is most apparent. In neither poetry nor the novel did Takuboku produce anything of sufficient substance to establish a literary reputation. His contribution to the history of modern poetry is significant for his introduction of new subjects for poetry, especially socialism. (p. 172)

As a novelist Takuboku failed to produce a work equal in quality to his tanka. His novels are read simply because they are his, not because of any particular intrinsic literary merit. Takuboku's novels did not pioneer new possibilities for the genre to the extent that his tanka did. Even his comparatively successful works such as *The Hospital Window, The Shadow of a Bird* and *Our Gang and He* are valuable only in the sense that they point to Takuboku's potential. In these novels he deals with ideas which are certainly ahead of their time, but his artistic accomplishment does not match that of such novelists as Ōgai, Tōson and Sōseki. The great irony of Takuboku's career is that he achieved lasting fame not through the novel, the form which he regarded most highly, but through the tanka, which he considered no more than a toy.

Even though Takuboku's poetry and novels can be disregarded in the evaluation of his position in modern Japanese literature, his essays must not be ignored. As Takuboku the artist is most clearly revealed in his tanka, so in his essays is Takuboku the critic most eloquently manifested.

Takuboku's essays reveal a remarkable sensitivity to the spirit of the age. Whether the issue was education, literature or politics, he intuitively saw through to the core of the problem and pointed it out fearlessly. Though often driven by impulse, he remained faithful to the dictates of conscience. His critical mind was kept active by a passion for new ideas for bringing forth a new world better than the present existing one. It is this zeal for the new, combined with a discriminating sensibility, that led him to develop his advanced views of life and literature and that enabled him to produce such a penetrating essay as "The Present State of the Age of Repression." It is only natural that Takuboku's farsighted view and unyielding voice calling attention to the injustices of an autocratic society should lead to his being posthumously placed in a position of mentor to the proletarian writers in the 1920s. The publication of "The Present State of the Age of Repression" gave them the courage to speak up for the weak and the oppressed. Concerning the literary impact of this essay upon the succeeding decade, Watanabe Junzō, one of the proletarian writers, has this to say:

> At the end of the essay Takuboku says that "criticism is what my literature seeks." A few years after Takuboku's death, namely around 1916 or 1917, a literary movement called proletarian literature came into existence for the first time in Japan. It was a literature produced from the viewpoint of the working class, which was to carry the future of Japan on their shoulders. . . . It was a literature born out of the

desire "to discover the necessity of tomorrow for our own sake." Further, it was naturally a kind of literature that declared war against "the present state of the age of repression." For the development of society and for the history of literature the rise of this type of literary movement was indispensable. In this sense, Takuboku's "The Present State of the Age of Repression" has given direction to the development of modern Japanese literature and proved itself to be the predecessor of the proletarian literary movement.

This essay along with "From Yumi-chō: Poems to Eat," an essay in a similar vein, sharpened for the proletarian writers the image of Takuboku as a writer for the common man. Takuboku thus came to be regarded as a person of profound sympathy for the poor as well as a strong exponent of freedom of the individual as the right of anyone regardless of social status. This passionate democratic sentiment places him among the most eloquent and foresighted critics Japan has produced in the last hundred years.

Along with Toki Aika, Takuboku is today considered a cofounder of the tanka group called *seikatsu-ha*, whose objective it was to sing about daily life. The group began to be so called after the publication of a magazine by Toki in 1913, *Life and the Arts*, a magazine intended to be in the vein of Takuboku's abortive magazine, *Tree and Fruit*. Its editorial policy was to attempt a narrowing of the gap between literature and life; Takuboku's tanka being an exemplar of what the magazine endorsed, he was regarded as the champion of the group. As a result tanka of similar style and subject matter to those of Takuboku and Toki since that time have been known as tanka of *seikatsu-ha*. The group stressed the importance of writing the tanka in three lines, and made it their motto to deal directly with the actualities of everyday existence, particularly with its hardships. Furthermore, in order to describe candidly such mundane details, they considered it imperative to bring poetic expression closer to the language of everyday conversation to generate a more immediate empathic bond between the reader and the situation presented in the tanka. Their style is thus individualistic and reflects a genuine attempt at reaching a wider reading public through the medium of the tanka. (pp. 172-74)

It is no exaggeration to say that not only Takuboku's contemporaries but succeeding generations of tanka poets whether they are aware of it or not write in the shadow of Takuboku. Takuboku's innovations changed the very nature of the tanka both in style and content. Today tens of thousands of people write tanka, and while maintaining the basic tanka form exhibit a greater flexibility in handling a variety of subjects. Many modern tanka deal with the concrete personal world of the poet, a trend which clearly displays the influence of Takuboku's *seikatsu-ha* sensibility. As long as this verse form remains, Takuboku's name as one of the great pioneers of modern tanka will be remembered by those who find pleasure and comfort in this form of poetry. (pp. 186-87)

Yukihito Hijiya, in his Ishikawa Takuboku, *Twayne Publishers, 1979, 205 p.*

MAKOTO UEDA   (essay date 1983)

[*Ueda is an educator and scholar specializing in Japanese literature. In the following excerpt, he discusses Takuboku's de-*

velopment as a poet and his failure as a fiction writer. Ueda especially focuses on Takuboku's daring experimentation with the tanka form.]

Since his death, Ishikawa Takuboku . . . has gained great fame as a poet, attracting many followers and admirers in succeeding generations. More books and articles have probably been written about him than about any other modern poet. His popularity, however, seems to depend less on his poetry than on the life that produced it. Takuboku's poems—many of them tanka—often sound trite or sentimental, or seem facile, when they are read as autonomous works of art. More appealing are the diaries that he kept intermittently from 1902 on, which honestly trace the vicissitudes of his restless mind. His life was a dramatic one, sprinkled with incidents that seem stranger than fiction. He had many failings: it is easy to accuse him of being irresponsible, overdependent, self-indulgent, emotionally unstable, or given to self-aggrandizement. Yet he was also brilliant, dynamic, and unremittingly honest with himself. He had explosive passions and a penchant for action, and seldom hesitated to do what he believed to be right. Seen against such a biographical background, his poems begin to breathe. They are a vital part of his life rather than independent works of art. For a tanka poet, the distance between life and art is usually short; for Takuboku, it hardly existed at all. (p. 95)

Takuboku published his first book of verse, entitled *Longing,* in 1905. It included 77 poems, all written in the shi form, their images and idioms much like those of the leading poets of the day, including Yosano Akiko, for whom the young Takuboku had great respect. The reactions of contemporary reviewers were mixed. Some praised the poems' youthful exuberance, flamboyant vocabulary, and precocious artistry; others condemned their pedantry, imitativeness, and self-indulgence. Today the collection is largely neglected, having been eclipsed by Takuboku's highly esteemed later volumes of verse: nevertheless, the book is a valuable document, for a number of its poems reveal Takuboku's early view of poetry in varying degree. (p. 96)

Takuboku was not able to sustain for very long the idealistic view of poetry he developed in his youth. Just before the publication of *Longing,* his father was excommunicated by the hierarchy of his Zen sect on the charge of failing to pay dues levied on his temple. The elder Ishikawa, an outcast priest at age 46, had no prospect of employment, and suddenly responsibility for supporting the family fell onto the shoulders of his only son. Another dependent was added when Takuboku's daughter Kyōko was born in 1906. The long and bitter struggle for survival that ensued not only changed Takuboku's life but affected his idea of poetry. (p. 99)

Takuboku's changing attitude toward literature was suggested in various writings at this time. In his diary entry for January 29, 1907, for example, he expressed disillusion with his former ideals:

> Poems written by the New Poetry Society and other schools of poets neither interest me nor impress me these days. I keep wondering what the reason could be. . . . Could it be because my heart has become rough and prosaic? More likely it is because poetry has plummeted from heaven to earth in my mind, because it has transformed itself from a melodious recitation in an auditorium to a chat in a shabby little room. I think of prose fiction day after day. I really must write a story.

A comment Takuboku made in 1908 reveals the poet's parallel fall into experience and sets out the specific realities he had come to consider the most appropriate material for poetry. In an essay called **"A Branch on the Desk,"** he observed that every person initially believes in his own capabilities, but when some painful experience forces him to realize his limitations, he concedes his defeat by nature and mutters to himself, "Whatever will be will be." Takuboku continued:

> However, nothing could sound as disgraceful as these words to a person who has had a profound confidence in himself and has prided himself on his dignity as an individual. Often, therefore, these words turn into a desperate wailing. Yet at other times, when a person carefully reconsiders them, he may conclude that defeat by nature is really a process by which to make that undefeatable power his own.

Although here Takuboku did not mention literature, he was talking about basic attitudes toward life that he thought should be the concern of all thinkers, including poets and novelists. According to him, these attitudes result in two types of literature. One is the "desperate wailing" of a person who has empirically learned human limitations; the other is a revelation of nature's forces, which, although intimidating, may benefit a person who can identify with them. The first mode is more lyrical, the second more naturalistic; both feature a man defeated by external forces. The proud poet confident in his extraordinary sensitivity is gone.

These two views of literature are embodied in *A Handful of Sand,* although the poems in that volume, being tanka, show the lyrical mode more clearly than the naturalistic. (pp. 100-01)

Takuboku's lyrical wailing can also be observed in some of his shi. Although his production in this genre markedly decreased after the publication of *Longing,* he did continue to write shi and planned to publish a collection in 1908. The short proem he wrote for this abortive collection expresses his new view of poetry, and can serve as a preface to all the lyrics he wrote after *Longing:*

> Sing out, when an everlasting struggle
> makes your tired joints ache,
> when a bitter grief almost overwhelms you,
> when your ailing child is on the verge of death,
> when you see your mother's image in a beggar,
> or when you are helplessly bored with your love.
> Gaze at the wordless sky
> and sing out, when those times arrive,
> O my starving friends!

Takuboku's poems were the outcries of a man suffering from the sorrow of life in this world.

Takuboku's naturalistic impulse is more pronounced in his prose fiction. He began writing stories in 1906, and wrote them with renewed fervor after his arrival in Tokyo in 1908, thereby fulfilling the desire expressed in his diary one year earlier. **"The Funeral Procession,"** one of his earliest stories, describes how the indifferent workings of death destroy the transcendent happiness of two insane lovers. **"Two Streaks of Blood"** also tells of death indiscriminately closing in on a lovely little girl and a dirty beggar woman. In **"The Plague"** the destructive force is dysentery, which attacks a village of peasants, and in **"The Window of a Clinic"** it is internal, the dark impulses of a newspaper reporter. Sinister forces become more numerous and complex in the longest of Takuboku's works in prose fiction, *The Birds,* which tells of the loves, griefs, and jealousies that envelop the residents of a rural town. In all these stories, the protagonists either passively surrender to fate or, after recognizing the inevitability of the surrender, begin leading lives of depravity.

Despite such naturalistic overtones, Takuboku's prose fiction was not well accepted in contemporary literary circles. Although early naturalist writers in Japan had tried to emulate the writings of Flaubert and Zola, by the time Takuboku turned to prose fiction in earnest the Japanese naturalistic novel had come to be an autobiographical genre in which the hero, closely modeled on the novelist, confessed his innermost impulses honestly and without verbal adornment. Takuboku was aware of the trend, but he was by nature too self-conscious to reveal his naked self in his stories, and preferred to depict dark impersonal forces manifesting themselves in characters distinctly different from himself. To contemporary readers used to confessional novels, his attitude seemed cowardly and dishonest. Moreover, his stories were often technically defective: the plot was weak, the theme was unclear, the characters were not fully developed, or the narrative viewpoint was not consistent. Sometimes he was not objective enough: he was either too sympathetic or too unsympathetic toward his characters. At other times his escapist impulse got the better of him, and he beautified his setting. In general, there was too much emotion and too little impartial observation.

His failure to become a successful novelist disheartened Takuboku, not only because it revealed his lack of talent in that genre, but also because it confirmed his failure to earn a livelihood through creative writing. (pp. 102-03)

The dark days of Takuboku's last years brought another significant change in his attitude toward poetry. Part of this can be viewed as a transference of his naturalistic impulse from prose fiction to verse: having failed as a novelist, he tried to do in poetry what he could not do in prose. His new stance is expressed in the essay **"Various Kinds of Poetry,"** written in 1910. There he remarked, tongue in cheek, that he envied a poet who did not possess "a mind that must scrutinize everything he does or says or contemplates throughout the very process of his doing or saying or contemplating, a mind that must challenge every problem squarely and reach its inmost core, or a mind that every day discovers many irrationalities and contradictions in himself and in the world, each discovery in turn intensifying further the irrationalities and contradictions in his life." Takuboku clearly wanted to become a poet who *did* have such a mind, one who scrutinized the forces operating in himself and in society. This is the type of naturalism he wanted to attain in his prose fiction, except that it places more emphasis on the mind of the writer himself. It is a more subjective, personal naturalism.

The same attitude can be detected in the most celebrated of Takuboku's critical writings, **"Poems to Eat,"** a short autobiographical essay published in 1909 that traces his growth as a poet. Its opening section is filled with negative rhetoric, vehemently rejecting the stance of Takuboku's younger days. He describes his early poetry as made of fantasies, childish music, a tiny intermingling of religious (or pseudoreligious) elements, and stereotyped sensibility. He then reveals how he became disillusioned with poetry during his days of struggle in Hokkaido [, the northernmost main island of Japan]. The latter part of the essay is an exposition of his newly discovered

poetic, whose essence can be seen in the excerpts below. At this stage in his life, Takuboku defined the poet as follows:

> A true poet must be as resolute as a statesman in reforming himself and in putting his philosophy into practice. He must be as singleminded as a businessman in giving a focus to his life. He must be as clearheaded as a scientist, and as straightforward as a primitive. He must have all these qualities and thereby make a calm, honest report on the changes of his psyche as they happen from one moment to the next, describing them without a word of adornment or falsehood.

In a corollary to the first definition, he defined poetry:

> Poetry must not be the so-called poetry. It must be a detailed report of changes that take place in a man's emotional life (I cannot think of a better word); it must be an honest diary. Hence, it must be fragmentary—it must not have unity. (Poetry with unity, namely philosophical literature, will turn into prose fiction when it takes an inductive form; into drama when it takes a deductive form. True poetry is related to fiction and drama in the same way daily reports of receipts and disbursements are related to a monthly or yearly balance sheet of accounts.) Furthermore, unlike a minister gathering material for his sermon or a streetwalker looking for a certain kind of man, a poet must never have a preconceived purpose.

The essay concludes with an appeal to his fellow poets, urging them not to be too imitative of Western poetry but to look intently at their own lives. (pp. 104-05)

In a sense, **"Poems to Eat"** expresses an idea of poetry to which Takuboku had unconsciously subscribed from the beginning, for if the essay's central thesis is an equation of poem and diary, he had been a diarist all along. Even as a teenage poet who gazed longingly at the sky, he sang about himself rather than about the sky. He was a diarist in the literal sense from an early age, too: his earliest surviving diary dates to the autumn of 1902, when he was sixteen; his last ends on February 20, 1912, a few weeks before his death. The surviving diaries cover much of the intervening ten years, the entire span of his literary career. The most moving of them all is known as *The Rōmaji Diary,* a diary of 1909 written in romanized Japanese because Takuboku did not want his wife and others to read the private thoughts he set down there. Clearly superior to any of his works in prose fiction, it provides ironic testimony that he was temperamentally less suited to be the novelist he wished to become than to be an author of diaries, which he wished to hide.

The Rōmaji Diary is a fine work of literature because it gives "a detailed report of changes that take place in a man's emotional life," the very quality Takuboku sought in poetry. It and the other diaries are sprinkled with poems, both tanka and shi, expressing the kind of psychological changes that cannot well be expressed in prose. (pp. 105-06)

One weakness inherent in this theory of composition is that the poem sometimes becomes so much a part of the author's diary that it loses its appeal to readers unfamiliar with the details of his life. To the poet, all his autobiographical poems are valuable because they are directly related to his personal life; however, unless they embody an experience rooted in universal human reality, they lose the means of relating themselves to readers. Unfortunately, some of Takuboku's later poems fall into this category: they have a measure of appeal to those who are thoroughly familiar with his biography, but they mean little to others. The fault lies less with the poems themselves than with Takuboku's poetic, his equation of poem and diary.

Takuboku himself was aware of this weakness. In a letter to a friend he once said: "At present I write tanka almost exclusively in the same frame of mind as I would have when keeping a diary. I suppose there are well- and ill-written diaries, depending upon the author's literary craftsmanship. But the merit of a diary should have nothing to do with the author's skill in writing. Indeed, a diary is valuable to no one but its author." Here Takuboku concedes that poetry is valuable to no one but the poet, that the value of poetry is entirely personal.

Such an admission implies a devaluation of poetry in relation to all other human activities. Takuboku recognized this. In an essay written in 1910, he compared a man of letters to a planner without the ability, opportunity, or financial resources to carry out his plans. He even compared literary composition to masturbation. . . . Ultimately, literature seemed too passive to him. He had learned from bitter experience how ineffectual it was in the real world, and he wanted to be more active, to become part of a force that directly participated in changing society.

Given such a pragmatic view of literature, it seemed that the only way poetry could play a positive role was by becoming overtly ideological in the service of a political movement. When poetry incites the masses to social reform, it can be said to have made a positive contribution to actual change. Takuboku's view of poetry seems to have been moving in this direction in his last years, especially after he became attracted to socialism in around 1910. (pp. 106-08)

The poems with socialist overtones, however, are only a small portion of Takuboku's later poetry. Of the 194 tanka that constitute *Sad Toys,* no more than a dozen overtly suggest his leftist beliefs. At least two reasons may explain this scarcity. One has to do with the nature of Takuboku's socialist beliefs. His socialism was more personal than political or philosophical, and therein lay its weakness, as well as its strength. It was an empirical belief deduced from a series of tragic experiences in actual life. When he discovered that no matter how hard he worked he was unable to support his family, he had to conclude that something was wrong with the existing capitalist society. On the other hand, he was not a systematic thinker who could, after sustained thought, arrive at a series of possible solutions for current social problems. Nor was he a political activist who could, through some drastic action, incite fellow workers to social reform if not to revolution. Socialism was a general direction in which his personal frustrations found an outlet. His belief in it was utterly sincere, but tended to be more emotional than ideological, more anarchist than Marxist.

That fact leads to the second possible explanation of why Takuboku did not write more political poems. He knew that poetry was of secondary value, that it was "masturbation"; yet he had to continue writing it because he had feelings too intense to contain. His dilemma was that of the poet who comes to hold a contemptuous view of poetry. . . . His unhappiness with being a poet sometimes made him take a sadistic attitude toward poetry. In fact, his abusive use of poetry began when he failed

to become a successful novelist. He told of his changing attitude then: "A husband who has lost a quarrel with his wife sometimes finds pleasure in giving a bad time to his child. I discovered that kind of pleasure in willfully abusing the tanka form." The same attitude is suggested in another of his metaphors for tanka, "sad toys." For Takuboku, poems became toys to which he would return whenever he was frustrated by his struggles in adult life; he could take out his frustrations on his toys.

Takuboku's last poetry collection, to which his friends posthumously gave the title *Sad Toys,* contains numerous tanka showing that attitude—so numerous, indeed, as to overshadow his leftist poems almost completely. . . . Takuboku, who wanted to reach a state of mind where he had no need to write poetry, never succeeded in that attempt. He was aware of his failure, and as a result a mixture of self-pity and self-contempt underlies his lyricism. He ended as a masochistic lyricist, a poet who tortured both himself and his form.

In conclusion, throughout his short and eventful career Takuboku consistently wanted to depict in his poetry fluid inner reality, the changes that occurred within his mind. Never greatly interested in external nature, he always sang of himself, depicting a vision of the self that constantly changed. At first he conceived of himself as a divine messenger from heaven, and accordingly he described the joys, hopes, and ecstasies of being a poet, the ethereal landscapes that were his inner reality at the time. Frustrations in his outer life quickly changed those landscapes, however. He came to see more shadows than sunlight, and subsequently he began to sing of the things that cast the darkest shadows. But singing did not remove the shadows, and he became increasingly aware of the powerlessness of poetry. He made an effort to restore its strength by absorbing the destructive energy of a revolutionary. Yet basically he remained a man of longing. Just as he longed to reach the far-off land of the Creator in his younger days, so he dreamed of a proletarian paradise that was to come after a wholesale destruction of the existing social order. When he tired of dreaming, he vented his impatience with himself by writing self-depreciating poems, or pitied his circumstances and wrote sentimental poems, or did a mixture of the two. He was a diarist in verse who was at times too dreamy, at times too wide awake. His poetry is a record of both those occasions, and as such it is intensely personal, honest, and alive. (pp. 109-12)

Makoto Ueda, "Ishikawa Takuboku," in his Modern Japanese Poets and the Nature of Literature, *Stanford University Press, 1983, pp. 95-136.*

ADDITIONAL BIBLIOGRAPHY

Iwaki, Yukinori. "An American Collection of Western Poems and the Early Career of Ishikawa Takuboku." *Comparative Literature Studies* XVIII, No. 2 (June 1981): 104-13.
> Discusses Takuboku's familiarity with English poetry and its possible influence on his writing.

Sesar, Carl. Introduction to *Poems to Eat,* by Takuboku Ishikawa, translated by Carl Sesar, pp. 13-18. Tokyo and Palo Alto, Calif.: Kodansha International, 1966.
> Discusses Takuboku's experimentation with the tanka form, stating that restoration of emotion, more colloquial language, and a sense of immediacy are his major contributions to Japanese poetry.

William James

1842-1910

American philosopher and psychologist.

One of the most influential figures in modern Western philosophy, James was the founder of Pragmatism as a philosophical school. The English philosopher Alfred North Whitehead called him "one of the greatest philosophic minds of all time," and despite formidable resistance to James's ideas during his lifetime, his works have become recognized as landmarks in the development of modern thought. In opposition to the tenets of scientific materialism and philosophic idealism, which had prevailed in Western philosophy throughout the eighteenth and nineteenth centuries, James attempted to comprehend and to describe human life as it is actually experienced, rather than formulating models of abstract reality far removed from the passion and pain of life. In James's philosophy of Pragmatism, the rationalist doubts of science as well as the nonrational certainties of mysticism are subordinated to the diverse moral and psychological needs of human beings.

Like psychologists Sigmund Freud and C. G. Jung and philosopher Henri Bergson, James was a highly original and often unorthodox thinker whose work has had an impact on various aspects of life and culture, including literature, religion, and psychology, as well as philosophic movements that emerged later in the twentieth century. In particular, his thought is considered a forerunner of the phenomenological movement in philosophy and psychology for its emphasis on the role of individual consciousness in the active creation, as opposed to the passive perception, of reality and meaning. As a psychologist in his first major work, *The Principles of Psychology*, James proposed the view of human consciousness as an unbroken process, rather than as a series of isolated thoughts and perceptions, a concept which provided the term "stream-of-consciousness" for describing the narrative technique of such modernist authors as James Joyce and Gertrude Stein. As a philosopher of religion, James offered an encyclopedia of spiritual beliefs in his *The Varieties of Religious Experience*, which argues for the acceptance of values derived from a stratum of human experience that is beyond rational discussion.

Among the best-known and most controversial examples of the tolerant and liberal spirit in James's work is "The Will to Believe." In this essay, as well as in his writings that expound the Pragmatic theory of truth, James attempted to resolve one of the oldest questions of philosophy—what can or cannot be known as "true"—by viewing any given truth as something that not only differs from person to person and is subject to change over a period of time, but also as something that may depend upon an individual's willing belief. This philosophy of the diversity and changeability of truths, which James later developed as the doctrine of "radical pluralism," stood in contrast to the monist absolutism of such thinkers of the time as F. H. Bradley, Charles Sanders Peirce, and Josiah Royce, who held that ultimate truth was unchanging and that reality was an immutable transcendent unity known as the absolute. These philosophers, who found James's view of the universe overly literal and materialistic, comprised one of two principal groups that attacked James's ideas. The other group was made up of such figures as G. E. Moore and Bertrand Russell, strict

The Bettmann Archive, Inc.

materialists and logicians who saw James's Pragmatism as simply indefensible in rational terms. While it was the doctrines of this latter group that would dominate Anglo-American philosophy throughout the twentieth century, rather than those of either James himself or his most illustrious successor, John Dewey, as an individual thinker James continues to be regarded among the most important in Western intellectual history.

Born in New York City and raised in various cities throughout New England and Europe, James was the eldest in a wealthy family of five children that included the novelist Henry James, Jr. and diarist Alice James. James's father, Henry James, Sr., was a deeply religious man who was trained to enter the Presbyterian ministry, but who became dissatisfied with the solutions of conventional religion to fundamental spiritual questions and eventually developed a system of beliefs based on the writings of the eighteenth-century Swedish mystic Emmanuel Swedenborg. Henry, Sr., believed that a divinity emanating from God was intrinsic to all human beings, and that conventions of society and organized religion largely served to blind individuals to their spiritual worth and to their absolute equality with one another. These beliefs were the source of his strong conviction that an individual should be allowed every opportunity to realize his or her personal qualities and abilities, a process that would ultimately result in a social utopia of diverse personalities unbent by the pressures of conformity, yet none-

133

theless capable of living together as equals. These principles were the basis for the culturally stimulating, liberal home environment in which William and his siblings were raised.

Because his father was as distrustful of educational institutions as he was of what he called "professional religion," James was educated at home in his early years, with sporadic attendance at various schools in England, France, Switzerland, and Germany. As a young student, he was divided between his strong attraction to both the natural sciences and to art. In 1860 he made a decision to study painting with noted Pre-Raphaelite painter William H. Hunt, but a brief period of study revealed to James that painting was not his field, for his pictorial talents were modest and did not develop significantly under Hunt's tutelage. Believing that to be a mediocre artist was a contemptible occupation, he abandoned art while still cultivating his sensitivity for the detail and abundance of the visible world. James next rediscovered his enthusiasm for natural science, entering the Lawrence Scientific School, Harvard, in 1861. There he studied chemistry, anatomy, and physiology under such professors as Charles W. Eliot and Louis Agassiz, and in 1864 transferred to the Harvard Medical School. While in medical school, James traveled to Brazil as an assistant on the Thayer expedition, a mission of exploration and study led by Agassiz. James greatly benefited from his close association with Agassiz, which, he later wrote, taught him "the difference between all possible abstractionists and all livers in the light of the world's concrete fulness."

While he continued to study medicine during the years 1867 and 1868, both at Harvard and in Europe, James suffered from a variety of what are widely considered to have been psychosomatic ailments—ocular sensitivity, pain in the lower back, and generalized lassitude. Accompanying these physical symptoms were frequent considerations of suicide and the feelings of acute anxiety which he later described in *The Varieties of Religious Experience,* where he disguised one particularly harrowing episode of "panic fear" as the testimony of an anonymous Frenchman. James's account details an experience of "a horrible fear of [his] own existence," a seizure of panic which summons the mental image of an epileptic patient he had seen in an asylum, "a black-haired youth with greenish skin, entirely idiotic, who used to sit all day on one of the benches. . . . He sat there like a sort of sculptured Egyptian cat or Peruvian mummy, moving nothing but his black eyes and looking absolutely non-human." The combination of this frightful image with James's abnormal fear gave rise to a personal revelation: *"That shape am I, I felt, potentially."* Elsewhere in *The Varieties of Religious Experience,* James wrote: "We are all *potentially* such sick men. The sanest and best of us are of one clay with lunatics and prison-inmates." This conviction, while losing the pathological force of the moment, became significant to James's later philosophy, which found an affirmation of human life meaningless without a recognition of evil and accident in the universe.

Although James's emotional and physical frailty persisted, he managed to keep up a demanding course of readings, both in medicine and now as a serious student of philosophy and psychology, and in 1869 he received his medical degree from Harvard. In 1870, the severity of James's neurasthenia abated when he read *Essais de critique générale* by the French philosopher Charles Renouvier, and thereafter resolved to achieve a greater measure of physical health and mental balance. James also credited Renouvier's philosophy of pluralism with freeing him of the "monistic superstition" of his earlier education and

revealing to him that "the world may *compose* a whole without being determined by it . . . that unity should not predetermine the many." An opponent of scientific determinism and an advocate of the doctrine of free will, Renouvier provided a particular focus—that of morality—which James praised for leading him out of a "paralysis of action occasioned by a sense of moral impotence." Believing now in his own power to oppose the malady which, as a moral evil, afflicted him, James determined to attain a state of health. "I finished the first part of Renouvier's second *Essais,*" he wrote in 1870, "and see no reason why his definition of free will—'the sustaining of a thought *because I choose to* when I might have other thoughts'—need be the definition of an illusion. At any rate, I will assume for the present—until next year—that it is no illusion. My first act of free will shall be to believe in free will." This belief in the benefits of a "posited" free will became a component of James's later philosophy, particularly in the doctrine of "The Will to Believe," which offered scientific and philosophical support for what had begun as a personal need.

James lived in a state of semi-invalidism until 1872, when he was appointed as an instructor at Harvard; his association with the university lasted until 1907. Noting that the first subject James taught at Harvard was physiology, scholars of his intellectual development often underline the significance of his background in the natural sciences in relation to his later career as a psychologist. When he became an instructor in psychology in 1876, he treated this field of study not as a branch of philosophy, one especially laden with metaphysical speculation, but as a natural science subject to the rigors of laboratory experiment. James's desire to eliminate metaphysics from future studies in psychology, and to consider this discipline strictly as a natural science, resulted in the innovative perspective of his first major work, *The Principles of Psychology.* Commissioned in 1878 to complete a textbook on this subject by 1880, James ultimately took twelve years to produce a monumental consideration of all knowledge in the field. Upon its publication in 1890, *The Principles of Psychology* was recognized as a landmark work of its kind, and although some of its conceptions—such as the distinction between metaphysical psychology and psychology considered as a natural science—aroused controversy, this treatise was nevertheless respected for its encyclopedic scope and the stimulating originality of its insights. Both as a focus of controversy and a vitalizing intellectual force, James's work as a psychologist predicted his later works as a philosopher.

In 1878 James married Alice H. Gibbens. Beginning with his first years of marriage, he entered a period of prodigious activity which established his popular image as a robust, adventurous, and above all open-minded investigator of human life and philosophic truth. For much of the time he was working on *The Principles of Psychology,* James was already an instructor of philosophy, shifting his interests from scientific inquiries about human behavior to philosophic questions of moral values, free will, and the reality of a spiritual dimension to life. Fascinated by the possibility of life after death, James joined the Society for Psychic Research in 1882, later serving as its president for a brief time. Regarding religious belief, James's ability to maintain both the skepticism of a trained scientist and a sympathetic open-mindedness is reflected in such early collections as *The Will to Believe, and Other Essays in Popular Philosophy, Human Immortality: Two Supposed Objections to the Doctrine,* and *The Varieties of Religious Experience.* With *The Will to Believe,* James began to establish himself as a philosophic iconoclast who presented a serious

challenge to the prevailing schools of rationalism and absolutism, until eventually he attained the stature of the most
important and most popular figure in American philosophy.
Each new volume became an occasion for attacks from his
critics and reaffirmed loyalty on the part of his supporters.
However, among critics and supporters alike James was respected and admired, and his friendships included illustrious
thinkers of diverse and often conflicting ideologies: Josiah Royce
and F.C.S. Schiller, Charles Sanders Peirce and Henri Bergson, F. H. Bradley and Theodore Flournoy. He was widely
regarded not only as a philosopher, but also as a poet, sage,
and mystic whose works and personal presence were inspirational as well as intellectually enlightening.

In the last decade of his life, James suffered from a heart
condition. Seeking rest and recovery, he traveled to Europe
with his wife in 1910, visiting his brother Henry in London.
Although biographers find there were basic frictions between
the personalities of the two renowned brothers—which may be
approximated by Henry's identification with an old, aristocratic
Europe and William's with a new, populist America—they held
each other, if not each other's works, in mutual respect and
affection. In the summer of 1910, William returned to America
and died not long after his arrival.

When *The Principles of Psychology* appeared in 1890 it was
immediately recognized as a major effort to assemble a massive
quantity of research from leading authorities of several nations,
and this contribution alone would have established its importance. In addition, James also proposed a number of particular
theories that have been received as pioneering concepts in the
field. As a researcher, James created the first laboratory for
psychological study in America, and his *Principles of Psychology* emphasizes the necessity for practical observation,
rather than metaphysical speculation, in attempting to understand the workings of the mind and emotions. Advocating the
abandonment of such concepts as "the soul, the transcendental
ego, the fusion of ideas and particles of mind stuff, etc.," he
pursued a definition and description of "mental states," considering the influence of the physical brain and of bodily experiences upon individual consciousness and emotions. Among
the most renowned of his conceptions in this area is the controversial James-Lange theory of emotion, which James and
Danish psychologist Carl George Lange developed independent
of each other. This theory states that it is a person's reaction
to a stimulus which causes an emotion rather than the emotion
causing the reaction; that is, we feel afraid because we run,
not run because we feel afraid. It was James's search for a
material answer to the function of emotions, as much as the
supportability of this particular theory, that was important for
the history of psychological study. Perhaps James's most famous contribution to psychology was his view of consciousness
as a physical process—a continuous flux of feelings, ideas,
and sensation—and not as a static condition in which isolated
thoughts and perceptions abruptly appeared and disappeared.
The chapter "The Stream of Thought" in *The Principles of
Psychology* revised traditional conceptions of human consciousness, particularly the idea that thought and feeling are
separable experiences not affecting each other, just as James's
opus in general undermined the view of psychology as the
"philosophy of the soul." James wrote that "the kind of psychology which could cure a case of melancholy, or charm a
chronic insane delusion away, ought certainly to be preferred
to the most seraphic insights into the nature of the soul." While
many of James's ideas were inevitably replaced by ones more
sophisticated and advanced, *The Principles of Psychology* is

still considered a masterpiece for its sensitive and inspired
articulation of human experience.

James's first collection of philosophical writings was *The Will
to Believe,* and the title essay of this volume elicited much of
the controversy surrounding James's value as a thinker. The
"belief" discussed by James is not specifically that of religion
but rather any general belief which facilitates moral decisions.
James contended that such beliefs, although without the support
of logic or science, could ultimately make true what was at
first merely believed to be true, as in the case of some task
the successful performance of which requires a strong faith in
the inevitability of success. Critics of this idea argue that, given
James's own admission of the potential fallibility of a belief
concerning the outcome of any action, there appears to be little
justification for such a moral program, which is equated with
wishful thinking or, in the sarcastic phrase of Dickinson S.
Miller, "The Will to Make-Believe." Some critics have suggested that James should have termed his concept "The Right
to Believe," especially as it applies to matters of religious
faith. Considering James an essentially agnostic thinker, George
Santayana wrote of him: "He did not really believe; he merely
believed in the right of believing that you might be right if you
believed." Defenders of "The Will to Believe," including
F.C.S. Schiller and William Barrett, praise James for offering
a liberating alternative to the restrictions placed upon human
will by doctrines demanding logical support as a prerequisite
for belief, doctrines which presuppose a deterministic, possibly
nihilistic reality. As in all his works, however, James's intention in the "The Will to Believe" was not to argue for the
adoption of a specific dogma, not even his own, but to encourage the exercise of ways of thinking that he believed could
improve human life. James's interest in various forms of belief
is also reflected in his writings on parapsychology and his
lectures on *Human Immortality,* reaching its culmination in
one of his most celebrated works, *The Varieties of Religious
Experience.*

Examining the sources and nature of religious belief, *The Varieties of Religious Experience* is considered the founding work
in the psychology of religion. Although this study was the first
to extensively document case histories of individual religious
experiences, critics have primarily regarded James's work as
more relevant to the philosophy of religion than to its psychological aspects. Recently, however, this view has been challenged by Gary T. Alexander, who finds that James significantly related his earlier study of psychology to his study of
religion, lending psychological as well as philosophical dimension to the later work. Subtitled "A Study in Human Nature," *The Varieties of Religious Experience* has as its premise
the idea that the persistence of religious feelings testifies to
their value in human life and to their importance to any serious
understanding of human behavior. This attitude was intended
as a counterpoint to the prevalent scientific view of the time
that strong religious feelings—such as those of spontaneous
mystical experience or a sudden religious conversion—are
pathological states meaningful only as they illuminate a subject's physical or psychological condition. After considering
such manifestations of religious feeling as "'once born' and
'twice born' characters," the morbid hypersensitivity of the
"sick soul," episodes of religious conversion, the lives of the
saints, and overwhelming mystical experiences of "cosmic
consciousness," James concludes that these phenomena indicate the existence of a real power or powers external to a
particular subject. However, while recognizing the religious
experience of individuals as the foundation of which the doc-

trines of organized religions are the superstructure, or "by-products" in the phrase of Jacques Barzun, James also concludes that no specific meaning can be attached to the varieties of religious experience that would uphold the dogma of any established religion. Summarizing his observations on religious experience, he stated: "The only thing that it unequivocally testifies to is that we can experience union with *something* larger than ourselves and in that union find our greatest peace." In the conclusion to the *Varieties,* as well as in the later work *A Pluralistic Universe,* James proposed the existence of a finite God or a plurality of gods. This being or these beings, while offering superhuman spiritual comfort, would not be vulnerable to the philosophic indictments against an all-loving, all-powerful god who, paradoxically, lacks the power to abolish evil in the world or who, malevolently, is unwilling to do so. The concept of a limited, pluralistic deity synchronizes with James's opposition, in such later works as *Pragmatism* and *Radical Empiricism,* to any form of absolute, preferring the "risk" that common sense finds inherent in the universe. "Common sense," wrote James, "is less sweeping in its demands than philosophy or mysticism have wont to be, and can suffer the notion of this world being partly saved and partly lost. . . . No fact of human nature is more characteristic than its willingness to live on a chance."

The body of ideas most readily associated with James are those of the philosophy known as Pragmatism, which was introduced in his 1898 lecture "Philosophical Conceptions." Critics have emphasized, however, that all of James's works are founded on the basic principles and attitudes of the Pragmatic philosophy. James's focus on concrete experience, rather than on abstract speculation, in *The Principles of Psychology,* his concern with the practical consequences of believing in *The Will to Believe,* and his refusal of absolutism in *The Varieties of Religious Experience* emerge as the major themes in the collection *Pragmatism: A New Name for Some Old Ways of Thinking.* While James traced the Pragmatic temperament—temperament being to James a major determinant of what ideas one will adopt and defend—back to Socrates, with Immanuel Kant, John Locke, and Francis Bacon among those included along the way, he acknowledged the immediate source of this philosophy to be C. S. Peirce's 1878 essay "How to Make Our Ideas Clear." Peirce was a colleague of James at Harvard and during the 1870s was a member, with James and others, of a philosophical society called the "Metaphysical Club." Peirce's essay outlined a method for determining solutions to philosophic and scientific questions through a systematic clarification of their meaning. He stated that "in order to ascertain the meaning of an intellectual conception one should consider what practical consequences might conceivably result by necessity from the truth of that conception; and the sum of these consequences will constitute the entire meaning of the conception." In his writings on Pragmatism, James extended Peirce's methodology beyond the original field of logical investigation it was intended to serve, developing it into a full-blown philosophy applicable to all areas of human experience, especially those outside the purview of logic and science, such as religious faith.

James asked: "What difference would it practically make to any one if this notion rather than that notion were true? If no practical difference whatever can be traced, then the alternatives mean practically the same thing, and all dispute is idle. Whenever a dispute is serious, we ought to be able to show some practical difference that must follow from one side or the other's being right." Implicit in this statement is James's

intention that Pragmatism should serve as a program for human action, as opposed to a method for organizing abstract problems of logic. A given "truth" is thus determined not exclusively according to whether or not it can be proven in rational terms; whenever a question of truth cannot be resolved by logic or present scientific knowledge, this question may be resolved by considering the benefits to an individual or society and including this as a factor in the decision for or against its truth. Hence, a given truth may change in light of circumstances which alter its beneficial consequences. James also specified another very important factor in the Pragmatic theory of truth: that the question of something being true or not must be a serious one and its resolution one way or the other "momentous," as in matters of religion or morality. Critics of the Pragmatic theory of truth have attacked its logical weaknesses, as well as remarking on the difficulties in arriving at an objective determination of the benefits of upholding a particular truth. Defenders of James's theory point out that it was not designed to serve the ends of logic or contribute to objective knowledge but to aid individuals in their adaptation to a world of change, and that the theory's value lies entirely in the area of subjective decisions and the consequences which result from them.

Fundamental to Pragmatism is James's rejection of all absolute truths and his belief that the universe is a pluralistic, not a monistic, reality. Nevertheless, he recognized the right of absolutists to believe in a unified reality in accordance with the needs of their temperament, which he called "tender-minded"—personalities who are "rationalistic (going by 'principles'), idealistic, optimistic, religious, free-willist, monistic, and dogmatical—as opposed to "tough-minded" individuals, who tend to be "empiricist (going by 'facts'), materialistic, pessimistic, irreligious, fatalistic, pluralistic, and skeptical." James also recognized the difficulties of promoting during his lifetime—which was an era of idealism and rationalism—a philosophy of pluralism in which "there appears no universal element of which all things are made." Writing of the concept of the absolute in Eastern mysticism, James remarked: "As compared with it, pluralistic empiricism offers a sorry appearance. It is a turbid, muddled, gothic sort of affair, without a sweeping outline and with little pictorial nobility." For James it was precisely these qualities of formless diversity and risk-filled possibility that constituted the essence and much of the appeal of the human condition.

Toward the end of his life James had plans, which remained undeveloped, of organizing the various themes and elements of his writings into a work of systematic philosophy, thereby clarifying many of the ambiguities and inconsistencies critics had found in his thought. He had often found it necessary in his works to address frequent and sometimes serious misunderstandings of his ideas on the part of his critics. In some cases his philosophical position was seen as the inverse of what he intended, as when Paul Elmer More found James's ideas to be those of a rationalist or F. H. Bradley described him as an idealist whose Pragmatism was "in harmony with views against which it is commonly understood to protest." The most common misconception about Pragmatism has been that it serves as a code, one nearly synonymous with America's capitalist system, that sanctions any method or behavior so long as it is efficient and profits the adherent. Such a misconception became outstandingly evident when Benito Mussolini credited James with teaching him the principles "to which Fascism owes a great deal of its success." Success divorced from a humanistic morality was in fact never a formula put forth by James, who coined the phrase "the bitch goddess, success" to castigate what he saw as a weakness among Americans for commercial advancement at the expense of moral integrity.

James's Pragmatism considered human emotions and subjective viewpoints as a necessary and much-neglected part of philosophy, and this perspective perhaps accounts for many of the problems early critics had in evaluating his works. The willingness to accept a philosophy in which feelings openly confront intellectual propositions has led to an increasing appreciation of James among later critics. In 1975 William Barrett, author of *Irrational Man*, a study of Existentialist philosophy, wrote of a James revival in his essay "Our Contemporary, William James." Studies by Jacques Barzun and Howard M. Feinstein are distinguished contributions to this revival and are among the most recent affirmations that James is the most important philosopher America has yet produced.

PRINCIPAL WORKS

The Principles of Psychology. 2 vols.   (treatise)   1890
*The Will to Believe, and Other Essays in Popular
    Philosophy*   (essays)   1897
*Human Immortality: Two Supposed Objections to the
    Doctrine*   (lectures)   1898; also published as *Human
    Immortality: Two Supposed Objections to the Doctrine*,
    1899 [enlarged edition]
*Talks to Teachers on Psychology and to Students on Some of
    Life's Ideals*   (lectures)   1899
The Varieties of Religious Experience   (lectures)   1902
Pragmatism: A New Name for Some Old Ways of Thinking
    (lectures)   1907
The Meaning of Truth: A Sequel to "Pragmatism"   (essays)
    1909
A Pluralistic Universe   (lectures)   1909
Memories and Studies   (essays)   1911
*Some Problems of Philosophy: A Beginning of an
    Introduction to Philosophy*   (unfinished treatise)   1911
Essays in Radical Empiricism   (essays)   1912
Collected Essays and Reviews   (essays and criticism)   1920
The Letters of William James. 2 vols.   (letters)   1920

JAMES MARK BALDWIN   (essay date 1891)

[*Baldwin was an American psychologist and educator. In the following excerpt, his consideration of* The Principles of Psychology *leads to a discussion of James's theory that, in Baldwin's phrasing,* "consciousness is a stream flowing in time." *Baldwin explains James's postulation that consciousness is not a series of discrete perceptions but an unbroken flow of perceptions, though he rejects the related idea that there is no distinction between feeling and thought. Baldwin's essay, originally published in 1891 in the* Educational Review, *is representative of contemporary reviews of* The Principles of Psychology, *many of which recognized it as an important work, while at the same time harboring serious objections concerning James's often iconoclastic theories. For other critical objections to James's psychological theories, see the excerpt by Charles Sanders Peirce (1891); for a later, more specialized view of* The Principles of Psychology, *see the excerpt by Bruce Wilshire (1968).*]

The fact that a recent issue of the *Revue Philosophique* mentioned [*The Principles of Psychology*] as the "long-announced treatise of Professor James," indicates that interest in it is not confined to this continent. I think it is safe to say that no book on psychology, in any language, has been so eagerly waited for in this generation, and it is as safe to say that no other book on psychology has appeared in this generation in English that was as well worth waiting for. (p. 371)

One of its most striking features is its breadth of reference to other writers in all languages. It is undoubtedly one of the most appreciative books of the work of thinkers everywhere that we have in English. Professor James has also given his book additional value by incorporating, *in locis,* full quotations from the most available and weighty authorities. The result is a book from which a reader, not versed in the history of thought, may get a pretty fair conception of the problems and schools of modern philospohy, so far as such problems rest upon psychological or physiological data.

In point of style Professor James is an acknowledged master, particularly as regards clearness, simplicity, and picturesque illustration. In this last respect he is surpassed, I think, by few writers on philosophical subjects now living. (pp. 371-72)

As to the method, Professor James advocates the positivist point of view of natural science, based both upon introspection and experiment, a method which late work has now fully justified. "This book, assuming that thoughts and feelings exist, and are vehicles of knowledge, thereupon contends that psychology, when she has ascertained the empirical correlation of various sorts of thoughts or feelings with definite conditions of the brain, can go no further—can go no further, that is, as a natural science. If she goes further she becomes metaphysical." (Preface.) That is, it is no longer *empirical* psychology. But Professor James' own treatment shows that interpretation is the essential need of the hour, even in empirical psychology. His greatest originality is not where he claims it—in the point of view. The present writer has advocated this point of view for several years, and half a dozen others could be named who have; but his originality is in his theoretical construction of data—in matters of interpretation.

In the same connection, under the phrase "psychologist's fallacy" . . . , Professor James emphasizes a point which in our day needs supreme emphasis. "The *great* snare of the psychologist is the *confusion of his own standpoint with that of the mental fact* about which he is making his report". . . . "he himself, knowing an object in *his* way, gets easily led to suppose that the thought which is *of* it, knows it in the same way in which he knows it, although this is often very far from being the case." This is the very bane of current speculative idealism, as far as its treatment of psychology goes. It reads into the child the speculative essentials of mind—self-activity, timeless identity, community with an absolute self-identical consciousness, etc. The first thoughts of a child are aware of the objects and of nothing else. But the psychologist, in looking at it, sees the "thought's object, plus the thought itself, plus, possibly, all the rest of the world. We must avoid substituting what we know (suppose) the consciousness *is* for what it is a consciousness of." So important is this warning of Professor James that I would not hesitate to devote all my space to sounding it out. Take this from Green: "A consciousness by the man of himself must be taken to go along with the perceptive act itself. Not less than this, indeed, can be involved in any act that is to be the beginning of knowledge at all. It is the minimum of possible thought or intelligence." On this assumption of the Greens and the Cairds and the Morrises, Professor James is not a whit too severe in this remark: "This is a perfectly wanton assumption, and not the faintest shadow of reason exists for supposing it true. As well might I contend that I cannot dream without dreaming that I dream, swear without swearing that I swear, etc., as maintain that I cannot know without knowing that I know." . . . Unity of treatment might have been brought into Professor James' account of "thought" if he had generalized the essentials of his theory in some such conception as that denoted nowadays by the word "apperception." I venture to think, subject to correction, that all of the author's theories concerning "knowledge about" a thing, as contrasted with mere "acquaintance with" a thing, are covered by the current conception of apperception. But before pressing this view, let us get hold, as clearly as we can, of his view of knowledge in general.

According to Professor James' way of thinking, what we have in consciousness is a stream flowing in time,—and empirical description of consciousness must begin with this stream, not with simple hypothetical sensations. This stream may be called, indiscriminately, Feeling or Thought, for there is no valid distinction between them. Feeling is immediately cognitive, *i.e.,* it has an object which it knows. What we are conscious of at any moment is a segment of this stream, a cut through it, so to speak, and this is our unit of division of the stream into parts. Each such conscious segment or cut is a Feeling or Thought of an object. This object may be a single simple thing, in which case the segment is a sensation, and knows the thing by "acquaintance," or it may be of different related external things or events, in which case it still has only a single object, the entire complex experience, but the Feeling or Thought is now a perception, conception, etc.; its knowledge is "knowledge about" the thing or things. Knowledge *about* a thing is knowledge of its relations. Acquaintance with it is limitation to the bare impression which it makes." . . . Following him I shall use the words Thought and Feeling simply for such a segment of the stream.

Now the present Thought may have as its object other Thoughts or segments of the stream, *i.e.,* it may know the past, and this is memory—the fact that a present Thought may know (cognize, feel) what has gone before in the same stream. The rule by which the exact segment of the past to be thus known is determined, is association, which is reduced to the single principle of contiguity. The reason that it is my own past that my present Thought knows (remembers) and no one's else past, we cannot say, except that my own past has a feeling of *warmth* (familiarity) to me, which no one's else past has to me, and by which I reach *self*-consciousness. "Remembrance is like direct Feeling; its object is suffused with a warmth and intimacy to which no object of mere conception ever attains. So sure as this present is me, is mine, so sure is anything else that comes with the same warmth and intimacy, and immediacy, me and mine." . . .

Further, in the stream of Thought there are nodal points, so to speak; points of emphasis (attention) "substantive Thoughts," and between these points of prominence there are transition portions, "transitive Thoughts," unattended to. . . . But there are no absolute divisions in the normal conscious life; that is, we are conscious of no breaks. When there are breaks, the two ends of the stream grow together vitally again. "Within each personal consciousness, Thought is sensibly continuous." "Even where there is a time-gap, the consciousness after it feels as if it belonged with the consciousness before it, as another part of the same self." . . . To expect this consciousness, to feel the interruptions of its objective continuity as gaps, would be like expecting the eye to feel a gap of silence because it does

not hear. . . . Transitive connections can always be found between substantive Thoughts; vague relationships by which the present Thought retains the tradition of the past. The stream of Thought is therefore continuous. There are no psychical atoms. In this supposition the associationist psychology makes itself ridiculous. "A permanently existing 'idea' or '*Vorstellung*,' which makes its appearance before the footlights of consciousness at periodical intervals, is as mythological an entity as the Jack of Spades." . . . Every such so-called "atom" has a "fringe" of transitive connections; it is prominent and vivid; its fringe is pale and washed-out. But in every case it has a fringe. The simplest Feeling has a ragged edge, and this ragged edge links on to the ragged edges of other feelngs higher up the stream and lower down. . . . The present Thought, therefore, is enriched by all the past experience of the individual, and the future Thought will be further enriched by what it inherits from the present.

In passing down the stream, Thought undergoes changes. The transitive may become substantive, and the reverse. The fringe may shine out in relief and the former object sink into dim suggestion only of feeling. These modifications in arrangement and disposition of the objects of Thought are due to the mental operations of "discrimination" and "comparison," of which no more can be said than that they are irreducible and fundamental characteristics of Thought.

Again, Thought is selective. Only a slight portion of one's past is held and utilized in the present. Our individual worlds are different, because by progressive selections we have built up our experiences differently. Perhaps nowhere else in psychological literature is the essential selective function of Thought so well developed and so richly illustrated as here.

The first peculiarity of this general conception is its use of terms. Feeling equals Thought, Feeling or Thought knows, Thought knows the past, etc. Does not this look like a subversion of the safest distinctions of current psychology? It does, indeed. But when we come to study the case more closely, we find it less revolutionary than it looks. We find that Professor James admits states of pure feeling in the ordinary sense, states which lack all "knowledge about," or relational quality. "In a new-born brain, this (strong sense stimulation) gives rise to an absolutely pure sensation." . . . Now whether or not we admit that such a state is cognitive, that is, is knowledge at all, the distinction is yet recognized between states purely or mainly affective, and states which involve relational constructions through discrimination and comparison. And I think Professor James is asking too much of us in requiring that we give up one of the few exact distinctions in terminology which descriptive psychology can boast, while at the same time he preserves the distinction in fact, and has no good terms to substitute for the traditional ones. Perhaps when he comes to treat of pleasure and pain he will give its usual meaning to the term feeling. (pp. 373-79)

James Mark Baldwin, "Shorter Literary Papers: Professor James' Principles of Psychology," in his Fragments in Philosophy and Science, *Charles Scribner's Sons, 1902, pp. 371-89.*

[CHARLES SANDERS PEIRCE]   (essay date 1891)

[*Peirce was an American philosopher and scientist. Called "the most original thinker of his generation" by William James, Peirce achieved his principal renown in such technical areas as logic and science. He also wrote numerous articles and essays on more*

Henry James, Sr., about 1880, from the portrait by Frank Daveneck.

general philosophical subjects, and one of these, entitled "How to Make Our Ideas Clear" (1878), introduced the term "Pragmatism." James later credited Peirce as the originator of this school of philosophy, though Peirce's concept of Pragmatism differed significantly from the philosophy James ultimately developed and popularized under that name. While Peirce did formulate the "Pragmatic test" that the meaning of a statement should be judged according to its practical consequences, James extended this idea beyond the original field of logical investigation it was intended to serve and applied it to all areas of human experience, especially those beyond the purview of logic and science such as religious belief. Aside from this concept of Pragmatism which links him to James in the history of American thought, Peirce was more closely related to the monist-absolutist branch of philosophy, which assumes a basic unity of all phenomena, than to James's pluralism, which finds no reason to posit a transcendent reality beyond the diversity of phenomena apparent to everyday perception. Peirce eventually renamed his philosophy "Pragmaticism" to distinguish it from James's Pragmatism. In the followng excerpt from a review of The Principles of Psychology, *Peirce rejects James's distinction between natural science and metaphysics, arguing that to label as metaphysical such conceptions as the "Soul," "Transcendental Ego," and "Ideas" (James's terms) is an unwarranted sacrifice of possible sources of knowledge. For a comparative study of James's and Peirce's philosophical thought, see the excerpt by Gail Kennedy (1956).]*

Prof. James's thought [in *The Principles of Psychology*] is highly original, or at least novel; but it is originality of the destructive kind. To prove that we do not know what it has been generally supposed that we did know, that given premises do not justify the conclusions which all other thinkers hold they do justify, is his peculiar function. For this reason the book should have

been preceded by an introduction discussing the strange positions in logic upon which all its arguments turn. Even when new theories are proposed, they are based on similar negative or sceptical considerations, and the one thing upon which Prof. James seems to pin his faith is the general incomprehensibility of things. He clings as passionately to that as the old lady of the anecdote did to her total depravity. Of course, he is materialistic to the core—that is to say, in a methodical sense, but not religiously, since he does not deny a separable soul nor a future life; for materialism is that form of philosophy which may safely be relied upon to leave the universe as incomprehensible as it finds it. It is possible that Prof. James would protest against this characterization of his cast of mind. Brought up under the guidance of an eloquent apostle of a form of Swedenborgianism, which is materialism driven deep and clinched on the inside, and educated to the materialistic profession, it can only be by great natural breadth of mind that he can know what materialism is, by having experienced some thoughts that are not materialistic. He inclines towards Cartesian dualism, which is of the true strain of the incomprehensibles and modern materialism's own mother. There is no form of idealism with which he will condescend to argue. Even evolutionism, which has idealistic affinities, seems to be held for suspect. It is his *métier* to subject to severe investigation any doctrine whatever which smells of intelligibility.

The keynote of this is struck in the preface, in these words:

> I have kept close to the point of view of natural science throughout the book. Every natural science assumes certain data uncritically, and declines to challenge the elements between which its own 'laws' obtain, and from which its deductions are carried on. Psychology, the science of finite individual minds, assumes as its data (1) *thoughts and feelings*, and (2) a *physical world* in time and space with which they coexist and which (3) *they know*. Of course these data themselves are discussable; but the discussion of them (as of other elements) is called metaphysics, and falls outside the province of this book. This book, assuming that thoughts and feelings exist, and are the vehicles of knowledge, thereupon contends that Psychology, when she has ascertained the empirical correlation of the various sorts of thought and feeling with definite conditions of the brain, can go no farther—can go no farther, that is, as a natural science. If she goes farther, she becomes metaphysical. All attempts to *explain* our phenomenally given thoughts as products of deeper-lying entities (whether the latter be named 'Soul,' 'Transcendental Ego,' 'Ideas,' or 'Elementary Units of Consciousness') are metaphysical. This book consequently rejects both the associationist and the spiritualist theories; and in this strictly positivistic point of view consists the only feature of it for which I feel tempted to claim originality.

This is certainly well put—considered as prestigiation. But when we remember that a natural science is not a person, and consequently does not "decline" to do anything, the argument evaporates. It is only the students of the science who can "decline," and they are not banded together to repress any species of inquiry. Each investigator does what in him lies;

and declines to do a thousand things most pertinent to the subject. To call a branch of an inquiry "metaphysical" is merely a mode of objurgation, which signifies nothing but the author's personal distaste for that part of his subject. It does not in the least prove that considerations of that sort can throw no light on the questions he has to consider. Indeed, we suspect it might be difficult to show in any way that any two branches of knowledge should be allowed to throw no light on one another. Far less can calling one question scientific and another metaphysical warrant Prof. James in "consequently *rejecting*" certain conclusions, against which he has nothing better to object. Nor is it in the least true that physicists confine themselves to such a "strictly positivistic point of view." Students of heat are not deterred by the impossibility of directly observing molecules from considering and accepting the kinetical theory; students of light do not brand speculations on the luminiferous ether as metaphysical; and the substantiality of matter itself is called in question in the vortex theory, which is nevertheless considered as perfectly germane to physics. All these are "attempts to explain phenomenally given elements as products of deeper-lying entities." In fact, this phrase describes, as well as loose language can, the general character of scientific hypotheses.

Remark, too, that it is not merely nor chiefly the "soul" and the "transcendental ego," for which incomprehensibles he has some tenderness, that Prof. James proposes to banish from psychology, but especially *ideas* which their adherents maintain are direct data of consciousness. In short, not only does he propose, by the simple expedient of declaring certain inquiries extra-psychological, to reverse the conclusions of the science upon many important points, but also by the same negative means to decide upon the character of its data. Indeed, when we come to examine the book, we find it is precisely this which is the main use the author makes of his new principle. The notion that the natural sciences accept their data *uncritically* we hold to be a serious mistake. It is true, scientific men do not subject their observations to the kind of criticism practised by the high-flying philosophers, because they do not believe that method of criticism sound. If they really believed in idealism, they would bring it to bear upon physics as much as possible. But in fact they find it a wordy doctrine, not susceptible of any scientific applications. When, however, a physicist has to investigate, say, such a subject as the scintillation of the stars, the first thing he does is to subject the phenomena to rigid criticism to find whether these phenomena are objective or subjective, whether they are in the light itself, or arise in the eye, or in original principles of mental action, or in idiosyncrasies of the imagination, etc. The principle of the uncritical acceptance of data, to which Prof. James clings, practically amounts to a claim to a new kind of liberty of thought, which would make a complete rupture with accepted methods of psychology and of science in general. The truth of this is seen in the chief application that has been made of the new method, in the author's theory of space-perception. And into the enterprise of thus revolutionizing scientific method he enters with a light heart, without any exhaustive scrutiny of his new logic in its generality, relying only on the resources of the moment. He distinctly discourages a separate study of the method. "No rules can be laid down in advance. Comparative observations, to be definite, must usually be made to test some preëxisting hypothesis; and the only thing then is to use as much sagacity as you possess, and to be as candid as you can."

[*Charles Sanders Peirce*], "*James's Psychology I,*" in The Nation, *Vol. LIII, No. 1357, July 2, 1891, p. 15.*

F.C.S. SCHILLER   (essay date 1897)

[*Schiller was an English philosopher who advanced a doctrine of neo-humanism. His opposition to the prevailing philosophy of rationalism in Anglo-American thought made him a natural ally and frequent defender of James's ideas. In the following excerpt, Schiller praises James's freedom from rationalist doctrines in* "The Will to Believe" *and thoroughly endorses James's conception of radical empiricism. For contrasting discussions of* "The Will to Believe," *see the excerpts by Dickinson S. Miller (1899) and George Santayana (1920); for critical analyses supporting the principles of James's essay, see the excerpts by Gail Kennedy (1956) and William Barrett (1975).*]

At the risk of seeming to use the language of extravagant eulogy I should like to call this collection of Prof. James' essays [*The Will to Believe; and Other Essays in Popular Philosophy*] a wholly admirable book, alike in form and in matter. That the form of any of Prof. James' literary productions should be deserving of the highest praise was indeed no more than would be anticipated by all who had ever enjoyed the grace of his style, the raciness of his phrases, the stimulus of his originality, in short the deftness of the manipulations whereby he is wont to charm the heavy indigestible dough of philosophic discussion to rise up into dainty shapes that need be disdained by no intellectual epicure. (p. 547)

The philosphic significance of the views sketched in Prof. James' present volume seems to me to reside chiefly in the fact that they mark a further step in the modern reaction against a one-sided and reckless rationalism—a reaction which bids fair ultimately to reconcile philosophy with common sense. That reaction has generally appealed to the *will* for a title wherewith to check the vagaries of the *"intellectus sibi permissus"*. The fashion was set by Schopenhauer's Will-to-live, continued in Mainläuder's Will-to-die, travestied in Nietzsche's Will-to-power, and last but not least, albeit in a somewhat different sense, Prof. James draws our attention to the importance of the Will-to-believe. For the selection of the title of the first essay to be the title of the whole volume is significant. That believe we must, but that as to the content and manner of our belief we are far freer than we have been taught to believe, is the pivot upon which Prof. James' thought revolves. Thus the book becomes a declaration of the independence of the concrete whole of man, with all his passions and emotions unexpurgated, directed against the cramping rules and regulations by which the Brahmins of the academic caste are tempted to impede the free expansion of human life. The great lesson it illustrates in various forms is that wisdom as well as dining is often a matter of great daring, and that there are not really any eternal and non-human truths to prohibit us from adopting the beliefs we need to live by, nor any infallible *a priori* test of truth to screen us from the consequences of our choice. Now that seems a most salutary doctrine to preach to a biped oppressed by many '-ologies,' like modern man, and calculated to allay his growing doubts whether he has a responsible personality and a soul and conscience of his own, and is not a mere phantasmagoria of abstractions, a transient complex of shadowy formulas that science calls 'the laws of nature'. As against the worship of such 'idols of the theatre,' Prof. James most opportunely reminds us that abstractions are made by men and for men and not men for abstractions, that they become not venerable but execrable when their origin is forgotten and the function for the sake of which they were formed is neglected. 'Pure' science in short is pure bosh, if by purity be meant abstraction from all human purposes and freedom from all emotional interest.

Prof. James himself describes his attitude as a "radical empiricism" . . .—*empiricism*, because he is "contented to regard its most assured conclusions concerning matters of fact as hypotheses liable to be modified in the course of future experience," and *radical*, because he will not take anything for granted, not even that the universe *is* a universe in any debatable sense. . . . For he will not allow that anything has been determined by calling the world a universe, so long as the infinite alternatives to which the term might apply are not rendered definite by a description of the particular universe intended. Hence he will not "dogmatically affirm monism as something with which all experience has to square," but accepts "the opacity of the finite facts as given," and "the crudity of experience remains an eternal element thereof". But if so, he must needs be a pluralist, on the ground that "there is no possible point of view from which the world can appear as an absolutely single fact. Real possibilities, real indeterminations, real beginnings, real ends, real evil, real crises, catastrophies and escapes, a real God, and a real moral life, just as common sense conceives these things, may remain in empiricism as conceptions which philosophy gives up the attempt either to 'overcome' or to reinterpret in monistic form." . . .

These are brave words and of the happiest augury; for they may mean the dawn of an era in which teleological postulates will be admitted to underlie all human activities, when consequently the postulates of man's knowing activities will be subjected to as candid a criticism as the implications of his feelings and actions, and when their subordination to the needs and aims of the whole organism will win due recognition.

The paper on **"The Will to Believe"** strikes Prof. James' keynote boldly by declaring that in all cases of genuine option between intellectual alternatives—that is in all cases where both alternatives appeal to us in any way—our decision not only lawfully may but must be made by our passional nature. It is idle in such cases to avoid decision by suspense of judgment; for though we may thus escape error, we also lose our chance of gaining truth. Very often, as is well illustrated by the Alpine climber in a desperate case, to refuse a decision is itself a decision; the climber must leap to safety or perish. . . . In such cases he who hesitates is lost, while conversely faith "creates its own verification," so that "the thought becomes literally father to the fact as the wish was father to the thought." . . . Hence Prof. James "cannot see his way to accept the agnostic rules for truth-seeking or wilfully agree to keep his willing nature out of the game". For "a rule of thinking which would absolutely prevent one from acknowledging certain kinds of truth, if those kinds of truth were really there, would be an irrational rule." . . . And the more so if it is realised that it is not really a question of intellect *versus* feelings, but of intellect *plus* one passion, "the horror of becoming a dupe," *versus* the rest. (pp. 548-49)

Biologically, the brain is primarily an exceedingly plastic organ for effecting exceedingly varied adaptations to the organism's ends and conditions of life: it would seem to follow at once that the mind's action must be teleologically vitiated throughout, and that there is not the slightest antecedent reason for supposing that it functions satisfactorily except with reference to the practical needs of the organism. If then there existed absolute truth, of which man was not the measure, it would be most natural that the human mind should prove inadequate to its comprehension. But fortunately there is no ground for the assertion of any such absolute truth. What passes for such is itself an abstraction, which may have its proper function in

the system of human ends, or may be perverted, like other aberrant instincts, into a mode of functioning useless, and even dangerous, to the whole organism. We are shut up then in a thoroughly anthropomorphic view of our experience. But it is an unwarrantable inference that such a view is *not* adequate to our needs. And it seems a most valuable suggestion of Prof. James' that we may often make it adequate by trying and by proceeding on the assumption that it is adequate. Whether *e.g.* the world is knowable or not may be, like the question whether life is or is not worth living . . . , one of the truths that become true by our faith . . . , one of the cases where "our personal response," the eye with which we regard the facts, may make all the difference. Certainly this suggestion will go some way towards explaining the strange divergence of the estimates of the world which are come to by different persons and in different sciences.

For it is not the least factor in the relief held out to us by Prof. James' doctrine that it emancipates us from the superstition that our sciences set forth a rigid, unbending and unhuman order of fact which our volitions and emotions fret against in vain. The sciences appear simply as methods of transmuting the givenness of facts into shapes subservient to our various purposes, and their 'principles' are adopted *ad hoc*. They may be as various as those purposes and as numerous as the sciences, though there is a natural tendency for the methods and assumptions of the predominant science to infect the rest. As Prof. James says, they are "chapters in the great jugglery which our conceiving faculty is for ever playing with the order of being as it presents itself" . . . , and it is a poor juggler that is taken in by his own tricks. There is no abstract sacrosanctity about the rules of science, and it may well be that "to the end of time our power of moral and volitional response to the nature of things will be the deepest organ of communication therewith we shall ever possess." . . . Such sayings should not be taken as derogatory to the majesty of science, but they contain a much-needed vindication of the rights of man, the maker of all sciences. (pp. 550-51)

> *F.C.S. Schiller, in a review of "The Will to Believe, and Other Essays in Popular Philosophy," in* Mind, *n.s. Vol. VI, No. 24, October, 1897, pp. 547-54.*

DICKINSON S. MILLER　(essay date 1899)

[*Miller was an American philosopher and a student of James's at Harvard whose reminiscences of James's pedagogical manner are included in* Great Teachers: Portrayed by Those Who Studied Under Them (1946). *While Miller held James in high personal regard, he was critical of James's lack of analytical rigor in his philosophy. The following excerpt is an attack on James's conception of the will to believe, "or to Make-Believe," as Miller renames it. However, while profoundly at variance with James's general principles and conclusions in the essay* "The Will to Believe," *Miller admires the personal courage of James and the adventurous quality of his thought. For another discussion critical of* "The Will to Believe," *see the excerpt by George Santayana (1920); for critical analyses supporting the principles of James's essay, see the excerpts by F.C.S. Schiller (1897), Gail Kennedy (1956), and William Barrett (1975).*]

[In **"The Will to Believe, and Other Essays,"** Mr. James] vigorously preaches the liberty of believing," "the lawfulness of voluntarily adopted faith," "the right to adopt a believing attitude in religious matters in spite of the fact that our merely logical intellect may not have been coerced." "I wish to make you feel," he says,—I take a form of his favorite declaration pitched upon almost at random,—"that we have a right to believe the physical order to be only a partial order; that we have a right to supplement it by an unseen spiritual order which we assume on trust, if only thereby life may seem worth living again." "The thesis I defend is, briefly stated, this: Our passional nature not only lawfully may, but must, decide an option between propositions whenever it is a genuine option that cannot by its nature be decided on intellectual grounds; for to say, under such circumstances, 'Do not decide, but leave the question open,' is itself a passional decision, just like deciding yes or no, and is attended with the same risk of losing the truth." "Faith based on desire," "believing by volition,"—thus he characterizes a mood of mind which he goes on to defend with inexhaustible resources of ingenuity and illustration, and with that well-known diction, straight from the hot-springs of an intense imagination, with which already, in his **"Psychology,"** he made alive whatever he touched.

There is something in Mr. James's stress upon the intellectual offices of will calculated to do essential service to philosophy in the forlornness of its present state; but only if clearly distinguished from the letter of his teaching. The literal precepts, as above, to which he lends his high authority are, I hold, among the formidable obstacles to progress in that disordered and distracted science. For my own part, I am of the old-fashioned conviction that such precepts are in effect an attempt to corrupt intelligence, that they aim a deadly blow at the vital instincts of the upright intellect. This is not the aspect of the matter that I should myself choose to put first. There is that to my own perception in honeyed theories of our place or prospects as men, in postulates of a golden solution of things fetched from whatever heaven of invention which are accredited because so eminently to our taste,—there is that in the sight of the constructive postulator, fancy-free, busy at his landscape-gardening in the infinite,—which is not so noticeably immoral as ridiculous. Desire strikes me as a quaint fortune-teller for man or the world. The defects in the appointments of this universe as a home for sensitive beings are only too obvious; but to rely for remedy upon the familiar human propensity to disbelieve in the existence of that which would be exceedingly disagreeable, seems a device past articulate comment. At such a medicine for its maladies, "the soul, if the soul had fingers, would snap them." But this JOURNAL is devoted primarily to ethical concerns; and Mr. James has himself raised the question of intellectual duty by scoffing long and heartily at the fantastic scruples of scientific purists and pedants who condemn the "faith" he defends as immoral. The charge is old. Moral distinctions are said to soften with age, and it even seems a return to the pragmatical sourness of a bygone controversial spirit and little in accord with the easy temper of speculative discussion at this hour to call a theory "immoral." That, in the feelings of large contemporary minds, is an epithet that should attach to disputed opinions only as a quotation from the Philistines and provincials. But thought is an agency; as Mr. James truly sets forth it may be guided, thwarted, or seduced by the will; it has goods to gain and evils to escape; and hence has its right and wrong. So far as intellectual emancipation permits us to retain intellectual conscience we still have the organ to discern that belief forcibly seized on is not honestly come by. The Will to Believe is a thing to be absolutely separated from the will to know the truth. The former is a desire for a purely subjective result, a state of our own consciousness that we seek in the first instance for its own sake, and may be willing to take an efficacious intellectual drug to produce. The latter is a desire that our convictions may correspond with reality, and naturally leads us to seek simply,

with inflexible directness, for the fact. Nor must we confound the will to believe with the wish, in itself blameless, natural, and even laudable, to find the truth congenial. As the author justly observes, "the most useful investigator, because the most sensitive observer, is always he whose eager interest in one side of the question is balanced by an equally keen nervousness lest he be deceived." The wish to find the truth congenial must first of all in consistency be a wish to find the truth. The Will to Believe is the will to deceive—to deceive one's self; and the deception, which begins at home, may be expected in due course to pass on to others. It is the will to hold that thing certain which now we feel to be uncertain; it says, "This thing seems to my best intelligence doubtful; but I will subject my mind to such a course of treatment; I will so tempt and beguile it by presenting this one matter for its credence and withholding rivals; I will so hypnotize it by keeping its gaze on this one brilliant object; that I shall presently find myself reposing in the peaceable possession of a full belief." (pp. 171-73)

[The] question arises whether the author means that we are to bring ourselves by use of will into a believing state of mind, an internal assent, or only that we are to act as if we believed. . . . In truth, much vigorous writing could be cited to either effect. We hear of our "right to believe" and also of our "right to adopt a believing attitude"; of "the right of the individual to indulge his personal faith at his personal risk," and again, of merely "acting on the assumption" of a certain tenet.

The author speaks of "those questions that belong to the province of personal faith to decide." If faith "decides," as in the case here referred to, a question of truth or falsehood, faith would appear to be the mental state of belief. Indeed, it is roundly said, "Faith means belief in something concerning which doubt is still theoretically possible; and," the writer goes directly on, "as the test of belief is willingness to act, one may say that faith is the readiness to act in a cause the prosperous issue of which is not certified to us in advance." Thus (though one does not gather why the thing should be identified with its test) it would seem that it is no mere outward scheme of living, without an *ex animo* ["sincere"] assent, that is recommended, but action flowing from and expressing a state of mind which is none the less belief because it rises superior to the evidence. However, there is much about risk boldly faced. "I have discussed the kinds of risk; . . . and I have pleaded that it is better to face them openly than to act as if we did not know them to be there." Faith "is in fact the same moral quality which we call courage in practical affairs." But the risk in question is the risk of being wrong, and to face that risk is to face uncertainty, to entertain doubt. And, as if to put us finally to confusion, comes the remark, to illustrate the courage of faith, that "there will be a very wide-spread tendency in men of vigorous nature to enjoy a certain amount of uncertainty in their philosophic creed, just as risk lends a zest to worldly activity."

The possible attitudes in this regard are not hard to classify. To believe a proposition is to hold it true. To believe it incompletely is to hold it more or less probably true, but possibly false. To recognize it as possibly false is so far to withhold belief from it. Belief is the appearance to the mind of truth in a proposition, reality in a thing. Belief and admission of falsity are, whether absolutely or in degrees, mutually exclusive. Now we may (as I said seemed the inevitable implication of terms the author puts in the foreground) deliberately make "good resolutions" of belief; we may resolve to kill a doubt we have and breed a belief we as yet have not; observation informs us that this can be done. In this case at the outset we face risk, the risk that our belief presently to be acquired may be false, that our doubts now being smothered may be justified. When, however, our course of self-treatment has been successful, and the belief is duly installed, the doubt by the force of the terms has vanished, and the uncertainty, though from the former point of view it was there and from some other mind's point of view may still be there, can by the mind in question be "faced" no longer. At this stage it is inapposite to quote, "the virtue to exist by faith as sailors live by courage; as, by strength of heart, the sailor fights with roaring seas," for in the exact measure in which faith is present, courage is not needed. At an earlier stage there may have been intellectual courage, though the species of courage involved in purchasing either mental comfort or mental exaltation, by shutting our eyes to sources of uncertainty, is much that of the ostrich that buries its head in the sand. A person who vigorously asserts a thing to himself because he wishes it to be true, is not commonly called a brave man for his pains. But note in any case that what is supposed to be courageous is not faith (if as Mr. James defined it "faith means belief"), but the will to acquire faith, the will to believe; and so far as that will accomplishes itself, the occasion for courage has passed.

The other alternative is the resolution not to believe, but to act as if certain propositions were true, from social motives, or ultimate personal preference, though we freely and mentally admit the while that they are entirely doubtful. There is no peculiarly intellectual courage here, because there is no intellectual interference of the will, but its practical application only. Under either alternative there may or may not, of course, be courageous practical conduct, but that is foreign to the question. Under this second alternative, however, it has to be noted, we may have a subtle approach to the first; for in controlling our conduct we may tend to control our imaginations, and so fix that habit of thought which constitutes belief.

The present case exhibits, I believe, both of these situations intermingled and not, I think, distinguished. In his preface Mr. James calls his attitude "empiricism." "I say 'empiricism,' because it is contented to regard its most assured conclusions concerning matters of fact as hypotheses liable to modification in the course of experience." There speaks to us the philosopher in wide contemplation of philosophic systems. Later, to the same effect, in the body of the book, "Faith is synonymous with working hypothesis. . . . A chemist, etc. . . . Now, in such questions as God, immortality, absolute morality, and free-will, no professed believer at the present day pretends his faith to be of a radically different complexion; he can always doubt his creed." Thus we should will to believe in default of evidence, but we are never to allow that will wholly to take effect. It is, perhaps, only the Will to Hope. Or is it that the multitude are humanely counselled to drown their doubts while the philosopher himself keeps his vision clear? Is this (unconsciously to the author) a gospel for spiritual weaklings delivered by a strong man who cannot find it in him to take advantage of it himself? Or are we all expected to have in us something of the multitude and a little of the philosopher; to know ourselves needy of faith and resolve recurringly to embrace it; to turn again and again with an access of resolve a set face of conviction to our world; to remember with return of self-consciousness that this is but our own attitude, taken at a risk of error; to act thus both the teacher of "wholesome doctrine" and the taught, deceiver and deceived, by turns or at once, and so appropriately illustrate our time?

About Mr. James himself there can be little question. For himself he is not one of those who, as Hume somewhere says, cover their eyes with their wings, their perceptions with their aspirations, like the angels in the Book of Revelation. Not wholly believing, or ever rejecting, he lives after all on the perilous edge, breathing the "eager air" of hazard to the last. And the temper that spurns agnosticism with its logical qualms and scruples and its spiritual penury, that gains "richness of result" by "indulging its personal faith," but all the while "enjoys a certain amount of uncertainty," is a fit birth of the *Zeitgeist* in an age of mental indecision. Mr. James's words had sometimes led us to picture him as one of a full habit of belief despising the water-gruel regimen of suspense and negation to which a pedantic rigorism would restrict us. But, no; he does not believe, albeit with the best will to believe (at times), in the world. He has the courage of his assumptions, but not their serenity. He has only a fighting faith (so to use the term for the moment), but no resting or reaping faith. . . . The late Sir James Stephen described Newman, in the midst of his subtle dealings with doubt in the "Grammar of Assent," as "a worm wriggling on a hook." But in our present author nothing evokes so potently as his suspense between belief and unbelief that something ardent, manful, and generous that escapes at all times from his pages. He has a frank and fearless exultation in his plight, a sense of sublimity as at the abyss's brink, an appeal to the pride of will and last "turnings of the character" which, profitless, perhaps, in their literal philosophic import, have in them something that rouses the blood like the peal and tucket of a bugle. His speculative attitude expresses his scorn of intellectual ease. Philosophy is for him a strenuous exercise and high adventure of the spirit,—at once a fortifying discipline and a test of our present quality.

If, now, I speak in this scanty space of the philosophic justification of the Will to Believe—or to Make-Believe—according to whatever interpretation, I must pass over most of Mr. James's points of argument and touch only on what is fundamental. My deepest philosophical difference with Mr. James may be put thus: It does not follow, because we cannot prove everything, because in the last resort we can prove nothing, that we are free to assume what we choose. He appears to conceive that with the surrender of what he terms Rationalism, Absolutism, etc., belief becomes a question of taste. This is the enviable liberty of what he pleasantly calls his Irrationalism. As soon as the lights of reason are turned down we may help ourselves in the dark to what we can lay hands on. Since there is no longer a rational warrant for belief, there is no longer a rational bar to assumption; one belief is just as good in that regard as another; so that we may deal with them on the single basis of our predilections, unconfused by the introduction of any alien standard. (pp. 183-88)

I cannot accept . . . Mr. James's name of "irrationalism." To ask of reason what it cannot here perform, to regard its inability as a discomfiture, a failure to meet due expectation, is entirely to misconceive the office and pretension of a subordinate engine of the mind. It is the function of reason to bring our minor and dependent beliefs into harmony with those that are fundamental and independent, to subject superficial tendencies to permanent instincts. Taken with its cerebral counterpart, it is, from the point of view of physiology, a form of inhibition; from the point of view of general biology, a means of checking first tendencies to reaction, and so preserving the organism alive in an environment full of traps. I cannot think it other than a misfortune that in a time when, despite or because of emancipations, both caprice and prejudice, in and out of philosophy, receive their liberal share of applause, the authority of reason should be deemed weakened because a confused theory calling itself "rationalism" falls to the ground. (pp. 188-89)

The will to believe is defined as a resolution to have faith in excess of the evidence. If this means in excess only of the tangible or producible evidence, it seems an abuse of terms. But the truth, as I have said, is that the author declines to take cognizance of the distinction between feeling a thing to be true, or, in a less degree, to be likely, and accepting it as congenial. Cravings and divinings with him are one. (p. 191)

I hold then—as this broken summary and these scattered suggestions would indicate—that there is a sufficiently firm basis in the conditions of life for the stern fact-facing temper for which Mr. James has so sorry an opinion. I feel it to be a declension from the heroics of "deliberate and courageous" faith; but after all one need not be put to confusion because the masters of speculative romance can "use grander language" than oneself; nor need one be envious of the scenic sublimities enjoyed by gentlemen who regard philosophy as an opportunity to express their taste in universes. We are told, indeed, that the quality of our own natures is shown by the scale and imperiousness of our "demands" upon the world we inhabit; but I cannot think it necessary, in order to clear one's character as a man, to commit a folly as a thinker. We are told, too, that all philosophic thought is an affair of one's demands, and that in disagreeing with so many of our opponents' opinions we make it evident that our own intellectual taste is essentially negative and destructive. There is an unspiritual energy of intellect whose love is for logic as a craft, and which animates a class of critical rigorists and precisians, extreme to mark what is done amiss in the minutiae of argument, but of a nature scarcely deep enough at root to feel the more far-reaching needs. To this I suppose there is little to be said. Not being of those who "enjoy a certain amount of uncertainty" in their religion, we cannot demonstrate by a postulating faith our depth of spiritual nature. For the rest, it may perhaps be taken as a confirmation of the charge that we are unanxious to rebut it. (pp. 194-95)

Dickinson S. Miller, " 'The Will to Believe' and the Duty to Doubt," in The International Journal of Ethics, *Vol. IX, No. 2, January, 1899, pp. 169-95.*

TH. FLOURNOY (essay date 1902)

[*Flournoy was a Swiss psychologist and philosopher and the author of* The Philosophy of William James *(1911). Like James, Flournoy opposed the contemporary trend of rationalism in philosophy, and this ideological sympathy led to a personal friendship between the two men. Flournoy's review of* The Varieties of Religious Experience, *excerpted below, originally appeared in the* Revue Philosophique *in 1902. In this review, Flournoy expresses an enthusiastic approval of James's study, particularly his willingness to view mysticism, which has often been regarded as a consequence of physical or mental pathology, as a valid groundwork for knowledge. For a contrasting view of* The Varieties of Religious Experience, *see the excerpt by H. Rashdall (1903). For other views of James's writings on religion, see the excerpts by Julius Seelye Bixler (1926) and Gary T. Alexander (1979).*]

James's philosophical originality lies not so much in the principles which he expounds, which are those of the most pronounced empiricism, as in his manner of applying them, and of following them up with a fidelity, a detachment from prejudice and an audacity which lead him into regions that are never reached by the vulgar practitioners of experimental philospohy, who are always prone, in spite of their noisy declaration of impartiality, to fall back into the old pedantic ruts.

This independence of spirit appears [in *The Varieties of Religious Experience*] from the very first chapter entitled "Religion and Neurology," in which James takes the bull by the horns and delivers a penetrating and in places a justly severe criticism of what he calls "medical materialism." This last is the view, much in vogue at present, that religion is irretrievably compromised by the mere fact that those whose experiences in this realm have been at all pronounced (that is to say "religious geniuses," the saints, prophets, mystics, and other humble souls possessed of a really personal and living faith) have generally exhibited symptoms of nervous instability, peculiarities of conduct, hallucinations, etc. They have been, in a word, eccentrics or psychopaths, from which fact it has been inferred that the religious phenomenon is nothing but a nervous disease which is of interest pathologically, but of no value in itself, and the very opposite of that great human ideal for which it has been taken.

James is so far from contesting the frequent combination of the religious genius and the psychopathic temperament, that he looks upon it rather as something quite natural and explicable. But he holds that to discredit the first by reason of the second is to confuse two entirely different questions, namely, the estimation of the *value* of things with the determination of their *origin* or cause. To make the origin the criterion of value has always been, it is true, a method dear to those prejudiced persons who take their ideas simply and solely from some authoritative source, ecclesiastical or traditional, without inquiring into either their content or their necessary consequences. But we have passed that stage, and the medical materialists are merely belated dogmatists, secularized theologues, when to-day they condemn certain phenomena of conscience and certain beliefs, on account of their morbid origin. To do this is not an empirical procedure. In science or politics we do not estimate a new idea or theory by the state of health of its author, but solely by its intrinsic value. We examine it for its direct utility and for its important implications. We ought to do the same in religion. The only criteria for a philosopher to employ in his criticism of religion are the wholly empirical criteria of its internal value, firstly, for the man who possesses it (his immediate happiness, the illumination it sheds upon his inner life), and secondly, of its tangible effects on individual conduct and collective progress.

It is only in a later chapter (that upon the "Value of Saintliness") that James enters into this appreciation of religion from the purely empirical point of view of its fruits. Before doing so, he found it necessary to review and describe its principal manifestations, including the morbid, which are often the most instructive. (pp. 219-22)

[From] the outset James's critical empiricism discarded, as methodologically unjustifiable, the estimates offered by medical materialism, quite as much as those offered by the theological profession. It is not by its roots and origins (whether one assigns them to the pathological condition of the organism or to revelation from on high) that one can judge of the value of religion in general, or of a given religion in particular, but only by its fruits, its consequences in the moral life of the individual and of humanity. This entirely practical and utilitarian valuation of the religious life is often mentioned by the author, and becomes the main theme of the fourteenth and fifteenth lectures, where he enters upon a critique of "The Value of Saintliness."

Nowhere else, perhaps, has James displayed a more exquisite sensibility or a more admirable delicacy of touch, in his twofold task as psychologist and moralist than in his delineation of the great classic traits in the physiognomy of the saints,—devotion, charity, purity, asceticism, heroism, etc. After having shown the grandeur and the defects, and made allowance for what human frailty and stupidity inevitably add by way of alloy, James, still using his purely empirical method and with no rhetorical artifices, concludes with a eulogy of saintliness, which in power of persuasiveness and real eloquence leaves the verbose apologies of the theologians far behind. Not only does a genuine experience of religion incomparably enrich the individual himself,—enlarging his vision and giving him strength, peace, and happiness,—but also it accelerates the evolution of humanity. The saints have indeed been the initiators of all moral progress, the heralds of a perfected state of society. We cannot reproduce in a few lines the impression left by these pages, in which moral insight vies with closely reasoned argument, and in which,—after a striking comparison between Nietzsche's super-man and its complete antithesis, the saint,—saintliness emerges absolutely justified from the "economic point of view," as representing an *ensemble* of qualities which are indispensable to the welfare of the world.

After this empirical justification of religion, there still remains the problem of its metaphysical value, and it is to this momentous question that James devotes his last chapters.

All religions suppose that the visible world forms a part of a more spiritual universe and derives its deepest significance therefrom, and that our real duty is to adjust ourselves to this higher universe; and further, that prayerful communion is a real means to that end, a truly efficacious act by which the spiritual energy of this other universe is brought to bear in our phenomenal world. But what are such beliefs worth? Are they anything but a subjective impression, a pure illusion? Do they correspond to an objective reality? (pp. 225-28)

One must . . . acknowledge the plain fact that there is no means of establishing rationally the objective validity of religious experience and its accompanying beliefs: but neither is there any means of refuting them, or of proving that mystical phenomena do not put the individual in contact with a higher reality.

Does this mean, then, that the understanding has no further place in this domain, and that thinking will not assist in solving religious problems? Certainly not, says James, but one must assign this work of the intellect to its proper place which is only secondary, being a subsequent reflection upon the immediate data of experience. Religious philosophy must start from religious phenomena accepted as such, and be content with classifying and analyzing their contents; in other words, from having been a theology that was metaphysical and *a priori* as it has hitherto been, it must become a critical and inductive science of religions. On such ground, it may hope some day to gain acceptance even by non-religious people, just as the facts of optics are acknowledged by those who are born blind. But just as optics would not exist were it not for the experiences of seeing individuals, in the same way the science of religions is based on the evidence afforded by religious persons; and it will never be in a position to decide whether in the end these experiences themselves are illusory or not. This last question of the objective and absolute significance of religious phenom-

Drawing by James of an American Indian, made during his expedition to Brazil as a medical student. From Four Papers Presented in the Institute for Brazilian Studies, Vanderbilt University, *by Charles Wagley, Octávio Gouvêa Bulhões, Stanley J. Stein, and Carleton Sprague Smith. Vanderbilt University Press, 1951. Reprinted by permission.*

ena will be impossible to solve scientifically, and it will always be for the individual either to leave it open or else to settle it by an act of personal faith.

James is among those who do not hesitate before this act of faith, and who stand for the metaphysical value of religion. And if you should object that in so doing he departs from the ways of science and of experimental philosophy, and goes over to the arbitrary and the individual, you would then find the "radical empiricist" a very formidable opponent. For he is neither to be duped by words, nor to be deceived by the pontiffs of modern "science" as to what constitutes true empiricism. He has seen and felt, better than any one else, the fundamental opposition which separates the so-called scientific from the religious point of view, and which revolves entirely about the question of personality and the reality of the Ego; and he declares that on this point, despite all objections, the religious man stands on the ground of actual experience and the scientific philosopher upon that of theory and prejudice. No summary can begin to do justice to the vivid and masterly pages which the American thinker devotes to this all-important issue. (pp. 229-31)

James's religious philosophy is characterized on the whole, as to method, by two intimately connected traits. First, it is empirical and always eager to take account of actually experienced facts, whatever they may be; for reality is far too rich and complex to be comprehended by a single individual, so that we can never expect every one to have the same religious experience or the same faith; and such diversity must be respected. And second, his philosophy is practical, that is to say, utilitarian, and rejects as vain all speculation that has no bearing on life. James formulated this second point in the principle of "pragmatism," which he adopted from his compatriot, too little known in Europe, the philosopher Peirce; it maintains that all belief is but a rule for action, and that its significance is consequently measured by the difference it can make in our conduct. This does away, at one stroke, with a host of idle questions, beginning perhaps with the controversies over the metaphysical attributes of God, such as his aseity, his necessity, simplicity, immateriality, etc.; for what difference does all this make to us and how could our conduct or our inner life be altered by the acceptance or rejection of such concepts? It is quite otherwise with the moral attributes of divinity, such as saintliness, justice, love, etc.; which react strongly upon us and whose significance and reality are guaranteed by their influence on our conduct.

His complete disdain of abstract metaphysics, and of ideas that have no practical bearing, makes James a typical representative of the genius of his race. Doubtless it was a similar inspiration, at bottom, which caused Kant to sweep aside all metaphysical lumber and to admit, by way of religious speculation, only what could be justified as a "postulate of the practical reason." But the older philosopher was unable to rid himself of the cumbersome machinery of scholastic argumentation, and it remained for the clear and keen common sense of the Anglo-Saxon, free of all pedantry, to formulate and apply the pragmatic principle with a simplicity and ease, one might almost say with a good humor, which make it instantly intelligible to readers unversed in dialectics. In this sense James is right in considering the tradition of English and Scotch analysts (of Locke, Hume, and the rest), to which he properly belongs, as representing far better than does the sage of Königsberg (with the metaphysical excesses whch he induced among his successors) the true critical method,—the "only method which

can make of philosophy a discipline worthy of a serious man," and the only one which works at all effectively against dogmatism and fruitless ratiocination of every kind. (pp. 241-43)

> *Th. Flournoy, "The Varieties of Religious Experience," in his* The Philosophy of William James, *translated by Edwin B. Holt and William James, Jr., Henry Holt and Company, 1917, 246 p.*

H. RASHDALL   (essay date 1903)

[*In the following excerpt, Rashdall criticizes* The Varieties of Religious Experience *as a compilation of pathological case histories that do not fully reflect the meaning and value of religion in human life and that also disparage the role that reason plays in religion. For a contrasting view of* The Varieties of Religious Experience, *see the excerpt by Th. Flournoy (1902). For other views of James's writings on religion, see the excerpts by Julius Seelye Bixler (1926) and Gary T. Alexander (1979) and the entry in the Additional Bibliography by James Dittes.*]

[*The Varieties of Religious Experience*] is not an easy work to review. The greater part of it is taken up with records of actual religious experience, mostly of abnormal kinds—remarkable cases of conversion, of exceptional saintliness, of religious exaltation and mystic insight. That the book is one of the highest interest, that extraordinary industry and research have been employed in collecting these records from the religious literature of all ages and faiths, that Prof. James's comments upon them are characterised by all his accustomed charm of style, vivacity and open-mindedness, is unquestionable. Nor can there be any doubt that it was well worth while to undertake such a task. They will at least be valuable as materials for Psychology and Philosophy, whatever may be thought of the use which Prof. James himself makes of them. It is good that philosophers should be reminded that there are sides of human nature and human experience which are too often undreamed of in the formal philosophy of the schools. It is well that the theologian should be compelled to recognise how ideas and experiences which he is in the habit of supposing to be peculiar to his own religion and perhaps to his own form of that religion are really, not indeed without characteristic differences and modifications but still to a large extent, common to many widely different faiths. But here we are obliged to ask what is the value of Prof. James's book, not merely as an interesting piece of literature, or even as a piece of psychological research, but as an actual contribution to Philosophy and particularly to the Philosophy of Religion.

I shall best perhaps answer this question by confining my detailed criticism to the chapter entitled "Conclusions." . . . I pass over the merely psychological part of Prof. James's conclusions—his mere summary of the leading characteristics of religious experience and his estimate of its partial utility and of the limitations of that utility. Against the fairness and general healthy-mindedness of his summing-up I have nothing to say. The only remark that seems called for is this—that Prof. James deals almost exclusively with abnormal and exceptional experiences. His own defence of this procedure is that the exceptional or extreme cases show more clearly than others what is the general character of the normal or ordinary cases. If the object be to test the existence of some specific faculty of spiritual insight, distinguishable from the ordinary operations of the reason, understanding, or moral consciousness, there may be much to be said for such a course. But when the question is as to the value of religion in life, its advantages are more questionable. Prof. James is quite alive to the defects of these abnormal types of character—the social uselessness and even perniciousness for instance of the more ascetic lives which he records. He fails to consider how far this is due to the very exaggeration or isolation of the qualities or tendencies in question. There is too little attempt to distinguish from an ethical or religious point of view between different kinds and varieties of the religious consciousness, though the feelings of most readers in the perusal of these ''human documents'' will probably range from the highest admiration and sympathy to a loathing and disgust relieved only by pity. He is right in demurring to the typical ''alienist's'' attempt to minimise the significance of all such experiences by a free use of such terms as ''morbid'' or ''neurotic''; but we may surely be allowed to protest also against a study of religion in which the sole interest of the inquirer in his subject seems to lie in their abnormal character. To take a concrete case, St. Paul was ''caught up into the seventh heaven'' and saw visions. Herein lies apparently for Prof. James the main interest of his ''case''. He is quite justified in treating St. Paul from this point of view as one of a numerous class of religious enthusiasts, and yet in pleading that that fact does not necessarily prevent our regarding those visions of St. Paul as sources of real ''revelation'' for the world. But he hardly seems to contemplate the possibility of a point of view from which the highest religious importance and significance of St. Paul may be held to lie, not in the fact that he saw visions, but in the fact that he was so very unlike the majority of persons who at various periods of the world's history have seen visions. Those visions, however we explain them, were no doubt, at that time and place, a condition of St. Paul's exceptional religious influence, and yet St. Paul the thinker, the spiritualiser of Jewish Theology and the rationaliser of Jewish Ethics, may be much more important than St. Paul the ecstatic visionary. Without denying the religious value of the vision which formed the turning-point in St. Paul's life, the most remarkable thing about St. Paul was not so much that he spake with tongues more than his converts, but that (unlike them) he attributed comparatively little importance to them in comparison with the higher and more rational gift of ''prophecy''. Prof. James's preoccupation with the marvellous and the abnormal almost inevitably conducts him to, if indeed it is not inspired by, a determination to find the essence of religion in feeling and emotion, and to belittle its rational or intellectual side.

But it is with Prof. James's metaphysical or philosophical conclusions that we are chiefly concerned here. He puts to himself the following questions:—

> First, is there, under all the discrepancies of the creeds, a common nucleus to which they bear their testimony unanimously?
>
> And, second, ought we to consider the testimony true?
>
> I will take up the first question first, and answer it in the affirmative. The warring gods and formulas of the various religions do indeed cancel each other, but there is a certain uniform deliverance in which religions all appear to meet. It of two parts:—
>
> 1. An uneasiness; and
>
> 2. Its solution.
>
> 1. The uneasiness, reduced to its simplest terms, is a sense that there is *something wrong about us* as we naturally stand.

> 2. The solution is a sense that *we are saved from the wrongness* by making proper connexion with the higher powers.

> The individual, so far as he suffers from his wrongness and criticises it, is to that extent consciously beyond it, and in at least possible touch with something higher, if anything higher exist. Along with the wrong part there is thus a better point of view, even though it may be but a most helpless germ. With which part he should identify his real being is by no means obvious at this stage; but when stage 2 (the stage of solution or salvation) arrives, the man identifies his real being with the germinal higher part of himself; and does so in the following way. He becomes conscious that this higher part is conterminous and continuous with a MORE of the same quality, which is operative in the universe outside of him, and which he can keep in working touch with, and in a fashion get on board of and save himself when all his lower being has gone to pieces in the wreck. . . .

I am quite willing to accept the positive side of Prof. James's contention—that these abnormal experiences do carry with them some probable evidence in favour of the reality of a spiritual world beyond the experiences themselves—in other words they do supply some evidence, to put the matter in a more definite and theological way than Prof. James himself would do, in favour of the existence of a God who is a moral being and of a future for the individual soul continuous with its present life, though I find it difficult to estimate the exact degree of weight which ought to be given to such experiences when taken in isolation from other arguments the validity of which would probably not be admitted by Prof. James. But Prof. James is not content with claiming consideration for the line of thought with which his book is occupied. He is prepared apparently to base religion entirely upon the evidence afforded by these abnormal experiences to the few who have gone through them. The rest of us must apparently depend entirely upon the external testimony of those who have experienced such things. Of all other arguments or metaphysical considerations Prof. James speaks with jaunty and light-hearted contempt. And no wonder: for his own metaphysical position, it would seem, is practically Hume's. It is clear that it would be useless for a reviewer who believes that Sensationalism was refuted once for all by Plato in the *Theaetetus* to enter into closer argument with a writer holding such a position—especially as neither old arguments nor new ones are adduced in support of his conclusion. Prof. James appears to rely exclusively upon that old topic of the Philistines, the disagreements of the Philosophers. ''I need not discredit Philosophy by laborious criticism of its arguments. It will suffice if I show that as a matter of history it fails to prove its pretension to be 'objectively' convincing. In fact, philosophy does not so fail. It does not banish differences; it founds schools and sects just as feeling does.'' . . . But do not Science and Politics found schools and sects, and is Prof. James prepared to hand over Science and Politics to the undisputed sway of subjective caprice or emotion, because there is not as yet a complete consensus as to the truth of Weismannism or the advantages of Democracy? There is one faith which all sects in Philosophy at all events have in common, except the sect to which Prof. James belongs, and that is faith in the validity of Reason, in the existence of truth and the duty of pursuing it. There is a faith which all religions as well as all philosophies have in common and that is the faith if a thing is really true, it must be true for you as well as for me. And that is just the truth which Prof. James categorically denies. I am not of course questioning the value or the partial and relative truth of many conflicting creeds, but they have their value just on one condition—that those who profess them really do believe them to be objectively true. They need not of course believe that they are infallible. We make mistakes in arithmetic, but we believe that *if* my answer to a problem in arithmetic be true, yours which differs from it cannot be true also. "To believe" means to think that a thing is objectively true. This is just the faith which Prof. James does his best to dethrone by inviting every one to believe just what caprice dictates. "The gods we stand by are the gods we need and can use, the gods whose demands on us are reinforcements of our demands on ourselves and on one another." ... All the Philosophies or Religions which believe in objective truth, no matter what their disagreements in other matters, have more in common with each other than they have with Prof. James's revived Pyrrhonism. Prof. James's position can only be described as a deliberate abandonment of the search for truth and a handing over of Religion and Morality (and why not Science?) to the sway of wilful caprice. To me at least to believe that my Religion or Philosophy was only true for me would be exactly the same thing as not believing it at all. Of course Prof. James is not consistent—no sceptic ever is. "In our Father's house are many mansions, and each of us must discover for himself the kind of religion and the amount of saintship which best comports with what he believes to be his powers and feels to be his truest mission and vocation." ... Beautifully put, but then this implies that there is an objective canon which makes one mission and vocation "truer" than another; it may be different in detail but the ideal by which its value is measured must be one and the same. I gladly recognise that my creed and the discrepant creed of my neighbour may both of them really be but approximations to or partial aspects of *the* truth, but to believe that both may be *equally* true is equivalent to not believing either to be true at all.

Prof. James's book is eminently one which "gives to think". As such it has a high value, intellectual and practical, and particular suggestions and ideas of it—for instance, its emphasis on the importance of the "subconscious self," to whose working the author attributes many of the religious phenomena which he studies—may contribute to the building up of a sober and rational philosophy of religion in the future. The candour and breezy optimism of his tone are attractive and stimulating. But to those who do not agree with it, its philosophy will seem (as a whole) flimsy and superficial. To such minds Prof. James's profound disbelief in Reason will suggest something more than a doubt whether in its real tendency the book is as edifying and religious as it evidently is in the intention of its author.

Prof. James insists much upon the fact that for the fortunate few who have undergone these immediate religious experiences they carry their own authority with them, and that therefore all inquiries into their objective validity are useless. That may be the case so long as reflective thought is excluded. But how often does it not happen that to those who have had, or thought they had, this immediate religious insight subsequent intellectual emancipation has brought doubt and disquietude? The very point that they doubt is whether their own emotions, intuitions, even visions were anything but the outcome of subjective wishes or a disordered brain. The world cannot be sharply divided, as Prof. James's wants to divide it, into those who possess immediate and self-sufficing insight and those who have had

no religious experience at all. There are thousands who will not and cannot trust whatever faculty of moral or spiritual insight they possess unless they are presented with a creed which satisfies their Reason. To be told to believe whatever they wish to believe only plunges them into a deeper scepticism. Such minds can only find the satisfaction that they require in a very different philosophy from that which underlies Prof. James's book. (pp. 245-50)

H. Rashdall, in a review of "The Varieties of Religious Experience: A Study in Human Nature," in Mind, *n.s. Vol. XII, No. 46, April, 1903, pp. 245-50.*

CHARLES M. BAKEWELL   (essay date 1907)

[*In the following excerpt, Bakewell enumerates the various doctrines of* Pragmatism *and contrasts them with the "old order" philosophical doctrines of rationalism (the assumption that logic and reason are the most valid means of gaining knowledge about the world) and monism, or absolutism (the assumption that the diverse aspects of matter and experience in some sense form a unified reality). Bakewell goes on to compare* Pragmatism *with the positivist philosophy of the nineteenth-century philosopher Auguste Comte, who advocated a strict dependence on scientific observation to gain and verify knowledge about the world and about human experience. Bakewell concludes with the objection that although* Pragmatism *avoids some of the more obvious pitfalls of past philosophies, it fails to offer a coherent method for arriving at intellectual judgments. For other discussions of* Pragmatism, *see the excerpts by Bertrand Russell (1908), F. H. Bradley (1908), Henri Bergson (1911), and John Dewey (1916). For other discussion of the contrasting philosophies of pluralism and monism, see the excerpts by Paul Elmer More (1910) and A. J. Ayer (1982).*]

When the philosophy which is now coming to be known as pragmatism first put in an appearance in the philosophical family, it was not given a very cordial welcome by its older brothers. It was, in fact, regarded as a sort of spurious product,—not a genuine birth, but a wind egg, as Plato would say. Or, to paraphrase Professor James's sub-title [*Pragmatism: A New Name for Some Old Ways of Thinking*], it was looked upon as simply a new name for some old and exploded errors of thinking. Philosophy, so it had generally been supposed, meant the rule of reason: here was a doctrine that held rationalism and intellectualism to be terms of reproach, and that sought its support in something that lay beyond the reach of reason and out of which reason itself was supposed to emerge. The attempt has often been made before. Every mystic has made it; many agnostics have made it; all misologists have made it. But, hitherto at least, the attempt by means of reason to get behind reason for reason's support has signally failed. Whether such support be sought in feeling, in ultimate 'fact' or 'datum', or in "temperament without a tongue," the outcome for philosophy has been the same: in the end they have led to the inculcation of the wise silence so far as philosophy's pet problems are concerned. Again, philosophy seeks to reduce the world of experience to unity: pragmatism fairly revels in pluralism. Philosophy tries to gather in all the loose ends of experience: pragmatism prefers an unravelled multiverse to a closely knit universe.

But, according to Professor James, the critics of pragmatism have indulged in much futile controversy which might have been avoided had they been willing to wait until the message was fairly out. The doctrine has been grossly misunderstood, and its advocates treated as if they did not even possess common ordinary intelligence. Our chief interest in [*Pragmatism*] must therefore be to find out exactly what the message is. (p. 624)

Pragmatism, as here presented, delights in making plain its scorn of all *a priori* constructions, talks much of 'facts,' and at every turn coquettes with science. In fact, it declares itself to be precisely on the level of the other sciences, having no peculiar method of its own and no superior claims to certainty, being even less certain of its results than the other sciences are of theirs, in proportion as its problems are vaster. It thus affects humility and eschews dogmatism. It knows nothing for sure except that no man can know anything for sure. It is the philosophy of the open doors. Emerson once wrote that the poets were to be the philosophers of the future, for they alone, defying the demon of consistency, are free to leave all doors open to the reception of truth in all its varied guises. The pragmatist claims the privilege which Emerson would reserve for the poets.

Another reason for the popularity of this philosophy is the sense of freedom that it appears to bring with it,—a freedom that many, no doubt, will be inclined to characterize as licence or lawlessness. But it undoubtedly *has* a democratic air. It reads like the philosophy of a 'new world' with a large frontier and, beyond, the enticing unexplored lands where one may still expect the unexpected. It appeals to one's sporting blood and one's *amour du risque,* for it is hospitable to chance. It is a philosophy in which one can take a gamble, for it holds that the dice of experience are not loaded. The older monistic philosophies and religions, as Professor James portrays them, seem to present by contrast stuffy closed systems and an exhausted universe. They seem to pack the individual into a logical straitjacket, and to represent all history as simply the unfolding of a play that was written to its very last line from the dawn of creation. These old monistic absolutisms go with the old order of things, and they and their advocates are treated by Professor James with scorn and contempt. Pragmatism is the philosophy of the *revolté,* and there is something of the *revolté* in us all. No inconsiderable portion of Professor James's book is polemical, and the gist of his polemics may be summed up in the phrases: *À bas* Hegel and all his tribe! *Conspuez* the Absolute! But it must be added that, in stating the views of his opponents, "the intellectualists," Professor James gives almost invariably a caricature of their views. He seems to recognize no other alternative to pragmatism save a soft and saccharine absolutism, which one may possibly find in the writings of a few of the mystics, and chiefly the oriental mystics, but which one cannot in fairness ascribe to any of the greater idealists, from Plato and Aristotle onward. Were pragmatism the only escape from such mystic monisms, we should all no doubt espouse the cause of pragmatism; for whatever may be the difficulties of the latter, the difficulties in the way of the former are greater far. To be sure, one can find in the writings of most idealists sentences that, wrested from their context, might seem to justify Professor James's strictures; but one has a right to expect of the pragmatist the same fairness in dealing with his opponents that he himself demands when he is the object of criticism.

Finally, pragmatism finds favor through its apparent simplicity. It is not a doctrine that hides its meaning in polysyllabic profundity. Its formulas can be stated in the vernacular tongue, and he who runs may read. And yet the complaint of the pragmatists that their critics uniformly show an inability to grasp their view suggests the doubt that this clearness may be more apparent than real.

Positively stated and briefly put, the significance of pragmatism, as I gather it from the book before us, is, that it is simply the modern analogue of positivism. The pragmatist, like Comte, repudiating metaphysics, seeks to substitute a philosophy which shall be nothing but the larger and more comprehensive science, having the same modesty and the same ambitions, and employing the same methods, as all the other empirical sciences, but dealing with more complex experiences. And the cue to the difference between positivism and pragmatism is found in the development which the natural sciences themselves have undergone in the past fifty years. In Comte's day physics was the fundamental science, and one somehow expected through it to reach the foundation stones of the universe. The sciences were supposed to give a transcript of reality, even though reality was called phenomenal. Once their work of simplification was accomplished, we should have traced reality to its lair, where we could behold it in its given primeval nakedness. But with the attempt to rest physics itself upon mathematics, science made its Copernican revolution, the significance of which is now coming to be clearly recognized. Science has become humanized. The real for science is not a world of independent or interdependent atoms, but a realm of experience. Science does not lead us to the concrete, but away from it. Its results do not give us transcripts of reality, but rather a compendious conceptual shorthand to describe our perceptions with, so many convenient short cuts across the fields of experience, which are valid so far as they are convenient, and so long as no more convenient short cuts have been found. Its reals are not static, but dynamic; not fixed, but fluent and plastic.

Now the pragmatist would apply all this to philosophy and her problems. The conception of God, for example, is valid in so far as it provides such a convenient short cut across the facts of experience, and so long as it continues to do so without at the same time blocking up other and more serviceable short cuts. And so with all the familiar problems. There is an undoubted fascination in such an undertaking. And to one who views the history of philosophy from the outside, and sees in it simply the record of exploded systems, this may seem to be the last word of philosophy. And if I may venture a prediction, it would be that pragmatism will rapidly gain in popularity in the next few years, but that it will continue to find favor, as it does at the present time, chiefly with those who are unacquainted, or but imperfectly acquainted, with the history of philosophy. For, like its predecessor positivism, it does not solve the difficult problems of philosophy; it simply ignores them. Of course I do not mean by this remark to bring against the pragmatists any wholesale accusation of ignorance of the history of philosophy. I am simply noting what I think is a patent and significant fact regarding the *Anhänger* of pragmatism,—those who sit on the bleachers and do the rooting.

Pragmatism, according to Professor James, "does not stand for any special results. It is a method only." . . . What then is the pragmatic method? It is "primarily a method of settling metaphysical disputes that otherwise might be interminable." Whenever a dispute arises, it asks for the practical consequences of the rival views. "What difference would it practically make to any one if this notion rather than that notion were true? If no practical difference whatever can be traced, then the alternatives mean practically the same thing, and all dispute is idle. Whenever a dispute is serious, we ought to be able to show some practical difference that must follow from one side or the other's being right." . . . Many philosophical disputes collapse into insignificance, Professor James thinks, when this test is applied. "There can *be* no difference anywhere that doesn't *make* a difference elsewhere—no difference in abstract truth that doesn't express itself in a difference in concrete fact and in conduct consequent upon that fact, imposed on somebody, somehow, somewhere, and somewhen. The whole function of philosophy ought to be to find out what definite difference it will make to you and me, at definite instants of our life, if this world-formula or that world-formula be the true one.'' . . . And again, Professor James writes: ''To attain perfect clearness in our thoughts of an object we need only consider what conceivable effects of a practical kind the object may involve—what sensations we are to expect from it, and what reactions we must prepare. Our conception of these effects, whether immediate or remote, is then for us the whole of our conception of the object, so far as that conception has positive significance at all.'' . . . (pp. 625-28)

All this contains undoubtedly much excellent advice which, if followed, would eliminate mere verbal disputes, would prevent the glorification of abstractions and check the tendency to make idols of names. But so far there would seem to be nothing in the ''pragmatic method'' that had to wait for the genius of pragmatism before being discovered. In fact, as Professor James says, it is as old as Socrates and Aristotle. The only thing that a philosopher of the intellectualist school could take exception to is the apparent implication that the practical effects are limited to ''the sensations we are to expect'' and ''the reactions we must prepare.'' But Professor James does not mean so to limit the method, for he holds that intellectual consequences are also practical effects. This being the case, it is hard to see how we have in this principle any philosophical method at all. For there is probably no philosophical dispute, however hypersubtle the distinction upon which it may turn, that has not somewhere and for some one had practical consequences. On the other hand, thoughts have a way of dying and getting buried in phrases which then come to be used as substitutes for thinking. This is a tendency everywhere found, even, I think, in the camp of the pragmatists themselves. And in so far as pragmatism is fighting the tendency to mere verbalism and to the misuse of abstractions, there is no reason why we should not all, whatever our philosophies, make common cause with her.

But Professor James tells us that the pragmatic method means *''the attitude of looking away from first things, principles, 'categories,' supposed necessities; and of looking toward last things, fruits, consequences, facts''* (italics the author's). It means ''the empiricist temper regnant and the rationalist temper sincerely given up.'' . . . Here is perhaps the parting of the ways. And yet I fail to find anything in the ''method,'' as Professor James has described it, which justifies these assertions. What if it should prove that looking toward ''first things, principles, 'categories,' supposed necessities'' is itself of value in helping us as we look toward ''last things, fruits, consequences, facts''? And, indeed, this is just what Professor James in his chapter on ''Common Sense'' and in his chapter on ''Pragmatism and Religion'' finds to be the case. There is an unfortunate antithesis in these assertions. Their *entweder—oder* implies the possibility of making a separation between first things and last things, principles and consequences, which would itself lead to the barren abstractionism of which Professor James complains, whichever horn of the dilemma one accepted. If, however, pragmatism does not mean to make this separation, if it is simply demanding of us all that we should be sober and patient, and show greater respect for the facts of experience, that we should never lose sight of the fact that our philosophies, one and all, are constructed to explain, to help us about in, experience, and that in building them up we all do start from

actual experience and must ever keep returning to experience,—then, once more, I should think that we could all get together, and even call ourselves pragmatists, if we liked that label, and cared to wear a new name for a good old way of thinking. (pp. 628-29)

That the so-called pragmatic method is not, strictly speaking, a method at all, comes out in the chapter where Professor James seeks to apply it to some familiar metaphysical problems. One illustration will suffice. Professor James is comparing abstract spiritualism with abstract materialism. According to both views the entire contents of the world are once for all given, the world is finished, it has no future. The pragmatist is asked to choose between the two theories. Since on either view the returns are all in, he finds them identical, and so he must hold that they both, ''in spite of their different-sounding names, mean exactly the same thing.'' . . . Now while in one respect these theories may be identical, and while Professor James, with certain practical purposes in view, may find them equally blighting, and hold that it is a matter of indifference which he believes, yet for all that, even pragmatically considered, they may reveal the greatest difference. For one man, holding to the one view, may find that it takes him off to the desert, there to spend the rest of his days doubled over, gazing at his umbilical and repeating the mystic ''om,'' while another, holding to the other view, may find that it takes him to his laboratory to study the properties and the behavior of matter. That is, if one only select one's point of view, every theory will reveal some sort of practical consequences. But there is another difficulty. Professor James, after pronouncing abstract spiritualism and abstract materialism identical, adds the significant words: ''I am supposing, of course, that the theories *have* been equally successful in their explanations of what is.'' But if the pragmatic method is to help us in deciding between these two views, it is just here that we want light; we want it to show us how we are to decide whether they have been equally successful in their explanation of what is. Perhaps Professor James could work this out on pragmatic principles, but in this chapter where he undertakes to show us the method in operation he does not do so. And I find it the same with all the other metaphysical issues that he discusses. So, while I am ready to give all honor to Professor James and his co-pragmatists for the service they are rendering philosophy in their wise cautions, in their insistence upon remaining near the concrete, avoiding barren abstractions and verbal disputes, respecting experience and learning of it, and recognizing the matter-of-fact instrumental character of thinking,—and these are virtues which we all aim to possess,— yet when all this is accomplished, the ''method'' is still to seek. (pp. 630-31)

Professor James's volume is interesting and stimulating throughout, and it is needless to add that it contains a deal of practical wisdom and much useful advice which all philosophers would do well to heed. And it seems to me to be much stronger in what it affirms than in what it denies. But as the positive doctrine stands, I think it lacks body. It needs the support of some more systematic philosophy than that which is here but roughly sketched. It could be taken up into and absorbed by idealism with mutual advantage both to pragmatism and to idealism. (p. 634)

Charles M. Bakewell, in a review of ''Pragmatism: A New Name for Some Old Ways of Thinking,'' in The Philosophical Review, *Vol. XVI, No. 6, November, 1907, pp. 624-34.*

BERTRAND RUSSELL   (essay date 1908)

[*Russell was an English philosopher and fiction writer who won the Nobel Prize for literature in 1950. His voluminous writings encompass many different areas and levels of intellectual concern, from the* Principia Mathematica *(1910-13), a work of theoretical mathematics written in collaboration with Alfred North Whitehead, to the learned but more generally accessible* History of Western Philosophy *(1945), to the many popular essays written throughout his career. As a mathematician and a technical philosopher, Russell is recognized as among the most significant of the twentieth century; as a writer concerned with general ideas in such fields as politics, psychology, and religion, Russell was advocate of progressive, sometimes radical ideas based on his rationalist, materialist view of existence. Summarizing his task as a philosopher attempting to comprehend the diversity of experience, Russell stated: "There is no one key: politics, economics, psychology, education, all act and react. . . . All I can do is make some men conscious of the problem and of the kind of directions in which solutions are to be sought." In the following excerpt from an essay originally published in* The Albany Review *of January 1908, Russell criticizes James's Pragmatic theory of truth on the grounds that, even assuming that beliefs which "pay" are true beliefs, there exists no method for deciding whether or not "the consequences of entertaining [a belief] are better than those of rejecting it." On this point, Russell concludes that "this question is one which is so difficult that our test of truth becomes practically useless." Russell elaborates this basic argument with demonstrations of the resultant problems involved in James's assumption of equivalence between truth and useful consequences. A similar position is developed by F. H. Bradley (1908). For a rebuttal of this line of argument, see the excerpt by John Dewey (1916), and for James's own rebuttal to Russell's critique, see the excerpt dated 1909. For other commentary in support of James's Pragmatic theory of truth, see the excerpt by Henri Bergson (1911), and for a general discussion of Pragmatism, see the excerpt by Charles M. Bakewell (1907).*]

The pragmatic theory of truth is the central doctrine of pragmatism. . . . William James states it in various ways, some of which I shall now quote. He says: 'Ideas (which themselves are but parts of our experience) become true just in so far as they help us to get into satisfactory relation with other parts of our experience'. . . . Again: 'Truth is *one species of good*, and not, as is usually supposed, a category distinct from good, and coordinate with it. *The true is the name of whatever proves itself to be good in the way of belief, and good, too, for definite, assignable reasons*'. . . . That truth means 'agreement with reality' may be said by a pragmatist as well as by anyone else, but the pragmatist differs from others as to what is meant by 'agreement', and also (it would seem) as to what is meant by 'reality'. William James gives the following definition of 'agreement': 'To "agree" in the widest sense with a reality *can only mean to be guided either straight up to it or into its surroundings, or to be put into such working touch with it as to handle either it or something connected with it better than if we disagreed*'. . . . This language is rather metaphorical, and a little puzzling; it is plain, however, that 'agreement' is regarded as practical, not as merely intellectual. This emphasis on practice is, of course, one of the leading features of pragmatism.

In order to understand the pragmatic notion of truth, we have to be clear as to the basis of *fact* upon which truths are supposed to rest. Immediate sensible experience, for example, does not come under the alternative of *true* and *false*. 'Day follows day', says James, 'and its contents are simply added. The new contents themselves are not true, they simply *come* and *are*. Truth is *what we say about* them'. . . . Thus when we are merely aware of sensible objects, we are not to be regarded as knowing

any truth, although we have a certain kind of contact with reality. It is important to realize that the *facts* which thus lie outside the scope of truth and falsehood supply the material which is presupposed by the pragmatic theory. Our beliefs have to agree with matters of fact: it is an essential part of their 'satisfactoriness' that they should do so. James also mentions what he calls 'relations among purely mental ideas' as part of our stock-in-trade with which pragmatism starts. He mentions as instances '1 and 1 make 2', 'white differs less from grey than it does from black', and so on. All such propositions as these, then, we are supposed to know for certain before we can get under way. As James puts it: 'Between the coercions of the sensible order and those of the ideal order, our mind is thus wedged tightly. Our ideas must agree with realities, be such realities concrete or abstract, be they facts or be they principles, under penalty of endless inconsistency and frustration'. . . . Thus it is only when we pass beyond plain matters of fact and *a priori* truisms that the pragmatic notion of truth comes in. It is, in short, the notion to be applied to doubtful cases, but it is not the notion to be applied to cases about which there can be no doubt. And that there are cases about which there can be no doubt is presupposed in the very statement of the pragmatist position. 'Our account of truth', James tells us, 'is an account . . . of processes of leading, realized *in rebus*, and having only this quality in common, that they *pay*'. . . . We may thus sum up the philosophy in the following definition: 'A truth is anything which it pays to believe.' Now, if this definition is to be useful, as pragmatism intends it to be, it must be possible to know that it pays to believe something without knowing anything that pragmatism would call a truth. Hence the knowledge that a certain belief pays must be classed as knowledge of a sensible fact or of a 'relation among purely mental ideas', or as some compound of the two, and must be so easy to discover as not to be worthy of having the pragmatic test applied to it. There is, however, some difficulty in this view. Let us consider for a moment what it means to say that a belief 'pays'. We must suppose that this means that the consequences of entertaining the belief are better than those of rejecting it. In order to know this, we must know what are the consequences of entertaining it, and what are the consequences of rejecting it; we must know also what consequences are good, what bad, what consequences are better, and what worse. Take, say, belief in the Roman Catholic Faith. This, we may agree, causes a certain amount of happiness at the expense of a certain amount of stupidity and priestly domination. Such a view is disputable and disputed, but we will let that pass. But then comes the question whether, admitting the effects to be such, they are to be classed as on the whole good or on the whole bad; and this question is one which is so difficult that our test of truth becomes practically useless. It is far easier, it seems to me, to settle the plain question of fact: 'Have Popes been always infallible?' than to settle the question whether the effects of thinking them infallible are on the whole good. Yet this question, of the truth of Roman Catholicism, is just the sort of question that pragmatists consider specially suitable to their method.

The notion that it is quite easy to know when the consequences of a belief are good, so easy, in fact, that a theory of knowledge need take no account of anything so simple—this notion, I must say, seems to me one of the strangest assumptions for a theory of knowledge to make. (pp. 116-19)

Another difficulty which I feel in regard to the pragmatic meaning of 'truth' may be stated as follows: Suppose I accept the pragmatic criterion, and suppose you persuade me that a certain belief is useful. Suppose I thereupon conclude that the belief is true. Is it not obvious that there is a transition in my mind from seeing that the belief is useful to actually holding that the belief is true? Yet this could not be so if the pragmatic account of truth were valid. Take, say, the belief that other people exist. According to the pragmatists, to say 'it is true that other people exist' *means* 'it is useful to believe that other people exist'. But if so, then these two phrases are merely different words for the same proposition; therefore when I believe the one I believe the other. If this were so, there could be no transition from the one to the other, as plainly there is. This shows that the word 'true' represents for us a different idea from that represented by the phrase 'useful to believe', and that, therefore, the pragmatic definition of truth ignores, without destroying, the meaning commonly given to the word 'true', which meaning, in my opinion, is of fundamental importance, and can only be ignored at the cost of hopeless inadequacy.

This brings me to the difference between *criterion* and *meaning*—a point on which neither James nor Dr Schiller is very clear. I may best explain the difference, to begin with, by an instance. If you wish to know whether a certain book is in a library, you consult the catalogue: books mentioned in the catalogue are presumably in the library, books not mentioned in it are presumably not in the library. Thus the catalogue affords a *criterion* of whether a book is in the library or not. But even supposing the catalogue perfect, it is obvious that when you say the book is in the library you do not *mean* that it is mentioned in the catalogue. You mean that the actual book is to be found somewhere in the shelves. It therefore remains an intelligible hypothesis that there are books in the library which are not yet catalogued, or that there are books catalogued which have been lost and are no longer in the library. And it remains an inference from the discovery that a book is mentioned in the catalogue to the conclusion that the book is in the library. Speaking abstractly, we may say that a property A is a *criterion* of a property B when the same objects possess both; and A is a *useful* criterion of B if it is easier to discover whether an object possesses the property A than whether it possesses the property B. Thus being mentioned in the catalogue is a *useful* criterion of being in the library, because it is easier to consult the catalogue than to hunt through the shelves.

Now if pragmatists only affirmed that utility is a *criterion* of truth, there would be much less to be said against their view. For there certainly seem to be few cases, if any, in which it is clearly useful to believe what is false. The chief criticism one would then have to make on pragmatism would be to deny that utility is a *useful* criterion, because it is so often harder to determine whether a belief is useful than whether it is true. The arguments of pragmatists are almost wholly directed to proving that utility is a *criterion*; that utility is the *meaning* of truth is then supposed to follow. But, to return to our illustration of the library, suppose we had conceded that there are no mistakes in the British Museum catalogue: would it follow that the catalogue would do without the books? We can imagine some person long engaged in a comparative study of libraries, and having, in the process, naturally lost all taste for reading, declaring that the catalogue is the only important thing—as for the books, they are useless lumber; no one ever wants them, and the principle of economy should lead us to be content with the catalogue. Indeed, if you consider the matter with an open mind, you will see that the catalogue *is* the library, for it tells you everything you can possibly wish to know about the library. Let us, then, save the taxpayers' money by destroying the books: allow free access to the catalogue, but condemn the desire to read as involving an exploded dogmatic realism.

This analogy of the library is not, to my mind, fantastic or unjust, but as close and exact an analogy as I have been able to think of. The point I am trying to make clear is concealed from pragmatists, I think, by the fact that their theories start very often from such things as the general hypotheses of science—ether, atoms, and the like. In such cases, we take little interest in the hypotheses themselves, which, as we well know, are liable to rapid change. What we care about are the inferences as to sensible phenomena which the hypotheses enable us to make. All we ask of the hypotheses is that they should 'work'—though it should be observed that what constitutes 'working' is not the general agreeableness of their results, but the conformity of these results with observed phenomena. But in the case of these general scientific hypotheses, no sensible man believes that they are true as they stand. They are believed to be true in part, and to work because of the part that is true; but it is expected that in time some element of falsehood will be discovered, and some truer theory will be substituted. Thus pragmatism would seem to derive its notion of what constitutes belief from cases in which, properly speaking, belief is absent, and in which—what is pragmatically important—there is but a slender interest in truth or falsehood as compared to the interest in what 'works'.

But when this method is extended to cases in which the proposition in question has an emotional interest on its own account, apart from its working, the pragmatic account becomes less satisfactory. . . . Take the question whether other people exist. It seems perfectly possible to suppose that the hypothesis that they exist will always work, even if they do not in fact exist. It is plain, also, that it makes for happiness to believe that they exist—for even the greatest misanthropist would not wish to be deprived of the objects of his hate. Hence the belief that other people exist is, pragmatically, a true belief. But if I am troubled by solipsism, the discovery that a belief in the existence of others is 'true' in the pragmatist's sense is not enough to allay my sense of loneliness: the perception that I should profit by rejecting solipsism is not alone sufficient to make me reject it. For what I desire is not that the belief in solipsism should be false in the pragmatic sense, but that other people should in fact exist. And with the pragmatist's meaning of truth, these two do not necessarily go together. The belief in solipsism might be false even if I were the only person or thing in the universe.

This paradoxical consequence would, I presume, not be admitted by pragmatists. Yet it is an inevitable outcome of the divorce which they make between *fact* and *truth*. Returning to our illustration, we may say that 'facts' are represented by the books, and 'truths' by the entries in the catalogue. So long as you do not wish to read the books, the 'truths' will do in place of the 'facts', and the imperfections of your library can be remedied by simply making new entries in the catalogue. But as soon as you actually wish to read a book, the 'truths' become inadequate, and the 'facts' become all-important. The pragmatic account of truth assumes, so it seems to me, that no one takes any interest in facts, and that the truth of the proposition that your friend exists is an adequate substitute for the fact of his existence. 'Facts', they tell us, are neither true nor false, therefore truth cannot be concerned with them. But the truth 'A exists', if it is a truth, is concerned with A, who in that case is a fact; and to say that 'A exists' may be true even if A does not exist is to give a meaning to 'truth' which robs it of all interest. Dr Schiller is fond of attacking the view that truth must correspond with reality; we may conciliate him by agreeing that *his* truth, at any rate, need not correspond with reality. But we shall have to add that reality is to us more interesting than such truth. (pp. 119-23)

It is chiefly in regard to religion that the pragmatist use of 'truth' seems to me misleading. . . . For their position, if they fully realized it, would, I think, be this: 'We cannot know whether, in fact, there is a God or a future life, but we can know that the belief in God and a future life is true.' This position, it is to be feared, would not afford much comfort to the religious if it were understood, and I cannot but feel some sympathy with the Pope in his condemnation of it.

'On pragmatic principles', James says, 'we cannot reject any hypothesis if consequences useful to life flow from it'. . . . He proceeds to point out that consequences useful to life flow from the hypothesis of the Absolute, which is therefore so far a true hypothesis. But it should be observed that these useful consequences flow from the hypothesis that the Absolute is a fact, not from the hypothesis that useful consequences flow from belief in the Absolute. But we cannot believe the hypothesis that the Absolute is a fact merely because we perceive that useful consequences flow from this hypothesis. What we can believe on such grounds is that this hypothesis is what pragmatists call 'true', i.e. that it is useful; but it is not from this belief that the useful consequences flow, and the grounds alleged do not make us believe that the Absolute is a fact, which is the useful belief. In other words, the useful belief is that the Absolute is a fact, and pragmatism shows that this belief is what it calls 'true'. Thus pragmatism persuades us that belief in the Absolute is 'true', but does not persuade us that the Absolute is a fact. The belief which it persuades us to adopt is therefore not the one which is useful. In ordinary logic, if the belief in the Absolute is true, it follows that the Absolute is a fact. But with the pragmatist's meaning of 'true' this does not follow; hence the proposition which he proves is not, as he thinks, the one from which comforting consequences flow.

In another place James says: 'On pragmatistic principles, if the hypothesis of God works satisfactorily in the widest sense of the word, it is true'. . . . This proposition is, in reality, a mere tautology. For we have laid down the definition: 'The word "true" means "working satisfactorily in the widest sense of the word"'.' Hence the proposition stated by James is merely a verbal variant on the following: 'On pragmatistic principles, if the hypothesis of God works satisfactorily in the widest sense of the word, then it works satisfactorily in the widest sense of the word.' This would hold even on other than pragmatistic principles; presumably what is peculiar to pragmatism is the belief that this is an important contribution to the philosophy of religion. The advantage of the pragmatic method is that it decides the question of the truth of the existence of God by purely mundane arguments, namely, by the effects of belief in His existence upon our life in this world. But unfortunately this gives a merely mundane conclusion, namely, that belief in God is true, i.e. useful, whereas what religion desires is the conclusion that God exists, which pragmatism never even approaches. I infer, therefore, that the pragmatic philosophy of religion, like most philosophies whose conclusions are interesting, turns on an unconscious play upon words. A common word—in this case, the word 'true'—is taken at the outset in an uncommon sense, but as the argument proceeds, the usual sense of the word gradually slips back, and the conclusions arrived at seem, therefore, quite different from what they would

be seen to be if the initial definition had been remembered. (pp. 124-25)

To sum up: while agreeing with the empirical temper of pragmatism, with its readiness to treat all philosophical tenets as 'working hypotheses', we cannot agree that when we say a belief is true we mean that it is a hypothesis which 'works', especially if we mean by this to take account of the excellence of its effects, and not merely of the truth of its consequences. If, to avoid disputes about words, we agree to accept the pragmatic definition of the word 'truth', we find that the belief that A exists may be 'true' even when A does not exist. This shows that the conclusions arrived at by pragmatism in the sphere of religion do not have the meaning which they appear to have, and are incapable, when rightly understood, of yielding us the satisfaction which they promise. The attempt to get rid of 'fact' turns out to be a failure, and thus the old notion of truth reappears. And if the pragmatist states that utility is to be merely a *criterion* of truth, we shall reply first, that it is not a useful criterion, because it is usually harder to discover whether a belief is useful than whether it is true; secondly, that since no *a priori* reason is shown why truth and utility should always go together, utility can only be shown to be a criterion at all by showing inductively that it accompanies truth in all known instances, which requires that we should already know in many instances what things are true. Finally, therefore, the pragmatist theory of truth is to be condemned on the ground that it does not 'work'. (pp. 129-30)

Bertrand Russell, "William James's Conception of Truth," in his Philosophical Essays, *Simon & Schuster, 1967, pp. 112-30.*

F. H. BRADLEY　(essay date 1908)

[*Bradley was an English philosopher who was one of the leading exponents of monist absolutism. However, although he asserted as an intuited fact that the ultimate nature of the universe was that of absolute unity, of apparent diversity resolved into a spiritual whole, his most influential work,* Appearance and Reality *(1897), emphasized the impossibility of confirming at a conceptual level this basic tenet of monist absolutism. Thus, rather than forming a system of proof for absolutism, Bradley's ideas served to encourage the spirit of inquiry among later thinkers who may or may not have shared his own philosophical assumptions. In the following excerpt, originally published in 1908 in the journal* Mind, *Bradley, like Bertrand Russell (1908), finds James's Pragmatic theory of truth undermined by the insurmountable difficulty of knowing the consequences of a belief, which in Bradley's view needs only to be understood as beneficial in order to render it a true belief. (For a rebuttal of this line of argument, see the excerpt by John Dewey (1916), and for James's own rebuttal to Russell's critique, see the excerpt dated 1909. Also see the excerpt by Henri Bergson (1911) for commentary in support of James's Pragmatic theory of truth.) Bradley ultimately finds, however, that this particular difficulty of the Pragmatic theory of truth is indicative of a general ambiguity which he considers an inherent quality of James's philosophy. This ambiguity allows Pragmatism to be construed as representing a variety of viewpoints, even that of its philosophical antagonist, Idealism. For a comparative discussion of the philosophical thought of James and Bradley, see the excerpt by A. J. Ayer (1982). For a general discussion of Pragmatism, see the excerpt by Charles M. Bakewell (1907).*]

While reading the lectures on Pragmatism, I, doubtless like others, am led to ask myself, 'Am I and have I been always myself a Pragmatist?' This question I still find myself unable to answer. The meaning of 'practice' and 'practical' is to my mind with Prof. James most obscure and ambiguous. On the

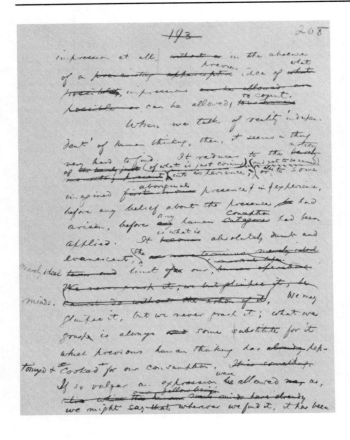

Holograph copy of James's manuscript of Pragmatism.
Courtesy of Alexander R. James.

one side he insists on a doctrine acceptable perhaps only to the minority. On the other side he extends so widely the limits of his creed that few indeed would in the end be left outside the fold. I will remark first on the wide and next on the narrow sense given to Pragmatism.

(i) One of the objections raised against Pragmatism has been its alleged degradation of truth. All value except of a borrowed kind has apparently been denied to theory. What it is which in the end has ultimate worth for the Pragmatist, has remained to myself a matter of mere inference and conjecture. But what has seemed certain is that theorizing has been condemned as worthless except as a means, while that which has value in itself has been left undetermined. Whether for instance the Pragmatist takes the world of art to belong to the region of the worthless-in-itself, I at least could not learn. This situation, surprising to myself, has on one understanding of Prof. James ceased, so far as he is concerned, to exist. For he takes the Good as a genus of which truth is one species. He denies or subordinates the distinction of theoretical and practical. Theory is one kind of practice, and so apparently is theoretical enjoyment. . . . And I suppose that fine art and the beautiful once more fall under this same head of 'practice'. And I conjecture that Prof. James would also include under 'practical' all human enjoyment. And, if this is so, who, except perhaps some narrow Hedonist, would wish to dissent? Life in all its main aspects is allowed to be the end, and none of these aspects is excluded and degraded to the level of a mere external means. Theory, besides its use in altering the course of events, may be pursued

independently within certain limits, may be allowed to satisfy its proper want, and to use its own criterion. And the same thing again will hold good in the case of fine art. I indeed may wonder what purpose is served by torturing everything that is good and valuable under the head of 'practice'. But, if the substance of all for which I have fought is conceded, I should think it unreasonable to dispute about a word.

In the ordinary sense of the word 'practice' therefore, according to Prof. James, truth need not be directly concerned with practice. Truth indeed must not become transcendent. It must not turn itself to some other world out of relation with the world of our perceptions and actions. But, so long as truth maintains its connexion, however indirect, with the sphere of our doing and suffering, the Pragmatist is satisfied. 'Any idea that helps us to deal, whether practically or intellectually, with either the reality or its belongings . . . will hold true of that reality'. . . . This denial of transcendence, this insistence that all ideas, and more especially such ideas as those of God or again the Absolute, are true and real just so far as they work, is to myself naturally most welcome. Most of us have, I think, now for some time accepted and tried to act on this principle. It hardly appears to me to be, at this time of day, revolutionary; but still, if this is what Pragmatism means, so much the better for Pragmatism.

And there is a further point on which Prof. James seems once more to endorse our ideas. I had been, I confess, led to think that, where the Pragmatist took successful practice as the test of truth, he meant this to hold of the individual agent. The idea that worked best in the furthering of my individual existence, I thought, was truth for me. I understood in short that good for the individual and true for the individual were much the same thing, and that further the individual could apply this criterion. And naturally I found that this led to difficulty. We speak, for instance, of a man's life being ruined by the useless discovery of some truth, say of his deceased wife's infidelity, and we hardly see our way to set down a truth of this kind as error. But the whole difficulty, we now learn from Prof. James, was manufactured by ourselves. It is a living witness to our blindness, our incompetence and injustice, not to use terms still more abusive. . . . For Pragmatism, I now understand Prof. James to say, does not pretend to hold of the individual. The idea that in a man's case does not work, or that works to his ruin, may for all that be true. For the true is 'the expedient in the long run and on the whole'. . . . And, this being understood, the whole difficulty so far disappears.

It is succeeded, however, I would urge, by fresh troubles. For what is 'the long run' and 'the whole', and how does the individual get to know about things like these, which seem really beyond him? On this vital matter Prof. James, it seems to me, leaves us without much assistance. We may conjecture that 'the long run' is the process that leads (if it really does lead) to the final victory of Good. We are reminded perhaps of that

> One far-off divine event,
> To which the whole creation moves.

But I am very far from sure that we are reminded rightly. And what 'the whole' is to mean seems, to my mind, beyond probable conjecture. Is it this or that set of beings inhabiting our planet, or is humanity but a small, a microscopical and an inconsiderable element among the beings that have value? In speaking of that which he terms 'humanism' Prof. James would have felt himself compelled, we might have supposed, to deal with such dangerous ambiguities and such distressing uncertainties. But another course unfortunately seemed to him more desirable. The result, however, so far as I see, is that 'the expedient in the long run and on the whole' remains unknown and unknowable. And yet it is this apparently by which the individual has to regulate his life.

And possibly Prof. James holds that the individual must walk here by faith. . . . The individual does not know and he cannot see that truth and goodness now are one, or how they ever will become one. But he must do what seems to him to be best, and again accept what seems to him to be true, and he must trust and believe that truth and goodness in the end will not be divergent. But, with this, the relative independence for us of truth, beauty and practical goodness, seems fully justified, and, so far as the practice of the individual is concerned, Pragmatism seems in short admitted not to work.

And with such a result I, in the main, naturally find myself in accord. To me, as to many others, it seems that in the end truth, fact and goodness are one, though I am forced to admit that we cannot perceive and verify this unity in detail, and that therefore in and for the individual a relative divergence must be recognized. Hence between Prof. James and myself the difference in the end would be practically trifling. But, on the other hand, theoretically, as soon as Prof. James attempts to deal with first principles, the case, I think, will be altered. For, as against our principle of immanent Reality, he seems to have adopted a transcendent Ideal. And that, I imagine, the history of philosophy has tended to show, is a thing which, as an ultimate principle, will not work.

(ii) If the above interpretation of Prof. James is correct, Pragmatism is no militant creed. It is in harmony with views against which it is commonly understood to protest, and to imagine that it portends a new dawn of philosophy . . . would be obviously ridiculous. And I hasten to add that I have not imagined that Prof. James would accept his doctrine as it is above interpreted. I think it at least possible that he takes the whole theoretical side of mind to be an instrument worthless in itself, used to gain a valuable end which he finds it convenient to leave in darkness. I am sure that the common antithesis of intellectual or theoretical and practical appears in his pages . . . , and that the former of these words is used derogatorily. The conclusion that, at least for the practice of the individual, Pragmatism is untrue, seems to me contrary to the whole tendency of Prof. James's teaching. And, if I rightly understand him, Pragmatism, far from being a view which tends to reconcile extremes, is committed to the denial of anything contrary to pluralism. It is committed to the assertion of the absolute mutability of the Universe and the absolute reality of individual disaster and evil. With regard to Prof. James's doctrine of human Freedom, here, as elsewhere, I find it impossible to decide what it means. But the pragmatic doctrine of Free Will, as it appears in this volume, seems to myself to be repeating that which I, for instance, under Hegelian influence sought to urge, in my *Ethical Studies,* more than thirty years ago. And Prof. James's view of Freedom, whatever else it may be, must, I assume, be something which leaves him at liberty to denounce Hegel and his followers.

The conclusion then which I would submit to the reader is that Prof. James's Pragmatism is essentially ambiguous, and that he throughout is unconsciously led to take advantage of its ambiguity. It can at discretion be preached as a new Gospel which is to bring light into the world, or recommended as that old teaching of common sense which few but fools have rejected. (pp. 127-32)

> *F. H. Bradley, "On the Ambiguity of Pragmatism,"*
> *in his* Essays on Truth and Reality, *Oxford at the*
> *Clarendon Press, Oxford, 1914, pp. 127-42.**

WILLIAM JAMES   (essay date 1909)

[*The following excerpt is a rebuttal to Bertrand Russell's argument (1908) that criticizes James's Pragmatic theory of truth.*]

Mr. Bertrand Russell's article, entitled 'Transatlantic Truth' [see excerpt dated 1908], has all the clearness, dialectic subtlety, and wit which one expects from his pen, but it entirely fails to hit the right point of view for apprehending our position. When, for instance, we say that a true proposition is one the consequences of believing which are good, he assumes us to mean that anyone who believes a proposition to be true must first have made out clearly that its consequences *are* good, and that his belief must primarily be in that fact—an obvious absurdity, for that fact is the deliverance of a new proposition, quite different from the first one and is, moreover, a fact usually very hard to verify, it being "far easier," as Mr. Russell justly says, "to settle the plain question of fact: 'Have Popes always been infallible?' than to settle the question whether the effects of thinking them infallible are on the whole good."

We affirm nothing as silly as Mr. Russell supposes. Good consequences are not proposed by us merely as a sure sign, mark, or criterion, by which truth's presence is habitually ascertained, tho they may indeed serve on occasion as such a sign; they are proposed rather as the lurking *motive* inside of every truth-claim, whether the 'trower' be conscious of such motive, or whether he obey it blindly. They are proposed as the *causa existendi* of our beliefs, not as their logical cue or premise, and still less as their objective deliverance or content. They assign the only intelligible practical *meaning* to that difference in our beliefs which our habit of calling them true or false comports.

No truth-claimer except the pragmatist himself need ever be aware of the part played in his own mind by consequences, and he himself is aware of it only abstractly and in general, and may at any moment be quite oblivious of it with respect to his own beliefs.

Mr. Russell next joins the army of those who inform their readers that according to the pragmatist definition of the word 'truth' the belief that A exists may be 'true,' even when A does *not* exist. This is the usual slander, repeated to satiety by our critics. They forget that in any concrete account of what is denoted by 'truth' in human life, the word can only be used relatively to some particular trower. Thus, I may hold it true that Shakespere wrote the plays that bear his name, and may express my opinion to a critic. If the critic be both a pragmatist and a baconian, he will in his capacity of pragmatist see plainly that the workings of my opinion, I being what I am, make it perfectly true for me, while in his capacity of baconian he still believes that Shakespere never wrote the plays in question. But most anti-pragmatist critics take the word 'truth' as something absolute, and easily play on their reader's readiness to treat his own truths as the absolute ones. If the reader whom they address believes that A does not exist, while we pragmatists show that those for whom the belief that it exists works satisfactorily will always call it true, he easily sneers at the naiveté of our contention, for is not then the belief in question 'true,' tho what it declares as fact has, as the reader so well knows, no existence? Mr. Russell speaks of our statement as an "attempt to get rid of 'fact'" and naturally enough considers it "a failure." . . . "The old notion of truth reappears," he adds—that notion being, of course, that when a belief is true, its object does exist.

It is, of course, *bound* to exist, on sound pragmatic principles. Concepts signify consequences. How is the world made different for me by my conceiving an opinion of mine under the concept 'true'? First, an object must be findable there (or sure signs of such an object must be found) which shall agree with the opinion. Second, such an opinion must not be contradicted by anything else of which I am aware. But in spite of the obvious pragmatist requirement that when I have said truly that something exists, it *shall* exist, the slander which Mr. Russell repeats has gained the widest currency.

Mr. Russell himself is far too witty and athletic a ratiocinator simply to repeat the slander dogmatically. Being nothing if not mathematical and logical, he must prove the accusation *secundum artem*, and convict us not so much of error as of absurdity. I have sincerely tried to follow the windings of his mind in this procedure, but for the life of me I can only see in it another example of what I have called . . . vicious abstractionism. The abstract world of mathematics and pure logic is so native to Mr. Russell that he thinks that we describers of the functions of concrete fact must also mean fixed mathematical terms and functions. A mathematical term, as *a, b, c, x, y,* sin., log., is self-sufficient, and terms of this sort, once equated, can be substituted for one another in endless series without error. Mr. Russell . . . [seems] to think that in our mouth also such terms as 'meaning,' 'truth,' 'belief,' 'object,' 'definition,' are self-sufficients with no context of varying relation that might be further asked about. What a word means is expressed by its definition, isn't it? The definition claims to be exact and adequate, doesn't it? Then it can be substituted for the word—since the two are identical—can't it? Then two words with the same definition can be substituted for one another, *n'est-ce pas?* Likewise two definitions of the same word, *nicht wahr,* etc., etc., till it will be indeed strange if you can't convict someone of self-contradiction and absurdity.

The particular application of this rigoristic treatment to my own little account of truth as working seems to be something like what follows. I say 'working' is what the 'truth' of our ideas means, and call it a definition. But since meanings and things meant, definitions and things defined, are equivalent and interchangeable, and nothing extraneous to its definition can be meant when a term is used, it follows that whoso calls an idea true, and means by that word that it works, cannot mean anything else, can believe nothing but that it does work, and in particular can neither imply nor allow anything about its object or deliverance. "According to the pragmatists," Mr. Russell writes, "to say 'it is true that other people exist' *means* 'it is useful to believe that other people exist.' But if so, then these two phrases are merely different words for the same propositon; therefore when I believe the one, I believe the other." . . . [Logic, I may say in passing, would seem to require Mr. Russell to believe them both at once, but he ignores this consequence, and considers that 'other people exist' and 'it is useful to believe that they do *even if they don't,*' must be identical and therefore substitutable propositions in the pragmatist mouth.]

But may not real terms, I now ask, have accidents not expressed in their definitions? and when a real value is finally substituted for the result of an algebraic series of substituted definitions, do not all these accidents creep back? Beliefs have their objective 'content' or 'deliverance' as well as their truth, and truth has its implications as well as its workings. If anyone believe that other men exist it is both a content of his belief and an implication of its truth, that they should exist in fact. Mr. Russell's logic would seem to exclude, 'by definition,' all such accidents as contents, implications, and associates, and would represent us as translating all belief into a sort of belief in pragmatism itself—of all things! If I say that a speech is eloquent, and explain 'eloquent' as meaning the power to work in certain ways upon the audience; or if I say a book is original, and define 'original' to mean differing from other books, Mr. Russell's logic, if I follow it at all, would seem to doom me to agreeing that the speech is about eloquence, and the book about other books. When I call a belief true, and define its truth to mean its workings, I certainly do not mean that the belief is a belief *about* the workings. It is a belief about the object, and I who talk about the workings am a different subject, with a different universe of discourse, from that of the believer of whose concrete thinking I profess to give an account.

The social proposition 'other men exist' and the pragmatist proposition 'it is expedient to believe that other men exist' come from different universes of discourse. One can believe the second without being logically compelled to believe the first; one can believe the first without having ever heard of the second; or one can believe them both. The first expresses the object of a belief, the second tells of one condition of the belief's power to maintain itself. There is no identity of any kind, save the term 'other men' which they contain in common, in the two propositions; and to treat them as mutually substitutable, or to insist that *we* shall do so, is to give up dealing with realities altogether. (pp. 146-50)

William James, in his The Meaning of Truth, *1909. Reprint by Cambridge, Mass.: Harvard University Press, 1975, 328 p.*

PAUL ELMER MORE   (essay date 1910)

[*More was an American critic who, along with Irving Babbitt, formulated the doctrines of New Humanism in early twentieth-century American thought. The New Humanists were strict moralists who adhered to traditional conservative values in reaction to an age of scientific and artistic self-expression. He is especially esteemed for the philosophical and literary erudition of his multi-volumed* Shelburne Essays *(1904-21). In the following excerpt, More criticizes James's doctrine of pluralism as elaborated in the collection* A Pluralistic Universe. *Examining pluralism along with the opposing doctrine of monism, More finds that both are projections of their proponent's private sensibility—the first of "personal change," the second of "personal identity"—and are equally undeserving of intellectual commitment. For other discussions of the contrasting philosophies of pluralism and monism, see the excerpts by Charles M. Bakewell (1907) and A. J. Ayer (1982).*]

It is one of the difficulties of coping with a philosophy of the flux, that no sooner have you come to grips with it than it flows into another form and eludes your grasp. To read the bold frontal attacks . . . and then to find that the adversary in a simultaneous publication has already slipped to one side, is to recall the Homeric wrestling match with the wily old man of the sea. No doubt he is Proteus still, and the contest is with the same foe, but the weapons must be changed and the grip altered. (p. 195)

There is something like the hilarity of sport in dragging out the inconsistencies, if not insincerities, of a philosopher who has tried to defend rationally a system which is professedly an attack on rationalism. For just that, and nothing more, is Pragmatism. It is easy to show that such a philosopher ought, so far as the correspondence of logic and reality goes, to be a complete skeptic. Well and good. But what will you do if, before the ink is fairly dry on your book, this Proteus of the lecture hall is before the world with a recantation of his errors and a frank retreat to just such logical skepticism as you denounced him for not confessing. In one sense, Professor James's Hibbert Lectures [collected in *A Pluralistic Universe*] are consistent with his past; they are in the right line of development from that temperamental impetus which by his own theory is the source of every philosophy, however he may have sloughed off various inconsistencies to attain this position. As a matter of fact, the word Pragmatism scarcely occurs in these lectures, and the attempt at their end to tack on a theory of creating, or even discovering, truth by the "practical reason" is purely perfunctory. Their central point, their crisis, so to speak, is the magnificent repudiation of the whole process of metaphysics:

> I saw [he says] that philosophy had been on a false scent ever since the days of Socrates and Plato, that an *intellectual* answer to the intellectualist's difficulties will never come, and that the real way out of them, far from consisting in the discovery of such an answer, consists in simply closing one's ears to the question. When conceptualism summons life to justify itself in conceptual terms, it is like a challenge addressed in a foreign language to some one who is absorbed in his own business; it is irrelevant to him altogether—he may let it lie unnoticed. I went thus through the "inner catastrophe"; . . . I had literally come to the end of my conceptual stock-in-trade, I was bankrupt intellectualistically, and had to change my base.

To such an inner catastrophe, not unlike one of the conversions he has described so luminously in his *Varieties of Religious Experience,* he was brought after long struggling with the problem of reason and after covering hundreds of sheets of paper with memoranda of his self-questioning. As the worldling under the stroke of heaven forswears the world, so now he is "compelled to *give up logic,* fairly, squarely, and irrevocably." (pp. 196-98)

[We] may regard the call from metaphysics to a philosophy of immediate experience as altogether wholesome. Abstract reason is not in its own field a false thing, nor is it without indispensable usefulness in the application of experience to life; nevertheless, not through it shall we come into intimate touch with reality, but through life itself; the truth for us is not what we have defined logically, but what we actually feel and will. It does not follow, however, that in accepting heartily this method we must equally accept Mr. James's statement of the relative values of what he reports as obtained by the method; we may even suspect that in his evaluation he is still imprisoned in the very error from which he is so eager to save us. Consciousness, he says, is not discrete, or divided into discontinuous moments, as it is presented to us by the reason, but is continuous; nor has it any conformity with the static void of monism. Time and change are of its essence, and if we wish to *know* reality we must "dive back into the flux itself." His

cry is like the command of Faust to leave the musty cell and throw one's self into the stream of the world—*Hinaus ins Freie!* There is grave irony as well as stirring exhortation in Mr. James's personal appeal to his audience:

> If Oxford men could be ignorant of anything, it might almost seem that they had remained ignorant of the great empirical movement towards a pluralistic panpsychic view of the universe, into which our own generation has been drawn, and which threatens to short-circuit their methods [of monistic dogmatism] entirely and become their religious rival unless they are willing to make themselves its allies. Yet wedded as they seem to be to the logical machinery and technical apparatus of absolutism, I cannot but believe that their fidelity to the religious ideal in general is deeper still. . . . Let empricism once become associated with religion, as hitherto, through some strange misunderstanding, it has been associated with irreligion, and I believe that a new era of religion as well as of philosophy will be ready to begin. That great awakening of a new popular interest in philosophy, which is so striking a phenomenon at the present day in all countries, is undoubtedly due in part to religious demands.

A pluralistic panpsychic view of the universe—that is to say: as our only knowledge is experience and our experience is an inner consciousness flowing with ceaseless change about endlessly differing sensations presented to it from without, so the truth of the world for us is not monism, but pluralism. We are *du réel dans le réel* ["of the real in the real"]; but this reality is an infinite group of interacting interpenetrating forces, over which no absolute law can be found to govern. And as these forces, like our states of consciousness, are in a constant mutation, so, like ourselves, they may very well be, in part at least, other streams of consciousness, meeting and embracing and repelling one another. How else, indeed, can they have any meaning or reality to us? The universe may thus be panpsychic, and one of the most interesting of Mr. James's lectures is a revival of Fechner's animism, with his vision of the world-soul enveloping and nourishing the souls of men. For the proof of such a theory Mr. James goes to what he deems the facts of experience:

> In a word, the believer is continuous, to his own consciousness, at any rate, with a wider self from which saving experiences flow in. Those who have such experiences distinctly enough and often enough to live in the light of them remain quite unmoved by criticism, from whatever quarter it may come, be it academic or scientific, or be it merely the voice of logical common-sense. They have had their vision and they *know*—that is enough—that we inhabit an invisible spiritual environment from which help comes, our soul being mysteriously one with a larger soul whose instruments we are.

By such steps the pragmatist, now rather choosing to be called the radical empiricist, arrives at the belief in a deity, who is by no means the static timeless absolute of the monist, with its foreignness from all things human, but a mighty God above other gods, "having an environment, being in time, and working out a history just like ourselves."

It is a seductive theory and has at least that quality of "thickness" which Mr. James, with his genius for phrase-making, contrasts with the "thinness" of idealism. It is charming, but then the dog that trails always at the heels of the pragmatist will have his bark: Is it true? This "pluralistic panspychic view of the universe," we are told, belongs to a "great empirical movement." We remember then that Mr. James himself has condemned the empiricists for "smashing the absolute" by means of a conceptualist logic, and we begin to wonder whether he is quite as free as he would have us believe from the rationalistic net. Somehow one cannot be quite at ease in this new pluralistic panpsychic Zion. . . . (pp. 204-08)

What, at bottom, is this Pluralism of Mr. James, but the same ancient presumption of the reason which he has himself so shrewdly denounced. His feeling for flux and change and multiplicity as an undeniable part of our conscious experience is a reality, a great and desirable reality, set over against the monist's exclusive sense of unity; but is it the whole of reality? How can one recall the innumerable witnesses of religion, or hearken to the self-revelation of the poets, how can one look into the mirror of one's own life, and not perceive that the sense of something immutable and unmoved exists in some way side by side with the sense of everlasting flux, that there is within us some

> central peace subsisting at the heart
> Of endless agitation?

Mr. James does, indeed, throw out hints that he has caught the meaning of this dualistic reality of experience, but, like other philosophers, he soon cowers at the imperious command of reason, and tries to hide the nature of his own submission to one horn of the dilemma by merriment over the writhing of Mr. Bradley on the other; meanwhile common-sense stands like *das Weltkind in der Mitte* ["the opportunist in the middle"]. We deceive ourselves if we believe that in Mr. James at last a mediator has been found "between the spirit and its environment, . . . between fate and faith, between the march of things and the impulsion of ideas, between the will of nature and the will of man, betwen science and religion." In attempting that mediation he has sought to supplant reason by immediate experience; in fact, he has been borne along by "the march of things," and, accepting these lower intuitions of change as the whole of experience, has straightway proceeded to build thereon his rationalistic theory of a universe which is altogether subject to mutability.

And if the Pluralism of Mr. James is no true substitute for dualism, but a rejection of the one for the many, so his Panpsychism commits the other error of metaphysics in translating a fact of inner experience into a theory of the universe at large. The comfortable belief in these world-souls and commingled spirits and finite Jehovahs is even a projection of our consciousness of personal change into the void, just as the monist's absolute abstraction is born of his consciousnes of personal identity. No doubt we are not alone in the universe. Forces beat upon us from every side and are as really existent to us as ourselves: their influence upon ourselves we know, but their own secret name and nature we have not yet heard—not from Mr. James, or Mr. Bradley, or another. Until that prophet has appeared, I do not see what better thing we can do than to hold our judgment in a state of complete skepticism, or suspension, in regard to the correspondence of our inner experience with the world at large, neither affirming nor denying; while we accept honestly the dualism of consciousness as the irrational fact. (p. 209-11)

Paul Elmer More, "The Pragmatism of William James," in his Shelburne Essays, seventh series, G. P. Putnam's Sons, 1910, pp. 195-212.

HENRI BERGSON   (essay date 1911)

[*Recipient of the Nobel Prize for literature in 1928, Bergson was a French philosopher whose reevaluation of the significance of time in human life was among the most revolutionary phases of modern thought. Bergson's philosophy—developed primarily in the volumes* Matter and Memory *(1896),* Time and Free Will *(1899), and* Creative Evolution *(1907)—is based on his observation that a scientific, analytical way of perceiving experience has fostered the conception of time as something measured, fixed, and artificial. This is a misrepresentation, Bergson thought, of how time is actually experienced: not measured in terms of discrete, spatial movements but moving in a continuous, unbroken flow; not fixed in a monotonous system of mensuration but active and changing; not an artificial construction of logic but, in the profoundest sense, real. Bergson termed this perception of time "lived time," or "duration," and the spontaneous, intuitive manner in which it is perceived exists as a valid means of acquiring knowledge about reality. In Bergson's philosophy, reality itself must be extended beyond the strictly physical confines of science. Consciousness is not identified with the physical brain, whose task it is to select or eliminate memories according to their usefulness, but is independent of matter. Thus, since consciousness is not physical and does not distinguish between past and present, all experience is preserved at a non-material, psychic level. Bergson's inspired, anti-scientific method of philosophy is similar to the Pragmatic thought of William James; like James's "stream-of-consciousness," Bergson's "duration" was an important influence on modern writers, most prominently Marcel Proust. In the following excerpt, originally published in 1911 as the introduction to the French edition of* Pragmatism, *Bergson endorses James's Pragmatic theory of truth as something "invented" and at the same time having its basis in objective reality. For a similar view of James's Pragmatic theory of truth, see the excerpt by John Dewey (1916). For contrasting views, see the excerpts by Bertrand Russell (1908), along with James's rebuttal (1909), and F. H. Bradley (1908). For a general discussion of* Pragmatism, *see the excerpt by Charles M. Bakewell (1907).*]

One would have a mistaken idea of James's pragmatism if one did not begin by modifying the idea usually held of reality in general. We speak of the "world" or the "cosmos"; and these words, according to their origin, designate something simple or at least well composed. We say "universe" and the word makes us think of a possible unification of things. One can be a spiritualist, a materialist, a pantheist, just as one can be indifferent to philosophy and satisfied with common sense: the fact remains that one always conceives of one or several simple principles by which the whole of material and moral things might be explained. (p. 248)

Most philosophies . . . restrict our experience on the side of feeling and will as at the same time they indefinitely prolong it on the side of thought. What James asks of us is not to add too much to experience through hypothetical considerations, and also not to mutilate it in its solid elements. We are absolutely sure only of what experience gives us; but we should accept experience wholly, and our feelings are a part of it by the same right as our perceptions, consequently, by the same right as "things." In the eyes of William James, the whole man counts. (p. 251)

It has at all times been said that there are truths which have to do with feeling as much as with reason; and that along with those truths we find already made there are also others we assist in the making, which depend in part on our will. But it must be said that in James this idea takes on a new strength and significance. Thanks to his particular conception of reality it blossoms into a general theory of truth.

What constitutes a true judgment? If an affirmation agrees with reality we say that it is true. But in what does this agreement consist? Our inclination is to see in it something like the resemblance of a portrait to the model: the true affirmation would be the one which would *copy* reality. (p. 253)

Even a philosophy like that of Kant, which insists that all scientific truth is relative to the human mind, considers true affirmations as given in advance in human experience: once that experience is organized by human thought in general, all the work of science consists, so to speak, in piercing the resisting envelope of the facts inside which the truth is lodged, like a nut in its shell.

This conception of truth is natural to our mind and natural also to philosophy, because it is natural to picture reality as a perfectly coherent and systematized whole sustained by a logical armature. This armature would be truth itself; all that our science does is to rediscover it. But experience pure and simple tells us nothing of the kind, and James confines himself to experience. Experience presents us a flow of phenomena: if a certain affirmation relating to one of them enables us to master those which follow or even simply to foresee them, we say of this affirmation that it is true. A proposition such as "heat expands bodies," a proposition suggested by seeing a certain body expand, means that we foresee how other bodies will act when exposed to heat; it helps us to proceed from a past experience to new experiences; it is a clue conducting to what will happen, nothing more. Reality flows; we flow with it; and we call true any affirmation which, in guiding us through moving reality, gives us a grip upon it and places us under more favorable conditions for acting.

The difference between this conception of the truth and the traditional one is plain to see. We ordinarily define the true by its conformity to what already exists; James defines it by its relation to what does not yet exist. The true, according to William James, does not copy something which has been or which is: it announces what will be, or rather it prepares our action upon what is going to be. Philosophy has a natural tendency to have truth look backward: for James, it looks ahead.

More precisely, other doctrines make of truth something anterior to the clearly-determined act of the man who formulates it for the first time. He was the first to see it, we say, but it was waiting for him, just as America was waiting for Christopher Columbus. Something hid it from view and, so to speak, covered it up: he uncovered it.—Quite different is William James's conception. He does not deny that reality is independent, at least to a great extent, of what we say or think of it; but the truth, which can be attached only to what we affirm about reality, is, for him, created by our affirmation. We invent the truth to utilize reality, as we create mechanical devices to utilize the forces of nature. It seems to me one could sum up all that is essential in the pragmatic conception of truth in a formula such as this: *while for other doctrines a new truth is a discovery, for pragmatism it is an invention.*

It does not follow, of course, that the truth is arbitrary. The value of a mechanical invention lies solely in its practical usefulness. In the same way an affirmation, because it is true, should increase our mastery over things. It is no less the creation of a certain individual mind, and it was no more pre-existent to the effort of that mind than the phonograph, for example, existed before Edison. No doubt the inventor of the phonograph had to study the properties of sound, which is a reality. But his invention was superadded to that reality as a thing absolutely new, which might never have been produced had he not existed. Thus a truth, if it is to endure, should have its roots in realities; but these realities are only the ground in which that truth grows, and other flowers could just as well have grown there if the wind had brought other seeds.

Truth, according to pragmatism, has come little by little into being, thanks to the individual contributions of a great number of inventors. If these inventors had not existed, if there had been others in their place, we should have had an entirely different body of truths. Reality would evidently have remained what it is, or approximately the same; but quite different would have been the paths we should have traced in reality, for our convenience in finding our way about in it. And this has to do not only with scientific truths. We cannot construct a sentence, we cannot even today pronounce a word, without accepting certain hypotheses which were created by our ancestors and which might have been very different from what they are. When I say: "My pencil has just fallen under the table," I am certainly not enunciating a fact of experience, for what sight and touch show me is simply that my hand opened and let fall what it held: the baby tied in his high-chair, who sees his plaything fall, probably does not imagine that this object continues to exist; or rather he has not the clear idea of an "object," that is to say, of something which subsists, invariable and independent, through the diversity and mobility of the appearances which pass before him. The first to venture to believe in this invariability and independence made a hypothesis: it is that hypothesis which we currently adopt every time we use a substantive, every time we speak. Our grammar would have been different, the articulations of our thought would have been other than what they are, had humanity in the course of its evolution preferred to adopt hypotheses of another kind.

The structure of our mind is therefore to a great extent our work, or at least the work of some of us. That, it seems to me, is the most important thesis of pragmatism, even though it has not been explicitly stated. It is in this way that pragmatism continues Kantianism. Kant had said that truth depends upon the general structure of the human mind. Pragmatism adds, or at least implies, that the structure of the human mind is the effect of the free initiative of a certain number of individual minds.

That, again, does not mean that truth depends upon each one of us: we might as well believe that each of us could invent the phonograph. But it does mean that of the various kinds of truth, the one which most nearly coincides with its object is not scientific truth, nor is it the truth of common sense, nor more generally truth of an intellectual order. Every truth is a path traced through reality: but among these paths there are some to which we could have given an entirely different turn if our attention had been orientated in a different direction or if we had aimed at another kind of utility; there are some, on the contrary, whose direction is marked out by reality itself: there are some, one might say, which correspond to currents of reality. Doubtless these also depend upon us to a certain extent, for we are free to go against the current or to follow it, and even if we follow it, we can variously divert it, being at the same time associated with and submitted to the force manifest within it. Nevertheless these currents are not created by us; they are part and parcel of reality. Pragmatism thus results in a reversal of the order in which we are accustomed to place the various kinds of truth. Apart from the truths which translate mere sensations, it is, according to pragmatism, the truths of feeling which would push their roots deepest into reality. If we agree to say that all truth is an invention, I believe we must, if we wish to remain faithful to the thought of William James, establish between the truths of feeling and the scientific truths the same kind of difference as there is, for example, between the sail-boat and the steamer: both are human inventions; but the first makes only slight use of artificial means,—it takes the direction of the wind and makes the natural force it utilizes perceptible to the eye; on the contrary, in the second the artificial mechanism holds the most important place; it covers the force it puts into play and assigns to it a direction which we ourselves have chosen.

The definition that James gives to truth therefore, is an integral part of his conception of reality. If reality is not that economic and systematic universe our logic likes to imagine, if it is not sustained by a framework of intellectuality, intellectual truth is a human invention whose effect is to utilize reality rather than to enable us to penetrate it. And if reality does not form a single whole, if it is multiple and mobile, made up of cross-currents, truth which arises from contact with one of these currents,—truth felt before being conceived,—is more capable of seizing and storing up reality than truth merely thought. (pp. 254-59)

> *Henri Bergson, "On the Pragmatism of William James: Truth and Reality," in his* The Creative Mind, *translated by Mabelle L. Andison, Philosophical Library, 1946, pp. 248-60.*

JOSIAH ROYCE   (lecture date 1911)

[In his lifetime Royce was the leading advocate of idealism in American philosophy. In such works as The Religious Aspect of Philosophy *(1885) and* The Conception of God *(1897), Royce supposed that the existence of imperfection and evil in the material world necessarily implies the existence of the Absolute, an omniscient consciousness which makes up the sole substance of the universe of apparently diverse phenomena. This philosophy stands at the opposite pole from the pluralism of William James, which assumes the diversity of phenomena has no "higher" unity and which recognizes the existence of imperfection and evil in the material world without seeking its dissolution on some transcendent plane of reality. James brought Royce to Harvard and was often his amiable antagonist in philosophical matters. In the following excerpt, Royce describes James as the "third representative American philosopher," along with Jonathan Edwards and Ralph Waldo Emerson, for his expression in philosophy of the spiritual life of the American people. This refers particularly to James's robust and frontiersman-like spirit of inquiry and his emphasis on the "cash value" of ideas. For a comparative discussion of the philosophical thought of James and Royce, see the excerpts by Ralph Burton Perry (1938) and A. J. Ayer (1982).]*

Fifty years since, if competent judges were asked to name the American thinkers from whom there had come novel and notable and typical contributions to general philosophy, they could in reply mention only two men—Jonathan Edwards and Ralph Waldo Emerson. (p. 3)

Fifty years ago, I say, our nation had so far found these two men to express each his own stage of the philosophy of our national civilization. The essence of a philosophy, in case you look at it solely from a historical point of view, always appears to you thus: A great philosophy expresses an interpretation of the life of man and a view of the universe, which is at once personal, and, if the thinker is representative of his people, national in its significance. Edwards and Emerson had given tongue to the meaning of two different stages of our American culture. And these were thus far our only philosophical voices.

To-day, if we ask any competent foreign critic of our philosophy whether there is any other name to be added to these two classic American philosophers, we shall receive the unanimous answer: "There is to-day a third representative American philosopher. His name is William James." For James meets the two conditions just mentioned. He has thought for himself, fruitfully, with true independence, and with successful inventiveness. And he has given utterance to ideas which are characteristic of a stage and of an aspect of the spiritual life of this people. He, too, has been widely and deeply affected by the history of thought. But he has reinterpreted all these historical influences in his own personal way. He has transformed whatever he has assimilated. He has rediscovered whatever he has received from without; because he never could teach what he had not himself experienced. And, in addition, he has indeed invented effectively and richly. Moreover, in him certain characteristic aspects of our national civilization have found their voice. (pp. 6-7)

Viewed as an American, he belongs to the movement which has been the consequence, first, of our civil war, and secondly, of the recent expansion, enrichment, and entanglement of our social life. He belongs to the age in which our nation, rapidly transformed by the occupation of new territory, by economic growth, by immigration, and by education, has been attempting to find itself anew, to redefine its ideals, to retain its moral integrity, and yet to become a world power. (pp. 16-17)

Our nation since the civil war has largely lost touch with the older forms of its own religious life. It has been seeking for new embodiments of the religious consciousness, for creeds that shall not be in conflict with the modern man's view of life. It was James's office, as psychologist and as philosopher, to give a novel expression to this our own national variety of the spirit of religious unrest. And his volume, **"The Varieties of Religious Experience,"** is one that, indeed, with all its wealth of illustration, and in its courageous enterprise, has a certain classic beauty. Some men preach new ways of salvation. James simply portrayed the meaning that the old ways of salvation had possesed, or still do possess, in the inner and personal experience of those individuals whom he has called the religious geniuses. And then he undertook to suggest an hypothesis as to what the whole religious process might mean. The hypothesis is on the one hand in touch with certain tendencies of recent psychology. And in so far it seems in harmony with the modern consciousness. On the other hand it expresses, in a way, James's whole philosophy of life. And in this respect it comes into touch with all the central problems of humanity.

The result of this portrayal was indeed magical. The psychologists were aided towards a new tolerance in their study of religion. The evolution of religion appeared in a new light. And meanwhile many of the faithful, who had long been disheartened by the later forms of evolutionary naturalism, took heart anew when they read James's vigorous appeal to the religious experience of the individual as to the most authoritative evidence for religion. "The most modern of thinkers, the evolutionist, the psychologist," they said, "the heir of all the ages, has thus vindicated anew the witness of the spirit in the heart—the very source of inspiration in which we ourselves have always believed." And such readers went away rejoicing, and some of them even began to write christologies based upon the doctrine of James as they understood it. The new gospel, the glad tidings of the subconscious, began to be preached in many lands. It has even received the signal honor of an official papal condemnation.

For my own part, I have ventured to say elsewhere that the new doctrine, viewed in one aspect, seems to leave religion in the comparatively trivial position of a play with whimsical powers—a prey to endless psychological caprices. But James's own robust faith was that the very caprices of the spirit are the opportunity for the building up of the highest forms of the spiritual life; that the unconventional and the individual in religious experience are the means whereby the truth of a superhuman world may become most manifest. And this robust faith of James, I say, whatever you may think of its merits, is as American in type as it has already proved effective in the expression which James gave to it. It is the spirit of the frontiersman, of the gold seeker, or the home builder, transferred to the metaphysical and to the religious realm. There is our far-off home, our long-lost spiritual fortune. Experience alone can guide us towards the place where these things are; hence you indeed need experience. You can only win your way on the frontier in case you are willing to live there. Be, therefore, concrete, be fearless, be experimental. But, above all, let not your abstract conceptions, even if you call them scientific conceptions, pretend to set any limits to the richness of spiritual grace, to the glories of spiritual possession, that, in case you are duly favored, your personal experience may reveal to you. James reckons that the tribulations with which abstract scientific theories have beset our present age are not to be compared with the glory that perchance shall be, if only we open our eyes to what experience itself has to reveal to us.

In the quest for the witness to whom James appeals when he tests his religious doctrine, he indeed searches the most varied literature; and of course most of the records that he consults belong to foreign lands. But the book called **"The Varieties of Religious Experience"** is full of the spirit that, in our country, has long been effective in the formation of new religious sects; and this volume expresses, better than any sectarian could express, the recent efforts of this spirit to come to an understanding with modern naturalism, and with the new psychology. James's view of religious experience is meanwhile at once deliberately unconventional and intensely democratic. The old-world types of reverence for the external forms of the church find no place in his pages; but equally foreign to his mind is that barren hostility of the typical European freethinkers for the church with whose traditions they have broken. In James's eyes, the forms, the external organizations of the religious world simply wither; it is the individual that is more and more. And James, with a democratic contempt for social appearances, seeks his religious geniuses everywhere. World-renowned saints of the historic church receive his hearty sympathy; but they stand upon an equal footing, in his esteem, with many an obscure and ignorant revivalist, with faith healers, with poets, with sages, with heretics, with men that wander about in all sorts of sheepskins and goatskins, with chance correspondents of his own, with whomsoever you will of whom the world was not and is not worthy, but who, by inner experience, have obtained the substance of things hoped for, the evidence of things not seen.

You see, of course, that I do not believe James's resulting philosophy of religion to be adequate. For as it stands it is indeed chaotic. But I am sure that it can only be amended by taking it up into a larger view, and not by rejecting it. The spirit triumphs, not by destroying the chaos that James describes, but by brooding upon the face of the deep until the light comes, and with light, order. But I am sure also that we shall always have to reckon with James's view. And I am sure also that only an American thinker could have written this survey, with all its unconventional ardor of appreciation, with all its democratic catholicity of sympathy, with all its freedom both from ecclesiastical formality and from barren freethinking. I am sure also that no book has better expressed the whole spirit of hopeful unrest, of eagerness to be just to the modern view of life, of longing for new experience, which characterizes the recent American religious movement. In James's book, then, the deeper spirit of our national religious life has found its most manifold and characteristic expression. (pp. 19-26)

Now one of the most momentous problems regarding the influence of James is presented by the question: How did he stand related to these recent ethical tendencies of our nation? I may say at once that, in my opinion, he has just here proved himself to be most of all and in the best sense our national philosopher. . . . Was not he himself restlessly active in his whole temperament? Did he not love individual enterprise and its free expression? Did he not loathe what seemed to him abstractions? Did he not insist that the moralist must be in close touch with concrete life? As psychologist did he not emphasize the fact that the very essence of conscious life lies in its active, yes, in its creative relation to experience? Did he not counsel the strenuous attitude towards our tasks? And are not all these features in harmony with the spirit from which the athletic type of morality just sketched seems to have sprung?

Not only is all this true of James, but, in the popular opinion of the moment, the doctrine called pragmatism, as he expounded it in his Lowell lectures, seems, to many of his foreign

William James and Josiah Royce in September 1903.

critics, and to some of those who think themselves his best followers here at home, a doctrine primarily ethical in its force, while, to some minds, pragmatism seems also to be a sort of philosophical generalization of the efficiency doctrine just mentioned. To be sure, any closer reader of James's **"Pragmatism"** ought to see that his true interests in the philosophy of life are far deeper than those which the maxims "Be efficient" and "Play the game" mostly emphasize. And, for the rest, the book on pragmatism is explicitly the portrayal of a method of philosophical inquiry, and is only incidentally a discourse upon ethically interesting matters. James himself used to protest vigorously against the readers who ventured to require of the pragmatist, viewed simply as such, any one ethical doctrine whatever. In his book on **"Pragmatism"** he had expounded, as he often said, a method of philosophizing, a definition of truth, a criterion for interpreting and testing theories. He was not there concerned with ethics. A pragmatist was free to decide moral issues as he chose, so long as he used the pragmatic method in doing so; that is, so long as he tested ethical doctrines by their concrete results, when they were applied to life.

Inevitably, however, the pragmatic doctrine, that both the meaning and the truth of ideas shall be tested by the empirical consequences of these ideas and by the practical results of acting them out in life, has seemed both to many of James's original hearers, and to some of the foreign critics just mentioned, a doctrine that is simply a characteristic Americanism in philosophy—a tendency to judge all ideals by their practical efficiency, by their visible results, by their so-called "cash values."

James, as I have said, earnestly protested against this cruder interpretation of his teaching. The author of **"The Varieties of Religious Experience"** and of **"The Pluralistic Universe"** was indeed an empiricist, a lover of the concrete, and a man who looked forward to the future rather than backward to the past; but despite his own use, in his "pragmatism" of the famous metaphor of the "cash values" of ideas, he was certainly not a thinker who had set his affections upon things below rather than upon things above. And the "consequences" upon which he laid stress when he talked of the pragmatic test for ideas were certainly not the merely worldly consequence of such ideas in the usual sense of the word "worldly." He appealed always to experience; but then for him experience might be, and sometimes was, religious experience—experience of the unseen and of the superhuman. And so James was right in his protest against these critics of his later doctrine. His form of pragmatism was indeed a form of Americanism in philosophy. And he too had his fondness for what he regarded as efficiency, and for those who "play the game," whenever the game was one that he honored. But he also loved too much those who are weak in the eyes of this present world—the religious geniuses, the unpopular inquirers, the noble outcasts. He loved them, I say, too much to be the dupe of the cruder forms of our now popular efficiency doctrine. In order to win James's most enthusiastic support, ideas and men needed to express an intense inner experience along with a certain unpopularity which showed that they deserved sympathy. Too much worldly success, on the part of men or of ideas, easily alienated him. Unworldliness was one of the surest marks, in his eyes, of spiritual power, if only such unworldliness seemed to him to be joined with interests that, using his favorite words, he could call "concrete" and "important."

In the light of such facts, all that he said about judging ideas by their "consequences" must be interpreted, and therefore it

is indeed unjust to confound pragmatism with the cruder worship of efficiency. (pp. 30-6)

[James] saw the facts of human life as they are, and he resolutely lived beyond them into the realm of the spirit. He loved the concrete, but he looked above towards the larger realm of universal life. He often made light of the abstract reason, but in his own plastic and active way he uttered some of the great words of the universal reason, and he has helped his people to understand and to put into practice these words.

I ask you to remember him then, not only as the great psychologist, the radical empiricist, the pragmatist, but as the interpreter of the ethical spirit of his time and of his people—the interpreter who has pointed the way beyond the trivialities which he so well understood and transcended towards that "Rule of Reason" which the prophetic maxim of our supreme court has just brought afresh to the attention of our people. That "Rule of Reason," when it comes, will not be a mere collection of abstractions. It will be, as James demanded, something concrete and practical. And it will indeed appeal to our faith as well as to our discursive logical processes. But it will express the transformed and enlightened American spirit as James already began to express it. Let him too be viewed as a prophet of the nation that is to be. (pp. 43-5)

> *Josiah Royce, "William James and the Philosophy of Life," in his* William James and Other Essays on the Philosophy of Life, *The Macmillan Company, 1911, pp. 3-45.*

JOHN DEWEY (essay date 1916)

[*Dewey was one of the most celebrated American philosophers of the twentieth century and the leading philosopher of Pragmatism after the death of William James. Dewey gave his Pragmatic philosophy the name "instrumentalism." Like James's Pragmatism, Dewey's instrumentalism was an action-oriented mode of speculation that judged ideas by their practical results, especially in furthering human adaptation to the changing circumstances of existence. Dewey criticized the detached pursuit of truth for its own sake and advocated a philosophy with the specific aim of seeking improvements in various spheres of human life. Much of Dewey's influence has been felt in the fields of education and political theory. In the following excerpt, Dewey examines James's Pragmatic theory of truth in terms of the dual criteria "that a belief is true when it satisfies both personal needs and the requirements of objective things." As Dewey points out, much of the controversy surrounding James's Pragmatic theory of truth derives from the charge that Pragmatists adhere to only the first criterion of truth, "that anything which is agreeable is true." This position forms the basis of the excerpts by Bertrand Russell (1908) and F. H. Bradley (1908). For other commentary in support of James's Pragmatic theory of truth, see the excerpt by Henri Bergson (1911), and for another discussion of Pragmatism, see the excerpt by Charles M. Bakewell (1907).*]

[In *Pragmatism*] Mr. James is most concerned to enforce, as against rationalism, two conclusions about the character of truths as *faits accomplis*: namely, that they are made, not a priori, or eternally in existence, and that their value or importance is not static, but dynamic and practical. The special question of *how* truths are made is not particularly relevant to this anti-rationalistic crusade, while it is the chief question of interest to many. Because of this conflict of problems, what Mr. James says about the value of truth when accomplished is likely to be interpreted by some as a criterion of the truth of ideas; while, on the other hand, Mr. James himself is likely to pass lightly from the consequences that determine the worth of a belief to those which decide the worth of an idea. When Mr. James says the function of giving "satisfaction in marrying previous parts of experience with newer parts" is necessary in order to establish truth, the doctrine is unambiguous. The satisfactory character of consequences is itself measured and defined by the conditions which led up to it; the inherently satisfactory quality of results is not taken as validating the antecedent intellectual operations. But when he says (not of his own position, but of an opponent's) of the idea of an absolute, "so far as it affords such comfort it surely is not sterile, it has that amount of value; it performs a concrete function. As a good pragmatist I myself ought to call the absolute truth *in so far forth* then; and I unhesitatingly now do so" . . . , the doctrine seems to be as unambiguous in the other direction: that any good, consequent upon acceptance of a belief is, in so far forth, a warrant of truth. [Dewey remarks in a footnote: Of course, Mr. James holds that this "in so far" goes a very small way. . . . But even the slightest concession is, I think, non-pragmatic unless the satisfaction is relevant to the idea as intent. Now the satisfaction in question comes not from the idea as *idea,* but from its acceptance as *true.* Can a satisfaction dependent on an assumption that an idea is already true be relevant to testing the truth of an idea? And can an idea, like that of the absolute, which, if true, "absolutely" precludes any appeal to consequences as test of truth, be confirmed by use of the pragmatic test without sheer self-contradiction? In other words, we have a confusion of the test of an idea as idea, with that of the value of a belief as belief. On the other hand, it is quite possible that all Mr. James intends by truth here is true (i.e., genuine) meaning at stake in the issue—true not as distinct from false, but from meaningless or verbal.] In such passages as the following (which are of the common type) the two notions seem blended together: "Ideas become true just in so far as they help us to get into satisfactory relations with other parts of our experience" . . . ; and, again, on the same page: "Any idea that will carry us *prosperously* from any one part of our experience to any other part, linking things *satisfactorily, working securely, simplifying, saving labor,* is true for just so much" (italics mine). An explicit statement as to whether the carrying function, the linking of things, is satisfactory and prosperous and hence true in so far as it executes the intent of an idea; or whether the satisfaction and prosperity reside in the material consequences on their own account and in that aspect make the idea true, would, I am sure, locate the point at issue and economize and fructify future discussion. At present pragmatism is accepted by those whose own notions are thoroughly rationalistic in make-up as a means of refurbishing, galvanizing, and justifying those very notions. It is rejected by non-rationalists (empiricists and naturalistic idealists) because it seems to them identified with the notion that pragmatism holds that the desirability of certain beliefs overrides the question of the meaning of the ideas involved in them and the existence of objects denoted by them. Others (like myself), who believe thoroughly in pragmatism as a method of orientation, as defined by Mr. James, and who would apply the method to the determination of the meaning of objects, the intent and worth of ideas as ideas, and to the human and moral value of beliefs, when these various problems are carefully distinguished from one another, do not know whether they are pragmatists in some other sense, because they are not sure whether the practical, in the sense of desirable facts which define the worth of a belief, is confused with the practical as an attitude imposed by objects, and with the practical as a power and function of ideas to effect changes in prior existences. Hence the importance of knowing which one of the three senses of practical is conveyed in any given passage.

It would do Mr. James an injustice, however, to stop here. His real doctrine is that a belief is true when it satisfies both personal needs and the requirements of objective things. Speaking of pragmatism, he says, "Her only test of probable truth is what works best in the way of *leading us,* what fits every part of life best and *combines with the collectivity of experience's demands,* nothing being omitted." . . . And again, "That new idea is truest which performs most felicitously its function of satisfying *our double urgency.*" . . . It does not appear certain from the context that this "double urgency" is that of the personal and the objective demands, respectively, but it is probable (. . . "consistency with previous truth and novel fact" is said to be "always the most imperious claimant"). On this basis, the "in so far forth" of the truth of the absolute because of the comfort it supplies, means that one of the two conditions which need to be satisfied has been met, so that if the idea of the absolute met the other one also, it would be quite true. I have no doubt this is Mr. James's meaning, and it sufficiently safeguards him from the charge that pragmatism means that anything which is agreeable is true. At the same time, I do not think, in logical strictness, that satisfying one of two tests, when satisfaction of both is required, can be said to constitute a belief true even "in so far forth." (pp. 320-25)

[*Pragmatism*] is more likely to take place as a philosophical classic than any other writing of our day. A critic who should attempt to appraise it would probably give one more illustration of the sterility of criticism compared with the productiveness of creative genius. Even those who dislike pragmatism can hardly fail to find much of profit in the exhibition of Mr. James's instinct for concrete facts, the breadth of his sympathies, and his illuminating insights. Unreserved frankness, lucid imagination, varied contacts with life digested into summary and trenchant conclusions, keen perceptions of human nature in the concrete, a constant sense of the subordination of philosophy to life, capacity to put things into an English which projects ideas as if bodily into space till they are solid things to walk around and survey from different sides—these things are not so common in philosophy that they may not smell sweet even by the name of pragmatism. (p. 329)

John Dewey, "What Pragmatism Means by Practical," in his Essays in Experimental Logic, *1916. Reprint by Dover Publications, Inc., 1953, pp. 303-29.*

GEORGE SANTAYANA (essay date 1920)

[*Santayana was a Spanish-born philosopher, poet, novelist, and literary critic who was for the most part educated in the United States, taking his undergraduate and graduate degrees at Harvard, where he later taught philosophy. His earliest published works were the poems of* Sonnets, and Other Verses *(1894). Although Santayana is regarded as no more than a fair poet, his facility with language is one of the distinguishing features of his later philosophical works. Written in an elegant, non-technical prose, Santayana's major philosophical work of his early career is the five-volume* Life of Reason *(1905-06). These volumes reflect their author's materialist viewpoint applied to such areas as society, religion, art, and science, and, along with* Scepticism and Animal Faith *(1923) and the four-volume* Realms of Being *(1927-40), put forth the view that while reason undermines belief in anything whatever, an irrational animal faith suggests the existence of a "realm of essences" which leads to the human search for knowledge. Late in his life Santayana stated that "reason and ideals arise in doing something that at bottom there is no reason for doing." "Chaos," he wrote earlier, "is perhaps at the bottom of everything." In the following excerpt from an intellectual profile of James, Santayana finds him to be an essentially agnostic thinker and focuses on what he considers the shortcomings of James's presumption of the will to believe. For another discussion critical of James's conception of the will to believe, see the excerpt by Dickinson S. Miller (1899); for discussions defending this idea, see the excerpts by F.C.S. Schiller (1897), Gail Kennedy (1956), and William Barrett (1975).]*

I think it is important to remember, if we are not to misunderstand William James, that his radical empiricism and pragmatism were in his own mind only methods; his doctrine, if he may be said to have had one, was agnosticism. And just because he was an agnostic (feeling instinctively that beliefs and opinions, if they had any objective beyond themselves, could never be sure they had attained it), he seemed in one sense so favourable to credulity. He was not credulous himself, far from it; he was well aware that the trust he put in people or ideas might betray him. For that very reason he was respectful and pitiful to the trustfulness of others. Doubtless they were wrong, but who were we to say so? In his own person he was ready enough to face the mystery of things, and whatever the womb of time might bring forth; but until the curtain was rung down on the last act of the drama (and it might have no last act!) he wished the intellectual cripples and the moral hunchbacks not to be jeered at; perhaps they might turn out to be the heroes of the play. Who could tell what heavenly influences might not pierce to these sensitive half-flayed creatures, which are lost on the thick-skinned, the sane, and the duly goggled? We must not suppose, however, that James meant these contrite and romantic suggestions dogmatically. The agnostic, as well as the physician and neurologist in him, was never quite eclipsed. The hope that some new revelation might come from the lowly and weak could never mean to him what it meant to the early Christians. For him it was only a right conceded to them to experiment with their special faiths; he did not expect such faiths to be discoveries of absolute fact, which everybody else might be constrained to recognise. If any one had made such a claim, and had seemed to have some chance of imposing it universally, James would have been the first to turn against him; not, of course, on the ground that it was *impossible* that such an orthodoxy should be true, but with a profound conviction that it was to be feared and distrusted. No: the degree of authority and honour to be accorded to various human faiths was a moral question, not a theoretical one. All faiths were what they were experienced as being, in their capacity of faiths; these faiths, not their objects, were the hard facts we must respect. We cannot pass, except under the illusion of the moment, to anything firmer or on a deeper level. There was accordingly no sense of security, no joy, in James's apology for personal religion. He did not really believe; he merely believed in the right of believing that you might be right if you believed.

It is this underlying agnosticism that explains an incoherence which we might find in his popular works, where the story and the moral do not seem to hang together. Professedly they are works of psychological observation; but the tendency and suasion in them seems to run to disintegrating the idea of truth, recommending belief without reason, and encouraging superstition. A psychologist who was not an agnostic would have indicated, as far as possible, whether the beliefs and experiences he was describing were instances of delusion or of rare and fine perception, or in what measure they were a mixture of both. But James—and this is what gives such romantic warmth to these writings of his—disclaims all antecedent or

superior knowledge, listens to the testimony of each witness in turn, and only by accident allows us to feel that he is swayed by the eloquence and vehemence of some of them rather than of others. This method is modest, generous, and impartial; but if James intended, as I think he did, to picture the *drama* of human belief, with its risks and triumphs, the method was inadequate. Dramatists never hesitate to assume, and to let the audience perceive, who is good and who bad, who wise and who foolish, in their pieces; otherwise their work would be as impotent dramatically as scientifically. The tragedy and comedy of life lie precisely in the contrast between the illusions or passions of the characters and their true condition and fate, hidden from them at first, but evident to the author and the public. If in our diffidence and scrupulous fairness we refuse to take this judicial attitude, we shall be led to strange conclusions. The navigator, for instance, trusting his "experience" (which here, as in the case of religious people, means his imagination and his art), insists on believing that the earth is spherical; he has sailed round it. That is to say, he has seemed to himself to steer westward and westward, and has seemed to get home again. But how should he know that home is now where it was before, or that his past and present impressions of it come from the same, or from any, material object? How should he know that space is as trim and tri-dimensional as the discredited Euclidians used to say it was? If, on the contrary, my worthy aunt, trusting to her longer and less ambiguous experience of her garden, insists that the earth is flat, and observes that the theory that it is round, which is only a theory, is much less often tested and found useful than her own perception of its flatness, and that moreover that theory is pedantic, intellectualistic, and a product of academies, and rash dogma to impose on mankind for ever and ever, it might seem that on James's principle we ought to agree with her. But no; on James's real principles we need not agree with her, nor with the navigator either. Radical empiricism, which is radical agnosticism, delivers us from so benighted a choice. For the quarrel becomes unmeaning when we remember that the earth is *both* flat and round, if it is experienced as being both. The substantive fact is not a single object on which both the perception and the theory are expected to converge; the substantive facts are the theory and the perception themselves. And we may note in passing that empiricism, when it ceases to value experience as a means of discovering external things, can give up its ancient prejudice in favour of sense as against imagination, for imagination and thought are immediate experiences as much as sensation is: they are therefore, for absolute empiricism, no less actual ingredients of reality. (pp. 74-80)

James fell in with the hortatory tradition of college sages; he turned his psychology, whenever he could do so honestly, to purposes of edification; and his little sermons on habit, on will, on faith, and . . . on the latent capacities of men, were fine and stirring, and just the sermons to preach to the young Christian soldier. He was much less sceptical in morals than in science. He seems to have felt sure that certain thoughts and hopes—those familiar to a liberal Protestantism—were every man's true friends in life. This assumption would have been hard to defend if he or those he habitually addressed had ever questioned it; yet his whole argument for voluntarily cultivating these beliefs rests on this assumption, that they are beneficent. Since, whether we will or not, we cannot escape the risk of error, and must succumb to some human or pathological bias, at least we might do so gracefully and in the form that would profit us most, by clinging to those prejudices which help us to lead what we all feel is a good life. But what is a good life? Had William James, had the people about him, had modern philosophers anywhere, any notion of that? I cannot think so. They had much experience of personal goodness, and love of it; they had standards of character and right conduct; but as to what might render human existence good, excellent, beautiful, happy, and worth having as a whole, their notions were utterly thin and barbarous. They had forgotten the Greeks, or never known them.

This argument accordingly suffers from the same weakness as the similar argument of Pascal in favour of Catholic orthodoxy. You should force yourself to believe in it, he said, because if you do so and are right you win heaven, while if you are wrong you lose nothing. What would Protestants, Mohammedans, and Hindus say to that? Those alternatives of Pascal's are not the sole nor the true alternatives; such a wager—betting on the improbable because you are offered big odds—is an unworthy parody of the real choice between wisdom and folly. There is no heaven to be won in such a spirit, and if there was, a philosopher would despise it. So Wiliam James would have us bet on immortality, or bet on our power to succeed, because if we win the wager we can live to congratulate ourselves on our true instinct, while we lose nothing if we have made a mistake; for unless you have the satisfaction of finding that you have been right, the dignity of having been right is apparently nothing. Or if the argument is rather that these beliefs, whether true or false, make life better in this world, the thing is simply false. To be boosted by an illusion is not to live better than to live in harmony with the truth; it is not nearly so safe, not nearly so sweet, and not nearly so fruitful. These refusals to part with a decayed illusion are really an infection to the mind. Believe, certainly; we cannot help believing; but believe rationally, holding what seems certain for certain, what seems probable for probable, what seems desirable for desirable, and what seems false for false.

In this matter, as usual, James had a true psychological fact and a generous instinct behind his confused moral suggestions. It is a psychological fact that men are influenced in their beliefs by their will and desires; indeed, I think we can go further and say that in its essence belief is an expression of impulse, of readiness to act. It is only peripherally, as our action is gradually adjusted to things, and our impulses to our possible or necessary action, that our ideas begin to hug the facts, and to acquire a true, if still a symbolic, signficance. We do not need a will to believe; we only need a will to study the object in which we are inevitably believing. But James was thinking less of belief in what we find than of belief in what we hope for: a belief which is not at all clear and not at all necessary in the life of mortals. Like most Americans, however, only more lyrically, James felt the call of the future and the assurance that it could be made far better, totally other, than the past. The pictures that religion had painted of heaven or the millennium were not what he prized, although his Swedenborgian connection might have made him tender to them, as perhaps it did to familiar spirits. It was the moral succour offered by religion, its open spaces, the possibility of miracles *in extremis*, that must be retained. If we recoiled at the thought of being dupes (which is perhaps what nature intended us to be), were we less likely to be dupes in disbelieving these sustaining truths than in believing them? Faith was needed to bring about the reform of faith itself, as well as all other reforms.

In some cases faith in success could nerve us to bring success about, and so justify itself by its own operation. This is a thought typical of James at his worst—a worst in which there is always a good side. Here again psychological observation is used with the best intentions to hearten oneself and other people; but the fact observed is not at all understood, and a moral twist is given to it which (besides being morally questionable) almost amounts to falsifying the fact itself. Why does belief that you can jump a ditch help you to jump it? Because it is a symptom of the fact that you *could* jump it, that your legs were fit and that the ditch was two yards wide and not twenty. A rapid and just appreciation of these facts has given you your confidence, or at least has made it reasonable, manly, and prophetic; otherwise you would have been a fool and got a ducking for it. Assurance is contemptible and fatal unless it is self-knowledge. If you had been rattled you might have failed, because that would have been a symptom of the fact that you were out of gear; you would have been afraid because you trembled, as James at his best proclaimed. You would never have quailed if your system had been reacting smoothly to its opportunities, any more than you would totter and see double if you were not intoxicated. Fear is a sensation of actual nervousness and disarray, and confidence a sensation of actual readiness; they are not disembodied feelings, existing for no reason, the devil Funk and the angel Courage, one or the other of whom may come down arbitrarily into your body, and revolutionise it. That is childish mythology, which survives innocently enough as a figure of speech, until a philosopher is found to take that figure of speech seriously. Nor is the moral suggestion here less unsound. What is good is not the presumption of power, but the possession of it: a clear head, aware of its resources, not a fuddled optimism, calling up spirits from the vasty deep. Courage is not a virtue, said Socrates, unless it is also wisdom. Could anything be truer both of courage in doing and of courage in believing? But it takes tenacity, it takes *reasonable* courage, to stick to scientific insights such as this of Socrates or that of James about the emotions; it is easier to lapse into the traditional manner, to search natural philosophy for miracles and moral lessons, and in morals proper, in the reasoned expression of preference, to splash about without a philosophy. (pp. 84-90)

George Santayana, "William James," in his Character & Opinion in the United States, *Charles Scribner's Sons, 1920, pp. 64-96.*

C. G. JUNG (essay date 1921)

[*Jung was a Swiss psychologist and creator of "analytical psychology," the theoretical basis of which grew out of his early study of psychoanalysis under Sigmund Freud. Disagreeing with Freud's theory of the unconscious sexual origin of neurosis, Jung developed a school of psychology based on the hypothesis that the source of human psychic life resides both in the individual's personal history, the "individual unconscious," and in the collective history of humanity, the "collective unconscious." Evidence for this theory is supplied by recurring motifs, termed "archetypes," in the recorded traditions of diverse cultures throughout human history. Examples of such motifs are the hero, the wise old man, and the spiritual quest. In Jung's psychology, archetypal patterns from mythology and folklore replace the unconscious sexual conflicts of Freud's system as a source of illumination for common patterns in human behavior. Jung also discerned archetypal patterns in modern literature, a practice that has led to a modern school of literary criticism. Another important concept of Jung's that has come into common usage is his famous distinction between "introverted" and "extraverted" personality types. In the following excerpt, originally published in Switzerland in 1921, Jung examines James's psychological categories of "toughminded" and "tender-minded," which he finds too generalized to be useful classifications of personality types. Jacques Barzun, in his critical study* A Stroll with William James *(1983), believes that "Jung honestly misunderstood James's terms. He did not even see that they do not amount to a through-and-through division of mankind, but only indicate tendencies." For a comparison of James's and Jung's respective personality theories, see the excerpt by P. Allan Carlsson (1973).*]

The existence of two types has also been discovered in modern pragmatic philosophy, particularly in the philosophy of William James. He says:

> The history of philosophy is, to a great extent, that of a certain clash of human temperaments.... Of whatever temperament a professional philosopher is, he tries, when philosophizing, to sink the fact of his temperament.... Yet his temperament really gives him a stronger bias than any of his more strictly objective premises. It loads the evidence for him one way or the other, making for a more sentimental or a more hard-hearted view of the universe, just as this fact or that principle would. He trusts his temperament. Wanting a universe that suits it, he believes in any representation of the universe that does suit it. He feels men of opposite temper to be out of key with the world's character, and in his heart considers them incompetent and "not in it," in the philosophic business, even though they may far excel him in dialectical ability.
>
> Yet in the forum he can make no claim, on the bare ground of his temperament, to superior discernment or authority. There arises thus a certain insincerity in our philosophic discussions: the potentest of all our premises is never mentioned.

Whereupon James proceeds to the characterization of the two temperaments. Just as in the domain of manners and customs we distinguish conventional and easy-going persons, in politics authoritarians and anarchists, in literature purists and realists, in art classicists and romantics, so in philosophy, according to James, we find two types, the "rationalist" and the "empiricist." The rationalist is "your devotee of abstract and eternal principles." The empiricist is the "lover of facts in all their crude variety." ... Although no man can dispense either with facts or with principles, they nevertheless give rise to entirely different points of view according to whether the accent falls on one side or on the other.

James makes "rationalism" synonymous with "intellectualism," and "empiricism" with "sensationalism." Although in my opinion this equation is not tenable, we will follow James' line of thought for the time being, reserving our criticism until later. In his view, intellectualism is associated with an idealistic and optimistic tendency, whereas empiricism inclines to materialism and a very qualified and uncertain optimism. Intellectualism is always *monistic*. It begins with the whole, with the universal, and unites things; empiricism begins with the part and makes the whole into an *assemblage*. It could therefore be described as *pluralistic*. The rationalist is a man of feeling, but the empiricist is a hard-headed creature. The former is naturally disposed to a belief in free will, the latter to fatalism. The rationalist is inclined to be dogmatic, the empiricist sceptical.... James calls the rationalist *tender-minded*, the empiricist *tough-minded*. It is obvious that he is trying to put his

finger on the characteristic mental qualities of the two types. Later, we shall examine this characterization rather more closely. It is interesting to hear what James has to say about the prejudices each type cherishes about the other . . . : (pp. 300-01)

They have a low opinion of each other. Their antagonism, whenever as individuals their temperaments have been intense, has formed in all ages a part of the philosophic atmosphere of the time. It forms a part of the atmosphere today. The tough think of the tender as sentimentalists and soft-heads. The tender feel the tough to be unrefined, callous, or brutal. . . . Each type believes the other to be inferior to itself.

James tabulates the qualities of the two types as follows:

Tender-minded
Rationalistic (going by "principles")
Intellectualistic
Idealistic
Optimistic
Religious
Free-willist
Monistic
Dogmatical

Tough-minded
Empiricist (going by "facts")
Sensationalistic
Materialistic
Pessimistic
Irreligious
Fatalistic
Pluralistic
Sceptical

(pp. 301-02)

In criticizing James' typology, I must first stress that it is almost exclusively concerned with the thinking qualities of the types. In a philosophical work one could hardly expect anything else. But the bias resulting from this philosophical setting easily leads to confusion. It would not be difficult to show that such and such a quality is equally characteristic of the opposite type, or even several of them. There are, for instance, empiricists who are dogmatic, religious, idealistic, intellectualistic, rationalistic, etc., just as there are ideologists who are materialistic, pessimistic, deterministic, irreligious, and so on. It is true, of course, that these terms cover extremely complex facts and that all sorts of subtle nuances have to be taken into account, but this still does not get rid of the possibility of confusion.

Taken individually, the Jamesian terms are too *broad* and give an approximate picture of the type antithesis only when taken as a whole. Though they do not reduce it to a simple formula, they form a valuable supplement to the picture of the types we have gained from other sources. James deserves credit for being the first to draw attention to the extraordinary importance of temperament in colouring philosophical thought. The whole purpose of his pragmatic approach is to reconcile the philosophical antagonisms resulting from temperamental differences.

Pragmatism is a widely ramifying philosophical movement, deriving from English philosophy, which restricts the value of "truth" to its practical efficacy and usefulness, regardless of whether or not it may be contested from some other standpoint. It is characteristic of James to begin his exposition of pragmatism with this type antithesis, as if to demonstrate and justify the need for a pragmatic approach. Thus the drama already acted out in the Middle Ages is repeated. The antithesis at that time took the form of nominalism versus realism, and it was Abelard who attempted to reconcile the two in his "sermonism" or conceptualism. But since the psychological standpoint was completely lacking, his attempted solution was marred by its logical and intellectualistic bias. James dug deeper and grasped the conflict at its psychological root, coming up with a pragmatic solution. One should not, however, cherish any illusions about its value: pragmatism is but a makeshift, and it can claim validity only so long as no sources are discovered, other than intellectual capacities coloured by temperament, which might reveal new elements in the formation of philosophical concepts. Bergson, it is true, has drawn attention to the role of intuition and to the possibility of an "intuitive method," but it remains a mere pointer. Any proof of the method is lacking and will not be easy to furnish, notwithstanding Bergson's claim that his "élan vital" and "durée créatrice" are products of intuition. Aside from these intuitive concepts, which derive their psychological justification from the fact that they were current even in antiquity, particularly in Neoplatonism, Bergson's method is not intuitive but intellectual. Nietzsche made far greater use of the intuitive source and in so doing freed himself from the bonds of the intellect in shaping his philosophical ideas—so much so that his intuition carried him outside the bounds of a purely philosophical system and led to the creation of a work of art which is largely inaccessible to philosophical criticism. I am speaking, of course, of *Zarathustra* and not of the collection of philosophical aphorisms, which are accessible to philosophical criticism because of their predominantly intellectual method. If one may speak of an intuitive method at all, *Zarathustra* is in my view the best example of it, and at the same time a vivid illustration of how the problem can be grasped in a non-intellectual and yet philosophical way. As forerunners of Nietzsche's intuitive approach I would mention Schopenhauer and Hegel, the former because his intuitive feelings had such a decisive influence on his thinking, the latter because of the intuitive ideas that underlie his whole system. In both cases, however, intuition was subordinated to intellect, but with Nietzsche it ranked above it.

The conflict between the two "truths" requires a pragmatic attitude if any sort of justice is to be done to the other standpoint. Yet, though it cannot be dispensed with, pragmatism presupposes too great a resignation and almost unavoidably leads to a drying up of creativeness. The solution of the conflict of opposites can come neither from the intellectual compromise of conceptualism nor from a pragmatic assessment of the practical value of logically irreconcilable views, but only from a positive act of creation which assimilates the opposites as necessary elements of co-ordination, in the same way as a coordinated muscular movement depends on the innervation of opposing muscle groups. Pragmatism can be no more than a transitional attitude preparing the way for the creative act by removing prejudices. James and Bergson are signposts along the road which German philosophy—not of the academic sort—has already trodden. But it was really Nietzsche who, with a violence peculiarly his own, struck out on the path to the future. His creative act goes beyond the unsatisfying pragmatic solution just as fundamentally as pragmatism itself, in acknowledging the living value of a truth, transcended the barren onesidedness and unconscious conceptualism of post-Abelardian philosophy—and still there are heights to be climbed. (pp. 319-21)

C. G. Jung, "The Type Problem in Modern Philosophy," in his The Collected Works of C. G. Jung:

Psychological Types, Vol. 6 *by C. G. Jung, edited by R.F.C. Hull, translated by H. G. Baynes, Bollingen Series XX, 1971. Reprint by Princeton University Press, 1976, pp. 300-21.**

JULIUS SEELYE BIXLER (essay date 1926)

[*Bixler was an American educator and theologian whose books include* Immortality and the Present Mood *(1931) and* A Faith That Fulfills *(1951). Bixler's* Religion in the Philosophy of William James *is a study covering broad areas of James's thought, with chapters devoted to the absolute, pluralism, the will, the deity, immortality, and mysticism. In the preface to this work, from which the following excerpt is taken, Bixler offers general commentary on James's contribution to the study of religion. While Bixler accords James a seminal position in the philosophy of religion, he views James as an outdated contributor to the study of the psychology of religion. This viewpoint—which is shared by many commentators on James's work, including James Dittes (see Additional Bibliography)—is challenged in the excerpt by Gary T. Alexander (1979).*]

The study of religion has made progress since James's death in 1910 but it has followed in general the lines which he pointed out. Particularly is this true of the philosophy as contrasted with the psychology of religion. In the latter field James was a pioneer, and the development of the subject since his time is due in large measure to the momentum which his efforts created. But his hypotheses as to the part played in religious experience by the subconscious self are out of date as a result of the great amount of attention which subconscious activity has received from investigators. In the field of the philosophy of religion, however, the situation is different. The issues which James raises here must form an integral part of any discussion of the subject, and the emphases he makes are of permanent importance.

The older rationalistic method of attacking religious problems is less in vogue today than formerly partly because of James's trenchant attacks upon it. In its place two main tendencies can be discerned in the religious thought of our time, each taking its cue from a special part of James's work. The first of these is the empirical, the method employed by James so successfully in his book on *The Varieties of Religious Experience*. The other is a modification of the empirical method and is usually called pragmatic. It follows the lines suggested in James's *The Will to Believe*, making postulates on the basis of experienced need, and it has much to say of human values and their possible identification with cosmic truth.

Two other less clearly formulated features of modern religious thinking which also point to James's influence deserve notice as well. The first of these, running parallel to a similar tendency in modern art, is toward realism. More is known about the universe today than ever before, and with this increase of knowledge has come an increase in sensitiveness to the tragedy of human suffering as well as a heightened sense of the futility of much human activity. As a result religion is looking the facts of life in the face with a gaze which in its unflinching and critical quality is new. In place of the older religious worldview with its rounded outlines and ultimate syntheses, with its conviction as to the beneficence of nature and the final triumphant destiny of man, modern religious thought envisages a universe with ragged and jagged edges, full of yawning abysses, calculated to fill man with a sense of the precariousness rather than the stability of his own position. With such an outlook James's pluralistic philosophy has much in common. The phrase "problem of evil" rarely appears on James's pages, but the idea is ever hovering in the background of his thought. To a generation which is still feeling the effects of the greatest calamity in history, and which regards much of the religious optimism of the past as based on illusion, James's awareness of the tragic element in life and refusal to eliminate it from his religious view of the world comes with a refreshing sense of reality.

But while our religious thinking is realistic in one respect in another it is romantic. This tendency can be seen in the attempt of some of the most recent writers to arrive at religious truth through an imaginative treatment of the *nuances* and subtleties which are involved in any venture at describing man's relation to his cosmic environment. The lure of the ultimate mystery, the fascination of the transcendent, and the possibility of socializing this fascination and turning it to practical account—such subjects as these are being brought to our attention in new and arresting fashion by some of the latest books on religion.

This way of approach dates back to James also, although it has developed a technique and consciousness of its own purposes which he did not have. He paved the way for it, however, in his empiricism, and especially in his implicit suggestion that the most satisfactory statement of man's place in the cosmos will be found in the most inclusive view of what human life really is. Experience is a many-sided thing and can be described from many points of vantage. The most complete truth about human life and its religious relationships will be found in that description of it which reaches out the farthest and at the same time penetrates the deepest. The meaning of the whole human struggle for existence and for value will be revealed most fully to that interpreter who with sympathy and insight sees the process as a many-sided whole and refuses to be content with any single formula or with a description which is made from any single point of view.

James was well qualified to be such an interpreter. Few have enjoyed the acute sensitiveness to value which was his and not many have been able as was he to envisage the larger relationships by which human life is encompassed. The fact may be worth dwelling on that James was particularly keenly aware of the importance and significance of human volitional activity. It is desirable to make this emphasis at a time like the present when certain scientific disciplines, claiming direct descent from James, are pressing the mechanistic view of human life. It is true that James has given us a scientific description of experience with the individual consciousness left out. But it is well to remember that no one has sketched more boldly than he the possibilities which can only be made actual through individual personal choice. (pp. viii-x)

> *Julius Seelye Bixler, in a preface to his* Religion in the Philosophy of William James, *Marshall Jones Company, 1926, pp. vii-xii.*

RALPH BARTON PERRY   (essay date 1938)

[*Perry was an American philosopher and biographer whose two-volume biography of William James won the Pulitzer Prize for that genre in 1935. One of James's students at Harvard, as well as a close friend, Perry became an adherent of Pragmatism and later developed his own version of this philosophy which he termed "neo-realism." In the following excerpt from his* In the Spirit of William James, *which contains essays on various aspects of James's work, Perry contrasts the personal and intellectual qualities of James and Josiah Royce. Whereas James is pluralistic, materialistic, utilitarian, and American in spirit, Royce is monistic,* absolutist, idealistic, and European in spirit. For commentary by Royce on James's thought, see the excerpt dated 1911; for another comparison study of the philosophical thought of James and Royce, see the excerpt by A. J. Ayer (1982).]

Both Royce and James were profoundly influenced by their religious inheritances. Both rejected the specific content of that inheritance and transformed it into a generalized attitude of sympathy and earnestness. Both were religious in feeling, although neither was attached to any orthodoxy or institution. But while Royce's religious inheritance came from his mother, James's came from his father; and while Royce's inherited religion was a literal evangelical piety, James's was a deeply original philosophical mysticism. This divergence had an interesting sequel. The religious philosophy of each resembled the parental prototype of the other.

Royce's mother was sustained during the perilous crossing of the continent by prayer and by a faith in providence. The family was unable to attach itself to any larger group and made their way alone, because their religious scruples forbade their travelling on the Sabbath. In moments of gravest danger Sarah Royce felt a sense of God's presence—"that calm strength, that certainty of One near and all sufficient." When her family was met by a rescuing party at the foot of the Sierras, she "stood in mute adoration, breathing, in my inmost heart, thanksgiving to that Providential Hand which had taken hold of the conflicting movements, the provoking blunders, the contradictory plans, of our lives and those of a dozen other people, who a few days before were utterly unknown to each other, and many miles apart, and had from those rough, broken materials wrought out for us so unlooked for a deliverance." The young Josiah was taught from the Bible, which with a copy of Milton and a small writing desk his devoted mother had brought with her from the old to the new home. He attended church with his parents until the time of his entering college. In after life his thought retained a flavor of biblical allusion and of homiletic eloquence. He took an interest in the problems of Christian theology and liked to translate his thought into the terms of Christian dogma. And yet, despite all this, the substance of his religon was philosophical rather than evangelical. God was defined as "an Absolute Experience transparently fulfilling a system of organised ideas." For Royce an idea was a purpose, and in the "Absolute Experience," everything in nature and history both has a purpose and finds that purpose concretely realized. There is no stark evil, but what appears on a finite view to be stark evil is seen as a phase of moral good. Each human soul embodies a unique purpose which is an indispensable part of the meaning of the whole. Death, which seems to be a sheer defeat of that purpose, is, in the final experience, found to be a victory in disguise.

James's father, on the other hand, was religious out of the depths of his own reflection and personal experience. Like all philosophical mystics he reached God by surmounting his own thought. He did, it is true, ascribe his personal salvation to Swedenborg; but he dissociated himself utterly from the Swedenborgian sect, and nourished his mind on metaphysics. His theology was a subtle rationalization of man's alienation and return to God through the perfecting of society. God's empire was never questioned. Suffering and sin were redeemed in the eternal triumph of which they formed subordinate and essential notes. Thus the elder James's personal religion was akin to the philosophy of Royce.

To his son, however, he transmitted not this "monistic" synthesis, this intellectualized certainty of cosmic goodness; but only a deep respect for the religious experience, as worthy of a hearing and as being a datum for which philosophy must supply a fitting hypothesis. And when it came to the hypothesis William found a very different way from his father's. Turning from the great theistic tradition of European philosophy, from Platonism, Thomism, Cartesianism, and Hegelianism, he found his hypothesis in morbid psychology and in that *parvenu* science known as psychical research. He took immortality to mean quite simply and literally a prolongation of individual life after the death of the body, and found arguments for it in the "transmission theory," according to which the brain does not produce the mind but lets it through from a beyond to which, after the brain's dissolution, it may again return. In Myers's doctrine of the subliminal consciousness he saw the possibility "that the conscious person is continuous with a wider self through which saving experiences come." He was not interested in any moralistic or other refined substitute for cruder religious phenomena. If he prophesied at all it was because he felt the "old Lutheran sentiment" in his bones. He identified religion with the specific religious "experiences," with the spiritual adventures of saints and martyrs—with the sense of conversion, exaltation and regeneration, and with the hope of resurrection. He looked for religion among the religious in their most unmistakably religious moments, and not among the philosopher's reflections *about* religion. He justified sheer faith. He defended a "'piecemeal' supernaturalism," or thought it the only defense of religion worth undertaking. Hence he could say to his latitudinarian friends who were much better churchgoers than himself that *he* was the methodist or evangelical, whereas they were the rationalists. It was thus James rather than Royce who could justify a literal acceptance of the piety of Royce's mother. (pp. 14-18)

Thus did Royce and James exchange parental inheritances. Royce's religious thought was akin to that of James's father; and that of James was a philosophical translation of the practical and emotional piety of Royce's mother. A similar inverse opposition of philosophy and inheritance appears in the relation of these two philosophers to their American nationality. Royce, the more American in his experience, is the more European in his philosophy; while James, the more European in his experience, is the more American in his philosophy.

Santayana once remarked that "America is a young country with an old mentality: it has enjoyed," he said, "the advantages of a child carefully brought up and thoroughly indoctrinated; it has been a wise child. But a wise child, an old head on young shoulders, always has a comic and unpromising side." Although Santayana did not at the moment have him in mind, Royce illustrates the point, both outwardly and inwardly. His head was disproportionate to his shoulders, and he was in his day the most notable exponent of what Santayana called "the genteel tradition." There has always been in America an old-world philosophy to which Americans of the new world have looked for edification and for a fundamental justification of their way of life. It was once Calvinism, then deism, then the Scottish philosophy of common sense, and finally, in Royce's day, the German transcendentalism of Kant and his metaphysical successors. Royce, like James, made the acquaintance of Goethe at an early age, but where James found a serene and objective naturalism that was easily assimilable to the American mind, Royce found the Germanic "building anew of the lost universe in the bosom of the human spirit." During his student days in Germany Royce studied Kant and Schopenhauer, and while at Johns Hopkins he gave much of his time to German literature of the Romantic period. He wrote a critical

essay on Schiller as early as 1878. Among philosophers Fichte, Schelling, and Schopenhauer, and to a lesser extent Hegel, became his masters, eclipsing the Mill and Spencer of his earlier years and the Anglo-American tradition to which James gave his permanent, though qualified, allegiance.

It thus transpired that, although Royce's was the characteristic American experience, it was left to James to develop an indigenous American philosophy, the first, perhaps, in which the American experience escaped the stamp of an imported ideology. Royce, bred and reared amidst what was most unique and local in American life, imported his philosophy from the fashion makers of continental Europe; while James, uprooted almost from infancy and thoroughly imbued with the culture of Germany and France, was a philosophical patriot, cutting the garment of his thought from homespun materials and creating a new American model. Royce, the product of a raw pioneer community, conceived his universe as a perfected Absolute; James, nourished on the refinements and stabilities of advanced civilization, depicted a cosmic wilderness "game-flavored as a hawk's wing."

All "classic," clean, cut and dried, "noble," fixed, "eternal," *Weltanschauungen* seem to me to violate the character with which life concretely comes and the expression which it bears of being, or at least of involving, a muddle and a struggle, with an "ever not quite" to all our formulas, and novelty and possibility forever leaking in.

Royce spent his early years in a region where people used their senses, learned by experience, and labored with their hands; his philosophy was rationalistic and *a priori*. James, born and bred among ideas, was the arch-empiricist, turning in his philosophy toward experience and practice. It was James's and not Royce's philosophical world that was "in the making"; it was James's and not Royce's conclusion, that "there is no conclusion." Royce took refuge in "the Eternal"; while for James time, flux, and chance constituted the very pulse of the living reality. Royce, feeling his physical impotence in a world of struggle, asked to have the victory written in the stars in order to contemplate and relive it in imagination. James, on the other hand, was the realist. To apply James's own expressions, it was Royce who in philosophy was "the tender-foot Bostonian," though he orginated even west of the Rocky Mountains; while James himself, who frequented Boston, Newport, and the capitals of Europe, was the philosophical "Rocky Mountain tough." James's "tough-mindedness," like the "tender-mindedness" of Royce, dwelt in the realm of philosophic thought, but his thinking took the form of an imaginative contrast to the comparative security of his actual condition. That which gave him "a sort of deep enthusiastic bliss" was a sense of "active tension," a sense, as he expressed it, "of holding my own . . .and trusting outward things to perform their part . . . but without any *guaranty* that they will."

That the American element in Royce's philosophy—his empiricism and his practicalism—is always in the last analysis subordinated to the requirements of his imported idealism, while James's nostalgic Americanism is dominant and incorrigible, appears in their philosophies of evil. James's dualism and meliorism is the view which might be expected of a man whose philosophy reflected the American conquest of nature and confidence in the future, Royce's optimistic monism is the speculative solution of a man steeped in the European tradition. (pp. 23-8)

The major philosophical difference between James and Royce is a difference of ethics. For both men even the truth of science is relative to the will of the thinker. To find the fundamental difference, then, we must look in that quarter. For Royce, the *a priorist* and absolutist, there is a will which transcends the natural inclinations, and which imposes upon them the principle of loyalty to the "whole." This is his *a priorism*. The moral ideal is metaphysically enshrined; the world *is* eternally what its temporal and finite parts aspire to be. This is Royce's absolutism. James, on the other hand, is a utilitarian—in the broad sense of that term. Moral value is rooted in the natural desires of men. The good rests on the experience of interests and of the means or objects by which they find themselves satisfied. The maximum of satisfaction, the "richer universe," the "more inclusive order," "the *best whole*, in the sense of awakening the least sum of dissatisfactions," is a regulative principle of conduct, and its realization is a future possibility contingent on the success of the moral will. The real world contains this aspiration and struggle, and does not exclude its attainment in time. But for James even the highest moral truths are empirical and experimental. (pp. 34-5)

> *Ralph Barton Perry, in his* In the Spirit of William James, *Yale University Press, 1938, 211 p.*

RONALD B. LEVINSON   (essay date 1941)

[*In the following excerpt, Levinson suggests that James's ideas in his "Stream of Thought" chapter in* The Principles of Psychology *may serve as a key to the radical linguistic experiments of Gertrude Stein, who was a student of James in the 1890s.*]

Readers of Miss Stein's more difficult productions, from *Tender Buttons* to *Operas and Plays* and beyond, have had thrust upon their attention numberless grammatical peculiarities, ranging from the violation of the conventional rules of punctuation to the complete structural disintegration of the traditional form of the English sentence. Examples abound. We may take as typical of Miss Stein's triumphs over grammar the following congeries of vocables—I dare not say sentences—from "Lynn and the College de France."

> Mary River. Pleases. In Harvest. It. Or rather. He
>   arranges. With it.
> By. Them. Or whether. There is an interruption.
> In hurriedly. Looking. For. Their door. To them.
> The college of France. Has learned.
> And will. All. Seats of learning.
> Which they do. Having. Been fought.

It is not our problem to determine the precise meaning, if any, of the preceding cryptogram. Ours is the far easier objective of suggesting, from the point of view of Miss Stein's interest in language, and her theory of its use, a definite purpose underlying her radical breach with the grammar of her native tongue.

A few years ago it was skillfully argued by Professor B. F. Skinner, in an *Atlantic Monthly* article entiled "Has Gertrude Stein a Secret?" [see excerpt dated 1934 in *TCLC*-6], that nothing rising to the dignity of a purpose is involved in these esoteric utterances of Miss Stein's. On Mr. Skinner's view (and the reader will find the hypothesis by no means lacking in the necessary documentation) the true and only begetter of these verbal patterns is Miss Stein's right arm, operating automatically, as if it had learned to do in the Harvard psychology laboratory in the middle nineties, when its owner was a student of psychology at neighboring Radcliffe. Mr. Skinner does not believe that *Three Lives* or *The Autobiography of Alice B.*

Toklas was written in this automatic fashion. These he would allow to be the products of the integral personality of Miss Stein; but such books as *Portraits and Prayers* and *Operas and Plays* he regards as in great part the cold and unmeaning products of Miss Stein's unhappy faculty of disengaging from her central self an "elbow" with nothing significant to say and with no power to import interest into the saying of it.

It is farthest from my mind to attempt a refutation of Mr. Skinner's interesting and valuable thesis. I think, however, that his view may require modification in such a way as to take into the reckoning certain quite definite stylistic doctrines of Miss Stein's which are on the conscious level of her mind, and which she has perhaps attempted to exemplify in the kind of writing that is in question. Some of these doctrines, dealing with the subtler issues of literary composition, are expressed with a degree of clarity that is not altogether usual in her writing, in her *Narration*, and related pronouncements appear quite explicitly in the slightly earlier *Lectures in America*.

It is now my turn to offer a hypothesis, which we briefly state before supplying any of the evidence available for its support. My suggestion is that most if not all of Miss Stein's writing which resembles in form and content the early automatic writing, is the attempt to put into practice some notions of the ideal function of language, notions which were in all probability derived from the distinguished teacher of her Radcliffe days, William James.

James' interest in language was, naturally, subservient to an overarching interest in the larger problems of psychology and philosophy. One finds, scattered here and there throughout his writings, many pregnant comments upon the nature of language, and the inadequacy with which it performs its important function in human life. We shall quote some of the more memorable of these, particularly those occurring in his *Psychology,* published shortly before Miss Stein's student days. In the famous chapter, "The Stream of Thought," we hear him voicing a complaint against the fixed and unchangeable character of names, particularly as they occur in our English speech, and against the resulting injury to the adequacy of our vision of the world. "What, after all, is so natural as to assume that one object, called by one name, should be known by one affection of the mind? But if language must thus influence us, the agglutinative languages, and even Greek and Latin with their declensions, would be the better guides. Names did not appear in them inalterable, but changed their shape to suit the context in which they lay." ... A little later we are further warned against the over-simplification in which the verbal christening of our thoughts is so eminently apt to land us. "Here again language works against our perception of the truth. We name our thoughts simply, each after its thing, as if each knew its own thing and nothing else. What each really knows is clearly the thing it is named for, with dimly perhaps a thousand other things. It ought to be named after all of them, but it never is." ...

But the climactic passage, marked by James' full genius for expression at once precise and picturesque, arrives on page 243, with its memorable metaphor of "flights and perchings." "As we take ... a general view of the wonderful stream of our consciousness, what strikes us first is this different pace of its parts. Like a bird's life it seems to be made of an alternation of flights and perchings. The rhythm of language expresses this, where every thought is expressed in a sentence, and every sentence closed by a period. The resting places are usually occupied by sensorial imaginations of some sort ...

the places of flight are filled with thoughts of relations, static or dynamic, that for the most part obtain between the matters contemplated in the periods of comparative rest.'' We are presently told that the ''substantive parts'' of the stream of our consciousness, *i.e.* the *perches,* lord it over the ''transitive'' flights, a tyranny which language assists in making possible. ''We ought to say a feeling of *and,* a feeling of *if,* a feeling of *but,* and a feeling of *by,* quite as readily as we say a feeling of *blue* or a feeling of *cold.*'' The result, James tells us, is a psychic impoverishment in which ''all *dumb* or anonymous psychic states have . . . been coolly suppressed, or, if recognized at all, have been named after the substantive perception they led to, as thoughts 'about' this object or 'about' that, the stupid word *about* engulfing all their idiosyncrasies in its monotonous sound. Thus the greater and greater accentuation and isolation of the substantive parts have continually gone on.''

This same standpoint James restated and reënforced in some of his very latest writings, those collected under the title *Essays in Radical Empiricism.* It is here that he expounded his distinctive doctrine that relations ''conjunctive as well as the disjunctive'' are just as much ''matters of experience as the things themselves.'' On that hypothesis it is obvious that conjunctions, prepositions, *et id genus omne;* need no longer feel any ontological inferiority to substances and adjectives, their traditional overlords. It is a corollary to James' position here, though he does not explicitly draw it, that a sentence without conjunctions and so forth to indicate its relations to the rest of reality is as metaphysically deficient as one which, while quite explicit in its relationships, is lacking a definite *something* to be ''about.''

All of the criticisms of language which we have cited from James can be matched by explicit pronouncements of Miss Stein's. To these let us now turn, restricting attention to the close parallels in one of the earlier mentioned *Lectures in America,* viz. ''Poetry and Grammar.'' As we read along, the first arrow to strike the target of our interest is the question on page 209 (punctuation and spelling hers). ''Do you always have the same kind of feeling in relation to the sounds as the words come out of you or do you not. All this has so much to do with grammar and with poetry and with prose.'' This query leads directly into a discussion of those parts of speech favored by some other authors and those favored by Miss Stein. She is rather sniffy about nouns. ''A noun,'' she tells us, ''is a name of anything, why after a thing is named write about it. A name is adequate or it is not. If it is adequate then why go on calling it, if it is not then calling it by its name does no good. . . . Nouns are the names of anything and just naming names is alright when you want to call a roll but is it any good for anything else. . . . Slowly if you feel what is inside that thing you do not call it by the name by which it is known. Everybody knows that by the way they do when they are in love and a writer should always have that intensity of emotion about whatever is the object about which he writes. And therefore and I say it again more and more one does not use nouns.''

As a corollary to this proposition about nouns follows the condemnation of adjectives. These are condemned for the company that they keep: ''adjectives are not really and truly interesting . . . because after all adjectives effect (sic) nouns and . . . the thing that effects a not too interesting thing is of necessity not interesting.'' . . .

Now for the first time we get into grammatical good company,—we are introduced to verbs and adverbs! Among the virtues attributed to them is the truly Jamesian excellence that they move and change, thus manifesting their relative adequacy to the changeful ''stream of consciousness.'' We read on page 212: ''verbs can change to look like . . . something else, they are, so to speak on the move and adverbs move with them and each of them find themselves not at all annoying but very often very much mistaken. That is the reason anyone can like what verbs can do.''

We need not pursue Miss Stein through the whole of her whimsical revaluation of the parts of speech. It is necessary for our purpose, however, to note her curious exaltation of prepositions and conjunctions. Let us hear her speak: ''Prepositions can live one long life being really being nothing but absolutely nothing but mistaken . . . I like prepositions the best of all.'' . . . ''Beside that there are conjunctions, and a conjunction is not varied but it has a force that need not make anyone feel that they are dull. Conjunctions have made themselves live by their work. They work and as they work they live. . . . So you see why I like to write with prepositions and conjunctions and articles and verbs and adverbs but not with nouns and adjectives. If you read my writing you will you do see what I mean.'' . . .

It remains to ask, what is the general purport of these grammatical doctrines of Miss Stein's, and how closely do they conform to the earlier presented gospel of grammar according to William James? In general it would seem safe to say that Miss Stein is urging a program of linguistic usage which, though definitely outrunning James' demands—one suspects that James would have found some of its features not a little extravagant— is nevertheless founded upon a conception of the ''stream of consciousness'' quite similar to that of James. Her accent on the more fluid and moving elements in language (the verbs and adverbs), her corresponding depreciation of the static moveless noun, what is this but the counterpart of James' plea in behalf of the ''flights'' as against the linguistic predominance of the ''perchings.'' And perhaps the most striking, though by no means the most fundamental, point of parallelism between them is the prominence they both accord to conjunctions and prepositions, the often unappreciated parts of speech. It is perhaps not wholly fanciful to discern in this doctrine of verbal equality a remote variation upon the theme of sturdy American democracy which is characteristic alike of James' *A Pluralistic Universe* and of Miss Stein's *The Making of Americans.*

In conclusion, I would not insist upon the literal derivation of Miss Stein of her grammatical predilections from William James. On the other hand it is difficult not to suppose at least an initial arousal and some permanent direction of interest toward the philosophy of grammar, as having passed from the persuasive teacher to the girl whom he evaluated as the most brilliant of all his feminine students. The substantial result of our inquiry, however, remains independent of the question of source. From whatever quarter the wind of doctrine blew, it propelled Miss Stein toward an appreciation of the potential interest to the literary craftsman of the subtle issues, half psychologic, half philosophic, which turn upon the finer categoreal analysis of the creative word. It is this intellectual concern with linguistic experimentation, though one may quite deny the success of the experiments, which may supply a clue for distinguishing the products of Miss Stein's literary workshop from those early automatic fruits of the Harvard laboratory of Psychology. (pp. 124-28)

Ronald B. Levinson, ''Gertrude Stein, William James and Grammar,'' in The American Journal of Psychology, *Vol. LIX, No. 1, January, 1941, pp. 124-28.**

ALFRED KAZIN (essay date 1943)

[*A highly respected American literary critic, Kazin is best known
for his essay collections* The Inmost Leaf *(1955) and* Contemporaries *(1962), and particularly for* On Native Grounds *(1942),
a study of American prose writing since the era of William Dean
Howells. Having studied the works of "the critics who were the
best writers—from Sainte-Beuve and Matthew Arnold to Edmund
Wilson and Van Wyck Brooks" as an aid to his own critical
understanding, Kazin has found that "criticism focussed many—
if by no means all—of my own urges as a writer: to show literature
as a deed in human history, and to find in each writer the uniqueness of the gift, of the essential vision, through which I hoped to
penetrate into the mystery and sacredness of the individual soul."
In the following excerpt, Kazin offers a general appraisal of James
and compares his temperament and writing style to those of his
brother, the novelist Henry James. For another comparison of
the brothers William and Henry, see the excerpt by F. O. Matthiessen (1948).*]

To the merely bookish, who would rather intone their knowledge than be shaped by it; to the merely devout, who would
rather worship their God than be transformed by Him; to the
formal logicians and contented monists, for whom the world's
disorder and depths are so easily sacrificed, William James has
always seemed loose or even vulgar because he preached that
an idea has meaning only as it is expressed in action and
experience. That he was so misunderstood is partly James's
own fault, since he *would* speak of "the cash-value" of an
idea in his characteristic attempt to reach the minds even of
those for whom cash-value was the only value. But it is largely
the fault of ourselves and our personal culture, since the rarest
thing in it is still moral imagination. For what James was
leading to in his pragmatism—once it had served as a theory
of knowledge—was moral in the classic sense of conduct,
moral in the enduring sense of the order and use of a human
life. Tell me, he seemed always to be saying to those who
were so content with ideas rather than with thinking, with
metaphysics rather than with morality, what is it you *know,*
what is it that is changed in you or by you, when you have
achieved your certainty or knowledge? What is it you live by,
appreciably, when you have proved that something is true?
James knew well enough, and could formulate the ends and
satisfactions of his opponents better than many of them could;
but that was only incidental to his essential aim. Knowledge
is for men that they may live—and men may live for ideal
ends. So is the monist happy in his all-enveloping unity, the
rationalist in his ideal symmetry, the mystic in his visions.
And all of these exist, said James; all of these must be taken
into our account of the human experience and the demands of
our nature. But do not confuse, he went on, your individual
need of certainty with the illusion that some supra-human order
is ascertained by it; do not confuse your use of reason—and
delight in it—with the illusion that what cannot be named or
verified by rationalism does not exist.

To say this is not to forget how treacherous James's ideal of
the provisional can be, and that he is particularly dissatisfying
when he merely brings us to the borders of moral philosophy.
He triumphed by disproving all the cults and systems which
ignored the shaping power of man's individuality, by threshing
his way through pre-scientific myths and post-scientific arrogance. But like so many American naturalistic thinkers, he took
a certain necessary definition of the good life for granted (or
confused it with the Elysian fields of the Harvard Department
of Philosophy?); whereas it is the unrelenting consciousness
of it that is most lacking. Yet what is most important here is
that the great particular for him, as for all the Jameses, was

the human self, and that out of it they made all their universals
(though it is always a question what Henry's universals were).
For the elder James the center of existence was the self that
seeks to know God and to be sublimated in Him; William's
theory of knowledge began with the knowing mind that *initiates*
the ideas to which the test of experience is to be applied; Henry
found his technical—and moral—triumph in the central Jamesian intelligence which sifts the experiences of all the other
characters and organizes them.... [In] an age when all the
materials through which William was running so eagerly demanded large positive answers, wholesale reconstructions and
a world view, Henry had quietly and stubbornly reproduced
his father's mystical integrity in the integrity of the observing
self. The novel for him was to be *histoire orale,* a branch of
history that sought the close textures and hidden lights of painting; but the highest morality was not so much in the story as
in the exercise of the creative principle behind it.

That devotion to a creative principle was the great epic of
Henry's integrity, as everything he ever sought or wrote was
a commentary on it. In most writers their works exemplify
their ambition; Henry's were about his ambition, as they were,
in one sense, only his ambition written large. Just as William's
vision always came back to a loose sea of empiricism in which
man could hold on only to himself, so Henry's was to define
and to fill out the moral history of composition. His theory of
art was not preparatory to a manipulation of experience; it *was*
his experience. His interest was fixed on writing about the
symbolic devotion of writing, as so many of his stories were
of writers (but only of depressed or unsuccessful writers: there
was no "dramatic process" in the surface of success). And
the central Jamesian intelligence, in all his disguises as "the
foreground observer," "the center of revelation," the artist
planning his effects, the critic "remounting the stream of composition," was always sifting and commenting in turn. "The
private history of any sincere work," he wrote once, "looms
large with its own completeness"; it was his symbol of man's
completeness. He studied his novels endlessly as he wrote
them, corrected them endlessly when they were published,
wrote a preface to each in which he summarized the history
of its composition, defined his every intent and use of means,
speculated on the general principles they illustrated, and at the
end, as he hinted to Grace Norton, might have written a preface
to the prefaces, commenting on *them* in turn. Secretions within
secretions, knowingness within knowingness: out of so self-
driven an integrity, as out of the intense interior life of his
characters, there could be grasped the central fact of the effort,
the search, the aura of devotion, that gave meaning to the
artist's life and form to his work. And always the thread remained firmly in the artist's hand, pulling it back to himself—
the story of Henry James was the story of Henry James writing
his novels.

Life for both always returned to the central self. Significantly,
it was always the richness of their personal nature that distinguished all the Jameses, and the overflow of life in them that
gave them their vascular styles. Ralph Barton Perry says of
the elder James that he felt his visions so intensely, and had
so many together, that he had to get them all out at once. The
elder James was always running over, laughing at himself for
it, and never stopped running over. Like William, he had so
many possible thoughts about so many things; and he had the
James exuberance (the seed *was* Irish) that always ran so high
in them despite the unending family history of illness. Superficially, of course, no two styles would seem to be so different
as William's and Henry's: the one so careful to be spontaneous,

the other so spontaneously labored; the one so informal in its wisdom, flinging witticisms, philosophical jargon, homeliness and hearty German abstractions about with a seeming care-lessness, protesting doubt at every point, yet probing with angelic friendliness in all the blocks of the human mind; the other so *made* a style, solemnly and deliciously musical, re-verberating with all the tones of all the books Henry had ever read, forever sliding into cozy French idioms, shyly offering the commonest spoken expressions in quotation marks—Henry always sought to be friendly. Yet both were great spoken styles, intimate and with an immense range of tone: the only difference being that William talked to friendly Harvard seniors and Henry later dictated to his secretary. What no one has ever said enough about Henry's style, of course, is that it was the family style become molten: like all the Jameses, he wrote instinctively out of his amplitude. He gushed in his letters and he purred in his novels, but there was always the James motor power behind him, their terrible need to seize and define everything within their range. And more, there was that "blague and benignity" in his style that Ezra Pound caught: the tricky interior changes of pace, the slow mandarin whisperings, the adjectives that opened all vistas for him like great bronze doors, the extaor-dinary *soundings* he could make with words, and covering them all, always his deceiving gentleness, the ceremonial diffidence, and his sudden barbs and winks.

To think of their styles is to be aware of the great innocence that was in all the Jameses, an innocence of personal spirit if not of moral perception. Financially secure, encouraged by their father to be different and uncontrolled, even to be without a profession, both ranged at will in what was still the household age of modern thought—a period when the security of their society encouraged those first studies in the naturalism of the psyche, and a voracious interior life. The only revolution either could envison was in new ways of knowing; and it is significant that William led the way to "the stream of consciousness." They all had the natural outpouring that came with innocence, the innocence that trusted in all the data of their inquiry, took the social forms for granted, and based life upon the integrity of the observing self. "In self-trust are all the virtues com-prehended." It was the Emersonian faith of their culture, in all its genteelism and instinctive trust in individuality. Just as the elder James's theology committed man, as it were, to be a recording angel, to seek the necessary revelation and inscribe it, so they were all recording angels, much as William said of Henry that under all his "rich sea-weeds" and "rigid barnacles and things" he cared only for making novels. Life was here and now, in all that system of relations between minds in which experience immediately consists; man *studied* it. The highest aim, somehow, was to be an author. But there is no very great sense of tragedy in any of them (compare them with the Ad-amses), no sense of that world process which is something more than William's metaphysical novelty and pluralism; the great depths of life are not in them.

In a time like our own, when men are so lost in themselves because they are so lost from each other, the Jamesian integrity can seem small comfort to us. We can take no social form for granted; we cannot possess or be possessed by those explo-rations in human consciousness which only parallel—or at best reveal—our quest for security. To say this is not to make a judgment on the Jameses, but to define our predicament. Our enforced sense of evil has nothing so creative in it as their innocence; and their legacy is still most precious for its sym-bolic integrity, its trust in mind, its superiority to our "failure of nerve." Even Henry James's greatest contributions to human

pleasure and self-comprehension, or his insistence on the in-tegrity of a work of art, are less important now than the emblem his pride raises before us. Even William's full devotion to realism, his imaginative projection of complexity, are less im-portant to us now than the respect he breeds in us for all the forms of reality and our necessary understanding of them. And it is this which is now most visible in them and most important to us: the simplicity of their respect for life and the intensity of their elucidation of it. They both worked in that period of modern history when the trust of man in his power to know was at its highest, when the revolution of modern political democracy, science and materialism carried along even those who were skeptical of the idea of progress. And if we feel at times that they are even greater than their thought, more far-ranging than the forms that contain them, it is because they burned with that indestructible zeal which we need so badly to recover—the zeal that cannot blind men to illusion, but must always rise above it, the zeal that cries that life does have a meaning: we seek to know. (pp. 216-18)

Alfred Kazin, "'Our Passion Is Our Task'," in The New Republic, *Vol. 108, No. 7, February 15, 1943, pp. 215-18.**

F. O. MATTHIESSEN (essay date 1948)

[*Matthiessen was an American educator and literary critic whose major studies examine American writers and intellectual move-ments. As a critic, Matthiessen believed that the examination of a given work of literature must also consider the social and his-torical context of that work. Concerning his study of American literature, Matthiessen stated: "I wanted to place our master-works in their cultural setting, but beyond that I wanted to discern what constituted the lasting value of these books as works of art." Matthiessen's works include* American Renaissance *(1941) and* Henry James: The Major Phase *(1944). In the following excerpt from his* The James Family, *Matthiessen compares the intellec-tual, artistic, and moral values of James with those of his brother, the novelist Henry James. Matthiessen illustrates the various di-vergences between them by viewing William as a romantic and Henry as a classicist. For another comparison of William and Henry James, see the excerpt by Alfred Kazin (1943).*]

"There is very little difference between one man and another," said WJ [William James], "but what little there is, *is very important.*" After contemplating all the divergences between the brothers' minds, the reader might well conclude that, on the contrary, the differences between these two men, born hardly more than a year apart, and exposed to the same en-vironment and to the same educational theory, were astonish-ingly great. All their other discrepancies in thought and ex-pression would seem to stem back to their contrasting conceptions of knowledge, since the knower as actor and the knower as spectator are bound to behold different worlds, and to shape them to different ends.

It will not do, however, to array WJ and HJ [Henry James] on opposite sides of their father's antithesis between *doing* and *being,* since Henry Senior's *being,* unlike Henry Junior's, was dynamic rather than static. The pattern of relationship is further complicated by HJ's kind of detachment and WJ's kind of immersion. The one led to aesthetic contemplation as the pri-mary mode of experience, the other to a view of life as an ethical proving ground for the will, where aesthetic standards were always subordinate. Here in particular the father would have found himself divided between his sons. His subordination of "moral" to "spiritual" put him on the side of contempla-tion, but his was the contemplation of the religious seer, not that of the artist. And when his attention was engaged with this world, Henry Senior had none of Henry Junior's aristocratic preferences; he was a more convinced equalitarian democrat even than WJ. Once again the basic differences are between modes of truth. For Henry Senior, truth was revelation, not something absorbed through the eyes and intelligence as it was for HJ, nor something made out of struggle as it was for WJ.

On such differences the changes could be rung indefinitely, and, as with other change-ringing, shortly to the point of stultification. But one other definition of the fundamental contrast between WJ and HJ is worth advancing, since it was first advanced by Santayana in his epoch-making formulation of "The Genteel Tradition in American Philosophy." Writing the year after WJ's death, his main point was the wide separation, from the time of Calvinism through that of transcendentalism, between the American mind and American experience, between the abstract intellect, pure and rarified, and the actual operative sphere of the pioneering will, aggressive and often brutal. Santayana cited Whitman as the one American writer who had "left the genteel tradition entirely behind." He instanced the James brothers as being "as tightly swaddled in the genteel tradition as any infant geniuses could be, for they were born before 1850, and in a Swedenborgian household. Yet they burst those bands almost entirely. The ways in which the two brothers freed themselves, however, are interestingly different. Mr. Henry James has done it by adopting the point of view of the outer world, and by turning the genteel American tradition, as he turns everything else, into a subject-matter for analysis. For him it is a curious habit of mind, intimately comprehended, to be compared with other habits of mind, also well known to him. Thus he has overcome the genteel tradition in the classic way, by understanding it. With William James too this infusion of worldly insight and European sympathies was a potent influence, especially in his earlier days; but the chief source of his liberty was another. It was his personal spontaneity, similar to that of Emerson, and his personal vitality, similar to that of nobody else. Convictions and ideas came to him, so to speak, from the subsoil. He had a prophetic sympathy with the dawning sentiments of the age, with the moods of the dumb majority. His scattered words caught fire in many parts of the world. His way of thinking and feeling represented the true America, and represented in a measure the whole ultra-modern, radical world. Thus he eluded the genteel tradition in the romantic way, by continuing it into its opposite."

There are many senses in which HJ is not a classicist and WJ is not a romantic, and these catch-all terms, almost exhausted of meaning by a century of hair-splitting conflict, are usually best excluded now from any critical discourse. But as Santayana employed them, they serve to distinguish the characteristic attitudes and productions of the brothers. WJ, to be sure, attacked the German romantic philosophers, and his radical empiricism held that experience was neither exclusively subjective, nor exclusively objective. But, as he announced in one introduction to his uncompleted metaphysics, "I prefer to start upon this work romantically"—that is to say, without formal justification, and in the mood of taking the open road to see where it would lead him. That had been the prevailing mood of his career, kindled by the animation and gusto of the intense individualist who was confident that what he found on the road would be worth finding. His delight in believing that Bergson had killed intellectualism was symptomatic of how he "continued the genteel tradition into its opposite." WJ escaped from

abstract thought by embedding thought in life, but, to the eyes of a more deliberate philosopher like Santayana, he also escaped from any exact processes of thought into the more exciting but confused realm of the fervent pragmatic will.

HJ too was romantic in his nostalgia for distant joys, in his attribution of so much glamour to the "otherness" of Europe. If he was classic in his desire for comprehension, in his belief that literature is "our sum of intelligent life," any strict classicist might take exception to his analysis of the inner life as disproportionate, and to the length of his forms as excessive. Yet HJ might seem to be giving his own version of Aristotle's dictum that form "is all of the boat that is not the wood" by saying that form "is substance to that degree that there is absolutely no substance without it." And as an artist he was on the side of the classic craftsman, the trainer of talent, against the romantic genius of prophetic inspiration. He was the objective practitioner, finding his subjects outside himself and regarding them as technical problems to be solved. When we hear him saying, in relation to *The Ambassadors*, that "One's work should have composition because composition alone is positive beauty.," we have reached the ground on which his work stands farthest from WJ's. For WJ's taste was for the unfinished and unformed as sources of further potentiality. (pp. 673-75)

The chief reason why HJ is capable of compelling our attention, despite the remoteness of his world from our own, is elucidated in his parable of the relation between the subject, the form, and the artist. "The house of fiction," he wrote in his preface to *The Portrait of a Lady*, "has not one window but a million." He then proceeded to expand this image and to drive its meaning home. At each of these windows hanging over the human scene "stands a figure with a pair of eyes. . . . He and his neighbours are watching the same show, but one seeing more where the other sees less, one seeing black where the other sees white, one seeing big where the other sees small, one seeing coarse where the other sees fine. And so on, and so on; there is fortunately no saying on what, for the particular pair of eyes, the window may *not* open; 'fortunately' by reason, precisely, of this incalculability of range. The spreading field, the human scene, is the 'choice of subject'; the pierced aperture, either broad or balconied or slit-like and low-browed, is the 'literary form'; but they are, singly or together, as nothing without the posted presence of the watcher—without, in other words, the consciousness of the artist. Tell me what the artist is, and I will tell you of what he has *been* conscious. Thereby I shall express to you at once his boundless freedom and his 'moral' reference."

That is the kind of talk, we are quickly reminded, to which WJ always kindled. Many of his sentences would fit directly into HJ's parable: for instance, the one about its being "the amount of life which a man feels that makes you value his mind"; or "a thing is important if anyone *think* it important"; or the one affirming that every philosopher worthy of the name must proceed from "a bias and a logic of his own." Only that last phrase happens to come from the preface to "The Figure in the Carpet" and to refer not to a philosopher but to an artist.

We are aware again, therefore, that no matter how wide the divergence between the directions taken by these brothers' minds, or between the curves of their reputations, they are held together by a solid core of values. Their kinship becomes even more striking when we recall the reasons HJ gave for using the symbol of the complex design in a Perisan rug to reinforce his plea for analytic appreciation. He was bent on making the point that you could not understand an artist's work if you approached it merely from outside. You had to enter imaginatively into its pattern as a whole, into the "special beauty" that "pervades and controls and animates it." This is not "the 'esoteric meaning,' as the newspapers say; it's the *only* meaning, it's the very soul . . . of the work."

Isn't this exactly the same plea that WJ made in *A Pluralistic Universe*? "Place yourself . . . at the center of a man's philosophic vision and you understand at once all the different things it makes him write or say. But keep outside, use your post-mortem method, try to build the philosophy up out of the single phrases, taking first one and then another and seeking to make them fit, and of course you fail. You crawl over the thing like a myopic ant over a building, tumbling into every microscopic crack or fissure, finding nothing but inconsistencies, and never suspecting that a centre exists."

Both brothers thus insist not only upon the necessity of having a point of view, but also upon the willingness to stand sympathetically inside other points of view. It was most natural for both of them to speak in terms of seeing, since, as we have noted again and again, both lived by their eyes. Both therefore took delight in introducing into their writing their fullest resources of visual imagery. The art of fiction allowed HJ to develop his pictorial gifts to greater lengths, but WJ, in the most extended image he permitted himself, writes as though for once he might be vying with HJ's breath-taking elabora-

tions. WJ wanted, in the exposition of his "Radical Empiricism," to instance the essential plurality of experience, how reality "is neither absolutely one nor absolutely many, but a stream whose parts coalesce where they touch," and then inevitably diverge. He made this conception as concrete as possible:

"*Prima facie*, if you should liken the universe of absolute idealism to an aquarium, a crystal globe in which goldfish are swimming, you would have to compare the empiricist universe to something more like one of those dried human heads with which the Dyaks of Borneo deck their lodges. The skull forms a solid nucleus; but innumerable feathers, leaves, strings, beads, and loose appendices of every description float and dangle from it, and, save that they terminate in it, seem to have nothing to do with one another. Even so my experiences and yours float and dangle, terminating, it is true, in a nucleus of common perception, but for the most part out of sight and irrelevant and unimaginable to one another."

The suspicion that WJ may have had HJ in mind is caused by the fact that, in all three of his late major novels, HJ had likened his social group to fishes held together "in a fathomless medium." Merton Densher had reflected, at the moment of Milly Theale's appearance in the Venetian palace, on how she seemed to "diffuse in wide warm waves the spell of a general, a beatific mildness. There was a deeper depth of it, doubtless, for some than for others; what he in particular knew of it was that he

Henry and William James. The Bettmann Archive, Inc.

seemed to stand in it up to his neck. He moved about in it and it made no plash; he floated, he noiselessly swam in it, and they were all together, for that matter, like fishes in a crystal pool.'' Such a comparison is ambivalent, since Densher also feels that he is ''immersed in an element more strangely than agreeably warm.'' He feels himself caught up, as does Strether somewhat less and Maggie Verver even more, in a densely involved and slowly circulating situation, all inescapably exposed to the observing eye.

To WJ such a world was far too static, far too attenuated in its aesthetic essences, for him to enter into it with much sympathy or even understanding. Though it is not likely that WJ was consciously directing his whole argument here against HJ, whom he would not have identified with ''absolute idealism'' or, indeed, with any strict philosophical position, nevertheless his image illustrates the essential relationship between them. For if many of HJ's phases were ''unimaginable'' to WJ, their minds came together in ''a nucleus of common perception.'' (pp. 679-81)

> F. O. Matthiessen, ''William James and Henry James,'' in his The James Family, Alfred A. Knopf, 1948, pp. 673-84.*

GAIL KENNEDY   (lecture date 1956)

[*Kennedy was an American educator and philosopher who taught at Amherst College. In the following excerpt, he reconsiders a longstanding controversy regarding James's conception of the will to believe, specifically the distinction between this doctrine and that of the ''right to believe.'' Kennedy explains that making this distinction clarifies the theoretical conflicts between James's philosophy Pragmatism and the similar philosophies of Charles Sanders Peirce and John Dewey. He also answers objections to* ''The Will to Believe,'' *such as those presented in the excerpts by Dickinson S. Miller (1899) and George Santayana (1920). For similar views of* ''The Will to Believe,'' *see the excerpts by F.C.S. Schiller (1897) and William Barrett (1975). For commentary by Peirce and Dewey on James's works, see the excerpts dated 1891 and 1916.*]

Peirce and Dewey were mistaken in regarding James's criteria of ''satisfaction'' as inconsistent with their own theories of truth, and also were mistaken in thinking James's essay, **''The Will to Believe,''** an attempt to justify attitudes of the sort which Peirce had described under the rubrics of ''tenacity,'' ''authority,'' and ''reasonableness.'' This error results from their failure to distinguish between two doctrines both of which James held: (1) the ''right to believe''—that under certain conditions belief in advance of all the evidence is justifiable and (2) the ''will to believe''—that under certain conditions a belief, i.e., a readiness to act, may be a factor in bringing about consequences different from those which otherwise occur. (p. 578)

[In **''The Will to Believe''**] James asserts two different propositions, not kept as distinct as they might have been either by him in that essay nor by his critics. The first is concerned with what should be called the ''right to believe'': it is, that under certain conditions one is entitled to believe in the existence of a fact in advance of having complete evidence. James says that this is the case where one is faced by an option not decidable on ''objective'' grounds alone which is live, forced, and momentous,—but obviously, in actual practice a right to believe is presumed, of necessity, far more extensively than these limitations would warrant. The second is concerned with what properly should be called the ''will to believe'': it is, that there

are certain cases where the belief in the future existence of a fact may itself help to produce that fact. As James puts it, there are ''cases where faith creates its own verification.'' The first of these propositions is the only one which is disputable. The second is a question of psychological fact which in any given instance may be true or false. Surely there *are* cases where belief in the possibility of a future fact may help to bring about the existence of that fact. For example, to enter into a marriage believing that it can be made a permanently successful union may well help to make it so.

James's conclusion for both cases is that when alternative beliefs are under consideration we have, within his stated conditions, a *right* to believe and act on the more *rational*, i.e., the belief which best meets the demands of our *whole* nature, intellectual, emotional and practical. ''Pretend what we may,'' he cries, ''the whole man within us is at work when we form our philosophical opinions. Intellect, will, taste, and passion cooperate just as they do in practical affairs; and lucky it is if the passion be not something as petty as a love of personal conquest over the philosopher across the way.''

The doctrine James expressed so eloquently in this volume aroused a controversy in which the right to believe and the will to believe were sadly confused. The first proposition refers to the ethics of belief, but the second asserts a possible fact. The right to believe may be legitimate in cases where no will to believe is involved, while where a will to believe *is* involved there is an *additional* reason for having a right to believe. The two last steps in James's faith ladder are:

> It shall be *held for true,* you decide; it *shall be* as if true, for *you.*

> And your acting thus may in certain special cases be a means of making it securely true in the end.

The first of these statements is an assertion of the right to believe, the second of the will to believe. Some critics, however, not noticing the difference, accused James of advocating a ''will to make-believe.'' This misunderstanding of James's thesis was subsequently read into his pragmatic theory of truth. (pp. 579-80)

The right to believe and James's subsequent pragmatism cannot be separated. In addition, the *will* to believe implies a world of real possibilities, one in which the future is in part indeterminate, and that some of these possibilities depend upon ourselves. So far as reality is indeterminate, ''truth'' must be so likewise. There is no prior absolute Truth; there are only truths in the plural. Our beliefs *become* true and we can in some degree make them come true. And so, when James later applies his pragmatic method to determine the meaning of the notion of ''truth'' itself, this is the result:

> The moment pragmatism asks this question, it sees the answer: True ideas are those that we can assimilate, validate, corroborate and verify. False ideas are those that we can not. That is the practical difference it makes to us to have true ideas; that, therefore, is the meaning of truth, for it is all that truth is known as.

For James, then, what is true is not *simply* whatever happens to satisfy a narrowly cognitive interest, but whatever works in the large and on the whole. The ''true'' is whatever is *right* in the way of belief. (pp. 581-82)

Here, apparently, is something different indeed from the original statement of pragmatism in Peirce's essay, "How to Make Our Ideas Clear" (1878). Both Peirce and Dewey thought so, and both rejected James's formulation of the doctrine. The disagreement about pragmatism as a theory of meaning and of truth stems, of course, from the opposition of their interests and backgrounds. Peirce had developed his pragmatism from studies of logic and scientific method under the influence of the scholastics and of Kant. James came to his formulation of pragmatism from the opposite direction, the study of psychology under the influence of the British empiricists and of Renouvier. And John Dewey arrived at his version of the doctrine—"instrumentalism" as he called it—from still a third starting point, that of neo-Hegelian idealism, partly through the influence first of James, the James of the *Psychology,* and later of Peirce. It is remarkable enough that, arising from such different backgrounds of interests and knowledge, their eventual positions so nearly converged; it is hardly surprising that they did not entirely coincide.

Peirce and Dewey were acutely conscious of the crucial ambiguity well expressed by A. E. Lovejoy's question: "Does the meaning of a proposition consist wholly in the future consequences predicted by it whether it is believed or not, or in the future consequences of believing it?" Both felt the barb in Josiah Royce's comment, "When a Jamesian pragmatist takes an oath what he should say is 'I promise to tell whatever is expedient and nothing but what is expedient, so help me future experience.'"

Peirce had disassociated his views from those of James before the book, *Pragmatism,* appeared. In an article entitled "Pragmatic and Pragmatism" written for Baldwin's *Dictionary of Philosophy and Psychology* (1902), he said:

> In 1896 William James published his *Will to Believe,* and later his *Philosophical Conceptions and Practical Results,* which pushed this method to such extremes as must tend to give us pause. The doctrine appears to assume that the end of man is action—a stoical axiom which, to the present writer at the age of sixty, does not recommend itself so forcibly as it did at thirty. If it be admitted, on the contrary, that action wants an end, and that that end must be something of a general description, then the spirit of the maxim itself, which is that we must look to the upshot of our concepts in order rightly to apprehend them, would direct us towards something different from practical facts, namely, to general ideas, as the true interpreters of our thought.

And in a subsequent article, "What Pragmatism Is," he added that the term knowing had now come to have a meaning "it was rather designed to exclude. So then, the writer, finding his bantling 'pragmatism' so promoted, feels that it is time to kiss his child good-by and relinquish it to its higher destiny; while to serve the precise purpose of expressing the original definition, he begs to announce the birth of the word 'pragmaticism,' which is ugly enough to be safe from kidnappers." Henceforth, Peirce always used the term pragmaticism to denote his own conception of the doctrine.

Dewey in an extended review of James's book *Pragmatism* tried to resolve the ambiguity which disturbed the critics. At times, he says, James "recognizes unequivocally" that only

> consequences which are actually produced by the working of the idea in cooperation with, or application to, prior existences are good consequences in the specific sense of good which is relevant to establishing the truth of an idea. . . . But at other times any good which flows from acceptance of a belief is treated as if it were an evidence, *in so far,* of the truth of the idea. This holds particularly when theological notions are under consideration.

James had fallen into this inconsistency, Dewey thinks, because he seems to be asserting "that since true ideas are good, any idea if good in any way is true." Dewey himself insists, along with Peirce, that no "satisfaction" is relevant to the truth of an idea "save *that* satisfaction which arises when the idea as working hypothesis or tentative method is applied to prior existences in such a way as to fulfill what it intends."

With this contention of Dewey's James really agreed. In a letter to Horace Kallen (1907) James says:

> As regards the "Will to Believe" matter, it should not complicate the question of what we mean by truth. Truth is constituted by verification actual or possible, and beliefs, *however* reached, have to be verified before they can count as true. The question whether we have a right to believe anything before verification concerns not the constitution of truth, but the policy of belief.

But this does not clear the matter up. The real question is, what are those relevant satisfactions? Writing to Ralph Barton Perry about an article by Perry, James gives his answer to this question:

> You speak, . . . as if the "degree of satisfaction" was *exclusive* of theoretic satisfactions. Who ever said or implied this? Surely neither Dewey, Schiller nor I have ever denied that sensation, relation, and funded truth "dispose," in their measure, of what we "propose." Nothing that we propose can violate them; but, *they satisfied;* what in addition gratifies our aesthetic or utilitarian demands best will always be counted as *more* true. My position is that, *other things equal,* emotional satisfactions count for truth—among the other things being the intellectual satisfactions. Certainly a doctrine that encourages immortality would draw belief more than one that didn't, if it were *exactly as satisfactory* in residual respects. Of course it couldn't prevail against knock-down evidence to the contrary; but where there is no such evidence, it will incline belief. And how can truth be *known* save as that which inclines belief?

Granted that James's language is often loose and ambiguous, are his conceptions of meaning and of truth so likewise? Were not Peirce and Dewey wrong in regarding James's criteria of "satisfaction" as inconsistent with their own theories of truth? Were they not also mistaken in thinking James's essay, **"The Will to Believe,"** an attempt to justify attitudes of the sort which Peirce had described in his essay, "The Fixation of Belief" (1877), under the rubrics of "tenacity," "authority," and "reasonableness"? And, if this is the case, does not their error result from a failure to distinguish between the two doctrines of the "right to believe" and "will to believe"? The first of these, the right to believe, is undeniably present in some degree or other wherever one must act upon insufficient evidence,—and this is the case with a great many practical decisions. Even the decision to undertake an arduous and expensive program of scientific experiments when it is not certain that these experiments will yield significant results can be an instance of the right to believe.

Now what James meant by the will to believe is not even mentioned in Peirce's essay. Peirce there discusses belief as the progressively forced adaptation of a wilful subject's propensities to an external reality. His argument is an explication of Spencer's thesis, the adjustment of inner to outer relations. What Peirce ignores in this paper is that, since experience is an *interaction* of organism and environment, his own doctrine of habit requires the interaction to be a two-way affair. Peirce, and Dewey also, would in fact agree with James as against Spencer that the person's activity can make a difference in those events which are the product of the interaction of the person with his environment. It is a question of fact as to what these differences are. And it would be difficult to deny that as a matter of fact in such practical affairs as participation in a common enterprise, being the member of an athletic team or entering into a marriage, the kind and degree of one's commitment does make a difference in what ensues. This is *not* to subscribe to the vulgar success formula, that "the power of positive thinking" can achieve miracles.

If the belief attitude of a person does in certain situations affect the consequences which ensue within that situation, then it will also be the case that a part of the *meaning* of the concepts which express this attitude are those consequences which are conceived to follow from that attitude. Peirce's definition of meaning is: "Consider what effects, that might conceivably have practical bearings, we conceive the object of our conception to have. Then, our conception of these effects is the whole of our conception of the object." But when we consider what can be meant by "practical bearings," it is clear that an interaction of the knower with the known is involved. Hence, there are *two* sorts of "conceivable effects": *(a)* acting on the simple belief that certain effects will occur; *(b)* acting on the belief that certain effects will occur *and* that a part of these effects can occur only as a result of the belief in the possibility of their occurrence. To Peirce's definition James would therefore add: *If a part of these conceivable consequences is dependent upon the belief, the particular sort of readiness to act, of the person, then the verification of the hypothesis here involved, which refers to the total predicted effects of the intended act, will include the "satisfaction" of having the belief in the possibility of those consequences realized.* This is what James meant by "satisfaction." Though his imprecision of language warrants the mistake, James's criteria of verification were not, as Peirce and Dewey supposed, hopelessly loose and ambiguous. (pp. 582-85)

Peirce and Dewey were trying to formulate a theory of meaning and of truth which looked to the model of disinterested scientific inquiry. James was concerned with concrete exigencies, the either-or decisions which are forced upon us, whereas Peirce and Dewey were thinking of the long-run consequences which would follow from repeated trials of a given hypothesis. It was their interest in the "standard observer" which led Peirce and Dewey to misunderstand James. James did not intend to alter Peirce's criteria of verification, he merely intended to extend their application. In doing so he was adhering to the view all three held, that experiencing, including the kind called processes of inquiry, is a two-way interaction of organism with environment as against Spencer's one-way "adaptation of inner to outer relations." In some instances, because of the nature of the problem, the subjective component will be more important than in others: one might then place opinions on a distribution curve as ranging from most to least affected by the subjective factor. In making James's extension there is no need, however, to alter the *method*. The difference is that Peirce and Dewey were interested in opinions on one side of the curve and James in those on the other. In consequence, they overlooked the fact that in the sphere of moral and practical affairs the subjective component is not irrelevant or a hindrance but an essential constituent of the situation within which the verificatory processes occurs. The "pragmatism" of James is not incompatible with Peirce's "pragmaticism" and Dewey's "instrumentalism." Each is appropriate for the sort of experience to which it should refer. (pp. 587-88)

Gail Kennedy, "Pragmatism, Pragmaticism, and the Will to Believe—A Reconsideration," in The Journal of Philosophy, *Vol. LV, No. 14, July 3, 1958, pp. 578-88.*

BRUCE WILSHIRE   (essay date 1968)

[*Wilshire is an American educator and philosopher whose works include* Romanticism and Evolution *(1968) and* Metaphysics: An Introduction to Philosophy *(1969). His* William James and Phenomenology, *from which the following excerpt is taken, represents one of the most important directions in modern Jamesian scholarship. After summarizing the views associated with the philosophical school of phenomenology, Wilshire discusses in what way James's* The Principles of Psychology *prefigured these views. For further study of the relationship between James and phenomenology, see the entries in the Additional Bibliography by Hans Linschoten and John Wild. For earlier views of* The Principles of Psychology, *see the excerpts by James Mark Baldwin (1891) and Charles Sanders Peirce (1891).*]

The central thesis of phenomenology is that the world is comprehensible only in terms of its modes of appearance to mind, and that mind cannot be conceived independently of the world which appears to it. Hence, despite Edmund Husserl's aversion to the word metaphysics, the phenomenological thesis generates implications concerning the structure of reality, and must be considered an outgrowth in the broadest sense of Kant's new metaphysics of experience. It is not that the world exists only in the mind, but that the world can be specified only in terms of what it appears to be to mind. Hence, as well, the phenomenological thesis generates a philosophy of mind: the relationship of mind to world is necessary and internal. Truths about the relationship are necessary and nonempirical and the discipline which discovers them is a nonempirical one. Mind cannot be conceived independently of the world which appears to it. Any phenomenological psychology derives from this fundamental philosophical background.

Probably more has been written about William James than about any other American philosopher. Thus it is startling that his pioneering work in phenomenology and his influence on Husserl went without proper notice for seventy years and has only just recently gained recognition. Husserl's own acknowledgment of James's influence is particularly revealing. He read the bulk of *The Principles of Psychology* in the 1890's and wrote, in 1900, that James's psychology had helped him find his way out of psychologism. This confining view held that since thought is a psychical activity, thought's object or what thought is about must be subject to psychological laws. Because all subject-matter areas are composed of objects-thought-about, psychologism held that psychology is the ultimate discipline.

No better initial stroke to sketch James's phenomenological psychology can be imagined than this admission by Husserl that James helped him overcome psychologism. The central thesis of a phenomenological psychology is that mind and thoughts cannot be conceived independently of the world which appears to mind, and that this phenomenal world can be conceived only through a philosophical investigation of the world's own structures (in Husserl's parlance, essences) as revealed to mind. For example, material objects and formal objects like numbers fall into different regional ontologies; if thought's objects are numbers, say, then at some point in the elucidation of the *thought* a mathematician will have to be called in, not just a psychologist. Although the object belongs to thought and thought is psychical, still the object of thought cannot be given an elucidation that is exclusively psychological. Hence psychology is derivative, not ultimate.

To be sure, modes of being are linked with modes of being presented to mind, but this linkage is not an external, contingent, or causal relationship (not merely factual), hence it cannot be the subject matter of any particular empirical science, e.g., psychology. The linkage is internal—exclusively conceptual. Truths about it are necessary in virtue of their very meaning, and it is apprehended by what Husserl calls a transcendental investigation.

Immanuel Kant first introduced the phrase transcendental exposition, by which he meant the demonstration of the necessary truth of conceptions or principles of judgment through the demonstration that other necessary truths, already in hand, are impossible without the presupposition of the conceptions or principles of judgment in question. What we begin with is actual; therefore that which makes it possible must be the case. The idea was adopted by Husserl and modified in line with his belief that essences (what some might call concepts) and connections of essences comprising necessary truths are *intuited* or seen in some sense. Kant had limited intuition to sensations. By pure phenomenology Husserl means transcendental phenomenology: an exposition of what must be the case in the way of essence if that which is actual in the way of phenomena is to be shown to be possible or intelligible. Husserl's goal is the intuition of necessary truths which lie at the foundation of knowledge. For example, we intuit this: that it is possible for a solid to present itself as a solid in the most fleeting of glimpses only because it is part of the essence of solid (of what we mean by "solid") that it be presented perspectively and incompletely to any given glance. Presuppositions of this sort, says Husserl, are grasped only in a transcendental or reversed method of investigation which goes against the natural empirical grain of the mind.

Indeed, the purpose of Husserl's famous "bracket" is to force investigations into the transcendental channel: to constrain us to give up the question, So we know this fact; now what other facts can we go on to know? and to ask instead, So we know what we take to be this fact; now how is this taking or intending—this *meaning*—possible? The procedure is comparable to Oxford philosophers' throwing language "out of gear." Their purpose in mentioning terms instead of using them and in working on concepts instead of with them is to grasp something about uses and concepts not graspable otherwise—their

inherent structures—which includes necessary connections between them.

Now I think that William James's *Principles of Psychology* is one of the best justifications for phenomenological psychology, and I think that Husserl's interest in the book is completely understandable. But it is a strange and often inconsistent work, all fourteen hundred pages of it. It justifies phenomenological psychology as much negatively as it does positively: both the pitfalls of departing from a phenomenological approach and the advantages of hewing to it are exhibited. James's program for the book calls for an autonomous, natural scientific psychology, replete with external, causal, and contingent relationships, and it acknowledges no special difficulty in describing and specifying mind or mental states. But as James progresses it gradually becomes clear that he cannot even begin to talk meaningfully about mental states unless he talks about them in conjunction with the world which appears to them; it becomes clear that he is caught in the phenomenological assumption concerning the mind-world relationship: that it is internal and noncontingent. It is thus absurd for him to talk of brain states causing mental states, as his program demands, before he knows what mental states are. We learn as much from the reversal of his program as we do from his phenomenological insights which occasion the reversal.

But this is not to minimize the fact that there are many of the latter. James achieves basic phenomenological insights which derive the meaningfulness of thought from the meaningfulness of the appearing world, a world he is often able to grasp *just* as it appears—no small accomplishment. Phenomenology has been called an exercise in seeing.

Yet it might be objected that if what is seen are just phenomena, just appearances, then phenomenology is much ado about nothing. It might be said that real knowledge of phenomena cannot be gained, but that this deficiency is unimportant because appearances are not reality, or it might be said that it is easy to know what appears to be the case, but hard to know what really is so; either way no discipline concerned with appearances is called for. But phenomenology rejects any such sweeping bifurcation of appearance and reality and maintains that grasping the phenomenon in its purity is difficult and requires a method.

Although James does not call his method phenomenological, his actual practice points in the direction of what Husserl later explicated. We are deceived about phenomena, James says, both by our practical concerns as men and by our theoretical concerns as scientists. Both concerns prompt us to pick out, before we know it, in the twinkling of an eye, what particular physical things *cause* the phenomenon. As men we are prompted for reasons of personal survival, as scientists for reasons of our theoretical projects. This produces the deception, James says. We then name or specify the phenomenon in terms of the single thing that causes it (for example, "an odor of violets," "a cheesy taste") and mask out the whole phenomenal field—the sense of the world's presence—in which the phenomenon is embedded, and for which, in its wholeness, the phenomenon should be named if it is to be specified adequately. Since we specify our thoughts in terms of the phenomena which are their objects, this also amounts to deception concerning thoughts.

Husserl took James's insight and formulated it thus: all judgments concerning physical things and causation are to be bracketed or suspended—not denied or ignored, but suspended, i.e., viewed within the environing context of meaningfulness which makes them possible as meaningful judgments, regardless of whether they be true or false. The seeing, which is phenomenological seeing, is difficult because what must be seen all at once is the total context of related phenomena, which render any particular phenomenon meaningful, a context which includes phenomena related not only to other phenomena but to ourselves as centers of consciousness. As phenomenology developed in the hands of Husserl, it became increasingly clear that the whole lived world (*Lebenswelt*) as the founding level of meaning is even more basic than the internal relationship of thought to thought's object (intentionality), since the specification of thought is parasitical on the specification of thought's object (phenomenon), and the specification of the latter is in turn parasitical on the sense of the whole lived world in which the particular phenomenon is embedded. James's thought anticipates in some ways this development.

The tradition in America has been to construe James's psychology as "functionalist." Unfortunately, like too much Jamesian scholarship, this construction conceals more than it reveals. It is all very well to say that James believed that mind performed a biological function in adjusting the organism to the environment; but if it is not added that he also believed that the function of mind cannot be rendered exclusively in biological terms, but requires irreducibly mentalistic ones expressing the way the environment appears to an organism conscious of its ends as its own, then more is concealed than revealed. Moreover, it must be added that James's conception of mentalistic terms is very different from that of an introspectionist. He is neither a pure functionalist, nor an introspectionist, nor a behaviorist; *if* he is any single thing, he is a pioneering phenomenologist.

John Watson, the founder of behaviorism, claimed that James's alleged functionalism was really subjectivistic and introspectionist. But both allegations are wrong, and showing how they are wrong throws added light on James's actual position. Watson and the intellectual communities in England and America were so ignorant of Husserl and of Continental thought that they usually lumped any talk about mental states or acts of thought in the category of introspective psychology: i.e., a psychology which attempted to develop a special vocabulary for the description of special nonphysical entities called thoughts or sensations; and which armed itself with its own units and modes of measurement so as to be adequate to "the other realm" of mind.

But a central doctrine of phenomenology is that mental states are intrinsically referential and worldly, that they cannot be specified in isolation as elements of another "realm," and that what they are as nonphysical entities (assuming this makes any sense at all) is at best a peripheral matter. For phenomenology, introspectionism is a displaced and misguided empiricism—and a disguised mimic of natural science—which is blissfully unaware of its own confusion. As E. G. Boring has pointed out, James's *radical* empiricism might have served as a basis for an American school of phenomenology, but it was simply never integrated into American psychology.

What distinguishes James's protophenomenology from functionalism, behaviorism, and introspectionism, is the idea of the intrinsic referentialness of mind, which snowballs in the *Principles* and turns that book in mid-course toward new intellectual horizons. (pp. 3-8)

> *Bruce Wilshire, in his* William James and Phenomenology: A Study of "The Principles of Psychology," *Indiana University Press, 1968, 251 p.*

P. ALLAN CARLSSON   (essay date 1973)

[*Carlsson is an American educator and philosopher. In the following excerpt, he compares James's division of "tender-minded" and "tough-minded" temperaments with C. G. Jung's personality types of "introverted" and "extroverted." While finding significant points of divergence between these respective psychological theories, Carlsson observes that James and Jung shared the fundamental assumption that "the individual holds a particular viewpoint because of his personality." For Jung's commentary on James's personality theory, see the excerpt dated 1921.*]

Among the nineteenth-century philosophers who considered the question why an individual adheres to a particular world-and-life viewpoint, there was a tendency to de-emphasize the personality of the individual himself. Comte and Kierkegaard, for example, advocated that the particular position an individual thinker happens to hold at any particular time is due to a developmental pattern through which each individual either passed or was capable of passing. For Comte, it depends upon whether the individual is thinking within a religious, metaphysical, or positive framework; each individual goes through the same development as does the human race, although both may be impeded and the individual may never progress. For Kierkegaard, it makes a difference whether the individual is in the aesthetic, ethical, or religious stage of life's way—Don Juan never advances beyond the aesthetic stage. On the other hand, Marx places the emphasis on the social/economic class to which the individual belongs.

In contrast to this, at the end of the nineteenth and beginning of the twentieth century, Jung and James were formulating a different approach. Each classified mankind into two world-and-life viewpoints, basing the distinction on the characteristics of the individual human personality. James used the notion of *temperament* while Jung used *general attitude types*. True, both Jung and James were psychologically oriented.

The only thinker to make much of this similarity between Jung and James is Jung himself. It appears interesting and it may even be important to analyze their similarities and differences. James, as a philosopher, was somewhat more theoretical in his approach to world-and-life viewpoints. Jung's chief interest was practical results. His goal was to aid his patients to see themselves and their world from a better perspective; in the process, he developed a type theory. Both thinkers, in attempting to make sense out of their own experiences, were able to perceive patterns emerging from the immense variety of the human personalities they encountered. James's theory classified philosophers into two groups, and he coined the terms *tender-minded* thinkers and *tough-minded* thinkers to label them. This division of man into two basic groups is Jung's connection point with James. Jung's terms are *introverted* and *extroverted*.

In order to show the emphasis Jung and James place on individual temperament, it will be necessary to comment briefly upon three points: (1) Jung's discussion of James's typology, (2) Jung's expanded typology, and (3) the respective roles the typologies play in the systems of these two thinkers.

Jung published *Psychological Types* in 1920 after struggling for some years to formulate a typology of man. He outlines a selected survey of human history to show that a two-fold dichotomy of human types has been rather common. This historical survey is the context in which Jung discusses James. Jung was acquainted with at least some of the writings of James and refers especially to *Varieties of Religious Experience* and *Principles of Psychology*. Interestingly enough, William James is the only philosopher discussed by Jung in *Psychological*

Types in the chapter on "The Problem of Types in Modern Philosophy." The discussion centers on the first part of James's essay, **"The Present Dilemma in Philosophy,"** where James sketched his two types of human temperaments. Since Jung discusses this dichotomy at length and thereby indicates the importance he attached to the distinction, it will be helpful to recall James's list of characteristics which he attaches to each of the types:

The Tender-minded.	The Tough-minded.
Rationalistic (going by "principles")	Empiricist (going by "facts")
Intellectualistic	Sensationalistic
Idealistic	Materialistic
Optimistic	Pessimistic
Religious	Irreligious
Free-willist	Fatalistic
Monistic	Pluralistic
Dogmatical	Skeptical

While there are few, if any, pure types, these characteristics clustered together into two basically different personalities.

In *Psychological Types* Jung attempts to trace the history of the idea of dividing mankind into two classes of people. It must be emphasized that he undertook the historical survey to reinforce his own ideas and not to expound on James's. The thesis Jung wished to support was inferred from the patients encountered in his psychoanalytic practice; with all their individual differences, people could be classified into types. This is the basis of Jung's division of mankind into two groups: the introverted person and the extroverted person. The crux of the distinction is the person's orientation. One individual may be more conditioned by the objects of his interest while another is more conditioned by his own inner self.

Jung calls this division of mankind into introverted and extroverted classes *general attitude types*. The introvert's habitual reaction is to protect the self; the psychic energy turns inward. The following words and phrases used to describe the introvert are culled from Jung's writings: feels lonely; dislikes society; becomes lost in large groups; sensitive; lacks social graces; either outspoken or overly polite; critical; quiet; pessimistic; overly-conscientious; works best alone or in small, familiar groups; lacks conventionality. On the other hand, the extrovert's habitual reaction is to direct his psychic energy toward the object of his attention. These words and phrases apply: sociable; likes organizations and groups; active; likes parties; keeps business and social life going; prefers to work in groups; optimistic; enthusiastic; tends to be superficial; tries to make a good impression; adaptable; very conventional. Jung indicates that his initial reaction on reading James is "to regard the tender-minded as introverted, and the tough-minded as extroverted," but he wished to scrutinize the issue before making a final judgment.

This scrutiny takes the form of a discussion which seems to hinge largely on James's first pair of opposing characteristics, the rationalist and the empiricist. The tough-minded empiricist is more dependent upon the external object for his orientation to the world and is, as such, regarded as connected with the extrovert. Now, if James's tough-minded is matched with Jung's extrovert and the intent is to harmonize both pairs, it naturally follows that tender-minded will be linked with the introvert. Jung does go on to discuss to some extent each of James's pairs of opposing characteristics, but the empiricist/rationalist dichotomy appears to be the key. Actually, much of Jung's

discussion at this point is not an attempt to analyze James but rather an opportunity to use the occasion as an associative springboard to discuss his own ideas. He does recognize that James is describing philosophical world-and-life viewpoints, while his own interest is somewhat broader, in that he wishes to provide a general classification for all human beings. Jung's scheme would, therefore, include James's. While James's dichotomy is technical, it, no doubt, could be generalized. Jung's point is that both were attempting to delineate the same dichotomy, and he offers James's work as evidence supporting his division of mankind into two basic personality types. (pp. 113-16)

[It] should be emphasized that both James and Jung thought their typologies were reasonably accurate descriptions of experience. James appeals to his audience; what he is saying is so obvious that its accuracy will be immediately recognized. Jung appeals to parallel accounts in history and to his own wide medical practice. In other words, both schemes are thought to be derived from experience.

My third topic, the roles the typologies play in these two systems, needs elaboration. The question why James chose to discuss typology in **"The Present Dilemma in Philosophy"** is important. He indicates that he introduces the typology at this particular point in his discussion because he wishes to offer the pragmatic method as a third alternative—a way to go between the horns of the dilemma. Due to the different orientations of the two world-and-life viewpoints, philosophers from each group are bound to hold differing positions. He uses labels which for his contemporaries graphically pictured the antagonism between the two types: "Bostonian tourist" and "Rocky Mountain tough." The pragmatic method could bypass the philosophical antagonism by focusing only on questions that had alternative answers—not merely verbal differences, but options that *really* differed from each other. These were the live, important questions for James. Even though the philosopher is prejudiced by his temperament, he should be able to see his present situation and the direction he wishes to go. The circumstances are shifted from a theoretical to a practical orientation. Incidentally, Jung recognized that this is James's purpose in discussing the typology. (p. 118)

Jung discusses James, as he does scores of others who classify people in at least two categories, in order to support his "introverted-extroverted" distinction. Jung's typology could be used in a theoretical approach to world views similar to James's, but Jung does not do this. Interestingly enough, Jung could parallel James even to the extent of introducing a possible way of communication and cooperation between differing groups through his concept of "wholeness." The individual who recognizes tensions within himself could theoretically recognize them in others.

Jung's emphasis on the hereditary components of the human personality is widely known, especially through his concept of the collective unconscious. James's position on this question is not so well known, but he also stresses inheritance of the basic world-and-life view orientation in the sense that the individual inherits a temperament and the world-and-life viewpoint he adopts must fit his temperament. The "marks" of the proper world-and-life viewpoint are discussed by James in "The Sentiment of Rationality."

Other than Jung's indication of his interest in James, I am not aware of any discussion which has noted the similarity of their approach. James's typology is well known to philosophers, who should not overlook Jung's treatment of world-and-life viewpoints. Both had a common orientation on this point: the individual holds a particular viewpoint because of his personality. (pp. 118-19)

P. Allan Carlsson, "Jung and James on the Typology of World Views," in The Journal of General Education, published by The Pennsylvania State University Press, University Park, Pennsylvania, Vol. XXV, No. 2, July, 1973, pp. 113-19.*

WILLIAM BARRETT   (essay date 1975)

[*Barrett is an American philosopher, literary critic, and social thinker. During the 1940s and 1950s, he was an associate editor of the* Partisan Review, *which was a leading forum in America for socialist political thought and modernist experimentalism in the arts. His best known work,* Irrational Man (1958), *is a highly regarded study of the literary and philosophical tradition of existentialism. This work, along with the more recent* Illusion of Technique (1978), *charts the philosophical reaction to the "deranged rationality" of modern analytical thought. Barrett provides a lucid and learned critique of the abstract nature of Western philosophy, which over the centuries has progressively narrowed its applications to the fields of science and technology rather than directly confronting the full range of human problems. In an interview, Barrett stated that "we have suffered a loss of primitive and direct perceptions, feelings, intuitions." Thus, such writers as Søren Kierkegaard, Friedrich Nietzsche, and the French existentialists represent an attempt to regain a sense of the most fundamental aspects of human existence. In the following excerpt from "Our Contemporary, William James," Barrett argues that James's sense of evil and insight into the "sick soul" gives him "a sense of actuality which makes him seem close to us." Barrett's central issue in his essay is defense of James's postulation of free will and the will to believe. For similar views of James's conception of the will to believe, see the excerpts by F.C.S. Schiller (1897) and Gail Kennedy (1956); for opposing views, see the excerpts by Dickinson S. Miller (1899) and George Santayana (1920).*]

I remember my disappointment as a young student years ago when I first read the classic essay, **"The Dilemma of Determinism."** The title led me to expect some objective and logical refutation that would once and for all impale the determinist on its prongs and leave him squirming there forever. I expected, I think, some new and surprising facts or some new logical relation of the facts that would finally settle the question in favor of freedom. Instead, James seemed to hurry past the objective question in order to get to the moral issues involved, and I was disappointed to find the bulk of the essay, as it seemed to me then, a moral appeal to the reader. For the dilemma of the determinist, as James presents it, is essentially a moral and not a metaphysical one. The objective question between freedom and determinism was thus left open and inconclusive as it had always been, and my young mind still felt dreadfully unsettled.

But of course this is where the question has to be left, and James is entirely right to hew to the line that he does. In this matter he is following the position of Kant a century before him. The firebreathers of determinism, like B. F. Skinner, who enter the dialectical fray convinced that they have seen the proof of determinism in their laboratory results last week, are greatly mistaken. The case for or against free will still stands where Kant left it. We have introduced all kinds of changes and refinements in terminology, but the objective merits of the case remain unaltered. Anything like a decisive proof for free will or determinism is unavailable. And where the matter is

thus logically inconclusive, practical concerns enter. It makes a great deal of difference, practically speaking, if we do believe in freedom. We are more likely to improve our character if we believe that the power to do so lies in the exertion of our will. Determinism, if really followed in practice, would tend to close off the will toward such striving. Thus it is to our practical advantage to believe that we are free beings, and our subjective decision in the matter does have objective consequences in our life. Faith in freedom produces future facts that confirm it—at least in its practical efficacy if not its ultimate metaphysical truth.

Freedom on such terms would seem to be a bald practical transaction, a cool *quid pro quo*. But what we have in the above summation is half, and less than half, of the Jamesian position. For if the belief in freedom is a moral choice on our part, it is ultimately for James also a religious act. Our moral life in the end makes sense only as an affirmation of some religious attitude toward the universe. Many of his pragmatist followers have sought to dilute this position; but it is nonetheless James's, persistently though sometimes waveringly held throughout the body of his writings. (pp. 56-7)

Freedom becomes fully real to us in those situations when it is literally a matter of life and death. We are *in extremis;* we have fallen into a black pit and we are gasping for breath as we struggle to crawl forward. Freedom is no longer an academic debate or the dizzying luxury of an indifferent choice between alternatives. The question of freedom has turned into a cry for help.

James knew this need in the only way in which it can be known—by direct personal experience. In 1870, when he was twenty-eight, he had a severe crisis that left him in a state of acute and paralyzed melancholy. We do not know exactly what circumstances may have precipitated this crisis. James's personality, despite his open and expansive manner, is shrouded in considerably more mystery than is commonly thought. He has left us an anonymous case in *The Varieties of Religious Experience* that is now taken to be largely a description of his own experience. Why this refuge in anonymity? Would it have seemed too mawkish and unmanly, too unashamedly personal, to make public confession of something so intimate? In any case, the passage describes the kind of experience around which much of his philosophizing turns; long as it is, we need to give it in full:

Whilst in this state of philosophic pessimism and general depression of spirits about my prospects, I went one evening into a dressingroom in the twilight to procure some article that was there; when suddenly there fell upon me without warning, just as if it came out of darkness, a horrible fear of my own existence. Simultaneously there arose in my mind the image of an epileptic patient whom I had seen in the asylum, a black-haired youth with greenish skin, entirely idiotic, who used to sit all day on one of the benches, or rather shelves, against the wall, with his knees drawn up against his chin, and the coarse grey undershirt, which was his only garment, drawn over him, enclosing his entire figure. He sat there like a sort of sculptured Egyptian cat or Peruvian mummy, moving nothing but his black eyes and looking absolutely non-human. This image and my fear entered into a species of combination with each

Caricature of James, by David Levine. Copyright © 1967 Nyrev, Inc. Reprinted with permission from The New York Review of Books.

other. *That shape am I,* I felt, potentially. Nothing that I possess can defend me against that fate, if the hour for it should strike for me as it struck for him. There was such a horror of him, that it was as if something solid within my breast gave way entirely, and I became a mass of quivering fear. After this the universe was changed for me altogether. I awoke morning after morning with a horrible dread at the pit of my stomach, and with a sense of insecurity the like of which I never knew before, and that I have never felt since. It was like a revelation; and although the immediate feelings passed away, the experience has made me sympathetic with the morbid feelings of others ever since. It gradually faded, but for months I was unable to go out in the dark alone.

We witness here such a convulsion and seizure by the unconscious that consciousness and its ideas would seem by comparison to exert only a feeble and peripheral force. Yet, on closer look, ideas play more of a role in this crisis than might first appear. It is hard for us today to recapture in imagination the stark and frightening power that the determinism embedded in physics had for the 19th-century imagination. "The molecules blindly run," the poet sang in his distress; and those molecules blindly moving would spin out our fate as they

would, whatever we appeared to will in the matter. That idiot will be me, and there is nothing I can do, if the particles are already irreversibly spinning in that direction. The imagination cowered before this prospect like a Calvinist shivering at the conviction of eternal damnation. And if this philosophical idea does not of itself beget the attack of acute depression, it nevertheless intensifies that depression because any way out seems to be barred beforehand. Ideas, as we see here, can have a most potent connection with the will, in this case a negative and frustrating one.

James was to find a more positive idea to help his will out of the impasse. In the spring of 1870 a turning point seems to come and he records in his diary:

> I think that yesterday was a crisis in my life. I finished the first part of Renouvier's second *Essais* and see no reason why his definition of free will—"the sustaining of a thought *because I choose to* when I might have other thoughts"— need be the definition of an illusion. At any rate, I will assume for the present—until next year—that it is no illusion. My first act of free will shall be to believe in free will.

In comparison with the murky and subterranean atmosphere of the previous excerpt, we are here in the daylight world of the mind and its ideas. Perhaps too daylight; perhaps the note here is too selectively intellectual, and there were other subliminal and more obscure forces at work floating James past his blockage. We have, however, to follow him to the letter: it is an idea—in this case the idea of free will—that opens the door out of his darkness. Yet James knows—though he had not yet written his great chapters on habit in the *Psychology*—that the idea by itself is not enough; that the links between idea and will, and between will and action, must be quickly and firmly established. He proceeds therefore to put the idea immediately into action:

> For the remainder of the year, I will abstain from the mere speculation and contemplative *Grublei* in which my nature takes most delight, and voluntarily cultivate the feeling of moral freedom, by reading books favorable to it, as well as by acting. After the first of January, my callow skin being somewhat fledged, I may perhaps return to metaphysical study and skepticism without danger to my powers of action. For the present then remember: care little for speculation; much for the form of my action; recollect that only when habits of order are formed can we advance to really interesting fields of action—and consequently accumulate grain on grain of willful choice like a very miser; never forgetting how one link dropped undoes an indefinite number. . . .

> Hitherto, when I have felt like taking a free initiative like daring to act originally, without waiting for contemplation of the external world to determine all for me, suicide seemed the most manly form to put my daring into; now, I will go a step further with my will, not only act with it, but believe as well; believe in my individual reality and creative power. My belief, to be sure, *can't* be optimistic—but I will posit life (the real, the good) in the self-gov-

erning *resistance* of the ego to the world. Life shall be built in doing and suffering and creating.

We have dwelt on this crisis of 1870 because it gives us the human and philosophic center around which James's life was to turn. In view of the extraordinarily productive and vigorous career that was to follow this breakdown, we could rate his as one of the prime cases of a victory over neurosis. Yet we do not conquer a neurosis unless we have learned from it and in some measure preserve within us the message it had to impart in the first place. For the rest of his days James remained sensitive to the desperation that lurks always at the core of even the best regulated lives. He could understand the ''sick soul'' and its morbid temperament because he himself was one of the morbid. He who has once had a terrifying vision will never doubt the existence of evil in this universe of ours. The torments of the sick soul, James tells us, if viewed objectively would be less than an adequate response to the abominable and loathsome things that take place in the world. Consequently James thereafter could never accept any idealistic philosophy that would make evil disappear through some ingenious feat of dialectic. All of which gives James a sense of actuality which makes him seem close to us.

More than this. The brief entries quoted from the journal for 1870 give us in compact outline the whole of the Jamesian philosophy that was to follow. The philosophy of *The Will to Believe,* twenty-seven years later, is already summed up in a single paragraph from the diary. Everything he was to write comes in some way out of the datum he had grasped in the crossing of this valley of the shadow. He was to become a moral philosopher essentially; but a moralist preoccupied with the scope, power, and above all the source of our moral will. Even a major work like his *Psychology* fits into this large design. For what James, coming from his studies in physiology, saw in the neural impulses was that consciousness is primarily connected with the discharge of energy, with action; and that motivation must therefore be a prime factor in human conduct. Happy the thinker who knows his direction so early.

''My first act of freedom will be to believe in freedom.'' How cheerful and courageous this note sounds after the discord and stress of his crisis. This simple utterance of the moment is the gist of the position later taken in *The Will to Believe.* Since freedom of the will is not ruled out on strictly logical grounds, one is therefore free to believe in it. But this belief, which is not itself a strict consequence of logic, nevertheless has distinct consequences in action. To believe in one's freedom has the advantages that it liberates the will and fosters action. Faith in freedom creates its own future facts, and thus confirms itself in action.

The argument is exactly the same, but in this later context James introduced an example from an altogether more extrovert and heroic domain of human effort than the one he had known in his crisis. Let us imagine, he tells us, a mountain climber who is caught in an impasse where he has to leap across an abyss to save himself. His way is barred behind; he must go forward or perish where he is. The jump is not too long that he cannot possibly make it; yet it is long enough that there is a chance he could fall short. Which then shall be believe? That he can make the leap or that it lies beyond his powers? If he believes he can do it, James argues, then his energies will be bolstered by that very faith, and he is much more likely to succeed in his leap. And afterward, when he stands safe on the other peak, his belief will have yielded confirmation of its truth.

This example, drawn from the daredevil and adventurous life of the out-of-doors, seems a far cry from the situation of James a quarter-century earlier sitting paralyzed and despondent in his father's house in Cambridge. But perhaps the two situations are not so different as they appear at first glance. The melancholic, to get past his despondency, has to make a leap as heroic and total in its own way as the mountaineer's jump from precipice to precipice. Only it is not done all at once, but day by day. That makes it more difficult, and should we not therefore say more heroic? There must be the slow and dragging accumulation of what James here calls ''willful choice'' until the sufferer emerges at last into the open air. And in both cases the choice is forced upon us: it is a matter of life and death, of individual salvation.

Ironically enough, the question of free will, in becoming real to us, has altogether changed its nature. It is no longer a question of alternative courses of action. We are no longer spectators at our own life dizzied by the gratuitous possibilities it affords. We are stuck in it up to our necks, and the question is whether we can go on at all. The question is no longer between the choice of A and B. A is life, and B death, or its moral equivalent. Everything in us cries out desperately for the choice of A, but do we have the will to make it? *The problem of free will thus becomes, more fundamentally, the problem of the will itself.* We need not go to the extreme situations of life—whether of the heroic mountain-climber or of the desperate melancholic—to see that this is so. We need only turn to the routines of ordinary life and the heavy load we must carry every day. The voice of Samuel Beckett intones: ''You must go on, I can't go on, I'll go on.'' That is the world in which each of us lives from day to day. The problem of the will thus becomes the problem of nihilism itself. And we are present here at what, underneath all the formal trappings of philosophy, must remain for most of us its fundamental question: Why live? Why go on? What meaning does it all have? James died before the virus of nihilism had passed from a few intellectuals into the democratic mass at large and become the epidemic of our time; and the one powerful statement of the question available to him, that of Nietzsche, he found distasteful and shied away from. Yet his sensitivity was such that the question is always there in the background for him; and that is one reason why he speaks to us at the present time.

The question of nihilism immediately places us on the terrain of the religious, whether or not we decide for or against religion. As soon as we give any utilitarian and naturalistic answers, they seem pallid beside the experience that provoked our question. Answer and question seem to pass each other by. Our will clamors for some deeper answer when its longing for freedom is in fact a cry for help. The longing for freedom is in fact a *prayer*—whether we actually voice that prayer or not. The question of morality becomes a religious one. And James, deciding at this early age to turn his intellectual energy henceforth to what he calls ''the moral impulse,'' was in fact committing himself to becoming a religious thinker. (pp. 59-61)

William Barrett, ''Our Contemporary, William James,'' in Commentary, *Vol. 60, No. 6, December, 1975, pp. 55-61.*

GARY T. ALEXANDER (essay date 1979)

[*In the following excerpt, Alexander demonstrates the way in which concepts discussed in* The Principles of Psychology *are applied and extended in* The Varieties of Religious Experience. *This view—that James significantly related his study of psychology to his study of religion, lending psychological as well as philosophical dimensions to the later work—contrasts with that of Julius Seelye Bixler (1926) and James Dittes (see Additional Bibliography). For another discussion of* The Varieties of Religious Experience, *see the excerpt by Th. Flournoy (1902). For an example of a phenomenological discussion of James's work, as mentioned in the excerpt by Alexander, see the excerpt by Bruce Wilshire (1968) and the entries in the Additional Bibliography by Hans Linschoten and John Wild.]*

It is a commonplace that William James's **The Varieties of Religious Experience** is seldom used in any substantive manner by current psychologists of religion, who, although often lauding the work as a creation of genius, tend to view it as primarily philosophical in nature. James Dittes has gone so far as to assert that, in fact, James "does not invoke in his discussion of religious experiences any of the psychological concepts he had labored through a decade earlier in his general psychology text" [see Additional Bibliography]. . . .

[One] important question which must be addressed in order adequately to interpret the **Varieties** is the extent to which it is psychological at all, that is, does it or does it not draw upon James's earlier psychology? My contention is that, while it may be true that James does not use his, or others', psychological categories systematically, it is emphatically not the case that he fails to make use of them at all. (p. 421)

One of the principal insights of those who have interpreted James's work as inherently phenomenological or philosophical-psychological is their awareness of his efforts to understand the meaning of human experience. For example, John Wild comments that in addressing the issue of free will James speaks "not as a strict scientist but rather as a phenomenological psychologist who recognizes that, while he must take account of the objective facts, there are also other facts of life which he must recognize, if he is to gain any understanding of human existence as it is actually lived in the world. . . ."

James attempts in the **Principles** to speak "as a strict scientist," although even he must finally admit that "when . . . we talk of 'psychology as a natural science,' we must not assume that that means a sort of psychology that stands at last on solid ground. It means just the reverse; it means a psychology particularly fragile, and into which the waters of metaphysical criticism leak at every joint, a psychology all of whose elementary assumptions and data must be reconsidered in wider connections and translated into other terms." Still, his aim in the **Principles** has been to consider experience primarily in terms of the "undivided 'mental state,'" which is to say that he seeks to have this state "accepted by my colleagues as the fundamental datum for their science." From the psychological point of view "we need a fair and square and explicit *abandonment* of such questions as that of the soul, the transcendental ego, the fusion of ideas or particles of mind stuff, etc." The agenda of the **Principles** is thus to examine the nature and function of this "mental state," while refraining from making evaluative or normative assertions as to its meaning—however difficult that may prove to be. Only in this manner, believed James, could psychology properly establish itself as an independent scientific discipline. To this end he defines psychology in the **Principles** as "the science of finite individual minds," which "assumes as its data (1) *thoughts and feelings,* and (2) *a physical world* in time and space with which they coexist and which (3) *they know.*" The psychologist's task is to establish "the empirical correlation of the various sorts of thought or feeling with definite conditions of the brain." This exercise having been accomplished, psychology "can go no farther . . . as a natural science."

The **Varieties,** on the other hand, is a text which does move beyond the constraints which James would impose on psychology as a natural science. No longer is he willing to treat the conscious individual strictly within the confines of the objective study of a "mental fact," for no longer is he significantly concerned with the nature and function of consciousness in relation to the brain. Now he is concerned with the "wider" experiential connections of consciousness, that is, with what he would term the "full fact" of religious experience, an experience which must be judged *"by the way in which it works on the whole"* rather than being reduced to its historical, physiological, or possible supernatural antecedents.

Rather, the experiencing individual of the **Varieties** is constituted in a significant respect by a sense of personal destiny and of playing a substantive role in the makeup of the larger cosmological context; that is, in this text the active, agentic consciousness is clearly viewed as a participant in the creation of a meaningful experience. This sense of participation is present in the above-mentioned "full fact" of human experience, which is comprised of the field of consciousness "*plus* its object as felt or thought of *plus* an attitude towards the object *plus* the sense of a self to whom the attitude belongs. . . ." This experienced full fact is crucial to our sense of living out a personal destiny and "is the one thing that fills up the measure of our concrete actuality. . . ."

This sense of an active, conscious self is entirely consistent with, and in fact draws on, James's discussions of the active character of consciousness which he presents in the **Principles,** namely that "*my experience is what I agree to attend to.* Only those items which I *notice* shape my mind—without selective interest, experience is an utter chaos." This initial psychological perspective is never abandoned; it is only expanded in the **Varieties** through the introduction of an individual's sense of living in active relationship with a "spiritual" dimension which, for many, gives meaning to their existence.

James, then, in examining religious experience, is looking at a full fact of human experience—an experiential datum which ideally involves raw experience, disciplined self-reflection, and specific actions derived from and given meaning in terms of the sense of self present within this experiential-reflective complex. Building upon his notion of the fundamental "mental state" which is set within the "stream of consciousness" and for which "selective interest" is a necessary aspect of self-expression, James in the **Varieties** extends his understanding of agency into the realm of lived, meaningful, religious experience. In the **Principles** the individual's self-experience is simply a datum, a portion of those elements of consciousness which the psychologist must take into account while striving to relate consciousness and brain functions. In the **Varieties** this self-experience stands as the basis of his analysis of religious experience per se. In short, James has shifted from what was primarily a formal discussion and description of the attributes and functions of the stream of consciousness in the **Principles** to an examination of the meaning of a particular mode of human experience, and this shift entails a more comprehensive method of inquiry than does that of his earlier psychological text.

It thus appears that both the object of James's concern and his method have been magnified considerably since the publication of the *Principles* in 1890. The *Varieties* offers an examination of lived religious experience by means of a method that moves well beyond the limits of a strictly natural science while . . . remaining consistent with observations derived from the latter perspective. In other words, whereas we can say that what has been termed the philosophical-psychology of the *Principles* is predominantly psychological in orientation, that of the *Varieties* is firmly committed to philosophical inquiry built on a consistent psychological anthropology. (pp. 422-24)

In James's view, the meaning of religious experience, and of experience in general, must finally be approached from the mutual perspectives of the psychology of individual consciousness on the one hand, and of philosophical reflection on the relationship that obtains between consciousness and reality on the other. Neither discipline alone is sufficient for an adequate investigation of the problem, that is, neither the psychological description of the sources and structures of religious experience, nor the exposition of a priori metaphysical or theological theories will allow for a full understanding of its meaning and value. To comprehend the meaning of religious experience demands the introduction of a type of philosophical argumentation which does not abandon the fundamental psychological orientation that grounds all of James's thinking, but which does, in fact, move well beyond the perspective of natural science. It is always individual experience, psychologically interpreted, which serves as the general context in light of which specifically religious experience is evaluated and out of which James later develops his ideas as to how the meaning of the universe itself may possibly be interpreted by a human consciousness that is actively engaged with it.

James has said in the *Principles* that the human individual is "born with a tendency to do more things than he has ready-made arrangements for in his nerve-centers." Hence the necessity of chossing plays a vital role in the formation of the individual self and likewise is at the core of his understanding of the religious individual. In his later philosophy James extends his model even further, arguing that this partial, active consciousness is embedded in what may be likewise characterized as a partial and incomplete universe—a cosmos that is itself constantly in the process of creation. James's pluralism, in short, is complete; for him the universe remains truly an open question. Reality, he insists, "MAY exist in distributive form, in the shape not of an all but of a set of eaches. . . ."

Viewed in this light, James's investigations of religious experience can be seen to provide a bridge from the descriptive, functional psychology of the *Principles,* with its leaking metaphysical joints, through the more explicitly philosophical-psychological method of the *Varieties,* and finally into his more broadly sketched explorations into the nature of the universe itself and of the individual's relationship with its reality. He has sought in the *Varieties* to demonstrate that religious experience is *real* experience and that it is reasonable when viewed in terms of the structure of human consciousness. This experiential reality, however, cannot be reduced to its psychological foundation. Another type of language is demanded in order to discuss adequately religious experience and this language, while remaining consistent with psychological findings, must also deal in distinctly philosophical modes of discourse as James endeavors to explore the relationship of agency and meaning within the experience of various individuals. In other words, James has shifted from seeing minds as objects to be studied and analyzed psychologically to attempting to describe the nature and significance of a particular kind of experience as it is meaningfully lived by specific individuals.

It is apparent that James makes direct use both in the *Varieties* and in his later philosophy of ideas derived from his earlier psychological text, most notably the field of consciousness, "imageless thought," and the active character of consciousness. Furthermore, even his introduction of the idea of a subliminal consciousness proves meaningful only when set within the context of a field of consciousness. The *Varieties* can thus be understood to represent a pivotal moment in the development of James's thinking, embodying as it does a tension between these descriptive psychological categories and more normative, philosophical modes of interpretation; while never allowing the necessary bond between the two perspectives to be severed. James, in short, understands human experience to become meaningful only as a result of the selective activity of an engaged consciousness; and he finds religious experience to represent one important way in which this process of the active organization of meaning is carried out. (pp. 432-34)

Gary T. Alexander, "Psychological Foundations of William James's Theory of Religious Experience," in The Journal of Religion, *Vol. 59, No. 4, October, 1979, pp. 421-34.*

A. J. AYER   (essay date 1982)

[*An uncompromising rationalist in the tradition of David Hume and Bertrand Russell, Ayer is an English philosopher whose first book,* Language, Truth and Logic *(1936), initiated the philosophical movement of logical positivism. The dominant strain in modern Anglo-American thought, logical positivism is concerned with the derivation of positive knowledge about the material world either by immediate perception of the senses or by analytical propositions of logic and mathematics, which must ultimately be grounded in empirical knowledge. These are, in Ayer's philosophy, two of three classes of statements about the world. A third class, which includes assertions of a metaphysical or mystical type, has no standing in the realm of knowledge and serves only as an indicator of the speaker's emotions. In the following excerpt, Ayer contrasts James's pluralistic philosophy with the monist-absolutist philosophies of F. H. Bradley and Josiah Royce. For commentary by Bradley and Royce, see the excerpts dated 1908 and 1911. For further discussion of the contrasting philosophies of pluralism and monism, see the excerpts by Charles M. Bakewell (1907) and Paul Elmer More (1910.*]

The main attraction of Pragmatism for James was that he saw it as illuminating and in a large measure resolving the principal issues of philosophical dispute. It allowed him to take one side in the debate, while leaving his opponents enough to save their honour. This was particularly true of his stand on the question of Monism and Pluralism. From a logical point of view his allegiance was wholly given to Pluralism, but he acknowledged the spiritual needs of those who wished to see the universe as One, and he thought that Pragmatism allowed for their indulgence.

The monism to which James was hostile was that of the contemporary followers of Hegel, in particular F. H. Bradley and James's Harvard colleague Josiah Royce. . . . Neither of these philosophers was an entirely orthodox Hegelian, nor did they wholly agree with one another, but they were alike in identifying Reality with a Spiritual Whole, which they called The Absolute. In Bradley's case, this was largely the result of his adopting the view, later to be discredited by G. E. Moore, that all relations are internal to their terms, with the result that he came to see everything as inextricably mixed with everything else. In Royce's case, it depended rather on his inability to see how our thoughts could refer to reality, whether truly or falsely, unless both the thinker and the object of his thought were themselves ideas in an all-knowing Mind, a doctrine which James characteristically parodied as the belief that a cat cannot look at a king unless some higher entity is looking at them both. Bradley and Royce were alike also in taking the Absolute to be perfect, with the difference that Bradley thought of it as necessarily transcending good and evil, whereas Royce believed that it held them in harmony, the existence of evil being, as he saw it, a necessary condition for that of the greatest good.

Theories of this type were offensive to James's feelings as well as to his reason. He was pleased by the show of variety in the world and resented its dismissal as mere appearance. He was morally shocked also by the blandness and callousness displayed in such remarks as Bradley's 'The Absolute is the richer for every discord, and for all the disunity which it embraces', with its implication that pain can be assumed to 'disappear into a higher unity'. Against this, he quotes with approval the protest of the anarchist writer M. I. Swift that when men commit suicide because they cannot find work to keep their families from starving, 'that slain man makes the universe richer, and that is philosophy. But while Professors Royce and Bradley and a whole host of guileless thoroughfed thinkers are unveiling Reality and the Absolute and explaining away evil and pain, this is the condition of the only beings known to us anywhere in the universe with a developed consciousness of what the universe is. What these people experience *is* Reality.' Neither was this only a moral question for James. He was intellectually opposed to a conception of reality which in any way divorced it from actual experience.

Nevertheless, as I said earlier, James did not lack sympathy for the spiritual yearnings which Absolute Idealism was partly designed to satisfy. In Royce's case at least, the underlying motive was overtly religious, and there are passages in *Pragmatism,* and still more in some of James's earlier writing, where James not only shows respect for this motive but appears even to concede that belief in the Absolute is justified by it. . . . But whatever sympathy he may have felt for the outlook of those to whom the idea of the absolute brought emotional satisfaction, it was not an outlook that he shared. This comes out in a characteristic passage from the earliest of his essays in *Essays in Radical Empiricism:*

> Since we are in the main not sceptics, we might go on and frankly confess to each other the motives for our several faiths. I frankly confess mine—I cannot but think that at bottom they are of an aesthetic and not a logical sort. The 'through-and-through' universe seems to suffocate me with its infallible impeccable all-pervasiveness. Its necessity, with no possibilities; its relations, with no subjects, make me feel as if I had entered into a contract with no reserved rights, or rather as if I had to live in a large seaside boarding-house with no private bedroom in which I might take refuge from the society of the place. I am distinctly aware, moreover, that the old quarrel of sinner and pharisee has something to do with the matter. Certainly, to my personal knowledge, all Hegelians are not prigs, but I somehow feel as if all prigs ought to end, if developed, by becoming Hegelians. There is a story of two clergymen asked by mistake to conduct the same funeral. One came first and had got no further

than 'I am the Resurrection and the Life' when the other entered. '*I* am the Resurrection and the Life,' cried the latter. The 'through-and-through' philosophy, as it actually exists, reminds many of us of that clergyman. It seems too buttoned-up and white-chokered and clean-shaven a thing to speak for the vast slow-breathing unconscious Kosmos with its dread abysses and its unknown tides.

One of the most interesting features of this passage is James's avowal of his suspicion that the motives of his philosophical 'faith' are fundamentally 'of an aesthetic and not a logical sort', and indeed it would seem that he always had a tendency to look upon philosophy as expressing some general attitude towards the world rather than as seeking, and if possible advancing, the correct solutions to a special set of problems. Thus, in the first of his lectures on Pragmatism he characterizes the history of philosophy as being 'to a great extent that of a certain clash of human temperaments'. He does not ignore the fact that philosophers most commonly advance arguments to support their theses, but he thinks that such arguments play a secondary role. The philosopher's temperament 'really gives him a stronger bias than any of his more strictly objective premises. It loads the evidence for him one way or the other, making for a more sentimental and a more hard-hearted view of the universe, just as this fact or that principle would.' Since these biases are not acknowledged, philosophical discussions have 'a certain insincerity'.

James thinks that this contrast between the more sentimental and the more hard-hearted view of the universe is to be found at work not only in philosophy but in 'literature, art, government and manners'. He presently expands it into his celebrated dichotomy of the tender and the tough-minded, the tender-minded being Rationalistic (going by 'principles'), Intellectualistic, Idealistic, Optimistic, Religious, Free-willist, Monistic, and Dogmatical: the tough-minded correspondingly being Empiricist (going by 'facts'), Sensationalistic, Materialistic, Pessimistic, Irreligious, Fatalistic, Pluralistic and Sceptical. James does not name any philosopher as fitting into either category, though it can fairly be assumed that he counted Hegel and his followers as tender-minded, while Hume and perhaps John Stuart Mill might serve as models for the tough. In most instances the strains are mixed, though one or other of them may predominate. Indeed, James himself is conspicuously such a mixture. In some ways he was very tough-minded: a radical empiricist, a sensationalist in his theory of being as well as in his theory of knowledge, a good deal of a materialist in his psychology and, if not a sceptic, not at all dogmatical. On the other hand, he was optimistic, temperamentally religious, anxious to find some opening for free will, and not a philosophical materialist. In sum, he was tough-minded in his approach to questions of natural facts but tender-minded when it came to morals and theology. It was not so much a question of his having a divided temperament as of there being a conflict between his sentiments and his reason. He wanted to retain his tender-minded beliefs, but not at the price of relaxing his intellectual standards. What chiefly attracted him to pragmatism was that it seemed to him the only philosophy that made this possible. (pp. 70-4)

A. J. Ayer, "Pragmatism," in his Philosophy in the Twentieth Century, *Random House, 1982, pp. 69-107.**

JACQUES BARZUN (essay date 1983)

[*Barzun is a French-born American man of letters whose wide range of learning has produced distinguished works in several fields, including history, culture, musicology, literary criticism, and biography. Barzun's contributions to these various disciplines are contained in such modern classics of scholarship and critical insight as* Darwin, Marx, Wagner *(1941),* Berlioz and the Romantic Century *(1950),* The House of the Intellect *(1959), and the recent biography* A Stroll with William James *(1983). Barzun's style, both literary and intellectual, has been praised as elegant and unpretentious. In the following excerpt from his biographical and critical study* A Stroll with William James, *Barzun offers a survey of James's major works and philosophical conceptions.*]

The work that James gave to the world in 1890 [*The Principles of Psychology*] is an American masterpiece which, quite like *Moby Dick,* ought to be read from beginning to end at least once by every person professing to be educated. It is a masterpiece in the classic and total sense—no need of a descriptive or limiting word before or after: not "of observation," or "of prose writing," not more "scientific" than "humanistic." One can point to these and other merits if one is so minded, but the fused substance defies reduction to a list of epithets. No matter how many unexpected qualities are found in it—wit, pathos, imaginative understanding, polemical skill, moral passion, cosmic vision, and sheer learning—the work remains always greater than their sum.

The book is again like *Moby Dick* in being the narrative of a search. When well launched on either, one reads on and on for the sake of the plot. At once simple and grandiose, it makes the vast erudition not merely easy to absorb but a bulwark of verisimilitude. And in James, the object of the pursuit is as elusive, as intimate, as momentous for Everyman as anything symbolized by the white whale: it is the human mind; or how, from multiple sensation—the 'one great blooming, buzzing confusion' of the infant's encounter with the world—comes such an extraordinary entity as the warm particular self each of us knows, with its perceptions, will, judgment, habits, emotions, preferences; and its undertermined powers: its capacity to abstract and remember, to suffer and utter in myriad languages, to create art and philosophize, to invent systems of writing and of algebra; and with the aid of puny limbs and muscles to bore through mountains, bridge abysses, and reach the moon.

It is no wonder the book is long, yet not so long as *War and Peace,* with which it shares one possibly obstructive feature. Readers of Tolstoy will remember how in their first acquaintance with *his* masterpiece the setting of the stage seemed long and dull—fifty pages of three-layered Russian names and no clear direction for our interest. Near the beginning of James's *Principles* there are also some pages that may at first seem rather dry. The opening proper is most enticing, but roughly between pages 30 and 65 with their diagrams and technical words the impression may arise that one is becalmed in a textbook. James had every reason—and Tolstoy no excuse—for putting us through this discipline. If we are interested, I will not say simply in the mind, but in conscious life, art, thought, the passions and the illusions of mankind, we must know something about the presumable seat of these activities. Hence the discourse about brain function and its physical conditions.

Nor is that subject as James treats it so much dull as temporarily forbidding by its terminology. But whoever happens to be ignorant of the neurology of the reflex arc will quickly become interested in learning why he drops the hot handle of the skillet and jumps up when he sits on a tack; while the sophisticated may be surprised to discover why it is inaccurate to speak of one's "reaction" to people or ideas, and why the familiar "conditioned reflex" is not a true reflex: it can be made to disappear by repeating the stimulus without reward—or, as Pavlov found out, by a sudden emergency, as when his trained dogs were caught in a fire.

The larger significance of the reflex arc is as the pattern or, better, as the scaffolding of our mental activity. Brain function is the physical response to the myriad stimuli that arouse it—the things we call "the world outside." The mind, which is not brain function, depends upon that response for its very different activity. The assumption is that 'every sensorial excitement propagated to a lower center tends to spread upwards and arouse an idea. Every idea tends ultimately either to produce a movement or to check one which otherwise would be produced.' What marks off the simple nerve-and-muscle mechanism of the reflex from the scaffolding above is that 'the lower centers act from present sensational stimuli alone; the hemispheres of the brain act from perceptions and considerations, the sensations which they receive serving only as suggesters of these.'

The originality of James's psychology is that it is written throughout from the empirical or naturalist's point of view without its being "reductive." He finds in experience alone the constituents of the mind and the explanations of its performance. But beware of taking "experience" too narrowly or equating it with one or another philosophy of knowledge or behavior. Not the least revelation of the *Principles* is its demonstration of what astonishing things do or do not occur in experience.

This being so, one looks back on those introductory pages and diagrams with something like the affection one feels for the unfamiliar rules that taught one a new game or the complex instructions for assembling a useful and diverting piece of equipment—except that here the game and the equipment have been ours from birth, and the wonder is that after so long a use we are learning to thread their intricacy for the first time. (pp. 34-6)

It is for Pragmatism that conventional opinion about James gives him the most ample credit—or discredit, as the case may be. Textbook summaries of his thought call Pragmatism the philosophy on which his fame is based. Yet some writers think it an idea unrelated to the rest of his work and which in no way affects his greatness as a psychologist and philosopher. Both views are baseless.

Pragmatism is not a philosophy; it is an attempt to explain how the mind ascertains truth. If correct, this explanation supplies a means of testing truths. Nor did James spend his life expounding Pragmatism; the volume of lectures called by that name was written only four years before his death, and so far from claiming particular merit for the idea, he gave to the published book the subtitle: "A New Name for Some Old Ways of Thinking." . . . (p. 83)

Historically, that is, for James, the term Pragmatism covers the steps we go through before we can say: "This is true; that is not." How do we know? One would suppose that the meaning of true and the signs of truth would have been settled long ago. Not so. All thinkers acknowledge that although mankind has always held many truths as permanent and unquestionable, these truths vary none the less, from place to place and mind to mind and especially from time to time. Science, which "makes progress" (i.e., varies), offers a good example of truths changing in time; religions and moral codes show truth's variability from place to place and mind to mind. This predicament calls for an investigation of truth, a bedrock statement of what it is. In the history of western thought two accounts have been repeatedly offered: that is true which copies or matches reality; that is true which is consistent with itself and other truths.

The copy or matching explanation is seen to have a fatal flaw from the moment one understands the stream of consciousness. "Copying reality" must mean that over there is a reality; here in the mind is a copy being made of it; to find the truth, see if the two match. Actually, no "copying" can take place, because no reaching out to "over there" is possible. What the mind sees, fells, gets hold of in whatever way, comes in one continuum —its own experience—not two. So there is nothing to match up, no direct testing of a "copy" with its original.

Consistency or coherence as a test proves just as false in the long run. For, in the first place, how are those earlier truths verified which demand consistency from the new one? And second, it often happens that two or more divergent schemes of thought show equal consistency and leave us wondering which is true. The possibility of different geometries based on opposite axioms is fatal to the test of consistency.

A system coherent within itself can also fail, because fresh experience upsets one part or another, or because the demonstration of coherence depends on words that hair-splitting mind may find ambiguous—double meanings, distinctions ad infinitum. Many proofs of the existence of God have succumbed in this way, though at first they satisfied not only the inventor but also his critics; the sharpest minds found no flaw.

The problem for James then was: how to account for the variability of truth and how to get around the weakness of the copy and consistency doctrines. It was not his problem alone. It was one of the great preoccupations of the men of his time. Read Nietzsche or Samuel Butler, Poincaré or Mach, or any other speculative thinkers and scientists after 1870, and you find the question recurring in many forms and contexts.

Responding in part to this agitation, the American Charles Sanders Peirce wrote a popular article in 1878 entitled "How to Make Our Ideas Clear." In it he suggested that a good way was to ask whether any practical difference would follow if some change were made in the statement of any idea. If the change left the consequences identical, then there was no difference between the two statements. To this rule of thumb he gave the name Pragmatism, from the Greek *pragma*, meaning "a thing done." Peirce was a neighbor in Cambridge whom James read and admired, corresponded with and befriended.

The word Pragmatism crystallized in James's mind all his own earlier inklings about a definition of truth and inspired him to set it forth under that name. After expounding his view in the Berkeley lecture of 1898, James presented a fuller account in eight lectures at the newly established Stanford University in 1906. He was there when the great San Francisco earthquake struck, but survived to repeat the lectures at Columbia University the following year; after which they appeared in the book entitled **Pragmatism.** In all these utterances James acknowledged his debt to Peirce, who ultimately would have none of it. James mentioned the influence of another friend,

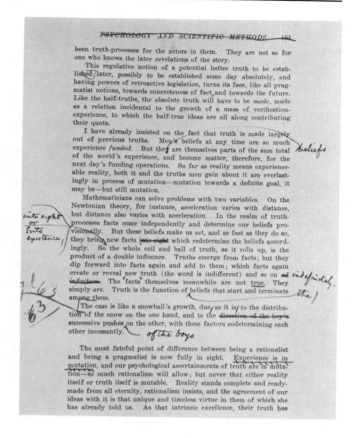

Printer's copy, with James's corrections, of Pragmatism.

the English philosopher Shadworth Hodgson, who also declined shared fatherhood.

What James did on his own, then, was to enlarge Peirce's and Hodgson's limited uses of the test into a description of all truth-seeking and -finding. When the natural purposiveness of the stream of mind is directed rationally for making sure that an idea is right, the search is "pragmatic" in the sense that it looks chiefly to what follows, not backwards to precedent or sideways to an "original." The mind perceives many bewildering things and frames many conceptions of them. To be called true, these ideas must correspond and must agree, as previous thinkers maintained, but with what? Agreement can only be found in the fitness of further experiences—objects seen or actions made possible.

James's description thus supplies the concreteness missing from both the copy and the consistency theories of truth. At the same time, the new definition supplies a standard of judgment: 'The true is only the expedient in the way of our thinking.' Or again: 'Truth is simply a collective name for verification processes, just as health, wealth, strength, etc. are names for other processes connected with life. Truth is *made*, just as health, wealth, and strength are made, in the course of experience.'

The making of truth might also be expressed as: "Go and see if experience *responds;* find out if later perceptions within the same field of interest bear out the interpretation, the formulation given tentatively at the outset. Note also whether the new idea fits in with earlier accepted ones." For 'loyalty to them is the first principle—in most cases it is the only principle.' This use of consistency is no return to an old error; it falls in at a different point in the handling of ideas. 'A new opinion counts as ''true'' just in proportion as it gratifies the individual's desire to assimilate the novel in his experience to his beliefs in stock. It must both lean on old truth and grasp new fact.' To sum up: 'Ideas (which themselves are but parts of our experience) become true just insofar as they help us to get into satisfactory relation with other parts of our experience.'

For example, when a stick is half dipped in water we see certain lines and colors that makes us think it broken—we know from past experience that that is how a broken stick looks. But if we have any doubt, we slide our hand along the stick in the water and feel no break: the idea ''broken stick'' is not true; it disagrees with a subsequent, relevant experience. The pragmatic test is repeated when we pull the stick out of the water, see it whole and lean on it—*not* broken.

In this sequence, the role of the idea is to lead us through action toward a fresh and fitting experience. Its power to do that is its truth-value. More generally about theories: 'none is absolutely a transcript of reality, but any one of them may from some point of view be useful. Their great use is to summarize old facts and to lead to new ones. They are only a man-made language, a conceptual shorthand, in which we write our reports of nature.'

In this version of how truths are made we find the explanation of the great variability of truth. The long life of errors, too, is accounted for: mistaken, incomplete views fitted well enough; they fitted all the facts known, all the experiences (or experiments) so far possible; they were useful as far as they went. From this human and historical condition, now or later, it is not likely that we shall emerge. (pp. 84-7)

James's test brought noble truth (often said to be naked, yet just as often clothed in a large capital letter) into the daily moil of practice, which unlike Theory is never perfect. The pragmatic analysis, the pragmatic test offer only variable, incomplete truths. What happens then to sacred, pure, absolute, and eternal Truth?

That question can be left hanging until someone shows where that truth is domiciled. In any case, the stated problem was not about this imaginary creature; it was about the evident variability of the truths we do have and the reason why we need them. First and last, then, the name Pragmatism, for all its Greek aura, was an unfortunate choice. It blurred the fact that the *question* of truth had been redefined, and not just the answer. His answer James had found hints of in many thinkers through the ages. But none gave it in full and none insisted as he did on the complexities—the rival claims of different kinds of evidence—along the path of discovering truth, let alone the difficulty of stating it unassailably. The pragmatic account of truth thereby disturbed many assumptions and caused much discomfort. It implied, for instance, that we ought to cease deploring the imperfect and approximate and accordingly abate our dogmatism, make room for a plurality of truths.

Naming such consequences only created the impression that here was a new and rather vulgar creed fishing for followers. Actually, what James had established was that all thinking creatures—scientists, philosophers, doctors, ditchdiggers, architects, lawyers, children—alike proceed pragmatically whether they know it or not. But if Pragmatism is not an ism one adopts like Marxism or Zen Buddhism, not a world-view but a description of the common path to truth, there is nothing to join and ''believe in.'' If the description is correct, everybody is a pragmatist, for the same reason that M. Jourdain in Molière's comedy had spoken prose all his life: there was no way he could do anything else. (pp. 87-8)

In watching James pursuing truth we have taken it for granted that Experience as its guarantor is a plain and simple thing. ''Everybody knows what is meant by experience.'' But do we? To think about it is to face a barrage of questions: How does experience come to us and where from? Is there anything behind it causing it to be as it is? Common sense tells us that we are in the universe, but common sense also puts experience of the universe inside us. We recall that James in his *Psychology* made it clear that our minds are directly aware of reality; they do not handle offprints of something out there, beyond reach, though objects are mainly perceived as independent of our thoughts about them. These various notions do not hang together. Common sense is a philosophy in disguise and one not quite well knit from end to end. It cannot explain, for instance, how the Empire State building, when you and I look at it, can be in your mind and also in my mind and also ''where it is,'' besides being in the mind of anybody in San Francisco who happens to think of it. (p. 109)

According to [Descartes], when we know objects outside, their only reality is their ''extension,'' their shape. Their other qualities—color, touch, sound, taste, smell—are not ''in'' them at all, but in the mind.

This view of knowing disposed of the uncertain, variable impressions we get of these ''secondary qualities''—they must be *our* doing; whereas extension is independent of us, reliable and permanent: it is ''matter,'' homogeneous, measurable, and hence the substratum of the universe that science can study with confidence. To be sure, Berkeley in the century after Descartes showed that this ''matter'' was pure supposition since it is by definition hidden from the senses; it serves only as an assumed support for the real and direct sensations of color, taste, and so on. By what logic should these be demoted in favor of a verbal entity? But Berkeley was generally misunderstood to mean that physical objects did not exist, and the role he ascribed to God as sustainer of things made him suspect to the men of science; so it was not until James that experience was put forth as the sole shape and presence of whatever there is to talk about.

But what is it made of, if not our old matter plus consciousness? What is this stuff whose character is neither one nor the other but neutral or general? 'There is no general stuff of which experience at large is made. There are as many stuffs as there are ''natures'' in the things experienced. If you ask what any bit of pure experience is made of, the answer is always the same: ''It is made of *that*, of just what appears—of space, of intensity, of flatness, brownness, heaviness, or what not.'' Experience is only a collective name for all these sensible natures, and save for time and space (and, if you like, for ''being''), there appears no universal element of which all things are made.'

This unaccustomed view of what happens is what James calls ''radical empiricism.'' An empiricist (as against a rationalist) is one whose philosophy explains the mystery of being by giving primacy to the part, the element, the individual, rather than the universal or the whole; 'it is a philosophy of plural facts,' which are not referred to Substance (matter) or to an Absolute Mind of which they are the emanation. To be ''radical,'' this empiricism 'must neither admit into its constructions any element that is not directly experienced, nor exclude from them any element that is directly experienced.' What is more, 'the relations that connect experiences must themselves be experienced relations and any kind of relation experienced must be accounted as real as anything else.'

One clear merit of this hospitable outlook, this 'taking everything that comes without disfavor,' is that it gets rid of the hide-and-seek of Appearance and Reality and the quarrels among their various classifiers. It puts ideas, feelings, sensations, perceptions, concepts, art, science, faith, conscious, unconscious, objects, and so-called illusions on a footing of equality as regards being real. There is of course the task of getting each "real" accurately described and its functions and relations charted. But 'a real place must be found for every kind of thing experienced.' Radical empiricism is, to begin with, a mind stretcher.

That merit is to some a demerit, because this openness confronts philosophy and the individual with a great deal more work than other schemes. Under it, all these bits of experience have to be examined and re-examined to ascertain how they hang together and what they may do or mean; there is no grand rule for grouping, subordinating, or throwing out. How can such an exceedingly loose-jointed and windswept abode constitute a universe? It does to the extent that experience offers us relations (including functions) already *there*. The philosophers' universes have 'always turned on grammatical particles. With, near, next, like, from, towards, against, because, for, through, my—these words designate types of conjunctive relation arranged in a roughly ascending order of intimacy and inclusiveness. We can imagine a universe of withness but no nextness; or one of nextness but no likeness, or of likeness but no activity, or of activity with no purpose, or of purpose with no ego. These would be universes each with its own grade of unity.'

Whatever anybody may mean by experience, it is clear that it comes well provided with all these conjunctions, or as they are often called, categories of thought. As we saw before, 'the organization of the Self as a system of memories, purposes, strivings, fulfilments or disappointments, is incidental to the most intimate of all relations, those of activity, change, tendency, resistance and the causal order generally.' So there is some order and system in the view of radical empiricism, even though it is not the perfect order and system that rationalists desire; like truth, it is not unity ready made but, when worked at, progressively achieved. The incompleteness of both universe and truth is in fact one and the same incompleteness, which a certain type of mind finds intolerably chaotic.

But there it is: 'No one single type of connection runs through all the experiences that compose it. If we take space relations, they fail to connect minds into a regular system. Causes and purposes obtain only among special series of facts. The self relation seems extremely limited and does not link two different minds together.' Anybody who wants to overcome these discouraging realities—discouraging to the beholder bent on finding the cosmos a grand, perfected system—must seek an Absolute that takes care of all the gaps and imperfections.' (pp. 110-12)

James turns his back on the absolutes of Matter and Idea and takes his stand in pure experience. In this phrase "pure" does not mean purified or distilled; it means sheer experience, raw experience. Nothing else is so unmistakably *given*—and given to everyone. Actually, 'only new-born babes or men in semicoma from sleep, drugs, illnesses, or blows may be assumed to have an experience pure in the literal sense of a *that* which is not yet any definite *what*, tho' ready to be all sorts of *whats*. Pure experience in this state is but another name for sensation. But the flux of it no sooner comes than it tends to fill itself with emphases, and these salient parts become identified and fixed and abstracted.'

This activity explains how experience, which is not any single stuff but is whatever comes, serves the familiar functions called subject and object, consciousness and "world outside." James offers an analogy with ordinary paint: 'In a pot in a paint shop, it serves in its entirety as so much salable matter. Spread on a canvas, with other paints around it, it represents on the contrary a feature in a picture and performs a spiritual function. Just so, I maintain, does a given undivided portion of experience, taken in one context of associates, play the part of a knower, of a state of mind, of consciousness; while in a different context the same undivided bit of experience plays the part of a thing known. In one group it figures as a thought, in another group as a thing.'

As he did with the copy theory of truth, James here preserves the outline of the dualism that we express in the words of common sense but, by specifying its contents, 'instead of being mysterious and elusive it becomes verifiable and concrete.' Knowing is then 'an affair of relations, it falls outside, not inside the single bit of experience.' By this account we are able to solve the riddle of reality "out there" as well as in the mind. The old theory that things shoot off a representation of themselves into each mind did not square with the many different and distorted pictures of those things and it violated the sense of life, the conviction of immediate seeing and believing. (p. 115)

[Experience] includes—and this is all-important—those "emphases" James so often alludes to—interest, purpose, conception, attention. These seem to work upon what the senses bring as well as upon the inner feelings and ideas. In fact, all forms of thought called higher or rational consist of breaking up the mass of sense impressions in accordance with those wants: 'we break them into histories and we break them into arts and we break them into sciences, and then we feel at home. We discover among its parts relations that were never given to sense at all—mathematical relations, logarithmic functions, etc., and out of an infinite number we call certain ones essential and ignore the rest.'

It is these discoveries and inventions that lead rationalists to invest their worshipful trust in ideas and to despise the world of sense. They see all that is interesting and valuable in life as the result of inner experience and conceptual effort. The rest is common stuff, most of which is ignored, any of which could be replaced by more of the same. Hence the plausibility of a Great Mind, whose perfect workings our smaller minds haltingly recapitulate as we discover what has been flawlessly arranged.

James's acknowledgment of an inner activity is no departure from his naturalist description of mind, but on the contrary an extension of it so as to cover what obviously occurs; after which, radical empiricism with its redefinition of consciousness as a function is confirmed: experience is protean: one part of it can act on another—know it, own it, share it, abstract from it, link it to make now a fact, now an idea. In these ways is the universe fashioned, a universe that changes independently of our thought and also changes in accordance with it, that exists outside us and inside too. We can follow all its doings if we posit experience raw and all-embracing in the Jamesian manner. (pp. 118-19)

The reader will remember that after James had given up medicine, his career embraced psychology and philosophy jointly, not in succession. This important fact strikes us again as we approach the birth of James's second masterpiece, *The Varieties of Religious Experience*. Delivered as the Gifford lectures in Edinburgh in 1901-1902, the book appeared in June of the latter year—those were the happy days of rapid publishing. The work is manifestly one of psychology; its subtitle is "A Study in Human Nature," and its subject matter and naturalistic method are in no way compromised by the application of James's three philosophic principles: radical empiricism, pluralism, and pragmatism. The first formal exposition of pragmatism, we remember, took place in 1898, and the first accounts of the other two doctrines also appeared in the late nineties, just preceding the systematic preparation of these lectures. (p. 227)

It is in effect Volume 3 of *The Principles of Psychology:* it has the requisite bulk (over 200,000 words); it is explicitly subtitled "A Study in Human Nature"; it deals extensively with the subconscious and the pathological; it adheres to the naturalistic tone; it is a piece of stupendous research; and like the pair of volumes that I call its thematic predecessor, it ranges freely over the world of human affairs and puts James's whole philosophy to work.

The seeming digressions about poverty and the social system, the quotations from Whitman and other poets, the literary and moral criticism, the uses of biological evolution and social history, the refutations of crude scientism and shallow philosophy, the fine discrimination among the nuances of emotion and their expressions—these and the sinewy, lucid, vernacular prose, full of its own varieties to match the varying subjects, make the work a fit sequel and conclusion to The Masterpiece.

The candor of James's opening remarks at once pacified the suspicious and forecast an engrossing investigation. His 'purely existential point of view,' says James, does not imply a devaluing of what it describes. He gives as his first example George Fox (an "enthusiast" if ever there was one) whose 'Quaker religion it is impossible to overpraise. In a day of shams, it was a religion of veracity rooted in spiritual inwardness. No one can pretend that in point of spiritual sagacity and capacity, Fox's mind was unsound. Yet from the point of view of his nervous constitution, Fox was a psychopath or *détraqué* of the deepest dye.' And James quotes evidence from Fox's *Journal*.

But—and this is the originality of the handling—James knows that the mere act of classifying facts to which affection is attached makes the feeling mind recoil, often justly. 'Probably a crab would be filled with a sense of personal outrage if it could hear us class it as a crustacean. "I am no such thing," it would say, "I am MYSELF, MYSELF alone."' The classifiers' search for essences threatens or negates worth; in explaining, they explain away—and incite others to do so: 'Fanny's extraordinary conscientiousness is merely a matter of over-instigated nerves. William's melancholy about the universe is due to bad digestion—probably his liver is torpid. Eliza's delight in her church is a symptom of her hysterical constitution. A more fully developed example of reasoning is the fashion quite common nowadays among certain writers, of criticizing the religious emotions by showing a connection between them and the sexual life.' All this medical materialism, the busy

'discrediting of states of mind for which we have an antipathy,' he calls 'a too simpleminded system of thought.'

It is true that modern psychology—James's own brand—does 'assume as a convenient hypothesis that the dependence of mental states upon bodily conditions must be thorough-going and complete. St. Paul certainly had once an epileptoid, if not an epileptic, seizure. But now, I ask you, how can such an existential account of facts of mental history decide one way or another upon their spiritual significance?' The same psychologizing would require that every state of mind be similarly regarded: 'Scientific theories are organically conditioned just as much as religious emotions are. When we think superior states of mind superior to others, is it ever because of what we know concerning their organic antecedents? No! it is always for two entirely different reasons. It is either because we take an immediate delight in them; or else it is because we believe them to bring us good consequential fruits for life.'

With reductivism set aside as unintelligent, James can go on to survey the vast intricacy of the religious record. He is interested only in individual testimony. Churches and theologies are not the subject matter of the psychologist and they themselves are by-products of the primary religious impulse. To the first question, What is the religious sentiment? the answer must be pluralistic and indefinite: it is a collective name for the many sentiments aroused in the religious life. This in turn consists of the experiences and acts of individuals when they feel themselves in some relation to whatever they deem the divine. And the illustrative case to single out here is James's incomparable treatment of Tolstoy's conversion and new life.

The mass of testimony, direct or from qualified observers, that James culled from the literatures of the West and East is marshaled around six great topics: the religion of healthy-mindedness; the sick soul; the divided self and its unification; conversion; saintliness; and mysticism. Nothing short of reading these chapters with their extracts and Jamesian sidelights will give an idea of the total effect. It is a revelation, in its palpitating reality, of mankind as a whole communing with the unseen; fearing, doubting, hoping, worshiping, sacrificing, praying. *The Golden Bough* yields something akin to this panorama, but its contents are necessarily without proportion, and the magical beliefs and practices that it recounts are too remote from ours to move us. Through James's eyes we see what the churches and sects themselves keep us from seeing—the religious spectacle as such, universal, yet not by virtue of an abstraction, as it was for the Deists, but by virtue of the feeling that the word enthusiasm records: the god at work within. (pp. 242-44)

Some thinkers are uncommonly truth-prone, not in the sense of telling the truth but of finding it. The gift is what makes the great scientists. They know the hang of things before the evidence comes in, and above all they know how to frame their intuitions so that these force the world to rethink. James made his revolutionary discoveries because he had, "ahead of time," an inkling of where the truth must lie. . . .

That some of James's formulations have been distorted and others taken too fragmentarily to be useful was to be expected. But much may be hoped from further studious accounts of the continuities between his mind and ours. Each return to his text in a fresh setting or through the prism of another mind discloses one more face of the mountain and better displays its mass and proportions. (p. 301)

Jacques Barzun, in his A Stroll with William James, *Harper & Row, Publishers, 1983, 344 p.*

ADDITIONAL BIBLIOGRAPHY

Allen, Gay Wilson. *William James: A Biography*. New York: Viking Press, 1967, 556 p.
    Most complete biography of James, making use of materials unavailable to Ralph Barton Perry (see Additional Bibliography) which enabled a fuller account of James's wife in his biography. Jacques Barzun, author of the critical study *A Stroll with William James* (1983) calls Allen James's "best biographer."

Ayer, A. J. "William James." In his *The Origins of Pragmatism: Studies in the Philosophy of Charles Sanders Peirce and William James*, pp. 183-336. London: Macmillan, 1968.*
    Section on James consists of a brief introduction and two chapters examining "The Will to Believe and the Pragmatic theory of truth" and "James's Doctrine of Radical Empiricism."

Blanshard, Brand, and Schneider, Herbert W., eds. *In Commemoration of William James, 1842-1942*. New York: Columbia University Press, 1942, 234 p.
    Collection containing essays on various aspects of James's life and works. Critics included in this volume are Dickinson S. Miller, John Dewey, Julius Bixler, Ralph Barton Perry, and Charles Morris.

Boutroux, Émile. *William James*. Translated by Archibald Henderson and Barbara Henderson. New York and London: Longmans, Green, & Co., 1912, 126 p.
    Highly laudatory study divided into sections that examine James's psychology, religious psychology, Pragmatism, metaphysical views, and philosophy of education. The general basis of Boutroux's admiration for his subject is that James "thought that philosophy, even in its boldest speculations, should maintain its bond with the soul of the thinker if it is not to degenerate into an empty assemblage of words and of concepts, devoid of all real content."

Brennan, Bernard P. *The Ethics of William James*. New York: Bookman Associates, 1961, 183 p.
    Study intended to answer the challenge that by definition Pragmatism is not concerned with ethics but only with expediency. Brennan finds that "morality plays a major role in the pragmatism of William James," and that although James did recognize an absolute moral code, in his ethical philosophy moral ideals have an objective validity "lodged in the *de facto* constitution of some existing consciousness."

——. *William James*. New York: Twayne Publishers, 1968, 176 p.
    Useful introductory study.

Browning, Don. "William James's Philosophy of Mysticism." *The Journal of Religion* 59, No. 1 (January 1979): 56-70.
    Questions whether or not James viewed mysticism as a support to moral action. Browning concludes that, as an experience which effaces individuality and pluralism, mysticism in James's philosophy eliminated the possibility of moral action on the part of individuals or groups.

Carus, Paul. "The Pragmatist View of Truth: A Problem without a Solution." *The Monist* XX, No. 1 (January 1910): 139-44.
    Highly critical review of *The Meaning of Truth*. Carus states that although James "misconstrues the philosophies of the past, though he lacks clearness of thought, the first requisite for a philosopher, his writings possess a charm that is unrivaled."

Chapman, John Jay. "William James." In his *The Selected Writings of John Jay Chapman*, edited by Jacques Barzun, pp. 203-07. New York: Farrar, Straus and Cudahy, 1957.
    Character sketch of James.

Cockerell, T.D.A. Review of *The Varieties of Religious Experience*, by William James. *The Dial* XXXIII, No. 394 (16 November 1902): 322-23.
    Calls *The Varieties of Religious Experience* "one of the great books of our time."

Compton, Charles H., ed. *William James: Philosopher and Man*. New York: Scarecrow Press, 1957, 229 p.
    Compilation of quotes and references in a variety of sources. Part One consists of quotations concerning James, many of them passing references made by such figures as Oliver Wendell Holmes, Theodore Roosevelt, and Adlai E. Stevenson. Part Two consists of references to James in 652 books by 344 authors.

Dittes, James E. "Beyond William James." In *Beyond the Classics? Essays in the Scientific Study of Religion*, edited by Charles Y. Glock and Phillip E. Hammond, pp. 291-354. New York: Harper & Row, 1973.
    Discussion of James's influence on the field of the psychology of religion. Dittes states that "James can be appropriately regarded as the founder of American psychology of religion not for the psychological theories or psychological data or psychological method he offered, but for his philosophical position or perhaps more accurately, philosophical temper or outlook." This judgement is disputed in the excerpt by Gary T. Alexander (1979).

Dooley, Patrick Kiaran. *Pragmatism as Humanism: The Philosophy of William James*. Chicago: Nelson-Hall, 1974, 220 p.
    Critic states that he has "attempted to articulate and defend the unity and coherence of James' philosophical vision," and finds the philosophy of humanism is the binding theme of James's works.

Feinstein, Howard M. *Becoming William James*. Ithaca, N.Y.: Cornell University Press, 377 p.
    Psychoanalytic biography of James up to the age of thirty, with particular emphasis on his relationship with his father.

Gordy, J. P. "Professor Ladd's Criticism of James's Psychology." *The Philosophical Review* I, No. 3 (May 1892): 299-305.
    Rebuttal to an attack on James's *The Principles of Psychology* (see entry in Additional Bibliography by George Trumbull Ladd).

Grattan, C. Hartley. "William James." In his *The Three Jameses: A Family of Minds*, pp. 108-207. 1932. Reprint. New York: New York University Press, 1962.*
    Biographical and critical study.

Hertz, Richard A. "James and Moore: Two Perspectives on Truth." *Journal of the History of Philosophy* IX (1971): 213-21.
    Examines Moore's critique (see Additional Bibliography) of James's theory of truth. Hertz finds that an essential disparity of perspective between the two thinkers—namely, the religionist orientation of Moore and the humanist position of James—led to their conflicting ideas of truth.

Hocks, Richard A. *Henry James and Pragmatistic Thought: A Study in the Relationship between the Philosophy of William James and the Literary Art of Henry James*. Chapel Hill: University of North Carolina Press, 1974, 258 p.
    Critic states that "the key which the thesis of this entire book turns on is above all else our grasping and understanding William's thought through Henry's own eyes." Hocks finds that Henry James had "an extraordinarily good grasp" of William James's philosophic thought and that in his later fiction he "actualized" the doctrine of Pragmatism.

Hoffman, Frederick J. "William James and the Modern Literary Consciousness." *Criticism* IV, No. 1 (Winter 1962): 1-13.
    Asserts that the "definition of an isolated self, its precise location in both space and time, its relationship to objects and to process" are the dominant concerns of modern literature, and that James's view of the self as a "process" in perpetual flux, rather than a "substance" with measurable qualities, served as an intellectual and literary influence on modern writers.

Hull, Byron D. "*Henderson the Rain King* and William James." *Criticism* XIII, No. 4 (Fall 1971): 402-14.

Finds Saul Bellow's novel *Henderson the Rain King* to be influenced by James's *The Principles of Psychology*. Hull contends that the initiation process that the protagonist undergoes is patterned after concepts in James's work, particularly the sort of therapeutic heroism in confronting evil which James often advocated.

Ladd, George Trumbull. "Psychology as So-Called 'Natural Science'." *The Philosophical Review* I, No. 1 (January 1892): 24-53.

Attack on James's conception of psychology as a natural science which excludes both metaphysics and physiology from its concerns. For a rebuttal to this essay, see the entry in the Additional Bibliography by O. P. Gordy.

Lee, Vernon. "Professor James and the *Will to Believe*." In her *Gospels of Anarchy, and Other Contemporary Studies*, pp. 193-231. London: T. Fisher Unwin, 1908.

Calls the essay of *The Will to Believe* "delightful and intolerable," stating that James's conception actually posits a "*need to believe*." Finding this basic contention untrue, Lee offers a description of an agnostic mind which does not hold belief to be a necessity. She also proposes the existence of both a will and a need *not* to believe.

Linschoten, Hans. *On the Way Toward a Phenomenological Psychology: The Psychology of William James*. Edited by Amedeo Giorgi. Pittsburgh: Duquesne University Press, 1968, 319 p.

Study of James's psychological theory based on the viewpoint that *The Principles of Psychology* "presupposes" concepts of the phenomenological school of psychology, specifically the idea that experience does not exist apart from a particular "experience-of-something."

Lovejoy, Arthur. *The Thirteen Pragmatisms, and Other Essays*. Baltimore: Johns Hopkins Press, 1963, 290 p.

Collects Lovejoy's writings on Pragmatism, including the essay "William James as Philosopher" (1911), which argues for James's often-impugned logical rigor and for the subtle complexities of what have commonly been considered easily understood works.

McDermott, John J. Introduction to *The Writings of William James: A Comprehensive Edition*, by William James, edited by John J. McDermott, pp. xiii-xliv. New York: Random House, 1967.

Survey of James's major works and philosophic concepts. Included in this edition is an important annotated bibliography of James's writings.

MacLeod, Robert B., ed. *William James: Unfinished Business*. Washington, D.C.: American Psychological Association, 1969, 106 p.

Collection of essays on James's psychological theories, including "William James's Humanism and the Problem of Free Will" by psychologist Rollo May.

Moore, Edward C. *William James*. New York: Washington Square Press, 1966, 194 p.

Introductory study designed for the general reader. Moore considers the full range of James's thought in order to avoid what he believes has been an undue emphasis placed on the essay "The Will to Believe" and the Pragmatic theory of truth.

Moore, G. E. "William James's 'Pragmatism'." In his *Philosophical Studies*, pp. 97-146. New York: Harcourt, Brace and Co., 1922.

Indictment of James's Pragmatic theory of truth in terms of its logical validity and coherence. Moore finds that James's dual criteria of usefulness plus verification do not result in a logically defensible theory. For a discussion of Moore's critique, see the entry in the Additional Bibliography by Richard A. Hertz.

Moore, John Morrison. "Experiential Religion in the Thought of William James." In his *Theories of Religious Experience, with Special Reference to James, Otto, and Bergson*. New York: Round Table Press, 1938, pp. 1-74.

Challenges James's assumption in *The Varieties of Religious Experience* that the objective forms of religion derive from the sub-

jective mystical experiences of individuals. Moore concludes that "it cannot be maintained that all of the rites, doctrines, and institutions of religion have originated in personal religious experience, for these external aspects of religion antedate and condition all the personal experience of which we have any record."

Morris, Lloyd. *William James: The Message of a Modern Mind*. New York: Charles Scribner's Sons, 1950, 98 p.

Introductory study designed for the general reader. Separate chapters describe and discuss James's central philosophical doctrines, including "The Pragmatic Method," "The Nature of Truth," and "A World of Pure Experience," while a closing chapter considers "The Influence of William James."

Otto, Max, and others. *William James: The Man and the Thinker*. Madison: University of Wisconsin Press, 1942, 147 p.

Centenary collection of essays which includes contributions by Dickinson S. Miller, John Dewey, and Julius Seelye Bixler.

Peirce, Charles Sanders. *Collected Papers of Charles Sanders Peirce*, Vols. V and VI. Cambridge: Belknap Press of Harvard University, 1960, 455 p.

Peirce's collected writings on Pragmatism, with several passing references to James's.

Pendleton, James D. "The James Brothers and 'The Real Thing': A Study in Pragmatic Reality." *South Atlantic Bulletin* XXXVIII, No. 4 (November 1973): 3-10.

Finds Henry James's short story "The Real Thing" to be "a literary embodiment of the major philosophic and scientific concepts of the late nineteenth century," specifically of William James's doctrine of Pragmatism. Pendleton argues that the two authors influenced each other's view of life.

Perry, Ralph Barton. *The Thought and Character of William James*. 2 vols. Boston: Little, Brown, and Co., 1935.

The first extensive biography of James, including many useful excerpts from letters and unpublished manuscripts.

Roth, John K. *Freedom and the Moral Life*. Philadelphia: Westminster Press, 1969, 157 p.

Studies the development throughout James's writings of the belief that individuals have the power and freedom to change themselves and their environment. In light of this freedom, Roth asks, what moral and ethical values would James advise adopting? Roth concludes that James's moral philosophy "stresses the pursuit of meaning through the extension of the values of freedom and unity," values which promote "an ordered existence and a sense of meaning that will not cease to grow."

Seigfried, Charlene Haddock. *Chaos and Context: A Study in William James*. Athens: Ohio University Press, 1978, 137 p.

Studies James's doctrine of relations, his idea that "the relations between things, conjunctive as well as disjunctive, are just as much matters of direct particular experience, neither more so nor less, than the things themselves." This direction of inquiry is accompanied by a consideration of James's doctrine of experience, which states that experience is never abstract but is always an experience of something particular, just as consciousness, in James's view, is always consciousness of something particular. Seigfried states in her conclusion that "the quasi-chaos of pure experience [Seigfried's modification of the "ordinary absolute chaos" posited by James] allows for tendencies and resistances which can be ignored only at our peril, since the flux of sensation has its own continuity, movement, and sense of direction. These experience tendencies are the basis for James's claim that relations are really experienced."

Skrupskelis, Ignas K. *William James: A Reference Guide*. Boston: G. K. Hall, 1977, 250 p.

Annotated bibliography of critical writings on James through 1974.

Strout, Cushing. "*All the King's Men* and the Shadow of William James." *The Southern Review* n.s. 6, No. 11 (Autumn 1970): 920-34.

Illustrates the influence of James's philosophic thought on Robert Penn Warren's novel *All the King's Men*.

————. "The Pluralistic Identity of William James: A Psycho-historical Reading of *The Varieties of Religious Experience*." *American Quarterly* XXIII, No. 2 (May 1971): 135-52.

> Follows the development of James's psychological, religious, and philosophic thought by a comparison with the development of the Swedenborgian thought of his father, Henry James, Sr.

————. "The Unfinished Arch: William James and the Idea of History" and "William James and the Twice-Born Sick Soul." In his *The Veracious Imagination: Essays on American History, Literature, and Biography*, pp. 44-56, pp. 199-222. Middleton, Conn.: Wesleyan University Press, 1981.

> The first essay discusses the implications of James's concept of Pragmatic truth for the writing of history. While stating that James replaced "an artificial rationalism with a pragmatic theory that tended to obscure the responsibility of truth-finding procedures," Strout speculates that James left uncompleted at his death a theory of cause and effect of potential value to the resolution of conflicting philosophical perspectives on historical events. The second essay on James in this collection is a biographical examination of James's emotional intellectual development which attempts to account for his eventual commitment to philosophy.

Thayer, H. S. "The Right to Believe: William James's Reinterpretation of the Function of Religious Belief." *The Kenyon Review* n.s. V, No. 1 (Winter 1983): 89-105.

> Recent defense of James's concept of the will to believe.

Wickham, Harvey. "Things Jamesian." In his *The Unrealists: James, Bergson, Santayana, Einstein, Bertrand Russell, John Dewey, Alexander and Whitehead*, pp. 29-67. New York: Lincoln MacVeagh, Dial Press, 1930.

> Unrelenting attack on the plausibility and coherence of James's philosophy.

Wild, John. *The Radical Empiricism of William James*. Garden City, N.Y.: Doubleday & Co., 1969, 430 p.

> Treats James as "an early member of that significant group of thinkers, scattered widely over the Western world, who became dissatisfied with the artificial abstractness of traditional systems of thought." Wild finds that James's later philosophic attitude of radical empiricism also informs the direction of his early works, most prominently *The Principles of Psychology*. This view accounts for James's avoidance of abstract systems of philosophical terminology, an intellectual policy which enabled him "to keep his thought in line with structures that could be found in the brute facts of existence." As such, James's thought anticipates the later school of phenomenological philosophy, which sought "not to construct but rather to find patterns in existence."

Vladislav (Felitsianovich) Khodasevich

1886-1939

(Also transliterated Chodasiewicz, Hodasevich, and Xodasevic) Russian poet, biographer, essayist, critic, and translator.

At the time of his death in 1939, Khodasevich was eulogized by Vladimir Nabokov as "the greatest Russian poet that the twentieth century has yet produced." However, until recently his writings have been largely unfamiliar to Western readers and critics, as well as to many specialists in modern Russian literature. He is best known as an ardent disciple of Alexander Pushkin, an important literary critic, and a poet who combined a knowledge of the classical tradition in Russian poetry with a modern ironic and pessimistic vision.

Khodasevich was born in Moscow to a middle-class family of Polish descent. The youngest of six children, he almost died in infancy and was plagued by poor health throughout his life. Khodasevich demonstrated literary interest and ability at an early age: he began to read at age three and by the age of six was writing poetry. A model student, Khodasevich attended Moscow's Third Gymnasium, which had a staunchly traditional curriculum that emphasized the study of the classics. While there, he acquired an appreciation of classicism in art that became a key stylistic feature of his major poetry. Also at the gymnasium, Khodasevich formed friendships with several students who would later become important in the Russian Symbolist movement, including Viktor Gofman and Alexander Bryusov, brother of Valery Bryusov, who was the leader of the movement and through whom Khodasevich was introduced to Andrey Bely and Aleksandr Blok. The Russian Symbolist movement was primarily derived from the French Symbolist school, which flourished in the late nineteenth century. While the Russian Symbolists led by Bryusov continued in the French tradition, stressing aestheticism and the irrelevance of didactic intent, another faction of the movement, headed by Blok, saw their craft as a form of mystical worship and themselves as mediators between the supernatural and the mundane. As a young poet, Khodasevich respected the work of these writers and was considerably influenced by their ideology and techniques. However, as he matured as a poet, Khodasevich developed an ironic, realist aesthetic that differed fundamentally from the idealist tenets of Symbolism, which attempted to make poetry into a spiritual absolute. Later in his life, Khodasevich criticized symbolism for its ambition "to turn art into reality and reality into art."

Although Khodasevich married three times, it was his second marriage, to the young poet Nina Berberova, that had the most impact on his career. Finding conditions under the new Soviet regime intolerable, he and Berberova decided to emigrate from Russia in 1922. Khodasevich hoped that the move would help restore his waning physical and mental health as well as provide Berberova with the artistic freedom he felt she needed in order to develop as a poet. However, tormented by feelings of homesickness and displacement, Khodasevich found it difficult living in Europe and moved more than forty times during the first five years of his emigration. In 1926 he settled in Paris, where he remained for the rest of his life. In the opinion of many commentators, emigration meant poetic decline for Khodasev-

ich, who wrote very little poetry after the publication of his collected poems in 1927.

Instead, he channeled his energy into the translation of the works of Polish, French, and Jewish writers he admired and into literary criticism, becoming one of the most important critics in the émigré community. His greatest achievements in this field are two important studies of Pushkin and a critical biography of the eighteenth-century Russian poet Gavriil Derzhavin, who, next to Pushkin, was the writer he most revered. During these years Khodasevich also wrote *Nekropol'*, his reminiscences of Bryusov, Blok, and others connected with the Symbolist movement. In his last years, Khodasevich's outlook on life, which had always been pessimistic, grew bleaker due to his steadily declining health, divorce from Berberova, and persistent anguish over his émigré status. Early in 1939, Khodasevich was diagnosed as having intestinal cancer, which proved fatal six months later.

Molodost', Khodasevich's first volume of poetry, is strongly marked by the influence of various Russian Symbolist poets, Bryusov in particular. As a young poet, Khodasevich had apprenticed himself to the Symbolist masters he admired, and *Molodost'* bears evidence that he was still imitating these writers and had not yet discovered his own authoritative poetic voice. The poems in this collection exhibit such traits of Symbolist style as rhetorical vagueness, morbid themes, and a general ambience of the other-wordly. Khodasevich's second collection, *Schastlivyi domik*, contains distinct signs of his movement away from the rhetorical characteristics of Symbolism and toward an ability to treat emotionally charged subjects in an unemotional and ironic fashion. Critics find that Khodasevich wrote his most distinctive poetry after *Schastlivyi domik*. It is in his third book, *Putem zerna*, that he fully established the ironic mode that is a distinctive aspect of his work. While the poems in this collection speak of anxiety, pessimism, and despair, these subjects are discussed with an aloof impartiality. Khodasevich's next major collection of poetry, *Tiazhelaia lira*, was composed in St. Petersburg shortly before his emigration. The poems in this work reflect his great love of this city and his depression over his impending departure. Some critics consider *Tiazhelaia lira* Khodasevich's most beautifully crafted work. In this book his bleak vision of existence is accentuated by descriptions of his severe poverty. However, this grim vision is characterized by an ironic perspective, achieved by bestowing hyperbolic significance upon commonplace objects and by describing cosmic elements in domestic terms. For example, in "Ballada" ("Ballad"), one of the most famous poems in this collection, the poet gazes up at a single, naked lightbulb in the ceiling and says, "I look into a plaster sky / at a sixty-watt sun." Through his skillful use of irony, Khodasevich described his sense of resignation before the hopelessness of the human condition, but avoided a self-pitying or complaining stance. *Evropeiskaia noch'*, Khodasevich's last major collection of poetry, appeared in his collected poems, *Sobranie stikov*, in 1927. Written during his years in exile, it is considered his most despairing work. In this collection, the poet looks back and mourns the losses of his past. Although Khodasevich's tone is characteristically impersonal and detached, the poems depict scenes of brutality, perversion, and anger, symbolizing the barbarity of being denied the freedom to create art. Several of the most powerful poems in *Evropeiskaia noch'* blend Khodasevich's memories of Russia with actual experiences in his émigré life. These poems are often concerned with death or abandonment, which some critics believe foreshadows Khodasevich's abdication of poetry.

Although Khodasevich received praise from many famous writers of his day, including Bely, Nikolai Gumilev, Maxim Gorky, and Osip Mandelstam, until recent years only a few scholarly articles had been written on his poetry. Some scholars believe that Khodasevich's previous neglect was due to the fact that he was largely a traditionalist during a time of experimentation in Russian poetry. Most commentators now agree that in the small quantity of poetry he produced, Khodasevich blended the themes and techniques of his poetic heritage and the ironic perspective of modern verse to produce one of the most distinctive contributions to Russian poetry in the twentieth century.

PRINCIPAL WORKS

Molodost' (poetry) 1908
Schastlivyi domik (poetry) 1914
Putem zerna (poetry) 1920
Stat'i o russkoi poezii (criticism) 1922
Tiazhelaia lira (poetry) 1922
Poeticheskoe khoziaistvo Pushkina (criticism) 1924
Sobranie stikov (poetry) 1927
Derzhavin (biography) 1931
O Pushkine (criticism) 1937

Nekropol' (memoirs) 1939
"On Sirin" (essay) 1970; published in journal *Triquarterly*
"Four Poems" (poetry) 1971; published in journal *The Russian Review*
"Thirty-four lyric poems" (poetry) 1974; published in journal *Russian Literature Triquarterly*
"Khodasevich's Gorky" (essay) 1976; published in journal *Yale Theatre*

Translated selections of Khodasevich's poetry and prose have appeared in the following publications: *A Second Book of Russian Verse; New Directions 1941: Anthology in Prose and Poetry; A Treasure of Russian Verse; A Little Treasury of World Poetry; The Complection of Russian Literature;* and *The Bitter Air of Exile: Russian Writers in the West, 1922-1972.*

NIKOLAI GUMILEV (essay date 1914)

[*Gumilev was one of the founders and major figures of the Acmeist movement in early twentieth-century Russian poetry. The Acmeists reacted against the earlier school of the Russian Symbolists, whose work they criticized as abstract, diffuse, and alienated by mysticism from the beauties and value of the physical world. Gumilev and other Acmeists, including his wife Anna Akhmatova and Osip Mandelstam, briefly established a poetics that demanded concise and concrete renderings of physical reality, emphasizing a neo-Classic formalism that contrasted with what the Acmeists considered the loose transcendental verbiage of the Symbolists. In the following excerpt, originally published in the Acmeist journal* Apollon *in 1914, Gumilev reviews Khodasevich's second poetry collection,* Schastlivyi domik.]

Vladislav Khodasevich's first book of poems came out in 1908, the second [**Happy Home**] only now. And after six years, he wanted to prepare only thirty-five poems. Such miserliness is very profitable for the poet. We do not grow accustomed to his dream or his intonation, he appears unexpectedly before us with interesting new words and does not stay too long, leaving behind him a pleasant feeling of not being fully satisfied and the desire for another visit. Both Tyutchev and Annensky were like that, and how they love them!

Khodasevich has the right to be such a nice guest. He is not dull; not dull to such an extent that he is not even paradoxical. When you do not agree with him and do not sympathize with him, you still believe and admire him. True, one would often like him to speak more confidently and to be freer in his gestures. A European in his love for the details of beauty, he is still a Slav in his sort of peculiar indifferent weariness and melancholy skepticism. Only hopes or sufferings can excite such a soul, and Khodasevich voluntarily, even with a certain arrogance, renounced both. . . . (pp. 147-48)

In Khodasevich's poems, with their somewhat flaccid rhythmics and not always expressive stylistics, much attention is devoted to composition, and that is what makes them beautiful. The reader's attention follows the poet easily, as if in a graceful dance, now dying away, now gliding, going deeper, or rising along the lines, which end harmonically, and which are new for every poem. The poet is either unable or does not wish to use all this energy from the rhythmic motion of ideas and images to create the temple of a new world-perception; he is for now only a ballet-master, but the dances he teaches are sacred dances. (p. 148)

Nikolai Gumilev, in a chapter in his On Russian Poetry, *edited and translated by David Lapeza, Ardis, 1977, pp. 140-49.**

VLADISLAV KHODASEVICH   (lecture date 1921)

[The following excerpt is from an essay written to mark the 84th anniversary of the death of Alexander Pushkin which was published in the journal Dom literatorov *in 1921. In this essay, Khodasevich reflects on the decline of modern Russian poetry, which he believed was indicated by a waning appreciation for Pushkin's poetry. He maintains that modern readers of Pushkin who value the form of his poetry but fail to consider its content are promoting a reverse "Pisarevism," referring to the critical attitude of Dmitri Pisarev, a nineteenth-century nihilist critic who attacked Pushkin's ornate and grandiose style and his lack of political and social content.]*

Much in Pushkin is almost incomprehensible to some of the younger poets, for the reason, by the way, that they are not always familiar enough with all that surrounds Pushkin; because the spirit and the style of his epoch are alien to them, and they have not come into contact with any remnants of his era. The same thing should be said of the language. Perhaps they even follow Pushkin's exhortation to learn the language from Moscow's women bakers of liturgical breads—but they themselves no longer speak the same language. Many shades of Pushkin's lexicon, so meaningful to us, to them are no more than archaisms. Some words with which a most valuable tradition is connected and which you introduce into your own poetry with great care, not knowing whether you have an inner right to use them—to such a degree they have an exceptional sacramental meaning for us—to prove to be simply pale in the judgment of the young poet—who does not even suspect what other things these words might mean to you, other than what they mean for everyone according to Dahl's dictionary. Occasionally whole series of the most cherished intimate thoughts and feelings prove to be inexpressible by means other than those found within the bounds of Pushkin's lexicon and syntax—and this, the most cherished, is seen only as "stylization."

One cannot help pointing at the same time to the recent resurgence of the tendency to sever form from content, and to the propagation of the idea of the primacy of form—much the way the primacy of content was preached during the first eclipse of Pushkin. Both the latter and the former are equally inimical to the whole spirit of Pushkin's poetry. Those who state that Pushkin is great by virtue of the virtuosity of his form, and that therefore his content is a secondary thing, because content in poetry has no meaning, are really "Pisarevites" in reverse. Not knowing this themselves, they are slanderers and secret enemies of Pushkin, acting in the guise of friends.

In saying all this I do not at all have in mind the Futurists, but rather the representatives of the more "moderate" literary groups. One could recount a large number of sad and curious anecdotes which prove that a direct elementary misunderstanding and ignorance of Pushkin is a phenomenon that is equally prevalent in young literary circles and among readers. All of this is the result of a growing inattentiveness to Pushkin. It arises from the fact that Pushkin's epoch is no longer our epoch, but he has not yet become a writer of antiquity, so that a scholarly study of Pushkin, whatever huge steps it may have taken, is still the legacy of a few. The importance and value of such study are not yet understood by either the mass reader or the mass writer. And thus the naive youth of our day, equally the reader and the young poet, decide that Pushkin is simply "old-fashioned."

The very fact that the cooling-off toward Pushkin is developed not in the flasks of the literary laboratory, that it is equally common to the reader and the writer, indicates that it feeds on the quotidian circumstances of reality. As in the days of Pisarev, the cooling-off toward Pushkin, the forgetting of Pushkin and insensitivity to him is supported by the mass of readers, that is, it arises for reasons that are, in the literary-social sense, organic. The reasons are not the same ones today that they were in the days of Pisarev, the aloofness from Pushkin now is motivated by other considerations, but it may prove to be more durable, spread wider, and last for a longer period of time, because it is prepared by historical circumstances of vast import and scope.

The Revolution brought much that is good. But we all know that together with the war it brought an as-yet-unseen bitterness and coarsening in all, without exception, strata of Russian people. A whole series of other circumstances leads to a situation wherein, no matter how we should strain toward the preservation of culture, a time of temporary decline and tarnishing of culture lies ahead. Together with culture the image of Pushkin will also tarnish.

But I would be insincere if, having once started talking of this, I did not express myself to the end. It may happen that the general twilight of our culture should disperse, but that phenomenon which I have called the eclipse of Pushkin will yet last longer and will not pass without leaving its mark. The historical rupture with the previous, Pushkinian epoch, will forever move Pushkin away into the depths of history. That closeness to Pushkin within which we grew up shall never again repeat itself . . .

Pushkin did not value popular adoration, for he did not believe in it. At best he had hoped to be liked by the people "for a long time"—but not "forever." "And long shall I remain liked by the people . . ." He saw the process of cooling-off as unavoidable, and outwardly expressed in two ways: either the crowd spits at the altar of the poet, that is, insults and hates him—or else it shakes his tripod in "childlike playfulness." In relation to Pushkin himself the first formula is already impossible: the "crowd" will never spit at the altar where his fire yet burns; but the next line: "And in childlike playfulness it shakes your tripod," will fully come to pass. We are already watching the advent of the second eclipse. And there will be more of them. The tripod will not fall for all ages, but it will be periodically shaken under the surging pressure of the crowd, which, playful and pitying nothing, is like history, like time. (pp. 66-9)

Times drives the crowd of people, who hurry to climb up on the stage of history, in order to play their role . . . and relinquish their place to others who are already shoving from behind. Making noise and crowding around, the mass shakes the tripod of the poet. We throw out most valuable possessions, our love for Pushkin, like a handful of sweet-smelling grass, into the fire of the tripod. And it will burn.

Moved back into the "smoke of centuries," Pushkin will arise in gigantic stature. National pride in him will flow into indestructible bronze forms—but that spontaneous closeness that heart-felt tenderness with which we loved Pushkin will never be known to coming generations. . . . Perhaps they will solve the riddles that we did not solve. But much of what was seen and loved by *us* they will never see.

That which I have spoken about is probably felt by many as a burning anguish, as something horrific, from which one may, perhaps, want to hide. Perhaps I too feel the pain, and I too feel like hiding—but what is to be done? History, generally speaking, *is* uncomfortable. "And from the fates there's no protection."

The heightened interest in the words of the poet which was felt by many people during the past several years arose, perhaps, from a premonition, from an insistent need: partly to decipher Pushkin while it is not yet too late, while the tie with his time is not yet lost forever; and partly, it seems to me, it was suggested by the same premonition: we are agreeing to what call we should answer, how we should communicate with each other in the oncoming darkness. (pp. 69-70)

> *Vladislav Khodasevich, "The Shaken Tripod,"*
> *translated by Alexander Golubov, in* Modern Russian
> Poets on Poetry, *edited by Carl R. Proffer and Joseph*
> *Brodsky, Ardis, 1974, pp. 61-70.*

ANDREI BELY (essay date 1922)

[*Bely is recognized as the most original and influential writer of the Russian Symbolist movement. A brilliant, restless, and undisciplined spirit, Bely consistently sought for spiritual meaning within the social and literary turmoil of pre-Soviet Russia. His enormous body of work, much of it autobiographical, presents a vivid impression of this quest. Bely's explorations of form and language served as a first step toward the modernist revolution in Russian verse, a call-to-arms by many young writers for more individual artistic freedom and the complete overthrow of traditional values and social criticism of the nineteenth century. Although he was hardly a popular writer—his work was too subjective and esoteric for the general public—Bely received great attention and acclaim as the standard-bearer for those Symbolists who felt that Symbolism was more of a world-view than a mere literary method. Bely's works are characterized by their verbal artistry, inner rhythm, and keenly developed style. In the following excerpt, originally published in the journal* Zapiski mechtatelei *in 1922, Bely praises the simplicity and deep spiritual knowledge evidenced in Khodasevich's poetry.*]

There is a rare happiness in writing—the opportunity of sharing a joy with one's reader in a natural manner; we have few joys, which is why one values them. Not so long ago I experienced a rare joy. I heard some poems, and I wanted to shout out: "How new this is, how true. This is what we need. This is what is newer than Futurism, Expressionism, and all the other schools!" The poems belonged to a poet who is not new, a poet without benefit of colorful plumage, simply a poet. There is one note in this poetry, but it will outlive the "latest," for the "latest" ages when the "very latest" appears. A sport has been popular in our poetry for about fifteen years, a sport of the "very latest" squeezing out the "latest," so no one has had time for a poet who was not the "latest" from the beginning. There was no time for him while Mayakovsky with such talent was "trousering" in the clouds and Esenin was calving in the sky with—what can you say?—talent also, and Kliuev poured Lake Chad into his teakettle and drank it down, cultivating his baobab trees in the North with so very much talent, almost with genius. We had no time to think about a simple baobabless poet whose truthfulness, shamefulness, and modesty seem to exclude him from the contest for the laurel wreath.

The wonder is that the laurel wreath has grown on him by itself.

Khodasevich is neither a new poet nor one who has received the approving glance of criticism. By standing in one place and not striving after novelty, he has traced and deepened his not especially colorful lines to the point of—classicism, stylization? No: to put the matter honestly, both for myself and for a poet who suddenly shines with simplicity in the midst of the motley colors and Persian carpets of modernism, I must ask, "What is this? Is it Realism brought to the point of harsh and somber prose, or is it the opening up of a spiritual world?"

> Ah, feel vexation's will
> And happiness (is that required?)
> When wondrously a chill
> Runs through our hair cold-fired.
> Your ear won't hear, your eye won't find.
> In secret fashion life is fine,
> The sky's infused, so deep, so whole,
> Into your almost ransomed soul.

Is this really poetry? A simple iambic meter, no metaphors, no colors—it's almost a report; but it is a report containing dispassionate spiritual knowledge about the process of artistic creation. Do you know the thing that magically illumines these clean lines? It is one line—more properly, one word: "almost." An "almost ransomed soul"—*pochti svobodnaya dusha.* As Tolstoy showed us in his article that the secret of art commences with that "certain little something," so here too is the magic beauty of truth in the "almost" of these lines. And this "almost" is the essence of Khodasevich's poetry. Take this poem:

> I look contemptuously through my portal.
> I look contemptuously through myself.
> I call forth weather's blows most mortal,
> Not trusting nature's help.
> Surrounded by the day's blue mesh
> I see but starless blackness.
> So wriggles in its bed too freshly made
> An earthworm severed by a spade.

The single stroke of these last two lines contains all the imagery of this eight-line poem; the poem, seen as a picture, leaves its frame and stands in relation to life.

Our era presents us an analogous example in the person of Baratynsky. In the previous century he was relegated to the twilight zone by, in turns, the poetry of Pushkin, Benediktov, Lermontov, Alexei Tolstoy, and Nadson. He was pushed into the background by both the great and the small, all so that in the twentieth century he could reveal his true giant stature. And Khodasevich may say, as Baratynsky said about his muse, that you would not call her a beauty, but she is striking for "the unusual expression of her face." This unusual expression holds the shadowy and harsh truth of a style similar to Rembrandt's: a spiritual truth. (pp. 224-26)

> *Andrei Bely, "On Vladislav Khodasevich," in* The
> Complection of Russian Literature: A Cento, *edited*
> *by Andrew Field, Atheneum, 1971, pp. 224-26.*

D. S. MIRSKY (essay date 1926)

[*Mirsky was a Russian prince who fled his country after the Bolshevik Revolution and settled in London. While in England, he wrote two important and comprehensive histories of Russian literature,* Contemporary Russian Literature *(1926) and* A History of Russian Literature *(1927). In 1932, having reconciled himself to the Soviet regime, Mirsky returned to the U.S.S.R. He continued to write literary criticism, but his work eventually ran afoul of Soviet censors and he was exiled to Siberia. He disappeared in 1937. In the following excerpt, Mirsky offers a descriptive appraisal of Khodasevich's major poetry.]*

The poets born after 1880 contributed little or nothing to the genuine achievement of symbolism. An exception is the case of Vladisláv Khodasévich. . . . Though in his technique he is almost free from symbolist influences, the general spirit of his poetry is much more akin to symbolism than to that of the younger school, for, alone of the younger poets, he is a mystic. His first book appeared in 1908, but he won general recognition only after the publication of his later, post-Revolutionary books, **The Way of the Grain** . . . and **The Heavy Lyre** . . . , which are full of mature and confident art. Khodasévich is a mystical spiritualist, but in the expression of his intuitions he is an ironist. His poetry is the expression of the ironic and tragic contradiction between the freedom of the immortal soul and its thralldom to matter and necessity. This eternal theme is expressed in his verse with a neatness and elegance rather reminiscent of the wit of an older age. Wit, in fact, is the principal characteristic of Khodasévich's poetry, and his mystical poems regularly end with a pointed epigram. This manner is very effective and goes home to the most unpoetical reader. He sprang into popularity in 1919-20, when, under the influence of their super-human suffering, the Russian intellectuals were more than usually open to the lure of mystic moods. But in spite of his mystical faith, he is a classicist, and his style is a skillful revival of the forms and fashions of the Golden Age of Púshkin. (pp. 475-76)

> D. S. Mirsky, "The Symbolists," *in his* A History of Russian Literature Comprising "A History of Russian Literature" *and* "Contemporary Russian Literature," *edited by Francis J. Whitfield, Alfred A. Knopf, 1973, pp. 430-84.*

Khodasevich in 1931. From The Italics Are Mine. *Copyright © 1969 by Nina Berberova. Reproduced by permission of Harcourt Brace Jovanovich, Inc.*

VLADIMIR NABOKOV (essay date 1939)

[A Russian-born novelist who emigrated in 1919 and who wrote most of his works in English, Nabokov was a prolific contributor to many literary fields and distinguished himself in particular as the author of the novels Lolita *(1955) and* Pale Fire *(1962). In his works Nabokov explored the origins of creativity, the relationships of artists to their work, and the nature of invented reality. Considered a brilliant prose stylist, Nabokov frequently entertains and simultaneously exasperates the reader with his intellectual and verbal play. Nabokov's technical genius as well as the exuberance of his creative imagination mark him as a major twentieth-century author. The following excerpt, from an essay entitled "On Hodasevich," first appeared in 1939 in a Russian émigré literary magazine published in Paris. In it, Nabokov assesses Khodasevich's stature in modern Russian poetry and remarks that his work possesses the mark of authentic poetry—the inseparability of its various "facets" (form, feeling, subject matter) from the whole poem.]*

This poet, the greatest Russian poet of our time, Pushkin's literary descendant in Tyutchev's line of succession, shall remain the pride of Russian poetry as long as its last memory lives. What makes his genius particularly striking is that it matured in the years of our literature's torpescence, when the Bolshevist era neatly divided poets into established optimists and demoted pessimists, endemic hearties and exiled hypochondriacs; a classification which, incidentally, leads to an instructive paradox: inside Russia the dictate acts from outside; outside Russia, it acts from within. The will of the government, which implicitly demands a writer's affectionate attention toward a parachute, a farm tractor, a Red Army soldier, or the participant in some polar venture (i.e. toward this or that externality of the world) is naturally considerably more powerful than the injunction of exile, addressed to man's inner world. . . . [If one] finds hard to imagine a poet, in the confines of Russia, refusing to bend under the yoke (such as, for example, declining to translate a Caucasian poetaster's jingles) and behaving rashly enough to put the muse's liberty above his own, one should expect to find more easily in *émigré* Russia plucky loners who would not wish to unite and pool their poetical preoccupations in a sort of communistery of the spirit.

Even genius does not save one in Russia; in exile, one is saved by genius alone. No matter how difficult Hodasevich's last years were, no matter how sorely the banality of an *émigré*'s lot irked him, no matter, too, how much the good old indifference of fellow mortals contributed to his mortal extinction, Hodasevich is safely enshrined in timeless Russia. Indeed, he himself was ready to admit, through the hiss of his bilious banter, through the "cold and murk" of the days predicted by Blok, that he occupied a special position: the blissful solitude of a height others could not attain.

Here I have no intention of hitting bystanders with a swing of the thurible. A few poets of the *émigré* generation are still on their way up and, who knows, may reach the summits of art—if only they do not fritter away life in a second-rate Paris of their own, which sails by with a slight list in the mirrors of taverns without mingling in any way with the French Paris, a motionless and impenetrable town. Hodasevich seemed to have sensed in his very fingers the branching influence of the poetry he created in exile and therefore felt a certain responsibility for its destiny, a destiny which irritated him more than it saddened him. The glum notes of cheap verse struck him more as a parody than as the echo of his collection, *Evropeyskaya Noch' (European Night),* where bitterness, anger, angels, the gulf of adjacent vowels—everything, in short, was genuine, unique, and quite unrelated to the current moods which clouded the verse of many of those who were more or less his disciples.

To speak of his *masterstvo, Meisterschaft,* ''mastery,'' i.e. ''technique,'' would be meaningless and even blasphemous in relation to poetry in general, and to his own verse in a sharply specific sense, since the notion of ''mastery,'' which automatically supplies its own quotation marks, turns thereby into an appendage, a shadow demanding logical compensation in the guise of any positive quantity, and this easily brings us to that peculiar, soulful attitude toward poetry in result of which nothing remains of squashed art but a damp spot or tear stain. This is condemnable not because even the most *purs sanglots* [''pure tears''] require a perfect knowledge of prosody, language, verbal equipoise; and this is also absurd not because the poetaster intimating in slatternly verse that art dwindles to nought in the face of human suffering is indulging in coy deceit (comparable, say, to an undertaker's murmuring against human life because of its brevity); no: the split perceived by the brain between the thing and its fashioning is condemnable and absurd because it vitiates the essence of what actually (whatever you call the thing—''art,'' ''poetry,'' ''beauty'') is inseparable from all its mysteriously indispensable properties. In other words, the perfect poem (at least three hundred examples of which can be found in Russian literature) is capable of being examined from all angles by the reader in search of its idea or only its sentiment, or only the picture, or only the sound (many things of that kind can be thought up, from ''instrumentation'' to ''imaginization''), but all this amounts to a random selection of an entity's facet, more of which would deserve, really, a moment of our attention (nor could it of course induce in us any thrill except, maybe, obliquely, in making us recall some other ''entity,'' somebody's voice, a room, a night), had not the poem possessed that resplendent independence in respect of which the term ''masterly technique'' rings as insultingly as its antonym, ''winning sincerity.''

What I am saying here is far from being new; yet one is impelled to repeat it when speaking of Hodasevich. There exists not quite exact verse (whose very blurriness can have an appeal of its own like that of lovely nearsighted eyes) which makes a virtue of approximation by the poet's striving toward it with the same precision in selecting his words as would pass for ''mastery'' in more picturesque circumstances. Compared to those artful blurrings, the poetry of Hodasevich may strike the gentle reader as an overpolishing of form—I am deliberately using this unappetizing epithet. But the whole point is that his poetry—or indeed any authentic poetry—does not require any definition in terms of ''form.''

I find it most odd myself that in this article, in this rapid inventory of thoughts prompted by Hodasevich's death, I seem to imply a vague nonrecognition of his genius and engage in vague polemics with such phantoms as would question the enchantment and importance of his poetry. Fame, recognition—all that kind of thing is a phenomenon of rather dubious

shape which death alone places in true perspective. I am ready to assume that there might have been quite a few people who, when reading with interest the weekly critique that Hodasevich wrote for *Vozrozhdenie* [an *émigré* daily in Paris before World War II] (and it should be admitted that his reviews, with all their wit and *allure,* were not on the level of his poetry, for they lacked somehow its throb and magic), simply did not know that the reviewer was also a poet. I should not be surprised if this person or that finds Hodasevich's posthumous fame inexplicable at first blush.... Be it as it may, all is finished now: the bequeathed gold shines on a shelf in full view of the future, whilst the goldminer has left for the region from where, perhaps, a faint something reaches the ears of good poets, penetrating our being with the beyond's fresh breath and conferring upon art that mystery which more than anything characterizes its essence. (pp. 83-7)

> *Vladimir Nabokov, ''On Hodasevich,'' in* The Bitter Air of Exile: Russian Writers in the West, 1922-1972, *edited by Simon Karlinsky and Alfred Appel, Jr., University of California Press, 1977, pp. 83-7.*

NINA BERBEROVA   (essay date 1952)

[*Berberova was a Russian poet and Khodasevich's second wife. Her autobiography,* The Italics Are Mine *(1969; see Additional Bibliography), provides numerous portraits of émigré authors. In the following excerpt from her essay ''Vladislav Khodasevich— A Russian Poet,'' she offers a general appraisal of Khodasevich's poetry and critical writings.*]

As a young university student and novice at poetry, [Khodasevich] was drawn into Moscow literary life, then dominated by Valery Brusov. It was an era of Russian thought rich in talent, in vigour, in fervor. After several decades of cultural stagnation, poets and writers of the symbolist school, painters, theatrical producers and musicians, all were *creating culture* before the very eyes of the public. Andrey Biely and Brusov in poetry, Stanislavsky, Alexander Benoit, Rachmaninov, in their respective spheres, shared in that memorable cultural renascence which had its counterpart in the social, economic, technical, and philosophical realms. Between 1905 and 1917, Khodasevich grew up mentally, his tastes matured, his creative ideas took shape. By the time of Russia's downfall, his personality was formed.

In the history of Russian poetry it is possible to discern, if one disregards the textbook definitions of ''classicism,'' ''romanticism,'' ''symbolism,'' two basic lines which ran parallel for two centuries, merging only once—in Pushkin. They have imparted to our poetry its unique richness and variety. One was born, as it were, of *wisdom,* the other, of *melody.* If we keep in mind that in poetry, as in any other art, substance and form are inextricably fused and that in a genuine work of art form is actually substance, we shall not be puzzled by the contradistinction of *wisdom* and *melodiousness,* an attribute of the substance and an attribute of the form. Wisdom was the point of departure of those poets who drew their inspiration from thought; melodiousness, of those who worked from sound and music. Derzhavin and Batushkov belonged to the first group; their poetry is wise, it is intellectual, while that of Karamzin and Zhukovsky is melodious and sensual. In Pushkin both trends are merged, with, perhaps, a slight predominance of the first. Lermontov, Fet, Balmont, Blok, Tsvetaeva, with seemingly nothing (or very little) in common, have carried the melodious line of Russian poetry to our own day. Boratynsky, Tutchev, Annensky, Khodasevich are links in the other chain;

their poetry is "profound" rather than "beautiful," rational rather than inspired, austere rather than musical. This intellectual quality, this keenness has been carried by Khodasevich to the limit; he is often prosaic, sometimes dry; he is pungent and replete with meaning; to create meant to him not so much *to sing* as *to mediate*. His poetry combined the poetic technique of the nineteenth century, revived and rejuvenated by him, with a modern acuteness of poetic perception and a daring imagery.

Very early in his poetic career he showed his preference for a sparing use of effects, for modesty of treatment, muted sonority, homely expressions, accents more intimate than declamatory. It may be assumed that the Russian literary environment after 1917 had suggested to him, by way of contrast, his own course as a poet. All around him there was noise and uproar—the gaudy and chaotic spectacle staged by the futurists. Five years, during which much of his best work was written, he spent in Soviet Russia in poverty, enduring hardships, distressed by the course of events, grieved by the loss of friends, appalled by the crudeness and wretchedness of the new mode of life. Nothing in his surroundings was in accord with his poetry—sombre, pure, austere, and profound. And yet, behind the coarse outward pattern he constantly caught glimpses of another reality, one that haunts all poets but is unrecognized or misunderstood by the multitude. For Khodasevich, this world was separated from that by a thin partition, through which it was given to him to see and to hear a great many things.

He never feared suffering, and every storm to him was a "beloved storm," sweeping away doubts, pity, pettiness. In his poem "The Automobile," he speaks of the frightful "gaps of the soul," corroded "as if by acids spilled on them," with everything tender, sweet, and gentle burnt out. Time and again he reminds us almost rudely, in harsh dissonances, of "the throbbing of another life," to which only chosen beings, steadfast, fearless, and intensely thirsting after truth, are granted access.

In February, 1921, the Writers' Club in Petersburg arranged one of its last literary soirées. The program was devoted to Pushkin. It was on that night that Alexander Blok made his famous and prophetic speech about poetry and the rabble—the rabble preparing to strangle poetry. Khodasevich, who also spoke, went even further. He said that the time was drawing near when "we shall have to cry out to each other in the wilderness," deprived of freedom to express our thoughts; we ought therefore to agree beforehand on some word of recognition, some "password" for poets who at any moment may be reduced to silence. Let the name of Pushkin be such a password, he said, to help us find one another in the dreary wilderness where soon we shall be lost.

This was hardly arrogance. Khodasevich at that time already had a clear foreboding of the doom awaiting Russian poetry. Did his awareness of the common fate threatening them all make him feel a close bond with all other poets of his generation? Hardly so; it was still too early for this. His poems at that period show him to be less concerned about his generation than about his personal peril and his fate as a poet; there is little "civic consciousness" in them. The dominant theme is that of his own, probable or improbable, salvation. If, to use Tutchev's words, his soul "was unable to find happiness through suffering," it was yet able "to find *itself* through suffering." Among all kinds of "petty truths" it sought the one great Truth. Often he dreamt, as Blok had done, of finding the thread that holds all things together and, by a single pull

at it, of transfiguring the whole cosmic order once and for all, so that in a flash the ultimate reality, the Truth worth living and working for, might be revealed. . . . Yet more than the cosmic act, the problem of the individual engrossed him. How to escape into that regenerated world? How to find one's way out of this our "grim and tense" existence into the other world? What helped him to bridge the chasm between the two worlds was poetic inspiration. (pp. 79-81)

Khodasevich collected three books of his poems into one slender volume and published them in Paris, in 1927. Of these three, the first, which appeared in Russia, in 1918, is the most philosophical; the second (1922), the most perfect in form; and the last (1927), the most tragic. In the first, entitled *Scattering of the Seed*, he searches for the paths down which the Fates lead us. In the opening poem he likens his own destiny and that of his country and nation to the fate of the seed that must be buried in fertile soil and must suffer death deep in darkness, before it returns to life and germinates anew.

In Russia, at the end of 1917, this poem sounded a note of hope; and, indeed, as long as the poet remained in his homeland, he never lost hope. (pp. 81-2)

The Heavy Lyre, his second book of poems, elicited the following comment from Andrey Biely: "Just as in his subject matter he adopts the themes and best traditions of our greatest poetry, so in his form he rises to the level of our glorious poets of old. And one rejoices; a poet of real stature has been born in our time. Such a birth is a rare event." In its integrity, its power, its acerbity and bitterness, this book is an extraordinary phenomenon in contemporary Russian poetry.

Its theme is the return "home" from the earthly inferno, not the voluntary return extolled by the romantics, but the enforced, inescapable fateful return; its theme is the end of the transient and visible world, the death of man and of things, after which there is nothing left but the faint breath of the spirit, powerful in its very weakness, eternal in its restless suffering and quest for self-perception. (p. 82)

The European Night, his third book of poems, was his last. During the last decade of his life, Khodasevich wrote no more than some fifteen poems. Earlier than many others, he saw the night descending on Europe. Horrified by what he had seen, he fell silent.

But only as a poet. During that last decade he became prominent in the Russian press of Paris as a literary critic. Week after week his critical articles appeared in the daily *Vozrozhdenie.* They were quite apart from the ordinary book reviews of new publications (in the U.S.S.R. and abroad), confined usually to an exposition and appraisal of the contents. Each of his essays was a profound and well-reasoned elaboration of a theme suggested by the literary work in question and bearing upon many contemporary problems, literary as well as philosophical, historical, and political. . . . Some of his favorite themes during those years were the common fate of Russian men of letters due to the realities of Russian life, the mission and purpose of literature, the ordeal of the poet, the painful yet consciously chosen path of the writer. The theme of the poet's vocation had been lightly touched upon in some of his poems; but only now did it receive a lucid and effective treatment in such articles as **"Bloody Repast,"** which today, after twenty years, appear as fresh and alive as when they first were written. (pp. 82-3)

Simultaneously with his journalistic activity, to some extent enforced, he devoted much time, as he had done all his life,

Khodasevich and Nina Berberova in 1925. From The Italics
Are Mine. *Copyright © 1969 by Nina Berberova. Reproduced by permission of Harcourt Brace Jovanovich, Inc.*

to the study of Pushkin. . . . In this field, it must be admitted, Khodasevich failed to achieve all he intended to do, and all that is left of his efforts is one book, *About Pushkin,* and a dozen or so historical-literary essays scattered about in various reviews. The biography of Pushkin he had dreamed of writing all his life remained unwritten.

But he did leave us another biography, that of the poet Derzhavin, which treats exhaustively the personality, the life, and the works of this poetic ancestor of Khodasevich himself. The eighteenth century, Catherine the Great, the rise of an obscure civil servant to the top ranks of the official hierarchy, the transformation of an obscure, provincial writer into a great Russian poet—all this has been presented by Khodasevich with simplicity, vividness, and a subtle understanding of an era and its people. It contains pages that reveal the author as a genuine master of Russian prose.

A few months before his death in 1939, his book *Necropolis,* a collection of his reminiscences of several writers and poets of his time, was published. These memoirs are distinguished from many others of the same kind by their lucidity, accuracy, and truthfulness. Nothing here is touched up, nothing embellished with fanciful flourishes. Blok, Gorky, Brusov, Sologub, and others, emerge before us life-sized, conjured up by the

author forcefully, precisely, while he keeps his own personality entirely in the background. This book is indispensable today for a clear understanding of these eminent literary figures of our recent past, all representatives of the short but brilliant period of Russian literature in the beginning of this century. (pp. 83-4)

A friend of Andrey Biely, Maxim Gorky, Z. N. Gippius, at various periods of his life, [Khodasevich] kept up a correspondence with these writers that will be of great value to the future student of our time. The words of W. Weidle, one of his closest friends and a faithful admirer, may serve to bring this unique Russian poet closer to the reader: "It may still be necessary to explain to some people what it is that links us to Khodasevich, and what he signifies to us. It may still be necessary to explain that he is truly *our own* poet. This is meant not only in the sense that he belongs to post-Pushkin Russia, to post-Goethe Europe, to our common uninterrupted history, but also on a deeper, more spiritual plane which makes him the most profound of all our contemporaries of the last decade."

Exile is always a tragedy, the fate of the émigré always a misfortune. To the poet, emigration can mean extinction, and Khodasevich realized only too well what was in store for him. When he left Russia, he knew what that Russia was; and living in Europe, he foresaw the doom of Europe and fully understood what the termination of a great historic epoch involved. He kept his thoughts to himself, never in all his life did he utter a single word for "the gallery," but several years before his death he had come to feel that, *this side of death,* the future held *nothing.* To talk of this in verse seemed indiscreet to him; if there is nothing, then what is the good of poetry? But in a private letter, written in 1932, he dropped two sentences: "I have nothing left. . . . It is time to bury all proud designs." (pp. 84-5)

Nina Berberova, "Vladislav Khodasevich—A Russian Poet," in The Russian Review, *Vol. 11, No. 2, April, 1952, pp. 78-85.*

RENATO POGGIOLI   (essay date 1960)

[*Poggioli was an Italian-born American critic and translator. Much of his critical writing is concerned with Russian literature, including* The Poets of Russia, 1890-1930 *(1960), which is one of the most important examinations of this literary era. In the following excerpt from that work, Poggioli discusses the salient features of Khodasevich's poetry. He especially concentrates on Khodasevich's economic use of words and ability to reveal life's pathos through domestic themes and images.*]

When compared to the *epigones* of prerevolutionary lyricism, or to the *neoteroi* of Soviet verse, feebly and briefly glimmering, like will-o'-the-wisps, in the darkening sky of Russian poetry, Khodasevich shines like a bright star, the light of which seems to come from another heaven or from another era. . . . [His poetry] remains, historically and critically, hard to classify, Khodasevich began his career at the apogee, or rather at the early decline, of the Symbolist movement; and while taking its achievements for granted, he felt rather detached toward its aesthetic creed. Formally and chronologically, his poetic ideal is more obviously related to that of the followers of both Acmeism and Clarism; yet despite this connection, his imaginative and moral world greatly differs from Kuzmin's, Gumilev's or Akhmatova's. His work escapes the pitfalls of Kuzmin's verse, all deriving from the whimsical fatuity of the author's caprice, to which Khodasevich opposes the high seriousness, and even ponderosity, of his own inspiration. Khodasevich showed that he was aware of this quality by defining his own poetry, in the title of his best collection, as a "heavy lyre." Gumilev's *engagement*, based on his view of art as action and of life as adventure, was equally foreign to Khodasevich, who treated both art and life as private and subjective experiences. Although nearer in spirit to Akhmatova than to any other poet, Khodasevich differs from her in his ability to submit emotion to the shock of reflection and to a detached comtemplation of things and events.

Despite other, and perhaps more important, divergences, Khodasevich must be placed in the triad he ideally forms with Mandel'shtam and Pasternak. It matters very little that he was hardly ever connected with the one or the other: his mature poetry, though so independent and distant, belongs with theirs. With Mandel'shtam, whose point of departure was the quasi-Parnassian reaction of Acmeism, Khodasevich shares, for instance, a classical taste and a spirited wit. With Pasternak, whose work proceeds from a neoromantic interpretation of the Futurist creed, he has in common a "rage for order," an urge to find some sense and design in the chaos of immediate experience. If there is something which sets him aside from Mandel'shtam and Pasternak, it is his dependence on tradition, which for him means in practice almost exclusively Pushkin's example. In this he followed precedents already established by Brjusov and Blok. For those two older poets, however, the Pushkinian tradition had been a point of arrival, while for Khodasevich it was a point of departure. And the Pushkin whom the latter chose as his model was the Pushkin of *Evgenij Onegin* rather than the romantic lyricist: in brief, the master who had captured the fleeting magic of feeling in the prosaic syntax of neoclassical verse. (pp. 303-05)

This best of all Pushkin's modern disciples seems to have understood as well as his master the secret of poetic economy. In his case, this means the deliberate choice of the speech of reflection to express a state of constant emotional tension. Formally and externally, his poetry takes well-beaten paths; it follows the standards of tradition and observes the norms of common sense. This does not imply a tendency toward the conventional and the commonplace; without indulging in either the gnomic or the epigrammatic, Khodasevich's poetry produces the effect of a mature wisdom and achieves an astonishing mastery of both imagery and thought. Classical in temper, always keeping his inspiration under control, Khodasevich is one of those rare modern poets who treat with prudent skepticism the very poetic power which is their birthright. He never exalts the muse or the artist within himself. He looks with great awe at the mystery of life, which may well "make vain all thoughts and words." A prosaic kind of verse seems to him a fitter tool than a high-flown poesy to convey his impersonal and objective vision of men and things. The poet sees himself as a man among men, as a bourgeois like everybody else, or, as he says in the poem "**Noon**," "a passer-by, a citizen, in a brown coat and a derby, the same as all the others...." Yet it is not without irony that in the same poem he magnifies his own physical size to convey the impression it makes on a boy playing at his feet. Still, instead of suggesting that contrast by comparing himself to Gulliver in the land of Lilliput, he prefers to describe his own person in terms of an inanimate and inarticulate landmark, as a huge and aged stone which has survived from an immemorial past.

This emphasis on the relative disproportion of things is one of Khodasevich's favorite motifs. Elsewhere he assigns a pre-

carious and provisional greatness to modest domestic objects, while reducing to their mean size and scope cosmic and elemental things. This reciprocal metamorphosis occurs in the central image of "**Ballad**," a poem in *The Heavy Lyre,* when the poet fixes his gaze on a lamp hanging from the ceiling, to contemplate, as he says, "a sixteen-watt sun in a stucco sky." Such an interplay between the domestic and the cosmic does not imply that the poet fails to distinguish between the different levels of man's experience of himself and of the world. As a matter of fact, Khodasevich keeps strictly separate the spheres of emotion and reflection from those of creation and life. His inspiration is often sparked by a recurring awareness of transcendental and metaphorical antinomies, of the external dualism ruling man's existence and the whole universe. Yet the very task of his poetry seems to be to reconcile those antinomies, and to bridge the gap that separates opposite realms of being. This is why he often bases his images on a witty and systematic antithesis of different philosophical categories, as when he describes the process of living as "breathing the space of time"; or when he defines hope as a "sweet memory of the future." In another poem he develops a simile of perfect symmetry, by treating time as if it were the fifth element, the unique medium of human life, where men live as naturally as birds in the air, fish in the water, worms in the earth, and salamanders in fire.

The poet views the universal dualism of all forms of being as a natural feature of the human condition, as a mysterious grace leading our body and our mind in contrary directions, which, as he says in the poem "**Ballad**," turns our feet toward the underground fire and our head toward the sky and its stars. It was on the premise of such a view that the poet wrote one of his best poems, "**Episode**," where he re-evoked in the first person what a psychiatrist would call a case of split personality. There Khodasevich reworked in his own way the Romantic theme of the Alter Ego, which had so deeply fascinated the imagination of many Russian writers, from Gogol' and Dostoevskij to Blok. The novelty of Khodasevich's treatment of this theme lies in the detachment with which he looks at his own double, whom he catches in the act of sleeping, and whom he describes with calm objectivity, as a purely material image rather than as a spiritual vision.

Despite his longing after a cosmic order, the poet feels the powerful attraction of the forces of destruction and disaster, which endanger the integrity of both life and the self. Thus, in a poem highly reminiscent of the so-called "President's Song" in Pushkin's play *The Feast During the Plague,* Khodasevich avows that he feels the pathetic seduction of all historical catastrophes or elemental cataclysms, since, as he says, "the heart of man sports as playfully as a child just awakened when revolt or plague crash upon us, throwing time as wide open as the sky." Khodasevich recognizes the presence of chaos not only in the world of history, but also in the narrow sphere of private, ordinary life. Nothing is more significant in this respect than the highly original "**Ballad**," which voices the tragedy of being within the four walls of a room. The highest grace of Khodasevich's poetry, in contrast with the transcendental ambitions of the Symbolists, is to be seen in this ability to express the pathos of life in small proportions, engraving it on matter as hard as a mosaic.

A poetry of this kind requires a frugal use of words and a sober employment of the poet's craft. Its double necessity is to open the way for introspection, and yet to restrain the flow of emotion. The poet achieves this difficult feat by adopting a moral attitude made of both candor and modesty. He may share the Decadent notion of poetic experience as a descent into a lower world; or the Symbolist conception of the poetic imagination as the soul's reminiscence of an earlier and higher existence. Yet his vision is neither apocalyptic nor mystic; Khodasevich ignores devils, angels, and even gods. He may treat man's life on earth as an exile of the soul, but by doing so he makes no less real either that life or this earth. It is this emphasis on the concrete that gives an objective quality to the revelations of his art, which, even more than spiritual, are ethical epiphanies. Such is the case with the beautiful poem **"The Monkey,"** where the poet tells how once he discovered the signs of supreme moral nobility in a monkey's hand, which, in a joking gesture of friendship, he shook as if it were a human one; and how, by a tragic chance and an ironic twist, all this took place on the very day when time got out of joint for all men: "That was the day that they declared the war." The contrast between the central vignette and the finale of this piece (probably inspired by "The Navigation," one of Turgenev's prose poems) is eloquent proof that Khodasevich's chamber music may achieve effects as magnificent as those of a church organ. (pp. 305-08)

> *Renato Poggioli, "The Poets of Yesterday," in his*
> The Poets of Russia; 1890-1930, *Cambridge, Mass.:*
> *Harvard University Press, 1960, pp. 276-315.**

WLADIMIR WEIDLÉ (essay date 1972)

[*Weidlé was a Russian émigré critic and a close friend and admirer of Khodasevich. In the following excerpt, he examines the ways in which seemingly contradictory qualities of Khodasevich's poetry—measured harmony and dissonant intensity—complement each other.*]

Among those who have pondered their own *ars poetica* most carefully, Khodasevich is one of the most self-conscious. He considers his *ars poetica* in his poetry too—though in what at first glance seems a contradictory way. He has two poems written almost simultaneously in 1923—one on February 4 (finally polished in May), the other March 24-27 (in 1927 the poet revised this one "as best I could," to use his own words, but remained dissatisfied even then, noting on his wife's copy "very bad"). Let us begin with the second poem:

> The spring babble will not soften
> The sternly clenched lines of verse.
> I've fallen in love with the iron gnashing
> Of cacophonic worlds.
>
> In the gape of yawning vowels
> I breath freely and easily.
> In the crowd of consonants
> I imagine a crush of stacked ice-floes.
>
> Dear to me—from the cloud of tin,
> Is the blow of a broken arrow,
> I love the singing and screeching
> Clangour of an electric saw.
>
> And in this life, dearer to me
> Than all harmonic beauties,
> Is a shudder rushing across my skin,
> Or the cold sweat of terror,
>
> Or the dream where, once whole,
> I explode and fly apart
> Like mud splattered by a tire
> Into alien spheres of being. . . .

There is nothing bad, let alone "very bad," about these lines. They have been given their final polish, as was everything that their author gave to the printer. **"Stacked ice-floes"** (*L'din vzgromozhdennykh)* is a fine, expressive, Derzhavinesque phonetic illustration of the object. "I love the singing and screeching / Clangour of an electric saw" is an even more graphic example of sound imitating and expressing sense. The whole poem strives to make this kind of connection—strives perhaps too insistently, perhaps its "sternly clenched" quality is somewhat artificial. This is probably what explains Khodasevich's dissatisfaction. But the other poem, written a month and a half earlier, and in a different key, is alien to everything "gnashing" and "clenched." The author expressed neither dissatisfaction nor satisfaction with the latter poem, but it hardly makes an insistent demand for us to appraise it higher—indeed we can scarcely appraise such "programmatic" verses using the same criteria we would use for poems not written at the behest of such an obvious authorial "order." But if we speak of the poetic and not poetry, it is precisely these two "orders," the difference between them which attracts our attention more than the quality of the two poems (which is approximately the same, and not among Khodasevich's finest). The first of these poems is quite unlike the second in everything except in its degree of saturation with poetry, a poetry characteristic of Khodasevich but not always present to an equal degree in all his verse:

> God is alive! Sensibly, but not trans-sensibly,
> I stroll among my lines of verse
> Like an unrelenting prior
> Among his humble monks.
> I pasture the obedient flock
> With a burgeoning staff.
> The keys to a mysterious garden
> Clink upon my belt.
> I am—a hoping, speaking creature.
> Trans-sensibly, perhaps, sings
> Only the angel appearing before God,
> But animals who haven't seen God
> Moo and bleat in transe-sense too,
> But I am not a favored angel,
> Nor a fierce snake, nor a dumb bull;
> I love my human tongue passed down
> To me from generation to generation:
> Its stern freedom,
> Its sinuous law . . .
> Oh, if only my mortal moan
> Could be cast in an ode of graphic form!

(pp. 339-41)

These two poems were not only written one right after the other, they were printed side by side on facing pages in the *European Night* collection (this was not published separately, but was part of the 1927 *Collected Poems*). It is as if the second is a corrective to, or at least an expansion on, the first. The poet seems to say, you thought my poetry was so tightly bridled, measured, striving toward harmony and reason, full of praise for transparency—then know now that in it I hear "iron gnashing," I see "the blow of a broken arrow," that "in this life, dearer to me / Than all harmonic beauties, / Is a shudder rushing across my skin, / Or the cold sweat of terror," and if this is true in life, the same is true in poetry; can't you see that I "explode" and "fly apart" here too, even in "sternly clenched" lines of verse. One cannot deny that this corrective to the "obedient flock" and to the glorification of law and intellect was indeed necessary. Too often, even much later, even after his death—people would repeat the concluding lines of a poem ("**Petersburg**") written three years later: "I grafted the classical rose: Onto the Soviet wilding." Just as, incidentally, on the other hand people too often saw in his poetry only the "mud splattered by a tire," only the "shudder" or "terror" of the themes characteristic of him. If we turn our attention to both of these 1923 poems simultaneously, we can cure both of these kinds of one-sidedness. However, even so they are completely cured only when we realize that the poems do not contradict each other, but speak of different things—and precisely for this reason they complement each other perfectly.

On first glance it might seem that unlike Horace or Verlaine, Khodasevich was bequeathing to posterity two different "Epistles to the Pisones," two different "arts poetiques." In fact in these two poems he set forth his unified but two-sided, double-edged poetics. First ("God is alive! Sensibly, but not trans-sensibly") he defined the character of his art; then ("The spring babble will not soften") its material, the soil (spiritual, of course) in which this art germinated and took root. "I explode," "I fly apart"—though the verbs are first-person, they refer to the man in the poet, not to the poet himself, not to the "speaking" "I" on whose belt the "keys to a mysterious garden" clink. *What* his poetry is about is one thing; what *kind* of poetry it is is quite another. However, this assertion still does not resolve one difficulty—one of the basic ones in the philosophy of poetry and art in general. Is this divergence of the "what" from the "how" justified? What is this connection between them supposed to be? Undoubtedly—and intentionally—I put it incautiously by saying that if in life the "terror" and the "shudder" are dearer to the poet than "all the harmonic beauties," the same is true in his poetry too. But is connection by similarity really unacceptable here, or is connection by contrast obligatory? Khodasevich was inclined toward the latter opinion. In conversation he liked to cite the Pushkin period *mot* (I couldn't find it in Pushkin, perhaps it's Vyazemsky) to the effect that there is no reason to write about a jolting wagon in jolting lines of verse. However, the *mot* strikes me as inaccurate, and in any case it should not be made a general rule. What then happens to everything that Radishchev, following the French, once so nicely called "descriptive harmony" (*izrazitel' naia garmoniia*)? After all, as we have just seen, Khodasevich himself quite artfully "imitated" (by tradition the post-Aristotelian "poetics" applied precisely this verb in the sections pertinent to this topic) meaning with sound. And all of his poetical forefathers did too, Pushkin above all. . . . True, however, and no less deserving of attention, is the fact that the desirability and possibility of such a direct correspondence between what is said and how it is said are by no means unlimited. In his poetics Khodasevich was inclined to formulate things either too narrowly or—as in the two poems I have cited—in the form of two conflicting principles, without noting with complete clarity how they are reconciled. But when using this poetics he achieved, in his best poems, just such a reconciliation of the irreconcilable in a way all his own and with unparalleled perfection. (pp. 342-44)

Khodasevich is best, he is most irreplaceable, most himself, when his poetics of blending terror with simplicity and quiet is done most thoroughly. "**The Blind Man**" is such a poem, "**From My Diary**," . . . "It was semi-dark in the street" (I am speaking only of the poems after *Heavy Lyre*); and some of his longer pieces belong here too—"**John Bottom**" and "**Sorrento Photographs**." It has always seemed to me that the whole cycle "**By the Sea**" remained short of this perfect bal-

Holograph copy of Khodasevich's poem "Sorrento Photographs." Courtesy of Ardis Publishers.

ance between despair and quiet. And now I will even say that "**Stars**," no matter how good the poetry, no matter how Khodasevich loved it ("Very good lines"—he was very parsimonious with such praise of himself), no matter how I continue to admire them, they seem to me—how shall I say—too emphatic, too flashy in their repulsiveness. I prefer "**Poor Rhymes**" and another similar poem—it wasn't the last, but it strikes me as the last nevertheless—"Through the drizzly winter day . . ." (*Skvoz' nenastnyi zimnii denek*). These two are his apogee. An unnoticeable apogee, but that's the way it had to be; their greatness, what Khodasevich was seeking in the depth of his being, what he wanted is this "unnoticeableness." That toward which his poetics was directed beginning with "**A Happy Little House**," that personal poetics which he had gradually felt out through three collections of verse and nurtured for many years. How much self-denial ("It's consoling to know that in the drugstore / They have sour pyramidon"), how many sacrifices, self-destruction even, were put into nurturing it like this! But then what tinsel too, at least next to these last two poems, is all of Valery Bryusov, for example, and how many of the works written by poets much more important than he! And now, tired, half-sick, such pain he wrote with—and such—seeming—haste (time, this time can be compressed and expanded) but nevertheless tormenting at night, first in one cafe, in Montparnasse, then another in Montmartre "with incredible effort"; "it was Sunday, disgusting." But "**Poor Rhymes**" had been written, ended with a simile which the Muse would not have bestowed on anyone else:

In a siphon bubbles can only
Go up and up, bubble with bubble. . . .

This was in the fall, in October. And in January of the next year, in another Parisian cafe "morning, in the darkness":

> Through the drizzly winter day
> —He has a suitcase, she has a bag—
>
> Across the parquet of Paris puddles
> Stump husband and wife.
>
> I strode after them a long while,
> And they went to the station.
> Wife was silent and husband was silent.
>
> And what is there to talk about, my friend?
> She has a bag, he has a suitcase . . .
> Heel clicked against heel.

(pp. 345-47)

"Bubble with bubble." "Heel clicked against heel." Period. The end. "Not with a bang, but a whimper," as another poet said. It could not be quieter or simpler. And nevertheless this is truly great lyricism, probably one of the last lyrical possibilities of the twentieth century. (p. 347)

> *Wladimir Weidlé, "A Double-Edged 'Ars Poetica':*
> *Vladislav Khodasevich," translated by Carl R. Prof-*
> *fer, in* Russian Literature Triquarterly, *No. 2, May,*
> *1972, pp. 339-47.*

VLADIMIR MARKOV (essay date 1973)

[*Markov is an American educator, critic, and translator special-izing in Russian literature. The following excerpt is from an essay originally published in* Triquarterly *in 1973 on Georgy Ivanov, who during his lifetime was considered by many to be the leading émigré poet, a position that Khodasevich holds today in the view of most critics. Markov maintains that Ivanov has been unfairly overlooked by critics and that Khodasevich's reputation as one of the most important émigré poets is based as much on literary politics as on the merits of his verse. An unexcerpted section of this essay offers a detailed comparison of Ivanov's and Khoda-sevich's poetry.*]

It is no secret that there is still an Ivanov "party" and a Khodasevich "party" and that the latter continues to be nu-merically stronger. Contemporaries like to choose, and perhaps have to, and it is only later that people begin to wonder why it was so necessary to choose between Nekrasov and Fet, Bra-hams and Bruckner, Tolstoy and Dostoevsky. One could quote Chekhov's Trigorin, who said, "Why jostle? There is enough room for everybody"—but in this case Ivanov does not get his due. Even his admirers avoid calling him the best at the expense of Khodasevich, whereas the Khodasevichites are often quite categorical in their preference. Vladimir Nabokov (who was praised by Khodasevich and murderously reviewed by Ivanov) considers Khodasevich "the greatest poet of our time" [see excerpt dated 1939]. Andrew Field recently called Kho-dasevich "the foremost poet of the emigration." And there is no doubt on which side Gleb Struve is in his book *Russian Literature in Exile*. . . . Both were "third generation" sym-bolists, both belonged to the literary establishment of the Rus-sian emigration, and both were, in a sense, "last poets" and were called such by critics. The poetry of each contains a great deal of acid, which means that both were essentially deca-dents—a fact Ivanov admitted in his verse more than once. One can also find identical motifs in their poetry, such as dreams, violence, and suicide. (pp. 141-42)

Gleb Struve blames Ivanov for inconsistencies with special gusto, and he seems to be right. It is enough to compare, e.g.,

such mutually exclusive poems on the "monarchist" theme as the deeply felt "Enameled cross in his buttonhole" and the sardonic poem on the double-headed eagle . . . (and either with the scathingly mocking "Here we are, more or less" . . .), to be inclined to agree with this. But the difficulty with Ivano is not his "inconsistency" but the fact that he often says the opposite of what he really means, or that he deliberately omits the essential. On the surface, "And people? What use have I for people?" . . . is an excellent foil for Khodasevich's "I love people, I love nature" . . . , but nothing could be more mistaken than a comparison of these two poems at face value. It is characteristic of the "nihilistic" Ivanov that he casually drops the line which could be used as a motto for his work, "I love life, my own as well as that of others," in a little-known poem not included in any of his collections. . . . His poetry is life affirming (which Khodasevich's certainly is not); it is about Man (*cf.* Khodasevich: "And Man? Isn't he there to be ignored by us?" . . .), about nature (not in Fet's sense, but who could forget Ivanov's branches and sunsets, among other nature im-ages—whereas Khodasevich simply does not notice nature), and, above all, about Art (which did not interest Khodasevich very much). (p. 143)

[Khodasevich] is a tragic poet, or, more precisely, the poet of the tragic impasse. Pushkin's Salieri (who, by the way, has more grandeur than his celestial counterpart) is tragic, too. Khodasevich fails as your life's companion; he is not for the desert island; his lyrical self is not attractive; his philosophy (but not his sensibility) is too dated; and his verse shows little grace (for which his laudable "classical" features are small compensation). Even his complexity is an old-fashioned split, rather than a more human interplay of tiny contradictions. D. S. Mirsky once called Khodasevich "the little Baratynsky from the underground, the favorite poet of all those who dislike poetry" and he is wrong only in his choice of epithet. Kho-dasevich did inhabit an underground of sorts, he does derive from Baratynsky, and he was *the* poet for newspaper critics and magazine publishers of the Russian emigration. Somehow he does satisfy the people who do not really love or understand poetry (as well as those who do, of course), but who approve of poetry if it contains "ideas." From their point of view, Khodasevich had the wrong kind of ideas, but ideas neverthe-less (which one could never say of Ivanov). In short, the sit-uation was not dissimilar to that of Apollon Maikov in the last century. Khodasevich's noble aversion to the avant garde played its part, too, and such deservedly respected critics as Weidlé and Terapiano could not but be attracted by him on these grounds also. After the onslaught of "mediocre" futurists who, at the beginning of the 1920's, appeared to constitute a possible literary establishment, it was a comfort to know someone who wrote "like Pushkin" and yet sounded contemporary. Kho-dasevich's "content" was appealingly profound and, at the same time, his "form" was so pleasingly "classical." The trouble, however, is that Khodasevich lacks charm, humanity, and freedom (just as Bryusov and Gumilyov do), and if one absolutely has to have these qualities in a favorite poet, there is no choice but Ivanov in the given context. After Khodase-vich's scorn, reading Ivanov is a relief, and one accepts his "non-profound" old-age grumbling (so similar to that of an-other quoter, Prince Vyazemsky) as something dear and hu-man. Even his poorer poems live, breathe, and are an indis-pensable part of the picture, whereas the best of Khodasevich is slightly dead and one wishes the worst had never been writ-ten—**"Sumerki,"** for instance, most of his Berlin verse, and **"Ballada."** But the most important thing is that Ivanov some-times tosses you behind the clouds with that rose . . . , whereas

Khodasevich is chained to this world in its most hateful aspects. This is why he wants another world so intensely—out of despair. This is why he wants another world so intensely—out of despair. In short, Ivanov may not be a greater or a better poet, but he is more of a poet (at least in this opinion). (pp. 151-52)

Vladimir Markov, "Georgy Ivanov: Nihilist As Light-Bearer," in The Bitter Air of Exile: Russian Writers in the West, 1922-1972, edited by Simon Karlinsky and Alfred Appel, Jr., University of California Press, 1977, pp. 139-63.*

ROBERT P. HUGHES (essay date 1973)

[*Hughes, an American educator and critic who specializes in Slavic languages and literature, has published articles on Osip Mandelstam, Vladimir Nabokov, and Alexander Blok. In the following excerpt, originally published in* Triquarterly *in 1973, he surveys the styles and themes in Khodasevich's major collections of poetry.*]

Although Khodasevich did not choose to have his first two volumes of poetry preserved in his *Collected Verse* (published in Paris in 1927), the second volume, at least, was considered more than juvenilia by contemporary readers and critics. *Youth* was published in 1908, *The Happy Little House* in 1914, both in Moscow. The latter was favorably received by the influential Nikolai Gumilyov in one of his omnibus reviews in the Acmeist journal *Apollon* (published in St. Petersburg) [see excerpt dated 1914]. Gumilyov praised Khodasevich's chary approach to writing (he thus does not wear out his welcome), and compares him in this respect to Tyutchev and Annensky; he finds him a promising poet, but lacking a certain sureness and freedom of gesture. This is followed by an astute characterization that remains valid for the remainder of Khodasevich's poetic career: "European in his love for the details of beauty, he is nevertheless very much a Slav in his rather particular indifferent weariness and melancholic skepticism. Only hope or suffering is capable of bestirring such a soul, but Khodasevich voluntarily, even with a certain arrogance, renounces the one and the other." Gumilyov approves of his attention to technical aspects, even though he finds stylistically inexpressive passages. He concludes with a vague statement that would seem to relegate Khodasevich to the ranks of the Symbolists: ". . . he is for now only a ballet-master, but the dances he teaches are sacred dances." (pp. 59-60)

Khodasevich's third volume, *The Way of the Grain*, published in Moscow just before he departed for Petrograd in 1920, is the first set of poems the poet and most of his critics considered mature verse. Among the most effective and unusual of the pieces in this collection are the longer narrative poems in blank verse. In **"Episode"** (1918), recalls a mystical event of three years before, when he was alone in his room on a dreary, wintry morning: he experiences a bifurcation of his self. For a brief moment he is simultaneously of the earth and beyond it, and he is able to see himself as if from the outside. Such a departure from his consciousness and the transformation of the ugly world became desirable to Khodasevich, and its attainment is also the subject of several short lyrics of this collection (e.g. **"Smolensk Marketplace,"** 1916 and **"Variation"**, 1919). There are other blank-verse narratives from this period. **"November the Second"** (1918), a view of revolutionary and civil war Moscow, concludes in restrained, prosaic sadness: "At home / I drank my tea, sorted out the papers / That had piled up on my desk during the week, / And sat down

to work. But, for the first time in my life, / Neither 'Mozart and Salieri,' nor 'The Gypsies' / That day could slake my thirst." **"Noon"** (1918) depicts the poet as he daydreams about a visit to Venice until he is interrupted by someone asking the time of day. **"An Encounter"** (1918) is another recollection of Venice. **"The House"** (1919-1920) comprises reflections on the transitory nature of human existence as the poet observes a deserted, ruined building. **"The Monkey"** (1919) . . . recalls a moment of epiphany experienced by the poet on the day World War I began. Immediately after the Revolution, Khodasevich did a brief stint as a functionary in various cultural organizations set up by the new Communist regime. His experiences are related with humor and foreboding in several sketches that were published in the nineteen-thirties and were later partially collected in his *Literary Essays and Memoirs*. . . . His bureaucratic career was shortlived and toward the end of 1920 he moved to Petrograd. (pp. 60-1)

Here Khodasevich wrote the majority of the poems that appeared in his fourth volume of verse, *The Heavy Lyre,* published both in Petrograd in 1922 and, after his emigration, in Berlin in 1923. [The poems in this collection] present a portrait of the artist dislocated both physically and spiritually. The discrepancy between appearance and reality, the imprisonment of his soul in a despised environment, that was a major theme of his earlier poetry is here both more intense and vastly more mature.

One other poem will demonstrate the aesthetic of Khodasevich at this juncture in his life:

> A burning star, the quivering ether—
> In spans of arches night is hiding.
> How is one not to love this world,
> This whole unlikely gift of Yours?
>
> You gave me five unsteady senses,
> You gave me all of time and space,
> At play in the mirage of arts
> Is my poor soul's inconstancy.
>
> And out of nothing I create
> Your seas, Your deserts, and Your hills,
> The total glory of Your sun,
> That is so blinding to our eyes.
>
> And suddenly at merest whim
> I wreck this splendid senselessness
> The way a tiny child pulls down
> A fortress that he's built of cards.

A poem of great simplicity (in iambic tetrameter, with alternating masculine and feminine rhymes), it offers a typical Khodasevich construction: a scene of tranquil beauty is cut short by questioning; the poet's function is examined; he comes solipsistically to doubt the existence of the phenomenal world (is it all his own creation?), and then concludes with a pointed metaphor. (pp. 61-2)

The Heavy Lyre . . . was highly praised by numerous critics, and it remains the favorite volume of most readers. The famous Symbolist poet and novelist Andrei Belyi wrote a lengthy and glowing review-article whose title is partially self-explanatory: "The Heavy Lyre and Russian Lyric Poetry" (*Contemporary Annals,* 1923). He traces Khodasevich's poetic pedigree to the greatest nineteenth-century poets, Pushkin, Tyutchev, Baratynsky, and Fet, and considers him a worthy successor to the tradition. (This was Belyi's second article in praise of Khodasevich; the first appeared in Volume 5 of his own miscellany, *Notes of Dreamers* [see excerpt dated 1922]. . . .)

A more restrained appraisal, and perhaps one of the most interesting and accurate views of Khodasevich in this period, is the one given by Osip Mandelstam in 1923 in his article on the poets of that period, "Storm and Stress":

> Russian Symbolism had its Virgils and its Ovids, and it had its Catulluses, not so much in seniority as in the type of creative work. It is here that Kuzmin and Khodasevich should be mentioned. They are typical younger poets, with all the purity and charm of sound that is peculiar to younger poets [. . .] Khodasevich cultivated Baratynsky's theme: "My gift is mean, and my voice not loud," and he played every possible variation on the theme of the stunted child. His junior lineage is traceble to the verse of the second-rank poets of the Pushkin and post-Pushkin period—amateur poets like the Countess Rostopchina, Vyazemsky, *et al.* Proceeding from the best period of Russian poetic dilettantism, from the family album, private verse epistles, workaday epigrams, Khodasevich brought right up into the twentieth century the intricacy and the tender coarseness of the folksy Moscow idiom that was in use in aristocratic literary circles of the last century. His verses are very folksy, very literary, and very elegant.

Khodasevich left the Soviet Union, accompanied by Nina Berberova, in June 1922. They settled at first in Berlin, where he wrote some of his cruelest and most terrifying poems: the four-poem cycle **"By the Sea," "Berlin," "From a Berlin Street," "An Mariechen," "No, no food shall I find today," "Summer Season," "Underground," "All is stone. . . ," "I arise enfeebled from my bed."** Some of the titles themselves indicate the desperate and cynical mood that seems finally to have taken possession of the poet. He was close for a time to Andrei Belyi and Maxim Gorky, with whom he edited a journal, *Colloquy*, that was intended—vainly—for distribution in the Soviet Union. He left Berlin in November 1923. His pillar-to-post existence—from Berlin to Prague to Rome to Gorky's villa in Sorrento for two lengthy visits—finally ended when he and his companion settled in Paris in 1925. There he was to spend the rest of his life. (pp. 62-3)

One of the best poems he was able to produce in this period is his **"Sorrento Photographs"** (1926). It is comprised of a double set of superimposed recollections. The first is of the funeral of a poor janitor in Moscow and a Good Friday procession through the winding streets of Sorrento. The depiction of the entrance of the procession with the effigy of the Virgin into the cathedral, and the candles and singing within, is one of the few ecstatic moments in Khodasevich's poetry. The second set of overlapping recollections comprises a view of Naples through the early morning haze and one of the Peter-and-Paul citadel in St. Petersburg reflected in the river Neva. These memories are grouped around the controlling metaphor of a double-exposed snapshot taken by a careless amateur photographer. The portrayal of the play of memory and the interpenetrating depictions of Italian landscapes and Russian scenes is a remarkable achievement. This long poem is one of Khodasevich's most successful—if untypical—efforts.

"Sorrento Photographs" and the widely anthologized **"Before the Mirror"** are probably the poetic high points of Khodasevich's fifth and final collection, ***European Night***, which was published in 1927 as the concluding section of his ***Collected Verse***. After this date Khodasevich wrote very few poems. Perhaps the finest are the poems written "on occasion," such as the elegy on the death of [his pet cat] Murr, the poem he dedicated to Katharine Hepburn after seeing her film performance as Mary Stuart (1936) and the magnificent fragment on the Russian iambic tetrameter (1938). An absolute master of this meter and deeply knowledgeable about the entire history of Russian poetry, the poet and his subject are a perfect match. (p. 64)

Khodasevich's death in 1939 marked the end of an era, both for European culture in general and for Russian *émigré* literature in particular. His passing was sadly observed with the posthumous publication of three poems and by two deeply felt appreciations of the man and his work by Nina Berberova and Vladimir Nabokov in *Contemporary Annals* (No. 69, 1939) [see excerpt dated 1939]. . . . Nabokov's contribution is a stirring defense against the poet's detractors, past, present, and future. Berberova's "In Memoriam Khodasevich" is also a valuable essay, not least in its intimate view of the poet and detailed knowledge of his life:

> . . . Khodasevich belonged to that generation which did not manage to have its say before 1917 and to which immediately after 1917 almost no one knew how to listen, the generation crushed first by the war and revolution, and then by exile. His contemporaries either died young, or they stopped writing. A huge number of them committed suicide. He too stopped writing verse, because, despite all his "classicism," he could not continue when there was no one with whom and for whom he could continue. This would have been too much "in the anthological genre."

> He himself traced his genealogy from Derzhavin's prosaicisms, from a few of the more harsh poems of Tyutchev, through the "very terrifying" lines of Sluchevsky about the old woman and the balalaika and through the "old man's intonation" of Annensky. There is much that is true in this, but the poison that is in Khodasevich's poetry, and what is the main thing—that precision and strength with which he poured this poison into his verse—is unique in Russian literature. Both Tyutchev and Annensky, if they had known his verse, would have come to meet him, because in their souls too there were those "holes burned by spilled acid" that were in Khodasevich's soul.

(pp. 65-6)

Robert P. Hughes, "Khodasevich: Irony and Dislocation, a Poet in Exile," in The Bitter Air of Exile: Russian Writers in the West, 1922-1972, *edited by Simon Karlinsky and Alfred Appel, Jr., University of California Press, 1977, pp. 52-66.*

EDWARD J. BROWN (essay date 1982)

[*Brown has written extensively on post-Revolution Soviet literature, including the standard work,* Russian Literature Since the Revolution. *In the following excerpt from that work, he discusses*

the viewpoint of the exiled persona in Khodasevich's European
Night.]

A beautifully moving statement of the exile experience is made
by Vladislav Khodasevich in his collection of poems entitled
European Night. . . . The exile's bitterness in those dark lyrics
is tempered only by consummate poetic mastery: no easy effort
at adjustment or optimism dilutes his poetic formulation of
anger and loss. But the collection as a whole belies the poet's
despairing statement, reported by Nina Berberova, that ''I cannot write there, I cannot write here.'' As a matter of fact he
could write here; and he wrote about us, in part.

In that same collection Khodasevich's long poem **''Sorrento
Photographs''** develops a striking metaphor for the divided and
confused consciousness of the exile, whose mixed images of
home and abroad have the effect of defamiliarizing—of making
strange in Shklovsky's sense—both the experience of exile life
and memories of home. Khodasevich compares the fantastic
results of this process to the double exposure of a film by an
absent-minded photographer. . . . (p. 346)

As the poet travels in and around Sorrento on a motorcycle he
has two memories of Russia which are superimposed, respectively, on a view of Amalfi and on Vesuvius and the Bay of
Naples. The first Russian memory is of a low and miserable
house in Moscow from the basement of which the body of a
floor polisher in his coffin is being carried to his grave; the
funeral procession seems to move through prickly agaves, and
the dead man's head ''swims in the azure air of Italy.'' And
in the second telescoping of memories the angel guardian which
crowns the Cathedral of Peter and Paul in St. Petersburg is

> reflected in the greenish waves
> of the Gulf of Castellamare,
> the mighty guardian of Tsarist Russia
> toppled headfirst.
> Ominous, fiery, brooding,
> so the Neva once reflected him
> and so he appeared to me—
> an error on the hapless film.

And Khodasevich, expectant of the further tricks memory may
play, ends his poem with a question concerning her caprices:

> Amid what losses and troubles
> after how many epitaphs,
> will she surface, airy,
> and what else, in turn
> will the shadow of Sorrento photographs
> cover, without covering.

So in Khodasevich's poems on exile dark images of a European
night give way to the bright paradox of Sorrento double ex-
posures, suggesting that something in the exile experience balances loss and disappointment. (p. 347)

> *Edward J. Brown, ''Exiles, Early and Late,'' in his*
> Russian Literature Since the Revolution, *revised edi-
> tion, Cambridge, Mass.: Harvard University Press,
> 1982, pp. 345-87.*

DAVID M. BETHEA (essay date 1983)

[*Bethea is an American critic and educator specializing in Slavic
languages and literature. In the following excerpt from his* Khodasevich: His Life and Art, *the most detailed study of the poet in
English, Bethea traces the major influences on Khodasevich's*

*poetry. He also examines the role of irony in Khodasevich's major
works.*]

The uniqueness of Khodasevich's poetic manner resides in his
startling fusion of Symbolism and post-Symbolism, ''idealism'' and ''realism,'' Pushkinian lapidary form and ever-questioning irony. Indeed, in Khodasevich's finest work an improbable balance—a sort of ''moving stasis''—is struck between
a private, ulterior sense of beauty and the process of ''living
down'' that beauty. Though Khodasevich may have some distinguished relatives in the Western poetic tradition (the names
of Laforgue, Hardy, and Auden come first to mind), there is
virtually no one, particularly if we consider his application of
the principles of modern ''unstable'' (the term is Wayne Booth's)
irony in lyric form, with whom he might be compared in Russia. (p. xvii)

Khodasevich's major period begins with the poems he wrote
from 1914 to 1920 and included in *Grain's Way* . . . , his third
collection. The agricultural metaphor that appears in the lead
poem and gives the volume its title is by now no longer decorative or iconographic; it informs and structures *Grain's Way*
(and has vital ramifications for *The Heavy Lyre* and *European
Night*, the collections to follow). Moreover, it shows Khodasevich to be a fully conscious harvester of poetic seeds sown
by other poets and other traditions—most notably, Pushkin and
Symbolism. Yet Pushkin and Symbolism, as the two great
sources feeding the immature collections [*Youth* and *The Happy
Little House*] were set to collide in the mature verse (less frequently, as it turns out, in *Grain's Way,* more and more frequently in *The Heavy Lyre* and *European Night*). This collision
. . . , is what makes some of Khodasevich's best work possible.
And this same collision produces a series of speakers who are
among the most ironic in modern Russian poetry. ''Irony,'' of
course, has favored status in modern critical idiom, and there
is no need . . . to quarry out a rigorous typology of irony's use
in lyric form. Still . . . it is worth taking a closer look at what
is perhaps its most distinctive quality.

To begin with, irony for Khodasevich was not simply the rhetorical ruse—the ''vicious dissimulation of one's political and
social powers'' for the purpose of escaping responsibility—
employed first by Demosthenes and Theophrastus. Rather it
was something much larger and thoroughgoing, something that
grew to be the only genuine way of dealing with a world that
gave one personal freedom at the cost of stripping one of
homeland and audience at the moment when, mature and confident, one was at the height of one's poetic powers. Khodasevich's use of irony is largely, as Wayne Booth would define
it, ''unstable.'' It opposes the stable weapon used by satirists
from Juvenal to Swift to Tolstoy, for it does not posit an implicit
moral standard against which to judge the literal meaning of
an ironic statement. Reading one of Khodasevich's later lyrics
does not involve ''seeing through'' the speaker's straw statement: there is no ''stepping up'' from the ground level of
factitious morality to the privileged height of genuine morality
hidden behind the lines. (pp. 103-04)

Khodasevich's sense of irony began with the view he took of
his own language. By the writing of *Grain's Way,* the sartorial
dandyism of his youth had become the linguistic urge to say
the most with the least. ''Stylistically speaking,'' says D. C.
Muecke, ''irony is dandyism, whose first aim, as Max Beerbohm, ironist and dandy, tells us, is 'the production of the
supreme effect through the means least extravagant.' '' ''Sophisticated'' rather than ''enthusiastic,'' content to use the
tradition at hand rather than insistent on plunging into the future

without it, Khodasevich was well aware of the dangers awaiting an "archaist" in a world of "innovators," and yet he believed that his language was neither so archaic, nor Mayakovsky's so traditionless, as was commonly held. Shortly after the publication of *Grain's Way* he wrote in one of his notebooks:

> Even those who understand and value my verse
> regret the archaic nature of its language. That
> is short-sighted. All the same, my verse will
> become the common domain only at that time
> when all our present-day language has grown
> profoundly old-fashioned, and the difference
> between Mayakovsky and me will be obvious
> only to the subtlest of philologists. I fear that
> by then the Russian language will have become,
> like Latin, "dead" also, and I will always be
> "for a few." And only that if they exhume me.

Thus, aside from personal skirmishes, Khodasevich had manifest artistic reasons for opposing Mayakovsky. Prosodically traditional, stylistically modest and understated, their tone intimate and chamberlike, their speakers ambivalent and multivoiced, the poems of *Grain's Way* and after are radically different from anything written by Mayakovsky. (pp. 106-07)

In *Grain's Way* Khodasevich refines a situational irony that would have been unthinkable in *Youth* or *The Happy Little House*. Several of the blank verse narratives, including **"The Monkey"** and **"2-go noiabria"** (**"The Second of November"**), function on one level "to present ironic situations or events to our sense of irony." Khodasevich's genius seems to gravitate toward the dramatic or situational—a development all the more noteworthy if one considers the atmospheric, sinuous, anti-dramatic verse of *Youth*. The speaker in **"The Monkey"** encounters a "beggarly beast" that manages, through a quaint handshake, to restore meaning to the chaos of history. "Humanity" is found where one would least expect it and the lesson learned seems a mighty triumph. Then, separated from the text, comes the bald, journalistic conclusion: "V tot den' byla ob"iavlena voina" (On that day war was declared). At least formally there is a narrative voice that should help us to interpret the statement, but in reality it is as if there is not. The absence of the speaker's response begs for comment and the artful juxtaposition of the monkey's lesson with the actuality of war flexes in impossible silence. (pp. 115-16)

Much of what Khodasevich writes after 1914 can be understood as coherent, complete, and stable . . . only if we appreciate it as ironic. Or to put the problem another way, the reader perceives the integrity in Khodasevich's verse only when he realizes that integrity in much modern poetry is closely related to anticlosure, or the tendency to leave major questions unanswered. Although a poetic experience is naturally "gratifying to the extent that those expectations that are aroused [by it] are also fulfilled," in a sense ironic poetry is gratifying because it fulfills the need to not be ultimately fulfilled. (p. 116)

Grain's Way is Khodasevich's "ripest" Moscow collection, and its final poems, which seem positioned where they are to underscore the all-important agricultural metaphor and the "harvesting" of a wisdom that affirms historical and biographical process, reveal a poet in touch with his place of birth, in firm possession of a homeland and an artistic heritage. What these poems suggest has recently been corroborated by Khodasevich's correspondence with the poet Boris Sadovskoy: like Blok and Bely, Khodasevich accepted the Revolution, but on his own unorthodox terms. If he later came to speak of the

Portrait of Khodasevich by his niece Valentina Khodasevich.

Bolshevik regime with bitterness, it was not because he was opposed on principle to revolutionary change but because the hopes placed on a coup "from below" were never realized. In a real sense, therefore, Khodasevich had to leave Moscow to survive. In Petersburg the living conditions were more tolerable and, perhaps no less important, the artistic freedom was greater. Yet Khodasevich's uprooting, begun in Petersburg and completed in various European cities, was to leave the sower of *Grain's Way* eventually disenfranchised. (pp. 117-18)

"Grain's Way" telescopes time—the cycle of one year, one generation, one lifetime. Other short lyrics in the collection align themselves to a specific time of day, which can also be viewed as a time in the life of the poet and his country. (The longer poems in blank verse . . . recapitulate this cyclical rhythm.) The general movement of the lyrics—from darkness to light to the edge of darkness again; from uncertainty about death to death itself to rebirth and reintegration into the cycle—appears to confirm Khodasevich's deliberate composition. Nearly all the poems written prior to the Revolution are included in the first half of the collection, while nearly all the poems written during the Revolution are included in the second half. But although the arrangement appears roughly chronological, a strict chronology is breached more than once in order that the larger structural rhythm be preserved. That Khodasevich indeed positioned subsequent poems with the cycle of **"Grain's Way"** in mind is further, and most convincingly, borne out by the choice to conclude the collection primarily with poems written or begun in the richly rewarding early months of 1918. Only through these poems, it seems, can the path taken by the grain be viewed as meaningful and complete. (p. 142)

The six narratives in blank verse that constitute the nerve center of *Grain's Way* are among Khodasevich's finest creations. Without them the volume would have, despite its impressive skeining of lyrics, an anthological character. But with them, and with the ballast provided by their deep, meditative character, *Grain's Way* is able to make a larger statement about the meaning of history. And in the midst of war and revolution, it was the question of this meaning that Khodasevich must have felt needed answering. Importantly, the first of these narratives begins shortly after the nightmarish dawn of **"In Petrovsky Park."** As becomes evident, the six poems present in microcosm the book's macrocosmic movement from death and psychic dislocation to life and reintegration. Thus, in keeping with the diurnal and seasonal models structuring the shorter lyrics, **"The Episode"** and **"The Second of November"** are darkly matinal, the first set in winter and the second in late autumn; they tell of the death of the poet and the death of his country, respectively. **"Noon"** and **"The Encounter"** are insouciantly midday, warm and summery; they celebrate life at its fullest. And **"The Monkey"** and **"The House"** reflect gradual change from afternoon to evening, warmth to coolness; they show life making peace with its own decline and with the eternal return of history's wheel.

Longer than the traditional lyric and shorter than the traditional *poema* (though Baratynsky wrote a *poema* of only a few pages), progressing through narrative time rather than expanding on some timeless present moment, as does the lyric, and written in a blank verse that conveys remarkably well the meditative character and the weightiness of their far-ranging subjects, these little masterpieces escape precise definition. Khodasevich of course was not the first to set down the musings of a peripatetic speaker in blank verse: Pushkin's great "Again I have visited," to name just one potential model, is a poem of which he surely was aware. But "Again I have visited" is primarily a lyrical piece, whereas these poems by Khodasevich are as dramatic as they are lyrical. For their use of dramatic principles in combination with one "lyrical" speaker they might be compared to Browning's dramatic monologues—with, however, the important disclaimer that Browning's group of multivoiced failed questers are both him and not him, while Khodasevich's speakers never appear to be anything other than transparent images of the ironic Khodasevich himself. (pp. 160-61)

Between 1914 and 1927 Khodasevich wrote almost all of the poetry on which he felt his reputation stood. In 1927 in Paris (by then his permanent residence in exile) he published the only edition of his collected verse to appear during his lifetime: this thin little book of less than two hundred pages consisted of *Grain's Way* and *The Heavy Lyre,* earlier collections now republished with slight variations in format, and *European Night,* poems collected during five years of emigration. Never prolific, always exacting, Khodasevich already seemed to sense that whatever place on the Russian Parnassus was to be his had been staked out by the hundred odd poems collected in this book. For by the late 1920s, despite the fact that Merezhkovsky hailed him as the Arion of Russian poetry and a number of influential critics (Aikhenvald, Bely, Mochulsky, Nabokov, Weidlé) recognized his poetry as among the most significant being written at the time, Khodasevich had begun to write very little verse indeed. (p. 186)

That Khodasevich's poetic output over these years was modest is not in itself an important fact; it merely points up his un-

derstanding of the relationship between poet and muse as something organic, unsponsored, necessary in its way, but never controlled by will. Moments of creativity or "secret hearing" came when it was time for them to come; they were not, à la Bryusov, oxen to be whipped onward by the poet's indefatigable lashings. This being said, it becomes a fact of some importance that Khodasevich wrote over half of the poems collected in his *Sobranie stikhov (Collected Verse)* between April 1921 (after he had moved to Petersburg and he had finally shaken a relapse of furunculosis) and September 1923 (after he had spent some fifteen months in emigration). This period of two and a half years saw the writing of nearly all of *The Heavy Lyre,* what may be Khodasevich's finest collection, and more than half of *European Night.* It was, in short, the most productive time in Khodasevich's otherwise unprolific career as a poet. (p. 187)

As was suggested . . . , the circumstances surrounding the writing of *The Heavy Lyre* were dramatically different from those surrounding the writing of *Grain's Way.* Now the setting is primarily Petersburg, Khodasevich's last home before a pillar-to-post existence in Western Europe. That Khodasevich saw Petersburg as a beautiful corpse and experienced the last months in Russia as a present in which *his* Pushkin no longer had a place [see excerpt dated 1921] and Blok died "gasping for air" certainly influenced the making of *The Heavy Lyre.* Khodasevich was living through a series of endings—privately, he was breaking with Anna Chulkova and falling in love with Nina Berberova; artistically, he was witnessing the eclipse of those traditions that had fed his poetry; historically, he was paying farewell to the city of Peter, soon to be the city of Lenin. All these endings make their way into *The Heavy Lyre.* The atmosphere is more heavy, the irony more trenchant, the grotesquerie more pronounced, the "zigzag of poetic truth," as Bely calls Khodasevich's play with light and shadow, more troubling and spasmodic. Khodasevich has, with one exception, turned away from the generously dilating form and philosophy of the poems in blank verse and turned inward to a short, intimate lyric form stressing the moment at the expense of narration through time. Structurally, *The Heavy Lyre* reads a good deal differently from *Grain's Way.* The earlier collection's overarching metaphor, with its implicit link between the psychic life of the poet and the psychic life of his country, is now plainly out of joint. It is replaced by the image of a lyric tradition grown almost too ponderous for the modern poet, yet one that can still be lifted and played at the *dusha's* ["soul's"] bidding. Add to the various endings involved in the making of *The Heavy Lyre* the fact that Khodasevich is parting with his *dusha,* the cherished source of otherworldly music (for by *European Night* this theme virtually disappears), and we as readers begin to grasp how poignantly "ultimate" is this collection for Khodasevich and for the modern poetic tradition in Russia. (pp. 208-09)

Khodasevich's much discussed traditionalism is always deceptive, and to argue, as the almost breathlessly computing Bely does, that Khodasevich's first cousins are Tyutchev, Pushkin, and Baratynsky is to omit at least half of the problem. Metrically, it is true, Khodasevich is not iconoclastic. But many of the words that Khodasevich weaves into a poem's ictic fabric and that the metrist scans and identifies (in a typical disposition) as Tyutchevian or Pushkinian are not words that Tyutchev or Pushkin would have used. Conscious stylistic deformation and dark, unstable, at times grotesque and absurd irony were not the stock-in-trade of Tyutchev and Pushkin. **"Ballada,"** perhaps Khodasevich's most famous lyric and the last poem in

The Heavy Lyre, begins with a stunned speaker gazing almost catatonically at a ceiling likened to a plaster sky and at a light in that ceiling likened to a sixty-watt sun—it is safe to say that no lyric written by Tyutchev or Pushkin commences with the assumption of so devastatingly barren a cosmos. Such ever-questioning irony and destructive use of detail were possible in Russian poetry only after, say, Annensky and Sluchevsky (who called the artist a "Doubting Thomas"), poets with whom the later Khodasevich easily shares as much as he does with Pushkin, Tyutchev, and Baratynsky. Thus, if the metrical form of Khodasevich's verse suggests to some a classical amphora, perhaps it is worth remembering that that vessel may contain semantic vitriol. Or, to use Khodasevich's metaphor for his artistic travails in *The Heavy Lyre,* what he achieved in his last months in Russia was a graft of "the classical rose [of nineteenth century tradition] to the Soviet wilding [of shattered, soon to be traditionless, postrevolutionary life]." (pp. 210-11)

"Ballada" may be the finest lyric that Khodasevich wrote, a poem that Vladimir Nabokov once described as attaining "the limits of poetic skill." Even alone, when first appearing, it had no small part in the making of Khodasevich's reputation. It is also the final poem in *The Heavy Lyre,* and, like "Grain's Way," another title poem, we may assume it is intended in some sense as that collection's frame. But just as "Grain's Way" saw time as benign or at least benignly indifferent, and therefore was "forward-looking," appropriately placed as frontispiece, so "Ballada" may be in some ways the opposite—"backward-looking" and ultimate. Correspondingly, if historical and personal time have become purposeless, destructive without being regenerative, then they cannot be joined in but must be overcome in some other way. . . . (pp. 237-39)

[In this poem, the] poet seems in some ultimate way to be moving inward—into his round prison of a room, into his position (presumably) at the center of the room, into, at last, himself. The first four stanzas, therefore, suggest themselves as a separate, enclosed semantic unit; it is in them that both the sound and sense of limitation, banality, "paltriness"—the persistent phonetic "rehearsing" of *skudost'* combined with its meaning—lead to a sort of impasse whose ultimate naming in the fourth stanza is an ending as well as a recognition of failure. (p. 245)

In a moment of desperation the poet embraces himself and his own lost lyricism. There is no change, aside from the rocking, in his external position: palingenesis, his birth into another time and space, must come, if at all, through some internal change wrought over his external state. . . . The metamorphosis takes place in the seventh stanza. . . . Importantly, what makes the change possible are the phonetic and semantic characteristics of the "music," or *mousikē,* and art over which the Muses preside. It is verbal music composed precisely of those elements of sound and sense, now in a way "turned inside out," that make poetry in other circumstances impossible.

The speaker is now able to grow out of his plaster sarcophagus, and himself. As we learn in another poem in *The Heavy Lyre,* perhaps the blade that pierces him is the one from whose incision will grow new wings. The last four stanzas, with their image of an open-ended, revolving dance, stand in contrast with the image of a closed, motionless circle of the first stanzas. . . . [They] reveal a poet whose life and surroundings have been filled with new movement . . . and who sees and hears both the physical footsteps and metrical feet of Orpheus. The latter's soul has undergone many reincarnations to reach the twentieth-century ironist. Like Orpheus and Dionysus Za-

greus, whose ritualistic deaths penetrated the mysteries of good and evil, the poet must forfeit his physical existence in order to be reborn into his music. And Orpheus' lyre is heavy because it has been lifted from the dross of a modern world. (pp. 246-47)

"Ballada" might be read, at least for Khodasevich, as an end to several things: the end of the Pushkin-Petersburg connection in Russian poetry; the end of lyricism in a state with no sense of resonant past; the end of the poet's Orphic role in such a state. . . . With an almost Blokian intuition of tragic finality, and with the Symbolist's view of another world seen through the demeaning details of this one, Khodasevich rises to the occasion, shifts from the minor key of his elegant chamber music to the major key of Blok's full-throated lyricism. Such a sense of momentary balance and cathartic release would not, at least in the same form, come again. By the time Khodasevich writes his second "Ballada," clearly a cruel mockery of the first, the possibility of a former lyricism is defiantly rejected. An image of dismemberment (a one-armed husband) is absurdly juxtaposed with an image of fertility (a pregnant wife) in the presence of an art form, the cinema, which Khodasevich regarded as philistine and culturally corrupt. The world of his last poems . . . is one in which the magic moment of Symbolism, capable of overcoming the present, indeed all temporal categories, is replaced by discrete, absurdly unrelated moments of lost time. It is a world that might be defined less by "irony" as a rhetorical device, what Barthes describes as "nothing but the question posed to language by language," than by "ironism" as an ontological state: for what eventually comes to underlie the semantic ambiguity is not a willing sense of play but a condition of being stripped of ultimate values (Pushkin, Petersburg, Russian poetry). Out of this state arises the bilious protest of the second "Ballada," when the poet, handed the same lyre of the earlier poem, cannot play it the same way. The absurdity is too great, and the speaker responds by taking a scourge (instead of the lyre) and whipping the angels, once happy messengers from his Orphic realm, for all he is worth. The second "Ballada" is one of the last poems in *European Night,* Khodasevich's last collection. The impasse alluded to in the first "Ballada" is now complete. And it is at this point that Khodasevich, an émigré in more ways than one, lapses into the almost total poetic silence of the last ten years of his life. (pp. 248-50)

It might be said that *European Night* is the most "unlyrical" collection of lyrics in the Russian language, if by "lyrical" we mean the *ta mele,* the "poems to be sung," of which the Greeks spoke. (p. 275)

[The] poems of *European Night* are, on many levels, a deliberate, often violent rejection of the *melos* of lyric poetry. Phonetically, they reject what is euphonious; semantically, what is the traditional or "grand" lexicon of poetic speech; thematically, what is related to psychic break-through or "inspiration." There are occasions in which the syntactic grace and balance of an earlier poem such as "The Soul" are now shattered by swarming verbs and adjectives. Moreover, the images in this collection are more optically precise than ever before: as Nabokov ingeniously put it in his review of the *Collected Verse,* there has gathered over the later poems a sort of "optical-pharmaceutical-chemical-anatomical deposit." Caught in a world that is totally conscious and "loathsomely material," the speakers of *European Night* observe their fallen state and take perverse pleasure in "singing the unsingable." Wladimir Weidlé has suggested that Khodasevich has now entered an "alien" (*chuzhoi*) realm, one that has little or nothing in common with the realms of **Grain's Way** and **The Heavy Lyre,** and the implication is that this alien element is not only linked with the Western European locale of the poems, but with their nature as poetic form. When he wrote of the ''other'' that was his *dusha,* Khodasevich was speaking of what was more essentially ''his'' (even though he could not possess it) than his body or his physical surroundings. But the element of otherness in **European Night** is entirely foreign and inimical to the poet. As we shall be seeing, the word-seeds that once fell into the ''black earth'' of a still vital Russian poetic tradition are cast, in Khodasevich's last collection, onto the alien pavement of European cities. Unable to take root, they harvest only the consciousness of the poet's failed role and, most painful for Khodasevich, the inevitable absence of poetic speech. (pp. 276-77)

Khodasevich, in ways that now seem bold, if not iconoclastic, actually went against the grain of the lyric tradition on which he was raised. Irony, at least in its ''modern,'' unstable, ever-questioning guises, is not a concept one generally associates with the dominant strain, righteous, *engagé,* doggedly searching for ''truth,'' of Russian literature. (Not surprisingly, exceptions such as Gogol or Chekhov were often—and still are—misunderstood for the irony in their works.) (pp. 346-47)

This aspect of Khodasevich's genius, the yoking of a self-ironizing, multi-voiced speaker with a prosodic profile that is traditional and a lexicon that is disarmingly simple, is finally receiving recognition. Misread, perhaps willfully so, by those such as Adamovich and Georgy Ivanov, Khodasevich's poetry demanded someone like Nabokov—whose own orientation was also toward irony rather than fierce ethical commitment and whose reputation also suffered attack for its ''un-Russian'' self-reflectiveness and playfulness (which actually, and *ironically,* went back to Pushkin)—to retrieve it from the neglect that ensued after Khodasevich's death. Not a few have been puzzled by Nabokov's categorical claim that Khodasevich is ''the greatest Russian poet that the twentieth century has yet produced''; they feel that this is another case of Nabokov's notorious mystification or *épatage.* (pp. 347-48)

How will posterity come to view Khodasevich, the symbolist-turned-ironist who fit into no niche during his lifetime and who subsequently, like Mandelshtam, Tsvetaeva, Bulgakov, and other important Russian modernists fully discovered only decades after their deaths, nearly ''fell through the cracks'' of literary history? To draw a parallel that he himself would probably not have understood, but one that removes him from the vicissitudes of literary politics and perhaps makes him more accessible to the Western reader, Khodasevich is a transitional figure who stands to the modern Russian lyric tradition as does Auden, *mutatis mutandis,* to that of England and America. He is a vital link between Symbolism and post-Symbolism, between the high lyricism and urgently eschatological visions of Blok and Bely, on the one hand, and the gradual foreshortening of that lexicon and those visions by poets, including the so-called Acmeists and Futurists, who rose to prominence in the prerevolutionary years, on the other. (p. 348)

Khodasevich's special blend of lyricism and irony, of Symbolism and post-Symbolism, was more than artistic device, though without its form it would have little meaning. It was his response to all that was being wrested from him and the literature he had served so well. (p. 350)

David M. Bethea, in his Khodasevich: His Life and Art, *Princeton University Press, 1983, 380 p.*

ADDITIONAL BIBLIOGRAPHY

Berberova, Nina. *The Italics Are Mine*. Translated by Philippe Radley. New York: Harcourt, Brace & World, Inc., 1969, 606 p.*
   A detailed memoir of Berberova's life from childhood until her emigration to the United States which includes a lengthy section devoted to her marriage to Khodasevich. For commentary by Berberova on Khodasevich's work, see the excerpt dated 1952.

Bethea, David M. ''Khodasevich's Poems in Blank Verse: The Pushkin Connection.'' *Topic: A Journal of the Liberal Arts* XXXIII (Fall 1979): 3-13.*
   Examines the influence of Pushkin on Khodasevich's poetry and notes ways in which Khodasevich's work marked the end of the ''golden age'' of Russian poetry and artistically severed the connection between Pushkin's classical poetics and the growth of modernism.

———. ''Sorrento Photographs: Khodasevich's Memory Speaks.'' *Slavic Review* XXXIX, No. 1 (March 1980): 56-69.
   In-depth discussion of one of Khodasevich's most famous poems. The critic concentrates on Khodasevich's blend of classicism and a modern ironical mode.

———. ''Following in Orpheus' Footsteps: A Reading of Xodasevic's 'Ballada'.'' *Slavic and East European Journal* XXV, No. 3 (Fall 1981): 54-70.
   A technical discussion of one of Khodasevich's most critically acclaimed poems.

Hagglund, Roger. ''The Adamovič-Xodasevič Polemics.'' *Slavic and East European Journal* XX, No. 3 (Fall 1976): 239-52.*
   Historical background of émigré literary scene in Paris and a detailed discussion of the debate between Khodasevich and poet-critic Georgij Adamovič. Hagglund maintains that the conflict between Khodasevich and Adamovič illuminates ''general problems of Russian émigré culture.''

Mandelstam, Nadezhada. *Hope Abandoned*. Translated by Max Hayward. New York: Atheneum, 1974, 687 p.
   A detailed memoir in which Mandelstam recalls Khodasevich at the height of his popularity in Russia. However, she evaluates him as a ''lost, tormented soul'' whose ''poetry brings no illumination. Inspired mainly by negativism and nonacceptance of life, there is a bitter infirmity of spirit about it.''

Smith, G. S. ''The Versification of Russian Émigré Poetry, 1920-1940.'' *The Slavonic and East European Review* LVI, No. 1 (January 1978): 32-46.*
   A technical comparison of the metrics of Russian émigré poetry and indigenous Russian poetry. Khodasevich's work is analyzed along with that of fourteen other émigré poets.

———. ''Stanza Rhythm and Stress Load in the Iambic Tetrameter of V. F. Xodasevic.'' *Slavic and East European Journal* XXIV, No. 1 (Spring 1980): 25-36.
   A technical discussion of the metrical variations in thirty-two poems written by Khodasevich between 1921 and 1924.

Struve, Gleb. ''The Double Life of Russian Literature.'' *Books Abroad* XXVIII, No. 4 (Autumn 1954): 389-406.*
   An evaluation of the Russian literary scene after the Communist Revolution of 1917 with a particular emphasis on the émigré writers. Struve calls Khodasevich ''one of the few genuinely pessimistic major Russian poets'' and claims that he had great influence on many young Parisian poets.

David Lindsay

1876-1945

English novelist.

Lindsay is considered an important influence on the development of modern fantastic literature. In his fiction, Lindsay introduced complex theories of spiritual evolution and explored the possibility and nature of a higher reality. Critics find that this emphasis on philosophical and moral themes distinguishes Lindsay's work from that of most previous authors in the fantasy genre and significantly influenced such later fantasists as C. S. Lewis and J.R.R. Tolkien.

Born in a suburb of London, Lindsay was the third child of Alexander Lindsay, a Scot, and Bessy Bellamy, an Englishwoman. Shortly after Lindsay's birth, his father abandoned the family, which was subsequently taken in by a widowed aunt. In his youth, Lindsay received a strict Calvinist religious education, which he rejected in adulthood when he began to study various forms of mysticism and metaphysical thought. Most critics note the profound effects of these two fields of study on Lindsay's fiction, specifically in his combination of Puritan moral values with esoteric mystical theories. Lindsay excelled in mathematics and composition, the two subjects upon which his diversified professional life would be based. He was a quiet, imaginative child, who avoided vigorous play and the company of others. This tendency toward reclusiveness and discomfort with social interaction grew more pronounced as he reached adulthood. Because of financial difficulties, Lindsay was unable to complete his formal education past grammar school, and at age sixteen he was apprenticed to a London insurance brokerage. Although Lindsay was successful in this career, he longed to devote himself to literature and metaphysics, and in his spare time he read deeply in the German philosophers he idolized, particularly Arthur Schopenhauer and Friedrich Nietzsche.

After serving in the British Army during World War I, Lindsay began his writing career in 1919 at age forty-three, three years after his marriage to Jacqueline Silver, a young woman he had met at a literary club in London. There is some difference in opinion as to the quality of Lindsay's marriage and its effect on his writing. Bernard Sellin states that Jacqueline's "youth, her enthusiasm and her unbounded faith made a writer out of a man who had been suffering from a psychological blockage," and that although she was later disillusioned when success eluded Lindsay, she was supportive and faithful in her belief in his writing career. But in the judgment of Colin Wilson, Jacqueline Lindsay "felt that she had made a mistake in encouraging [her husband] to give up his business career for the heartbreaking profession of literature," and that their marriage steadily deteriorated, which contributed to Lindsay's withdrawal and depression. Because a number of critics have commented on the ambivalence toward women and marriage in Lindsay's novels, discussion of Lindsay's marriage is significant. In most of Lindsay's work, earthly marriages and romantic unions are unsatisfactory, with his characters finding harmonious partnerships only in the sublime realm to which all Lindsay's heroes and heroines aspire. From 1919 to 1926

Lindsay wrote and published four novels. The first of these, originally entitled *Nightspore in Tormance,* was written in eleven months and found a publisher immediately upon completion, although Lindsay was requested to cut 15,000 words from the manuscript and change the title. The novel, published in 1920 as *A Voyage to Arcturus,* received marginal critical approval but commercially was a complete failure. Yet, compared to the commercial and critical failure of the novels that followed, *Arcturus* was Lindsay's most successful work.

After he had completed his second novel, *The Haunted Woman,* in 1922, Lindsay immediately began to write *Sphinx* and simultaneously worked on his most uncharacteristic novel, *The Adventures of Monsieur de Mailly,* a historical romance. *Sphinx* was published in 1923, but *Mailly,* also completed that year, was rejected for publication until 1926, after it had undergone extensive revision. The failure of these novels to produce a sufficient income depleted Lindsay's savings and forced him to sell his large house in Cornwall. In 1929, Lindsay moved his family to a modest dwelling in the Sussex village of Ferring, a remote location that perfectly suited Lindsay's reclusive temperament. However, Jacqueline Lindsay desired more social contact than did her husband, and in 1938 she persuaded him to buy a boarding house near Brighton, a popular seaside resort. Although Lindsay was concerned about his privacy, the move promised additional income and an opportunity to be near E. H. Visiak, one of Lindsay's few literary friends. Visiak also wrote fantastic fiction and later authored one of the first in-depth studies of Lindsay's work. During his years at Brighton, Lindsay continued to write. The last of his books to be published in his lifetime was *Devil's Tor,* a sprawling, problematic novel which he wrote in the late twenties and published in 1932. Lindsay completed *The Violet Apple* and worked on *The Witch* until 1939, when he abandoned his efforts on the lengthy, frustrating manuscript. By this time Lindsay's neglect of his health had left him severely anemic. His fundamental distrust of the medical profession prevented him from seeking attention for a seriously abscessed tooth, which caused gangrene and a fatal hemorrhage. His last two novels, *The Violet Apple* and *The Witch,* were published for the first time in 1976, thirty-one years after his death.

Lindsay's first novel, *A Voyage to Arcturus,* is undoubtedly his best-known and most important. In *Arcturus,* Lindsay presented the themes and philosophic vision upon which the rest of his novels are based, utilizing such devices of fantastic fiction as space travel, which prompted C. S. Lewis to remark that Lindsay was the first writer to show him "what other planets in fiction are really good for; for *spiritual* adventures." Spiritual adventure is the primary motivation for the characters in *Arcturus* and the novels that follow it. *Arcturus* stands as an indictment of the false values of modern society and the longing for spiritual transcendence. In this sense, Lindsay's work has much in common with the Scottish fantasy writer George MacDonald, whose writings had considerable influence on Lindsay. Generally, however, Lindsay's fiction was much more affected by the philosophical thought of Schopenhauer and Nietzsche. From Schopenhauer, Lindsay acquired the concepts of the Will as essence of power and of the sublime, which Lindsay, unlike Schopenhauer, perceived as a real condition. Lindsay considered the sublime a state of heightened spiritual, moral, and intellectual awareness that could be attained by individuals who possessed extraordinary character and fortitude. In *Arcturus,* and in the rest of his novels, Lindsay sends his protagonist in quest of the sublime. The emphasis in *Arcturus,* however, is not on the attainment of the sublime, but on the various physical and moral dimensions the hero discovers during his quest. These physical and moral realms radically contradict each other, signifying the illusory and relative nature of reality. Nietzsche's influence can be found in the didactic tone and in the nihilistic attitude that Lindsay displays toward mundane reality throughout *Arcturus.* It is this fiercely judgmental idealism and tortured desire to believe in a transcendent reality that would give meaning to life that Lindsay's defenders claim infuses his writing with genius.

In the novels which followed *Arcturus,* Lindsay attempted a more detailed exposition of the sublime. Such books as *The Haunted Woman, Sphinx,* and *The Violet Apple,* show men and women living conventional, shallow lives in the mundane world and their subsequent transcendence into the world of higher reality. Although after *Arcturus* Lindsay never again used the device of space travel as a means to propel characters on their spiritual quest, he utilized other devices, such as secret chambers, towers, and dream machines, to allow the transcendence to take place. In the sublime realm, the characters acquire perfect knowledge and an awareness that is unattainable in the material world. Here Lindsay's characters frequently find absolute affinity with their true mates, always people with whom they are not paired in the tainted, confused material world. An additional factor marking the attainment of the sublime is the loss of individuality, which in the sublime reality is a trite non-truth. Individuality is shed by redemptive pain, self-sacrifice, and, ultimately, death of the earthly self. To cling to pleasure and life indicates attachment to the physical world, and such attachment prohibits admission into the sublime. The characters in Lindsay's novels who attain the sublime are those who hurl themselves toward destruction for the sake of loved ones or a higher ideal. In this way, Lindsay's philosophy blends fundamental Puritan belief in self-denial and the Christian virtue of martyrdom with his adaptation of German mysticism.

Critical appraisal of Lindsay's work varies widely. Most objections are aimed at his prose style, which has been consistently termed amateurish. Some critics believe that Lindsay embarked on a literary career too late in life to develop a comfortable relationship with writing. The major critical controversy regarding Lindsay's prose is whether it is simply awkward because of his lack of skill as a novelist or if its stilted, odd quality is an aspect of his intention to mirror other-worldliness. Although Lindsay's staunch defenders acknowledge some problems with his prose style and narrative structure, they generally minimize the severity of these flaws and praise the overall quality of thought demonstrated in his novels. Of *A Voyage to Arcturus* Harold Bloom said, "Nothing else in English since Blake and Shelley, that I know of, has found its way back so surely to that early romance world where gods and men meet and struggle as equals or near-equals." Lindsay has never been a widely read fantasy writer, but his work has gained a cult status and its contribution to the genre is regarded as undeniably significant.

PRINCIPAL WORKS

A Voyage to Arcturus   (novel)   1920
The Haunted Woman   (novel)   1922
Sphinx   (novel)   1923
The Adventures of Monsieur de Mailly   (novel)   1926; also
    published as *A Blade for Sale,* 1927
Devil's Tor   (novel)   1932
**The Violet Apple and The Witch*   (novels)   1976

*The Violet Apple was written in 1934 and *The Witch* was unfinished
  at the time of the author's death.

THE TIMES LITERARY SUPPLEMENT   (essay date 1920)

[*The following excerpt is taken from a disapproving review of* A Voyage to Arcturus.]

However much one may resent such a book as **"A Voyage to Arcturus,"** one must pay tribute to the cleverness which enables Mr. David Lindsay to capture the elusive quality of the worst kind of nightmare. He does not content himself with giving us a vivid description of life as it conceivably might be on another planet; we are transported to remote regions of space in order that the riddle of human existence may be studied in true perspective; and the solution thence afforded is very much what one might expect a temporarily unbalanced mind to arrive at if an anaesthetic were potent for just one critical instant longer—which, mercifully, it never is. Mr. Lindsay's imagination is prolific rather than powerful, and he has not controlled it towards any coherent result. For instance, the hero of the adventure, Maskull, encounters on his journey in Arcturus a number of entities—human, superhuman, and diabolic—whose relation to him and to each other never becomes clear; nor can we find any connecting link between the startling and often gruesome episodes which mark his progress. There may be an intention of allegory in what appears to be simply the riot of morbid fancy; but we doubt whether many readers will be inclined to pursue the possible hidden meaning over a quagmire and through a noisome fog. For the book is, at any rate, consistent in respect of its uniform unwholesomeness; the keynote being struck in the opening chapter, which recalls Baudelaire, or Poe in his most grisly vein. It is, no doubt, a legitimate aim of the writer of fiction to make the flesh creep; scarcely, we think, to make the gorge rise.

A review of "A Voyage to Arcturus," in The Times Literary Supplement, *No. 976, September 30, 1920, p. 637.*

C. S. LEWIS   (essay date 1940)

[*Lewis is considered one of the foremost Christian and mythopoeic authors of the twentieth century. Indebted principally to George MacDonald, G. K. Chesterton, Charles Williams, and the writers of ancient Norse myths, he is regarded as a formidable logician and Christian polemicist, a perceptive literary critic, and—most highly—as a writer of fantasy literature. Lewis also held instructoral posts at Oxford and Cambridge, where he was an acknowledged authority on medieval and Renaissance literature. A traditionalist in his approach to life and art, he opposed the modern movement in literary criticism toward biographical and psychological interpretation. In place of this, Lewis practiced and propounded a theory of criticism that stressed the importance of the author's intent, rather than the reader's presuppositions and prejudices. In the following excerpt, composed in 1940 and published*] *in 1947 in* Essays Presented to Charles Williams, *Lewis comments on the necessity of suspense and impending danger in successful adventure stories. He cites* A Voyage to Arcturus *as being an outstanding example of how an author effectively draws readers into an improbable narrative by promising unpredictable and dangerous situations for the protagonist.]*

I have sometimes wondered whether . . . 'excitement' may not be an element actually hostile to the deeper imagination. In inferior romances, such as the American magazines of 'scientifiction' supply, we often come across a really suggestive idea. But the author has no expedient for keeping the story on the move except that of putting his hero into violent danger. In the hurry and scurry of his escapes the poetry of the basic idea is lost. In a much milder degree I think this has happened to Wells himself in the *War of the Worlds*. What really matters in this story is the idea of being attacked by something utterly 'outside'. As in *Piers Plowman* destruction has come upon us 'from the planets'. If the Martian invaders are merely dangerous—if we once become mainly concerned with the fact that they can *kill* us—why, then, a burglar or a bacillus can do as much. (p. 10)

It is here that Homer shows his supreme excellence. The landing on Circe's island, the sight of the smoke going up from amidst those unexplored woods, the god meeting us ('the messenger, the slayer of Argus')—what an anticlimax if all these had been the prelude only to some ordinary risk of life and limb! But the peril that lurks here, the silent, painless, endurable change into brutality, is worthy of the setting. Mr de la Mare too has surmounted the difficulty. The threat launched in the opening paragraph of his best stories is seldom fulfilled in any identifiable event: still less is it dissipated. Our fears are never, in one sense, realised: yet we lay down the story feeling that they, and far more, were justified. But perhaps the most remarkable achievement in this kind is that of Mr David Lindsay's *Voyage to Arcturus*. The experienced reader, noting the threats and promises of the opening chapter, even while he gratefully enjoys them, feels sure that they cannot be carried out. He reflects that in stories of this kind the first chapter is nearly always the best and reconciles himself to disappointment; Tormance, when we reach it, he forbodes, will be less interesting than Tormance seen from the Earth. But never will he have been more mistaken. Unaided by any special skill or even any sound taste in language, the author leads us up a stair of unpredictables. In each chapter we think we have found his final position; each time we are utterly mistaken. He builds whole worlds of imagery and passion, any one of which would have served another writer for a whole book, only to pull each of them to pieces and pour scorn on it. The physical dangers, which are plentiful, here count for nothing: it is we ourselves and the author who walk through a world of spiritual dangers which makes them seem trivial. There is no recipe for writing of this kind. But part of the secret is that the author (like Kafka) is recording a lived dialectic. His Tormance is a region of the spirit. He is the first writer to discover what 'other planets' are really good for in fiction. No merely physical strangeness or merely spatial distance will realise that idea of otherness which is what we are always trying to grasp in a story about voyaging through space: you must go into another dimension. To construct plausible and moving 'other worlds' you must draw on the only real 'other world' we know, that of the spirit. (pp. 11-12)

C. S. Lewis, *"On Stories,"* in his On Stories and Other Essays on Literature, *edited by Walter Hooper,*

Harcourt Brace Jovanovich, Publishers, 1982, pp. 3-20.*

C. S. LEWIS   (essay date 1947)

[In the following excerpt, from a 1947 letter to poet Ruth Ritter, Lewis expresses his indebtedness to Lindsay's A Voyage to Arcturus, *calling it the "father" of his science-fantasy* Perelanda, *the second volume of the Ransom trilogy. Lewis also credits Lindsay with showing him that interplanetary travel can be used to demonstrate spiritual adventures.]*

Can you bear the truth—*Voyage to Arcturus* is not the parody of *Perelandra* but its father. It was published, a dead failure, about 25 years ago. Now that the author is dead it is suddenly leaping into fame; but I'm one of the old guard who had a treasured second hand copy before anyone had heard of it. From Lyndsay [sic] I first learned what other planets in fiction are really good for; for *spiritual* adventures. Only they can satisfy the craving which sends our imagination off the earth or hurtling it another way. In him I first saw the terrific results produced by the union of two kinds of fiction hitherto kept apart: the Novalis, G. Macdonald, James Stephens sort and the H. G. Wells, Jules Verne sort. My debt to him is very great: tho' I'm a little alarmed to find it so obvious that the affinity came through to you even from a talk about Lyndsay [sic]. For the rest, *Voyage to A* is on the borderline of the diabolical: i.e. the philosophy expressed is so Manichaean as to be almost Satanic. Secondly, the style is often laughably crude. Thirdly, the proper names (Polecrab, Blodsombre, Wombflash, Tydomin, Sullenbode) are superb and perhaps Screwtape owes something to them. Fourthly, you must read it. You will have a disquieting but not-to-be-missed experience.

C. S. Lewis, in a letter to Ruth Pitter in 1947, in C. S. Lewis: The Art of Enchantment *by Donald E. Glover, Ohio University Press, 1981, p. 33.*

ROGER LANCELYN GREEN   (essay date 1958)

[In the following excerpt, Green comments on the dreamlike quality of A Voyage to Arcturus. *According to Green,* Arcturus *is unlike traditional allegories, because clues to its meaning lie "somewhere in the subconscious mind."]*

To read *A Voyage to Arcturus* is indeed to enter a bewildering dreamland, almost a land of nightmare, but, as in Tormance, there is an intensity of light which makes everything vividly real. It is not possible, or desirable, to give a précis of this astonishing book . . . for Tormance is a world of the spirit, rather than a planet like any other before or since. Nor is it an allegory in the sense that *Pilgrim's Progress* is, for its haunting, terrifying quality lies in the fact that the meaning seems clear somewhere in the subconscious mind, but eludes the conscious with the numbing horror which we sometimes experience in seeking to recapture a dream which lingers somewhere in our being—vividly real but frighteningly incomprehensible. (pp. 180-81)

Roger Lancelyn Green, *"Tormance and Malacandra,"* in his Into Other Worlds: Space-Flight in Fiction, from Lucian to Lewis, *Abelard-Schuman, 1958, pp. 177-84.**

BRIGID BROPHY   (essay date 1963)

[Brophy is an Anglo-Irish novelist, dramatist, and critic. Influenced by Freud and Shaw, she creates witty social satires of middle-class morality and hypocrisy strongly marked by elements of farce and word-play. As a literary critic, Brophy is known for her provocative and acerbic remarks, particularly the iconoclasm of Fifty Works of English and American Literature We Could Do Without *(1967) in which she attacks such works as* Hamlet, Wuthering Heights, *and* Moby Dick. *In the following review of* A Voyage to Arcturus, *Brophy calls Lindsay "a master of bathetic ineptitudes." Brophy finds that* Arcturus *frustrates the reader because the structure and intent of the work is inconsistent; as an example Brophy notes that sex is a primary concern of the novel, but that the topic is repressed in "a fluid of metaphysics."]*

[*A Voyage to Arcturus* is one of] the first fruits of a series called 'Rare Works of Imaginative Fiction'. 'Rare,' the publishers explain, implies out of print and unobtainable—which is fair enough; but 'imaginative' provokes an instant's resentment. I should have thought it a case for Coleridge's distinction. Fanciful, even fantastic, these are. But if you label such wizened and often sawdusty old gourds 'imaginative fiction', what have you left for *Anna Karenina*? (p. 904)

The technique of *A Voyage to Arcturus* might have been rejected as too creaking by the *Strand Magazine* in the youth of Sherlock Holmes, but in fact the book dates from 1920. The blurb . . . admits 'David Lindsay was by no means a great writer'. He proves a master of bathetic ineptitudes, with a grasp on this world so clumsy that it's just as well when, after a prelude of minimal relevance, he gets his urrocket off to another. But even then he's unhandy enough to introduce an inhabitant of the other world as 'a woman who knows her way about the world'. The very title is inept, since the space voyage is not to Arcturus but to its satellite, Tormance, 'the residential suburb of Arcturus'. (Can it be this, the only amusing line in a leaden book, which inspired Firbank to 'Chedorlahomor, a *faubourg* of Sodom'?)

Tormance, which is governed by two supernatural powers, casts the traveller into a perplexity of metaphysics. He is forever changing his mind about which is the good and which the bad power, or whether they are in fact identical. All he can actually *do* is explore the surrealist landscape, asking the names and properties of districts and their inhabitants—a form of story which, condemned to surprises instead of suspense, quickly uses up the reader's attention. At the start, the main question is which inhabitants can grow what extra sense organs or even extra limbs for special embraces. But soon even this nastily plastic symbolism is more or less discarded and the inquiry settles down to which district is inhabited by men only, which by men-women, which by an all-female woman (who is, significantly, lethal to most men, and who possesses neither soul, personality nor even features until a man's love gives them to her), which by a living statue of a youth with 'the beauty of a girl' and which by a third sex for which not only a new organ but a new pronoun and adjective (*ae* and *aer*) have to be invented. 'It is your *sex* that interests me,' says the traveller to an example of the last category. 'How do you satisfy your desires?' For answer the creature points to 'the concealed organ on aer brow'. It's pretty clear that it is sex which interests the author, too, and that the two ambiguous, interchangeable supernatural powers on the planet represent the author's view of the sexes. But his interest is repressed under, though still visible in, a preserving fluid of metaphysics. A displeasing smell of repression, of morbid hygiene, pervades the book—which is

a genuine curio, but aesthetically of the same order as an embryo pickled in a bottle. (pp. 904-05)

> Brigid Brophy, in a review of "A Voyage to Arcturus," in New Statesman, Vol. LXV, No. 1683, June 14, 1963, pp. 904-05.

KINGSLEY AMIS   (essay date 1963)

[A distinguished English novelist, poet, essayist, and editor, Amis was one of the Angry Young Men, a group of British writers of the 1950s whose writings expressed bitterness and disillusionment with society. Common to the work of the Angry Young Men is an anti-hero who rebels against a corrupt social order in a quest for personal integrity. Amis's first and most widely praised novel, Lucky Jim *(1954), is characteristic of the school and demonstrates his skill as a satirist. Amis has since rejected categorization or alliance with any literary group and maintains that he is only interested in following his artistic instincts. Throughout his career, Amis has also sustained an interest in science fiction. He was coeditor of the* Spectrum *science fiction anthologies and was the author of one of the first major critical surveys of the genre in* New Maps in Hell *(1960). In the following excerpt, Amis reviews* A Voyage to Arcturus *and claims that it does not fall into the science fiction genre. He classifies the novel as being closer to religious allegory, but without a reliance on "some great public myth" which might have attracted a larger, more interested, readership.]*

["**A Voyage to Arcturus**"] has probably always been more talked about than read, and its diffusion among general readers may prove the death-blow to its reputation. It is the kind of rambling fantasy, rich in ambiguous symbolism, which slightly repels the many who like novels to make solid sense, and violently attracts the few who enjoy dredging them for deep, dark, mysterious secrets about Life and the Universe. The secrets extractable from this book, as is usual in such cases, will be different for different readers and even, perhaps, for the same reader in different moods. . . .

In very rough outline this is a science-fiction adventure. After an incredible (but otherwise unremarkable) incident at a spiritualist séance in London, the hero, one Maskull, boards an outsize torpedo made of crystal and is conveyed to Tormance, described as the one inhabited planet of the star Arcturus. Here he spends a lot of time searching vaguely for a being (variously named Surtur, Faceny, Crystal-man and Shaping) who is perhaps possessed of divine attributes of one kind or another. At an early stage Surtur appears to Maskull in person and, after haranguing him about the stern, eternal rhythm of their environment, says he wants Maskull to serve him. Maskull agrees, but little more is heard of this project, and he ultimately dies on Tormance with his search not only unaccomplished but—for me at any rate—still undefined.

In the meantime we have been treated to an abundance of cheapjack marvels. Non-human novelties include a camel-sized ten-legged flying reptile, self-generating plant-animals and an armor-plated horse-sized insect with jaws like scimitars.

The story is scattered with allegorical-sounding proper names: Matterplay, Jotwind, Spadevil, Wombflash. And there is much metaphysical jargoning between Maskull and his various guides. . . . But the most that emerges with any clarity is the necessity of duty and the danger of pleasure. We knew about that already. Some kinds of reader will be interested to detect a keen, though resolutely non-pornographic, interest in bisexuality and hermaphroditism. But the nature of Lindsay's possible psychological disturbances, like that of his spiritual ones, remains a matter for speculation at most.

This is not science-fiction, which is a realistic genre. It is in intention, perhaps, a religious allegory, but, to be intelligible and satisfactory, such writing does well to rest upon some great public myth—in our literature, upon Christianity. Without such underpinning it will fall, as here, into whimsy, into mere dream. And other people's dreams are not interesting.

Kingsley Amis, "Adventures on a Distant Star," in *The New York Times Book Review, November 24, 1963, p. 60.*

J. B. PICK (essay date 1964)

[*In the following excerpt, Pick discusses the salient themes and motifs of* A Voyage to Arcturus. *Pick attributes Lindsay's neglect by critics and the reading public to the fact that both were largely unable to recognize the visionary nature of his work.*]

Once a man has begun his book, if he has anything in him it will come out. If he hasn't much in him, and realises it, he will strike an attitude to disguise the fact. The attitude may take the form of "stylistic originality" or something of that sort, which the literati, who are easily deceived, may well admire.

It is no wonder that David Lindsay was never found generally acceptable. He had actually *seen* something, and his masterpiece *A Voyage to Arcturus* is a vivid account of the vision. We require from a witness not a display of educated sensibility but an account of what happened, and this is what David Lindsay gives us. The literati have often proved to prefer a display of educated sensibility. If nothing important has happened, to display educated sensibility is the only possible reason for only giving an account at all.

David Lindsay's tragedy—and his literary life was really that—is the tragedy of a man who has seen something, tells people and they don't listen or don't understand what he is talking about.

Lindsay had worked as a Lloyd's underwriter for fifteen years before he wrote his first novel. During this time he had filled notebooks with observations, reflections, perceptions and aphorisms, which all slanted in one direction and culminated in the explosive vision which became *A Voyage to Arcturus,* as soon as he left his job and settled in Cornwall to write. The book sold only a few hundred copies and its reception is typified by a review in the *Times Literary Supplement,* dated September 30th 1920 [see excerpt above]. . . . (p. 171)

The book is nothing whatever like Baudelaire or Poe, in whatever vein they may be writing, but the reviewer had several detective novels to deal with and no time for reflection. *Arcturus* was not reissued until 1945 and by that time David Lindsay was dead.

Lindsay, a strong, reserved man of Scottish Calvinist background, a solitary walker, a mountaineer, devoted to German metaphysics and to music, was not primarily an artist. He was concerned ruthlessly with his vision of truth, with his bitter and profound experience of spiritual reality. Panawe, the artist in *A Voyage to Arcturus,* says: "Nothing comes of it [art] but vanity." In his notebook Lindsay writes: "The first preliminary for all metaphysical thinking is to produce within oneself the sense of *reality.*" Lindsay had this sense; he did not need to "produce it within himself."

If the reality behind his vision had been acknowledged on the appearance of *Arcturus,* perhaps his grip upon our human life here on earth would not have weakened so sadly in his later work. *Arcturus* proved too weird and strange both for critics and public.

No wonder. Its keywords are "wildness" and "grandeur." Its impact is powerful, its message at the same time tonic and terrible. The book is *there,* as a whole, violent and compelling. It is not anything so crude as an allegory, it is an imaginative fire in which years of thought are burned up. In *Devil's Tor* the painter says: "A symbol is a mystic sign of the Creator. An allegory is a wall decoration with a label attached." *A Voyage to Arcturus* is no wall decoration.

Later books needed "composing" from scraps of discontinuous perception, from ideas and observations. None has the singleness of *Arcturus,* none gives the same impression of overwhelming, unified power. The "story" is often forced, and has insufficient means of locomotion. Lindsay in some of the books seems like a lithe, muscular man in a very ill-fitting suit. The savagery has gone, the grandeur is more abstract and the "sublimity" seems more deliberately sought.

In *Arcturus* the wildness is naked. Pleasure and pain are seen contemptuously as vulgar and trivial. (p. 172)

The book begins as if Lindsay intends to set his story in the here and now. He introduces a set of characters who assemble for a seance. They are all fully described, as though they were the chief runners in a marathon. In fact they disappear like bubbles on a stream and never return after the first chapter. Two rough, wild strangers, Maskull "a kind of giant, but of broader and robuster physique than most giants," and Nightspore, "of middle height, but so tough looking that he appeared as if trained out of all human susceptibilities" enter the house just when the medium is about to conduct a materialisation. The medium succeeds in producing a beautiful, supernatural youth. A thick, muscular, ugly, yellow-faced man with an expression of "sagacity, brutality and humour" bounds in and twists the youth's neck round. "A faint, unearthly shriek sounded, and the body fell in a heap on the floor . . . The guests were unutterably shocked to observe that its expression had changed from a mysterious but fascinating smile to a vulgar, sordid, bestial grin." So much for the wiles of Crystalman, the god of this world.

From that moment everything is vision, and only occasionally does deliberate invention intrude. The story of Maskull's pilgrimage pulses and flows. The savage latecomer, Krag, who is in fact an emissary of Muspel, the hidden eternal light, and who on earth takes on the aspect of redemptive Pain, draws Maskull and Nightspore aside and persuades them to accompany him on a voyage to Tormance, one of the planets of the star Arcturus. (p. 173)

My guess is that the characters assembled for the seance were to have been the leading figures in a novel of the same oddly polite, disturbing kind as the later *Sphinx* and *Violet Apple,* but at the point of Krag's entry, the vision exploded in a huge pattern of light, the novel disappeared, and an extravagant masterpiece took its place. From then on the tale drives forward with reckless directness.

Despite the metaphysical intention, everything is concrete. We start from fruits and colours, not from abstractions. The nature of a fruit unknown on earth is "hard, persistent, melancholy." . . . The imagery, often drawn from music, is burning and impressive. The descriptions have tremendous imaginative force, and a vivid hallucinatory quality. Lindsay uses words violently, sometimes uncouthly, is occasionally ponderous, and cares nothing for grace. (pp. 173-74)

Sometimes, when words have to be put into the mouths of the strange, living, symbolic figures, and the vision provides no words, he makes them up from what he knows—bald, direct and without the glow of vision. At other times their utterances have a gnomic, pithy conciseness and an aphoristic force which strike home to the heart. . . .

The tale itself is the account of Maskull's pilgrimage on Tormance, in search of Muspel, about which he knows nothing except that he seeks it. Maskull is a Prometheus figure who "came to steal Muspel-fire, to give a deeper life to men, never doubting if your soul could endure that burning." Krag and Nightspore desert him. He goes through a series of remarkable, violent, terrifying adventures in a world of extraordinary reality, led onwards towards Muspel by mysterious drumbeats. These drumbeats are indications that the other world of Muspel in truth exists. (p. 174)

Maskull's nobility and daring make it possible for him to receive intimations that beyond this world there is another, which alone is real. But Maskull is human, and can be led in many directions. Nightspore is Maskull's "new man" who awakes only when Maskull, the everyday self, dies. The nature of the true god becomes revealed after terrible suffering, for the Devil is the God of this world and idealism, philosophy, pleasure, love are all the toys with which Crystalman deceives his victims. Most forms of mysticism, too, seek union only with Crystalman (or Shaping) and never realise the existence of the hidden Muspel. (p. 175)

Any description of the book must give an uncouth, bizarre impression, and this is not unjust. But what emerges after several readings is something quite other—a sense of the remarkable profundity and coherence of the vision and its message. The message is terrible in its uncompromising purity, and is more likely to repel casual readers than to attract. But the achievement of the book exactly balances the astonishing ambition of its intention. This, surely, is most exceptional. (p. 176)

Everything that David Lindsay wrote is the work of a man who cannot help but see what others do not, the true nature of what he calls "the vast shadow-house of earth and sky." To find an individual Scottish novel comparable with *A Voyage to Arcturus* in force and strangeness—and it is in no way comparable in depth and scope—you would have to go back as far as *The Confessions of a Justified Sinner*. It is odd that the most extraordinary Scottish novelist of this century should have been so neglected. (p. 182)

J. B. Pick, "The Work of David Lindsay," in Studies in Scottish Literature, *Vol. 1, No. 3, January, 1964, pp. 171-82.*

E. H. VISIAK (essay date 1970)

[*An English writer of fiction and expert on mysticism, Visiak was a close personal friend of Lindsay and one of his first critics and biographers. In the following excerpt, he discusses Lindsay's use of Christian dogma in* A Voyage to Arcturus.]

Lindsay himself would have disliked, and probably rebutted, the assertion, but the significance of *A Voyage to Arcturus,* is

dogmatically Christian. Only the aspect is different. Muspel, the 'sublime light', is God; Crystalman, the loathsome incubus who intercepts and perverts the sublime rays as they enter the souls, is Satan; and Krag, who saves the souls from sinking into the abominable abyss, is the Redeemer.

In the case of Crystalman and Krag, the joint presentation is inverted. Crystalman, in his incarnation in Tormance, is a charming personality, like a cultured English gentleman, who is also a poet (Lindsay was allergic to poetry); a vital, vitalising character. His voice is as lulling as sweet music; or it can be as a thrilling summons. This was excellently brought out on the radio in dramatising the work; Crystalman accosts Nightspore, the voyager to *Arcturus;* 'Nightspore!' It is as if he had cried, *'Nightspore, wake up! Arise from the dead!'*

He was a fake, the shadow of selfhood—itself a shadow. Behind his ingratiating amenity is the inane mime. In addressing Nightspore, he is mimicking the exalted words 'I came that ye might have *life,* and that ye might have it more abundantly'; in modern terms, 'I have come to *electrify you*!'

And Crystalman has all the various sorts and conditions of Arcturans in his net, whether they are idealists, intellectuals, hedonists, masochists, sadists, or good, kindly—even self-sacrificing—souls. However hard and sincerely any of them strive after righteousness, when they die, his vulgar rictus comes out in their faces in derision. All that Muspel—who is 'fighting for his life'—can avail, apparently, is, with Krag's help, to prevent by the ministry of pain, the perverted souls from sinking into abominable dissolution. Nightspore is given a dreadful glimpse of it. At the sight, he is appalled, and he too becomes, like Krag, a Redeemer.

Nor is this additional Redeemer un-Christian since Christ himself, according to St. Paul, was the 'forerunner of many brethren'.

But the chief and most debatable parallel between Lindsay's *tour de force* and dogmatic Christianity is his ascription to Crystalman of beauty. Here indeed there is a scriptural difference! Christ appreciated the 'lilies of the field'; in *Arcturus,* even the ethereal hues of dawn belong to Crystalman. In regard to beauty in art, it is not so disparate; Christ apparently discouraged architectural enthusiasm. At any rate, he pointed out the transitory condition of the 'great buildings' his disciples admired; while in the Old Testament, we read 'the hand of the Lord shall be upon all pleasant pictures'. In the main point, however, the fiction and religion are at one; sublimity is the ultimate. It relates to the spirit; beauty relates only to the senses. If beauty obscures sublimity, it is evil; the meretricious substitute of the 'second best', as I have noted.

Lindsay held that beauty and art—art as a means of beauty— were not only evil in this way; he saw them also as causes of perversion. They are the products of Crystalman. Here, there seems to be some sort of spiritual refraction, and we are in metaphysical profundities; for the mystery of Crystalman is the mystery of evil itself. He is an illusion, and the producer of illusions, as the Christian Devil is the 'father of lies', a lie himself, 'who never was, and now is not'.

It is an enigma analogous to that of materialistic phenomena; a paradox like that of the Neo-Platonic proposition of 'Bound and the Infinite'. 'Bound' implies form; form involves physical space, matter, and restriction or limitation. Yet the Infinite cannot logically admit of spatial demarcations, any more than Eternity can admit of being measured off by time and motion (perhaps time and motion are swallowed up in Einstein's principle of Relativity—I am not, in Lindsayan language, *to know*). Nor are Infinitude and Eternity the ultimate concepts. They must presumably be twin-aspects, corresponding to 'space-time', uniting in a transcendental synthesis; the *mystic sublime*. But space and time are elemental, natural, and Lindsay virtually equates Crystalman with Nature, which Blake very accordingly asserts is evil—it and its energy. 'All energy is evil'—which accords in one way with the Hindu *mot*, 'Do nothing and everything is done'. Crystalman in his incarnation, as we have seen, is extremely energetic—'full of vim', in the hearty phrase.

But here again we are perplexed; for how could Crystalman, shadow without substance, illusion, or the Devil, or Nature, be incarnated—embodied, that is to say, in a specific individual? He may be regarded as an abstraction in the negative sense, as darkness is the negation of light, disease of health. But even Muspel, the 'Divine Light', could not be incarnated, or canalised, in that way. Muspel could only be manifested, on the principle of the 'One and the Many', in facets and scintillations countless as the stars.

There are no Churches in Tormance, no symbology or ceremonial—which seems a pity. Otherwise, it might have been shown how that kind of beauty, on Lindsay's argument, obscures sublimity by sentimentalising it, as in pictures on sacred subjects even by the Great Masters. Again, there are no Saints. Even the most integral Arcturans, the most assiduous and well-intentioned, betray at death Crystalman's vulgar grin. Only, Krag, the administrator of redemptive pain, and Maskull, the voyager to *Arcturus*, are *bodhisattvas;* they defer their own celestial felicity in order to save others. Maskull, or *Nightspore*, as he has then become, decides on following this course, after a glimpse of the abominable waste of putrefaction Crystalman's influence has caused, the horror of which is as that hinted in Poe's story of the Inquisition, *The Pit and the Pendulum*. (pp. 109-11)

> E. H. Visiak, "'Arcturus' and the Christian Dogma," in The Strange Genius of David Lindsay: An Appreciation *by J. B. Pick, Colin Wilson & E. H. Visiak, John Baker, 1970, pp. 109-11.*

J. DERRICK McCLURE (essay date 1974)

[*In the following excerpt, McClure discusses* The Adventures of Monsieur de Mailly, *a historical romance, which he believes has been unfairly ignored because it is so different in setting and structure from Lindsay's fantastic novels. McClure argues that* Mailly's *differences are superficial and that Lindsay's technique and philosophy, as demonstrated in this novel, are similar to those in his other works.*]

[David Lindsay's *Adventures of Monsieur de Mailly*] is a vastly entertaining book: colourful in its setting, abounding in vividly portrayed characters, rapid and lively in its action, at times riotously funny; and also providing, to an astonishing degree, the pleasure which arises from seeing a device of brilliant ingenuity which is at once totally unexpected and totally logical. It is certainly the most immediately likeable of all his works, and the one which might have been least expected to lapse into near oblivion. At a first reading, moreover, it seems as dissimilar to the unearthly fantasies of *A Voyage to Arcturus* as to the quieter probings of *The Haunted Woman* and *Sphinx*. Yet to dismiss it as a mere pot-boiler, and to suggest that it stands wholly apart from the rest of Lindsay's work, are alike unperceptive. Though it contains virtually no supernatural ele-

ments . . . , it deals no less than his other novels with the questions of illusion and reality: to what extent those can be distinguished, and whether an ultimate reality in fact exists. And here as elsewhere, Lindsay firmly asserts a positive answer to the latter question; but not before treating the reader to such a degree of inversion, reversal, turning inside out and general mangling of his assumptions that his whole concepts of truth and pretence are called in question. *Mailly* is a historical romance to the same extent that *Arcturus* is a science-fiction novel and *The Haunted Woman* a ghost-story: it is a penetrating and disturbing philosophical speculation in the superficial disguise of a common literary genre; and I at least, on completing the book, felt scarcely less shaken, though much more pleasantly, than after my first reading of *Arcturus*. (pp. 226-27)

Mailly, in its chronological position in the sequence of Lindsay's works, represents a natural stage in the development of his thought, or of his use of fiction to reveal his thought. In *Arcturus,* he systematically demolishes each of the possible attitudes which may be used as defences against reality, and finally presents a terrifying picture of the universe as it appears when all comforting delusions are gone. The protagonist wanders from one false position to another, adopting the attitudes of the characters he meets in each successive episode, only to find that altruism, egoism, moral dedication, domesticity, devotion to art, religious fervour, and sexual infatuation are alike useless in the face of the real world. . . . *The Haunted Woman* (which is certainly no more like *Arcturus* than *Mailly* is like either) is much less far-reaching; but conveys with no less success, through the medium not of an episodic fantasy but of a low-toned novel constructed with classical regularity, the notion of another world—beautiful, enticing, dangerous, but "real"—behind the conventional masks which constitute life for most people: the author repeats in a much less spectacular form part of the previous book's message, as if to emphasize its relevance to the lives of his readers. *Sphinx* at first sight seems to be merely a more elaborate and cumbrous treatment of the same theme; and certainly the supernatural element is used for virtually the same purpose as in *The Haunted Woman*, namely to provide glimpses of the reality behind formal social patterns. It differs noticeably from its predecessor, however, in placing much greater emphasis on the delusions which exist within the natural world. By depicting a social milieu in which the guiding principle (at least for the females) seems to be that each person must maintain his-or-her own mask intact while trying his-or-her level best to penetrate behind that of everybody else—and in the full awareness that everybody else is acting with precisely the same purpose—Lindsay is able to suggest that not one but several layers of error may overlie the ultimate truth. . . . As in *Arcturus* but without the machinery of fantasy, and certainly without the same attempt at differentiating and categorizing the various poses, Lindsay explores the complex fankles of error which must be passed through before reality is reached. . . . *Mailly* simply represents the next logical step: in this novel Lindsay focusses his whole attention on the misconceptions and misunderstandings that can occur in ordinary life, and the attempts of one man to discover reality, or create his own reality, in a world of posing and intrigue; and without invoking a supernatural world suggests that whatever the ultimate truth may be, several co-existent realms of fraud remain steadily in front of it. (Is it an accident that the story is set in the Paris of Louis XIV, where social ceremonial was developed to a degree rarely surpassed? . . .). . . . As much as in any of the earlier novels, the reader is left wondering, after several enforced reconsiderations of the evidence presented to him, precisely what he has in fact seen and whether he has interpreted it correctly. Undoubtedly the book is much more light hearted in tone than its predecessors (though it is typical of Lindsay's refusal to conform to convention in literature any more than he does in philosophy that an episode of stark and completely unexpected tragedy occurs in the middle of the novel), and it is unusual too in that the protagonist is in complete control throughout the book of whatever situation presents itself to him; but these features are by no means sufficient to exclude the book from consideration in an assessment of Lindsay's achievement.

The second of the novel's four virtually self-contained episodes provides a clear illustration of the author's method: the surface effect of delightful comedy is obtained by the presentation of an intricate network of misconstructions arising from a casual joke, in which each of the participants has his own distinct interpretation of the real circumstances. (pp. 227-29)

A superb comic story, but not only this. Every character has put his own interpretation on the facts, and the various interpretations are neither accurate nor mutually consistent. The final coup involves a guarantee that all the illusions will be superseded not by realization of the truth but by a new illusion. . . . As in *Arcturus,* Lindsay conducts his characters, and readers, through a maze of events in which fact and fiction are inextricably jumbled. And at the very end, a new aura of unreality is added to the whole affair by the revelation that it need never have happened. . . . (pp. 231-32)

The last and most elaborate of the four "adventures," which takes up more than half the book, is of a complexity which almost defies analysis. Against the deceptively reassuring background of solidity and stability provided by the intense clarity, detail, and realism of Lindsay's visual descriptions (a feature invariably present in his work, whether he is describing an unearthly dream world, a stately English manor-house, a pleasant path beside a river, or a domestic interior in Paris) and the meticulous precision with which he enumerates each gesture, and the exact moments of entrance and exit, of the various characters, a story is played out which involves a sequence of deceptions, cross-purposes, mistaken identities and misinterpreted motives so intricate that long before the end a reader is liable either to have fallen several steps behind or to have given up all attempt to do anything but enjoy the story as a simple thriller. Yet the plot is entirely self-consistent, and the logic of events flawless. Lindsay—almost unfairly—also reinforces the devastating effect of the story on the reader's intellect by ensuring that the action is so rapid and exciting as to give him no time, or inclination, to pause and disentangle the growing complexities of the plot. What he achieves in *Arcturus* by his remarkable imagination he achieves here by his gift for sheer drama: the reader is swept along by the appeal of the book to one level of enjoyment so that the questions which it raises are pushed into the background of his mind, providing a disturbing undercurrent while he is in process of reading the novel and emerging, cumulatively reinforced, into full consciousness when he has completed it. The question in his mind while absorbed in the novel is: can Mailly's audacity and wit carry him unscathed through a very dangerous situation? It is not until he closes the book that a deeper question forces itself on his awareness: what precisely *was* the situation? (pp. 234-35)

Lindsay's concern, in this book no less than in his others, is with fact and fantasy; with the simultaneous existence of several worlds, or at least of several views of the world, each of which may be attractive or even unavoidable to the people who hold it but not all of which can be valid. He may, as in *Arcturus,*

examine each of them in turn, or, as in *Sphinx* and to a greater extent in *Mailly,* focus on their complex interaction; he may end by destroying all illusions or by stating the necessity of maintaining at least one . . . ; but his basic theme is the same. The ending of *Mailly* might be seen as a particularly grim example of a deception maintained: the hero has triumphed and confidently expects further successes; but this may be the gravest error of all, as few readers can be unaware that the imminent war referred to, in which he will be commanding a regiment, resulted in disastrous defeat for France. However, Mailly is unique among Lindsay's protagonists in that, though the world in which he moves is shifting and unstable, he himself is not affected. His adroitness, audacity, and self-possession remain absolutely consistent, and sufficient for the handling of any situation which presents itself (correctly or otherwise) to him. We need not doubt that he will cope equally well with anything that may arise in his subsequent career.

Lindsay is not a writer whose works would appeal to all; this may be admitted at once. Yet the almost total neglect of such a remarkable and gifted novelist is astonishing; though less so, unhappily, in Scotland than it would be elsewhere. His connection with the Scottish literary tradition is at first sight tenuous, certainly: he owes as little to tradition as any man could; but his interest in the supernatural is shared by, among others, Scott, Hogg and Stevenson; and, more importantly, his intense and persistent questioning of the nature of reality is of the same kind as that which gives rise to much that is characteristic in Scottish literature. The case for a revival of interest in his work has been cogently argued elsewhere, though of course the best case is contained in his novels themselves. Yet *Adventures of Monsieur de Mailly* has been virtually ignored even by those who have written with admiration and insight on his other books. Enough has been said here, I hope, not only to call attention to the novel as a fascinating work in its own right, but to suggest that it is much more characteristic of its author than has been supposed. (pp. 235-36)

> *J. Derrick McClure, "'Purely As Entertainment'? 'Adventures of Monsieur de Mailly' As a Representative Work of David Lindsay," in* Studies in Scottish Literature, *Vol. XI, No. 4, April, 1974, pp. 226-36.*

J. D. McCLURE (essay date 1974)

[*In the following excerpt, McClure discusses the ambiguity of Lindsay's language and logic in* A Voyage to Arcturus. *He argues that Lindsay deliberately constructed the novel to thwart probability, realism, and the reader's logical assumptions, thus creating a disorienting effect similar to that experienced by the main character in his adventure on a planet where earthly physical laws are inoperable.*]

On the most obvious level, the profoundly disturbing effect of [*A Voyage to Arcturus*] results in part from the extraordinary fecundity of the author's imagination. The abundance and variety of outlandish plants, animals, landscapes and weather conditions on the planet Tormance convey the impression of a world to which the laws of nature as known on Earth are simply irrelevant. Against this dauntingly alien background, the behaviour of the characters, who in most cases are logical extensions of recognisable human types, stand out with discordant familiarity: yet even in this field, anomalies are visible. Oceaxe doubts whether the rugged, bearded hero of the book is sufficiently masculine to be her lover; yet her husband is the dainty, boyish Crimtyphon. Strong and masterful figures like Oceaxe and Spadevil seem to be at the mercy of such obviously inferior creatures as Tydomin and Catice. . . . Lindsay is thus able to write a story in which nothing is predictable, even on the grounds that the unexpected is what will probably happen: where normal standards are neither accepted nor defied but wholly abrogated, the concept of the unexpected has no meaning.

Not only the scenes and events described in the book, but also the construction of the book itself, deviates strangely from orthodox standards. The first chapter naturally causes the reader to assume that the story will centre on some at least of the several vividly individualised characters who are immediately introduced; yet after the seance episode they are never heard of again. Despite the novel's title, the actual voyage is treated most perfunctorily, and in a way which, if this were science fiction, would surely have seemed unconvincing even in 1920: a torpedo pointed at the apparent position of Arcturus in the visible sky. After filling the story with cryptic clues to his final meaning, the author concludes with a passage in which it is stated with brutal directness—and shown to have been already suggested and apparently rejected half-way through the book. Lindsay is clearly determined that no assumptions or presuppositions whatever—not even ones which parts of the book lead a reader to form about other parts—shall survive a reading of this novel.

Evidently, Lindsay does not merely create a new and strange world: he causes the reader to experience something like the destruction of the universe he knows, with the spiritual distress and fear which this entails. No amount of mere physical or behavioural oddity exhibited by the scenes and characters of the book, however, could have this effect; and the cause for the violent shock sustained by any reader of *Arcturus* must be sought at a deeper level. It can be found, I suggest, in Lindsay's use of language. For example, a striking feature of the novel is the proliferation of strange names: supernatural beings, people, places and inanimate objects are all identified by weird and memorable labels. Of these names, some refer with naive clarity to attributes of the entities which they denote (Hator, Faceny, Matterplay). Some are composed of one element of which the same is true and another of which it cannot be said (*Joi*wind, *Brood*viol, Al*ppain*). Others, though bearing no literal applicability to their referents, have some degree of metaphorical or associative appropriateness, either in whole (Maskull, Nightspore, Oceaxe) or in part (*Dream*sinter, Gang*net*). Others again are concocted from real words but seem to have no connection with the things which they name (Branchspell, Swaylone, Digrung). Finally, some are entirely meaningless (Tydomin, Leehallfae). There are no grounds, that I can discern, on which the choice of name-type on any given occasion could be predicted. A reader's natural tendency to look for order and consistency is therefore a guarantee that he will be led astray: because most of the names look as if they should be meaningful, and some clearly are, the inclination is to look for meaning in them all, and to be puzzled and confused when meanings cannot always be found. Lindsay artfully encourages this tendency by giving an obviously appropriate name to Joiwind, the first Tormantic character to appear, and making her say that names in her world 'follow nature'. At times, too, he provides other false clues by seeming to select names in accordance with principles which are applied on single occasions only. . . . The reader is thus led to use his powers of reasoning continuously to no purpose (and the greater his literary sophistication the more deep-rooted will be his tendency to do this), with the result that the reading experience entails something comparable on the intellectual plane to the pain which

'act(s) as a lower sympathetic note to all (Maskull's) other sensations'. (pp. 29-31)

The same disconcerting mixture of sense and nonsense is conspicuously present in the metaphysical conversations which Maskull holds with the people he meets. Corpang's observations on the primary colours . . . provide one illustration of this. 'Blue is existence. It is darkness seen through light; a contrasting of existence and nothingness'. The blue of the sky is the visible result of light diffraction, and beyond it is the darkness of space: this statement thus contains a hint of plain physical fact. 'Red is feeling. When we see red we are thrown back on our personal feelings'. Red is, in Europe at least, associated by a long tradition with passion and excitement, and to that extent the statement bears some relation to reality: however, it has surely not the same objective truth that is suggested by the description of blue. 'Yellow is relation. In yellow light we see the relation of objects in the clearest way'. This looks like a statement referring solely to the sensually-perceived world; and as such, it is false, given any intelligible meaning of the words. That is, of the three comments, one has some measure of objective validity, another a hint of subjective validity, and the third no validity at all. Yet they are all together in a single utterance, and no hint is given that they are regarded by either the speaker or the hearers as in any way different from each other.

Corpang's philosophical tenet that existence, relation and feeling, analogically comparable to length, breadth and depth, are three separate worlds each with its governing deity is expressed in language which again combines meaning and meaninglessness (Ch. 17). 'The first world is visible, tangible Nature. It was created by Faceny out of nothingness, and therefore we call it Existence'. If it is allowed that the word *existence* can be used to mean not *the fact of existing* but *that which exists,* so that the statement can be reworded as 'The universe was created, therefore we say that it exists', this utterance is seen to be in fact a tautology, as *create* means *cause to exist.* 'The second world is Love', and this world of 'Love, or Relation' is shown to be contradictory to the first on the grounds that 'A natural man lives for himself; a lover lives for others'. This last statement is not the expression of a logical necessity or a physical law, but it is recognisable as an observation on an aspect of human behaviour which, though artificially polarised and simplified, is as far as it goes valid. Finally, 'Just as depth is the line between object and subject, feeling is the line between Thire and man'. This is a recognisable definition of *depth* only when the word is used in a specialised and restricted sense, namely the illusion of distance from foreground to background in a picture: it does not relate to the normal usage of the word. And the comparison adds nothing to a reader's understanding of Corpang's concept of *feeling,* which he has already defined as 'the need of men to stretch out toward their creator'. The concept which is common to both sides of the analogy is that of a *line:* but as abstract a concept as this loses all touch with reality if it is not drawn from a physical referent, as it is not here. That is, the information content of the sentence is nil. Yet it looks like an analogy, and the inclination to assume that any analogy is reasonable and helpful is well entrenched in popular thought. The fact that the words *depth* and *feeling* regularly appear in collocation ('depth of feeling') gives the pseudo-analogy a further subtle air of being natural and proper, though of course this fact is completely irrelevant to Corpang's argument. Here again, in other words, his three statements differ from each other in kind and in degree of validity and relevance. Lindsay is in fact writing, with great skill, meaningless verbiage which touches on logic and physical reality frequently enough to give it the specious appearance of reasoned argument based on factual observation. And when, a couple of pages later, Corpang states that 'Thire cannot exist without Amfuse, and Amfuse cannot exist without Faceny', and Maskull replies: 'That must be so . . . Without life there can be no love, and without love there can be no religious feeling', the evident simplicity and truth (on a superficial level) of Maskull's statement further encourages the delusion that Corpang's, of which it is supposedly an interpretation, and by implication everything else that Corpang has said about the three deities and their worlds, is also simple and true. Other examples of this deliberate confusion of the reader abound in the book. Leehallfae's explanation of Faceny's nature is one: 'He faces Nothingness in all directions . . . He draws his inspirations from it'. This statement is by any standards strange; but a natural first reaction would be to make the obvious concession that some deviation from normal linguistic usage is permissible, indeed unavoidable, in metaphysical statements. However, even metaphysical language may not include logical contradictions. This sample does. 'Nothingness' is a term of which no positive can be predicated: to say that 'nothingness' has directions, or can be a source of inspiration, is logically meaningless. Leehallfae's statement therefore has no contact with reality whatever. This does not mean that it cannot be responded to imaginatively, but it does mean that as language it has no content: it says nothing about anything. That it *can* be responded to imaginatively is a fact on which Lindsay relies: it stirs the imagination by its strangeness, and deludes the reader (if he is not on his guard) into thinking he has heard something very profound. . . . When such tricks of false reasoning occur in the speech of the sensual and egocentric Oceaxe ('Isn't the whole world the handiwork of innumerable pairs of lovers?' 'You think me wicked? . . . Leave all other mad and wicked people as well. Then you'll find it easier to reform the rest') or the cunning and vicious Tydomin ('Perhaps it will ease your mind to carry it. There's only one relief for remorse, and that's voluntary pain'. 'If you come to grief, your thoughts will hardly have corresponded with the real events of the world, which is what you boast about'), the reader is inclined to see them as revelations of character—which, of course, they are—and not to take them at their face value. Corpang, Leehallfae and Panawe, however, are characters of a higher type: intellectuals dedicated to things beyond themselves: and therefore the tendency is to take their statements as real information given by the author. Lindsay plays effectively on the common frailty of failing to consider what is said apart from the person who says it. By such devices, he achieves the same disturbing effect on the reader's intellect as his remarkable descriptions of the external world of Tormance have on his imagination.

Another subtly disconcerting feature of the book is that the viewpoint from which the events are narrated is at times varying and ambiguous. As a general rule, the story is told by an omniscient narrator and the focus is on Maskull: what is related is Maskull's sense-data and his reactions to them. This viewpoint is maintained consistently enough for such departures from it as '. . . it grew intensely cold. None noticed it'. (where 'none' includes Spadevil and Tydomin as well as Maskull), 'Joiwind opened her eyes, smiled, and slumbered again' (at a point when Maskull and Panawe, the only other characters present, are sleeping), 'His stern eyes saw nothing ahead but an alluring girl and a half-infatuated man' (the focus suddenly shifting to Corpang) and the conversation which Oceaxe and Tydomin hold when Maskull is out of earshot, to stand out prominently. A jarring effect is also provided by the sudden

switching of attention to Maskull after the first chapter, in which even when present he is no more prominent than any of the other characters. . . . Once Lindsay's meaning is understood, the latter 'switching of attention' is seen to be no switching of attention at all: however, it looks sufficiently like one to have the desired effect of giving the reader something of a shock. Lindsay is using the traditional device of describing very extraordinary events through the eyes of a very ordinary man; but, clearly, with variations. (pp. 31-5)

Related to the shifting viewpoint, but more continuously present and considerably more disturbing, is Lindsay's seemingly random blend, in his descriptive passages, of objective observations and subjective impressions. Many examples of this can be found as a result of his habit of using adjectives in groups of three. Sullenbode's voice, for instance is 'rich, slow and odd'. 'Slow' refers to plain physical fact, and is unambiguous: certainly it is a relative and not an absolute term, but whether a voice (or rather, an utterance) is slow or not is not, in terms of any normal usage of the word, a matter for debate. 'Rich' also refers to sensually perceptible facts, but it is a much more impressionistic term: just what, objectively, are the physical characteristics of a 'rich' voice is difficult to state precisely, and not all hearers would necessarily agree that the label 'rich' was appropriate to a given voice. 'Odd' has no objective reference at all: it records a subjective reaction and says nothing whatever about the external factors which produced that reaction. (p. 35)

The clouds over Sant are 'evil-shaped': there is of course no such thing as an evil shape, and this can only mean that their shapes reminded somebody of things felt or known to be evil. The question thus arises: whose impressions and interpretations do these adjectives record? Maskull's, presumably, on the level of the story, with his experiences and their effects on him. The implications of this, however, are fairly far-reaching. A man who, on this planet and under normal circumstances, exhibited behaviour as erratic as Maskull's would be regarded as certifiable. (Of course, Maskull's behaviour on Earth is the epitome of normality, and his Tormantic adventures are designed precisely to demolish the social conventionality on which he at first relies: this, however, does not affect the present point.) His intellect and morality are at the mercy of his emotions, and those at the mercy of his senses. His senses themselves do not operate as on Earth: Lindsay is astoundingly successful in suggesting the weird synaesthetic experiences and mutually confusing effects of the senses and the other mental functions which he undergoes. In nearly every episode he has new sense organs, with corresponding changes in his perceptions and attitudes. At various times he is compared to a man in a dream or said himself to doubt whether he is dreaming or awake, and once . . . he considers that he has been 'labouring under a series of heavy enchantments'. Precisely how reliable, therefore, are his impressions? At times they are overtly demolished, or shown to have been inappropriate, almost as soon as they are recorded. The peninsula where at first he sees 'coolness and delicate shade' and 'wild and charming seclusion' is immediately revealed as the location where the abominable Crimtyphon is amusing himself by turning a man into a tree. . . . The whole book is a chronicle of Maskull's wanderings from one illusion to another. Can we, as readers, therefore accept accounts of his impressions and judgments at their face value? (If it is suggested that the implication of the subjective descriptions is that they indicate not Maskull's impressions but those which the reader, if present, would have formed, this does not get rid of the question; for the reader is an Earth creature who on Tormance would have been served by his Earthly faculties no better than Maskull was by his. And this is certainly not a book of which the reader is invited, or permitted, to watch the events with unmoved detachment.) Obviously, when reading fiction we 'believe' what the author tells us. But in this book the situation is complicated by the fact that it is impossible, until the very last episode, to know what the author is telling us. Superficially, *Arcturus* is a tale of an Earth traveller's strange experiences on another planet. But the traveller is himself aware that his experiences, or at least his impressions of them, are untrustworthy. By narrating what seems to Maskull to be happening, and at the same time showing that Maskull's judgments and perceptions are unstable, Lindsay completes the effect which he wishes to achieve of causing the ground to vanish from under the reader's feet: he makes it impossible for us not only to accept the implications of what we have seen, but to be certain that we have in fact seen it.

Lindsay's style has been consistently attacked by his critics; and it is undeniable that sentences like 'Both were buried in their own painful thoughts' or 'The cliffs were soon scrambled up' add nothing to the book as a sample of prose technique. However, if my reading of the novel is correct, such things as use of emotionally loaded descriptions, switching of the viewpoint and mingling of the subjective and the objective are not in this book faults, but positive and deliberate contributions to the total effect. C. S. Lewis's comment that '. . . scientifically it's nonsense, the style is appalling, and yet this ghastly vision comes through' . . . is strangely inept: it is not a question of 'and yet'. The scientific absurdities are at times made to seem speciously reasonable by reference to actual well-known facts: Nightspore's evidence for the reality of back-light is an example of this: 'Unless light pulled, as well as pushed, how would flowers contrive to twist their heads around after the sun?', and so is Corpang's suggestion that Tormance has more primary colours than Earth because it is lighted by two differently-coloured suns. The reader is thus caused momentarily to doubt his own scientific knowledge. In the same way, the attack on his reason and emotions could not have been made so effectively without the oddities of style discussed here: certainly they are not, in the abstract, marks of good writing, but they are used intentionally and for a specific purpose. The 'ghastly vision' could have been explained as an intellectual concept, but could not have been expressed with anything like so powerful an effect, in a work which adhered to the orthodox rules of style. And indeed, would it not have been a gross inconsistency if a book which suggests that all pleasures are delusions and traps had been written with grace and elegance? Lindsay's aim . . . is to persuade not the senses, but the soul. (pp. 35-8)

> *J. D. McClure, "Language and Logic in 'A Voyage to Arcturus'," in* Scottish Literary Journal, *Vol. 1, No. 1, July, 1974, pp. 29-38.*

COLIN WILSON (essay date 1976)

[*Wilson is an English novelist, critic, and philosopher. His first book,* The Outsider *(1956), began a series of works, both fiction and nonfiction, the central purpose of which has been to investigate mental and spiritual faculties of an exceptional kind latent in certain individuals. These faculties, which Wilson characterizes as those of the visionary, have as their basis the capacity and need to experience a sense of meaning and purpose in human life. The frustration of this need, according to Wilson, is observable in the predominantly negative tone of modern authors such as*

Samuel Beckett and modern philosophers such as Jean-Paul Sartre. Whereas Sartre's philosophy of existentialism demands a recognition of the basic absurdity and futility of human existence, Wilson's "new existentialism" proposes that "Man should possess an infinite appetite for life. It should be self-evident to him, all the time, that life is superb, glorious, endlessly rich, infinitely desirable." In the following excerpt, Wilson maintains that Lindsay had genius, but that he was a "genuinely incompetent writer." He traces the development of Lindsay's vision and themes from his first novel, A Voyage to Arcturus, *to his last,* The Witch. *Wilson places Lindsay in a group of other highly imaginative and misunderstood artists, including Paul Cezanne, Vincent Van Gogh, and Charles Ives, but states that Lindsay's true tragedy was that he had profound, visionary genius "without the powers to convey it to other people."*]

Lindsay is a paradox in the most genuine sense of the word. Nowadays we are inclined to use the word paradox to signify an apparent contradiction—truth standing on its head to attract attention, as Chesterton said. But a real paradox is a truth with two faces, and the faces continue to stare in opposite directions, even when they have been analysed and explained. Well, the truth is that Lindsay is a visionary, a man of Beethoven-like sublimity, a truly original genius. The history of philosophy and mysticism are full of such names—J. L. Hamann, Max Stirner, Constantin Brunner, Theodore Lessing. . . . But Lindsay differs from most of these in being also a genuinely incompetent writer. He should be an inspiration to every American student who has ever sweated his way through a Creative Writing course, for he proves so conclusively that it *is* possible to write like an amateur and still be a man of genius. And, what is more, still produce books that are worth reading.

The other face of the paradox is that most of his books are genuinely bad, stylistically speaking. . . . Even *Arcturus,* the greatest of all his books, would have benefited from the labours of a good editor. . . . *The Witch* and *Devil's Tor* are not so much flawed masterpieces as shattered masterpieces, like those crystals a car windscreen dissolves into if you hit it with a hammer. What is worse, the faults are not the kind you can skip, like some of the romantic excrescences in Thomas Wolfe or Faulkner. Such faults spring from too much fluency, while Lindsay is like a man with a bad stammer. You cannot accept his style as some peculiar eccentricity, like Henry James's, and concentrate on the content. All you can do is to accept that he wrote all his life with an embarrassing clumsiness that most would-be writers outgrow at seventeen. (pp. 4-5)

But having recognised this, we also have to acknowledge that Lindsay's clumsiness *is* actually bound-up with the nature of what he is saying. *The Violet Apple* contains this important sentence:

> He was not shrinking from her eyes because of their contained moral censure, but because they . . . could only communicate with his frightful, earthy, mortal nature, which was like an invitation to share a common coffin.

This is the problem that runs obsessively through all his books—most notably, through *The Haunted Woman, Sphinx* and *The Violet Apple:* this feeling that all our activities, all our social relations, *falsify* the reality inside us. It is as if man lived in a world of distorting mirrors. He *knows* the reflection he sees is false; yet since he has never seen a plane mirror, he can only have the faintest idea of what he actually looks like.

Now in the above sentence, the words about 'their contained moral censure' are an example of Lindsay's infelicities; he would have done better to say 'the censure in them' (the word moral is actually irrelevant here). But Lindsay's clumsiness is not always of this willful nature. In the opening paragraph of *Devil's Tor,* we sense another problem:

> No sooner had they quitted the sunken lane, with its high banks and overshadowing trees, and entered upon the long stretch of open road, bordered at first by walls of piled stones, but soon running unconfined for mile upon mile across the rising moor, than the full menace of the advancing storm struck them. The young girl Ingrid Fleming turned her head towards her male companion with an inquiring look, as by a sort of sympathy they came to a dubious standstill.
>
> "What shall we do? Go back?"

That opening sentence is too long. But you get the feeling that it is too long because Lindsay is unwilling to leave the description of the moor—which suits him—to focus on the human beings with their petty personal problems. . . . But then, a novel has to have people in it; there's no help for it. So you have to come out of the world of overshadowing trees and stormy skies to the world where girls give men 'inquiring looks.' Lindsay is much more at home in the world of the double star Arcturus, where the characters are as alien as the landscape, and the conversation can achieve a high level of philosophical content with a minimum of merely social exchange. (pp. 5-6)

In one of his letters, Lindsay suggests that there are two kinds of novelist: those who describe the world, and those who try to explain it. . . . Trollope and Jane Austen obviously belong among the describers, while Dostoevsky, John Cowper Powys and Lindsay himself are explainers. But then, the *events* in Dostoevsky and Powys are also tremendous, to match their themes, the classic material of tragedy: murder, incest, seduction, violence. Dostoevsky's *Devils,* for example, contrasts the rather silly, shallow social world of a small provincial town with the lives of human beings—Kirilov, Shator, Stavrogin—for whom the world is an enormous mystery of good and evil. Lindsay's trouble is that he lacks the temperament for this type of writing. When he sets out to portray the world we live in, he is as confined by his social class as Trollope or Jane Austen were by theirs. No Raskolnikovs, no Rastignacs or Vautrins, not even a Stephen Dedalus or Julien Sorel. For a man of genius who wanted to be a novelist, Lindsay was singularly ill-equipped. The kind of people he seems to find himself writing about, again and again, *are* the kind you would find in the first act of a fashionable comedy. The women may have sparkling blue or brown eyes (like the two heroines of *The Violet Apple*), but the male characters always address them rather formally, and you can tell that Lindsay would be scandalised at the idea of anyone getting raped, or even seduced. Dostoevsky can make us understand what it feels like to be a murderer, Powys what it feels like to be a sadist, Joyce what it feels like to be an adulterous wife. . . . By comparison, Lindsay has no power of empathy. In social atmosphere, his novels have a certain resemblance to those early novels of Bernard Shaw, before he had discovered his true metier: they are all about rather wooden ladies and gentleman. (pp. 7-8)

This, again, immediately suggests what was wrong with Lindsay, not simply as a novelist, but as a human being. In a book about Shaw, I pointed out that those five 'novels of his nonage' were all attempts to establish a *self-image,* to discover the sort of person he wanted to be. In the fifth of them, *An Unsocial Socialist,* he finally created an archetypal Shavian character, Sidney Trefusis (on whom he later based the hero of *Man and Superman*). . . . In *A Haunted Woman,* Isbel Loment looks into a mirror which shows her her true self; her face is wiser, maturer and somehow tragic. In many ways, Lindsay and Shaw were close together. They wrote about the same themes. But Lindsay never established a self-image. Maskull, the hero of *Arcturus,* has no character; he is just a large bearded figure. *A Haunted Woman* has a heroine rather than a hero; its chief male character, Henry Judge, is again a wooden nonentity. Besides, he is too old to provide his creator with a possible self-image. And so it goes on: Nicholas Cabot in *Sphinx,* Saltfleet of *Devil's Tor* . . . , Anthony Kerr of *The Violet Apple:* all are typical Lindsay males, although the explorer Saltfleet has more dash than most of them. In short, Lindsay himself had no idea of what kind of person he wanted to be. . . . So, to some extent, these books of Lindsay spring out of his own frustration, his sense of not being able to express the person he basically felt himself to be. . . . Nietzsche, a philosopher Lindsay deeply admired, talked about 'How one becomes what one is'. It was a secret Lindsay never discovered.

Some critics might feel that all this leaves nothing much to be said about the later novels, from *A Haunted Woman* to *The Witch;* if they express a purely individual frustration, and do it rather clumsily, what point is there in dwelling on them? Such a view would be superficial. Lindsay's genius never found complete self-expression; but it was so considerable that even its incomplete self-expression provides material for endless discussion. It is not ultimately important that he found no satisfactory self-image. What is astonishing is that in spite of this, he managed to express his remarkable vision so fully. (pp. 8-9)

Lindsay was deeply influenced by Nietzsche, and also by Nietzsche's great mentor, Schopenhauer. 'The world as Will and Illusion' would be an apt sub-title for a book on Lindsay. Like all visionary idealists, he is troubled with the essentially *trivial* nature of everyday life—what Heidegger calls 'the triviality of everydayness'. The path of human beings lies on the horizontal plane. And if this world—which satisfies most people—were the only world, then men of genius like Lindsay would want to commit suicide. But we have glimpses of an intensity of consciousness that make everyday consciousness appear to be a shabby illusion. *All* men of genius, no matter how different the nature of their insight, have this in common. . . . (p. 9)

The man of artistic genius attempts to create a kind of road to another level of reality; he wants to travel vertically rather than horizontally. Lindsay likes to use the image of some immense stairway, symbolised by the rising chords at the opening of Beethoven's Seventh Symphony. And he likes to speak of this 'other reality', this *real* reality, as the 'sublime'.

Like Nietzsche, Lindsay is a master of the history of ideas. And, like Schopenhauer, he is inclined to see most of these ideas as various forms of illusion. . . . *Arcturus* is a book about these illusions—false ideas of reality. The hero, Maskull, is 'Everyman', and he travels to the double star with his alterego, Nightspore, and a curious, sneering character called Krag, who at first strikes us as a brutal cynic. On the planet Tormance, Maskull finds himself deserted—and then meets a series of characters who all have totally different views of reality. It sounds like a boring allegory; in fact, the creative invention is so dense that an adequate commentary on the book would be longer than *Arcturus* itself. Most of the people Maskull encounters accept the idea that God is a synonym for goodness and beauty, and that his name is Crystalman. Lindsay is saying that such an idea is false and trivial. In *Arcturus*, beauty is inclined to deflate like a punctured balloon into something grotesque and sickening—the 'Crystalman grin'. It *would* be possible to find cultural parallels for the various philosophies expressed in *Arcturus:* i.e. Joiwind is a kind of Blakeian mystic . . . , her husband Panawe a Platonic idealist, Oceaxe and her husband symbols of the Nietzschean Will to Power, Spadevil a kind of Miltonic stoic, and so on. But it is doubtful that Lindsay was thinking in these terms when he wrote *Arcturus*. He seems to have written in a kind of imaginative trance. Tormance is as real as Tolkien's Middle Earth; the result is that the book can be read again and again, as you might visit a real place. Towards the end, we begin to grasp that Lindsay regards *all* existence as an illusion. Nevertheless, there *is* an ultimate reality—Muspel—which somehow lies beyond existence. This becomes manifest in what is perhaps the greatest scene in the book—in the underground land of Thire, where three apparently genuine visions of God appear to Maskull, then are all shown to be 'human, all too human'. At the end of the book, the sneering Krag is revealed to be the representative of Muspel—God rather than the devil. And Lindsay expresses his own basic view of the world as a deep conflict of good against evil: not conventional good against conventional evil, but a cold and sublime reality fighting for its life against a sweet and cloying beauty that masquerades as goodness.

Arcturus is Buddhistic in its vision. My own basic feeling is that it is too sweepingly negative. But it is a masterpiece—in form as well as content, being constructed like a series of Chinese boxes, one inside the other. If it had been as 'true' as Lindsay believed, it would have left him nothing more to say. But Lindsay himself certainly believed he had more to say.

Readers who turn to *The Haunted Woman* after reading *Arcturus* are bound to be puzzled and disappointed. *Arcturus* is clumsily written, but after the first few chapters, you cease to notice this, completely absorbed in Lindsay's visionary world. In the remaining books, you are always aware of the clumsiness. The odd thing is that, in spite of this, they draw the reader back to them. When I first read *The Haunted Woman* I thought it simply a mistake that would be best forgotten. Harold Visiak, on the other hand, thought it Lindsay's best book. . . . On re-reading, I can see why Visiak thought so highly of it; it is, in its own way, a masterpiece.

Again, the subject is reality versus illusion. And he finds a peculiarly effective symbol for it. Isbel Loment is an intelligent and vaguely dissatisfied young woman who is engaged to be married to a fairly satisfactory young man. She goes to visit an old house that is for sale. Alone in the hall, she finds an old flight of stairs that lead to an upper storey—a storey that dates from the time of the Vikings, and now no longer exists. (It shares this characteristic with 'Muspel'.) . . . There she meets Henry Judge, the man who is selling the house. The two recognise themselves as soul-mates; in this 'other' world, their essence can find expression; the false personality has been left down below. Their problem now is that when they both go downstairs—by different routes—they remember nothing whatever of what they have experienced in the upper storey. . . . Lindsay has found the perfect symbol for the states of sudden intensity and insight experienced by poets and mystics—and their frustration at being unable to take even a mem-

ory of it back to ordinary consciousness. Isbel and Judge even try writing notes and leaving them in their pockets; but when they get back to the 'downstairs' world and discover the notes, they find them incomprehensible.

I personally get the feeling that, having developed this situation, Lindsay had no idea of how to resolve it, so the strange, tragic ending of the book is not its logical conclusion. (pp. 9-12)

When we consider the tremendous sweep of [Lindsay's] work, from *Arcturus* to *The Witch*, it seems incredible that such a high level of sustained creativity and insight could be achieved in the face of such total indifference [by publishers and critics]. Of course, there *have* been many similar tragedies in the arts—Cezanne, Van Gogh, Charles Ives. Yet there have been few major writers on whom the gods have played such an apparently malicious trick: to grant such a profound vision, without the powers to convey it to other people.

Or so I felt when I wrote my first long essay on David Lindsay, seven or eight years ago. What has surprised me is that I *have* periodically gone back to Lindsay's 'unsuccessful' books, and each time found them more satisfying. For years I kept *Arcturus* by my bed, and often read a chapter at random before falling asleep; every time I discovered things that I had not noticed before. When I re-read *The Haunted Woman*, it struck me as a beautiful and poetic work, full of smells of autumn and spring, glowing gently with its own life. *Sphinx* I have never possessed—I borrowed Visiak's copy—so have never had a chance to re-read it. But when I came to re-read *Devil's Tor* in order to write my section of *The Strange Genius*, I found it so haunting and disturbing that I had the whole book duplicated—at considerable cost—and then bound. And recently, as soon as I began to read the typescript of *The Violet Apple*, the old magic reasserted itself, and I found myself deliberately reading slowly, so as not to finish it too quickly. *The Witch* has left me slightly dazed—yet not as much as I expected to be. . . . [In] fact, once you have got used to Lindsay's cast of mind, it is surprisingly clear and straightforward; as in *Arcturus*, you know you are in the hands of a man who knows where he is going. One day, no doubt, enthusiastic Lindsayites will insist that the whole manuscript should be printed, complete with its different endings. . . . (pp. 16-17)

Colin Wilson, in an introduction to The Violet Apple & The Witch *by David Lindsay, edited by J. B. Pick, Chicago Review Press, 1976, pp. 1-18.*

JOHN HERDMAN   (essay date 1976)

[*In the following excerpt from a favorable review of* The Violet Apple and The Witch, *Herdman defends Lindsay's prose style, which has been harshly attacked by Brigid Brophy (1963), Kingsley Amis (1963), and Colin Wilson (1976). Herdman claims that Lindsay's problems as a novelist are formal rather than stylistic. According to Herdman, Lindsay's creative perception was too alienated from the established social order of his day to be adequately expressed in the novel form created for and endorsed by that social order.*]

Anthony Kerr, the playwright in David Lindsay's *The Violet Apple,* laments the fate of the writer who 'dares to exhibit in black and white an immeasurable personality—one that refuses to fit itself to common standards . . . I say that the function and purpose of literature is to assist the enlargement of the soul. But that is what critics and editors have once for all decided to make their role, and the unfortunate author who takes upon himself to violate the unwritten edict will run up against the fact as soon as his first notices appear. . . .'

These words were surely spoken from Lindsay's heart. The daring and devotion of his commitment to such a view of literature brought him nothing but neglect during his lifetime, and oblivion for his work; these two novels appear for the first time thirty-one years after his death, *The Violet Apple* half a century after its completion. Yet both of them, for all their awkwardnesses and difficulties, eminently fulfil the criteria for 'a true book' proposed by a character in *The Witch:* 'And so Felix's principle was that a true book, being quickened by the ray of pure intelligence in the reader, must display its authenticity by the repeated sounding within the soul of a sudden note, like sharp music. And such books, that need not be the best written, or the most immediate transcript of actual life, were those which could permanently expand and ennoble the spirit of man, whereas the other sort were like a cargo of corpses'. (pp. 14-15)

If in *A Voyage to Arcturus* Lindsay achieved his most vivid and coherent embodiment of the perception that the familiar, phenomenal world is a deceptive veil of illusion, in his later works he strove to give form to his overwhelming consciousness that behind this illusory façade there lies another world of sublime and terrible reality, which in *Arcturus,* under the name Muspel, looms mightily but is never realised.

The view cannot be admitted that the subsequent books merely recapitulate in less satisfactory terms what was said once and for all in the first novel. For, not content to leave the Muspel world a vague and ungraspable postulate, Lindsay set himself to confront the questions: In what does the sublime world consist? To what degree, if at all, can it be experienced in this life? The novels after *Arcturus* are all explorations of these questions, but it is only with *The Witch* that Lindsay works his way through to answers that are more than tentative. The seriousness and persistence of his questing in the face of public indifference and private unhappiness make his achievement the more moving.

Commentators on Lindsay seem to have reached a consensus that he was an awkward and inept user of words. . . . Lindsay's syntactic idiosyncrasies, however, which are usually cited in support of such a contention, seem to me to come into a very different category from the awkwardness of much of his dialogue and his handling of social reality, and to spring from a quite different source. I believe that a case could be made out—and I shall return to this later—that Lindsay was, in terms of his peculiar intentions and methods, a consummate master of a highly individual style. For him the world of dreams is a token of the more real spiritual world which underlies that of appearances, and his peculiarities of syntax can be seen as standing for, or corresponding to, the strangeness of the dream world, what he often calls its 'glamour'. In the same way as, for the Lindsay of *The Witch,* a base of silent, passional 'music', or inspiration, lies behind the grosser, humanly composed music which can be heard by the physical ear, his stylistic idiosyncrasies, in what they communicate emotionally, stand for the passional ground which underlies a purely semantic meaning.

Lindsay's difficulties and limitations as a novelist are not stylistic but formal. They spring from the unsuitability of a form which, historically, was created by and had as its main function the celebration and exploration of, a particular kind of social system, for a writer who by temperament and by the nature of

his perceptions was completely alienated from any kind of social 'reality'. (pp. 15-16)

His difficulties as a novelist arise, in the main, from the problems involved in finding a structure which could bring together, so as to make plain the relationship between them, Crystalman's world of surface 'reality' and the Muspel world of sublime reality. *A Voyage to Arcturus* succeeds so triumphantly in its artistic purpose for a reason which is oddly ironic. By sheer imaginative power Lindsay creates a world which, in its strangeness and spirituality, suggests to us what he meant by the 'sublime world'; yet it stands, by his conscious intention, not for that world but for *this* one. Therein lies the shocking power of its conclusion; but within the paradox dwells an artistic flaw, namely that the depth and complexity of the book cannot be fully experienced except with the aid of information which is withheld from us until its ending. For that reason it appears an incomparably finer achievement at a second reading than at the first. In *Arcturus,* the sublime world remains unuttered, except indirectly through the suggestiveness with which Lindsay imbues the world of Crystalman—an effect which cuts across his conscious intention.

In *The Haunted Woman,* his next book, he seems to suggest that the sublime world cannot at all be attained or apprehended in this one, that any spiritual state which appears to embody it is a sham. . . . In the same way that the bulk of *Arcturus* can only be understood in the light of its ending, *The Haunted Woman* can only be understood in the light of *Arcturus;* and Lindsay's third novel *Sphinx,* Colin Wilson suggests, stands in a similar relation to *its* predecessor [see excerpt dated 1979].

Lindsay must have come to realise, however, that his absolute refusal to allow the least penetration of the life of earth by the sublime world was ultimately a dead end, and artistically self-defeating. In particular he seems to have been dissatisfied that the three areas which he believed most clearly intimated to men the existence of a sublime world—namely music, dreams, and ideal love between the sexes—should be seen only as manifestations of Crystalman.

The Violet Apple, then, embodies a rather more optimistic version of his philosophy than the novels which preceded it. The determination to permit a fruitful penetration of one world by the other, however, makes the problem of form particularly acute. The first half of the novel cannot be regarded as other than bad. All the characters, but particularly the protagonist Anthony Kerr, are given to an intolerably mannered, affected and artificial habit of speech, and the depiction of upper middle class social life is extraordinarily stiff, laboured and formal. It could be argued that Lindsay is intentionally expressing and emphasising the shallowness of such a life, in order to contrast it with the spiritual life which is destined to erupt in its midst; but if such a conscious intention exists, there is too little in the early part of the book by which to measure it. It is more likely that Lindsay's faults and inadequacies in dealing with the social world are simply expressive of its complete unreality to him, and are consequently inseparable from the sources of his greatness.

It is true, again, that in the books which followed *Arcturus* its author, shaken by the cool reception of that masterpiece, introduced an element of what Colin Wilson has called 'potboiling' [see excerpt dated 1979], but which might be better described as an attempted masking of his real intentions, so that the ordinary reader is not aware of what is happening to him until it is too late. As a means of finding acceptance this ploy was doomed to failure by the fact that Lindsay was unable to conceal the evidence of his own integrity. No reader could be fooled into supposing, even in its early pages, *The Violet Apple* to be a novel of manners. Throughout all the conventional descriptions and the wooden cocktail-party chit-chat a certain quality of intentness is maintained, hard to localise but unmistakable, by which its ultimate seriousness is never in doubt. The novel records the slow impingement upon the social world of the real, spiritual world, and the final penetration of the one by the other through supernatural agency.

Anthony Kerr, a bachelor in his middle thirties, is a fashionable playwright whose art is 'cynical in its underlying essence'. . . . His friend Jim Lytham is engaged to Haidee Croyland, and more because it is expected of him than out of any profound feeling, Anthony himself becomes engaged to Jim's sister Grace, likewise a friend of long standing.

Haidee, however, has in the past been attracted to Kerr, and now, almost without her own volition, she feels compelled to pursue him in defiance of the social conventions, to his embarrassment and the anger and perplexity of Jim and Grace. Through her persistence and with the help of a series of coincidences in which we are invited to see the interest of fate, Anthony and Haidee come closer together. . . . (pp. 16-18)

Anthony has inherited a family heirloom, a finely wrought glass serpent brought back by a distant ancestor from the Crusades, and containing a seed traditionally held to be from the Tree of Knowledge in the Garden of Eden. When the ornament is accidentally broken, the seed is potted for Anthony by Grace's half-sister Virginia, an implacable enemy of Haidee. In due course the seed grows into a miniature apple tree which produces two violet fruits, and, in the course of a quarrel with Virginia, Haidee steals one of the apples, and at a crucial stage in her relationship with Anthony eats it before returning to London from the country. As a result she experiences extraordinary spiritual sensations, and in a parallel to Eve's temptation of Adam she writes to Anthony insisting that he should himself eat the second fruit. (p. 18)

When, after some hesitation, he eats the apple, a succession of overwhelming spiritual insights breaks in upon him. By this time all the woodenness and awkwardnesses have been put by, and Lindsay is in his element, the world of inner perceptions, and writing with immense clarity and exactness. In the midst of Anthony's strange experience Grace has entered, and Lindsay describes how she 'could only communicate with his frightful, earthy, mortal nature, which was like an invitation to share a common coffin'. She is a representative of 'a remote life', while he now lives in an atmosphere compounded of Haidee's being.

Lindsay was perennially fascinated by women, seeing in them the supreme conjunction of animality, as represented by sex, with spirituality. Kerr now sees the eating of the fruit of the Tree of Knowledge as symbolic of 'the first rising of man and woman from a world of unconscious animals', and sex shame as 'no more than the derivative, or sympathetic base, of [a] nobler shame which concerns the soul alone; . . . inasmuch as to be an animal at all is shameful while sex is the extreme manifestation of animalhood'.

At this point he hears a voice sounding in his ear, 'Haidee is not a woman; she is a spirit!' He is aware that this is a hallucination: 'His intuitions, breaking away one by one from their moorings in the depths, were beginning in the violence of their ascent to overshoot the walls of his conscious brain,

and to rebound towards him from outside as sense perceptions'. He goes on to meditate this intuition, 'not poetically, but literally'. The love of which he is now aware between Haidee and himself is of a different order from that of earth, for it belongs to 'that spirit world, that so-distant yet possibly contiguous field of actually existing life, no doubt far solider than the solid world of matter, which he had ever known to be its travesty and mockery!' (p. 19)

Haidee has thirty hours previously experienced corresponding spiritual exaltations, centring even more closely on Anthony than his on her. With the wearing off of the narcotic effects of the drug, however, she has undergone a profound reaction: not only has she lost the spiritual insights just gained, but even the aesthetic perceptions she previously possessed seem to have disappeared, or altered in nature. When Anthony, still in a state of ecstasy, goes to see her, no communication between them is possible. Subsequently Anthony experiences an equivalent disintegration of his exalted vision, and returning to the common world goes to the country to reoffer his hand to Grace as a matter of honour, but is refused. He goes for a walk in the woods, where he realises that 'the sudden mysterious failure of his artistic ideals and metaphysical flashes of insight had diminished something of his intellectual pride'. He now sees his experience in this way: 'A drug falsely stimulates my brain for a few hours, and I am deceived into imagining that this artificial exaltation corresponds to something real . . . I am well out of it'.

It seems at this point as if the effect of the eating of the apples has been nothing but another of Crystalman's illusions. Anthony determines on a fresh start in life. Art now appears to him 'a still-born travesty of life' arising from 'a perverted instinct of motherhood', and representing 'a mere dead symbol of an impossible isolation and repose'. He decides to abandon his career as a playwright and his London life, and buy some land to work in Cornwall, where he will live alone, devoting himself to 'a simpler and better faith'.

At this point Anthony happens upon the original of a scene in a painting he possesses, in which the form of a Cross seems to emerge from the trees beside a pool. It is Easter Sunday. At the same instant he sees Haidee. As they talk it becomes apparent that what their experience has done is to bring home to them the shallowness and artificiality of their lives, and in obliging them to set aside their petty concerns to make possible their regeneration. They will not allow what was granted them to disappear entirely from their sight, but will seek to win it back by will and effort. . . . (pp. 19-20)

Thus *The Violet Apple* suggests that though the ideal world is not attainable in this life, intimations of it may yet fructify mundane existence and inject it with value: 'we can continue to move *towards* the other, in full confidence that we shall never attain the full perfection in the body—though, let us trust, in another world'. Haidee will marry Anthony and go away with him to a new life. . . . The book ends with the consideration that 'the fruit was eaten in pride and independence, while the Cross was representative of the dying pride upon which every man must be miserably extended who wishes to imitate Christ'. *The Violet Apple* projects a view of life which is closer to Christian orthodoxy than that of any other of Lindsay's works.

Between *The Violet Apple* and Lindsay's last, unfinished novel, *The Witch,* stands *Devil's Tor,* which deals with the coming together of a man and woman fated to engender a mystic avatar whose destiny it will be to deflect the world from its present course of ignobility and mediocrity. This book places much stress on the concept of a Great Mother, or Life, who lies between 'The Ancient' and the living forms of the created world.

Devil's Tor however is a reworking of *The Ancient Tragedy*, which was written before *The Violet Apple*, and J. B. Pick maintains that *The Witch* is closer in spiritual atmosphere to the latter. It can, indeed, be seen as a logical extension of the earlier book, an attempt to penetrate deeply the nature of the sublime world of which *The Violet Apple* offers no more than tantalising glimpses. Its protagonist, Ragnar Pole, has much in common with Anthony Kerr. . . . Like Kerr he is a vaguely dissatisfied man, and the opening of the book finds him in a state of undefined expectation precipitated by the music played by a Mrs Toller, which raises in him an 'emotional apprehension of a stir of new life, until almost he could have sworn that something was round the corner for him, the first faint roots already acted'. The odd diction helps to make evident to us the proximity of a strange world.

In many ways *The Witch,* in spite of its incomplete state, is the most carefully and effectively structured of Lindsay's works in its bringing together of two metaphysical worlds. In *Arcturus* the transition is crude and abrupt, the early scenes on earth being largely irrelevant to what follows; in *The Haunted Woman, Sphinx,* and *The Violet Apple* the various means of translation, within their contexts of a shallow social existence, place an inevitable strain on credulity. In *The Witch,* however, the solid world is penetrated from the start by the spiritual, through the enchantment worked on Ragnar by the witch Urda Noett and her subordinates Mrs Toller and Mme Klangst, by which his perception of reality is subtly altered. We are thus prepared for far-reaching strangeness, culminating in Ragnar's journey to heaven while still in life. The meaning of Ragnar's enchantment is slowly unfolded as the book progresses, so that there is never a disablingly wide gap between the enactment of events and our apprehension of their significance. It is a measure of the book's ambition that Urda, whom we first encounter as a living figure in a drawing room, is nothing less than a manifestation of the Ancient, the ultimate source of the universe.

Besides the scale and nobility of its ambition, which attempts no less than the imaginative construction of a total view of the nature of reality, what is most immediately striking about *The Witch* is the fecundity of Lindsay's metaphysical perception, his ability to give intellectual form to recognisable intuitions, and his faculty of expressing them exactly, either abstractly or by means of analogy. The book's effects are inseparable from the sonorous majesty of the language, and I have already indicated my belief that what is usually taken as clumsiness or idiosyncrasy makes its positive contribution to the emotional power generated by the language. That the book is unfinished is less damaging to its integrity than might be supposed. Essentially, its aims are realised, and its climax attained in the high though dense rhetoric of the closing pages of what exists. It is probable that what Lindsay could not face was the task and implications of bringing Ragnar back to earth. For such was to be his fate after his living foretaste of the world to come: 'he, alone of men alive in the world was to be brought beyond the prison of earth to the dreadful "outness" by another way than the personal gate of death; sealed to some purpose by the experience he might return for a further while to prison'. That purpose, as later revealed to Ragnar by Mme Klangst, is simply 'to bear witness to these matters among men'. (pp. 20-2)

I do not know what I can say in praise of *The Witch;* it seems to me an extraordinary and profoundly moving work of genius, a greater book than *Arcturus,* but little of its quality can be conveyed by criticism—it has to be read. I shall end this essay by reverting to the question of language for I believe that in this area Lindsay is still misunderstood even by his admirers. Colin Wilson [see excerpt dated 1976] describes him as 'a genuinely incompetent writer' and most of his books as 'genuinely bad, stylistically speaking'; while J. B. Pick speaks of 'particularly stilted and peculiar' diction in *The Witch* and of 'the oddities of syntax which grew on Lindsay in his later years'.

In the first place I do not think that these oddities merely "grew on" Lindsay; they are to some degree evident throughout his work, and are most evident when he is talking directly and abstractly about the spiritual world. (pp. 23-4)

It is in *The Witch,* where Lindsay is dealing almost entirely with spiritual realities, that such tendencies are most marked, and it is noteworthy that in its more naturalistic scenes he is quite capable of writing with a bare lucidity. I would defend his stylistic oddities, therefore, by suggesting that they stand as a figure for the 'otherness' which he is trying to convey: the slight shock of finding words used in an unusual, yet an oddly appropriate way, corresponds to the suggestive distortions of reality in a dream. I do not mean that Lindsay did this by a consciously arrived at intention, for creativity does not work that way; but that it is his intuitive method of communicating strangeness, of injecting 'glamour' into abstraction. (p. 24)

The rhythmic integrity of prose, and especially of Lindsay's kind of prose, can be as important as that of poetry: semantic meaning is not all. (p. 25)

> *John Herdman, "The Previously Unpublished Novels of David Lindsay," in* Scottish Literary Journal, *No. 3, Winter, 1976, pp. 14-25.*

COLIN WILSON   (essay date 1979)

[*In the following excerpt, Wilson discusses the strengths and weaknesses of Lindsay's later novels. He particularly focuses on Lindsay's characterization, noting that Lindsay frequently created protagonists who exhibited frustrations and attitudes similar to his own. Besides tracing Lindsay's philosophical beliefs to Friedrich Nietzsche and the Manichees, a religious sect which rejected everything in the world as evil, Wilson also links Lindsay with writers of his age—including T. S. Eliot, D. H. Lawrence, and T. E. Hulme—who shared a similarly pessimistic view of twentieth-century society.*]

It is easy to miss the point of Lindsay's last three novels if one fails to consider that there have been many attempts to do what he was trying to do, and that few—or none—have succeeded. What he is trying to do is to write about "two worlds", and to convey his rejection of "this world" by the evocation of another. There have been dozens of romantic and post romantic writers who have attempted the same thing, none with complete success. (p. 38)

In reading *The Haunted Woman, Sphinx* and *Devil's Tor,* the reader must focus clearly on the underlying intention. Then they will be seen as impressive achievements in a great tradition. To judge them as realistic novels somehow gone wrong is to completely miss the point. For the point is the feeling underlying them, this passionate attempt to communicate an intuition that "this world" is in some deep sense unsatisfying, but that this is not the end of the matter. There *is* something else, the something of which Poe's haunted tombs and Yeats's fairylands are only a symbol. For nearly two centuries now, ever since Blake, the world has been trying to articulate this "something else", from the vague nature-yearnings of Wordsworth and Byron and Shelley and the exotic occultism of Huysmans, Crowley and Montague Summers to Powys, D. H. Lawrence and T. S. Eliot. Writers who seem to have as little in common as Hemingway and Firbank are united by this same urge to transcend the communal life-world. No one who read Yeats's early poetry actually believes in fairies; the reader simply focuses upon the emotion for which the fairies are an "objective correlative". And this is also the trick of reading Lindsay's novels.

[E. H.] Visiak rightly points out that *Sphinx* lacks magic; all the same, it is an absorbing book. *The Haunted Woman* may have been unsuccessful as a conventional novel, but it had given Lindsay the confidence to think of himself as a novelist. Perhaps only readers who have actually tried to write a novel can appreciate the feeling of its opening pages, with the train pulling into the country station, the hero with his trunk, about to embark on a new stage of his life. A novelist gets as fascinated by his own story as he might by somebody else's. He waits eagerly to see what will happen next. In a sense, he is not inventing. He is playing a game according to the rules, and anything might happen. The rule is to place oneself in a situation, and to look around as if one were in a real place, trying to describe what one sees. The aim is "realism"—to render with reality. (This is true even in fantasy.) (pp. 39-40)

In *Sphinx,* Nicholas Cabot comes to live with a family in a country village. He is working on a machine for recording dreams. (Both Visiak and J. B. Pick have objected to this as preposterous; but with a little trouble, Lindsay could have made it sound plausible; if instead of his "recording machine", he had talked about an electro-encephalograph that somehow picks up "brain waves" and translates them back into their basic images as a record translates a wavy line back into music, it would have sounded convincing enough.)

The "heroine" of the book, insofar as it has one, is a composer, Lore Jensen, who has given up writing serious music to compose sentimental trifles with titles like "Pamela in the Rose Garden". From Lindsay's remarks about the sickening music of the waltz at the end of *Arcturus,* one can imagine his attitude to this. One of the daughters plays an early piece of Lore's called "Sphinx", and Nicholas is impressed:

> The opening was calm, measured and drowsy. One could almost see the burning sand of the desert and feel the enervating sunshine. By degrees, the theme became more troubled and passionate, quietly in the beginning, but with a gradually rising storm—not physical, but of emotion—until everything was like an unsteady sea of menace and terror. Towards the end, crashing dissonances appeared, but just when he was expecting the conventional climax to come, all the theme threads united in a sudden quietening, which almost at once took shape as an indubitable *question.* It could then be seen that all that had gone before had been leading the way to this question, and that what had appeared simple and understandable had been really nothing of the sort, but, on the contrary,

> something very mysterious and profound. . . . Half a dozen tranquil and beautiful bars brought the little piece to a conclusion.

Nicholas objects to Evelyn's interpretation that the question of the Sphinx is simply "Why are we alive?"; he believes the Sphinx was the goddess of dreams, and explains that there are dreams that we are unable to remember afterwards, but which amount to visions of reality. This states the central theme of the book, and also indicates its basic outline. Just as, in *The Haunted Woman,* the reader waits to find out what each new trip to the "haunted rooms" will bring, so in *Sphinx,* he waits for experiments with the dream machine. This is obviously an excellent basic plot, guaranteed to hold the interest; it would take a thoroughly incompetent writer to spoil it; and Lindsay, while clumsy, is not incompetent. This is why *Sphinx,* while no masterpiece, *is* an interesting and readable novel. Read slowly with ears attuned to Lindsay's themes, it is a rewarding experience. (pp. 40-1)

Perhaps the chief fault of *Sphinx*—and one that nobody would expect from Lindsay—is that it has a pervading atmosphere of triviality. This is partly because of its subject. When Nicholas moves into the Sturt's house, he has entered a little whirlpool of gossip and intrigue. A character called Maurice Ferreira—a smart, shady would-be Casanova with a talent for engineering—is in love with Lore Jensen, and is also flirting with one of the Sturt girls, Evelyn. . . . Nicholas wastes a great deal of time involved in these intrigues. (pp. 41-2)

But when one has pushed aside the undergrowth of plot, the theme emerges as identical with that of *The Haunted Woman,* although with variations. Nicholas's recordings of his own dreams reveal a Lore who is in agony, and who needs help. . . . At a casual reading, it seems that it is her involvement with Ferreira that is causing her torment, and this interpretation seems to be strengthened by a description of Ferreira (as seen in a dream):

> He was leaning against a tree, smoking. . . . He was wearing ordinary clothes, but his face was the face of a *devil!* Dead-white, sneering and smiling, it was at the same time cruel and childish; and the childishness imparted such an aspect of degradation to it that the cruelty seemed almost a redeeming element.

There is so much of Crystalman in this description that one suspects deeper meanings here. I am inclined to believe this would be a mistake. In a dream-speech made after her death, Lore dismisses him as completely unimportant.

Lore's death is announced at a fete in the local manor house. Her body is found in a deep stream. Ferreira had gone to the fete with the intention of quarrelling with her—she has dismissed him and announced her marriage to an effete little music critic. Ferreira is even carrying a revolver to threaten her. But it emerges later that her death was suicide, and was nothing to do with Ferreira. "I thought I was running from him, but I was running *towards* something all the time"—Lindsay's death romanticism again.

In the last chapter of the novel, Evelyn makes a "recording" by the bedside of her sleeping father, and then plays it back. The dream reveals the duality of Lore's nature. She is symbolically trapped under water. But her suicide, as she flings herself into the water, releases her "other self", which is able to escape from the water. Moreover, in this final dream, Nicholas appears on horseback, holding another horse by the mane. Lore mounts, and the two of them ride off over the sea. It is after this dream that Evelyn rushes to Nicholas's bedroom, and finds him dead.

What is one to understand by all this? . . . Its meaning—the meaning Lindsay intended (the point of this distinction will appear in a moment)—can only be grasped by someone who has read *The Haunted Woman*. Lore and Nicholas are in the same position as Isbel and Henry Judge, her lover. Social conventions and the messy confusion of everyday life hide from them their basic affinity. (Their first meeting is a quarrel; Lore imagines that Nicholas is sneering at her for writing cheap pot-boilers, and tells him to mind his own business.) Lindsay's thesis—with which almost any psychologist would agree—is that deep dreams may reveal things unknown to the waking consciousness. He also believes that minds with deep affinities can communicate in dreams: this is obviously why Lore appears in Nicholas Cabot's dreams. (pp. 42-3)

Lindsay was obsessed by the falseness imposed on us by society, and the difficulties experienced by people of integrity in "becoming what one is" (to use Nietzsche's phrase). Lore and Nicholas would be ideal for one another; his taciturnity and seriousness are exactly what she needs in a husband. . . . More important, his fortune will enable her to write serious music instead of turning out pot-boiling confections to support herself. (Money is obviously one of her problems; at one point, her father had to support her in a flat.)

But the book leaves one curious problem. *Why* is Lore in such agony? Her sensitivity about her pot-boiling makes it clear that she feels guilty about it, and does it against her will. She turns out a sugary song for one of the sisters, and admits to Nicholas that she composed it in a few minutes to have a reason for calling.

And this song is the occasion of an exchange that again reveals their fundamental closeness. The poem is about a scottish bard who has been to a hilltop to watch the dawn, but is unhappy and frustrated, and a peat cutter who has not raised his eyes from his dreary work all morning, yet who is happy because the work satisfies him. Nicholas objects: "Peat cutting may be more *necessary* than mountain climbing, but, after all, it is the mountain climbers who have built up civilization. Columbus was a mountain climber, and so were Newton and Darwin."

Is Lore's unhappiness due to her awareness that she is, by nature, a mountain climber, and that she is wasting her life? At the garden fete, where a rather dull piece of her music is performed, Lore remarks: "My day's done. I have this afternoon to thank for being able to realize it at last." This would seem the most likely explanation.

I suspect that this is only half the truth. When one views Lindsay's life and work as a whole, a more sinister interpretation suggests itself. Like Lore Jensen, Lindsay is fundamentally a tragic figure. One feels sorry for him, as one might feel sorry for an attractive girl with a hare lip or cleft palate. *Arcturus* reveals him as a man of formidable genius. His other books reveal him as a hopelessly clumsy writer, always tripping over his own feet. The writing is too self-conscious, and totally devoid of grace. When one has read *Devil's Tor*, his last tremendous bid for recognition, one cannot help feeling that the whole thing was a terrible miscalculation. The book is full of elements of greatness, all counterbalanced by the old awkwardness and inability to make anyone speak or act naturally.

Somewhere, there is an odd neurosis—or it may be a lack of self-knowledge. Visiak remarks: "He was radically unhappy, dissatisfied, hungry for recognition in the literary world." How can this be true of the stern, Calvinistic author of *Arcturus*? Yet it is. Lindsay was thoroughly self-divided. *Arcturus* has the strange maturity and perfection that sometimes happens early in the career of an artist. . . . When this happens, the artist's personality has to catch up with his intellectual development. But while man's imagination can mature through intensity and will-power, his total personality needs another important element—experience. (pp. 44-5)

That Lindsay experienced this fear cannot be doubted. Like Lore, he tried to compromise, to add a pot-boiling element to *The Haunted Woman* and *Sphinx*. It made no difference; they failed to attract attention. The same reserve and shyness that made him sometimes socially awkward made the surface of his writing incompetent, amateurish, and it was this amateurishness that prevented critics taking him seriously. The pot-boiling of *The Haunted Woman* and *Sphinx* made no difference. Lindsay attempted no more pot-boilers. (I am leaving *M. de Mailly* out of account because it is written purely as entertainment.) *Devil's Tor* and *The Witch* are wholly serious; but the seriousness made no difference; they were failures.

This is why Lore Jensen's predicament in *Sphinx* is so serious. Lindsay was a strange compound of genius and naivete, and the result was an invisible trap that he could not understand or escape. The reader of *Sphinx* finds it hard to grasp why Lore should be so tormented, why she should finally be driven to suicide to escape the invisible barriers that prevent her from becoming "who she is". Lindsay was so deeply involved in his own precisely parallel situation that he failed to realize that Lore's despair would seem unmotivated. (pp. 45-6)

What of *Devil's Tor*, that immense, ponderous block of German metaphysics and pagan mysticism, nearly a quarter of a million words long. J. B. Pick says "The book has a stodgy feel", and E. H. Visiak told me that it was almost unreadable. However, when he re-read it, Visiak acknowledged that he found it unexpectedly fascinating. . . . The odd thing about Lindsay was that he could write so patiently about boring people. Most good novelists feel the need to people their books with striking characters. Lindsay is comparable to Dostoevsky as a writer of ideas; but to think of Dostoevsky is to think of an incredible gallery of obsessed men, grotesques, demonic women, alcoholics, murderers, saints. If he occasionally includes a conventional character—Varvara Petrovna in *Devils*, of example—it is to provide a contrast to the demonic drives of the other characters. Lindsay's characters are all relatively conventional. It is boring to be in their company for nearly five hundred pages. On the other hand, it has memorable pages and even chapters, when Lindsay can get away from his characters.

The book's opening makes the problem quite plain. Its heroine, Ingrid, and her cousin Hugh Drapier, are taking a walk on Dartmoor when a storm comes down. All this passage—nearly forty pages of it—is magnificent; Lindsay is in his element. (pp. 46-7)

Apart from this, Lindsay is writing as clumsily as ever. (p. 48)

At one point in *Devil's Tor*, Peter Copping, the artist, remarks: "This business threatens to drag on indefinitely." This is the chief fault of the book; personal complications drag on and on. Yet in conception, it comes close to being a masterpiece, and even its maladroit execution cannot entirely spoil it.

Its basic philosophy seems to differ from that of *Arcturus*. Lindsay's obsession is still his feeling that "this world" is unreal, and that we receive clear glimpses of the real world that lies behind it. But his "real world" has become more positive than the featureless Muspel, something closer to the Shavian life-force or Lawrence's sexual-creative principle. And in other ways, Lindsay has moved closer to Lawrence. Like Lawrence, he feels that we are living at the end of an era, on the point of total collapse into decadence. Democracy is one of the signs of this decadence. Like the Lawrence of *The Plumed Serpent*, Lindsay looks back nostalgically to the primitive—to the ages when the savage inhabitants of Britain recognized that the creator of the world was an emanation from God called the Great Mother. As embodied in the Great Mother, the principle of femininity meant creation, and protection of her children. It has gradually been degraded into sexuality. Woman has come to think of herself as a temptress whose job is to persuade some man to undertake her lifelong support; she has accepted a degraded subordinate role.

It should be noted that this view of women is inherent in all Lindsay's novels. The women he approves of are indifferent to sexuality, gripped by more important urges: Joiwind, Lore and Ingrid, even Sullenbode and Isbel. He obviously feels an irritable distaste—blended with fascination—for the seductresses—Oceaxe, Celia Hantish. (pp. 48-9)

What hope does Lindsay see in this decadent world? This is the point of *Devil's Tor*. The answer lies in an Avatar, a new Christ or Buddha. Lindsay points out with grim satisfaction that Christ, Mahomet and the rest were not Avatars of peace but of war. "After their vanishing sprang up always hatred, wars, massacres, the stake, the rack, the scourge." This is the voice of Krag from *Arcturus,* and it echoes some of Lawrence's more irritable pronouncements—the kind of thing that led Russell to call him a fascist.

How will the Avatar appear? This is the subject of *Devil's Tor*. The Earth Mother is stirring in her sleep. She causes the storm that breaks open the Devil's Tor, revealing her tomb, and she brings together the three men who possess the broken halves of a magical stone which, when united, will allow these ancient, long-buried forces to express themselves again. And one of the men, an explorer called Saltfleet, will ultimately become the husband of Ingrid, the virgin destined to bring forth the Avatar.

Everything depends upon the two halves of the stone being joined. Lindsay manages to prevent this from happening for about four hundred and fifty pages by various twists of the plot. When the halves are finally joined, they seem to explode into stars (in the hands of the man who joined them). Saltfleet and Ingrid recognize that it is their destiny to produce the Avatar, and the novel ends with a resounding burst of thunderous prose.

No doubt this attempt at a summary is unfair. This is inevitable, for reasons I have explained. Apart from *Arcturus*, Lindsay wrote only one satisfactory novel, the light-weight *M. de Mailly*. One can either concentrate on his failure to accomplish his aim, or upon the aim itself. At the head of all Lindsay's work could be set the lines from the end of *Faust:*

> All things transitory
> Are but reflection . . .

In *Devil's Tor,* he also accepts the rest of this chorus: . . .

> The eternal womanly / Leads us upward and on.

This position is not consistent with that of *Arcturus*, but we may presume that it represents the result of deeper reflection. *Devil's Tor* is an attempt to dedicate a monument to the "Eternal womanly." . . . If this aspect of the book is accepted, then it will be seen as something of a masterpiece, in spite of its longueurs. It is closer to poetry than to the novel, and it must be admitted that page after page succeeds in sounding those oddly deep notes, like the 'cello in *The Haunted Woman,* that have the authentic poetic effect of making the muscles of the skin contract.

All the same, it cannot be denied that Lindsay's final position was deeply pessimistic, as a mysticism based upon violent rejection of "the world" is bound to be. . . . The negative is a vortex into which it is too easy to get sucked. I find that if I proceed to criticise a writer or philosopher, trying to put my finger on his failings, it becomes increasingly difficult to add reservations, to explain that, in spite of all this, I may regard him as an important and worthwhile figure. It is like running away downhill; it becomes increasingly hard to stop. This also seems to be Lindsay's trouble. *Arcturus* is a Manichean book— the Manichees were a sect who believed that everything to do with "this world" is evil, and that only Heaven is good, so that their philosophy was a thoroughgoing rejection of all life. Everything is rejected. In subsequent works, Lindsay tried to retreat from the edge of this chasm, and the positive values of *The Haunted Woman* and *Sphinx* are closer to the values of any idealist. He obviously also feels that Lore Jensen's early piano piece, "Sphinx", is a valuable piece of art; it asks an ultimate question. In *Arcturus*, this piano piece would have been dismissed as a delusion of Crystalman. Lindsay once said "Music is the higher speech; so that if truly there are angels and they converse with one another, it must be in music". How has music managed to escape the power of Crystalman? (pp. 51-3)

The position taken by Shaw in [*Man and Superman*] is surprisingly close to the Lindsay of *Arcturus*. In the third act, Don Juan and the Devil engage in a long argument. Hell is a place where people talk of nothing but beauty, sublimity, nobility and the rest. (pp. 53-4)

But Shaw contrasts this world of cloying sweetness (in which even music is dismissed as "the brandy of the damned") with the great evolutionary drive. He wants to go to heaven, not for happiness, but for work—to "help life in its struggle upwards".

It is Lindsay's lack of an evolutionary vision that leads him into pessimism. His work after *Arcturus* shows him retreating from his Manicheeism, into recognition that "the Aryan Brahmins, the Stoics, the Christian saints and martyrs" had justified the destruction of the Tertiary animals. But he fails to think out what this change of position implies. Instead, he falls into a facile pessimism about the evils of civilization, and turns his face nostalgically to the past. . . . (p. 54)

J. B. Pick has said: "Lindsay's tragedy—and his literary life was really that—is the tragedy of a man who has seen something, tells people, and they don't listen or don't understand what he is talking about", and several times more in the course of his excellent essay [see excerpt dated 1964], he speaks of Lindsay as a man with a vision who failed to communicate it. This is quite a long way from the truth, for it implies that Lindsay's vision was personal and unique. It wasn't. *Man and Superman* springs from a similar vision, and is dated 1901-3. T. E. Hulme also took up a similar position before the 1914 war. . . . According to Hulme, man is born in a condition of hopeless delusion and weakness called Original Sin, and his only hope of minimising its effects is not to follow his heart or his feelings, but to submit himself to rigorous discipline. For "discipline" substitute "pain", and you have the view presented by Krag. (pp. 54-5)

In Lindsay's belief in the redeeming power of pain—and consequently of war and conflict—one also catches echoes of Nietzsche. . . . And Nietzsche's glorification of war and violence is again a corollary of his evolutionism. He dislikes more peace because he thinks it turns men into fleas; if man will not mount the evolutionary ladder willingly, he must be flogged up it. Nietzsche was not a consistent evolutionist either; he counterbalanced his doctrine of the superman with a belief in eternal recurrence that means virtually that this world is a delusion and free will impossible. (p. 56)

What I have tried to show . . . is that Lindsay was not really a solitary visionary. He was expressing the spirit of the age as much as Eliot, Hulme, Lawrence (both D. H. *and* T. E.—the latter had very much in common with Lindsay), Wyndham Lewis, and the European existentialists. He undoubtedly misunderstood his talents when he decided to become a novelist, for the novel for Lindsay meant people; people wrangling and interacting and quarrelling. And he was not really interested in people. (pp. 61-2)

Lindsay was simply not cut out for writing about the endless and boring complications between Ferreira and Lore Jensen and Saltfleet and Arsinal. They actually bored him as much as the reader. But he didn't know that. He assumed he would find no one to accept his vision undiluted, and that the pill had to be sugared. In fact, the best thing that could happen to Lindsay now is that some enterprising publisher should publish his late works in one volume—*The Haunted Woman, Sphinx, Devil's Tor, The Violet Apple, The Witch* and the philosophy manuscript—edited ruthlessly so as to cut out all the "complications". It would not be too difficult, for, like Melville in *Moby Dick,* he tends to intersperse chapters of major statements with padding. With Lindsay's major thoughts then between two covers, it should be possible to see that he deserves to be included in any list of the important names in literature in the first half of this century. (pp. 62-3)

> *Colin Wilson, in his* The Haunted Man: The Strange Genius of David Lindsay, *The Borgo Press, 1979, 63 p.*

JOY POHL   (essay date 1981)

[*In the following excerpt, Pohl discusses the dualistic elements of* A Voyage to Arcturus, *contending that Lindsay meticulously selected and juxtaposed opposites to create a world of randomness and illusion on Tormance. In encountering dual systems of reality which have equal validity, the hero experiences a "spiritual journey" which will lead him to resolve the duality of his own nature.*]

In *A Voyage to Arcturus* . . . David Lindsay has created a metaphysical quest-romance, a spiritual journey in search of some insight into the ultimate nature of being, through a world in which events have a symbolic rather than realistic significance. In Tormance, his "residential suburb" of the star Arcturus, Lindsay constructs a world replete with spiritual dangers, whose physical strangeness renders more compelling the interior conflicts he portrays. C. S. Lewis has called the book "shattering, intolerable, irresistable"; Eric Rabkin, "soul-wrenching and mind-distorting," both attesting to its power to mirror an inner

reality, to evoke the life of the spirit. What Lindsay has achieved is, in the words of C. S. Lewis, "a lived dialectic" [see excerpt dated 1947], and he has achieved this through a systematic examination of dualities within a moralized landscape. It is this which in large measure gives *A Voyage to Arcturus* its haunting qualities.

Appropriately, the central figure is himself a dual character. Maskull, the protagonist throughout most of *A Voyage to Arcturus,* is mask and skull—the everyday, rational, exterior aspect of the self. He is a Promethean figure come to Tormance (a telescoping of "torment" and "romance" prefiguring the pleasure/pain dualism on which the plot revolves) "to steal Muspel-fire, to give a deeper life to men." Nightspore, Maskull's doppelgänger whose name, connoting both darkness and propagation, life and death, ironically prefigures his ultimate role. He is the "new man" who emerges when Maskull, the everyday self, dies. Nightspore is Maskull's essential self, the pneuma or spirit brought forth when the mask is stripped off and the restraining skull split open, when the rational exterior is exposed as but another illusion preventing the comprehension of essential reality.

Paralleling the dual nature of the hero is the double sun of the planet Tormance, a double sun which affects the protagonist Maskull in spiritually contradictory ways. Branchspell, whose name suggests its capacity to foliate and embroider reality and hence to hold man under various illusory enchantments, is the sun of the everyday world. It is the sun under which Maskull travels on his spiritual odyssey, its withering, electric-white light throwing the moralized landscapes of Tormance into greater relief, rendering by its intensity what Maskull might otherwise perceive as illusory "dreamland," "vividly real." . . . Branchspell's light is the light of man's world.

Alppain, whose name indicates the spiritual heights to which Maskull rises and the pain to be endured thereof, is the sun toward which Maskull moves. It lights the world of the spirit, its dawn representing not "mystery"—an acknowledgment of the limitations of reason—but "wildness," a total release beyond the constraints of reason. . . . The power of Alppain's light is such that even within its sunset Maskull, the rational man, experiences "a feeling of disintegration—just as if two chemically distinct forces were simultaneously acting upon the cells of his body" and wonders, in the effect of its afterglow, if he can face Alppain itself and live. . . . These "violent sensations," however, are the product of "the struggling of wills" within Maskull, the pull of the world of external reality, of the physical world, and the pull of the world of the spirit. (pp. 164-65)

Because Arcturus produces two kinds of light, the light of the physical world and the light of the spirit, Tormance has two sets of primary colors, a third duality whose ramifications Lindsay explores. As with his dual protagonist and dual sun, this duality also delineates the world of the spirit and the world of physical reality. Branchspell produces blue, yellow, and red—blue "delicate and mysterious, yellow clear and unsubtle, and red sanguine and passionate". . . . Later Maskull learns that Branchspell's blue is existence, its yellow is relation, and its red is feeling. . . . Alppain, on the other hand, produces *ulfire,* "wild and painful," *jale,* "dreamlike, feverish, and voluptuous," as well as blue. . . . Here *ulfire* represents existence, blue stands in the middle and represents relation, and *jale* is feeling. . . . Thus as the yellow sun of Branchspell shows the "clear and unsubtle" relation of objects in the real world, the blue sun of Alppain indicates the "delicate and mysterious" nature of relationships in the spiritual world. By creating two new primary colors, Lindsay more than expands his spectrum. In positing a dual set of primary colors and juxtaposing them as antithetical triads, he vivifies the distinction between the real and the symbolic, between the physical and the spiritual.

A fourth duality which Lindsay explores is the masculine/feminine dichotomy. By systematically varying this dualism through a series of fantastic Tormancian cultures, he seeks to grasp its ontological implications. Lindsay's first handling of this theme of male/female dualism comes with the artist Panawe of Poolingdred. Lindsay here postulates a culture in which each individual's sex is determined by the winner of a struggle between the male and female contained within the same body. Hence the conflict or tension caused by the presence of two sexes is resolved at or near birth. (pp. 165-66)

In other Tormancian cultures, the male/female dichotomy is resolved through partnerships or pairings in which the women are as openly assertive as the men or equally aggressive seekers after truth. An exception is the land of Sant, a religious community whose adherents, followers of Hator, rigorously exclude females on penalty of death. Women are regarded as despised objects whose propensity for softness and capacity for love render them unfit for the austerities and asceticism of Sant's guiding principle: the renunciation of all pleasure. (p. 166)

In his final treatment of this dichotomy, Lindsay postulates a culture in which the masculine and feminine principles are wholly antithetical and come together only at the greatest risk of peril for the male. Haunte, a hunter of Sarclash, is a pure male for whom "all laws are female." . . . Sullenbode, the semi-amorphous embodiment of the female principle, possesses neither soul, nor personality, nor even features unless transformed by love. Love, however, between a pure male and a pure female is impossible, Haunte states, pointing out that "when Maskull loves a woman, it is Maskull's female ancestors who are loving her." . . . Deprived of his protective masculine stones, Haunte, driven by desire, seeks out Sullenbode and is destroyed by her. Maskull's kiss, however, transforms her into a living soul, one who "is perfectly willing to disappear and become nothing for the sake of the beloved" . . . , an act in which Sullenbode indulges so that Maskull might continue his search for Muspel. Thus Lindsay concludes his investigation of this dualism with a highly maudlin, certainly conventionalized treatment of the male as a questing figure and the female as civilizing earth-mother. (pp. 166-67)

Throughout his pilgrimmage on Tormance, Maskull embraces new lifestyles and philosophies, experiencing physiological transformations which provide new modes of perception and "new perspective on the chain of life." These experiences form an implicit exposition of the many versus the one duality, of the multiplicity which denies Maskull the essential unity he seeks. Moreover, these adventures within heavily moralized landscapes are themselves paired off and juxtaposed in the form of dualities.

In his first Tormancian culture, Poolingdred, Maskull encounters an innocent world whose inhabitants feed off *gnawl* water and find even the thought of eating fruit terrible. Located in the middle of his forehead, Maskull finds a *breve* (a fleshy protuberance) which enables him to read thoughts, in his chest a heart tentacle for stroking, and on either side of his neck, *poigns* (knoblike organs) which enable him "to understand and sympathize with all living creatures." . . . Admirably equipped then to empathize in a world in which all physical needs are provided, Maskull experiences contentment. He finds nothing

beyond love in this environment and needs no understanding beyond mysticism.

Juxtaposed to this selfless and giving world is the world of Ifdawn Marest. Here the will rules and Maskull's *breve* becomes a *sorb*, a third eye which has the capacity to absorb others. . . . The heart tentacle becomes a third hand for grasping. Even the land reflects the impulsive and arbitrary nature of its inhabitants, constantly and unpredictably erupting or dropping off into the abyss. Here Maskull learns that there is more to life than the somewhat sentimentalized humanity of Poolingdred, that indeed passage through such an environment equipped as a resident of Poolingdred is tantamount to suicide. Maskull is inevitably led then to compare the two societies, one whose central thrust is power versus one whose central thrust is empathy. (pp. 167-68)

However, the explorations of these dualities, organized as adventures within moralized landscapes, are finally each revealed as illusion, revelations not of the one which Maskull seeks but of the many. Even a final experience in which Maskull is vouched ideal love is revealed as illusion, albeit one which maintains its beauty even when its illusory nature is realized. This dichotomy between the one and the many, the real and the illusory, is ultimately explained via a cosmic dualism. On the cosmic level, the dichotomy is between Surtur, the god of Muspel, for whom Krag is the embodied form, and Crystalman, variously known as Shaping and Faceny, for whom Gangnet is the embodiment. Muspel, the hidden eternal light, pure spirit, Lindsay had earlier called "the primeval world of fire; existing before heaven and earth, and which will eventually destroy them." Crystalman feeds off this Muspel-stream, his shadow form acting as a prism, shivering pure spirit into millions and millions of life forms, each possessing via the transformation an ineffable and grotesque sweetness. Some particles of Muspel emerge unaltered "by reason of their extreme minuteness." . . . Krag is thus "a spirit compounded of those vestiges of Muspel which Shaping [Crystalman] did not know how to transform." . . . Trying to undo Crystalman's work, Krag brings redemptive pain into the world; and thus while Crystalman masquerades as a god in the guise of pleasure, Krag, who is also Surtur, is frequently mistaken for the devil.

Maskull completes the first stage of his journey back to spirit by renouncing his self-life, his false and private world of "dreams and appetites and distorted perceptions" and embracing the whole, great world of Crystalman. . . . At the end of his odyssey, he is told by Krag, "You have run the gamut. What else is there left to live for?" . . . Indeed he has lived all the illusions, embraced all the lifestyles which the strange world of Tormance provides. Tormance then becomes a metaphor for those systems, both philosophical and theological, which man imposes on the overt world and which encapsulate his spiritual being. With Maskull's death, the dormant Nightspore is aroused. Nightspore represents thus the enlargement of personality (i.e., Maskull's personality) necessary to assimilate the vital world of the spirit which Muspel symbolizes. Nightspore is then literally the reborn Maskull, and the "gamut" which Maskull runs creates the inner amplitude which allows this spiritual transformation. In the final moments of the story, Nightspore discovers "Muspel consisted of himself and the stone tower on which he was sitting." . . . Having run the gamut, his duality is resolved, and he is capable of perceiving reality without illusion. (p. 169)

Joy Pohl, "Dualities in David Lindsay's 'A Voyage to Arcturus'," in Extrapolation, *Vol. 22, No. 2, Summer, 1981, pp. 164-70.*

BERNARD SELLIN   (essay date 1981)

[*In the following excerpt, Sellin discusses Lindsay's philosophy of the Sublime World and traces the manifestation of this philosophy in the content and structure of his novels.*]

David Lindsay is an ideologist rather than a philosopher, as the reader will be quick to notice. If it is the invention, the exoticism and the strange that make the first impression, one soon discovers, behind these flights of fancy, a kind of thought that lacks neither richness nor interest. While his novels gravitate towards imaginary worlds, the writer's thinking, in itself, leaves the beaten track, and takes the form of intuition of a vivid intensity. All Lindsay's determination is needed to ensure that his plots adhere to the reality of this world. As a general rule, the realistic picture gives way to intimations of the hereafter. (p. 174)

The whole of Lindsay's writing is based upon the experience of duality, or the feeling that life as we know it, whilst being scarcely enriching, contains elements which testify to a possible grandeur. Being lonely, and the prisoner from birth until death of a few years' existence, as well as a composite mass of atoms exposed to the dangers of an impersonal world, man is nothing. Nevertheless, he is not destitute of grandeur, as is evident in his tenacity in surmounting unhappiness, his intelligence and his aspirations. From this point of view, man asserts his place in some superior order of things. This model, as some kind of ideal, Lindsay calls the Sublime.

The theory of the Sublime constitutes the ultimate point of the whole of Lindsay's ideology. Its importance is considerable, since it claims to be nothing more nor less than an explanation of the universe. It is accordingly essential to understand it properly. Lindsay himself repeatedly insists upon the importance he attaches to this theory, which he also considers to be one of the most original aspects of his thinking. He adds that his entire ideology, in his view, must be an exposition of the Sublime.

Before examining the content of this doctrine, it is necessary to resolve an ambiguity as to the word itself, which differs, when used by Lindsay, from current usage. According to Lindsay, the term was chosen, for want of anything better, to denote a certain transcendent world. The interpretation is accordingly his own.

The word is one of long standing, since it is found, for the first time, in the third century A.D., in the writings of a Greek orator called Longinus, author of *On the Sublime*. It is principally in the eighteenth and nineteenth centuries, however, that the term achieved its period of glory, thanks notably to thinkers such as Boileau and Edmund Burke. Burke's definition, that the Sublime was founded upon profusion, irregularity, pain and darkness, as opposed to the Beautiful, sets the tone for a whole stream of literature, typified particularly by the 'Gothic novel'.

Kant takes up the term, and then comes Schopenhauer. His theory of the Sublime is taken directly from Kant, but it embodies the conception of free will, unique to the author. (pp. 174-75)

Lindsay's admiration for Schopenhauer is known. One of his characters in *Devil's Tor,* Uncle Magnus, bears a likeness, both physically and morally, to the German philosopher. . . . Lindsay parts company from his mentor, however, when it comes to the Sublime. He does not hesitate to criticise Schopenhauer's conception of the Sublime as being 'the contemplation of Beauty under threatening circumstances'. Is it enough for a beautiful woman to be surprised by a storm to make the scene a Sublime one? Lindsay poses this question by reducing Schopenhauer's theory to its essentials. He then adds that, in his view, 'The Sublime is not beauty but something else, which is related to beauty, yet transcends it.' . . . (pp. 175-76)

The conception of the Sublime did not come to David Lindsay through reading such philosophers as Kant and Schopenhauer. It is more accurate to say that it established itself through contact with the world, and that it was born out of the very experience of the author. Lindsay indefatigably repeats that the Sublime world, in his view, is more real than the tangible world. 'The Sublime world is not a metaphysical theory but a terrible fact, which stands above and behind the world, and governs all its manifestations'. Far from being immaterial, and populated by ghosts and illusions, the Sublime has a body whose substance is more real, and more solid, than 'this coloured, cubic and heavy world of ours'. (p. 177)

The first approach of the Sublime is met in *A Voyage to Arcturus.* This is the picture of Muspel, which is hardly precise, because the book tries, above all, to denounce the pitfalls of the conscious world. The choice of the Scandinavian myth of Muspel, as a symbol of the Sublime, was determined by other reasons. Besides the symbolic use to which Muspellsheim, the world of fire of Nordic mythology, lends itself, it did not escape Lindsay that Muspel was, according to legend, the original world. The giant, Ymir, father of the human race, united fire and ice. Lindsay returns to the idea of a world that existed before the Earth and Heaven, and imbues the legend with a certain Platonism and Gnosticism, in order to arrive at an original conception of a pre-existing world, whose actual universe would only be a much inferior derivative. By the device of the myth of Muspel, Lindsay similarly explains the end of the world, and the reconquest of the Sublime world. (p. 178)

In order to justify the pre-eminence of the Sublime world, Lindsay affirms that the explanations of the universe by earlier religions and philosophies are scarcely satisfactory. The message of *A Voyage to Arcturus* is the negation of traditional codes, and the discovery of a new principle of explanation in the Sublime. According to Lindsay, theories of evolution, the virtues of education, human fraternity, and the idea of God, are all deceits which have had the sole effect of concealing from men's eyes the existence of the Sublime world. The only true explanation that remains is that of Schopenhauer, making the will, or powers striving towards something, the basis of existence. All our unhappiness arises out of that. The will to live is tyrannical and sad. The misery of man on earth comes from the overriding necessity to satisfy the demands of the will. All privation is painful to it. Starting from there, Lindsay adds that a world whose insufficiencies are so evident can present no interest whatsoever. Its limitations are explicable by its nature. The tangible world is secondary, created from an ideal model which is itself set free from the servitude of will.

The history of the world, and of humanity in particular, is the story of a disgrace. This degradation, it must be stressed, however, has nothing to do with the Christian conception of the Fall. The three standards of this evolution are the Sublime, the self and morality. The Sublime state is the example of an entirety that is free from all imperfection. The transition from the Sublime to the self is due to the interference of the principle of individuality that Lindsay likens to Nature. Morality, for its part, particularly appears as a repressive force of the self. . . .

Such, in broad terms, are the principal lines of Lindsay's ideology. (pp. 178-79)

The Sublime is not of this world, repeats Lindsay. The conquest of the Sublime, therefore, begins by detachment from the world. In *A Voyage to Arcturus,* after long preparation, it is necessary to await the death of Maskull in order to begin to reach for the Sublime. . . . In *Devil's Tor,* it is the storm which acts as the catalyst of the Sublime. The walk taken by Hugh and Ingrid is an ascent, far removed from the everyday world. Already separated by distance and height, they are still more isolated by the tempest which rages around them. The rain encloses them like a prison. It forms a wall between them and the rest of the world. . . . Nevertheless, it is a false prison, as the isolation is the first of the conditions necessary to be free. The storm reveals a new mode of existence of which Hugh and Ingrid have previously had only a vague intuition. Within a few minutes, the significance of life is overthrown. Values commonly accepted, such as life, love and fraternity, lose their importance. All that is human becomes obliterated in the face of the terrible grandeur of the Sublime world.

One solitary experience of the Sublime is enough to transform the course of existence, as if something at the very foundation of oneself has been broken. The pessimism of Lindsay and his heroes has no other source than this impossibility of seeing the tangible world as our reason for existence. (pp. 179-80)

The experience of the Sublime engenders more anguish than satisfaction, because it disturbs one's life. Anguish is a component of the Sublime. In contrast to the Christian Paradise, which one need only await in tranquillity and virtue, the Sublime has the effect of making man depressive. It is accompanied by 'disturbance, sullenness, infinite longing, sadness, despair'. . . . Sublimity is nothing but the subconscious desire of the soul to regain its origin, and a nostalgia to return to the intangible world, or the Paradise Lost from which our real world emanated. The dissatisfaction is that of 'the outsider', who knows that he belongs to the hereafter. 'Men, you see, are not only men, they are also and essentially *spirits*. The world is not their right place . . . Accordingly, in their unconscious depths, men are unhappy in the world, which is not their place, and which confines them.' What some call 're-demption' is no more, in Lindsay's eyes, than the soul's return to its first condition.

The instrument of learning is the soul or the spirit. Truth does not lie within the gift of the senses. It is only discovered inwardly, by an effort to free oneself from surrounding influences, in order to respond to a transcendent need. Between the human soul and the driving force of the world, there is an identity of nature which explains that knowledge of the world concerns only a part of man, his eternal soul. Men are 'also and essentially spirits', writes Lindsay, meaning that human nature combines a mental life with an organic one. Of these two, only the former is of interest in enabling one to discover a fundamental knowledge of life. David Lindsay begins, therefore, by dividing his characters into two categories. On the one hand, there are the initiates of the body, and, on the other, those of the soul. The doctor, as a servant of the body, is placed in the ranks of latter-day charlatans. Women, unceasingly preoccupied with dress, ornamentation, beauty and bodily cares, do not escape criticism. Lindsay denounced barbarity, and the return to animalism. Man has lost his soul, he cries, and is no longer anything more than a 'human biped, whose stomach is paramount in the existence of a mystic universe'. . . . At the polar opposite are found nearly all Lindsay's heroes and heroines, such as Hugh Drapier, Lore Jensen, Ingrid Colborne and others, each of them being almost without substance, for whom the body scarcely exists. (pp. 180-81)

Without examining it very deeply, David Lindsay takes up . . . the philosophy of Plato, with its contrast of two worlds; the creation of the world by a Demiurge, the human soul considered as part of the Universal Soul, the traps of the tangible world, the possibility of man recovering his divine, eternal origin, and the unhappiness of man on earth, subjected to this nostalgia for his first existence. In spite of this borrowed philosophy, Lindsay loses no time in parting company from his illustrious predecessor. To the Platonic theory, there are now added other currents of thought, particularly Stoicism, Eastern philosophy and Gnosticism.

Man is aware of existing independently of the world which surrounds him. Experience proves to him his individuality. This division constitutes, in Lindsay's eyes, the first stage of the Sublime. Individuality is the opposite of the Sublime, and Sublimity represents, to a large extent, the effort of man to regain the whole. Human experience, in the sense that it is narrowly linked to individuality, is, in the nature of things, anti-Sublime. (pp. 181-82)

The method to which Lindsay adheres . . . [consists of] *aban-doning* individuality altogether. The conquest of the Sublime is achieved by a renunciation of the self, which has long been seen as one of the foundations of any mystical quest. The necessary condition for all progression towards Divinity, and any kind of illumination, is moral detachment. This abandonment of the principle of individuality is presented to us in several forms, including sacrifice, acceptance of Fate, magnanimity and altruism.

The most spectacular of these gifts of oneself is sacrifice. This is one of the most baffling aspects of *A Voyage to Arcturus*. Several times in this book, characters disappear by jumping into a void, from the top of a cliff. (pp. 182-83)

Sacrifice, says one of the characters in *A Voyage to Arcturus,* is not utilitarian, but a ransom that one pays. . . . It constitutes, therefore, the first step towards the discovery of the Sublime, in the sense that this sacrifice is both a gift and a renunciation. If one accepts that the Sublime is not of this world, man must agree to die, the will to live being the manifest proof of attachment to this world. Whosoever wishes to rise above life, indeed 'above mysticism', must be ready to sacrifice his own material existence. That which constitutes the nobility of life, and which gives a meaning to life, is this faculty to give, of one's own free will, that which man will see forcibly removed in death. (pp. 183-84)

The second form taken by abnegation of the self is the acceptance of the decrees of Fate. The theme scarcely appears in *A Voyage to Arcturus*. It will be remembered, however, that it is present in *The Haunted Woman*. The love of Judge and Isbel totally overwhelms them. When they meet in the haunted room, they act in defiance of good sense and convention. They are drawn towards one another, as if by a magnet. Finally, in *Devil's Tor,* there reigns a fatalistic atmosphere. Men are the playthings of forces which overtake them. The different intrigues are improbable. There are too many coincidences, and too many unexplained events. The book would have scarcely any value if there were not, behind the improbability, the principle of an inexorable Fate. The actions of the characters are explicable by intuitions, and by impulses that are but little understood. (pp. 185-86)

Coincidences, chance, luck and intuitions are just so many modern forms of that Fate which the ancients knew so well. The improbability of *Devil's Tor* . . . conceals the very ambitious plan of restoring some nobility to the idea of Fate, which has not ceased to be degraded over the course of centuries. The ancients had a sharp sense of the existence of this superior world which both surrounded men and governed their actions. This world in which the ancients believed would be one form of the Sublime world. The Sublime world has disappeared, and with it the idea of Fate, replaced by the conception of an all-powerful God, this modern 'insipid' form of determinism, created by a people incapable of accepting the idea of an inexorable Fate. . . . The beliefs and values of David Lindsay involve pain and suffering, which take the form of endurance or sacrifice. In itself, suffering has nothing Sublime about it, but it is the instrument of the Sublime. 'If one were set the problem of causing men to acquire their original Sublime nature, no other means could be found than by making them *suffer*. Thus pain is justified', writes Lindsay, in his *Philosophical Notes*. Lindsay's ideas approximate to certain trends in asceticism and stoicism, whilst always retaining their own originality.

In order fully to understand Lindsay's use of the term 'Sublime', one must refer to the nature of the Sublime. Nearly all definitions of the Sublime, whether by Kant, Burke or Schopenhauer, stress the violence involved therein. In all cases, there is a contrast between opposites. A Sublime spectacle is at once attractive and agonising. It evokes as much fear as pleasure. . . . When he conceives his Sublime world, Lindsay starts from this same idea. He imagines an order of things in which pain and pleasure would be united. The degradation that has characterised the transition from the Sublime world to the actual world would only be the dissociation of pleasure and pain, which were formerly united. . . . Man feels either pleasure or pain, but rarely both at the same time. When these two feelings are joined, we are in the presence of the Sublime, and of a return to the first condition of man. (pp. 186-87)

To regain his Sublime origin, man has no better means than to submit himself to the beneficial effect of pain. Pain becomes the 'solvent of pleasure'. It must be clearly understood that it is not a matter of replacing pleasure with pain, but to attain, through the effect of pain, a union with the interior pleasure of the Sublime. The Sublime state does not separate them.

The arguments used by Lindsay to justify the positive value of pain are certainly not lacking. Without pain, pleasure is insipid. . . . Moreover, adds Lindsay, pain brings satisfaction, since pain brings the benefit of inducing man to surmount it. It impels change. While certain people benefit from pleasure, others seem to flourish much more under the influence of pain. Their nobility in no sense diminishes. (pp. 187-88)

David Lindsay takes as his own the axiom of Baudelaire, expressed as 'You are a happy man. I pity you, sir, for being so easily happy.' Like Baudelaire before him, Lindsay sees pain as being 'the divine miracle for our impurities'. He also denounces those people who laugh too easily, to the neglect of self-discipline. Happy people are the slaves of modern times, satisfied with monotony and meagre rewards. For the true 'aristocrat of the universe', something more than half-measures is needed. Either one must abandon oneself to an orgy of pleasure or else one must eschew all forms of pleasure.

Between these two extremes, Lindsay has made his choice. The supreme blessing is pain, and he goes on to explain his reasoning. Failure represents the best springboard to success.

Man is like a boxer. He must train himself to receive blows. He must accept insult and injustice without faltering. . . . In order to remain above the conflict, one must never show oneself to be troubled, if one is a wise man. In moments of acute emotional upheaval, feelings must be hidden. . . . Without this ruggedness and determination, he adds elsewhere, man remains a dilettante who can scarcely be taken seriously.

It is towards the philosophy of endurance, therefore, that Lindsay's preference is directed. (p. 189)

Between *A Voyage to Arcturus* and *Devil's Tor,* more than ten years intervene. In the latter work, the thinking is more refined, and the intuition of the former is confirmed. The theory of the Sublime has been considerably developed. In *Devil's Tor,* the Scandinavian myth of Muspel has been relegated to the background with only a few references to recall what was, in *A Voyage to Arcturus,* representative of the ideal transcendent world. At the same time, this suprasensible reality is brought considerably nearer, assuming the solidity and consistency of real life. The plan is much more ambitious than in the earlier book. Lindsay attempts nothing less than the reconstruction of the world in his own style, from its very beginnings until the end of time. The Muspel of *A Voyage to Arcturus* has become 'The Ancient'. As for Surtur, the defender of Muspel, he has been replaced by a Demiurge who is female.

David Lindsay's interpretation has its origin in the simple statement that it is impossible to imagine a male God. Such a male Creator of the Universe could not have prevented himself from giving the product of his creation certain characteristics of his own. Now, reasons Lindsay, one need only open one's eyes, and look about one, to notice that the world is essentially female. 'All the great elements of the world, the universal and all-powerful incentive of love, the enormous fact and cult of beauty, the endless production of children to supply the wastage by death, the seasonal mating of free animals, and annual rebirth of vegetation, the orbits of planets and comets, the doubtless curved paths of the stars, the tides, not only of the sea, the purely-instinctive existences of all creatures, save the moral among humans, and even of them, everything of this was so peculiarly of the female stamp, emotional, blind, repetitive, that it was as if he had found himself in a house whose every room contained women's clothes, needlework, flowers, stuffs, silken draperies, fragile furniture, infants' toys and garments; and were asked and required to consent that the residence had been equipped for his own use by a man.' . . . (pp. 193-94)

Nature, by common consent a divine creation, is, according to all the evidence, essentially female, especially as only curved lines are to be found there. To-day, psycho-analysis has come to support this interpretation, by giving to nature a maternal image. The most important human function, that of reproduction, is female. Without it, the world would long since have ceased to exist.

In conclusion, according to Lindsay, nearly all the components of the universe bear witness to belonging to this femininity. After love, women, children, beauty, nature, civilisation and art, what is left? Work and war are two activities that one readily associates with men, but also with unhappiness, pain, and even hatred. Work and war are such glaring examples of imperfection that it would be senseless to regard them as derivatives of a perfect being, the creator of the universe. We are led, both by evidence and absurdity, to the only possible interpretation; that the universe has not been created by a male God, but by a female Demiurge. (pp. 194-95)

Lindsay's Demiurge [a Great Mother figure,] can be cruel and bloodthirsty, when necessary. In this respect, the depiction still conforms to the studies of this cult, which have shown the Great Mother to be a bellicose Goddess, presiding equally well at the production of living beings as at their destruction. Suffering is a reality that nobody can escape, not even the Creator. Between the world and its Creator, there is an identity of nature, both being based upon suffering. (p. 195)

Human misery . . . , according to Lindsay, is largely a consequence of the degradation of the feminine values embodied in the Ancient and the Great Mother. This evolution occurred partly because patriarchal societies replaced primitive matriarchal societies, and partly because the female ideal was corrupted. It is this latter aspect that should now be considered.

The problem presenting itself to Lindsay is a simple one. How is it possible to reconcile the conception of women as the source of all perfection with his own evidence of the frivolities and limitations of the 'weaker sex'?

This paradox shows that there has been continuity between the Ancient and twentieth-century woman, albeit a gradual debasement. From that, the question arises as to whether this corruption was inevitable, whether time is the cause of erosion and especially whether some happening intervened, at one stage or another, to influence the course of events. It is towards this last solution that Lindsay inclines. The Ancient, he writes belonged to 'femaleness', without being 'womanly', making the distinction that Lindsay establishes between 'female' and 'woman'. . . . The female finds itself dissociated here from female sexual characteristics. At the beginning of humanity, there was femininity. The appearance of man occurred simultaneously with that of woman, in circumstances that remain quite obscure, but which permit the assertion that the human tragedy is bound up with the emergence of the bisexual condition. All evil stems from this 'unnatural' divison. There can be no clearer proof of life's imperfection than the need to 'choose' a sex, which confronts us at birth. Man, just as much as woman, is condemned to be an actor on the world stage, playing a rôle imposed upon him by his own sex, compelled to lie, and to dissemble in the presence of the other sex.

Just as with Christianity, Lindsay conceives a Fall from the divine state to the human state, but here the divine state is a maternal one. The Fall is nothing else than the passing from the maternal state to the bisexual state. (pp. 195-96)

To a large extent, David Lindsay discovered the Sublime through his own personal experience, and especially through music. This last point is one that needs to be emphasised, especially as earlier studies have not dealt with this fundamental aspect. (p. 203)

Although he played no instrument, and could not even read a musical score, he had reached a stage where music held few secrets for him. He was never a theorist, however. He lived music, and, according to his friend, Rober Barnes, whose musical education was certainly more comprehensive, Lindsay's musical judgments showed insight. While music, for most people, is a pleasant diversion, Lindsay made it a veritable art, superior to all other artistic forms. Scorning the eye, as being the organ of illusions, he regarded the ear as a divine organ, and truly the narrow door leading to ultimate reality. . . . (pp. 203-04)

In order to understand the importance that Lindsay attached to music, there is no need to look very far, and just one sentence sums up his thinking. 'Music is the experience of a supernatural world.' . . . As 'the experience of a supernatural world', music is definitively a revelation of the Sublime. The attraction of music, therefore, stems from its power of emancipation from the Earth. Music constitutes a world apart, far removed from the imperfections and falsities of our present lives. To put it more precisely, music is the proof, and the product, of a parallel world. Lindsay scarcely develops this idea, contenting himself, it seems, with drawing the conclusions to which his personal experience has led him. It is not known whether Lindsay was content to adopt the interpretation of Schopenhauer, who saw, in music, the revelation of another world, whose existence would have preceded the emergence of the present world. According to Schopenhauer, music speaks of a 'world' that is completely independent of the world of free will. It is a message coming directly from the hereafter, free of interference from the world of phenomena, unlike the other arts. As will be noticed, this interpretation is quite close to that of Lindsay.

It is possibly because it suggests the world of our origins that music is associated more with nostalgia than with Nietzschean jubilation. Anything else would be surprising. It is primarily as a release that music appears, this 'power as a releasing factor' of which Ingrid speaks, at the very beginning of *Devil's Tor*. 'You seemed under an enchantment. I fancy you were not merely held, but seriously disturbed. Where were you?' Hugh asks Ingried, to which the young girl replies 'In a strange sphere, unsuggested by the music, I expect. Music is never more than a releasing factor for me; and that's why I am cold to nine-tenths of music, for it doesn't release. I can secure the same emancipation from things without music at all, much more slowly, but retentively on that account, as up here, alone and at peace with everything actual. I've told you something about that. *It must be the beginning of the Sublime.*' . . . (pp. 204-05)

Of all the arts, music alone is truly Sublime. Hence, this writing, which is presented, above all, as a conquest of the Sublime, is permeated with this philosophy of music, which is both the catalyst of the journey to the source of life and the proof of Paradise Lost. Since it operates to suggest the other world, Lindsay knew how to use music. Thunder, another manifestation of the parallel world, is 'the greatest music'. . . . The magic stone that has fallen from the sky seems to emit music. Death, gateway to the hereafter, is accompanied by 'solemn music'. . . . The mystic union of Ingrid and Saltfleet takes place against a background of 'mystical music'.

Far from being a mere prop, music is the very pillar upon which rests Lindsay's writing. In view of this, it is scarcely surprising to find, amongst all the characters in search of another world, an exceptional number of musicians. . . . There is no book by Lindsay which does not contain a piece of music that, in some way, sets the style. Each one begins with the performance of a piece, as if the author wanted to fix the tone of the novel. (p. 205)

So great is Lindsay's love of music that it ends in dominating the ideological background, to become a technique of expression, and a style in itself. This writer may span the world, without really seeing it, and emphasis has already been given to the impoverishment of his power of realistic narration, but music is the one thing that does not pass unnoticed. (pp. 206-07)

'Only a very few people will ever read *A Voyage to Arcturus*, but, as long as even two or three people will listen to Beethoven, two or three people will read it', declared Lindsay, with that mixture of humility and arrogance that is so characteristic of his personality. In order to write, he had to use words, but the artist in him was closer to the musician. He contemplated the world in philosophical terms, and tried to convey his intuitions and reflections in the way a musician would have been able to do. His undeniable guide was Beethoven, whose symphonies, too, encroach upon the present in order to confront man with his metaphysical destiny. The rhythm of Lindsay's books draws its inspiration from the unfolding of a musical work, consisting of a slow introduction, followed by characteristic themes, a staccato passage, and a finale which is sometimes clear, and sometimes vague, as if the book ended with a question. The music is not only descriptive, but interrogates, suggesting bridges between the world down here and the hereafter. It is a form of expression, but also a form of life, to the point that, when he comes to describe the metamorphoses of the soul, in search of its origins, Lindsay will have recourse to the 'three musics', these being, respectively, liberation from the everyday world, discovery of the soul, and incorporation of the human soul with the Absolute. . . . (pp. 208-09)

> *Bernard Sellin, in his* The Life and Works of David Lindsay, *translated by Kenneth Gunnell, Cambridge University Press, 1981, 257 p.*

HAROLD BLOOM   (essay date 1982)

[*Bloom is one of the most prominent of contemporary American critics and literary theorists. In* The Anxiety of Influence *(1973), Bloom formulated a controversial theory of literary creation called revisionism. Influenced strongly by Freudian theory, which states that "all men unconsciously wish to beget themselves, to be their own fathers," Bloom believes that all poets are subject to the influence of earlier poets and that, to develop their own voice, they attempt to overcome this influence through a process of misreading. By misreading, Bloom means a deliberate, personal revision of what has been said by another so that it conforms to one's own vision: "Poetic influence—when it involves two strong, authentic poets—always proceeds by a misreading of the prior poet, an act of creative correction that is actually and necessarily a misrepresentation. The history of poetic influence . . . is a history of anxiety and self-serving caricature, of distortion, of perverse, wilful revisionism." In this way the poet creates a singular voice, overcoming the fear of being inferior to poetic predecessors. Bloom's later books are applications of this theory, extended in* Kabbalah and Criticism *(1974) to include the critic or reader as another deliberate misreader. Thus, there is no single reading of any text, but multiple readings by strong poets or critics who understand a work only in ways that allow them to assert their own individuality or vision. In addition to his theoretical work, Bloom is one of the foremost authorities on English Romantic poetry and has written widely on the influences of Romanticism in contemporary literature. In the following excerpt, Bloom explains his theory of literary fantasy, which states that "the cosmos of fantasy . . . is revealed in the shape of nightmare and not of hallucinatory wish-fulfillment." Bloom places Lindsay in the line of great masters of High Romantic fantasy-quest, which includes William Blake and Percy Bysshe Shelley, and praises* A Voyage to Arcturus *for challenging the reader's identification with concepts of narcissism and Prometheanism, upon which traditional fantasy depends. According to Bloom, who himself wrote a fantasy modeled after* Arcturus, *Lindsay's book belongs "at the very center of modern fantasy."*]

I intend to offer here only the opening move or swerve of what might become a theory of literary fantasy, or perhaps might join itself to some existent theories of that mode. As motto or

epigraph I take from my personal favorite among modern fantasies the plangent sentence spoken by Nightspore to Krag over the corpse of the Promethean quester, Maskull: "Why was all this necessary?", to which Krag replies with his customary angry abruptness: "Ask Crystalman. His world is no joke." "All this" is nothing less than the most Sublime and spiritually terrifying death-march in all of fantastic literature, in some respects even overgoing similar journeys from Dante on to Browning's *Childe Roland to the Dark Tower Came.* David Lindsay's *A Voyage to Arcturus* . . . is a very unevenly written book, varying in tone from preternatural eloquence to quite tedious bathos. Yet I will assert for it a greatness that few contemporary critics might grant, and part of that greatness is the book's near-perfection in a particular kind of romance invention, as once it would have been called, that kind we have agreed to call fantasy. (p. 1)

Fantasy is a literary sub-genre, by which I do not mean to deprecate it, but rather to state this formula: what is good in fantasy *is* romance, just as anything good in verse *is* poetry. Historically, the eighteenth century, and subsequently Romanticism, replaced the heroic genre by romance, even as the concept of the Sublime replaced theology. If Freud, as I now believe, extended and rationalized Romanticism rather than replaced it, we can aver that the literary element in dream, as expounded by Freud, is always romance. In the anxiety of belatedness that the eighteenth century waning of the Enlightenment passed on to Romanticism (and to Freud), can be found the repressed source of modern literary fantasy, because fantasy beckons as a release to any sense of belatedness. (p. 2)

I phrase [the Clina Men, or opening Lucretian swerve of a theory of fantasy] in this formula: *fantasy, as a belated version of romance, promises an absolute freedom from belatedness, from the anxieties of literary influence and origination, yet this promise is shadowed always by a psychic over-determination in the form itself of fantasy, that puts the stance of freedom into severe question.* What promises to be the least anxious of literary modes becomes much the most anxious, and this anxiety specifically relates to anterior powers, that is, to what we might call the genealogy of the imagination. The cosmos of fantasy, of the pleasure/pain principle, is revealed in the shape of nightmare, and not of hallucinatory wish-fulfillment.

My formulaic swerve, and immediate subsequent remarks may give the impression that I am deprecating literary fantasy or at least describing its apparent strength as its implicit weakness, but my intention is exactly the reverse; I speak descriptively, but indeed of fantasy's true strength and of its use for the literary mind in our belated age. To illustrate my formula and the role of fantasy as a belated Sublime, I turn . . . to David Lindsay's *A Voyage to Arcturus,* recalling as I turn that the Sublime originally meant a style of "loftiness," of verbal power conceived agonistically, against all rivals. (p. 6)

Criticism begins in the lived experience of a text, meaning both the fondness of reading, and the ambivalences that fondness calls forth, including those ambivalences that play through relationships between texts in many of the ways they play through human relationships. In regard to Lindsay's *A Voyage to Arcturus,* I have experienced a relationship marked by a wild fondness and an endless ambivalence, itself productive of my own first attempt at literary fantasy, published in 1979 as *The Flight to Lucifer,* a book very much in the Arcturan shadow. Shadow is the great closing trope of Lindsay's book, as Nightspore, the *pneuma* or spark of the dead Promethean, Maskull, confronts the Demiurge Crystalman, from the standing-point of a tower beyond death:

> The shadow-form of Crystalman had drawn much closer to him, and filled the whole sky, but it was not a shadow of darkness, but a bright shadow. It had neither shape, nor colour, yet it in some way suggested the delicate tints of early morning. It was so nebulous that the sphere could be clearly distinguished through it; in extension, however, it was thick. The sweet smell emanating from it was strong, loathsome, and terrible. . . .

This demiurgic shadow has a profound literary anteriority, and historically can be identified with the Aesthetic Movement in England (circa 1870-1900), which we associate with Swinburne, Whistler, Beardsley, the young Yeats, but above all others, with Pater and Wilde. Crystalman's bright shadow, with its delicate tints of early morning, has its clear source in the high purple of Pater's vision of the Renaissance. (pp. 6-7)

Lindsay, like Pound and Stevens, must have read Pater's first essay *Diaphaneite,* where the artist is called a crystal man, transparent and Apollonian, more than human in his perfection. Against Crystalman as Paterian Demiurge Lindsay sets his most imaginative creation, the grotesque but stalwart god of redemptive pain, strikingly named Krag in what I take to be a tribute to Carlyle's isolated hill farm in Dumfriesshire, the rugged Craigenputtoch, where *Sartor Resartus* was written, it being the book from which the religious vision of *A Voyage to Arcturus* is quarried. In *Sartor Resartus,* the post-Calvinist Lindsay found most of the ingredients of his Gnostic myth, presented by Carlyle however with his characteristic German High Romantic irony and parodistic frenzy of despair. Carlyle's outrageous ontological fable has the humor that Lindsay could not attain, yet it lacks the final frenzy of absolute literary fantasy, which past all opening swerves must stage its own death-march beyond the pleasure/pain principle. We can cite here Carlyle's own Professor Teufelsdröckh's quotation from Friedrich von Schlegel: "*Fantasy* is the organ of the Godlike," and on that basis prepare to turn again to Lindsay's quest for fantasy's simultaneous stance of freedom and over-determination. (pp. 7-8)

[Readers,] friends and students, whom I have urged to read *A Voyage to Arcturus,* have tended to be severely divided in their reaction to the book, and to literary fantasy in general. When, in my disappointment, I have probed the negative reactions of readers I trust, I have found that they do center uncannily on what I take to be the true critical issue here: why do books promising aesthetic freedom (and I know no fantasy wilder than *A Voyage to Arcturus*) seem to labor under such apparent aesthetic bondage? Why might a sensitive reader come to believe that Lindsay's book is a vivid nightmare, at best, rather than the absolute vision that I keep discovering in it?

A Voyage to Arcturus begins rather weakly, I would concede, as a kind of parody of science fiction, more or less in the mode of Jules Verne. Yet even in that hopeless first chapter, "The Séance," the Uncanny enters the book with the leaping advent of Krag. Still, it is not until Chapter VI, when Maskull wakes up on Tormance, that the Sublime proper begins, as in this book it must: by, through and in suffering. Shelley suggested, as Longinus had, that the Sublime existed in order to induce the reader to abandon easier pleasures for more difficult pleasures. In Lindsay's savage fantasy, the Sublime has passed

through Carlyle's Everlasting No and Centre of Indifference, leapfrogged over his Everlasting Yea, and then culminated by turning his Natural Supernaturalism inside out, to produce a Supernatural version of a Darwinian Naturalism. Lindsay seems to have invested himself in the most peculiar chapter of *Sartor Resartus,* "Symbols," and to have taken literally Carlyle's grand injunction there:

> A Hierarch, therefore, and Pontiff of the World will we call him, the Poet and inspired Maker; who Prometheus-like, can shape new Symbols, and bring new Fire from Heaven to fix it there. . . .

That Fire from Heaven Lindsay names Muspel-fire, taking the name "Muspel" I suspect from *Sartor Resartus* again, where Carlyle writes of "the Adam-Kadmon, or Primeval Element, here strangely brought into relation with the *Nifl* and *Muspel* (Darkness and Light) of the antique North." Carlyle's juxta-position is of the Kabbalistic Primal Man with the Niflheim or mist-home, the Northern night, and with Muspelheim or bright-home, the Southern realm of light. Lindsay reverses these mythological *topoi,* in one of his many instances of a kind of natural Gnosticism. It may be, though, that here Lindsay followed Novalis, who in Chapter 9, "Klingsohr's Tale," of *Heinrich von Ofterdingen* placed the realm of King Arcturus in a northern region of light. Maskull lands on Tormance in its south, and always goes due north, but dies just before the gateway of Muspel, which he then enters in his spiritual form as Nightspore. But that raises the issues both of quest and questers in this daemonic fantasy, and I need to remark on these issues before I can relate the narrative patterns of *A Voyage to Arcturus* to my incipient theory of literary fantasy.

Novalis and Shelley are the two greatest masters of High Romantic fantasy-quest, and Lindsay descended from both of them. . . . (pp. 8-9)

Lindsay's remorseless death-drive is so much darker than anything in Novalis, even than the *Hymns to the Night.* Shelley is the closer prototype for Maskull's drive beyond the pleasure/pain principle, a prototype that begins in *Alastor,* proceeds through *Prometheus Unbound* and *Epipsychidion,* and culminates in *Adonais* and *The Triumph of Life.* The protagonists of Shelleyan quest are all antithetical beings, set against nature and every merely natural value or affection. I venture the surmise that Shelley's verse-romances had much to do with establishing the theoretical pattern for most of the prose-fantasies that move in the Promethean tradition from Mary Shelley's *Frankenstein* on to Lindsay's *Arcturus.* I would call this pattern a Narcissistic one, in both the Ovidian and the Freudian sense, because the assimilation to one another of the unlikely duo of Narcissus and Prometheus is central to this internalized kind of fantastic quest-romance. Indeed, that curious assimilation, ensuing in a narcissistic Prometheus or Promethean narcist, is the direct cause of what I have been calling the *clinamen* or opening swerve, or ironic reaction-formation, of a theory of literary fantasy. The aggressivity of Promethean quest, turned quite destructively inwards against the self, results from a narcissistic scar, a scar inflicted by nature upon the questing antithetical will. One consequence of this scar is the aesthetic bafflement of literary fantasy, its ironic or allegorical conflict between a stance of absolute freedom and a hovering fear of total psychic over-determination. Shelley's Poet in *Alastor,* like his wife's Victor Frankenstein, is haunted by his *daimon* or dark double, in Frankenstein's case the creature he has made. The Shelleyan wandering Poet, and Frankenstein, and Lindsay's Maskull are all unable to get beyond self-destruction because their profound Narcissism is indistinguishable from their Prometheanism. Like Ovid's Narcissus, every protagonist of fantasy, even the greatest among them, say Don Quixote and Lewis Carroll's Alice, conclude by crying out: "my image no longer deceives me" and "I both kindle the flames and endure them." To state this another way, the Shelleyan quester, the Don, Alice, Maskull, Frankenstein, any true hero or heroine of literary fantasy discovers at last that the only fire they can steal is already and originally their own fire. (p. 10)

The compounding of Narcissism and Prometheanism produces the swerve that begins literary fantasy, a swerve that calls into question [Stanley] Cavell's notion that a fictional tale is a history over which the teller has absolute authority. Neither narcist nor Promethean can transcend human limitations, and the story of Narcissus is as much the tragedy of human sexuality as Prometheus is of human aspiration. . . . [Again] I turn back to read *A Voyage to Arcturus* as a fantasy that triumphantly becomes a narcissistic yet Promethean tragedy.

All through this discourse I keep verging upon an entrance into Lindsay's Tormance, and find great difficulty in negotiating that threshold, so I will allow myself to become more personal even than usual, in order to account for my difficulties on a cognitive as well as an affective basis. Reading Lindsay's book (and I have read it literally hundreds of times, indeed obsessively I have read several copies of it to shreds) is for me at once an experience of great freedom and of tormented psychic over-determination or nightmare. I know of no book that has caused me such an anxiety of influence, an anxiety to be read everywhere in my fantasy imitating it, *The Flight to Lucifer*. . . . Repeated readings have confirmed my initial sense that no other fictional work inflicts such spiritual violence upon its audience. E. H. Visiak . . . accurately observed this strange tonality of *A Voyage to Arcturus:*

> This effect, whatever may be the cause of peculiar subconscious energy that was involved, is violently disturbing. The reader's very intellect is assailed; his imagination is appalled. . . .

I would to a step further than Visiak, and say that Lindsay's violence directly assaults what Freud called the bodily ego, the self's or personality's investment of libido in its own ego, which perhaps by such investment creates the Narcissistic ego. Like Blake's, Lindsay's aim is precisely apocalyptic: our relation to the natural world and to ourselves as natural men and women is to be broken, once and for all. (pp. 11-12)

The four central beings of Lindsay's narrative are Krag, whose hidden name is Surtur; Crystalman, whose other name is Shaping; Maskull, the Promethean quester; and Nightspore, who so mysteriously is Maskull's friend upon earth, but who on Tormance cannot come into existence until Maskull dies. As a fourfold, these have their rather precise equivalents in the mythologies of Blake, Shelley, Yeats and Freud, and to list the equivalents is highly instructive. Krag is Blake's Los, or what Yeats in *A Vision* calls Creative Mind, or Freud the achieved Ego, beyond the narcissistic investment, and so in touch with the Reality Principle, or what Shelley's Prometheus will become only after he is unbound. Crystalman is Blake's Satanic Urizen, or Yeats's Will, the Freudian Superego or the Jupiter of *Prometheus Unbound*. Maskull is Blake's Orc, and rather fascinatingly his name in Yeats's *Vision* is also the Mask, at once the Freudian narcissistic libido and the Shelleyan Pro-

methean. Nightspore, perhaps Lindsay's most surprising personage, is akin to the driving instinctual force or urge that Blake calls Tharmas, Yeats the Body of Fate, Shelley Demogorgon, and Freud the Id, agency of the Unconscious. But further allegorization of Lindsay's narrative must wait until I have clarified its weird shape as narrative. (p. 13)

After the rather unconvincing opening séance, the narrative is puzzlingly inconclusive until the moment that Maskull wakes up in the Arcturan night, to find his companions gone. He will never see Nightspore again, because Nightspore is his own spiritual form, who cannot function upon Tormance until his natural aspect, embodied in Maskull, has died. And there is not the slightest doubt but that Maskull is doom-eager. . . . He is also astonishingly violent, and awesomely capable of enduring the really unbearable climates, regions and beings of the accursed world of Tormance. The typical inhabitant of Tormance is summed up in the description of one particular ogre as someone "who passed his whole existence in tormenting, murdering, and absorbing others, for the sake of his own delight." Since Maskull is hardly interested in his own delight, but only in his own possible sublimity, a very curious narrative principle goes to work as soon as Maskull starts walking due North upon Tormance. It is that singular kind of nightmare some of us dream obsessively, in which you encounter a series of terrifying faces, and only gradually do you come to realize that these faces *are terrified,* and that *you* are the cause of the terror. Maskull himself is at once the most remarkable and most frightening consciousness upon Tormance, and Maskull after all is technically a lost traveller, cut off in space and time. (pp. 13-14)

Lindsay's narrative thus has the shape of a destructive fire seeking for a kindlier flame, but finding nothing because it burns up everything in its path. As we discover only in the book's last scene, after Maskull is dead, there is no Muspel or divine flame anyway, because Nightspore's true encounter with the Sublime, beyond death, results in his beautiful realization "that Muspel consisted of himself and the stone tower on which he was sitting. . . ." By then, the exhausted reader has transferred his identification from Maskull to Nightspore, from Prometheus-Narcissus to what Blake called "the real Man the imagination." It is the progressive exhaustion of the reader, through violence and through identification with Maskull, which is the true plot of Lindsay's narrative, as I will demonstrate by breaking into the text at Chapter XIV, which is Maskull's third morning on Tormance.

By then, Maskull has had a career of endless catastrophe, having suffered four murderous enchantments the previous day, and having been instrumental in at least four murders. Once away from the beings completely entranced by Crystalman, the Pater- or Wilde-like aesthetes Panawe and Joiwind, Maskull plunges into the problematic world of Ifdawn, where he breaks the neck of the hideous Crimtyphon, fails to prevent the murder of Oceaxe by Tydomin, is saved by Krag from being sorbed by Tydomin, himself sorbs Digrung, and then needlessly executes Tydomin and Spadevil. This sequence of disaster is followed by Maskull's vision in the Wombflash Forest, where he sees himself murdered by Krag, and then is shocked unconscious when he attempts to follow Nightspore. When the reader stands with Maskull in the subsequent idyll of the encounter with the gentle fisherman Polecrab and his uncanny wife, Gleameil, then the reader, like Maskull, badly needs a rest. And, for a very few pages, we are rested, but only to be set up for an extraordinary violence, unlike any other narrative effect I have known. With daemonic cunning, even a kind of narrative cruelty, Lindsay introduces children for the first and only time in his book, and they are presented as being the least narcissistic beings upon Tormance, in another reversal of earth-psychology. Each child's ego seems wholly unparanoid, and in no way formed by the self's narcissistic investment. Confronted by children who have never known a narcissistic scar, and whose reactions to their mother's voluntary departure and almost certain death are so much more dignified than any earthly child could manifest, the reader is lulled into an ontological security, a delusive sense that the book's worst violence is past.

This sense is literally detonated upon Swaylone's Island, where the Paterian dictum that all the arts aspire to the condition of music is answered by a vision of music as the most destructive of all the arts. After Earthrid's music has murdered Gleameil, and failed to rid Tormance of Maskull, the quester from earth plays his own music upon the circular lake called Irontick. Maskull forces the Muspel-light to appear, but strains too hard to contract it into a solid form. His intention is to compel Surtur, the true or alien God who actually is Krag, to appear, but if he were successful, surely he would materialize Nightspore, his own spark or *pneuma*, as the Gnostics would have said. Despite the dangerous power of his extraordinary will, Maskull's success is limited. His music kills Earthrid, yet his fire destroys the lake, Earthrid's instrument. When the Muspel-light vanishes, it is because the waters of the lake have fallen through, thus breaking the instrument, the waters in their descent having met Maskull's fire. The category of the aesthetic and the reader's response to the final pastoral element in the narrative have been broken together. Maskull, and the reader, are left exhausted, waiting for the fourth daybreak upon Tormance.

That exhaustion, and the textual violence provoking it, are the uncanny or Sublime splendor of Lindsay's book, and place the book, I would argue, at the very center of modern fantasy, in contrast to the works of the Neochristian Inklings which despite all their popularity are quite peripheral. Tolkien, Lewis and Williams actually flatter the reader's Narcissism, while morally softening the reader's Prometheanism. Lindsay strenuously assaults the reader's Narcissism, while both hardening the reader's Prometheanism and yet reminding the reader that Narcissism and Prometheanism verge upon an identity. Inkling fantasy is soft stuff, because it pretends that it benefits from a benign transmission both of romance tradition and of Christian doctrine. Lindsay's savage masterpiece compels the reader to question both the sources of fantasy, *within the reader,* and the benignity of the handing-on of tradition. Fantasy is shown by Lindsay to be a mode in which freedom is won, if at all, by a fearful agon with tradition, and at the price of the worst kind of psychic over-determination, which is the sado-masochistic turning of aggressivity against the self.

Reluctantly, I forbear further commentary upon Maskull's misadventures, and move on to the instructive moment of his death: instructive, particularly in regard to a theory of fantasy, but highly problematic as to its meaning in the book. The ultimate romance model is certainly the curious wasting-away into death of Shelley's Poet in *Alastor*, yet that death seems a less equivocal triumph than Maskull's ebbing-away into sublimity. With Crystalman barely disguised as the Oscar Wildean Gangnet on one side of him, and the glowering Krag hammering away on the other, Maskull stands for the dignity of the Promethean human caught between contending divinities. But Lindsay ne-

gates the Promethean by an occult triumph, crucial for his dialectic:

> "What is this Ocean called?" asked Maskull, bringing out the words with difficulty.
>
> "Surtur's Ocean."
>
> Maskull nodded, and kept quiet for some time. He rested his face on his arm.
>
> "Where's Nightspore?" he asked suddenly.
>
> Krag bent over him, with a grave expression.
>
> "You are Nightspore."
>
> The dying man closed his eyes, and smiled. Opening them again, a few moments later, with an effort, he murmured, "Who are you?"
>
> Krag maintained a gloomy silence.
>
> Shortly afterwards a frightful pang passed through Maskull's heart, and he died immediately.
>
> Krag turned his head round. "The night is really past at last, Nightspore. . . . The day is here." Nightspore gazed long and earnestly at Maskull's body.
>
> "Why was all this necessary?"
>
> "Ask Crystalman," replied Krag sternly. "His world is no joke. He has a strong clutch . . . but I have a stronger. . . . Maskull was his, but Nightspore is mine."

I quoted the end of this great passage at the beginning of my discourse, and come full circle back to it now, but in I trust the finer tone of a *clinamen,* a swerve into the start of a theory of literary fantasy. What kills Maskull? In an earlier vision, he had seen Krag murdering him, whereas Krag, at the start of the final voyage, prophesies that Crystalman as Gangnet will be the cause of Maskull's death. Lindsay equivocates, as he has to. Every other corpse in this book of endless corpses has the vulgar Crystalman grin upon it, even that of the beautiful High Romantic Sullenbode, who has died for love of Maskull. But Maskull's corpse disappears, without our knowing what final expression it carried. Krag speaks two utterly contradictory truths: to Maskull: "You are Nightspore," and to Nightspore: "Maskull was his." In death, Maskull becomes Nightspore; in life the Narcissus in him kept him Crystalman's. The discursive contradiction is at the heart of the fantasy mode: Promethean freedom or striving for freedom implicates quester, writer, and reader more deeply in the bondage of Narcissus, and a form that promises under-determination takes on both the strength and the nightmare quality of over-determination.

I cannot leave *A Voyage to Arcturus* . . . without a few words of sheer praise for a book that has affected me personally with more intensity and obsessiveness than all the works of greater stature and resonance of our time. Nothing else in English since Blake and Shelley, that I know of, has found its way back so surely to that early romance world where gods and men meet and struggle as equals or near-equals. (pp. 14-17)

Harold Bloom, "'Clinamen': Towards a Theory of Fantasy," in Bridges to Fantasy, *George E. Slusser, Eric S. Rabkin, Robert Scholes, eds., Southern Illinois University Press, 1982, pp. 1-20.**

ADDITIONAL BIBLIOGRAPHY

Rabkin, Eric S. ''The Fantastic and Escape.'' In his *The Fantastic in Literature*, pp. 42-73. Princeton: Princeton University Press, 1976.
> Discusses the serious issues addressed in *A Voyage to Arcturus*, such as the relativity of morality, the nature of heightened perception, and the development of existential nihilism, which set the novel apart from many other works of fantasy.

Raff, Melvin. ''The Structure of *A Voyage to Arcturus*.'' *Studies in Scottish Literature* XV (1980): 262-67.
> Discusses each day of Maskull's journey in *A Voyage to Arcturus* in relation to his physical and spiritual transformations. Raff maintains that Lindsay's novel is structured so that the reader might follow the process of Maskull's discovery of the true nature of existence.

Schofield, Jack. ''Cosmic Imagery in *A Voyage to Arcturus*.'' *Extrapolation* XIII, No. 2 (May 1972): 146-51.
> Explicates the allegorical intent of *A Voyage to Arcturus*, concentrating on the Promethean myth that is central to the work and the dual natures of the supernatural beings.

Scholes, Robert, and Rabkin, Eric S. ''*A Voyage to Arcturus*.'' In their *Science Fiction: History, Science, Vision*, pp. 207-13. New York: Oxford University Press, 1977.
> An examination of the ways in which Lindsay utilized the conventions of science fiction and fantasy in *A Voyage to Arcturus* to create a powerful moral odyssey which questions the fundamental nature of reality.

Sykes, Christopher. ''Looking Back at Novels.'' *Books and Bookmen* XXIII, No. 11 (August 1978): 42-3.*
> Praises the storyline of *The Violet Apple* but also notes the stilted, dated style of Lindsay's prose.

Wolfe, Gary K. ''David Lindsay and George MacDonald.'' *Studies in Scottish Literature* XII, No. 2 (October 1974): 131-45.*
> Discusses the influence of the Scottish fantasy writer George MacDonald on Lindsay. While Wolfe finds many similar themes and devices in the works of the two writers, he notes that MacDonald was more successful than Lindsay at adapting his fiction to the public's taste. Wolfe considers both writers worthy of more critical study than they have received.

————. *David Lindsay*. Starmont Reader's Guide, edited by Roger C. Schlobin, no. 9. Starmont House, 1982, 64 p.
> Outlines the development of Lindsay's career and presents a synopsis of his major novels.

Liu E

1857-1909

(Also transliterated Liu T'ieh-yün; also wrote under the pseud-onym of Liu Ngo) Chinese novelist.

Liu is best known for his novel *Lao Ts'an yu-chi (The Travels of Lao Ts'an)*, which critics consider one of the finest examples of observation and description in early twentieth-century Chinese literature. Conforming to a narrative tradition prominent during the Ch'ing Dynasty (1644-1912), *The Travels of Lao Ts'an* is told through the eyes of a wandering scholar-author who pro-vides detailed, often satirical, descriptions of the places and events he encounters.

Liu was born into a family that traced its lineage to the Sung Dynasty (1127-1163). An energetic, curious child, he dis-played interest in a wide range of subjects, and later engaged in passionate, erratic periods of study of medicine, music, poetry, astronomy, and military science. After his father's death, Liu went to Yangchow where he lived a monastic life and studied with a teacher of the T'ai-ku religious sect, which combines the philosophies of Confucianism, Buddhism, and Taoism. This period of religious commitment and study sub-dued Liu's impetuous nature to a degree, and developed in him a strong sense of social responsibility and compassion for his fellow human beings. For a period of time after leaving Yangchow, Liu pursued a career in medicine, with which he soon became disenchanted, and then devoted his energies to starting a printing house in Shanghai. When this venture failed, Liu was forced to return to his childhood home in Huaian, Kiangsu. In the following year, 1888, the Yellow River flooded the nearby Honan region and Liu pioneered an innovative flood-control project. As a result, he was appointed flood control adviser of three provinces, which began his career in public service. Progressively minded, he attempted to persuade gov-ernment officials to build a railway system across China to promote industrial growth and commerce. His ambition and foresight made him several powerful conservative enemies in the government who were suspicious of his motives for de-veloping a railway and disapproved of the foreign intervention such a project would require. In 1900, when a wide-spread famine occurred during the Boxer Rebellion, Liu purchased rice from Russian soldiers encamped in a Peking granary and distributed it to starving citizens. This philanthropic act further aggravated his enemies, who saw it as a presumptuous mis-appropriation of government property. After the Rebellion Liu invested in numerous business ventures, many of which failed, and became involved in several archeological projects that proved of crucial importance to the study of early Chinese history. Between 1903 and 1907 he negotiated to purchase a large tract of land with the intention of opening a railroad. Government officials who were envious of Liu's shrewd and profitable ma-neuver accused him of buying land to encourage foreign in-tervention in China's economy. This charge was made re-peatedly with little effect until it was brought in conjunction with a charge concerning the grain distribution incident of 1900. In 1908, Liu was arrested and sent to a remote province in Chinese Turkistan, where he died the following year.

The Travels of Lao Ts'an, originally published in thirty-four magazine installments between 1904 and 1907, is typical of late Ch'ing Dynasty fiction in that it is a loosely-constructed, episodic work that presents action in a series of vignettes. Some critics have doubted that Liu actually wrote the entire novel, speculating that it was completed by a young male relative. *Travels* is both autobiographical and allegorical in nature. Liu modeled the hero, Lao Ts'an, after himself, making him a physician with an interest in engineering and giving·him keen critical faculties that are frequently aimed at the injustices dealt the citizenry by unscrupulous government officials. In the first chapter, for example, China is allegorically represented by a large ship that is in danger of sinking under the weight of old and new masts, which symbolize the country's cumbersome old and new bureaucracy. The other prominent characters in *Travels* were largely drawn from individuals connected with China's political scene in Liu's day, as well as his personal friends and enemies.

Because of its structure and sophisticated method of social criticism, *Travels* has been compared to Voltaire's *Candide* and other works of Western satire. The philosophy Liu presents in it resembles that of T'ai-ku, though an additional aspect of the moral and philosophical vision in *Travels* is a Western endorsement of individual enterprise and success, which in turn contributes to an enhanced quality of life for the entire society. *Travels* was immediately popular upon publication in serial form, because it was perceived as a prophetic work anticipating the civil unrest and cultural change China would experience in the twentieth century. In expressing Lao Ts'an's disillusion-ment over the corruption of the Manchu empire, Liu was ac-tually revealing his own intuitive grasp of China's social sit-uation and its impending revolution. *Travels* has been praised by critics for the broad scope of its commentary and the pre-cision of its descriptive passages. Critics especially note Liu's facility at describing poetical and musical performances, which provide passages of lyrical beauty in what is predominantly a social critique written in vernacular language.

Although Liu wrote several other fictional works, none of them approached the level of accomplishment or popularity of *Trav-els*. It is upon this work alone that his literary reputation was made and rests.

PRINCIPAL WORKS

*Lao Ts'an yu-chi (novel) 1925
  [*Mr. Derelict* (abridged version), 1948; *The Travels of Lao Ts'an*, 1952]

*This work first appeared serially in magazines from 1904-1907.

H. Y. YAND AND G. M. TAYLER (essay date 1948)

[*Yand and Tayler are the translators of* Mr. Derelict, *an abridged version of* The Travels of Lao Ts'an. *In the following excerpt from the preface to* Mr. Derelict, *they interpret the work as an expression of Liu's sadness over China's decadent state, and note the ways in which he used autobiographical and historical material in the creation of characters and the development of themes.*]

In one life-time Liu Ngo had achieved not a little. His work on the Yellow River, the opening of the Shansi iron-mine, the distribution of rice to starving people in Peking, the discovery of the oracle bones and the writing of **Mr. Derelict** were achievements any single one of which might have made a man proud. But active, creative and at times even luxurious as was his life, it was tinged throughout with bitterness and melancholy, the melancholy of all far-sighted Chinese of that period, who, while they might lead the life of cultured epicureans themselves, could not fail to realise that their traditional society with all that they valued was passing away, and the future offered no hope. Thus although Liu Ngo's actions were the positive expression of clear-sighted patriotism, his book was an expression of a deep pessimism, for he knew that all his efforts could only serve to patch up something that was beyond repair. In his own introduction to **Mr. Derelict** he explained that the book was wrung from him as a cry of anguish: *Now we grieve for our own life, for our country, for our society and for our culture. The greater our grief the more bitter our outcry; and thus this book was written. The game of chess is drawing to a close and we are growing old. How can we refrain from lamentation?* So he expressed his sadness at the decadence of China.

This novel is largely autobiographical, for the hero is easily recognisable as Liu Ngo by his profession of physician, his interest in the Yellow River and his attitude towards officialdom in general. The first chapter of the book is allegorical. Huang Jui-ho (the character "huang" meaning yellow in Chinese) symbolises the Yellow River, whose sickness broke out every year and could not be cured by ordinary physicians. The boat in danger of being wrecked is China, the four men at the helm being the four ministers of war, the six old masts standing for the six old departments of war and the two new masts for the two newly created departments. The length of the boat was two hundred and forty feet, symbolising the twenty-four provinces of China, while the thirty feet on the north-east side were the three north-eastern provinces of Manchuria, and the ten feet on the east stood for Shantung province. China in the past had relied upon experience and precedent in guiding the ship of State, but such methods would not serve in time of crisis, and the gift of a compass to the pilot symbolises the scientific spirit of the West which would enable statesmen to set a definite course and take effective steps to follow it. The description of those who instigated trouble and advocated a resort to violence suggests that the writer was against revolution.

Of the other characters in the novel, Yü Hsien was drawn from life, being the leader of the Boxer Rising who won fame as an official in Shantung; while Chang Yao, the Governor of Shantung, is the Governor Chang of the novel, and Shih Shan-ch'ang, Liu Ngo's chief antagonist in river conservancy, is probably the Inspector Shih of the book. (pp. 10-12)

The unique literary merit of **Mr. Derelict** lies largely in the descriptive passages. Apart from the first chapter of **Private Lives of the Chinese Scholars (Ju Lin Wai Shih)** which contains certain fine descriptive passages, traditional Chinese novels are confined in general to narrative and dialogue, and in this respect Liu Ngo excels all his predecessors, for his sketches both of people and of scenery are unsurpassed. (pp. 12-13)

H. Y. Yand and G. M. Tayler, *in a preface to* Mr. Derelict *by Liu Ngo, George Allen & Unwin Ltd., 1948, pp. 7-13.*

HAROLD SHADICK   (essay date 1952)

[*Shadick is an American educator and translator specializing in Chinese literature. In the following excerpt, taken from the introduction to his translation of* The Travels of Lao Ts'an, *Shadick discusses Liu's moral philosophy and the criticisms of the Chinese political system presented in the novel.*]

From the point of view of worldly career Liu T'ieh-yün's life was a failure, and **The Travels of Lao Ts'an** is the expression of his disillusionment. In the author's preface he compares himself with the ancient author of the famous poem *Li Sao* ("Encountering Sorrow") and other writers of novels and dramas, saying that he wrote in tears to express his lifelong sorrows. It would be wrong, however, to infer that the book is a long complaining wail. The prevailing mood is rather one of genial interest in life in all its forms, with a realization of the suffering that human beings inflict—mainly through ignorance or thoughtlessness—on one another. Whatever he writes about, Liu T'ieh-yün shows keen observation of reality and brings to his description a mellow mind steeped in literature and refined by music and art. He is a happy fusion of the man of action and the meditative man. Mr. Liu Ta-shen tells that no matter how occupied his father might be with business or politics, he never failed in the evening to light his pot of incense, play on his *ku ch'in* (the long horizontal lute, instrument par excellence of the scholar), and read some poetry or classics. Though Lao Ts'an, who represents the author, is an educated man and well received in official circles, and, though he enjoys whiling away an hour reading poetry, is always interested in painting and calligraphy, and goes about covering inn walls with poems of his own composition, he is as far removed as possible from the conventional literary man of the official class, dressed in silks and furs, who sits over his books and is afraid to soil his hands. He wears cotton clothes and refuses to accept a gown lined with fox; he is equally at home talking with high officials and talking with innkeepers. He buys some bean curd, peanuts, and wine and is not ashamed to carry these to his inn himself. The plight of people ruled by a tyrannical official arouses his anger, and when his intervention has resulted in the release of a father and daughter wrongfully accused of murder, he feels as though he has "eaten of the fruit of immortality."

After the literary renaissance began, and especially after 1925, when the Ya Tung edition of **The Travels** was published with a long critical introduction by Hu Shih, the literary merits of the book, its masterly use of the vernacular, and its descriptive power became recognized; it has now achieved a secure place of honor among the novels of China. It is hardly possible to open one of the school anthologies of Chinese literature published during the last twenty years without finding several excerpts included as models of style. (pp. xvi-xvii)

Liu T'ieh-yün makes his novel a vehicle for expressing his ideas on a variety of subjects. His moral philosophy is most fully revealed in the words of the maiden Yü Ku, and Yellow Dragon, the eccentric sage, in the four-chapter episode (chapters viii to xi) of Shen Tzup'ing's visit to the Peach Blossom Mountain. Some Chinese critics have dismissed this section of the book as foolish fantasy. The foreign reader will find it interesting as an example of the jejune pedantry that Chinese writers are often given to; he will also find some profound insights in it.

The author's philosophy—it is almost a religion with him—is a fusion of Confucianism, Buddhism, and Taoism. Most educated Chinese, of course, move freely among these three systems of thought, but Liu is unusually positive in asserting that morality is really a simple matter and that these systems are nonessential elaborations. The important thing for him is to do good and to be unselfish. This is stated in chapter ix, and reiterated most forcibly in chapter xi, where he says that in heaven and earth there are only two parties. "One party preaches the common good: they are the sages and Buddhist Holy Ones, subject to Shang Ti. The other party preaches private interest: they are evil spirits and devils, subject to Ah Hsiu Lo." Doing good is not a matter of following particular rules and observing petty restrictions. Nor is it a matter of repressing the natural desires and inclinations of man. In this he is strongly opposed to the teaching of Chu Hsi who sums up his theory of morals in these words: "The thousands and ten of thousands of words of the Sages all amount to teaching man to hold fast to *t'ien li* (heavenly reason, i.e. innate moral principles) and to subdue *jen yü* (human desires)."

Liu is willing to trust spontaneous human desires and is apprehensive of the tyranny of the reason, which so easily becomes a projection of individual prejudice. He gathers together in a rather arbitrary way passages from the classics to support an ideal of naturalness and sincerity. He daringly applies this to the subject of sex, admitting a freedom of relationship that avoids crass sensuality, though it seems to allow proximity and even physical intimacy, and is raised by intellectual and spiritual companionship to something comparable to, though different from, Western romantic love. This theme is more fully developed in the second part of the novel, *A Nun of T'aishan*.

He is prepared to face the facts of human experience and sees that apparent evil may contribute to ultimate good. The references in chapter xii to the overabundance of life and the necessary destruction of the surplus, as also to the key position of Force Supreme, show the influence of Darwinian biology and Western physics. The naturalism or positivism of Western scientific philosophy can easily be accommodated to Liu's Taoistic thought, which views life from an unsentimental and almost amoral point of view. Safeguarded from all dogmatism and fanaticism, it gives its blessing to anybody who lives freely and fulfills his destiny without encroaching on the freedom of others.

One reason for the early popularity of *The Travels* was that on the strength of the conversation in chapter xi it was accepted by many people as a prophetic book written between 1894-1900 that foretold accurately the Boxer Rebellion in 1900. Since that "prophecy" was fulfilled, it was natural to expect that the great events promised for 1910 and 1914 would materialize. The novel was actually written between 1904 and 1907, but the "prophecy" of a revolution in 1910 (though the author, of course, thought that the revolution would fail) was a very near guess, as the monarchy was actually overthrown in 1911. The author was not, however, really attempting to write prophecy, but was expressing his intense awareness of impending internal changes in China, and was even thinking in terms of a new world culture in which China would take her place.

Liu T'ieh-yün was opposed to doctrinaire extremes and to violent revolution. This is clear from his description of the du-

plicity of a revolutionary demagogue in the allegory in chapter i, and from the attack on the Boxers and revolutionaries in chapter xi. Satire on office-hunting, jealousy, and other corruptions among officials which forms the staple of the *Revelations of Official Life* plays a much smaller part in *The Travels*, but a great deal is suggested by a few words. Thus, in the first part of chapter iv we have a picture of selfish office-seekers that could only have been drawn by one who had been in the hurly-burly of official life himself.

The main political criticism in the book is reserved for the type of official who is honest and conscientious but bigoted, narrow, and without the suppleness of mind that will enable him to evaluate actual situations and make allowances for human nature. Honest officials in China have for hundreds of years been described as *ch'ing kuan* (pure officials), and as Hu Shih points out in his Introduction to *The Travels*, where honesty has been joined with intelligence as in men like Pao Cheng of the eleventh century, such men are admirable in every way. But where a man is pure and at the same time bigoted and stupid, his honesty makes him all the more dangerous since he is liable to be trusted and given high position. . . . Many chapters of the novel are devoted to the maladministration of justice of Yü Hsien (chapters iv, v, vi) and Kang Pi (chapters xv-xviii). The limitations of such "honest" officials are summarized when the wise Prefect Pai, having proved by a little common sense and ingenuity that Kang Pi's snap judgment in a murder case was wrong, proceeds to diagnose his weakness: "The pure and incorruptible man naturally arouses our admiration, but he often has one bad characteristic: he thinks that all other people in the world are little and mean, and that he is the only superior man."

If Liu T'ieh-yün opposes revolution, his positive recommendations for the political reform of China would seem to be these:

(1) A high standard of intelligence as well as honesty should be required of officials;

(2) The freemasonry of officials should not prevent the cashiering of the incompetent. This idea appears in Lao Ts'an's conversation with Governor Chuang (chapter xix);

(3) Foreign advice should be sought and foreign techniques adopted. (pp. xvii-xx)

(4) Over-energetic government should be avoided. All positive reforms should be gradual, moderate, and adapted to existing conditions. (p. xx)

Judged by the Western conception of a novel, the book lacks unity both of plot and subject matter. It is the author's one attempt at this type of writing and was written in installments when he was about fifty years of age. This probably accounts for occasional carelessness and inconsistency in the text. In spite of its desultoriness, however, the book has a unity of feeling produced by the author's tireless interest in people and things, his moral integrity, and his pervading sense of humor. Seen through his keen and sympathetic eyes, nothing is too humble to hold interest.

As in most Chinese literature before the revolution, whether in the classical or the vernacular language, the influence of tradition is everywhere present. Precedents could be found for almost every incident and every theme. The dream in the first chapter has its counterpart in the supernatural setting of the prologues to most Chinese novels. The idyllic, otherworldly atmosphere of Shen Tzu-p'ing's night in the Peach Blossom

Mountain is a typical Chinese fantasy apt to be introduced into otherwise realistic tales. Poisoned cakes, "planted" stolen goods, and accusations of theft based on the measurements of a piece of stolen cloth occur in earlier stories. The theme of inviting a mountain recluse to assist in the government goes back to Chu-ko Liang, 181-234 [A.D.], and earlier. . . . The book preserves the form of the traditional novel which purports to be a series of installments of a storyteller's narrative. Thus each chapter begins with a formula like "It is further told" and ends in suspense, with the promise that the suspense will be relieved in the next chapter, that is, the next recitation.

In the opinion of Hu Shih, the unique achievement of the author is in the descriptions of scenery and of music. In place of the stereotyped descriptions to be found in the earlier novels which reflect the sedentary bookishness of the Chinese scholar and the too-great wealth of ready-made phrases available to him from centuries of nature poetry and artistic prose, Liu T'ieh-yün attempts to express with precision and in his own words what he has seen and heard. The result is a direct yet imaginative style that convinces the reader of the reality of the experiences described. (pp. xxi-xxii)

Apart from such elaborate passages of description the book abounds with fine touches which produce an impression of reality. The account of the arrival of Shen Tzu-p'ing at the mountain villa and the description of everything he saw there (chapters ix and x) employ subtle art to create an atmosphere in which the natural and the supernatural are blended. This unearthliness is something which can be felt even by the Westerner if he responds with sympathetic imagination to the influence of Chinese scenery and architecture, reinforced by literary and mythological associations. Similarly anyone who has traveled through the towns and villages of the great North China plain will recognize the authenticity of Lao Ts'an's descriptions of life in the inns and yamens and on the roads of Shantung. (p. xxii)

> *Harold Shadick, in an introduction to* The Travels of Lao Ts'an *by Liu T'ieh-yün (Liu E), edited and translated by Harold Shadick, Cornell University Press, 1952, pp. vii-xxiii.*

JOHN D. COLEMAN   (essay date 1976)

[*In the following excerpt, Coleman discusses how the disintegration of Confucian values in nineteenth-century Chinese society affected* The Travels of Lao Ts'an, *illustrating the ways in which Liu E maintained a traditional stance by expounding values of Confucianism which were no longer a vibrant part of Chinese culture. Coleman begins by comparing* Travels *to Wu Ching-tzu's famous satire* The Scholars, *which was written at the beginning of the Ch'ing dynasty, when the Confucian tradition dominated Chinese culture.*]

The Scholars and **The Travels** [*of Lao Ts'an*] stand as acknowledged literary landmarks, the former near the beginning, the latter near the end of the Ch'ing dynasty. In the interim the Ch'ing passed through the familiar cyclical pattern of dynastic consolidation and decline. The fall of the Ch'ing dynasty, however, was not just the end of another dynasty. In the past the Confucian world view had always survived dynastic decline and fall, and had, with few interruptions, continued to function both as a state doctrine and, in fact, as perhaps the principal mainstay of Chinese civilization itself. But this privileged and unique role of Confucianism did not ultimately survive the impact of the West following the Opium War (1839-42), and

Confucianism, as a viable philosophical, social and governmental system, perished together with the Ch'ing dynasty. This was a break of unprecedented severity in the continuity of Chinese civilization and, necessarily, all areas of Chinese culture were profoundly affected. Standing as landmarks at opposite ends of the same dynasty, *The Scholars* and **The Travels** are, nevertheless, separated by the gulf left by the demise of Confucian tradition, and precisely because of this gulf we should not be surprised that the differences between the two novels prove more revealing than the similarities. In this paper, I mean to examine some of the differences in style and content between *The Scholars* and **The Travels,** and to relate these differences to the gradual waning of the Confucian tradition during the Ch'ing dynasty.

Wu Ching-tzu wrote *The Scholars* during the High Ch'ing, a time of cultural unity, self-confidence, and unprecedentedly strong imperial power. Then, as in the past, China viewed itself as the absolute center of civilization, surrounded on its periphery by lesser peoples, with little to offer China culturally. The dominant political world view of the time, we may say, was Chinese "culturalism." According to this doctrine, the emperor, as *t'ien-tzu* . . . , son of heaven, ruled in the name of Chinese culture over *t'ien-hsia* . . . , all under heaven, i.e., in theory at least, over the entire world. . . . At the core of Chinese culturalism we find, of course, the Confucian imperial system, with its emphasis on Confucian *li* . . . , ritual. During the High Ch'ing, Chinese culturalism seemed as unassailable as did the son of heaven himself. Wu's value system, we shall see, and in turn *The Scholars* itself, rested upon this intact premise of culturalism, not yet disturbed in any of its essentials by the impact of the West. Both, therefore, reflect the *consonance* of the times themselves.

Consonance is carried over, too, into the style of *The Scholars.* Wu Ching-tzu continued most of the Ming-Ch'ing novelistic conventions, and we may therefore call the style of the novel traditional. There are, however, also major stylistic innovations, such as the eschewal of poetry and the use in its place of lyrical prose descriptions. Another innovation is the striking refinement of characterization techniques.

Indeed, the major feature of the style is its innovativeness, its creativity. Does this contradict the label, "traditional"? Not at all. In fact, the one implies the other, for to truly continue a tradition requires "a combination of reverence for the society's symbols with freedom of revision; it presupposes a state of tension which leads to development within a tradition." When a novel, like *The Scholars,* furthers a tradition, it may be said to be moving in harmony with the developmental current of that tradition and so to stand in a relationship of *consonance* to it.

Liu T'ieh-yün wrote **The Travels** on the eve of the collapse of the Ch'ing Dynasty. With the Ch'ing, Chinese "culturalism" also collapsed, having been gradually and painfully replaced by Chinese nationalism, based on the relatively later concept of *kuo-chia* (nation). Liu's value system, and in turn **The Travels** itself, are naturally products of this wrenching cultural and political transformation, and inevitably reflect, therefore, the *dissonance* of those times.

Dissonance is also reflected in the style of **The Travels.** Like Wu, Liu T'ieh-yün continued many of the Ming-Ch'ing novelistic conventions, but we must, nevertheless, call Liu's style *traditionalistic,* rather than traditional. Of traditionalistic authors, D. H. Lawrence wrote: "They keep up convention, but they cannot carry on a tradition. There is a tremendous difference between the two things. To carry on a tradition, you must add something to the tradition.'' There are, to be sure, stylistic innovations in **The Travels**. As examples the prose passages which describe nature or music are usually singled out. But on a more fundamental level, Liu appears to cling tenaciously to the bulk of Ming-Ch'ing stylistic conventions, which, in the context of the times, lends the novel a peculiarly anachronistic air. Peculiar, because despite the fact that in **The Travels** the author often insightfully grapples with modern exigencies and thus, at least at times, looks forward in content, in style he looks back to a more comfortable past. When a novel, like **The Travels**, clings to tradition rather than furthering it, it may be said to be occluding the developmental current of that tradition and so to stand in a relationship of *dissonance* to it.

Why then, given that both *The Scholars* and **The Travels** are episodic in nature, does *The Scholars* appear cohesive, whereas **The Travels** does not? The thesis of this paper is that *The Scholars* maintains cohesiveness because Wu Ching-tzu possessed a value system, both unified within itself and viable in relation to its time, which he successfully embodied in both the content and style of *The Scholars*; *The Travels* lacks cohesiveness and ultimately flounders, because the value system which Liu embodied in the content and style of the novel is neither unified within itself nor viable in relation to its times. (pp. 62-4)

In his introduction to his translation of **The Travels** [see excerpt dated 1952], Harold Shadick makes the following general evaluation of the novel:

> In spite of its desultoriness, the book has a unity
> of feeling produced by the author's tireless interest in people and things, his moral integrity,
> and his pervading sense of humor.

The combination of traits mentioned by Shadick is, to be sure, present in **The Travels**, but the traits are not, in my opinion, sufficient to make the novel cohesive. Nor is it simply a question of desultoriness. Rather, the desultoriness is, in the case of **The Travels**, itself symptomatic of a contradiction in Liu T'ieh-yün's value system so fundamental that it perforce ruled out the possibility of **The Travels**' being cohesive. This contradiction arises from the conflict, on the one hand, between Liu's desire that China change in order to cope with the perilous situation then confronting it, and, on the other hand, that China remain the same in order to preserve traditional Confucian values. Liu's thinking constitutes, I believe, a late reflection of the *t'i-yung* . . . substance-function controversy expressed by Chang Chih-tung, among others, several decades before **The Travels** was written. The *t'i-yung* formula was an attempt to devise a rationale whereby a degree of Westernization could be sanctioned (*yung*), mostly in ''peripheral'' areas such as warfare and technology, while carefully preserving intact Confucian tradition and values (*t'i*). We know from history that neither the *t'i-yung* formula, nor any other formula for that matter, was ultimately able to preserve the *t'i* of Confucian tradition. . . . As Confucian values gradually failed in practice, and were replaced by Western values or Chinese-Western syncretisms, attempts were made by some thinkers to preserve Confucian values in limbo, as it were, apart from any practice. But, in effect, this was tantamount to embalming these values. Here we can speak of the substitution of romantic traditionalism for real tradition, substitution of an emotional yearning for a traditional matrix of values for real traditional values.

Liu desired change, then, in order to cope with modern exigencies, but hoped that this change would be minimal and peripheral, leaving the traditional core of Confucian values intact. Basically, we have said, this desire recapitulates the *t'i-yung* formula, and also reflects therefore the latter's contradiction. Let us now turn to Liu T'ieh-yün's value system, as expressed in **The Travels**, to see how it reflects the contradictions outlined above.

We are on much surer ground in trying to ascertain the author's values in **The Travels** than was the case in *The Scholars*. **The Travels** is full of overt didacticism, and there are in addition many lengthy direct statements, which may be taken as statements of the author's values. There is no need therefore to resort to indirect methods. We may begin by examining two topics which represent the opposite poles of the *t'i-yung* contradiction as it appears in **The Travels**: Liu's moral philosophy (*t'i*) and his patriotic concern with the state of the nation (*yung*).

The very first chapter of **The Travels** immediately involves us in Liu's profound concern for the plight of China and its citizenry on the eve of the 1911 revolution. In the first chapter we find Lao Ts'an's pointedly didactic, but nevertheless, moving dream about the Ch'ing ship of state:

> It was a great ship, twenty-three or twenty-four
> *chang* long, but there were many places in which
> it was damaged. On the east side was a gash
> about three *chang* long, into which the waves
> were pouring with nothing to stop them . . . No
> part of the ship was free from scars. The eight
> men looking after the sails were doing their
> duty faithfully, but each one looked after his
> own sail as though each of the eight was on a
> separate boat: they were not working together
> at all.

Asked what should be done about the ship's distress, the hero, Lao Ts'an, replies:

> As I see it the crew have not done wrong intentionally; there are two reasons why they have
> brought the ship to this intolerable pass. What
> two reasons? The first is that they are accustomed to sailing on the Pacific Ocean and can
> only live through 'pacific' days. When the wind
> is still and the waves are quiet, the conditions
> of navigation make it possible to take things
> easy. But, they were not prepared for today's
> big wind and heavy sea and therefore are bungling and botching everything. The second reason is that they do not have a compass. When
> the sky is clear, they can follow traditional
> methods, and when they can see the sun, moon
> and stars they can't make serious mistakes in
> their course. This could be called 'depending
> on heaven for your food.' Who could have told
> that they would run into this overcast weather
> with the sun, moon and stars covered up by
> clouds, leaving them with nothing to steer by?

To attempt to remedy this situation, Lao Ts'an and his friends row out to the larger ship in order to supply it with a compass. But, so great is the confusion and xenophobic panic of the crew and passengers that their reaction seems only to insure the ship's final destruction. (pp. 71-3)

This very disquieting passage is notable because it poignantly and realistically depicts the dilemma of late Ch'ing society. Traditional methods of governance are clearly no longer adequate to cope with modern conditions. The ship of state has become damaged in the fray, and what is worse, has lost its bearings, since it no longer had adequate means of navigation. A compass, which here seems to indicate reliance on the artifices of Western technology, is needed to replace the more natural navigation by the stars, i.e. orientation by means of tradition. Liu seems to acknowledge here that a certain amount of Westernization is necessary if China is to survive. Yet, he also accurately depicts the tragic disorientation resulting from the waning of tradition. Panic and violence, a sense of profound impotence and intense grief, characterize this disorientation. (p. 74)

Having successfully sketched the broad outlines of the crisis in Ch'ing society, Liu extends his concern to some lesser, but nevertheless critical national problems as well. The important subject of flood control, an area where Liu himself made substantial contributions, is dealt with at great length in *The Travels*. Like Wu Ching-tzu, Liu also has much to say about the immense harm done to society by corrupt officials, but in a new twist he also points out that principled, but myopically overzealous officials can be equally harmful.

The above sections of *The Travels* reflect the *yung* side of the *t'i-yung* contradiction within Liu's thinking. These sections show real insight into and deep concern with the many facets of the national crisis. Furthermore, they are all characterized by directness and unquestioned relevance to the problems being discussed.

Because China's laborious and painful transition from *t'ien-hsia* (all under heaven) to *kuo-chia* (nation) is from the outset depicted by Liu with such relevance, insight and passion, we expect the novel to develop along these same lines, and to maintain the tone of serious inquiry into the national dilemma. The expectations are soon disappointed, however, for we find that Liu can sustain relevance only as long as none of his deeper Confucian values (*t'i*) are threatened. The moment these values are threatened, traditionalistic topics infiltrate Liu's thinking, thereby occluding the real issues at hand.

An example of this phenomenon is the long discourse given on revolution by the old sage, Yellow Dragon. Yellow Dragon begins by contrasting the short-lived Boxers to the more serious, long-term threat of revolution. Understandably, revolution was a volatile and threatening topic to Liu, who was vitally concerned with preserving tradition, and so we are not surprised when Yellow Dragon proceeds to analyze at length the nature of revolution in terms of the *Book of Changes*. The entire explanation is unalloyed traditionalism and is totally lacking in relevance. Moreover, because the problem itself is so urgent and the explanation offered so inadequate, the effect of this entire passage is highly disconcerting. In passages such as this, we see, not the author's artistic grasping of his nation's dilemmas but, on the contrary, his strong personal need to block those threatening aspects of reality, so that his more traditional views (*t'i*) need not be sacrificed.

Liu's moral philosophy, we shall find, is also based on such evasion of reality. To begin with, the context in which Liu chooses to introduce his philosophical views itself points toward evasiveness. In chapters eight through eleven, Shen Tzu-p'ing visits Peach Blossom Mountain, the lofty retreat of Yellow Dragon and Yü Ku, and there engages in long-winded

philosophizing with these two quasi-immortal beings. This section of the novel has as a stylistic precedent the numerous interludes in earlier Ming-Ch'ing novels which take place in heaven, and it seems thus to be airily and disturbingly detached from the realistic concerns of the rest of the novel. What kind of philosophy do we find expounded here? Liu's philosophy appears to be a traditionally syncretic fusion of Confucianism, Taoism and Buddism, much like the creed of the T'ai-ku sect, to which Liu belonged for a time. Of the three philosophies, Confucianism is decidedly the most important:

> "If the Confucian school is the greatest, wherein lies its greatness? I venture to ask you to explain." The maiden (Yu Ku) said, "Their similarity consists in encouraging man to be good, leading man to be disinterested. If all men scheme for private advantage, then the Empire is in chaos. Only Confucianism is thoroughly disinterested."

Yü Ku goes on to qualify this by explaining that she has in mind pre-Sung Confucianism only. Here Liu seems to be influenced by the Han learning and New Text Movement of the late Ch'ing era.

Liu's moral philosophy apparently engendered a considerable degree of discomfort in Harold Shadick, for in his introduction Shadick has this to say about Liu's philosophy:

> The foreign reader will find it interesting as an example of the jejune pedantry that Chinese writers are often given to; he will also find some profound insights in it.

Discomfort arises because instinctively we feel that despite its occasional profound insights Liu's philosophizing is nothing but philosophizing in the clouds, serving principally as temporary relief from the oppressive reality of earth. It is, in short, an obfuscation.

A similar situation obtains when we examine some of the lyrical descriptive passages, such as the one at the beginning of this paper. There are many passages in *The Travels* which are highly lyrical and skillfully crafted. But in the end these passages are, like Liu's moral philosophy, jejune traditionalism, because they too are detached and simply float above the rest of the novel like pleasant irrelevancies. Since they do not relate directly to the primary if often unconscious concern of the novel, namely the impending collapse of Confucian tradition, they necessarily obfuscate this concern. To realize how much of a distraction these scenes really are, we have only to think of Dostoevsky's novels. Dostoevsky, too, struggled with waning tradition. So preoccupied was he with the cultural and religious crisis of the nineteenth-century West, that we find practically no descriptions of nature at all in his novels, let alone lyrical descriptions. Descriptions of nature would merely have been a distraction.

The various facets of content and style examined above do not work together to produce a cohesive whole. Some reveal and elucidate the burden of the novel, others obfuscate it. The reason for this lack of cohesion, we have seen, is that Liu's value system reflected the *t'i-yung* contradiction, and was therefore not unified.

The times in which Liu lived contributed significantly to his failure. Liu's times were dissonant, in that a major cultural transformation, the collapse of China as *t'ien-hsia* (all under heaven) and the rise of China as *kuo-chia* (nation), had already been under way at least since the time of the Opium War. This all-encompassing transformation led to a schism within Liu's thinking. . . . The times demanded that the imminent demise of tradition be faced. Liu was not able to do this (as did Dostoevsky, for example, in the West) and remained mired in contradictions. We should not judge him too harshly for this, however. Later Chinese writers such as Lu Hsün did face the crisis more directly, but even in Lu Hsün, ambivalence and disorientation resulting from the loss of tradition are still remarkably strong. (pp. 74-7)

We sense in reading *The Travels* that the author had to struggle to maintain optimism. This is so, I believe, because on some level Liu had realized the gravity of the situation of late Ch'ing China and the futility of the *modus vivendi* between tradition and flux which his values represented. In *The Travels,* therefore, we find an underlying sense of impotence, pessimism and grief which the author's traditionalism could gloss over, but was powerless to allay. (p. 77)

> *John D. Coleman, "With and without a Compass: 'The Scholars', 'The Travels of Lao Ts'an', and the Waning of Confucian Tradition during the Ch'ing Dynasty," in* Tamkang Review, *Vol. VII, No. 2, October, 1976, pp. 61-79.*

DONALD HOLOCH   (essay date 1980)

[*In the following excerpt, Holoch discusses the allegorical structure of* The Travels of Lao Ts'an. *He maintains that Liu's allegorical technique serves to unify the novel and imbue it with lyrical beauty, while presenting complex social and political commentary. Holoch also analyzes the way in which the main character, Lao Ts'an, functions as the ideal narrator, being primarily a symbol of a heightened, sensitive intellect that observes and records events but remains unchanged by them.*]

If the whole work (and not just the dream episode of the ship of state) is read as an allegory, many otherwise puzzling or unintelligible aspects of *Travels* become functional. Features fundamental to allegory as a form are all prominent in the construction of *Travels:* personification; striking attention to the particulars of visual imagery matched by a deep concern for abstract concepts; action interspersed with extensive commentary; episodic structure and the repetition of similar incidents; the extended metaphor of the journey; and the central contradiction between static accumulation of incident and dynamic movement tending toward change. [In a footnote, the critic states: The characterization is drawn from G. Clifford, *The Transformations of Allegory* (London, 1974), pp. 5, 9, 22, 23, 34.] Since the dream episode is generally accepted as allegory, I will start with that, to show that the allegory does not end when Laocan awakes.

In a brief *wenyan* preface, the author asserts that the essence of mankind is its spiritual nature, which accounts for sorrow; he invokes a series of works written over the millennia purportedly for the purpose of expressing sorrow, and indicates that their meaning must be sought below the surface; he includes his own novel in this elegiac tradition.

The narrative, set in Shandong in the decade before 1900, begins in chapter 1. This chapter has, for purposes of analysis, nine units, the last of which is resolved at the start of chapter 2. We come to realize that chapter 1 is a prologue and that its central figure, Laocan, has symbolic importance. (p. 131)

The settings for chapter 1 have mythical overtones. The town of Qiancheng, recorded in early medieval times, no longer

exists; and Penglai is a utopia associated with immortality. The prologue has two central allegorical events: the treatment of the Yellow River and the vision of the ship of state. Mr. Huang Ruihe is a pun on *Huang he,* Yellow River; the disease is the annual breaking of the dikes, as is evident when Laocan invokes the great Yu, mythological controller of floods, as the originator of the cure. Similarly we know that the sailing ship is a symbol from the inordinate detail of its description and from the sequence of events on board. That the allegory of the ship of state is actually a dream (which began after Huang's feast) we realize only at the start of chapter 2, when Laocan wakes up.

Since the central figure of both allegories is Laocan, and since he wakes from an allegorical dream to an allegorical reality, the nature of the rest of the text is suggested and it is important to specify what Laocan symbolizes in order to get the author's meaning. . . . Laocan is a symbol of the ideal. We know this from a series of contrasts in the prologue. He is distinguished from common people by his learning, from educated officialdom by his honesty, and from top levels of administration by his appreciation of modern technology. Not involved in the questionable practices of bureaucracy, he is always willing to tackle the real problems of China. He can do so with success, in the case of traditional problems, by his familiarity with tradition and particularly those aspects of it which have undeservedly fallen out of practice. He is a man of uncommon vision, for while others celebrate the successful treatment of a traditional problem (river control), he worries about even more serious modern problems. Here his proposals are based on a thorough analysis; unlike more radical proposals they are neither foolishly hasty nor unscrupulous. Laocan is clearly not meant to represent a group or class—he is a socially uncontaminated pure ideal, a selfless morality applied to politics.

The content of Laocan's political vision is essentially this: though China has many problems, the crucial one is the new one posed by the aggression of modernized nations; the solution is the application of technology rather than changes in social structure. The vision is a response to the preceding decade of China's history: defeat in the Sino-Japanese War and consequent competition among imperialist nations to carve out spheres of influence; the Reform Movement which attempted to counter the threat but met government opposition and was succeeded by revolutionary groups.

The allegory of the ship of state is a reactionary rendition of that history. (pp. 132-34)

[In] its judgment of bureaucrat's and revolutionary's treatment of people it is so disingenuous that one wonders if Laocan (who makes the judgment) isn't meant to represent a partial view, narrower than that of the narrator who intends to expose his limitations. But no, Laocan does represent the ideal. It is the ideal of a technocratic elite, which must sustain itself by idealizing the rationality of the ruling group and discrediting all forms of dissent as selfish disregard of national (= technical) progress. The ideal is politically reactionary but under conditions recognized as quite modern—historically a transitional position. (p. 134)

Political power is subjectively regarded, in terms of motive. The prologue re-examines Chinese tradition not only for what is most amenable to technical innovation, but also to establish the moral superiority of the ideal. The reader is meant to like Laocan as a character: the ideal has an ethical as well as a political aspect. Besides being affable, modest, helpful, intelligent, and unaffected, Laocan is a man of principle; and there is a suggestion of the tragic about him, since the likelihood (in the dream allegory) is that his solution for China's key problem will not gain acceptance. . . .

We can expect Laocan, the political symbol, to embody the moral ideal of a sensitive and tragic perception of human experience; the dramatic structure of the prologue—with Laocan, in the midst of a celebration, having visions of a troubled future—suggests that this will be the case. One anticipates a reflective and philosophic novel. (p. 135)

Laocan responds to situations and scenes but is not changed by them; his prime role is as viewer, auditor, commentator, in short as focus of consciousness. . . . What we have in this novel is a series of ideological units . . . linked, through the device of the journey, by an ideal commentator. (pp. 135-36)

There is no dispute about Liu E's preeminence as a lyrical *prose* stylist. Hu Shi and C. T. Hsia observed that Liu E uses prose poetically and in so doing achieves effects worthy of great poetry and far superior to the novel's own passable verse. In *Travels* he attempted to develop, through the 'humble' medium of vernacular prose, aesthetic effects of 'high' *wenyan* literature, of both the reflective essays and the nature lyric.

The poetic element of the novel, however, seems to me to be neither virtuoso display nor diversion from the political content and mimesis of society: it is not something confined to detachable descriptions. The linguistic resources of lyric poetry— rich allusion, coherence of imagery, significant parallelism, all in conjunction with scenic depiction—are at work in the prose of this novel, whether setting is evoked or social interaction is portrayed. That the author does not resort to poetic cliché (as even hostile critics agree) indicates his successful development of lyrical procedures in the medium of prose. (pp. 144-45)

The entire novel can then be interpreted as an allegorical structure with two parallel cycles in which the first, ambiguous, political resolution of the protagonist's concern with injustice is eventually replaced by a more satisfactory metaphysical understanding of the dilemma first posed in the allegorical events of the prologue.

Travels is a product of its times in the prominence of political themes and the exposé of officials. These features are not the central ones, however. We can accept Hsia's view of the novel as 'political' only if we specify that it is profoundly antipolitical, rejecting political action as useless. It is a retreat from the process of change, which seems, in the conservative perspective of the narrative, beyond rational comprehension. The alternative is a concern with cultural values, which are

seen to be, like the Chinese state, under attack. These unchanging values need to be recovered from the great repository of Chinese tradition by a critical intelligence undaunted by orthodox doctrine. They need to be preserved in practice, enacted in a world of individual human relations, where suffering is perennial and perennially in need of remedy. The discord between the ahistoric idealism of the first preface and the historical engagement of the prologue is resolved in the course of the novel by showing that political acts do not achieve the good results intended. An enveloping melancholy is the price of abandoning politics. The lyricism of the novel is elegiac.

The complex and sophisticated conservatism expressed in Liu E's fiction is fully aware that the preservation of values is not automatic and requires a struggle. In turn-of-the-century China, where cataclysmic change stared the intelligentsia in the face, if a theoretical reformulation of 'China' were rejected, then the familiar situations and traditional texts had to be scrupulously re-examined to discover their true nature, and the essential China could be preserved on the basis of recovered truth.

Liu E's artistic method expressed the need to grasp and master the actual detail in a world where all things would otherwise dissolve, to see things as they were so that truth would be revealed. His conservative impulse in a dynamic historical context led to aesthetic innovation. The unprecedented mimetic quality of his descriptions was necessary to embody his overriding ideological concerns. The abandonment of cliché and the new accuracy of detail have diverted critics into discussing the novel in terms of verisimilitude: autobiographical value, accurate representation of objects, imitation of the effects of music, fidelity to contemporaneous social conditions, literalness of the Shandong scenery. Of course Liu E provided ample basis for this critical activity; my aim is not to deny or diminish his mimetic skill. The point is simply that here mimesis is at the service of allegory, and that this relationship is the key to the unity of the novel. (pp. 145-46)

Donald Holoch, " 'The Travels of Laocan': Allegorical Narrative,'' in The Chinese Novel at the Turn of the Century, *edited by Milena Doleželová-Velingerová, University of Toronto Press, 1980, pp. 129-49.*

ADDITIONAL BIBLIOGRAPHY

Review of *The Travels of Lao Ts'an,* by Liu E. Choice IV, No. 10 (December 1967): 1122.
    A favorable review of the novel.

Jack London

1876-1916

(Born John Griffith London) American novelist, short story writer, essayist, journalist, autobiographer, and dramatist.

London was a popular Naturalist whose fiction combined high adventure, socialism, mysticism, Darwinian determinism, and Nietzschean theories of race. Of the fifty books published during his brief career, *The Call of the Wild* is the most famous and widely read. London's fiction, particularly *The Call of the Wild, The Iron Heel, The Sea-Wolf,* and the short stories "Love of Life," "To Build a Fire," and "Bâtard," are considered classics in American literature, and have often been compared with the stories of Joseph Conrad and Rudyard Kipling.

London was born in San Francisco to Flora Wellman, who had been abandoned by her common-law husband of one year. Nine months after the child's birth, Wellman married John London, for whom the infant was named. The family moved often, living on farms and attempting several unsuccessful business schemes at the insistence of London's mother, a proud, erratic, somewhat unstable woman whose actions went unchecked by her gentle but ineffective husband. London's mother inspired in him a pride of race and the will to succeed, but for affection he had to turn to his stepfather and sister. After completing grammar school in Oakland, London worked in a cannery and as a longshoreman; he also became a nocturnal scavenger on San Francisco Bay, styling himself as the "Prince of the Oyster Pirates." While still in his teens he tramped around the country viewing the seamy side of life, which he later depicted in *The Road.* In his spare time London read widely in literature and philosophy, but was most profoundly influenced by the works of Herbert Spencer, Karl Marx, Kipling, and Friedrich Nietzsche. At the age of nineteen he enrolled in high school, completing the course work in one year, then entered the University of California, where he also joined the Socialist Workers Party. After one semester he had to leave college because of lack of money. He went to the Klondike during the gold rush of 1898; a year later he returned to San Francisco penniless, but with a wealth of memories that provided the raw material for his first collection of short stories, *The Son of the Wolf,* which contains violent, colorful adventures about men and animals fighting for survival amidst the "white silence" of the pitiless Yukon wilds. These stories were immensely popular, and several other stories and novels set in Alaska followed, written in the simple, vigorous style that distinguishes London's work. *The Call of the Wild* and *White Fang,* the most highly regarded of these Alaskan books, are characteristic in their exploration of the struggle between the conflicting calls of barbarity and civilization.

In 1900, confident that early success promised impending greatness, London married with the expectation that his wife would cure his wanderlust by providing a stable, well-disciplined family environment that would enable him to produce serious literary works. His wife, however, soon resented the weekly gatherings of intellectuals, hangers-on, and assorted "characters" that London arranged in order to amuse himself with games, pranks, and heated debate. In this setting he met the independent, talkative Charmian Kittredge. She fulfilled London's ideal of the comrade-mate that he depicted in nu-

merous stories and novels. After three years of marriage London and his wife separated, and London married Charmian within a day of his final divorce decree.

In addition to his popular and highly remunerative fiction, London also wrote for various magazines as a journalist. Among other assignments, he was a widely syndicated correspondent during the Russo-Japanese War of 1904-05. He continually sought first-hand experience for his writings, the most important instance being the period in 1902 when he wandered the slums of England disguised as a derelict; he later recorded his observations of poverty and degradation in *The People of the Abyss.* The highest paid writer of his day, London earned more than a million dollars; but financial naiveté and poor judgment were compounded by mismanagement by his trusted employees. The thousands of dollars he poured into labor and materials for his boat, the "Snark," and his dream home, Wolf House, are the most striking examples of his ill-advised faith in his business sense. The destruction of Wolf House, a case of suspected arson, was a devastating event from which London never recovered. In his last years, he was despondent about his failure to produce a male heir, and mounting financial obligations drove him to maintain the by-now taxing thousand-word-a-day writing schedule he had established at the onset of his career. Suffering from constant pain and depression brought on by various maladies, including liver and intestinal disease, London tried to mask his symptoms with drugs and alcohol in order to keep up the self-imposed public image of the invincible man of action. It has been conjectured that his death from an overdose of painkiller was suicide.

The wide variety of experiences and readings that fed London's literary imagination produced the seemingly contradictory world views found in his works. His high regard for the writings of Charles Darwin and Nietzsche is demonstrated by the doctrines of rugged individualism and of the amoral *übermensch* (''superman'') that dominate such early adventure stories as *The Call of the Wild* and *The Sea-Wolf*. *The Call of the Wild* differs drastically from the overly sentimental animal stories popular during London's early career, with his dog protagonist Buck existing unrestrained by the human emotions and morality that limited portrayal of the savagery of nature in other popular novels. Buck's brutality and complete avarice are at the same time repelling and alluring to readers who vicariously participate in his conquests without guilt. In later short story collections such as *South Sea Tales*, London's evolutionary theory took on the sinister aspect of white supremacy reflected in characterizations of Nordic or Anglo-Saxon heroes as conquerors of ''inferior'' island races. Yet, at the time that London was writing these celebrations of the Great Blond Beast, he was also producing thoughtful socialist novels and essays in which he advocated the solidarity of the working class for the betterment of humanity. *The Iron Heel*, a futuristic dystopia, is the most notable example of his political fiction; in this work, London drew upon his experiences as a laborer and his reading of Marx to portray a vision of the rise of fascism in America. Marxist critic Leon Trotsky called the novel ''astonishing'' in its ''prophetic vision of the methods by which the Iron Heel will sustain its domination over crushed mankind.'' As in most of his works, the author projected his own political sympathies into the novel, making his protagonist a socialist leader who champions the cause of labor reform. These paradoxes in London's fiction mirror the contradictions of his personal and political life; he once told a reporter, ''I am a white man first and a socialist second.''

London also declared that such works as *The Sea-Wolf* and the autobiographical *Martin Eden* were written to refute the doctrines of individualistic supermen, an argument many critics have been unable to reconcile upon examination of the texts. In *The Sea-Wolf*, the Nietzschean sea captain, Wolf Larsen, bears London's nickname and his past and shares his favorite authors and philosophical beliefs. He also echoes London's insistence upon facing the reality that life is totally meaningless as opposed to accepting the comforts of moral convention and traditional religious faith. Many critics consider these and other criteria unmistakable evidence of London's admiration for Wolf Larsen. In *Martin Eden* on the other hand, London created what some critics regard as a self-conscious, self-pitying, romanticized portrait of the author as a young man. Early critics dismissed the novel as a minor work replete with embarrassing revelations and stylistic flaws, and regarded the protagonist's ultimate suicide as absurdly unaccountable. However, more recent critics view the suicide as a natural consequence of Eden's discovery of nihilistic truths he is emotionally unfit to face—not unlike the reaction of Wolf Larsen. Though each man secretly desires to return to a paradise of ignorance, the dark knowledge can only be escaped through ''the long sickness'' or death.

London believed that all great fiction blended fact with romantically rendered beauty, power, brutality, and other vigorous attributes. Accordingly, he romanticized autobiographical experiences in his works. Many critics believe that an egotistic narcissism drove him to project himself into the strongest, hardest working, most intelligent protagonists in his works, while the physically extraordinary, unconventional helpmates in such later novels as *The Valley of the Moon* and *The Little Lady of the Big House* idealize the qualities he most admired in his wife Charmian.

Most critics agree with H. L. Mencken's estimate that London's ''too deadly industry'' produced a ''steady emission of half-done books'' that the author did not rework. However, most also agree that despite stylistic clumsiness and didactic intent, there remain in London's works moments of brilliance. His innovative, simple style, descriptive skill, and adherence to the principles of Naturalism laid the groundwork for such later writers as Sherwood Anderson, Ring Lardner, and Ernest Hemingway. In Earle Labor's estimation, London's stature as an artist derives from ''his 'primordial vision'—the mythopoeic force which animates his finest creations and to which we respond without fully knowing why.'' Carl Sandburg defined the basis of the attraction when he stated: ''The more civilized we become, the deeper is the fear that back in barbarism is something of the beauty and joy of life we have not brought with us.'' London's works offer this vicarious alternative, as Robert Barltrop observed, because ''their material does not reflect—indeed, it provides an escape from—life as the mass of people know it.''

(See also *TCLC*, Vol. 9; *Dictionary of Literary Biography*, Vol. 8: *Twentieth-Century American Science Fiction Writers*; Vol. 12: *American Realists and Naturalists*; and *Something about the Author*, Vol. 18.)

PRINCIPAL WORKS

The Son of the Wolf (short stories) 1900
The God of His Fathers, and Other Stories (short stories) 1901
A Daughter of the Snows (novel) 1902
The Call of the Wild (novel) 1903
The Kempton-Wace Letters [with Anna Strunsky] (novel) 1903
The People of the Abyss (essay) 1903
The Sea-Wolf (novel) 1904
The Game (novel) 1905
War of the Classes (essays) 1905
White Fang (novel) 1906
Before Adam (novel) 1907
Love of Life, and Other Stories (short stories) 1907
The Road (essays) 1907
The Iron Heel (novel) 1908
Martin Eden (novel) 1909
Lost Face (short stories) 1910
Revolution, and Other Essays (essays) 1910
The Cruise of the ''Snark'' (essays) 1911
South Sea Tales (short stories) 1911
John Barleycorn (autobiography) 1913
The Valley of the Moon (novel) 1913
The Mutiny of the ''Elsinore'' (novel) 1914
The Strength of the Strong (short stories) 1914
The Scarlet Plague (novella) 1915
The Star Rover (novel) 1915
The Little Lady of the Big House (novel) 1916
The Turtles of Tasman (short stories and drama) 1916
The Red One (short stories) 1918

Island Tales   (short stories)   1920
Letters   (letters)   1965

JONATHAN HAROLD SPINNER (essay date 1970)

[*In the following excerpt, originally published in 1970, Spinner discusses the autobiographical novel* Martin Eden, *which he regards as one of the first bleakly existentialist anti-hero novels in American literature. For further discussion of the autobiographical element and existentialism in London's works, see the excerpts by Abraham Rothberg (1980) and Michael Qualtiere (1982).*]

Martin Eden is one of the first novels that documents the disintegration of the American success story, the final collapse of the Horatio Alger legend, the great fall of the Gospel of Wealth myth. Yet it also marks one of the first scenes in a new American drama, that of the existential dilemma of the modern anti-hero. If the book is seen only as a final chapter in the annals of the American success story, then it seems to be two separate, distinct, and unintegrated halves, with Martin Eden's behavior after becoming a successful novelist seemingly inexplicable. But by considering the novel as presenting some of the opening lines of the modern existential problem, *Martin Eden* becomes a complete and solid piece of work, and an enduring American novel.

The Horatio Alger-Gospel of Wealth myth was the American statement to the world. The last quarter of the 19th century was imbued with it, the literature of the time is flooded with it. London's novel, written in the opening years of the 20th century appears, in its first chapters, to be yet another reflection of that guiding beacon of American thought. Martin Eden fully intends to succeed. The American dream of success is his dream of success. (pp. 114-15)

Eden, like any other young American, knows that through hard work, he will emerge victorious. Yet it is Eden's misfortune and folly, from the viewpoint of the traditional American dream, that he has chosen a course fraught with introspective perils, that of writing. Nor does Eden limit himself to magazine editing, or newspaper work; his ambition is fine writing and the rarified atmosphere of the mind. It is this attempt by Eden that leads him from the narrow, sure channels of the American dream to the broad, uncertain depths of the existential dilemma. One wonders if London realizes that Eden's introspectiveness is self-destructive. I doubt that he does, however, because of the parallelism in London's own life. As I intend to show, an unconscious thread of introspection as an avenue of death for those not strong enough to accept the discoveries that it presents, runs throughout the novel. But I believe it to be unconscious and unknown to London.

The modern existential dilemma, that overworked phrase, can be defined as the loss of identity, the feeling of alienation, the lack of faith so well-documented in so much of modern literature. . . . Although the existential dilemma was hidden for three-quarters of a century in America behind the twin facades of the westering myth and the Horatio Alger legend, the myths of escape and success, *Martin Eden* breaks through as one of the first fictional statements of American existentialism.

Eden is the perfect name for an American Adamic hero who falls after eating of the Tree of Knowledge. If Eden is Adam, then his Eve is Ruth Morse, who bids him eat of the forbidden

fruit of introspective self-awareness. Satan, if he does not whisper in Ruth's ear, speaks to her heart in more direct ways. Ruth sees Martin as a full-blooded, lower class, sexual Minotaur, with his "heavy corded, almost bull-like (neck), bronzed by the sun, spilling over with rugged health and strength." And although Ruth considers Eden's strength "gross and brutish," she is surely and steadily drawn to his phallic power. Freud would have been delighted.

It is ironic that the fragile, innocent Ruth Morse should tempt Eden, yet the apple she offers is, like Eve's, forbidden to Eden and so much desired. From his humble, lower-working class viewpoint, the bourgeois world-view is all encompassing and grand. Yet Eden does not accept Ruth's, or the middle class' view of obtaining wealth. From the first, he is intrigued by bourgeois education and knowledge, and not by the material goods that they possess. He intends to get that education and knowledge, for the middle class students in school with him, although physically his inferiors, could talk Ruth's "talk—the thought depressed him. But what was a brain for? . . . What they had done, he could do."

Thus far we have all the beginnings of an Horatio Alger story, a poor-boy-makes-good theme. Yet Eden has taken a fatal turn, for instead of turning outward toward the wealth and position of a Mr. Butler, he turns inward the bitter loss of faith of a Mr. Brissenden. We cannot carry the comparison of Brissenden and Eden too far, for Eden has been tempered in different fires, yet the comparison exists. Both are artists, both are disillusioned, and both are destroyed by the society and the intellectual climate that surrounds them. Both, as strong as they appear, are brittle, although both have been through much. Brissenden has been through sickness, through tuberculosis. Eden has been through Cheese Face and the laundry.

The Cheese Face and the laundry episodes are the most powerful in the novel. They have similar qualities, and are, indeed, extremely similar experiences. They are hard physical experiences, and Eden survives them both because of his endurance and ability to withstand physical pain. Yet as toughening as these experiences are, they do not prepare Eden for the mental toughness that the new industrial-scientific-existential age demands. It is interesting to note that Eden recalls the Cheese Face incident when he is at the bottom, when rejection slip after rejection slip has totally defeated him for the moment, when the Horatio Alger myth has been shattered, when long, hard work has brought no reward. It is then that he recalls his greatest triumph, it is then that he reminds himself that he can withstand any physical pain. After his reminiscent dream, he tells himself that he will succeed. However, there is a note of uncertainty in it, as though Eden realizes that this is a different battle he is in because as he tells himself, "You can't stop here. You've got to go on. It's to a finish, you know."

Similarly, the laundry is another test of Eden's physical endurance. Again his mind is overwhelmed by the physical, and as he fought like a brute against Cheese Face, so he works and lives like an animal in the laundry. As in the Cheese Face incident, Eden's mind, his introspective tool, is shattered. It is impossible for Eden to work like an animal and think on a high level at the same time. Physically, Eden is fairly well up to it, mentally he is destroyed by it. After three months of working at the laundry during the week, and bicycling to San Francisco to see Ruth on the weekends, Eden gets drunk with his partner Joe. "He forgot, and lived again, and living, he saw . . . the beast he was making of himself—not by the drink, but by the work." As he drunkenly realizes, it was not by being a "toil-beast" that he could succeed. This was the whiskey's message. "The whiskey was wise. It told secrets on itself."

Thus, on both occasions, it is work, hard work, that brings on a mental shattering in Eden. For Eden, Horatio Alger is proven wrong, hard work does not lead to success, but to death, a spiritual and intellectual one. These are premonitions of the stresses that Eden will soon face, they are indications of what Eden lacks, mental toughness. They are turning points in the book, because they both denote the destruction of the Horatio Alger myth, and the development of the existential dilemma that Eden is soon faced with. These two incidents are the links in the novel between the two opposite philosophical statements. If Eden cannot cope with Horatio Alger, how will he be able to cope with Jean Paul Sartre?

It is precisely because of Eden's introspection, the natural result of his profession, that the events of the second half of the novel occur. By some editorial miracle, totally unexplainable by either Eden, London, or ourselves, Eden's work becomes, suddenly, acceptable, and he becomes rich, famous, wanted. It would appear that Horatio Alger was right all along, success comes with hard work. Yet for Eden, material success has the taste of ashes, because it is based on "work performed." As he tells the Morses and their middle class friends at dinner, it is because he now has money and is famous that they dote on him, and not because "I'm Martin Eden, a pretty good guy and not particularly a fool . . . And it was all done long ago; it was work performed, . . . when you spat upon me as the dirt under your feet." (pp. 115-17)

Eden refuses to be objectivized, to be made an "it" by others, as all of us tend to do to people. He will not be "pigeon-holed" as an artist, he wants to be taken as a man. Yet what truly crushes Eden, what really shows his lack of emotional strength, and reveals the depth of his existential problem, is Brissenden's death. . . .

Neither Brissenden nor Eden have the mental strength required by an existential age of the introspective writer. They both search desperately for answers, they are both overwhelmed by the thought of man as little more than nothing in the chaos of the universe. . . . Introspection has reinforced their knowledge, gained by first-hand physical experience, of man's nothingness, physically and spiritually. . . .

There are other signs throughout the novel that Eden is heading toward a dilemma of existence, a problem of alienation. Loneliness is a continuously stated problem for Eden throughout the book. Because he is entranced and possessed by the fruit of the middle class, knowledge, Eden breaks off relations with the lower class, his first paradise. He finds the lower class too coarse, ill-mannered, and stupid, at first, to remain with them. Even after his disillusionment with the middle-class, he finds it impossible to return to the lower class, to find a woman like Lizzie Connolly satisfying and fulfilling. He recognizes her virtues and her beauty, but he is too far alienated from her surroundings to stay with her. Eden realizes he is not a brute and is "a damn poor Nietzscheman," that he would marry Lizzie if he could "and fill her quivering heart full of happiness." But Martin Eden cannot, "and it's a damn shame." (p. 118)

Eden's relationship with Ruth is indicative of his whole relationship with middle class society. Ruth, an ironical name to give to a woman who is far from ready or willing to go wherever Eden would lead her, is at once afraid and drawn to Eden,

primarily for the same reasons American "polite" society is both drawn to and afraid of him—his vitality and power are repulsive, yet magnetic to the middle class. Eden realizes this and refuses to be used. Now he finds the bourgeois "sickening," and realizes that what he dreamed in his innocence, "that the persons who sat in the high places, who lived in fine houses and had educations and bank accounts, were worthwhile," is the great lie of the Horatio Alger success story.

He moves toward the socialists, the labor unions, the radicals, but because he is already alone, because he is already divorced from two classes, he cannot accept their theories. His star is the hero, the Nietzschian superman, and socialism, while fine for the mob, is not for Martin Eden. With Brissenden's suicide, he is truly alone, alienated, the classic existential anti-hero in the classic existential dilemma. It is then that he longs for paradise again, to which he can never return, the paradise he knew as a poor sailor in Tahiti. There, he and Moti, the chief's son, wait for "the rush of a big breaker whereon to jump the reef." Eden relives those thrilling moments of breakthrough, of fierce physical enjoyment, of youthful pleasures, of agrarian order so that he can escape from the "disorder of his squalid room," from the disorder of his existential dilemma in the modern industrial world.

Eden has gone from order to disorder, from paradise to hell, from being at one with the universe to alienation from it and from his fellow man. The "Moti" dream is an aspect and outgrowth of the westering myth of escape. It is then that he attempts to return to the South Seas, to go west, to escape from his existential reality. But suicide can be spiritual as well as physical. Eden attempts death through myth, through dream, and perhaps, realizing this on a subconscious level, kills himself physically on route to his spiritual death. Because, as we have seen, he lacks the necessary mental toughness to survive in this existential world, Eden cannot face the loss of paradise to which his introspectiveness has led him. Suicide, from this desert of emotions, from this spiritual hell, becomes a positive act for Eden. He conquers the absurd natural order by imposing his human will on it, forcing himself to death. (p. 119)

Martin Eden is a rude shock to a literature overwhelmed with the Horatio Alger-Gospel of Wealth myth. I find no other American novel of the era is so hopeless, so empty, so awful in its view of man as this one is. Long before the terminology came into existence, London had written an existential novel, had given America one of its first existential anti-heroes. Like Eden just before his death, one sees in this novel a terrible vision of self-knowledge, of self-awareness for America in the 20th century. . . . (p. 120)

Jonathan Harold Spinner, "Jack London's 'Martin Eden': The Development of the Existential Hero," in Jack London: Essays in Criticism, edited by Ray Wilson Ownbey, Peregrine Smith, Inc., 1978, pp. 114-20.

EARLE LABOR   (essay date 1974)

[*Labor, an American educator, is considered an authority on London and taught the first courses on London offered at an American university and in Western Europe. The author of several published articles on London, Labor is also the editor of* Great Short Works of Jack London (1965). *In his critical study* Jack London, *Labor discusses the author's diverse, prolific career, using representative works to illustrate London's thematic concerns, literary style, and temperament, and arguing for his inclusion among the world's great writers. In the following excerpt*] *from that work, Labor examines the early Klondike stories, for which London is best remembered. Thematically, these stories illustrate the importance of comradeship to survival in a hostile natural environment, and the necessity of an ethical code based on the authority of individual conscience.*]

Specific titles of London's works may be blurred among our other dim memories of youth, but few persons who have ever encountered his tales can totally forget the lonely traveler who dies unmourned in the awesome cold of the Arctic winter because he has accidentally wet his feet and failed to build a fire; the lost miner who wanders across the Arctic waste land in a nightmarish odyssey of starvation and exposure, sustained solely by an incredible will to live; or either of the magnificent dogs: Buck, captivated by the call of the Northland Wild, and White Fang, tamed by the loving-kindness of a gentler master. There is something timeless about these stories. At the turn of the century, when they first appeared, there was also something very timely about them.

A reading public that had dieted on propriety and pap for more than a generation and whose appetite for strenuous action had been whetted by the colorful melodramas of Kipling and by the melodramatics of Theodore Roosevelt was hungry for the meaty fare of Jack London's Northland. The opening sentence of **"An Odyssey of the North"** is the harbinger of a new kind of American fiction: "The sleds were singing their eternal lament to the creaking of the harnesses and the tinkling bells of the leaders; but the men and dogs were tired and made no sound." Others had already used the Klondike materials for profit, but their writings lacked the vividness and poetic cadence of London's style, a style which fused the vigorous and the picturesque. Furthermore, his was a fresh breed of fictional heroes—not the maudlin gentlemen who scalded flowers with their tears or who emasculated themselves on the altars of sentimental caprice—but "a lean and wiry type, with trail-hardened muscles, and sun-browned faces, and untroubled souls which gazed frankly forth, clear-eyed and steady." . . . Kipling had introduced a kindred type the decade before, and London was quick to acknowledge his debt to the master of the "plain tale."

But the Klondike argonauts were not merely copies of those leathery cockneys and Irishmen in the Queen's Army whose individualism was subverted to the uses of British Imperialism and whose sporting ethic was at times gratuitously cruel. London's Northland heroes were, by contrast, a ruggedly independent yet a remarkably compassionate breed who paid allegiance only to the inexorable laws of nature and to the authority of conscience, but who also possessed a capacity for selflessness and comradeship very much like the *agape* of primitive Christianity. Theirs was a situational ethic, predicated on integrity, charity, and pragmatism. They had invaded a hostile land where the ruling law was "survival of the fittest" and where the key to survival was adaptability, but this did not simply mean physical fitness or brute strength: "The man who turns his back upon the comforts of an elder civilization, to face the savage youth, the primordial simplicity of the North, may estimate success at an inverse ratio to the quantity and quality of his hopelessly fixed habits," explains the narrator in his prologue to the story **"In a Far Country."** . . . (pp. 49-50)

This code of the Northland, with the mystique of comradeship at its heart, is dramatized in **"To the Man on Trail,"** the first of Jack's Klondike stories which had so excited the editors of the *Overland Monthly*. A Yuletide story, it is trimmed with the rich assortment of symbols, pagan as well as Christian,

Seventeen-year-old Jack London photographed in Yokohama while serving in the crew of the "Sophia Sutherland." Courtesy of the Trust of Irving Shepard.

appropriate to the occasion. The setting is Christmas Eve in the cabin of the Malemute Kid, who dominates *The Son of the Wolf* collection as high priest of the code. Gathered together are representatives from a dozen different lands who are swapping yarns, reminiscing about home, and sharing the heady Christmas punch concocted by Kid. At midnight the convivialities are suddenly interrupted by the jingling of bells, "the familiar music of the dogwhip, the whining howl of the Malemutes, and the crunch of a sled"; then comes "the expected knock, sharp and confident" and the entrance of "the stranger." . . . (p. 51)

Jack Westondale, the stranger, explains that he is pursuing a gang of dog thieves. While the guest is eating the Christmas snack hospitably prepared for him, Kid studies his face and finds him worthy. . . . (p. 52)

Westondale apparently embodies all the vital traits of the code hero; and, while he is taking a quick nap before again taking to the trail, the impression is confirmed by Kid: "Been in going on three years, with nothing but the name of working like a horse, and any amount of bad luck to his credit. . . . The trouble with him is clean grit and stubbornness." . . . A short three hours later Kid rouses the young giant and—Magus-like—sends him on his way with fresh provisions and wise counsel. Fifteen minutes later the festivities are stopped a second time—by a nearly exhausted stranger who wears the red coat, not of St. Nick, but of the Royal Canadian Mounted Police. He demands fresh dogs and information about Westondale, who is running—he discloses—not for, but *from*, the law after having robbed a Dawson gambling casino of forty thousand dollars!

Though the revelers have kept silent according to Kid's example, they furiously demand an explanation after the Mountie has gone: why has Kid given sanctuary and aid to a man who has doubly violated the code by robbery and by deception? . . .

> Don't jump a dog when he's down. You've only heard one side. A whiter man than Jack Westondale never ate from the same pot nor stretched blanket with you or me. Last fall he gave his whole clean-up, forty thousand, to Joe Castrell, to buy in on Dominion. To-day he'd be a millionaire. But white he stayed behind at Circle City, taking care of his partner with the scurvy, what does Castrell do? Goes into McFarland's, jumps the limit, and drops the whole sack. Found him dead in the snow the next day. And poor Jack laying his plans to go out this winter to his wife and the boy he's never seen. You'll notice he took exactly what his partner lost,—forty thousand. Well, he's gone out; and what are you going to do about it?'' . . .

Without belaboring his symbolism, London has provided a fitting epiphany to the conclusion of his Christmas carol; moreover, the situational ethic which informs the story was sure to appeal to a reading public less than one generation removed from frontier justice.

The mystique of comradeship is obversely dramatized in the fourth story in *The Son of the Wolf* collection, **"In a Far Country,"** which had first appeared in the June, 1899, issue of the *Overland Monthly*. In this tale about "two Incapables" named Carter Weatherbee and Percy Cuthfert, who elect to spend the long Arctic winter snugly marooned in a deserted cabin rather than suffer the hardships of breaking trail with their comrades for the thousand remaining miles to Dawson, London reiterates the idea that survival is not primarily a matter of physical fitness.

Both Incapables are healthy, husky men, whereas Merritt Sloper, the wiry little argonaut who functions as moral norm in this and in several other Klondike episodes, weighs less than a hundred pounds and is still yellow and weak from the fever he had picked up in South America. . . . Sloper predicts the Incapables' fate as he and the remaining members of the party pull out from the cabin: "[Ever] hear of the Kilkenny cats?" he asks Jacques Baptiste, the party's half-breed guide. "Well, my friend and good comrade, the Kilkenny cats fought till neither hide, nor hair, nor yowl, was left. . . . Now, these two men don't like work. They won't work. We know that. They'll be all alone in that cabin all winter,—a mighty long, dark winter." . . . (pp. 52-4)

At first, Sloper's prophecy appears to be wrong, for the Incapables seem determined to prove their compatibility; in addition, they are plentifully stocked with food and fuel. But, representatives of a degenerate society, they are fatally undersupplied in the moral staples needed for subsistence in the Northland. Weatherbee, formerly a clerk, is an unimaginative, materialistic fool who has joined the gold rush to make his fortune; Cuthfert, opposite as well as apposite, is the overripe cultural dilettante afflicted with "an abnormal development of sentimentality [which he mistakes] for the true spirit of romance and adventure." . . . Moreover, the two men lack that "protean

faculty of adaptability"—the capacity to slough off the callus of "self" along with the specious comforts of civilization—which is the most vital insurance against the dangers of the wilderness.

After an overeager show of industrious cooperation, they abandon the austere discipline of the code. Their spiritual degeneration, as they succumb to each of the Seven Deadly Sins, is initially dramatized in their social relationship. First, pride is manifest in a foolish arrogance which precludes the mutual trust requisite to survival in the wilderness. . . . (p. 54)

Next appears lust, as they consume with sensual promiscuity their supply of sugar, mixing it with hot water and then dissipating "the rich, white syrup" over their flapjacks and breadcrusts. This is followed by sloth, as they sink into a lethargy which makes them "rebel at the performance of the smallest chore," including washing and personal cleanliness—"and for that matter, common decency." . . . Accelerated by gluttony, their moral deterioration now begins to externalize itself in their physical appearance. . . . Covetousness and envy appear when they divide their sugar supply and hide their shares from each other, obsessed with the fear of losing the precious stuff.

The last of the cardinal sins, anger, is delayed awhile by another trouble: "the Fear of the North. . . . the joint child of the Great Cold and the Great Silence," . . . which preoccupies each man according to his nature. (p. 55)

The symbolism grows richer as the drama moves toward its ghastly climax. Though London had not yet read the works of Sigmund Freud, his metaphors reveal an instinctive grasp of dream symbolism, particularly of the unconscious associations of sexual impotency and death. Cuthfert is obsessed with the absolute stillness of the phallic, arrow-shaped weathervane atop the cabin. . . . The metaphors of potency-life versus emasculation-death coalesce in the story's vivid climax, as anger completes the allegoric procession of the deadly sins. Thinking that his companion has pilfered his last tiny cache of the symbol-laden sugar, Weatherbee attacks Cuthfert in the cold fury of insanity and severs his spine with an axe, thereby fulfilling the premonition of symbolic emasculation; and then falls heavily upon him as the bullet from his victim's Smith & Weston explodes in his face.

The closing tableau—a grotesque inversion of the primal scene—dramatically reveals London's pre-Freudian intuitions: "The sharp bite of the axe had caused Cuthfert to drop the pistol, and as his lungs panted for release, he fumbled aimlessly for it among the blankets. Then he remembered. He slid a hand up the clerk's belt to the sheath-knife; and they drew very close to each other in that last clinch." . . . Passages like this one apparently substantiate Maxwell Geismar's observation that London seemed to be more at home in the "world of dream and fantasy and desolate, abnormal emotion . . . than the world of people and society" and that "his best work was often a transcript of solitary nightmares" [see *TCLC,* Vol. 9]. But such an assessment, notwithstanding the brilliance of Geismar's Freudian interpretation of London's life and work, is too limited. Though a considerable amount of his fiction does fit into this category, London's best is something more than "a transcript of solitary nightmares": it is the artistic modulation of universal dreams—*i.e.,* of myths and archetypes. (pp. 56-7)

Earle Labor, in his Jack London, *Twayne Publishers, Inc., 1974, 179 p.*

JAMES I. McCLINTOCK (essay date 1975)

[*McClintock's* White Logic: Jack London's Short Stories, *examines the themes, motifs, and artistic techniques London employed during what he regards as the three phases of the author's career. In the following excerpt from that work, McClintock discusses the critical climate in American letters during the early years of London's career to determine the degree to which the blend of romance and realism in his short stories reflected his desire to be commercially successful on the one hand and his desire to shock complacent and sentimental readers on the other.*]

During his apprenticeship, Jack London was not only seeking an adequate form and style for his short stories, but also defining his literary attitudes in relation to the continuing debate between realism and romance. Although he thought of himself as a realist, he was actually struggling to uncover a literary theory that would transcend deficiencies he perceived in both the realist and romantic traditions by uniting the best qualities of each. Since, for him, "the thought is the thing," he needed a literary perspective consistent with his "working philosophy of life," his third prerequisite for "success as a writer" in addition to a knowledge of life and of commercial literature. Somehow that perspective would have to account for the dark truths about nature and man's position in it thrust upon him by his fascination with evolutionary thought. And, simultaneously, that perspective would have to be consistent with a deeply felt intuition that man is noble and that humanly sustaining ideals can be validated. (p. 35)

Jack London began writing when the most influential short story theorists and commentators had fallen under the spell of realistic technique; Brander Matthews, for example, was a disciple and ardent defender of William Dean Howells. London learned from the realists "how to forbear the excesses of analysis, to withhold weakly recurring descriptive and caressing epithets, to let the characters suffice for themselves," to be "dramatic" rather than "tediously analytical." . . . These emphases upon depersonalized narration and scenic method would seem to place London with the realists. Moreover, London used most of the realists' catchwords like "facts," "truth," "reality," and "honesty" to characterize his own intention and practice and to praise the works of other writers whom he admired most. He noted with pride, for instance, that his materials came from experience, making them "real" ("like 90% of my stories, **'The Benefit of the Doubt'** is based upon actual experience"). (pp. 35-6)

But London's "near-at-hand" truth and his autobiographical materials came from the Klondike, the high seas, and the tropics—familiar places to him but not to his readers. The places and characters are "not impossible" and no doubt were "real" to London, but not real in the Howellsian sense of the "average" or the "commonplace" which were hateful words to London. The experiences London used as the stuff for his fiction had sprung from his lower class existence and included the crude, the violent and the sordid, all "average" to him, but not to Howells who assumed the middle class American as the norm for perception. Literature written from a Howellsian perspective bored London; it was bloodless. He wanted his stories to "live and spout blood and spirit and beauty and fire and glamor." These attitudes and characteristics, the appeal to intensity, seem to make a romantic out of London. Indeed, his fiction has sometimes been called "romantic realism," which, unfortunately, is not a revealing phrase. (p. 36)

His literary theory parallels an eclectic compromise between realism and romance implicit in the reviews written by the more fashionable popular magazine critics; and it is strikingly similar to the concepts of literary naturalism formulated by recent academic critics like Charles Walcutt and Donald Pizer.

Virtually every American magazine that printed reviews or literary gossip at the turn of the century had staff members and outside contributors who took part in the battle between romance and realism. . . .

By the turn of the century, the skirmishing was nearly completed; the major areas of contention defined and almost settled. Intellectually, the battle had gone to Howells and the realists, but the popular victory had gone to the critics who favored stories which in some way managed to combine elements of realism and romance. From this compromise London took his cue, demonstrating his sensitivity to the popular arguments. (p. 37)

The view that triumphed, if the repeated testimony in its behalf is the measure of its acceptance, was a combination of what was felt to be the essence of the two positions. The popular critics of both persuasions would accept as artistic any work which combined materials from the world, even though unsavory in isolation, if they were shot through with some kind of idealism. (p. 39)

This magazine compromise is the fundamental critical conception behind Jack London's short stories. And an attempt to combine idealism with the rough external world he observed, to balance a vital emotional life with the truths of scientific observation, is a recurrent theme in both London's life and his work. . . . Martin Eden's literary theory is a statement of London's own. Early in his career Martin learns to avoid both romantic and realistic clichés in his works but to combine the best elements of both realism and romance. . . . (p. 40)

Like the popular magazine critics, London objected to the "too great singleness of sight and purpose" shown by both sides. On the "clod" side, he objected to the Zolaesque "brute-savageness" if it existed for its own sake. On the "god" side, he objected to a sentimental view of human nature.

At first glance, though, London's fiction would seem to make him an apostle of the sensationally shocking. Joan London noted that "he soon became a pioneer of American 'realism.' He broke every writing tradition long revered in America, seemed . . . ultramodern and shocking" because, like Martin Eden, he used "scenes that were rough and raw, gross and bestial." . . . He had contempt for the avoidance of violence and the artistic capitulation to feminine sensitivities. He agreed with Crane's sentiment, "Tradition, thou art for sucklin children, / Thou art the enlivening milk for babes; / But no meat for men is in thee . . ." Nevertheless, London agreed with the realist and romantic critics who deplored the cataloguing of sordid experience, or, indeed, any kind of detail which did not have a clear relevancy to the fates of the characters. (p. 41)

But where would the emphasis lie in that broad territory between the utter brute and the utter saint? In fixing the proportions of the saintly and the brutish, he favored the positive: "Surely I have learned how vile [man] can be," he remarked, "But this only strengthens my regard, because it enhances the mighty heights he can bring himself to tread."

That optimistic, affirmative impulse, surprisingly, was in part a product of his exploration of scientific thought which was helping him formulate the philosophy of life that demanded a new literary theory and attracted him to that critical compromise theorists were groping for. . . . London was captivated by the evolutionary optimism of two social Darwinists, one English and the other German. In the exchanges between London and his literary confidant Cloudesly Johns throughout 1899 and 1900, the grand philosophical speculations of Herbert Spencer and Ernst Haeckel are often at center stage. (p. 43)

Jack London was more Lamarkian than he knew, not surprisingly perhaps, since so were Darwin, Spencer, Haeckel and Marx. All subscribed to the notion of "acquired characters," believing that beneficial characteristics acquired during the struggle for existence would be transmitted genetically to the following generations.

London, then, had what he would consider a scientifically responsible justification for imbuing sordid materials with idealism. He had an intellectual framework and a literary theory he synthesized from magazine criticism, both of which encouraged him to dramatize "spirit groping" and "soul searching" characters pursuing "heaven-sent dreams and divine possibilities" while being true to biology that was altering old conceptions of nature and man's place in it and insisting that struggle was at the core of experience. "Thought, mind, soul" have a place in the natural order; men are not necessarily unthinking, vicious animals driven by amoral instincts.

He had reason to attempt to infuse sordid materials with idealism, ugly truths with self-sustaining values, when he began to compose the Alaskan stories. By 1899, when he broke into *The Overland Monthly* with **"To the Man on Trail,"** the "clods" (Zola's disciples) had rejected a belief in the possibility of achieving personal fulfillment in a universe scientifically described. (p. 45)

London may have thought of himself as a realist because he believed that he was engaged in recording truth honestly and would have agreed with Howells that the goal of the writer is to describe reality and that "all tells for destiny and character." But London's conceptions of truth, reality and character were remarkably different from the realist's. Holland was correct in assuming that "the deeper philosophical points of departure always color the work and interweave themselves into the story and set the pace and determine the impact of the fiction." Something happens to London's fiction when he promotes ideas. Jack London was seriously recording truth, but not mere truth. He desired to present "strong truth," and to make absolutely clear to his reader his own conception of that truth. To him, a neglect of either the external or of man's subjective experience would be an abandonment of that truth-seeking: the realist's "fact" had to be converted into a romantic "truth." It is this impulse to didacticism, his compelling desire to communicate "strong truth" forcefully, that leads to the romantic intensity of his fiction. (p. 51)

London's "god" and "clod" eclectic literary theory demonstrates that like Whitman he wished to embody in his fiction both matter and spirit, both the body and the soul, and to forge a new relationship between them. With Whitman, and other serious romantics, London shared a sense of active participation in a dynamic cosmos that was lacking in Howellsian realism. . . . London hoped to shock his readers into a sense of active, masculine forces shaping their characters and destinies and to drag them bodily into an awareness of new values. Like Whitman, he felt the prophetic impulse and lurked egotistically in and behind his stories, exuding a self-conscious intensity and recommending a new approach to life. And if Whitman used prose-poetry to evoke a sense of cosmic power, London employed a poetic prose style to infuse his grand landscape

with mythic significance. In many ways London was seeking to do for prose what Whitman had done at mid-century for poetry.

The comparison with Whitman is a little too flattering. London's dogmatically expressed theories and good intentions are not always consistent with his practice. He might deride the conventionalities of sentimental romance or commonplace realism, but both find places in the nineteen volumes of collected short stories. Even in work which cannot be described a hack, he would glaze his strenuous idealism with sentimental platitudes or lace his evocative prose with insignificant detail.

But by no means was the young Jack London without insight, profundity and real understanding. His visions of nightmare and glory as they erupt from his Alaskan stories prove that his fiction is more than popular art. Although he did learn from the magazines and handbooks that there would be a market for fiction that presented bold materials—the adventurous, violent, even sordid—if they were shot through with idealism and that critical acclaim went to those stories which were presented dramatically and created a single impression, his short fiction is more than a prefabricated construction built from the commentaries of magazine critics. The union of his personal experiences, his individual understanding of Spencer's and Haeckel's ideas as they bore upon a redefinition of man's potential in a scientifically describable nature, and his willingness to dramatize those strong truths by concentrating upon mythic settings and characters struggling to affirm meaningful values, differentiates his work from both his predecessors and from countless practitioners whose stories appeared in the magazines London studied. (pp. 53-4)

James I. McClintock, in his White Logic: Jack London's Short Stories, *Wolf House Books, 1975, 206 p.*

ROBERT BARLTROP (essay date 1976)

[*Barltrop, a member of the Socialist Party of Great Britain, claims a strong identification with his working class background. He is the author of* The Monument: Story of the Socialist Party of Great Britain (1975), *and editor of* London's Revolution: Stories and Essays (1978). *In the following excerpt from his* Jack London: The Man, the Writer, the Rebel, *Barltrop notes that many of the novels on which London's reputation rests were either considered risky or were not well received at the time of publication. The critic attributes this to the grimly realistic nature of London's works, which presented unsentimental animal stories in such works as* The Call of the Wild, *horrific portraits of prison life and the American judicial system in* The Road *and* The Jacket, *and a pessimistic attack on the middle class in* Martin Eden.]

What is remarkable about the two-thirds of Jack's work on which his popularity rests is the extent to which it was ahead of the taste or the mood of his time. He achieved fame quickly as a writer of vigorous, lucid adventures in the frozen north and at sea. With this reputation as a story-teller established, nothing he wrote was likely to be rejected. Nevertheless, the fact is that the Jack London books which are the most widely read and esteemed today were all doubtful properties when they were published. *The Call of the Wild* and *The People of the Abyss* were successful against expectations. *The Iron Heel, The Road, Martin Eden* and *The Star Rover (The Jacket)* were received either coolly or with actual disparagement. One reason why Charmian says little about the last four is that they were still uncelebrated at the time she wrote her biography. Yet without these he would not be famous: known perhaps as an excellent short-story writer, but without major works to his credit.

The reason for doubting whether the public in 1903 would find *The Call of the Wild* acceptable has been noted—its departure from the convention of sentimentality in animal stories. Leaving aside *The Iron Heel,* because it is a special case in every sense, something similar can be said of the other books that either did not expect or did not find favour in Jack's lifetime. *The Road* and *The Jacket* both describe prison life in horrific terms. That, indeed, is the fascination of *The Jacket.* Its historical fantasies vary from the ordinary to the wishy-washy, but the background of the punishment cell grips the reader's imagination. In the early nineteen-hundreds this was fundamentally unsuitable material. A sentimental account of a prison episode, such as Wilde's in *The Ballad of Reading Gaol,* was thought sufficiently daring as the alternative to Dickensian pictures of the wicked receiving their desserts. In showing the brutality of prisons, with more than an implication that justice was a sham anyway, Jack London was a generation in advance of his time.

Martin Eden was disliked for its pessimism, the hero's inability to be happy. Having overcome the odds against him, he finds himself without a creed or a relationship he can trust. Half a century later, in a popular literature without happy endings, the theme was unexceptional and comprehensible; it was acceptable in the nineteen-twenties; but in pre-1914 America it suggested only unhealthy introspection. Likewise, attacks on middle-class conduct and the success-myth were to become fashionable later. When *Martin Eden* was published, their effect was to alienate the magazine- and novel-reading public. Why should a young man with the world at his feet be contemptuous of society and success, and finally decide on suicide?

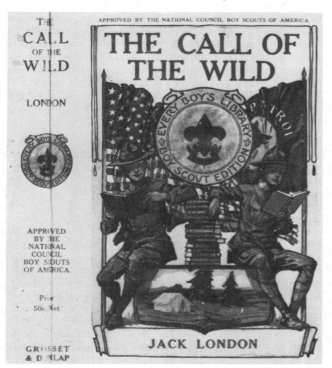

Dust jacket of the edition of The Call of the Wild *endorsed by the Boy Scouts of America. Courtesy of the Trust of Irving Shepard.*

Jack London's themes were taken directly from his own experiences, and his treatment of them took no account of being 'nice'. Many of his stories are autobiographical, narrating incidents in his life either openly in the first person, as in *The Road* and *John Barleycorn,* or with slight disguises of names and circumstances. Not infrequently he used the names of people he had known in a way which would be unthinkable to libel-haunted English writers. (pp. 180-81)

His stories appear to be true. In matters of detail they undoubtedly were true. At times when he was challenged over authenticity he was always able to reply with the certainty of first-hand experience. . . .

Yet the use of existing people and true events is not in itself realism. The fact is that Jack London's stories have their persistent appeal because, ultimately, they are not realistic at all: they are romantic fantasy. It is not just the case that they bring a world of distant excitement to town-dwellers; the world is adapted to be as the reader wants it, rather than as he would have found it. The drinking and gambling in Klondike saloons are without the misery which follows them in real life—it is all part of a swashbuckling, virile existence for strong men and beautiful women. The heroes combine superb physique with outstanding intellectual powers. Martin Eden and Ernest Everhard both have muscles which almost burst their clothes. Elam Harnish is 'a striking figure of a man . . . he had lived life naked and tensely, and something of all this smouldered in his eyes'. In the Tivoli saloon he puts down every man in arm-wrestling across the bar. The minor characters are in the same mould. . . . (p. 182)

Nevertheless, Jack London's fantasies are not the same as the fantasies created by most popular writers. He had created them for himself. In practically everything he did in his life, romantic images obscured what things and people were really like. The failures in his personal relationships and his projects were certainly due to this; the idealisation of his experiences in his stories was not simply a selective view from a safe distance, but expectations he had taken into—and, apparently, preserved through—those experiences. One reason is that the experiences of oyster-pirating, the sea, tramping and the Klondike were all short-term, enabling him to feel a member of an exalted and glamorous brotherhood without the disenchanting effects of time. He entered and left them with mental pictures formed by his boyhood reading.

His vision was the same as his readers'. Just as they envisaged a northland full of manly adventures and populated by such characters as the Malemute Kid, so did he. He voiced their feeling that it was far above the life led by the majority of people, that it bred a higher type of man. . . . A number of the stories represent extremes of fantasy. The beautifully-told '**The Night Born**' is an example: the sort of sexual episode away from civilisation that most men daydream of at some time.

No doubt many thousands of people in Jack's own time half-believed they might have such adventures, given the opportunity. The legend of the frontiersmen was still potent. Jack's reputation for realism came partly from this belief, and also because his stories had a full measure of toughness. Death is frequent in them, usually by violence; disease, frostbite and scurvy appear regularly, and leprosy is used in several of the South Seas stories. In fact this is another aspect of romanticism. What is signified is the 'law of life' which Jack laid down. It replaces explanation and makes human efforts redundant: 'this is how it is', the author is saying.

Several of the stories are built round this principle. Perhaps the best is a boxing story, **'A Piece of Steak'.** Its chief character is a hard-up, ageing fighter who is matched with a rising younger man. His skill just fails to master the other's greater strength and speed. As he walks home, he thinks how narrow a thing it was and how he could have won if he had been able to afford a piece of steak beforehand. The excellence of the story comes from leaving it there, without expressions of sentiment: in time the same thing will happen to the younger man. While we know it is true, there is the feeling that the writer likes the idea of it being true—'the law' is like God, disposing of man regardless of what he proposes.

This overlaying of romantic concepts on vivid, often harsh, experience produced inconsistency. Some of Jack London's stories fail because of his inability to break through the concepts and perceive what men and women would think and feel in such situations. **'An Odyssey of the North',** for all its thrilling pursuit, fails in this way. Even **'Love of Life',** one of the most powerful of his stories, comes close to bathos at the end when the man is rescued and among other human beings recovering from his ordeal. (pp. 183-84)

[Jack's best work] is to be found in a number of short stories which establish him as one of the masters of that form. A collection of these outstanding stories would include **'The Apostate', 'The Mexican', 'Love of Life'**—the ending is an irrelevance rather than a weakness, **'A Piece of Steak', 'The Night Born',** and **'To Build a Fire'.** There are six or seven others which are very good by any standard. . . . (pp. 184-85)

The reason why these have, on the whole, been denied literary importance is their subject-matter. Whatever the quality of Jack London's stories, they are not taken seriously because their material does not reflect—indeed, it provides an escape from—life as the mass of people know it. This applies not only to the Klondike and the South Seas stories, but to those which are about boxers and tramps; equally, these represent attractive, disreputable sub-worlds of fantasy. Comparison can be made with American writers of the early part of this century—Sinclair Lewis, for example—who, with narrative ability inferior to Jack London's, won critical praise for their pictures of the known contemporary world. Since that world changes, there is no reason why London should not be recognised as a writer of high order. The place for him in literature is much on a level with Maupassant's. His view was too restricted for the place to be a topmost one, but in the field of imaginative storytelling his work cannot be bettered. (p. 185)

> *Robert Barltrop, in his* Jack London: The Man, the Writer, the Rebel, *Pluto Press, 1976, 206 p.*

ABRAHAM ROTHBERG (essay date 1980)

[*In the following excerpt, Rothberg gives a psychoanalytic interpretation of* The Sea-Wolf, *tracing the novella's characters and situations to London's childhood, domestic problems, and artistic and commercial aims. Although London stated that the work was meant as an attack upon the individualistic superman, Rothberg contends that Wolf Larsen and Humphrey Van Weyden are in fact doubles who display the two contrasting aspects of London's personal temperament and desires. For other views of London's reflection of his own personality and of existentialism in his works, see the excerpts by Jonathan Harold Spinner (1970) and by Michael Qualtiere (1982), who consider such self-revelation in London's works intentional.*]

The Sea-Wolf is one of the most controversial of Jack London's novels and critics have disagreed violently not only about its merits but about its meaning. London himself declared his intentions: "In *The Sea-Wolf* there was, of course, the superficial descriptive story, while the underlying tendency was to prove that the superman cannot be successful in modern life. The superman is anti-social in his tendencies, and in these days of our complex society and sociology he cannot be successful in his hostile aloofness." This public declaration must be treated with skepticism for, in life as in his work, London was not altogether in touch with his intentions either personally or artistically, nor was he above lying about them, but it must not be dismissed out of hand either. Because *The Sea-Wolf* deals with conflicts in himself and in his society that London felt powerfully and profoundly, conflicts between what he was and wanted to be, between a public persona he sought to foist on others and the private self of which he was painfully, even agonizingly aware, conflicts between his "socialist convictions" and his "capitalist career," between the urgings of his talent and the demands of the literary marketplace of his time, one must consider the novel with all the available resources—biographical, historical, psychological and literary—if the novel is to make sense and its place in London's life and work understood. (p. 569)

One of the ways London had of coming to terms with his experience was to write fiction based on it, thus dealing with both myth and reality, past and present, simultaneously. (p. 576)

Wolf Larsen's character may initially have been based on newspaper stories of Alexander McLean and bolstered by London's recollections of Melville's Ahab and Milton's Lucifer; and Humphrey Van Weyden may be warp of Harvey Cheyne in Kipling's *Captains Courageous* and woof of Ross Wilbur in Frank Norris's *Moran of the Lady Letty,* but Larsen and Van Weyden are special creations of Jack London, of his conscious choices and subconscious necessities. *Consciously,* London was using those literary resources in combination with parts of his past and present life and temper, the able-bodied seaman of seventeen, fierce and rebellious, frightened and uncertain, who made the sealing voyage in 1893, the twenty-seven-year-old newly arrived writer who was a troubled man, husband, father and son, trying to negotiate the passage to maturity, to a decision about his wife and family and his mistress.

Unconsciously, London was carried even further back into his earliest life in Flora London's household, with all its difficulties, back into the most basic problems of his extraordinary nature. To anyone who knows London's public life and work, it is evident that he reserved the name "Wolf" to himself. He signed his letters that way, he had a wolf's head on his bookmarks, he called his dream house the "Wolf House," he loved people to call him by that name and wanted others to consider him tough enough to deserve such a sobriquet. Surely Wolf Larsen spoke for that tough part of London's conscious character; but there was also the private, shy, uncertain, fearful and epicene Jack London, the reader and writer of books, not the sailor, boxer and adventurer, the man London wanted very much to keep hidden. That aspect of him is perhaps not so consciously embodied in the character of Humphrey Van Weyden, a writer though only a critic, a dilettante not a professional, a man writing for reputation not cash, a coddled bourgeois with an income, the kind of man Jack London had once and in some measure still aspired to be.

Larsen and Van Weyden London's antithetical selves are in open conflict, Larsen having London's *conscious* desire to be a superman, to find answers to life's questions by reading, to regret ever "having opened the books" which, instead of providing answers, brought only profound melancholy—"the long sickness"—suicidal impulses and despair, and, at last, death. Like Larsen, London had endured a difficult, deprived childhood. Like Larsen, London was and wanted to be skipper of the ship, and looked down on those below him. Like Larsen, London was the "wolf" on the prowl who despised women, but lusted for them sexually. On the other hand, Van Weyden is the Jack London who loved to read, who wanted to be a writer and a good one, who was physically frail and often ill, who was afflicted by his often poetic sensitivity and melancholy introspection, who was racked by homosexual longings.

This "doubling" of characters is one way of turning against the self, the respectable, inhibited, bourgeois London turning against the outlaw, hedonist, worker Jack; in short, Van Weyden is London's superego acting against the unrestricted activities and desires of his id. In this *literary* doubling, London as author is able to kill that id as *literally* as he was to do in his subsequent suicide, the literary "splitting" offering him a defensive strategy, a way for the superego to deal with the libidinal release that, in 1903, London was indulging in his affair with Charmian Kittredge, to deal with his violating the respectability that Flora London had so deeply ingrained in her son and that was filling him with guilt for having ruptured his marriage and left his wife and children. (pp. 576-78)

Psychoanalytically, if the *Ghost* is a paradigm of Flora's household, then the man who runs the ship is not only Jack London, the Oedipal son, but also his father, John London, the sexual father who is hated and admired and with whom Humphrey Van Weyden as the passive, effeminate son is vying for the love of Maud [Maw-awed?]. Wolf, the father, will not permit Hump [!], the son, to have the mother until he grows up, that is until he becomes a violent, aggressive and sexual man— *i.e.*, until he wants to kill his father. Van Weyden, when he sees Maud "crushed in the embrace of Larsen's arms," finally fights Larsen, stabs him and is prevented from killing him only by Maud's pleas not to, "For my sake." (pp. 578-79)

After days on an open boat, Van Weyden and Maud find an island which is a seal rookery, and where "the seals hauled out, and the old bulls guarded their harems, while the young bulls hauled out by themselves." Van Weyden, the young bull who has taken his harem from the old bull Larsen, however, manages, despite their being on a rookery to live in the most chaste style, a point London insists on in the text, ostensibly to please the *Century*'s editor and readers, but there is a more profound logic involved as well. The son may steal the mother and take her to an island, and for the mother's sake not kill the father, but the incest taboo nonetheless continues to keep him from sexual relations with the mother. Moreover, Larsen, that released id, is a transposed part of Van Weyden, that inhibiting superego, so that he, too, as double, is punished for indulging in incest, witnessing the primal scene, by being made blind, a symbolic castration, and impotent. Not until Larsen is dead and dumped over the side can Van Weyden and Maud declare their love for one another. (p. 579)

The double . . . is not only the self turned against another, antithetical self, but turned against the introjected selves of parental figures and surrogates so that, in his fiction, London is projecting the introjected parental selves on whom his own selves are modelled. Larsen, thereby, is not only the punitive father figure, the role-reversed mother (Flora London), from whom one must learn to be tough and aggressive and suc-

cessful, and who must be feared and admired, but also Maud Brewster, the role-reversed father, from whom one must learn to love and be passive. Yet with neither may one have sexual relations because of the incest taboo, though one may, acceptably, express the most extravagant, sex-tinged admiration for either or both.

These earlier role models were overlaid and intensified by the corresponding figures so important to London in the year 1903: Bessie Maddern London, Charmian Kittredge and George Sterling. In marrying Bessie, Jack took his best friend Fred Jacobs' fiancée, a woman for whom he did not feel profound sexual passion, who was to stabilize his life and bear him children. Bess was to be the good, nourishing, sexually pure mother, and Charmian became the erotic seductive one, that feminine saint-and-sinner dichotomy endemic to Victorian sensibility and literature to which London was by no means immune. Charmian was more like Flora, "masculine" and "aggressive," and in leaving Bessie for her, Jack was in his deepest recesses violating the incest taboo as well as the conventionalities that, ironically, Flora had inculcated in him. In London's feelings for George Sterling, and Van Weyden is in good measure modeled on that effete poet, London was demonstrating in life much the same homoerotic impulses that were fictionally made manifest between Van Weyden and Wolf Larsen.

Though disguised in expression, the homosexual feelings between the captain and his mate are made explicit in a variety of ways. London has Van Weyden describe Larsen's body with a sexual intensity that is remarkable for 1903. At the beginning of the novel, the action has Larsen assigning Van Weyden to the very lowest rank on his ship, cabin boy—traditionally a

London in his study. Courtesy of the Trust of Irving Shepard.

homosexual role—and cook's helper—traditionally a feminine role—until gradually Van Weyden works his way up to the second highest rank on the ship, mate to Wolf Larsen. The sexual implication of mate is clear enough, but is further reinforced by the biographical fact that London and Charmian called each other *Mate* as a term of endearment and as a genderless substitute for the words *husband* and *wife*. Van Weyden performs such domestic tasks for Larsen as making his bed, dressing his wounds, nursing him when he is ill, and admiring his body with sensual yearning. . . . When Larsen notices that Van Weyden is admiring his physique, he commands Van Weyden to feel his muscles. Admiringly, Van Weyden does so, observing, "They were hard as iron." Simply to compare London's description of Maud Brewster as "positively bewitching, and, withal, sweetly spirituelle, if not saintly," with that of Larsen is to do more than note London's desire to please the *Century*'s audience. Immediately after this muscle-feeling scene, Larsen promotes Van Weyden to be his mate.

From the very beginning, Van Weyden's effeminacy and passivity are stressed. When the ferry is rammed and sinking, he "behaves like a woman": he panics; he does nothing to help himself or others; he cannot swim; he faints; he does not even call out to the passing *Ghost* to be saved from the waters of the Bay, and only Wolf Larsen's sharp eye rescues him. The red-faced man goes about the ferry, buckling life-preservers on passengers, doing what he can to help, though he has artificial legs. London makes much of this leg symbolism: the very day Van Weyden is saved from the sea, he is swept off his feet in a storm, hits the deck and hurts his knee so that he must hobble around; before that, when the ferry was sinking, the red-faced man, though he has lost both his legs, shows that he has more "leg to stand on" than does Van Weyden; when Larsen, who has plucked Van Weyden from the waters sets about "making a man of him," he points out that Van Weyden has never had to work for a living, that his father left him the money he lives on. "You stand on dead men's legs," Larsen declares. . . . London extends the imagery of hurt, burned or lost limbs so that an underlying castration symbolism emerges. London uses the classical castration symbol of blindness for Larsen when the "Wolf" at last is defeated, just as he uses Mugridge's loss of a foot to a shark in the same way. Forrey shrewdly points out that when Larsen has lost his ship to his brother Death and is cast adrift in the *Ghost,* it is in a *dis*masted ship, symbolic of castration, and that Van Weyden's symbolic achievement of masculinity and victory is capped in his raising the masts. (pp. 580-83)

There was and is a form of male "admiration" for women which is so fulsome as to reveal the essential hostility of its emotional origins. Such admiration and hostility run through all of *The Sea-Wolf* from its very beginning, where the women on the sinking ferry behave hysterically, to its very end, in which Maud Brewster, after remarkable exertions for any human being, is made to confess, "I am only one small woman," the diminutive clearly sentimental derogation, though London would likely have apologized that it was to gratify the great "American Prude." That derogation is carried over into London's contempt for Van Weyden's (and his own) "effeminacy," for his hysteria, his weak muscles, his failures of physical courage, his general ineptitude, all these signs of weakness, dependence, inferiority. London permits Van Weyden the reflection that men without women—*i.e.,* sailors—become brutes—"Coarseness and savagery are the inevitable results."—because women make men capable of softness, tenderness and compassion. London makes the conventional "nod"

in the direction of women's "spirituality" unbelievably fulsome: ". . . not one of [the sailors] . . . had been in contact with a good [sic!] woman, or within the influence or redemption which irresistibly radiates from such a creature."

When Van Weyden first sees Maud Brewster, he is moved to enthusiasm: "She seemed . . . like a being from another world. I was aware of a hungry outreaching for her, as of a starving man for bread. . . . I know that I was lost in a great wonder, almost a stupor—this, then, was a woman?" (pp. 585-86)

Maud Brewster leaves the *Ghost* with Van Weyden in an open boat 600 miles from nowhere, and while Van Weyden rests and sleeps, she steers that boat for seven consecutive hours. At that juncture what Van Weyden is moved to admiration by is her "femininity" in searching for a hairpin! . . . When they have landed on the island they call Endeavor, Maud works with him to build a shelter, gathers driftwood, cooks, and helps Van Weyden to kill bull seals for meat. Consequently, Van Weyden loves her for being "one small woman," and his virility is bolstered by having someone "weaker" than he dependent on him for protection. . . . Shortly thereafter, as Forrey astutely points out, Van Weyden resumes his feminine role by making breakfast for Maud, who then accuses him of usurping her role. Van Weyden is both relieved and delighted by her firm insistence that "*she* is going to play the feminine role." (pp. 586-87)

The "socialist" London makes his hero responsible for "one small woman," but is unable to move his hero to help save Leach or Johnson, or to help the sailors in the forecastle kill Larsen, to give only two important examples. This "hardening" as a result of love makes Van Weyden realize that the "death which Wolf Larsen . . . had made me fear, I no longer feared. The coming of Maud Brewster into my life seemed to have transformed me." The delicate, ethereal Maud Brewster also devolves until she can help Van Weyden club seals to death and also save him from Larsen's suffocating embrace—psychoanalytically another obvious conflict between Van Weyden's homosexuality and heterosexuality—by knocking Larsen unconscious with a seal club. Having done so, she becomes the "mate-woman" not the "one small woman," and Van Weyden exults: "Truly she was my woman, my mate-woman, fighting with me and for me as the mate of a caveman would have fought, all the primitive in her aroused, forgetful of her culture, hard under the softening civilization of the only life she had ever known."

London kept his promise to the *Century*'s readers and the great "American Prude" but at a considerable cost. Though Van Weyden and Maud spend days in an open boat, and weeks on a deserted island, there is no sex between them. Their natural functions are never referred to and, in fact, they are depicted as virtually bodiless. The love affair between them is pale, sexless, and utterly unrealistic, though it is pitched on a high rhetorical plane. (pp. 587-88)

Despite London's stated intentions for the novel, Vernon L. Parrington saw *The Sea-Wolf* as the "frankest statement in American literature of the unbridled will-to-power, egoistic, amoral. A malignant ferocity in a philosophical, herculean sea captain, whose body is destroyed by paresis, but whose malignancy is unconquered." Assuming that the writer knew what he was doing, and Parrington—and many other critics and readers—knew what they were reading, how could intention and achievement be so far apart? Technically, London was telling the truth when he claimed he had *intended* to write an attack on the "super-man philosophy"; the "superficial story" does on a superficial reading attest to the decline and fall of Wolf Larsen, but the "underlying tendency" works the other way. As in *Call of the Wild,* London had written a philosophical and political allegory in *The Sea-Wolf,* and very likely as unwittingly, in which "the little floating world" of the *Ghost* was to convey the larger one as he saw and felt it. That world was run by cruel "captains" of industry, like Larsen. Larsen and his kind of capitalism are eventually done to death by the newer industrialists who, like his brother Death, use new machinery—the steamboat not the sailboat—and give the crew a bigger share of the profits (London uses the sea term *lay,* which carries the sexual double entendre), for which they desert the *Ghost* for the *Macedonia.*

The workers of that world, the sailors, are too inferior, weak, undisciplined and cowardly to be able to overthrow these "captains of industry," supported as they are by the guns of the hunters, police and military force. Such leaders of the workers as arise—violent, hating ones like Leach, or those like Johnson who are "swayed by idea, by principle, and truth, and sincerity,"—are soon isolated and killed for their independence and rebelliousness; the rest are reduced to passivity, indifference, or the kind of servility that the Mugridges stand for.

Capitalism is the hell ship where the intellectuals, like Van Weyden, are forced to be the "mates," but even when they act as helmsmen, they steer where the captain directs and they obey his orders. Although they are sympathetic to the cause of the workers, such intellectuals are neither tough enough nor brave enough to join the workers in overthrowing their captains' tyranny, so they make do with sentiment and poetry, love and books. (pp. 589-90)

To Larsen, London gives an intensity of being, imbuing him with all his own energy, pride, intelligence and lust for domination. Wolf Larsen dominates the book and all its characters. (p. 591)

There was then, for profound psychological reasons, a confusion between London's professed intention and his actual achievement. Just as Milton unquestionably wished to justify God's ways to man yet imbued Satan with much of his own pride and grandeur, so too London probably wanted to show Wolf Larsen's depravity and defeat but instead emphasized his pride and grandeur. Because Larsen was so much a projection of tumultuous forces in London's own personality, he could do no other. . . . To Larsen, London gave his own name, "Wolf," his own poverty and deprivation and hard work as a child. Larsen was a sailor too, with all the strength, courage and good looks London wanted others to think he had, and in some measure did have. London gave Larsen the same melancholy, the same materialist philosophy, the same intense hostility for and aggression against men and society that he himself had. In places he even gives him the same language, phrases that were to be repeated in interviews, letters and other books, even that bitterly reiterated, "My mistake was in ever opening the books." Unconsciously, too, in his description of Larsen's mind and temperament, he gave a penetrating criticism of his own mind and temperament. "He betrayed the inaccuracies of the self-read man, and, it must be granted, the sureness and directness of the primitive mind. The very simplicity of his reasoning was its strength." . . . Unfortunately, that simplicity was not strong enough to sustain London's art, or his beliefs, or his marriage, or, finally, his life. (p. 593)

Abraham Rothberg, "Land Dogs and Sea Wolves: A Jack London Dilemma," *in* The Massachusetts Review, *Vol. XXI, No. 3, Fall, 1980, pp. 569-93.*

JAMES DICKEY   (essay date 1981)

[*Dickey is considered one of America's foremost contemporary poets. He is also the author of the bestselling novel* Deliverance *(1970). In the following excerpt from an introduction to* The Call of the Wild, White Fang, and Other Stories, *Dickey discusses the symbolic and personal significance of the wolf in the author's Arctic stories and other works. Unlike other critics, Dickey regards London's depictions of dogs and wolves in his stories as mythic rather than realistic, and considers the stories convincing examples of the "connection between the creative powers of an individual writer and the unconscious drive to breed and survive, found in the natural world."*]

"Primeval" is a word often used to describe Jack London's work, his attitude toward existence, and his own life. From the beginning of the intensive self-education he undertook early in his adolescence through the end of his life at the age of forty, he prided himself on his "animality," and identified with his chosen totem beast, the wolf. His gullible friend, the California poet George Sterling, called him Wolf, he referred to his wife as Mate-Woman, named his ill-fated mansion in the Sonoma Valley Wolf House, and created his most memorable human character, Wolf Larsen, in *The Sea Wolf.* Larsen exemplifies all of the characteristics London admired most: courage, resourcefulness, ruthlessness, and above all, a strength of will that he partly bases on that of Milton's Satan in *Paradise Lost.* Larsen's favorite lines from Milton are "To reign is worth ambition, though in hell: / Better to reign in hell than serve in heaven," a sentiment with which London certainly concurred.

This attitude toward the *figure* of the wolf—a kind of Presence, an image, a symbolic and very personal representation of a mythologized human being—is pervasive throughout all of London's Arctic tales and is implied in many of his other fictions. The reader should willingly give himself over to this interpretation of the wolf, and conjure the animal up in the guise of the mysterious, shadowy, and dangerous figment that London imagines it to be. We should encounter the Londonian wolf as we would a spirit symbolic of the deepest forest, the most extremely high and forbidding mountain range, the most desolate snowfield: in short, as the ultimate wild creature, supreme in savagery, mystery, and beauty.

The mythic wolf that London "found" in his single winter spent in the Canadian North during the Klondike Gold Rush of 1897-98 and imbued with strangeness and ferocity bears in fact little resemblance to any true wolf ever observed. In studies by biologist Adolph Murie and researchers like L. David Mech and Boyce Rensberger, the wolf emerges as a shy and likable animal with a strong aversion to fighting. (pp. 7-8)

And yet London's wolf is very much a part of the consciousness of many people, and as the wolf's habitat continues to shrink under the pressure of oil pipelines and other industrial encroachments, its mystery and its savage spirituality increase, now that vulnerability has been added. We need London's mythical wolf almost as much as we need the wildernesses of the world, for without such ghost-animals from the depths of the human subconscious we are alone with ourselves.

That Jack London, the Klondike, the wolf, and the dog should have come together in exactly the circumstances that the gold-fever afforded seems not so much a merely fortunate conjunction of events but a situation tinged strongly with elements of predestination, of fate. Born in poverty only a little above the truly abject, London displayed almost from the beginning such a will to dominate as might have been envied by Satan himself, or for that matter, by Milton. (pp. 8-9)

During his later travels and his battles for survival in the economic wilderness, he came quickly to the belief that knowledge is indeed power. In his case, knowledge was more than the simple and too-abstract word "power" implied; it was muscle, blood, teeth, and stamina; it gave the force and direction that the will must take. When he landed in the Yukon in 1897, he had already read, with virtually superhuman voraciousness, hundreds of books and articles, principally in the fields of sociology, biology, and philosophy. He was alive with ideas and a search for ultimate meaning that amounted to an obsessively personal quest, and shared with the pre-Socratic philosophers . . . a belief that the great All is single and can be known. As he moved farther into the winter wilderness of the northern latitudes, he came increasingly to the conclusion that the "white silence" of the North is the indifferently triumphant demonstration of the All, the arena where the knowable Secret could most unequivocally be apprehended and, as the conditions demanded, lived. The snowfields, mountains, forests, and enormous frozen lakes were to London only the strictest, most spectacular, and unarguable symbols of the universal abyss, the eternal mystery at the heart of nothingness, or the eternal nothingness at the heart of mystery, as Herman Melville saw it in *Moby Dick*. (pp. 9-10)

London's scattered but deeply *felt* reading had so imbued him with Darwinian principles that he looked on the landscape of the Yukon as a kind of metaphysical arena in which natural selection and the survival of the fittest were enacted unendingly, illustrating (though to no perceiver but the casual) the "Law." The North is a background that determines character and action, bringing out in men certain qualities from the psychic depths of the race of all living beings. London does not attempt, as Melville does, to strike through the "mask." The "mask" in London's tales is more the classic mask of the actor, the mask that each participant feels rising to his face from the setting of the drama, the frozen features that *rerum natura* has always reserved for it.

As George Orwell has remarked, London's instincts "lay toward acceptance of a 'natural aristocracy' of strength, beauty and talent." Few writers have dwelt with such fixation on superlatives: "the strongest," "the biggest," "the handsomest," "the most cunning," "the fiercest," "the most ruthless." One cannot read these stories without agreeing with Orwell that "there is something in London [that] takes a kind of pleasure in the whole cruel process. It is not so much an approval of the harshness of nature, as a mystical belief that nature *is* like that. 'Nature red in tooth and claw.' Perhaps fierceness is the price of survival. The young slay the old, the strong slay the weak, by an inexorable law." London insists, as Melville does not, that there is a morality inherent in the twin drives of animal evolution; brute survival and the desire of the species to reproduce itself are not primary but exclusive motivations.

In this savage theater of extremes, this vast stage of indifference, where "the slightest whisper seemed sacrilege," London felt himself to be a man speaking out of the void of cosmic neutrality and even to it and for it, wearing, really, no mask but his half-frozen face, from which issued in steam and ice the truth of existence: the way things are.

The actors are men and dogs. (pp. 10-11)

London's anthropomorphizing of animals is well known, and the instances in which he overindulges this tendency are frequent and sometimes absurd. He was no Rilke or Lawrence, seemingly able to project his own human point of observation into another entity, either living or inorganic, and *become* the contemplated Other. He could not and certainly would not have wanted to know, as Aldous Huxley said Lawrence did, "by personal experience, what it was like to be a tree or a daisy or a breaking wave or even the mysterious moon itself. He could get inside the skin of an animal and could tell you in the most convincing detail how it felt and how, dimly, inhumanly, it thought." London had no wish to negate himself in favor of becoming an animal; the London dog or wolf is presented not as itself but as London feels that *he* would feel if he were embodied in the form of a dog or a wolf. The self-dramatizing Nietzschean is always very much present. In the canine battle scenes, for example, London analyzes with an almost absurd and quite human confidence the various "tactics" employed by the participants.

> But Buck possessed a quality that made for greatness—imagination. He fought by instinct, but he could fight by head as well. He rushed, as though attempting the old shoulder trick, but at the last instant swept low to the snow and in. His teeth closed on Spitz's left fore leg. There was a crunch of breaking bone, and the white dog faced him on three legs. Thrice he

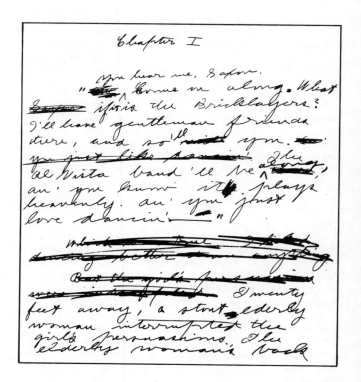

Holograph copy of the first page of London's The Valley of the Moon. *Courtesy of the Trust of Irving Shepard.*

tried to knock him over, then repeated the trick and broke the right fore leg.

Anyone who has ever seen dogs fighting knows that such subtleties as "the old shoulder trick" do not occur; if the affair is not merely one of a good deal of threatening noise, then one dog just goes for the other in any way possible. When London describes what dogs *do* rather than what they "think"—how they *look* when listening, how they appear when in repose, how they pace when restless or hungry—he is very good. When he makes a primitive philosopher of the dog in the same sense in which the author is himself a primitive philosopher, the result is less convincing. One believes of Bâtard that in five years "he heard but one kind word, received but one soft stroke of a hand, and then he did not know what manner of things they were." It is quite conceivable that a dog that had never received such treatment would not know how to respond. On the other hand, Buck's mystique of racial fulfillment, his metaphysical musculature, are . . . plainly impossible. . . . Likewise, White Fang's encounter with the Californian electric streetcars "that were to him colossal screaming lynxes" is not the product of a first-rate imagination. London merely knew that, since White Fang had lived in the Arctic and lynxes also lived there, and since lynxes sometimes make noises and streetcars also make them, he could feel justified in combining these items in a figure of speech the reader would be inclined to take as reasonable because neither reader nor lynx nor London nor streetcars could prove it was not. A moment's reflection, however, should disclose how farfetched the image is; the dog would simply have been bothered by the utter *unfamiliarity* of the machine, would simply have apprehended it as a large noise-making *something*, though assuredly no lynx.

White Fang was conceived as a "complete antithesis and companion piece to *The Call of the Wild*." London averred that "I'm going to reverse the process. Instead of the devolution or decivilization of a dog, I'm going to give the evolution, the civilization of a dog—development of domesticity, faithfulness, love, morality, and all the amenities and virtues." Yet, why is *White Fang*—more than twice as long as *The Call of the Wild* and a good deal more virtue-bent in the human sense of intention, a story in which the animal protagonist ends not as the leader of a pack of wild wolves but crooning his "lovegrowl" amidst a chorus of city women rubbing his ears and calling him the Blessed Wolf—why is it so markedly inferior to the story of reversion? Largely, I think, because the events depicted in *The Call of the Wild* are closer to what one *wants* to see happen: because we desire the basic, the "natural," the "*what is*" to win and not the world of streetcars and sentimentalism that we have made. Thus, in a sense, if we accede to London's narrative we also are approving of God and his white, mocking malevolence, his "Law" maintaining sway over all the irrelevances and over-subtleties of mechanized life. We like the author for putting the perspective in this way, and especially in a way as forthright, inexorable, exciting, and involving as he commands.

The key to London's effectiveness is to be found in his complete absorption in the world he evokes. The author is *in* and committed to his creations to a degree very nearly unparalleled in the composition of fiction. The resulting go-for-broke, event-intoxicated, headlong wild-Irish prose-fury completely overrides a great many stylistic lapses and crudities that would ordinarily cause readers to smile. As Orwell notes, "the texture of the writing is poor, the phrases are worn and obvious, and the dialogue is erratic."[3]

True, but it is nonetheless also true that London has at his best the ability to involve the reader in his story so thoroughly that nothing matters but *what* happens; in this sense he is basic indeed. His primary concern is action, with no pause to allow the savoring of verbal nuances or subtleties of insight. "La vérité, c'est dans la nuance," said Flaubert. London would have left that notion behind in the dog blood crystallizing on the ice floe, the eddying plume of a miner's frozen breath. His style is in presenting what *is,* and that only. As a writer London is at his most compelling in "presentational immediacy"; the more the passage relates to the nerves and feelings of the body, the more effective it is. (pp. 12-15)

He is an artist of violent action, exemplifying what the American poet Allen Tate meant when he said: "I think of my poems as commentaries on those human situations from which there is no escape." Once caught in London's swirling, desperate, life-and-death violence, the reader has no escape either, for it is a vision of exceptional and crucial vitality. London's most characteristic tales have the graphic power of the best cinema. . . . [The] quintessential Jack London is in the on-rushing compulsiveness of his northern stories. Few men have more convincingly examined the connection between the creative powers of the individual writer and the unconscious drive to breed and to survive, found in the natural world. (p. 16)

> *James Dickey, in an introduction to* The Call of the Wild, White Fang, and Other Stories *by Jack London, edited by Andrew Sinclair, Penguin Books, 1981, pp. 7-16.*

MICHAEL QUALTIERE (essay date 1982)

[*In the following excerpt, Qualtiere compares the character Wolf Larsen's mental and physical deterioration to Nietzsche's symptoms during his "long sickness." Qualtiere concludes that Larsen's perception of Nietzsche's intention in his "Revaluation of Values," his brain disease, his recurring headaches, blindness, and paralysis parallel Nietzsche's deterioration in a way that defies coincidence. Qualtiere considers this sufficient evidence that London was aware of the potential destructiveness of introspective discoveries that lead to rejection of traditional morality. For contrasting views of London's treatment of this theme in his works, see the excerpts by Jonathan Harold Spinner (1970) and Abraham Rothberg (1980).*]

This study will suggest that the complex mental life of Wolf Larsen, [*The Sea-Wolf*'s] central figure, was expressly designed to reflect Nietzsche's personal psychological history. (p. 261)

For this discussion, the most significant aspect of Wolf Larsen's philosophy is the way it follows, point by point, Nietzsche's Revaluation of Values. For example, the cornerstone of the Revaluation is Nietzsche's violent repudiation of altruism. The German scholar insisted that human pity and compassion—values traditionally held in high regard—are actually *immoral;* he described them as "decadent values," sins against oneself. . . .

In *The Sea-Wolf,* this "revaluation" of altruism is the principal theme of the novel's opening section. "Then you don't believe in altruism?" narrator Humphrey Van Weyden asks Wolf Larsen. Larsen's reply, "I do wrong always when I consider the interests of others," echoes Nietzsche's sentiment exactly. Altruism? Larsen scoffs, "I wouldn't stand for that." . . . (p. 262)

Larsen's rejection of altruism is but one of a series of Nietzschean considerations that emerge from the recurring incident-questioning-revaluation pattern of the narrative. First, Van Weyden is exposed to and threatened by a gratuitous brutality—some incident that challenges his traditional values. Second, he engages Larsen in a discussion of the event, one that inevitably leads to a questioning of those values. Third, in every instance, Wolf Larsen repudiates the values, vehemently rejecting any moral conception of life. "We sail away right *over* morality," wrote Nietzsche in *Beyond Good and Evil,* "we crush out, we destroy perhaps the remains of our own morality by daring to make our voyage...."

Note the similarity between Nietzsche's imagery and that of *The Sea-Wolf.* Nietzsche used a recurring metaphor in his discussion of the Revaluation and of its associated psychological trauma, the long sickness: that of a small ship far removed from the security of land, tossed about on stormy and uncharted seas. This imagery is found throughout *Thus Spake Zarathustra, Fate and History,* and *The Joyful Wisdom,* and is seen even in *The Birth of Tragedy* and *Beyond Good and Evil.* (p. 263)

Nietzsche's imagery, with its allusions to psychological "homesickness" and "longing for the land," is the central metaphor of *The Sea-Wolf.* It is aboard the *Ghost,* a small ship tossed about on uncertain seas, far removed from the security of land, that the lengthy intellectual discussions between the narrator and his principal antagonist take place. The voyage of the *Ghost,* under the careful tutelage of Wolf Larsen, becomes Neitzsche's "voyage" of Revaluation....

Each time Van Weyden takes one of his many grievances or concerns to Wolf Larsen, he enters the conversation armed with a theretofore unquestioned moral conception of life. He insists on interpreting life in terms of transcendent concepts—purpose, truth, virtue, right and wrong, eternal life—, in his words, those "dreams, radiant flashing dreams" ... that have traditionally given aim and meaning to human existence.

Nietzsche's Revaluation of Values flatly rejected such idealism. (p. 264)

Wolf Larsen, with Nietzsche, regards the concept of eternal life as mere "slush and sentiment." ... According to Larsen, there is no higher "Truth," no higher *anything.* The concepts of "Truth," "God," "human soul," he says, arise from "the drunkenness of life, the stirring and crawling of the yeast, the babbling of the life that is insane with consciousness that it is alive." ...

With Nietzsche, Larsen insists on moving beyond good and evil. The concepts of sin, virtue, and of right and wrong, he says, are simply "human fictions." ...

Life, Larsen maintains, is no more than a festering yeast, something that lives and moves simply because it is the inclination of life to live and move. And, with Nietzsche, Larsen denies any "aim" or "purpose" in existence—any "reason" to live or move. Pointing to his crew, Larsen says, "They move in order to eat in order that they may keep moving." ...

Van Weyden's response sounds the first strains of the "long sickness." "But the hopelessness of it," he protests.

"I agree with you," replies Larsen. (p. 265)

Nietzsche predicted the long sickness as the inevitable psychological consequence of his Revaluation. This sense of despair and hopelessness follows rejection of the concepts that once provided focus and significance to human existence. Without the sustenance of these principles, life becomes a meaningless

struggle in a valueless world, a hopeless effort carried on for no apparent reason. (pp. 265-66)

Nietzsche's prediction of the long sickness was based largely on personal experience; the German scholar suffered acutely from the psychological after-shock of his own Revaluation. "My existence is a *fearful burden*," he wrote in 1880. "What shall I do? Every morning I despair of outliving the day" (1885). "Night and day, I am in a state of unbearable tension and oppression ... Nothing is sick, but the poor soul" (1888)....

Wolf Larsen has similarly "pulled out" those concepts once used, in Nietzsche's words, "to project some value into the world." In their absence, the same unyielding melancholy of Nietzsche's long sickness emerges at the core of Larsen's psychological profile. (p. 266)

Shortly after being taken hostage aboard the *Ghost,* Van Weyden—now "afflicted with Wolf Larsen's repulsive ideas" ...—begins to exhibit all the symptoms of the long sickness. The narrator finds that "[l]ife had become cheap and tawdry, a beastly and inarticulate thing, a soulless stirring of the ooze and slime." ... As he gradually beings, in his own words, "... to find in Wolf Larsen's forbidding philosophy a more adequate explanation of life than I found in my own...." ... he realizes that he is losing "all that was best and brightest in life." ... "Where was the grandeur of life," laments Van Weyden....

The sentiment evident in Van Weyden's quote "the sooner over and done with the better," the conviction that life has been so devalued that even death seems a better option, is the primary symptom of the long sickness. This sentiment occurs thematically throughout the initial section of *The Sea-Wolf.* Minutes after arriving aboard the *Ghost,* Van Weyden witnesses the burial of a man whose features "had frozen into a diabolical grin at the world he had left and outwitted." ... Later, Wolf Larsen openly predicts that crewmember Johnson will kill himself out of despair of living in this "little floating world." "And as for you, Johnson," taunts Larsen, "you'll get so tired of life before I'm through with you that you'll fling yourself over the side. See if you don't." ... Finally, the entire crew deserts Wolf Larsen and his "forbidding philosophy" in favor of his symbolically named brother—Death Larsen—because, simply, Death offered them a better deal. "He gave them a bigger lay," says Larsen of Death. (p. 267)

No one aboard the *Ghost,* however, is as deeply affected by the psychological after-shock of Revaluation than is Wolf Larsen himself. Having negated the traditional concepts, Larsen is faced with an empty, meaningless existence and, like Nietzsche before him, is beset by "black moods," ... "primal melancholy," ... and unyielding despair....

Significantly, London clearly indicates that it is Wolf Larsen's philosophy, his rejection of human fictions and illusions, that has led him to despair. Larsen has, in effect, *reasoned* himself into depression. Immediately following a lengthy discussion during which the sea captain once again rejects tradition and asserts his own Nietzschean philosophy, Van Weyden diligently notes Larsen's mood and is specific as to its origins: "The old primal melancholy was strong upon him. He was quivering to it. He had reasoned himself into a spell of the blues...." (p. 268)

Wolf Larsen ... has pulled out the sustaining concepts, leaving his world empty and valueless. The consequent mental anguish which besets him would therefore seem, by Nietzsche's own definition, to be a studied example of the long sickness. (p. 269)

With his philosophical predecessor, Larsen falls prey to the profound conflict between intellectual conviction and emotional longing. "I often doubt," he confides to Van Weyden,

> "the worthwhileness of reason. Dreams must be more substantial and satisfying. Emotional delight is more filling and lasting than intellectual delight; and, besides, you pay for your moments of intellectual delight by having the blues. Emotional delight is followed by no more than jaded senses which speedily recuperate. I envy you. I envy you."
>
> (p. 270)

However, despite the psychological pressures of Revaluation, Larsen holds fast to his intellectual convictions, regretfully explaining that it is too late for him to change....

Although shaken himself by inner conflict, Friedrich Nietzsche likewise clung to his philosophical theories, thus laying the groundwork for an explosive psychic struggle....

Nietzsche did in fact suffer a dramatic mental-physical breakdown. An overview of public reaction to this breakdown suggests that the widespread notoriety and speculation surrounding Nietzsche's collapse significantly influenced London's writing of *The Sea-Wolf*.

The most persistent theory at the turn of the century speculated that the strain of his philosophic efforts and the tremendous pressure of his psychic conflict played a critical role in Nietzsche's collapse. This opinion, based on the initial medical and psychological diagnoses, was later popularized by the scholarly opinions and publications of the academic community, the hundreds of magazine articles written about Nietzsche prior to and immediately after his death in August of 1900, and his earliest biographers. (p. 271)

Apparently, Jack London believed that the inference, at least, was a valid one. London believed that Nietzsche (as was emphasized in the case of Wolf Larsen) had, in a manner of speaking, *reasoned* himself to his final condition. In *The Iron Heel,* London wrote of

> Friedrich Nietzsche, the mad philosopher of the nineteenth century . . . who, before he was done, reasoned himself around the great circle of human thought and off into madness.

When London's wife, Charmian, praised the philosophy of Nietzsche's *Thus Spake Zarathustra,* Jack answered by recalling the German scholar's eventual collapse. Charmian later described the incident: "I called attention to the wholesome philosophy of Zarathustra. In return I was reminded by Jack of Nietzsche's ultimate fate."

This background brings us to what may be the most important, if undiscovered, Nietzschean element of *The Sea-Wolf*—Wolf Larsen's mysterious collapse. Nietzsche's inner turmoil led to his slow decline and eventual breakdown. The philosophical and psychological events of Wolf Larsen's life closely parallel Nietzsche's personal history, and he also suffers a gradual decline and breakdown—one remarkably similar to that of the German scholar. Did Jack London, aware of the specific details of Nietzsche's collapse and enticed by the symbolic potential of historical fact, choose to translate Nietzsche's own symp-

toms into the symptoms and the symbols of Wolf Larsen's decline?

Examination of the collapse of each supports this suggestion. Nietzsche and Larsen are both felled by a mysterious "brain breakdown." Nietzsche to the end remained uncertain as to the exact origin and nature of his illness. "It is very difficult," he wrote, "to diagnose what is wrong with my brain...." There was no question, however, that his illness did involve some sort of breakdown of the higher nerve-centers, and that Nietzsche was, in his own words, "in the throes of a serious disease of the brain." Speaking of an "inflammation of the brain," and of the "cerebral *coup de grace*" he feared close at hand, Nietzsche wrote, "I have had to give up doubting. The malady which has attacked me is cerebral...."

Wolf Larsen is also uncertain of the exact diagnosis of his illness, but concedes that it is as Van Weyden has suggested, "some sort of brain breakdown." ... "But how can you account for it?" the narrator asks. "Where is the seat of your trouble?"

"The brain," Larsen answers immediately, echoing Nietzsche's own words.... (pp. 272-74)

The symptoms of their respective cerebral disorders are likewise strikingly similar. Nietzsche and Larsen share violent, recurring headaches. Nietzsche's adult life was plagued by a constant battle against headaches—headaches which, in his own words, were "of the most violent kind lasting for several days." (p. 274)

Wolf Larsen also suffers violent, recurring headaches lasting for several days and rendering him senseless and bedridden until they pass....

In Van Weyden's poignant description of Larsen's headaches, we glimpse the German scholar himself—dazed and reeling from the shattering attacks....

In the slow process of decline, Nietzsche and Larsen experience a gradual loss of vision. (p. 275)

The imagery of vision becomes symbolic when, foreshadowing his fate, Larsen admits he sometimes wishes that he were "blind to the facts of life" . . .—all the while insisting, however, that his understanding, his *perception* of those facts is accurate. His repeated explanations and philosophical arguments typically employ this idiomatic sense of "to see:"

> "As I see it, I do wrong always when I consider the interests of others. Don't you see?" ...
>
> "I wouldn't stand for that . . . [altruism]. Couldn't see the necessity for it, nor the common sense." ...
>
> "Because I am a bigger bit of the ferment than you? Don't you see? Don't you see?" ...

Finally, it is Wolf Larsen who does not "see"; his eyes are glazed and twisted, his vision grows weaker and eventually fails him altogether.

The illness of both Friedrich Nietzsche and Wolf Larsen is also marked by a severe "paralytic disturbance." Nietzsche's final collapse in 1889 was at first characterized as a "paralytic stroke." A diagnosis of "progressive paralysis" was later entered under the section *Disease* at the head of the record and signed by the noted psychiatrist Wille who examined Nietzsche at the time of his admittance to the Basel Psychiatric Clinic. Nietzsche's progressive decline, during which he became an invalid, confined to bed or chair, seemingly confirmed that he was indeed, as Dr. Binswanger of the Jena Mental Hospital had diagnosed, suffering from a "psychic paralytic disturbance."

Wolf Larsen suffers the same physical decline. Progressive paralysis cripples Larsen's body and destroys his once indomitable will until he too lies completely immobile and mute. (p. 276)

In his selection of paralysis as one of the symptoms—one of the symbols—of Wolf Larsen's decline, London appears to have drawn on the peculiar irony of Nietzsche's fate. Nietzsche had often used paralysis as a metaphor, both to emphasize the frustration of nineteenth century existence, and to warn of the potential consequence of Revaluation and the long sickness. "Paralysis of the will;" he wrote in *Beyond Good and Evil*, "where do we not find this cripple sitting nowadays!" And yet, even as he cautioned his readers, warning that his philosophy had the effect of "paralyzing and breaking the weak," ironic foreshadowings began to appear in Nietzsche's own life as early as 1880.... As the "progressive paralysis" of his later years overtook him, Nietzsche himself became broken and crippled. Thus Nietzschean scholar Walter Kaufmann writes, "Without seeking to explain away Nietzsche's illness, one can hardly fail today to consider it also symbolical."

A similar irony is witnessed in the progressive paralysis of Wolf Larsen. Larsen . . . denies those traditional concepts which would give "aim" or "purpose" to human activity. "We want

to live and move," he insists, "though we have no reason to. . . ." It was this particular life-view to which Nietzsche referred when he wrote, "There is one great paralysis: to work *in vain*, to struggle in vain." Wolf Larsen, who believes that it *is* all in vain, that there is no "aim," no "reason" to live and move, eventually, and symbolically, becomes paralyzed. Van Weyden comments on the irony: "'To be' was all that remained to him—to be, as he had defined death, without movement. . . ." (p. 277)

It is difficult to imagine that, in constructing the downfall of the novel's Nietzschean figure, Jack London selected a "Revaluation of Values" followed by a mysterious brain breakdown, violent, recurring headaches, gradual loss of vision, and progressive paralysis—the supposed cause and exact symptoms of the collapse of Friedrich Nietzsche—by chance alone. (p. 278)

Michael Qualtiere, "Nietzschean Psychology in London's 'The Sea-Wolf'," in Western American Literature, *Vol. XVI, No. 4, Winter, 1982, pp. 261-78.*

JOAN D. HEDRICK   (essay date 1982)

[*Hedrick is an American educator and the author of* Solitary Comrade: Jack London and His Work. *In the following excerpt from that work, Hedrick seeks to illustrate London's inability to integrate his political insight with his emotional limitations in such "socialist" works as* The Iron Heel.]

After London established his literary reputation, he had more latitude in the material the editors would accept, and he experimented, especially in the period between 1905 and 1909, with stories that had a political point of view. It is fair to wonder if London did not bring a different consciousness to bear in the stories he wrote not for the literary marketplace but to further the cause of socialism. Three of these stories are especially revealing of London's relationship to the working class. They are **"The Apostate,"** . . . **"The Dream of Debs,"** . . . and **"South of the Slot."** . . . A fourth, **"The Strength of the Strong,"** . . . is notable for its eloquent expression of the goal of a cooperative commonwealth.

Much can be inferred about London's relation to his material by the persona that he adopts in the telling of his stories. **"The Strength of the Strong,"** like **"South of the Slot,"** is an extraordinarily controlled and well-wrought piece. In it London adopts the parable form and with it a formal distance from his material. He employs a third-person narrator, but the events of the tale, which concern the rivalry between two primitive tribes, the Meat-Eaters and the Fish-Eaters, are told by Long-Beard, patriarch of the Fish-Eaters. This story-within-the-story technique further distances author and reader from the material, as does the story's unfolding in the dawn of human history. London's narrative stance in **"The Strength of the Strong"** is very like that characteristically adopted by Hawthorne in his allegories of the human heart: there is an evenhandedness in the portrayal of characters, and personality is subordinated to psychological and social types. This is appropriate to their exploration not of one person's consciousness but of the dynamics of social intercourse. (p. 169)

[**"The Strength of the Strong"**] is perhaps London's finest expression of his socialist consciousness. The distancing achieved by his formal devices allows him to deal forthrightly with the institutions of his society. The parable is a disguise of sorts, but it is an accepted literary device through which dangerous and seditious views may be expressed. In that it is an accepted

Holograph copy of the final page of The Valley of the Moon. *Courtesy of the Trust of Irving Shepard.*

and "public" device, it differs from the private dream-language that characterizes London's more covert attempts to subvert his readers. The "public" quality of London's narrative stance is responsible for the high degree of control he exercises on his material. With complete awareness of what it is about, **"The Strength of the Strong"** juxtaposes what is with what should be. Yet it must be said that, like Hawthorne's allegories, this parable appeals primarily to the intellect, not the emotions. It lacks the power of *The Call of the Wild* and does not seem to engage London's and the reader's desires on the deepest level. Still, it is a more humanistic vision than London ordinarily brought to his stories of human beings, which perhaps has to do with the fact that the Fish-Eaters are suspended between the animal world and the modern world of industrial capitalism.

"The Apostate" is the most directly autobiographical of the four stories. Though London is predictably closer to his material, he still exercises a high degree of control over his story. Perhaps because the factory life of Johnny, a "work-beast," so clearly represented an earlier, discarded self, London was able both to understand his character and to feel distant from him. (pp. 170-71)

London could not have described Johnny's working-class life in such convincing detail had he not experienced the same mind-and-body-destroying factory rhythms; yet London attributes to his character a consciousness more limited than his own, and this discrepancy distances London from his creation. London's detachment is apparent in his description of Johnny as he walks away from his home and his job, never to return: "He did not walk like a man. He did not look like a man. He was a travesty of the human. It was a twisted and stunted and nameless piece of life that shambled like a sickly ape, arms loose-hanging, stoop-shouldered, narrow-chested, grotesque and terrible." . . . This description comes as a shock, even though the distortion of Johnny's body by his work has been completely accounted for. The reader can believe that the industrial labor has extorted a terrible human price; what is unacceptable and disturbing about London's description of Johnny as "a twisted and stunted and nameless piece of life" is that it seems to totally deny him humanity; he lacks even the glimmering illusions that made London's dray horse labor on. He is only a piece of flesh. In London's reduction of his character to this material basis he makes him less than human in the very moment that he asserts himself against the system that has dehumanized him. London can empathize with Johnny in his victory over his mother, but in this story neither Johnny nor his author break through to a fully human consciousness. Neither does the story transcend the immediate power relationships of the family to mount a critique of the social relations of capitalist production. (pp. 175-76)

In **"The Dream of Debs"** a general strike has paralyzed the whole country. . . . The major difference between this story and others in which London has portrayed the working class is that here they are superbly organized and disciplined, and, far from being beastly and degraded, they take destiny into their own hands and bring capital to their terms before the strike is over. . . . But the emotions that London might have brought to this collective struggle are singularly absent. London's use of an upper-class narrator who is victimized by the strike denies the reader direct participation in the working-class victory, and his dead-pan narration kills much of the vitality of the story. Clearly, as McClintock has suggested, London intended to satirize the limited consciousness of this Mr. Cerf,

whose final comment on the events is that the "tyranny of organized labor is getting beyond human endurance," and "something must be done." But it is significant that London was unable to imagine himself part of this working-class struggle. In this dream of working-class triumph, London allied his consciousness with that of a deposed upper-class victim. (p. 176)

In **"South of the Slot"** London creates an alternative to the scenario he had worked out in *The Sea-Wolf*. In that novel the bourgeois narrator triumphed over Wolf Larsen by refusing to look at the reality of capitalist society. In **"South of the Slot,"** the working-class persona triumphs over the middle-class Freddie Drummond, and, because Bill Totts is engaged in a collective struggle, he is associated not with the pessimistic materialism of Wolf Larsen but with unity, strength, and emotional wholeness. It is perhaps the only happy ending London ever wrote that was not sentimental and false, with the notable exception of *The Call of the Wild*. (p. 177)

If **"South of the Slot"** was Jack London's most self-aware socialist story, his most ambitious contribution to socialist literature was *The Iron Heel*. Insofar as *The Iron Heel* is compelling, its energy comes from what Trotsky [see *TCLC*, Vol. 9] called the "powerful intuition of the revolutionary artist." Ernest Everhard, the hero of this book, is able to see further than his contemporaries; before others are fully aware of the oligarchic tendencies of capitalism, Everhard prophecies the coming of the Iron Heel. London's power as a political visionary is the mainspring of a book that lacks novelistic interest yet deeply reveals the consciousness and identity of Jack London. (p. 188)

[By] focusing on the way *The Iron Heel* fails as a novel, we can perhaps better understand London's inability to integrate the political and the personal in his own consciousness. Better than any other single work, *The Iron Heel* reveals the radical disjunction between London's political insight and his emotional limitations. (p. 189)

The first scene in *The Iron Heel* is in outline precisely parallel to the opening scene of *Martin Eden;* the proletarian hero is brought to an upper-class home and introduced to the bourgeois heroine, who immediately falls in love with him. Both heroes make "a rather incongruous appearance." . . . The hero's powerful workingclass physique exercises its fascination on Avis. . . . Seated at dinner in the midst of Avis and her father, who is a university professor, and his preacher friends, who are skilled metaphysicians, Ernest not only knows how to use a knife and fork, he effortlessly triumphs in debate, and does it without even alluding to humiliations inflicted on him by his working-class background. (pp. 192-93)

Everhard is the scientific socialist, reasoning from the world to his ideas about the world; the ministers are the metaphysicians, reasoning from their consciousness to the world. But never does London suggest to his readers what some of these "facts" of working-class life were, for specificity would puncture the daydream. The purpose of this scene is not to enlighten the readers to the realities of working-class life but to impress upon them the superiority of Ernest Everhard. "How the scene comes back to me!" exclaims Avis. "I can hear him now, with that war-note in his voice, flaying them with his facts, each fact a lash that stung and stung again. And he was merciless." . . . The pleasure that we are meant to take in this triumph is covertly sado-masochistic. Everhard's intellectual battles with the capitalist class and their flunkies are repeatedly described in terms of physical violence ("sometimes he exchanged the rapier for the club and went smashing amongst their thoughts right and left'' . . .), and the pleasure Ernest takes in these victories is fraught with unhealthy and seemingly very unsocialistic emotions. Here he is at the Philomath Club, pausing in his blows to scrutinize the expression of his victim, Col. Van Gilbert, a tough corporation lawyer: ''Ernest paused for a moment and regarded him thoughtfully, noting his face dark and twisted with anger, his panting chest, his writhing body, and his slim white hands nervously clenching and un-clenching.'' . . . Though we are privy to these scenes sugges-tive of repressed sexuality, nowhere do we see Everhard ex-pressing tender and sexual feelings toward Avis. The closest he comes to it is the ''bold'' look he gives her at their first meeting: ''You pleased me,' he explained long afterward; 'and why should I not fill my eyes with that which pleases me?''' . . . Avis is delighted to be the object of his will, but her pleasure in his mastery is destined to be vicarious; in her erotic fantasies she prefers to see him mastering other men—in debate—to being herself sexually overpowered. . . . Her vicarious enjoy-ment of Ernest's powers makes her a perfect mate, for in the few scenes in which they are together, he is so exhausted from doing battle with the oligarchy that he is reduced to infantile dependence. . . .

> He paused and looked at me, and added:
>
> ''Social evolution is exasperatingly slow, isn't it, sweetheart?''
>
> My arms were about him, and his head was on my breast. ''Sing me to sleep,'' he murmured whimsically. ''I have had a visioning, and I wish to forget.'' . . .

Reminiscent of the scene in *The Sea-Wolf* when Maud tucks Humphrey into bed, this passage may also be compared to the scene in *Lady Chatterley's Lover,* when Clifford, the impotent husband of Lawrence's heroine, allows himself to be bathed and cared for by Ivy Bolton. Clifford Chatterley, a gentleman-artist whose war wound has not permitted him to be a real husband to his wife, has by this late point in the novel trans-formed himself into a hard-driving industrialist who achieves extraordinary production from his miners. . . . The perverse and infantile emotional relationships that Lawrence ascribes to his capitalist are identical to the ones London, in a much less self-conscious way, ascribes to his revolutionary. Both Law-rence and London describe relationships in which sexual feel-ings are displaced onto work and then replaced by pregenital, narcissistic emotions. In this scenario women allow men to sink back into a state of blissful unawareness. Ernest Everhard, whose X-ray vision crowds his consciousness with more reality than ordinary men experience, has particular need of this escape from thought.

Thus London's revolutionary hero has a very unrevolutionary consciousness. The contradictions here are acute: Everhard builds his vision of a new society by pumping iron in the oppressive social relationships of the capitalist society he wishes to over-throw. London's awareness of the contradictions of manhood in capitalist society was neutralized by his ignorance of the contradictions of womanhood. Like Hemingway, he writes about ''men without women.'' Even though London's heroes are sometimes with women, his understanding of them does not include their relationships with women. He is at his best when describing oppression in the male spheres of work, saloon, and prison. When he attempts to write about women's spheres, which he identifies with romantic love and the upper class, he

is too aware of his own victimization to understand the peculiar ways in which women, too, are victims. Like Charmian Lon-don, Avis Everhard takes pride in her ability to make her husband happy. . . . Ernest is simply too tired to extend the revolutionary struggle into the politics of his domestic life. But if we were to reply to Avis's rhetorical question—what greater joy could have blessed her than to provide her husband for-getfulness—we might suggest that she urge him to struggle with the politics of his own sexuality. (pp. 193-96)

If Ernest Everhard was too weary to take up this subject, he was doubtless also too threatened. The feelings associated with sexual politics are so intense as to require great personal cour-age to face. The intensity of London's feelings—in particular the intensity of his unconscious revulsion from women—may be suggested by a revealing slip of the pen. This occurs just after Ernest's initial triumph over the churchmen at the Cun-ningham's dinner table, in which Avis's father took great de-light. ''After the guests had gone, father threw himself into a chair and gave vent to roars of Gargantuan laughter. Not since the death of my mother had I known him to laugh so hear-tily.'' . . . Clearly Avis means ''not since *before* the death of my mother,'' but the elision conflates the two incidents, the death of the mother/wife and the confounding of the bourgeois metaphysicians. In this unconscious association, both events give rise to one long laugh of triumph. This slip may be com-pared to London's comments in *The Road* about the stories he made up about his past, for the consumption of his ''marks.'' Invariably he presented himself as an orphan, and he delighted in disposing of his mother through deadly disease: ''Heart disease was my favorite way of getting rid of my mother, though on occasion I did away with her by means of con-sumption, pneumonia, and typhoid fever.'' . . . London did not always wish death upon his mother figures, but, as Kevin Starr has observed, ''The shaming of an upper class woman appears as a frequent motif in London's stories.'' (p. 196)

In one further way *The Iron Heel* is suggestive of Jack London's consciousness and identity. Chapter 19 is entitled ''Transfor-mation,'' and here the common naturalistic device of a radical change in class identity is employed in the service of a guerila war against the Iron Heel. Avis assumes the identity of a daugh-ter of the oligarchy: she becomes Felice Van Verdighan. As a double agent, she gives secret signals to both the revolution-aries and the mercenaries of the oligarchy. ''As agents-prov-ocateurs, not alone were we able to travel a great deal, but our very work threw us in contact with the proletariat and with our comrades, the revolutionists. Thus we were in both camps at the same time, ostensibly serving the Iron Heel and secretly working with all our might for the Cause.'' . . . Her work ''in both camps at the same time'' is suggestive of the posture London maintained throughout much of his life, writing for the bourgeois press but attempting secretly to subvert their principles. In order to accomplish this, Avis is commanded by Ernest, ''You must make yourself over again so that even I would not know you—your voice, your gestures, your man-nerisms, your carriage, your walk, everything.'' Avis ob-eys. . . . London even imagines surgeons trained in the revo-lutionary art of plastic surgery. . . . But if one must become the enemy in order to destroy him, is the game worth the candle? London seems never to have asked this question in *The Iron Heel,* but it drives his hero to suicide in *Martin Eden.* (pp. 198-99)

Joan D. Hedrick, in her Solitary Comrade: Jack Lon-don and His Work, *The University of North Carolina Press, 1982, 265 p.*

MARY ALLEN (essay date 1983)

[*In the following excerpt from her* Animals in American Literature, *Allen examines London's Klondike stories, and argues that the author differed from the mainstream of Naturalistic writers because he depicted Darwinist theory literally, through his animals, rather than symbolically, through human protagonists. Allen also discusses London's obvious admiration for the wild and independent beast over the tamed animal, exemplified in* The Call of the Wild *and* White Fang.]

London has been placed both in and out of the naturalistic tradition in American literature. Charles Walcutt includes him on the basis of his advocacy of Spencer's *First Principles,* that blind, inexorable law is the operating force of the universe. Walcutt discovers, however, the discrepancy between London's ideas and the naturalistic use he makes of them. In a version of unfeeling nature in which man's death is insignificant, London's snow works as mechanistically as Crane's ocean in ''The Open Boat.'' But against that snow a subtle distinction exists in the death of London's characters: they commit a misstep of pride, an error in judgment. If naturalism precludes free will, London is not one of its followers. While his characters are limited by the conditions of the Klondike, they are there by choice. And it is possible to adapt. If they were doomed on arrival, the critical test of survival would not exist, a struggle that follows not as the unfolding of sheerly deterministic forces but as a result of individual instinct, imagination, and will.

Vernon Parrington excludes London from the naturalistic tradition on the basis of his revolutionary Nietzschean spirit that contradicts determinism, which Parrington sees as the key tenet of naturalism. And he is correct in doing so. The grim cosmos of Crane, Norris, and Dreiser, where Darwinism is applied almost exclusively as a social principle, shows man as an inevitably debased and defeated animal in an urban jungle. London's animalistic humans, even in the wilds where they are more visceral than city man, do resemble Norris's McTeague and similar hairy beasts. But London's men and other animals flare with will. While a prime determinant of the naturalistic protagonist's doom is his sexual appetite, that instinct is strikingly absent in most of London's people. Their physical drive is for food, a quest that does not always lead to disaster.

What most dramatically sets London apart from the mainstream of naturalism in his Klondike stories—something so obvious it is surprising to find it so rare—is that he makes Darwinism literal and presents the *animal characters themselves.* Jay Gurian makes the case that since ''a *wholly* naturalistic human hero is an impossibility,'' London solves a dilemma by creating the nonhuman hero, thus fulfilling a ''romantic necessity'' in naturalistic literature. But the very creation of a genuine hero dispenses with naturalism itself. The rare survivor in deterministic fiction, if considered heroic at all, is a cynical remnant of the struggle: Sister Carrie, for example.

London creates, instead, romantically realistic heroes in his dogs—and naturalism is dispelled. It is his socialistic works that reek of pessimistic determinism. His dogs not only survive but they triumph. Within the realm of actual behavior, the exceptional dog is capable of deeds that humankind finds noble. Because adaptability is more important than sheer savagery, the triumphant animal is much more than the most powerful predatory beast. On the other hand, where he does follow the laws of survival that offend the morality expected of the human hero, he may be excused.

Cover of The Owl, *the magazine in which London's first short story appeared in 1897. Courtesy of the Trust of Irving Shepard.*

Had London decided upon dogs sheerly for illustration of his Darwinist views, he could not have presented them more successfully. Yet he maintains he was simply writing stories about dogs, and his least ideological writing is his best. In response to the reader who finds a human allegory in his animal characters, London maintains that when he created them he was ''''unconscious of it at the time. I did not mean to do it.'''' London's affection, respect, his *passion* for dogs makes them better characters than his supermen, whose superiority is always in doubt and who must mouth ideas. In releasing his lushest poetry with his animals London is further removed from naturalism, in which emotions are as pared off as opportunities are. He not only makes Darwinism literal (interpreting survival as partially a matter of will), but in his writing of dogs London shares the exultant spirit of Darwin himself, a spirit that was darkly altered by naturalism as his theories were applied to social man.

The story of a dog that comes closest to the pessimistic conclusions of naturalism is **''Diable—A Dog,''** . . . in which the animal is conditioned to viciousness by a vicious master. A better Pavlovian example in fiction would be difficult to find. No one shows us more effectively than London not only *that* an animal develops in response to stimuli but just *how* that development takes place, as a natural process occurring in the dog's association with man rather than as a controlled experiment.

Motivated by hate for the meanest of the litter, Black Leclère purchases the pup Diable. . . . Unlike Diable's reactionary brutality, Leclère's hatred is a product of "understanding and intelligence." In mutual animosity man and dog roll on the ground tight as lovers. But while the dog's part in the struggle is a credible defense, Leclère's imitation of a beast is ludicrous. One is inclined to smile when a man bites back at a dog.

Leclère's will to dominate is all too darkly believable. His cruelty to the dog successfully fosters ferocity, whereas "with a proper master the puppy might have made a fairly ordinary, efficient sled dog." . . . Still, Leclère's drive to make Diable "wilt in spirit and cringe and whimper at his feet" . . . fails. Heredity and conditioning count for much in his behavior, but an individual will drives him on where another dog would be broken.

In an attack on the "nature" writing of his time, London denounces the view that all animals below man are "automatons and perform actions only of two sorts—mechanical and reflex—and that in such actions no reasoning enters at all." The belief that man is the only animal capable of reasoning, he says, "makes the twentieth-century scientist smile. It is not modern at all. It is distinctly mediaeval . . . homocentric." (pp. 78-80)

If *The Call of the Wild* is not London's most perfect work, it is as powerful as anything he wrote, with a mystique that, if anything, deepens the more civilized we become. Although written from Buck's point of view, the story is faithful to the accurate behavior of a dog. The tendency to enter the animal's consciousness in a well-developed portrayal is almost unavoidable, and London achieves that point of view with varying degrees of success. The awkward beginning, "Buck did not read the newspapers, or he would have known that trouble was brewing," gives the impression that the reader might have expected that the dog could read. To say that Buck is sent north to help men find "yellow metal" rather than gold does not solve the narrative problem of the nonverbal animal, for he no more knows the words *yellow* or *metal* than he knows the word *gold*. While one does not doubt that Buck "could not understand what it all meant" . . . when he is choked and thrown into a cage-like crate—either because such cruelty is incomprehensible *or* that a mere dog cannot grasp its meaning—this explanation lends a juvenile cast to a story which rises to much more than that. The terminology selected to represent the dog's mental processes, however, is carefully chosen according to the following theory: "I wrote, speaking of my dog-heroes: 'He did not think these things; he merely did them,' etc. And I did this repeatedly, to the clogging of my narrative and in violation of my artistic canons; and I did it in order to hammer into the average human understanding that these dog-heroes of mine were not directed by abstract reasoning, but by instinct, sensation, and emotion, and by simple reasoning."

After one's initial skepticism in response to an author's entry into a dog's consciousness, Buck's point of view soon becomes acceptable, unobtrusive. He is forever a real dog, while most of his emotions, particularly his passion for freedom, are convincingly drawn. If London is guilty of the occasional cliché in *The Call of the Wild*—Buck "was beaten (he knew that); but he was not broken" . . .—it is so fused with a passionate and original story that it may be forgiven. When London's fires

of injustice rage, as they do for the beaten and caged Buck, that reader would be hard who did not feel something for him. The buoyant emotions that triumph in the dog despite his acquaintance with the brutality of man and nature—which make most modern protagonists cynical—may be accepted as genuine, for the animal does not simulate emotions.

Buck is that classic American frontier hero—rugged, male, celibate, and free. As Raymond Benoit points out, in his escape to freedom Buck is as American as Rip Van Winkle. But while Rip's call of the wild is an escapist's fantasy, Buck makes the dream of going into the wilderness actual. What is more, London ingeniously makes him a *proletarian* hero. Uncommonly versatile, Buck may be domestic or wild, restrained or impassioned, accepting or rebellious. While adaptability is his overall strength, a quality potentially damaging to his individuality, Buck maintains his integrity by holding to obedience under necessity without becoming subservient: "a man with a club was a lawgiver, a master to be obeyed, though not necessarily conciliated." . . . (pp. 81-2)

Exemplar of Darwinism, Buck also becomes a revolutionary for the working class before London had officially put Marxism to work. Through it all Buck emerges as that rarity—a fulfilled character. The "me" generations of the latter twentieth century in the quest for physical and psychological wholeness, even in the search for vocational fulfillment, might find in Buck a kind of perfection, a sense of self-completion that reaches to joy according to that Greek definition of happiness—the exercise of vital powers along lines of excellence in a life affording them scope. Buck also touches the case of the modern in another powerful way: his experience is a triumph over a subtle but significant dread—the fear of fat living.

All of this is achieved through Buck within the bounds of a realism that revolutionized popular fiction in the 1900s. London defends his faithfulness to factual reality against a charge of "'gross falsifying of nature's records,'" of *nature fakery*, by a reader none other than the president of the United States, Theodore Roosevelt (whose charge that *White Fang* [1906] errs in having the lynx kill the wolf is based on a misreading—it is the other way around). London maintains that his books about dogs are "a protest against the 'humanizing' of animals, of which it seemed to me several 'animal writers' had been profoundly guilty." His chief target is John Burroughs, the popularizer of animal lore, who despite "well-exploited and patronizing devotion" to the "lower animals" considers them "disgustingly low." His homocentric view follows from the "self-exalted ego" that requires a vast distance between man and the other animals. London's strong fellow feeling for dogs is evident, but even more striking is his respect for them as remarkable individuals—capable of pain and fear, surely, but creatures unlike and often superior to man.

Only in the Alaskan frontier do London's dogs reach their fullness, a frontier whose time came perfectly for the wildly adventurous young man who went for gold and admittedly found himself in the Klondike. (pp. 82-3)

[Buck's] old life is remembered as one of boredom; there he was easily king of the whole realm of house and kennel. Now he must earn his place at the top. He waits, and when the time is right he defeats the team's head dog, Spitz, in a death struggle that calls not only for every ounce of his new-found strength but for great ingenuity as well.

As Buck's powers increase and the inhibitions of civilization are sluffed off, this mighty young male character lacks one thing that might certainly be expected in a return to nature, particularly an animal's return to nature—an uninhibited sexual life. Yet not only does Buck escape the entanglements of mating, but he is free from the bothersome urge altogether. His unquestionable sense of virility is evidenced instead through size, strength, prowess as a fighter, and the sheer energy of his joyful gallop across the snow which takes the place of breeding as the perpetuation of life. Buck's purifying passage to the primitive calls for the abandonment of all encumbrances (such as the woman who adds the last impossible weight to the sled). No troublesome female will travel with his pack.

The threat of the female is made emphatic in the example of the dog Dolly who goes ''suddenly mad,'' announcing her condition by a ''heartbreaking wolf howl that sent every dog bristling with fear.'' She goes straight for Buck, who knows only that ''here was horror, and fled away from it in panic'' with the frantic female ''panting and frothing, one leap behind.'' Nor does she ''gain on him, so great was his terror.'' Buck is never so frightened as he is here—and nowhere else does he run away. Even when he was kidnapped he did not panic. The spirit of the neurotic, destroying female is at large even in the Klondike, and Buck must go deeper into the wilderness to escape her—plunging through woods and across channels ''in desperation.'' . . . He is safe only when the dog-driver crushes Dolly's head with an ax.

If in the American grain Buck is predictably powerful, wilderness-loving, and celibate, he is uniquely a proletarian hero at the same time. The fact that the necessity for dogs in the Klondike took them both to the frontier and to unbearable working conditions allows for a call of the wild along with an appeal to workers of the world—in this case those who are literally enchained. When the dogs are first harnessed to the sleds they go at their task eagerly, suited as they are for long journeys in the cold. A team of huskies raising a spray of snow as they rip a sled out of place is a thrilling sight—and a triumph for them. When the dogs are fresh, all ''passiveness and unconcern'' disappear; they become ''alert and active, anxious that the work should go well, and fiercely irritable with whatever, by delay or confusion, retarded that work.'' . . . (pp. 84-5)

But extenuating labor is a greater killer than the cold. Buck turns rebel to incite the other dogs to protest their conditions and to overthrow the tyrannical leader, Spitz, a sort of class revolution that backfires into friction within the group. . . . Yet when Buck becomes head dog himself (a more just leader than Spitz, but an authority figure, nevertheless), being at the front of the sled only means more debilitating toil than before.

Most of London's dog-drivers do not learn the rule of the trail: that a man must first care for his dogs and then for himself. The old-timer knows for practical fact, not sentiment, that ''as with our dogs, so with us.'' It would be difficult to imagine a place where people were more dependent on animals than in the Klondike of the late 1890s, where sled dogs were *the* form of transportation, food consisted mainly of meat (at least it would seem so in London's work), a fur coat was a necessity, not to mention leather moccasins, and the dogs also provided entertainment by fighting and racing. . . . Buck would likely have died under the whip if John Thornton had not intervened to keep him in his camp. Together they watch as the foolhardy and cruel driver forces the remaining dogs across the spring ice—where the sled cracks through, taking dogs, men, and that extra weight, the woman, down to a justified death.

The stages leading to Buck's freedom, ironically set in motion when he is kidnapped from the sweet bondage of home, take

a new turn in his allegiance to Thornton, a loyalty that is the exception for the animal in American literature. To the credit of the many-faceted Buck, he is capable of affection and devotion, and in this he resembles the dog of traditional lore, man's best friend. This passage in Buck's life is saved from sentimentality by the harsh struggles that precede it and the salutary rush to the wilds which follows. Buck's loyalty to Thornton, too, has in it the honoring of a debt. As conditions are turned to opportunities with Buck, his association with Thornton presents the occasions for the dog's most spectacular feats. The dramatic rescue of his master from the river comes closer than any other episode to the expected role of the dog hero of juvenile literature. But it is nicely held in bounds as Buck pulls Thornton only part way across the torrent and the full rescue requires help from the men on shore.

Buck's most wonderful performance is breaking out the sled weighted with a thousand pounds of flour at sixty degrees below zero. Not only is this more essentially a London event than the river episode because of the author's special touch with the cold, but being centered in self-fulfillment rather than altruism, it flares with his Nietzschean spirit. Buck may not know that Thornton's one thousand borrowed dollars are on the line, not to mention his pride, and the dog may get into the harness as an act of loyalty. But once he is there, the challenge is everything. (pp. 85-7)

That Buck's supremacy should become a matter of public record is appropriate and satisfying. But at the same time the episode reminds us that only humans need applause. The event also reveals the weakness of vanity in Thornton, who boasts of his dog with no idea of how much weight he can pull. Thus Buck is given a kind of moral edge over his master. Plus—in saving face and money for him, the dog more than pays his debt in full. Although the prize goes to Thornton, the fact that Buck earns $1,600 for five minutes' work clearly raises him from the ranks of proletarian laborer.

If Buck had stayed with Thornton, the call of the wild would have remained a myth. No matter how far into the wilderness the two might go, the dog would still be bound to the man. Growing restless, Buck strays from Thornton to hunt with a wolf, sensing a new blood longing and pride. . . . When he returns to find Thornton slain by Indians, in a frenzied attack Buck kills them too.

And so the mighty dog is free at last for the passionate, essential life of the wild, which for him becomes literal and absolute. . . . (p. 87)

No form of tooth and claw savagery is more ecstatic than London's version of the life of animals. While the violence of men may be secretly approved by some who write of it, human brutality is rarely, if ever, so completely sanctioned. So volatile is the life of London's animals that other versions of violence, Kipling's cult of savagery, for example, which was a major influence on London, is tame by comparison. The Anglo-Indian's jungle animals do lead an enviable life beyond the rule of men, but that life is civilized, almost gentle in tone. It is a jungle society that turns back on man. Animals are referred to as ''Free People,'' and the bad animals are those who refuse to submit to authority, the antithesis of the ultimately anarchic Buck.

The bloody violence that London injected into the pale literature of his time is generally considered a law of ''club and fang'' for all animals alike. But the approach to the brutality of men and of the other animals varies sharply. Rather than being tragic or even well motivated, the killing of man by man, especially in the Klondike where life is so scarce, is incredibly foolish. **"In a Far Country"** ... shows a man axing his cabin mate for accidentally taking sugar from the wrong bag. This rash act is not to be equated with the survival of the fittest, for the murderer is more irked than hungry. Given the power of reason to investigate, he is the stupid animal for not using it. In another instance a bride-to-be refuses to marry the man who will not kill. The bloodthirsty woman prevails, and he presents her with the heads of four of his tribesmen. Suicide is even more absurd. A hustler from California carries a thousand dozen eggs north that sell at a dollar and a half apiece, and when they turn out to be spoiled he hangs himself, a denouement more amusing than it is awful.

The physical abuse men inflict upon animals carries a power of another order. London's most flawed characters not only attempt to manipulate animals for economic purposes, but they are often sheerly sadistic. No sign of a deeply flawed human character announces itself more certainly than the gratuitous abuse of a dog.... If one didactic thread runs through London's Klondike stories, it is that a man who ill uses dogs will suffer for it. (pp. 88-9)

The form of violence that is exhilarating in London's work is the kill of one wild animal by another, especially in the world apart from man. London's dogs justifiably wound men—their teeth against his clubs, cages, the whip—although they almost never kill humans. But it is the hunt for food that exhilarates. Motivated by a hunger not so severe as to debilitate—and hunger is a subject London knows well from his poverty-ridden days of "meat hunger" as a child—the wild animal's energized attack is a sight of raw beauty. As being a killer in the wilds is the epitome for Buck, so is it for White Fang, who takes up where Buck leaves off.

Reversing Buck's story, London takes the three-quarter wolf, one-quarter dog from the primitive Far North to California. And as *The Call of the Wild* rises to a climax, *White Fang* dies down from one. What the author intends as the virtue of adaptation comes across instead as the case of a character who sells out, at least so it seems to the American reader. The case for civilization is apparently viewed differently in Europe, however, where *White Fang* outsells *The Call of the Wild*. (p. 90)

The conversion to domesticity represses rather than alters White Fang's basic nature; the wild creature is never truly at home again. In the North his abdication to the society of man inspires hatred from his own kind, and the civilized dogs arriving in the Yukon want to destroy him from envy. Although he is exhibited as "The Fighting Wolf" by his Indian owner, organized battle is an atrocity set up for human entertainment. As a result of a decisive defeat by a bulldog, White Fang is purchased out of mercy and taken to California, where opportunities for sanctioned violence are almost nil. There his wildness is thoroughly frustrated, as he is punished for stealing chickens and taught not to respond to his urge, and ostracized when he takes food from the other dogs.

The ultimate squelch of his wild spirit comes from the female, Collie, who "took advantage of her sex to pick upon White Fang and maltreat him." ... Like "a policeman following him," this "pest" ... nudges like a prickly conscience, never forgiving him for the chicken-killing episode. Although White Fang's father One Eye had been pursued and restricted by the female in a similar manner, his role as father required that he be a better hunter than ever, so his essential nature was fulfilled. Many are the restraints of White Fang's new environment, but Collie is "the one trial" ... in his life. He is doomed. The pursuant female triumphs: one afternoon White Fang "ran with Collie." ... How discreet—how bland—how asexual. What puritans are London's mighty male dogs.

Thus the final door is closed on the splendor of White Fang. The next time we see Collie she is snarling her timid mate away from the inevitable litter. A fellow cannot fool around once without becoming responsible for a family. And society is ever present here to make sure a male does his duty, whatever tame activities that entails. A last contrived episode allows for White Fang's ferocity—he attacks an escaped convict. But he is pretty much out to pasture when he weakly drags toward his family at the novel's end, closing a story that is finally as much a testament to wildness as *The Call of the Wild*. (pp. 92-3)

> *Mary Allen, "The Wisdom of the Dogs: Jack London," in her* Animals in American Literature, *University of Illinois Press, 1983, pp. 77-96.*

CHARLES N. WATSON, JR.   (essay date 1983)

[*Watson, an American educator, has taught university courses about London and his works. In his* The Novels of Jack London: A Reappraisal, *he discusses nine works considered among London's best, examining the sources, literary techniques, and personal and professional influences that effected London's art. In the following excerpt from that work, Watson discusses* The Valley of the Moon, *commenting upon London's depiction of the male and female protagonists in the throes of marital strife, his preoccupation with barrenness and procreation, his changing opinions about the working class and economics, and his emphasis on the alternatives the West offers for escape from congested Eastern cities.*]

[*The Valley of the Moon*] derives not only from the vogue of "back to the land" stories but also from deep stresses in London's creative and marital life. In early 1911, as he cranked out one potboiler after another, he fretted about his "going out of vogue" and his "natural and inevitable deterioration as a writer." His discouragement over his continuing childlessness, moreover, no doubt contributed to the tensions that came close to destroying his marriage during the miserable winter in New York. Surely it was his and Charmian's preoccupation with barrenness and fertility that led him to make a significant departure from his source in [LeRoy] Armstrong's "The Man Who Came Back," in which the narrator and central figure is the husband. In *The Valley of the Moon,* prominent as Billy Roberts is, London subordinates him to Saxon, from whose point of view the action is presented. At first, in fact, London intended to have Saxon narrate the story herself. Though he quickly abandoned that device in favor of third-person narration, the focus remains on Saxon throughout the best portions of the novel, books One and Two.

This narrative method and its interpretive consequences have not been clearly recognized. London's earlier attempt to create a female protagonist—Avis Everhard in *The Iron Heel*—was a failure. *The Valley,* too, is a highly uneven novel, but here that unevenness has nothing to do with the centrality of the woman. On the contrary, unlike Avis, Saxon is characterized with penetration and sensitivity. Important misinterpretations have arisen from the failure of critics to recognize that Saxon's is the normative point of view, which serves as a corrective to Billy's emotional gyrations and egotistical bluster. Indeed,

An article written by London for the San Francisco Examiner *during the Russo-Japanese War. Courtesy of the Trust of Irving Shepard.*

Book Three is weaker than its predecessors largely because at that point Saxon is relegated to the background.

Before that falling-off, London skillfully etches the scenes of working-class life, such as the opening episode in the laundry, which contrasts carefree youth with the gritty realities of a lifetime of sweatshop labor. Mary and Saxon's girlish chatter about "gentlemen friends" and a "heavenly" danceband is suddenly interrupted by an elderly woman, pregnant with her eighth child, whose back—"loose, bulging, and misshapen"—begins a "convulsive heaving." Screaming, "Gawd! O Gawd!," she flings "wild glances, like those of an entrapped animal, up and down the big whitewashed room that panted with heat and that was thickly humid with the steam that sizzled from the damp cloth under the irons of the many ironers." After making a partial recovery, the woman collapses on the floor, her "long shriek rising in the pent room to the acrid smell of scorching cloth." Lying on her back, "drumming her heels on the floor," she shrieks "persistently and monotonously, like a mechanical siren," until two other women drag her into an adjoining room and her screams are drowned out by the "vast, muffled roar of machinery." . . . (pp. 194-95)

At the end of the workday, Saxon returns to a home that promises no relief from the fierce discord of the laundry. Like the Higginbothams' house in *Martin Eden*, the dingy dwelling of her brother and sister-in-law offers Saxon only a choice of nightmares. Greeted by the "screeching reproach" of the front gate, she negotiates the narrow walk and missing doorstep,

then enters the kitchen with its sparse furnishings, stained plaster, and stove "worn through and repaired with a five-gallon oil-can hammered flat and double." The dinner awaiting her consists of a plate of "cold beans, thick with grease," which she rejects in favor of a slice of buttered bread and a cup of "cold tea that had been steeped so long that it was like acid in her mouth." Throughout the meal, she must endure the carping of her sister-in-law, Sarah, "middle-aged, lop-breasted, hair-tousled, her face lined with care and fat petulance" . . . , whose incessant voice Saxon cannot escape even in the privacy of her bedroom.

In her hypocrisy, self-pity, and violent hysteria, Sarah recalls Crane's Mary Johnson, who harangues Maggie for daring to grasp at the hope of escape offered by Pete, much as Sarah raves about the disgrace of Saxon's keeping company with a prizefighter. Next she terrifies her young child with visions of "the mother that bore you" confined to a padded cell, "with the lunatics screechin' an' screamin' all around, an' the quick-lime eatin' into the dead bodies of them that's beaten to death by the cruel wardens." . . . When Tom comes mildly to Saxon's defense, Sarah turns on him a stream of accusations and aggressive self-pity: "An' what have you ever did for me? That's what I want to know—me, that's cooked for you, an' washed your stinkin' clothes, and fixed your socks, an' sat up nights with your brats when they was ailin'." . . . Tom pleads with her to be calm, but he succeeds only in precipitating her complete emotional disintegration: "In response, slowly, with utmost deliberation, as if the destiny of empires rested on the certitude of her act, she turned the saucer of coffee upside down on the table. She lifted her right hand, slowly, hugely, and in the same slow, huge way landed the open palm with a sounding slap on Tom's astounded cheek. Immediately thereafter she raised her voice in the shrill, hoarse, monotonous madness of hysteria, sat down on the floor, and rocked back and forth in the throes of an abysmal grief." Though Saxon feels "incensed, violated," she consoles Sarah by stroking her forehead with "slow, soothing movements" . . . , working desperately to restore a measure of peace before Billy arrives.

Lurid as this scene is, London keeps it from melodramatic excess. Sarah remains a horrifying yet plausible figure, the counterpart of the screaming woman at the laundry. Both women, London makes clear, have been ground down in the relentless mill of urban squalor, their lives unrelieved by the slightest gleam of hope. Tom, it is true, manages to maintain an unassuming, ineffectual saintliness. Yet his is the easier life. It is the women, London implies, whose lives are the dreariest, whose burden of childbearing and domestic toil is frequently doubled by the necessity of labor in a stifling laundry or factory.

Equally effective are the crowd scenes: the games and brawls at the Bricklayers' picnic in the early chapters, and later the battle between the strikers and the scabs and police. The latter scene is particularly stunning, the violence exploding suddenly into the tranquil neighborhood of white picket fences, where children are playing in the street and housewives idling in doorways and windows. It is the children, in fact, who begin the battle by stoning the scabs, and from that moment Saxon is transfixed by the "rapid horror before her eyes that flashed along like a moving picture film gone mad." . . . The nightmare is epitomized for her by a grotesque fat man, the leader of the scabs, whose "head had become wedged at the neck between the tops of the pickets of her fence. His body hung down outside, the knees not quite touching the ground. His hat had fallen off, and the sun was making an astounding high light on his bald spot. The cigar, too, was gone. She saw he was looking at her. One hand, between the pickets, seemed waving at her, and almost he seemed to wink at her jocosely, though she knew it to be the contortion of deadly pain." . . . Helplessly she watches as Bert is shot and as Chester Johnson, with whom she had danced before her marriage to Billy, backs a scab onto the fence and pounds his face with a revolver butt. When Chester is in turn shot by the fat man, Saxon finds "the bodies of three men hung on her picket fence" like laundry on a line. . . .

With incredible swiftness, the eruption passes before her and is gone; and "moving as in a dream," she comes down her front steps, her eye taking in images of dislocation surrealistically magnified and yet strangely trivial: "The round-bellied leader still leered at her and fluttered one hand," and "the gate was off its hinges, which seemed strange, for she had been watching all the time and had not seen it happen." . . . In its suddenness and decisive carnage, and in its destructive effect on a young marriage, the scene recalls the climactic battle between the ranchers and the marshall's posse in Norris's *The Octopus.*

Yet such naturalistic set-pieces are important primarily as stages in Saxon's experience. Though only the final journey in Book Three is explicitly a "pilgrimate" . . . , the entire novel depicts Saxon's quest for her portion of happiness. The road to that happiness lies through the vicissitudes of marriage, which here is not permanent bliss but a process of painful growth and

change. Much as Oakland itself is "just a place to start from," the little Pine Street cottage, with its neat geranium beds and picket fence, suggests the naive conventionality of Saxon's vision of an eternal honeymoon—a vision shattered when the battling strikers and scabs knock the front gate off its hinges, trample the flowers, and strew the fence with corpses. Her seemingly invulnerable domestic life has been shockingly violated, and the nature of the violation is confirmed by the death of her premature child and the disintegration of her marriage.

This quest for marital happiness is also a quest for the fulfillment of certain ideas and values. Most prominent of these is the struggle to recover the westering impulse which London associated with the Anglo-American spirit. Equally important, Saxon is searching for an acceptable form of religious belief. By some not-too-convincing process of cultural osmosis, she has absorbed the nineteenth-century crisis of faith, sensing the decline of old certitudes and the need for new sources of religious inspiration. If the answers she finds are not always credible, London writes convincingly of her desperate need to find them.

This religious anxiety emerges early, when Saxon and Mary nervously discuss Bert Wanhope's atheism. Intrigued though finally dissatisfied by Bert's negations, they struggle to articulate their own conceptions of the deity. (pp. 196-99)

From the beginning London stresses the psychological and quasi-religious nature of Saxon's racial attitudes. Finding the orthodox God remote and puzzling, Saxon discovers credible surrogates in the heroic figure of her father, a captain of cavalry who had died before she could know him; and especially her mother, a poet and an equally heroic California pioneer who had crossed the plains in a covered wagon and died when Saxon was a child. In the daguerreotype of her mother, her "deeply religious" nature finds a "concrete" object of worship. Her mother "meant to her what God meant to others"; and the relics of her mother's life—the daguerreotype, the manuscript poems, and the chest of drawers that traveled across the plains—have become her "high altar and holy of holies." . . . The poems are sacred scriptures containing an elusive "clue" with which "all would be made clear," . . . and she handles all her mother's possessions "with the deep gravity and circumstance of a priest." . . .

This idealized "mother-myth" . . . obviously originates in an orphaned girl's longing for the dimming figure of her memories. But Saxon's myth-making is more than a hunger for lost security. It is an espousal of her mother's qualities of mind and character—the raw courage, the "grit," . . . of the true pioneer who shepherded the family across the plains and held them together when they reached California. What especially arises in Saxon's mind like an imagined tapestry is the great adventure of westering, "palpitating and real, shimmering in the sun-flashed dust of ten thousand hoofs, . . . across a continent, the great hegira of the land-hungry Anglo-Saxon," through which, like "a flying shuttle, weaving the golden dazzling thread of personality, moved the form of her little, indomitable mother." . . .

Many readers, viewing Saxon's emotions in the light of later manifestations of Germanic and Anglo-American racism, will find her adulation of the "land-hungry Anglo-Saxon" ominous. Saxon does not, indeed, entirely escape the taint of racism, nor does London himself. Notions of Anglo-Saxon supremacy were in their heyday, and London's fiction often reflected—and perhaps contributed to—their advance. Yet the

London's yacht the "Snark," anchored off Somoa in 1908. Courtesy of the Trust of Irving Shepard.

attitudes of these characters should at least be recognized as a perennial form of working-class paranoia, which is aggravated during periods of economic hardship when the competition for jobs is the most fierce. The same impulse appears in Bert and Billy's lament for their kind as "the last of the Mohegans," . . . an echo of Cooper's elegiac record of the passing of an earlier frontier in the Leatherstocking Tales. (pp. 199-200)

London carefully distinguishes, moreover, between Saxon's pride of ancestry and the more belligerent chauvinism of Billy and Bert. When Bert rants about the fate of the "old white stock," . . . Saxon holds herself aloof; nor does she chime in with Billy's tirade against socialism as the haven of "a lot of fat Germans an' greasy Russian Jews." At times, indeed, she is unable to allow such racial posturing to go unreproved. When Billy, observing the dense concentration of Portuguese farms near San Leandro, grumbles that "the free-born American ain't got no room left in his own land," Saxon replies, "Then it's his own fault." Billy, in turn, insists that Americans could easily farm like the Portuguese if they wanted to, but that they "ain't much given to livin' like a pig offen leavin's." Saxon remains unimpressed: "Not in the country, maybe. . . . But I've seen an awful lot of Americans living like pigs in the cities." . . . To be sure, her rejection of Billy's statements seems at times the result more of gentility than of true conviction, and occasionally she joins Billy in his xenophobia, envisioning the true "Americans" crushed by hordes of more

provident and industrious "foreigners." But her sense of proportion and decency more than once offsets the extremes of Billy's racism, and hers is the dominant point of view throughout the novel. (pp. 201-02)

By the time she and Billy leave Oakland, . . . [Saxon] is ready to exchange the urban frontier for a resumption of the pioneers' search for open land, where her ancestral heritage and her marriage to Billy can be fruitfully united.

Even as her courtship begins, Saxon has before her, in Sarah and Tom, an instance of a marriage fallen into hopeless chaos. After Sarah's hysteria has subsided, Tom's reflections offer Saxon a lesson she would do well to heed. Urging her to enjoy herself while she can, Tom observes ruefully that she will "get old, and all that means, fast enough." Then, almost as an afterthought, he muses: "Hell! Think of it! Sarah and I used to go buggy-riding once on a time. And I guess she had her three pair of shoes, too. Can you beat it?" . . . But Saxon, who has defended her right to three pairs of shoes and is about to go buggy-riding with Billy, draws no parallel between Tom's past and her own future: "Fresh from the shattering chaos of her sister-in-law's mind, Billy's tremendous calm was especially satisfying, and Saxon mentally laughed to scorn the terrible temper he had charged to himself." . . . The irony of her naive reflections will be apparent soon enough.

Though Saxon never sees in Tom and Sarah's troubles any forecast of her own future, she is more wary of the friction between Mary and Bert. From the beginning Bert is "very possessive with Mary, almost roughly so," . . . and as a result Mary remains edgy and defensive. Even before their marriage they struggle for power, Mary insisting that "I'll lead the man around by the nose that marries me" and Bert rejoining, "I'll be everlastingly jiggerooed if I put up for a wigwam I can't be boss of." . . . When the two couples dine together, Bert's scathing cynicism and Mary's "unconcealed hostility" cause Saxon to be "concerned over the outcome of their marriage." . . . On a later visit Billy becomes aware that he is "making comparisons": Bert and Mary's house has no "satisfying atmosphere." . . .

But although Billy and Saxon avoid open acrimony, they do engage in a quieter power struggle of their own. After denying that she would ever attempt to rule her husband, Saxon maneuvers Billy into accepting her idea of how their wedding ring should be inscribed. Mary is quick to point out that Saxon is "having her own way and leading [Billy] by the nose already," . . . and Saxon momentarily acknowledges the justice of the charge. The lesson is soon reinforced by Mercedes Higgins, who insists that "the greatest of the arts is the conquering of men" . . . and from whom Saxon learns the guile she will need to get Billy out of Oakland, salvage her foundering marriage, and gain a full partnership in their work.

Mercedes is a preposterous but fascinating character. Acting as Saxon's mentor throughout Book Two, she exerts a powerful influence on the younger woman's attitudes toward marriage and on her religious and social beliefs. That influence is predominantly negative, though nonetheless insidiously attractive. She speaks for the dark side of London's vision, grim, cynical, nihilistic, yet full of the Dinoysian energies of life and love. She is a demon that must be exorcised before Saxon's (and London's) more optimistic spirit can reassert itself in the agrarian dream of Book Three. (pp. 202-03)

Her rage for life proceeds directly from her vision of death, which appears in one of the most horrific images London ever created: the gruesome specter of the salt vats, where the corpses of paupers await dissection. Visions of maggoty cadavers and grinning skulls had always lurked at the periphery of London's consciousness, but this particular *mememto mori* has a special force because it combines the vision of death with London's other nightmare image, the social pit. The salt vats exist only for the poor—only for those who lack the price of a proper burial. The vats are also a special hell for women, a Gothic chamber of horrors in which Mercedes has glimpsed "the things men may do with your pretty flesh after you are dead." . . .

Her terror of the salt vats leads Mercedes to the religion of living passion. When Saxon asks her whether she believes in God, she answers, "Who knows?" . . . ; she fears only the salt vats. It is she who elevates the washing of "dainties" into a "true sacrament of beauty," . . . in which she acts as the priestess of a cult of love, performing her ablutions as if she were conducting a high mass. The apparent absurdity of this ritual, with its disquieting undertone of masculine fetishes, should not be permitted to obscure its importance for Saxon, who has been searching for the totems and incantations with which to worship her husband as she once worshipped her mother. Before long, she is indeed striving with a "fervor almost religious" . . . to make Billy's life perfect.

But although Saxon accepts much of what Mercedes teaches, an important difference remains. Mercedes's creed is all ego, an ethic of self-fulfillment which occasionally calls for the sacrifice of others. She indulges her expensive tastes while denying similar luxuries to her husband; and when she promises to sell Saxon's fine needlework for a small commission, she cheats Saxon out of part of the price. Discovered in her subterfuge, Mercedes invokes the salt vats: "To escape the vats I would stop at nothing—steal the widow's mite, the orphan's crust, and pennies from a dead man's eyes." . . . This self-serving ethic eventually becomes a full-blown Nietzschean creed of power. When two scabs are beaten by a mob, she look on without pity. "Most men are born stupid," she declares. "They are the slaves. A few are born clever. They are the masters." . . . (pp. 204-05)

Saxon, however, cannot accept an anarchic world without purpose, without justice, with no goal but self-fulfillment. Though desperately anxious for her own portion of happiness, she conceives of it only as something shared. She can fulfill herself only through Billy. (p. 205)

The best part of the novel is the series of chapters in Book Two tracing the disintegration of Saxon's marriage, beginning with the battle between the strikers and scabs and culminating in Saxon's nervous breakdown while Billy is in jail. When the conflict erupts, Billy naturally sides with the strikers. Saxon, however, sees the larger tragedy, in which men die and families are destroyed on both sides. Recalling Mercedes's cynicism, she wonders whether Billy, too, is merely "a wild beast, a dog that would snarl over a bone." . . .

The gradual estrangement of Billy and Saxon is almost wholly convincing, the more so because London presents it from Saxon's point of view. While Billy remains blind to the forces destroying their marriage, Saxon can see them with a painful clarity while remaining powerless to halt them. She is thus an increasingly divided person, one part of herself experiencing and suffering while the other half remains detached, a spectator of her own tragedy. She feels triply bereft, mourning the loss of her baby, the deaths or departures of her friends, and Billy's growing preoccupation with the strike. (p. 206)

Saxon's emotional breakdown is vividly portrayed, its bodily symptoms reflecting her psychic desolation. Her moments of delirium provide little escape from her present trouble. . . . (p. 207)

The ruins of London's estate Wolf House, which was destroyed by fire. Courtesy of the Trust of Irving Shepard.

But Saxon's personal distress also signals a crisis of the outer society—of both its economic system and its religious faith. Saxon's description of her feeling of "goneness," of "loss of self," of being "a stranger to herself," is the language not only of psychopathology but, more important, of spiritual alienation. . . . What Saxon glimpses . . . is not so much the romantic vision of splendidly savage nature as the earlier Enlightenment conception of the world as a great "frictionless" machine, in which all motion is governed by immutable laws. The romantic notion that everything is wild and free gives way to the impression that everything is orderly and rational. The tide ebbs and flows, the sun rises and sets; and even the west wind, that capricious favorite of romantic poets, comes "regularly" into the bay to command the sailboats to obey its unwavering laws of force.

What Saxon is offered, in short, is a choice of machines: the grindingly destructive machine of industrial society or the harmonious beauty of the machine of nature. The breakdown of social justice is soon made painfully vivid. . . . She cannot understand . . . a world in which some men possessed so much food that they threw it away, paying men for their labor of spoiling it before they threw it away." . . . But to recognize the insanity of such a society is to call into question the benevolence of God. Remembering Mercedes's tales of almost incredible social injustice, she can only conclude that God does not exist at all. . . . (pp. 207-09)

But Saxon cannot accept this bleak view for long. Life may be a trap, but she is determined to escape it—to grasp her "small meed of happiness" before succumbing to the "black grave" or the "salt vats." . . . She has long since recognized that Billy's disintegration was but a symptom of the larger social disease, not a sin for which he could be held responsible. Saxon, too, refuses to believe she is either sinful or stupid. After the inspiriting sojourn with the young sailor revives her courage, she wakes the next morning feeling "her old self" and begins "putting the neglected house in order." . . .

Up to this point, London has written a coherent and often affecting novel of a young woman's struggle for happiness in a world that seems to conspire against her. Unfortunately, his didactic impulse soon leads him astray. When Saxon's search for the bluebird of happiness goes on the road, the narrative becomes little more than a combination of agricultural pamphlet and California travelogue—and not even an interesting travelogue, at that. (p. 209)

For Saxon, however, the agrarian dream, shorn of its racism and with due allowance for its portion of sentimentality, offers an attractive if somewhat simplistic answer to the discontents that have plagued her life in the city. . . .

[Thus, the] lyrical description of the entrance into the Sonoma Valley suggests that though the land is no longer free, it still promises values that the will can make real. The ethic of nihilism and power, embodied earlier in Billy and Mercedes, has been defeated by the civilizing impulses of Saxon, whose healed marriage offers yet another instance of London's struggle to close the divisions in his own mind and life. (p. 210)

> *Charles N. Watson, Jr., in his* The Novels of Jack London: A Reappraisal, *The University of Wisconsin Press, 1983, 304 p.*

ADDITIONAL BIBLIOGRAPHY

Beauchamp, Gorman. "Resentment and Revolution in Jack London's Sociofantasy." *The Canadian Review of American Studies* 13, No. 2 (Fall 1982): 179-92.
> Discussion of *The Iron Heel* and other dystopian works by London. Beauchamp contends that London's attraction to socialism and his depiction of revolution in his works are directly related to the resentment the author harbored against bourgeois society and his desire to violently destroy it.

Braybrooke, Patrick. "Jack London and the Unexpected." In his *Peeps at the Mighty*, pp. 113-29. 1927. Reprint. Freeport, N.Y.: Books for Libraries Press, 1966.
> Discussion of "The Unexpected." Braybrooke considers this short story an illumination of London's personal philosophy, which views life's unexpected occurrences as tests which some pass and others fail.

Brooks, Van Wyck. "Jack London." In his *Sketches in Criticism*, pp. 248-52. New York: E. P. Dutton, 1932.
> Biographical sketch. Brooks attributes what he considers London's "abnormal" self-assertiveness and will-to-power to an exaggerated sense of inferiority that drove him, and finally killed him.

Cantwell, Robert. "Jack London: Melodrama." In his *Famous American Men of Letters*, pp. 161-70. New York: Dodd, Mead & Co., 1957.
> Biographical sketch. Cantwell recounts familiar details about London's early life and discusses the circumstances surrounding the writing and publication of *The Call of the Wild*.

Cook, May Estelle. "Nature Books for the Holidays." *The Dial* XLI, No. 491 (1 December 1906): 387-90.*
> Review of *White Fang*. Cook contends that while many readers prefer the strong ending of *The Call of the Wild*, *White Fang* is a superior work that ends happily and therefore all but erases the cruelty depicted throughout.

Feied, Frederick. "*The Road*: Jack London." In his *No Pie in the Sky: The Hobo as American Cultural Hero in the Works of Jack London, John Dos Passos, and Jack Kerouac*, pp. 23-40. New York: Citadel Press, 1964.
> Discussion of *The Road* and earlier socialist articles. Feied traces the influences of this book to London's personal experiences and to earlier works on the subject by lesser authors.

Graham, Don. "Jack London's Tale Told by a High-Grade Feeb." *Studies in Short Fiction* 15, No. 4 (Fall 1978): 429-33.
> Critical discussion of short story "Told in the Drooling Ward." Graham regards the short story as unique among contemporary English-language stories that concern the insane.

Graham, Stephen. "Jack London." In his *The Death of Yesterday*, pp. 53-61. London: Ernest Benn, 1930.
> Biographical and psychological discussion of London's life and works. Graham calls London a "feminine" man, noting his use of female characters to voice his own personal thoughts in his works and what Graham regards as the "near hysteria" of his writing, which he considers a female, rather than a male, trait. Graham concludes that his weak ideas and extravagances are diminished because London was an exceptional talent, "an awaker, an annunciator, a wall-shatterer" who spoke to the yet unsettled young man.

London, Charmian. *The Book of Jack London*. 2 Vols. New York: Century Co., 1921.
> An intimate portrait of Jack London written by his second wife. His personal life is the focus of this biography, which includes extensive quotations from private conversations and numerous excerpts from London's correspondence.

London, Joan. *Jack London and His Times*. Seattle: University of Washington Press, 1939, 385 p.

Describes the economic and political backdrop against which Jack London pursued his literary career. The author, London's daughter, concentrates upon the rise of industrialism, the concommitant popularization of socialist and labor politics, and the influence of both upon London's work.

Martin, Ronald E. "Jack London: Radical Individualism and Social Justice in the Universe of Force." In his *American Literature and the Universe of Force*, pp. 185-214. Durham, N.C.: Duke University Press, 1981.
    Examines the influence of Edmund Spenser's philosophy on London's works.

Ownbey, Ray Wilson, ed. *Jack London: Essays in Criticism*. Santa Barbara, Salt Lake City: Peregrine Smith, 1978, 126 p.
    A collection of critical essays by Clarice Stasz, Sam S. Baskett, Earle Labor, and others.

Perry, John. *Jack London: An American Myth*. Chicago: Nelson-Hall, 1981. 351 p.
    Biography. Perry seeks to retrace London's ancestry and life, dismantling the myths which London and his biographers helped create.

Portelli, Alessandro. "Jack London's Missing Revolution: Notes on *The Iron Heel*." *Science-Fiction Studies* 9, Part 2, No. 27 (July 1982): 180-94.
    Critical discussion. Although earlier critics regarded the narrative framework of *The Iron Heel* as unimportant in view of the novel's prophetic scientific and social analysis of revolutionary thought, Portelli posits that the tri-partite narrative frame and the types of actions and results each illicits serve several important functions in the novel.

Sinclair, Andrew. *Jack: A Biography of Jack London*. New York: Harper & Row, 1977. 297 p.
    The first biography of London written after examining his personal papers.

Stone, Irving. *Sailor on Horseback: The Biography of Jack London*. Cambridge: Houghton Mifflin Co., 1938, 338 p.
    A sympathetic biography.

Tavernier-Courbin, Jacqueline. *Critical Essays on Jack London*. Boston: G. K. Hall, 1983. 298 p.
    Includes essays by Tavernier-Courbin, H. L. Mencken, Anatole France, Earle Labor, Susan Ward, and others. The collection is divided into sections on London's life, his works in general, specific works, and writing techniques.

Walcutt, Charles Child. "Jack London: Blond Beasts and Supermen." In his *American Literary Naturalism, A Divided Stream*, pp. 87-113. Minneapolis: University of Minnesota Press, 1956.
    Discussion of London's adventure stories. Walcutt contends that because London found the struggle to survive implied in the theories of Darwin and Spenser so appealing, he cast primitive, strong-minded heroes as exaggeratedly self-conscious extensions of himself in his works. His moral idealism about social injustice equated the hero with courage and the villain with cowardice.

Walcutt, Charles Child. *Jack London*. American Writers Pamphlet, no. 57. Minneapolis: University of Minnesota Press, 1966, 48 p.
    Biographical and critical essay, covering most of London's work.

Walker, Franklin, *Jack London and the Klondike*. San Marino, Calif.: Huntington Library, 1966, 288 p.
    Relates London's Klondike adventures to their fictional counterparts in his Arctic tales.

Ward, Susan. "Jack London and the Blue Pencil: London's Correspondence with Popular Editors." *American Literary Realism 1870-1910* XIV, No. 1 (Spring 1981): 16-25.
    Examination of London's thoughts regarding publishers and editors who censored his works. Ward uses examples from correspondence to support the contention that London wrote primarily to please public taste and thereby make money. However, she considers the longevity of his works and reputation testimony to the artistic nature of his work.

Leopoldo Lugones

1874-1938

Argentinian poet, short story writer, essayist, and novelist.

Lugones is considered one of the most important poets and fiction writers of the *modernista* movement in Spanish American literature. While his mentor, Rubén Darío, is credited with initiating this revival in Spanish literature, the first since the seventeenth century, Lugones's technical virtuosity is considered even greater than that of his predecessor. His experimental use of metaphors, symbolism, meter, rhyme, and visual imagery in such early collections as *Las montañas del oro* and *Lunario sentimental* displays the influence of such poets as Victor Hugo, Walt Whitman, and Jules Laforgue, one of the French *vers libre* poets who abandoned formal literary conventions in his works and greatly influenced the work of such modernist poets as T. S. Eliot and Ezra Pound. Lugones later moved toward more traditional poetic forms, a trend firmly established with the publication of *Odas seculares,* a collection of nationalistic poems commemorating the Argentinian centennial. In addition to his innovations in poetry, influential short stories in Lugones's *Las fuerzas extrañas* introduced science fiction to Argentinian literature and inspired imitation by such writers as Jorge Luis Borges. More than any other writer of the *modernista* movement Lugones strove to establish an independent Latin American form of expression by synthesizing the most unique and expressive elements of Romanticism, Realism, Naturalism, Symbolism, and Aestheticism.

Lugones was born in the village of Rio Seco in the province of Cordoba and as a youth moved with his family to the city of Cordoba. There he attended a Catholic secondary school, which he left in protest against both strict discipline and church dogma. In 1893 he moved to Buenos Aires, where he became one of the dominant figures among the school of *modernista* writers led by Rubén Darío. Darío's high regard for Lugones's first poetry collection, *Las montañas del oro,* insured the young poet's place among the leaders of the avant-garde movement, and after Darío left Argentina, Lugones's leadership was indisputable. As a journalist and a member of the socialist group Centro Socialista de Estudios, Lugones wrote articles expounding political views that sometimes served as the themes of his poetry as well. However, he soon shifted from socialism to a conservatism that grew increasingly reactionary and nationalistic, ending in fascism. He held several government posts, serving as the director of the library of the National Council of Education from 1914 until his death, and also as Argentina's representative to the Committee on Intellectual Cooperation of the League of Nations. Lugones's drastic political changes are reflected in his later works, where nationalism and historical themes are developed. Argentinian intellectuals once led by Lugones attacked these later works, accusing him of opportunism, imitation, and even plagiarism. Even after his style turned to more traditional forms, Lugones continued to experiment with metaphors and imagery. This experimentation has been viewed as Lugones's search for a standard of stability in his work that was lacking in his emotional life. This search culminated in disillusionment and despair, and in 1938 Lugones took a fatal dose of cyanide.

With the appearance of his first poetry collection, *Las montañas del oro,* Lugones's reputation as the most innovative of the *modernista* poets was established. In a grandiose style indicative of youthful vigor and bombast, the poems call for a revolution of poetic conventions, and also define the poet as a prophetic visionary uniquely qualified to lead a social revolution, thus establishing a relationship between the poet's artistic and political goals. The experimental use of free verse in this collection exhibits the influence of the French *vers libre* poets and of Walt Whitman; it also displays elaborately sensual visual imagery that has been regarded as both beautiful and shocking. The tone of *Los crepúsculos del jardín,* Lugones's second collection, is quieter and more detached, moving from the spacious mountain settings of *Las montañas del oro* to the confines of small gardens. Here the poet is characterized as a loner who is divided by his superior vision from the masses by a gulf of misunderstanding. This detachment is complemented by an emphasis on emotion rather than style and by the use of metaphors that display a mastery of the interplay between sound and meaning. Lugones's final work of his *modernista* phase is *Lunario sentimental,* considered his masterpiece and his most influential work. Metaphors that juxtapose unlike elements and original rhymes in the collection were praised and imitated. Many critics also note the influence of Laforgue on *Lunario sentimental* in the ironic, irreverent humor of the collection.

In *Odas seculares* only vestiges of French influences remain. This epic celebration of pastoral Argentina abandons the explosive virtuosity of the earlier collections, turning to classical poetic models. In the villages and plains, ordinary objects and scenes are illuminated by the poet's observant eye. "A los ganadosy las mieses," representative of the poems in the collection, honors the poor minorities who seek refuge in the grassy pampas. This celebration of traditional modes of living praises rural life and displays a growing conservatism that would characterize later collections. In these subsequent works, Lugones warned against the encroachment of industrialization and modernization that threatened the farmlands. Despite the somewhat monotonous nature of the traditional rhymes used in the works, Lugones's imaginative power persists in new manners of expression that some critics have called "Latin-Americanisms." *Romancero del río seco*, published posthumously, contains Lugones's most intimate poems, formed from memories of his youth in Cordoba, that extoll the virtues of love, patriotism, and courage embodied in the laborers, artisans, and gauchos of the recent past. The gaucho is also honored in *La guerra gaucha,* a collection of historical vignettes that present romantic pictures of heroism. These patriotic tales depict freedom fighters opposing supporters of Spanish rule. Natural imagery informs the work, symbolising suprahuman support of the gaucho's cause; sunlight in particular, one critic has observed, implies the blessing of an Incan deity.

In addition to his influential poetic innovations, Lugones also affected the course of Argentine fiction. His most well-known short stories, collected in *Las fuerzas extrañas,* introduced science fiction to Argentine literature. By using the names of real scientists and alluding to factual innovations in contemporary science, Lugones made the far-fetched stories more credible, confusing the delineation of fact and fiction. This use of realistic elements and references to current scientific knowledge would be used by other writers, including Borges, an early commentator on Lugones's work who praised this collection as containing some of the best fiction in Hispanic literature. Some critics contend that the maudlin point of view and obsessive concern with death in the tales shows the influence of Edgar Allan Poe, while others note that the two writers chose distinctly different points of view for their work. In contrast to the first-person confessions of Poe's horror tales, Lugones's stories are typically narrated by an observer and often demonstrate the two-pronged nature of scientific discovery—the pleasure of acquiring valuable knowledge and the fear of delving into the unknown. In "El psychon," the recent discovery of the process of liquifying gases is employed by Lugones to depict a doctor who produces pure thought in liquid form. "La lluvia de fuego" depicts the growing horror in ancient Gomorrah as a volcanic rain of incandescent copper particles slowly destroys the city. The confusion and fear of the farm animals, who cannot understand what is happening, is juxtaposed with the terror of the humans, who fully comprehend the situation. Lugones's interest in science fiction eventually waned, but his fascination with the unknown led to stories dealing with the occult, Egyptology, theosophy, and Argentinian superstitions. Most critics argue that these stories, including those in *Cuentos fatales,* do not have the verisimilitude of the science fiction tales. The writer's involvement with his subject is thinly veiled with weak plots, and the stories are longer and more diffuse. Others believe that his entire body of fiction was of secondary importance to Lugones, and therefore not as carefully revised and finely wrought as his poetry, for which he had a higher regard.

Lugones has been praised as a poetic innovator who more than any single poet helped create a uniquely Latin American form of literary expression. His knowledge of world languages and literature aided him in selecting the most modern terms and techniques in poetry, and allowed him to assimilate components from disparate schools of thought in the creation of an individual voice.

PRINCIPAL WORKS

Las montañas del oro   (poetry)   1897
La guerra gaucha   (novel)   1905
   ["Death of a Gaucho" published in *Tales from the
      Argentine* (partial translation), 1930]
Los crepúsculos del jardín   (poetry)   1905
Las fuerzas extrañas   (short stories)   1906
Lunario sentimental   (poetry)   1909
Odas seculares   (poetry)   1910
Historia de Sarmiento   (history)   1911
   ["Sarmiento the Educator" published in *The Green
      Continent: A Comprehensive View of Latin America by
      Its Leading Writers* (partial translation), 1944]
El libro fiel   (poetry)   1912
"Como hablan en las cimas" ("How the Mountains Talk")
   (poem)   1915; published in journal *Stratford Journal*
El libro de los paisajes   (poetry)   1917
"A Good Cheese"   (short story)   1920; published in
   journal *Inter-America*
"Shepherd Boy and Shepherd Girl"   (short story)   1920;
   published in journal *Inter-America*
Las horas doradas   (poetry)   1922
Cuentos fatales   (short stories)   1924
Romancero   (poetry)   1924
"Luz" ("Light")   (poem)   1927; published in newspaper
   Christian Science Monitor
Poemas solariegos   (poetry)   1928
Romancero del río seco   (poetry)   1938
Antología poética   (poetry)   1941
"Autumn Sweetness"   (poem)   1942; published in journal
   Commonweal
"Death of the Moon"   (poem)   1943; published in journal
   Poetry
Obras poeticas completas   (poetry)   1948
"Yzur"   (short story)   1963; published in *Classic Tales
   from Spanish America*

Translated selections of Lugones's poetry have appeared in the following publications: *Argentine Anthology of Modern Verse, The Epic of Latin American Literature, Hispanic Anthology, Literature of Latin America, The Modernist Trend in Latin American Poetry, Some Spanish American Poets,* and *Translations from Hispanic Poets.*

JOHN EUGENE ENGLEKIRK   (essay date 1934)

[*In the following excerpt from his* Edgar Allan Poe in Hispanic Literature, *Englekirk provides evidence of Poe's strong influence on the themes, style, and subject matter of Lugones's early poetry, particularly in the collection* Las montañas del oro. *Englekirk also notes Poesque techniques and themes in the short story collections* Cuentos fatales *and* Las fuerzas extrañas.]

As is the case of almost every initial work of the Modernista poets, the influences that tended to shape [Lugones' *Las mon-*

tañas del Oro], this first volume, chronologically speaking, of modern Argentine poetry are very much in evidence. With convincing unanimity most critics call attention to the two men whose influences are easily discernible and of greatest moment, Hugo and Poe. . . . Although many critics may fail to comment on Hugo's influence, mentioning other authors, such as Whitman and D'Annunzio, they are invariably constant in referring to the Poesque source. . . . José G. Antuña claims that Lugones imitated Poe, and Arturo Torres-Rioseco comments on the fact that no one has pointed out Poe's influence. Darío's reference to the "mental genealogy" of his young protégé is well known. . . . (pp. 279-80)

Amado Nervo suggested one phase of Poe's influence over Lugones in his reference to "el horror lógico de Poe." But quite as palpable as this element of Poesque horror is the almost absolute subservice of the Argentine poet to both the verse technique and prose style of Poe's work. These two aspects of Poe's influence led Lugones on to the exaggeration of which Alfredo Ortiz Vargas speaks: "—its (*Las montañas del Oro*) greatest merit consisted in bringing into relief by exaggeration the new tendencies that were bound sooner or later to be accepted."

Although Hugo's theme of the poet's lofty mission, and many of the figures of speech and much of the vocabulary of the French romantic poet, prevail in the introductory poem, **"Las montañas del Oro,"** one cannot fail to note already the horror and desolation of the fabulous landscape of Poe's **"Silence,"** the Biblical prose poem that seems to have captivated completely the youthful fancy of Lugones. This element of horror, whether originating directly from Poe in every case or not, is couched in a manner and style so decidedly Poesque that it is impossible not to attribute to him most of Lugones' inspiration in this theme. In many instances the nature of this horror recalls the treatment of Baudelaire or of Maeterlinck. In others, however, there are marked allusions to those works of Poe in which the horrible predominates. (pp. 280-81)

In spite of the very apparent reference to Baudelaire in the selection **"á Histeria,"** Alfredo Ortiz Vargas did not fail to note Lugones' indebtedness to Poe. . . . The description of the "selva temblorosa" ["trembling forest"] through which Lugones and his beloved one pass is of the inordinately weird fantasy of Poe; and similarly terrifying is the profound abyss into which they fall and which proves to be her tomb. It is especially in the final lines that one senses both the Baudelairian and the Poesque source. The references to the "flores del Mal" ["flowers of evil"] and to the Satanic spark of the eyes and the vocabulary, imagery, symbolism, and style of the poem present an interesting intermingling of the characteristics of those two related spirits whose influence has been so prominent in modern poetry. . . . (pp. 281-82)

[Attention] should be called to the repetition of a theme that is the leitmotif of most of these poems of horror: the Poesque theme of the death of a beautiful woman, rendered in an atmosphere of metaphysical horror to the aria of "love within the tomb." It is the recurrence of this note that, in spite of the many carnal strains of Baudelaire, testifies to the constant influence of Poe. Accordingly, one comes to the same conclusion as to the Poesque source of the poem, **"nebulosa Thulé,"** the very title of which calls to mind that "ultimate dim Thule" of Poe's "Dreamland." The Argentine's exaggerated treatment of this same theme is characteristic of his compositions **"la vendimia de Sangre"** and **"rosas del Calvario."**

The weird alcoholic vision of **"metempsicosis"** is the very consummation of horrible fantasy à la Poe. It is another splendid example of the tendency of the impulsive Lugones to attune a Poesque theme and a Poesque milieu to the extravagant temper of his own youthful art. The poem was obviously inspired by Poe's tale of metempsycosis, "Metzengerstein." This "potro colosal" ["colossal horse"] of Lugones, this fantastic charger who was first portrayed in **"á Histeria"** . . . , is the colossal charger of Poe's tale. In "Metzengerstein" this unearthly steed stands forever outlined against the fiery background of that final scene:

> The fury of the tempest immediately died away, and a dead calm sullenly succeeded. A white flame still enveloped the building like a shroud, and, streaming far away into the quiet atmosphere, shot forth a glare of praeternatural light; while a cloud of smoke settled heavily over the battlements in the distinct colossal figure of— *a horse.*

Lugones silhouettes him against a black promontory that rises above the waters. . . . The setting for the macabre description of the terrifying dog in the poem is unquestionably Poesque. (pp. 283-85)

It is easy to account for the biblical style that predominates in the collection of prose poems that come under the general caption of "Segundo ciclo" and that is much in evidence throughout the entire volume. The similarity of the technique employed by Lugones to Poe's manner in "Silence" is indicative of the principal source. . . . (p. 286)

Undoubtedly the parallelisms and repetitions that abound in Poe's poetry had much to do with the shaping of the unduly exaggerated technique Lugones uses in *Las montañas del Oro*. But these *jeux d'esprit* do not spring entirely from contact with Poe alone. The young Argentine poet seems to have been an enthusiastic admirer of the innovator Silva; and at least one of his poems attests to his imitation of the verse technique employed by the French Symbolists. I refer to the appropriately-named selection "antifona". . . . However, Poe's ultimate influence in the matter cannot be gainsaid. (pp. 287-88)

[*Los crepúsculos del jardín*] was the second product from the pen of Lugones. It is well-nigh impossible to recognize the earlier poet in this volume. Lugones had attained the crest of the over-wrought symbolism and artificial gleaning of the poetic tendencies then in vogue. Because of these exaggerated characteristics, there is little in his poetry of this period to remind one of Poe. There are vague reminiscences of the author of "The Raven" in those poems that lament the departure and absence of love, poems the melancholy spirit and shadowy atmosphere of which are in conformity with the title of the work. **"La alcoba solitaria," "El solterón," "Melancolía," "Canto del amor y de la noche,"** and **"Canto de la tarde y de la muerte"** may be cited as the more convincing poems of this type. Many lines from the two last-mentioned selections and from **"Elegía"** are very reminiscent of Poe.

"El buque" and **"A tus imperfecciones"** are the only poems of the volume that seem to have been definitely and directly influenced by Poe. Lugones was probably indebted to the American for the parallelisms, refrain, and repetition of rhyming words of the former; the latter reveals the Poesque note of despair and fatality. **"A tus imperfecciones"** is not Poesque in theme; but through its prevalent note of inevitable despair it produces effects that parallel those of Poe's characteristic elegies. The Argentine poet laments the denial of love, and not its loss through death as does Poe. The poem ends with the realization of the fact that destiny will thwart the fulfillment of the poet's dream of love. . . . (pp. 288-89)

Very Poesque is the strange tale Lugones entitled **"La novia imposible."** The hero is of the type encountered in Poe. He suffers from the same morbid, supersensitive madness that characterizes Poe's creations. There are very palpable reminiscences of "William Wilson" in the account of the strange friendship this Poesque character cherished as a boy. . . . This decadent character is wildly enamored of the Moon; he meets his death through his insane yearning to sleep with Her in the liquid cristal of the pool. The entire atmosphere created by the madman's final ravings is strongly suggestive of Poe.

"Francesca" is a forerunner of those two fine collections of tales, *Cuentos fatales* and *Las fuerzas extrañas,* wherein one is constantly aware of the spirit that moved Poe to write some of his best tales. Lugones would have us believe that he came into possession of a thirteenth century parchment which revealed the true story of those immortal Italian lovers. In all seriousness and with minute attention to every detail so as to captivate completely the credulity of his readers, Lugones fascinates us with an examination of its contents. His theme, his treatment, and his attitude are all reminiscent of the Poe who enjoyed a good hoax. (pp. 292-93)

The spirit of mystery, of fatalism, and of the extraordinary; symbolism and highly-imaginative themes; and a show of facts and of vast learning to gain credence for his tales are the outstanding characteristics of the *Cuentos fatales* of Lugones. Because of the prevalence of the above-mentioned traits, it is easy to account for the many resemblances in these tales to those of Poe. (pp. 296-97)

This spiritual resemblance to Poe, which is so very apparent in the prose of Lugones, is not a passing characteristic of the Argentine intellectual. It has made itself evident in works that represent his literary labors over a long period of years. Time has emphasized the delineation of this trait; so much so that in one of his latest works, **"El ángel de la sombra,"** Lugones makes his reader not only Poe-conscious but also very sensible of a resemblance to certain works of Poe. His first novel is, in the main, but a lengthened version of his tales **"Los ojos de la reina"** and **"El puñal,"** clothed, however, in a deeper note of mystery and of fatality. About the figure of the heroine, Luisa, there hovers that "phosphorescence of decay" of the heroines of Poe. She seems to be the reincarnation of all of Poe's ethereal women. She is as mysterious as her rebirth out of the past of the Middle Ages is incredible. Very characteristic of the spirit of the work is the passage that reveals her identity in a previous existence. . . . When her lover learns that she is destined to die early, he longs passionately for death, believing that "Amarse en la muerte era poseerse en la eternidad" ["In death we will possess our love for eternity"]. How reminiscent of Eleonora's parting are the comforting words of the dying Luisa. . . . After her death, he, like Poe, experiences material sensations of the Beyond.

So much for the prose of Lugones. There remains for consideration but one volume of verse, *El libro fiel,* published in Paris in 1912 and dedicated to his wife. Two poems of this collection seem to have been definitely influenced by Poe. The first of these selections contains lines that are very suggestive of the symbolism of Poe's "Ulalume." . . . (pp. 298-300)

It is, however, when he meditates on the possible death of his "señora" that he most approximates Poe. The expression of the anguish he suffers takes form in his poem **"El canto de la angustia."** . . . The atmosphere and effect created in this portrayal of the terror and despair of a lonely lover are very reminiscent of Poe. . . . (pp. 300-01)

After the publication of *El libro fiel,* Lugones turned a deaf ear to the allurements of the foreign muses and cultivated the national and traditional theme and manner, already essayed in *Odas seculares* . . . , in his later works, *El libro de los paisajes, Las horas doradas,* and *Romancero.* It is useless to search for influences here. Patriotic themes, folklore, and popular verse forms make these volumes stand out in startling contrast to the earlier works of Lugones. And yet there are moments in the reading of the first two books particularly when one feels that the Argentine poet has, consciously or unconsciously, subscribed to a verse esthetics that is, in some respects, allied to Poe's. (p. 302)

Throughout *El libro de los paisajes* there is a monotonous repetition of certain rhyme combinations that is in some measure reminiscent of Poe's verse. While in Poe's case it is an open question as to whether this repetition is largely the result of an effort to produce effects or whether it is due, in the main, to rhyme poverty, with Lugones it is evident that this is his way of expressing the monotonous beauty and peace of his native pampas. In the same volume there are many attempts at onomatopoeia, especially in the group of poems that come under the general title of **"Alas."**

It would be difficult to prove with any degree of certainty that Poe was instrumental in the shaping of the poetic theories and technique of Lugones, were it not for a very illuminating confession of the Argentine poet himself, in which he pays Poe the highest of compliments while voicing some general conceptions on poems and poetry. . . . The fact that Lugones considers Poe the supreme type of poet who unites in just proportions the various elements that constitute a poem, would seem to indicate that Poe has lost none of the prestige he first enjoyed in *Las montañas del Oro* of almost a quarter of a century ago. (p. 304)

John Eugene Englekirk, "Poe's Influence in Spanish America," in his Edgar Allan Poe in Hispanic Literature, *Instituto de las Españas, 1934, pp. 152-417.**

DOROTHY McMAHON   (essay date 1954)

[*In the following excerpt, McMahon contends that the shifting styles and thematic concerns of Lugones's works throughout his career are indicative of his search for a stable system of values, rather than of ever-changing imitations of other authors.*]

[Leopoldo Lugones], an admittedly outstanding Argentine poet, has been nonetheless a controversial figure. For Rufino Blanco-Fombona he was a poseur, a shameless imitator or even a plagiarist, a man so completely lacking in personality and convictions that he should be classified as an actor rather than as an author, for every new reading made him don the personality of the most recent object of imitation. For Carlos Obligado his personality, moral and diamond clear, is reflected in the wealth of invention and the heartfelt sincerity of his poetry exalting home and country. For Pedro Miguel Obligado, Lugones, in spite of his frequent changes in attitude, was always fundamentally the same, for he was basically sincere, so much so that when he finally reached the conclusion that the world was a battleground in which it was not worth while to struggle, that his desire for justice and beauty and peace could not be satisfied, in short, that no ideal was worthy of his faith, he died by his own hand.

But rather than the chameleon versifier, rather than the bard of home and country, rather than the frustrated champion of noble causes, the works of Lugones to me bespeak the man in search of roots. He was seeking a set of values to which he could cling, a force that would give him a longed-for stability. Viewed in this light, the changing emphases of his poetic work—outcries against injustice, rejection of the rational, praise of country, praise of home and wife, descriptions of nature, descriptions of the people and customs of his native region—are all but different means of seeking the same end, a feeling of stability. His shifting political beliefs—from radicalism to socialism to democracy to ultraconservative militarist nationalism—are but another manifestation of his quest for what he could accept as truth. He was primarily concerned not with the consistent defense of his established beliefs but rather with the establishment of the beliefs themselves. His feverish dedication at intermittent intervals to research in history and language and mathematics is but further evidence of that gnawing desire which prompted him to attempt to learn, Why is man? and Why is Lugones?

As a child Lugones had lost his sense of security. His family, through a series of reverses, saw itself obliged to leave its ancestral lands in Río Seco and move to the city of Córdoba. (p. 196)

In Córdoba, Lugones attended the Catholic secondary school, but, rebellious against both discipline and dogma, he soon left school and church with what Pedro Miguel Obligado describes as a ''portazo teatral'' [''theatrical slam of the door'']. As a result of this break with the teachings of his childhood, Lugones was left in early adolescence with the problem of attempting to fill the void left by his displaced beliefs, and, from this time on, his whole emotive and intellectual energy was directed toward seeking a set of beliefs to sustain him. It was his personal tragedy that he never found any he could really accept.

Blanco-Fombona raises the question as to which was the genuine Lugones: the Lugones-Hugo, the Lugones-Herrera y Reissig, the Lugones-Laforgue, the Lugones-Pascoli, the Lugones-Virgil? (p. 197)

But other than to point to his ''verbal magnificence'' and his gift for poetry, Blanco-Fombona offers no real explanation as to why Lugones often excels the apparently disparate poets whose work he accuses him of imitating. The reason lies, I believe, in the fact that Lugones had much in common with all the poets whose works his own at different periods resembles. Hugo, the apostle of revolt and champion of the downtrodden, had also been the victim of an insecure childhood marred by domestic strife and difficulty and numerous changes of residence. The same feelings which prompted Hugo to cry out against injustice prompted Lugones to utter the same cry in his *Montañas del oro* (1897). The same innate pride prevented both youthful poets from complaining of their personal woes and caused them to sublimate their wounded sensibilities in an anguished plea for social justice for all. The Lugones-Hugo period springs not from superficial imitation but from a common mainspring of emotion.

Some eight years later *Los Crepúsculos del jardín* (1905) reflects the same sensitive and wounded poet who now seeks stability through a partial withdrawal from a society which does not understand his superiority and through an objectivity more apparent than real, for the objectivity is in the nature of a defense-mechanism rather than in that of a genuine detachment. In this volume of verse, one sees plainly that Lugones is sad and that ambivalence is the keynote to his emotional nature. . . . The similarities between Lugones' *Los Crepúsculos del jardín* and Herrera's *Los Extasis de la montaña* (1904) are so marked that even a very superficial reading of the two could scarcely fail to reveal them. It is not my purpose to attempt to prove which date of composition is earlier, for the two poets were simply reacting in a similar way to their bitter disenchantment with a life whose joys both would have liked to savor to the full. Julio Herrera y Reissig (1875-1910) was the victim of poor health. He felt strongly, and in true modernist fashion he resented so deeply, the failure of others to recognize his superiority that he incased himself in his *Torre de los panoramas* (the garret of his father's home commanding a view of Montevideo Harbor) and sought happiness in the perfection of his verses and the company of a few kindred souls. Lugones did not withdraw physically from society, but for a while he did withdraw psychologically in an effort to find stability through the cultivation of perfection of form and detachment from emotional entanglements.

These same withdrawal tendencies are apparent to a much greater degree in what Blanco-Fombona has called the ''Lugones-Laforgue'' period. Jules Laforgue (1860-87) was a young man of great talent, and of even greater sensibility, whose feelings of insecurity were increased by the death of his mother (1877), the subsequent changes in the family's mode of living, and finally the death of his father (1881), which left him, as one of the older members of the family, not only completely on his own but also with the additional responsibility of caring for numerous younger brothers and sisters. Laforgue felt a great need for something he could cling to. . . . Because Laforgue was never able to feel the security he desired, he sought to establish a psychological bulwark for himself by keeping aloof and disdaining his fellows. The culmination of this attitude occurs in his *L'Imitation de Notre Dame la Lune* (1886), with its complete rejection of the human, the rational, and its emphasis on ridicule and skepticism.

Lugones by 1909, the year in which his *Lunario sentimental* appeared, had experienced feelings similar to Laforgue's and had as a result attempted to find the answer to his unhappiness in the same way—by a rejection of the rational in favor of the irrational, the leitmotiv of his *Lunario sentimental*. The work is similar to Laforgue's not because it is an imitation as such but because Lugones was seeking stability along the same path which Laforgue had already traversed.

Lugones, however, did not find in withdrawal and rejection of the rational the roots he craved, and so he turned to other means of seeking them, among them the one used by Giovanni Pascoli. Pascoli (1855-1912) was dominated by a great love of family. When he was very young, his sense of security was shattered by his father's murder and several additional deaths soon afterward in his immediate family. He found solace in describing the scenes of family life, the little everyday things which make up daily living, the minor aspects of nature as seen in his native region, which for him constituted an extension of his own personality. Pascoli did not take pleasure in nature in general. It is nature in its commonplace aspects in his corner of the world which interests him, which gives him his feeling of life, of belonging, of having roots. Lugones, too, tried this means of achieving the stability he was seeking so desperately and so gave rise with his *Libro de los paisajes* (1917) to the Lugones-Pascoli period. The work of the two poets was similar because both were striving for the same goal in the same way. Pascoli always used the same means; Lugones whenever he failed to achieve what he sought by one means began casting about for another, until all had been exhausted. His "imitations" of other poets are examples of his having tried the same means which had appealed to other poets of like temperament in that they too had seen their security threatened and were attempting to retain it or establish it. It is this quest for a stabilizing force which provides the common element in Lugones, Hugo, Herrera y Reissig, and Pascoli and which makes it possible for Lugones to surpass at times his "models."

There is a Virgilian ring to Lugones' *Odas seculares* (1910), but, rather than an "imitation" of Virgil, this work is an attempt to find the desired stability through an extension of personality by identifying himself with Argentina. In this work Lugones describes the various elements which make up Argentina, the products, the industry, the people; and he does a masterful job of capturing the essence through a description of the components. Then, in the concluding lines of the principal poem, "A los ganados y las mieses," of *Odas seculares,* he identifies himself with Argentina by reference to a family celebration of Independence Day during his childhood. . . . Lugones in *Odas seculares* was attempting to provide himself with roots by identifying himself with the patria whose centennial celebration of independence he felt as something very personally his, perhaps all the more so because of his previous unsuccessful quests for stability through protest (*Las Montañas del oro*) and withdrawal or rejection (*Los Crepúsculos del jardín* and *Lunario sentimental*). The identification of self with some other element must have yielded a degree of satisfaction to Lugones, even though it was not complete, because two years later in *El Libro fiel* (1912) he uses the same technique, but with his wife and domestic felicity as the objects with which he identifies himself. "Patria," perhaps, had been too impersonal a concept to permit Lugones to enjoy a sense of full identification with it, and so he turned to substituting something more tangible, more personal. But once more the object of identification proved to be something less than fully satisfying as a means of affording stability, for human life is fleeting, and Lugones realized that the loved object could die and leave him anchorless once more. . . . (pp. 197-200)

While love for wife and home persisted, the search for another force to afford him inner security had to persist also, for he could not find it in an individual. And so we find the poet turning to what Blanco-Fombona has designated his Lugones-Pascoli period, in which he produced *El Libro de los paisajes* (1917) and *Las Horas doradas* (1922). In a sense Blanco-Fombona's point that Lugones' interest in nature is nationalistic is well taken. . . .

Lugones was describing nature not because it evoked in him pleasurable emotions to which he wished to give expression but because he was seeking in the everyday aspects of nature in his own country the roots he needed. He was trying to see in nature an extension of his own personality, and to achieve such an end nature in general was of no use to him. It had to be nature in the region with which he could identify himself, just as it did in the case of the Italian Pascoli.

Since nature at best is an impersonal element, it is not surprising that Lugones eventually turned his attention from a region itself to the people who inhabited it. By 1927 he had composed *Poemas solariegos,* in which he sings of the inhabitants, past and present, of Río Seco, his *patria chica,* in his effort to identify himself with something real and lasting. . . . In this work he conceives of the lowly and the humble (cf. "**Los Ínfimos**") as constituting the real realities of life, and he concludes his enumeration of the humble things to which he sings with a reference to his native town. (p. 200)

Lugones, however, was not one of those simple, uncomplicated beings whom he described so lovingly in his attempt to convince himself that he was.

He could not find real satisfaction in any of the devices which he applied so diligently in his effort to find beliefs to sustain him, roots to support him. And when he could no longer find any new path to pursue in the hope of attaining the inner security he desired so earnestly, he could no longer endure a life turned irrevocably meaningless for him.

An ardent seeker after truth, Lugones, for the sake of his own peace of mind, could not afford to admit discouragement even to himself, which is why there are so few overt examples in his poetry of a desire to regress to an earlier, happier state of mind or to change personalities by being someone or something else. His apparent assurance, however, springs from a whistling-in-the-dark attitude, for there are evidences throughout the whole gamut of his poetic production of his basic emotional instability. (p. 201)

Lugones cannot believe in God as He was presented to him in his childhood; yet he cannot find any suitable substitute, and a substitute he must have to achieve peace. As a consequence of this attitude, the poet, who for him is the one who seeks the answers to the riddle of life, in part by challenging established beliefs, is both a source of light and a source of doubt. Because of inner confusion, the overt expression of one emotion is sometimes a mask for another more intimate, frightening emotion whose existence Lugones is afraid to admit even to himself. Self-contradiction becomes a means of pushing on toward ultimate truth.

It is this contradictory element in Lugones' work which gives rise to the accusation that he is inconsistent, for it recurs time after time as each new hope of finding roots proves false, and he must perforce reject it in favor of another. His admiration for the grand gesture, for dying well, is an indication of his unfulfilled love for stability. What greater proof of inner tranquillity can one manifest than to relinquish life calmly? (p. 202)

For a valid judgment Lugones' poetry should be considered on the basis of its intensity of feeling, and this is not always, or even often, what it appears to be on the surface. He was not really praising Argentina, or nature, or marital felicity, or Río Seco per se. He was looking for fulfilment in them, and therein lies the emotional impact of his poetry, as well also as the reason for its sometimes being adjudged artificial. Lugones was a neurotic personality, and while the neurotic may be personally miserable, he is capable of producing the most appealing of poetry, for he gives expression to the fears and feelings, exaggerated in him, common to all of us. Despite the apparent restraint of Lugones' poetry, it was the outpouring and the searching of a tortured and bewildered soul which never achieved that inner tranquillity it sought so fervently. (p. 203)

Dorothy McMahon, "Leopoldo Lugones: A Man in Search of Roots," in Modern Philology, *Vol. LI, No. 3, February, 1954, pp. 196-203.*

JANICE SANDERS MORENO (essay date 1963)

[*In the following excerpt, Moreno examines the various meanings of silence as a persistent and flexible symbol in Lugones's poetry.*]

Silence often appears in the works of contemporary poets as a symbol of tranquility or as a symbol of ruin and despair. The meanings of silence in the poetry of Leopoldo Lugones are particularly subtle and profound. A study of Lugones' use of silence reveals that it is, like Darío's "princess," a personal symbol. This symbol communicates his most intimate thoughts, and these thoughts evoke feelings that lie beyond the immediately accessible poetic experience.

Because silence functions to reveal the poet's most intimate thoughts, it is necessarily subjective, but when silence is observed in context, that is, when it is associated with objective words, it is possible to describe silence, to ascertain its characters, its personality.

Using a Symbolist technique, Lugones assigns color to silence. Silence is shown again and again as pale, clear, white, silver, and gold. These adjectives give silence weightless, fragile, vague, and ethereal qualities. Reminiscent of the effect produced by Darío's "blue," these adjectives which modify silence, also create for it a setting of a dream-like world of immateriality, a world of **"La blanca soledad,"** where the "soft body of silence can sweetly rest."

Most important in the creation of this dream world is clearness or brightness. In **"Paseo matinal,"** . . . dawn brings a quiet, peaceful, uncluttered atmosphere. Here, clearness, brightness, becomes a quality within which silence can suspend itself and can impose the beauty of its immensity. In **"La novia imposible,"** a poetic fantasy in prose, the moon, divinely silent, is a liquid clearness which impregnates the atmosphere with a pale gold, giving silence a dream-like home.

Lugones frequently alludes to the moon and stars in an effort to illustrate the personality and character of silence. Celestial bodies often represent the ineffable, the inexplicable, the exotic. Transferred to silence, they give it the same qualities.

In Lugones' poetry, the moon and stars have an added function, also characteristic of silence: they create a vacuum-like atmosphere—an abyss where all things fall and are removed from themselves. For example, in **"La blanca soledad,"** the moon, cooperating with silence, creates a white abyss of quiet into which shadows fall and live like ideas. . . . And again in **"Paisajes,"** . . . the calmness of silence disengages man's soul and it escapes him as a languid tear escapes from the eyes, or as a petal falls from its flower. . . .

The moon seems to represent for Lugones, the epitome of silence. In **"El Pierrot negro (Pantomina),"** . . . Pierrot, a Picasso-like clown, is on the moon, and the silence he finds there frightens him. There the silence is so profound and so engulfing that it makes all expression, pantomime, all movements, grotesque. . . . (p. 760)

Using the symbol of a cat, he implies that feline silence is distrustful and meditative, and he assigns these aspects to his own personal symbol. So, in **"Himno a la luna,"** . . . cats walk on paws of distrustful silence, and in **"Quimera lunar,"** . . . a meditating shadow has the silence of a cat.

But silence also has the characteristics of a dog. In **"Paisajes,"** . . . silence walks like a long greyhound. The significance of this image is not readily accessible, but one may infer that silence, like the greyhound, moves gracefully, through a series of ripples of silver-grey. The image of a dog further illustrates the loyalty of silence. In **"Delicia otoñal,"** . . . Lugones walks through an elm park and following his footsteps is a loyal silence on tip-toe.

Lugones associates silence with water. In **"Silencio,"** . . . there is a fountain, the symbol of silence, that drips endlessly, quietly, and lazily. And the objects around it are infected with its qualities: the brim of stone surrounding the fountain also seems to drip mutely, and ivy stretches out slowly and infinitely. This poem illustrates the power of silence for, like the fountain, silence infects its subjects with its atmosphere and the products of this atmosphere are made eternal.

When Lugones identifies rain with silence, it is to illustrate the eternal nature of both. For instance, in **"El canto de la angustia,"** . . . silence, like a soft and sighing rain, falls slowly, immemorial and eternal.

Clocks and pendulums and even just the marking of time play an important part in showing the eternal quality of silence for, while the death of a clock's silence may or may not be near (See **"El solterón"** . . .), silence itself, Lugones' silence, endures. (pp. 760-61)

The characterization of silence is enhanced by the moon, rain, and white. The evaluation of silence is not a different process, for qualities and concepts associated with silence explain and illustrate silence's goodness.

For example, in **"La violeta solitaria,"** . . . silence offers protection, and in **"Luna de los amores,"** a "grato silencio de amistad" ["pleasant silence of friendship"], . . . puts everyone at ease. (p. 761)

Love is also a concept which Lugones associates with silence. Indeed, the love which Lugones most extols is the love that exists in silence. Silent love is, for Lugones, the bravest love and the most profound love. . . .

A silent love is more profound because it has as its only witness that which is eternal and pure; and the silence which witnesses this love exerts its power and makes love eternal.

An unrequited love, if it is to be brave, must also be sung silently or secretly. . . .

The concept of silent love carries with it in Lugones' poetry a certain fascination with death, at times heightened to the point of being a premonition of death's arrival. It is not unusual, therefore, to find an atmosphere of death surrounding and engulfing the silent love which Lugones praises. Indeed, it is a natural phenomenon in Lugones' poetry. . . .

Death alone is sometimes a part of silence, but only when death is good—when it is submissive or voluntary, and in Lugones' opinion, consequently brave. In **"A los ganados y las mieses,"** . . . Lugones compares the death of a small goat and a lamb: the goat dies, bleating mournfully, while the lamb, as if in a sacrificial rite, gives of himself in silence, and his death is a white and silent gaze. . . . Even a river, silence's symbol, dies voluntarily, for in **"Delectación morosa,"** . . . a river runs without murmur or complaint toward death. And silence even sweetens winter, Nature's voluntary death, for winter reaches its climax without grief, in a golden silence of dead leaves. (**"El dorador"** . . .). (p. 762)

That Lugones, in his poetry, should associate his notion of death with his personal symbol is not surprising, for Lugones, the man, deeply believed in a voluntary, a silent death. . . .

Holograph copy of Lugones's poem "Holocausto." From Homenaje a Leopoldo Lugones. Academia Argentina de Letras, *1975. Reproduced by permission of the publisher.*

And in 1938, the Argentine poet, as if descending from the pulpit to carry out what he had consistently preached, "se alejó voluntariamente de la vida . . ." ["moved voluntarily from life"]. . . . (pp. 762-63)

The personal departure of Lugones—a leave-taking in a white ship of silence—delivered him into a world of beauty and purity, a personal world of silence. But the silence which Lugones created is not a silence which we are denied, for it is also a part of life. Silence is an acute awareness of all things and of ourselves; it is a state of profundity, a state of vision where objects and people are seen in a "claridad triunfante" ["triumphant clarity"].

A state perhaps at first entered out of the boredom of being "simply" mortal, or because of a desire to leave an enemy world of voices, silence is an escape from reality, but an entrance into a profound reality, a reality beyond. Pierrot, the clown, a symbol of base reality, was unhappy on the moon but, caught up in an atmosphere of silence, he soon began to look at the world through a telescope and the world took on new shape and meaning. And reigning in silence was the "conformidad grave de la vida" ["burdensome resignation of living"]. But it is harmony that triumphs in silence—a result of a profound knowledge of all things, it is the harmony the world seeks, a harmony which gives wings to ecstasy.

And man enters Lugones' white abyss of silence where life, death, and love exist in harmony, and he, like Lugones, is removed from himself, but his solitude is comforting for silence is even more profound than death. Silence holds the memory of the unknown, it guards the secrets of deep thought, and it cradles eternal life. (p. 763)

Janice Sanders Moreno, ''Silence in the Poetry of Leopoldo Lugones,'' in Hispania, *Vol. XLVI, No. 4, December, 1963, pp. 760-63.*

MANUEL BELLONI   (essay date 1969)

[*An Argentine author, Belloni was a founding member of the El Hombre Nuevo group, and a frequent contributor to* Américas. *In the following excerpt from that journal, Belloni traces Lugones's career and discusses early influences on his poetry, his mastery of poetic technique and language, and his role as "torch-bearer" of modernism as an independent Latin American literary movement.*]

Leopoldo Lugones was the first Argentine writer; that is, the first intellectual totally dedicated to letters, the first *homme des lettres* who as such heralded a step forward in Argentine culture. It was not mere coincidence that he should be, at the same time, the torchbearer of Modernism, whose mantle he had inherited from Rubén Darío, and should head the first really independent movement in Latin American literature. This innovation has not been given the revolutionary value it deserves, as it perhaps defines the form of Latin American culture as eclectic and recompilative of all Western culture and, at the same time, the source of a wave of culture from Latin America to Europe that foretold the prominence of the New World in the realm of ideas. . . . Lugones' effect on Spain was similar to that of Benjamin Franklin on France a century before, renewing the nation's repertoire of ideas. Nevertheless, he was clearly original in his ecumenical effort of New World gathering, assimilating, ruminating, and creating. (p. 15)

Lugones is the search, through the word, for eternal beauty. And for this search he must master verse technically and language formidably in order to win in this battle of giants. His stylistic signs are metaphor, vocabulary, golden brilliance, the voluptuousness of the baroque movement, sylvan spiral and volute, Latin Americanism in his great figures of speech, rocky dryness in conceptual synthesis, sparkling jewelry. We would almost say that to read him one ought to wear sunglasses. His sensual rhythm has Whitmanesque swells, and he uses repetition to embed one wave on another, with his nutritive, telluric touch: *Emigre la semilla de la siembra / del genésico horror de las matrices / Emigre la semilla de la siembra.* (Let the seed depart from the sown field / from the generative horror of wombs / Let the seed depart from the sown field.) (*Las Montañas de Oro*).

There is always an agrarian and nourishing tone in his sweeping visions, as we see in his **"Oda a los Ganados y las Mieses (Ode to the Cattle and Pastures),"** his greatest poem in *Cantos Seculares* [*Secular Songs*], published in 1910, one century after the May Revolution. This deep-lying patriotic feeling made him the intellectual head of the Centennial, the federal *caudillo,* youthfully attacking everything. He entered the Plaza de Mayo in Buenos Aires with his poems like any other provincial conquistador and soon dominated its literary circles. He boasted of his homeland, was dazzled by big-city ideas, and turned to socialism. He knew his own dignity and did not join the scramble for the top of the pyramid, and his silence, and his poems, made him the leader. He knew Darío, who, leaving for Europe, tacitly named him his heir in the realm of Modernism.

What did Modernism signify? A declaration of independence for Latin American intelligence, without rejecting valuable support from the outside. The brain was liberated in that it made decisions *per se* and without fearing the authority of foreign criticism. . . . All categories were cultivated passionately, fruitfully. Selective eclecticism united the new cosmovision and the emphasis on nature of Romanticism; the search for the concrete truth and avoidance of the unreachable metaphysical of Positivism; the valiant capture of reality as it is, of Realism; the descriptive bent toward the low and the ugly, of Naturalism; the expressive capacity of the particular or the symbol's induction toward the general, of Symbolism; a certain disdain for the commonplace and a search for the rare and strange of Aestheticism (*Los Raros,* The Strange Ones, was one of Darío's key books). (pp. 15-16)

Modernism rejected nothing and, without intending to, gave an original and Latin American note to everything. To the antagonistic European world it was the integrative Latin American reply, and by foreswearing the choice of factions, it inaugurated a new and different world. It wrung the neck of the *purely* romantic swan, but preserved exoticism, orientalism, traditionalism and romantic sentimentalism. It selected from every movement and made a sensational Creole stew that would nourish, even politically, half the twentieth century. . . .

Lugones not only symbolized the Taoist pendulous swing as an aesthetic guide, but he himself, in his own works, showed such a Laotian spiral. The socialist would become aristocratic; the extremist, moderate; the epic, lyric; the traditionalist, futurist; the esoteric, open; the feminine transcendent from spiritual intuition would become the eminently humanist masculine intelligence. And thus the condor would fly over the whole continent with his wings tinted with the solar gold of beautiful truths. All nature would remain at his feet like a visible sign of the world conquered by the heights. All human gambits, even parapsychology, would be frazzled by the unsleeping eye. Epic glory would make our hair curl with the heroism of his stories like *La Guerra Gaucha* [*The Gaucho War*], a sensational description of Güemes' guerrillas. He was demoniacally baroque and Apollonianly classical, unmeasured and balanced, volcanic and supportive, realistic and numinous, chiaroscuro and luminous, beautiful and supremely ugly. Because Modernism and its chief refused to select and reject, because to choose is to cut something from reality and throw the rest away, and they preferred to synthesize all and fire it in an earthborn and experimental passion. (p. 16)

Argentina strove forcefully to fill the half-century with the powerful wingbeats of Lugones, in all categories. His condor's wings cover the poem with *Los Crepúsculos del Jardín* [*Dusk in the Garden*], *Poemas Solariegos, El Libro de los Paisajes* [*The Book of Landscapes*], *Odas Seculares,* and *Romances del Río Seco* [*Romances of the Río Seco*]. His voice is made complete in an eclectic book, a sentimental Lugonariad of prose and poetry, or in a robust historical exposition in *Historia de Roca* [*History of Roca*] or *Historia de Sarmiento* [*History of Sarmiento*] where he sees like a profound and ontologic poet and carves a masterful and rotund prose, among the most perfect of Argentine literature. He is aware of his mission, and he writes: *El poeta es el astro de su propio destierro. / El tiene su cabeza junto a Dios, como todos, / Pero su carne es fruto de los cósmicos lodos, / De la Vida . . .* (The poet is the star of his own exile. / He has his head next to God, as all do, / But his flesh is the fruit of the cosmic mud, / Of life . . .).

Installed on Parnassus, Lugones occupied it for a quarter of a century with his sacred poet's work. He was gallant and fine, sumptuous and plastic, rigorous and terse, ample in Olympian gesture and language. He had one of the widest vocabularies in Spanish literature and was a renewer of the classics and of words. He was a master of grammar, to the boundary of rhetoric. To be the teacher of generations it was necessary to learn everything and then to forget it when it had become part of one. Thus having mastered technique to its depths, one can be free of constant watchfulness and vacillations.

Lugones was a sculptor whose every stroke was precise. He wrote forty books and expended enough effort on magazines and newspapers for at least another ten. He was never in a hurry and wove his fabric with the tenacity and brilliance of a silkworm in its cocoon. He completed ten books of poetry. A metaphysical investigator who was proud of his origins, he wrote in *Romances: esto no es para extranjeros, / cajetillas ni pazguatos* (this is not for foreigners, / wealthy *porteños* or simpletons). Neither did he write for an acquiescent public; he wrote because it was his means of expression and he required the public to mount his stairs of philosophy, history, mythology, language, philology, Latin, Greek, and Spanish to reach him. It was his lofty manner of respecting the public. Everything he did had a Creole flavor to the marrow. He was moved emotionally by the achievements of the Gauchos of Salta Province and he makes us weep with their integrity and humble heroism.

He possessed the sacred destiny of making the daily act transcendent through its inherent symbol and this is the essence of art; to rescue the day from its precariousness and to praise its meaning to eternity. And without meaning to he was to be a democratic knight, as leaders are always men in perfect contact with their people and their best interests rather than those foreign to them. The whole human race passed before him and he powdered the earth and recognized his favorite son. He tamed the language and achieved the supreme skill of saying exactly what he wanted, without cuts or additions. He is comparable in simplicity only to Goethe. (p. 17)

How much he says, and how economically; how rich and how severe, the ox rises beyond his inanity and attains a definite place, with the definitive strength of art like a Michelangelesque statue on the hazy pampa. Lugones is one of those traitorous poets whom our spoiled palate often offends, believing them deaf or simple; but if we let their honey fall into our mouths, closing our eyes, we will taste the nectar of Mount Hymettus and will find again the line that comes from Theocritus through Virgil, Greco-Latin to the core. And Lugones knows it. By instinct. *Llevo en mí lo mejor / De mi padre y mi madre, que en mí es vida gloriosa, / Y lo mejor del hijo y de la esposa, / Y así está en mí todo el amor. / Lo que en mi madre fue belleza / y en mi padre vigor y nobleza, / En la esposa fe segura / Y en el hijo ternura, / Ilumina mi corazón / Con esplendor absoluto.* (I carry in me the best / Of my father and my mother, which in me is glorious life, / And the best of son and wife, / And thus in me all is love. / What in my mother was beauty / and in my father vigor and nobility, / In my wife confident faith / And in my son, tenderness, / Illumines my heart / With splendor absolute.)

From such possession by poetry he becomes hearty and countryish and is not frightened of the common side of humanity. (p. 19)

Thus he passed from anecdote to action, from Virgil to Homer, and he could have been the French poet Banville, or the Ecuadorian Olmedo. All previous poetry met in him; and all subsequent came from him. (pp. 19-20)

Only Sarmiento can be compared with Lugones in sweep, with his command of prose that Unamuno admired so much. Thus from his native homeland this rocky man came down to show us the country and to unify the Gaucho wisdom of Hernández and the sweeping power of Sarmiento, to join in a still unrecognized miracle of synthesis, the Aeolian harp with summoning drum, the pastoral flute with the bugle of war, thunder with the blond curls of a pretty girl. Goethe said that the true poet does not describe things but is them. Herein lies Lugones' complicated simplicity in making us fall in love with the pampa: *infinitamente gimen los ejes broncos / De lejanas carretas en la tarde morosa. / A flor de tierra entre los negros troncos, / La luna semeja un hongo rosa.* (Infinitely squeak the hoarse axles / Of distant carts in the laggard evening. / A flower of earth between the black trunks, / The moon appears to be a rosy mushroom.) . . .

All poetry has the tint of Lugones, the precursor who opened up all of the paths for spiritual conquest, the golden condor. (p. 20)

Manuel Belloni, "Leopoldo Lugones: 'The Golden Condor'," in Américas, Vol. 21, No. 1, January, 1969, pp. 15-17, 19-20.

JOAN E. CIRUTI (essay date 1975)

[*Ciruti is an American educator. In the following excerpt she discusses several of Lugones's uncollected short stories to illustrate the immense knowledge he displays of such wide ranging subjects as physical and biological science, religion, and the occult. Despite the variety of his themes and subject matter, Ciruti contends that a search for universal truth unites much of Lugones's work.*]

The short stories of Leopoldo Lugones have not yet been fully appreciated for what they can tell us of the man and of his contributions to Spanish-American prose fiction. That he wrote short stories all his life is well known, for he published collections at intervals in his career. He is recognized also as one of the originators of the "cuento fantástico," a type that has flourished in his native Argentina. The collected stories of Lugones, nevertheless, number fewer than half of those he wrote, and even they have not received the critical attention they deserve. Scholars and critics tend to dismiss his short stories with brief comments, as they judge his narrative skill on the basis of the baroque prose of *La guerra gaucha*. The short stories, however, differ markedly from *La guerra gaucha*, and afford insights into the thought processes of the artist from age twenty, in 1894, to his death, in 1938. (p. 134)

A chronological ordering of the short stories shows that Lugones' most active period in the genre was from 1897 to 1899, twenty-six stories being published in the latter year alone. These are, of course, years that Rubén Darío was in Buenos Aires, and the young *modernistas* gathered around him, Lugones outstanding among them, were extremely productive. Another peak is reached in the years 1906-1909, when Lugones was an active collaborator in the weekly news and literary review *Caras y Caretas*. The remaining years of his career see the publication of isolated stories. . . . As one would expect from a *modernista* writer, the subject matter of these short stories is varied. Nevertheless, as will become evident, certain themes and preoccupations continue throughout the years.

Love, in many guises, ranging from the innocent to the diabolical, is a recurring motive especially in the stories of Lugones' early years, before he was thirty. More often than not the plots concern a candid attraction between adolescents who scarcely comprehend the emotion they feel; frequently there is

a humorous twist, in which the lovers are protected in their innocence by some higher power. Five of the seven stories in the collection *Cuentos* are of this type, and similar story lines are found in four additional narrations. Typical of the plots is "**Las manzanas verdes,**" . . . in which Bradlio communicates his love for Naira by pasting cut-outs on green apples so that, when they ripen, the skin shows a heart pierced by an arrow. But one apple has a skull and crossbones, representing Naira's guardian, and the insult narrowly avoids detection when the girl bites off the incriminating design. Where love is concerned, innocence, faithfulness and sincerity are apparently of great importance to the author. Even the Lugones version of Don Juan Tenorio emphasizes a certain candor and sincerity. In "**El secreto de don Juan**" . . . , the spirit of Don Juan himself appears at the end to confirm that his secret lay in his sincerity. . . . (pp. 135-36)

In other stories a lack of selfless faith produces tragedy. Such is the case in "**Piuma al vento**" . . . , in which his sweetheart's skepticism about his feather-balancing act leads a clown to commit suicide. And in "**Los principios de moral**" . . . , Lugones goes so far as to present a woman frivolous in her infidelity. In a conversation between two dogs, reminiscent of Cervantes' *Coloquio de los perros*, the satire is biting. (p. 136)

Love for Lugones, then, is not always untarnished or happy. A number of his stories relate details of an illusive or melancholy love, the unnatural frequently playing a part as in "**¿Una mariposa?**" . . . , the first story Lugones published in Buenos Aires. And three of the four stories in *Lunario sentimental*—"**Inefable ausencia**" . . . , "**La novia imposible**" . . . and "**Abuela Julieta**" . . .—suggest that sadness and suffering may be an integral part of love. Sometimes the torment of love is more than melancholy; it is satanic. The title of "**Amor de nieve**" . . . at first suggests purity, but the story ends by aptly describing a "belle dame sans merci" who finds a worthy adversary. Her honor already tarnished by a subterfuge that makes it appear her cousin has seduced her, Aurelia receives him for one week in a strange, frigid love affair, then cleanses her stained honor with blood, as the code demands. (pp. 136-37)

The range of motives in the stories treating of love already reveals a duality that is present throughout Lugones' short story production. On the one hand, he is attracted by a simple life where goodness prevails, and, on the other, he is fatally drawn to the mysterious, where there is always a hint of evil. This preoccupation with what Lugones himself called "las fuerzas extrañas"—the occult, the inexplicable, the powers beyond man's control or comprehension—predominates in his two best-known collections, *Las fuerzas extrañas* and *Cuentos fatales*, and, consequently, it is the tendency for which he has been most recognized. The stories contained in these two collections are, indeed, typical of this aspect of Lugones' short story production, but when seen within the larger perspective, they may be categorized differently and reevaluated with regard to their importance in judging Lugones as a short story writer.

Perhaps most impressive in *Las fuerzas extrañas* are the five science-fiction stories that make up roughly half of the collection. The procedure in much contemporary science fiction is to suggest an alternate reality in which the reader becomes enveloped. Lugones, a typical *modernista* spirit that rejected limitations, provides an adventure beyond the usual boundaries of man's reality. The narrator, typically, participates in the story as a knowledgeable observer, which gives him a perspective from which to judge the events, and Lugones has ample opportunity to display his considerable scientific knowledge. He also uses the technique, later so important in the stories of Jorge Luis Borges and others, of mentioning the names of real men of science along with fictional characters, thereby blurring the line between the real and the unreal. These stories can be all the more frightening, as Lugones intends, for having an aura of truth about them. . . .

[The] first was "**El psychón.**" . . . Suggested by the recent discovery of the process for liquefying gases like hydrogen, the story recounts Dr. Paulin's production, in the laboratory, of pure thought in liquid form. In "**La metamúsica**" . . . , Juan, the narrator's friend, succeeds in projecting on a screen the colors of music and achieves the poet's ideal of being able to interpret the universe. (p. 137)

Lugones, in these stories of science fiction, feels that he has a window looking onto the abysm of more complete knowledge than man possesses, perhaps of total comprehension. This feeling is at once marvelous and frightening. The narrator of "**El espejo negro**" also expresses the hesitation and fear he feels. . . . Lugones, like the characters of these stories, is curious to decipher the mysteries of the universe, but he is afraid that man cannot venture into the unknown with impunity. Each of these stories, with the possible exception of "**Viola acherontia,**" ends with the destruction of the invention or the inventor. In "**Viola acherontia,**" where the outcome of the experiment is left in doubt, the mad biologist is described as a criminal and ''un perfecto hechicero de otros tiempos,'' which is to say that he represents evil present in the real world. Lugones maintains a greater distance from him: the narrator is no friend of the experimenter, merely an interviewer.

Lugones' venture into science fiction ends with this group of stories written about the turn of the century, but his preoccupation with the unknown continues all of his life. His attention, from this point on, is concentrated on phenomena that are not empirically verifiable. A number of his stories deal with the occult sciences, particularly as practiced in the Middle East. He was an early disciple of Madame Blavatsky and was well versed in her theosophy. "**Un fenómeno inexplicable**" . . . was originally published with the title "**La lycanthropia**" in the monthly theosophical magazine *Philadelfia*. In this story, while traveling in a deserted area of the provinces of Santa Fe and Córdoba, the narrator meets an elderly, solitary Englishman, whose meditations had led to an awareness of a dual personality, and a desire to see his double produce the form of a horrible monkey that shadows him continually. Another early story, "**Kabala práctica**" . . . , has a similar plot.

By the early 1920's Lugones' interest has turned to Egyptology, which provides the theme for three of the *Cuentos fatales,* as well as for "**Nuralkamar**" . . . , one of his last stories. (pp. 138-39)

Of all the short stories Lugones wrote, these on the occult sciences tend to be the longest and most diffuse. The plots are complicated and lack the unity that normally characterizes his narrations. More often than not, the flimsy story line serves primarily as a vehicle for extensive expositions on the history and occult beliefs that presumably form the background for the story. He does not manage, as in *Las fuerzas extrañas,* to create a plausible fictional situation in which to incorporate his erudition. Perhaps in his zeal to pass these off as histories rather than stories, he suppresses the truly fictional. Perhaps his attraction to the occult is so great that he can only conceive of it as reality.

Lugones' liking for the exotic beliefs of distant lands does not cause him to neglect the superstitions of the Argentine gaucho. "**El escuerzo**" . . . , originally published as "**Los animales malditos,**" illustrates the belief that a dead *escuerzo,* a kind of toad, must be burned or it will resuscitate and take revenge on the person who killed it. In "**Águeda**" . . . , a romantic legend of a bandit, the superstitious beliefs are incidental to the plot, but still of prime importance in the total effect of the story.

Inexplicable appearances and dead people provide the subject matter for a number of stories. (p. 140)

With the exception of "**El hombre del árbol,**" all of [the] stories of ghosts and the dead were published in 1907. This seems to indicate . . . that Lugones reached a turning point around 1906 or 1907, in which the irrational became more fascinating to him than the science fiction that had occupied him for several years. Further support for this conjecture may be found in three short stories, also published in 1907, which seek to define insanity. In "**El descubrimiento de la circunferencia,**" Clinio Malabar's unique madness, like that of the man who believed he was dead, consisted of maintaining that the circumference was the key to human life and that death could not come so long as he was enclosed in a circle. The protagonist of "**Un sujeto ilógico,**" on the other hand, defines insanity as a lack of concordance between logic and the will. And the third story, "**El 'definitivo,'**" leaves insanity in the realm of the inexplicable: it is something that is at once undefinable and ''definitive.''

Along the same general lines of treating the unnatural, a substantial block of stories narrates myths. (p. 141)

The most outstanding of the Hellenic myths, and one of Lugones' better stories, is "**Los caballos de Abdera.**" . . . The proud inhabitants of Abdera, a Thracian city justly famous for its horses, treat their animals so well that the horses begin to humanize: they become vain, fall in love with humans, and develop a conscience. Finally, they rebel, and it takes the divine intervention of Hercules to save the humans. As the inventors in the science fiction stories created machines that killed them, so the inhabitants of Abdera unwittingly produced a beast that could overpower them. The frightening part is that the horses' destructive desire develops along with their humanization. As happened with the chimpanzee Yzur, acquisition of the power to think was no blessing.

Myth, by its very nature, affords Lugones the opportunity to use his imagination to the fullest, without being fettered by convention or reality. Three narrations with fairy-tale atmospheres relate flowers and the life of man: "**La muerte de la señorita Clementina**" . . . , "**La rosa y la espina**" . . . and "**El culto de la flor.**" . . . Another large category of myths treats of biblical and religious themes. Most were written early in Lugones' career, and in some the sentiment overpowers the artistic value. Several of the stories end with miracles, another version of the strange and inexplicable forces that always interest Lugones. (pp. 141-42)

One of the most interesting stories of *Las fuerzas extrañas* is "**La lluvia de fuego,**" which bears the sub-title ''Evocación de un desencarnado de Gomorra.'' Told from the perspective of an elderly recluse whose only vice now is gluttony, the story manages to capture the progression from curiosity to sheer horror, as incandescent copper particles rain down on Gomorrah. In capturing the horror of the situation, Lugones makes effective use of animals. The first indication that the volcanic rain is not a passing thing comes from the reaction of the birds. And finally, as virtually all life has been extinguished, a pride of thirst-crazed lions is the vehicle for describing the terror of the incomprehensible destruction. The animals' terror is instinctive, from not understanding; man's horror stems from comprehending too well.

Although many of the short stories already discussed at least imply a lesson to be learned, there is a sizeable group that explicitly proposes a standard of conduct or sets forth a system of values. Some take the form of fables; others have modern settings and characters taken from contemporary life. A few present abstract principles, but the majority are, on a personal level, concerned with the moral character of the individual. . . . **"La defensa de la ilusión"** . . . and **"Cosas de gansos"** . . . take on political overtones as they present plots in which the consequences of the actions men take are unimportant so long as a principle is being defended. Among those stories that are more personal, several comment on human faults, the criticism softened by humor. (p. 142)

The tone of the stories becomes more serious as Lugones moves from general to more specifically Christian themes. In **"Verano"** . . . , a monk's devotion before a crucifix produces a new Garden of Eden that is once again destroyed by carnal love. The result of the original fall from grace is the subject of **"El carnaval negro"** . . . , which makes its point through a dantesque vision. Another dantesque vision is the motive of **"La biblioteca infernal"** . . . , important for the insights it gives into Lugones' own moral code. As the narrator turns the last page of a book that has given him a vague impression of fear, a vision begins in which he descends into the library of Satan. In the rooms of Pride, he finds books that glorify suffering and tyranny, all the codes of force. The rooms of Avarice contain volumes that produce money and measure out hunger among the peoples. The shelves of Lust, he says, are the ones preferred in Hell, and he describes them in terms of serpents. Then he mentions some of the books contained there, from Petronius and Apuleius to the moderns. . . . The rooms of Anger, Gluttony, and Envy are crossed rapidly, and he descends to the area of Stupidity, where he finds all the newspapers of the world, all the products of rational philosophy, all the books against God. Finally, the entire library seems to come together to form a gigantic Satan, and he slams shut the covers of the book he is perusing. (p. 143)

If Lugones seems to provide answers in the form of moral guides in many stories, there are others in which the motive is clearly a search: for happiness, for beauty, for the ideal. These values in the life of man can be as illusive as was love in some of the first stories discussed, or as mystifying as the forces of the Great Beyond. (p. 144)

Lugones also is preoccupied with the search for beauty. In **"El hallazgo de la belleza"** . . . , the caliph who lives in a splendid palace is told that he must find beauty within himself. In his youth, however, Lugones was concerned with exterior beauty, as is evidenced by three short stories, all published in 1899 and all notable for their symbolist style. **"Misa de primavera"** . . . , a symphony of color, is the most lyrical of the three. It is a fantasy of a mass celebrated each spring in which all the characters are birds, and they move in an environment beautifully decorated with flowers. . . . [In] **"El paraíso de buen tono"** . . . , Lugones treats of what might be described as a *modernista* paradise. Ismenia is a young lady given to traveling through fantastic regions in her dreams. . . . (pp. 144-45)

The depiction of such an elegant, sophisticated society—"de buen tono" ["in good taste"]—that is so frequently taken as the standard of the *modernista* generation, is not characteristic of the short stories of Leopoldo Lugones. His preference is, obviously, for a simpler, pastoral existence. Nature, especially animals, appears with great frequency in his stories, making many of them like fables or apologues. Born and raised in the province of Córdoba, in the village of Río Seco, Lugones knew and had a healthy respect for natural things. In an early story, **"Los buscadores de oro"** . . . , two adventurers, attempting to collect the gold uncovered by the ocean in Tierra del Fuego, narrowly escape death from an angry sea that takes them on "hombre a hombre" ["man to man"]. Similarly, **"La ley natural"** . . . illustrates that nature can defend itself against the domination of man.

Taking into account the role of nature in Lugones' stories, and the uncomplicated characters that populate the majority of them, it is not at all surprising that he had in process at the time of his death a series of *criollo* stories, the "cuentos serranos" ["mountain tales"]. Animals and gauchos are the protagonists of these eight narrations. (p. 145)

"Sangre real" . . . , one of the "cuentos serranos" and Lugones' last published story, has a majestic condor as its protagonist. Because the drought is bringing out the scavengers, the worst of them the condor, the *patrón* and a youth seek out the bird's nest. At first, Lugones carefully delineates the destructive power of the condor, but, as the male returns to protect his young, the attention is turned to the beauty of his flight, and, finally, the bird's bravery and nobility are so impressive that the gauchos decide to let him live. The description of the condor's flight is as sensitive and the prose as harmonious as anything Lugones had written before. . . . (p. 146)

Lugones was a humanist concerned more with the moral than the social. In the "cuentos serranos," as in so many of his earlier stories, he is extolling such virtues as loyalty, faith and courage. The characters, animal as well as human, are unpretentious, and display a warmth of human affection that Lugones, evidently, prized highly. In many of his earlier stories, the Argentine setting is of little consequence; the events could have taken place almost any place in the world. The fact that Lugones now finds in typically Argentine characters and situations the same universal values that he has esteemed all along is simply a confirmation of his *modernismo*. The *modernistas*, although frequently accused of neglecting their own countries and continent in their literature, in truth, never did. They were guilty only of not permitting themselves to be bound by a too narrow nationalism: they viewed America in more universal terms, as part of a larger world.

The style of Lugones' short stories tends to be conversational, although it can vary from the erudite to the lyrical. A frequent structure has the narrator talking to someone, a friend or a disciple, and it is common for the narrator to speak from experience as a participant in, or as an observer of, the action. Lugones, sometimes accused of a lack of intimacy in his poetry, in his short stories strives to achieve the effect of nearness to the action. In stories dealing with the unnatural and the unreal, he tries to convince the reader that the events actually happened. This leads him to be one of the first to use the names of real people in his stories, a technique later much imitated. His writing is spontaneous, without evidence of a lot of polishing. In the album of clippings that was reproduced as *Las primeras letras de Leopoldo Lugones*, he sometimes annotated, with corrections, on stories he intended to publish again. The corrections tend to make changes in language, not in content, and, on the whole, are not extensive. Spontaneity suffers at times, however, when he seems to want to overwhelm his reader and lectures at length. The stories of *Cuentos fatales* are the worst offenders in this respect. For the most part, his stories are very short, and he is adept at creating suspense. (pp. 146-47)

In his short stories Lugones is constantly searching for some universal truth to which he can cling. The reality of Argentina and other places, the Bible and church history, legends, the physical and biological sciences, the occult sciences, theosophy, everything comes under his scrutiny. Like the boy/man/old man of **"El pájaro azul,"** Lugones learns many things along his route, and, as in the story, there is the hint that the ideal is unobtainable. He seems to suggest, by the attention he gives in his short stories to unpretentious, good people leading a pastoral existence, that happiness and contentment lie in an uncomplicated life where there is no consciousness of the limitations of man or his status in the universe. Such is the life Lugones seems to long for, but his curiosity continues to draw him to the mysterious in spite of the intranquility of the soul with which it leaves him. The desire to return to his origins that is inherent in the "cuentos serranos" of his last years is perhaps one of the clearest manifestations of the longing he had felt throughout his adult life. (p. 148)

It is now clear that *Las fuerzas extrañas* and *Cuentos fatales,* the collections most widely read, convey a distorted conception of Lugones as a short story writer. *Las fuerzas extrañas,* the better of the two, contains some masterful representations of his talent and illustrates that his interests covered science fic-tion, the occult, Hellenic and religious myths. But even it gives no indication of the more romantic side of his character, or of the continuing search that is so evident when all of the short stories are considered. . . . Lugones may not have considered his short stories on a par with his poetry, and, for that reason, may have left so many of them dispersed in journals. Perhaps, for the same reason, he labored less over them, with the result that his personality comes through more easily. In any case, the image of himself that Leopoldo Lugones left in his short stories is clear, and it shows us a multi-faceted man at once a part of his generation and an individual. (p. 149)

Joan E. Ciruti, "Leopoldo Lugones: The Short Stories," in Revista Interamericana de Bibliografía: Inter-American Review of Bibliography, *Vol. XXV, No. 2, April-June, 1975, pp. 134-49.*

ADDITIONAL BIBLIOGRAPHY

Franco, Jean. "The Discovery of the New World." In his *An Introduction to Spanish-American Literature*, pp. 158-92. London and New York: Cambridge University Press, 1969.*
    Brief discussion of poetic themes and influences.

Mudrovic, Mike. "The Speakers Position in Some Poems of Machado and Lugones." *Kentucky Romance Quarterly* XXVII, No. 3 (1980): 281-88.*
    Compares and contrasts the function of the observer in poems of similar themes by Antonio Machado and Lugones.

George Orwell

1903-1950

(Pseudonym of Eric Arthur Blair) English novelist, essayist, critic, and journalist.

The following entry presents criticism of Orwell's novel *Nineteen Eighty-Four*. For a complete discussion of Orwell's career, see *TCLC*, Volumes 2 and 6.

George Orwell and the year 1984 have become closely identified in the public imagination since the publication of his classic novel *Nineteen Eight-Four*, an attack on totalitarianism and a warning that absolute power in the hands of any government can deprive a people of all basic freedom. While the novel is based in part on the Soviet example, it is set in England to underscore Orwell's conviction that unchecked power even in the hands of a Western democracy could result in a repressive regime. Various terms used in the book, such as ''Newspeak'' and ''double-think,'' have passed into common usage—and are often misused according to Orwell's definitions—while ''Big Brother,'' perhaps the work's most famous coinage, has become synonymous with oppressive government. Lawrence Malkin has noted that ''no political book, whether fiction or nonfiction—and the essence of Orwell's success is that no one is ever sure whether *1984* is one or the other—has passed more thoroughly into the English language and the popular consciousness of the Western world than Orwell's dark masterpiece.''

Orwell's first major critical and popular success as an author came with the publication of *Animal Farm* in 1945. His income from the book's sales, though not great, enabled him in the spring of 1947 to rent a house on the Scottish island of Jura, where he began work on a new novel. In December of 1947 Orwell was hospitalized for treatment of the tuberculosis from which he had suffered since his mid-thirties. He spent the first half of 1948 in Hairmyres Hospital in Glasgow, and on his release returned to Jura to complete the novel, tentatively entitled *The Last Man in Europe* but ultimately called *Nineteen Eighty-Four*. Although very ill and under a doctor's orders to work no more than an hour each day, Orwell was unable to find a typist willing to come to the isolated island, so he prepared the final manuscript of *Nineteen Eighty-Four* himself. He collapsed almost immediately upon completing the task, and was bedridden for the remaining two years of his life. Many critics contend that the overwhelming pessimism of *Nineteen Eighty-Four* is directly related to Orwell's fatal illness, a position supported by Orwell's remark that the novel ''wouldn't have been so gloomy if I hadn't been so ill.'' Friends and acquaintances of Orwell, however, have emphatically maintained that *Nineteen Eighty-Four* was not meant to be Orwell's last book, or his last word as an assessment of the future. Orwell was a prolific writer who had lived by his pen for years, and often spoke of plans for essays and for another novel he hoped to write upon his recovery. He also remarried just three months before his death, telling his friend T. R. Fyvel that the marriage would give him another reason to live.

Nineteen Eighty-Four was identified by Geoffrey Stokes as the first major twentieth-century dystopian novel, which is a modern variation of the traditional utopian novel. The utopian novel

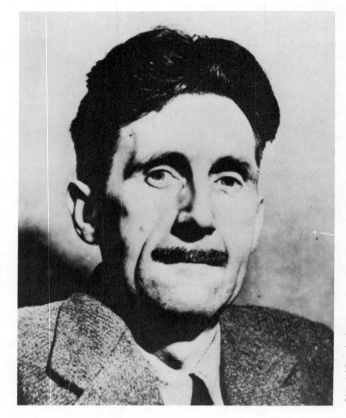

has been an established genre since the appearance of Sir Thomas More's *Utopia* in 1516. Until the early twentieth century, works of this sort commonly expressed a belief in humanity's potential for individual and social perfectibility. These ideal societies were usually depicted as lying not in the future but in some remote geographical area. Following World War I, anti-utopian, or dystopian, novels began to appear. These works frequently projected contemporary social, political, and economic trends into a foreseeable future. Probably the two best-known dystopias before *Nineteen Eighty-Four* are Yevgeny Zamyatin's *We* and Aldous Huxley's *Brave New World,* with which *Nineteen Eighty-Four* is often compared. However, Orwell's novel differed from Zamyatin's and Huxley's in that he did not posit any technological advances—often a staple of futuristic fiction—but only adapted existing technology in the creation of such devices as the telescreens and speakwrites.

Nineteen Eighty-Four vividly portrays life in Oceania, a totalitarian state controlled by a mysterious Inner Party that exacts blind devotion to the Party and to its leader, Big Brother, by means including constantly rewritten history (which retrospectively proves the Party infallible) and two-way telescreens monitored by Thought Police. The world is divided into three superstates—Oceania, Eastasia, and Eurasia—that are continually realigning and continually at war. The constant warfare cripples the productive capabilities of each superpower so that the population of each exists in poverty and ignorance, kept in a state of patriotic frenzy aided by reports of glorious victories on the battlefields, parades of captured enemy soldiers, and frequent public executions of spies and traitors to the State. The novel recounts the brief revolt of one man, Winston Smith, against the control of the Party, and his eventual, inevitable defeat. In one of the novel's most often quoted passages, Smith writes in his diary that he understands "how" but not "why" the Inner Party maintains its absolute control over the past and over the minds of the inhabitants of Oceania. The "why" is not revealed until near the end of the novel in a dialogue between Smith and his betrayer O'Brien, an Inner Party official who has pretended to belong to an underground movement dedicated to overthrowing the Party and Big Brother. In this scene, Orwell employs the fictional device of an extended dialogue between an adherent of the old order and a proponent of the new, a device which enables the author to present to the reader a closely reasoned explication of the inner logic of the society under discussion. O'Brien tells Smith that the Party seeks power for its own sake, thus differing from totalitarian states of the past, such as those that existed in Stalinist Russia or Nazi Germany, which at least employed the pretense of serving the people whom they subjugated. The Inner Party in *Nineteen Eighty-Four* offers no moral justification for its actions.

Beginning with the earliest reviews of *Nineteen Eighty-Four*, critics have tended to interpret the novel in one of three ways: as a satire of the contemporary social and political scene; as an attack on a specific political party or system (most often thought to be Stalinist Communism); or as a general warning about the dangers of totalitarianism, which could result if any government assumed absolute power. The last interpretation was Orwell's own, and he issued a statement to this effect through his publisher, Fredric Warburg, after noting that many early reviews of the book—particularly in the United States—assumed that the novel was meant as a pointed attack on a particular government. Despite Orwell's disclaimer, which included the remark that the novel was set in Britain "in order to emphasize . . . that totalitarianism, if not fought against, could triumph anywhere," some critics have applied a narrower interpretation to *Nineteen Eight-Four*. Mark Schorer, for example, early interpreted the novel as an attack upon aspects of British socialism, and a *Life* magazine review of the novel in 1949 indicated that the novel warned against the rise of "left-wing totalitarianism." As recently as 1980 Isaac Asimov wrote that *Nineteen Eighty-Four* "was clearly an anti-Soviet polemic," a picture "of Stalinism, and Stalinism only." V. S. Pritchett was one of the earliest reviewers of the novel to theorize that despite the futuristic setting, *Nineteen Eight-Four* actually satirized Orwell's own milieu—post-World War II England. Many of the details of life in Oceania correspond to situations in Orwell's essays and letters describing life in England during the 1930s and 1940s—in particular the drab living conditions, inadequate food, bombed-out buildings, and the shortage, at one time or another, of nearly every commonplace household item.

After his involvement in the Spanish civil war—in which he fought on the side of the Loyalists—Orwell committed himself to making political writing into an art. In his 1946 essay "Why I Write" he stated that "every line of serious work that I have written since 1936 has been written, directly or indirectly, *against* totalitarianism and *for* democratic Socialism, as I understand it." *Animal Farm*, Orwell continued, was the first book in which he consciously fused artistic and political pur-

pose, and he wrote that he hoped to do the same in his next novel. Because of the political nature of the book, and because it has been from the first such an enormous success, various politically oriented groups have sought to claim *Nineteen Eighty-Four* as a manifesto of their own views, and to annex Orwell as an ideological blood brother. Paul Schlueter predicted that the eponymous year would bring with it much politicized writing about *Nineteen Eighty-Four*, "with now one group and then another group clutching Orwell to its collective breast." True to his prediction, a resurgence of critical writing about the novel began in 1980 and a number of factions have been contesting earnestly in print for the privilege of claiming Orwell as their ally. One of the most vociferous and controversial of these groups are those essayists, critics, and political analysts who term themselves neoconservatives. Gordon Beadle has noted that "American conservatives are not generally given to celebrating the political wisdom of English left-wing socialists, yet this has been the curious fate of George Orwell." The neoconservative position on Orwell is prominently represented by Norman Podhoretz, who calls *Nineteen Eighty-Four* "one of the great prophetic warnings against the threat of Soviet totalitarianism." The neoconservative interpretation of *Nineteen Eighty-Four* also extends to a reexamination of Orwell's own political beliefs. Podhoretz maintains that Orwell abandoned many of his Socialist beliefs during his lifetime and even theorizes that Orwell may have "insisted on clinging so tenaciously to his identity as a man of the Left" to add authority to his criticism of left-wing political thought. This supposition is dismissed by Robert Hitchens, who insists that Orwell's "identity as a 'man of the Left'" was something he fought for and evolved over a period of decades. Many other commentators on Orwell's life and works conclude that he was highly critical of leftist political thought precisely because he did associate himself with the political Left and therefore wished its precepts to be as valid as possible. In addition, friends of Orwell who have written about him maintain that while he certainly developed politically throughout his life, he did not change his essential political beliefs and he consistently regarded himself as a left-wing socialist. Fyvel has noted that Orwell "became and remained a Socialist" and that he "regarded himself as belonging to the radical wing of the British Labour Party and continued to believe that its measures could make the life of the British working class somewhat more humane and better."

When *Nineteen Eighty-Four* first appeared at the height of the Cold War it was perhaps natural to interpret the novel, as many did, as a denunciation of the Soviets. Popular perception of the novel has shifted, however, in the years since its publication. Asimov is among those critics to have noted that the term "1984" has come to stand "not for Stalinism or even for dictatorship in general—but merely for government." Now any overly intrusive government program or policy is likely to elicit the adjective "Orwellian," while Paul Grey finds that "merely mentioning the date can convey muzzy criticism of whatever the speaker happens to dislike." The year 1984 is inextricably linked in the minds of millions of readers with the concept of oppressive government, and the novel has, in John H. Barnsley's words, "become part of the common imaginative heritage of the Western world."

(See also *Contemporary Authors*, Vol. 104; *Dictionary of Literary Biography*, Vol. 15: *British Novelists, 1930-1959;* and *Something about the Author*, Vol. 29.)

GEORGE ORWELL   (letter date 1948)

[*In the following excerpt from a letter to his publisher, Fredric Warburg, Orwell discusses the last stages of the writing of* Nineteen Eighty-Four *and his proposed titles for the novel.*]

I shall finish the book . . . early in November, and I am rather flinching from the job of typing it, because it is a very awkward thing to do in bed, where I still have to spend half the time. Also there will have to be carbon copies, a thing which always fidgets me, and the book is fearfully long, I should think well over 100,000 words, possibly 125,000. I can't send it away because it is an unbelievably bad MS and no one could make head or tail of it without explanation. On the other hand a skilled typist under my eye could do it easily enough. If you can think of anybody who would be willing to come, I will send money for the journey and full instructions. I think we could make her quite comfortable. There is always plenty to eat and I will see that she has a comfortable warm place to work in.

I am not pleased with the book but I am not absolutely dissatisfied. I first thought of it in 1943. I think it is a good idea but the execution would have been better if I had not written it under the influence of TB. I haven't definitely fixed on the title but I am hesitating between **"Nineteen Eighty-Four"** and "The Last Man in Europe".

> *George Orwell, in a letter to F. J. Warburg on October 22, 1948 in his* The Collected Essays, Journalism and Letters of George Orwell: In Front of Your Nose, 1945-1950, Vol. IV, *edited by Sonia Orwell and Ian Angus, Harcourt Brace Jovanovich, Inc., 1968, p. 448.*

[JULIAN SYMONS]   (essay date 1949)

[*Symons holds two highly praised literary reputations: that of the serious biographer and that of the detective novelist. His popular biographies of Charles Dickens, Thomas Carlyle, and his brother A. J. A. Symons are considered excellent introductions to those writers. Symons is better known, however, for his crime novels, particularly* The Progress of a Crime (1960). *Symons and Orwell met in 1944 when Orwell was literary editor of the socialist weekly* Tribune, *to which Symons was a frequent contributor. Prior to their first meeting, Orwell had commented in an article in* Partisan Review *that Symons wrote "in a vaguely Fascist strain"—a comment for which he apologized to Symons and which he later retracted in the* Partisan Review. *The two remained friends for the rest of Orwell's life. In the following excerpt Symons finds that in the fifteen years between the writing of Orwell's first novel,* Burmese Days, *and* Nineteen Eighty-Four, *Orwell tended to reduce characterization in favor of examining ideas in his novels. (This interpretation is challenged by Harold J. Harris (1959), who maintains that* Nineteen Eighty-Four *"depends more upon character and plot development than upon discursive statement.") Symons characterizes* Nineteen Eighty-Four *as a serious examination of power and corruption, marred by a somewhat "schoolboyish" sensationalism. In a letter of 16 June 1949 Orwell thanked Symons for his "brilliant as well as generous review" of* Nineteen Eighty-Four, *agreeing that the "Room 101" episode was crudely presented: "I was aware of this while writing it, but I didn't know another way of getting somewhere near the effect I wanted."*]

It is natural that such a writer as Mr. Orwell should regard increasingly the subject rather than the form of his fictional work. **Burmese Days** is cast fairly conventionally in the form of the contemporary novel; this form had almost ceased to interest Mr. Orwell in 1939, when, in **Coming Up For Air**, the form of the novel was quite transparently a device for comparing the England of that time with the world we lived in before the First World War. In **Coming Up For Air**, also, characterization was reduced to a minimum: now, in **Nineteen Eighty-Four**, it has been as nearly as possible eliminated. We are no longer dealing with characters, but with society.

The picture of society in **Nineteen Eighty-Four** has an awful plausibility which is not present in other modern projections of our future. In some ways life does not differ very much from the life we live to-day. The pannikin of pinkish-grey stew, the hunk of bread and cube of cheese, the mug of milkless Victory coffee with its accompanying saccharine tablet—that is the kind of meal we very well remember; and the pleasures of recognition are roused, too, by the description of Victory gin (reserved for the privileged—the "proles" drink beer), which has "a sickly oily smell, as of Chinese rice-spirit" and gives to those who drink it "the sensation of being hit on the back of the head with a rubber club." We can generally view projections of the future with detachment because they seem to refer to people altogether unlike ourselves. By creating a world in which the "proles" still have their sentimental songs and their beer, and the privileged consume their Victory gin, Mr. Orwell involves us most skilfully and uncomfortably in his story, and obtains more readily our belief in the fantasy of thought-domination that occupies the foreground of his book. . . .

The central figure of **Nineteen Eighty-Four** is a member of the Outer Party and worker in the records department of the Ministry of Truth, named Winston Smith. Winston is at heart an enemy of the Party; he has not been able to eliminate the past. When, at the Two Minutes' Hate sessions the face of Emmanuel Goldstein, classic renegade and backslider, appears on the telescreen mouthing phrases about party dictatorship and crying that the revolution has been betrayed, Winston feels a hatred which is not—as it should be—directed entirely against Goldstein, but spills over into heretical hatred of the Thought Police, of the Party, and of the Party's all-wise and all-protecting figurehead, Big Brother. . . .

Sexual desire has been so far as possible removed from the lives of Pary members; and so Winston sins grievously and joyously with Julia, a member of the Junior Anti-Sex League.

The downfall of Winston and Julia is brought about through O'Brien, a friendly member of the Inner Party, who reveals that he, too, is a heretic. They are admitted to membership of Goldstein's secret organization "the Brotherhood," which is committed to the overthrow of the Party. But O'Brien is not in fact a member of "the Brotherhood"—if indeed that organization is not simply an invention of the Inner Party—and the benevolent-seeming proprietor of the junk shop belongs to the Thought Police. Winston is arrested and subjected by O'Brien to physical and mental coercion; its effect is to eradicate what O'Brien calls his defective memory. . . .

The corrosion of the will through which human freedom is worn away has always fascinated Mr. Orwell; **Nineteen Eighty-Four** elaborates a theme which was touched on in **Burmese Days**. Flory's criticism of Burma might be Winston Smith's view of Oceania: "It is a stifling, stultifying world in which to live. It is a world in which every word and every thought is censored. . . . Free speech is unthinkable." And Flory's bitter words: "Be as degenerate as you can. It all postpones Utopia," is a prevision of Winston saying to Julia in his revolt against Party asceticism: "I hate purity, I hate goodness! I don't want any virtue to exist anywhere." But in **Nineteen Eighty-Four** the case for the Party is put with a high degree of sophistical skill in argument. O'Brien is able easily to dispose of Winston in their discussions, on the basis that power is the reality of life. The arrests, the tortures, the executions, he says, will never cease. The heresies of Goldstein will live for ever, because they are necessary to the Party. The Party is immortal, and it lives on the endless intoxication of power. "If you want a picture of the future, imagine a boot stamping on a human face—forever."

Mr. Orwell's book is less an examination of any kind of Utopia than an argument, carried on at a very high intellectual level, about power and corruption. And here again we are offered the doubtful pleasure of recognition. Goldstein resembles Trotsky in appearance, and even uses Trotsky's phrase, "the revolution betrayed"; and the censorship of Oceania does not greatly exceed that which has been practised in the Soviet Union, by the suppression of Trotsky's works and the creation of "Trotskyism" as an evil principle. "Doublethink," also, has been a familiar feature of political and social life in more than one country for a quarter of a century.

The sobriety and subtlety of Mr. Orwell's argument, however, is marred by a schoolboyish sensationalism of approach. Considered as a story, *Nineteen Eighty-Four* has other faults (some thirty pages are occupied by extracts from Goldstein's book, *The Theory and Practice of Oligarchical Collectivism*): but none so damaging as this inveterate schoolboyishness. The melodramatic idea of the Brotherhood is one example of it; the use of a nursery rhyme to symbolize the unattainable and desirable past is another; but the most serious of these errors in taste is the nature of the torture which breaks the last fragments of Winston's resistance. He is taken, as many others have been taken before him, to "Room 101." In Room 101, O'Brien tells him, is "the worst thing in the world." The worst thing in the world varies in every case; but for Winston, we learn, it is rats. The rats are brought into the room in a wire cage, and under threat of attack by them Winston abandons the love for Julia which is his last link with ordinary humanity. This kind of crudity (we may say with Lord Jeffrey) will never do; however great the pains expended upon it, the idea of Room 101 and the rats will always remain comic rather than horrific.

But the last word about this book must be one of thanks, rather than of criticism: thanks for a writer who deals with the problems of the world rather than the ingrowing pains of individuals, and who is able to speak seriously and with originality of the nature of reality and the terrors of power.

[Julian Symons], "Power and Corruption," in The Times Literary Supplement, *No. 2471, June 10, 1949, p. 380.*

JAMES HILTON   (essay date 1949)

[*Hilton was an English journalist and novelist who had his greatest successes with the novels* Lost Horizon *(1933) and* Goodbye, Mr. Chips *(1934). He moved to the United States in 1935 and collaborated on writing the scripts for the popular film versions of these two best-selling novels. He became widely known to American audiences as a book reviewer and radio announcer. In the following excerpt, Hilton praises the timeliness of* Nineteen Eighty-Four, *noting that "Mr. Orwell has not invented too much"— that many of the details of life under the repressive totalitarian regime presented in* Nineteen Eighty-Four *had in fact occurred in various countries.*]

Mr. Orwell who in **"Animal Farm"** wrote a short deft satire on certain modern trends, has now looked ahead to see where those trends are pointing, and the result is a fictional forecast of the sort of England and the sort of world that await today's children. It is not a pretty story and one could hope that it is not a likely story either. Fascinatingly dreadful from first word to last, it represents an end-product of that long line of novels about the future that began by being Utopian and idealist, and passed through the social criticism of Erewhon to H. G. Wells's warnings of the shape of things to come. But even the Wellsian future did not blueprint the breakdown of the human soul; Aldous Huxley came nearer to it in the mid-twenties, though his brave new world was so called in mockery. But today Mr. Orwell does not mock.

Briefly, the situation by 1984 is as follows. England has become Airstrip One of Oceania, which comprises America, the Atlantic islands, Australia and South Africa. Oceania is always at war with other Eurasia or Eastasia, the other two conglomerates that share the rest of the world. . . . Warfare is constant, but (for England) mainly distant, though rockets fall on London at frequent intervals—not atom bombs, because they have been barred by tacit agreement as being dangerous to the totalitarian structure of all three governments. Which touches the core of the thesis—that (according to Mr. Orwell) the totalitarian state's only aims are power and survival, so that it must organize permanent war as a means of wasting the products of its advanced technology, since if these products were ever to be used for raising the citizen's living standard, the essence of a hierarchical society would be destroyed.

Mr. Orwell gives us his argument through the story of Winston Smith, a minor official and Party-member in the Records Department of the Ministry of Truth (Minitrue, in the Newspeak jargon which by 1984 is fast supplanting old-fashioned English). . . .

Winston, of course, is only a small cog in the gigantic machine. . . .

In this degraded world Winston commits the infinite crime of writing entries in a private diary, urged to do so by some faint and vestigial stirring of historical conscience—heresy indeed; and from then to the final page is the story of how he is spied on, inveigled, discovered and tortured, until at the appalling finish his multiple confessions are not only abject but sincere— because by that time he really does love Big Brother. For after all, to make people just do things is naive work for a tyranny equipped with all the modern technique of propaganda, drugs, shock-therapy, and hypnosis; making people want to do things is much more subtly successful.

This is the deep horror of Mr. Orwell's story, compared with which Mr. Wells's prophecies of atomic bombs, astonishingly accurate though they were, seem mere adventure yarns. For by 1984 physical warfare has ceased to be important—indeed, there is even a sinister suggestion that war may not be actually happening, and that the rockets that fall from time to time on big cities are sent by the rulers themselves to uphold the myth which is the necessary psychological background for their own continuance in power. The real warfare is the unceasing struggle in and for the human soul—the attempt to eradicate the last traces of free thought and of the truly scientific spirit, to mould human nature into a gray, glum image, and to foul the sources (this is Winston's job) that would leave any basis for historical comparison between present and past. . . .

"Nineteen Eighty-Four" will be widely read and energetically discussed; it may also be conveniently misinterpreted by those who are themselves already influenced by the cult of Minitrue.

But as a major insight into the crisis of our age it will stand acute analysis from any number of viewpoints; to take but one example, its appraisal of sex in the totalitarian scheme takes shrewd account of the killjoy motive—i.e. that the hearty enjoyment of pleasure is bad for Big Brother mythology, whereas frustrations help it. Mr. Orwell's intelligence plays so phosphorescently into so many exiting issues that it is hard to treat the book as a novel at all; perhaps it isn't, or at any rate the characters in it are the exact opposite of those whom you feel you know; they are, like the world they live in, phantasmally impelled.

Yet for those who comfortably think that no such total change could take place within our own lifetime, the answer is that the beginnings of such changes have taken place and are taking place. Epidemics of spying and counter-spying, debasement of word-currency and the spread of slogans, jingles and thought-avoidance, myth-building by screen and radio, regimentation of children, the debauching of science and the falsification of history—all these symptoms have been seen in one country or another during our own generation. So Mr. Orwell has not invented too much; mostly he has orchestrated tunes already heard. And yet—perhaps because of some lingering romanticism—one is inclined to remember with affection Philip Guedalla's remark that nearly all the important things in history very nearly didn't happen. Historians will also ask whether, granting that the Oceania of 1984 might come to pass, it could make itself immune from the ordinary laws of change and upset. Is it possible for a tyranny to rivet itself so firmly as to be practically indestructible?

Even Mr. Orwell sees a ray of hope in the *proles* though little enough in the intellectual. . . .

"**Nineteen Eighty-Four**" is a remarkable book; as a virtuoso literary performance it has a sustained brilliance that has rarely been matched in other works of its genre. But what gives it importance is its timeliness; it is as timely as the label on a poison bottle.

> *James-Hilton, "Mr. Orwell's Nightmare of Totalitarianism," in* New York Herald Tribune Weekly Book Review, *June 12, 1949, p. 3.*

MARK SCHORER (essay date 1949)

[*Schorer is an American critic and biographer. In his often anthologized essay "Technique as Discovery," Schorer put forth the argument that fiction deserves the same scrutiny, the same close attention to diction and metaphor, that the New Critics had been lavishing on poetry. He determined that fiction viewed only with respect to content was not art at all, but experience. For Schorer, only when individuals examine "achieved content," or form, do they speak of art, and consequently, speak as critics. Schorer also argued that the difference between content and art is "technique," and that the study of technique demonstrates how fictional form discovers and evaluates meaning, meaning that is often not intended by the author. In the following excerpt from a review of* Nineteen Eighty-Four, *Schorer interprets the novel as Orwell's attack not only on totalitarianism but also upon aspects of British Socialism. In the course of his discussion, he examines Orwell's method of making his fictional world live for the reader.*]

James Joyce, in the person of Stephen Daedalus, made a now famous distinction between static and kinetic art. Great art is static in its effects: it exists in itself, it demands nothing beyond itself. Kinetic art exists in order to demand: not self-contained, it requires either loathing or desire to achieve its function. . . .

George Orwell's new novel, "**Nineteen Eighty-Four**," is a great work of kinetic art. This may mean that its greatness is only immediate, its power for us alone, now, in this generation, this decade, this year, that it is doomed to be the pawn of time. Nevertheless it is probable that no other work of this generation has made us desire freedom more earnestly or loathe tyranny with such fulness.

"**Nineteen Eight-Four**" appears at first glance to fall into that long-established tradition of satirical fiction, set either in future times or in imagined places or both, that contains works so diverse as "Gulliver's Travels" . . ., Butler's "Erewhon," and Huxley's "Brave New World." Yet before one has finished reading the nearly bemused first page, it is evident that this is fiction of another order, and presently one makes the distinctly unpleasant discovery that it is not to be satire at all.

In the excesses of satire one may take a certain comfort. They provide a distance from the human condition as we meet it in our daily life that preserves our habitual refuge in sloth or blindness or self-righteousness. Mr. Orwell's earlier book, "**Animal Farm**," is such a work. Its characters are animals, and its content is therefore fabulous, and its horror, shading into comedy, remains in the generalized realm of intellect, from which our feelings need fear no onslaught. But "**Nineteen Eighty-Four**" is a work of pure horror, and its horror is crushingly immediate.

The motives that seem to have caused the difference between these two novels provide an instructive lesson in the operations of the literary imagination. "**Animal Farm**" was, for all its ingenuity, a rather mechanical allegory; it was an expression of Mr. Orwell's moral and intellectual indignation before the concept of totalitarianism as localized in Russia. It was also bare and somewhat cold and, without being really very funny, undid its potential gravity and the very real gravity of its subject, through its comic devices. "**Nineteen Eighty-Four**" is likewise an expression of Mr. Orwell's moral and intellectual indignation before the concept of totalitarianism, but it is not only that.

It is also—and this is no doubt the hurdle over which many loyal liberals will stumble—it is also an expression of Mr. Orwell's irritation at many facets of British socialism, and most particularly, trivial as this may seem, at the drab gray pall that life in Britain today has drawn across the civilized amenities of life before the war.

One hesitates to write this, to seem to equate physical discomfort with moral outrage, yet for the novelist as a practicing being, the equation is not unreal, and, in fiction, physical discomfort can give texture and body and feeling and finally force to even the gravest moral issue, and it can, apparently, give it even the fearful vitality that characterizes "**Nineteen Eighty-Four**."

As Winston Smith comes home for lunch from his office (we do not yet know that he works at the Ministry of Truth) on an April day thirty-five years from now, we are first of all aware of the depressing seediness of things—the "gritty dust" in the street, the smell of "boiled cabbage and old rag mats" in the corridor, the elevator that seldom works because electricity must be saved, Winston's skin "roughened by coarse soap and blunt razor blades," the festering varicose ulcer on his ankle.

Such physical details, even as the outlines of the horrendous moral world that Smith inhabits become clear, create the texture, the immediate reality of the novel, and as the dust of broken plaster settles into the pores of his skin, as he eats his dispirited way through many tasteless, sodden, public meals, as he drinks the raw, burning stimulant called Victory Gin, he is seen in one area after another of his lonely and never private life more and more deeply submerged in the gray squalor of a world which is without joy or love and in which desultory but still destructive war is the permanent condition. It is always the atmosphere created by these details that heightens and intensifies, that signifies, indeed, the appalling moral facts. (p. 1)

One cannot briefly outline the whole of Mr. Orwell's enormously careful and complete account of life in the super-state, nor do more than indicate its originality. He would seem to have thought of everything, and with vast skill he has woven everything into the life of one man, a minor Party member, one of perhaps hundreds of others who are in charge of the alteration of documents necessary to the preservation of the "truth" of the moment.

Through this life we are instructed in the intricate workings of what is called "thoughtcrime" (here Mr. Orwell would seem to have learned from Koestler's "Darkness at Noon"), but through this life we are likewise instructed in more public matters such as the devious economic structure of Oceania, and the nature and necessity of permanent war as two of the great super-states ally themselves against a third in an ever-shifting and ever-denied pattern of change. But most important, we are ourselves swept into the meaning and the means of a society which has as its single aim the total destruction of the individual identity.

To say more is to tell the personal history of Winston Smith in what is probably his thirty-ninth year, and one is not disposed to rob the reader of a fresh experience of the terrific, long crescendo and the quick decrescendo that George Orwell has made of this struggle for survival and the final extinction of a personality. It is in the intimate history, of course, that he reveals his stature as a novelist, for it is here that the moral and the psychological values with which he is concerned are brought out of the realm of political prophecy into that of personalized drama.

No real reader can neglect this experience with impunity. He will be moved by Smith's wistful attempts to remember a different kind of life from his. He will make a whole new discovery of the beauty of love between man and woman, and of the strange beauty of landscape in a totally mechanized world. He will be asked to read through pages of sustained physical and psychological pain that have seldom been equaled and never in such quiet, sober prose. And he will return to his own life from Smith's escape into living death with a resolution to resist power wherever it means to deny him his individuality, and to resist for himself the poisonous lures of power.

"Nineteen Eighty-Four," the most contemporary novel of this year and who knows of how many past and to come, is a great examination into and dramatization of Lord Acton's famous apothegm, "Power tends to corrupt and absolute power corrupts absolutely." (p. 16)

> Mark Schorer, "An Indignant and Prophetic Novel," in The New York Times Book Review, *June 12, 1949, pp. 1, 16.*

GEORGE ORWELL   (letter date 1949)

[*The following is an amalgam of two slightly different forms of a letter from Orwell to Francis A. Henson that appeared in* The

New York Times Book Review *and* Life *magazines. The original letter has been lost. In this excerpt, Orwell stresses that the totalitarian society depicted in* Nineteen Eighty-Four *was not meant as an attack upon any specific political system or party, but rather was meant as a warning that such a totalitarian society could arise anywhere. Both Orwell and his publisher Fredric Warburg felt it necessary to issue such a disclaimer after numerous reviews of* Nineteen Eighty-Four, *particularly in the United States, misinterpreted the novel as an attack on the Soviet state, the British Labour Party, or any other single political group. For an example of such a review, see the entry from* Life *magazine in the Additional Bibliography.*]

My recent novel [*Nineteen Eighty-Four*] is NOT intended as an attack on socialism or on the British Labor Party (of which I am a supporter) but as a show-up of the perversions to which a centralized economy is liable, and which have already been partly realized in Communism and fascism. I do not believe that the kind of society I describe necessarily will arrive, but I believe (allowing of course for the fact that the book is a satire) that something resembling it *could* arrive. I believe also that totalitarian ideas have taken root in the minds of intellectuals everywhere, and I have tried to draw these ideas out to their logical consequences. The scene of the book is laid in Britain in order to emphasize that the English-speaking races are not innately better than anyone else and that totalitarianism, *if not fought against,* could triumph anywhere.

> George Orwell, in an extract from a letter to Francis A. Henson on June 16, 1949, in The Collected Essays, Journalism and Letters of George Orwell: In Front of Your Nose, 1945-1950, Vol. IV, *edited by Sonia Orwell and Ian Angus, Harcourt Brace Jovanovich, 1968, p. 502.*

V. S. PRITCHETT   (essay date 1949)

[*Pritchett is a highly esteemed English novelist, short story writer, and critic. Considered one of the modern masters of the short story, he is also one of the world's most respected and well-read literary critics. He writes in the conversational tone of the familiar essay, a method by which he approaches literature from the viewpoint of a lettered but not overly scholarly reader. A twentieth-century successor to such early nineteenth-century essayist-critics as William Hazlitt and Charles Lamb, Pritchett employs much the same critical method: his own experience, judgment, and sense of literary art are emphasized, rather than a codified critical doctrine derived from a school of psychological or philosophical speculation. His criticism is often described as fair, reliable, and insightful. In the following excerpt, Pritchett finds fault with those critics who dismiss* Nineteen Eighty-Four *because it portrays an unlikely future. Pritchett approaches the novel not as a cautionary tale but rather as a satire upon present conditions.*]

Nineteen Eight-Four is a book that goes through the reader like an east wind, cracking the skin, opening the sores; hope has died in Mr. Orwell's wintry mind, and only pain is known. I do not think I have ever read a novel more frightening and depressing; and yet, such are the originality, the suspense, the speed of writing and withering indignation that it is impossible to put the book down. The faults of Orwell as a writer—monotony, nagging, the lonely schoolboy shambling down the one dispiriting track—are transformed now he rises to a large subject. He is the most devastating pamphleteer alive because he is the plainest and most individual—there is none of Koestler's lurid journalism—and because, with steady misanthropy, he knows exactly where on the new Jesuitism to apply the Protestant whip. . . .

Mr. Orwell's book is a satirical pamphlet. I notice that some critics have said that his prophecy is not probable. Neither was Swift's *Modest Proposal* nor Wells's *Island of Dr. Moreau*. Probability is not a necessary condition of satire which, when it pretends to draw the future, is, in fact, scourging the present. The purges in Russia and, later, in the Russian satellites, the dreary seediness of London in the worst days of the war, the pockets of 19th-century life in decaying England, the sordidness of bad flats, bad food, the native and whining streak of domestic sluttishness which have sickened English satirists since Smollett, all these have given Mr. Orwell his material. The duty of the satirist is to go one worse than reality; and it might be objected that Mr. Orwell is too literal, that he is too oppressed by what he sees, to exceed it. In one or two incidents where he does exceed, notably in the torture scenes, he is merely melodramatic: he introduces those rather grotesque machines which used to appear in terror stories for boys. In one place—I mean the moment when Winston's Inquisitor drives him to call out for the death of his girl, by threatening to set a cageful of famished rats on him—we reach a peak of imaginative excess in terror, but it is superfluous because mental terrorism is his real subject.

Until our time, irony and unnatural laughter were thought to be the duty of the satirist. . . . (p. 646)

But disgust, the power to make pain sickening, the taste for punishment, exceed irony and laughter in the modern satirist. Neither Winston Smith nor the author laughs when he discovers that the women of the new State are practised hypocrites and make fools of the Party members. For Mr. Orwell, the most honest writer alive, hypocrisy is too dreadful for laughter: it feeds his despair.

As a pamphleteer Orwell may be right in his choice of means. The life-instinct rebels against the grey tyrannies that, like the Jehovah of the Old Testament, can rule only as long as they create guilt. The heart sinks, but the spirit rebels as one reads Mr. Orwell's ruthless opening page. . . . But though the indignation of *Nineteen Eighty-Four* is singeing, the book does suffer from a division of purpose. Is it an account of present hysteria, is it a satire on propaganda, or a world that sees it itself entirely in inhuman terms? Is Mr. Orwell saying, not that there is no hope, but that there is no hope for man in the political conception of man? We have come to the end of a movement. He is like some dour Protestant or Jansenist who sees his faith corrupted by the "doublethink" of the Roman Catholic Church, and who fiercely rejects the corrupt civilisations that appear to be able to flourish even under that dispensation. (pp. 646, 648)

> *V. S. Pritchett, in a review of "Nineteen Eighty-Four," in* The New Statesman & Nation, *Vol. XXXVII, No. 954, June 18, 1949, pp. 646, 648.*

SAMUEL SILLEN (essay date 1949)

[*The following excerpt, taken from the now-defunct Communist magazine* Masses and Mainstream, *demonstrates the violently negative Communist reaction to* Nineteen Eighty-Four. *Mentioned in the excerpt is Victor Kravchenko, a Russian government official who defected to the United States and later wrote* I Choose Freedom (1946), *which criticizes Stalin's dictatorship.*]

Like his previous diatribe against the human race, *Animal Farm*, George Orwell's new book [*Nineteen Eighty-Four*] has received an ovation in the capitalist press. The gush of comparisons with Swift and Dostoyevsky has washed away the few re-maining pebbles of literary probity. Not even the robots of Orwell's dyspeptic vision of the world in 1984 seem as solidly regimented as the freedom-shouters who chose it for the Book-of-the-Month Club, serialized it in *Reader's Digest,* illustrated it in eight pages of *Life,* and wrote pious homilies on it in *Partisan Review* and the New York *Times*. Indeed the response is far more significant than the book itself; it demonstrates that Orwell's sickness is epidemic.

The premise of the fable is that capitalism has ceased to exist in 1984; and the moral is that if capitalism departs the world will go to pot. The earth is divided into three "socialist" areas, Oceania, Eurasia and Eastasia, which unlike the good old days of free enterprise are in perpetual warfare. The hero, Winston Smith, lives on Airstrip One (England) and balks at the power-crazed regime. He is nabbed by the Thought Police, tortured with fiendish devices, and finally he wins the privilege of being shot when he learns to love the invisible dictator.

Orwell's nightmare is also inhabited by the "proles," who constitute a mere 85 per cent of Oceania and who are described with fear and loathing as ignorant, servile, brutish. (p. 79)

As a piece of fiction this is threadbare stuff with a tasteless sex angle which has been rhapsodically interpreted by Mark Schorer in the New York *Times* as a "new discovery of the beauty of love between man and woman" [see excerpt dated 1949]. This new discovery is well illustrated by the following scene in which Winston Smith makes love to Julia, a fellow-rebel against the dictatorial regime:

> 'Listen. The more men you've had, the more I love you. Do you understand that?'
>
> 'Yes, perfectly.'
>
> 'I hate purity, I hate goodness. I don't want any virtue to exist anywhere. I want everyone to be corrupt to the bones.' . . .

Or consider this: Orwell's hero, who is supposed to awaken what the reviewers call "compassion," is interviewed by a man whom he believes to be the leader of the underground resistance to the tyrannical regime:

> 'You are prepared to cheat, to forge, to black-mail, to corrupt the minds of children, to distribute habit-forming drugs, to encourage prostitution, to disseminate venereal diseases—to do anything which is likely to cause demoralization and weaken the power of the Party?'
>
> 'Yes.'
>
> 'If, for example, it would somehow serve our interests to throw sulphuric acid in a child's face—are you prepared to do that?'
>
> 'Yes.'

The author of this cynical rot is quite a hero himself. He served for five years in the Indian Imperial Police, an excellent training center for dealing with the "proles." He was later associated with the Trotskyites in Spain. . . . During World War II he busied himself with defamation of the Soviet Union.

And now, as Lionel Trilling approvingly notes in *The New Yorker,* Orwell "marks a turn in thought." What is the significance of this turn? The literary mouthpieces of imperialism have discovered that the crude anti-Sovietism of a Kravchenko is not enough; the system of class oppression must be directly upheld and *any* belief in change and progress must be frightened out of people. (p. 80)

The bourgeoisie, in its younger days, could find spokesmen who painted rosy visions of the future. In its decay, surrounded by burgeoning socialism, it is capable only of hate-filled, dehumanized anti-Utopias. Confidence has given way to the nihilistic literature of the graveyard. Now that Ezra Pound has been given a government award and George Orwell has become a best-seller we would seem to have reached bottom. But there is a hideous ingenuity in the perversions of a dying capitalism, and it will keep probing for new depths of rottenness which the maggots will find "brilliant and morally invigorating." (p. 81)

> Samuel Sillen, "Maggot-of-the-Month," in *Masses & Mainstream*, *Vol. 2, No. 8, August, 1949, pp. 79-81.*

ROBERT HATCH   (essay date 1949)

[*In the following excerpt from the liberal weekly* The New Republic, *Hatch demonstrates himself to be virtually alone among early reviewers of* Nineteen Eighty-Four *in interpreting the novel as an improbable work of fiction displaying misanthropic and conservative fears that are not to be taken seriously.*]

Right now, the sort of people who write books are feeling depressed and those who embark for utopia are ending up at unpleasant places. Aldous Huxley's Southern California of *Ape and Essence* was a degraded and disgusting community; George Orwell's London of *Nineteen Eight-Four* is even worse. In fact, the tale his imagination has to tell is so alarming that editorials are being written on the subject and there seems to be a general feeling that steps will have to be taken. Before the panic becomes too widespread, it should perhaps be pointed out that Orwell is just playing a new version of "let's pretend." The future may be bright or it may be black; it won't be a straight projection from the present.

(In simplest terms, the author of *Nineteen Eighty-Four* has pushed what he considers the iniquitous power of the modern state, England, say, under the present Labour Government, to an ultimate conclusion.) He feels that we are being deprived of too many freedoms, that there is too much interference in our private lives, and he foretells the day when we shall have no liberty and no privacy whatever. It is historically true that we have given up a lot of freedom: to knock our neighbor over the head, for instance; or, more recently, to raise our children in pristine ignorance. And it is a fact that an internal revenue inspector, or an FBI agent, feels entitled to ask impertinent questions. Orwell doesn't like this (who does?) and he calls the deteriorating situation to our attention by supposing that the time will come when we shall forfeit the right to enjoy our marriage beds and when two-way telescreens and hovering police helicopters will spy into our most private and trivial moments. He even puts a date to it—1984—and that perhaps is what makes his prophecy so chilling.

Surely, nobody can object to Orwell's employing his imagination in any manner he sees fit, and since he is blessed with an ingenious one, nobody can deny that his book is entertaining in a repulsive way. The only thing to guard against is taking it too seriously, for as a guide to the future *Nineteen Eight-Four* is a blind alley. (p. 23)

Is this a "mad scientist" story, one of those horror yarns in which a deranged doctor turns men into manikins? The laboratory trappings make it look so, but that doesn't seem to be

Orwell's point. He has observed that totalitarian countries show a cavalier attitude toward verifiable reality, and he is imagining the day when all logic, all evidence will be swept aside by omnipotent power. Such tyranny is real in the world; we have current examples. Maintaining the delicate balance between human dignity and bureaucratic efficiency, between freedom and security, is the critical problem of our age. The dangers of a proliferating state are evident even without the examples of Germany and Russia. But we cannot make it wither away, and we must discover therefore how to master it, confine it, use it for our purposes.

The objection to *Nineteen Eighty-Four* is not that it is too bizarre, but that it is not bizarre enough. The author is obviously warning us that we face extinction, that the course we are embarked upon will lead in the near future to an abdication of humanity in favor of the governing machine. From the nationalization of coal to the elimination of the human soul is only a short step, but to take it Orwell must make one very broad assumption: that men are a thoroughly contemptible race of beings incapable of holding their place in the world. His aloofness is more than aristocratic disdain; it appears as an embracing misanthropy that dries the springs of sympathy and makes his book a logician's exercise rather than a work of art.

Whatever Orwell's intention, the effect of *Nineteen Eighty-Four* is to make us stop in our tracks, to try no more experiments lest they destroy our fragile humanity, to retreat if we can from the abyss. But we cannot retreat and the abyss is not there. Orwell's pit of universal dissolution is outside the pattern of human relationships. It demands a new race, a tribe of super ants, to usurp the future, and the threat of that chimera is no more useful a guide to present conduct than warnings that we are presently to be the victims of a celestial collision.

In all probability, 1984 will be a difficult year—most presidential-election years are. But by New Year's Day, 1985, if not sooner, Orwell's utopia will be over on the fantastic fiction shelf where it belongs. (p. 24)

> Robert Hatch, "George Orwell's Paradise Lost," in *The New Republic, Vol. 121, No. 5, August 1, 1949, pp. 23-4.*

MARTIN KESSLER   (essay date 1957)

[*In the following excerpt, Kessler examines the way power is maintained in the dystopias created by Aldous Huxley in* Brave New World *and by Orwell in* Nineteen Eighty-Four. *Kessler finds that* Nineteen Eighty-Four *is usually perceived by readers as more realistic and more horrifying than* Brave New World, *because the police-state tactics of Orwell's novel are within the realm of human experience, while Huxley's vision of conspicuous consumption and complete psychological conditioning has never been realized. Kessler, however, like Huxley himself (see excerpt dated 1958) believes that a* Brave New World-*like future is the greater danger in the United States.*]

The late Lord Keynes once described his fellow economists as "the trustees, not of civilization, but of the possibility of civilization." In this, as both Aldous Huxley and George Orwell tell us in effect, Keynes showed himself a true son of the Victorian Age. For, it is the unique feature of the twentieth century that the material requisites for the "possibility of civilization" are at hand. "From the moment when the machine first made its appearance," Orwell's Goldstein (Trotsky) writes, "it was clear to all thinking people that the need for human inequality had disappeared." And in Huxley's *Brave New World* the Controller informs the Savage that ''there isn't any need for a civilized man to bear anything that is seriously unpleasant.'' While Orwell bases the oligarchical collectivism of 1984 on conspicuous production, and Huxley his Brave New World on conspicuous consumption, they both start from the same premise, that science has solved the problem of production. Indeed, the means whereby these rulers of the not-so-distant future choose to dispose of the surpluses created by a phenomenally efficient productive machine offer the key to their power.

The production problem is thus incidental to the economy of abundance that Huxley and Orwell are describing and in this more than anything else lies their pessimism. Ever since man first started to seek the kingdom of heaven here on earth, the cartographers of the perfect state have been obliged to devote a good deal of time to the question of *how* to provide Utopia's subjects with the means for the enjoyment of perfection. Through the application of science to the production of goods, through the redistribution of existing income and property relationships, through the abolition of ''costly'' and wasteful desires, the Utopians of the last five centuries had hoped to construct a perfect society in which men and women could enjoy that ultimate degree of happiness which, it was implied, they were denied through the folly and wickedness of their present rulers. (pp. 565-66)

By the late nineteenth century, indeed, the rapidly accelerating tempo of scientific discovery encouraged the more vulgar of the Utopians to envisage the perfect society solely in terms of the strange and wonderful gadgets which it would have at its disposal. The prophetic novels of Jules Verne, H. G. Wells, and others, all, to a greater or lesser extent, glamorized their Brave New Worlds in terms of the material conveniences and comforts science would put at the disposal of man. The quality of life in such an environment of abundance was either ignored (as in Jules Verne), or, as in the early Wells, described in altogether glowing terms.

As science has transformed fiction into fact (often ahead of schedule), it has become apparent that the remaining material obstacles to Utopia have been—or in the underdeveloped areas of the world are in the process of being—surmounted. It is of course true that there is no certainty that the ''subsistence barrier'' has been conquered for all time. The Malthusian dilemma will probably continue to be (though perhaps on a ''higher plane'') a limiting factor to economic expansion. There is every reason to believe, indeed, that the application of limited resources to unlimited desires will continue to challenge man's ingenuity. But—and it is an important but—the emphasis will shift, according to both Huxley and Orwell, from the absolute or relative increase of resources (that is, from problems of production and distribution) to the restriction, control or ''guidance'' of unlimited desires. From the stomach, the art of politics will move to the psyche.

As a result, the whole quality of existing super- and sub-ordination systems will undergo—and, judging from Huxley's and Orwell's other writings, is already undergoing—something of a sea change. Both men are concerned with those aspects of modern science (Pavlonian biology, eugenics and narcotics with Huxley; electronic communications media and cybernetics with Orwell) which will enable future élites to ''freeze'' the *status quo.* Up to now the élite class in political society has never been secure in its power; changes in the mode of production, wars, votes, intrigues (depending on the kind of society in operation) have constantly threatened it. . . . [The]

political structure was never hermetically sealed for all time. Even India and China, where the *status quo* had enjoyed apparently unbreakable religious and institutional sanctions, were ultimately forced to submit to a reconstruction of their social fabric.

Indeed, the absolutely ''closed society'', to borrow Karl Popper's useful phrase, has existed only in the day dreams of rulers and, more usually, of their ideologists. For, to attribute power to an individual or class is one thing; to exercise that power is infinitely more difficult; to exercise it absolutely is (or rather has been up to now) impossible. . . . The twentieth-century democratic state, based on popular consent and with carefully circumscribed powers, is able to: (1) conscript and maintain mass armies, (2) effectively regulate the external and internal flow of goods and individuals, (3) impose *and* collect undreamed of per capita tax revenues, (4) obtain almost instantaneous compliance for its directives, and so on. In the case of contemporary totalitarian countries, where the state's power in law is never less than its power in fact (where the potential is always the actual), we have the nearest thing to the absolute exercise of absolute power known in the history of political society. And in the society of the not-so-distant future, Huxley and Orwell somewhat gloatingly tell us, science will have made the power of the state ''absolutely absolute'', while man—happily shaking off responsibility according to satirist Huxley, unhappily deprived of personal volition according to moralist Orwell—will have created a society where that power will be instantaneously applied.

The important thing to remember about the ''distopias'' of both Huxley and Orwell is that they posit a perfectly malleable (and hence perfectly predictable) human nature incapable of experiencing any emotion or exercising any judgment outside of the prevailing (and, in Orwell, continuously changing) frame of reference. The destruction of personal identity in objective reality is thus complete—or nearly complete, for being romantics at heart, both Huxley and Orwell introduce exceptions. (pp. 566-68)

In analyzing the ''technology'' of power available to the rulers of the Brave New World and 1984—and the use (''technique'') they make of this power—one becomes uncomfortably aware that neither Huxley nor Orwell assumes a level of technology much more advanced than what is already enjoyed in the more industrialized nations today. Thus Orwell's television screens, which enable a probably nonexistent ''Big Brother'' to keep tabs on every aspect, private and public, of the lives of his subjects, are already being widely used by industry for quality-control purposes, by military establishments to insure better communications and by state police to track down traffic violators. (pp. 568-69)

Examples like [this] could be adduced for almost every scientific method or technical gadget found in either *Brave New World* or **Nineteen Eighty-Four.** Certainly, the key to the power of the élite in both instances depends only indirectly on technology. While it is unquestionably true that industrial technology (and, even more important, the social and economic consequences of that technology) has made the exercise of absolute power *possible,* there is no reason to believe—as Huxley apparently does—in a necessary correlation between technological progress and an increase in the actual use of technology for socio-political ends.

Actually, the application of technology and science forms only a small (though extremely important) part in the techniques of power of these two books. Technology merely makes possible the realization of an operational philosophy designed to "freeze" the existing social structure in perpetuity. As such, it is introduced primarily for literary and pedagogic effect. . . . In Orwell, where reference to technology is . . . indirect and where the effect sought is realism rather than satire, technology is rarely hilarious and in one or two instances—as when Julia and Winston are discovered in their hideaway by the television screen—it is positively frightening. The reason why *Nineteen Eighty-Four* seems so much closer to home is that our experience has been almost exclusively with the conspicuous-production and police-state kind of dictatorship Orwell is describing. We have no historical experience with a conspicuous-consumption dictatorship based upon an economy of plenty and absolute psychological conditioning—although this may well come to be the more serious danger in countries like the United States.

An operational political philosophy can have no objective beyond the purely pragmatic one of effectiveness. Asked to justify distopia, Mustapha Mond in *Brave New World* and O'Brien in *Nineteen Eighty-Four* both answer, in effect, "It works"; when asked, to what end, both must answer in terms of stability and order—or, in less polite language, the maintenance of existing power relationships. . . . [O'Brien] does not even bother to justify his exercise of power to Winston. Power for him is its own justification. (pp. 569-70)

The horror of *Nineteen Eighty-Four* is much more direct [than that of Huxley's *Brave New World*], for we have all had experience (most of it happily indirect) with the kind of society Orwell is describing. It is merely the twentieth-century totalitarian state made absolute by carrying the political principles of twentieth-century totalitarianism to their logical conclusion. A pessimist might observe that *Nineteen Eighty-Four* is the only alternative to *Brave New World*.

What is its animating political principle? Fear, misery and repression, the obverse of *Brave New World* whose animating principle, as we have seen, is happiness through instantaneous gratification of every conditioned desire. The moralist in Orwell is very apparent in all this. For, if the state is forced to deny, repress and distort in order to maintain its power, then there must be something to deny, repress and distort. If the state must corrupt man, then he is not corrupt to begin with. Unlike *Brave New World*, the state in *Nineteen Eighty-Four* cannot control the condition of human existence. It can only condition the future of his existence. Instead of the gift of life, the state can offer only the punishment of death—a serious limitation in its power.

For Orwell was always a great believer in the essential "decency" (a favorite term of his) of man and this belief never left him even when, depressed and sick with tuberculosis, he retired to the Hebrides to write this last and most profoundly pessimistic of his novels. True, Winston Smith (the name is a tribute to the uncommon Englishman, Churchill, and the common Englishman, Smith) is finally destroyed, for not even the strongest man can withstand the new state. But there will be others. They will be crushed, of course, but still the cells and torture chambers of the Ministry of Love will never be empty. Most of the rebels will be unwilling, like Parsons and Ampleforth, and will oppose the state in spite of themselves. No matter, man will still be worth saving even when salvation is no longer possible. To the end, Orwell retained his Western faith in man—not natural man or civilized man, but "man who

is born of woman" and "whose days are filled with trouble". He remained a humanist.

That, however, is the extent of Orwell's optimism. For, granted that man will continue to be worth saving, he can't be saved in 1984. The *proles,* who constitute 85 per cent of the population of Oceania and who are left free by telescreens and thought police to enjoy their misery, will not rise. . . . The full force of the totalitarian state of 1984 is brought to bear only against the remaining 15 per cent, the party members who staff the offices of the Ministries of Truth (propaganda and the arts), Peace (war), Love (law and order), Plenty (economic affairs). It is these who are the potential candidates for rebellion.

The fundamental problem for the modern repressive dictatorship is how to maintain full employment and at the same time retain the scarcities on which that dictatorship depends. Restricting the output of goods is obviously no solution, for the idleness and privations resulting from a deliberate policy of economic stagnation are obviously unnecessary and will inevitably lead to rebellion. On the other hand, it is equally clear (to old-fashioned meliorist Orwell at least) that an all-round increase in living standards would—given the capacity of industrial technology—make the continued existence of a hierarchical dictatorship impossible since the state depends upon institutionalized instrumentalities to do the repressing. (The Brave New World, on the other hand, is self-regulating. Except for the need of industrial technology for divison of labor, the Alpha, Beta, Epsilon differentiation is politically unnecessary for the perpetuation of the "happy" dictatorship. Mustapha Mond, for example, is really a superflous figure.)

In *Nineteen Eighty-Four* this dilemma of the repressive dictatorship is solved in the conventional manner, that is, through war. Other forms of conspicuous production (useless production of statues, wilful destruction, spoilage or hoarding), while they would accomplish the same end, are not satisfactory psychologically. War is not only "a way of shattering to pieces or pouring into the stratosphere, or sinking in the depths of the sea, materials which might otherwise be used to make the masses too comfortable and hence in the long run too intelligent"; it also stimulates an emotional atmosphere in which Doublethink can best flourish. As a result, the three superstates of the book—Oceania (the Americas, the British Isles and Atlantic islands, Australasia and South Africa), Eurasia (most of the Eurasian continent) and Eastasia (China, Mongolia, Tibet, Japan and the Pacific islands)—are engaged in continuous warfare with one another. Alliances keep shifting and the wars themselves, while they induce strong emotions, cause few actual casualties and are confined mostly to uninhabited borderlands and floating fortresses. Since none of the three superstates can be conquered by the other two in combination and since, moreover, there is nothing in a material sense left to fight about (each state being economically self-sufficient), wars become artificial techniques whereby the ruling élites in the three states can, in a psychologically acceptable manner, use up the products of the machine without raising living standards.

It would be impossible, however, for the repressive dictatorship to realize the full benefits of this mode of conspicuous production without "Doublethink"—a discovery that antedates 1984. "Doublethink", as Goldstein, Orwell's orthodox heretic, defines it, "is the power of holding two contradictory beliefs in one's mind simultaneously, and accepting both of them." Without Doublethink the party would not function. For, when the party intellectual lies, it is essential that he both know that he is tampering with reality and at the same time genuinely believe in his lie. Only thus is it possible to arrest the course of history. Only thus is it possible for the party to "change" objective reality by tacitly denying its very existence. The constant tampering with history (Winston's job consists in revising historical announcements to fit into the current party line), for example, is part of this massive attempt to destroy the individual's relationship with objective reality altogether. In a sense, as Orwell realizes, the freedom to say that two plus two makes four is the most essential freedom. And while Winston in the end is brainwashed into believing— actually believing—that two plus two equals five, Orwell leaves one with the impression that truth, while it will never prevail, will persist and will have to be continuously brainwashed out of human consciousness. Even Newspeak, the language of 1984 especially designed to encourage Doublethink, will never be totally successful in stopping Thoughtcrime from arising, even though it may be able to suppress the "crime" once it has appeared. (pp. 573-76)

> Martin Kessler, "Power and the Perfect State: A *Study in Disillusionment As Reflected in Orwell's* 'Nineteen Eighty-Four' and Huxley's 'Brave New World'," in Political Science Quarterly, Vol. LXXII, *No. 4, December, 1957, pp. 565-77.**

ALDOUS HUXLEY   (essay date 1958)

[*Known primarily for his dystopian novel* Brave New World (1932), *Huxley was a British-American man of letters and novelist of ideas. The grandson of noted Darwinist T. H. Huxley and the brother of scientist Julian Huxley, he was interested in many fields of knowledge, and daring conceptions of science, philosophy, and religion are woven throughout his fiction. Continually searching for an escape from the ambivalence of modern life, Huxley sought a sense of spiritual renewal and a clarification of his artistic vision through the use of hallucinogenic drugs, an experience explored in one of his best-known later works,* The Doors of Perception (1954). *Twenty-seven years after writing* Brave New World, *Huxley wrote* Brave New World Revisited, *in which he demonstrated instances that seemed to foretell the imminent approach of a completely organized society similar to that of the novel. The following excerpt from that work compares* Nineteen Eighty-Four *with* Brave New World *and finds that the future will more likely resemble Huxley's vision than Orwell's. A similar conclusion is reached by Martin Kessler (1957).*]

George Orwell's *1984* was a magnified projection into the future of a present that contained Stalinism and an immediate past that had witnessed the flowering of Nazism. *Brave New World* was written before the rise of Hitler to supreme power in Germany and when the Russian tyrant had not yet got into his stride. In 1931 systematic terrorism was not the obsessive contemporary fact which it had become in 1948, and the future dictatorship of my imaginary world was a good deal less brutal than the future dictatorship so brilliantly portrayed by Orwell. In the context of 1948, *1984* seemed dreadfully convincing. But tyrants, after all, are mortal and circumstances change. Recent developments in Russia and recent advances in science and technology have robbed Orwell's book of some of its gruesome verisimilitude. A nuclear war will, of course, make nonsense of everybody's predictions. But, assuming for the moment that the Great Powers can somehow refrain from destroying us, we can say that it now looks as though the odds were more in favor of something like *Brave New World* than of something like *1984.*

In the light of what we have recently learned about animal behavior in general, and human behavior in particular, it has become clear that control through the punishment of undesirable behavior is less effective, in the long run, than control through the reinforcement of desirable behavior by rewards, and that government through terror works on the whole less well than government through the non-violent manipulation of the environment and of the thoughts and feelings of individual men, women and children. Punishment temporarily puts a stop to undesirable behavior, but does not permanently reduce the victim's tendency to indulge in it. Moreover, the psycho-physical by-products of punishment may be just as undesirable as the behavior for which an individual has been punished. Psychotherapy is largely concerned with the debilitating or anti-social consequences of past punishments.

The society described in *1984* is a society controlled almost exclusively by punishment and the fear of punishment. In the imaginary world of my own fable punishment is infrequent and generally mild. The nearly perfect control exercised by the government is achieved by systematic reinforcement of desirable behavior, by many kinds of nearly non-violent manipulation, both physical and psychological, and by genetic standardization. (pp. 4-5)

It is worth remarking that, in *1984,* the members of the Party are compelled to conform to a sexual ethic of more than Puritan severity. In *Brave New World,* on the other hand, all are permitted to indulge their sexual impulses without let or hindrance. The society described in Orwell's fable is a society permanently at war, and the aim of its rulers is first, of course, to exercise power for its own delightful sake and, second, to keep their subjects in that state of constant tension which a state of constant war demands of those who wage it. By crusading against sexuality the bosses are able to maintain the required tension in their followers and at the same time can satisfy their lust for power in a most gratifying way. The society described in *Brave New World* is a world-state, in which war has been eliminated and where the first aim of the rulers is at all costs to keep their subjects from making trouble. This they achieve by (among other methods) legalizing a degree of sexual freedom (made possible by the abolition of the family) that practically guarantees the Brave New Worlders against any form of destructive (or creative) emotional tension. In *1984* the lust for power is satisfied by inflicting pain; in *Brave New World,* by inflicting a hardly less humiliating pleasure. (pp. 26-7)

> *Aldous Huxley. in his* Brave New World Revisited, *1958. Reprint by Harper & Row, Publishers, 1965, 118 p.*

HAROLD J. HARRIS   (essay date 1959)

[*In the following excerpt Harris discusses the relationship between Orwell's essays and his fiction—specifically examining themes and ideas from a number of essays that were later developed in* Nineteen Eighty-Four. *Harris contends that character and plot development in the novel remain more important than the introduction of analytical elements. For a contrasting opinion, see the excerpt by Julian Symons (1949), who finds that characterization in the novel is subordinate to the development of ideas.*]

George Orwell used the essay for a number of different purposes, but mainly for the purposes of political and literary comment. At the same time, the essay served his creative work in much the same way that notebooks served more self-consciously literary artists like James and Hawthorne. In his essays can be found many of the raw materials which were later to be reworked—or in some cases carried over without real reworking—into the fictive world Orwell called *1984*. For that reason the relationship between Orwellian essay and novel is worth exploring.

More than almost any other important writer of his time Orwell was an enemy of the needlessly abstract and overly intellectualized. Himself very much the intellectual, he nevertheless saw clearly that the great mass of men do not live primarily along the level of ideas, and that the life of those who do is almost invariably thin and attenuated. Our thoughts and feelings, he felt, are conditioned more by what we eat and the surroundings in which we eat it than by high-powered ideas which have been transmitted to us. Writing about the English public school he attended, in the essay entitled **"Such, Such Were the Joys,"** Orwell at a remove of some twenty-odd years felt his way back into the school along a grim corridor of bedwetting and physical bullying and bad smells. . . . So too the world of 1984, the Oceanic world, is constructed primarily in terms of the sensory. (The sense of smell is perhaps given greater artistic expression by Orwell than by any other significant twentieth-century novelist.) Almost the first thing that we learn about Winston Smith is that a varicose ulcer is making his thirty-nine years miserable. And even before we find out about his ulcer, we discover that he moves through a region of boiled cabbage and old rag mats—the two distinguishing features of the hallway in the Victory Mansions he lives in. (pp. 154-55)

This, then, is what living in the totalitarian society means: dressing shabbily, eating badly, and living as well as working in drab-grey, wholly unaesthetic surroundings. The point that Orwell makes is unmistakably that except for the most spiritual or the most ideological of us, we are concerned most of the time—and rightly so—with the so-called creature comforts. The intellectual may disregard them but he does so only when he is able to take them completely for granted. Existing without the slightest bit of freedom, Orwell shows us, is a terrible thing; existing without any opportunity to see or smell or taste beautiful things, or even tasteful ones, is just as terrible. (p. 155)

Winston does not stand off from the flaking plaster, the ersatz gin, and the boiled cabbage in order to provide either himself or the reader with an objective account of them, nor does he point out (even to himself) the relationship between these things and the kind of society that Big Brother's brand of totalitarianism has produced. Instead, Orwell has so made his plot that those elements which in an essay had served as another signpost along the way to an objectively rendered part of the past, in *1984* constitute the whole physical world—the *only* one attainable in the present, and almost the only conceivable one—for Winston and for all those with whom he comes in contact. The sense of smell and even the basic attitude toward reality may be the same in both essay and novel, but the need to develop a character in a fictive situation required Orwell's using the same raw materials in significantly different fashions.

It is not only food, gin, and cigarettes that are ersatz in the "utopia" Orwell unfolds before us. The language of Oceania, too, is thoroughly phony; it is deliberately designed to conceal reality wherever possible, to distort it. For the purposes of concealment and distortion the semi-mythical Big Brother and his cohorts have created a new language, Newspeak, and gone systematically about the destruction of standard English (which they have dubbed Oldspeak). Out of Newspeak have come such brilliant slogans as "War is Peace," "Freedom is Slavery," and "Ignorance is Strength," all of course reversals of Oldspeak slogans. So successful has been the process of changing

the language (and with it the corollary process of changing the past) that the people living in 1984 have reached the stage where formulating ideas hostile to the orthodox ones has become difficult. (pp. 155-56)

There is a striking parallel between the view of language that emerges from *1984* and that found in Orwell's essay **"Politics and the English Language."** "Now, it is clear," he says right near the beginning of the essay,

> that the decline of a language must ultimately have political and economic causes: it is not due simply to the bad influence of this or that individual writer . . . A man may take to drink because he feels himself to be a failure, and then fail all the more completely because he drinks. It is rather the same thing that is happening to the English language. It becomes ugly and inaccurate because our thoughts are foolish, but the slovenliness of our language makes it easier for us to have foolish thoughts.

Later on in the essay Orwell has some interesting remarks to make about the cliché. . . . The attitude expressed [in **"Politics and the English Language"**] is reflected generally in the novel through the medium of the stereotyped language that issues from the mouths of "Big Brother" and the inner party member and is echoed by the outer party people with whom Winston comes in contact. But *1984* is something more than a schematized treatise on language and politics; altogether somewhat sparse in point of characterization—only Winston Smith exists in any real depth—Orwell's novel nevertheless depends more upon character and plot than upon discursive statement. (The flagrant exception to this generalization is the solid block of pages given over to Winston's reading of what he thinks to be the Brotherhood's bible.) Orwell is particularly good at catching off, rather in the manner of Dickens, the portrait of an easily recognized and quickly sounded type. Such are the intellectual Syme, the old prole from whom Winston tries to get something about the pre-Big Brother past, and the old prostitute named Smith who is shoved into Winston's cell in the Ministry of Love. Such too is the outer party functionary who always takes his meals in the cafeteria when Winston does. . . . True the nameless functionary comes to life for only a moment, but that moment is solidly imbedded in the novel's total fabric. . . . Thus the essayist's insight into how the cliché acts as a depersonalizing force is made over into the novelist's terrifying glimpse of the completely depersonalized person in the totalitarian society. (pp. 156-57)

Harold J. Harris, "Orwell's Essays and '1984'," in Twentieth Century Literature, *Vol. 4, No. 4, January, 1959, pp. 154-61.*

C. M. KORNBLUTH (essay date 1958?)

[*Kornbluth was one of the earliest science fiction writers to forego speculation about what might exist in outer space and to focus instead on depicting a dystopian future on earth. His widely read and translated novel* The Space Merchants (1953), *coauthored with Frederik Pohl, was one of the first works of science fiction to extrapolate a horrifyingly possible future from existing social, political, and economic trends. In an unexcerpted portion of the following essay, Kornbluth maintains that the science fiction novel has never been an effective means of social criticism because works in this genre tend to incite contemplation rather than action. Kornbluth examines several works that he considers science fiction containing both implicit and explicit social criticism, includ-*

ing Jonathan Swift's Gulliver's Travels *(1726), his and Pohl's* The Space Merchants, *and Orwell's* Nineteen Eighty-Four. *In the following excerpt, first published in 1959, the year following Kornbluth's death, Kornbluth concludes that, despite its many readers, Orwell's novel has done nothing to combat tyranny. He then provides a psychological interpretation of the symbolic content of* Nineteen Eighty-Four, *contending that the horrors of this world stem from the horrors of Orwell's childhood. For a differing psychological interpretation of* Nineteen Eighty-Four, *see the excerpt by Marcus Smith (1968).]*

I can prove that Orwell was consciously, deliberately, writing *1984* as propaganda—and I say propaganda without apologies. There is nothing evil about the thing itself, and unless social criticism is also propaganda, it is mere whimpering. Toward the end of his life Orwell knew exactly who he was and what he was doing. His essays tell us that everything he wrote was polemic and political. He did novels and he also did the odd jobs he thought should be done which nobody else was doing. He did critical studies of comic postcards and boys' newspapers in a spirit of deliberately humorless intensity. He wanted to find out what these media had to say about the English working class and what their implications were for his primary tasks of combatting tyranny and establishing socialism. He delved into the structure of the English language and wrote an essay on how to write about politics without being nonsensical; this to him was also related to combatting tyranny and establishing socialism. We may take it for granted that he wrote *1984* to help combat tyranny and establish socialism.

The second part of his program was little noticed, which was an old story to Orwell; his earlier books, *Animal Farm* specifically, said that the rulers of Russia were no damned good; that the final proof of this was you could hardly tell the Russian rulers from the rulers of Germany and England. Nobody seemed to notice this; they merrily went ahead and used the book as a stick to beat Russia with.

Now, has *1984,* with its enormous circulation, done anything to combat tyranny? . . . I can only say that I think it did not. Call me Procrustes and let's move along.

The book is an almost arrogantly good novel. The prose is the prose of a man with an English public school education, and I have noticed that these old Eton and Cambridge boys can write rings around anybody unfortunate enough not to have attended a public school and an ancient university. The book has structure; a beginning, middle and end, balanced and proportionate. It has fully realized characters and, as it "should" be in a novel, these are protagonist, antagonist, heroine, comic relief (that's Parsons) and spear-carriers. It is an added pleasure to read a book that matter-of-factly accepts formal limitations and works within them at high intensity. The reporting could not be improved on; Orwell selects the relevant detail every time, knows the importance of trivia, bangs sense-impressions at us until we see, hear, taste, feel and smell the world of *1984.*

Orwell is the writer in a hundred thousand who notices and remarks that not only the taste but the texture on the tongue of coffee with sugar is different from the texture of coffee with saccharine.

The book is unusual in that it is written on one literal and two symbolic levels, one apparently semi-conscious and the other I think wholly unconscious. On the semi-conscious level *1984* is almost an allegory of growing up in middle-class England. We know from Orwell's long essay **"Such, Such Were the Joys,"** that he did not think his childhood was an easy one,

and this could readily be inferred also from *1984.* We have only to think of Winston Smith as a boy and of the inquisitor O'Brien as his father for many things to fall kaleidoscopically into a sudden new design.

Sexual activity is forbidden to Winston Smith as it is to a boy under pain of dire punishment.

There are no laws or clear-cut rules of conduct for Winston Smith to obey; he, like a child, may transgress without meaning to. He must not only do what is right, he must *be good*.

The uncanny O'Brien always knows what Winston Smith is thinking. (pp. 88-90)

O'Brien is large and powerful; Winston is small and weak.

O'Brien practices incredible brutalities on Winston in the name of "education"; Winston believes this and continues to like O'Brien. At any moment during the torture one expects the inquisitor to say "This hurts me more than it hurts you," but that would have given the game away.

And in one damnably strange passage, O'Brien says to Winston: ". . . is there anything that you wish to say before you leave? Any message? Any question?" At this point Winston's mind should be boiling with a thousand questions about the mysterious Brotherhood he has just joined, but he asks none of them. What he does ask is: "Did you ever happen to hear of an old rhyme that begins Oranges and lemons, say the bells of St. Clement's?"

"Again O'Brien nodded. With a sort of grave courtesy he completed the stanza:

". . . When I grow rich, say the bells of Shoreditch."

Tell me a story, Daddy.

This symbolic level, the level of boyhood, I have described as semi-conscious. The many parallels between Winston Smith as an adult in London and Eric Blair (Orwell's real name) as a schoolboy at "Crossgates" described in **"Such, Such Were the Joys"** could hardly have escaped the creator of them both. To Winston Smith, O'Brien's "face seen from below looked coarse and worn, with pouches under the eyes and tired lines from nose to chin." This is just how young Eric sees adults, almost word for word. Young Eric confusedly believes that every adult is in league with the school's headmaster and will drop everything to report him if he misbehaves—paralleling the Thought Police and the swarming amateur informers. Young Eric suffered from the school's squalor and lack of privacy, and what Winston Smith desperately wants is just a little cleanliness and a room of his own with no spying telescreen. It is clear that Orwell deliberately drew on recollections of his childhood for *1984,* and we should note that he explicitly equipped Winston Smith with a complicated feeling of guilt about his mother. I sense, however, both in his essay and the novel a failure to come to grips with the relationship between father and son. In the essay his memories of his father are unbelievably meagre—father was just an irritable man who always said "Don't!" Similarly Smith's father is curiously absent from his consciousness.

So far we have cruised the surface of the novel and taken a short submarine tour through its depths. I now invite you to join me in the bathysphere and descend to the ocean floor.

Let us consider first a curious architectural feature of *1984* introduced to us in the following passage: ". . . in the side wall, within easy reach of Winston's arm, (was) a large oblong slit protected by a wire grating. This last was for the disposal of waste paper. Similar slits existed in thousands or tens of thousands throughout the building, not only in every room but at short intervals in every corridor. For some reason they were nicknamed memory holes. When one knew that any document was due for destruction, or even when one saw a scrap of waste paper lying about, it was an automatic action to lift the flap of the nearest memory hole and drop it in, whereupon it would be whirled away on a current of warm air to the enormous furnaces which were somewhere in the recesses of the building.''

The same devices can be found in the fictional future of Robert Heinlein. Heinlein, however, by analogy with a term out of mediaeval architecture and because of their function, calls them ''oubliettes''—from the French verb oublier, ''to forget.'' This is the sensible thing to call them. Orwell calls them the exact opposite of what they are. Perhaps on one level this harmonizes with the culture of the time—Freedom is Slavery, Ignorance is Strength, War is Peace. Perhaps the name has another level of meaning, which I shall take up shortly.

Before I do, let us look at Room 101, the torture room in the Ministry of Love. I suggest that Room 101 is Orwell's unconscious symbol for the uterus. My reasons are:

Room 101 is obviously the first room in the numbering system; the starting place.

It is a room below ground in the center of a white, windowless pyramid named the Ministry of Love—female symbolism can scarcely go further than that.

The three numerals 101 displayed on a page constitute a naive sketch of the female genitalia seen from below.

''Room'' is a pun for ''womb,'' underscored by the two ''w'' sounds which crowd along after it, as if to correct the ''r'' sound. (pp. 90-3)

Now let us look at those slits protected by liftable skirts ''for some reason . . . nicknamed memory holes.'' I suggest that the illogical name is an unconscious pun for femaleness. ''Memory'' is close to ''mammary''. The first syllable, ''mem'' is the Anglo-Indian word for ''lady,'' and Orwell was born an Anglo-Indian. And there is a whole cluster of childhood names for mother which are more or less close to ''memory''—''mum,'' ''mummy'' and so on.

The memory holes and Room 101 have this in common: they symbolize torment and destruction in the womb. The question we must face is, why does the uterus symbolize for Orwell a place of torment where destruction and ''the worst thing in the world'' happens to everybody? The uterus is supposed to be the place of warmth and safety. I cannot help wondering whether Orwell's birth was a long and painful one, and whether his mother suffered a near miscarriage or two while pregnant with him.

We are now almost outside the area of literary criticism, but not quite. I believe that some readers may find *1984* meaningful and compelling or unreal and revolting on an unconscious basis of agreement or disagreement with Orwell's image of the uterus as a place of torment.

I hope nobody will conclude that I am deprecating Orwell's work or character by discussing it in this fashion. I say this only because some time ago the critic Anthony West of the *New Yorker* wrote on Orwell. To his own satisfaction he traced most of Orwell's themes back to his unhappy school experi-

ences [see *TCLC*, Vol. 2]. Unless I misread him, he concluded that because of this Orwell's work and even Orwell's manhood were so much the less. I regard this conclusion as a howling non sequitur. I think Orwell was a great writer and led as useful and noble a life as can be imagined for a twentieth century man. (pp. 94-5)

C. M. Kornbluth, ''The Failure of the Science Fiction Novel As Social Criticism,'' in The Science Fiction Novel: Imagination and Social Criticism *by Basil Davenport, Richard A. Heinlein, C. M. Kornbluth, Alfred Bester, and Robert Bloch, second edition, 1964. Reprint by The Folcroft Press, Inc., 1969, pp. 64-101.**

RUSSELL KIRK (essay date 1968)

[*An American historian, political theorist, novelist, journalist, and lecturer, Kirk is one of America's most eminent conservative intellectuals. His works have provided a major impetus to the conservative revival that has developed since the 1950s. The Conservative Mind (1953), one of Kirk's early books, describes conservatism as a living body of ideas ''struggling toward ascendancy in the United States''; in it he traced the roots and canons of modern conservative thought to such important predecessors as Edmund Burke, John Adams, and Alexis de Tocqueville. Kirk has also been a trenchant critic of the decline of academic standards in American universities:* Decadence and Renewal in the Higher Learning *(1978), in particular, is a forceful denunciation of the ''academic barbarism'' which he states has replaced the traditional goals of higher education—wisdom and virtue—with the fallacious ones of ''utilitarian efficiency,'' relaxed admissions, and innovative forms of education. The result, in Kirk's view, is that ''the higher learning in America is a disgrace.'' Kirk's detractors have sometimes been skeptical of the charges he levels against liberal ideas and programs, accusing him of a simplistic, one-sided partisanship. His admirers, on the other hand, point to the alleged failure of liberal precepts—in particular those applied in the universities—as evidence of the incisiveness of Kirk's ideas and criticisms. In the following excerpt Kirk defines what he considers the conservative, reactionary nature of Orwell's radicalism, insisting that his socialism was essentially a sentimental reaction to the conditions of life. Kirk insists that Orwell was essentially a misanthrope who, because he rejected Christian orthodox dogma, conveyed a vision of despair.*]

In the twentieth century, no novelist has exerted a stronger influence upon political opinion, in Britain and America, than did George Orwell. Also Orwell was the most telling writer about poverty. In a strange and desperate way, Orwell was a lover of the permanent things. Yet because he could discern no source of abiding justice and love in the universe, Orwell found this life of ours not worth living. In his sardonic fashion, nevertheless, he struck some fierce blows at abnormality in politics and literature.

''There is no such thing as genuinely non-political literature,'' Orwell wrote in his essay on **''The Prevention of Literature''** (1945), ''and least of all in an age like our own, when fears, hatreds, and loyalties of a directly political kind are near to the surface of everyone's consciousness. . . . It follows that the atmosphere of totalitarianism is deadly to any kind of prose writer, though a poet, at any rate a lyric poet, might possibly find it breathable. And in any totalitarian society that survives for more than a couple of generations, it is probable that prose literature, of the kind that has existed during the past four hundred years, must actually *come to an end*.'' Soviet Russia supplies the proof: ''It is true that literary prostitutes like Ilya Ehrenberg or Alexei Tolstoy are paid huge sums of money, but the only thing which is of any value to the writer as such—his freedom of expression—is taken away from him.''

George Orwell was a left-wing professional journalist, with some of the faults which that unhappy conjunction encourages. Occasionally he wrote hastily and carelessly; he was bitter and arrogant; desiring men to be as gods, he despised them because they had the effrontery to be loud and smelly and stupid. But also Orwell was much more than a left-wing professional journalist. He was fearless, kind, honest, consumingly earnest, and very English. He was the latest representative of the English radical tradition which extends through Langland, Bunyan, Cobbett, Dickens, and Chesterton—a paradoxical radicalism rooted in the experiences and the prejudices of a strong people. In a number of ways—his origins, his poverty, his pessimism, his mingled hatred and pity for the poor, in the subjects of his books—he resembles George Gissing, who died at a similar age of similar causes after a similar life. Orwell's radicalism was that which is angry with society because society has failed to provide men with the ancient norms of simple life—family, decency, and continuity; the sort of radicalism which does not mean to disintegrate the world, but to restore it. (p. 21)

Like all true satirists, Orwell, was allergic to *people*. He adored the Platonic idea of a man; he could not abide the vulgarity of the flesh. What he really hated about modern society was its ugliness, its monotony, its cheapness, its commonness. These are like the opinions of Ruskin, but they are not the impulses of a typical collectivistic revolutionary.

If Hume was a Tory by accident, Orwell was a leftist by accident. His instincts were more aristocratic than egalitarian; and, like the genuine aristocrat, he held a thoroughgoing contempt for commercialism and crassness. (p. 22)

Orwell's Socialism was that meager and contradictory Socialism which so often pops up upon the Labour back-benches, astounded at the bill for nationalizing steel or enraged at petty interferences with Her Majesty's subjects. Orwell frankly disliked and feared ''scientific'' Marxists; he sympathized with the confessedly muddled socialism of the ordinary British working-man, who thought of Socialism simply as shorter hours, better wages, and less bossing about. Of such a workingman he wrote in *Wigan Pier:* ''Often, in my opinion, he is a truer Socialist than the orthodox Marxist, because he does remember, what the other so often forgets, that Socialism means justice and common decency.''

The is the sort of socialism which literary men like William Morris and Cunninghame Graham stood for—a socialism perfectly impractical, hopelessly sentimental, but generous, intensely human, and not unlike Tory radicalism. When a man like Orwell begins to see what State Socialism really must become in the age that is dawning, he writes *1984,* grits his teeth, and dies.

He loathed the Utiopianism of H. G. Wells much as William Morris was infuriated at the Utopianism of Edward Bellamy. Orwell despised, indeed, nearly all his fellow-socialists. (pp. 22-3)

Orwell's socialism, then, scarcely can be called a position at all, but only an agonized leap in the dark, away from the pain of consolidated, uniform, industrialized modern existence. Orwell was acutely and miserably class-conscious, as perhaps only a poor and puzzled Englishmen can be, to a degree most Americans find difficult to understand; he thought of himself always as distinctly middle-class, and he wished he were noth-

ing of the sort. So the best solution which occurred to his mind was the merging of all orders of society into a vast inchoate proletarian dbody. He predicted in *Wigan Pier,* half in despair, half in hope, that the hard-pressed British bourgeoisie would be reduced to the condition of the working-people:

> And then perhaps this misery of class prejudice will fade away, and we of the sinking middle-class—. . .—may sink without further struggles into the working class where we belong, and probably when we get there it will not be so dreadful as we feared, for, after all, we have nothing to lose but our aitches.

Yet Orwell was not candid here. Actually, he was appalled at the idea of being assimilated by the amorphous mass of sweating, cursing, humdrum, unthinking humanity. What he really thought of working people, in the flesh, is suggested by various descriptions of the ''proles'' in *1984.* They are not the paragraphs of a man who loves common people with a vast gregarious joviality. Orwell would no more have called Walt Whitman *camerado* than he would have adored Big Brother.

At heart, Orwell hated all innovation. The most ingenious feature of his last book, over which he must have labored with a mordant pleasure, is his burlesque of recent endeavors to revise out of recognition the English language. I refer, of course, to the appendix on ''The Principles of Newspeak.'' To dehumanize man altogether, Ingsoc has stripped and mutilated the language, converting it into a propagandist's pidgin-English.

What Orwell yearned after was not the gray egalitarian future, but old England, ante-bellum England, England before the automobile and the council-house and the troubles of our times. His praises of English tradition are almost in the tone of Burke. In *Coming up for Air,* Orwell expresses himself through George Bowling, a lower-middle-class, middle-aged man who tries to revisit the scenes of his youth and finds that the country he knew as a boy has been obliterated by suburbia, and then smashed by bombs. . . . (pp. 23-4)

The past, Orwell thought, was gone irretrievably; and yet the decent people in his books are reactionaries, men who try to turn back to the old ways. Little of the past survives for them to recapture—hardly more than rags and tatters of nursery-rhymes, as in *1984.*

As for the present, Orwell found it intolerable. He thought of it as the Great Depression of his early years in England: the dole and massive unemployment. He became a Socialist because he believed (knowing very little about economics) that under ''capitalism'' there must be perpetual unemployment on a vast scale. Worse than the material privations of life on the dole was the damage done to character; he had known many decent workingmen, he said, who had disintegrated morally after a few weeks or months on the dole: denied work, they felt useless, rejected by society, and fell to pieces. They would not be worth hiring again.

The migrant farm-laborer and the London beggar were the subjects of his second novel, *A Clergyman's Daughter.* . . . There has been no truer or more dreadful writing about the lot of the destitute and the outcast. The scene of the derelicts—men and women—in Trafalgar Square at night was the wild power of *Lear.* Yet it is possible to conceive of a degradation worse than this.

For if the present is Purgatory, the probable future will be Hell. Orwell foresaw the approach of a totalist society from which faith, custom, common sense, justice, order, freedom, brotherhood, art, literature, and even sexual love would be eradicated. The new "socialist" oligarchy would live for the intoxication of brutal power; the administrative and technical people, party members, would live in terror and stupor; the proletarian masses would exist on the level of beasts. This new society never will end, says O'Brien, the *agent provocateur* in *1984*: it will writhe eternally, its energizing spirit the lust for power. Religion will be dead, but materialism will have failed; freedom will have been exchanged for security, and then security will be chucked through a "memory hole" into the central incinerator. O'Brien is candid with his victim Winston:

> Do you begin to see, then, what kind of world we are creating? It is the exact opposite of the stupid hedonistic Utopia that the old reformers imagined. A world of fear and treachery and torment, a world of trampling and being trampled upon, a world which will grow not less but more merciless as it refines itself. . . . But always—do not forget this, Winston—always there will be intoxication of power, constantly increasing and constantly growing subtler. Always, at every moment, there will be the thrill of victory, the sensation of trampling forever on an enemy who is helpless. If you want a picture of the future, imagine a boot stamping on a human face—forever.

This terrifying passage raises a question; and Orwell did not answer that question. Such a triumph of *pleonexia* is more than conceivable: we see it dominating China's "Cultural Revolution," in which the whole heritage of civilization is denounced and destroyed, and in which the only gratification remaining even to the masters of society is stamping upon a human face. But here is the question: what force or appetite, immensely stronger than human wishes, inspires the ambition to trample forever upon an enemy who is helpless?

Just such a culmination of sin is described in Christian orthodoxy. It is called the reign of the Anti-Christ. And it is produced by the intervention of a supernatural hatred, working upon human depravity. It is the overthrow of the normal by the abnormal. It is the apotheosis of Satan.

Orwell saw the Church in disrepute and disorder, intellectually and morally impoverished; and he had no faith. He could not say how the total corruption of man and society would be produced; he could not even refer to the intrusion of the diabolical; but he could describe a coming reign of misrule wonderfully like the visions of St. John the Divine. He saw beyond ideology to the approaching inversion of humanitarian dogmas. All the norms for mankind would be defied and defiled. Yet because he could not bring himself to believe in enduring principles of order, or in an Authority transcending private rationality, he was left desperate at the end. A *desperado*, literally, is a man who has despaired of grace. (pp. 24-5)

> *Russell Kirk, "George Orwell's Despair," in* The Intercollegiate Review, *Vol. 5, No. 1, Fall, 1968, pp. 21-5.*

MARCUS SMITH (essay date 1968-69)

[*In the following excerpt, the critic finds that the presentation of Winston Smith as the victim of an Oedipal psychological disorder is central to the structure of* Nineteen Eighty-Four. *The sequences in which O'Brien tortures Winston in the Ministry of Love are compared to a series of psychoanalytic sessions, with the "cure" of Winston, the analysand, as the ultimate goal. Smith concludes that Winston's ostensible acceptance of Big Brother at the novel's close merely represents the transfer of his feelings for his missing mother. For a different psychological interpretation of the novel, see the excerpt by C. M. Kornbluth (1958).*]

In stressing the political and social ideas in *1984*, Orwell's critics have neglected the psychological development of the protagonist, Winston Smith. This is a very serious distortion, for *1984* is not simply an externally developed portrait of an anti-Utopian society; rather it deals with the inexorable conflict between an ultra-rational, totalitarian social ideal and the irrational neurotic reactions of an individual human being. Previous studies have either ignored Winston's characterization or have considered merely *what* happens to him on the level of plot. But Winston is clearly and carefully developed along familiar Oedipal lines and an accurate understanding of *1984* must take this into account and consider *why* he behaves the way he does and how this affects the total meaning of Orwell's novel.

The Party's slogan is "Who controls the past controls the future; who controls the present controls the past." This explains the Party's obsession with adjusting history to accord with the "facts" of the moment, and on the historical level of the facts and figures the Party completely controls the past. But the past which the Party has not yet dominated so efficiently is the past as it operates in the human unconscious, individual and collective. The Proles, for instance, have clung to their "ancestral code" . . . and the Party both subjugates and defers to their blind animal energy by allowing them sex, pornography, real coffee, beer and their archaic language. Yet as Winston notes, *"Until they become conscious they will never rebel, and until after they have rebelled they cannot become conscious."* . . . Thus, while the Proles pose no revolutionary threat to the Party's control of Oceania, they are nevertheless a quantitative obstacle to the ultra-rationalism which characterizes the Party's thought and aims, especially the Inner Party. At one point O'Brien asserts that "Reality exists in . . . the mind of the Party, which is collective and immortal." . . . But this should be contrasted to the symbolic Prole woman outside Charrington's shop. . . . This archetypal earth mother causes Winston to observe that "The future belonged to the proles" and this possibility is never entirely overturned by anything that happens in *1984*.

This theme of an independent collective memory and an evolutionary possibility is, however, only hinted at. There is good reason for this since it is difficult to imagine a viable way to dramatize it. As a novelist Orwell must work scenically and with individualized figures. Thus he focuses on a representative individual, Winston Smith. And Orwell shows in developing Winston that the past (as it operates in and through the unconscious) is independent of the rational control of either the Party or Winston himself. The main issue in *1984* is whether or not the individual's intractable unconscious can somehow be "rationalized." This is suggested in the Ministry of Love when Winston asks O'Brien, "But how can you stop people remembering things? . . . It is involuntary. It is outside oneself. How can you control memory? You have not controlled mine!". . . . O'Brien implies by his answer that the Party has perhaps rejected the concept of an autonomous unconscious: *"You* have not controlled it. That is what has brought you here. You are here because you have failed in humility, in self-discipline.'' . . . This is a crucial exchange, for O'Brien is saying that the individual mind can be completely dominated by the rational will. But if we review Winston's path to the Ministry of Love, we find that it was neither pride nor lack of discipline which caused his downfall, but rather impulsive actions quite beyond his conscious control.

This is apparent in the opening chapter when Winston starts his diary, ostensibly his first act of overt political rebellion. Winston does not attach any hope to his act, because "Either the future would resemble the present, in which case it would not listen to him, or it would be different . . . and his predicament would be meaningless.'' . . . Lacking any clear external motive (and facing almost certain death if caught), why does Winston even bother with a diary? The answer Orwell supplies is that the diary is a compulsive act and that the lay-out of Winston's room and the diary itself are the causes of his rebellion:

> To one side of it there was a shallow alcove. . . .
> By sitting in the alcove, and keeping well back,
> Winston was able to remain outside the range
> of the telescreen. . . . *It was partly the unusual
> geography of the room that had suggested to
> him the thing that he was now about to do.*
>
> But *it had also been suggested by the book* that
> he had just taken out of the drawer. It was a
> peculiarly beautiful book. Its smooth creamy
> paper, a little yellowed by age, was of a kind
> that had not been manufactured for at least forty
> years past. (. . . italics added)

The alcove and the book are not just incidental stimuli, but are part of a pattern of stimuli to which Winston is responsive throughout *1984*.

The alcove, for example, is a haven, one of several which figure in Winston's memory and actions. He dreams of his mother and sister together "in some subterranean place—the bottom of a well . . . or a very deep grave." . . . The room above Charrington's shop awakens in Winston "a sort of nostalgia, a sort of ancestral memory." He finds this room "curiously inviting," a place in which he could be "utterly alone, utterly secure." . . . Later he describes it to Julia as "a pocket of the past" where "no harm could come to them." . . . Winston's obsession with safe, womb-like pockets has obvious Freudian overtones and throughout *1984* his quest for security takes the form of mother substitutes.

Similarly, Winston tries to flee into the past by means of old objects, persons from the past, archaic rhymes and riddles, and relationships—all of which he associates with his childhood and ultimately his lost mother. The diary is at least forty years old. Winston is thirty-nine. (pp. 423-25)

Winston's self-destructive flight into the past and his quest for a haven cannot be explained as deliberate, conscious "escapism" from the political nightmare of Big Brother's world. Time and again Orwell stresses the involuntary nature of Winston's acts. The main cause lies in Winston's unconscious and is the result of a childhood trauma and its subsequent guilt. Orwell establishes this early in *1984* during one of Winston's dreams:

> At this moment his mother was sitting in some
> place deep down beneath him, with his young
> sister in her arms. . . . Both of them were look-
> ing up at him. They were down in some sub-
> terranean place. . . . He was out in the light and

air while they were being sucked down to death, and they were down there because he was up here. . . .

The source of this dream (and Winston's guilt-ridden mother-complex) is an incident which happened when he was a boy living with his mother and sister. His mother had brought home a chocolate ration and Winston had selfishly demanded the entire piece. Even though he was given the larger share, he viciously grabbed all of the chocolate and ran down the stairs. When he returned after several hours his mother and sister were gone and he never saw them again. His last vision of them establishes a basic image to which Winston tries to return throughout the novel: "His sister . . . had set up a feeble wail. His mother drew her arm round the child and pressed its face against her breast." . . . This image of protection and security is deeply embedded in Winston's unconscious and all his actions are attempts to expiate his guilt and thereby regain the protective shelter of his mother's arms.

Thus, when we go back and consider the content of Winston's diary, what we find is not a statement of political rebellion. . . . The diary . . . is not a record of Winston's rebellious thoughts; instead it is an outlet for the fears and guilt fantasies which press upon his conscious mind.

Again and again Winston is drawn back to the theft of the chocolate and the loss of his mother. When he meets Julia in the forest (another haven), she gives him a piece of chocolate which stirs up "some memory which he could not pin down, but which was powerful and troubling." . . . After Winston tastes the chocolate the association (though still obscure) becomes even more compelling: "There was still that memory moving round the edges of his consciousness, something strongly felt but not reducible to definite shape. . . . He pushed it away from him, aware only that it was the memory of some action which he would have liked to undo but could not." . . .

Thus very early in their relationship, Julia is associated in Winston's unconscious mind with his mother. This helps to explain, I think, how despite his initial disgust at Julia's physical attractiveness . . . , Winston is able to respond to her sexually. Before she gives him the chocolate, Winston is impotent . . . , but after he eats the chocolate he can make love to her, which he interprets as "a political act." . . . We must distinguish, however, between Winston's conscious interpretation of his own actions and their unconscious causes. It is true that the Party forbids fornication, but it is more important that Winston finds in Julia a temporary mother substitute and, as in the case of the diary, it seems to me that the main motivation stems from his unconscious mind.

Winston's unconscious is also involved in his strange relationship with O'Brien. Like Julia, O'Brien enters the novel in the opening chapter during the Two Minutes Hate. [The critic adds in a footnote that: "Whereas Winston's first reaction to Julia is disgust, because of her obvious sexuality, he feels 'deeply drawn' to O'Brien's virile strength and thinks he is 'a person that you could talk to'." . . .] Winston ostensibly turns to O'Brien in order to enter a politically significant conspiracy against the Party. Yet at the end of their first interview, Winston reveals quite a different response when he cannot think of any further questions to ask: "Instead of anything directly connected with O'Brien or the Brotherhood, there came into his mind a sort of composite picture of the dark bedroom where his mother had spent her last days, and the little room over Mr. Charrington's shop, and the glass paperweight, and the steel engraving in its rosewood frame." . . . Thus O'Brien, too, is merged with Winston's other images of refuge and security.

Winston, of course, is mistaken about O'Brien, just as he is mistaken about the room over Charrington's shop. O'Brien is a loyal Party member, the engraving conceals a telescreen and Charrington is a member of the Thought Police. And as Winston is dragged away to the Ministry of Love the futility of his fetishism and quest for haven is exposed when one of the policemen smashes the glass paperweight and reveals that the mysterious object in its center is merely a "fragment of coral, a tiny crinkle of pink like a sugar rosebud from a cake." . . . Indeed, from the very instant he bought his old notebook from Charrington (perhaps even before that), Winston has lived under the all-observing gaze of the Party. His "rebellion" has never amounted to anything but a pathetic and foredoomed groping. But this, ironically, is of little or no significance. In the world of *1984* it is not the defeat and destruction of the individual that is important. What is, is whether there are any limits to the Party's extension of power.

In the Ministry of Love, Winston is psychologically torn to pieces and then systematically made over into the image and likeness of the Party—at least apparently. The crucial irony, however, is that the final transformation in Winston's personality does not occur until the last page of the novel and that even then the mechanism of change lies outside the Party's control.

In the Ministry of Love Winston's unconscious is the object of attention, especially his mother complex. This is suggested in the opening scene of the third section. In the cell with Winston are several people. One of them, "an enormous wreck of a woman, aged about sixty," drunk and vomiting, is dumped into Winston's lap:

> She put a vast arm round his shoulder and drew him towards her, breathing beer and vomit into his face.
>
> "Wass your name, dearie?" she said.
>
> "Smith," said Winston.
>
> "Smith. . . . Thass funny. My name's Smith too. Why," she added sentimentally, "I might be your mother!"
>
> She might, thought Winston, be his mother. She was about the right age and physique, and it was probable that people changed somewhat after twenty years in a forced-labor camp. . . .

It is irrelevant to wonder whether or not this woman is indeed Winston's mother: she never appears again. But we must not overlook the importance of this apparently accidental encounter and we must realize that this woman's role is important symbolically. Her literal history is unimportant; she is obviously one more manifestation of Winston's messy and intractable unconscious which follows him even into the sterile, super-egotistic Ministry of Love with its concealed floodlamps endlessly spilling light into the white porcelain rooms.

Much of what happens to Winston in the Ministry of Love resembles psychotherapy. O'Brien is the analyst. . . . O'Brien also becomes at one point another surrogate for Winston's mother. This happens when O'Brien forces Winston to admit (with the help of electro-shock torture) that two-and-two make anything the Party wishes: "Abruptly he was sitting up with O'Brien's arm round his shoulders. . . . For a moment he clung to O'Brien like a baby, curiously comforted by the heavy arm round his shoulders. He had the feeling that O'Brien was his protector." . . . After more pain and more responsive adulation by Winston, O'Brien explains that "We do not destroy the heretic because he resists us; so long as he resists us we never destroy him. We convert him, we capture his inner mind, we reshape him." . . . But does the Party ever capture Winston's "inner mind." its stated goal? The last part of the novel seems to say that it does not.

Some twenty-five pages after O'Brien's declared intention, Winston seems on the conscious level to be a changed person. When given a slate he scribbles the orthodox Party epigrams: Freedom is Slavery, Two and Two make Five, God is Power. . . . Yet he still somehow clings to his heretical fantasies: "He dreamed a great deal all through this time, and they were always happy dreams. He was in the Golden Country, or he was sitting in the sun, talking of peaceful things." . . .

This distinction between the conscious, orthodox Winston and his unconscious resistance to the Party is made even clearer after Winston screams out Julia's name in his sleep. . . . When O'Brien appears a few moments later, he asks Winston what his true feelings are towards Big Brother and the latter replies, "I hate him." Winston is then taken to Room 101 to learn to love Big Brother and appropriately Room 101 is "as deep down as it was possible to go" in the Ministry of Love. . . .

In Room 101 Winston is forced to confront the "worst thing in the world." . . . For him this is a mask-like cage of rats which O'Brien fits over his face. . . . But before the rats are released, Winston panics and screams out, "Do it to Julia!" Julia is the only object he can think of to interpose between himself and the unendurable threat of the rats.

How does this scene fit in with our examination of Winston's mother-complex? The relationship is rather obscure, which explains why critics have attacked or ignored it. But Orwell does suggest a connection. Winston's fear of rats in Room 101 is anticipated when a rat appears in the room over Charrington's shop. Winston cringes in fear. . . . Julia had been saying that London was "swarming" with rats: "Did you know they attack children?" . . . (pp. 426-30)

The chain of association is obviously complex, but I see it as follows. Julia triggers powerful guilt feelings in Winston with her remark about rats attacking children: Winston deserted his mother and sister and left them to the rats. Or perhaps he even identifies himself with the rats. . . . Winston's guilt derives from his tongue and mouth which selfishly devoured his sister's chocolate. And in his unconscious he links this act in a causal fashion with his mother's and sister's disappearance and presumed death. The rats are the "worst thing in the world" because they destroyed his mother and sister but they are also the appropriate agents of expiation since his offending mouth will be punished. Winston's confrontation is something he has both feared and yet wanted, because until he expiates his guilt he cannot regain his mother and the security of her embrace.

Regardless of whether this is the precise meaning of the rat scene, it is obvious that Winston's actions in Room 101 are due to his unconscious fears and desires. O'Brien emphasizes this when he says:

> "Do you remember . . . the moment of panic that used to occur in your dreams? There was a wall of blackness in front you, and a roaring

sound in your ears. There was something terrible on the other side of the wall. You knew
that you knew what it was, but you dared not
drag it into the open. It was rats that were on
the other side of the wall.'' . . .

Despite O'Brien's explanation, the rat cage and Winston's apparent capitulation, the scene in Room 101 is merely a pen-
ultimate step in Winston's long and agonized mother quest.
His surrender does not occur until the last page of *1984*. In the
final chapter the scene shifts to the Spreading Chestnut, a bar-
cafe, where Winston comes every day to work out chess problems and stupify himself with Victory Gin. Ironically, however, despite everything that has happened to him, he still
wavers between total orthodoxy and his old heretical fantasies.
(p. 431)

A trumpet call then announces an imminent victory bulletin
and Winston, seized by the excitement, makes his peace with
Big Brother: ''the final, indispensible, healing change had never
happened, until this moment.'' . . . This change, however, is
remarkably ironic, for after a series of unsatisfactory mother
substitutes, Winston turns to the ultimate surrogate, Big Brother
himself: ''He gazed up at the enormous face. Forty years it
had taken him to learn what kind of smile was hidden beneath
the dark mustache. O cruel, needless misunderstanding! O stubborn, self-willed exile from the loving breast!'' . . . . Winston
has learned to love Big Brother. On the surface this seems a
victory for the Party, but actually it is a hollow triumph, for
the Party has failed in its stated purpose. This irony is implied
by the hyperbolic style of the last paragraph, and it emerges
clearly when we consider that the Party's object was to cure
Winston, to make him sane. . . . ''We do not destroy the heretic
because he resists us,'' says O'Brien. ''We convert him, we
capture his inner mind, we reshape him.'' . . . But it is obvious
that Winston's ''inner mind,'' his unconscious, is never captured or reshaped. Instead Winston's neurosis prevails. At the
end of *1984* Winston has not been essentially changed, only
now he has managed to transfer his irrational burden to the
massive power symbol of Big Brother.

Modern literature abounds in Freudian ''types'' and considered
by itself Winston's Oedipal characerization is commonplace
despite its complexity. What is remarkable and important is
the way Winston's characterization affects the meaning of *1984*.
The Party, says O'Brien, is ''interested solely in power.'' . . .
And the key to power is control of the past, not just the external
past of history, but also the past as it operates in the individual
unconscious. Since the Party never does capture Winston's
unconscious, its quest for power is frustrated.

At one point, in fact, O'Brien admits that Winston is a ''flaw
in the pattern'' . . . , though he claims that Winston is
''alone.'' . . . But Julia is obviusly another ''flaw'' and so are
the two Party stalwarts, Ampleforth and Parsons, who are brought
to the Ministry of Love. Like Winston, their crimes were involuntary. Ampleforth needed a rhyme for ''rod'' and allowed
the word ''God'' to remain in his definitive edition of Kipling,
and Parsons was turned in by his daughter for screaming out
in his sleep, ''Down with Big Brother!''

Rebellion in *1984* is not a deliberate, conscious activity. It
occurs accidentally or in one's sleep or because of impulses
and reactions stemming from the individual's unconscious. To
eliminate rebellion, then, the Party must do no less that radically change the nature of man. This major premise of the Party
is explicitly stated by O'Brien: ''. . . we create human nature.

Men are infinitely malleable.'' . . . But in the case of Winston
Smith, the Party fails to change ''human nature'' and the last
paragraph suggests ironically that it is precisely the flexibility
of human nature that limits the Party's power. At the start of
1984 Winston is searching for a substitute mother and at the
end of the book he ''finds'' her in Big Brother. At best the
Party has achieved a stalemate. Winston is never a threat to
the Party's control, but Big Brother as well as the individual
must confront and acknowledge the intractable nature of man,
that wall of blackness. (pp. 432-33)

*Marcus Smith, ''The Wall of Blackness: A Psycho-
logical Approach to '1984','' in* Modern Fiction
Studies, *Vol. XIV, No. 4, Winter, 1968-69, pp. 423-33.*

ISAAC ASIMOV (essay date 1980)

[*Asimov is one of the best-known, most prolific, and most popular
of modern science fiction writers. His career began during what
is termed the ''Golden Age'' of science fiction, a period during
the 1920s and 1930s when pulp fiction magazines such as John
W. Campbell's* Astounding Science Fiction *provided a forum for
the early scientific and speculative fiction of writers such as Robert
A. Heinlein, Poul Anderson, and Theodore Sturgeon. Asimov has
written a number of works that are considered classics in the
field, including* I, Robot *(1950), the* Foundation *series, consisting
of the* Foundation *trilogy (1951-52) and the concluding novel*
Foundation's Edge *(1982), as well as the short story ''Nightfall,''
which was voted the best work of science fiction ever in a poll
conducted by the Science Fiction Writers of America in 1971.
Since coauthoring a biochemistry textbook in 1950, Asimov has
written numerous science texts and articles that display his talent
for popularizing scientific writing. He is also the author of children's books, humorous and mythological pieces, and critical
studies of the Bible and the works of Shakespeare. In the following
excerpt, originally published in 1980, Asimov applies a biograph-
ically oriented analysis to* Nineteen Eighty-Four. *He writes that
after Orwell was wounded during the Spanish civil war, he devoted the rest of his life to a private campaign against Stalinist
communism, ''determined to win in words the battle he had lost
in action.'' Asimov finds that the novel functions only as a denunciation of Stalinist totalitarianism. It is a failure as prophesy
and as science fiction, Asimov writes, because the Party's methods
of control would fail if put into practice, and because Orwell
''lacked the capacity'' to imagine such technological advances
as computers and robots, which would be necessary to maintain
the totalitarian society of* Nineteen Eighty-Four.]

[*1984*] attempted to show what life would be like in a world
of total evil, in which those controlling the government kept
themselves in power by brute force, by distorting the truth, by
continually rewriting history, by mesmerizing the people generally.

This evil world was placed only thirty-five years in the future
so that even men who were already in their early middle age
at the time the book was published might live to see it if they
lived out a normal lifetime. (p. 275)

[*1984*] described society as a vast worldwide extension of Stalinist Russia in the 1930s, pictured with the venom of a rival
left-wing sectary. Other forms of totalitarianism play a small
role. There are one or two mentions of the Nazis and of the
Inquisition. At the very start, there is a reference or two to
Jews, almost as though they were going to prove the objects
of persecution, but that vanishes almost at once, as though
Orwell didn't want readers to mistake the villains for Nazis.

The picture is of Stalinism, and Stalinism only.

By the time the book came out in 1949, the Cold War was at its height. The book therefore proved popular. It was almost a matter of patriotism in the West to buy it and talk about it, and perhaps even to read parts of it, although it is my opinion that more people bought it and talked about it than read it, for it is a dreadfully dull book—didactic, repetitious, and all but motionless.

It was most popular at first with people who leaned toward the conservative side of the political spectrum, for it was clearly an anti-Soviet polemic, and the picture of life it projected in the London of 1984 was very much as conservatives imagined life in the Moscow of 1949 to be.

During the McCarthy era in the United States, *1984* became increasingly popular with those who leaned toward the liberal side of the political spectrum, for it seemed to them that the United States of the early 1950s was beginning to move in the direction of thought-control and that all the viciousness Orwell had depicted was on its way toward us. (pp. 277-78)

Even if Stalinism and McCarthyism are disregarded, however, more and more Americans were becoming aware of just how ''big'' the government was getting; how high taxes were; how increasingly rules and regulations permeated business and even ordinary life; how information concerning every facet of private life was entering the files not only of government bureaus but of private credit systems.

1984, therefore, came to stand not for Stalinism, or even for dictatorship in general—but merely for government. Even governmental paternalism seemed ''1984ish'' and the catch phrase ''Big Brother is watching you'' came to mean everything that was too big for the individual to control. It was not only big government and big business that was a symptom of *1984* but big science, big labor, big anything. (p. 278)

Many people think of *1984* as a science fiction novel, but almost the only item about *1984* that would lead one to suppose this is the fact that it is purportedly laid in the future.

Not so! Orwell had no feel for the future, and the displacement of the story is much more geographical than temporal. The London in which the story is placed is not so much moved thirty-five years forward in time, from 1949 to 1984, as it is moved a thousand miles east in space to Moscow.

Orwell imagines Great Britain to have gone through a revolution similar to the Russian Revolution and to have gone through all the stages that Soviet development did. He can think of almost no variations on the theme. The Soviets had a series of purges in the 1930s, so the Ingsoc (English Socialism) had a series of purges in the 1950s.

The Soviets converted one of their revolutionaries, Leon Trotsky, into a villain, leaving his opponent, Joseph Stalin, as a hero. The Ingsoc, therefore, convert one of their revolutionaries, Emmanuel Goldstein, into a villain, leaving his opponent, with a moustache like Stalin, as a hero. There is no ability to make minor changes, even. Goldstein, like Trotsky, has ''a lean Jewish face, with a great fuzzy aureole of white hair and a small goatee beard.'' Orwell apparently does not want to confuse the issue by giving Stalin a different name so he calls him merely ''Big Brother.''

At the very beginning of the story, it is made clear that television (which was coming into existence at the time the book was written) served as a continuous means of indoctrination of the people, for sets cannot be turned off. (And, apparently,

in a deteriorating London in which nothing works, these sets never fail.)

The great Orwellian contribution to future technology is that the television set is two-way, and that the people who are forced to hear and see the television screen can themselves be heard and seen at all times and are under constant supervision even while sleeping or in the bathroom. Hence, the meaning of the phrase ''Big Brother is watching you.''

This is an extraordinarily inefficient system of keeping everyone under control. To have a person being watched at all times means that some other person must be doing the watching at all times (at least in the Orwellian society) and must be doing so very narrowly, for there is a great development of the art of interpreting gesture and facial expression.

One person cannot watch more than one person in full concentration, and can only do so for a comparatively short time before attention begins to wander. I should guess, in short, that there may have to be five watchers for every person watched. And then, of course, the watchers must themselves be watched since no one in the Orwellian world is suspicion-free. Consequently, the system of oppression by two-way television simply will not work.

Orwell himself realized this by limiting its workings to the Party members. The ''proles'' (proletariat), for whom Orwell cannot hide his British-upper-class contempt, are left largely to themselves as subhuman. (At one point in the book, he says that any prole that shows ability is killed—a leaf taken out of the Spartan treatment of their helots twenty-five hundred years ago.)

Furthermore, he has a system of volunteer spies in which children report on their parents, and neighbors on each other. This cannot possibly work well since eventually everyone reports everyone else and it all has to be abandoned.

Orwell was unable to conceive of computers or robots, or he would have placed everyone under nonhuman surveillance. Our own computers to some extent do this in the IRS, in credit files, and so on, but that does not take us toward *1984,* except in fevered imaginations. Computers and tyranny do not necessarily go hand in hand. Tyrannies have worked very well without computers (consider the Nazis) and the most computerized nations in today's world are also the least tyrannical.

Orwell lacks the capacity to see (or invent) small changes. His hero finds it difficult in his world of 1984 to get shoelaces or razor blades. So would I in the real world of the 1980s, for so many people use slip-on shoes and electric razors.

Then, too, Orwell had the technophobic fixation that every technological advance is a slide downhill. (pp. 279-80)

This is not science fiction, but a distorted nostalgia for a past that never was. (p. 281)

Nor was Orwell particularly prescient in the strictly social aspects of the future he was presenting, with the result that the Orwellian world of 1984 is incredibly old-fashioned when compared with the real world of the 1980s.

Orwell imagines no new vices, for instance. His characters are all gin hounds and tobacco addicts, and part of the horror of his picture of 1984 is his eloquent description of the *low quality* of the gin and tobacco.

He foresees no new drugs, no marijuana, no synthetic hallucinogens. No one expects an s.f. writer to be precise and exact

Political division of the world in Nineteen Eighty-Four.
Reprinted by permission of Stanford Alumni Association.

in his forecasts, but surely one would expect him to invent *some* differences.

In his despair (or anger), Orwell forgets the virtues human beings have. All his characters are, in one way or another, weak, or sadistic, or sleazy, or stupid, or repellent. This may be how most people are, or how Orwell wants to indicate they will *all* be under tyranny, but it seems to me that under even the worst tyrannies, so far, there have been brave men and women who have withstood the tyrants to the death and whose personal histories are luminous flames in the surrounding darkness. If only because there is no hint of this in *1984,* it does not resemble the real world of the 1980s.

Nor did he foresee any difference in the role of women or any weakening of the feminine stereotype of 1949. There are only two female characters of importance. One is a strong, brainless "prole" woman who is an endless washerwoman, endlessly singing a popular song with words of the type familiar in the 1930s and 1940s (at which Orwell shudders fastidiously as "trashy," in blissful non-anticipation of hard rock).

The other is the heroine, Julia, who is sexually promiscuous (but is at least driven to courage by her interest in sex) and is otherwise brainless. When the hero, Winston, reads to her the book within a book that explains the nature of the Orwellian world, she responds by falling asleep—but then since the treatise Winston reads is stupefyingly soporific, this may be an indication of Julia's good sense rather than the reverse.

In short, if *1984 must* be considered science fiction, then it is very bad science fiction.

Orwell's *1984* is a picture of all-powerful government, and it has helped make the notion of "big government" a very frightening one.

We have to remember, though, that the world of the late 1940s, during which Orwell was writing his book, was one in which there had been, and still were, big governments with true tyrants—individuals whose every wish, however unjust, cruel or vicious, was law. (pp. 281-82)

Orwell, however, had no time for either Mussolini or Hitler. His enemy was Stalin, and at the time that *1984* was published, Stalin had ruled the Soviet Union in a rib-breaking bear hug for twenty-five years, had survived a terrible war in which his nation suffered enormous losses and yet was now stronger than

ever. To Orwell, it must have seemed that neither time nor fortune could budge Stalin, but that he would live on forever with ever increasing strength. —And that was how Orwell pictured Big Brother.

Of course, that was not the way it really was. Orwell didn't live long enough to see it but Stalin died only three years after *1984* was published, and it was not long after that that his regime was denounced as a tyranny by—guess who—the Soviet leadership.

The Soviet Union is still the Soviet Union, but it is not Stalinist, and the enemies of the state are no longer liquidated (Orwell uses "vaporized" instead, such small changes being all he can manage) with quite such abandon. . . .

Big Brothers *do* die, or at least they have so far, and when they die, the government changes, always for the milder.

This is not to say that new tyrants may not make themselves felt, but they will die, too. At least in the real 1980s we have every confidence they will and the undying Big Brother is not yet a real threat. (p. 283)

In addition to the immortality of Big Brother, Orwell presents two other ways of maintaining an eternal tyranny.

First—present someone or something to hate. In the Orwellian world it was Emmanuel Goldstein for whom hate was built up and orchestrated in a robotized mass function.

This is nothing new, of course. Every nation in the world has used various neighbors for the purpose of hate. This sort of thing is so easily handled and comes as such second nature to humanity that one wonders why there have to be the organized hate drives in the Orwellian world.

It needs scarcely any clever psychological mass movements to make Arabs hate Israelis and Greeks hate Turks and Catholic Irish hate Protestant Irish—and vice versa in each case. To be sure, the Nazis organized mass meetings of delirium that every participant seemed to enjoy, but it had no permanent effect. Once the war moved onto German soil, the Germans surrendered as meekly as though they had never Sieg-Heiled in their lives.

Second—rewrite history. Almost every one of the few individuals we meet in *1984* has, as his job, the rapid rewriting of the past, the readjustment of statistics, the overhauling of newspapers—as though anyone is going to take the trouble to pay attention to the past anyway.

This Orwellian preoccupation with the minutiae of "historical proof" is typical of the political sectarian who is always quoting what has been said and done in the past to prove a point to someone on the other side who is always quoting something to the opposite effect that has been said and done.

As any politician knows, no evidence of any kind is ever required. It is only necessary to make a statement—any statement—forcefully enough to have an audience believe it. No one will check the lie against the facts, and, if they do, they will disbelieve the facts. Do you think the German people in 1939 *pretended* that the Poles had attacked them and started World War II? No! Since they were told that was so, they believed it as seriously as you and I believe that they attacked the Poles.

To be sure, the Soviets put out new editions of their Encyclopedia in which politicians rating a long biography in earlier editions are suddenly omitted entirely, and this is no doubt the germ of the Orwellian notion, but the chances of carrying it as far as is described in *1984* seems to me to be nil—not because it is beyond human wickedness, but because it is totally unnecessary.

Orwell makes much of "Newspeak" as an organ of repression—the conversion of the English language into so limited and abbreviated an instrument that the very vocabulary of dissent vanishes. (pp. 284-85)

As a matter of fact, political obfuscation has tended to use many words rather than few, long words rather than short, to extend rather than to reduce. Every leader of inadequate education or limited intelligence hides behind exuberant inebriation of loquacity. . . .

We are therefore in no way approaching Newspeak in its condensed form, though we have always had Newspeak in its extended form and always will have. (p. 285)

Although Orwell seemed, by and large, to be helplessly stuck in the world of 1949, in one respect at least he showed himself to be remarkably prescient, and that was in foreseeing the tripartite split of the world of the 1980s.

The international world of *1984* is a world of three superpowers: Oceania, Eurasia, and Eastasia—and that fits in, very roughly, with the three actual superpowers of the 1980s: the United States, the Soviet Union, and China. (p. 286)

He also foresaw a permanent state of war among the three; a condition of permanent stalemate with the alliances ever-shifting, but always two against the strongest. This was the old-fashioned "balance of power" system which was used in ancient Greece, in medieval Italy, and in early modern Europe.

Orwell's mistake lay in thinking there had to be actual war to keep the merry-go-round of the balance of power in being. In fact, in one of the more laughable parts of the book, he goes on and on concerning the necessity of permanent war as a means of consuming the world's production of resources and thus keeping the social stratification of upper, middle, and lower classes in being. (This sounds like a very Leftist explanation of war as the result of a conspiracy worked out with great difficulty.)

In actual fact, the decades since 1945 have been remarkably war-free as compared with the decades before it. There have been local wars in profusion, but no general war. But then, war is not required as a desperate device to consume the world's resources. That can be done by such other devices as endless increase in population and in energy use, neither of which Orwell considers.

Orwell did not foresee any of the significant economic changes that have taken place since World War II. He did not foresee the role of oil or its declining availability or its increasing price, or the escalating power of those nations who control it. I don't recall his mentioning the word "oil."

But perhaps it is close enough to mark Orwellian prescience here, if we substitute "cold war" for "war." There has been, in fact, a more or less continual "cold war" that has served to keep employment high and solve some short-term economic problems (at the cost of creating long-term greater ones). And this cold war is enough to deplete resources.

Furthermore, the alliances shift as Orwell foresaw and very nearly as suddenly. When the United States seemed all-powerful, the Soviet Union and China were both vociferously anti-

American and in a kind of alliance. As American power decreased, the Soviet Union and China fell apart and, for a while, each of the three powers inveighed against the other two equally. Then, when the Soviet Union came to seem particularly powerful, a kind of alliance sprang up between the United States and China, as they cooperated in vilifying the Soviet Union, and spoke softly of each other.

In *1984* every shift of alliance involved an orgy of history rewriting. In real life, no such folly is necessary. The public swings from side to side easily, accepting the change in circumstance with no concern for the past at all. (pp. 287-88)

To summarize, then: George Orwell in *1984* was, in my opinion, engaging in a private feud with Stalinism, rather than attempting to forecast the future. He did not have the science fictional knack of foreseeing a plausible future and, in actual fact, in almost all cases, the world of *1984* bears no relation to the real world of the 1980s.

The world may go communist, if not by 1984, then by some not very much later date; or it may see civilization destroyed. If this happens, however, it will happen in a fashion quite different from that depicted in *1984* and if we try to prevent either eventuality by imagining that *1984* is accurate, then we will be defending ourselves against assaults from the wrong direction and we will lose. (p. 289)

Isaac Asimov, " 'Nineteen Eighty-Four'," in his Asimov on Science Fiction, *Doubleday & Company, Inc., 1981, pp. 275-89.*

MURRAY SPERBER (essay date 1980)

[*In the following excerpt Sperber offers a psychological interpretation of* Nineteen Eighty-Four, *finding that the novel represents Orwell's lifelong feelings about and responses to authority figures and externally applied controls.*]

George Orwell's *1984* has sold over eleven million English language copies; it has so penetrated the culture that most people can tell you that Big Brother is watching and that the year of the title is ominous. But *1984* seems better known and commented upon—there are hundreds of book chapters, articles, and reviews—than carefully read. Particularly overlooked is its plot or rhetorical structure: Orwell's design for the work and his design upon us, his readers. This lack of commentary is a tribute to Orwell's rhetorical success: because *1984* is horrifying and suspenseful, its writing strong and polished, readers are caught inside and gain little distance on its structure.

Most critics have focused on *1984*'s politics, how the book reflects certain political concerns of its author, its time, and the entire modern age. Many writers have also connected the work to Orwell's previous writings as well as the genre of dystopian fiction, and a few have discussed it in terms of its author's physical and psychological condition when he wrote it. No writer, however, has connected Orwell's plan for the book to his lifelong psychological feelings, especially his responses to authority and control, or discussed how the author manipulates his readers' feelings in the most profound way and for definite psychological ends.

Analysis of *1984* generally begins and finishes with political and literary interpretations. If we focus, however, on Orwell's rhetorical and psychological strategy, we might explain the book and its power more fully. Orwell explains his rhetorical plan for *1984* within the book itself (and rhetoric, how writers manipulate words and readers, was one of his favorite, at times, obsessive subjects). In describing Winston's reaction to Goldstein's book, he offers both a definition of literature and a clue to his plan for *1984*:

> The book fascinated him . . . In a sense it told him nothing that was new, but that was part of the attraction. It said what he would have said, if it had been possible for him to put his scattered thoughts in order. It was the product of a mind similar to his own, but enormously more powerful, more systematic, less fear-ridden. The best books, he perceived, are those that tell you what you know already.

The author of Goldstein's book is to Winston as the author of *1984* (and Goldstein's book) is to us. Orwell wants to tell us what he thinks we already know, fear, and have not articulated. The glass paperweight that fascinates Winston is a crucial metaphor. . . . The paperweight symbolizes the enclosed world that Winston and Julia try to create at Charrington's and, since the Thought Police have constructed that world, the enclosed world of Oceania. In a wider sense, the paperweight can stand for our relationship to the book: to read *1984* is to enter Orwell's sealed world.

From the very first sentence—"the clocks were striking thirteen"—we know that this world is askew, and we move through it, alongside what appears to be a traditional hero, Winston Smith, without knowing exactly where we are going. . . . Orwell wants his reader to experience life in Oceania, and in lieu of waiting for the world of 1984—indeed, as a way of warning against it—he places his reader within his fictive world.

1984 is filled with clues, double-meanings, false leads, false hopes, all carefully planted and nurtured by the author. The book has its Thriller as well as Boys' Adventure aspects—Orwell was very interested in these popular forms—and during our initial reading, we are caught up in the suspense and action of the plot. Only toward the end of the book do we begin to see how Winston, and we, have been tricked and manipulated. O'Brien tells Winston that "For seven years I have watched over you," . . . and later Winston acknowledges "that for seven years the Thought Police had watched him like a beetle under a magnifying glass." . . . (pp. 213-15)

Our hopes for Winston and Julia had brushed aside the many warnings. (p. 215)

From the beginning, with the two minutes of hate, we are repulsed by the mob and in sympathy with the odd-person-out. Winston appears as the traditional hero of fiction, and we empathize with his struggle, his romance, his entire life. Like Winston, we are attracted to O'Brien and trust him. There are clues that he/we are wrong. . . . Throughout the meeting with O'Brien, there are foreshadowings of doom, but partly because O'Brien is such a persuasive figure and the idea of rebellion so right, we cannot truly believe in Winston's imminent destruction.

Who is O'Brien and why is he doing these things? He seems to be the perfect organization man—or in contemporary parlance, the gamesman executive—for he knows the score but keeps playing the game, indeed, keeps the game playing. O'Brien admits that he needs Winston as much as the latter needs him—interesting rebels like Winston make life and power in Oceania worthwhile. At some level, O'Brien even resembles Winston—they are the only two persons whom we encounter who can

articulate the concept of rebellion—and possibly O'Brien needs to squash Winston's rebellion to justify his own acquiescence to the system, to prove again to himself the wrongness of his rebellious feelings.

Winston is enlightened by the book that O'Brien gives him; later, O'Brien claims part authorship, but the book reads like an authentic revolutionary document. In *1984*, both statements could be true. Winston luxuriates in the physical pleasure of solitude and reading. We share this pleasure because we are also readers and because Winston is the only person in Oceania who is doing something from our world. The book contains foreshadowings of his destruction, but toward the end of his reading, with Julia next to him, he has "a strong, sleepy, confident feeling. He was safe, everything was all right." . . . (pp. 215-16)

The lovers are from traditional romance, and Julia is little more than a stereotypical sex object: they try to overcome great opposition, seek a place to be alone, and when they appear to succeed, they gain hope. But Orwell brings them, and us, to the most optimistic moment in the book immediately before he sends them low. Winston hears the washerwoman singing her Cockney song, and he thinks about how the proles will win in the end and how intellectuals, like himself, will die away. "'We are the dead,'" he tells Julia. Again, the double meaning. "'You are the dead,' said an iron voice behind them." . . . A single meaning: the dream ends and permanent nightmare begins. Orwell tells us, "Unthinkable to disobey the iron voice from the wall." . . . (p. 216)

All of the double-meanings unravel from the arrest. We see the blindness of Winston's and Julia's pleasure: every moment was watched, possibly choreographed by the Thought Police. Winston is not only brought low when he is most hopeful but when he is most vulnerable. He is in bed, naked with his lover. His arrest reverberates back through all of the scenes in the room and suggests that all safe and comforting places are traps. (pp. 216-17)

Like Winston, we have been manipulated. We are attracted to Charrington's shop and the room above—it is a place of peace and comfort in the violent 1984 world, and it is from our world. Mr. Charrington seems to represent English decency, and he even gives a speech about privacy and the importance of "common courtesy." [Charrington] is out of the great English fiction tradition of caricature, and, because we recognize him, we trust him and are comforted.

Orwell provides clues about Charrington. If we ignore them, he suggests, if we are so foolish and sentimental as to believe in obsolete people like Charrington, we might never make it through the modern political age and will end up in Oceania. Winston's ongoing interest in the nursery rhyme about the bells of London is crucial: the first verses are nostalgic and comforting, and Charrington is able to help him with them; the conclusion, recited to Winston immediately upon arrest, tells him, "Here comes a chopper to chop off your head." Orwell implies that if we are too ignorant to remember the whole rhyme, we become the naive child in the children's game played to the rhyme. We deserve to get our heads or emotions chopped off.

Yet, for all of the rhetorical preparation, we are still not ready for the torture scenes. The prisoners and our emotions are manipulated by standard tricks—the starving prisoner appeals to Winston's sense of pity—and by the psychological threat of Room 101. Orwell makes every reader try to concieve of his or her worst fears, although he gives Winston, not "some quite trivial thing," . . . but the more general fear of rats.

Winston's fate is the final trap for the reader. He ends lobotomized, living out his death. The hero neither wins (Melodrama) nor dies (Tragedy); he is condemned to live in stasis. Winston's fate short circuits our feelings for him. We do not feel pleased nor purged, merely chilled and depressed.

Throughout *1984,* Orwell tries and often succeeds in rendering the horrors of a subjective universe. But, at times, especially during the torture scenes, rather than convince us by sleight of plot, he seems to want to fasten us to the table as O'Brien does Winston.

A rhetorical analysis of *1984* presents a series of paradoxes: the author condemns authoritarian deception but tightly manipulates his hero and reader; the author condemns brutality and torture but moves his hero and reader through some of the most vivid torture scenes in the language; and the author condemns brainwashing but reworks his hero's mind and through literary devices tries to reshape his readers'. These paradoxes are not solved, however, by further rhetorical analysis. Relentlessly they point to the psychological level of the book, what *1984* meant to its author when he wrote it and what it means to us when we participate in his fiction.

How autobiographical is *1984;* is Winston Smith, George Orwell? Certainly not in a literal one-to-one sense, but probably in a fictive, projective way. Orwell, sitting down in the late 1940s and imagining the world of *1984,* seems to have asked himself, as most of us would, how he or a person very similar to him would do in that world. With that idea as a point of departure, both back into his private history and forward with his creative imagination, he moves his projection, Winston Smith, around his very un-brave new world.

Like Orwell, Winston is a writer who spends much of his time mocking or despairing the decline of literacy. Winston dislikes the Party intellectuals, especially their power lust, as Orwell distrusted the leftist intellectuals of his era. But, in *1984,* dislike is met with betrayal. . . . (pp. 217-18)

When Winston first thinks of keeping a diary, Orwell tells us "All he had to do was to transfer to paper the interminable restless monologue that had been running inside his head for years." . . . This is true of the author and his composition of *1984.* The bind between Winston and Orwell extends beyond the act of writing: Winston is the last hero in Orwell's almost continuous line of isolated heroes, odd-persons-out, a line that includes not only fictional characters like Flory, Dorothy Hare, Gordon Comstock, and George Bowling, but Orwell's narrative persona in his essays and memoirs.

When Orwell was working on *1984,* his only other major piece of writing was his memoir of childhood and adolescence, "Such, Such, Were the Joys. . . ." Orwell relates how, as a child, he was obsessively aware of his body and its awkwardness; Winston mirrors this concern. In both works, Orwell describes the brutality of children and the fear that they can generate. The Brotherhood, the secret organization, seems to connect to schoolboy fantasies and fears: is it real, how widespread is its membership and power? Its very name, as well as the litany that Winston and Julia swear on its behalf, echo the world of fearfulness and cruelty in "Such, Such Were the Joys. . . ."

The analogies between the memoir and the fiction are numerous and extend to the way that Winston is taught by O'Brien: if we substitute for O'Brien's dial and his electric torture ma-chine, the silver pencil and the riding crop with which the headmaster hit Orwell at school when he did not recite his lessons absolutely correctly, we can see Winston's reeducation as a mirror of Orwell's own education. (pp. 218-19)

Orwell was fascinated by schooling. *1984* is an education for its hero and reader; its course title is the possibilities of betrayal: political, the Party and its former and present members; familial, children turning in parents and vice versa; sexual, Julia and Winston; and personal, Winston's self-betrayal. "Such, Such" contains the same theme: schoolmates betraying each other and the system betraying the individual. In Orwell's world, with schooling comes punishment: for Winston's stupidity, Room 101; for ours, the disappointment at the denouement.

To say, however, that what Orwell "did in *1984* was to send everybody in England to an enormous Crossgates to be as miserable as he had been," as Anthony West charges [see *TCLC,* Vol. 2], is to minimize the point of Orwell's fiction. His plan is much grander than an attack on his old school. Orwell transforms his experiences—some based on adolescence but most from earlier childhood and later adult events—into a world of fears and fantasies that will encompass all people, during all periods of their lives, for all of history. (p. 219)

George Orwell, because of his very acute sense of political, psychological, and even physical persecution in the late 1940s, was interested in exploring the world of human persecution, walking around inside of it, and reproducing it in literary form. Orwell, like most people, had some paranoid feelings; but, unlike most people, he did not turn away or repress his paranoid feelings; rather, he explored them and recreated a version of them in *1984* (he even conceived a *1984* word for repression: Crimestop, which "means the faculty of stopping short, as though by instinct, at the threshold of any dangerous thought.") . . . (pp. 220-21)

1984, with its telescreens, Thought Police, thoughtcrime, and Big Brother always watching is a persecuting, paranoid-inducing world. Wartime and postwar London oppressed Orwell, and he turned it into the surface details of oppression in *1984;* political events, the Socialist government in Britain, the Stalinist governments in the East, and the Cold War mongering ones in the West, depressed him, and he turned them into the political oppression of *1984;* and even literary events, especially the publishing problems with his previous book, *Animal Farm* (it was turned down by a number of publishers, Orwell believed for political reasons) disgusted him and contributed to the writing machines, the end of literacy in *1984.* Add to this, his slow death from tuberculosis, his decision to live and work on the Jura Islands off the coast of Scotland—a cold, damp place, exactly the worst climate for tuberculosis—and we see the world of real and imagined persecution surrounding and permeating the composition of *1984.* We also begin to understand why Orwell transmuted this world into his fiction, and why he felt impelled to place his reader inside of it—in part to share his horror, in part to warn against it.

Very early in *1984,* we learn that "somewhere or other, quite anonymous, there were the directing brains who coordinated the whole effort and laid down the lines of policy." . . . We never see the anonymous "they," nor even find hard evidence of their existence, but we have a constant feeling, connected to Winston's fear and love of Big Brother, that "they" exist. . . .

[In] *1984,* the source of persecution is the father figure, Big Brother, and the father surrogate, O'Brien (these seem analogous to Schreber's God and Dr. Fleichsig). From his first appearance, O'Brien seems to be the good loving father whom Winston seeks. But in fact, he "was directing everything . . . He was the tormentor, he was the protector, he was the inquisitor, he was the friend." . . . Charrington also appears kindly and paternal, but later he literally removes his mask. Good fathers do not exist in the *1984* world. (p. 221)

Like most artists, Orwell explored and expressed his emotions, but in *1984,* because of his circumstances while writing the book, he worked more deeply and thoroughly than ever before. Wisely, he chose fantasy as his vehicle—not his usual essay, memoir, or realistic fiction—and this provided the mask and the distance for his fullest expression of personal vision. *1984* is ostensibly about the future, but much of the psychological intensity comes from the author's past, not only his feelings about school but much earlier experiences as well.

Winston is in search of his past: O'Brien, the apparently good father, has the key. . . . [Winston's] desire to rediscover and repair the past impels him, in part, to Charrington's and to his inevitable destruction.

Family love, human love, is impossible in the *1984* world. Because the past does not exist, neither does a childhood of pleasure and growth. Winston finds the Oceanic version of childhood in the cellars of the Ministry of Love, O'Brien's "place": "In this place you could not feel anything, except pain and the foreknowledge of pain." . . . And Room 101, "many meters underground, as deep down as it was possible to go," . . . is Winston's unconscious, his memories as well as his present and future prospects. Winston has made a brave attempt to become sane—to understand his past and to change his present—but in an insane world, his attempt is doomed. In Oceania, the psyche has permanently fragmented: the Party is super-ego; the proles, id; and all ego functions—what Winston seeks—have been destroyed.

Winston's search for loving parents is futile. The only permitted parents are the Party. Throughout *1984,* there is an implied equation between the Party's control over people and parental control over children. Frequently we can substitute the word *parent* for Party: "she [Julia] had grasped the inner meaning of the Party's [the parents'] sexual puritanism . . . the sex instinct created a world of its own which was outside the Party's [the parents'] control and which therefore had to be destroyed if possible." . . . If one has sexual relations, one might love an outsider, esteem oneself, break out of the insane family, and develop autonomy. The psychological meaning, however, cannot and should not be isolated from the political, literary, rhetorical, and even local meanings of the passage: the reference to the puritanism in Stalinist Russia; the literary trope of parental opposition to lovers; the rhetorical device, lovemaking in Oceania as a crime to heighten Winston's and Julia's fears of persecution; and, the local reference, the ongoing puritanism of England. This brings everything back to George Orwell who grew up in a puritanical English household and boarding-school. After Winston and Julia make love for the first time, Orwell writes, "Their embrace had been a battle, the climax a victory. It was a blow struck against the Party." . . . (pp. 222-23)

The goal of Oceanic society is to make people into fearful, obedient children, existing within a totally subjective and irrational universe. *Newspeak* is the language of the childish,

allowing minimal verbal expression. The attempt to break out of permanent childhood and construct an individual life becomes, in the insane world of *1984,* a schizophrenic act: Julia "realized that she herself was doomed, that sooner or later the Thought Police would catch her and kill her, but with another part of her mind she believed that it was somehow possible to construct a secret world in which you could live as you choose." . . . (pp. 223-24)

In the cellars of the Ministry of Love, Winston learns that "There is only one offense" in Oceania—opposing the Party . . . Winston's arrest and torture confirm the pessimism, as well as the rhetorical structure, of the entire book: all rebellion is doomed, all parents evil and omnipotent. In the beginning, Winston had thought that "in any case the Party was invincible. It would always exist, and it would always be the same. You could only rebel against it by secret disobedience." . . . Winston is a bad child, a rebel; he must learn how to act, how to become a permanent and obedient child—thus O'Brien's reindoctrination of him. Winston must be broken down, his growth toward autonomous adulthood—greatest after reading Goldstein's book—must be reversed; his earliest childhood fears must be realized and placed in permanent control of his psyche.

In *1984,* Orwell captures well the return to the source of all fears and fantasies, including paranoid ones, the time when parents are omnipotent and children powerless. . . . Under torture, Winston regresses until he is a whimpering infant. . . . (pp. 224-25)

The reindoctrination process is a means for Winston to learn his lessons correctly this time, to internalize the Party/parental control so that no outside force is needed. The process is successful. . . . Like a child, he cries and then is comforted—it was all right, everything is all right—and he is reunited at last with the omnipotent parent.

This is a chilling end, a world where no one attains autonomous, rational adulthood, where we are always the victim of brutal parents. Apparently, this was George Orwell's greatest fear; this is the bottom stratum of *1984.* (p. 225)

Orwell portrays the irrational demands of the parental world, and he understands Winston's childishness. But, at this juncture, he separates himself from his hero. Orwell was never going to be like the others; he is not Winston. The latter joyfully embraces permanent childhood; Orwell places his "boyhood" in the past and condemns himself to isolated maturity.

Orwell's novel, devastating in its demonstration of how easily we can be tricked and controlled, is nonetheless the testimony of a person willing to carry the pain and grief of not being tricked, of seeing through the traps and self-betrayals, of refusing to be joyful at the price of Big Brother's embrace. What we get, as readers, is not Winston's joy but Orwell's pain: thus the book is an honest warning. The world of *1984* can be prevented if we know and resist the wish in ourselves to be comfortable, to be like the rest, with the father. But resist or not, it will be very painful: the politics of individualism are hard.

George Orwell, unlike Winston Smith, always spoke up; indeed the act of writing the novel was his last protest. Winston never finished his diary; Orwell wrote *1984.* He wanted to break through the noise and claptrap, especially government propaganda, of his age, and he chose a most extreme rhetorical form as his vehicle. The success of *1984* validates the wisdom of his choice. (pp. 225-26)

Murray Sperber, " 'Gazing into the Glass Paper-weight': The Structure and Psychology of Orwell's '1984'," in Modern Fiction Studies, *Vol. 26, No. 2, Summer, 1980, pp. 213-26.*

BERNARD CRICK   (essay date 1980)

[*Crick was the first biographer to be granted unrestricted access to the private papers held by Sonia Orwell, Orwell's second wife; for that reason his* George Orwell: A Life *is generally regarded as the most reliable account of Orwell's life. Many commentators, however, maintain that in his strictly factual account of Orwell's life Crick fails to convey any sense of the man's personality. In his introduction to the biography Crick defends his biographical approach, writing "I do not think that one can look into Orwell's mind . . . or anyone else's. The best that a biographer can do is to understand the relationship between the writer and the man . . . by examining their journey together in detail, always remembering that what they did and how they reacted to what happened along the way will tell us more than constantly analysing and reanalysing their 'characters' and the difference between them." Crick maintains that he has tried "simply to write as straightforward and informative a life as possible." In the following excerpt, he discusses the political nature of Orwell's writings, characterizing him as a left-wing intellectual and placing him among the three most important political writers in English history.*]

I saw and still see Orwell as someone who fully succeeded, despite his tragically early death, in the task he set himself in mid-career. He succeeded in such a way that he moved, even in his lifetime, from being a minor English writer to being a world figure, a name to set argument going wherever books are read. In 1946 he wrote in **"Why I Write"**: "What I have most wanted to do throughout the past ten years is to make political writing into an art," adding that "looking back through my work, I see that it is invariably where I lacked a *political* purpose that I wrote lifeless books and was betrayed into purple passages, sentences without meaning, decorative adjectives and humbug generally."

Orwell came to see himself as a "political writer", and both words were of equal weight. He did not claim to be a political philosopher, nor simply a political polemicist: he was a writer, a general writer, author of novels, descriptive works that I will call "documentaries", essays, poems and innumerable book reviews and newspaper columns. But if his best work was not always directly political in the subject matter, it always exhibited political consciousness. In that sense, he is the finest political writer in English since Swift, satirist, stylist, moralist and stirrer, who influenced him so much. (pp. xiii-xiv)

Orwell's reputation and influence have increased since his death and show no sign of diminishing. The actual life of such a writer is, alas, only half the story. His greatest influence has been posthumous and has been for liberty and tolerance, but not as passive things to be enjoyed, rather as republican virtues to be exercised: the duty of speaking out boldly ("the secret of liberty," said Pericles, "is courage") and of tolerating rival opinions not out of indifference, but out of principle and because of their seriousness. And plain speaking always meant to him clear writing: communality, common sense, courage and a common style. He saw his literary and his political values as perfectly complementary to each other, he could not conceive of them being in contradiction—even if plain style sometimes limited the kind of literature he could enjoy as well as the development of his own more theoretical ideas. His own style became a cutting edge which, with much trial and error, by fits and starts, he slowly forged into a weapon of legendary strength. He made common words sharp, made them come to life again until under his spell one thinks twice before one uses any polysyllables, still less neologisms.

So in the term "political writer" the second word is as important as the first. Obscure, pretentious or trendy language was to Orwell always a sign of indecision or of deceit, as much when used by private men as by party hacks. (p. xiv)

He became a Socialist (somewhat later than people think) and denied fiercely, whether in reviewing a book by Professor Hayek or in the story of **Animal Farm,** that equality necessarily negates liberty. On the contrary, he stood in that lineage of English socialists who, through Morris, Blatchford, Tawney, Cole, Laski and Bevan, have argued that only in a more egalitarian and fraternal society can liberties flourish and abound for the common people. It was a tradition that stressed the importance of freely held values, to which the structural arguments of Marxism were, at best, only marginal. Yet his influence has been to reprove backsliding socialists, to sustain democratic Socialists (he always capitalised it thus) and to win back Communist fellow-travellers rather than to convert non-socialists. Many liberals seem unimpressed by Orwell's socialist values, taking what they want from him, admiring him rather abstractly as a *political* writer, but not wanting to come to terms with the content of his politics, with his actual views about the needs of humanity (always humanity, and not just Europeans) and the constraints of a capitalist, acquisitive society. Some either ignore his socialism or espouse a legend that by 1948 and in **Nineteen Eighty-Four** he had abandoned it. . . . Part of his anger against the Communists was not only that they had become despots who squandered human life and despised liberty, but that they were also discrediting democratic Socialism. There is really no mystery about the general character of his politics. From 1936 onwards he was first a follower of the Independent Labour Party and then a *Tribune* socialist; that is, he took his stand among those who were to the Left or on the Left of the Labour Party: fiercely egalitarian, libertarian and democratic, but by Continental comparisons, surprisingly untheoretical, a congregation of secular evangelicals.

What was remarkable in Orwell was not his political position, which was common enough, but that he demanded publicly that his own side should live up to their principles, both in their lives and in their policies, should respect the liberty of others and tell the truth. Socialism could not come by seizure of power or by Act of Parliament, but only by convincing people in fair and open debate and by example. He would take no excuses and he mocked pretentious talk of "ideological necessity". Truth to tell, he made rather a name as a journalist by his skill in rubbing the fur of his own cat backwards. At times he was like those loyal and vociferous football supporters who are at their best when hurling complaint, sarcasm and abuse at their own long-suffering side. Sometimes, of course, it is deserved; and it may always be said to keep them on their toes. Small wonder that some of Orwell's fellow socialists have at times been tempted, like Raymond Williams . . . [see TCLC, Vol. 6], or like Isaac Deutscher in his polemic against **Nineteen Eighty-Four** [see *TCLC,* Vol. 2], to doubt whether he should be on their terraces at all. But he chose to and he was, whether they like it or not or would prefer quieter spectators. At most times there was a touch of the true Jacobin about him rather than the John Stuart Millite.

Certainly to call Orwell a supreme political writer, both for what he said and how he said it, is to point only to his major talent and influence. There were other good things as well. He began as a novelist and was planning a new novel when he died. Later he repudiated his early novels, except *Burmese Days* and *Coming Up For Air.* (pp. xiv-xv)

He developed as an essayist. Much critical opinion now locates his genius in his essays. There is much to be said for this view, especially if *Down and Out in Paris and London, The Road to Wigan Pier,* and *Homage to Catalonia* can be treated as long essays, since they are all as unusual a mixture of description and speculation as one of them is of fact and fiction. His best essays are by no means all political, though those on politics and literature, language and censorship have become classics of English prose, anthologised and translated throughout the world, even where they are not supposed to be read. A small history could be written of *samizdat* and illegal translations of such essays and of *Animal Farm* and *Nineteen Eighty-Four* (read behind the Iron Curtain as angry satire rather than a pessimistic prophecy). (pp. xv-xvi)

While angry at injustice and intolerance, he never seemed to ask too much of ordinary people: his anger centred on the intellectuals, precisely because they hold or influence power and should know better. His politics were Left-wing, but many of his prejudices were conservative. And he wrote about many positive values that have nothing directly to do with politics, love of nature above all: he did not wish to live in a world in which everything could be manipulated, even for the public good. (p. xvi)

His patriotism is important. He was almost alone among Left-wing intellectuals in stressing the naturalness and positive virtues of loving, not exclusively but none the less intensely and unashamedly, one's native land. He held this view because of his rather old-fashioned radicalism that links his "Tory anarchist" or individualist phase to his final socialist period. . . . He was, indeed, a "revolutionary patriot". For he saw our heritage and the land itself as belonging to the common people, not to the gentry and the upper middle classes. . . . He held this view before the War, even in his anti-militarist, quasi-pacifist mood: it was neither an overreaction to accepting the necessity of war in September 1939 nor a lapse back to Edwardian jingoism. . . . But part of his anger was reserved for those intellectuals who had yielded the native field without a fight, departing for a shallow cosmopolitanism or, worse, staying at home to mock. He was intellectually but never socially intolerant of pacifists on this score. He detested their policies but defended their principles and liked their company. (pp. xvii-xviii)

Orwell was careful, amid all his diatribes, to distinguish between *patriotism,* as love of one's own native land (so that anyone who grows into that love can be a patriot), and *nationalism,* as a claim to natural superiority over others (so that States must naturally consist of one nation and seek to exclude others). It is typical that he makes this distinction, which is of extraordinary importance, briefly and almost in passing, neither elaborating it theoretically nor exploring its implications. But it is clear, deliberate, and it is there in his essay "Notes on Nationalism" of 1945.

Certainly there was a gentler patriotism in Orwell which preceded his socialism and stemmed from his love of English literature, customs and countryside. In many ways he remained socially conservative, or as his friend Cyril Connolly put it in a famous aphorism, "a revolutionary who was in love with the 1900s". Orwell said of himself in **"Why I Write"** of 1946, the same essay that declared himself to be a political writer:

"I am not able, and do not want, completely to abandon the world-view that I acquired in childhood. So long as I remain alive and well I shall continue to feel strongly about prose style, to love the surface of the earth and to take pleasure in solid objects and scraps of useless information." (p. xviii)

He is a specifically English writer and a specifically English character, both in his seeming amateurism—sometimes truly amateurish—and in his eccentricities. He lived and dressed as simply as he came to write, and in some ways as oddly. But he was never insular. He was steeped in French and also in Russian literature through translation, though hardly at all in German. He knew more about European and colonial politics in the 1930s and 1940s than most of his literary contemporaries, or politicians for that matter. He followed contemporary American writing closely but knew little about American history and politics—had he known more he might have avoided misunderstandings when *Animal Farm* and *Nineteen Eighty-Four* were published in America. His other best works also came to be reprinted and translated well and widely. He had things to say which are still of universal significance, more so than those of some far more systematic philosophical and academic thinkers. And something of his characteristic style, discursiveness and colloquial ease, the buttonholing directness, the zeal to write for a broad, rather than a purely intellectual public, must come across even in translation, for his style has influenced a generation of young writers in Germany, Japan and Italy, for instance, who do not all read him in the original. Throughout the world "Orwellian" means this English essayist's manner as well as the quite different connotation that "Orwellian" has gained from *Nineteen Eighty-Four*.

He is also, perhaps in the very security of his Englishness (it is Englishness, not Britishness, incidentally), a writer of historical stature on English national character. (pp. xviii-xix)

Some literary friends in Orwell's last years of fame never understood his politics nor accepted the importance he attached to politics in general. Cyril Connolly, for instance, often urged Orwell to get away from his political journalism and back to the writing or real novels. Such English intellectuals themselves represented that divorce of political and literary sensibility which Orwell's life contradicted and which so many of his essays railed against. (p. xix)

[As] well as a political writer, Orwell was a political thinker of genuine stature. *Nineteen Eighty-Four* can be seen as a "development model", of a kind familiar to economic historians and social scientists, and every bit as tightly organised, logical and internally consistent as Thomas Hobbes' *Leviathan,* the masterpiece of English political philosophy. The governing regime is a wickedly clever and plausible synthesis of Stalinism and Nazism. *Nineteen Eighty-Four* is to the disorders of the twentieth century what *Leviathan* was to those of the seventeenth. Orwell chose to write in the form of a novel, not in the form of a philosophical tractatus. He would, indeed, have been incapable of writing a contemporary philosophical monograph, scarcely of understanding one. . . . To theorise about political developments in the form of a novel rather than as a treatise has advantages in reaching a wider public and for intuitive understanding, but disadvantages in credibility and explanatory precision.

Hobbes believed that a breakdown in good government would cause a return to a hypothetical state of nature, a condition of violent anarchy where "the life of man is solitary, nasty, brutish and short". Orwell believed that a breakdown in good government (by which he meant a breakdown in liberty, tolerance and welfare) could cause a leap forward into a hypothetical world order of one-party total power, a kind of State that the world had never seen before. He thought it would be novel in that the last vestiges of genuine ideology, whether Communist or Fascist, would have withered away and yet merged in a single hierarchy of oppression and propaganda motivated by a desire for power for its own sake: "If you want a picture of the future of humanity imagine a boot stamping on a human face—forever."

Orwell had first formulated the concept of totalitarianism shortly after his escape from Spain. He argued that common factors were emerging in Stalinism and in Nazism concerned with the retention and extension of power by the inner party elite. These lead the State to mobilise all society as if for perpetual and total war, a common process more important than the vestigial and nominally antagonistic ideologies. (p. xx)

If one takes the term "political writer" in its broadest sense to include philosophers, statesmen, publicists and pamphleteers who might claim to be secure in the canon of English literature, three names seem indisputably preeminent: Thomas Hobbes, Jonathan Swift, and George Orwell. The intellectual historian might make some claims for Edmund Burke, J. S. Mill or William Morris, but Burke and Mill, while fine writers indeed, seem too narrow in their range, sonorous but pedestrian compared to the nominated three; and to read Morris after Swift and Orwell is to condemn him as being too consciously literary by far, however original and influential were many of his ideas. Hobbes was a philosopher, grinding and grounding every point, but also indulging in a vast polemical irony that makes *Leviathan* a masterpiece of baroque prose. Swift was a pamphleteer and the supreme satirist, able to satirise knowledgeably philosophy and theology as well as party politics, but not himself philosophical; and his style was a forceful blend of classical form and of colloquial diction, so that *Gulliver* is a masterpiece of Augustan prose. Orwell in one work approached the importance and the scale of Hobbes, but he had none of his philosophical knowledge or disposition; and in many others of his works he learned consciously from Swift how colloquiality and formality can be mingled both for comic and polemic effect, and in so doing evolved his own flexible plain style which, while not the most beautiful modern English prose, is certainly the best model of English writing for a hundred and one different purposes. Orwell's common style rested on the questionable assumption that all knowledge can be reduced to common sense. But if he did not have the philosophical sophistication of Hobbes, yet his common sense saved him from Swift's bitter pessimism, at times hatred of humanity. For the thing about common sense is that one believes that other people, quite ordinary people, have it too.

The achievement is more important than the man. The main theme of a biography might therefore simply be how he came to hold the original and heterodox views of *Homage to Catalonia, Animal Farm* and *Nineteen Eighty-Four*. But that would be too narrow, excluding not only a picture of the life he led but also the achievement of the writer. Many of the best essays would get lost. And the essays raise at once the peculiarly Orwellian problem of the image of the writer and the character of the man. The very image he came to exhibit or established is complex, for such a simple man (so it is said). To hold Orwellian views and to write in an Orwellian manner mean different things. How could the essayist Orwell, revelling in natural variety, produce the Orwellian vision of a totally ma-

chined society? The common-sense answer is that being a writer of great ability, he adopted another style and mode of writing when he wanted to warn against the *possibility* of something happening. But if one reads *Nineteen Eighty-Four* before any other book of Orwell's or is told that it was his last testament, then one may well believe that it is a prophecy or forecast of the future, not simply an awful warning. Then there is, indeed, a contradiction between the two images of Orwell, and so people have presumed a change of character and of values in his last years. I examined this view very carefully, since it was commonly held and important, but I am bound to say that I found no evidence for it.

Some people still underestimate him as a writer. Why identify the final and utter pessimism and defeat of Winston Smith with the milder pessimism of the author? Why identify the shallow and imperceptive nostalgia of George Bowling in *Coming Up For Air* with George Orwell's loving, but knowing and measured, even half-ironic nostalgia? Mere names mislead. With what other novelist would so many readers and critics so confidently identify characters with author? Is the man so simple or does his art lull or gull some of his readers into simplicity? Perhaps the trouble arises from the nature of the essayist who appears to talk about himself so much, about *his* experiences and *his* prejudices. How closely related is that "George Orwell" to Eric Blair who became known as George Orwell? The art of the colloquial essayist, himself constantly and amusingly breaking the normal divide between fact and fiction, between the real person and the persona, this is well enough understood; but it can make things difficult when the same man is also a novelist; it can actually encourage critics and readers to think of Winston Smith as what Orwell thought he himself might become. Suppose there was, however, an Orwell mask that got stuck upon the private and modest person, Eric Blair? Does that diminish the performance?

"Orwell" sets many traps both for himself and for his readers. The question is only important, of course, if one is primarily concerned with the man. Some have said that the man is more important than his writings, meaning the example of the life he led. I do not share this view. A biographer should not, in any case, accept such absolute disjunctions between "character", "circumstances" and "works". Also the view diminishes his works. I suspect that when his old friend, Sir Richard Rees (in his *George Orwell: Fugitive from the Camp of Victory . . .*), called him "almost saintly", it was because he was never as happy with the content of Orwell's writing as he hoped to be.

Some have found an easier solution to this problem of the literary Orwell and a real Orwell. But I have found no evidence that a man called Eric Blair changed character when he came to call himself for the publication of his first book, "George Orwell". I have observed, however, a more subtle and gradual process, that Julian Symons first noted, by which Blair came to adopt the Orwell part of himself as an ideal image to be lived up to: an image of integrity, honesty, simplicity, egalitarian conviction, plain living, plain writing and plain speaking, in all a man with an almost reckless commitment to speaking out unwelcome truths: "liberty is what people do not want to hear." But a public image of Orwell grew up even in his lifetime which was like a vulgarised version of this somewhat ideal image. It presented Orwell as the corporal of the awkward squad, that perennial difficult fellow who speaks unwanted home truths out of order, asks embarrassing questions, pricks the bubbles of his own side's occasional pomposity, who goes too far in all this, making the whole Labour movement sound like a swarm of pacificist, naturist, fruit-juice-drinking cranks, and loses his own sense of humour when he cannot appreciate that a pack of lies is ideological necessity, or that an election address is necessarily humbug. (pp. xx-xxii)

Bernard Crick, in his *George Orwell: A Life*, Little, Brown and Company, 1980, 473 p.

JOHN H. BARNSLEY (essay date 1981)

[*In the following excerpt Barnsley notes some weaknesses in Orwell's imaginative projection of a totalitarian state. He questions the efficacy of controlling an entire population through the methods presented in the novel, and disagrees both with Orwell's presentation of the proles as a homogeneous mass and with his pessimistic vision of technology as a tool of repression.*]

In his essay on Henry Miller, **'Inside the Whale'**, George Orwell commented that 'The first test of any work of art is survival.' By this, his own criterion, his novel *Nineteen Eighty-Four* has done quite well. . . . It has become part of the common imaginative heritage of the Western world.

One reason for its influence is Orwell's style: concrete, observant, intelligent and readily accessible to the average reader, not least in schools and colleges. Good prose, he believed, is, or should be 'like a windowpane' and he followed a policy of easy intelligibility. Secondly, Orwell is notable for his empathy with the common man—or perhaps with *l'homme moyen éclairé*, the enlightened common man. All his five novels, and also his essays and documentaries, are written from that perspective. And so it is with *Nineteen Eighty-Four*. It is written from the viewpoint of a 39-year old worker in the Records Department in the Ministry of Plenty, the ironically-named Winston Smith. Like all Orwell's novelistic heroes—Flory, George Bowling, Dorothy Hare, and Gordon Comstock—Smith is an unexceptional person, possibly less gulled and dehumanised than the majority, but otherwise without any special merit or distinction. The tone is set on the first page, where 'a varicose ulcer above his right knee' constrains him to walk slowly up the seven flights of stairs to his flat in the (again ironically-named) Victory Mansions. As he moves to the window he is described as 'a smallish, frail figure, the meagreness of his body merely emphasized by the blue overalls which were the uniform of the Party.'

Smith's unexceptionality serves a dual purpose: it allows the ordinary reader to identify with him and it allows Orwell to describe the future as *experienced*, internally and personally, by the proverbial 'man in the street', and not merely as an external construct. In this, the novel differs both from modern futurology and most science-fiction accounts of the future.

Further, the landscape of *Nineteen Eighty-Four*—emotional as well as physical—is a recognisable one, drawn not from any futuristic vision but from recent history. It is the world of the 1930s and '40s that haunts the book; a landscape of dreary urban decay. (p. 30)

It is a world of shortages, of shoddy goods and constant privation. This is a world familiar from memory to the older generation and from historical accounts—not least Orwell's own—to the younger one.

But the success of the book must be related also to its specific plot and to the political world it conjures up. Here Orwell's novel is a monstrous denunciation, by the method of *reductio*

ad absurdum, of totalitarianism. It is also a vision that has clearly touched upon the fears and apprehensions of many in successive generations of the postwar world. It articulates these fears in concentrated, prismatic form. As a consequence the very word 'Orwellian' has taken on its modern connotations and expressions like 'Big Brother', 'Newspeak', 'Ministry of Truth', 'Thought Police', 'Hate Week' and 'Doublethink' have entered the political lexicons of at least the more sceptical.

Some have contended that *Nineteen Eighty-Four* is to be treated as merely an imaginative artistic work with no predictive intent. But, *pace* these commentators, Orwell made it quite clear that he saw the world of *Nineteen Eighty-Four* as a possibility for any centralised economy, not least in the 'free' West. As he wrote:

> My recent novel is *not* intended as an attack on Socialism or on the British Labour Party . . . but as a show-up of the perversions to which a centralised economy is liable. (And he added): I do not believe that the kind of society I describe necessarily *will* arrive, but I believe . . . that something resembling it *could* arrive [see excerpt dated 1949].

Given this, one must note that the generality of relevance of *Nineteen Eighty-Four* has, since he wrote those words, become more heightened not less so. In the book all economic activity, save a few proletarian enclaves (local shops and pubs), is organised by the 'Ministry of Plenty'. The abolition of private property had occurred in 'the middle years of the century'. We find a similar tendency in reality. In the postwar period the long-term trend of all Western countries, without exception, has been a centralising one. In each the state has considerably expanded its size and functions and the public sector has grown at the expense of the, now more closely regulated, private sector.

Further, the technological base for Orwell's society has also largely been provided. . . . Even the omnipresent 'telescreens', which abolish privacy in *Nineteen Eighty-Four,* are under development as gas-discharge panels. Further, some technologies Orwell did not predict have distinctly Orwellian implications. This is particularly true of the computer and of microelectronic technology.

In view of this, it is useful and indeed comforting to point to some weaknesses in *Nineteen Eighty-Four*. The first observation to be made is that the novel essentially accepts the efficacy of a behaviourist psychology embodied in totalitarian politics. Manipulation of an entire population is portrayed as both possible and effective. Rebellion is a failed hope, just as Winston Smith's own rebellion is (and he has, apparently, been under observation for seven years). To be sure, Orwell exposes the grim mechanics of this manipulation: the political abuse of language ('War is Peace', 'Freedom is Slavery', 'Ignorance is Strength' and the creation of 'Newspeak' wherein heretical thoughts will be unutterable); the literal re-writing of history by the Ministry of Truth; the continual mobilisation of the population to face some new wartime 'emergency'; the adoption of advanced technologies of continuous surveillance, particularly the two-way 'telescreens' capable of registering a human heartbeat; and in the last event the use of torture and 'elimination'. But such tactics, while deprecated, are still presented as effective.

This is a determinist nightmare *à la* B. F. Skinner. But as Skinner's critics exemplify, the majority of psychologists and social scientists adopt a more voluntarist perspective, allowing for the role of free-will and imposing limits on the extent to which people are 'conditionable' into an absurd conformity. Further, one is bound to ask that if two members of the Outer Party, Smith and his girlfriend Julia, both relatively 'ordinary' people, can resist such manipulation, why not thousands of others?

Secondly, and related to this, we have Orwell's perception of the 85 per cent majority, the 'Proles', as an undifferentiated 'mass', apathetic, apolitical, and readily manipulable. (pp. 31-2)

It is true that Winston Smith believes, prior to his 'rehabilitation', that 'If there was hope, it *must* lie in the proles, because only there . . . could the force to destroy the Party ever be generated'. But the development of the book provides no support whatever for this hope. The image of an unthinking, easily-swayed majority occurs centrally also in **Animal Farm.** But applied to humans in the latter part of the 20th century it is a largely fictitious stereotype. Orwell would have done well to adopt a more analytic approach to the logic of in industrialism and to the class structure. For what has in fact happened is that the majority—'Proles' least of all in their own self-conceptions—have become *more* not less differentiated. They have become differentiated by education, skill, status level, and type and location of work. So much so that the very term 'working class' or 'proletariat' has, *pace* Marx, lost a good deal of its former structural relevance. The rise of the service industries and the mechanisation (and later automation) of the primary and secondary sectors have also whittled down the involvement of workers in purely manual tasks, and inflated the stratum of 'white-collar' workers. (p. 32)

Thus, the central image in **Nineteen Eighty-Four** of an homogenised 'mass', comprising more than four-fifths of the population, is an unconvincing one. Further, his omission of worker 'resistance' in the form of trade-unionism contributes to the unconvincing stereotype of the 'Proles'. Mention of trade-unionism is a lacuna in all Orwell's political writing—though he comments in **The Road to Wigan Pier** that 'the English working class do not have much capacity for leadership, but they have a wonderful talent for organisation. The whole trade union movement testifies to this'. But by ignoring the purely economic force of organised labour—let alone its political manifestations—he failed to anticipate a substantial segment of postwar European economic and political history, and not least that of Britain, the setting of his novel.

Finally, there is Orwell's attitude to technology in **Nineteen Eighty-Four.** In the Orwellian future the 'empirical method of thought' is restrained and science is turned to thoroughly dystopic ends. 'Technological progress', he writes, 'only happens when its products can in some way be used for the diminution of human liberty'. Further, 'There are . . . two great problems which the Party is concerned to solve. One is how to discover, against his will, what another human being is thinking, and the other is how to kill several hundred million people in a few seconds without giving warning beforehand. In so far as scientific research still continues, this is its subject matter'. Advances in communications technology, he believed, and this is a central point neglected by critics, supplied the necessary, if not sufficient, conditions for this form of totalitarianism. . . .

There is in Orwell none of the fascination with the positive advances of science that we find in, say, Francis Bacon or H. G. Wells or, today, in such writers as Herman Kahn and

Arthur C. Clarke. His other writings attest to his concern that technology could threaten nature and tradition. . . . (p. 33)

But his pessimism was overdrawn and derives, we suggest, from a very traditional humanistic disdain for and recoil from science and technology and all their products. As in C. P. Snow's 'two cultures', science and technology are viewed as almost inescapably opposed to humanist values and pursuits. Given this, the opposing case needs to be put: namely that science and technology can contribute to human freedom and dignity, often accidentally so. For instance, the industrialisation of India has helped breach the caste system, that of South Africa has weakened apartheid, and that of the southern states of America has encouraged racial integration. Industrialisation is in many ways inherently democratising.

Orwell's negative depiction of technology and its implications, then appear unconvincingly one-sided. Though it is also true that a couple of passages in **Nineteen Eighty-Four** express a suppressed optimism about technology. Here is one of them:

> From the moment when the machine first made its appearance it was clear to all thinking people that the need for human drudgery, and therefore to great extent for human inequality, had disappeared. If the machine were used deliberately for that end, hunger, overwork, dirt, illiteracy, and disease could be eliminated within a few generations.

But he allowed his pessimism to overcome this *sotto voce* optimism and hence we have an unrealistic picture of stultified science and dystopic technology.

But these criticisms aside, **Nineteen Eighty-Four** is an important book. It is probably the best-known anti-totalitarian novel and, as with other possible dystopias, is most usefully regarded as a critical benchmark against which contemporary developments may be assessed. Its admonitory world is thoroughly anti-humanist: Winston Smith is described by his Party interrogator, O'Brien, as 'the last man'. 'Your kind is extinct,' O'Brien comments, 'we are the inheritors'. And Orwell did originally intend to title the book *The Last Man in Europe.* (pp. 33-4)

> *John H. Barnsley, '''The Last Man in Europe': A Comment on George Orwell's '1984',''* in Contemporary Review, *Vol. 239, No. 1386, July, 1981, pp. 30-4.*

PATRICK REILLY (essay date 1982)

[*In the following excerpt Reilly contends that in* Nineteen Eighty-Four *Orwell discredited humanism as a valid creed for modern times. For another discussion of the creed of humanism within the text of* Nineteen Eighty-Four, *see the excerpt by Ian Watt (1983).*]

Nineteen Eighty-Four has always been a scandal. It was denounced as a surrender to the mysticism of cruelty, a weapon in the Cold War, an item in our own hate-week, a capitalist horror-comic whose author was another lost leader in the tradition of Wordsworth. Its special offence was its alleged renegade politics, its repudiation of all that 1917 stood for. Yet the scandal is in fact far greater, for the book transcends politics to repudiate not just the Revolution but humanism itself. It is not a capitalist horror-comic—the porn manufactured by Big Brother has found a cosier home in the capitalist West than behind the Curtain—but its enemies might well have described it as a religious horror-comic. It enacts a struggle between two religions, humanism, the religion of the past, with Winston as its last advocate, and totalitarian sadism, the religion of the present and, the book's pessimism insists, of the future, with O'Brien its prophet-fanatic.

'Struggle' is, of course, obsequiously honorific. Winston's humanism has as much chance of checking the new savage god as biscuits strewn before tanks. Suspense comes, if at all, not from wondering whether he can elude, far less overthrow, Big Brother, but whether he can sustain defiance to the modest extent of dying for the faith, winning the martyr's crown: 'the object is not to stay alive but to stay human'. Even this limited victory, Winston joining Spartacus and More, Hus and Bonhoeffer, is finally seen as a fantasy, as much a piece of wish-fulfillment as Jack the Giant-Killer. Here the Giant wins; the dissident loses everything except his life in the book's appalling conclusion.

The privilege of heroic death is as obsolete as Shakespeare and the paperweight, and humanism is denied even a martyr. Right from the start Winston is a dubious candidate for the honour. His faith is less than rockfast. What he most fears as lunatic, heretic, minority of one, is that there *is* no truth to die for, and the book confirms his dread. Winston versus O'Brien, humanism versus power-worship, is an absolute mismatch which no self-respecting Board of Control would ever have sanctioned. Relying on the spirit of man, Winston might just as well have trusted in Poseidon or Thor or the exploded God of Christian mythology. The real affront to modern pieties is in the implication that the defeat of humanism is somehow disconcertingly related to the death of the God whose obituary the nineteenth-century humanists so authoritatively announced. Some, like Nietzsche and Feuerbach, hailed his demise, but even when regretted, it was not seen as calamitous. George Eliot, having thrown her clod into the grave, consoles the bereaved: since heaven is no longer there to help us, we will, because we must, help and love each other all the more. It is this religion of humanity that *Nineteen Eighty-four* consigns to the dustbin of discredited mythologies.

Three gods appear in the book: O'Brien's savage deity; the god of traditional religion that Winston rejects; and the god he claims to serve, the spirit of man that will, somehow, finally defeat Big Brother. Instead, Winston is demolished along with his humanist hopes. We can, if we wish, soften this conclusion by seeing it as the debacle of a very flawed individual and a defective creed whose failure leaves the true doctrine intact, thus wrenching the text away from the despair-of-a-dying-man view to that of a cautionary tale for progressives, an optimistic exhortation to those who share the faith not to repeat the blunders. Yet the inadequate Winston is the only liberal champion textually present, the last of his kind, as O'Brien taunts him—is that in itself an implied judgement on the kind he represents? (pp. 19-20)

We may describe Winston as inadequate humanist, provided we do not assume on Orwell's behalf, in defiance of the text, an implied adequate humanism which Winston unfortunately mislaid, importing into the book another tougher strain (our own, naturally) which would have sustained Winston if only he had found it. Poor, misguided Winston—why couldn't he be like us? The fallacy is the graver when we reflect that he *is* like us, that he is the universal representative, his defects not those of an individual or group, but, at crucial points, of humanity itself as seen by Orwell.... Where *Animal Farm* merely shatters the hopes of Revolution, *Nineteen Eighty-Four* shatters those of autonomous man, lending itself easily to the

religious view that atheism inevitably leads to the worship of Big Brother.

The ritual of the Two-Minute Hate, hell-fire sermon and *auto-da-fe* combined, exhibits the power of the new religion, as the woman responds to the telescreen image of the Saviour, like St Teresa to Christ, while Winston hides from the other face of God—Jehovah, ineluctable avenger. His defiance is as futile as that of Marlowe's Faustus; the Thought Police will get him whether he writes or destroys the diary—God is not mocked. What the old religions only aspired to, the new one has achieved. Big Brother *is* infallible to a degree undreamt of by the most fervid of ultramontanes. He can annihilate and create too, as Comrade Ogilvy demonstrates when called into existence as miraculously as Adam, hagiographic equivalent of the legendary saints, an example of total dedication, a eunuch for Oceania's sake. Julia, by contrast, is a sexual heretic, rebel from the waist downwards, with sex for its own sake the extent of her particular *non serviam*. Winston also commits sexcrime, but his root sin is ownlife, the heresy of individualism, depriving him of the faith to see that London is a thriving city, laden with provisions. Both lovers are like the obsessed sinners of traditional religion, feverishly digging their own pits, for, as Julia says, every sinner confesses; confession, however, as O'Brien insists, is as good for the soul in the present religion as Catholic apologists have claimed it to be in the old.

The new god spurns loveless obedience as inefficacious unto salvation. The function of Room 101 in Oceanic theology is to eradicate every possible competing passion, in line with Christ's insistence that to love father or mother is to hate him: thou shalt love the lord thy God with thy whole heart and thy whole mind, no corner, however tiny, reserved for inferior loyalties. In Room 101 one learns to value God above all else, to devote one's whole life *ad maiorem gloriam dei* ["to the greater glory of God"]. Winston, loving Julia as Milton's Adam loves Eve, wilfully rejects creator for created, and the sinner must be taught to detest his error, for what good is a forced obedience? Satan could have been barred from Eden, Winston arrested the moment he bought the diary, but to what purpose? How is the sinner to be redeemed unless first permitted to sin? Charrington's shop, like the tree in Eden, is placed in the sinner's path and he falls that he may be cleansed.

Mere outward conformity is a scandal to the puritans who control Oceania; one must love God *because* he chastises—Winston, miscasting himself as Prometheus, must be schooled to his proper role as Job. *Areopagitica* is obscenely parodied in the argument that good only comes via evil, that only a loving obedience is worthwhile. The moment of expulsion from Eden is terrifying, as is that moment when the bliss of Winston's room is shattered by the accusatory voice from behind the picture, but no more for Winston than Adam is paradise irretrievably lost. O'Brien, playing Michael to Winston's Adam, describes the three stages in the sinner's regeneration—learning, understanding, acceptance—and warns that the first two are necessarily painful. But the pain is purgatorial, God being cruel to be kind. O'Brien receives Winston with all the sad reproach of a father forced to chastise an erring child, calling him affectionately by his first name, employing the classic opening gambit of every father so situated: 'You knew this, Winston.... Don't deceive yourself. You did know it—you have always known it.' The only omission is the assurance that this is going to hurt him even more than the culprit.

The new God declines to lose a single soul.... Hell has no place in the theology of Oceania, for hell is God's shame, his admission that there are wills too stubborn, evils too obdurate, even for his love to overcome—every hellbound soul is the devil's victory. The devils of *Nineteen Eighty-Four,* ownlife, sexcrime and the rest, win no victories, are indeed permitted to exist simply to demonstrate the futile folly of seduction, in exalting God the more by their humiliating impotence. Winston, misinterpreting himself as rebel, is really acting out his role in an Oceanic *felix culpa.* The Christian God (it is perhaps the chief accusation against him) is a committed liberal who allows Satan to compete by refusing to coerce men into heaven. The new, unscrupulous God rejects this puerile notion of fair play as another vestige of gutless liberalism, repudiating the public schoolboy image for that of a surgeon cutting out a cancer with no nonsense about giving it a sporting chance. The operation is always successful. Winston dreams he hears, perhaps does hear, O'Brien's consoling voice assuring him that he is at last in the hands of the omniscient, infallible healer; O'Brien refers to Julia's perfect conversion as a text-book case—redundantly, since there is no other kind in *Nineteen Eighty-Four:* 'Everyone is washed clean.' No one is lost in this perfected model of Christian salvation.... (pp. 20-2)

The new religion's power is most frighteningly displayed in its disciples' fanaticism. The tired, ageing O'Brien is transfigured as he chants his paean to power. Winston cowers before the enormous face 'filled with a sort of exaltation, a lunatic intensity', the face of the mystic as seen by the bewildered, fearful outsider. The new creed totally repudiates the whole Christian-humanist ethos. 'Above all we do not allow the dead to rise up against us', and the vetoed resurrection makes unpersons of Christ, Shakespeare and all the other champions of man's allegedly unconquerable spirit. Humanism is as dead as the Galilean and the implication is that the two deaths are related. O'Brien denounces hypocritical totalitarians like Dostoyevsky's Grand Inquisitor who pretend that power is only a means to happiness, incurring the guilt of power like Christ assuming sin so that men may be happy, claiming absolute freedom for themselves on the pretext of bringing absolute happiness to others. O'Brien lambasts this along with the doublethink of the liberal totalitarians, those willing, like Winston, to commit atrocities in order to set men free. O'Brien's honest totalitarianism is by contrast, based on de Sade, power as an end, exercised for its own sake: 'We are the priests of power . . . God is power.' The *agape* gives way to a vision of a boot forever crushing a human face.

Even as O'Brien rhapsodises, Winston is struck by the tired, ageing face of the speaker, impotence in its most absolute form of death overcoming the power-worshipper. But, by allowing O'Brien an insight into the cruel discrepancy between his words and his state, Orwell deliberately renounces the opportunity for ironically subverting the rhetoric as absurd. O'Brien, as always reading Winston's mind correctly, dismisses his own approaching dissolution as trivial when set against the immortality of his adored collective; who cares about individual decay when 'the weariness of the cell is the vigour of the organism'? Winston, by contrast, collapses when forced to confront his physical ruin—his God fails where O'Brien's triumphs.

We are on the fringe here of what Orwell referred to as the major problem of our time: the tragedy of human finitude. He has been rebuked for avoiding in his work this paramount problem of lost faith, but a careful reader will often detect it lurking below the secular surface. (p. 23)

[*Nineteen Eighty-Four*] does deal with his major problem, and its darkness is inseparable from his failure to solve it in a way he could endorse, and, worse still, its solution in a form he finds totally abhorrent. Winston's humanistic solution is brushed aside as contemptuously by O'Brien as Gulliver's jingoistic nonsense by the Giant King. O'Brien tackles and 'solves' the problem where Winston conspicuously fails. 'Alone—free—the human being is doomed to die, which is the greatest of all failures.' So asserts O'Brien, solving Orwell's major problem by denying the value of the individual, for the body survives though the cell dies. However repugnant to Christian-humanist principles, O'Brien's solution works, enabling him to transcend his personal weakness, giving a sense of purpose to individual existence. Orwell knew that men live by myths as long as they believe them true, like the British after Dunkirk, still irrationally assured of their invincibility. O'Brien's fanaticism is akin to this atavistic patriotism, and it makes him, like the British, an opponent difficult to resist, far less overcome. His adversary will require an equivalent fervour to survive.

It is easy to expose Winston's limitations, harder to determine why Orwell cooperates with O'Brien in doing so. It looks as if Orwell has sold out to power, except that Winston is attacked as a member of a group detested by Orwell: the power-worshipper posing as freedom-fighter. When O'Brien, catechising Winston, asks him, like a schoolmaster coaching a star pupil, how one man asserts his power over another, Winston, freely and after reflection, gives the scholarship answer: 'by making him suffer'. It is a compromising answer, betraying an innate authoritarianism, and Winston does pass from adversary to pupil, learning, albeit painfully, the facts of life. O'Brien similarly changes from draconian instructor to protector and father, to whom Winston clings with all the trust of a suffering child. Winston is, finally, as much a power-worshipper as O'Brien, though his devotions are performed in the catacombs of his mind while his teacher's are those of the established church. Orwell uses O'Brien to force Winston to burn in public the incense to the God he secretly, unconsciously, adores—for it is Winston's discovery that 'if you want to keep a secret you must also hide it from yourself'.

This explains the passage where Winston agrees to commit all manner of atrocities to help overthrow Big Brother, the very atrocities which make Big Brother so detestable in the first place. It is easy to condemn Winston's doublethink, harder to select someone entitled to throw the first stone, for Dresden, Hiroshima, Vietnam, the whole urban guerrilla sprawl, all in some way represent a deal with our own O'Briens and we are all, in some degree, Winston. Making this deal, Winston has, the book demonstrates, already lost the moral chess-game awaiting him in the Ministry of Love. O'Brien has him taped and, at a crucial point in their confrontation, explodes the claim to moral superiority by playing back the diabolic commitment agreed by the purportedly moral man. Defeated intellectually, Winston protests that something in the universe, 'some spirit, some principle', will never succumb to Big Brother. O'Brien, for once misreading (deliberately?) Winston's mind, proposes God as the likeliest candidate, only for Winston to repudiate the transcendent God of traditional religion. The God he means is the God of nineteenth-century humanism, the God in man, totally immanent, reclaimed by Feuerbach from the heaven where his creator, man, in an immature act of self-alienation, has mistakenly exiled him.

The trap is set when O'Brien lures Winston into declaring that he too, as man, participates in godhead—if humanity is God, all men are divine. But, as the tape recording makes plain, there is nothing, morally, to distinguish Winston from O'Brien, nor, presumably, his God from O'Brien's savage deity. No need to dispute Winston's rhetoric when the enemy has on tape the voices of the last, self-proclaimed man swearing to throw acid in a child's face and a full-length mirror to reveal the revolting bag of filth that is the alleged last guardian of the human spirit. Winston's faith, however attractive, fails, the humanist ethos crumbles under pressure: *animal rationale* is the consoling dream, Yahoo the sickening reality. Instead of Blake's human form divine, there is a stinking animal, and all three defeats, moral, intellectual and physical, are interrelated. Winston weeps uncontrollably at the sight of his ruined body because, broken intellectually and morally, he has only the body left, and it is here that the hazard of rejecting a transcendent God becomes so evident. (pp. 24-5)

Winston's final bankruptcy suggests how frail are his beliefs in an age of fanaticism, and, paradoxically, it is precisely their rationalism that convicts them of ineptitude. Few readers of Mann's *The Magic Mountain* leave the long debate between the violently irrational Naphta and the liberal humanist Settembrini convinced that the latter has won, and the confrontation, minus the intellectual high jinks, recurs in Winston versus O'Brien, with humanism even more clearly the loser. True, O'Brien, unlike Naphta, can use torture to boost his arguments, but it would be wrong to ascribe his victory simply to this. Winston very soon senses his own intellectual inferiority, is convinced that his opponent 'was a being *in all ways* larger than himself'. Feuerbach's humanism, Winston's own argument, is ironically turned against him: 'nothing exists except through human consciousness—outside man there is nothing.' The God in man is steadily humiliated as Winston struggles in vain to resist not the torturer but the logician, is reduced finally to intellectual tantrums, a childish insistence that Big Brother cannot endure because Winston could not endure it, that things must get better simply because they are so bad now, an argument anticipated by Rupert Brooke's fish—'"This life cannot be all," they swear, / "For how unpleasant if it were!"'

Rehabilitation begins long before Room 101. Winston starts as heretical mind disguised as conformist; his session with O'Brien ends with his mind now orthodox but the inner heart still recalcitrant and, as he believes, inviolate. Room 101 ensures the transition to perfect orthodoxy of mind and heart together, when, having lagged behind emotionally, he finally catches up with his completely cured intellect. The humanist is destroyed and it is pointless to fault human nature rather than his creed, since religion has always attacked humanism for its wild overestimation of fallen man, like expecting a cripple to sprint. Pascal argues that to know one's corruption without knowing God means despair; *Nineteen Eighty-Four* promotes such despair in its exhibition of human wretchedness, man's inability under stress to be other than sickeningly selfish.

It strikes Winston that 'in moments of crisis one is never fighting against an external enemy, but always against one's own body', and it is the pain-shunning body, swelling to fill the universe, that betrays the would-be idealist. In battle the great, noble issues give way to brute preservation; self-transcendence is restricted to comfortable armchairs. . . . In the Ministry of Love a skull-faced man, dying of starvation, is given some bread by a fellow-prisoner, who is at once brutally beaten by a guard for his act of charity. The skull-faced man, ordered to Room 101, begs obscenely to be reprieved, and, searching frantically for a substitute victim, naturally fixes upon his bene-

factor, hysterically accusing him of having whispered treason as he gave the bread. Orwell's modern rendition of the parable focusses less the charity of the Good Samaritan than the degradingly selfish fear of the recipient. If the greatest proof of self-transcendence is to die for another, the nadir of selfishness is to use the benefactor's body as a shield.

Nor is the skull-faced man to be regarded as a monster of depravity; for he is a normal man acting as all men do when put to the test, as the Good Samaritan will act too when *he* is summoned to Room 101—we may feel ashamed only on condition of recognising the guilt as universal. Room 101 is where humanity is exposed, not where cowards are separated from heroes. In *Nineteen Eighty-Four* there are no heroes, simply pain, and 'nothing in the world was so bad as physical pain'. Martyrs are simply the mistakes of an inefficient penology, of blundering executioners who take them at their word that they prefer death when they are really like fake suicides, inadvertently killing themselves through obstinacy or an over-prolonged attempt to make it look real. It is essentially a matter of chronology, of being on hand at the inevitable moment when the martyr is screaming to be saved from himself. Nothing is finally more important than one's own skin. 'All you care about is yourself', says Julia, explaining her treachery as a single instance of a universal law, and Winston, taught by his own experience, agrees. Peter weeps and reforms, Judas hangs himself; Orwell's characters act as they must and despise themselves for it. Gulliver concludes his long list of human depravities by remarking that all this is 'according to the due course of things' and is ready to overlook these 'natural' defects, provided man renounces pride. Winston and Julia meet, finally, the Gulliverian stipulation. They are the deed's creatures and what they have done makes the erstwhile lovers despise themselves in despising the human animal.

We can, of course, protest that Orwell's is a ferocious examination, its passmark fixed to ensure universal failure, and go on to redraft the questions to suit ordinary human beings rather than the moral senior wranglers he blames us for not being. But, after all, it is his examination, and if we think the despair comes from impossible expectations, we arrive too late to persuade him to change his mind. Winston's reverence for the prole mother as the human image is finally as shattered as the glass paperweight broken by the Thought Police—such reverence, like paperweight and diary, humanism and God, Shakespeare and tragedy, belongs with all the other beautiful rubbish of the past, a mere rubbish heap of details, like the old prole's memory. Instead, we have the present, disgusting but real. Winston's fitful, irrational hope in the proles—*credo quia impossible est*—flickers against his more usual, 'realistic' view of them as urbanised Yahoos, animal rather than human (warned by a prole of an approaching rocket, he immediately takes cover, despite hearing nothing himself, because the proles possess an instinct denied to rational beings). He patrols the prole districts, like a behaviourist observing rats, fascinated by the teeming life of the slums, the sexual instinct in its most blatant form, noting the sordid, swarming life of the streets, the smell of urine and sour beer, watching the women rioting over a shortage of pans, the men squabbling over the one public event that engages them, the national lottery. It is not so much London in 1984 as any British city fifty years earlier. The attitude of reverence, spasmodic and fragile, cannot be sustained amid such reality without recourse to mysticism belonging to the past as much as the paperweight; and reverence gives way to a Swiftian disgust with the human animal, the prole mother to Parsons excreting into a defective pan, his stink polluting the whole cell.

Winston is, of course, not Orwell, is indeed a prime target of Orwell's attack, but, in our anxiety to protect him from what for us is a discreditable association with his 'hero', to keep him, for his sake and ours, pleasingly on the side of the progressive angels, we avert our eyes from the book's pessimism. Winston's attitudes and revulsions, at least occasionally, are those of his creator; despite a deep sympathy with common people, an affection for the minutiae of everyday life, there are moments when Orwell exhibits the furious despair of the militant reformer outraged by the blind irresponsibility of ordinary men. . . . The final despair of *Nineteen Eighty-Four* is surely shared by Orwell, since Winston's inadequacy in Room 101 is the inadequacy of everyman.

It would be impertinent to apologise for Orwell; reading his life, we could do worse than treat him with the reverence Winston felt towards the prole woman. But reading his last book, we must acknowledge its despair—the real insult is to doctor what he writes in the interests of our own self-assurance. Yet life and art do seem here so strangely mismatched. The essay on Swift supplies the answer. Despite condemning Swift as a diseased writer, Orwell kept returning to the source of infection—clearly, there was a Swift in himself that he found irresistible. However unbalanced or one-sided, Swift does, for Orwell, present a view of life which, if limited, is nevertheless true and is the more obligatory because we prefer to ignore it. It can even be occasionally invigorating—Orwell praises one of Swift's most outrageous poems for exploding the fraud of feminine delicacy. There follows this revealing comment: 'Part of our minds—in any normal person it is the dominant part—believes that man is a noble animal and life is worth living; but there is also a sort of inner self which at least intermittently stands aghast at the horror of existence.' In *Nineteen Eighty-Four* the Swift in Orwell has taken over, the inner self, uncensored, records the horror of existence. God is dead, Nietzsche reported; Orwell's last communiqué adds Man to the casualty list. (pp. 26-30)

> *Patrick Reilly, " 'Nineteen Eighty-Four': The Failure of Humanism," in* Critical Quarterly, *Vol. 24, No. 3, Autumn, 1982, pp. 19-30.*

T. R. FYVEL (essay date 1982)

[*Fyvel is an English essayist, journalist, and editor. He was introduced to Orwell by their publisher, Fredric Warburg, and they remained friends through the last ten years of Orwell's life. Together they edited a series for Secker & Warburg entitled Searchlight Books, the first volume of which was Orwell's* The Lion and the Unicorn. *In 1982, Fyvel published* George Orwell: A Personal Memoir. *This memoir is divided into three sections: in the first, Fyvel examines Orwell's life and career up to the year they met; in the second, he writes about Orwell during the decade of their acquaintance; and in the third, he assesses Orwell's work in terms of his personal knowledge of Orwell. In the following excerpt from that work, Fyvel discusses Orwell's feelings about* Nineteen Eighty-Four *and, while concurring with the many critics who find autobiographical elements in the novel, notes that "out of his private* nightmare *Orwell . . . produced a book profoundly and prophetically related to the* public *problems of the time." Robert Christgau (1983) similarly interprets the novel as a private nightmare of the author's which nonetheless has significance for more than just Orwell. Walter Kendrick (1983), on the other hand, maintains that the novel has no significance except to Orwell—and to other white upper-middle-class British males—dismayed*

by the waning of old standards of gentility. Fyvel also examines the enormous impact Nineteen Eighty-Four *has had on twentieth-century thought, concluding that it has "more than any other book published since 1945, subtly affected the popular impression of the way history has been proceeding."*]

Orwell was very worried because in America *Nineteen Eighty-Four* was being billed in Right-wing circles as an all-out attack on socialism, which had never been his intention. As I remember it, my comment was more or less that one could easily see how such a misunderstanding could arise—I also had pondered about the name 'Ingsoc' Orwell gave to his future society. But of course *Nineteen Eighty-Four* was *not* a savage attack on socialism; it was a warning about a possible type of state tyranny which called itself socialist. In **'Writers and Leviathan'**, Orwell had written that it was a weakness of the Left to suppose that with the overthrow of capitalism, something like democratic socialism would inevitably take its place. There was no such inevitability: with the abolition of capitalism, who knew what régime might follow? *Nineteen Eighty-Four* was an allegorical warning against the worst possible consequence. Taking political questions calmly as was my wont (except about the European Jews) I said that Orwell need not worry; his novel was far too good to be made merely an object of extreme Right-wing propaganda; such publicity would soon die down and the book would find its place in modern thought on its merits. . . .

[Orwell's publisher Fredric] Warburg did indeed issue a press statement protesting against the depiction of *Nineteen Eighty-Four* not as a warning but as an attack on socialism. He said that he had put out the statement at Orwell's special request. . . . (p. 165)

[Orwell was] a prophet whose work posthumously became part of the literary folklore of the late twentieth century and in this process his position became transformed. In the essays he wrote during his lifetime, he addressed the small groups of intellectual readers of small-scale magazines like *Horizon* and *Polemic*. Since his death, he has become a writer with an impact upon the imagination of the mass reader and there has been no halting this transformation. *Animal Farm* and *Nineteen Eighty-Four* have sold internationally in millions of copies. Their slogans, continually quoted, have become a regular part of the modern political idiom. (p. 174)

The impact of Orwell's thought has also transcended frontiers. One notes how some situations under Communism have been variously described as 'Orwellian' by Soviet writers like Solzhenitsyn. East European intellectuals, indeed, have often expressed surprise that Orwell, who had never visited a Communist country, should so faithfully have understood the essence of life under Communism. As for the US, as just one among countless examples, an American professor told me that at the start of her course in political science, she regularly asked her students as their first task to read, and to comment on, Orwell's essay, 'Politics and the English Language'. I have recently been told how in many West German schools, Orwell's essays feature prominently in studies of modern English writers.

And so on. A point to note is that Orwell's impact has seemed to grow regardless of criticisms levelled against his work, and this goes for some leading Marxist critics. For instance, in the essay he called **'Nineteen Eighty-Four:** The Mysticism of Cruelty', Isaac Deutscher, that eminent biographer of Trotsky and one-time guide of the New Left, tried in 1954 to put Orwell in his place as a talented but politically naive outsider [see *TCLC*, Vol. 2]. It was unfortunate, he wrote, that poor Orwell encountered Communism at such a bad moment in 1937, the time of Stalin's Moscow treason trials and the Communist propaganda lies about the POUM ["'Partido Obrero de Unificación Marxista''—(United Marxist Worker's Party)] in Spain. Not being a systematic political thinker, Orwell let the picture of Communism in his mind become stuck in this particular moment. He did not realize, as he, Deutscher, as a trained Marxist historian did, that beyond Stalin's dictatorship, the Soviet system was bound to develop either towards Bonapartist adventurism, or more likely towards great liberalization.

Neither of these developments has of course taken place within the rigid Soviet Union. Looked at today, Deutscher's essay reads already like the tired and dated political journalism of the fifties. By contrast, Orwell's reflection of that ominous moment of world history in 1937, which he caught in *Homage to Catalonia* and *Nineteen Eighty-Four* , remains as grave a warning as ever. Somehow, the impetus of Orwell's writing has effortlessly survived this and similar Marxist critiques.

Attempts to explain this impetus and pin Orwell down in a phrase have proved tempting. He has been described by one notable critic [V. S. Pritchett] as a writer who went native in his own country. This is only partly true. He did seek to fashion some sort of native English proletarian life-style for himself and he did rough it with English tramps. But he roughed it only for a brief while and then largely in search of material. (pp. 174-75)

He has been described as 'the wintry conscience of his generation'. Again, yes and no. His exact contemporaries—Greene, Powell, Muggeridge, Waugh, Koestler—were fully able to make up their own consciences, as were 'Auden & Co.', who followed three or four years later. Orwell's major appeal has on the contrary been to the conscience of the generation that has grown up since his death and quite remarkably so on all sides of the political spectrum. . . .

Were I personally to venture a one-sentence judgement, I would say that more than any writer I can think of, Orwell by sheer concentration and drive transcended the limitations which he partly inherited but also partly created. I remember him as determinedly leading his would-be proletarian existence, keeping a blinkered gaze firmly fixed on popular mass culture and on major contemporary issues of political morality—and on little else. It seems to me that in this way he excluded large areas of the artistic and aesthetic imagination from his life. (p. 176)

While as a journalist and novelist he had considerable gifts of description, he was also handicapped by gaps in his imaginative powers. Apart from satire, he found it hard as a novelist to draw rounded characters (unless, of course, they were those of animals). He found it particularly hard to draw the characters of women and to see his heroines as independent human beings, not just social influences impinging on an Orwellian anti-hero. Since he liked to write love scenes, this was a major shortcoming which he also had to fight against.

There was another limitation he had to transcend. As I saw him, Orwell set himself to write of the limitless immorality of totalitarianism without having any close knowledge of, or even as it could seem a special interest in, Hitler and Hitlerism and Nazi Germany—the supreme revolutionary force for evil active in his lifetime. (p. 177)

Orwell's prestige rests in the end on *Animal Farm* and *Nineteen Eighty-Four* , and as I read the two books again I was struck by their contrast. *Animal Farm*, which he wrote in 1943-4,

when reasonably happily married and with Eileen an appreciative listener as he worked on it, seems a sunny tale of the countryside. By contrast, *Nineteen Eighty-Four,* which he wrote four years later when struggling against illness on Jura, is all inferno, a story of permanent metropolitan darkness. (p. 193)

The world has lived very nicely with *Animal Farm* but uneasily with *Nineteen Eighty-Four.* It is fair to say that Orwell's last work has, more than any book published since 1945, subtly affected the popular impression of the way history has been proceeding. The book contains obvious elements of his private nightmare—the hero's loneliness and guilt, memories of London's wartime squalor, his phobia about rats, images of a boot on a face . . . And yet, out of his *private* nightmare Orwell by his supreme effort produced a book profoundly and prophetically related to the *public* problems of the time, an allegory that after his death has become like a measuring rod of history.

This impact is all the more remarkable because at first sight, as one reads it today, *Nineteen Eighty-Four* has a few very evident faults. True, the imaginary future Orwell wrote about back in 1948 still has a very ingenious look—he had good insight into the shape of history to come. The world of 1984 which Orwell drew was dominated by three totalitarian super-states—Eurasia (Soviet Union), Eastasia (communist China) and Oceania (the US) and for a writer looking ahead in 1948 this was not a bad guess. He saw Britain as Oceania's Airstrip One—again not a bad guess, but then the American connection simply drops out of his story, leaving Britain alone as a totalitarian Oceania. As such, in Orwell's picture, it is ruled to the last detail by the all-powerful Party, which is headed by Orwell's nice invention of a mythical protector, Big Brother, the fount of all wisdom and virtue—and of absolutely total ruthlessness. (Well, we have since Orwell's death seen the temporary rise of some similar figures.) The Party is divided into the mysterious privileged minority of the Inner Party and Orwell's chosen victims (his own social class), the harassed Outer Party members who are constantly watched over by the Thought Police for deviation, dissenters being tortured within the Ministry of Love and vaporized.

In this coherent inferno, the watching is done through ubiquitous telescreens—Orwell's single mechanical invention for the future—through which the Party simultaneously broadcasts lying propaganda and has everybody watched all the time for possible heresy. (Again, this is not a bad broad forecast of today's mounting Government supervision of citizens by computer storage of information.)

But now we come to the Proles, the vast working-class majority of the population who do not count in Orwell's Britain of 1984; and here he seemed to stumble. His picture is of a completely demoralized British working class:

> The Proles were born, they grew up in the gutters, they went to work at twelve, they passed through a brief blossoming period of beauty and sexual desire, they married at twenty, they were middle-aged at thirty, they died, for the most part, at sixty. Heavy physical work, the care of home and children, petty quarrels with neighbours, films, football, beer, and above all, gambling filled up the horizon of their minds.

This picture has not only little connection with the real organized and motorized British worker of the eighties, taking their holidays in Florida; it was an old-fashioned view even at the time when Orwell wrote in 1948. Since he severely censured

Kipling for writing patronizing poems about soldiers who dropped their aitches, his own laboured attempts to reproduce Prole cockney speech are curious. Altogether, it is odd that Orwell, when writing on Jura in 1948, should in his Proles produce a picture of the British workers that looks like one taken from his childhood. Other faults in the book strike the reader. Orwell presents his totalitarian Party as deliberately unideological, neither nationalist nor Communist, which seems unlikely. His dirty, run-down London of 1984 with its bomb gaps is no city of the future but the bombed wartime London he remembered. The sinister canteen in the Ministry of Truth where the hero Winston eats is obviously based on the innocent wartime canteen of the BBC, which he also remembered.

And so on. Yet these faults hardly matter. The point is that the reader is soon caught by the sheer power and cohesion of Orwell's nightmare vision of a savage, totalitarian society—above all, one in which nothing can change. Orwell's Party rules Oceania by a system of *doublethink* under which two opposed opinions can be held simultaneously. Thus, while it derides every principle of English socialism, Orwell has the Party call its philosophy 'Ingsoc'. . . . Within the nightmare, life is forever unchanged. The clocks of London strike thirteen. Big Brother glares from giant posters and his eyes watch the citizens through the telescreens. In his cubicle in the Ministry of Truth, the hero Winston Smith sits forever changing and falsifying past copies of *The Times* in keeping with current Party edicts, because the Party maintains that whoever controls the past controls the future. (pp. 196-99)

Into this nightmarish vision of the future, in which all details dovetail, Orwell has as it were projected himself into the story in the shape of his wretched hero Winston Smith. Whereas in Orwell's other novels the ending is implicit in the telling, Winston's doom is conveyed *explicitly* from the start. He is described as knowing himself doomed when he defies Party rules to keep an individual diary. Doom comes nearer to him and his girl Julia when they start to have an affair. It becomes inevitable when they visit Inner Party member O'Brien and offer to join the traitor Goldstein's army. When arrested, Winston is tortured and brainwashed by O'Brien within the Ministry of Love. His final and ultimate doom arrives when he is taken to room 101 'where the worst thing in the world happens', the worst thing in Winston's case being that a cage of rats is placed over his face, whereat he collapses, totally recants and becomes an automaton, loving Big Brother.

Since I first read *Nineteen Eighty-Four*, a neat *ad hominem* critique of it has been put forward by Anthony West, who noted the similarity between Winston Smith's fate in 1984 and Orwell's memories of St Cyprian's as told in **'Such, Such Were the Joys'** [see *TCLC*, Vol. 2]. As Mr West saw it, the mounting pattern of fear in which Orwell envelops Winston paralleled the fears which he himself recalled feeling at St Cyprian's, leading to the climax of the dread summons to the headmaster's study for the inevitable beating. Mr West goes on: 'Whether Orwell knew it or not, what he did in *Nineteen Eighty-Four* was to send everyone to an enormous Crossgates (St Cyprian's) to be as miserable as he had been.'

The critique is neat, but, firstly, Mr West was in part discovering the known. I recall how Orwell himself told me (although I don't think he wrote this anywhere) that the sufferings of a misfit boy in a boarding school were probably the only English parallel to the isolation felt by an outsider in a totalitarian society. Secondly, and more important, since Orwell always wrote autobiographically, touches of his private nightmare do

recur in his writings. As I have myself suggested, one can if one likes find memories of his own loneliness as a boy woven into the sense of isolation felt by Winston Smith. Perhaps without the neuroses of Eric Blair the works of George Orwell might never have been written, but to reduce Orwell's achievement to these neuroses is naive.

After all, when composing *Nineteen Eighty-Four,* he was touching on the problems of very real dictatorship while writing in the horrendous dictatorial age of Hitler, Stalin and others. With a tremendous, exhausting psychological effort, adding no doubt elements of his private nightmare, he tried through the experiences with which he endowed the hapless Winston Smith to look deeply into the collectivist future he saw ahead. As I have said, his immediate model for his totalitarian Oceania was Stalin's Soviet Union, but I think his vision was much wider. As he wrote in the book, by the fourth decade of the twentieth century, all the main currents of political thought were authoritarian. The earthly paradise had been discredited at exactly the moment when it had seemed, through technology, to become realizable. These words in *Nineteen Eighty-Four* are put into the mouth of the rebel Goldstein, but there is no reason to think they are not Orwell's own. In previous writings he had stressed that bourgeois individuality was going, the bonds of family, locality, religion, craft and profession were going. In their place a new collectivism was spreading in society, whether in work or life or leisure. But it also appeared to Orwell in 1948 that the new collective did not bring the earthly paradise any nearer. Not only that, it appeared to him that under the threat of violence and the nuclear terror, the new collective could become grotesquely dehumanized. It is as a permanent warning against the danger of the dehumanized collective in our society that *Nineteen Eighty-Four* has survived and should be seen to have survived.

Two concluding points. When Orwell told me that because he thought ill health had affected it, he was dissatisfied with *Nineteen Eighty-Four* (he wrote to Julian Symons that he had 'ballsed it up') I think that his dissatisfaction was mainly directed at the third part of the book, where Winston is interrogated and tortured by O'Brien. From my first reading, one passage had particularly remained in my mind, that in which O'Brien explains that to Big Brother and the Party, power and the infliction of torture on victims are not only justified for their own sake. They are also justified for ever. (pp. 199-201)

I remember how at my first reading I had thought that here Orwell was really piling on his private nightmare a bit, yet the words must have made an impact on readers and been specially remembered. I found the passage used as comment in articles on the tenth anniversary of the Soviet crushing of Dubcek's liberal Communist Czech régime and on the twenty-fifth anniversary of the Soviet crushing of the Hungarian revolution; and on the occasion of the crushing of Solidarity in Poland in 1981-2, I found it said in the press that to Comrade Brezhnev, the Soviet boot must be on the face of the satellite countries forever. Like other Orwellian sayings, it has proved to be prophetic.

My last point concerns the Appendix on 'Newspeak'. The American Book of the Month Club at first wanted him to omit it. Fortunately he resisted, for his account of how his Party rulers in Oceania were busy eliminating large numbers of common English words from existence and substituting newly knocked-up words for others in order to make heretical thought impossible—this is almost the best touch of satire in the whole book. (pp. 201-02)

I noticed how in her splendid autobiographical account of her political imprisonment under Stalin, the Soviet author Eugenia Ginzburg referred to Orwell's comments on totalitarian society with an apparent certainty that her references would be understood. When I mentioned this to a Russian friend—well, she was lucky enough to have come out of the Soviet Union five years ago—she said: 'What do you mean? With his *Newspeak* and *Doublethink,* Orwell wrote for us! No Westerner could understand him as intimately as we in the Soviet Union felt he understood our lives.' (p. 202)

His judgements might not be precisely correct every time, but I think it is his sceptical agnosticism which in particular appeals to readers who grew up after Hitler and Stalin had drawn their line across history, in that second half of the twentieth century he never saw. They were readers who had lost their own illusions, about the United Nations or the promises of the Soviet paradise, about unreal expectations of freedom in the Third World and even the hope that social democracy at home in the West could do more, as Orwell said, than improve society by a small measure.

As an agnostic—and here again lies his appeal—he was a great anticipator of the shape of things to come. *Nineteen Eighty-Four* showed that he was fascinated not only by the future but by the question of the past. Today we seem afloat amid a facile nostalgia for the fashions and artifacts of the past, but this is a relatively new attitude. When Orwell was writing, in the sombre forties, the past seemed to lie behind one like a heap of dull wreckage. Orwell was among the first to try to resurrect the legitimate values of the past, even to indulge himself with a certain nostalgia. If he had long left his upper-middle-class background behind, he never thought that its ideals of public service and patriotism were simply to be mocked and rejected. He endowed all the heroes of his novels, even Winston Smith wandering amid fantasies in the year 1984, with that nostalgic memory of a 'golden country' of rabbit-cropped pastures, an overgrown copse and a still pool with fish, a memory which he had himself treasured since childhood. (p. 205)

In *Nineteen Eighty-Four* he tried to show how the future needed the past with Winston's concern over half-forgotten nursery rhymes and his purchases of a ledger of beautiful old white paper and a water-coloured Victorian paperweight. (p. 206)

One of his crucial anticipations was, of course, of the way in which totalitarian Communist societies would develop. Admittedly the Soviet society of today is no longer monolithically totalitarian as it was at the peak of Stalin's great terror. Still, in its rigid insistence on the central bureaucratic control of everybody and everything, in its enduring restriction on individual expression and in the use of KGB police force against dissidents, it can still be reasonably described by the adjective 'totalitarian', and Orwell's forecast of the world dangers inherent in such Communist totalitarianism was a major piece of political thinking. . . . He wrote his *Nineteen Eighty-Four* long before Czeslaw Milosz in his Nobel Prize-winning *The Captive Mind* described the enforced Soviet imposition of a distorted political mass fantasy upon a captive population.

He not only knew Communist life in his own time; he had an image of its future. In O'Brien's interrogation of Winston by shock treatment in the Ministry of Love, there is a point where he shifts dramatically from merely accusing Winston of political *thoughtcrime* in daring to oppose the Party. He says that in his puny individual opposition, Winston has simply shown himself as *insane*—and the purpose of his torture was to cure

him of his insanity. It is as though Orwell had anticipated the switch of the KGB from Stalin's former mass purges to the present method of singling out Soviet political dissidents and incarcerating them in psychiatric hospitals like the Serbsky, where they are treated by drugs against exaggerated belief in their individuality and against paranoid delusions of reforming the Soviet system. (pp. 206-07)

But to return to the central theme of Orwell's thought, to his main message as expressed in his essays and *Nineteen Eighty-Four.* It was a simple, straightforward message. In spite of his nostalgia for his childhood pleasures and his appreciation of the virtues of his early background, he had travelled far from the whole culture and way of life of his conservative, very English, one-time imperial, native upper-middle class. As he liked to say, it was all up with this class. (pp. 207-08)

Instead, he became and remained a socialist. He regarded himself as belonging to the radical wing of the British Labour Party and continued to believe that its measures could make the life of the British working classes somewhat more humane and better.

And yet, he was profoundly afraid of what he saw as a larger, inevitable social change which was simultaneously in progress: the growth of a dehumanized, technological collective life lying ahead, particularly within the Big Soviet State in the East, but for that matter also within the State of depersonalized Big Business in the West. (The machines mechanically turning out 'prolefeed' novels for the masses in *Nineteen Eighty-Four* are a satire directed against American-style pulp fiction.) He was afraid of the loss of personal freedom as the collective society took over. He was afraid of violence as the moral checks of the old bourgeois order crumbled—see the essay **'Raffles and Miss Blandish'.** And he was of course afraid of the implications of nuclear terror.

And so we come to the crux of what he strove for in life. Both in his own life and his writings, he expressed the basic dilemma of his time, and also of our time which has followed after his death. The dilemma was that with Hitlerism and Stalinism, with two world wars and the nuclear arms race, an end had unmistakably come to that optimistic belief in man's inevitable progress, about which he had still read and been taught in early youth. The outlook of his English imperial upper-middle class, the glaring inequalities of Western capitalism—from these he turned with a weary shrug: he was formally a socialist. Yet at the same time he knew that the Marxist Utopia was hollow. He felt deeply pessimistic about the new collectivist manipulation of men and women which technical progress made possible in the society taking shape.

And so, in this dilemma, he called for the practice of the only possible virtues which he thought were possible in our time. He called for the reassertion of belief in personal freedom of speech; for the use of precise, truthful language in politics; for the equality of all citizens before the law; above all, for common decency and compassion in the conduct of political affairs. Simple virtues perhaps; his genius lay in his knowledge that in the dilemma of our time, these simple virtues might well be all we had to cope with the problems of our time crowding in upon us. It is as the great anticipator of our modern dilemma and the advocate of the only virtues at our disposal that I like to remember Orwell. (pp. 208-09)

T. R. Fyvel, in his George Orwell: A Personal Memoir, *Macmillan Publishing Co., Inc., 1982, 221p.*

NORMAN PODHORETZ (essay date 1983)

[*In the mid-1950s Podhoretz established a reputation for literary criticism that incorporated a left-wing political orientation. As editor of* Commentary *since 1960, he shifted the focus of that periodical from current Jewish issues to a broader concern with many aspects of American culture. His early criticism, gathered in* Doings and Undoings: The Fifties and After in American Writing *(1964), displays his tendency to relate external social and political issues to the literary work in question. In two autobiographical works,* Making It *(1968) and* Breaking Ranks: A Political Memoir *(1979), Podheretz chronicles his gradual change in political orientation from left-wing radicalism toward conservatism. In recent years Podhoretz has completely abandoned his Leftist position to become a leading neoconservative political essayist. His recent books include the controversial* The Present Danger: Do We Have the Will to Reverse the Decline of American Power? *(1980) and* Why We Were in Vietnam *(1982). In the following excerpt from one of the most controversial discussions of Orwell in recent years, Podhoretz attempts to demonstrate that if Orwell had lived into the 1980s his political views would have undergone a shift from democratic socialism to neoconservatism. For contrasting opinions, see the excerpts by Gordon Beadle (1984), who challenges Podhoretz on the grounds that his arguments rest upon judiciously edited quotations taken out of context, and Robert Christgau (1983), who dismisses all such speculation about a living Orwell's possible political orientation as "silly."*]

Normally, to speculate on what a dead man might have said about events he never lived to see is a frivolous enterprise. There is no way of knowing whether and to what extent he would have changed his views in response to a changing world; and this is especially the case with a writer like Orwell, who underwent several major political transformations. On the other hand, the main issues that concerned Orwell throughout his career are still alive today, often in different form but often also in almost exactly the same form they took when he wrote about them. This is why so many of his apparently dated journalistic pieces remain relevant. Even though the particular circumstances with which they deal have long since been forgotten, the questions they raise are questions we are still asking today and still trying to answer.

If this is true of much of Orwell's fugitive journalism, it becomes even more strikingly evident when we consider some of his major works: *Animal Farm* and *Nineteen Eighty-Four* among his novels, and among his discursive writings, [*Down and Out in Paris and London, The Road to Wigan Pier,* and *Homage to Catalonia*] . . . , not to mention many of the wonderful essays collected in [*Inside the Whale, Dickens, Dali and Others,* and *Shooting an Elephant*]. . . . So relevant do all these works seem today that to read through them is to be astonished, and a little depressed, at the degree to which we are still haunted by the ghosts of political wars past. (pp. 30-1)

The two main groups contending over Orwell today are the socialists on the one side and, on the other, the disillusioned former socialists who have come to be known as neoconservatives. The socialists, of whom Crick is a leading representative, declare that Orwell was a "revolutionary" whose values can only be (as Crick puts it) "wilfully misunderstood . . . when he is claimed for the camp of the Cold War." For their part, the neoconservatives deny that Orwell was a revolutionary; they think of him instead as a major critic of revolutionism. And they do indeed claim him for "the camp of the Cold War" in the sense that they see in his work one of the great prophetic warnings against the threat of Soviet totalitarianism. Thus the Committee for the Free World, an organization made up mainly

of neoconservative intellectuals (and with which I am associated), publishes material under the imprint "Orwell Press" and in general regards Orwell as one of its guiding spirits.

As a writer, Orwell is most admired, and rightly so, for the simplicity and straightforwardness of his style. "Good prose," he said, "is like a window pane." He valued such prose for its own sake, on aesthetic grounds, but he also believed that in political discourse clarity was a protection against deceit. . . . Since Orwell wrote about politics in a language that . . . succeeded marvelously in the art of calling things by their proper names and confronting questions with plainness and precision, one might think that nothing would be easier than defining his point of view. The problem is, however, that he wrote so much and changed his mind so often—mostly on small issues but also on large ones—that plausible evidence can be found in his work for each of the two contending interpretations of where he stood.

As a very young man, Orwell was, by his own account, a "Tory anarchist." But at the age of thirty or thereabouts he converted to socialism and kept calling himself a socialist until the day he died. Crick therefore has no trouble in piling up quotations that support the socialist claim to possession of Orwell. He does, however, have a great deal of trouble in trying to explain away the side of Orwell that has given so much aid and comfort to antisocialists of all kinds. For, avowed socialist though he certainly was, Orwell was also a relentless critic of his fellow socialists from beginning to end. (p. 31)

[While] he still regarded the Communists as comrades in the struggle for socialism, he went to fight against Franco in the Spanish Civil War. There he learned two things: that the Spanish Communists were more interested in furthering the aims of Soviet foreign policy than in making a socialist revolution at home, and that the left-wing press in England (and everywhere else) was full of lies about what was actually going on in Spain. For the next few years, much of his writing was devoted to attacks on the Stalinists and their fellow travelers, who, in those days of the "Popular Front," included almost everyone on the Left.

These attacks were written from what can loosely be described as a Trotskyist or revolutionary-socialist perspective based on, among other things, the proposition that England was hardly, if at all, better than Nazi Germany. But with the outbreak of World War II, a new Orwell was born—Orwell the English patriot. "My Country, Right or Left," he now declared in one of his most memorable phrases, and went on to excoriate the "anti-British" attitudes that had been so fashionable on the Left throughout the 1930s and to which he himself had temporarily subscribed.

Then, toward the end of the war, and with the defeat of fascist totalitarianism in sight, Orwell began brooding more and more on the possibility that communist totalitarianism might turn out to be the inevitable wave of the future. In *Animal Farm,* written while the Soviet Union was still a wartime ally of the Western democracies, he produced a satire on the Russian Revolution so unsparing that it could be and usually was interpreted as a repudiation of all hopes for a benevolent socialist revolution. Like *Homage to Catalonia* before it, the manuscript was rejected as too anti-Soviet by the first few publishers to whom it was submitted. One of the publishers in this case was no less a personage than T. S. Eliot, whose own aggressive conservatism did not prevent him from doubting that Orwell's was "the right point of view from which to criticize the political situation at the present time."

Finally there was *Nineteen Eighty-Four,* which came out just at the height of the Cold War and very shortly before Orwell's death. In that novel, Orwell portrayed the England of the future as a totalitarian society ruled over by a Communist-like party in the name of "Ingsoc" ("newspeak" for English socialism). He later explicitly denied that in using this term he had intended to cast any aspersions on the British Labour Party, of which he was a (highly critical) supporter, let alone that he was attacking socialism itself [see Orwell excerpt dated 1949]. Nevertheless, neither in *Animal Farm* nor in *Nineteen Eighty-Four* was there any trace of the idea that a socialist revolution could be accomplished without a betrayal of the ideals of liberty and equality to whose full realization socialism was in theory committed.

No wonder Crick has so much trouble staking the socialist claim to Orwell. No wonder too that other socialists of varying stripe like Isaac Deutscher and Raymond Williams have said that Orwell was not really one of them.

If Orwell was a great political writer—and I think he was, though I would not place him quite so high as Crick does—it is not because he was always right in his strictly political judgments. The plain truth is that he was more often wrong than right. For example, he predicted that the British Conservatives (the "Blimpocracy") would never go to war against Hitler; then, when they did, he refused to believe, and he doubted "whether many people under fifty believe[d] it either," that England could "win the war without passing through revolution."

In addition to making many mistaken political predictions, he was also capable of serious errors of political valuation, as when he joined briefly in the fashionable cry of the mid-1930s to the effect that there was no difference between fascism and liberalism. And even after correcting errors of this kind, he was capable of backsliding into such similar absurdities as saying that British rule in India was as bad as Hitler's rule in Europe, or that British policy toward Greece in 1945 was no different from "the Russian coercion of Poland."

Wrong though he so often was about particular events, however, Orwell in every stage of his political development was almost always right about one thing: the character and quality of the left-wing literary intellectuals among whom he lived and to whom he addressed himself as a political writer. More than anything else, the ethos of the left-wing literary intelligentsia was his true subject and the one that elicited his most brilliant work. Indeed, whatever ideas were fashionable on the Left at any given moment were precisely the ones he had the greatest compulsion to criticize. And the fact that he criticized them from within only added authority to the things he said—so much so that I wonder whether this was why he insisted on clinging so tenaciously to his identity as a man of the Left.

It is largely because of Orwell's relation to the left-wing intelligentsia that I believe he would have been a neoconservative if he were alive today. I would even suggest that he was a forerunner of neoconservatism in having been one of the first in a long line of originally left-wing intellectuals who have come to discover more saving political and moral wisdom in the instincts and mores of "ordinary" people than in the ideas and attitudes of the intelligentsia. "One has to belong to the intelligentsia to believe things like that," he wrote in 1945 after listing several egregious examples relating to the progress

of World War II; "no ordinary man could be such a fool." This remark has become especially well known in recent years, but it is only one of many passages of similar import scattered throughout Orwell's writings.

Nor was it only on political issues that Orwell defended the "ordinary man" against the left-wing intelligentsia. Even in the mid-1930s, during his most radical period, he attacked Cyril Connolly's novel *The Rock Pool* for suggesting that "so-called artists who spend on sodomy what they have gained by sponging" were superior to "the polite and sheep-like Englishman." This, he said, "only amounts to a distaste for normal life and common decency," and he concluded by declaring: "The fact to which we have got to cling, as to a lifebelt, is that it *is* possible to be a normal decent person and yet to be fully alive."

This streak of populism, always strong in Orwell, became even more pronounced with the outbreak of World War II, when it took the form of a celebration of England and the English character. As a corollary to becoming a wholehearted patriot—and in coming to see patriotism as a great and positive force—Orwell lashed out more ferociously than ever at the British intelligentsia:

> . . . the really important fact about so many of the English intelligentsia [is] their severance from the common culture of the country. . . . England is perhaps the only great country whose intellectuals are ashamed of their own nationality. In left-wing circles it is always felt that there is something slightly disgraceful in being an Englishman and that it is a duty to snigger at every English institution. . . . All through the critical years many leftwingers were chipping away at English morale, trying to spread an outlook that was sometimes squashily pacifist, sometimes violently pro-Russian, but always anti-British. . . . If the English people suffered for several years a real weakening of morale, so that the Fascist nations judged that they were "decadent" and that it was safe to plunge into war, the intellectual sabotage from the Left was partly responsible.

Is it any wonder that the neoconservatives see Orwell as a guiding spirit when everything he says here has been echoed by them in talking about the American intellectuals of today? (pp. 32, 34)

Another and related reason for thinking that Orwell would be a neoconservative if he were alive today lies in his attitude toward pacifism. For a very brief period in his youth Orwell flirted with pacifism, but nothing could have been more alien to his temperament and he soon broke off the affair. . . . [In] 1940, when a British defeat seemed likely [Orwell wrote]: "There is nothing for it but to die fighting, but one must above all die *fighting* and have the satisfaction of killing somebody else first."

Moved by such feelings, Orwell came to write about pacifism with an even fiercer edge of scorn and outrage than before. Later he would regret using the term "objectively pro-Fascist," but that is what he now accused the pacifists—or "Fascists," as he called them—of being (for, "If you hamper the war effort of one side you automatically help that of the other"); he also attacked them for "intellectual cowardice" in refusing to admit that this was the inescapable logical implication of their position; and he said that they were hypocritical "for crying

The hate rally. Still from the motion picture 1984, *directed by Michael Radford. Virgin Films.*

'Peace!' behind a screen of guns.'' But in trying to imagine where Orwell would have stood if he were alive today, the key sentence in his attack on pacifism is this: ''Insofar as it takes effect at all, pacifist propaganda can only be effective *against* those countries where a certain amount of freedom of speech is still permitted; in other words it is helpful to totalitarianism.''

Everything I have just quoted was written at a time when Nazi Germany was the main totalitarian enemy. But here is what Orwell said about pacifism at the very moment when the defeat of Hitler was imminent and when the Soviet Union was about to replace Nazi Germany as the most powerful embodiment of totalitarianism in the world:

> Pacifist propaganda usually boils down to saying that one side is as bad as the other, but if one looks closely at the writings of the younger intellectual pacifists, one finds that they do not by any means express impartial disapproval but are directed almost entirely against Britain and the United States. Moreover they do not as a rule condemn violence as such, but only violence used in defense of the Western countries. The Russians, unlike the British, are not blamed for defending themselves by warlike means. . . .

The ''real though unadmitted motive'' behind such propaganda, Orwell concluded, was ''hatred of Western democracy and admiration for totalitarianism.''

It is hard to believe that the man who wrote those words in 1945 would have felt any sympathy for the various ''objectively'' pacifist antidefense movements of today, about which the very same words could be used without altering a single detail. I can even easily imagine that Orwell would have been still angrier if he had lived to see so many ideas that have been discredited, both by arguments like his own and by historical experience, once again achieving widespread acceptability. It goes without saying that he would have opposed the unilateral disarmament that is now the official policy of the British Labour Party. . . . But I think he would also have opposed such measures as the nuclear freeze and a unilateral Western pledge of no-first-use of nuclear weapons. Given the conception of totalitarianism he developed in *Animal Farm* and *Nineteen Eighty-Four* as a totally closed system in which lies become truth at the dictate of the party, the notion that a verifiable disarmament agreement could be negotiated with the Soviet Union would surely have struck him as yet another pacifist ''illusion due to security, too much money and a simple ignorance of the way in which things actually happen.''

As for no-first-use, Orwell surely would have seen this as a form of unilateral disarmament by the West (since it would make Soviet superiority in conventional military power decisive on the European front) as well as a euphemistic screen behind which the United States could withdraw from its commitment to the defense of Western Europe under the hypocritical pretext of reducing the risk of nuclear war.

Nor is it likely that Orwell would have been reconverted to pacifism by the fear of nuclear weapons. As a matter of fact, he thought that "the worst possibility of all" was that "the fear inspired by the atomic bomb and other weapons yet to come will be so great that everyone will refrain from using them." Such an indefinite Soviet-American stalemate, he predicted, would lead to precisely the nightmare he was later to envisage in *Nineteen Eighty-Four* ("the division of the world among two or three vast totalitarian empires unable to conquer one another and unable to be overthrown by any internal rebellion").

This does not mean that Orwell contemplated the possibility of a nuclear war with equanimity, or that he did not on other occasions say that it could mean the destruction of civilization. Nevertheless, in 1947, the very year in which the Cold War officially began, Orwell wrote: "I don't, God knows, want a war to break out, but if one were compelled to choose between Russia and America—and I suppose that is the choice one might have to make—I would always choose America." (pp. 34-5)

To understand the force and the courage of Orwell's forthright repudiation of the idea that there was no significant moral difference between the United States and the Soviet Union, we have to remind ourselves that neither anti-Americanism nor neutralism was confined exclusively to the pro-Soviet Left. . . .

[There] can be no doubt that Orwell did belong in "the camp of the Cold War" while he was still alive. Nor can there be much doubt that if he were alive today he would have felt a greater kinship with the neoconservatives who are calling for resistance to Soviet imperialism than with either the socialist supporters of détente or the coalition of neutralists and pacifists who dominate the "peace movement" in Europe and their neoisolationist allies in the United States.

For consider: Orwell's ruling passion was the fear and hatred of totalitarianism. Unlike so many on the Left today, who angrily deny that there is any difference between totalitarianism and authoritarianism, he was among the first to insist on the distinction. Totalitarianism, he said, was a new and higher stage in the history of despotism and tyranny—a system in which every area of life, not merely (as in authoritarian regimes) the political sphere, was subjected to the control of the state. Only in Nazi Germany and the Soviet Union had totalitarianism thus far established itself, and of the two the Soviet variety clearly seemed to Orwell to be the more dangerous. (p. 36)

When Orwell wrote about the dangers of totalitarianism, then, whether in his essays or in *Nineteen Eighty-Four,* it was mainly the communist version he had in mind. To be sure, he followed no party line, not even his own, and he could always be relied on to contradict himself when the impulse seized him. At one moment he would denounce any move to establish good relations with the Russians, and at another moment, he might insist on the necessity of such relations.

But these were transient political judgments of the kind that, as he himself ruefully acknowledged, were never his strongest suit. What he most cared about was resisting the spread of Soviet-style totalitarianism. Consequently he "used a lot of ink" and did himself "a lot of harm by attacking the successive literary cliques" that had denied or tried to play down the brutal truth about the Soviet Union, to appease it, or otherwise to undermine the Western will to resist the spread of its power and influence.

If he were alive today, he would find the very ideas and attitudes against which he so fearlessly argued more influential than ever in left-wing centers of opinion (and not in them alone): that the freedoms of the West are relatively unimportant as compared with other values; that war is the greatest of all evils; that nothing is worth fighting or dying for; and that the Soviet Union is basically defensive and peaceful. It is impossible to imagine that he would have joined in parroting the latest expressions of this orthodoxy if he had lived to see it return in even fuller and more dangerous force.

I have no hesitation, therefore, in claiming Orwell for the neoconservative perspective on the East-West conflict. But I am a good deal more diffident in making the same claim on the issue of socialism. Like Orwell, most neoconservatives began their political lives as socialists; and most of them even followed the same course Orwell himself did from revolutionary to democratic socialism. Moreover, those neoconservatives who were old enough to be politically active in 1950, the year Orwell died, would still at that point have joined with him in calling themselves democratic socialists. About thirty years later, however, most of them had come around to the view expressed by the philosopher William Barrett in explaining why he had finally given up on his long and tenaciously held faith in "democratic socialism" (the telling quotation marks are Barrett's):

> How could we ever have believed that you could deprive human beings of the fundamental right to initiate and engage in their own economic activity without putting every other human right into jeopardy? And to pass from questions of rights to those of fact: everything we observe about the behavior of human beings in groups, everything we know about that behavior from history, should tell us that you cannot unite political and economic power in one center without opening the door to tyranny.

The question is: would Orwell, in the light of what has happened in the three decades since his death, have arrived eventually at a position similar to Barrett's? Crick is certain that he would not—that he would have remained a socialist, and a militant one. I am not so sure.

Orwell was never much of a Marxist and (beyond a generalized faith in "planning") he never showed much interest in the practical arrangements involved in the building of socialism. He was a socialist because he hated the class system and the great discrepancies of wealth that went with it. Yet he also feared that the establishment of socialism would mean the destruction of liberty. . . . The trouble is that capitalism, which "leads to dole queues, the scramble for markets, and war," is probably doomed. (It is indeed largely as a result of the failure of capitalism that the totalitarian world of *Nineteen Eighty-Four* comes into being.)

Suppose, however, that Orwell had lived to see this prediction about capitalism refuted by the success of the capitalist countries in creating enough wealth to provide the vast majority of their citizens not merely with the decent minimum of food and housing that Orwell believed only socialism could deliver, but with a wide range of what to his rather Spartan tastes would have seemed unnecessary luxuries. Suppose further that he had lived to see all this accomplished—and with the year 1984 already in sight!—while "the freedom of the intellect," for whose future under socialism he increasingly trembled, was if anything being expanded. And suppose, on the other side, he had lived to see the wreckage through planning and centralization of one socialist economy after another, so that not even at the sacrifice of liberty could economic security be assured.

Suppose, in short, that he had lived to see the aims of what *he* meant by socialism realized to a very great extent under capitalism, and without either the concentration camps or the economic miseries that have been the invariable companions of socialism in practice. Would he still have gone on mouthing socialist pieties and shouting with the anticapitalist mob?

Perhaps. Nothing has been more difficult for intellectuals in this century than giving up on socialism, and it is possible that even Orwell, who so prided himself on his "power of facing unpleasant facts," would have been unwilling or unable to face what to most literary intellectuals is the most unpleasant fact of all: that the values both of liberty and equality fare better under capitalism than under socialism.

And yet I find it hard to believe that Orwell would have allowed an orthodoxy to blind him on this question any more than he allowed other "smelly little orthodoxies" to blind him to the truth about the particular issues involved in the struggle between totalitarianism and democracy: Spain, World War II, and communism.

In Orwell's time, it was the left-wing intelligentsia that made it so difficult for these truths to prevail. And so it is too with the particular issues generated by the struggle between totalitarianism and democracy in our own time, which is why I am convinced that if Orwell were alive today, he would be taking his stand with the neoconservatives and against the Left. (pp. 36-7)

> *Norman Podhoretz, "If Orwell Were Alive Today,"*
> in Harper's, *Vol. 266, No. 1592, January, 1983, pp.*
> *30-2, 34-7.*

IRVING HOWE   (essay date 1983)

[*A longtime editor of the liberal magazine* Dissent *and a regular contributor to* The New Republic, *Howe is one of America's most highly respected literary critics and social historians. He has been a socialist since the 1930s, and his criticism is frequently informed by a liberal social viewpoint. Howe is widely praised for what F. R. Dulles has termed his "knowledgeable understanding, critical acumen and forthright candor." Howe has written: "My work has fallen into two fields: social history and literary criticism. I have tried to strike a balance between the social and the literary: to fructify one with the other: yet not to confuse one with the other. Though I believe in the social approach to literature, it seems to me peculiarly open to misuse; it requires particular delicacy and care." In the following excerpt, originally published in* The New Republic, *January 3, 1983, Howe reprises many of his earlier critical comments on* Nineteen Eighty-Four *(see Additional Bibliography and TCLC, Vol. 2). He finds that the novel remains horrifying not because it has proven to be an accurate prophecy, but because the concept of a totally controlled society ruled through terrorism by a self-perpetuating elite now seems quite plausible. Howe also addresses many commonly posed questions about the work, including whether or not it is a novel or a satire, how Orwell viewed the proles, and whether or not Orwell would still be a socialist today.*]

It is a common experience to fear that the admirations of youth will wear thin, and precisely because *1984* had so enormous an impact when it originally came out more than thirty years ago, I hesitated for a long time before returning to it. I can still remember the turbulent feelings—the bottomless dismay,

the sense of being undone—with which many people first read Orwell's book. My fear now was that it would seem a passing sensation of its moment or even, as some leftist critics have charged, a mere reflex of the cold war. But these fears were groundless. Having reread *1984,* I am convinced, more than ever, that it is a classic of our age.

Whether it is also a classic for the ages is another question. What people of the future will think about Orwell's book we cannot know, nor can we say what it might mean to those who will remember so little about the time of totalitarianism they will need an editor's gloss if they chance upon a copy. But for us, children of this century, the relation to *1984* must be intimate, troubled, nerve-wracking. In 1938 or 1939 the idea of a world divided among a few totalitarian superpowers, which Orwell made into the premise of his book, had not seemed at all far-fetched. . . . When Orwell published his book a decade later, in 1949, one felt that, despite his obvious wish to unnerve us with an extreme version of the total state, he was presenting something all too familiar, even commonplace.

Also familiar, though in a somewhat different sense, was the body of detail about daily life in Oceania that Orwell built up. Many of the descriptive passages in *1984* were simply taken over, with a degree of stretching here and there, from Orwell's earlier books or from his life-long caustic observations of twentieth-century England. (pp. 3-4)

As it turned out, the unfuture of Oceania had some pretty keen resemblances to the immediate past of England.

Resemblances, also, to the years of Stalinist terror in Russia. The grilling of Winston Smith by the Oceania authorities, the alternation between physical beatings and sympathetic conversations, the final terrifying appearance of O'Brien, master of power—all these recall or parallel Arthur Koestler's account in *Darkness at Noon* of how the NKVD interrogated its victims. Koestler's description, in turn, anticipated closely what we have since learned about the methods of the Soviet secret police. It was to Orwell's credit that he understood how the imagination flourishes when it is grounded in common reality.

He knew, as well, that to make credible the part of his book which would spiral into the extraordinary, he had first to provide it with a strong foundation of the ordinary. Or to put it another way, he knew that his main problem was to make plausible—which, one might remember, is not the same as the probable—his vision of how certain destructive tendencies of modern society could drive insanely forward, unbraked by sentiments of humaneness or prudence.

Yet while rereading *1984,* I have come to recognize still another way in which it all seems decidedly familiar—but *this* familiarity causes shock.

The very idea of a totally controlled society in which a self-perpetuating elite rules through terror and ideology no longer strikes us as either a dim horror or a projection of the paranoid mind. In the few decades since Orwell wrote, we have gone a long way toward domesticating the idea of the total state, indeed, to the point where it now seems just one among a number of options concerning the way men live. The thought that totalitarianism is a constant, even commonplace possibility in the history of our time—this may prove to be as terrifying as the prospect that we might sooner or later be living under an Orwellian regime. No sensible person could have taken *1984* as an actual prediction; even those who read the book with malice or loathing knew it had to be taken as a warning, no doubt a fearful warning. That in its fundamental conception it should now seem so familiar, so ordinary, so plausible, is—when you come to think of it—a deeply unnerving fact about the time in which we live. But a fact it is.

To ask what kind of book *1984* is may seem a strange, even pedantic question. After all, you might say, millions of people have read the book and appreciated it well enough without troubling their heads about fine points of genre. Yet the question is neither strange nor pedantic, since in my experience there remains among Orwell's readers a good portion of uncertainty and confusion about what he was trying to do. People will often say, "Look, we're getting close to the year 1984 and we aren't living in the kind of society Orwell summoned; doesn't that mean he was exaggerating or perhaps that he was morbid?" To this kind of complaint there is a simple enough answer: It's in the very nature of anti-utopian fiction to project a degree of exaggeration, since without exaggeration the work would be no more than still another realistic portrait of totalitarian society.

Other complaints, being more sophisticated, take on a "literary" edge. Some of them, still often heard, are that the book contains no "real characters," or that there isn't enough of a credible social setting, or that the psychological vision of the story is somewhat rudimentary. Such complaints have really to do with genres or misunderstandings of genres; they reflect a failure to grasp the kind of fiction Orwell was writing and what could legitimately be expected from it. When a critic like Raymond Williams says that *1984* lacks "a substantial society and correspondingly substantial persons," he is (almost willfully, one suspects) missing the point. For the very premise of anti-utopian fiction is that it sketch an "inconceivable" world in such a way as to force us, provisionally, to credit its conceivability; that it project a world in which categories like "substantial society . . . substantial persons" have largely been suppressed or rendered obsolete. In actuality a society like that of Oceania may be impossible to realize, but that is not at issue here. A writer may, in the kind of fiction Orwell was composing, draw the shadows of "the impossible" as if they were real possibilities—if only in order to persuade us that finally they are not possible. As it happens, we have come close enough during the last half century to a society like Oceania for the prospect of its realization to be within reach of the imagination. And that is all a writer of fiction needs.

There are kinds of fictions that should not really be called novels at all: think of Voltaire's *Candide,* Swift's *Gulliver's Travels,* Peacock's *Crotchet Castle.* In *Anatomy of Criticism,* Northrop Frye, hoping (probably in vain) to check the modern tendency to lump all fictions as novels, describes a kind of fiction he calls Menippean satire, "allegedly invented by a Greek cynic named Menippus." This fiction "deals less with people as such than with mental attitudes . . . and differs from the novel in its characterization, which is stylized rather than naturalistic. . . ."

A quarter of a century ago, when first writing about *1984,* I thought this a satisfactory description of the kind of book Orwell had composed; but now I would like to modify that opinion. Almost everyone has recognized how brilliant Orwell was in finding symbolic vehicles and dramatic instances through which to render the "mental attitudes" about which Frye speaks. Think only of Newspeak and Big Brother, Hate Week and memory hole, all of which have entered our speech and consciousness as vivid figures. . . . There remains, then, good

reason to see *1984* as an instance of "Menippean satire"—but only in part.

For in going back to the book, I have learned to appreciate parts that now strike me as novelistic in the usual sense. Especially those parts in which Winston Smith and Julia try to find for themselves a patch, a corner where they can be alone and make love. Here bits of individuality begin to make themselves felt: Julia's boldness, for instance, in arranging their escapade to the country, where they can be free of the hated telescreen, or her charming indifference to all ideologies, as when she falls asleep during Winston's excited reading from the forbidden book, Emmanuel Goldstein's *Theory and Practice of Oligarchical Collectivism.*

I now think that *1984* ought to be read as a mixture of genres, mostly Menippean satire and conventional novel, but also bits of tract and a few touches of transposed romance. Such a description may be helpful, although not because anyone is foolish enough to want exact categories; it may train us, at the least, to avoid false expectations when we read.

An anti-utopian fiction must have a touch or two of excess. There has to be a story which takes the familiar conventions of the once-fashionable utopian novel and stands them on their heads. Elsewhere I've described that touch of excess as "the dramatic strategy and narrative psychology of 'one more step' . . . one step beyond our known reality—not so much a picture of modern totalitarianism as an extension, by just one and no more than one step, of the essential pattern of the total state." But this excess can of course consist of more than one step; it might be two or three, yet not many more steps than two or three, since then the link of credence between writer and reader might be broken by a piling on of improbabilities.

What has especially struck me in rereading *1984* is that, yes, it's true that in an anti-utopian fiction the writer can afford at most a few steps beyond our known reality, but he is likely to achieve his strongest effects precisely at the moment when the balance teeters between minimal credence and plummeting disbelief. For at such a moment we ask ourselves: Can things *really* go this far? And it is then that our deepest anxieties are aroused. Is it conceivable that the total state could be so "total," could break and transform human beings so far beyond what "human nature" may be expected to endure? We think and hope not, but we cannot be certain. We know that the total state has already done things earlier generations would have supposed to be impossible.

One such moment occurs in *1984* when Orwell turns to sexuality in Oceania. Members of the Outer Party—we remain in the dark about the Inner Party—are shown to be trained systematically to minimize and deny the sexual instinct, certainly to separate the act of intercourse from sensual pleasure or imaginative play. There can be no "free space" in the lives of the Outer Party faithful, nothing that remains beyond the command of the state. Sexual energy is to be transformed into political violence and personal hysteria. (pp. 4-8)

It remains a fascinating question whether Orwell had captured here an essential part of the totalitarian outlook or had gone too far beyond "one more step." We know that in the years of Stalinism the Soviet Union favored, at least publicly, a prudish, sometimes a repressive anti-sexuality. But there is no evidence that during those years—and this is the period upon which Orwell drew for his book—Communist Party members were forced to suffer greater sexual repressiveness than the rest of the population. If the evidence is skimpy, Orwell was nonetheless touching on something very important here; he was taking an imaginative leap from totalitarian "first principles" concerning, not so much sex, certainly not sex in its own right but the threat of "free space," that margin of personal autonomy which even in the worst moments of Stalinism and Hitlerism some people still wanted to protect. And it was this margin that Orwell took to be the single great "flaw" of all previous efforts to realize the totalitarian vision. Whether a complete or "total" totalitarianism is possible, or possible for any length of time, is not, I want to repeat, the question. All that matters, for our purposes, is that it be plausible enough to allow a fictional representation.

Winston Smith's journey from rebellion to breakdown is a doomed effort to recover the idea, perhaps even more than the experience, of a personal self; to regain the possibility of individual psychology and the memory of free introspection. And this occurs in *1984*—I think it is one of Orwell's greatest strokes—not so much through ratiocination as through an encounter between two bodies. When Winston Smith and Julia make their first escapade out of London, carefully finding a patch in the woods where they can make love, they are not "in love," at least not yet. What happens between them is only—only!—the meeting of two eager bodies, animal-like if you must, but wonderfully urgent, alive, and good. They are free from the grip of the Party; this moment is theirs.

In this and a few other sections Orwell writes with a kind of grieving, muted lyricism, a hoarse lyricism which is about as much as, under the circumstances, he can allow himself. I have found myself moved, far more than when I first read the book, by these brief and unabashed celebrations of the body. A little freer in our language than in 1949, we would now say that Julia is a woman who likes to fuck, and it seems important to put it exactly that way, since in the wretched precincts of Oceania just about the best that anyone can do is fucking.

Bolder still than Orwell's strategy of "one more step" in treating sexuality is his treatment of power. He tends to see the lust for power as a root experience, something that need not or cannot be explained in terms other than itself, and here too, I think, the passage of time has largely confirmed his intuitions. Let me draw upon your patience for a minute as I recall certain criticisms made by admiring critics of Orwell soon after *1984* came out. Philip Rahv, in a fine essay-review of the book, said that in one respect Orwell may have surpassed even Dostoevsky in grasping "the dialectic of power" [see *TCLC*, Vol. 6]. *The Brothers Karamazov* shows the Grand Inquisitor as a tyrant ruling from benevolent intent: he believes man to be a weak creature, who needs the lash for his own good and can be happy only when the burden of freedom is lifted from his back. During the interrogation conducted by O'Brien, Winston Smith, hoping to please his tormentor, repeats the Grand Inquisitor's rationale for the holding of power:

> ... that the Party did not seek power for its own ends, but only for the good of the majority. That it sought power because men in the mass were frail, cowardly creatures who could not endure liberty or face the truth.... That the choice for mankind lay between freedom and happiness, and that, for the great bulk of mankind, happiness was better. That the Party was the eternal guardian of the weak, a dedicated sect doing evil that good might come, sacrificing its own happiness to that of others.

All of this strikes O'Brien as mere cant; he scorns it as "stupid." Turning up the dial of the machine that regulates Winston Smith's pain, he chastises him in these memorable words:

> The Party seeks power entirely for its own sake. We are not interested in the good of others; we are interested solely in power.... One does not establish a dictatorship in order to safeguard a revolution; one makes the revolution in order to establish the dictatorship. The object of persecution is persecution. The object of torture is torture. The object of power is power....
>
> ... Power is in inflicting pain and humiliation. Power is in tearing human minds to pieces and putting them together again in new shapes of your own choosing.

This exchange forms a key passage in *1984*, perhaps in the entirety of modern political discourse. (pp. 9-11)

Can we now be so certain that Orwell was wrong in giving O'Brien that speech about power? I think not. For we have lived to witness a remarkable development of the Communist state: its ideology has decayed, far fewer people give credence to its claims than in the past, yet its power remains virtually unchecked.... Not many educated Russians, including those highly placed within the party, can be supposed still to "believe" they are building the Communist society first expounded by Marx and Lenin. But the party remains.

What then do the apparatchiks believe in? They believe in their apparatus. They believe in the party. They believe in the power these enable. That a high Soviet bureaucrat might now talk to an imprisoned dissident in the bluntly cynical style that O'Brien employs in talking to Winston Smith does not therefore seem inconceivable. It does not even seem far-fetched. (pp. 13)

I take it as a sign of Orwell's intuitive gifts that he should have foreseen this historical moment when belief in the total state is crumbling while its power survives. Whether such a condition signifies an explosive crisis or a period of low-keyed stability, we do not yet know. But there is now at least some ground for lending credence to Orwell's admittedly extreme notion that the rulers of the total state no longer need trouble to delude themselves, perhaps because they no longer can, about their motives and claims. The grim possibility is that they now have a realistic view of themselves as creatures holding power simply for the sake of power, and that they find this quite sufficient.

The most problematic, but also interesting, aspect of *1984* is Orwell's treatment of the proles. (pp. 13-14)

Winston looks for some agency or lever of rebellion that might threaten the power of the Party. *"If there is hope,"* he writes in his notebook, *"it lies in the proles ..."* If ... and then the paradox that even in the half-forgotten era of capitalism used to bedevil Socialists: *"Until they [the proles] become conscious they will never rebel, and until after they have rebelled they cannot become conscious."* Orwell knew of course that traditionally Marxists had offered a "dialectical" resolution of this dilemma: the imperatives of action stir people into consciousness, and the stimulants of consciousness enable further action. A powerful formula, and millions of people have repeated it; but like other left-wing intellectuals of his day, he had come to feel dubious about its accuracy or usefulness. In writing *1984*, however, Orwell was wise enough to leave slightly open the question of whether the proles could exert a decisive power in modern society.

Here, if anywhere, Orwell made his one major error. The proles are allowed more privacy than Party members, the telescreen does not bawl instructions at them, and the secret police seldom troubles them, except occasionally to wipe out a talented or independent prole. What this must mean is that the Inner Party judges the proles to be completely crushed and tamed, no threat to its power either now or in the future, quite demoralized as individuals and helpless as a social class.

But the evidence of history—which ought, after all, to be crucial for a writer of an anti-utopian fiction—comes down strongly against Orwell's vision of the future. Europe this past half century has been convulsed by repeated, if unsuccessful, rebellions in which the workers (or proles) have played a major role, from East Berlin in 1956 to France in 1968, from the Hungarian Revolution to the rise of Solidarity in Poland. (pp. 14-15)

If the "ruling circles" of Poland, Czechoslovakia, and Hungary could talk in private to O'Brien, they would tell him that, lucid as he may be on the subject of power, he may well be making a mistake in his view of the proles.

An aura of gloom hangs over *1984;* the book ends with a broken Winston Smith drinking Victory Gin and blubbering his drunken love for Big Brother. He has made his "adjustment."

"If there is any hope, it lies in the proles," Winston Smith had said. But is there any hope? That is not a question Orwell is obliged to answer; he need only ask it, with sufficient honesty and the despair that shows him to be a man of his century. The gloom that hovers over the book has been "explained" by some critics as a symptom of the grave illness Orwell was suffering at the end of his life, at the very time he wrote *1984.* Perhaps there is a small measure of truth in this, but basically it seems to me a rather stupid idea. A merely sick or depressed man could not have written with the surging inventiveness that shapes *1984*—and, in any case, where have these critics kept themselves this past half century? Haven't they heard the bad news? No, the gloom of *1984* is real and justified; but it is an energizing and passionate gloom.

If the extremism of Orwell's vision derives from a close responsiveness to the idea of a world in which human life is shorn of dynamic possibilities, it also reflects his growing distaste for politics itself, at least a politics that leaves no margin for anything but itself. And this may also account for the streak of conservatism in Orwell's outlook—a conservatism less of politics than of sensibility: that is, an appreciation for the way people actually live, the strengths of received ties and feelings. One of the most affecting parts of *1984* is Winston Smith's recurrent effort to recall fragments of the past, the days before the Party took power. (pp. 16-17)

This conservatism of feeling, already present in Orwell's earlier books, is taken by some readers to conflict with his democratic socialist convictions. That would be true only if socialism were seen—as indeed both authoritarian left and reactionary right see it—as a total expurgation of the past, an attempt by a bureaucratic elite to impose "utopia" through terror. Orwell understood, however, that democratic socialism is an effort to extend what is valid in the past, to enlarge our freedoms and deepen our culture. The conservative sentiments Orwell reveals in *1984* not only aren't in conflict with his socialist opinions, they can be seen as sustaining them. Or so, at least, one hopes.

While writing this essay I have been asked several times by an editor of an American magazine eager for a quick word: "If Orwell were still alive, would he have remained a socialist?" The question is absurd on the face of it, since no one can possibly know. But this much can be said: Within his generation of left-wing writers and intellectuals, some have turned to the right, some have tried to refine their socialist values toward a greater stress on democracy, and others have abandoned their interest in politics entirely. Which of these directions Orwell might have taken it would be foolish to say, except that it's hard to imagine him dropping his interest in politics entirely.

We do know that Orwell publicly repudiated efforts to use *1984* as a piece of anti-socialist propaganda [see Orwell excerpt dated 1949]. (p. 17)

This is simply Orwell's opinion, and we know that writers often don't grasp the full implications of their work. It is quite possible, therefore, for some readers to say that while Orwell did not intend his book to be an attack on the socialist idea, it can be read that way.

And so it can. The vision of things Orwell presents need not necessarily lead to any one political conclusion, except a stress upon the urgency of democratic norms. Liberals, conservatives, and socialists can all argue from Orwell's text in behalf of their views, though the more sophisticated among them will recognize that a political position must be justified in its own terms, independently of any literary text.

Orwell understood that there is a profound tendency within modern society toward economic collectivism; that this tendency can take on a wide range of political colorations, from authoritarian to democratic; and that it can be deflected or modulated but probably cannot simply be annulled. The interpenetration of state and society, government and economy is simply a fact of modern life, quite as industrialization and urbanization have been. In correspondence from 1940, Orwell wrote, "There is [little] question of avoiding collectivism. The only question is whether it is to be founded on willing cooperation or on the machine gun"—that is, whether it will be democratic or authoritarian. This puts the matter with admirable precision. *1984* shows us what might happen if "the machine gun" triumphs; but the other choice remains to us. (p. 18)

Irving Howe, "1984: Enigmas of Power," in "1984" Revisited: Totalitarianism in Our Century, edited by Irving Howe, Harper & Row, Publishers, 1983, pp. 3-18.

ERIKA MUNK (essay date 1983)

[*In the following excerpt Munk examines Orwell's attitudes toward women and criticizes him for not specifically addressing women's issues in* Nineteen Eighty-Four. *Elaine Hoffman Baruch (1983) and Daphne Patai (Additional Bibliography) similarly find fault with Orwell's lack of a feminist perspective.*]

On the face of it, the role of women is not a promising subject to take up when considering *1984.* Throughout his career, Orwell the political journalist had nothing to say about women, and Orwell the novelist is in this realm, for the most part, a stone best left unturned. The subject of women simply didn't catch Orwell's attention. It never became a part of his egalitarianism, his vaunted fairness. . . .

[In] Orwell's picture of Oceania, each prophetic element is imagined with great care: surveillance's iron control; the brutal rigidity of class; the mechanization of masscult; Newspeak's decimation of language; technology's failure to make life either better or easier; a science reduced to fashioning military and psychological tools; constant mobilization for a constant state of war; nasty, shoddy food, clothes, and housing; ever present torture and execution; the systematic rewriting of history; above all, doublethink, one terse concept which nails down false logic, false philosophy, false politics, and the internalized lie. But the effect of such a world on half its population is meagerly depicted; a social structure has been described in which woman's place is basically unexamined.

Yet a love affair is central to the novel's plot, and the repression—more accurately, deflection—of eroticism analyzed as Oceania's most profound method of social control. Orwell wasn't concerned with women as a social group, but he certainly was concerned with sexuality. After Winston and Julia make love the first time he writes, "Their embrace had been a battle, the climax the victory. It was a blow struck against the Party. It was a political act." At least, that is what Winston thinks; Orwell's own opinion seems, from the evidence of the novel, more ambivalent, misty, tangled. It is worth trying to unravel because finally, and perhaps unintentionally, *1984* has something useful to say about women in a male future, and both men and women in a society of sexual repression.

The relationship of males and females in Oceania's social, economic, and political structures is only occasionally mentioned; it is hard to shape even a simple outline. Winston and Julia are Party members of low-middling status. In this class, marriage is of a fairly standard kind—the women apparently do the housework and the home care of children. When there are no children, separation is countenanced but there is no divorce; Orwell doesn't explain whether this was meant to discourage alliances or prevent too much childbearing. Society is stratified primarily on hereditary lines, father to son. Children are indoctrinated and regimented outside the home, and encouraged to inform on their parents. Most women seem to hold jobs, but never powerful ones; the telescreens are often inhabited by females with strident brassy voices, directing calisthenics or singing patriotic songs. Women seem to be treated as social inferiors—when Winston and Julia met with O'Brien, who is powerful in the Party, he "almost ignored Julia, seeming to take it for granted that Winston could speak for her." Winston has not one conversation of substance with a woman.

Sexual life for these Party members is rigidly puritanical. In Newspeak, "goodsex" means "normal intercourse between man and wife, for the sole purpose of begetting children, and without physical pleasure on the part of the woman; all else was 'sexcrime' . . . [which] covered fornication, adultery, homosexuality, and other perversions, and, in addition, normal intercourse practiced for its own sake." This must be why there is no mention of contraception or abortion, though one wonders what Julia—who fornicated regularly for its own sake—used to prevent pregnancy.

We aren't told whether the Party's Inner Circle, who are granted some material privileges, have to follow the same sexual code as lesser members, but probably they do—for the Party's goal in all this repression is to use the thwarted erotic energy as fuel for mass hatred of the enemy, a hatred which obscures their subjection, while at the same time, disruptive affectionate ties are prevented. . . .

For the proles, things are different: divorce, prostitution, pornography, and promiscuity, not to mention perfume and makeup, are permitted at the bottom. . . .

In Orwell's total state, the sexual and cultural lives of the poor have changed only in that they are more deprived, more manipulated, more anomic than in 1948, and the social status of Party women is not unlike that of middle-class women in World War II England, though gloomier. The alienation and brutalization of children is an old accusation against statism of the right or left; Orwell hasn't rethought it, or made it important in his scheme. His most striking concept is the deliberate rechanneling of desire, though it was not a new idea. The mere sight of a Nazi rally suggests it, Reich and other psychologists of fascism had explored it, different novelists worked on this theme. Here, in Orwell's own idiosyncratic way, it is the heart of the book. The three Party slogans—War Is Peace, Freedom Is Slavery, Ignorance Is Strength—are upheld by an unspoken fourth: Love Is Hate.

When Winston and Julia fuck it is indeed a rebellious political act. Yet Julia is a peculiar rebel. "I'm not interest in the next generation, dear, I'm interested in us.' 'You're only a rebel from the waist downwards,' he told her. She thought this brilliantly witty and flung her arms around him with delight." Julia has a certain practical shrewdness and is devoted to Winston; beyond that, she is neither intelligent nor idealistic. . . . Julia likes makeup and hates other women. Her survival tactics are commonplace: "Always yell with the crowd, that's what I say. It's the only way to be safe." She does, however, have some virtues that Winston doesn't appreciate. One thing that astonished him about her was the coarseness of her language—you'd think he'd enjoy it after all that Newspeak. More important, "She would not accept it as a law of nature that the individual is always defeated. . . . She did not understand that there was no such thing as happiness."

Winston does accept these grim propositions, making him as peculiar a rebel as Julia, and he clearly saw her shallowness, which makes his particular rebellion odd too. (Of course, he has two forms of dissent to her "women-live-for-love-alone" one.) He doesn't like Julia much and knows little more about her than I've sketched above. There is no description of their lovemaking, or passionate feeling, of bodies; we are barely told what Julia looks like. This in a book which delights in nature when it can and lushly details the horrors of spongy pink meat in an ersatz stew, the ulcer on Winston's leg, a severed hand in the gutter, and, at length, torture. Winston isn't even lecherous; the seduction is Julia's, overcoming his sexual diffidence, his self-consciousness about age and bad health. . . . Winston fucks Julia as an attack on his society; he wants sex not only because it's outlawed but because he thinks it's corrupt, impure, bad, and will rot Oceania's foundations.

When Julia breaks under questioning, there's no surprise. She's a sensualist and a realist. When Winston breaks, it shouldn't be surprising either: he must end up loving Big Brother—because he's human and has been tortured, of course, but more profoundly because the Party hates sex, and Winston also hates it, the Party transmutes sexuality into hostile power, and Winston used his lovemaking with Julia as a form of hostile power. When Winston first sees Julia, he fantasizes torturing, raping, and murdering her. When he first meets O'Brien, the Party official who entraps and tortures him, he is immensely drawn. Toward the end, when O'Brien has beaten him down, Winston thinks: "O'Brien was a person who could be talked to. Perhaps one did not want to be loved so much as to be understood. It did not matter whether O'Brien was a friend or enemy." The beginning and the end fit; Winston, one way or another, has been the regime's creature from the start, without knowing it.

There is another notable aspect to his rebellion which connects to the whole question of women and sex. Winston's dissent—whether fucking or writing—is individual and personal, a mode dictated by the constant surveillance and drastic punishments of his society. He is a paranoid loner, and he is right. This dissent, however, is further shaped by longing for the past, and remains untouched by any vision of a possible, different, better future. The truths he'd like to save are historical. When O'Brien, pretending to be an anti-State conspirator, suggests a toast to the future, Winston counters with one to the past. He is moved to buy his diary, and begin his rebellion, in an antique store, where he and Julia later make a love nest and where they are trapped (the owner is an agent). Winston's conscious, egalitarian, socialist, inner slogan is that salvation will come from the Proles, but almost every move he makes shows he wants a return to capitalist democracy, circa 1912.

The two women for whom he feels "mystic reverence" are a working-class mum and his own mother, suffering, stalwart, archetypal. Julia's carnality is modern, his squeamish yen for purity is old-fashioned. One consequence of his attitude, is that women's dreary situation in 1984 London—even drearier than the men's—is not as distressing to Winston as, say, Newspeak or the Hate sessions, because it's a continuation of the old ways rather than a drastic extrapolation from them or a total change. For better or worse, all Winston's grievances are regressive.

Winston's description of Oceania parallels Orwell's analysis of Europe's possible, even probable, fate though not its inevitable doom; the novel's a cautionary satire rather than a prediction. Is it also necessary to accept Winston's sexual attitudes and emotions as Orwell's own? It would be gratifying to be able to say that Orwell left women's 1984 social conditions in many ways the same as they were when he wrote, in order to make a conscious statement that they were already repressive enough, thank you. Or to say that Julia's blank mind and stunted character were the deformations of Oceania's sexist society, that Winston's priggishness, his morbid focus on violence, his ambivalent attraction to male authority, his impotent fixation on nostalgia, were laid out in the book as examples of what conditioning does even to a dissenter in a totalitarian system. Unfortunately, none of this rings true for a second. (pp. 50-2)

There are some clear historical reasons for Orwells' curious lack of attention to women as either social force or social problem when he envisioned Oceania's overall structure. The '30s and '40s in England were a thin period for feminist thought and women's politics, during which the radicalism of earlier years was replaced by a conventional, middle-class liberalism. . . . Left-wing women gave their energies to working-class and anti-Fascist movements whose issues they saw as more urgent; others who felt radically about women's oppression had nowhere to go, in a situation where socialist groups were dismissive and feminist groups conservative. As a result, feminist concerns were simply not part of the left-wing discourse of the time.

This explanation is, of course, not an excuse. It was also a rotten time for democratic socialism, which Orwell passionately affirmed (and which, in its earlier development in England, considered women's emancipation an important issue). It must have taken considerable effort on Orwell's part to ignore

the large presence of the woman in question in Nazi and Stalinist ideologies, and of women's oppression in their realities; it is a bit surprising that he overlooked the way this oppression was expressed through puritanism, motherhood, and the family.

The hibernation of feminism was terrific good luck for him: if a vigorous feminist movement had existed when he wrote, he would have had to fight its challenges tooth and nail. Orwell thought women's issues were trivial—when he wrote, at great length, about English character, community life, moral values, and daily culture in **"The Lion and the Unicorn,"** he took no note of sex, children, or the family; when he summarized recent British social history he never mentioned suffrage or changes in sexual mores. . . . Orwell qualmlessly ignored women as a social question. (p. 52)

Reticence in writing about erotic behavior is evident throughout his novels. (Orwell's greatest feat of reticence, however, is in **"Inside the Whale."** Discussing Henry Miller at great length, he never talks about Miller's sexual attitudes or writing!) Loathing of the flesh, of dirt, of anything squishy, messy, damp permeates the work. Every element of Winston's feelings about women and the body occurs in other novels: what we encounter in *1984* is not sexual thought and behavior postulated for a totalitarian future, but a concentrated expression of the sexual thought and behavior met in all Orwell's writing—much less transformed—than Stalin was in becoming Big Brother, or the British Ministry of Information when it turned into the Ministry of Lies. . . .

1984 failure to include any detailed models of totalitarian family and sexual life leaves a hole in its surface reality. Winston's love of purity, his worship of sacrificial drudging motherhood—values which Orwell seems to share—mar the book's politics: those values were central to the propaganda of the totalitarian states whose existence prompted Orwell's warning. Orwell's hostility to feminism and his apparently willful disregard of women's unjust treatment are infuriating to anyone who admires his style and ideas. They nibble away at his righteous persona. They buttress the left's long, stubborn blindness. And they make *1984* less useful as the urgent warning it was meant to be. Winston's distaste for the sexual, Julia's philistine stupidity, and the lack of any sensuous eroticism to counteract the novel's brutal and shabby imagery make sexual love as a gesture of rebellion not merely doomed (which it might well be) but weightless, inconsequential. Orwell seems to be writing passionately about the perversion and destruction of a pleasure he doesn't really like and may not even believe in.

All this said, there is still no denying that *1984* forces us to look at authoritarian puritanism, at woman-hating and body-hating, at the manipulative alchemy which society uses to turn our desires into power-lust, buying-lust, death-lust, and the abnegation of our loving selves. Orwell's own muddle can become a part of *1984*'s lesson. (p. 52)

> *Erika Munk, "Love Is Hate: Women and Sex in '1984'," in* The Village Voice, *Vol. XXVIII, No. 5, February 1, 1983, pp. 50-2.*

ROBERT CHRISTGAU (essay date 1983)

[*Christgau is an American music, film, and literary critic. In the following excerpt, he dismisses as "silly" the speculative attempts to determine what Orwell's political opinions would be today (see the excerpts by Norman Podhoretz and Gordon Beadle, 1983).*

Christgau notes that Orwell was regarded during his lifetime for his independence and humanism, and not for his political or social acuity. In a discussion of Nineteen Eighty-Four, *Christgau finds Orwell's presentation of the Party's desire for power for its own sake the most terrifying aspect of the novel.]*

In the silly tug-of-war over the current political affiliation of a man who died three years before Stalin, *1984* and *Animal Farm* are the chief exhibits for the opposition—Norman Podhoretz in *Harper's*, for instance [see Podhoretz excerpt dated 1983]. Those leftists who don't believe he and Podhoretz deserve each other reply that Orwell never stopped calling himself a socialist, or thinking like one. But they're clearly more comfortable with the Orwell who wrote *Homage to Catalonia* in the late '30s—the freedom fighter whose commitment to working-class revolution snapped into place at the same time as his opposition to the Soviet Union, during the Spanish Civil War.

It's silly to speculate about where Orwell would stand in today's politics because we don't prize him for his position—we prize him for his independence. His understanding of economics was sketchy, he seemed unaware that women (much less homosexuals) might constitute an oppressed group, and although he was a passionate and prophetic anti-imperialist, it's hard to imagine him feeling any less disdain for the mess of third-world politics than, let us say, V. S. Naipaul. But he hated repression of any sort (not just totalitarianism) so viscerally that it's equally hard to imagine him mouthing neoreactionary rationalizations in which torturers are transformed into the bad best hope of Latin American democracy. So as he approached 80, Orwell would no doubt still be a maverick, valued most of all, as always, not for his political content but for his attitude, his persona, and his writing itself.

Since Orwell believed very emphatically in letting "the meaning choose the words, and not the other way about," this may seem needlessly paradoxical. But in fact Orwell's obsessive ideas about prose constituted a metaphysic that was the ground of his authority. Springing as it did from his deepest political convictions, this metaphysic was the source of his political credibility. The clarity, candor, and common sense of Orwell's style made a kind of transcendent ideal out of ordinary English decency. Amid the rhetoric and romanticism of literary Marxism he strove to speak for plain people whose lives were dedicated mostly to getting on. A colonial and Etonian with a taste for slumming, he probably never knew those people as well as he wanted or claimed—V. S. Pritchett once commented that he had "'gone native' in his own country." But if only because it was in him to try, he got a lot closer to them than most of his peers, and you could feel that in his words. Thus his forebodings about authoritarianism always seemed more down-to-earth than those or Arthur Koestler (or later, Hannah Arendt). And thus would-be populists of the left and right still think he's worth squabbling over.

Because Orwell died the year after *1984* was published, it's come to seem his last word on man's fate, which it wouldn't have been, if only because most of its prophecies were incorrect. . . . In 30 years . . . nobody has matched both the scale and the sadism of Hitler's and Stalin's lust for control. Small comfort, and I'm not holding my breath. But I'm not predicting that the Hitler/Stalin spirit must inevitably dominate the planet, either. *1984* did.

Yet as it happens the truth value of this proposition is beside the point, because regardless of its realism or lack of same, regardless of how it distorts Orwell's best message, a fixation on the will to power is the secret of the novel's artistic triumph.

And it's this triumph, of course, that well-meaning leftists wish they could pick holes in. In *1984,* even more than in the relatively digestible (and dismissible) *Animal Farm,* Orwell achieves the popular contact his political instincts always drove him toward: to attribute the novel's enormous, unflagging appeal to the machinations of anti-Soviet propaganda barons is to indulge in the left's customary cultural elitism and myopia. Where *Darkness at Noon* now seems a terrifying period piece, *1984* reveals less as a satire than as a feat of pop sensationalism not all that different in effect from such sci-fi dystopias as Richard Fleischer's *Soylent Green* or John Brunner's *The Sheep Look Up.* Insofar as the novel escapes the usual critical insults—"manipulative," "melodramatic," etc.—it's protected by Orwell's serious and humane persona. He's so obviously a high middlebrow on the same level as those who favor such antipopulist rhetoric that he's immune to charges of commercialism, though not to ad hominem speculations about his dark fascination with the sadistic and the authoritarian—speculations that as far as I'm concerned might just as well be true, because I make it an article of faith that books which carry a real emotional charge tap something deeper in a writer than mere craft. And the hold of this book is so widely acknowledged that I suspect those who resist it of having something to hide, like those who claim to be bored by pornography.

Perhaps what they're hiding (or hiding from) is the old paradox of power on the left—seeking it in order to dismantle it. There would seem to be a logic, after all, in which those who succeed in dismantling their own power will ultimately fall under the control of those who don't, or who never intended to in the first place. This premise is what makes *1984* even scarier than the typical futuristic horror-show, although Orwell, like any good thriller writer, doesn't reveal it until he's 30 pages from the end: "The Party seeks power entirely for its own sake. We are not interested in the good of others; we are interested solely in power. Not wealth or luxury or long life or happiness; only power, pure power." The idea that a version of this premise might be true, or even possible, is the Room 101 of left intellectuals, and some of them will never forgive Orwell for making it come alive.

But nobody suffers more under Ingsoc (Newspeak for English socialism) than Orwell himself: *1984* is a nightmare of his own devising, a suffocating, self-enclosed system that embodies all his worst fears, every one of which proceeds or at least gains plausibility from the notion that "the object of power is power." Orwell's attachment to the abiding details of daily life, his conviction that change must begin with the needs and desires of ordinary people, and above all his faith in clarity, candor, and common sense—all are turned on their heads. Because the Party won't utilize technology for "the good of others," there are no simple comforts under Ingsoc—everything is cheap, broken, stunted, ersatz, unavailable, as if the deprivations Orwell experienced on the down-and-out side of the Depression have imposed their texture on all of history. The people have become the proles, as incapable of improving their lot without leadership, which is methodically and gleefully weeded out from above, as were the lumpen with whom a younger Orwell roughed it. And for someone who lives through language, the world of *1984* is worse than a nightmare: it's a madhouse without doors or windows at zero gravity, with nothing, nothing at all to hold on to.

Clearly, then, the physical and social dimensions of Orwell's nightmare can be dismissed as one man's bad dream, although certain specifics make more sense than they usually get credit for—notably the joyously expedient carnality of Winston Smith's love affair with Julia and the condescending depiction of the proles (who are always viewed through the eyes of Smith, a slummer like Orwell with more excuse). But while it makes some sense to accuse Orwell of metaphysical crudity—a priori and a posteriori get confused in the book's argument at times—his linguistic analysis grounds the novel as decisively as his will-to-power premise, and it's just as substantial. Given the author's fervent belief that meaning precedes language, the process whereby Smith is persuaded that a photograph he just saw never existed or that two plus two equals five obviously terrified Orwell beyond all reason, but it's an evasion to pass off his terror as irrational. (pp. 54-5)

For left intellectuals to pretend that plain Americans are brainwashed into fearing repression above all else is a hideous distortion—if anybody's brainwashed it's the American plain and fancy who don't. In short, both the power and the paradoxes of *1984* are worth taking very seriously. It's a cautionary image of a world we don't want to make. And if we think we're safe just because it hasn't literally come true, we don't deserve to call ourselves leftists *or* intellectuals. (p. 55)

> Robert Christgau, "Writing for the People," in The Village Voice, Vol. XXVIII, No. 5, February 1, 1983, pp. 54-5.

WALTER KENDRICK   (essay date 1983)

[*In the following excerpt Kendrick finds that* Nineteen Eighty-Four *amounts to nothing more than Orwell's upper-middle-class distaste for shabby living conditions, the working classes, and the growing disregard for old standards of gentility. T. R. Fyvel (1982) and Robert Christgau (1983) also find that* Nineteen Eighty-Four *evolved from Orwell's private fears, but maintain that the novel has a broader application and deeper meaning than a mere expression of the author's personal anxieties.*]

This book should have been called *1948;* it has far more to tell us about middle-class paranoia after World War II than about any possible future. Even when, aged about 12, I read *1984* for the first time, I knew that Orwell's nightmare wasn't mine; except for Winston Smith's rat phobia (I still get a chill from that), the novel's horrors struck me as quaint and rather hysterical, though I couldn't have said why. Now I can: Orwell's nightmare is simply that of an overfastidious member of the British haute bourgeoisie who sees gentility crumbling. Dirty streets, the smell of cabbage in the halls, the proletarization of England—what a nightmare!

Reading *1984* again, I find it strangely similar to *Lord of the Rings.* Both have about the same relation to reality, but I won't belabor that; both also take their origin from fantasies about language. Tolkien, an Old English scholar, began by inventing his own archaic language, then devised a fable to embody it. Orwell, a man of letters in the Johnsonian-Arnoldian tradition, saw that tradition waning and had a bad dream about what would happen to Standard English if low-class hands got hold of it. The result was Newspeak, the language of 1984. The masters of Oceania commit many crimes, but torture and brainwashing are minor compared to the ultimate travesty of Newspeak. The rest is props; if Newspeak fails, *1984* does.

They fail. In an appendix, "The Principles of Newspeak," Orwell tells us that this artificial language, intended to replace Oldspeak (Standard English) completely by 2050, was designed so that "a heretical thought—that is, a thought diverging from the principles of Ingsoc—should be literally unthinkable,

at least so far as thought is dependent on words." Newspeak invents some words, but its major technique is to reduce the polyvalence of pre-existing Oldspeak words. . . .

Does the concept of intellectual freedom exist before the words that name it, or are we able to conceive of "intellectual freedom" because the rules of Standard English (Newspeak, too) allow those words to be combined that way? So long as there are adjectives and nouns (Newspeak retains both), the two will combine with or without any speaker's volition. Orwell wants us to be horrified at the prospect of a language which, in and of itself, makes heresy impossible; yet every example he gives shows that linguistic freeplay is as operative in Newspeak as in any other language—spinning out heresy, nonsense, and poetry.

Big Brother is ungood can be said in Newspeak, as can *All mans are equal;* but the first is "a self-evident absurdity," while the second is possible "only in the same sense in which *All men are red-haired* is a possible Oldspeak sentence.". . . The restraints upon thought that Orwell's nightmare would locate in Newspeak itself could never be inherent in any language, no matter how stripped down; they would have to be imposed from outside, by an authority which acknowledges the possibility of heresy every time it judges that one thought is thinkable and another is not. Such authority is resistible, and the very existence of language guarantees that resistance will arise.

The real horror of Newspeak, for Orwell, has nothing to do with intellectual freedom: the language is crude, simplistic, and almost wholly Germanic in etymology and grammar. Fancy Greek and Latin derivations have been purged; instead of "have a full emotional understanding," Newspeakers grunt *bellyfeel.* All preterits and plurals are regular (or "weak," as old grammar books call them): *thinked* replaces "thought," *mans* replaces "men." Opposites and comparatives are formed with prefixes: "bad" becomes *ungood,* "worse" and "worst" turn into *plusungood* and *doubleplusungood.* There's nothing abhorrent about all this except its clumsy appearance and porcine sound; even a supposedly deplorable sentence like *Oldthinkers unbellyfeel Ingsoc* has a kind of barnyard lyricism about it. But Newspeak is definitely a language for proles (or Prussians), and that scares Orwell more than anything else.

It's a shame that *1984* has become a lightning rod for everybody's vague anxieties about things to come. Unless you're British, male, lower-upper-middle class, and stuck fast in 1948, you can't possibly sympathize with it. As a period piece, *1984* still holds some interest, but you're an idiot if you imagine that it can tell you anything about the future.

> Walter Kendrick, "Newspeak Double-Think," in The Village Voice, Vol. XXVIII, No. 5, February 1, 1983, p. 55.

ELAINE HOFFMAN BARUCH   (essay date 1983)

[*In the following excerpt Baruch provides a discussion of Orwell's approach to love and sex in the totalitarian society of* Nineteen Eighty-Four. *She finds that Winston Smith's delight in the domestic activities engaged in with Julia in the room above Charrington's shop, and his glorification of the prole woman in the yard below, amount to a "romanticization of the domestic" that explains the negative reactions of feminist reviewers of the novel, including Erika Munk (1983) and Daphne Patai (Additional Bibliography). However, Baruch explains why this romanticization is a healthy reaction on the part of Smith.*]

Early in *1984* Winston Smith has a dream:

> Suddenly he was standing on short springy turf, on a summer evening when the slanting rays of the sun gilded the ground. The landscape that he was looking at recurred so often in his dreams that he was never fully certain whether or not he had seen it in the real world. In his waking thoughts he called it the Golden Country. . . .

A girl with dark hair comes toward him across the field and with a single movement tears off her clothes. (p. 47)

Later, the dream comes true.

There are precedents for Orwell's "Golden Country." In Huxley's *Brave New World,* it is the reservation that preserves the green world of nature and wildness. In Yevgeny Zamyatin's *We,* which Orwell knew and praised highly, it is the land beyond the Green Wall that represents freedom and forest. And, of course, long before that, there was Arcadia. . . .

It is not only the external world of nature that provides a setting for love in anti-utopia. There are internal shelters as well. In Zamyatin, it is the house of antiquity with its blazing colors unlike the glass architecture of the rest of the One State. In Orwell, it is the room above Charrington's junk yard that is the twentieth-century love grotto. It contains that ancient shrine, a double bed. In anti-utopia, ordinary life itself becomes utopia—utopia, that is, in the sense of a longed-for ideal.

Anti-utopians believe that there was a union of passion and thought before the state takeover. (pp. 47-8)

Anti-utopian authors locate the source of freedom from the state in romantic love. Here too they differ from feminist writers, who often see it as a source of oppression—for women. Winston says, "Not love so much as eroticism was the enemy. . . ." Women too sometimes see eroticism as the enemy, not because it is a threat to the state, as in *1984,* but because it is a threat to the self.

But just how erotic is Winston and Julia's relationship? Of their first meeting in the wood, we read:

> She stood looking at him for an instant, then felt at the zipper of her overalls. And, yes! It was almost as in his dream. Almost as swiftly as he had imagined it, she had torn her clothes off, and when she flung them aside it was with that same magnificent gesture by which a whole civilization seemed to be annihilated. Her body gleamed white in the sun.

Enough to please a Lawrence—and with the emphasis on the woman for a change. But then what do we hear? "'Have you done this before?'" asks the hero.

Consistently, there occurs a deflation of the erotic. When they make love again, Orwell writes: "He pressed her down upon the grass, among the fallen bluebells. This time there was no difficulty." And another time: "'It's all off,' she murmured as soon as she judged it safe to speak. 'Tomorrow, I mean. . . . It's started early this time.'" It is hard to believe that so trivial an impediment as menstruation would deflect such supposedly passionate lovers. (pp. 47-9)

There is much that is bourgeois about Orwell's romance—perhaps working class is a better term. That is where Winston's sympathies lie, after all: with the proles. (p. 49)

Yet what is amazing is how much feeling the understated passages in *1984* are still able to carry. And no doubt that was part of Orwell's point:

> [Winston] wondered vaguely whether in the abolished past it had been a normal experience to lie in bed like this, in the cool of a summer evening, a man and a woman with no clothes on, making love when they chose, talking of what they chose, not feeling any compulsion to get up, simply lying there and listening to peaceful sounds outside. Surely there could never have been a time when that seemed ordinary.

In his nostalgia for ordinary pleasures, Winston even glorifies the prole woman hanging up diapers and singing cheap popular songs. (How different from Orwell's earlier *Tribune* articles, which contrast the susceptibility of working-class women to "wealth fantasies" in the "love books," i.e., women's papers, with the reality of their physical pain. Now it is his hero who is sentimentalizing those very women.) In the bleak world of *1984,* what Orwell gives us is a romanticization of the domestic.

No wonder feminists don't like him.

In his treatment of women and love there is much to fault Orwell, if one is so minded. Winston has violent fantasies of raping and killing Julia when he thinks he cannot have her. "It was always the women, and above all the young ones, who were the most bigoted adherents of the Party, the swallowers of slogans, the amateur spies and nosers-out of unorthodoxy." Later he not only dreams but is able to live out the ancient fantasy of having a beautiful young creature declare that she loves him before he even knows her name—he with his varicose veins and false teeth—and then be utterly unresisting. "He could do what he liked with her." We never do learn what her last name is, although we get much detail about her use of cosmetics and desire to wear silk stockings and high-heeled shoes. "'You're only a rebel from the waist downwards,'" Winston tells Julia. As if to prove it, she falls asleep when he reads excitedly from Emmanuel Goldstein's revolutionary manual.

But matters aren't so simple. Winston's initial murderous fantasies are all too explicable in the light of Wilhelm Reich's *The Mass Psychology of Fascism,* which notes that "every inhibition of genital gratification intensifies the sadistic impulse." Reich also makes clear why Winston's charge that women are politically orthodox is less that of a sexist than a realist: women and adolescents are always willing to heed political reaction, says Reich, because they are so sexually repressed. Since the main thrust of the anti-sexual conditioning in *1984* is directed to the women, those bearers of the red sash of chastity, Julia, who provides a deliberate foil to Winston's absent and sexually impoverished wife, is all the more remarkable in her rebellion. Like Zamyatin's I-330, Julia rejects the uniform and pallor of the Party. The use of cosmetics, like the sex act itself, can represent either bondage or liberation, depending on the norms of the society. In Tommaso Campanella's seventeenth-century utopia, *City of the Sun,* wearing cosmetics or high heels is punishable by death. Severe restrictions seem to apply in *1984* as well. In such a society, to wear makeup represents an act of freedom, not the capitulation to patriarchy it might be in ours. Sex is unquestionably the key political issue in *1984:*

> Unlike Winston, she had grasped the inner meaning of the Party's sexual puritanism. It

was not merely that the sex instinct created a world of its own which was outside the Party's control and which therefore had to be destroyed if possible. What was more important was that sexual privation induced hysteria, which was desirable because it could be transformed into war fever and leader worship.

Religions and tyrannical political systems, as Reich points out, provide excitement that is both anti-sexual and a substitution for sexuality. Julia recognizes this before Winston does.

Finally, Julia's identification with sexuality may have less to do with woman's traditional association with the body than with something more important. It is not only dystopias that repress sexual love; most utopias do also. Even when they allow promiscuity, they do so to reduce the claims of individual passion against the state. . . . In traditional utopias, the characters never reach a state of complete individuation. It is the giant state that is the main character, like the parent or parent surrogates of one's childhood. Utopia represents a state before adult genitality. In such a world, sexual rebellion, if it ever occurs, constitutes separation from authority figures, the mythic journey to adulthood, growth of consciousness, and total individuation. The more severe the prohibition overturned, the greater the heroism. In this light, there is no question that the most courageous and admirable figure in the society of *1984* is Julia. (pp. 49-51)

Not all utopian planners exclude [elements of sex, love, self-ishness, and fantasy]. Women's utopias, which are anarchic rather than authoritarian, do not see a split between the individual and the community. They are much more inclusive of feeling, of fantasy (although not the traditional kind), and art—as, for example, in Doris Lessing's *Marriages Between Zones Three, Four, and Five.* Why these differences? Perhaps because the Oedipus complex operates with far greater force among men, the traditional male utopia is confining, constricting, rigid. In male utopias, women are deprived of their ancient power. In dystopia, they are granted it back again, with approval.

Despite the attempt of the mathematical world of Zamyatin's *We* to eliminate the unconscious, all the old mythology is apparent in the hero's responses to women. Like much of Western culture before him, he splits the sexual object, and has two lovers: O-90 and I-330.

Although the roseate O-90 with her eyes of blue crystal has an appealing sensuality—she talks of spring when the hero speaks of formulas—there is no doubt that she comes from a long line of childlike, submissive heroines. Yet she too is subversive in that she insists on becoming an illegal mother. Then there is the ambiguous I-330, who is fire and ice, a sting and honey—and brilliant, a rebel against the existing order intellectually as well as physically. Unquestionably, D is afraid of her, and her seductive enchantments as well as her intellect, her ability to overpower him, to erase thoughts of all else in a kind of drowning. She comes from the *femme fatale* tradition of dangerous and alluring sorceresses. She represents freedom from the state but also erotic enslavement. Yet it is I-330 that D prefers—here in dystopia in a way that he perhaps would not feel free to prefer her in the real world, where the O's tend to win out. At the end, however, he is saved for the One State by a fantasiectomy—the operation that removes imagination.

Orwell, in contrast, treats only one woman. He doesn't split women into the good versus the seductive, the antithesis that

Freud treats in his "On the Universal Tendency to Debasement in the Sphere of Love" (unless Winston's shadowy wife should be considered one side of the split). Yet in reversing the values of the old sexual definitions—"I hate purity, I hate goodness"—is he not tied to the old mythology after all? At least Winston can be congratulated on rejecting the traditions of the seduced and abandoned heroine: "The more men you've had, the more I love you." "Not merely the love of one person, but the animal instinct, the simple undifferentiated desire," is what he says delights him in Julia. Actually, the relationship of Orwell's lovers is as faithful as anyone of the old world could have wished. Would Winston have responded with the same fierce jealously as the Savage in *Brave New World* had he found Julia with someone else? Probably not, though it is doubtful that he actually wants the promiscuity of *Brave New World.* His desire that everyone be corrupt to the bones has meaning only where it is impossible of fulfillment. Sexual freedom in *1984* is a political act. In a state of sexual permissiveness, it would cease to be that, indeed, would become a sign of submission.

Part of the significance of Orwell's treatment of love is that, once consummated, it doesn't depend on fantasy. In fact, it is as if Winston has had a fantasiectomy himself. He has none of D's dependence on dualistic images of woman as child/mother or temptress/destroyer. Since so many feminists are trying to eliminate these polarities, perhaps they should praise Orwell, who keeps nothing of the sado-masochistic elements of the *We* lovers either. But while Orwell eliminates the dangerous lure of I's sexuality in his treatment of Julia, he also eliminates I's intellectuality, and this women will not be so quick to forgive. . . . It is [I-330] who is a member of the underground resistance that actually seems to exist in *We,* and she who leads the hero to a momentary political rebellion.

It is this relationship between the sexes that Orwell reverses, when he might have equalized it. Why? Is it because, despite his rejection of fantsy, Orwell is a sexist after all? Or because Winston Smith is the outsider from the beginning, the man with political consciousness unlike Zamyatin's hero, who starts out as the good man of the One State, gifted in mathematics but something of a naif otherwise? Or because such a shift makes more poignant Winston's betrayal of Julia at the end, his regression and defeat? (pp. 52-4)

What [Orwell's] treatment of love and sex in *1984* indicates is that he would have been happy with traditional love. But this is not an option that remains. The only love that is allowed in *1984* is the love for the leader. What Freud said about the attraction of the group to the leader of the Church and the army applies to the leader of the totalitarian state as well. It is a libidinal tie, grounded in the child's love for the father. Instead of being an object relationship, it is a regressive bond, an identification, which is something far more primitive and therefore potentially dangerous. Recently, some critics have indicated that Orwell's sexism prevented him from seeing that the power relationships in *1984* are based on the model of sexual polarization. I would make a different claim: The domination of male over male in *1984,* that of O'Brien over Winston, for example, is far more severe than the domination of male over female. Polarization need not be sexually based; indeed it is not in *1984* where the opposition is between the ruling class and the ruled, and ultimately between one leader and his followers. Here the basic model is not male/female but rather parent/child, as it is in most political groups. Winston is passively masochistic and submissive to O'Brien in ways that Julia never is to her lover. Whether we like his depiction or not, Orwell's sexual love provides the only escape from male domination of males in *1984,* the only escape from the reversion to Freud's primal horde. Insofar as Winston and Julia are able to meet "for the purpose of sexual satisfaction, in so far as they seek for solitude, [they] are making a demonstration against the herd instinct, the group feeling," in Freud's terms.

But by the end of *1984,* there is no idyllic nature (there is no mother in the old sense), and there is no sex, let alone sexual love. Now it is just possible that we could get rid of these traditional sources of pleasure and still remain human. Pascal said: "There is nothing that cannot be made natural. There is nothing natural that cannot be lost." Then too what seems utopia to one sex might well be dystopia for another. It is surely of some significance that the loss of home, marriage, romantic love, and the replacement of motherhood by *in vitro* reproduction that Huxley so deplores in *Brave New World* are posited as the very terms of liberation in Shulamith Firestone's *Dialectic of Sex,* one of the most influential books to come out of the women's movement. The crucial questions are: To what use would a society put these changes, and what kind of society can we expect?

The answer Orwell gives is horrifying. In his review of Zamyatin, Orwell claimed that *We* was superior to *Brave New World* because of its "intuitive grasp of the irrational side of totalitarianism—human sacrifice, cruelty as an end in itself, the worship of a Leader who is credited with divine attributes. . . ." In *1984* O'Brien says: "the old civilizations claimed that they were founded on love and justice. Ours is founded upon hatred." Not quite so. There is an affective tie that remains and Winston confesses it at the end: "He loved Big Brother." He is therefore able to participate vicariously in the power that intoxicates the Inner Party. Traditional sexual love has been transformed into a sublimated homosexuality, which may in fact be part of all patriarchal institutions—but which is here pushed to its furthest extreme. Looking at such a world from the outside—and we are still outside, even if getting closer—who would not lament the loss of "the Golden Country"? (pp. 55-6)

> Elaine Hoffman Baruch, "The Golden Country: Sex and Love in '1984'," in "1984" Revisited: Totalitarianism in Our Century, edited by Irving Howe, Harper & Row, Publishers, 1983, pp. 47-56.

IAN WATT (essay date 1983)

[*Watt is one of the twentieth century's most significant contributors to the study of the novel form. In his seminal work* The Rise of the Novel: Studies in Defoe, Richardson, and Fielding, *he argues that the novel is above all a realistic genre and that its unique appearance in the eighteenth century, specifically in the works of Daniel Defoe, Samuel Richardson, and Henry Fielding, was influenced by, as well as contributed to, the general movement toward "philosophical realism" in Western civilization after the Renaissance. For Watt, two characteristics define the novel in its completed form: one is "presentational realism," or the technique of rendering particular moments and events believable to the reader; the other is what he calls "realism of assessment," which consists of the kind of moral authority and control an author exercises over a narrative. Watt concludes in his study that either one or the other of these characteristics were lacking in the works of Defoe, Richardson, and Fielding, and that it wasn't until the stories of Jane Austen that the novel achieved its complete form. In the following excerpt Watt examines Orwell's characterization of Winston Smith, defining Smith as a humanist. Watt describes*

Smith as having "a constellation of special intellectual, aesthetic, and literary values," including a love of and desire to maintain the moral values of the past. For a discussion of Smith as "an inadequate humanist" and of Nineteen Eighty-Four *as a portrayal of the failure of humanism, see the excerpt by Patrick Reilly (1982).*]

Winston Smith's sensibility . . . can be seen as representing a constellation of special intellectual, aesthetic, and literary values. There is the love of what Newspeak calls *oldthink,* that is, the ideas grouped round the equally outmoded concepts of "objectivity and rationalism" and of old folk rhymes. There is, further, his love of the particular and the detailed in other things. . . .

Behind these aspects of Winston's inner sense of values is the larger idea that individual feeling is the most essential and desirable reality available. It is this idea that leads Winston, at his first and only real meeting with O'Brien until his arrest, to propose his toast, "To the past." The Party has persuaded people that "mere impulses, mere feeling, were of no account"; on the other hand, Winston is loyal to the values of an earlier generation—like his mother, who had assumed that "what mattered were individual relationships, and a completely helpless gesture, an embrace, a tear, a word spoken to a dying man, could have value in itself." It is also the rights of individual feeling which cause Winston to conclude that he must continue on his present course to the end; as he put it, if your "object was not to stay alive but to stay human, what difference did it ultimately make?" After all, he reflects, "They could not alter your feelings; for that matter you could not alter them yourself, even if you wanted to."

One term to describe this constellation of private thoughts and feelings in Winston Smith would be Humanism. The term has many diverse and not wholly clear meanings; but in the inner life of Winston Smith Orwell certainly describes both some main characteristic features of the earliest manifestations of Humanism in the history of the West, and some of the essential meanings the term has acquired more recently. (p. 108)

The nearest Greek equivalent to the Latin *humanitas* was *anthropismos;* and the early development of the notion, like that of its analogue *philanthropia,* had its basis in the close practical relationship in the life of fourth-century Athens between four forces which we would now call freedom of speech, the rule of law, the political freedom of the city, and the individual's right to make his own moral and political decisions. Humanism, then, arose in a society which was radically opposite to that of *Nineteen Eighty-Four.* For Isocrates (436-338 B.C.), who is commonly regarded as the chief precursor of Humanism, persuasion through speech was the key instrument of a free society. . . .

It was left to the Romans to develop the ideas of humanitas in education and to give it a more systematic development. (p. 109)

In Renaissance Europe, the term Humanism took on a rather new meaning. It is specifically applied, in the *Oxford Dictionary*'s definition, for instance, to the study of "the language, literature, and antiquities of Rome, and afterwards of Greece." Renaissance Humanism began as the educational spearhead of the revival of learning in the fifteenth century, but eventually it acquired the general sense of the classical, and mainly secular, education which was established in high schools and colleges during the sixteenth, seventeenth, and eighteenth centuries. The "good art" became defined as the *litterae humaniores* (more humane letters) of Oxford and other universities on the grounds that the great authors of Latin and Greek literature were more worthy of study than those of other languages.

The final stages in the development of the concept of Humanism came to the fore in the twentieth century. On the one hand, the classical tradition lost much of its power; and on the other, Humanism was colored by the scientific, secular, and empirical attitudes of the period. The idea that man should limit his knowledge to the enquiries, objectives, and limitations of the individual human mind was developed as a specific school of thought by F.C.S. Schiller and William James. The scientific and experimental attitude which they systematized under the name of Humanism no longer survives as a movement, but it has supplied some of the term's secular connotations in its present use.

Winston Smith cannot be considered a humanist in any of its earlier senses, if only because he makes no mention of Greek or Latin, and we are told nothing about his schooling. On the other hand, his hostility to Newspeak, his obsession with language, and his need for a free exchange of ideas show him as beginning at exactly the point where the founders of Humanism began. Winston Smith holds fast both to the value of Oldspeak and to the ultimate rationale of the early humanist position—the achievement of individual freedom. This freedom, threatened in the days both of Isocrates and of Cicero, no longer exists at all in the society of *Nineteen Eighty-Four;* but it remains Winston's basic need, and it is essentially that need for free intellectual interchange that explains his obsession with meeting O'Brien, and that had led him to start his diary.

There is a little more to say about the relation of Winston Smith's ideas to Humanism, but first we should, perhaps, consider the question of whether his author, George Orwell, could have had any specifically humanist intention for *Nineteen Eighty-Four.* He would not willingly have affixed any ideological label to himself; but on the other hand it is an important part of his distinction as a writer that he took nothing for granted, and as a result he was often both well behind the times and well ahead of them. (pp. 110-11)

[An example] is how very old-fashioned Orwell was in his attitude to language, and it wasn't just a question of his advocacy of the plain style. It was a lifelong passion. As he revealed in his essay **"Why I Write,"** Orwell, at the age of "about sixteen . . . suddenly discovered the joy of mere words, i.e., the sounds and associations of words." . . . Orwell wrote that he did not wish "completely to abandon the world view that I acquired in childhood"; and the first feature of it that he mentioned was to "continue to feel strongly about prose style."

This attitude to language is old-fashioned because neither the capacity to remember the "accurate and significant" use of words, nor how they are spelled, nor even a genuine concern with "prose style," were much more common then than they are today. For Orwell, however, they remained central; and this was not wholly for literary and stylistic reasons, but because he was also alive, as few other writers have ever been, to the moral and political importance of the notion that, in Keats's words, "English ought to be kept up." In such essays as **"Politics vs. Literature: An Examination of *Gulliver's Travels*,"** **"Politics and the English Language,"** and **"Inside the Whale,"** Orwell demonstrated the necessary connections between literature, language, and the collective life with a fine intensity; and there, as in many other essays, he makes us realize that relatively simple things such as the use of truthful

or untruthful language are connected with the greatest issues of social value, political decency, and—ultimately—with the existence of human freedom or of its opposite.

These simple meanings—not unlike the basic views of Isocrates or Cicero—Orwell certainly intended, and indeed consciously and persistently pursued, throughout his life. Especially in *Nineteen Eighty-Four.* One reason for the clarity of this theme in the novel may be that, whatever conflicts may have existed between Orwell the radical and Orwell the traditionalist in his treatment of political problems, there was no conflict in regard to language.

Nor did Orwell's education stop short with his capacity to write. At school, Orwell was something of a social rebel and a political radical, but he was certainly a traditionalist in his studies. At his prep school, and later at Eton, Orwell was a student of the classics, of what amounts to a school version of the *litterae humaniores;* and later he chose Greek, Latin, and Drawing as his three optional subjects for the Civil Service examination that sent him to Burma as a policeman. He paid tribute, later, to the fact that Eton, despite its many faults, had "one great virtue . . . a tolerant and civilized atmosphere which gives each boy a fair chance of developing his own individuality." One wouldn't claim Orwell as a man who read the classics consistently throughout his life; and one must admit that he was bitterly contemptuous of St. Cyprian's, his prep school, and unenthusiastic about many aspects of Eton; nevertheless it was there that he received an education based on the old humanistic classical tradition, a tradition which he never attacked.

It is, therefore, just possible that Orwell, having some conception of the humanist tradition, deliberately used some of its values to inform the positive aspects of Winston's sensibility. This tendency, it must be conceded, goes only as far as is plausible, given the kind of society depicted in the novel and Winston's own lack of educational opportunity; in any case, Winston Smith is not a conscious nor a heroic protagonist of moral and intellectual convictions. One remembers, for instance, his betrayals. They began with his earliest guilty memory of the last moment in which he saw his mother before she disappeared, when, overpowered by desperate childish greed, he had stolen the last quarter of the family's rare and precious two-ounce ration of chocolate from his helpless little sister, and with it fled from his home. At the end Winston betrays Julia—"Do it to Julia," he says, when faced by the rats; and he betrays himself when the novel finishes with Winston's succumbing to the overpowering pressures of the collective ideological machine, and discovering that "He loved Big Brother."

O'Brien affirms that "We"—the Party—"create human nature," and it is, of course, part of Orwell's warning in *Nineteen Eighty-Four* to show that "they" cannot be beaten. Winston learns that he and Julia were wrong when they thought that "They can't get inside you." They can, and, therefore, Winston does not even have the consolation of being able to say, as he once did, "if you can *feel* that staying human is worthwhile, even when it can't have any result whatever, you've beaten them." Orwell's picture of the future defines the villain as the general tendency of modern bureaucratic control to lead to a cripplingly anti-humanist monolithic collectivism; and so Winston Smith must be ignominiously defeated.

Not much, I believe, has been written about Winston's character; and there is obviously some truth in Irving Howe's concession that "there are no credible or 'three-dimensional' characters in the book.'' But, as Howe says, Orwell was trying to portray a society in which ''the leviathan has swallowed man'' and so ''the human relationships'' that are normally ''taken for granted in the novel are here suppressed.'' Nevertheless, Winston Smith is worth our attention as a crucial test example, and he is in some respects a worthy one. His worth is suggested by his given name, Winston, and perhaps by his sharing Shakespeare's initials of W. S. In any case, Winston Smith has a legitimate love of the traditions of the past, and that love is combined with a genuine concern for the language and literature of Oldspeak, and for the right to independent thought. The critics have not made much of this side of the novel, but Winston Smith is, in the hated jargon of Newspeak, a martyr to the *ownlife*, meaning ''individualism and eccentricity.'' He is even obsessed, in the typical humanist way, with unanswerable questions, and particularly the question of ''Why?'' As he writes in his diary, ''I under stand *HOW:* I do not understand *WHY*.'' That he eventually succumbs to the police and O'Brien doesn't weaken the truths of what he thinks and does in the first two parts of the novel. ''Truisms are true, hold on to that!'' Winston reflects, and writes down in his diary as a credo: ''Freedom is the freedom to say that two plus two make four. If that is granted, all else follows.''

That is not granted, but we can still say that, however grim his end, Winston Smith is the only person in the novel who makes any sort of stand for the simple intellectual and moral values which, for over two millenia, have had the majority of the literate and the decent on their side. O'Brien three times calls Winston ''the last man,'' with increasing irony at this professed ''guardian of the human spirit''; and this is reflected in the original title for the book, ''The Last Man in Europe.'' Considering how little there is about Europe in the book, ''The Last Humanist Man'' might have been a more accurate title, although *Nineteen Eighty-Four* is no doubt better for other reasons. (pp. 111-13)

> *Ian Watt, ''Winston Smith: The Last Humanist,'' in On ''Nineteen Eighty-Four,'' edited by Peter Stansky, W. H. Freeman and Company, 1983, pp. 103-13.*

MARTIN ESSLIN (essay date 1983)

[Esslin, a prominent and sometimes controversial critic of contemporary theater, is perhaps best known for coining the term ''theatre of the absurd.'' His The Theatre of the Absurd *(1961) is a major study of the avant-garde drama of the 1950s and early 1960s, including the works of Samuel Beckett, Eugene Ionesco, and Jean Genet. Esslin worked with Orwell in the British Broadcasting Corporation's wartime propaganda department for two years. In the following excerpt he maintains that the use of the mass media to control public opinion in* Nineteen Eighty-Four *resembles the media manipulation of the wartime BBC. Esslin also expresses surprise that Orwell failed to grasp the potential of television as a powerful tool of mass manipulation, noting that the telescreens in* Nineteen Eighty-Four *are most usually depicted as either transmitting images from each household to secret watchers, or else as broadcasting audio rather than visual images. Regarding this, Esslin finds that the most terrifying and Orwellian aspect of modern American life is the power of media to manipulate public tastes, desires, and knowledge.]*

Orwell's *Nineteen Eighty-Four* is dominated by the mass media, and so is the actual, real life 1984 that has now dawned. To that extent, Orwell was right.

But the mass media—the cheap mass-circulation press, mechanically produced romantic novels and pop songs, war films,

radio, and television—are not a mere fictional element in Orwell's negative utopia. It can be—and has frequently been—asserted, with some force, that the whole book was engendered by Orwell's own experience within one of the most powerful media organizations of his time—the wartime BBC.

I happen to have shared some of that experience with George Orwell and I can testify to the truth of this assertion from firsthand experience. (p. 126)

It is no coincidence that Winston Smith in *Nineteen Eighty-Four,* exactly like George Orwell in 1943, should be working in a propaganda organization dedicated to manipulating public opinion and faking the image of history. Orwell based his description of this process mainly on what had already happened in the Soviet Union. Smith's job consists in rewriting history in the light of current—and constantly changing—political circumstances. This systematic eradication of the past was a feature of Stalinism. Fervently idealistic supporters of the Soviet revolution in the West had been deeply dismayed when they saw how, after the great purges, the formerly revered leaders of the revolution—men like Trotsky, Bukharin, Kamenev, Zinoviev, Radek—had been expunged from the history books, their features obliterated even on historical photographs. The articles devoted to them were deleted from the official encyclopedia and new pages supplied to replace those that subscribers were ordered to cut out.

But there are indications that Orwell had found similar tendencies nearer home as well—in the British propaganda effort. The work Orwell had to do as an editor in the Indian section of the Empire Service of the BBC was not quite as drastic as the Soviet obliteration of past history. But to a man of his political sensibility and anticolonialist views (which stemmed from his first job with the British police in Burma), many of the directives that reached him from the higher regions of the policy makers in the British government and the BBC must have been hard to swallow and execute. (pp. 128-29)

The abrupt reversals that followed changes in the war situation were all too similar to the sudden remodelings of the shape of the past described in *Nineteen Eighty-Four:* from 1939 to 1941 Stalin had been a villain who had made a pact with Hitler and carved up Poland, our ally. But on the evening of the day Hitler invaded the Soviet Union, Winston Churchill was on the air offering Britain's hand of friendship to Stalin. Suddenly the BBC's propaganda stressed the sturdiness of the Russian people, the heroism of the Red Army, and Stalin's genius as a war leader. And then, when the war was over, the cold war started and Stalin was reconstituted as a sinister villain.

Much of the role of the mass media in *Nineteen Eighty-Four* also derives from Orwell's familiarity with the propaganda technique of Goebbels, the mastermind behind the German psychological warfare offensive. The German radio broadcasts of special announcements of victories were preceded by lengthy bursts of martial music and fanfares, in exactly the same manner as described in *Nineteen Eighty-Four*. . . . The principles of Newspeak in *Nineteen Eighty-Four* certainly owe much to the study of German propaganda that formed part of the daily routine of those working in the British propaganda effort. The manipulation of the masses by the media in *Nineteen Eighty-Four* thus is clearly an amalgam of the practices Orwell had encountered in Soviet and Nazi propaganda before and during the war, and his own experience as a propagandist in the BBC's English-language service to India.

As a politically minded writer Orwell was aware of the contrasts between the totalitarian propaganda methods of the Nazis and Stalinists and those followed by Britain; he later praised the BBC's scrupulous adherence to truthfulness in its news broadcasts. But even inside Britain wartime propaganda sometimes indulged in deception. (p. 129)

If Orwell's forecast for the Britain of 1984 has proved off the mark, his vision of what the Communist world would be like on the other hand appears astonishingly accurate.

The drabness of daily life in the countries of Eastern Europe may not be quite as depressing as that in *Nineteen Eighty-Four,* but drab and colorless it certainly is. The division of the population into party members and ''proles'' is as marked as Orwell foresaw it. So also is the dullness and uniformity of the output of the mass media, whether newspapers, television, or radio. The incessant stream of predictable propaganda produces in members of the lower levels of the party the same indifference expressed in *Nineteen Eighty-Four* by Julia, ''who knew it was all rubbish, so why let one be worried about it?'' Even the hate sessions of *Nineteen Eighty-Four* have their parallel in the party meetings in present-day Eastern European countries at which attendance is compulsory, and members must display at least the outward signs of anti-American and anticapitalist feelings.

Orwell proved far too pessimistic, however, in anticipating that the boredom and indifference provoked by this incessant bombardment with predictable political slogans would lead to a total acquiescence of the population with the regime. The risings of ''proles'' and nonparty as well as party intellectuals in East Germany (1953), Hungary (1956), Czechoslovakia (1968), and Poland (at various times, but most notably in 1980-81) and the continuing dissidence among intellectuals in the Soviet Union itself prove that the totalitarian manipulation of popular feelings and ideas by the mass media is far less effective than Orwell had imagined.

Perhaps in 1984 we can see with greater clarity that the annihilation of the past can never be as effective as Orwell imagined it. In a society with the remnants of an educational system the total eradication of the literature of the past, as envisaged by Orwell, would be well-nigh impossible. There are in Orwell's book youth organizations modeled on the Hitler Youth and the Soviet Young Pioneers, but schools and universities barely get a mention. And yet, in a society as highly industrialized and geared to armaments production as that of Orwell's Oceania, there must have been institutions designed to train these specialists, not to speak of subliterary technicians such as Winston Smith himself. The continued availability of the classics in the Soviet Union, for example, to this day acts as a powerful antidote to the totalitarian manipulation of culture. A critical and humanistic tradition remains active and is the inspiration behind the major works of art produced by dissident writers, painters, and composers. It also inspires those who, while remaining within the establishment, continue to say a great deal between the lines in works that pass through the official censorship. Even if a total eradication of the literature of the past were possible, Orwell underestimated the time it would take. What Orwell imagined fully accomplished within some thirty years after the Ingsoc revolution in Britain has not as yet even begun to happen in the Soviet Union a full sixty-five years after the Bolshevik revolution.

In the developed Western world, Orwell's pessimism about the demise of parliamentary democracy and the disappearance of any laissez-faire economy has, up to now at least, not been vindicated by events; and the general atmosphere of life in the industrialized countries of the Western world looks very different in 1984 from what Orwell imagined. Yet even here Orwell, while seemingly wrong at the surface, may, in many ways, have been right at a deeper level.

Britain and America—the hub of Orwell's Oceania—have reached an unprecedented degree of affluence in 1984; in spite of high unemployment and large budget deficits, the standard of living has reached levels that were unimaginable in 1949. There is still parliamentary government. Nevertheless, here too the trend toward mass apathy and mass manipulation Orwell foresaw certainly is present and subtly, if gradually, transforming society.

There is, after all, not that much difference between a society that floods the masses with cheap, novelettish romance, raucous and sentimental pop music, and pornography to keep them amused and politically inert and one that does the same thing for commercial gain—but with the identical ultimate political result: apathy, ignorance of real issues, and acquiescence in whatever the politicians are doing. And does not commercial television do just that?

In other words, the division of society into the manipulators and the manipulated which Orwell rightly diagnosed as the sinister side of Stalinist and Nazi totalitarianism, and thus as a primarily political phenomenon, might be in the process of coming to pass in the ''free,'' nontotalitarian societies of the developed world simply by the operation of the mass media—through the incessant advertising of products in a manner all too suggestive of the blandishments and threats of Big Brother. (We love you if you buy our product! But woe to you if you do not buy it: your wife will hate you, you will have itching hemorrhoids, bad breath, slipping dentures, and a host of other terrible misfortunes!) It might be argued also that the media is well on the way toward transforming politics too into a mere appendage of the hard-sell advertising industry. This, ultimately, would result in a state of affairs very similar to that in the totalitarian countries: a population brainwashed into almost total apathy toward the political process, blindly following the slogans emanating from the mass media, above all television.

Orwell, so preeminently a literary man of the thirties, saw the process of the vulgarization of the masses almost entirely in terms of the printed word. It is odd, considering that he had worked in radio, that he did not rate the impact of that medium more highly. More astonishing, however, is his failure to foresee the nature and impact of television. At the time he was writing *Nineteen Eighty-Four,* television had already been a feature of British life; the BBC opened the world's first regular television service in 1936. (pp. 130-32)

And Orwell was aware of television. What fascinated him, however, was not its potential for providing entertainment to be watched, but its possible use as an instrument for watching people unawares in their homes. The telescreens in *Nineteen Eighty-Four* are cameras that transmit the picture of the room they are surveying to a center where policemen watch individual citizens. The telescreens are omnipresent in the homes of members of the Party in *Nineteen Eighty-Four,* but with the exception of an early morning gymnastics broadcast there is scarcely a mention of visual programming. Repeatedly Orwell refers to the sound of statistics being read out and propaganda speeches being heard from the telescreens. In other words,

Orwell saw the telescreens largely in terms of radio receivers with the capacity to transmit pictures to secret police watchers, but not as what they have actually become, the omnipresent, constant providers of highly colorful visual entertainment for the broad masses.

In spite of Orwell's awareness of the need for cheap entertainment to keep the proles happy, it is particularly remarkable that he should have failed to recognize in television the ideal provider of such shoddy hypnotic amusement. His interest in the new medium is fixed on its capacity to transmit from the individual home to the center, not on its capacity to provide the most powerful psychological stimuli through visual programming. "The great majority of the proles did not even have telescreens in their homes." The analysis of the state of society in Ingsoc Britain in Goldstein's secret book does refer to the fact that "the invention of print . . . made it easier to manipulate public opinion and the film and the radio carried the process further. With the development of television, and the technical advance which made it possible to receive and transmit simultaneously and on the same instrument, private life came to an end."

And as the proles do not have television, the proles are, in fact, allowed to have a private life. They are not worth watching. Behind this elitist view that only the members of the Party—i.e., the intellectuals—are significant enough to be watched and to be deprived of a private life, there lurks a residue of the Old Etonian's contempt for the lower classes.

Many critical observers maintain that in the developed industrial societies of the Western world, television, principally in its commercial form, has come to play the part that thought control, Newspeak, and the whole manipulative apparatus in the hands of the Party perform in *Nineteen Eighty-Four*. Commercial television in the United States has become a multi-billion-dollar enterprise which in effect is making the population progressively more stupid, incapable of sustained thought and concentration, and politically more apathetic. And all this with the expressed purpose and explicit justification that it is advertising through the mass media which keeps the economy of mass-production going. In other words: it is the television industry that operates under the implicit assumption that "ignorance is strength."

It might even be argued that the two other slogans of Oceania—"freedom is slavery" and "war is peace"—also express some of the basic principles and practices of a society dominated by the television medium: after all, the obfuscation of the masses' minds by television and the political apathy it seems to produce might well be seen as a form of slavery—an abdication of the exercise of genuine democratic decision making by the masses; and it might also be argued that the way the international situation is handled by the media creates the illusion of peace while bloody and destructive wars are being waged around the globe.

This may seem an extreme way of putting the matter. But, on reflection, it should become clear that our situation in 1984 contains at least the germs of a development in this direction. The image of Big Brother is absent from the affluent West, yet it remains a fact that politicians here too are now sold by image through television advertising, the intellectual level of which certainly is no higher than the slogans that advertise Big Brother in *Nineteen Eighty-Four*. Nor is the image of the hated adversary, Goldstein, absent from our screens, where he assumes the multifarious shape of the terrorist, the spy, the sub-

versive element, or, indeed, that eternal adversary, the rival superpower whose position as the perpetual enemy has become accepted as unquestionable and axiomatic.

It is moreover possible to assert that reasoned argument has been severely reduced in political discussion and debate, that the level of political knowledge among the masses is deplorably low, and that in many democratic countries the percentages of votes cast in elections are decreasing at an alarming rate. It can thus be argued that, albeit over a somewhat longer time span than Orwell envisaged, the masses might well decline to the status of disenfranchised and politically castrated proles.

This danger seems particularly acute in the United States, where commercial and advertising interests dominate television and radio, leading to the elimination of most "cultural" subjects from broadcasting. In those countries where television and radio are partly or wholly run as public services, there is considerable evidence that, in fact, the electronic media can be used to bring about a gradual improvement in the levels of taste in fields like drama and music, and that they may even be able to raise the political awareness of the population. But it is equally evident that this process is extremely slow and might, at best, merely increase what will always remain a small minority of highly educated and politically conscious individuals. This consideration is moot in the United States, where the deplorable state of television tends to be accepted as an immutable fact of life, almost a law of nature. The provincialism of this attitude, which ignores the evidence even of such a close neighbor as Canada, whose strong, publicly run broadcasting service has been able to a certain extent to maintain the presence of culture on the air in radio and television, is one of the sinister symptoms for the drift of the United States toward *Nineteen Eighty-Four*. On the other hand, the example of the use of the mass media in some European countries—Scandinavia, Holland, West Germany, Britain—provides at least a glimmer of hope.

That in 1984 television, in all the developed industrial countries of the Western world, has become mainly responsible for supplying the masses with cheap fiction, vicarious excitement, and mentally debilitating soft porn is too evident to need much elaboration. What may seem less obvious is the fact that Newspeak in 1984 takes its shape from the language of television advertising. Examples of tautological pseudo-logic like: "This powder washes whiter because it contains a special ingredient that washes whiter" have become commonplace on TV advertising. That such a statement should be considered convincing enough to warrant inclusion in an expensively produced commercial is striking evidence that the principles of Newspeak can debase the language to a point where genuine thought becomes impossible. And once the effectiveness of this attack on logical thought has been established by commercial advertising, inevitably political advertising follows suit. We may be well on the way toward reaching that point. Election commercials in the United States have almost totally eliminated reasoned argument and rely more and more on the mere appearance of the candidate. The effect of this technique on the level of political oratory even in contexts where reasoned argument might be possible—public meetings, press conferences, debates in Congress—has become painfully apparent in recent years and campaigns.

Orwell was among the first to formulate one of the basic facts about totalitarian politics and its manipulation of the masses: Large masses of people can best, and most completely, be controlled and manipulated to the extent that they can be removed from contact with reality. As their ideologies are distortions of reality, totalitarian regimes have to create a fantasy world that corresponds to their picture of reality. O'Brien tells Winston in one of their last confrontations:

> You believe that reality is something objective, external, existing in its own right. You also believe that the nature of reality is self-evident. When you delude yourself into thinking that you see something, you assume that everyone else sees the same thing as you. But I tell you, Winston, that reality is not external. Reality exists in the human mind and nowhere else.
>
> (pp. 132-36)

Television is a powerful instrument for projecting an alternative reality into the minds of its audience. Most of what is seen on television is staged or at least edited, including even those elements that are perceived as most real, such as the news. (p. 136)

In actuality, television presents a highly artificial, edited, staged, and therefore unrealistic picture of the world. This is true not only of openly fictional fare—situation comedies, police series, feature films—but also of the news, sports broadcasts, talk and game shows, and political debates. The very fact that cameras were in position to record a news event shows that its filming had been anticipated and staged. And in the great majority of cases it must subsequently have been edited and rearranged to give the maximum dramatic effect. In that sense much of the news is theater. Orwell, unresponsive as he was to the potential of television, imagined the rulers of *Nineteen Eighty-Four* distorting reality by means of radio broadcasts and newspapers. Television, because it is photographic and gives the illusion of a direct transmission of real events, has proved an infinitely more powerful medium for the creation of artificially distorted perceptions of the real world. In that sense the reality of 1984 far surpasses what Orwell imagined.

The political effects of this state of affairs may be more indirect, more gradual, and less readily perceived. They might well, for that very reason, be more insidious in the long run. For they operate in an atmosphere of affluence rather than of scarcity (as it exists in *Nineteen Eighty-Four* and in today's Communist world) and that in itself may be a more dangerous factor: affluence and contentment are a more effective means of gaining the acquiescence of the manipulated masses than discontent and deprivation. The long-term political effects on the masses of living in a fantasy environment, as I have suggested, might well spell the end of participatory democracy as we now know it in the Western world.

Despite the implications for the future, on the surface of daily life Orwell's vision has *not* come true in the non-Communist developed world. In the so-called Third World, however, there are numerous features of daily life that closely resemble the situation in Orwell's Britain—"Airstrip One." (pp. 136-37)

If Orwell's vision of the situation in the developed Western world is so much farther off the mark, this is perhaps due to the fact that he greatly underestimated the speed of change. Winston Smith is thirty-nine years old in 1984, which means that he was born in 1945, the year World War II ended. Orwell thus chose the year 1984 simply because he tried to imagine what the world would be like when the generation born after the end of the war had reached maturity. One generation is a very short time span on the scale of history. But we must forget that Orwell, in his mid-forties when he wrote *Nineteen Eighty-*

Four, knew that he was mortally ill and would not long survive the publication of his book. To a dying man even the nineteen-sixties must have appeared unconscionably far distant, in an almost mythical future.

Most utopias and anti-utopias are set centuries or even millenia ahead. Orwell took a considerable risk in describing a future that many of the readers of the first edition of his book would actually live to see. That is why, as far as the mass media are concerned, we in 1984 can merely discern the potential for the emergence of tendencies that might ultimately develop into what Orwell envisaged on a much longer time scale. In *Brave New World* Aldous Huxley imagined a population drugged into apathy by chemical means, pills of "soma." Writing almost twenty years after Huxley, Orwell came much nearer to a possible reality by seeing that it was much more likely that this type of apathy might be produced by the mass media (although he obviously underrated the power of television). Prophets of evil things to come tend to hope that their predictions will not come true, precisely because of their fear of what they have prophesied and warned against. Through its impact on millions of readers Orwell's *Nineteen Eighty-Four* has surely already done much toward averting the evils it predicted.

As regards the media, however, these warnings are still most pertinent; radio and television are among the most powerful and potentially beneficial inventions of the human spirit—in their effect over centuries to come as decisive for the development of civilization as the invention of writing itself, or the art of printing. Because Orwell as a writer was involved in the political use of the media, he saw the negative possibilities of radio and TV for the next generation. But radio, and above all television, can also become powerful positive influences to raise levels of awareness, knowledge, and culture; they have much to contribute toward the goal of a more humane humanity. Orwell's dire warnings are perhaps even more relevant in 1984 than when they were first uttered. (pp. 137-38)

> *Martin Esslin, "Television and Telescreen," in On "Nineteen Eighty-Four," edited by Peter Stansky, W. H. Freeman and Company, 1983, pp. 126-38.*

JOHN ATKINS   (essay date 1984)

[*Atkins is an English literary critic and novelist. He served as literary editor of the socialist weekly* Tribune *before Orwell accepted that position in 1943 and was friends with Orwell during his last years. In the following excerpt Atkins characterizes Orwell as a socialist, though he believes that Orwell felt that theoretical socialism had failed.*]

I doubt if any writer at any time has annexed a year so firmly and convincingly for himself as George Orwell. Except for him, 1984 would be no more significant than 1974 or any other year you can think of. In Orwellian terms, 1984 means menace; it stands for the triumph of Totalitarianism—a useful word with which Orwell familiarized us, preferring it to either Communism or Fascism because it covered both.

Orwell himself stood for Socialism—but immediately we are involved in semantic confusion. For is not Communism a brand of Socialism? Many use the terms interchangeably. One of the most essential ingredients of Socialism for Orwell was democracy. Was he therefore—and more importantly, from my point of view in this paper, would he have been today—a Social Democrat? But what is Social Democracy? The inner meaning of *democracy,* without being too fastidious, is relatively clear. But *social*? Does it mean Socialist? Might not the term Democratic Socialism be more exact? There seems to be little agreement on the point. To add to the confusion, the first Marxist party in Orwell's homeland, Great Britain (although he would probably have used the more limited term England) was Hyndman's Social Democratic Federation. Most of us, including Orwell, roughly identified Marxism with Communism, and in his day this meant the Soviet variety (there are many others and they seem to spawn annually). But Communism, except in its curious Newspeak understanding of the term, is not democratic. Some of the bitterest in-fighting in the history of Socialism and its derivatives has been between the Communists and the Social Democrats. (pp. 34-5)

We know, from his many biographers and commentators, that until Orwell went to Wigan [to gather material for a book on mining conditions] he had only the haziest idea of Socialist theory. Richard Rees said that he spent more than three years trying, unsuccessfully, to convert his friend to Socialism. When the conversion finally came, it was the result of intense feeling (disgust mingled with outrage), not of doctrinaire theory. . . . In fact, it was an extremely worldly event, one which might well have been anticipated by anyone knowing Orwell's character: human suffering and injustice moved him on a scale that could not be matched by argument. (p. 35)

[What] are the qualities of traditional Socialism (or English Socialism, as some of us like to call it) that attracted Orwell? [Orwell biographer Bernard] Crick lists them in his biography as egalitarian, non-Marxist (which means partly non-systematic and partly non-biblical), moralist, craft-conscious (not class-conscious); and deeply concerned with the balance between "town and country." In other words, English Socialism was not specially designed for the urban proletariat, like Marxism. To be more precise, it was not "specially designed" at all. It grew. It was organic. Later readers of Orwell did not always get the point. *Animal Farm,* for instance, was treated as an attack on Socialism. It was nothing of the kind. It was an attack on Totalitarianism, with the Soviet variety used as a model. (pp. 35-6)

In 1983 a new political party, the Social Democratic Party, contested a General Election in Britain. Would Orwell have supported it? Its name would have encouraged him but he was too wise a bird to be taken in by such simplicities. He would have wanted to know who these new Social Democrats were. They were for the most part Labour Party members who could no longer accept the activities of the Left. They were naturally dismissed as renegades, even concealed Tories, by the simon-pure Marxists. (pp. 36-7)

Always in discussing Socialism we are bedevilled by the absence of firm definition. That words should have exact meanings (in public discussion, that is—the rules are different for poetry) and should be used meaningfully was central to Orwell's thought. The meaning of Fascism is another example. Most Socialists between the Wars regarded Fascism as "advanced capitalism" even the last resort of capitalism. This view still persists in some quarters, especially among what are now called Left Wingers, who increasingly refer to Mrs. Thatcher's government as Fascist. But if the word is to have meaning, how can it describe at one and the same time Mussolini's single-party, socialist-bashing, castor-oil republic and a system where four main parties send representatives to Parliament, where views of every possible complexion are openly expressed, and Habeas Corpus still applies? Orwell saw Fascism as a grim

perversion of Socialism—as was Communism. Fascism for him was a genuine mass movement, with an elitist philosophy and a popular appeal. (p. 37)

If we wish to compress Orwell's views into a single proposition (admittedly, a very risky procedure, but probably necessary in a world where slogans rule) it could be this: *Theoretical* Socialism has failed; or, alternatively, Socialism cannot usefully be theoreticized. (Not, please note, theorized, a different matter altogether.) In an article entitled **"Our Own Have Nots"** (*Time and Tide,* 27 Nov. 1937) Orwell wrote that he wished to overcome "the tragic failure of theoretical Socialism, to make contact with the normal working classes." He saw the "normal working" people as likely to respond to human warmth, sympathy and understanding but to be quite unmoved by such remote notions as *dictatorship of the proletariat* or *economic determinism.* (p. 38)

It was the modern way of life Orwell loathed, a way not really challenged by Marxism. Marxism simply wishes to make it more efficient. (As D. H. Lawrence once wrote, Marxism and Capitalism resemble a racing car and an express train each trying to reach the same destination before the other.) Orwell's rebellion grew out of revulsion; it was cultural, not political. He distrusted so many of his apparent "Socialist" colleagues because they promised improvements which bore no relationship to their methods. His picture of the contemporary world ("everything slick and streamlined, everything made out of something else. Celluloid, rubber, chromium-steel everywhere, arc lamps blazing all night, glass roofs over your head, radios all playing the same tune, no vegetation left, everything cemented over. . . . .") would flourish equally well under Marxism-Leninism as under Toryism. (p. 39)

If we are to give a name to Orwell's politics it would be the politics of despair. The dominant tone is pessimism. The early Socialists did not despair because they had their Socialism to feed their hope. Orwell's despair was based on the knowledge that much of this "Socialism" had in practice become debased and corrupted. *Happiness of the people* had been replaced by *victory of a system*—a system no longer critically examined by those that support it. There was no way back. . . . Today, in 1984, a few Orwellians have broken away from the Labour Party in a desperate attempt to refloat the old values. They have invoked the precious word *democratic* and they have qualified it with *social.* The words are right, but is the faith that moves mountains still there?

In one respect I think Orwell was mistaken. (His honesty and concern for people can never be questioned.) *1984* is unrealistically pessimistic. If we look at the world around us we may agree that his vision has already been realized: we are at the mercy of the super-powers who play war-games with other people. But Orwell's picture of a dreary though apparently satisfied proletariat is false. He imagined that groups in public houses singing updated versions of *Knees Up Mother Brown* and *Down at the Old Bull and Bush,* all contently supping Victory Gin, would be the social norm. The bosses, from Big Brother downwards, would use fear and oppression to maintain their power. But this will not happen and is not happening. The modern British worker wants a "new second-hand" Ford Cortina. Once he gets it, he's happy. Add to this holidays in Benidorm or the Costa Brava, and he feels he is in a Workers' Paradise that makes the Soviet version dull and insipid. This life represents the kind of synthetic texture that Orwell abhorred, but it is winning. Pessimism is justified, but a different kind

Orwell's home on the island of Jura, where he wrote Nineteen Eighty-Four. *The Orwell Archive, University College London.*

of pessimism from Orwell's. (There is, of course, another option: atomization.) There is absolutely no point in governing through pain when it is so much easier and less stressful to govern through pleasure. Ultimately, *Brave New World* is a more accurate picture of a predictable future than *1984*. Huxley's mistake was to project his vision six hundred years into the future, thus turning it into a fairy tale.

There is little point in attempting to guess how Orwell would have voted in 1983, or what he would advocate in an actual 1984. But he was a man we admired, whose opinion was welcomed and respected, and it would bring political comfort to be able to say: He would have said or done thus or thus if he were still alive. One thing we do know. He would have resisted mere theory and recipes that remind us of Eastern Europe (e.g., two hundred more nationalized companies, subservient trade unions, a nationalized press). He would have urged policies that give the individual the feeling that he is being considered. He did not know the exact, mathematical answers any more than anyone else but he did know that progress must be piece-meal. If something goes wrong, it can be put right without too much damage. When something goes wrong with a centralized plan, however, the whole world will know about it. Like ripples in a pool, the process cannot be limited. Or to change the metaphor, cut through one beam and the house will fall down. (pp. 41-2)

> John Atkins, "Orwell in 1984," *in* College Literature, *Vol. XI, No. 1, 1984, pp. 34-43.*

GORDON BEADLE (essay date 1984)

[*Beadle challenges the claims of both Norman Podhoretz (1983) and Robert de Camara (see Additional Bibliography) that Orwell either became or would have become a proponent of conservative political thought. Such a view can only be supported, according to Beadle, by first ignoring the distinctions between socialism, communism, and Marxism, and then by assembling "carefully selected quotes from some of Orwell's more pointed attacks on the Soviet Union, Communists, Marxists, authoritarian socialists, and pacifists." Further, the critic maintains, Orwell's own political actions throughout his life must be disregarded in order to support the neoconservative argument.*]

American conservatives are not generally given to celebrating the political wisdom of English left-wing socialists, yet this has been the curious fate of George Orwell. From the very beginning of his literary success in this country, the creators of the myth of the conservative Orwell would appear to have deliberately ignored Orwell's own interpretation of his work. Although Orwell lay dying of tuberculosis while the American conservative crusade gathered momentum, he insisted upon issuing "a sort of *démenti*" against what he took to be a deliberate misreading of *1984* [see Orwell excerpt dated 1949]. . . .

Orwell's interpretation of *1984* went largely unnoticed, but the enormous commercial success of *Animal Farm* and *1984* gradually brought Orwell's lesser known works back into print. Collections of his essays, journalism, and letters began to appear and by the late 1960s Orwell had become a kind of cult figure of the liberal anti-Communist left. Americans were now confronted with the Orwell who had fought with an army of the extreme left against Franco in Spain. Conservatives had to reckon with the Orwell who was convinced that only a socialist revolution could save Britain from defeat in World War II and the Orwell whose fervent anticommunism was rooted in the suspicion that communism was "merely a particularly vicious form of state capitalism." (p. 71)

Now, suddenly, American conservatives, under the new banner of "neoconservatism," have once again attempted to claim Orwell. Why, one might ask, should they turn for comfort to a revolutionary socialist such as Orwell at this late date? Norman Podhoretz recently provided the answer [see excerpt dated 1983]. After taking note of the remarkable posthumous rise in Orwell's reputation as an essayist, Mr. Podhoretz concludes that "it is, after all, no small thing to have the greatest political writer of the age on one's side: it gives confidence, authority, and weight to one's own political views." Orwell, as Podhoretz readily admits, is a writer "well worth stealing." Stealing or willfully bowdlerizing? According to Podhoretz, Orwell was never much of a socialist—"beyond a generalized faith in 'planning' he never showed much interest in the practical arrangements involved in the building of socialism." It seems that he was no revolutionary either. Neoconservatives "deny that Orwell was a revolutionary: they think of him instead as a major critic of revolution." Having detached Orwell from socialism and revolution, Mr. Podhoretz has no difficulty in presenting Orwell as one of the "guiding spirits" of the neoconservative Committee for a Free World.

Well, if Orwell was neither a socialist nor a revolutionary, then what was he doing in Loyalist Spain in 1936, where he went to write and stayed to fight in the ranks of an army representing the most revolutionary section of the Spanish working class? Orwell leaves the reader of his moving memoir of the Spanish Civil War [*Homage to Catalonia*] with little doubt as to his motives for fighting in Spain.

> I came to Spain with some notion of writing newspaper articles, but I had joined the militia almost immediately, because at that time and in that atmosphere it seemed the only conceivable thing to do. . . . The revolution was in full swing. . . . There was much in it that I did not understand, in some ways I did not like, but I recognized it immediately as a state of affairs worth fighting for.

Orwell's revolutionary Barcelona, with its gutted churches, collectivization extending down to cafés and bootblacks, strictly enforced economic equality, and absence of well-dressed people, surely comes close to a description of the ultimate neoconservative political nightmare. Yet the figure "guiding spirit" of the Committee for the Free World "recognized it immediately as a state of affairs worth fighting for."

After Spain, Orwell's personal war with communism began in earnest. But the nature of Orwell's opposition to communism was always revolutionary, not conservative. In their frequent references to Orwell's anticommunism, neoconservatives forget (or deliberately omit) the fact that his bitter condemnation of communism was based on the belief that communism was a reactionary force dedicated to the suppression of any genuine social and economic revolution. The Communists in Spain, Orwell insisted, betrayed the workers by deliberately prevent-

ing a real revolution from taking place . . . Orwell's *Homage to Catalonia* was written largely with the intention of exposing the Communist betrayal of the revolution in Spain. Yet Orwell emerged from the Spanish Civil War less disillusioned with socialism than conservatives generally assume. "I have seen wonderful things," he wrote shortly before leaving Spain, "and at last really believe in Socialism, which I never did before."

George Orwell was not one of those English socialists of the 1930s who loudly supported revolutionary socialism abroad and lived contentedly with capitalism at home. "I do not see how one can oppose Fascism," he concluded in January 1937, "except by working for the overthrow of capitalism, starting, of course, in one's own country." Now Podhoretz contends that "with the outbreak of World War II, a new Orwell was born—Orwell the English patriot," and he cites "My Country, Right or Left" as one of "his most memorable phrases. . . ." However, Orwell the patriot remained very much Orwell the revolutionary. **"My Country, Right or Left"** is actually the title of an essay in which Orwell declared that "only a revolution can save England," and he did not shrink from the possibility of violence to achieve it: "I dare say the London gutters will have to run with blood. All right, let them, if it is necessary. But when the red militias are billeted in the Ritz I shall still feel that the England I was taught to love so long ago and for such different reasons is somehow persisting."

Orwell's renewed sense of patriotism led to a series of sharply worded attacks upon Marxists, pacifists, and other elements of the Socialist left whose motives he questioned. But this was not really a "new Orwell." It was more like a heightened version of the old Orwell of the highly controversial *Road to Wigan Pier*. He took his self-appointed role of critic and conscience of the left very seriously, even if he was not always fair in his criticism. Indeed, Orwell sometimes sharply condemned views and positions that he himself had only recently abandoned. But he could certainly turn a memorable phrase, and neoconservatives have frequently attempted to trade on his wit and integrity by quoting him out of context. For example, Norman Podhoretz and Jeffrey Hart are fond of using the vivid description of the social deviants of the English socialist movement that appears in *The Road to Wigan Pier:* "One sometimes gets the impression that the mere words 'Socialism' and 'Communism' draw towards them with magnetic force every fruit-juice maker, nudist, sandal-wearer, sexmaniac, Quaker, 'Nature Cure' quack, pacifist, and feminist in England." Very amusing from the neoconservative point of view, but Podhoretz and Hart take care not to point out that *The Road to Wigan Pier* is in fact a sustained argument in favor of a socialist society. (pp. 71-3)

Orwell warned the reader that he was "arguing FOR Socialism, not AGAINST it." He was simply admitting that "as with the Christian religion, the worst advertisement for Socialism is its adherents." Orwell feared that the Marxists and the crank elements of the English socialist movement were discrediting the cause of socialism in the eyes of the common people he celebrated in his novels. The central thesis of *The Road to Wigan Pier* was that socialism had "been buried beneath layer after layer of doctrinaire priggishness, party squabbles and half-baked 'progressivism' until it is like a diamond hidden under a mountain of dung." The diamond must be recovered. Socialism must stand for "justice and liberty" and regain its anticapitalist revolutionary posture. Well said, but not exactly a neoconservative message. (p. 73)

To assume, as Orwell did, that only a socialist revolution could save Britain from defeat in World War II seems absurd or at best naive in retrospect. But we must remember that revolution was in the air. . . . Toward the end of 1944 Orwell admitted with characteristic honesty that in taking the view that "the war and the Revolution are inseparable," he had made "a very great error." He attributed this rather gross misreading of the political climate of Britain to wishful thinking.

With victory now in sight, Orwell turned his attention to the impending General Election and the practical arrangements of building a democratic society in the postwar era. . . . Orwell was pleased with the Labour victory of 1945, but not with the behavior of the Labour government. In one of his London newsletters to the *Partisan Review,* he insisted that no Labour government really "means business" unless it "(a) nationalises land, coal mines, railways, public utilities and banks, (b) offers India immediate Dominion Status (this is a minimum), and (c) purges the bureaucracy, the army, the diplomatic service, etc., so thoroughly as to forestall sabotage on the Right." By nationalization of the land, Orwell meant that the state should "certainly impose an upward limit to the ownership of land (probably fifteen acres at the very most), and . . . never permit any ownership of land in town areas."

Orwell had previously advocated the strict "limitation of incomes" on such a scale that "the highest tax-free income in Britain does not exceed the lowest by more than ten to one." He called for a "reform of the educational system along democratic lines" that should begin by immediately "abolishing the autonomy of the public schools and older universities and flooding them with State-aided pupils chosen simply on grounds of ability." A Labour government that "meant business" would also abolish the titles of the "so-called aristocracy," close the House of Lords, and disestablish the Church of England. Orwell rather grudgingly favored "retaining the Royal Family," but only because "modern people can't, apparently, get along without drums, flags and loyalty parades" and "it is better that they should tie their leader-worship onto some figure who has no power."

This is not the place to evaluate the political viability or wisdom of Orwell's proposals. I merely wish to point out that Orwell did in fact take considerable interest in "the practical arrangements of Socialism." But again, it is not the sort of prescription for human progress that one would expect from one of the "guiding spirits" of neoconservatism.

Another area of embarrassment for the neoconservatives lies in Orwell's unremitting war against the Roman Catholic church. As early as 1932, Orwell was taking "great pleasure" in taunting Catholic theologians and converts to the faith. But his real quarrel with the Roman church turned on his belief that "its influence is and always must be against freedom of thought and speech, against human equality, and against any form of society tending to promote earthly happiness." Accepting the Catholic point of view meant "accepting exploitation, poverty, famine, war and disease as part of the natural order of things." The Catholic church was not only opposed to humanitarian reforms, it was "pro-Fascist, both objectively and subjectively." In Spain, Orwell was pleased to discover that "churches were pillaged everywhere and as a matter of course, because it was perfectly well understood that the Spanish Church was part of the capitalist racket." During the dark days of World War II, he virtually accused the English Catholics of plotting treason. (pp. 73-4)

Catholicism was also seen by Orwell as a sinister influence in the literary world. He was convinced that the destruction of intellectual liberty that went with "Orthodox Catholicism" had "a crushing effect upon certain literary forms, especially the novel." Orwell accused Catholic writers from Chesterton to Graham Greene of debasing their talents and ruining their work by becoming Catholic propagandists. (p. 74)

Given the radical nature of Orwell's politics and the ferocity of his attacks on Roman Catholicism, one would logically expect Mr. Buckley's ultra-rightist *National Review* to look upon George Orwell as a kind of unholy cross between Jane Fonda and Bertrand Russell.

But not so. In May of 1983, the *National Review* featured an essay in which Mr. Robert de Camara paid very respectful "Homage to Orwell" [see Additional Bibliography]. Mr. de Camara concludes that the "forces of darkness have huge armies, a bigger and better arsenal, liberation movements, and the whores' allegiance. The forces of light have Orwell on their side and draw strength from it." Perhaps so, provided one can properly distinguish "the forces of light" from "the forces of darkness."

Now before the discovery of Orwell-the-neoconservative escalates into a right-wing literary cottage industry, it might be well to briefly describe just how this seemingly impossible shell game is played. The usual method, with some interesting minor variations, is to ignore or deliberately blur the distinctions between socialism, communism, and Marxism and then string together carefully selected quotes from some of Orwell's more pointed attacks on the Soviet Union, Communists, Marxists, authoritarian socialists, and pacifists. The conservative conclusion becomes fairly obvious, provided that Orwell's own revolutionary program is carefully concealed and the real nature of his criticism of the Soviet Union and communism is largely ignored. But the Orwell of the '30s cannot be entirely ignored, so he is said to have undergone a patriotic conversion at the beginning of the war or, as Mr. de Camara would have it, "with the Goths at the gates, the leftist swaggering stopped." Here the strained credibility of the neoconservative argument turns on one's willingness to accept the notion that conservatives have such a monopoly on patriotism that patriotic utterances can be equated with a "conversion" to the conservative cause. But the problem here is that the patriotic Orwell was initially convinced that only a radical socialist revolution could save Britain from "the Goths at the gates." As the war progressed, his "leftist swaggering" found concrete expression in the series of radical socialist reforms that I have outlined. And Orwell, of course, never understood the "conservative" implications of his patriotism and went on calling himself a socialist until his death in 1950. (p. 75)

Political converts, like religious converts, not only sing the loudest; they also assume that everyone is ripe for conversion to their cause. But anyone who takes the trouble to read his published work carefully is likely to conclude that George Orwell was no more ripe for a conversion to neoconservatism than, say, Alfred Kazin, after his return from a neoconservative revival meeting at the Plaza. It seems more likely that Orwell would have dismissed neoconservatism as merely another one of those "smelly little orthodoxies which are contending for our souls." (p. 76)

Gordon Beadle, "George Orwell and the Neocon-
servatives," in Dissent, *Winter, 1984, pp. 71-6.*

ANDRÉ BRINK (essay date 1984)

[*Brink is one of the leading figures in modern Afrikaans literature. The author of many novels, Brink has also written dramas and volumes of critical essays, and has translated into Afrikaans the works of William Shakespeare, Henry James, Graham Greene, Lewis Carroll, Albert Camus, Georges Simenon, and Miguel Cervantes. In the following excerpt Brink prefaces his discussion of several apocalyptic South African novels with an analysis of Orwell's* Nineteen Eighty-Four. *He concludes that the past-tense narrative of Orwell's novel indicates that the novel ends not in "despair and the triumph of Big Brother, but in the vindication of the creative act, the written word."*]

Any examination of apocalyptic visions or tendencies in post-modern fiction must proceed from an acknowledgment of the terms in which George Orwell defined the power and the (apparently) ultimate triumph of Big Brother. It is significant that the stranglehold of his regime on the lives and loves and minds of individuals is made possible, in the first instance, only by the existence of a counterforce which turns out to be a mirror image of the original: without the "total onslaught," to use the term current in South African Newspeak, Big Brother loses his own raison d'être. If necessary, the adversary, the heretic, has to be invented. . . .

The perpetuation of Big Brother's power, once it has been imposed, depends on the maintenance and celebration of the Lie: Orwell's "doublethink," the incessant reinvention of the past in order to control future and present. . . . The final triumph of the Lie, when two plus two can be made to signify either five or anything else, is also the final eclipse of freedom. Hence Orwell's profoundly moving formula: "Freedom is the freedom to say that two plus two make four. If that is granted, all else follows." (p. 189)

In these totalitarian conditions the only forms of revolt, all of them contained within the notion of "thoughtcrime," are private and individual. Sex is revolutionary. . . . So is writing: nothing precipitates the confrontation with Big Brother so fatally as Smith's insistence on thinking for himself—and on committing his thoughts to his diary. In itself, the private revolt may appear absurd, guaranteeing nothing but the extermination of the dissident himself; yet there is a blind form of hope in the Sisyphean act: "I don't imagine that we can alter anything in our own lifetime. But one can imagine little knots of resistance springing up here and there—small groups of people banding themselves together, and gradually growing, and even leaving a few records behind, so that the next generation can carry on where we leave off."

Nineteen Eighty-Four is generally seen as demonstrating the futility of this hope: no "small group" is allowed to survive; the few intrepid rebels are obliterated, not by killing them but by turning them into blind, thoughtless supporters of Big Brother. That, after all, is the note on which the book ends. The end of the book, however, is not the end of the story. It seems to me that a fascinating "deconstruction" of the text can be undertaken from the point of view of time and tense. It is well known that Orwell wrote his book in 1948 and used the same figures to arrive at the "anagram" 1984: in other words, purporting to "look ahead" into the future, he was really affirming the existence, the omnipresence, of that future in the present, in every "now." But he goes much further. The book, from "It was a bright cold day in April, and the clocks were striking thirteen" (which in itself does to conventional notions of time almost what Ionesco does in the opening scene of *La cantatrice chauve*) to "He loved Big Brother," is written in the past

tense. I cannot accept this as mere adherence to narrative tradition: and even if it were, it may yet *function* in a wholly unconventional way. The narrator is writing about Winston Smith from a vantage point much further into the future than "1984," looking back at events already concluded—something he could conceivably do only if Big Brother's regime has become extinct in the meantime. The narrator lives, writes and judges from a framework of values radically different from that of Big Brother. (Cf. this remark in the appendix on Newspeak: ". . . the word *bellyfeel*, which implied a blind, enthusiastic acceptance difficult to imagine today.") Interrogated by the torturer-traitor O'Brien, Smith sees again the newspaper fragment he himself destroyed earlier by feeding it into a "memory hole": contrary to everything he has been led to believe, evidence is *not* destroyed; so the accumulated evidence from his life and the lives of other would-be rebels must have survived for the narrator to draw his text from it. Belying what Orwell himself said about the "new" dictatorships faced by the world in his time ("The terrifying thing about the modern dictatorships is that they are something entirely unprecedented. Their end cannot be foreseen. In the past every tyranny was sooner or later overthrown"), *Nineteen Eighty-Four* ends not in total despair and the triumph of Big Brother, but in the vindication of the creative act, the written word. (pp. 189-90)

> *André Brink, "Writing against Big Brother: Notes on Apocalyptic Fiction in South Africa," in* World Literature Today, *Vol. 58, No. 2, Spring, 1984, pp. 189-94.**

ALFRED KAZIN (essay date 1984)

[*A highly respected literary critic, Kazin is best known for his essay collections* The Inmost Leaf *(1955) and* Contemporaries *(1962), and particularly for* On Native Grounds *(1942), a study of American prose writing since the era of William Dean Howells. Having studied the works of "the critics who were the best writers—from Sainte-Beuve and Matthew Arnold to Edmund Wilson and Van Wyck Brooks" as an aid to his own critical understanding, Kazin has found that "criticism focussed many—if by no means all—of my own urges as a writer: to show literature as a deed in human history, and to find in each writer the uniqueness of the gift, of the essential vision, through which I hoped to penetrate into the mystery and sacredness of the individual soul." In the following excerpt Kazin discusses the political nature of Orwell's works and in particular of* Nineteen Eighty-Four.]

In Orwell's novel [*1984*] thirty rocket bombs a week are falling on the capital; nothing more is said of them. Like the "atom bomb" that explodes over Oceania's "Airstrip I"—England—and by destroying a church provides a hiding place in the belfry for the lovers in an "almost deserted stretch of country," all these bombs are abstractions in a book that, except for the hardships of daily living borrowed from the 1940s, is meant to be an abstract of a wholly political future. Orwell was an efficient novelist not particularly interested in fiction; he used it for making a point. Bombs in *1984* symbolize Orwell's pent-up rage about everything in the political world from the mass unemployment of the 1930s (which continued well into the war period) to the ignorance of the left intelligentsia justifying Stalinism because the Russian people were pouring out their blood. By 1948, when Orwell was finishing the novel he had conceived in 1943, he was also maddened by the postwar division of the world, the atom bombs on Japan, and England's dependency on America. The ex-radical neo-conservative proponents of America-as-ideology now trying to claim Orwell overlook the fact that England's currency in *1984* is American. England is Oceania Airstrip I. We know whose airstrip it is.

Winston Smith and his fellows in the Ministry of Truth spend their days rewriting the past: "Most of the material you were dealing with had no connection with anything in the real world, not even the kind of connection that is contained in a direct lie." Not Orwell's novel is fiction but the world itself. Fiction as deliberate abstraction from life is what this terror society lives on. By political fiction Orwell means a society that has no meaning. A collectivized insanity is what a wholly tendentious politics has reduced us to. *We* have become the vacuum. Appearance has replaced reality, and appearance is just propaganda. In this future emptiness any two of the three great powers dividing the world (Orwell was grimly sure there would soon be two) may be officially but only symbolically at war. This is a war without end, because it is probably being waged in the "Ministry of Peace." Or if it is really going on, like the present war between Iran and Iraq, the belligerents may not recall why they went to war. Truckloads of enemy prisoners are regularly shown to London, but they may not be prisoners or even enemies. Bombs do occasionally fall on the city, but like Somoza [of Nicaragua], or Assad [of Syria], the rulers of this society probably bomb their own people to keep them cowed. (p. 13)

The thirty bombs falling each week in *1984* are symbols of the routine terror that Orwell imagined for the end of the century. Politics for him had become the future as complete domination. Pervasive injustice had certainly become his vision of things. In *1984* only the utter disregard of the masses by the Party (a theme fundamental to the book but not demonstrated as fully as the devastation of language and the elimination of the past) shows Orwell's compassion struggling against his shuddering vision of the future. "Work and bed," I used to hear English factory workers complain. "Might as well be dead." The deadly fatigue of 1939-1945 is captured in one line about Winston Smith's neighbor Mrs. Parsons. "One had the impression that there was dust in the creases of her face."

What Orwell would not transfer from 1945 to 1984 was the positive and liberating aspects of wartime controls. England was in many respects more fully mobilized for war than Nazi Germany. A general improvement in national health and social services convinced many people that such efficiency called for widespread nationalization. An impatient drive for a better life increasingly filled the atmosphere as Germany finally went down to defeat. To the amazement of many people in the "movement," this brought the Labour party to power with the greatest majority in the history of British socialism. Orwell's writings of the period reflect little of this. It is true that he was ailing with the lung disease that was to kill him in 1950, that his wife Eileen had died in March 1945 when he was in Germany as a correspondent, that he was still writing for the left-wing *Tribune*. It is also true that the author of the wickedly brilliant satire on Stalinism, *Animal Farm,* continued to proclaim himself a supporter of the Labour party and a libertarian Socialist.

Nevertheless, the bread-and-butter issues that brought Labour to power did not get into the novel that made Orwell's name a symbol for the fear of socialism. The tyranny in this book is called "Ingsoc," English Socialism. Like so many Americans on the left, Orwell was more concerned with what Russia portended for socialism than with the actual struggles of the working class. "Socialism" in America is just a rumpus between nostalgic and former radicals. In England it was a na-

tional movement, a government in power, an aroused consciousness. What was more on Orwell's mind, despite his undiminished sympathy for Labour, was the issue of domination which he knew so well from his upper-class background, though he derived, he said, from the lower part of it. Or as Lenin put it, Who Whom?—who's going to run the show and drive the rest of us?

Socialism to George Orwell, as to the utopian reformers and idealists of the nineteenth century, was not an economic question but a moral one. The welfare state little interested Orwell. He was naive, or perhaps just literary, when he wrote in *The Road to Wigan Pier,* his documentary of British poverty in the Thirties, "economic injustice will stop the moment we want it to stop, and no sooner, and if we genuinely want it to stop the method adopted hardly matters." To the twenty-six-year-old Karl Marx writing in the *Economic and Philosophical Manuscripts* (1844), the purpose of socialism was to end, for once in human history, the economic struggle for existence that has always kept man from "reappropriating" his essence. Exactly a century later Orwell wrote in a book review, "The real problem of our time is to restore the sense of absolute right and wrong when the belief that it used to rest on—that is, the belief in personal immortality—has been destroyed. This demands faith, which is a different thing from credulity."

Just at the moment when twentieth-century technology had shown itself capable of feeding the hungry, when everything in sight justified Marx's testimony in *The Communist Manifesto* to the power of new productive forces and Whitehead's praise of "the century of hope" for "inventing invention," socialism in its original meaning—the end of tribal nationalism, of man's alienation from his own essence, of wealth determining all values in society—yielded to the nightmare of coercion. What drove Orwell into an opposition all his own, what made for the ominousness of *1984,* for a deadliness of spirit that fills the book and helped to kill him at forty-six, was his inability to overlook the source of the nightmare. Lenin had seized the state in the name of the long-suffering working class. Thomas Hobbes in 1651 had called Leviathan "the mortal God." He ascribed its power over men to their fear of violent death at each other's hands in the brute state of nature. Fear causes men to create a state by contracting to surrender their natural rights and to submit to the absolute authority of a sovereign. By the social contract men had surrendered their natural liberties in order to enjoy the order and safety of the organized state. But under the total domination of the socialist state men could be just as afraid of violent death at each other's hands as they had been in the state of nature.

"Socialism" was not a fetish to Orwell. . . . With his dislike of absolutist intellectuals, he would not have been astonished to see the ease with which so many former radicals have managed to overcome their disillusionment in the arms of the Pentagon, the CIA, the National Security Administration, and other current examples of how to get "the State off our backs." No great admirer of the United States, which he never cared to visit, Orwell would have made note of the fact that last year the average American household watched television for seven hours and two minutes each day, that households with cable now watch fifty-eight hours a week, and that in this year of 1984 readers of a liberal weekly could read the following:

> Is Big Brother watching? If you are tired of
> Gov't . . . tired of Big Business . . . tired of
> everybody telling you who you are and what
> you should be . . . then now is the time to speak

out. . . . Display disgust and declare your independence. Wear a Big Brother Is Watching Shirt today, Tee shirt $10/ . . . Canadians remit $US. Big Brother is Watching LTD, Neenah WI . . .

Orwell thought the problem of domination by class or caste or race or political machine more atrocious than ever. It demands solution. Because he *was* from the upper middle class and knew from his own prejudices just how unreal the lower classes can be to upper-class radicals, a central theme in all his work is the separateness and loneliness of the upper-class observer, like his beloved Swift among the oppressed Irish. Everyone knows by now that he was born in India, that he was brought up to the gentility, snobbery, and race-pride of the British upper classes, especially in the more anxious forms of class consciousness dictated by genteel poverty. He was put through the scholarship mill for Eton and revolted against the system by not going on to Oxford or Cambridge, choosing instead to become a policeman in Burma.

After five years of this, furiously rejecting British imperialism, he threw himself into the life of the *Lumpenproletariat* in Paris and London, the "people of the abyss" as his admired Jack London put it. In England he lived the life of a tramp for months at a time in spite of his weak lungs, and after publishing his first book, *Down and Out in Paris and London* (1933), he went out to the mining districts of the North to do his extraordinary firsthand investigation of working-class life and poverty, *The Road to Wigan Pier* (1937).

Hostile critics of *1984* have eagerly picked on the fact that despite his attempt to immerse himself in workingclass life, Orwell did not commit himself to socialism until he returned to England in 1937, after being wounded in the Spanish Civil War and hunted by Loyalist police for having fought with the proscribed anti-Stalinist POUM. It was the wonderful fraternalism of the anarchists and other obstinate idealists on the left that gave Orwell his one image of socialism as a transformation of human relationships. In Catalonia, for a brief season after Franco's revolt in 1936, the word "comrade" really meant something. In *Homage to Catalonia* Orwell recited with wonder the disappearance of the usual servility and money worship. What a glorious period that was—until the nominally socialist government in Madrid, instigated by the communists, frustrated every possibility of social revolution from within. Even before Franco conquered in 1939, the old way of life had been restored in Catalonia.

Orwell never forgot what he had seen in Catalonia. This was more than "socialism with a human face," it was socialism as true and passionate equality. Socialism, he wrote near the end of his life, can mean nothing but justice and liberty. For Orwell socialism was the only possible terminus—where? when?—to the ceaseless deprivations suffered by most human beings on earth. But since he equally abominated the despotisms still justified by many English and American left intellectuals, he made a point in *1984* of locating the evil in the thinking of the leading Thought Policeman, O'Brien.

Political intellectuals on the left, the ex-left, the would-be left, the ideological right, can be poison. By the time he summed up all his frustration and rage in *1984,* Orwell had gone beyond his usual contempt for what he called "the boiled rabbits of the left." He was obsessed by the kind of rationale created by modern intellectuals for tyranny by the state. O'Brien's speeches to the broken Winston Smith in the Thought Police's torture chamber represent for Orwell the core of our century's political hideousness. Although O'Brien says that power seeks power and needs no ideological excuse, he does in fact explain to his victim what this power is.

The power exerted and sought by political intellectuals is that they must always be right. O'Brien is frightening because of the way he thinks, not because of the cynicism he advances. Dostoevsky in *The Possessed* said of one of his revolutionist "devils"—"When he was excited he preferred to risk anything rather than to remain in uncertainty." O'Brien tells his victim: "You are a flaw in the pattern, Winston. You are a stain that must be wiped out. . . . It is intolerable to us that an erroneous thought should exist anywhere in the world, however secret and powerless it may be."

Every despotism justifies itself by claiming the power of salvation. Before salvation by the perfect society, there was salvation by the perfect God. One faction after another in history claims to represent perfection, to the immediate peril of those who do not. My salvation cannot tolerate your disbelief, for that is a threat to my salvation.

O'Brien tortures Winston Smith because of O'Brien's necessary belief that the mind controls all things. There is in fact no external reality. The world is nothing but man and man nothing but mind. Winston, not yet electro-shocked into agreeing to this, protests from his rack: "The world itself is only a speck of dust. And man is tiny—helpless! How long has he been in existence? For millions of years the earth was uninhabited." O'Brien: "Nonsense. The earth is as old as we are, no older. How could it be older? Nothing exists except through human consciousness. . . . Before man, there was nothing. After man, if he could come to an end, there would be nothing. Outside man there is nothing."

That is the enemy in *1984,* and against it the exhausted and dying English radical, in the great tradition of English commonsense empiricism, is putting forth his protest that the world is being intellectualized by tyrants who are cultural despots. They are attempting to replace the world by ideas. They are in fact deconstructing it, emptying it of everything that does not lend itself to authority which conceives itself monolithically, nothing but consciousness.

George Orwell's explicitly old-fashioned view is that reality does start outside of us; it is in fact political. Because we are never really alone, whatever introspection tells us, power is always exerted in the name of what we have in common. Life is lived, little as some of us recognize it, as manufactured and coercive loyalties, unmistakable threats and terrible punishments, violent separations from the body politic. The sources of social control and domination are swallowed up in our anxiety, which in an age of psychology deludes itself as being wholly personal, and are embedded in a consumer society professing the elimination of all wants and having no other goal but satisfaction. Actually, we are creatures of society, which is why the tyrant state arises in answer to some mass deprivation. Then the tyranny that afflicts us in our name attempts to reconstitute us by forces so implacable that we internalize them. This is the aim of the Party in *1984.*

Nineteen Eighty-Four is in one respect an exception to the methodical social documentation that was Orwell's usual method. The most powerful details in the book relate to our identification with compulsion. The book is a prophecy, or, as Orwell said, a warning about a future terrible because it rests on a fiction and so cannot be substantiated. It would never occur to

Orwell's unwearied enemy on the British left, Raymond Williams, that every pious mouthful he still utters about "Socialism" is the merest abstraction couched in the in-house vocabulary of a religious sect. Orwell's attack on O'Brien as the Grand Inquisitor of an enforced solipsism has not been widely understood. Unlike nineteenth-century individualists, who still had some perspective on the society that was forming around them, we no longer recognize the full extent of the social controls *for* which we more and more live. Orwell would have enjoyed the irony. Our media culture confirms Einstein's belief that the history of an epoch is represented by its instruments. Yet nothing in the sensationalist discussion of Orwell's novel has been so mindless as television's pointing with alarm at the telescreen in *1984* peeking into our bedrooms. You would think that the telescreen had invented itself.

Orwell had the peculiar ability to show that social coercion affects us unconsciously. It become personal affliction. In *Down and Out in Paris and London* and in *The Road to Wigan Pier* he showed poverty not just as destitution but as the crippling of the spirit. In *Homage to Catalonia* and in *1984* he demonstrated the extent to which a state at war must hold its own people hostage. (pp. 13-14, 16)

Orwell's passion for the social detail—politics is how we live, how we are forced to live—was of the kind that only resistant solitary minds are capable of. "Not one of us," indeed. The social coercion that most people are no longer aware of became his fated subject because he took coercion as his personal pattern. The clue to his blunt style, with its mastery of the single sentence meant to deliver a shock, is its constant aggression on the reader. Orwell is always telling the reader how innocent everyone is about the reality of society. Orwell's speciality is his awareness of limits in all things, not least the limits of his own talent and interest. "Truth" is his writer's ace in the hole, not imagination. Only Orwell, shot through the throat, would have made a point of saying in *Homage to Catalonia,* "I ought to say in passing that all the time I was in Spain I saw very little fighting."

He clearly made up his mind very early that his ability as a writer was his ability to absorb truth in the form of pain and to give it back. In "Why I Write," a 1946 statement at the head of his *Collected Essays, Journalism and Letters,* he said that even as a boy "I knew that I had a facility with words and a power of facing unpleasant facts, and I felt that this created a sort of private world in which I could get my own back for my failure in everyday life." Writing he imagined as a "continuous" story about himself, "a sort of diary existing only in the mind." When he began writing actively, it consisted for him as "a descriptive effort almost against my will, under a kind of compulsion from the outside, . . . [it] always had the same meticulous descriptive quality."

Orwell remains the best commentator on his own work because he could never modify the sense of fatality behind it. Without grandiosity and without apology, he knew himself to be, vis-à-vis the unending storm of political compulsion and terror, in an exceptionally vulnerable position. "His subject matter will be determined by the age he lives in—at least this is true in tumultuous, revolutionary ages like our own—but before he even begins to write he will have acquired an emotional attitude from which he will never completely escape." But this sense of fate made him perhaps one of the few lasting writers produced by the 1930s. Unlike Silone, Malraux, or Koestler, Orwell was never a true believer and so had nothing to repent of.

Like the stronger and more drastic Solzhenitsyn, Orwell knew why literature in the face of totalitarianism will be documentary. He knew how to face a reality entirely political. In a way, he knew nothing else. But unlike the communist writers formed by the 1930s, Orwell also knew that good writing must be entirely consistent, that the merest touch of eclecticism or a message is fatal. Literature in an age of political atrocity, as the exiles and dissidents from Eastern Europe are showing us, may take the form of fable, but the fable is designed to embarrass, to impart a sense of infliction. Orwell's sense of literature always focused on the unbearable detail. In life as in his books, he delighted in extreme gestures. In the bitter postwar winter of 1946, when fuel was scarce, Orwell actually chopped up his son's toys. But anyone who thinks that the extreme gesture in our day is found more in private life than in our relation to the state has not been aware of the Holocaust, the Gulag, and the latest from the war between Iran and Iraq. This Orwell foretold in *1984,* just as brooding on Stalin as Big Brother he also imagined Khomeini. In Brazil I heard a government minister say, "We have a hundred million people in this country, most of whom we do not need." More and more leaders of the third world talk that way. In private many of us dream that *for* the billions of the third world.

Orwell admitted that he was too ill when writing *1984* to round it all out. But of course it succeeds, it threatens, it terrorizes, because it represents a wholly oppositionist point of view that calls for the downright and repeated emphases of the great pamphleteer rather than the subtly developing action within a novel. Orwell's marked tendency to directness, flatness, laying down the law, along with his powerful anticipation of fact, belongs to a radical and adversary tradition of English pamphleteering not practiced by American writers—the tradition of Swift, Tom Paine, Hazlitt, Blake, Cobbett, Chesterton, Shaw, founded on some enduring sense of injustice, on the need to break through those English class prejudices that Orwell called "a curse that confronts you like a wall of stone." Edmund Wilson used to say that the English Revolution took place in America. In Britain literature has been the revolution. Orwell represents this for the first half of our century as none of his countrymen do. As always, the revolution stays in just one head at a time.

Nevertheless, the great pamphleteers are the great issue raisers. Issues became Orwell's writing life, which is why even when he was near death he could never resist accepting still another book for review. His "I Write as I Please" column for the *Tribune* makes up the central section of his work; the four volumes of his collected essays, letters, jounalism are more interesting to me than his novels. *Nineteen Eighty-Four,* novel or not, could have been conceived only by a pamphleteer who in his migratory life insisted on keeping his extensive collection of English pamphlets. His way of writing is always more or less an argument. His writes to change your mind. Socialism, which had meant justice and liberty, in its regression now forced him to choose liberty in *1984* as the response of "the last man in Europe" (the original title for the book) to the State's organized atrocities against a man alone.

But that is not the whole story behind *1984,* as Orwell bitterly insisted, just before he died, against all those attempting to turn him into a defender of the system he described in *The Road to Wigan Pier.* "We are living in a world in which nobody is free, in which hardly anybody is secure, in which it is almost impossible to be honest and to remain alive. . . . And this is merely a preliminary stage, in a country still rich with the loot of a hundred years. Presently there may be coming God knows what horrors—horrors of which, in this sheltered island, we have not even a traditional knowledge.'' Rosa Luxemburg, the critic on the left most trenchant on Lenin's despotism, warned before she was murdered in 1919 that true victory lay ''not at the beginning but at the end of revolution.'' The true radicals are those who conceive the beginning but cannot bear the end. Ignazio Silone as an exile in Switzerland used to lament: ''We are the anti-fascists, always anti! anti!'' Orwell's problem was no doubt that, like so many of us, he knew best what he was against. All the more reason to take him seriously at a time when it has become unfashionable and even dangerous to be ''against.'' (pp. 16, 18)

> *Alfred Kazin, '''Not One of Us','' in The New York Review of Books, Vol. XXXI, No. 10, June 14, 1984, pp. 13-14, 16, 18.*

GORMAN BEAUCHAMP (essay date 1984)

[*The following excerpt is taken from a paper originally delivered at a conference on ''The Future of Nineteen Eighty-Four'' in 1983, at which several scholars, including Beauchamp, Ejner J. Jensen, Bernard Crick, Eugene J. McCarthy, and W. Warren Wager presented papers on various aspects of Orwell's novel. These essays were later expanded for publication. Beauchamp examines the relationship between* Nineteen Eighty-Four *and Orwell's 1947 essay* ''Such, Such Were the Joys.'' *Many critics, most notably Anthony West (see TCLC, Vol. 2), have found a connection between Orwell's depiction of the harsh conditions at the boarding school that he attended and life under totalitarianism in 1984 Oceania. West, in particular, concluded that Big Brother is merely a larger version of the wife of Orwell's headmaster. Many critics have dismissed West's psychoanalytic reading, and Beauchamp is in agreement with that dismissal; however, Beauchamp does believe that the sadism depicted at Orwell's boarding school is different only in degree and not in kind from the sadism of a totalitarian state. In the following excerpt, Beauchamp discusses the nature of that sadism.*]

Bingo is the nickname given to the wife of the headmaster at Crossgates (really St. Cyprian's) in Orwell's autobiographical essay **''Such, Such Were the Joys.''** Since the publication of Anthony West's attack [see *TCLC* Vol. 2] . . . on Orwell's political thought, this essay has become a crux in interpreting his critique of totalitarianism generally and ***Nineteen Eighty-Four*** in particular. The deepest understanding of totalitarianism at which Orwell could arrive, West contends, was to imagine it resembling a very bad boys' school. ''Whether he knew it or not, what he did in ***Nineteen Eighty-Four*** was to send everybody to Crossgates to be as miserable as he had been.'' Since most of his misery at Crossgates emanated from the cruel caprice of Bingo, she became, West asserts, Orwell's model of the totalitarian tyrant of his novel. ''Big Brother, the feared dictator whom everyone pretends to love, is really Bingo.''

Most critics have dismissed West's essay as fatuous psychological reductionism, a response with which I have much sympathy. But leaving aside its parlor Freudianism, I want here to accept its basic premise and argue for a different conclusion: not West's own conclusion that the identification of Crossgates with Oceania and Bingo with Big Brother trivializes and thus undermines Orwell's depiction of totalitarian tyranny but, rather, the conclusion that this identification extends and universalizes the sadistic power drives that crystallize in the Caesarean environment of totalitarianism. Put most simply, Crossgates *is* a microcosm of Oceania, Bingo *is* Big Brother in miniature: only the scale, not the essence, differs. There is nothing inherently

implausible in Orwell's identification of Crossgates as Oceania writ small, nothing preposterous about presenting Bingo as a prototype of Big Brother. . . . (pp. 66-7)

Orwell is not suggesting, of course, that all schools are microcosms of despotism nor that all schoolmasters—or their wives—are cryptototalitarian, but he does seem to suggest that a place like Crossgates offers an image of pointless persecution of the weak by the strong, of a cruelly arbitrary exercise of dictatorial power, that, much magnified, reflects the modus operandi of the totalitarian state. (p. 67)

Thus, given that the essay is a far slighter work than ***Nineteen Eighty-Four,*** one finds adumbrated in it a number of the motifs developed more fully in Orwell's final novel. Even though a school for upperclass students, Orwell's Crossgates is marked by an atmosphere of deliberate dirtiness, dinginess, and deprivation—exactly the atmosphere that permeates Oceania. . . . The many critics who have viewed the sordidness of Airstrip One in 1984 only as a reflection of the actual and unavoidable conditions of wartime London have not paid sufficient attention to [Orwell's] description of an environment kept *intentionally* harsh and dismal. As explained in Goldstein's *Theory and Practice of Oligarchical Collectivism,* the ends of the totalitarian state, which depends on hierarchical differentiation, are served by keeping all but a small elite in a state of constant deprivation. (pp. 6-8)

Oceania is marked by shortages, shoddiness, a pervasive grimness and grime: the atmosphere of Crossgates—something cold and evil-smelling—encompassing a whole world. Bingo and Sim (Mr. Wilkes) justify their parsimony on the grounds that deprivation builds character, while their true motive is greed; likewise Big Brother imposes a regime of permanent austerity, ostensibly for national defense but really to ensure the inequality on which the power of the Party rests.

Though there are no laws in Oceania, everyone lives with a constant sense of guilt; the same atmosphere permeates Crossgates. ''Guilt seemed to hang in the air,'' Orwell wrote, ''like a pall of smoke.'' . . . Bingo repressed the erotic instincts of her charges with all the rigor exhibited by the Party's Junior Anti-Sex League. She anticipates one of the tactics of Oceania's Thought Police in accusing the boys of *facecrime,* an appearance that reveals one's guilt.

> ''Have you looked in the glass lately, Beacham?'' said Bingo. ''Aren't you ashamed to go about with a face like that? Do you think everyone doesn't know what it means when a boy has black rings around his eyes?''. . .

Indeed, the boys at Crossgates—and I must reemphasize that we are concerned with Orwell's perception and not necessarily the literal reality of St. Cyprian's—live, like their counterparts in Oceania, with the sense of being under constant surveillance, under the eye of their own Big Brother. (p. 69)

Such conditions of life at Crossgates conspire to create in the Orwell persona an intense ambivalence toward Sim and Bingo: a feeling of hatred compounded by the guilt experienced in hating them, his ''benefactors.''. . . It is this guilt-ridden ambivalence that West identifies as the origin of Winston Smith's hate-love relationship with Big Brother—or, more precisely, with the Big Brother surrogate, O'Brien.

> How difficult it is for a child to have any real independence of attitude could be seen in our behavior toward Bingo. I think it would be true

to say that every boy in the school hated and feared her. Yet we all fawned on her in the most abject way, and the top layer of our feelings toward her was a sort of guilt-stricken loyalty. . . .

While the pre-echoes here of Winston's tortured psychomachia are palpable, the Orwell persona nevertheless triumphs over Bingo by leaving Crossgates with his hatred for her still intact. She had damaged but had not destroyed him, and writing ill of her (as Winston wants to of Big Brother) proved the best revenge. But then Crossgates lacked, of course, the true terror tactics of Oceania, which succeed in violating even "the few cubic centimeters inside your skull" that Winston thought inviolable and in converting his hatred of Big Brother into "love."

In reading **"Such, Such Were the Joys"** as a prolegomenon to *Nineteen Eighty-Four,* the danger lies in distorting the scale, making small affairs loom too large to bear comparability with great ones. Still, it seems to me undeniable that the essay provides—if not a secret code that explains away *Nineteen Eighty-Four* as residual adolescent animus, as West claims— a microcosm in quotidian life of *l'univers concentrationnaire* of totalitarianism. . . . If we recall Orwell's concentration on political subjects in his writing after 1936, and particularly his obsession with totalitarianism, then his using even the relatively trivial and peculiarly English genre of schoolday reminiscences to show the cryptototalitarian personality functioning in spaces outside the walls of the Reichstag or the Kremlin will not surprise us.

My point thus far has been not to represent Bingo as exceptional, but rather as all too typical of that particular personality that can be called the power seeker. As already noted, Orwell was at once fascinated and repelled by this type, which he saw as increasingly dominating the ideological life of the modern world. (pp. 70-1)

In *Nineteen Eighty-Four* Orwell provides, of course, the apotheosis of bully worship, a scenario of the future where brute power provides the only social bond and thus where the power-seeking personality, incarnated in the mythical figure of Big Brother and the mundane one of O'Brien, rules without any of the traditional restraints on power. Oceania serves as Orwell's ultimate Caesarean environment and allows for a degree of tyranny that the cruelest of Roman emperors would have envied.

In this context, Orwell advances a motive for the exercise of power that has proven the most controversial crux of *Nineteen Eighty-Four.* "I understand HOW" Winston Smith writes in his thoughtcriminal diary, "I do not understand WHY". . . : why, that is, the Party has deliberately constructed a world hard, ugly, and brutal. In a famous passage, O'Brien, a member of the Inner Party, explains WHY.

> The Party seeks power entirely for its own sake. We are not interested in the good of others; we are interested solely in power. Not wealth or luxury or long life or happiness; only power, pure power. . . .

Tutored in the torture chambers of the Ministry of Love, Winston does begin to understand O'Brien's message: that one asserts power over another by making him suffer. . . .

> If you want a picture of the future, imagine a boot stamping on a human face—forever. . . .

This terrible image epitomizes what, for Orwell, was the real, if often disguised, motive force that underlay the exercise of power—sadism. Men seek power in order to dominate, humiliate, and torture others.

Clearly, this is an appalling conclusion, one that, if true—or to the degree that it is true—would undermine the legitimacy of any form of rule of some men over others. Isaac Deutscher, who characterizes this pessimistic conclusion as "the mysticism of cruelty," claimed that "at heart Orwell was a simple-minded anarchist" in whose eyes "any political movement forefeited its *raison d'être* the moment it acquired a *raison d'état*" [see *TCLC*, Vol. 2] There is, without doubt, an unmistakable streak of the Prudhon-Bakunin mentality in much of Orwell's political thought; and, if O'Brien's credo truly reveals the motive for the gaining and deploying of power, then anarchism, in some degree or other, would indeed seem the only possible antidote—a conclusion that should come as no surprise to any reader who recalls Orwell's praise in *Homage to Catalonia* of the anarchism in Barcelona in the early days of the Spanish Civil War. But it is not any imagined alternative to but rather the indictment of power that stands at the center of *Nineteen Eighty-Four,* and the indictment demands consideration.

In **"Raffles and Miss Blandish,"** Orwell declares, "The interconnection between sadism, masochism, success worship, power worship, nationalism and totalitarianism is a huge subject whose edges have barely been scratched, and even to mention it is considered somewhat indelicate." He continues,

> Fascism is often loosely equated with sadism, but nearly always by people who see nothing wrong in the most slavish worship of Stalin. The truth is, of course, that the countless intellectuals who kiss the arse of Stalin are not different from the minority who give their allegiance to Hitler or Mussolini. . .nor from the older generation of intellectuals . . . who bowed down before German militarism. All of them are worshipping power and successful cruelty. It is important to notice that the cult of power tends to be mixed up with a love of cruelty and wickedness *for their own sakes.* . . .

Obviously Orwell saw that the most persuasive evidence for O'Brien's credo of power-as-sadism was provided by the twin totalitarianisms of the 1930s and 1940s—Fascism and Communism. Some of the investigations into the psychological substructures of these phenomena—for instance, Erich Fromm's *Escape from Freedom*—indeed bear out much of Orwell's analysis of the totalitarian mentality; and inhabitants of Eastern Europe, Czeslaw Milosz testifies in *The Captive Mind*, "are amazed that a writer who never lived in Russia should have so keen a perception into its life." But Orwell's point in **"Raffles and Miss Blandish"** is that the cult of power, with its love of cruelty for its own sake, is in no wise peculiar to totalitarian regimes—though most obvious there, since its manifestations are writ so large—but had become a pervasive feature of twentieth-century life. The essay, after all, specifically examines a Western pop-cult phenomenon—the detective story—that Orwell found increasingly brutal in its contents and its appeal. That the English reading public had made a best-seller of a work of "intellectual sadism" like *No Orchids for Miss Blandish*—"Carlyle for the masses," he called it—Orwell saw as symptomatic of the times, symptomatic of the power worship that seemed universal.

People worship power in the form in which they are able to understand it. A twelve-year-old boy worships Jack Dempsey. An adolescent in a Glasgow slum worships Al Capone. An aspiring pupil at a business college worships Lord Nuffield. A *New Statesman* reader worships Stalin. There is a difference in intellectual maturity, but none in moral outlook.

Thus, as Bingo prefigures Big Brother and Crossgates Oceania, so the ethos of power that eventuates in O'Brien's declaration of sadism appears in less virulent forms, Orwell believed, at all levels of life: in England and America, for instance, no less than in Russia or Germany. (pp. 72-4)

The proposition that a sadistic desire to dominate and degrade underlies *all* exercise of power, however, evokes strong resistance. Isaac Deutscher argues in "The Mysticism of Cruelty" that this view indicates Orwell's tendency to judge the world in terms of simplistic, ahistorical generalizations. And George Kateb, to cite just one other example, levels much the same criticism [see Additional Bibliography]. (p. 74)

While such criticisms are not without merit, several things should be said in Orwell's defense. First, *Nineteen Eighty-Four* belongs to the literary genre called the anti-utopia or dystopia, an extrapolation of certain negative features of the author's own day into the future. The dystopia functions as a *Gedankenversuch* or "what if" novelistic formula that allows for the spinning out of speculative possibilities to their ultimate conclusion. . . . Like all dystopias, then, *Nineteen Eighty-Four* is an admonitory satire, warning of dangers that lie ahead. And the warning consists precisely in drawing out totalitarian ideas "to their logical consequences." Put another way, Oceania is the logical consequence, the pure idea, of the totalitarian mentality—the truly Caesarean environment where power operates without constraint—and not an attempt at historical mimesis. . . . Orwell offers a negative Platonic ideal—an archetype of the unjust state which, in its pure evil, corresponds to no known historical reality. . . . Oceania can be seen as the perfection of totalitarianism, an ahistorical *idolum* in which all other motives for power except its essentially sadistic one are purged away by imagination: it is the *ideally unjust* state. (pp. 75-6)

If *Nineteen Eighty-Four* is a dystopian extrapolation of totalitarian potentialities carried to their logical extreme and not an analysis of historical totalitarianism, still the extrapolation, to have ideological significance, must be based on some perceived truth about the real-world phenomenon. But the problem is that we do not know the truth—or even if there *is* a truth—about the motives of totalitarianism. . . .

In short, no consensus exists on any feature of totalitarianism, particularly on so controversial a subject as the psychological motives of its adherents. But this very uncertainty means that Orwell's theory of power-as-sadism, insofar as it is drawn from the historical phenomenon, cannot be dismissed as a distortion of *the* truth, for it is just such a fixed truth about totalitarianism that we lack. Indeed, as Irving Howe notes, none of Orwell's critics "has yet been able to provide a satisfactory explanation for that systematic excess in destroying human values which is a central trait of totalitarianism" [see Additional Bibliography]. Deutscher, Kateb, and like-minded critics notwithstanding, sadism offers as logical an explanation of the motives of totalitarian rulers as any other that has been advanced. (p. 76)

In summary, then, these two things can be said about Orwell's theory of sadism as it relates to historical totalitarianism. First, that it is intended as a deliberate exaggeration—a dystopian extrapolation—of totalitarian practice into a "pure" or ideal form. As Howe puts it, "the world of 1984 is *not* totalitarianism as we know it, but totalitarianism after its world triumph. Strictly speaking, the society of Oceania might be called post-totalitarian." Second, that while so little agreement obtains about the nature of the real-world phenomenon, Orwell's imputation of sadism as the power motive in totalitarianism seems as reasonable as any other and finds support in the analytical literature on the subject. The extrapolation of *Nineteen Eighty-Four,* then, is an extrapolation of the brute reality that in our century (as Orwell wrote in 1940) "human types supposedly extinct for centuries . . . have suddenly reappeared, not as the inmates of lunatic asylums, but as the masters of the world. . . . O'Brien's credo of sadism is thus merely the logical extension of the experience of Auschwitz and Buchenwald, his boot stamping on a human face forever the ideal of the totalitarian modus operandi perfected and extended into the future, crushing the whole world beneath it.

I argued earlier that for Orwell the Big Brothers are merely exaggerations of the Bingos, that the Caesarean tyrant represents the ordinary power seeker magnified by the environment. Concomitantly, the impulse that motivates the totalitarian Caesars—sadism—must be the same impulse that motivates all power seekers, however limited their sphere of action. In other words, the underlying motive of all power is the desire to dominate as an end in itself, making others suffer serving as the purest sign of one's dominance. All other rationales for power, then, are simply so much camouflage disguising the essentially sadistic motive. This would seem to be the implicit corollary of Orwell's position in *Nineteen Eighty-Four,* the corollary of the power worship that he saw as "a universal religion" of our age. If the Bingos are all incipient Big Brothers, then their basic drive is the same, differing only in the degree of opportunity it has to manifest itself. (pp. 77-8)

In the best early review of *Nineteen Eighty-Four,* Philip Rahv compared Orwell's analysis of power favorably with that of Dostoevsky in *The Brothers Karamazov* [see *TCLC*, Vol. 6]. . . . The Grand Inquisitor [in Dostoevsky's novel] offers the classic statement of totalitarian paternalism: that a ruling elite justifiably monopolizes power to benefit, not itself, but weak, helpless subjects incapable of determining their own social destiny and willing to sacrifice freedom in exchange for a childlike security. Winston assumes that O'Brien, too, will offer such a justification for the Party's exercise of power. In response to O'Brien's catechistic question, "Why should we want power?" Winston gives what he thinks is the Party line: "You are ruling over us for our own good. . . . You believe that human beings are not fit to govern themselves, and therefore—." . . . At this point O'Brien increases the voltage of torture: "That was stupid, Winston, stupid!" O'Brien rejects, that is, the self-serving, self-deluding apology of the Grand Inquisitor as naive—the rationalization of a seeker after total power unwilling to face the truth about his own motives—and offers instead the explanation quoted above: "Power is not a means; it is an end. . . . The object of power is power." Rahv—and I agree with him—finds O'Brien's explanation more truthful than that of the Grand Inquisitor, but he seems to restrict its applicability to totalitarian regimes alone. (pp. 79-80)

The temptation is to see what is revealed by the analyses of totalitarianism as inapplicable to other, more moderate systems. Let me take a final example, again from Erich Fromm but this time from his instructive essay printed as an afterword to *Nineteen Eighty-Four*. Here Fromm several times makes the salutary point that "it would be most unfortunate if the reader smugly interpreted *1984* as [only] another description of Stalinist barbarism, and if he does not see that it means us, too" [see Additional Bibliography]. Fromm notes a number of significant parallels between the "predictions" of Orwell and the actual developments in the West since 1948: the growth of militarism, of doublethink, of mind control. All of this, surely, "means us, too." But O'Brien's revelation about the universal motive for power—does that mean us, too? Fromm does not say. (p. 80)

For *Nineteen Eighty-Four* to make the indelible impression that it does, we must feel that its power-as-sadism premise is not altogether false, or not false all the time; that the part Orwell abstracts from the whole does exist, though we shrink from mentioning it; that political behavior *is* often as he describes it, although he refuses to admit more important factors. All in all, this seems like a fair and accurate assessment of *Nineteen Eighty-Four*. Like the political cartoonist. . .Orwell draws a caricature that is an exaggeration, no doubt a gross exaggeration, but there is a truth to it—not the *whole* truth, but *a* truth—and we confront it with the shock of recognition. (p. 81)

[*Nineteen Eighty-Four*] surely ranks as one of the half dozen most important books of this century, arguably—for all its artistic and ideological limitations—the most influential one. . . Our perception of politics has been permanently altered by it. . . . But if the brooding image of a fictional Big Brother or the inquisitorial doctrine of O'Brien, entering our collective consciousness, has restrained the practices of their real-life avatars or alerted us to resist the dangers, then Orwell will have succeeded in his purpose even if he had to exaggerate a single truth about the hidden nature of power in order to do it. (p. 82)

> Gorman Beauchamp, *"From Bingo to Big Brother: Orwell on Power and Sadism," in* The Future of "Nineteen Eighty-Four," *edited by Ejner J. Jensen, The University of Michigan Press, 1984, pp. 65-85.*

GEORGE WOODCOCK (essay date 1984)

[*Woodcock is an author, editor, and currently a professor of English at the University of British Columbia. He is most widely known for his literary criticism and for his biographies of George Orwell and Thomas Merton. Woodcock also founded Canada's most important literary journal,* Canadian Literature, *and has published widely on the literature of Canada. From 1940 to 1947 he was the editor of the literary journal* Now. *In a 1942 letter to* Partisan Review, *Orwell attacked* Now *and several other magazines for wartime pacifist inclinations and ties to fascist politics. Woodcock denied Orwell's charges, which led to an argumentative and heated correspondence between the two men. They next met sometime later, an "odd" meeting as Woodcock describes it: "I got on a London double decker bus in Hampstead, and when I climbed to the top deck I saw a crest of dark brown hair that I remembered. Orwell turned around and waved me to the seat beside him. . . . Almost immediately he looked at me earnestly. 'You know, Woodcock,' he said, 'It's all very well to quarrel on paper, but that shouldn't make any difference to one's personal relationships.'" The two remained friends for the rest of Orwell's life. Woodcock later wrote* The Crystal Spirit, *one of the most penetrating and important studies of Orwell's personality and writings. In the following excerpt, Woodcock disagrees with American conservatives (see the excerpt by Norman Podhoretz dated 1983) who try to claim Orwell as one of their own. Instead,*

Woodcock places him in a distinctly English line of literary radicals that includes Jonathan Swift and Charles Dickens.]

[Orwell's] last two books, the ones that earned him the fame he had never enjoyed before, had been swept into the propaganda of the cold war in such a way that he had come to be regarded as a socialist-hating conservative rather than a socialist who wished to save his beliefs from the aberrations of the Russian communists.

Orwell is still largely misunderstood in North America, where the modern neoconservatives happily claim as their own, and this I think is because he belongs so firmly in the English tradition of literary radicalism. The fact that he shared the insights of contemporary continental European writers, mainly ex-communists like Arthur Koestler, Franz Borkenau, and Ignazio Silone, who had seen through the Soviet myth, does not detract from the fact that he expressed his insights in a peculiarly English way, adopting Swift's *Gulliver's Travels* as his distant model for *Animal Farm*.

Herbert Read once said that "Defoe was the first writer to raise journalism to a literary art; Orwell perhaps the last." And, limiting though the definition may seem, it does place Orwell clearly in the line of dissenting didacticism to which he belongs, a line that continued in the radical tradition from Defoe to Cobbett and Dickens, to Gissing—that sad failure in whom Orwell saw so much of himself—and to H. G. Wells.

Orwell grew beyond the facile, shiny, Utopian side of Wells, and this may explain why, when the master and the disciple met, they quarrelled, and Wells memorably denounced Orwell as "that Trotskyite with big feet." But the Wells of the negative Utopias, like *The Sleeper Awakes* and *The Island of Dr Moreau*, is strongly present in Orwell's vision, and so also is the Wells of the lower-middle-class genre novels, *Kipps* and *Mr Polly* and *Tono Bungay*.

Dickens was probably Orwell's favourite among the Victorian novelists, and though Orwell sought for a prose far less decorated than that of Dickens, there is no doubt that the emotional if not the aesthetic affinities were considered. Orwell wrote a long and particularly fine essay on Dickens, and I have always felt that the pen portrait of the novelist at the end of that piece characterized Orwell as well as his subject: "He is laughing, with a touch of anger to his laughter. It is the face of a man who is always fighting against something, but who fights in the open and is not frightened, a type hated with equal hatred by all the smelly little orthodoxies which are now contending for our souls."

Orwell treated Dickens as a nineteenth-century liberal with all the generous urges and angers of his kind, and though the times made him describe himself as a socialist, it was in Dickens's company that he really belonged. There was nothing of the modern-day conservative about Orwell, but a great deal of the Tory in William Cobbett's sense: the man of social conscience who sees the ancient values of community and decency foundering and who seeks in some radical way to reassert them. And here one sees another line of English writing to which Orwell certainly belongs, that of the great moralistic essayists, whose concern for justice accorded with their search for the clearest prose in which to write of it. Hazlitt as well as Cobbett stands among Orwell's ancestors—Hazlitt who claimed, "I never wrote a line that licked the dust."

It has often been said that Orwell was more important as a man than as a writer. I do not think this is true, or that one can make facile distinctions of that kind in the case of any writer, but the fact remains that he possessed a strange and compelling character and projected more than most writers the image of a deeply moral man. Sixteen years after Orwell's death our common friend Herbert Read wrote to me, "His personality, which remains so vivid after all these years, often rises like some ghost to admonish me." (pp. xi-xiii)

George Woodcock, in an introduction to Remembering Orwell, *edited by Stephen Wadhams, Penguin Books, 1984, pp. v-xiii.*

ADDITIONAL BIBLIOGRAPHY

Allen, Francis A. "*Nineteen Eighty-Four* and the Eclipse of the Private World." *Michigan Quarterly Review* XXII, No. 4 (Fall 1983): 517-40.
Discusses the individual's loss of privacy as the most horrifying aspect of the future society presented in *Nineteen Eighty-Four.*

Ashe, Geoffrey. "Second Thoughts on *Nineteen Eighty-Four.*" *Month* n.s. 4, No. 5 (November 1950): 285-300.
Early interpretation of *Nineteen Eighty-Four* as an attack on left-wing progressive thought. Ashe writes that the novel is a horror story whose politics are incidental.

Barr, Alan. "The Paradise Behind *1984.*" In *English Miscellany: A Symposium of History, Literature, and the Arts,* edited by Mario Praz., pp. 197-203. Rome: British Council, 1968.
Examines some religious parallels and allusions in *Nineteen Eighty-Four.*

Beauchamp, Gorman. "Of Man's Last Disobedience: Zamiatin's *We* and Orwell's *1984.*" *Comparative Literature Studies* X, No. 4 (December 1973): 285-301.*
Compares the plots of both *We* and *Nineteen Eighty-Four*—each involving an individual rebelling against the omnipotent State—with the Christian myth of Adam's primal disobedience against God.

Bolton, W. F. *The Language of 1984: Orwell's English and Ours.* Nashville: The University of Tennessee Press, 1984, 256 p.
Discounts Orwell's reputation as a master of English prose.

Chilton, Paul, and Aubrey, Crispin, eds. *Nineteen Eighty-Four in 1984.* London: Comedia Publishing Group, 1983, 120 p.
Collection of essays focusing primarily on aspects of current social and political life that resemble those portrayed by Orwell in his novel. Included are essays by the editors on "The Making of *1984,*" David Widgery on "Reclaiming Orwell," Paul Chilton on "Newspeak: It's the Real Thing," and Colin Ward on "Big Brother Drives a Bulldozer."

College Literature XI, No. 1 (1984): 1-113.
Issue devoted to studies of *Nineteen Eighty-Four,* including essays by Gorman Beauchamp on "*1984:* Oceania as an Ideal State," Joan Weatherly on "The Death of Big Sister: Orwell's Tragic Message," and Paul Schlueter on "Trends in Orwell Criticism, 1968-1983." An essay by John Atkins is excerpted in the entry above.

Crick, Bernard. *George Orwell: A Life.* Boston: Little, Brown, 1980, 473 p.
The authorized biography. Crick was the first biographer granted access to private papers held by Orwell's widow. A portion of Crick's introduction to this work is excerpted in the entry.

Cronkite, Walter. Preface to *Nineteen Eighty-Four,* by George Orwell, pp. 1-3. New York: New American Library, 1984.
Notes the many terms from the novel that have passed into common use. Cronkite also stresses that the novel was meant not as prophesy but as a warning in the form of political satire.

De Camara, Robert C. "Homage to Orwell." *National Review* XXV, No. 9 (13 May 1983): 566-74.
Maintains that Orwell, deeply skeptical of socialism, abandoned many of his socialist beliefs during his lifetime. The critic offers an interpretation of *Nineteen Eighty-Four* as "a profoundly pessimistic vision" of the world after the triumph of socialism.

Dyson, A. E. "Orwell: Irony as Prophecy." In his *The Crazy Fabric: Essays in Irony,* pp. 197-219. London: Macmillan and Co., 1965.
Applies aspects of Orwell's 1946 essay on Jonathan Swift to Orwell's own works and particularly to *Nineteen Eighty-Four.*

Elsbree, Langdon. "The Structured Nightmare of *1984.*" *Twentieth Century Literature* 5, No. 3 (October 1959): 135-41.
Finds that the structure of *Nineteen Eighty-Four* is derived from dreams, nightmares, and reveries, resulting in a world lacking objective external realities.

Feder, Lillian. "Selfhood, Language, and Reality: George Orwell's *Nineteen Eighty-Four.*" *The Georgia Review* XXXVII, No. 2 (Summer 1983): 392-409.
Finds Winston Smith's struggle to maintain his individuality against the oppression of the Party to be the central conflict of *Nineteen Eighty-Four.* Feder interprets the novel as a prediction of the dangers inherent in the programmatic attempt to deprive language of its referential function.

Fialka, John J. "The Time has Come for Deciding if 1984 Will Resemble *1984.*" *The Wall Street Journal* LXIII, No. 166 (7 June 1983): 1, 20.
Examines some ways in which *Nineteen Eighty-Four* is received and interpreted by modern readers.

Fromm, Erich. Afterword to *Nineteen Eighty-Four,* by George Orwell, pp. 257-67. New York: New American Library, 1983.
Afterword is reprinted from 1961 edition of the book. Fromm places *Nineteen Eighty-Four* in relation to other dystopic novels, including Aldous Huxley's *Brave New World* and Yevgeny Zamyatin's *We.*

Geering, R. G. "*Darkness at Noon* and *Nineteen Eighty-Four:* A Comparative Study." *The Australian Quarterly* XXX, No. 3 (September 1958): 90-96.*
Compares Koestler's fictionalized account of the Moscow Purges during the Russian Revolution with Orwell's novel of a fictional totalitarian state.

Gray, Paul. "That Year is Almost Here." *Time* 122, No. 23 (28 November 1983): 46-56.
Overview of Orwell's life and career, with emphasis upon the enormous impact the novel *Nineteen Eighty-Four* has had, particularly upon American popular culture.

Greenblatt, Stephen Jay. "George Orwell." In his *Three Modern Satirists: Waugh, Orwell, and Huxley,* pp. 37-73. New Haven, Conn.: Yale University Press, 1965.
Biographical and critical essay discussing various critical approaches to Orwell's novels.

Gross, Miriam, ed. *The World of George Orwell.* New York: Simon and Schuster, 1972, 182 p.
Eighteen brief biographical and critical essays, including contributions by William Empson and Malcolm Muggeridge, and a discussion of *Nineteen Eighty-Four* by D.A.N. Jones.

Hamilton, Kenneth M. "G. K. Chesterton and George Orwell: A Contrast in Prophecy." *The Dalhousie Review* 31, No. 3 (Autumn 1951): 198-205.*
Compares *Nineteen Eighty-Four* and Chesterton's *The Napoleon of Notting Hill.* Hamilton dismisses Chesterton's novel as a romantic fable, while calling Orwell's novel realistic prophecy.

Harris, Roy. "The Misunderstanding of Newspeak." *The Times Literary Supplement,* No. 4214 (6 January 1984): 17.
Analysis of the term Newspeak, which in *Nineteen Eighty-Four* was applied to a deliberately distorted language, but, Harris finds, is commonly applied to any obfuscated technical jargon. Harris

maintains that Orwell developed the concept of Newspeak out of a logophobia, or fear of words, that stemmed from his awareness of the ease with which words can be used to misrepresent or to obscure reality.

Hitchens, Christopher, and Podhoretz, Norman. "An Exchange on Orwell." *Harper's* 266, No. 1593 (February 1983): 56-58.
Hitchens's response to Podhoretz's January *Harper's* article on Orwell (see Podhoretz excerpt, 1983), followed by comment from Podhoretz. Hitchens questions several of Podhoretz's contentions regarding Orwell's political attitudes, and attacks Podhoretz's implication that Orwell maintained his identity as "a man of the Left" only to give weight to his criticism of left-wing political thought. Podhoretz responds with selected quotes from Orwell's essays to support his contentions.

Howe, Irving. "Orwell: History as Nightmare." In his *Politics and the Novel*, pp. 239-55. Greenwich, Conn.: Fawcett, 1957.
Argues that usual literary categories do not apply to *Nineteen Eighty-Four*, which is a unique attempt to create a world lacking in any individualism. Howe describes Orwell's technique in constructing his fictional society as "the dramatic strategy of 'one more step'"—the result of observing current conditions and then making a logical supposition about what might happen next.

————, ed. *Orwell's Nineteen Eighty-Four: Text, Sources, Criticism*. New York: Harcourt Brace Jovanovich, 1982, 450 p.
Valuable compendium. The volume contains the text of the novel *Nineteen Eighty-Four*, excerpts from other major dystopian novels of the twentieth century, and a number of critical articles, some of which are excerpted in the entry above. Included are essays by Lionel Trilling on "Orwell of the Future" and "George Orwell and the Politics of Truth," Arthur Koestler on "A Rebel's Progress: To George Orwell's Death," and Hannah Arendt on "Ideology and Terror: A Novel Form of Government."

————, ed. *1984 Revisited: Totalitarianism in Our Century*. New York: Harper & Row, 1983, 276 p.
Collection of original essays about Orwell and the major themes and ideas of *Nineteen Eighty-Four*. Included are essays by Mark Crispin Miller on "The Fate of *1984*," Bernard Avishai on "Orwell and the English Language," and Robert Nisbet on "*1984* and the Conservative Imagination."

Hunter, Lynette. *George Orwell: The Search for a Voice*. Stony Stratford, England: Open University Press, 1984, 242 p.
Examines Orwell's narrative voice in his major works.

Jensen, Ejner J., ed. *The Future of Nineteen Eighty-Four*. Ann Arbor: University of Michigan Press, 1984, 209 p.
Collection of essays originally delivered at a 1983 University of Michigan conference designed to examine the significance of *Nineteen Eighty-Four* as the year of the title approached. Included are essays by Bernard Crick on "*Nineteen Eighty-Four: Satire or Prophecy?*", Richard W. Bailey on "George Orwell and the English Language," Alex Zwerdling on "Orwell's Psychopolitics," and Joseph Addison on "The Self and Memory in *Nineteen Eighty-Four*.

Kalechofsky, Roberta. *George Orwell*. New York: Frederick Ungar, 1973, 149 p.
Discussion of Orwell's major works.

Karel, Thomas A. "George Orwell: A Pre-1984 Bibliography of Criticism, 1975-1983." *Bulletin of Bibliography* 41, No. 3 (September 1984): 133-47.
Extensive bibliography covering Orwell criticism published from 1975—the cut-off date for material listed in Jeffrey and Valery Meyers's 1977 bibliography—through December of 1983.

Kateb, George. "The Road to 1984." *Political Science Quarterly* LXXXI, No. 4 (December 1966): 564-80.
Examines some possible reasons for the overwhelming pessimism of *Nineteen Eighty-Four*.

Kegel, Charles H. "*Nineteen Eighty-Four*: A Century of Ingsoc." *Notes and Queries* 10, No. 4 (April 1963): 151-52.

Advances several theories about why Orwell chose the year 1984 as the date and title of his final novel. The critic notes that just one century earlier—in 1884—three major English socialist organizations formed: the Fabian Society, the Social Democratic Federation, and the Socialist League. Paul Gray notes that Orwell's manuscript shows that 1980 and 1982 were also considered (see Additional Bibliography).

Labedz, Leopold. "Will George Orwell Survive 1984? Of Doublethink & Double-Talk, Body-Snatching & Other Silly Pranks, I and II." *Encounter* LXIII, Nos. 1 and 2 (June 1984; July-August 1984): 11-24; 25-34.
Extensive examination of the trends in past and present critical interpretations of George Orwell's political attitudes as evinced in *Nineteen Eighty-Four*. Labedz focuses especially on the critical tendency to interpret the novel as a left-wing polemic, which he views as a misinterpretation of Orwell's intent. Labedz maintains that Orwell's attitudes in the 1940s, if transplanted into the 1980s, would be representative of right-wing political thinking.

Lee, Robert A. *Orwell's Fiction*. Notre Dame, Ind.: University of Notre Dame Press, 1968, 188 p.
Important examination of Orwell's novels as works of fiction, not as fictionalized autobiographies or social criticism.

Leif, Ruth Ann. *Homage to Oceania*. Columbus: Ohio State University Press, 1969, 162 p.
Study of Orwell's political beliefs as evinced in his works.

"The Strange World of 1984." *Life* 27, No. 1 (4 July 1949): 78-85.
Review article interpreting *Nineteen Eighty-Four* as a warning against "left-wing totalitarianism," to which both Orwell and Arthur Schlesinger, Jr., responded in the next issue of *Life* (see Orwell excerpt dated 1949 and Schlesinger entry in Additional Bibliography). Passages from the novel are reprinted and illustrated by Abner Dean.

Malkin, Lawrence. "Halfway to 1984." *Horizon* XII, No. 2 (Spring 1970): 33-9.
Finds the most frightening aspect of *Nineteen Eighty-Four* to be its depiction of "the totalitarian threat to individual freedom from collectives of the right or left."

McNamara, James, and O'Keefe, Dennis J. "Waiting for 1984: On Orwell and Evil." *Encounter* LIX, No. 6 (December 1982): 43-8.
Summarizes *Nineteen Eighty-Four* as Orwell's vision of the world after the destruction of capitalism. McNamara and O'Keefe examine critical reaction to the novel and define *Nineteen Eighty-Four* as "a moral treatise."

Meyers, Jeffrey, ed. *George Orwell: The Critical Heritage*. London: Routledge & Kegan Paul, 1975, 392 p.
Collection of reviews and critical studies with an excellent introduction by Meyers discussing Orwell's career and the dominant themes of Orwell criticism.

Meyers, Jeffrey, and Meyers, Valerie. *George Orwell: An Annotated Bibliography of Criticism*. New York: Garland Publishing, 1977, 132 p.
Most thorough bibliography to date.

Modern Fiction Studies 21, No. 1 (Spring 1975): 3-136.
Issue devoted to Orwell criticism. Included are essays by Martin Green on "Orwell as an Old Etonian," Melvyn New on "Orwell and Antisemitism: Toward *1984*," and James Connors on "Zamyatin's *We* and the Genesis of *1984*."

New, Melvyn. "Ad Nauseam: A Satiric Device in Huxley, Orwell, and Waugh." *Satire Newsletter* VIII, No. 1 (Fall 1970): 24-8.*
Discusses Orwell's use of nauseating images in *Nineteen Eighty-Four* to express his own moral indignation over conditions in Oceania without overt moralizing.

Orwell, George. *Nineteen Eighty-Four: The Facsimile of the Extant Manuscript.* Edited by Peter Davidson. New York: Harcourt Brace Jovanovich, 1984, 381 p.
> Reproduction of the existing one hundred ninety-seven pages of original manuscript of *Nineteen Eighty-Four,* including Orwell's hand-written additions and corrections. Each manuscript page is faced with the editor's typed transcript. The introduction details the circumstances surrounding the writing of *Nineteen Eighty-Four* and provides extensive physical descriptions of the manuscript pages.

Patai, Daphne. "Gamesmanship and Androcentrism in Orwell's *1984.*" *PMLA* 97, No. 5 (October 1982): 856-70.
> Examines the Party's pursuit of power for its own sake in *Nineteen Eighty-Four* in the terms of game theory.

Ranald, Ralph A. "George Orwell and the Mad World: The Anti-Universe of *1984.*" *The South Atlantic Quarterly* LXVI, No. 4 (Autumn 1967): 544-53.
> Interprets *Nineteen Eighty-Four* as a satire intended to alert readers to the possibility of totalitarianism.

Rankin, David. "Orwell's Intention in *1984.*" *English Language Notes* XII, No. 3 (March 1975): 188-92.
> Summarizes some critical interpretations of the political nature of *Nineteen Eighty-Four* as well as Orwell's own explication of his intent.

Roazen, Paul. "Orwell, Freud, and *1984.*" *The Virginia Quarterly Review* 54, No. 4 (Autumn 1978): 675-95.
> Compares the lives and political attitudes of Orwell and Freud. Roazen finds that Freud's system of psychoanalysis is "remarkably similar" to the way of life the Party inflicts on the residents of Oceania in Orwell's novel.

Sarris, Andrew. "Chronicles of a Decent Man: Why He Wrote." *The Village Voice* XXVIII, No. 5 (1 February 1983): 47-49.
> Surveys some recent critical approaches to Orwell's life, work, and political and social attitudes.

Schlesinger, Arthur, Jr. Letter to the Editor. *Life* 27, No. 4 (25 July 1949): 4.
> Response to *Life* magazine review of *Nineteen Eighty-Four* in which the novel is interpreted as a warning against "left-wing totalitarianism" (see Additional Bibliography). Schlesinger concurs with Orwell's own view that the novel warns against the possible rise of totalitarianism anywhere.

Smyer, Richard I. *Primal Dream and Primal Crime: Orwell's Development as a Psychological Novelist.* Columbia: University of Missouri Press, 1979, 187 p.
> Discusses Orwell's novels as manifestations of sexual guilt.

Sperber, Murray. "The Author as Culture Hero: H. G. Wells and George Orwell." *Mosaic: A Journal for the Interdisciplinary Study of Literature* XIV, No. 4 (Fall 1981): 15-29.*
> Overview of Orwell's life, career, and reputation, tracing the reasons why Orwell has attained an extra-literary status as a major twentieth-century figure.

Stansky, Peter, and Abrahams, William. *The Unknown Orwell.* New York: Alfred A. Knopf, 1972, 316 p.
> Biography of Orwell's first thirty years. This is the first volume of a proposed three-volume biography.

――――. *Orwell: The Transformation.* New York: Alfred A. Knopf, 1980, 302 p.
> Biography of Orwell from the publication of his first novel to his involvement in the Spanish civil war. This is the second volume of a proposed three-volume biography.

Steinhoff, William. *George Orwell and the Origins of 1984.* Ann Arbor: University of Michigan Press, 1975, 288 p.
> Demonstrates by means of extensive quotes from Orwell's works that *Nineteen Eighty-Four* represents the culmination of the development of Orwell's political beliefs.

Stewart, Ralph. "Orwell's Waste Land." *The International Fiction Review* 8, No. 2 (Summer 1981): 150-52.
> Finds that T. S. Eliot's poetry, particularly that of *The Waste Land,* was a direct influence upon Orwell's novel *Nineteen Eighty-Four.*

Stokes, Geoffrey. "The History of the Future." *The Village Voice* XXVIII, No. 5 (1 February 1983): 4-5.
> Examines the history and tradition of utopian and dystopian novels. Stokes finds that until the 1920s novels that projected into the future were unfailingly optimistic. *Nineteen Eighty-Four* was "the precursor of a virtually unbroken stream of dystopias that dominated futuristic writing until quite recently."

Wain, John. "From Diagnosis to Nightmare: Koestler and Orwell on the Totalitarian Mind." *Encounter* LXI, No. 2 (September-October 1983): 45-50.*
> Demonstrates that the functioning of a society such as Orwell depicted in *Nineteen Eighty-Four* would be physically and psychologically impossible.

Winnifrith, Tom, and Whitehead, William V. *1984 and All's Well?* London: Macmillan Press, 1984, 104 p.
> Examination of some aspects of modern popular culture with some comparison with the way of life described in *Nineteen Eighty-Four.* The authors conclude that few aspects of modern life resemble 1984 Oceania.

Woodcock, George. "George Orwell and the Living Word." *Queen's Quarterly* 91, No. 3 (Autumn 1984): 501-15.
> Examines the development of Orwell's commitment to fresh and precise use of language, concluding with a discussion of his conception of Newspeak in *Nineteen Eighty-Four.*

World Review n.s. Nos. 11-16 (June 1950).
> Issue devoted to essays about Orwell. Included are essays by Bertrand Russell, T. R. Fyvel, Malcolm Muggeridge, Stephen Spender, Tom Hopkinson, and Herbert Read.

Dorothy L(eigh) Sayers

1893-1957

(Also wrote under pseudonym of Johanna Leigh) English novelist, short story writer, essayist, poet, translator, dramatist, and critic.

Sayers is known as an accomplished Dante scholar, a respected writer on Christian themes, and as the creator of Lord Peter Wimsey, the sophisticated detective-hero of such acclaimed mystery novels as *Murder Must Advertise, The Nine Tailors,* and *Gaudy Night.* In these last-named works, Sayers attempted to fuse the detective story with the novel of manners. In so doing, she not only lent literary respectability to the genre of detective fiction, but also helped pioneer new directions for writers in that field. As a scholar, Sayers is most noted for her translation of Dante's *Divina Commedia.* Her interest in religious history and devotion to orthodox Christianity led her to write several learned chancel dramas as well as a highly successful radio-play cycle on the life of Jesus Christ, *The Man Born to Be King.*

Sayers was born in Oxford, where her father was headmaster of the Cathedral Choir School. Tutored at home as a child, she mastered French, Latin, and German at an early age. Years later, she won a scholarship to Somerville College, Oxford University, receiving both her bachelor's and master's degrees in 1920 and graduating among the first group of women to be granted degrees by the University. After leaving Oxford, Sayers held several jobs, including those of French teacher and reader for Blackwell's publishing house. She also published two small volumes of poetry, *Op. I* and *Catholic Tales and Christian Songs,* the latter of which includes a short religious play written during Sayers's Somerville years. In 1922 Sayers found long-term work as a copywriter for an advertising firm in London. She held this job for nine years while writing several of the Wimsey novels in her spare time. In 1928, five years after the publication of her first detective novel, *Whose Body?,* Sayers and author Anthony Berkeley founded the London Detection Club, of which she later became president. By 1931, the financial success of Sayers's Lord Peter Wimsey series allowed her to quit the advertising job and become a full-time writer. Her non-Wimsey novel *The Documents in the Case,* which was modeled on Wilkie Collins's psychological mystery *The Moonstone,* had already appeared, signalling the author's gravitation toward the novel of manners. In the years ahead, Sayers gradually adopted a more in-depth, psychological approach to her characters, particularly Wimsey, and also began limiting the centrality of murder to the plot. When her murderless mystery, *Gaudy Night,* was published in 1935, Sayers believed that she had achieved her goal of fusing the mystery with the novel of manners.

Sayers turned to drama the following year and, after producing one last novel about Wimsey, *Busman's Honeymoon,* concentrated primarily on religious themes. She was convinced that the stage was the artistic medium best-suited for presenting an emerging concern of hers—Christian history and belief—in an understandable, stimulating way to the general public. In her first verse drama, *The Zeal of Thy House,* which Sayers wrote for the Canterbury Festival in 1937, she selected a lesser-known personage from religious history, the 12th century French ar-

chitect William of Sens, to afford a modern exploration of sinful pride. In general, all of Sayers's chancel dramas—like those of T. S. Eliot, Christopher Fry, and Charles Williams—adopted similar approaches, blending the past with the present and interpreting historical events in a contemporary light. Her approach to translating Dante's *Divina Commedia* was very similar in this sense. But before she assumed this massive project, she produced what is considered her greatest achievement in drama, *The Man Born to Be King,* originally broadcast as a BBC radio series in 1941 and later published in book form. Throughout her career Sayers wrote numerous thought-provoking articles, essays, and books on a variety of subjects, many of them religious, and many have received considerable critical attention. *The Mind of the Maker,* possibly her most famous work of nonfiction, draws an analogy between the three-fold creative act of writing (conception, execution, and reader response) and that of the Holy Trinity. Sayers dedicated the majority of her last decade to translating the *Divina Commedia,* which she titled *The Comedy of Dante Alighieri the Florentine,* a project toward which she had been steered by friend and fellow author Charles Williams. Sayers died in Witham, Essex in 1957 while still working on the final section, *Paradiso.* Her colleague Barbara Reynolds later completed the translation. The entire work, part of the Penguin Classics series, is recognized for its accomplishment and is still used in many college classrooms today.

Sayers's early Wimsey novels have been shown to be heavily influenced by the works of Sir Arthur Conan Doyle and by E. C. Bentley's experimental mystery classic *Trent's Last Case*. Her detective hero, Lord Peter, though ostensibly modelled on the archetypal sleuth Sherlock Holmes, was also characterized in these stories as a dandified clubman reminiscent of P. G. Wodehouse's comical Bertie Wooster. But Sayers's deepest influences lay with two early masters of mystery, namely, Collins and Sheridan Le Fanu. Sayers believed that "if the detective story was to live and develop it must get back to where it began in the hands of Collins and Le Fanu, and become once more a novel of manners instead of a pure crossword puzzle." Consequently, Sayers developed Lord Peter into the sensitive, serious individual of the later novels and began to introduce weighty, humanistic themes, one of her most prominent being that of personal integrity in one's work, one's relationships, and one's attitude toward God. Sayers's aptitude for authentically detailing interesting milieus, such as the advertising world in *Murder Must Advertise* or England's fen country in *The Nine Tailors*, and intertwining these settings with adept criticism of contemporary life, as well as her introduction of a significant love element (heroine Harriet Vane) beginning in *Strong Poison*, established Sayers as an effective writer of the classic, psychological mystery novel. In the best of Sayers's short stories, many critics believe the author at least equalled, if not exceeded, the same high standards she demonstrated in her greatest novels.

In her dramas Sayers sought to present Christian truths to what she believed was primarily a religiously uneducated public. In the plays, she interpreted such personages as Emperor Constantine, Faustus, Mephistopheles, and Jesus Christ, and such subjects as guilt, sin, and redemption. All the dramas share the orthodox Christian message that human redemption from sin and spiritual death is through acceptance of God's forgiveness, made possible through Jesus' life, propitiatory death, and resurrection. In the radio play cycle *The Man Born to Be King*, the image of Jesus assumes central importance. The drama was a breakthrough in religious dramatization because Parliament, at that time, forbade the stage representation of any divine being. Although the plays were broadcast over radio and not produced on the stage, vigorous protests were lodged by groups such as the Lord's Day Observance Society. It is now commonly recognized that Sayers succeeded in conveying Jesus' life and teachings in modern, everyday language to the public, and thus paved the way for such later modernistic religious dramas as *Godspell* and *Jesus Christ Superstar*.

There has been conflicting critical reaction to nearly all of Sayers's canon. Some scholars, including Edmund Wilson, have belittled the Wimsey novels for their superfluous detail and dialogue and for their general lack of distinction, while others have praised the mysteries for their finely structured plots, engaging themes, and erudite prose. Sayers's book-length philosophical essay *The Mind of the Maker* has been criticized by some as thematically unsound and stale; by others as inspired and compelling. Despite much controversy, the importance of Sayers's work is evidenced by the increasing amount of critical attention it receives. The majority of Sayers scholars affirm the writer's high stature as a writer of fiction. Furthermore, they recognize her as a preeminent authority in the detective-mystery field for her numerous articles on the nature and history of the genre, particularly her esteemed introductions as editor to the *Great Short Stories of Detection, Mystery, and Horror* series. As to Sayers's Christian apologetics in her dramas, lectures, and essays, even her most fervent antagonists concede that her works possess a forceful, craftsmanlike expression of her thought. Finally, Sayers's translation of the *Divina Commedia*, though faulted for its blending of archaic and modern diction and for its controversial rhyme scheme, still manages to capture the essence of Dante's work in a way that critics find especially appealing to the modern reader. Although Sayers was initially remembered primarily for her novels concerning Lord Peter Wimsey, she is now more commonly regarded as a Christian humanist who left a mark of high accomplishment in each artistic area to which she turned.

(See also *TCLC*, Vol. 2; *Contemporary Authors*, Vol. 104; and *Dictionary of Literary Biography*, Vol. 10: *Modern British Dramatists, 1900-1945*.)

PRINCIPAL WORKS

Op. I (poetry) 1916
Catholic Tales and Christian Songs (poetry and drama) 1918
Whose Body? (novel) 1923
Clouds of Witness (novel) 1926
Unnatural Death (novel) 1927; published in the United States as *The Dawson Pedigree*, 1928
Great Short Stories of Detection, Mystery, and Horror [editor] (short stories) 1928; published in the United States as *The Omnibus of Crime*, 1929
Lord Peter Views the Body (short stories) 1928
The Unpleasantness at the Bellona Club (novel) 1928
Strong Poison (novel) 1930
The Five Red Herrings (novel) 1931; published in the United States as *Suspicious Characters*, 1931
Great Short Stories of Detection, Mystery, and Horror, second series [editor] (short stories) 1931; published in the United States as *The Second Omnibus of Crime*, 1932
Have His Carcase (novel) 1932
Hangman's Holiday (short stories) 1933
Murder Must Advertise (novel) 1933
Great Short Stories of Detection, Mystery, and Horror, third series [editor] (short stories) 1934; published in the United States as *The Third Omnibus of Crime*, 1935
The Nine Tailors; Changes Rung on an Old Theme in Two Short Touches and Two Full Peals (novel) 1934
Gaudy Night (novel) 1935
Busman's Honeymoon; A Love Story with Detective Interruptions [with Muriel St. Clare Byrne] (drama) 1936
Busman's Honeymoon (novel) 1937
The Zeal of Thy House (religious drama) 1937
The Devil to Pay; Being the Famous History of John Faustus, the Conjurer of Wittenberg in Germany; How He Sold His Immortal Soul to the Enemy of Mankind, and Was Served XXIV Years by Mephistopheles, and Obtained Helen of Troy to His Paramour, with Many Other Marvels; And How God Dealth with Him at the Last (drama) 1939
In the Teeth of the Evidence (short stories) 1939
Begin Here (essays) 1940
The Man Born to Be King (religious dramas) 1941
The Mind of the Maker (religious essay) 1941
The Just Vengeance (religious drama) 1946
Unpopular Opinions (essays) 1946
The Comedy of Dante Alighieri, the Florentine: Hell [translator] (poetry) 1949

Creed or Chaos? (essays) 1949

The Emperor Constantine (religious drama) 1951

The Comedy of Dante Alighieri, the Florentine; Purgatory [translator] (poetry) 1955

The Song of Roland [translator] (poetry) 1957

The Comedy of Dante Alighieri, the Florentine: Paradise [translator] (poetry) 1963

Christian Letters to a Post-Christian World (essays) 1969; also published as *The Whimsical Christian: 18 Essays,* 1978

Are Women Human? (essays) 1971

''The Dogma in the Manger: A Reply to Kathleen Nott'' (essay) 1982; published in journal *Seven: An Anglo-American Literary Review*

*This work was completed by Barbara Reynolds.

THE TIMES LITERARY SUPPLEMENT (essay date 1917)

[*In the following excerpt, the critic notes the skill evident in the poems of* Op. I, *even though finding some marred by their "strained preciosity."*]

The title [**"Op. I"**] is, perhaps, a little ambitious—perhaps we may see in it the fervour of youth; and the first poem will show that Miss Sayers is not without something of the true fire. The theme of **"Alma Mater"** is Helen of Troy, recalling her great past to her young son Idaeus, and presenting in a contrast rich with eloquence and passion the love of the son and the more momentous passion of the lover. . . .

The failing of Miss Sayers is a strained preciosity—observable in the stanzas about Oxford under the title **"Lay,"** and in **"The Lost Castle,"** apparently celebrating the close of Oxford life in a number of songs representing different phases of thought, or life, or letters. **"The Gates of Paradise"** is a good essay in the mystical religious ballad (though the confusion of ''Hell'' with ''Paradise'' seems to mar it a little). The writer's capricious taste in titles baffles us in the case of **"A Man Greatly Gifted"** and **"The Elder Knight,"** which follows it, should surely be entitled ''The Younger Knight.'' Nevertheless there is not a poem in this collection which one can neglect; and with **"Hymn in Contemplation of Sudden Death"** towards the end, we get quite away from sophistications to a calm, simple utterance of singular charm.

> A review of ''*Op. I.,*'' in The Times Literary Supplement, *No. 784, January 25, 1917, p. 47.*

WILL CUPPY (essay date 1929)

[*In the following excerpt Cuppy, who frequently reviewed mystery fiction for the* New York Herald Tribune, *favorably appraises the short story collection* Lord Peter Views the Body.]

This department remains faithful to the mystery works of Dorothy L. Sayers—they're always delightful. Those who may charge Miss Sayers with mere flippancy because she trifles with wit and humor are all wrong, as the force of these twelve stories [in **Lord Peter Views the Body**] amply proves, she is funny, to be sure, but she knows her thrills much better than the ponderous boys. Lord Peter Wimsey, the exquisite sleuth, gambols through the tales, which deal with such marvels are

the man with the copper fingers . . . and a modern cave of Ali Baba, with cyanide, jewels, a roast chicken, a classic cross word puzzle and what not as clews. Most of the tales stress the fantastic, grotesque and macabre.

> *Will Cuppy, in a review of ''Lord Peter Views the Body,'' in* New York Herald Tribune Books, *March 31, 1929, p. 11.*

MARY McCARTHY (essay date 1936)

[*McCarthy is an American novelist, essayist, short-story and travel writer whose works are noted for their sophistication, wit, satire, and a caustic frankness that also characterizes her literary and drama criticism. Much of her criticism focuses on the weakness of playwrights and novelists, and exhibits a distaste for modern literature. In the following excerpt from a negative review of* Gaudy Night, *McCarthy dismisses the novel as an unfortunate attempt by a mystery writer to write a conventional novel.*]

''This mystery is also a novel. This novel is also a romance.'' So the blurb-writer for Messrs. Harcourt, Brace announces **"Gaudy Night,"** a new detective story by Dorothy Sayers. This statement has a rather pathetic and desperate candor, the candor of the unregenerate bluffer who hopes by putting a bold face on it to convert a liability into an asset. The facts are that **"Gaudy Night"** as a romance is cloudy and longwinded; as a novel it has moments of atmospheric interest; but as a detective story it is a thoroughgoing, dismal flop. This tale of the terrorization of an Oxford woman's college commits at least three unforgivable detective-story sins. In the first place, there is no murder; and while some detective-story readers like few murders and some like many, all detective-story readers like *one* murder. In the second place, there is no action: almost 275 pages of the conversation of female dons must be leafed through before the Shrewsbury College Menace becomes anything more than mildly annoying. In the third place, there is no problem, and therefore, really, no mystery. It is true that the identity of the culprit is shielded until the last few pages of the novel, but more than this is needed to make a mystery story truly mysterious. The essence of the pure detective story is that it should present a central problem, or problems, which seems, on the face of it, impossible of solution: the mystery of the locked room and the mystery of the perfect alibi are the problems most frequently used and therefore most familiar to detective-story readers. In the perfect mystery the murderer avoids detection, not because the detective cannot physically lay his hand on him, but because the criminal has so cleverly distorted and thereby camouflaged his crime that it is impossible for the detective even to grasp its nature and meaning, let alone its perpetrator. Dorothy Sayers has, in the past, produced excellent examples of the pure detective story, but in the hybrid **"Gaudy Night"** she has given us a primer mystery in which the criminal escapes her pursuers only by being slightly fleeter of foot.

The metamorphosis of Dorothy Sayers is interesting, even though a little unfortunate. It may be that from the very beginning Miss Sayers, the brilliant detective-story writer, was a frustrated novelist. Certain it is that in successive mysteries she has been edging, more and more boldly, into the novelist's territory, until with **"Gaudy Night"** she has flatly put her foot in it, in more senses than one. Miss Sayers as a detective-story writer was considered, quite rightly, a stylist, a wit, a psychologist, a scholar. Since the standards by which a novelist is measured are inevitably more severe, Miss Sayers as a novelist can now lay claim to scholarship alone. She can still quote aptly from Burton, Drayton, Sir John Harington, Sir Thomas

Browne, Sir Philip Sidney, but laid bare in a full-length novel her style seems prosy, her wit over-prim and spinsterish, her psychology slightly antiquated and mechanical. Her venture into the novelist's field is exactly as regrettable and as awkward as the stage debut of a drawing-room mimic. The novel has gained no new Aldous Huxley, and the mystery story has, temporarily, at any rate, lost one of its most able practitioners. (p. 458)

> *Mary McCarthy, "Highbrow Shockers," in* The Nation, *Vol. CXLII, No. 3692, April 8, 1936, pp. 458-59.*

DOROTHY L. SAYERS (essay date 1937)

[*Sayers's essay "Gaudy Night," composed in 1937, is deemed by critics an extremely insightful criticism of her detective fiction. In the following excerpt from this essay, Sayers explains the development of her novels and of Lord Peter Wimsey.*]

Taking it all in all, I think it is true that each successive book of mine worked gradually nearer to the sort of thing I had in view [for the detective novel]. *The Documents in the Case,* which is a serious "criticism of life" so far as it goes, took a jump forward rather out of its due time; *The Five Red Herrings* was a cast back towards the "time-table" puzzle-problem. *Strong Poison,* to which I shall have to return later, rather timidly introduced the "love-element" into the Peter Wimsey story. I think the first real attempt at fusing the two kinds of novel was made in *Murder Must Advertise,* in which, for the first time, the criticism of life was not relegated to incidental observations and character sketches, but was actually part of the plot, as it ought to be. It was not quite successful; the idea of symbolically opposing two cardboard worlds—that of the advertiser and the drug-taker—was all right; and it was suitable that Peter, who stands for reality, should never appear in either except disguised; but the working-out was a little too melodramatic, and the handling rather uneven. *The Nine Tailors* was a shot at combining detection with poetic romance, and was, I think, pretty nearly right, except that Peter himself remained, as it were, extraneous to the story and untouched by its spiritual conflicts. This was correct practice for a detective hero, but not for the hero of a novel of manners. At this point you will begin to suspect that Peter was fast becoming a major problem to his inconsiderate creator, and so indeed he was.

It is amazing how recklessly one embarks upon adventures of the most hideous toil and difficulty, and that with one's eyes wide open. I had from the outset, of course, envisaged for Peter a prolonged and triumphal career, going on through book after book amid the plaudits of adoring multitudes. It is true that his setting forth did not cause as great a stir as I had expected, and that the adoring multitudes were represented by a small, though faithful, band of adherents. But time would, I hoped, bring the public into a better frame of mind, and I plugged confidently on, putting my puppet through all his tricks and exhibiting him in a number of elegant attitudes. But I had not properly realized—and this shows how far I was from understanding what it was I was trying to dŏ with the detective novel—that any character that remains static except for a repertory of tricks and attitudes is bound to become a monstrous weariness to his maker in the course of nine or ten volumes. Let me confess that when I undertook *Strong Poison* it was with the infanticidal intention of doing away with Peter; that is, of marrying him off and getting rid of him—for a lingering

instinct of self-preservation, and the deterrent object-lesson of Mr. Holmes's rather scrambling return from the Reichenbach Falls, prevented me from actually killing and burying the nuisance.

Two things stood in the way of my fell purpose. First, in accordance with the general contradictoriness of things, just when I had decided that I could not do with Peter for a single moment more, the multitudes began, though rather sparsely and belatedly, to roll up and hang hopefully about along the route, uttering agreeable cheers and convinced that the show was billed to continue. Some of them even did a little mild adoring, and I was quite pathetically grateful to them and disposed to give Peter a little longer run. But what really stayed my hand was something still more unexpected, and in a sense more creditable. I could not marry Peter off to the young woman he had (in the conventional Perseus manner) rescued from death and infamy, because I could find no form of words in which she could accept him without loss of self-respect. I had landed my two chief puppets in a situation where, according to all the conventional rules of detective fiction, they should have had nothing to do but fall into one another's arms; but they would not do it, and that for a very good reason. When I looked at the situation I saw that it was in every respect false and degrading; and the puppets had somehow got just so much flesh and blood in them that I could not force them to accept it without shocking myself.

So there were only two things to do: one was to leave the thing there, with the problem unresolved; the other, far more delicate and dangerous, was to take Peter away and perform a major operation on him. If the story was to go on, Peter had got to become a complete human being, with a past and a future, with a consistent family and social history, with a complicated psychology and even the rudiments of a religious outlook. And all this would have to be squared somehow or other with such random attributes as I had bestowed upon him over a series of years in accordance with the requirements of various detective plots.

The thing seemed difficult, but not impossible. When I came to examine the patient, he showed the embryonic buds of a character of sorts. Even at the beginning he had not been the complete silly ass: he had only played the silly ass, which was not the same thing. He had had shell-shock and a vaguely embittered love affair; he had a mother and a friend and a sketchy sort of brother and sister; he had literary and musical tastes, and a few well-defined opinions and feelings; and a little tidying-up of dates and places would put his worldly affairs into order. The prognosis seemed fairly favorable; so I laid him out firmly on the operating-table and chipped away at his internal mechanism through three longish books. At the end of the process he was five years older than he was in *Strong Poison,* and twelve years older than he was when he started. If, during the period, he had altered and mellowed a little, I felt I could reasonably point out that most human beings were altered and mellowed by age. One of the first results of the operation was an indignant letter from a female reader of *Gaudy Night* asking, What had happened to Peter? he had lost all his elfin charm. I replied that any man who retained elfin charm at the age of forty-five should be put in a lethal chamber. Indeed, Peter escaped that lethal chamber by inches.

But I was still no further along with the problem of Harriet. She had been a human being from the start, and I had humanized Peter for her benefit; but the situation between them had become still more impossible on that account. Formerly, she could not marry him to live on gratitude; now he had advanced to a point where he could not possibly want her to do anything of the kind. Her inferiority complex was making her steadily more brutal to him and his newly developed psychology was making him steadily more sensitive to her inhibitions. Clearly, they could not go on like this; and time was passing with alarming rapidity, at this rate they would be grey-headed before they were reconciled. At all cost some device must be found for putting Harriet back on a footing of equality with her lover. It was clear that it would be of great help to her to receive a proposal from another, and entirely disinterested man; but this, by itself, was not enough. About this time I was playing with the idea of a ''straight'' novel, about an Oxford woman graduate who found, in middle life, and after reasonably satisfactory experience of marriage and motherhood, that her real vocation and full emotional fulfilment were to be found in the creative life of the intellect. While investigating the possibilities of this subject, I was asked to go to Oxford and propose the toast of the University at my College Gaudy dinner. I had asked myself exactly what it was for which one had to thank a university education, and came to the conclusion that it was, before everything, that habit of intellectual integrity which is at once the foundation and the result of scholarship.

Having delivered myself of these sentiments in a speech, the substance of which (stripped of its post-prandial rhetoric) was later embodied in an article in the official organ of the Oxford Society, I discovered that in Oxford I had the solution to all my three problems at once. On the intellectual platform, alone of all others, Harriet could stand free and equal with Peter, since in that sphere she had never been false to her own standards. By choosing a plot that should exhibit intellectual integrity as the one great permanent value in an emotionally unstable world I should be saying the thing that, in a confused way, I had been wanting to say all my life. Finally, I should have found a universal theme which could be made integral both to the detective plot and to the ''love-interest'' which I had, somehow or other, to unite with it. (pp. 209-13)

By one of those curious ironies which provide so wholesome a check to the vanity of authors, *Gaudy Night* [has] been loudly condemned by some critics for lack of construction. It would be truer to say that it is the only book I have ever written which has any construction at all, beyond a purely artificial plot-construction. Some of the blame is undoubtedly mine for not having made the construction more explicit (though I thought I was laying its articulations bare with an openness verging on indecency). I really think, however, that the construction was obscured by the conviction, still lingering in many people's minds that a detective plot cannot bear any relation to a universal theme.

In the sixties of the last century there was still no divorce between plot and theme. *Man and Wife* is a mystery story built on the theme of the unequal marriage laws of the Three Kingdoms; and that theme provides the mainspring of the plot. It is only of recent years that we have had detective stories composed entirely of plot, without theme, or with the theme a mere incidental embroidery. We have even had stories divorced from their settings; bodies are discovered (for instance) in churches, theatres, railway stations, ships, aeroplanes, and so forth, which might just as well have been discovered anywhere else, the setting being put in only for picturesqueness and forming no *integral* part either of theme or plot. To make an artistic unity it is, I feel, essential that the plot should derive from the setting, and that both should form part of the theme. From this point

of view, *Gaudy Night* does, I think, stand reasonably well up to the test; the setting is a women's college; the plot derives from, and develops through, episodes that could not have occurred in any other place; and the theme is the relation of scholarship to life. I am sure the book is constructed on the right lines, though I am naturally conscious of innumerable defects in the working. (pp. 216-17)

I was once challenged, in a circle of writers, to account for the sales of *Gaudy Night*. I had not the honesty to say that I thought it sold because it was a good book. I do think it sold because it was a sincere book upon a subject about which I really had something to say. I think, too, it sold because it dealt in a knowledgeable way with the daily life of a little-known section of the community. Readers seem to like books which tell them how other people live—any people, advertisers, bell-ringers, women dons, butchers, bakers or candlestick-makers—so long as the detail is full and accurate and the object of the work is not overt propaganda. Finally, of course, there was Peter, who, escaping annihilation and surviving a drastic surgical operation, has lived to see himself surnamed ''the Incomparable.'' (p. 218)

> *Dorothy L. Sayers, ''Care and Feeding of the Who-dunit: 'Gaudy Night','' in* The Art of the Mystery Story: A Collection of Critical Essays, *edited by Howard Haycraft, revised edition, Simon and Schuster, 1947, pp. 208-21.**

ASHLEY DUKES   (essay date 1939)

[*Dukes was an important English dramatist and drama critic during the first half of the twentieth century. He is most noted for his writings on modern European theater, particularly poetic drama. He had a broad knowledge of continental drama and, both as a translator and as the manager of his own theater, introduced English audiences to the work of several important French and German dramatists, including Ernst Toller, Georg Kaiser, and Lion Feuchtwanger. In the following excerpt, Dukes pronounces Sayers's Canterbury Festival play* The Devil to Pay *a failure due to its unoriginal conception of the Faustian legend.*]

[*The Devil to Pay*] advertises itself under the caption 'there must be some meaning in this tormented universe', and having thus related the theme of Faustus to the world of today in the spectator's mind, it presents him with an action and an argument valid only to those who accept wholeheartedly the mediaeval-Christian proposition. I for one do not quarrel with a religious play demanding unconditional assent, whether it be played in the Chapter House of Canterbury or in His Majesty's Theatre. It is a condition of all religious drama to ask for such assent; and the men who played dramatic mysteries on the steps of churches started with the inestimable advantage that their audiences agreed with them. (So, for that matter, did the Greeks who played dramatic myths on a hillside.) Those writers of religious drama, like Eliot, who give pleasure both to the just and the unjust, are in number few and in spirit tortuous. Maybe the writer of *The Devil to Pay* would herself like to give such catholic pleasure, and it is true that the wit of humanism and the humor of humanity play over this curious scene in which Hell's jaws gape on one side of the stage and Heaven's stairway winds upward on the other, with fragments of Wittenberg, Innsbruck and Rome in between them.

The play is devoted and sincere; why then does it strike me at the same time as perverted and immodest? Not only because great parts (they remain great parts) are acted with small imagination; nor because the 'mansions' into which the stage is divided are trivial and pictorial where the 'mansions' of mediaeval drama were creations of poetry; nor even because mediocre blank verse, that most tiresome medium which can be used by a writer of our time, rises in a series of peaks, regularly formed, above a plain of even more mediocre and sometimes facetious prose. These are faults of execution that could be readily forgiven, if only the great tale of Faustus were in some way refreshed in conception, brought into harmony with our common experience. But 'Faustus is faced with the final, ineluctable choice between the evil and the good. . . . Mephistopheles too is the Devil as the Ages of Faith saw him—at once evil and grotesque, miserable and triumphant, fascinating and abominable, the cheater and the cheated, the jester and the laughing-stock of eternity.' It is all terribly, flatly true. An authoress of ingenious fiction, gifted with a sense of humor and as convinced as any curate of her spiritual unity with the Ages of Faith, has unfortunately presumed to tell us again about Faust and the Devil. Before going into the theatre one said to oneself 'You know, it would be hard to fail with this subject.' Coming out, one realized it can be even harder to succeed. Not only worldly possessions can make difficult the passage of the needle's eye; spiritual obsessions blandly owned by certain minds are as awkward an obstruction.

I am sorry to regard *The Devil to Pay* as a lamentable setback to the cause of poetic drama, and maybe to the cause of good drama in general. For much as we want the unfamiliar and serious audience that Eliot (for example) brought into the theatre, we do not want them in a theatre that is itself a bore. The problem of the religious play is to compel the assent which is its own foundation. A poet compels this assent, at least for the space of time that the listener remains under the spell of his work of art. Other sorts of writers not only fail to compel it, but evoke a dissent as vigorous as mine has been to this year's Canterbury drama, so unwisely brought to the regular stage. (pp. 706-07)

> Ashley Dukes, ''Summer Seasons: The English Scene,'' in Theatre Arts Monthly, Vol. XXIII, No. 10, October, 1939, pp. 704-08.*

RUPERT HART-DAVIS　　(essay date 1939)

[*Hart-Davis, an English author and editor, directed his own highly respected publishing company for over twenty years. In the following excerpt from a review, Hart-Davis concludes that nearly all the stories found in* In the Teeth of the Evidence *are predictable and unsatisfying.*]

In the Teeth of the Evidence contains seventeen short stories, almost all unsatisfying. The detective story was born as a short story, and remained so through the reigns of Edgar Allan Poe, Conan Doyle (with a few exceptions) and G. K. Chesterton; but now, curiously enough, we have little patience with really short stories of detection. Miss Sayers's new volume opens well, with Lord Peter Wimsey in the clutches of an Old Wykehamist dentist, but only two stories deal with his Lordship's activities. There follow five episodes in the life of a colourless commercial traveller called Montague Egg, and the rest of the book contains miscellaneous crime stories. Among them are an amusing account of a barber's brainwave, and an excellent, almost surrealist, story called *The Leopard Lady;* but the majority of the stories in the book seem to have escaped unwillingly from popular magazines. They have little twists in their tails, but one can almost always anticipate them. Remembering

The program distributed at the first performance of the drama Busman's Honeymoon, *an adaptation of Dorothy L. Sayers's novel. This particular copy was autographed by both authors. From* Dorothy L. Sayers: Nine Literary Studies, *by Trevor H. Hall. Archon Books, 1980. Reproduced by permission of Trevor H. Hall.*

some of Miss Sayers's more elaborate backgrounds, one almost wishes she had supplied a little more padding. (p. 880)

> Rupert Hart-Davis, ''Murder with Padding,'' in The Spectator, Vol. 163, No. 5816, December 15, 1939, pp. 878, 880.*

HILAIRE BELLOC　　(letter date 1940)

[*At the turn of the century, Belloc was considered one of England's premier men of letters and a provocative essayist. His characteristically truculent stance as a proponent of Roman Catholicism and economic reform, and his equally characteristic clever humor drew either strong support or harsh attacks from his audience. But critics find common ground for admiration in his poetry; Belloc and his longtime friend and collaborator G. K. Chesterton have been lauded by W. H. Auden as the best light-verse writers of their era, with Belloc's* Cautionary Tales *(1907) considered by some his most successful work in the genre. And in such collections as* On Nothing *(1908) and* On Everything *(1909), Belloc proved that he could write convincing and forceful essays on nearly any subject, as either controversialist or defender of the status quo, in a prose style marked by clarity and wit. Closely linked to*

Belloc's Catholic beliefs was his proposed economic and political program called Distributism, a system of small ownership harking back to Europe's pre-Reformation period and fully described in the controversial 1912 essay The Servile State. *Because he looked to the past—particularly to the Middle Ages—for his ideals, Belloc has not been widely read by modern readers; his desire to return to the values of an authoritarian epoch, as well as recurrent flashes of anti-Semitic comment in his works, have contributed to his eclipse as an important literary figure. In the following excerpt from a letter, Belloc finds* Creed or Chaos? *to be very well written but lacking in an essential point: a definition of the creed that informs and substantiates Sayers's views.*]

I have read Miss Sayers' pamphlet [*Creed or Chaos?*] and I agree with you that it is very well written, for especially is it concise. The main thesis is one with which of course all those of my way of thinking are so familiar that they take it for granted. But her exposition of her thesis seems to me to lack one essential point. She does not say what creed gives the religion to which she is attached nor on what authority that creed should be received. (p. 292)

It seems to me that in the case of this very able pamphlet, as in the case of the great mass of less able similar expositions, there is a lack of definition which is fatal. There is no answer to the question *Quid de ecclesia?* Which may be put more shortly, *Ubi Christus?* The orthodox answer is that the Church is the union of all the faithful, that is of all who accept her doctrines whether explicitly or implicitly. Those who accept them explicitly are of the visible Church, those who accept implicitly by their conduct and their morals are of the invisible Church, which includes any number of people who have never admitted an explicit faith at all or even heard of it, but serve God.

A thing only *is* because it is one. Now it seems evident to me that people who write as this very clear writer does write are avoiding the main issue. *They avoid the issue of unity.* For I think that those who write under the conditions of this country, of its institutions and of its central tradition, have two loyalties in mind—one which implies the visible Church and its unity, but another incompatible with this (which is I think at heart the religion of all English people), the worship of the nation. To abandon the institutions to which they are attached is to go into exile, and that is the hardest condition to which human beings can be subjected. (p. 293)

Hilaire Belloc, in a letter to Guy Dawnay on July 4, 1940, in Letters from Hilaire Belloc, *edited by Robert Speaight, Hollis & Carter, 1958, pp. 292-93.*

CLIFTON FADIMAN (essay date 1941)

[*Fadiman became one of the most prominent American literary critics during the 1930s with his insightful and often caustic book reviews for* The Nation *and* The New Yorker *magazines. He also reached a sizeable audience through his work as a radio talk-show host from 1938 to 1948. In the following excerpt, Fadiman briefly outlines the thought contained in* Begin Here.]

You may know of Dorothy L. Sayers as one of the best (I do not say the best, for I have had enough irate correspondence lately) of living detective-story writers. **"Begin Here"** is not a thriller but a brief "statement of faith," with a certain amount of wisdom and much courage. For Miss Sayers, an English-woman, the future is here and now, as it always is, and she is among those who believe this the time to think about it. A downright lady who knows her own mind, she has no patience with what she calls "grandiose" schemes for postwar federal

unions. She is a disciple not of H. G. Wells but of G. K. Chesterton. Her blueprints do not involve world air armadas, an international language, and other specifics. They have to do with the human soul and with its liberation from the fetish of Economic Man, a fetish in which she believes many of our modern ills are rooted. Her brief book is a plea for a non-economic society, but how this is to be reconciled with her obvious desire to retain the British Commonwealth intact is not entirely clear. There is, by the way, nothing mystical about Miss Sayers, though there is something very religious. The New Aesthetes, who have fallen in love with the wave of the future as the old ones fell in love with incense and medieval Latin, will get little comfort from her. (pp. 65-6)

Clifton Fadiman, in a review of "Begin Here," in The New Yorker, *Vol. XVII, No. 12, May 3, 1941, pp. 65-6.*

CHARLES WILLIAMS (essay date 1941)

[*Williams was a writer of supernatural fiction, a poet whose best works treat the legends of Logres (Arthurian Britain), and one of the central figures among the literary group known as the Oxford Christians or "Inklings." The religious, the magical, and the mythical are recurrent concerns in his works, reflecting his devout Anglicanism and lifelong interest in all aspects of the preternatural. Although his works are not today as well known as those of his fellow-Inklings C. S. Lewis and J.R.R. Tolkien, Williams was an important source of encouragement and influence among the group. He was a close friend of Sayers, who occasionally attended the weekly meetings of the Inklings. In the following excerpt, Williams discusses Sayers's thesis in* The Mind of the Maker.]

Miss Sayers has done a very interesting thing [in *The Mind of the Maker*]. She has (1) discussed the mind of the artist—particularly of the writer, (2) discussed it in relation to the statements about the nature of God as Creator made in the Christian creeds. I admit that I approach any such analogy with the highest reluctance and suspicion. I am too like the Areopagite to be anything but gloomy about analogies with the Uncreated; the damage they do is incalculable. I admit, however, that Miss Sayers all but converted me; she converted at least all that is convertible. This was due not to the way she runs her analogy but to the way she does not run it. She has always had a very high sense of human folly—no doubt, like most of us, from her experience of it both without and within; and whatever opinion any reader may hold of the Trinitarian formula he will at least admit that her realism is sound and her rationality accurate.

My respect for Miss Sayers and my personal adoration of the Blessed Trinity prevent me from doing more than indicate the analogy she presents. She says that every work of art—say, for convenience sake, every book, is threefold; there is the Idea (or "the writer's realization of his own idea"); the Energy or Creativity (without which the Idea is not known, but which "is conscious of referring all its acts to an existing and complete whole"); and the Creative Power, which is the thing "which flows back to the writer from his own activity and makes him, as it were, the reader of his own book", and also the means by which a response is produced in other readers. Miss Sayers says here: "It is at this point that we begin to understand what St Hilary means in saying of the Trinity: 'Eternity is in the Father, form in the image, and use in the Gift'." Miss Sayers and St Hilary together threw, for me, a sudden light on what

St Thomas meant when he said that the proper name of the Holy Ghost was Gift.

I admit that I am not at all sure that Miss Sayers was right to publish this book. It will, I fear, often return to her as anything but the Power which is the Gift. It will be, in spite of her passionate protest, used all over the country, (1) to show that one of our greatest creative artists is a Trinitarian, (2) that really the Trinity is quite easy and simple—shamrocks and so on, (3) that Art is the handmaid of Religion, (4)—but Miss Sayers's introduction, by no means the least profitable part of the book, has already denounced the "distortion of facts and deliberate falsifications" which harass the unfortunate writer—among Christians especially. It remains that the judicious reader (if there is one) will be edified and encouraged by the book, especially by the chapter on Scalene Trinities, Gnostic dramatists, the son-ridden activity of James Joyce, and the Patripassionism of *In Memoriam*. And I hope Miss Sayers will invite me to lunch one day to discuss whether Milton is not father-centred after all. (pp. 689-90)

> Charles Williams, "Renovations of Intelligence," in Time & Tide, *Vol. 22, No. 33, August 16, 1941, pp. 689-90.**

RAYMOND CHANDLER   (essay date 1944)

[*Chandler was an American novelist and screenwriter who, along with his mentor Dashiell Hammett, elevated the genre known as the hard-boiled detective story into an American art form. His first and perhaps most famous novel,* The Big Sleep, *introduced the detective hero Philip Marlowe, one of the most memorable characters in the field. In the following excerpt, Chandler takes exception to Sayers's ideas on detective fiction as expressed in her introduction to the first* Omnibus of Crime.]

In her introduction to the first **Omnibus of Crime,** Dorothy Sayers wrote: "It [the detective story] does not, and by hypothesis never can, attain the loftiest level of literary achievement." And the reason, as she suggested somewhere else, is that it is a "literature of escape" and not "a literature of expression." I do not know what the loftiest level of literary achievement is: neither did Aeschylus or Shakespeare; neither does Miss Sayers. Other things being equal, which they never are, a more powerful theme will provoke a more powerful performance. Yet some very dull books have been written about God, and some very fine ones about how to make a living and stay fairly honest. It is always a matter of who writes the stuff, and what he has in him to write it with.

As for "literature of expression" and "literature of escape"—this is critics' jargon, a use of abstract words as if they had absolute meanings. Everything written with vitality expresses that vitality: there are no dull subjects, only dull writers. All men who read escape from something else. (pp. 56-7)

I think what was really gnawing at Miss Sayers's mind was the slow realization that her kind of detective story was an arid formula which could not even satisfy its own implications. It was second-grade literature because it was not about the things that could make first-grade literature. If it started out to be about real people (and she could write about them—her minor characters show that), they must very soon do unreal things in order to form the artificial pattern required by the plot. When they did unreal things, they ceased to be real themselves. They became puppets and cardboard lovers and papier-mâché villains and detectives of exquisite and impossible gentility.

The only kind of writer who could be happy with these properties was the one who did not know what reality was. Dorothy Sayers's own stories show that she was annoyed by this triteness; the weakest element in them is the part that makes them detective stories, the strongest the part which could be removed without touching the "problem of logic and deduction." Yet she could not or would not give her characters their heads and let them make their own mystery. It took a much simpler and more direct mind than hers to do that. (p. 57)

> Raymond Chandler, "The Simple Art of Murder," in The Atlantic Monthly, *Vol. 174, No. 6, December, 1944, pp. 53-9.**

ELLERY QUEEN [PSEUDONYM OF FREDERIC DANNAY AND MANFRED BENNINGTON LEE]   (essay date 1951)

[*Ellery Queen was the joint pseudonym of Frederic Dannay and Manfred B. Lee. The two wrote a distinguished body of mystery fiction portraying the adventures of the detective Ellery Queen, contributing some of the world's finest mystery and detective fiction to the genre. In the following excerpt, Dannay and Lee highlight Sayers's achievement in fusing the detective story with the novel of manners and praise* Lord Peter Views the Body *as one of the most important books in the mystery field.*]

Miss Sayers has done more to add literary tone to crime fiction than most of her contemporaries, and it is to her infinite credit that she attempts to wed the detective story to the legitimate novel of manners with the utmost deliberation—almost, it might be said, with the malice aforethought. While some critics share the belief that she "has now almost ceased to be a first-rate detective writer and has become an exceedingly snobbish popular novelist," one should not forget Howard Haycraft's subtle compliment to her larger aims—"her very errors do her honor" [see *TCLC*, Vol. 2].

> Ellery Queen [pseudonym of Frederic Dannay and Manfred Bennington Lee], "The First Moderns: 'Lord Peter Views the Body'," in their Queen's Quorum: A History of the Detective-Crime Short Story As Revealed by the 106 Most Important Books Published in This Field since 1845, *Little, Brown and Company, 1951, p. 82.*

DUDLEY FITTS   (essay date 1955)

[*An American poet, critic, educator, and translator, Fitts is one of the twentieth century's foremost translators from the ancient Greek. He has been especially praised for his modern colloquial translations of Aritsophanes's plays, particularly* The Birds. *In the following excerpt, Fitts discusses Sayers's errors with rhyme and diction in her translation of Dante's* Divina Commedia. *For further discussion of Sayers's translations, see the excerpt by Janet Hitchman (1975).*]

Miss Sayers' success with the first two *cantiche* of [*The Comedy of Dante Alighieri the Florentine*] is considerable. She is scholarly enough and discriminating enough to give us what must be given as background and commentary for this difficult poem. I find her most effective when she is simply informative; her philosophical and theological reflections are too unfocused for my taste, too sentimentally patronizing in the homiletic manner of Mr. C. S. Lewis.

She is not, I should say, an accomplished poet; but she does handle verse intelligently, and there are moments when she seems to me singularly happy in suggesting the tone-changes, the special nuances, of certain passages. The general progression, the cumulative sense of journey, the grand design—here, in inevitable diminution, is the clear apprehension agreeably transmuted for us. I am almost persuaded: and yet!

Miss Sayers has chosen to write in *terza rima*, the stanza of the original. In Italian, a language that practically rhymes itself, this form is normal and uncoercive. In English, however, which does not rhyme spontaneously, it is either a fatal clog or a distorting force. Miss Sayers is frequently successful with it in neutral passages where dilution or perversion is of minor importance, but in the taut, hard-driving passages she is pushed into all sorts of odd positions.

The triumphs may well be tours de force, but they are won at the expense of constant disasters that need not have happened if the second line of each tercet had been left blank, with no attempt to reproduce the coronal rhyme. Her second failure, just as serious, proceeds from her faulty diction. She has considered, as she tells us, the "whole range of intelligible English speech," and she has decided, correctly, to employ any word or phrase, however "unpoetic," to solve the problem of the moment. I could not be more in agreement.

We find, however, that she really thinks that "the intimate *tu* and the ceremonial *voi*" can be rendered by English pronouns. And so we get "thou," which is so ceremonial in English that it has become comic, and, of course, brings all its hideous verb forms. And when this ceremonial discord coincides with even a mild colloquialism, like,

> O me, Angel! how art thou
> changed! they said;
> Nor 'tother nor which! nor
> single nor a pair!,

a kind of linguistic delirium sets in. Or a cantankerous flatness. Unhappily, these faults are so nearly pervasive that they reduce the impact of a work generously conceived and lovingly elaborated.

> Dudley Fitts, "An Urge to Make Dante Known," in The New York Times Book Review, November 6, 1955, p. 59.

C. S. LEWIS (essay date 1958)

[*Lewis is considered one of the foremost Christian and mythopoeic authors of the twentieth century. Indebted principally to George MacDonald, G. K. Chesterton, Charles Williams, and the writers of ancient Norse myths, he is regarded as a formidable logician and Christian polemicist, a perceptive literary critic, and—most highly—as a writer of fantasy literature. Lewis also held instructoral posts at Oxford and Cambridge, where he was an acknowledged authority on medieval and Renaissance literature. A traditionalist in his approach to life and art, he opposed the modern movement in literary criticism toward biographical and psychological interpretation. In place of this, Lewis practiced and propounded a theory of criticism that stresses the importance of the author's intent, rather than the reader's presuppositions and prejudices. Like Charles Williams, Lewis was a friend of Sayers and a member of the Oxford Christians, a literary group with which Sayers herself was occasionally associated. In the following excerpt from a panegyric he wrote for Sayers's memorial service (but was unable to deliver), Lewis discusses his friend's life and work.*]

The variety of Dorothy Sayers's work makes it almost impossible to find anyone who can deal properly with it all. Charles Williams might have done so; I certainly can't. It is embarrassing to admit that I am no great reader of detective stories: embarrassing because, in our present state of festering intellectual class consciousness, the admission might be taken as a boast. It is nothing of the sort: I respect, though I do not much enjoy, that severe and civilized form, which demands much fundamental brain work of those who write in it and assumes as its background uncorrupted and unbrutalised methods of criminal investigation. Prigs have put it about that Dorothy in later life was ashamed of her 'tekkies' and hated to hear them mentioned. A couple of years ago my wife asked her if this was true and was relieved to hear her deny it. She had stopped working in that genre because she felt she had done all she could with it. And indeed, I gather, a full process of development had taken place. I have heard it said that Lord Peter is the only imaginary detective who ever grew up—grew from the Duke's son, the fabulous amorist, the scholar swashbuckler, and connoisseur of wine, into the increasingly human character, not without quirks and flaws, who loves and marries, and is nursed by, Harriet Vane. Reviewers complained that Miss Sayers was falling in love with her hero. On which a better critic remarked to me, 'It would be truer to say she was falling out of love with him; and ceased fondling a girl's dream—if she had ever done so—and began inventing a man.'

There is in reality no cleavage between the detective stories and her other works. In them, as in it, she is first and foremost the craftsman, the professional. She always saw herself as one who has learned a trade, and respects it, and demands respect for it from others. . . . She aspired to be, and was, at once a popular entertainer and a conscientious craftsman: like (in her degree) Chaucer, Cervantes, Shakespeare, or Molière. I have an idea that, with a very few exceptions, it is only such writers who matter much in the long run. 'One shows one's greatness', says Pascal, 'not by being at an extremity but by being simultaneously at two extremities.' Much of her most valuable thought about writing was embodied in *The Mind of the Maker:* a book which is still too little read. It has faults. But books about writing by those who have themselves written viable books are too rare and too useful to be neglected.

For a Christian, of course, this pride in one's craft, which so easily withers into pride in oneself, raises a fiercely practical problem. It is delightfully characteristic of her extremely robust and forthright nature that she soon lifted this problem to the fully conscious level and made it the theme of one of her major works. The architect in *The Zeal of Thy House* is at the outset the incarnation of—and therefore doubtless the *Catharsis* from—a possible Dorothy whom the actual Dorothy Sayers was offering for mortification. His disinterested zeal for the work itself has her full sympathy. But she knows that, without grace, it is a dangerous virtue; little better than the 'artistic conscience' which every Bohemian bungler pleads as a justification for neglecting his parents, deserting his wife, and cheating his creditors. From the beginning personal pride is entering into the architect's character: the play records his costly salvation.

As the detective stories do not stand quite apart, so neither do the explicitly religious works. She never sank the artist and entertainer in the evangelist. The very astringent (and admirable) preface to *The Man Born to Be King*, written when she had lately been assailed with a great deal of ignorant and spiteful obloquy, makes the point of view defiantly clear. 'It was assumed', she writes, 'that my object in writing was "to do good". But that was in fact not my object at all, though it was quite properly the object of those who commissioned the plays in the first place. My object was *to tell that story* to the best of my ability, within the medium at my disposal—in short, to make as good a work of art as I could. For a work of art that is not good and true *in art* is not true and good in any other respect. (pp. 91-3)

The architectonic qualities of this dramatic sequence will hardly be questioned. Some tell me they find it vulgar. Perhaps they do not quite know what they mean; perhaps they have not fully digested the answers to this charge given in the preface. Or perhaps it is simply not 'addressed to their condition'. Different souls take their nourishment in different vessels. For my own part, I have re-read it in every Holy Week since it first appeared, and never re-read it without being deeply moved.

Her later years were devoted to translation. The last letter I ever wrote to her was in acknowledgement of her *Song of Roland,* and I was lucky enough to say that the end-stopped lines and utterly unadorned style of the original must have made it a far harder job than Dante. Her delight at this (surely not very profound) remark suggested that she was rather starved for rational criticism. I do not think this one of her most successful works. It is too violently colloquial for my palate; but, then, she knew far more Old French than I. In her Dante the problem is not quite the same. It should always be read in conjunction with the paper on Dante which she contributed to the *Essays Presented to Charles Williams.* There you get the first impact of Dante on a mature, a scholarly, and an extremely independent mind. That impact determined the whole character of her translation. She had been startled and delighted by something in Dante for which no critic, and no earlier translator, had prepared her: his sheer narrative impetus, his frequent homeliness, his high comedy, his grotesque buffoonery. These qualities she was determined to preserve at all costs. If, in order to do so, she had to sacrifice sweetness or sublimity, then sacrificed they should be. Hence her audacities in both language and rhythm.

We must distinguish this from something rather discreditable that has been going on of recent years—I mean the attempt of some translators from Greek and Latin to make their readers believe that the *Aeneid* is written in service slang and that Attic Tragedy uses the language of the streets. What such versions implicitly assert is simply false; but what Dorothy was trying to represent by her audacities is quite certainly there in Dante. The question is how far you can do it justice without damage to other qualities which are also there and thus misrepresenting the *Comedy* as much in one direction as fussy, Miltonic old Cary had done in the other. In the end, I suppose, one comes to a choice of evils. No version can give the whole of Dante. So at least I said when I read her *Inferno.* But, then, when I came to the *Purgatorio,* a little miracle seemed to be happening. She had risen, just as Dante himself rose in his second part: growing richer, more liquid, more elevated. Then first I bagan to have great hopes of her *Paradiso.* Would she go on rising? Was it possible? Dared we hope?

Well. She died instead; went, as one may in all humility hope, to learn more of Heaven that even the *Paradiso* could tell her. For all she did and was, for delight and instruction, for her militant loyalty as a friend, for courage and honesty, for the richly feminine qualities which showed through a port and manner superficially masculine and even gleefully ogreish— let us thank the Author who invented her. (pp. 93-5)

C. S. Lewis, ''A Panegyric for Dorothy L. Sayers,'' *in his* On Stories and Other Essays on Literature, *edited by Walter Hooper, Harcourt Brace Jovanovich, Publishers, 1982, pp. 91-5.*

PETER DICKINSON (essay date 1964)

[*Dickinson is a British novelist, poet, and former editor of* Punch *who is considered an eclectic and original writer, respected for both his young-adult fantasies and adult mysteries. He has expanded the limits of both genres, blending his imagination with a strong historical and cultural sensibility and demonstrating his interest in anthropology through his emphasis on the importance of custom and ritual. Dickinson is praised for his storytelling ability, and for the economy and liveliness of his prose style. In the following excerpt from a review of* The Lord Peter Omnibus, *he praises Sayers's Lord Peter stories for their power to prompt repeated re-readings over the course of years.*]

Between 1923 and 1937 Dorothy Sayers wrote eleven full-length Wimsey detective stories, starting with *Strong Poison* and ending with *Busman's Honeymoon.* This makes quite a compact and coherent body of work, developing along standard lines, from the early euphoria, through a workmanlike, trade-learning period, to a group of high, classic whodunits, which were followed by a romantic decline. The same course can be traced, more drawn-out, in the work of Miss Sayers's nearest rival, Margery Allingham. . . .

Rereadability is a curious thing. It does not necessarily depend on the literary value of the book. There are certain writers— Buchan, Conan Doyle, C. S. Forester, Trollope, for instance— who are almost infinitely rereadable, much more so than Proust or Joyce or even the borderline Dickens. This may have something to do with the reader: those lazy-minded enough to prefer reading what they've already read also prefer a certain sort of book. But Miss Sayers is in this class. . . .

This is doubly odd. One wouldn't have thought that an art-form dependent on a surprise ending would stand much repetition. . . . And one wouldn't have thought that one could bear to read another syllable of Wimsey's omniscient superiority. It is possible that Miss Sayers would have argued, as Ian Fleming does about Bond, that her creation was intended to have a few unsympathetic traits, but (as with Bond/Fleming) it is hard not to believe that she adored him. . . .

On the other hand, this bizarre passion plays an important part in creating an essential element of rereadability: Barchester, Hornblower's navy, Holmes's London are remote worlds, ideal for escapists, and Wimseyland, with its inverted, Edwardian vulgarity, in which the only claret is Lafite and the only Sauterne Yquem (''it's rather decent,'' comments his Lordship) and the only books worth collecting are incunabula, must have been just as remote, even when Miss Sayers was writing. In its weird light the appalling passages, such as Wimsey's breakdown over having helped to hang a man at the end of *Busman's Honeymoon,* became tolerable.

That isn't enough, of course. The great, shamus-riddled world of the Chandler-imitators is as remote and weird as anything Miss Sayers dreamed up, but very few of their books are re-readable. With her, as a person walks round the grounds for the second time, there is the continual astonishment at the amount of hard work she put in. The jokes are good jokes, for the most part; the backgrounds are carefully thought out and worked in; and the plots are both ingenious and practical, often involving both a legal and medical complexity. She was a great stopper of holes; nearly always, about halfway through the book, there are long passages of dialogue in which Wimsey and Parker, or Wimsey and Harriet, thresh round various other solutions to the problem, elaborating and discarding, but generally showing why they won't work. Even in [*The Lord Peter Omnibus,*] which contains three of the minor works (*Unnatural*

Death, The Unpleasantness at the Bellonna Club and *Clouds of Witness*), she continually tests and examines the structure of her plot in a way which few modern thriller-writers would dare to.

Peter Dickinson, "The Great Rereadable," in Punch, Vol. CCXLVI, No. 6457, June 10, 1964, p. 871.

THOMAS HOWARD   (essay date 1970)

[*An American educator, critic, and essayist, Howard has written important critical studies on the works of C. S. Lewis and Charles Williams, in addition to his own spiritual autobiography,* Christ the Tiger *(1968). In the following excerpt he favorably reviews* Christian Letters to a Post-Christian World, *noting with approval the essays' tone of unabashed confidence in Christianity.*]

Dorothy Sayers might waggishly be called the Carry Nation of secularism, and especially of the obsequious attempts on the part of the modern church to make its dogmas tasty to a world that has no taste whatever for its wares. She had nothing but scorn and contempt for the mumbling apology offered by secularist theology for a towering drama of events that is at least the most exciting thing ever thought of, in her view, quite apart from whether or not one *believes* it. Roderick Jellema's selection of her essays [*Christian Letters to A Post-Christian World*] constitutes a series of *frappes* on behalf of the robust Christian orthodoxy.

In one essay, for instance, called **"The Greatest Drama Ever Staged,"** after having given a lively account of the Christian story, she finishes "So that is the outline of the official story— the tale of the time when God was the underdog and got beaten. . . . This is the dogma we find so dull—this terrifying drama of which God is the victim and hero. If this is dull, then what, in Heaven's name, is worthy to be called exciting? The people who hanged Christ never, to do them justice, accused Him of being a bore. . . . We have very efficiently pared the claws of the Lion of Judah certified Him 'meek and mild.'"

There are several essays of this sort, plumping hard and brilliantly for an unabashed orthodoxy. There are essays on the subject which seemed to lie at the center of her concerns—that of the *imago Dei* shining especially through man the creating creature. There are studies of Dante and Charles Williams, in which the notion of Christian imagination is thrown into relief against the rather bleak background of secularist criticism.

In one very funny spoof of modern Biblical scholarship, she crawls myopically through Conan Doyle's "The Red-Headed League," bringing to that story the canons critics have brought to bear on the record of the Evangelists. The most amusing essay in the book is one in which she offers a liturgical calendar, revised for the benefit of post-Enlightenment man. (pp. 40-1)

Thomas Howard, "Old Truths and Modern Myths," in The New York Times Book Review, March 15, 1970, pp. 40-1.

JULIAN SYMONS   (essay date 1972)

[*Symons holds two highly praised literary reputations: that of the serious biographer and that of the detective novelist. His popular biographies of Charles Dickens, Thomas Carlyle, and his brother A.J.A. Symons are considered excellent introductions to those writers. Symons is better known, however, for his crime novels, particularly* The 31st of February *(1950) and* The Progress of a Crime *(1960), which was an Edgar Allan Poe Award from the*

Mystery Writers of America in 1960. In the following excerpt he concludes, after studying several of Sayers's novels, that the author's short stories are more carefully written and enjoyable than her longer fiction.]

Of Dorothy (Leigh) Sayers . . . it is not easy to write fairly. For her wholehearted admirers, a diminished but still considerable band, she is the finest detective-story writer of the twentieth century; to those less enthusiastic, her work is long-winded and ludicrously snobbish. The early books are as ingenious as the later ones, and differ from them chiefly in her attitude to Lord Peter Wimsey. It is from a point of view a long way short of idolatry that they are discussed here.

Her merits were rare among the crime writers between the wars. Her mind was clear and incisive, and she had read very widely in crime literature. Her introductions to the first two volumes of *Detection, Mystery and Horror,* published in 1928 and 1931 show an acute intelligence at work. She was the first writer to place five of Poe's stories rather than three within the canon, the first to acclaim the merits of Le Fanu in this field. Everything she says calls for respect, even though some of it may prompt disagreement. And in reading her novels and short stories it is impossible not to admire the careful craftsmanship with which they have been made. Her plots are organized with care; the details she produces about a means of murder are often original and always carefully researched. She took pains to make sure that the details in her stories were right, or at least she tried to make sure, not always with success. In the best of her early novels, *Unnatural Death* . . ., murders are committed by the injection of an air bubble into an artery, which stopped the circulation and so caused an apparently natural death. A medical opinion given a few years later was that although the entry of air into the circulation *may* cause death, this "would be unlikely with a hypodermic syringe, which rarely holds more than 2-3 cc." It would be pernickety, though, to condemn a book which is a compendium of clever touches (who else has thought of making not one set of false footprints, but three, as the villain does here?) on such a ground. The method was at least possible, and it would be ungenerous to demand certainty. *The Unpleasantness at the Bellona Club* . . . is partly concerned with the decision about an inheritance involved by the question of whether General Fentiman or Lady Dormer was the first to die, and similarly cunning strokes can be found in most Sayers books.

The case against Dorothy Sayers rests chiefly upon the same evidence that admirers would cite in her favor. It is based upon the way in which she wrote, and upon the character of her detective. Edmund Wilson called a later novel, *The Nine Tailors,* "one of the dullest books I have ever encountered in any field" [see *TCLC,* Vol. 2], and there can be no doubt that by any reasonable standards applied to writing, as distinct from plotting, she was pompous and boring. Every book contains an enormous amount of padding, in the form of conversations which, although they may have a distinct connection with the plot, are spread over a dozen pages where the point could be covered in as many lines. This might be forgivable if what was said had some intrinsic interest, but these dialogues are carried on between stereotyped figures (her English yokels are particularly to be deplored, with facetious professional men running them close) who have nothing at all to say, but only a veiled clue to communicate. These people, like the clubmen in the *Bellona Club* or the minor upper-class characters in *Clouds of Witness* are indeed conceived in the terms of a sketch for *Punch,* and *Unnatural Death* shows her flinching away from anything more serious. The multiple murderess here detests men (she shows an "uncontrollable revulsion of the flesh" when kissed by Wimsey) and has distinct power over clinging women. She is clearly a lesbian, but because of Sayers's inability to convey this, the portrait of her is inadequate. Of course the conventions of the time did not permit description of physical lesbian acts, but there is something coarsely wrong about the way in which this woman first tries to murder Wimsey and then desperately attempts to force herself to make love to him.

It would be charitable to think that Wimsey, like Sheringham, was conceived as a joke, but unhappily there is every indication that Sayers regarded him with the most tender feelings. Lord Peter, the second son of the Duke of Denver, is a caricature of an English aristocrat conceived with an immensely snobbish loving seriousness. His speech strongly resembles that of Bertie Wooster, slightly affected by Arthur Augustus d'Arcy in the *Magnet*. He sometimes wears a monocle, or at least this is a fact sometimes mentioned, and it would seem that it may have been either a real monocle or a powerful magnifying lens. He drops the last letters of words, and says things like "I'll drop in on you later and we'll have a jolly old pow-wow, what?" and asks of a man following him, "Is the fellow a sahib?" At times his self-conscious humor is excruciating. . . . (pp. 107-10)

The development of Dorothy Sayers can be charted best from an essay she wrote in 1937, in which she says that she had always wanted her books to be "novel[s] of manners instead of pure crossword puzzle[s]," so moving back to the tradition of Collins and Le Fanu. She had "indulged in a little 'good writing' here and there" and had been encouraged by its reception. With this encouragement, she had introduced a love element into *Strong Poison* . . . , produced a "criticism of life" in *Murder Must Advertise* . . . , and at last in *Gaudy Night* . . . had as she thought succeeded in "choosing a plot that should exhibit intellectual integrity as the one great permanent value in an emotionally unstable world" and so managed to say "the thing that, in a confused way, I had been wanting to say all my life."

There is a breath-taking gap here between intention and achievement. Wimsey remains essentially unchanged. He still says things like "What-ho! that absolutely whangs the nail over the crumpet," and a snobbishness outrageous even for Sayers has provided him with a pedigree and a family history which, together with a long biographical note, act as preface to the new editions of each book. The books themselves show, with the exception of the lively *Murder Must Advertise*, an increasing pretentiousness, a dismal sentimentality, and a slackening of the close plotting that had been her chief virtue. *Gaudy Night* is essentially a "woman's novel" full of the most tedious pseudo-serious chat between the characters that goes on for page after page. Mrs. Q. D. Leavis seems perfectly right in placing this later Sayers beside Marie Corelli and Ouida, and in saying that she performed the function of "giving the impression of intellectual activity to readers who would very much dislike that kind of exercise if it was actually presented to them," [see *TCLC*, Vol. 2]. Sayers is hardly likely to have agreed with this attack, but after *Busman's Honeymoon* . . . , which was frankly subtitled "A love story with detective interruptions," she turned away from the hero of whom she had said, " I can see no end to Peter this side of the grave." In the last twenty years of her life, she wrote no more detective novels. When, a few years before her death, her American publishers asked for a new introduction to accompany an omnibus volume, she refused it, saying that she had written the

books only to make money and had no further interest in them. (pp. 128-29)

Dorothy Sayers's short stories treat their subjects with an ease that most of the novels lack, and they are free from the worst excesses of Wimsey. Within the space of thirty pages, there is mercifully no room for Wimsey-Bunter dialogue, although there is still some stuff that must seem strange to those who regard Sayers as a semi-realistic writer. "Go back to your War Office and say I will not give you the formula" cries a French Royalist Count to Wimsey. "If war should come between our countries—which may God avert!—I will be found on the side of France." This is from a preposterous but rather enjoyable story called **"The Bibulous Business of a Matter of Taste,"** in which three Wimseys appear at a French château and have their credentials tested by a prolonged session of vintage and date naming. The collection that contains this story, *Lord Peter Views the Body* . . . , includes also the genuinely terrifying **"The Man with the Copper Fingers"** and **"The Adventurous Exploit of the Cave of Ali Baba,"** which opens with a newspaper account of Wimsey's death, followed by his enlistment in some unspecified secret society. *Hangman's Holiday* . . . includes the clever **"The Image in the Mirror"** and a funny, quite uncharacteristic Sayers (no detective appears in it) called **"The Man Who Knew How."** *In The Teeth of the Evidence* . . . offers two good stories in which Wimsey appears rather mutedly and several odds and ends, including the delightful **"The Inspiration of Mr. Budd."** Altogether, the short stories suggest that Dorothy Sayers might have been a better and livelier crime writer if she had not fallen in love with her detective. (p. 170)

Julian Symons, in his Mortal Consequences: A History—From the Detective Story to the Crime Novel, *Harper & Row, Publishers, 1972, 269 p.*

MARGOT PETERS AND AGATE NESAULE KROUSE (essay date 1974)

[*In the following excerpt, Peters and Krouse uncover sexist characterizations and situations in the Wimsey novels. For further discussion of Sayer's female characters, see the excerpt by Virginia B. Morris (1983).*]

Critics of the British detective novel have generally agreed that it is a conservative genre. The detective functions as the guardian of the status quo: he brings to justice criminals who have threatened middle-class stability by threatening the foundation of that stability—money. Not surprisingly, the genre itself is a product of the nineteenth century, for only this century saw the triumph of a class into which an outsider could buy his way—as he could not into the aristocracy—if only he could get his hands on capital. The getting of capital, therefore, motivates most criminals to murder in detective fiction, and the detective is worshiped by the middle classes who understand that their wealth and position will eventually be safe in his hands.

Given the conservatism of the genre, one can further predict that stereotypes of character will seldom be violated. Thus, upon opening an Allingham, a Sayers, or a Christie, one finds many of the familiar sexist attitudes toward women that one might otherwise expect these women writers to avoid. Christie offends the least, but still offends.

Allingham and Sayers have a fetish in common that makes their fiction even more conservative than usual: hero-worship of the aristocracy. To make one's detective a policeman like

Maigret, or a private detective like Holmes or Poirot, is realistic. To envision Britain being saved by Albert Campion and Lord Peter Wimsey, two highfalutin aristocrats who run about with their butlers, limousines, monocles, and hundred-year-old bottles of port, puts the detective novels of Allingham and Sayers cloud-high in the realms of reactionary fantasy. This is surely the reason why these intelligent women sin in their depiction of women: where you have knights you've got to have ladies. (p. 144)

Like Allingham, Sayers worships aristocracy. Although Peter Wimsey is odd-looking, garrulous, silly, and often downright asinine, he commands immediate worshipful respect from country yokels, servants, and single working women. Such respect for "his Lordship" does not reflect Sayers's awareness that the internalized inferiority produced by the class system is painful: instead, she treats her working class people as comic. Their naïve conversations are calculated to make the gentle reader smile indulgently.

In this conservative world, women have their place. Lord Peter keeps the "Cattery," an office of single, poor, but highly competent women who do the tedious drudgery necessary for successful detection: they type, answer fraudulent advertisements, and accept domestic and clerical positions to collect evidence. They also show great resourcefulness and courage. In *Strong Poison,* for example, Miss Climpson insinuates herself into the Wayburn household by ingeniously faking her powers as a medium. At considerable risk and danger to herself, Miss Murchinson picks a lock to memorize the contents of a legal file. Wimsey munificently rewards one and all with everything but public recognition. After Miss Climpson has stoutly held out against a jury determined to convict Harriet Vane, Wimsey promises her a dinner and even greater delights: in spite of a heavy growth of beard, he will take her around the corner and kiss her. He never indicates that the successes for which he is repeatedly congratulated rest on the work of women; nor does Sayers remind us of that fact on appropriate occasions.

Sayers deserves some credit for creating Harriet Vane, an intelligent, spirited, and successful professional writer, a woman who could be Wimsey's equal if not his superior. Harriet even has some sexual autonomy: she has lived with Philip Boyles without being married to him, and she offers to do the same with Wimsey. On closer examination, however, Harriet is not a feminist ideal: she does not appear very often, nor is she treated quite fairly by Sayers; her class and her sex make her impotent, a realistic enough view. Furthermore, Sayers celebrates rather than deplores Harriet's gradual progress into insignificance as a two-line entry in his lordship's biography: "*Married,* 1935; Harriet Deborah Vane, *daughter* of Henry Vane M.D." Harriet's books are omitted, but not her baby, "*one son* (Bredon Delagardie Peter), *born* 1936." Wimsey's bibliography, his coat of arms, and even his clubs rate three lines each.

One reason Harriet resists marriage to Peter through three entire novels is that she fears the loss of her independence, as well she might. (pp. 147-48)

Harriet also resists marriage because she feels unworthy of Peter, an opinion in which Sayers seems to concur. Although Peter claims to love Harriet's integrity, intelligence, and ability to stick to the point, he high-handedly completes a sonnet she has had trouble with and left forgotten in a notebook. Though no novelist himself, he tells her how to write her current novel, and Harriet compliantly follows his advice with good results.

In fact, she is pleased because she thinks that shows he takes her work seriously and is not the protective male: "He was being about as protective as a can opener" (*Gaudy Night*). But she is simply unable to see both sides of a bad penny, which she mistakes for a can opener. Even though Harriet has spent six months in residence at Shrewsbury Women's College (a name as unfortunate as the "Cattery"), she is unable to solve the mystery of vandalism and poison-pen letters; Peter walks in and solves the problem in a matter of days. Sayers comments omnisciently that Harriet Vane—scholar, novelist, and respected intellectual equal of the brilliant women scholars at Shrewsbury—is simply not as smart as Wimsey. "Peter's intelligence could always make rings around her own more slowly moving wits" (*Gaudy Night*). No wonder Harriet's sense of self-esteem is extremely low. She even goes so far as to apologize for dying: remembering that Peter will be annoyed if she gets killed obeying a mysterious phone call, she stops on her way to possible death to scribble an apology to Peter for her rash decision.

Harriet's independence is often only a grimace or a mannerism. Even her sexual autonomy is finally negligible. Wimsey magnanimously ignores her aberration from conventional sexual morality, and he is right in doing so. By the conventions of romance, Harriet's experience can be discounted because she did not love the man. In fact, Sayers makes it clear that Harriet didn't even have any fun. Wimsey loves her and inevitably masters her. The order of his major gifts is aptly suggestive: first a dog-collar for protection, then an antique chess set for beauty rather than utility since Harriet is an indifferent player, and finally, of course, a house. A happy ending.

Sayers's one redeeming quality is her accurate recording of the problems—but not the victories—of single, intelligent, independent women. She includes a number of details that are implicitly feminist: the poverty of women's colleges, an observation which would have pleased Virginia Woolf; the self-doubt of intellectual single women; the wasted talents of a brilliant scholar married to a farmer; the necessity that women make a choice no man has to make between marriage and career. In other novels Sayers can even make feminist points through humor: a corpse sits unnoticed for hours at Wimsey's club—a wonderful joke about the liveliness of these male sanctuaries (*The Unpleasantness at the Bellona Club* . . .). In view of such details, one is tempted to forgive all, but one has no right to do so. Sayers does treat Harriet Vane and other intellectual, independent women shabbily, in striking contrast to her excessive admiration for Wimsey. It is also noteworthy that Sayers's only committed feminist, Miss Hillyard, is interested in the rights of women and critical of male privileges simply because she has no man of her own: We've heard that one too often before. (pp. 148-49)

Margot Peters and Agate Nesaule Krouse, "Women and Crime: Sexism in Allingham, Sayers, and Christie," in Southwest Review, *Vol. 59, No. 2, Spring, 1974, pp. 144-52.**

JANET HITCHMAN (essay date 1975)

[*In the following excerpt, Hitchman surveys Sayers's fiction and dramas, concluding with some generally favorable commentary on her translations of Dante's* Divina Commedia. *For further discussion of Sayers's translations, see the excerpt by Dudley Fitts (1955).*]

As the Wimsey books are all detective stories, it is not easy to discuss them without giving away their plots. They are all still in print, and there are many people who like their mystery stories to remain mysteries until the end. . . .

[*Clouds of Witness*] concerns the trial of a peer for murder, and gives a good description of a now obsolete ceremony. The right of a peer to be tried by his peers was abolished later, and probably because of this the book seems much more old-fashioned than its date would suggest. . . . (p. 72)

Clouds of Witness embodies all those things which made critics so furious with Dorothy L. Sayers. Firstly, her snobbery—the whole clue to the mystery is contained in a letter in French which is read to the lords without translation, the assumption being that all members of the upper house were fluent in the language. There is a translation in the book, but one feels it is only there at the publisher's insistence. (p. 73)

Clouds of Witness was followed . . . [by *Unnatural Death* and then] *The Unpleasantness at the Bellona Club*.

This last-named book does more to invoke the disillusion of the twenties than any social tract could do. . . . (p. 74)

The Unpleasantness at the Bellona Club is, in my opinion, one of the best Wimsey books, chiefly because it is straightforward in the telling. It does not go off into side issues, nor is it tainted with the worst of Dorothy's prejudices. It also contains some wildly comic ''Bloomsbury'' dialogue. (pp. 74-5)

The book for which Dorothy is supposed to have done the most meticulous research is *The Nine Tailors*. (pp. 81-2)

The story goes along at a cracking pace, and the book was, deservedly, a runaway best-seller. (p. 85)

If I think *The Nine Tailors* was Dorothy's best book, I find its successor, *Gaudy Night,* certainly her worst. It has quite a good idea behind it, the tracing of a poison pen writer in a women's college—the revenge theme. There are some splendid characters, and some very good isolated scenes. Dorothy herself called it ''an overgrown monster,'' as it is nearly 350 pages long, and adds:

> It is the only book I have written which embodies any kind of ''moral'' and I do feel rather passionately about this business of the integrity of the mind—but there it is—it's the book I wanted to write and I have written it. . . . I wouldn't claim that it was in itself a great work of great literary importance; it is important to me.

The ''integrity of the mind''—but was she exercising that integrity to use the format of a detective novel to preach a sermon? Here was a captive, and captivated, audience, already in love with her characters, and wham! they are hit over the head with a treatise on ultimate truth. There is not even a corpse! Dorothy might have argued that truth should be proclaimed everywhere, and by any means, but her readership felt cheated. That was not likely to encourage people in the search for truth. Along with this theme is Dorothy's perennial highlighting of the damage which can be done by sexually frustrated females. (p. 86)

Looking back over the whole range of the Wimsey books one can see trends in them now which were certainly not apparent to the reader at the time they were written, and may have been only dimly realized by the author. Dorothy needed money, and

The coat of arms of Lord Peter Wimsey, drawn by C. W. Scott-Giles. Copyright 1977 C. W. Scott-Giles. Reproduced by permission of the Estate of C. W. Scott-Giles OBE.

primarily that is why the books were written; but toward the end they became more than ever like morality plays—good against evil, the terrible retribution that evil exacts. She was an upholder of the law, and the law demanded death for the murderer. It is evident that this aspect of her work troubled her conscience, and she meets it head on in the last chapter of *Busman's Honeymoon*. Even then she had to make the murderer full of hatred, unrepentant and uncaring—a person who justly deserved his fate. (p. 111)

[Soon Sayers] found another passion—the theater. She never stood on the edge, but dived right into anything which caught her interest. She adored all the trappings of the stage, picked up the jargon, and worshiped anyone connected with it. (p. 112)

In 1936 Dorothy was approached by the Friends of Canterbury Cathedral to write a play for their festival of 1937. She chose for a subject not one of the better-known bishops or martyrs but William of Sens, the architect who rebuilt the cathedral after the disastrous fire of 1174. It is written in blank verse, and is an exploration of the sin of pride—the pride of William, not for himself, but for his work; his raging zeal for the house of God, missing out God Himself. (p. 113)

The play is well argued, even if it does seem to make God somewhat petty-minded and guilty of the very sin He condemns in William. From the theatrical point of view it is extremely ''actable''—the only jarring note is the dragging in of an unlikely love interest. (p. 114)

The Zeal of Thy House is a splendid play in the genre of religious drama, and it is a pity that it is no longer very highly rated.

Dorothy's Canterbury play of 1939 was not so successful. Called *The Devil to Pay,* it is a version of the Faustus story. What she intended doing was to supply ''some kind of human interpretation to a supernatural legend.'' It was too much ''in the mind'' for the average playgoer and had only a four weeks' run. (pp. 115-16)

Dorothy did not do another stage play until 1946, when she wrote *The Just Vengeance* for Lichfield Cathedral's 750th anniversary. It was directed by Frank Napier, with music composed by Antony Hopkins. It is obviously a play written for a special occasion and a special place, and it never really comes to life. But Queen Mary, who had her accommodation nearby, liked it. . . . [Her last stage play, *The Emperor Constantine*] was anything but successful; I think it has a great many of the faults of the Wimsey books: over-discursive, setting off at angles, hammering home points already made plain and ignoring obscure ones. (p. 116)

Of the radio serial plays title *The Man Born to Be King,* there is little new to be said. They are of a uniform excellence, and they *were* a breakthrough in religious broadcasting. They did bring Christ the Man and Christ the Son of God into the household, speaking a language all could understand. . . . (pp. 136-37)

One cannot but agree that without *The Man Born to Be King,* we should never have reached *Jesus Christ Superstar* via *Godspell*. . . . (p. 137)

That Dante was the last love of [Sayers] life is evident from the great pains she took, not only with the translation, but also with the verification of every fact, studying medieval astronomy and so forth, and even with the actual layout of the books. (p. 155)

It is certainly possible that the reader without formal classical or literary training can learn more about theology, medieval history, and Renaissance Italy from Dorothy L. Sayers's Dante than from any other source. Her introductions and notes alone are more informative than another's scholarly treatise. As to the poetry, how much of it is Sayers and how much Dante, I am unable to judge. . . . (pp. 158-59)

Some lines are, I feel, a little awkward, and the use of certain words questionable in the context. Dorothy said she had tried "to avoid the poles of 'quotha! and 'sez you!'" and I think it was a mistake to make a character in Purgatory speak in what she calls "Border-Scots" because the "dialect bears something of the same relation to English as Provençal does to Italian." It is never wise to write in Scots dialect if you happen not to be a Scot, and in this particular context the effect is dreadful. But some of the lines are beautiful, particularly the rendering of the Lord's Prayer by the penitent Proud in Purgatory. (p. 159)

It was a tragedy that Dorothy was unable to see the final outcome of her last great love affair; for it was that. As much as she had loved any man or friend, she loved Dante, and this love comes through her many articles and essays, through the hundreds of letters she wrote about the work in progress, through the work itself. Whatever its merits or demerits as a translation, a work of scholarship or a poem in its own right, it stands as a monument to this great love. (p. 160)

> Janet Hitchman, *in her* Such a Strange Lady: A Biography of Dorothy L. Sayers, *Harper & Row, Publishers, 1975, 177 p.*

LIONEL BASNEY (essay date 1979)

[*In the following excerpt, Basney emphasizes the pivotal importance of* The Nine Tailors *in Sayers's evolution from mystery writer to novelist, judging it one of her most successful and complex works.*]

[*The Nine Tailors*] was the tenth of Dorothy L. Sayers's 12 mystery novels. It came at a crucial point in her career; according to her own testimony, *Murder Must Advertise* . . . was the first novel in which she approached serious fiction—a "criticism of life" along with the murder, the detection, and Peter Wimsey's charming flippancy. In this she was only partially successful. The novel's analysis of modern commercial motives is clear enough, and congruent with what she would say later in her wartime social commentary. But the thought is not completely integrated with the mystery. The story's excitement, and Lord Peter's charm, seem to float above the heavy business of the theme.

In contrast, the book following *The Nine Tailors, Gaudy Night* . . . , is not a murder mystery at all. Harriet Vane and Oxford dominate the story; Lord Peter proposes, and Harriet accepts, as we knew she would. Plot and theme are thoroughly integrated here; but the whole project is clearly an outright novel, and ought to be judged as such.

Between these books—the murder mystery with theme attached, and the serious novel with mystery attached—came *The Nine Tailors,* the most successful of Sayers's stories at integrating detective interest and a seriously intended "criticism of life." This makes it a definite achievement, one of the very few mystery stories that may be considered an interesting novel as well. A detective story is not often expected to carry intellectual or ethical implication. It is, wrote W. H. Wright, "a complicated and extended puzzle cast in fictional form" in which style and thought are out of place. On the contrary, Sayers's fiction had always had style. In *The Nine Tailors,* moreover, it is the murder mystery's essential ingredient—the murder and its detection—which initiates a coherent and moving statement about the nature of human experience.

Despite this, the book's reputation has always been shallow. Among casual mystery readers it is rumored a masterpiece. Among purists it tends to be dismissed as "that book about campanology." The lore of English change-ringing is, in fact, central to the story, and accounts in part for its instantaneous popularity. But the book is "about" campanology in roughly the same way as *King Lear* is "about" the weather. The storms that whip through the tragedy are impressive stage business; but insofar as they have metaphoric value they are, by definition, about something else. Similarly, bells and bell-ringing are part of the materials of *The Nine Tailors,* which is clearly about something else altogether.

The book's real impact arises not from its materials but from skillful invention and construction; Sayers succeeded in making both narrative momentum and conceptual substance flow naturally from the same set of circumstances. The novel's deepest concerns are functions of its perfection as a murder mystery. (pp. 23-4)

The plot satisfies beautifully the two main requirements of a mystery "gimmick": it is virtually unguessable, and utterly convincing. In the best tradition of detective writing, it turns on a bit of evidence which has been unmistakably present throughout the story, and has been ignored for very familiarity. The murder is committed by no one, or rather by several people, as innocently and indifferently as if it were a natural catastrophe. The murderers are nine bell ringers, who get their man by ringing an eight-hour peal in the church of Fenchurch St. Paul. Their victim, tied in the bell chamber itself, can neither escape nor make his presence known. He is killed by the anatomical effects of long-continued noise in the closed space of the belfry. The people responsible for his death are ignorant of his presence; the people responsible for his presence have no part in the peal that kills him; the direct agents of death are the bells, which do nothing that is not mechanically dictated to them by the skilled but unknowing hands below. (p. 24)

It is, to say the least, an unusual crime. But in judging it we must distinguish between the rules of detective writing and its normal conventions. Sayers has carefully obeyed the rules; the solution to the mystery is always at hand. The murder is no more technical than homicide by an unknown aboriginal poison, and a good deal more credible than homicide by a slingshot icicle (this is not an invented example). The book contains a number of suspects, and no "Australian cousins" turning up at the last moment to solve an otherwise insoluble crime. If Wimsey's solution of the mystery is finally somewhat by chance, he does solve a number of subsidiary mysteries by the normal route of clues and logic; too, the final discovery of things by a concurrence of events beyond Wimsey's foresight is fully in line with a story that began with coincidence, and contributes importantly to the meaning of the whole tale.

On the other hand, Sayers rode hard but confidently over a number of mystery writing's conventions. First, Wimsey is as much involved in the death as the other bell ringers. Here we see Sayers arranging ahead of time for Wimsey's customary loss of detachment. Unless, like Chesterton's Father Brown, he has a special moral vocation, the classical detective tends to remain "objective," personally detached from the crimes to be investigated. Holmes himself is a "consulting detective" whose professionalism guarantees his neutrality; he is there to solve puzzles. But Wimsey is in this affair from beginning to end, robbed involuntarily of his detective's distance and objectivity. His responsibility for the death in the belfry is immediate; it is not a matter of empathy, or of delicate social situations, as when he must investigate friends or family, or even of personal sympathy with the murderer. It is a matter of complicity; his hands are as red as anyone's.

Second, and perhaps even more important, there is no single murderer on whom all the guilt of murder may be laid. The scapegoat theory of murder mysteries will not work here: no individual can expiate society's corruption by being executed. Further, none of the people involved with the murder has a murderer's conscious guilt to hide. They are all, in various ways, innocent and responsible at the same time. Again Sayers violates a convention. As Chesterton wrote: "The chief difficulty [with the mystery novel] is that the detective story is, after all, a drama of masks and not of faces. It depends on men's false characters rather than their real characters." Sayers made the same observation more than once in her criticism of the form. But in *The Nine Tailors* this is not true, or it is true only in limited fashion. The true murderers have nothing to hide, being unconscious of their deed. They therefore wear no masks. We live and move among ordinary men who have killed one of their kind, and we see their real faces. Wimsey sees them too, and becomes their friend—is, in the essential sense, one of them.

The death's third consequence is not in violation of a convention, but requires the special use of one. Some varieties of the detective story—particularly those featuring a scientist or policeman—depend upon esoteric knowledge for solutions. The murder by unknown poison cannot be explained by a layman. Sometimes the detective's display of knowledge seems miraculous, solving an utterly opaque mystery in a way no reader could have done; in these cases it is a defect in the story's

construction. *The Nine Tailors* appeals to unusual knowledge, the lore of change-ringing. But the information is not sprung on us, nor is it Wimsey's long-secret specialty come suddenly to light. Wimsey learns about the bells from a pamphlet quoted in the text, and so may we. Finally, moreover, the technicalities of change-ringing are not necessary to the central mystery, though Sayers uses them to solve subordinate ones (here she is scrupulously fair) and to remind us of the bells' presence and importance.

The murder actually occurs by force of cumulative coincidence. But no one knows this, and as a result Sayers is free to heighten the mystery by any means available. For this purpose the bells provide an almost inexhaustible source of eerie suggestion. Her specific technique is a discreet touch of pathetic fallacy. Have the bells some dim preternatural consciousness? Several characters testify to their strangeness; they seem almost alive. What Sayers is doing is equivocating about the agents and meaning of the murder. (pp. 25-6)

In the business of detection, like most of Sayers's books, *The Nine Tailors* is most satisfactory. But its special interest . . . arises when this business impinges on deeper thematic concerns. How are the two levels to be united? One tactic for this is Sayers' use of a consciously literary, allusive style. In *The Mind of the Maker*, for instance, Sayers assembled 10 quotations which "were obviously hovering in my memory when I wrote a phrase in *The Nine Tailors*." The passage describes the church roof as Wimsey stands beneath:

> Incredibly aloof, flinging back the light in a dusky shimmer of bright hair and gilded outspread wings, soared the ranked angels, cherubim and seraphim, choir over choir, from corbel and hammerbeam, floating face to face uplifted.

It is a Paradisal vision; it quiets even the invincibly secular Wimsey. Behind it Sayers ranges quotations from the Bible, Milton's *Nativity Ode* ("The cherubick host in thousand guires"), Keats, Browning, T. S. Eliot, and Donne ("a bracelot of bright hair"). Though she modestly points out the disparity between sources and use, the allusions have something concrete to do with the passage's excitement. The allusive richness images an aesthetic excellence which is itself the image of a deeper exultation.

Another example, unconfessed, is more interesting because it is not part of a descriptive set piece:

> The air was so heavy with water, that not till they had passed Frog's Bridge did they hear the sweet, dull jangle of sound that told them that the ringers were practising their Christmas peal; it drifted through the streaming rain with an aching and intolerable melancholy, like the noise of the bells of a drowned city pulsing up through the overwhelming sea.

Along with the Atlantis image and (perhaps) a glance toward Claude Debussy's *La Cathedrale engloutie*, the passage is enriched by its deliberate echoing of *Hamlet* III.i.162 ("Like sweet bells jangled, out of tune and harsh"), itself parodied in its own century by Thomas Shadwell (*The Virtuoso*, 1676). The passage seems to mingle archetypes: bell, temple, flood, sea. Where Sayers uses Biblical quotation or style, this archetypal depth also appears. . . . "And over all, the bells tumbled and wrangled, shouting their alarm across the country. . . .

awake! make haste! save yourselves! The deep waters have gone over us!"

That the novel's style can open out to this sort of connotation does not detract from its more usual clear, witty narrative tone. The allusions undergird the style, at crucial points giving us to know that the story goes deeper than its surface bustle. But this stylistic development of certain of the story's features is also essential to the significance of the murder mystery itself. Sayers's use of a semipastoral village setting connects the murder with a representative human community; suggestions about religious mystery, as in the image of the bells and the Biblical allusions, help to work out the murder's ethical complication. For the murder was, in a sense, a corporate action of the community in its human agents both conscious and unconscious of the circumstances, and in the bells, which are an image for the village's common life. To this, religious allusion adds a delicate if undefinable sense of purpose. The bells seem to be implying something else, an impersonal justice beyond the capacities of any of the humans to grasp. (pp. 29-31)

It is in the community . . . that the murder's ambiguities come to rest. The community is responsible. Here also we come to Sayers's basic theme and her most striking alteration of detective story convention. As W. H. Auden wrote in his fine essay, "The Guilty Vicarage" (1946), the discovery of a murderer usually leads society from a state of apparent innocence to one of true innocence. Evil is identified and rooted out, because responsibility for it is placed on a single agent, who is then disposed of. But this moral simplification is the very thing Sayers is working to destroy. She achieves a more difficult and realistic vision than this. Her representative society, the village, moves from apparent innocence toward the realization of true guilt.

The genre's limits are nevertheless present. The villagers as a group do not grasp the murder's implications. The book is, in fact, about Wimsey's own perceptions, and secondarily about Fenchurch St. Paul. He understands; he is the village's surrogate, and his insight is ours also. Deacon's death has been "doubly determined." It was caused by the chance that ties him in the bell chamber and prevents his being freed; also, by the mute but actual justice of the event, which Sayers will neither state nor ignore. (pp. 31-2)

As with other aspects of *The Nine Tailors* . . . its resolution falls partially within and partially outside the normal boundaries of mystery fiction. Sayers makes a deeper use of the genre's conventions, drawing her thematic concerns out of the mystery's typical preoccupation with event and circumstance. But most detectives manage to retain scientific (or aesthetic) detachment from their cases; they have a neat, *a priori* and, in their terms, adequate response to tragedy. They "solve" mysteries, resolving tension and reinstating the primacy of induction. Wimsey, on the other hand, loses his detachment. His solution reinstates not reason but charity, the necessary sharing of pain and guilt. One cannot explain death without to some degree explaining it away. For this reason, Wimsey's identification with both parties to the murder makes the most suitable closing to the novel's ambiguous case. Other viewpoints are offered. The district constable simply closes the investigation. Venables raises the old superstitions about the bells. But Wimsey's profound discomfort remains the most realistic and humane response. It completes, without releasing us from, the moral tension of the murder itself. (pp. 34-5)

> *Lionel Basney, "'The Nine Tailors' and the Complexity of Innocence," in* As Her Whimsey Took Her:

Critical Essays on the Work of Dorothy L. Sayers, edited by Margaret P. Hannay, The Kent State University Press, 1979, pp. 23-35.

ALZINA STONE DALE (essay date 1979)

[*Dale is an American free-lance writer and editor who is the author of biographies of G. K. Chesterton and Sayers (see Additional Bibliography). In the following excerpt she discusses* The Man Born to Be King, *noting the devices employed by Sayers to construct a cohesive middle section to the Gospel story, which bridges the gap between Jesus' birth and the events of Passion Week with stories of miracles and parables.*]

There is still a great tendency on the part of her critics to divide Dorothy L. Sayers, like all Gaul, into three parts. Some seem to feel that she could not be a successful writer of mysteries, an effective playwright, and a masterly translator of Dante, while others assume that she grew, or was converted, from one category into the next. What these people all miss when they try to pigeonhole Miss Sayers is that her sly, whimsical sense of humor, her remarkable ability to translate ideas from one generation to another, and her Christian convictions appear in everything she wrote. What she learned in one aspect of the craft of writing she applied to any other job she undertook, for part of her peculiar genius was to see connections and similarities between situations and concepts that to ordinary people might appear widely different. This trait is nowhere better illustrated than in her creation of the plot of *The Man Born to Be King*. (p. 78)

The Christianity she believed in was not her personal invention but the faith of the historical Christian church. Discovering that so many of her contemporaries were unfamiliar with the source of their own religious and ethical convictions, she began to put more of her time into translating these statements into modern idioms, in as many ways and in as many places as she could. As a result she became one of the great popularizers of Christianity. (p. 79)

The more her translations worked, the more we take them for granted. This is particularly true of *The Man Born to Be King*, in which Miss Sayers created the plot structure, and in so doing, translated the Gospels into modern terms. . . .

The plays that make up *The Man Born to Be King* were an outstanding popular success, but it is easy to take her success for granted and not look too closely at the methods she used to achieve her purpose. Hunting for clues among her copious notes makes one startling thing clear: both her plot and its protagonists, Jesus Bar Joseph and Judas Iscariot, were not really present in her source material, for which, true to her Oxford education, she had gone back to the Greek New Testament as the primary source. She passed lightly over the enormous body of secondary commentary and refused to be limited by its current conventional wisdom. The world she created within these plays grew from her own capacious brain, and its dramatic structure was the result of her own engineering, but its purpose, always, was to tell the Gospel story compellingly. The chief reason this series of plays is not always recognized as having her most successful plot is that the Gospel story is considered a "given," but she did do what she said she did: flesh out an existing tale.

In writing these plays she had been assigned a job for which there were "no modern precedents to offer a guide as to treatment or to prepare the minds of the critics and audience for what they were to hear." She had to write 12 plays to be heard a month apart by a general audience, originally children, who might listen to one or two, or get sufficiently interested to keep tuning in. She had material "that began with the birth in Bethlehem and ended with Passion Week in Jerusalem," with the rest of Christ's so-called "life" nothing but a "string of parables, a bunch of miracles, a discourse, a set of sayings, a flash of apocalyptic thunder—here a little, and there a little." (p. 80)

The first clue to her own creation lies in the fact that she called these plays a "play-cycle," but it is necessary to consider and dismiss several meanings for "cycle" before her point is clear. Two dictionary definitions of "cycle" do not fit *The Man Born to Be King.* They are a "recurring succession of events" and "a group of plays treating the same theme." The third definition from *Webster's Collegiate Dictionary,* however, is "a series of narratives dealing typically with the exploits of a legendary hero."

The Man Born to Be King fits this third definition perfectly. Miss Sayers had been familiar since her college days with the famous medieval cycles dealing with legendary figures like Roland, the nephew of Charlemagne. But it is the Matter of Britain, or the story of Arthur and its accrued legends like the Holy Grail, which is the closest match.

Like the life of Christ, the Arthurian legend has a highly dramatic birth story complete with royal parents, indicating that this baby is "born to be king," as well as an account of the hero's obscure upbringing by Merlin and Sir Ector. Then Arthur as a young man is recognized as king in the dramatic episode of the sword in the stone. At the end of Arthur's life, parallel to the Passion of Christ, there is the story of the Morte d'Arthur, which begins with his betrayal by Guinevere and Lancelot, includes Mordred's treason and the last great battle of Camlann, and ends with Arthur's disappearance to the Isle of Avalon, where he awaits Britain's call. Each story gains depth and universality from these mythic elements, but also makes both heroes sound like legendary demigods, an effect Miss Sayers was far from wishing to create with her own plays.

For her, anyhow, the significant parallel in terms of plot construction was the fact that "between the Nativity and the Passion, there is no real story at all." In the Arthurian legend, the middle becomes separate tales of his knights' adventures, while in the Gospels, the middle of the Ministry, especially in the synoptic Gospels, is arranged more according to topic than chronology.

Fortunately, the job of making up a "middle" was one for which Miss Sayers was well qualified. She knew the difference between getting a bright opening idea, such as a body in a bath, and working out the story to dramatize that curious event. She also not only liked mental puzzles, but was a master of the "divided mind," in which the author knows what is really happening but the reader does not. (pp. 81-2)

She found her greatest single help in the Gospel of John, who always showed a logical connection between events, and often their chronological order as well. (p. 83)

Once she had her outline of events, she developed her system of using minor characters as "tie-rods"; that is, having them appear early and later on, which allowed them growth and logic as characters instead of mystery play walk-on parts. By this device she also reduced the confusion of the "number of persons who flit" through the Gospels, and she snatched every

change to tighten her dramatic construction by "combining" people.

That her invented character, Proclus the centurion, is present at Herod's court in the nativity play, has a sick servant for Jesus to heal in the fourth play, is on duty in Jerusalem during Passion Week, and is finally stationed at the Cross, seems so natural that we take it for granted. In some cases she borrowed traditional identifications, such as Mary Magdalen and Mary of Bethany, the sister of Lazarus, which had been approved by St. Augustine. Others like Shadrach, the colleague of Nicodemus and Joseph of Arimathea, were given names and personalities as she went along.

All authors use this economy of characterization; but these plays represent a master craftsman's performance, for Miss Sayers took each and every chance for such doubles, from Claudia's Tyro-Phoenician handmaiden Eunice, who is also the foreign woman with the sick child, to her remarkable decision to identify *all* of Christ's major disciples with those who had first followed John the Baptist. In addition, she doubled up like parables on the logical grounds that their similarity shows that Jesus, like any good teacher, used His own materials over and over.

These "tie-rods" also served her ultimate purpose of making Jesus Bar Joseph realistic by showing Him in convincingly dramatic situations. They let her demonstrate that His goodness was not static, that "there was that clash between His environment and Himself which is the mainspring of drama." But her basic plot sprang also from her conviction that Jesus did not deliberately stage His fulfillment of prophecies about the Messiah, both because that made a story that could not be acted and a character who was a fraud who "produced" his own life.

So like any detective story writer, she did precisely what her character Harriet Vane said was the proper way to write such plots: begin at the end. For dramatic purposes, Miss Sayers took the beginning of Passion Week, or Palm Sunday, as the beginning of the end. By that point in the Gospel, the die is clearly cast. Jesus is not popular with the rulers of this world, whether they are Jewry, as represented by Caiaphas, Pharisees, Sadducees or Scribes, or Rome. His refusal to provide free bread and circuses has made Him less of a charismatic, populist leader, too, but to the Zealots, still hoping for a sudden, successful armed rebellion, He is still a possible hope. Then, at that precise moment, Judas is suddenly center stage in the Gospel story, egotistically convinced that either Jesus is betraying him or that only he, Judas, can weld the sources of power and support together to bring in the Kingdom.

Miss Sayers reasoned that because the original records did not show that the disciples knew where the ass came from for the procession into Jerusalem, that need not mean there was no logical explanation for its appearance. So she had the ass there because Baruch the Zealot was hoping to get a clearcut sign from Jesus that He was willing to be the leader of an uprising. Baruch had been in touch with Judas behind Jesus' back, trying to learn what sort of person Jesus was. While the other disciples were surprised but accepted an ass ready to ride, she made Judas see it as damning proof of his worst suspicions that Jesus was a traitor. In that moment, filled with irony for us looking on, Judas is given the motivation to betray Jesus.

Next Miss Sayers followed her own rule and worked backward to establish the circumstances in which her Judas would think her Jesus might sell out. Her characterization of Judas was in fact her real creation, for the Gospel account is lacking any explanation of his motives, apart from the magical idea that it was "written" that one of His own would betray Him and the suggestion that Judas was a thief whose personality Jesus understood. She needed her Judas three-dimensional so that he could help her characterize her Jesus Bar Joseph.

She realized that Judas's connection with the Zealots was not just another "tie-rod," but the mainspring of her plot. She also saw that she was free to make anything she liked out of Judas, so long as he fitted into her Palm Sunday ending and contributed to the characterization of her other protagonist. Judas's validity, therefore, was determined by her success in "translating" Jesus out of the Gospel account into a real, believable person, for the two characters depend upon one another. In Judas, as she developed him, she had her "unreliable narrator" who was highly intelligent but morally deficient, who like Othello could only see clearly what he had destroyed after he killed it.

As she explains in the notes to the actor, he must play Judas "real," not go off into a stock Richard III stance of "I am determined to prove a villain." If Judas was bad because he was born that way with no reasons given, then his choice as a disciple makes Jesus look like a fool, and that in turn will destroy her chances of making Him real and compelling. But so far as her Gospel sources are concerned, Judas is an enigma, who appears abruptly, near the close of the story, "all set for villainy." As she said, "we are not told how he came to be a disciple, nor what motives drove him to betray his Master [but] when he had done his worst and saw what he had done, he brought back the reward of iniquity and went out and hanged himself. He seems a strange mixture of the sensitive and the insensitive." She therefore took her cue from the modern world and made Judas not only an intellectual with strong opinions on how to do good, but also an organization man, intrigued by power and determined to wield it.

Her first brilliant stroke in Judas's characterization was to bring him into the story early in a place where he fits quite naturally, but never appeared in any Gospel versions. In her second play, "The King's Herald," Judas, like Peter, Andrew, James and John, appears as a disciple of John the Baptist. Like them, he was involved in the Ministry from its beginning and he is first shown to us as a capable organization man, herding converts down to the Jordan. (pp. 83-6)

Dorothy Sayers said that she deliberately chose to make Judas not only a modern, but "one of us," that is, a part of the intellectual elite. Since Jesus spoke of him sternly, far more so than He did of Peter and his impetuous sins, she deduced that Judas was guilty of the deadly corruption of the proud virtues, or, as we would say, of tremendous gifts of intelligence and leadership. As he appeared in her plays Judas is a very realistic portrait of a political animal we have seen often in the twentieth century. He is not only determined to save Israel from itself at all costs, but also well aware of his superior status as the star pupil, first of John the Baptist, and then of Jesus Himself. . . . [Miss Sayers] put him in the forefront of the action in the second through tenth plays and gave her audience plenty of opportunity to see him as the kind of bright young man who has haunted our recent political campaigns, smarter than his charismatic puppet candidate, self-righteously angry at the squandering of campaign money on perfume when it might have been used for buying votes. His kind have ended up in court on SDS charges, or as defendants at Watergate, quite surprised at the turn events have taken. (pp. 86-7)

But while she was busily creating her Judas, Miss Sayers also had to fight the fact that "at the name of Jesus every voice goes plummy, every gesture becomes pontifical, and a fearful, creeping paralysis slows down the pace of the dialogue," while she must also make it plain that, "of course the minute you take Christ as somebody real, you've landed in theology—[but] you've got to translate the thing into terms of life and action. . . ." Her first step was to give Him a real name like the other characters, calling him Jesus Bar Joseph, not Jesus Christ, and letting Him appear onstage without any supernatural effects such as heightened language like poetry, or lead-ins, until the last play, in which His Resurrection appearances are deliberately heralded by angels or occur with a magical quickness that scares His own followers. (p. 87)

In seeking to dramatize for us that "clash between His environment and Himself which is the mainspring of drama," she hit upon the magnificent device of making Judas the kind of person who can give Jesus dramatic opportunities to demonstrate this clash. Not only does Judas fill the need of any great leader for someone who is capable of understanding what he is doing, but potentially, he is the one best suited to carry out the Gospel afterwards. In *The Man Born to Be King*, Judas emerges as someone who might easily have become a Saint Paul. In dramatic terms, moreover, a dialog or an argument between these two, carried on in front of the other disciples who act as a kind of chorus, is a very natural way of seeing what is happening. Each stage of the Ministry is shown in this way with Judas's assumptions and reservations illuminating Jesus Bar Joseph's mission. (pp. 87-8)

During the fifth, sixth and seventh plays before the Passion begins, we grow accustomed to having Judas understand what Jesus is saying, to having him understand everything except Whom he is dealing with, an understanding that, ironically, comes to the other major disciples quite naturally at the Transfiguration. When Jesus' message becomes harder and they lose followers, He can say to Judas, teasing him, "At any rate, Judas it does not look like being a popular doctrine. The crowd is drifting away. Comfort yourself with the reflection that they are not likely to crown me king today." As we have come to expect, Judas understands Him, even though he is also misled by the fact that Jesus recognizes his anxieties into false suspicions. Judas becomes more watchful and more distrustful as he and Jesus talk to one another over the heads of the other disciples. Judas expects Jesus also to take nothing on faith and question all motives, just as he is also developing a good case for a martyr who will help the cause, an ironic but understandable inversion of the real meaning of the Cross. (p. 89)

It is [Miss Sayers's] creation of him as a character with that kind of sweep and depth, matching the personality of her Jesus Bar Joseph (watched by an audience who know Who He is and how the story must end), that makes these plays work dramatically. We have all seen other men of great gifts worship themselves to their own and others' destruction.

These plays represent a triumph of dramatic development made from static materials of such symbolic nature that the modern world did not take them seriously. Without her character of Judas to involve Jesus closely with someone whom He can neither convince nor control, she could not have succeeded in making her Jesus Bar Joseph real. By creating her "workmanlike" plot, hidden from the participants until the end, while gradually revealed to us, colored by the irony of the story's familiarity, she did far more than she admitted when she said, "To make an *adequate* dramatic presentation of the Life of

God . . . would require superhuman genius. . . . Nevertheless, when a story is great enough, any honest craftsman may succeed in producing something not altogether unworthy. . . .'' But in fact we have here a very superior craftsman, and when she is onstage in her favorite persona of the ''writer Dorothy L. Sayers,'' then, as she pointed out in her analysis of Dante the author and Dante the character, we must be careful not to confuse the two and refuse to give credit to the author for his own creation. (p. 90)

> Alzina Stone Dale, '' 'The Man Born to Be King':
> Dorothy L. Sayers's Best Mystery Plot,'' in As Her
> Whimsey Took Her: Critical Essays on the Work of
> Dorothy L. Sayers, edited by Margaret P. Hannay,
> The Kent State University Press, 1979, pp. 78-90.

MARY BRIAN DURKIN, O.P. (essay date 1980)

[In the following excerpt, Durkin emphasizes that Sayers's Christian humanism is the most important factor in her work.]

On the Sayers Commemorative Tablet at her alma mater, Somerville College, Oxford University, are the words, ''Praise Him that He hath made man in His Own Image, a maker and a craftsman like Himself.'' As a maker and craftswoman, Miss Sayers held, and enunciated vigorously, her convictions about the sacramentality of work and the obligation of every person to utilize his or her talents so that works and actions reflect the triadic nature of the Divine Trinity. In *Begin Here* she states: ''Man is never truly himself except when he is actively creating something. To be merely passive, merely receptive, is a denial of human nature.'' Explained at length in *The Mind of the Maker* and in numerous essays, her views on the creative approach to life and to work have a persuasive force today when all too frequently, the pressures of social and economic conditions compel considerations of the financial remunerations of a position or job rather than the more valid concern: ''the worth of the work.'' It is a measure of her own creativity and her concern to inculcate right attitudes toward work that she injected her ideals into so many of her writings: it is the theme of the short story **''Blood Sacrifice,''** the key concept in many lectures, the thrust of many notes accompanying her translation of the *Inferno*. The sins of Dante's age, she insists, are those of today or of any age when individuals refuse to acknowledge that they are made in God's Image and hence are duty-bound to be God-bearing images, witnesses of the truth which they profess to believe. In those powerful essays, **''The Dogma Is the Drama,'' ''Strong Meat,'' ''Creed or Chaos?''** and **''The Greatest Drama Ever Staged,''** she expresses her dynamic faith in Christianity, not as an optional philosophy or way of life, but as the criterion of all philosophies, the clue to the riddle of the universe. (p. 174)

At the Memorial Service held in January 1958 at St. Margaret's, Westminster, the eulogy, written by C. S. Lewis [see excerpt dated 1958], praised her as ''an artist and an entertainer who respected her craft.'' This respect, which she herself might have termed ''intellectual integrity,'' is a hallmark of her thoughts. She had a brilliant mind, a scholar's training and love of learning, an esteem for all that concerned the right use of the intellect. In one of her earliest poems, called simply **''Lay,''** she expresses the idea that because Oxford is an intellectual center, it is therefore ''a sanctified city,'' meriting reverence. This esteem for scholarship and places devoted to its development is notable not only in *Gaudy Night,* but also in numerous lectures and essays where she speaks out against

mental slovenliness so blatantly evident in popular illiteracy, the slipshod use of language, religion posing as a consolatory panacea instead of the rigorous, demanding way of life it should be. Clear-minded, forthright, facile, witty, at times truculent in expressing her disgust over intellectual laziness, she used her talents to instruct and to entertain, to encourage and to admonish. She was particularly vocal about the proper use of the gifts of the mind. ''I do not know whether we can be saved through the intellect,'' she told Charles Williams, ''but I do know that I can be saved by nothing else. I know that if there is a judgment I shall have to say, ''This alone, O Lord, in Thee and in me I have never betrayed; and may it suffice to know and to love Thee after this manner for I have no other love, knowledge, or choice.' ''

In pondering these statements is there perhaps a danger that undue emphasis is given to certain aspects of her life and work, her Christian ideals, for instance, while neglecting other facets? She would be the first to deplore any effort to portray her as one without faults; she was no model of saintly patience, no paragon of virtue—and never pretended to be—but she faced her faults and her trials in life with fortitude and faith, believing firmly in the truth she states in *The Just Vengeance*, ''Whoso will carry the Cross, the Cross will carry him.'' Out of her tribulations, she had the consolation of knowing that she possessed a gift from the Giver of All Gifts; she recognized her talents, stating forthrightly: ''I am a writer, and I know my craft.'' In her lifetime, she had the pleasure of seeing her novels gain recognition: ''No single trend in the English detective story of the 1920's,'' wrote Howard Haycraft, ''was more significant than its approach to the literary standard of the legitimate novel, and no author illustrates this trend better than Dorothy Sayers, who has been called by some critics the greatest of living writers of this form [see *TCLC*, Vol. 2]. Whether or not everyone agrees with this view, no one can dispute, he claimed, ''her preeminence as one of the brilliant and prescient artists the genre has yet produced. (pp. 174-76)

''A great work of art,'' she once commented, ''has vitality only when it speaks to our condition.'' She would have chortled loudly, no doubt, at the idea of calling her novels ''great'' works of art, but despite her rather scoffing attitude toward these ''breadwinners,'' as she termed them, her letters to Mr. Gollancz reveal her attitude toward her fiction, for she stated more than once that she would never turn out a shoddy piece of work. This is clearly evident, for the same artistry that marks the translations of which she was so justly proud, *Tristan in Brittany, The Song of Roland,* and *The Divine Comedy,* is notable in the careful construction of *The Man Born to Be King,* in the dramatic enactment of the Nicene Council in *The Emperor Constantine,* and the weaving together characterization and authentic details of background essential to the plot in *Gaudy Night, Murder Must Advertise,* and *The Nine Tailors.* Her best writings in each genre that she attempted attest to her commitment to utilize her intellect, imagination, and creativity to glorify the Divine Maker and to atone for whatever she lacked through human frailty. (p. 176)

At the present time it is safe to say that Sayers's work as an essayist, and as a scholar and translator of Dante merits the greatest acclaim. When her friend Dr. Barbara Reynolds completed the translation of the *Paradiso,* she wrote in the Foreword: ''It was evident from the beginning that she was bringing to Dante studies in this country a new and vitalizing force . . . in her lectures, in her introductions and commentaries on *Hell* and *Purgatory,* and in her translation itself, she brought Dante within the reach of thousands of readers for whom he would otherwise have remained unintelligible.'' (p. 177)

One of the significant facts that emerges from a close study of Miss Sayers's works is that in her fiction, dramas, essays, and translations there are key concepts which give unity and force to her entire canon. A writer of minor stature, yet she made important contributions to the development of the detective story, to radio drama, and to Dante scholarship. Blessed with a keen intellect, driving energy, a creative imagination, and sincere love for Christian truths, Dorothy L. Sayers was an entertainer, dramatist, scholar, theologian, translator, and above all else, a Christian humanist whose works epitimize her artistic credo: ''The only Christian work is good work well done.'' (p. 178)

Mary Brian Durkin, O.P., in her Dorothy L. Sayers, *Twayne Publishers, 1980, 204 p.*

JOHN R. ELLIOTT, JR. (essay date 1981)

[*In the following excerpt, Elliott discusses Sayers's scholarly work on medieval drama.*]

It has always been surprising that with her wide interest in all forms of medieval literature Dorothy L. Sayers wrote so little on the subject of medieval drama. Her own plays, particularly *The Man Born to Be King,* and *The Just Vengeance,* show an assured knowledge of, and an instinctive sympathy with, the techniques of the English mystery plays, yet Dr Sayers devoted

Holograph copy of a poem written by Dorothy L. Sayers in 1911. From Dorothy L. Sayers: A Literary Biography, *by Ralph E. Hone. The Kent State University Press, 1979. By permission of Anthony Fleming.*

the majority of her scholarly writing to other medieval genres—allegory, romance, epic—and of course to Dante.

Some years ago, while doing research into the modern revival of medieval plays in England, I came across the first part of an article published by Sayers in 1952 entitled **"Types of Christian Drama."** This was an attempt to relate the contemporary revival of religious drama in England, in which she herself played so conspicuous a part, to its roots in the medieval mystery, morality, and miracle plays. . . .

"Types of Christian Drama" may have had its origin in a lecture which Sayers gave on **"Church and Theatre"** at St Anne's House, Soho, in June 1943 as part of a series of talks on **"Christian Faith and Contemporary Culture"**. . . . The text of that talk has not come to light but its impetus must have been the broadcast of her radio-play, *The Man Born to Be King,* during Holy Week of that year. Some idea of its contents may be gleaned from the Introduction which Sayers wrote for the published text of that play. (p. 81)

[Here] Sayers remarked that ''the medieval mysteries'' offered no useful ''precedent'' to a modern Christian playwright, since not ''one listener in ten thousand'' could be assumed to be familiar with them. The unexpected popular success of the 1951 York Festival changed this situation to the point where Sayers could confidently bring up the subject of the mystery cycles before a general audience in the autumn of that year without fear of obscurantism. She was, though, one of a tiny minority among the spectators at York the previous summer who were already familiar enough with the plays to be able to spot theological errors in Martin Browne's staging. Hers was virtually the sole voice raised in criticism of the production, which was showered with praise by the reviewers, the only other exception being Herbert Read, who complained that he did not hear enough Yorkshire accents in the cast and that only Satan should have had a London one. Sayers was also the only commentator on the production to quote evidence from medieval sources in order to suggest more authentic methods of staging. . . . Her thumb-nail summary of what a mystery cycle was actually like in the Middle Ages remains to this day perhaps the most accurate one yet written, surprisingly perceptive, for its date, on such features as anachronism and comedy, aspects of the cycles which still puzzle some readers and audiences today.

Equally informative are her comments on the proper style for contemporary religious drama. These are all the more refreshing when compared with the prevailing ideas on the subject at the time, to be found in such standard handbooks as Martin Browne's *The Production of Religious Plays* (1932) and A. H. Debenham's *Religious Drama* (1935). Such works advised the prospective producer of a religious play, especialy if it was to be performed in a church, to adopt rules of decorum identical to those followed by the celebrants and congregation at a divine service. They also assumed that the usual criteria of the professional theatre had no place in a play with a religious purpose. It was to such notions that Sayers was addressing herself when she wrote that ''it is far more important that the actors should be good actors than that they should be good Christians,'' and that ''no amount of pious intention'' will make up for the dullness of a dull play. That such shibboleths were much on her mind at this time may be seen elsewhere, as in the coy programme-note that she wrote for a performance of her play, *Christ's Emperor,* at the Colchester Festival in July 1951:

The presentation of a play in this Church is an offering to Almighty God, in which you partake by your presence. Your laughter and applause are an act of courtesy to your fellow-men and the actors, and as such cannot surely by displeasing to our most courteous lord.

Such ideas seemed "advanced" in the England of 1951, though in essence they were medieval. Now we tend to take them for granted. It is always timely, however, to be reminded that Christianity, if it is to survive, must be "vital, tough, relevant to life and intellectually urgent," and that it cannot be successfully evangelised by means of "bad stained glass, sentimental tunes, tweety little poems and pictures, and woolly undramatic plays." (pp. 82-3)

> *John R. Elliott, Jr., in an introduction to "Dorothy L. Sayers and the Other Type of Mystery," in* VII: An Anglo-American Literary Review, *Vol. II, 1981, pp. 81-3.*

DAWSON GAILLARD (essay date 1981)

[*In the following excerpt, Gaillard explores the theme of responsibility for one's actions in Sayers's fiction.*]

In January 26, 1940, in **"Wimsey Papers—XI"** of *The Spectator,* Lord Peter pleads with his wife to speak to the people, to tell them that they were waging a war that could be won on the battlefield and lost at home. He tells her to arouse them and "make them understand that their salvation is in themselves and in each separate man and woman among them. . . . [The] important thing is each man's *personal responsibility*." Sayers's detective fiction dramatizes her gradually developing acknowledgement of Lord Peter's imperative.

Sayers's readers not only follow a densely populated trail of clues; we also participate in the almost magical process of literature, the pull of an artistic design toward gradually increasing awareness of a truth about humanity beyond the event of the puzzle. By the end of *The Nine Tailors,* for example, we not only understand the title as an allusion to the death of an unidentified man, we also realize its significance. Taken as a whole, the novel heightens the injunction that we ask not for whom the bell tolls. Vividly we are reminded that it tolls for each of us. We recognize our experience in Sayers's and in John Donne's before her.

If the artist is faithful to her art, she presents a truth that "is new, startling, and perhaps shattering—and yet it comes to us with a sense of familiarity." It is new because the artist creates it and we witness the design in the making. It is familiar because we share her discovery, which becomes ours. The true artist, Sayers affirmed, cries, "Look! recognize your own experience in my own." First, though, Sayers had to learn what her own was.

Sayers's detective fiction gave her a way to discover her times and society. Her last works, for example, include actual places that she had known—the advertising agency, the Fen country, and Oxford. Sayers's detective writings share with her readers her gradual recognition of the values that she associated with these places: the mixture of economic necessity and psychological strategy that characterizes the advertising world, the close association of the natural and divine worlds in the Fen country of her childhood, the significance of intellectual standards and work that she had witnessed as a student at Oxford. What Sayers had blithely begun in order to earn money and to enjoy herself also revealed to her significant connections among the loss of integrity, traditional woman-man relationships, and war.

Her fiction does not dope the reader into irresponsibility over the conduct of life. Although the detective form always punishes the criminal, Sayers was not eager to reassure her audience that such a comfortable pattern of poetic justice characterizes human life. As *The Nine Tailors* dramatizes, we are all members of one another; we are all responsible.

Looking back from the perspective of a second world war, Sayers argued that to categorize war or crime as problems to be solved in the manner of a detective novel leads people astray. They begin to think of death as the evil, whereas they ought to pay attention to the chaos that war brings to the survivors. If they do not, they will direct all their resources "to evading war at all costs, rather than to dealing intelligently with the conditions of life which cause wars and are caused by wars." That evasion, she said, characterized her society between World Wars I and II. In her detective fiction of the twenties and thirties, as we have seen, conduct and the conditions of human life had always been central.

Later, after she had stopped writing detective stories and retired her characters from fiction, she brought them back during the first years of the second world war to speak for her in *The Spectator,* as Lord Peter does when he asks Harriet to use her talents to arouse the citizens. And in an excerpt from a supposed sermon on Armistice Sunday, Sayers spoke through the persona of the Reverend Theodore Venables, who concluded that "the whole interval between this war and the last had been indeed a period of armistice—not peace at all, but only an armed truce with evil."

Looking back over Sayers's detective fiction, we find that it dramatizes one source of the evil—faulty attitudes toward work. The right attitude manifests itself in creative joy and vitality, a touch of the eternal. For example, Peter Wimsey's work of detecting usually intoxicates him. The excitement he shares with Charles Parker as they follow the movements of the Person Unknown in *Clouds of Witness* and that he and Harriet share as they decode the cipher in *Have His Carcase* emanates as much from the love of creating order out of fragments of information as from his respect for the truth and work well done.

His intoxication resembles that of the change ringer. To the onlooker, the narrator of *The Nine Tailors* explains, the eight intense faces in the spellbound circle of ringers may seem to be absurd. However, their concentration signals the "solemn intoxication that comes of intricate ritual faultlessly performed." Lord Peter's capers and energetic conversation signify his intoxication. Like the change ringers who find pleasure in making music, Lord Peter finds pleasure in making sense. There is one major difference, of course. His work results in the life or the death of someone, the gravity of which, as we have seen, Lord Peter likes less and less. Nevertheless, he does his job with dedication. (pp. 89-91)

Admirable people in Sayers's fictional world follow a code of right behavior. Superintendent Kirk of *Busman's Honeymoon* expounds on Lord and Lady Wimsey's code that "when things ain't done, they won't do 'em—and that's the long and short of it." The same can be said for all of Sayers's good characters. They uphold codes of honor and integrity about their work. (p. 93)

The villains or questionable characters misuse their work. They do not serve it. Mr. Garrick Drury of **"Blood Sacrifice,"** in

In the Teeth of Evidence, violates his theatrical art. As an actor, he wants only those vehicles that appeal to the public. As a producer, he takes advantage of the young playwright John Scales, who needs money. Drury turns Scales's honest play into a sentimental pleasure dome for the public. Scales complains; he thinks of the money he receives as "wages of sin"; nevertheless, he takes it.

In *Strong Poison,* Norman Urquhart abuses his position as family lawyer and trustee of an estate. Similarly, Dr. Penberthy of *The Unpleasantness at the Bellona Club* takes advantage of his authority as General Fentiman's physician. In *Unnatural Death,* Mary Whittaker uses her nursing skills to commit murder. Julian Freke diabolically uses his surgical skills to flaunt his crime.

By misusing their work, Sayers's criminals sin against God. They disrupt the divine pattern of creative energy, at least temporarily. Although evil cannot be abolished, it can be redeemed by creative power. To Sayers, creativity meant synthesis, making something new out of the materials that one has. One does not destroy in order to create, one assimilates the old with the new. Sayers's belief applied to her view of art as well as to her view of society. "The good that emerges from a conflict of values cannot arise from the total condemnation or destruction of one set of values, but only from the building of a new value, sustained like an arch, by the tension of the original two," she stated.

The marriage between Harriet Vane and Peter Wimsey concretely dramatizes a synthesis of values—Peter's aristocratic, male-dominated heritage with Harriet's contemporary, feminist views. Individually, they are dedicated to their work—Harriet to shaping words; Peter to shaping facts. Together, they provide models for the social revolution that, in *Gaudy Night,* Lord Peter foresees. (p. 94)

We rejoice in the universe that Sayers created in her detective fiction in celebration of creation itself. In the back of an antique shop in *Gaudy Night,* Peter and Harriet sing together—"tenor and alto twined themselves in a last companionable cadence." In the most exuberant scene in *Busman's Honeymoon,* Peter and Harriet sing, "Here we sit like BIRDS in the wilderness" with Mr. Puffett, Miss Twitterton, and Mr. Goodacre.

At the New Year's Eve service in *The Nine Tailors* another community joins in song. At first, the congregation seems lost in the large church of the Fen country. Then the people begin to sing. They are joined with each other and with the divine presence evident in the cherubim and seraphim that echo the human voices from high above. "My God!" exclaims Lord Peter. His expletive appropriately expresses the majesty of the hymn, "Let everything that hath breath praise the Lord." Celebration and praise of the glory of creation characterizes Sayers's works. (pp. 102-03)

For the artist, as for any worker, the creating is a continuous process. Sayers explained in *The Mind of the Maker* that it was no accident that her novel *Gaudy Night* and her play *The Zeal of Thy House,* written soon after it, should have the same themes. Although the former signals the end of one development, the detective novel, and the latter signals the beginning of another, Christian drama, together they illustrate the continuing creativity of Dorothy L. Sayers. (p. 103)

Dawson Gaillard, in his Dorothy L. Sayers, *Frederick Ungar Publishing Co., 1981, 123 p.*

VIRGINIA B. MORRIS (essay date 1983)

[*In the following excerpt, Morris explores Sayers's approach to female criminals in her novels. For further discussion of Sayers's female characters, see the excerpt by Margot Peters and Agate Nesaule Krouse (1974).*]

Although Dorothy L. Sayers was a highly conventional writer who saw in the detective novel a celebration of the triumph of law and order and the preservation of the status quo, her conservatism did not extend to her treatment of fictional women criminals. Like many other novelists, Sayers created women characters who were accused not only of breaking the law but also of defying sexual mores. But unlike other detective writers, typified by the puritanical Raymond Chandler, Sayers does not condemn the sexuality she describes; rather, she uses it to demonstrate the popular biases that defined the role of the woman criminal both in fiction and in life.

Typically, Sayers' criminal women and women suspects are one way or another sexually unconventional, either because of their illicit sex or homosexuality or because of overwhelmingly obsessive or repressed love. However, by placing her characters in particular social environments Sayers provides cultural explanations for their deviance; and by treating each one as an individual, she avoids cliche. But . . . her treatment of female criminals modifies convention without totally denying it.

Sayers draws on extensive literary, theoretical, and historical precedent in linking female crime and illicit love. Both the popular literature of the nineteenth and early twentieth centuries and the serious fiction and drama of the period perpetuated the notion of a causal relationship between illicit sex and female criminality. Furthermore, contemporary social scientists, including criminologists and psychologists, repeatedly pointed to the unconventional sexual habits of women criminals as one of the characteristic behavioral patterns of these deviants.

Sayers uses the theme of illicit love most dramatically in *Strong Poison,* in which an innocent Harriet Vane is accused of murdering her lover, and in *Documents in the Case,* in which a calculating, adulterous woman instigates her husband's murder. And although neither woman is convicted, the suspicions which residually cling to them stem from their indecorous sexual liasons.

In *Gaudy Night,* the most complex and in many ways the best of her novels, Sayers examines the subject of women criminals in . . . [a most] provocative way. Two psychological motivations for crime are considered in the novel, both having to do with sexual drives: the effects of denying sexuality and the consequences of submerging the self so completely in the beloved that injury to one becomes injury to both. Despite two pointed but unsustained jibes at psychoanalytic (specifically Freudian) theory, the novel is a serious, sustained examination of the purported sexual roots of feminine deviance.

Harriet Vane confronts the problems of a psychologically disturbed woman when she is asked to uncover the source of a series of malicious and increasingly dangerous pranks which are plaguing her alma mater, Oxford's fictional Shrewsbury College. Five years away from her own horrible encounter with the law, Harriet is still personally drawn in contradictory directions: on the one hand, she yearns for the intellectual stimulation and personal isolation of the scholarly life; on the other, she is increasingly attracted by the promise of sexual and domestic pleasure with Peter Wimsey. Unable, even after so many years, to escape completely from the notoriety of being accused of murdering her lover, Harriet is not able to resolve her own emotional and sexual needs until the events at Shrewsbury force her to confront them directly.

In keeping with the deeper examination of criminal motives, Sayers makes the crimes in the novel more atypical as well. Instead of murder or robbery, the perpetrator engages in apparently wanton acts: destroying personal and college property; sending anonymous, obscene notes; and, in the most overtly violent action, assaulting Harriet after mistaking her in the dark for Miss de Vine, the College's Research Fellow. But the harassment is not trivial. One bright but troubled student, plagued with thirty or more of the abusive notes, tries to drown herself in the river, and Miss de Vine, widely known to have heart trouble, is no doubt intended to die from the trauma of the attack that stuns the hardier Harriet.

Because the College dreads the unpleasant—even ugly—publicity that the perpetrator is obviously trying to force on it, the dons are hesitant to consult the police and depend on Harriet to unravel the mystery. Her conclusion, that the actions must be the work of a member of the academic staff, is based to a certain extent on the evidence, and to a much more profound extent on her own deep fears, that in choosing the celibate life of the mind the women she admires and would like in some ways to emulate have denied a vital, healthy part of themselves. This denial, she supposes, can result in mental disturbance and crime.

She equates sexual frustration or denial with perversion and madness and the capacity to threaten and perhaps even to harm other women. (pp. 489-90)

Harriet's willingness to believe that the culprit is one of the professional women is fostered by her conversations with one of the college housemaids, Annie Wilson. Annie's view that "some of these clever ladies are a bit queer.... Funny, I mean. No heart in them" ... plays directly to Harriet's own fears. But Annie's views are more conventional than that. She insists that women do not need a college education—much less a college—because books do not teach them how to be good wives, which should be a woman's occupation. In a later conversation, Annie makes an even stronger claim that women should not take men's jobs because it is not fair to make it even harder for men to find work; again she insists that a woman's job is to be a good wife and mother. Such reactionary views, the opposite of Sayers's own, are made credible from this working-class woman at least in part because she is so articulate. But Harriet, although unpersuaded, is disconcerted by Annie's vehemence.

Of all the outrages, Harriet is most disturbed by the harassment of the student Newland, which drives the girl to attempt suicide when she should be preparing to do brilliantly on her exams. No motive seems adequate to the consequences in this case. The desire to bring scandal and disgrace to the college might explain defacing the library; a personal vendetta might underlie destroying a scholar's manuscript; a perverted mind might explain obscene notes. But what could—even to a disturbed mind—justify torturing someone apparently selected at random? The incident stands, even at the conclusion of the novel, as one of the clearest indications of the deeply disturbed mind of the culprit because it represents the depersonalization of the vendetta.

Newland's torture suggests that the perpetrator is capable of real violence and must be found swiftly, even if it means getting outside help. When Harriet turns to Peter Wimsey, she has made a critical decision crucial to the novel's theme. Her need

for him interlaces their private story with the broader relationship between men and women, particularly the relationship of sex and responsibility.

This interweaving makes the novel more deeply satisfying to the reader because the issues which define the culprit are also relevant to the novel as a whole. Just as Peter learned in *Strong Poison* about the marriage plans of his friends when he was falling in love with Harriet, so here the issues of women's independence and self-sufficiency, as well as the consequences of recognizing the weaknesses or culpability of one's beloved, are played out on many levels. For as Peter soon suspects, blindly adoring love rather than sexual denial is the key to the disturbances at the college, and it is not long before his suspicions are confirmed.

Sayers brings the question into focus by having Miss de Vine recall an experience in which a historian applying for a professional post had submitted an essay in which he failed to reveal his knowledge of a letter contradicting his thesis; as a member of the hiring committee, Miss de Vine knew the letter and determined that the applicant did as well. Not only did he fail to get the job, but he was stripped of his M.A. and, to all intents and purposes, excommunicated from the academic world. Unable to cope with his disgrace, he turned to drink and then to suicide, leaving a destitute wife and two small children.

After her murderous attack on Harriet, the maid Annie finally is identified as the disgraced historian's wife and as the culprit. (pp. 490-91)

In Annie's view the real crime is the destruction of women's traditional, sex-defined roles of wife and mother and its concomitant effect on the status of men, particularly her own man. Ironically, to avenge the crime against Robinson, Annie assumes many of the qualities she so despises in her enemies. Rather than being her husband's helpmate or his accomplice, she is his avenger. She defines the role on her own initiative and willingly seeks out her victims, intending to do them psychological and physical harm. One popular theory of early twentieth-century female criminality asserted that violence and aggression, alien to the inherent nature of women, were possible only by denying female sexuality. In choosing the unfeminine, that is, in depending on intelligence and passion to carry out criminal actions, women criminals reaffirm their deviance. Annie would have rejected this theory, but to criminologists Annie would represent an excellent model in support for it. (p. 492)

In the evolution of the woman criminal in Sayers' novels, Annie is clearly the culmination of an increasingly serious and innovative view of the forces that drive quite ordinary human beings—particularly women—to acts of violence. (pp. 493-94)

The variety of characters [found in *Gaudy Night,* as well as in *Strong Poison, Documents in the Case,* and *Unnatural Death*] and the complexity of their criminal actions mark Sayers as a seminal force in the creation of fictional women criminals. More profound in her characterizations than Agatha Christie, and much more interested in women than her contemporary male mystery writers, Sayers has had a lasting influence on the nature of these characters in detective novels.

I am not suggesting that Sayers' chief objective in her work was to alter her reader's perceptions of the woman criminal, but it is evident that her innovations have become part of the literary tradition. In reading Josephine Tey, Ruth Rendell, and P. D. James, one can discover examples of serious attention paid to women who commit murder or other crimes of violence and fraud. Sexual indiscretion or deviance in these novels continues to signal the potential guilt of the women, but these writers follow Sayers' lead in adding criminological and psychological dimensions to their characters and by drawing on actual criminal cases as the basis of their work. Furthermore, the women in Tey's, Rendell's, and James's novels are complex characters, not simple functionaires of men or sexual predators.

[Sayers'] use of convention and her ability to go beyond it are clear. In **Strong Poison** and **Documents in the Case,** she began with traditional portraits of women criminals following literary and historical precedents. But within the convention she dramatized the issues of public and judicial prejudice, the presumption of guilt, and the importance of decorum, especially sexual decorum, in the disposition of cases. In doing so, she succeeded in separating criminality from sexual indiscretion. Nothing illustrates this more clearly than Harriet Vane's innocence.

In the other pair of novels, **Unnatural Death** and **Gaudy Night,** Sayers is even less limited by convention. She addresses the frustrations and insecurities of women coping on their own with a changing world, particularly a world in which women have opportunities—including those for crime—which had not been available to them before. By adding psychological dimensions and a social context to the depiction of her characters, particularly when she examines the relationship of their criminality and their sexuality, she provides in her best novels a fine distinction between conventional woman criminals and criminals who are women. (pp. 494-95)

> *Virginia B. Morris, ''Arsenic and Blue Lace: Sayers' Criminal Women,'' in* Modern Fiction Studies, *Vol. 29, No. 3, Autumn, 1983, pp. 485-95.*

BARBARA REYNOLDS   (essay date 1984)

[*Reynolds, an English essayist, translator, and longtime Cambridge lecturer in Italian, met Sayers in 1946 when the latter came to Cambridge to lecture on Dante. A friendship developed that lasted the remainder of Sayers's life, during which time the two kept in constant contact regarding Sayers's translation of the* Divina Commedia. *At the request of Penguin Books, Reynolds finished the three-volume work after Sayers's death. She later became a founding editor of* VII: An Anglo-American Literary Review, *which is devoted to study of the works of Sayers, C. S. Lewis, J.R.R. Tolkien, Charles Williams, G. K. Chesterton, Owen Barfield, and George MacDonald. In the following excerpt, she compares and contrasts Sayers's literary theory, outlook, and craft as a mystery writer with those of her infrequently mentioned influence, Chesterton.*]

In October 1925, G. K. Chesterton had on his desk a stack of recent detective stories to review for his journal, *G. K.'s Weekly.* For some reason he did not do so. Perhaps he had no great opinion of them for he merely gave them a brief mention and went on instead to write an article, ''How to Write a Detective Story.'' It was published in the 17 October, 1925 issue of *G. K.'s Weekly.* (p. 136)

[John] Cournos at once posted to Dorothy Sayers the copy of *G. K.'s Weekly* which contained the article. On October 18, writing from her flat in Great St. James's Street, London, she thanks him for it and for saving her ''six useful pennies''; and she goes on to discuss the article in detail. This letter is the earliest evidence we have of her opinion on Chesterton as a theorist and practitioner of the craft of detective fiction. . . .

By the autumn of 1925 Dorothy Sayers was already the author of two detective novels and several short stories. . . . It is, therefore, as a fellow professional that she comments on Chesterton's advice. (p. 137)

In his article Chesterton regards detective fiction as a game. He speaks of the ''craft or trick of writing mystery stories. . . . For the detective story is only a game; and in that game the reader is not really wrestling with the criminal but with the author.'' In 1925, Dorothy Sayers agreed with him:

> There is 'meat', too, in his calling it not only a trick but a 'craft'. . . . It does give just that curious satisfaction which the exercise of cunning craftsmanship always gives to the worker. It is almost as satisfying as working with one's hands. It is rather like laying a mosaic—putting each piece—apparently meaningless and detached—into its place, until one suddenly sees the thing as a consistent picture.
>
> (p. 138)

About the *craft* of detective fiction, Dorothy Sayers learned a good deal from Chesterton, but she progressed in ways which diverged from him in important respects. She took the detective genre more and more seriously. It ceased to be a game. In a sense, it had always been more to her than that. From the outset, she had hoped to raise detective fiction to the level of the novel of manners, a criticism of life, with believable and interesting characters. This had been achieved by Wilkie Collins in *The Moonstone,* in her opinion ''probably the very finest detective story ever written.'' She admitted that the genre could never attain the highest level of literary achievement:

> it rarely touches the heights and depths of human passion. . . . It does not show us the inner workings of the murderer's mind—it must not; for the identity of the murderer is hidden until the end of the book. . . . A too violent emotion, flung into the glittering mechanism jars the movement by disturbing its delicate balance. The most successful writers are those who contrive to keep the story running from beginning to end upon the same emotional level, and it is better to err in the direction of too little feeling than too much.

The difficulty became acute when the murderer had been shown to be a likeable human being:

> A real person has then to be brought to the gallows, and this must not be done too lightheartedly. Mr. G. K. Chesterton deals with this problem by merely refusing to face it. His Father Brown (who looks on sin and crime from the religious point of view) retires from the scene before the arrest is reached. He is satisfied with a confession. The sordid details take place ''off''.

Dorothy Sayers had been aware of this problem from the beginning. (pp. 139-40)

The dilemma, a moral as well as a technical one, continued to be a concern to the author and became an important ingredient in the development of her novels.

She handled the matter in various ways. In ***Whose Body?*** . . . , the moral aspect is faced in general terms. Technically, as regards the balance of the work, involvement with the ultimate fate of Sir Julian is rightly avoided. We learn that he is arrested before he can commit suicide but not before he has made a written confession. In ***Clouds of Witness*** . . . , Lord Peter's involvement is intimately personal: the two main suspects are his brother and his sister, while a third suspect was planning to elope with his sister. (It is scarcely surprising that he should seek release from tension at the end of the story by getting drunk!) No-one is brought to justice, however, for the suspect murder turns out to be suicide. Nevertheless, the dilemma has been brought home to Lord Peter, this time as an *argumentum ad hominem*.

In ***Unnatural Death*** . . . , the dilemma acquires a new dimension. This is the novel which Dorothy Sayers mentioned to Cournos two years before its publication, saying she was rather nervous of it because it showed signs of becoming "round." In other words, serious concerns, such as moral responsibility, were threatening to unbalance the work. And indeed we do find that Lord Peter is much troubled in his conscience. His "beastly interference," as he puts it, has led to two further murders—of Bertha Gotobed and Vera Findlater. Was the first murder, that of hastening an old lady's death, an old lady dying of cancer, such a serious crime? Was he justified in investigating it? He seeks the advice and reassurance of Mr. Tredgold, the priest of St. Onesimus. Miss Climpson, too, has a crisis of conscience: should she reveal what she had no right to read?

Dorothy Sayers's hope, as she said in her letter to Cournos, was to keep the story "in no more than high relief." She treats both cases of troubled conscience with as light a touch as she can without trivialising them. The conversation between Lord Peter and the priest is skillfully managed. The dilemma is discussed solemnly, in a religious context and setting, without evasion, and the burden is shifted. Lord Peter feels free to pursue his enquiries and, as it turns out, he is in time to save Miss Climpson's life. Miss Climpson, with her fussy scruples, which are easily overcome by her inquisitiveness and by her loyalty to Lord Peter, is left as a faintly comic character. Yet there is also something heroic about her; she is not afraid to incur danger to herself.

The culprit, Mary Whittaker, commits suicide. Involvement in the emotions of a trial and execution is thereby avoided. The novel is well balanced and the technical problems are solved. Nevertheless, the dilemma was still not settled in the author's mind; the case comes up again for discussion in the much more serious context of ***Gaudy Night*** . . . . The question of moral responsibility [here takes] on dimensions far beyond those suggested in ***Whose Body?*** or even in ***Unnatural Death*** itself. But this is to anticipate. (pp. 141-43)

[*The Unpleasantness at the Bellona Club*] is the first of the two novels in which the culprit is offered an honourable way out. Dr. Penberthy is gently persuaded by Lord Peter to write a confession, clearing Ann Dorland. Another member of the club leaves a revolver handy in the library and Penberthy shoots himself. The tragedy is kept at a distance. A final touch is in keeping with the title of the book. The club complainer, Wetheridge, rushes into the bar:

> I say, you fellows . . . here's another unpleasantness. Penberthy's shot himself in the library. People ought to have more consideration for the members.

The balance of the novel is so contrived that we accept the consequence. Lord Peter (and the reader) are more interested in the vindications and future of Ann Dorland than in the fate of the culprit.

In ***Strong Poison*** . . . , as in ***Clouds of Witness,*** Lord Peter is personally involved. He has fallen in love with the accused, Harriet Vane, and hopes to marry her. He therefore has no scruples about hunting down the culprit. His detachment from the murderer's fate is credible, as well as functional. As in Chesterton's stories, the novel ends with the arrest and the sordid details take place "off."

In ***The Five Red Herrings*** . . . , a puzzle novel, in which characterisation is at a minimum, the culprit, Ferguson, will probably get off on a plea of self-defence or justification homicide. Of all the Sayers novels, this is the most markedly two-dimensional and, to many of her readers, for this reason, the least attractive.

In ***Have His Carcase*** . . . , the situation between Lord Peter and Harriet has developed but their feelings are not involved with the fate of the murderer and his confederates. The investigation is clearly shown to have been justified. But, like Father Brown, the investigators leave the scene before the end. . . . (pp. 143-44)

In ***Murder Must Advertise*** . . . , the culprit, Mr. Tallboy, is to some extent also a victim. Like Dr. Penberthy in *The Unpleasantness at the Bellona Club,* he is offered an honourable way out. Some readers dislike the sight of Lord Peter "playing God" in this way and this suggests that he is becoming a credible human being, or "round," as Dorothy Sayers expressed it in 1925, someone to be taken seriously, too seriously, perhaps, for the balance of the novels. Some development has certainly taken place since the earlier book. Lord Peter is more deeply involved with Tallboy's fate than with Penberthy's and is unable to celebrate with Parker when the drug-smuggling ring is rounded up. Even so, the novel ends on a light note. (p. 144)

[*The Nine Tailors*] is perhaps the most profound of all the Sayers novels in its treatment of guilt. The question has been well discussed by Professor Lionel Basney [see excerpt dated 1979]. The moral responsibility for the suspected murder is shared by the whole community. Will Thoday, who inadvertently brings about Deacon's death, atones for it with his own life in an attempt to save a man from drowning. Good comes of Lord Peter's investigations (he is in no doubt this time), but he is overwhelmed by the thought of Deacon's terrible death. The horror is diminished by the serene acceptance of divine judgment expressed at the end by the Rector, Mr. Venables.

The problem of whether to bring her characters (and the reader) face to face with the consequences of detecting crime, a problem which seemed in 1925 chiefly a matter of technique, occupied more and more of Dorothy Sayers's attention. Finally, in *Gaudy Night* . . . the matter is thrashed out thoroughly in the discussion in the Senior Common Room at Shrewsbury College. In relation to the plot, the discussion is a device to reveal the attitude of the dons to the establishment of truth, at whatever cost, and this is itself the main theme of the book. By now, she has achieved a detective story which far transcends the "trick" or "craft" of mystery writing. In structure, theme, characterisation, criticism of life, *Gaudy Night* belongs more to the category of a serious novel than to detective fiction. That there is a mystery to be solved is of minor importance.

The last novel, **Busman's Honeymoon** . . . , began as a play devised in a light-hearted mood of enquiry into a technical problem, namely, how to reveal an essential clue to an audience without their being aware of it. As it turned out, it contains the deepest emotional involvement of Lord Peter in the consequences of his activities as a detective. His distress at Frank Crutchley's imminent execution is overwhelming. But this is not unique. We learn from Bunter's conversation with Harriet that his master has often suffered in this way; that he has visited the condemned in prison and asked their forgiveness. Lord Peter himself tells Harriet that he witnessed a hanging once to see if it would cure him of ''meddling,'' as he calls it. (There are hints of this state of mind also in **Gaudy Night,** as recalled by Harriet.) He does all he can to ensure a fair trial for Crutchley, engaging Sir Impey Biggs as Counsel for the Defence. He does what he can also for Polly Mason or, rather, when it comes to the point, he has to ask Harriet to write to Miss Climpson for him. Such powerful and poignant treatment of the situation would have unbalanced the earlier novels. It is acceptable here as part of the deepened characterisation of Peter and Harriet and of their love for each other. And, significantly, it is the last of the novels. No story about them done 'in the flat, on rather broad lines'' is acceptable after this. The short stories which follow are proof of this. (The subsequent novel, *Thrones, Dominations,* was left unfinished.) The most believable continuation of their story is to be found in *The Spectator* ''Wimsey Papers,'' reflecting Lord Peter's war-time activities. By bringing him to life as a credible human being, his creator killed him off as a detective.

One novel remains: **The Documents in the Case.** . . . Constructed as a series of letters and documents, it presents different technical problems from those of the other novels. Here, everything, not only the sordid details, takes place ''off''. Even so, the consequences of selfishness and wrong-doing are clearly shown. The horror of the victim's lonely death by poisoning is more gruesomely suggested than in any of the others. Jack Munting's distress at having to betray his talented friend, Harwood Lathom, is never really a dilemma and the reader feels at the end that justice has been done.

From this brief survey, it might appear that Dorothy Sayers was, or became, a more serious writer of detective fiction than G. K. Chesterton. It remains to test this idea. (pp. 144-46)

It is perfectly true, as she said, that Chesterton avoids the final reckoning of arrest, sentence and execution. (p. 146)

Structurally, the device is convenient, particularly in a short story. Chesterton's use of it does not necessarily mean that he takes a less serious view than Sayers of the consequences of crime and its detection. As we have seen, she had recourse to similar methods. It could be argued, on the contrary, that Chesterton is the more serious writer of the two. The moral concern of his stories extends beyond the plot and the solving of the mystery. Father Brown is a priest. His business is with the soul, not with the tidying-up processes of the law. He is saddened by evil but not surprised or overwhelmed by it. He expects it. His nerves are stronger than Lord Peter's. From a knowledge of himself, he arrives at a knowledge of the potential for evil-doing in all human beings. He also knows the potential for good in the most evil characters. Flambeau, the French master criminal, known formerly as ''Le Roi des Apaches,'' turns private detective (and *he* feels no scruples about bringing criminals to justice). These is no such extreme conversion in the Sayers stories. The nearest approach to it is the case of Mr. Rumm in **Strong Poison,** the safe-breaker turned evangelist

and hymn-singer, who teaches Miss Murchison how to pick a lock.

Both Chesterton and Sayers are conjurors. That is part of their stock in trade. The quickness of the hand deceives the eye, the entertaining patter distracts attention from the essential clue. Both make skillful use of surprise. Both Father Brown and Lord Peter are placed by their circumstances at an angle from which observation is unusual; both have the advantage of camouflage. In addition, Chesterton is a master of paradox: things are seldom what they seem. (pp. 146-47)

Yet the similarities between the two writers outnumber the differences. Though separated by a generation, they were both typical English products of much the same period. They draw upon a common stock of jokes, many of their allusions are identical and Sayers takes over several of Chesterton's quips and mannerisms. She obviously loved *Biography for Beginners,* those delightful rhymes invented by E. C. Bentley (the Clerihews, so called from his second name), which his friend Chesterton illustrated. The sub-title of this little book is: ''Being a Collection of Miscellaneous Examples for the Use of Upper Forms.'' That is indeed the nature of the rhymes: schoolboy humour, but the humour of brilliant, well-read, sophisticated schoolboys like Chesterton and Bentley and their friends at St. Paul's School, as G. K. describes them in his *Autobiography.*

Schoolboy humour it may have been, but it appealed strongly to English intellectuals of the 1920s. Dorothy Sayers gives her own pleasure in it to Lord Peter. . . . In **Busman's Honeymoon,** Lord Peter quotes the Clerihew about the great Duke of Wellington who reduced himself to a skellington. Readers who do not know their Bentley must think that Sayers is making Lord Peter needlessly callous and trivial, whereas she is simply making him a man of his time. Like herself, he is someone who enjoys having fun with words, in the tradition of Lear and Carroll and of the Rhyme Club which she and her friends founded at Oxford and which is echoed in **Murder Must Advertise,** where the nimble-witted copy-writers try to find rhymes for Balliol. (pp. 148-49)

Of the period jokes enjoyed by both writers, one must suffice. In **The Unpleasantness at the Bellona Club,** Lord Peter says:

> I'm not here to make trouble. *Au contraire,* as the man said in the Bay of Biscay when they asked him if he'd dined.

Chesterton uses this joke in his *Autobiography* in quite a serious context. He is speaking about his experience of good and evil and refers to a friend who understood it:

> He was a most distinguished psycho-analyst, of the most modern and scientific sort. He was not a priest; far from it; we might say, like the Frenchman asked if he had lunched on the boat, *au contraire.*

The novel preceded the *Autobiography* by eight years, but this does not mean that Chesterton copied the joke from Sayers. It was typical of what might be called the educated vulgarity of English people of their time. And that is something else which the two writers had in common: unashamed vulgarity. ''Vulgar people are never mad. I am vulgar myself and I know,'' says Dr. Bull in *The Man Who Was Thursday.* Chesterton also speaks in ''The Blue Cross'' of the ''sublime vulgarity'' of man. And Dorothy Sayers, charged by a journalist with being vulgar, robustly acknowledged the accusation in a lecture, ''The Importance of Being Vulgar,'' in which she said:

It is, of course, all too easy to be vulgar without
being great; it is not nearly so easy to be great
without being vulgar—indeed it is almost impossible in any activity which brings one into
contact with one's fellow creatures.

Combined with defiance of this nature, we find in both writers
a deliberate philistinism, a rejection of intellectual pretentiousness and literary snobbishness. "We all owe much sound morality to the penny dreadfuls," says Chesterton in *Orthodoxy*.
And in **Strong Poison,** Sayers gives to Lord Peter the assertion
that detective stories are the most moral literature we have.
(pp. 149-50)

As literary artists they had much in common. They both loved
and valued the restrictions of artistic form. "The artist loves
his limitations: they constitute the *thing* he is doing," says
Chesterton in *Orthodoxy*. Even as a young writer, Sayers loved
the fixed form. Her earliest poems, **Op. I** and **Catholic Tales
and Christian Songs,** reflect this pleasure, especially the series
of poems entitled *Lay,* written in accordance with the rules laid
down by the fourteenth-century French poet, Eustache Des-
champs in his *L'Art de Dictier*. The challenge of intricacy
stimulated her to develop her skills, just as she later rejoiced
in the challenge of Dante's *terza rima*. A comparison of Chesterton and Sayers as poets would be worth undertaking. He
evidently approved of an early poem of hers, **"Rex Doloris,"**
for he published it in the *Eye-Witness* in April 1918. She later
included it in **Catholic Tales and Christian Songs.** The rollicking, defiant tone of much of Chesterton's poetry appealed to
her and she knew a lot of it by heart. (pp. 151-52)

Both Sayers and Chesterton resisted current fashions in thought.
They were sceptics, odd men out. In the same article, Sayers
says:

> I have no use whatever for Enlightened Opin-
> ion, whose science is obsolete, its psychology
> superficial, its theology beneath contempt and
> its history nowhere . . . the sincerest efforts
> after virtue produce only chaos if they are di-
> rected by a ramshackle and incoherent philos-
> ophy.

This brings us to the link between Chesterton and Sayers as
Christians. Dorothy Sayers said on several occasions that she
owed a great deal to Chesterton's *Orthodoxy*. Of the many
tributes which she paid to this work, the last and perhaps the
most cogent is to be found in her preface to Chesterton's play,
The Surprise, which was published after his death, in 1952. . . .
The Surprise deals with the freedom of the will as understood
by a creator of characters. This was something that fascinated
both writers. In *Orthodoxy* Chesterton had said: "God was a
creator, as an artist is a creator." This is a concept which
Dorothy Sayers developed brilliantly in **The Mind of the Maker.**
(pp.153-54)

She had first read *Orthodoxy* "as a sulky teenager." Five years
before her death she still remembered the effect it had on her.
This is perhaps the most significant link between G. K. Chesterton and Dorothy L. Sayers. (p. 155)

> *Barbara Reynolds, "G. K. Chesterton and Dorothy
> L. Sayers," in* The Chesterton Review, *Vol. X, No.
> 2, May, 1984, pp. 136-57.**

ADDITIONAL BIBLIOGRAPHY

Basney, Lionel. "God and Peter Wimsey." *Christianity Today* XVII,
No. 24 (14 September 1973): 27-8.
  Traces Lord Peter Wimsey's "conversion" process in Sayers's
  novels, from a flat character to a complete human being.

Campbell, SueEllen. "The Detective Heroine and the Death of Her
Hero: Dorothy Sayers to P. D. James." *Modern Fiction Studies* 29,
No. 3 (Autumn 1983): 497-510.*
  Studies Harriet Vane and her relationship to Lord Peter Wimsey
  in *Gaudy Night*.

Dale, Alzina Stone. *Maker and Craftsman: The Story of Dorothy L.
Sayers*. Grand Rapids, Mich.: William B. Eerdmans, 1978, 158 p.
  A straightforward biography written to introduce Sayers and her
  works to young people.

Durkin, Mary Brian, O.P. "Dorothy L. Sayers: A Christian Humanist
for Today." *The Christian Century* XCVI, No. 37 (14 November
1979): 1114-19.
  Contains a biographical summary, followed by an examination of
  several works, especially emphasizing Sayers's essays.

Hall, Trevor H. *Dorothy L. Sayers: Nine Literary Studies*. London:
Gerald Duckworth & Co., 1980, 132 p.
  Contains various studies possessing a historical or factual, rather
  than interpretive or critical, emphasis. Hall includes several recollections and impressions of Sayers by her acquaintances.

Hannay, Margaret P., ed. *As Her Whimsey Took Her: Critical Essays
on the Work of Dorothy L. Sayers*. Kent: Kent State University Press,
1979, 301 p.
  Contains fifteen essays covering the full scope of Sayers's canon,
  and addends an annotated checklist of various collections of unpublished manuscripts and letters.

Hone, Ralph E. *Dorothy L. Sayers: A Literary Biography*. Kent: Kent
State University Press, 1979, 217 p.
  Combines biographical information with critical commentary on
  the majority of Sayers's works.

Marshall, Donald G. "*Gaudy Night:* An Investigation of Truth." *VII:
An Anglo-American Literary Review* IV (1983): 98-114.
  A close reading of *Gaudy Night*. Marshall concludes that the novel
  offers a wide variety of meanings and interpretations.

Mascall, E. L. "What Happened to Dorothy L. Sayers That Good
Friday?" *VII: An Anglo-American Literary Review* III (1982): 9-18.
  Defends Sayers's Christian orthodoxy.

Moorman, Charles. "The Suburbs of the City: T. S. Eliot, Dorothy
L. Sayers." In his *The Precincts of Felicity: The Augustinian City of
the Oxford Christians*, pp. 101-36. Gainesville: University of Florida
Press, 1966.*
  Examines the portrayal in Sayers's fiction of Civitas Dei (the City
  of God) and Civitas Terrena (the Earthly City), noting Sayers's
  debt to Charles Williams.

Nott, Kathleen. "Lord Peter Views the Soul." In her *The Emperor's
Clothes*, pp. 253-98. Bloomington: Indiana University Press, 1958.*
  Attacks C. S. Lewis and Sayers as a pair of "fundamentalists"
  whose thought and works are philosophically unsound. Writing
  from the viewpoint of a scholarly atheistic materialist, Nott argues
  that Lewis and Sayers are "braver and stupider" than other contemporary Christian writers, who are themselves "less pin-
  headed" than they.

———. "The Emperor's Clothes Invisible? An Open Letter to Richard
Webster." *VII: An Anglo-American Literary Review* III (1982): 19-33.*
  Defends her arguments against C. S. Lewis's and Sayers's thought.
  Nott's essay was written in reply to a rebuttal by Richard Webster
  (see Additional Bibliography) of the philosophical and literary
  arguments raised in her *The Emperor's Clothes*. "We speak,"
  Nott states, "different languages across an unbridgeable gap."

————. ''A Debate Deferred: Notes Towards a Reply.'' *VII: An Anglo-American Literary Review* III (1982): 45-8.

   Answers Sayers's essay ''A Debate Deferred: The Dogma in the Manger,'' a reply to Nott's *The Emperor's Clothes* (see Additional Bibliography).

Orwell, George. *The Collected Essays, Journalism and Letters of George Orwell*, Vol. 1, edited by Sonia Orwell and Ian Angus, pp. 160-62. New York: Harcourt Brace Jovanovich, 1968.*

   Reviews *Gaudy Night*. Orwell remarks that Sayers's detective stories, considered as such, are quite bad.

Patterson, Nancy-Lou. ''Beneath That Ancient Roof: The House As Symbol in Dorothy L. Sayers' *Busman's Honeymoon*.'' *Mythlore* 37, No. 3 (Winter 1984): 39-48.

   Examines Sayers's portrayal of Lord Peters' and Harriet's house, in *Busman's Honeymoon*, as a symbol that unifies the images of idea, husband, and wife.

Stewart, J.I.M. ''The Mysterious Mystery-writer.'' *The Times Literary Supplement*, No. 3949 (2 December 1977): 1398.

   Favorably critiques Sayers's unfinished biography of Wilkie Collins.

Symons, Julian. *The Detective Story in Britain*. London: Longman, Green & Co., 1962, 48 p.*

   Deems unsuccessful Sayers's attempt to evolve the detective story into a novel of manners. Symons states that in Sayers's later novels she submerged the detective story to the point that it ceased to exist.

Taylor, D. J. ''Meaning and The Mind of the Maker.'' *VII: An Anglo-American Literary Review* III (1982): 49-62.

   Compares the ''mind'' of the modern computer with the mind of the human creator as described in trinitarian terms in *The Mind of the Maker*.

Webster, Richard. ''The Emperor Clothed and in His Right Mind?'' *VII: An Anglo-American Literary Review* II (1981): 11-31.*

   A rebuttal of Kathleen Nott's philosophical and literary position in her essay ''Lord Peter Views the Soul'' (see Additional Bibliography).

Youngberg, Ruth Tanis. *Dorothy L. Sayers: A Reference Guide*. Boston: G. K. Hall & Co., 1982, 178 p.

   A selected bibliography of writings on Sayers and her work, spanning the years 1917-1981.

Robert W(illiam) Service

1874-1958

English-born Canadian poet, novelist, and autobiographer.

During the early twentieth century, Service was one of North America's most popular poets, and his work is still widely read today. He is best known for his jauntily rhythmic verses that celebrate life and adventure in the Yukon, particularly "The Shooting of Dan McGrew" and "The Cremation of Sam McGee." Because of the marked influence of Rudyard Kipling's work on his verse, Service has often been called "the Canadian Kipling."

Born in England and educated in Glasgow, Service moved to Canada when he was twenty years old. He traveled extensively in British Columbia and worked at a variety of jobs until he was hired by a Vancouver bank in 1902. Two years later, Service was assigned to a Yukon branch, where he remained for eight years and gathered material for his ballads. His first volume of verse, *Songs of a Sourdough* (also published as *The Spell of the Yukon*), was published in 1907 and was an instant success. The royalties from this book enabled Service to retire and compose more verse and his first novel, *The Trail of Ninety-Eight: A Northland Romance*. Service worked as a war correspondent for a Toronto newspaper during the Balkan War of 1912-13; he later covered events in France during World War I and also worked as an ambulance driver. After the war, Service married a French woman and remained in France, where he wrote most of his remaining verse and novels. In 1940, when the Nazis invaded France, Service was forced to leave and return to Canada. While in North America he spent time in Hollywood, where he wrote his two-volume autobiography. After World War II, Service returned to France and lived in retirement on the French Riviera until his death in 1958.

A poet who deliberately omitted the word "poem" from his book titles, Service was quoted as saying, "Verse, not poetry, is what I was after—something the man in the street would take notice of and the sweet old lady would paste in her album; something the schoolboy would spout and the fellow in the pub would quote." Considering the wide and continuing popularity of his verse, it would seem that he succeeded in this objective; for example, by 1940 *Songs of a Sourdough* had sold more than two million copies. The most famous poems in *Sourdough* are "The Shooting of Dan McGrew" and "The Cremation of Sam McGee," which mythologize the adventure and masculine vigor of life during the Klondike Gold Rush at the turn of the century. In these poetic ballads, which are designed as dramatic monologues, Service incorporated popular Yukon slang of the day with a memorable cadence and rhyme scheme. After the publication of *Sourdough* and another volume of verse, *Ballads of a Cheechako*, Service wrote his first novel, *The Trail of Ninety-Eight*, which was published in 1910 and was also extremely successful. Service intended it to be, in his words, "the only fictional record of the gold rush." He modeled the novel's main character, Athol Meldrum, after himself. Meldrum is a romantic dreamer and drifter, who, in spite of his outcast role, has considerable moral fiber and courage, but, unlike Service, is destined to fail rather than

succeed. *The Trail of Ninety-Eight* was later produced as a movie, as were several of Service's other novels.

In addition to the poetry and prose inspired by the Yukon, Service wrote books based on his experiences in the bohemian circles of Europe before World War I. The most popular work he wrote about this period is *The Pretender: A Story of the Latin Quarter*, which was published in 1914. This novel is a high-spirited, if slightly cynical account of avant-garde life in Paris. During the war years in France, Service's employment as a reporter and ambulance driver provided him with inspiration for one of his best-known books of verse, *Rhymes of a Red Cross Man*. It was this volume that enabled Service to gain a degree of distinction as a poet in his own right, and not merely as a devotee of Kipling, as critics had hitherto alleged. Many critics praised *Rhymes of a Red Cross Man* for displaying a genuine empathy with the common soldier's circumstances and for evoking deep feelings of patriotism in the reader. The volumes of verse Service wrote after the Second World War are more autobiographical and opinionated than any of his previous collections. *Songs of a Sun-Lover*, published in 1949, was Service's first postwar book of verse. In it he demonstrated his distinctive brand of rhyme-making, but also presented his opinions on such serious issues as poetry, politics, human nature, and religion. The bulk of Service's later verse was published under the title *More Collected Verse* in 1955. But it is his earlier ballads that are responsible for his continuing fame.

Because his poetry is deliberately anti-intellectual, Service has been alternately attacked or ignored by literary critics. Several recent scholarly articles on his work, however, have argued that the literary standards by which it has been judged are inapplicable, because Service's verse falls into an oral, folk-loric tradition, and its formal aspects are of secondary importance. Written to appeal to the unsophisticated and the traditionalist, Service's verse is widely anthologized and continues to find a large and receptive audience.

(See also *Something about the Author*, Vol. 20.)

PRINCIPAL WORKS

Songs of a Sourdough (poetry) 1907; also published as
     The Spell of the Yukon, 1907
Ballads of a Cheechako (poetry) 1909
The Trail of Ninety-Eight: A Northland Romance (novel)
     1910
Rhymes of a Rolling Stone (poetry) 1912
The Pretender: A Story of the Latin Quarter (novel) 1914
Rhymes of a Red Cross Man (poetry) 1916
Ballads of a Bohemian (poetry) 1921
The Collected Verse of Robert Service (poetry) 1930
The Complete Poems of Robert Service (poetry) 1933
Bar-Room Ballads: A Book of Verse (poetry) 1940
Ploughman of the Moon: An Adventure into Memory
     (autobiography) 1945
Harper of Heaven: A Record of Radiant Living
     (autobiography) 1948
Songs of a Sun-Lover (poetry) 1949
Rhymes of a Roughneck: A Book of Verse (poetry) 1950
Lyrics of a Lowbrow: A Book of Verse (poetry) 1951
More Collected Verse (poetry) 1955
Later Collected Verse (poetry) 1960

THE SEWANEE REVIEW   (essay date 1909)

[*In the following review, the anonymous critic discusses Service's poetic style, remarking that, although it shows considerable skill and vigor, his poetry deals too rawly with the harsh realities of life in the Yukon.*]

As records of actual experience in the West and farthest North, [the verses in *The Spell of the Yukon*] exhibit considerable skill and are well worth reading. The "Spell," however, we must admit, is rather that of the new matter, than of its artistic treatment. To us, to speak quite plainly, it seems ragtime verse, and we are yet unconvinced that a barrel organ tune is the fit means of memorializing the crude and terrible experiences of man face to face with the wilderness and the Arctic cold. Verse, is intended to drop a veil of illusion between the facts and us, that we may perceive their diviner significance. A violent insistence, therefore, upon crude verbal colour and literal rendering of line for line from nature in fierce without atmosphere garishness, seems to us a mistaken method, the more to be deplored as Mr. Service lays occasional claim to other than the venal favors of the journalistic muse. More than one line and stanza, indeed the conception of several of the entire poems, have sufficiently impressed us, to make the desire quite hearty

that Mr. Service would henceforward seek poetic truth, and not the veridicity of the kodak snap-shot; and go for his athletic schooling to poets of better pedigree than Rudyard Kipling. (pp. 381-82)

A review of "The Spell of the Yukon and Other Verses," in The Sewanee Review, *Vol. XVII, No. 3, July, 1909, pp. 381-82.*

THE SPECTATOR   (essay date 1915)

[*In the following review, the critic synopsizes* The Pretender, *applauding the novel's energy and humor.*]

[*The Pretender: A Story of the Latin Quarter*] is not a story of the '15 or the '45. The bizarre wrapper as well as the sub-title make that sufficiently clear. The pretending in which the hero of Mr. Service's new novel indulges is that common to all children, and, according to Miss Jane Harrison, it is characteristic of youth. But in the case of James Horace Madden it was temperamental and ineradicable. He was always under the spell of his histrionic imagination, and, to make matters worse, he had been for a while on the stage. When we first make his acquaintance as "the happiest young man in Manhattan" at the age of twenty-six, he was already at the close of the sixth period of his life, each inspired by a dramatic conception of himself. . . . But though consciously dramatic, Mr. Madden was also conscious of his limitations. Although he had achieved fame and was making a handsome income, he knew that he was simply repeating himself and trading on his initial success. He overhears two of his friends, a precious poet and an atrabilious critic, discussing his books at the club. The poet calls him "the Indiana idol, the Boy Bestseller-monger." He is "a perfect bounder as regards Art. But he knows how to truckle to the mob." And the critic more subtly attributes his success to the fact that "he *is* the public, the apotheosis of the vulgar intelligence." Hence his sudden resolve—inspired, as usual, by his histrionic imagination—to sink his individuality, disappear, and achieve success on his own merits. Hence a steerage passage to Europe, drudgery in London, a precipitate marriage to a French girl, and a long struggle in the Latin Quarter. In the end, after his MSS. have come boomeranging back with great regularity, the tide turns and liberal fees come rolling in. All this time, be it noted, he has discarded the pen-name under which he achieved his repute as a "best-seller" and assumed a new *alias*. Also we are given to understand that he has become infected with the artistic spirit of his environment. But with the best of intentions he was unable to escape success. He was "doomed to popular applause." . . . The story of this adventure is told with great gusto and abundant humour. The flaw, from a moral point of view, is that in obstinately carrying out his scheme he does so not only at the cost of his own comfort, but at the expense of his devoted wife, and comes very near losing her in the process, though at any moment in the game he could have saved the situation by revealing his identity to his literary patrons. So that while we are attracted by his exuberant and engaging personality, we are, at times, repelled by his self-centred egotism. The heroic qualities are monopolized by the wife, who is a miracle of thrift, industry, and uncomplaining devotion. Thus, for all its extravagance and high spirits, the story is a real tribute to French womanhood, as it is also an act of unqualified homage to the immortal charm of Paris, and a brilliant picture of latter-day and *ante-bellum* Parisian Bohemia, emphasizing its joyous *camaraderie,* while not overlooking its sinister and even horrible aspects. *The Pretender* is, in fine, a gay, high-spirited, audacious book, with moments of frank indecorum inevitable in any attempt to paint the life of the Latin Quarter, and one or two episodes which we would have wished away; but no grown person could take mischief from its pages. Here at least is a novelist who construes his functions in the spirit recommended by a writer in the *Contemporary Review*, and has no desire to exchange the rôle of an entertainer for that of a war critic. (pp. 818-19)

> *A review of "The Pretender," in* The Spectator, *Vol. 114, No. 4537, June 12, 1915, pp. 818-19.*

WITTER BYNNER   (essay date 1916)

[*An American poet, critic, and translator, Bynner was known for his expertise in Oriental art and literature. His translation of verse of the T'ang dynasty,* The Jade Mountain (1929), *was the first volume of Chinese poetry completely translated by an American poet. Bynner was first recognized by the general public as one of the perpetuators of the Spectra hoax. Along with Arthur Davison Ficke, Bynner, a traditional lyric poet who disapproved of the experimental movements in early twentieth-century verse, pseudonymously published a book entitled* Spectra (1916), *which was received by the literary community as a serious work but was actually intended as a parody of Imagist poetry. In the following excerpt from a review of* Rhymes of a Red Cross Man, *Bynner assesses Service's popularity and indebtedness to Kipling and notes Service's ability to accurately depict life on the battlefield.*]

Robert W. Service has been a poetic phenomenon. More or less ignored by the critics, he has won a vast following. And it seems to me time for a fellow-craftsman to protest that in this case the public is right. During these years while **"The Spell of the Yukon"** has accumulated a staggering sale of five hundred thousand copies and while the wells of Kipling have been growing muddy or dry, the professors of poetry and the dilettanti have been paying attention to Imagists and Spectrists, leaving Service—they thought—to school-boys. But the popularity of this poet need not have hurt him in the eyes of the discerning nor need his debt to Kipling have injured him in their ears.

It happens that I had just read and reviewed "Spectra," the latest expression of "the new verse," and been struck with it as a strange phosphorescent crest of impressionism, when there came into my hands the volume by Service, **"Rhymes of a Red Cross Man,"** two hundred pages of sturdy sentimental realism. And I started up with a gasp. Here was "the old verse." Here was something actual, intimate, human, alive.

I will grant at the outset, to such as incline to disagree with my estimate, an occasional familiar crudeness in the book and the mawkishness of poems like **"Our Hero," "Son,"** and **"The Convalescent."** But the crudeness is the kind you grasp hands with heartily and the mawkishness is the kind you look away from respectfully, and what's left, by far the greater part, you thrill and laugh over like a boy.

Here, as in the earlier poems, is an implicit acknowledgment of the debt to Kipling. It reaches even to free use of the phrase, "thin red line of 'eroes" or to the refrain, "For I'm goin' 'ome to Blighty in the mawnin'" echoing the refrain of "Danny Deever." But such echoes are the proper salute of kinship; for this latest book confirms Service not as Kipling's imitator only but as his successor. **"The Ballads of a Cheechako"** and **"Rhymes of a Rolling Stone"** were a disappointment to those who suspected their author of a true and important gift; for they contained nothing of the calibre of **"The Spell of the Yukon,"** that big poem which distinguished his first volume,

"Songs of a Sourdough," and has become the title-poem of its later editions. Nor did the general contents of his two intermediate volumes bear out the general promise of the first or prepare one for the vigor and sweep and human emotion of these poems of the War. The poems are dedicated to Service's brother, "killed in action, August 1916," but the emotion in them is not melancholy or bitter. It is not *against*; it is *for*. And it is not for a kingdom on earth or in heaven, but for your home and your fellows; and there's a recurrent feeling that your fellows may, after all, be Germans.

The best of the poems are long narratives in dialect, Cockney or Scottish. There are **"The Odyssey of 'Erbert 'Iggins," "The Whistle of Sandy McGraw," "Bill the Bomber," "The Haggis of Private McPhee," "The Coward," "Only a Boche," "My Bay'nit,"** and **"My Mate."** (pp. 531-32)

[The] book is not in its best element a commentary or a conclusion, it is an emotion; and therein, in emotion and in action, lies its strength. It is what Kipling might have made of the War, had his genius still been young. Though the master would have written with surer artistry and less sentiment, the pupil has an advantage or two. Kipling showed what discernment genius could give an imperialist; Service shows what discernment sympathy can give a democrat. And where the Englishman used technical terms with an impressive proficiency sometimes confusing to the layman, the Scotsman uses the slang of the trench so casually and fitly that the picture and the action is on the instant clear-cut and unmistakable. Detail after detail of life at the front takes its place in the various narratives, adding touches of excitement, pathos, terror, tenderness, or humor, and in the end imbuing this particular reader with a closer sense of life in the Great War than any correspondent, novelist, or poet has yet given him—making it so natural, straightforward, first-hand, vibrant, that if you are like me you will close the book with the painful silence in the ears that follows great sound and the flush in the head that comes from the sight of broken bodies and the squeeze in the throat that comes in the presence of honest human emotion. It is not a criticism from without, but a cry from within—dignifying even "Tipperary." We have been inquiring for the poetry of the War. In my judgment, here it is. (p. 532)

> *Witter Bynner, "Poetry from the Trenches," in* The Dial, *Vol. LXI, No. 731, December 14, 1916, pp. 531-32.*

H[ARRIET] M[ONROE]   (essay date 1917)

[*As the founder and editor of* Poetry, *Monroe was a key figure in the American "poetry renaissance" which took place in the early twentieth century.* Poetry *was the first periodical devoted primarily to the works of new poets and to poetry criticism, and from 1912 until her death Monroe maintained an editorial policy of printing "the best English verse which is being written today, regardless of where, by whom, or under what theory of art it is written." In the following excerpt, Monroe praises the vigor and accuracy of Service's war poems in* Rhymes of a Red Cross Man.]

After noting Mr. Witter Bynner's praise of [*Rhymes of a Red Cross Man*] in the *Dial* [see excerpt dated 1916], his generous acclaim of this adventurous Yukon trailer as a poet of a high order, I read the book through, almost persuading myself the while that I agreed: perhaps Mr. Bynner was right, perhaps Mr. Service's large public was right—here was indeed a younger Kipling, racing through war's marching rhythms and rising to lyric flights of song. Could it be?—was this Red Cross man from the Yukon the real thing? Then I happened to open [the anthology] *Soldier Poets* and turn to a chance song of a soldier now dead, Captain [Julian] Grenfell of the Royal Dragoons; and as I read *Into Battle . . .*, part of it as lyric as the song of a thrush, Mr. Service's deliberate rhyming fell to its own lower place. Poignant and sympathetic as he is, keen and racy, pathetic and humorous, in his presentation of the life and feelings of the rank and file, his poems are, after all, talk about it and about—in none of them does he utter the very heart-cry of the emotion.

On the lower plane, of poetry made rather than sung, some of the **Red Cross Rhymes** are very good indeed. (p. 272)

> H[arriet] M[onroe], *"War Poems,"* in Poetry, *Vol. X, No. V, August, 1917, pp. 271-78.*

DONALD OGDEN STEWART   (essay date 1921)

[*In the following excerpt, Stewart reviews* Ballads of a Bohemian. *Although he considers the book one of Service's weaker efforts, he notes that it contains several memorable passages. For further discussion of* Ballads of a Bohemian, *see the excerpt by Louis Untermeyer (1922).*]

Having successfully disposed of the Yukon and the Great War, Mr. Service now rents a garret in the Parisian Latin Quarter and tells us about this thing called Bohemia.

Rhymes of a Red Cross Man

BY

ROBERT W. SERVICE

Author of "The Spell of the Yukon," "The Ballads of a Cheechako," "Rhymes of a Rolling Stone," etc.

NEW YORK
BARSE & HOPKINS
PUBLISHERS

The title page of Rhymes of a Red Cross Man. *Courtesy of the Estate of Robert W. Service.*

One does not, of course, expect poetry from Mr. Service. But [**Ballads of a Bohemian**] must seem a little flat even to those debutantes and clerks who felt so strongly moved by the red blooded virility of the versifier's earlier works. When, for instance, he chants of the joys of being poor—when he glorifies the attic room, the ragged coat, the last ten sous—one is reminded of various recent glorifications of life in the army by patriotic lady authors. Through a hole in Mr. Service's ragged coat one catches a glimpse of silk underwear.

There are, however, as usual with Mr. Service, many quotable gems in this collection—many lines which linger deliciously, like the taste of garlic, after one has closed the book—my particular favorite being the following four lines from Noctambule:

> Full am I with cheer;
> In my heart the joy stirs;
> Couldn't be the beer,
> Must have been the oysters.

Musing over these lines one is minded to think of that other great Bohemian ballad writer, François Villon; one is almost tempted to hope that Mr. Service's emulation of that early bard will apply not only to Villon's method of enjoying this Bohemian life but also to his imagined manner of leaving it.

> Donald Ogden Stewart, *"So This Is Bohemia!"* in The New Republic, *Vol. XXVI, No. 338, May 25, 1921, p. 384.*

W. A. WHATLEY   (essay date 1921)

[*In the following excerpt, Whatley discusses the two major divisions of Service's work: the poems written before World War I, which focus on life in the Yukon, and those written during the war, which deal with the soldier's experience. Whatley also examines the influence of Rudyard Kipling on Service's poetry and maintains that while Service's Yukon verse is highly imitative of Kipling, his war poems are original and personal.*]

The work of Robert W. Service falls naturally into two divisions. The first of these consists of his entire poetic output prior to the Great War. The major theme of the verse of this period is the interpretation of the life of the Great North, with its pendulum-sweep from the heroic to the mean, and its direct contact with the primary forces of Nature; it is to this verse that Service owes his title of "the Kipling of the Northwest." The second division of Service's work is made up of poems written during the war and dealing with soldier life at first hand, being the direct result of the author's experiences in trench, camp, and hospital while in active service with the Red Cross at the Front.

In the pre-war verse of Service, the influence of Kipling is unmistakably and universally manifest. The poems of this period are, in the main, poems of adventure which are modeled, either consciously or unconsciously, upon the lines of the Kipling poem of the "Rhyme of the Three Sealers" type. In the **Ballads of a Cheechako,** the **Rhymes of a Rolling Stone,** and **The Spell of the Yukon,** the Kipling attitude toward the life of the wild and the primitive is the prevailing *motif.* Service, as well as Kipling, looks upon the North as the last stronghold of the hostile forces of Nature, into which man penetrates only as a rash and audacious intruder, but in which he has no legitimate place or standing.

This identity of feeling and spirit which characterizes the work of Kipling and Service is evident upon the most cursory examination of representative poems. (p. 300)

The Arctic scenes of both poets are drawn in the same light, are shaded with the same colors; the reactions of both to the inspiration of the North are in the same spirit.

In addition to this parallelism, there are other and more technical evidences of the influence of Kipling in Service's earlier work. His metrical forms and rhyme-schemes show a marked similarity to those of Kipling. . . . The ballad form is a prime favorite with Service; and in this, as in more minute features of his verse, the Kipling influence is evident.

Only in the matter of diction is there any appreciable difference to be noted; and the distinction here lies in something which is difficult to define, but which permeates the style of Service and serves to differentiate it subtly from that of Kipling. The style of both poets is spontaneous and virile; but there is an innate *American* quality in the diction of the one which distinguishes it from that of the other. It would be difficult, or rather impossible, to point out the exact nature of this difference without having recourse to minute and exhaustive analysis; the difference lies more in the nice shadings of habitual and local usages of language than in anything else, and its presence is more easily felt than pointed out. Service acquired his knowledge of the North through intimate and hard experience, and the language in which he celebrates its splendors and terrors is the *bona fide* speech of the North. Kipling's acquaintance with the North is at second hand, or at the best was made from the deck of a steamer. The difference in the degree of familiarity has left its trace upon the diction of both poets, if not upon the spirit of their works.

There is a tendency on the part of the general reader to class Service as a simple American echo of Kipling; and in so far as his early poetry is concerned, it is to be frankly acknowledged that Service is deeply in Kipling's debt. But Service is really more than a mere imitator—rather, he is an enthusiastic follower. He is a kindred spirit, an American continuation of the Kipling tradition—if such a thing as a Kipling tradition may be said to have come into existence so soon. (pp. 301-02)

As a war poet, Service has definitely assumed the position which Kipling, in view of his past achievements, might have been expected to occupy. One of the many surprises which were brought in by the year 1914 and its immediate successors was the complete and dismal failure of the greatest living English poet to live up to the spirit of the occasion. . . . [It] was left to Service, hitherto a simple follower of the elder poet, to sing the saga of the trenches, the hospital, and the camp.

The war-verse of Service is sincere and vital; it does not leave the impression, as is the case with the large majority of Kipling's poems, of having been written for a purpose. It is not tainted with the evidence of propaganda. It is a spontaneous interpretation of the spirit of the war through the lips of one who experienced it, throughout the various phases of its four years of conflict and toil, at first hand. It is instinct with the life of the "carry-on" spirit, the determination to make the best of conditions which were well-nigh unbearable, to see the stupendous task through to a definite and satisfactory ending.

The influence of Kipling is not so universally noticeable in this verse as in that of the pre-war period; the vividness of his experience of the Great Adventure seems to have inspired Service to break away into more individual and original lines. A number of these poems, nevertheless, show the old influence as plainly as do their predecessors; such productions, for instance, as "**Going Home,**" which is as evident an adaptation of "**Danny Deever**" as is "**The Song of the Mouth-Organ**" of another famous Kipling poem. "**The Red Retreat,**" "**A Song of Winter Weather,**" and "**Funk**" are reactions to trench life and campaign incident which show the influence of the *South African Ballads,* in structure, diction, and spirit; while "**Jean Desprez**" is equally traceable to such Kipling influences as "The Ballad of East and West" and "The Ballad of the King's Mercy." "**The Man From Athabaska**" marks the transition from the poetry of the North to that of the war, and is not lacking in evidences of the influence of Kipling, being somewhat reminiscent of the latter's "M.I."

In a second class of war poems, the Kipling influence is less evident. These have a more intimate, personal ring; and in this they show a marked departure from the Kipling model. In truth, Kipling is surprisingly neglectful of the individual for a poet of his magnificent range. He is interested in the interpretation of the type, and either fails to attempt or is incapable of the expression of individual reactions. Service, on the other hand, has a deeper personal sympathy; and where Kipling depicts the soldier class as an entity, *en masse,* Service develops the reaction of the individual soldier himself. (pp. 302-04)

There is a final group of poems among the *Rhymes of a Red Cross Man* which show no appreciable Kipling influence. These are purely personal reactions of the poet himself to the war, and the influences to be traced between their lines are anything but Kiplingesque. If anything, they are more reminiscent of the work of Rupert Brooke than of that of any other recent poet. Of these, "**Tricolour**" and "**The Lark**" are perhaps the best, although "**The Fool**" is almost equally good. (p. 306)

Thus Service, while he may be the inferior of Kipling in original gift of poetic genius and in versatility, is at least not justly condemned as an imitator and nothing more. That he is indebted to Kipling in no small degree, no one can deny; but it is equally undeniable that his work possesses merit of its own, which is not attributable to any exterior influence, and is only to be credited to the possession of native poetic genius. (pp. 307-08)

> *W. A. Whatley, "Kipling Influence in the Verse of Robert W. Service," in* The Texas Review, *Vol. VI, No. 4, July, 1921, pp. 299-308.*

LOUIS UNTERMEYER   (essay date 1922)

[*A poet during his early career, Untermeyer is better known as an anthologist of poetry and short fiction, an editor, and a master parodist. Horace Gregory and Marya Zaturenska have noted that Untermeyer was "the first to recognize the importance of the anthology in voicing a critical survey of his chosen field." Notable among his anthologies are* Modern American Poetry *(1919),* The Book of Living Verse *(1931),* New Modern American and British Poetry *(1950), and* A Treasury of Laughter *(1946). Untermeyer was a contributing editor to* The Liberator *and* The Seven Arts, *and served as poetry editor of* The American Mercury *from 1934 to 1937. In the following excerpt, he sarcastically names Service and Edgar A. Guest North America's poet laureates, and offers tongue-in-cheek "praise" for* Ballads of a Bohemian. *For further discussion of* Ballads of a Bohemian, *see the excerpt by Donald Ogden Stewart (1921).*]

The spell of Service is less local [than that of Edgar A. Guest] and far more potent. Is there an elocutionist that has not shrieked the tale of "**A Madonna of the Streets**" or a doughboy that has not heard (for the seventeenth time) **"The Shooting of Dan McGrew"**? . . . "The book **'Songs of A. Sourdough'**, subsequently called **'The Spell of the Yukon'"** (I am now quoting the author's bird's-eye view of himself) "reached its seventh edition before the date of publication." . . . His **"Rhymes of a Red Cross Man"** had, as their text,

> Have faith! Fight on! Amid the battle hell,
> Love triumphs; Freedom beckons—all is well. . . .

Witter Bynner, President of the Poetry Society, was roused to write, "It is what Kipling might have made of the War, had his genius been still young. . . . Excitement, pathos, terror and tenderness or humor and, in the end, imbuing this reader with a closer sense of life in the Great War than any correspondent (*pace* Gibbs), novelist (such as Barbusse), or poet (*vide* Sassoon) has yet given" [see excerpt dated 1916].

But it is possible to appraise the popularity of Guest and Service more directly. Both have recently appeared with new collections of verse in "two sizes of type pages, various bindings and richly illustrated slip-covers". (p. 482)

The paper jacket of Robert W. Service's new collection, **"Ballads of a Bohemian"**, . . . has the figure of a man holding a pipe as its central motif. But the scene, in spite of the elegant red smoking jacket, is much less domestic. In the smoke that drifts through the room, the figures of five smiling young ladies are seen, evidently visions of the smoker's bohemian past. They are grouped about a table in traditional attitudes of adoration and abandon; one is a dancer, one a model, one a midinette, the other two seem to be professional magazine-cover bohemians. So with the poems they epitomize. Temporarily abandoning the red-blood-and-guts style which he carried off so jauntily, turning away from his borrowings from Kipling, from "the lusts that lure us on, the hates that hound us", Service, thinly disguising himself as an obscure free lance in Montparnasse, gives us a series of seventy-five ballads and verses connected by shreds of prose. It is a gay, mad life he pictures— and such a startlingly original one! It is as faithful to life as Puccini's sugared opera, as Villonesque as Henry K. Hadley's correctly mincing "In Bohemia". Here we have the Latin Quarter with its procession of libertine artists and dangerously beautiful models; its murderous *apache* lovers who forsake their haunts and lead honest lives as soon as their child is born; its half-sentimental, half-cynical *boulevardiers;* its sewing-girls who queen it in Moscow, Rome, and the Argentine and then come back to die in the gutters of Paris; its parade of absinthe-drinkers, dandies, grisettes, Philistines. . . . It is all so refreshingly novel! The treatment of these unusual themes is consistently individualized. The famous story of the tame flea (the one that escapes and, after a search of the guest of honor, is handed back to its owner who cries, "That isn't my Lucille!"), this story is told in the metre of Gilbert's "Yarn of the Nancy Bell". . . . (pp. 483-84)

"The Pencil Seller" (beginning, "A pencil, sir; a penny— won't you buy?") and others of the same parlor genre are told in the rich declamatory idiom of "The Face on the Bar-room Floor". And when he leaves the Parisian background, Service's adaptability grows even more varied. He can be as lyrical as Noyes imploring one to come down to Kew in lilac-time, in lilac-time, in lilac-time. . . .

Eugene Field? Why not? The little toy soldier placed on a shelf by Little Boy Blue becomes:

> I'll put you away, little Teddy Bear,
> In the cupboard far from my sight;
> Maybe he'll come and he'll kiss you there,
> A wee white ghost in the night.

Naturally, Mr. Service, living in petulant Paris, lacks Edgar A. Guest's unflagging buoyancy. But he can also cheer his (according to the sales sheets) great army of readers by writing verses like **"The Joy of Little Things"**, **"The Contented Man"**, and **"The Joy of Being Poor"**. Technically, Service is incalculably Guest's superior even though he tries to rhyme such ill-mated pairs as "lyric—hysteric" and "rondel—respond well". But it is his paeans of Paris that will win him the admiration of all those who found his other verses so restrained and true to life. This is the life!—here amid the tinkling patter of the Boul' Mich', the Café de la Paix, the imbibing of countless Pernods, the plashing of the Fontaine de Medicis, the ever-fascinating poet's garret—this is the life of the true bohemian! We recognize it at once, we who have read "The Parisienne", who have seen a dozen ateliers in comic operas, we who find Merrick so much more effective than Murger. It is a rapidly growing gallery that Service is filling. Pictures of the Yukon, the War, the Red Cross, the Latin Quarter. It is almost time for the American laureate to rediscover his (and our) America. (p. 484)

Louis Untermeyer, "Our Living Laureates," in The Bookman, *New York, Vol. LIV, No. 5, January, 1922, pp. 481-84.**

LORNE PIERCE (essay date 1927)

[*In the following excerpt, Pierce credits Service's poetry with depicting the essence of the Yukon spirit and states that his poetry has an entertaining, though unrefined, quality.*]

Whatever may be said of [Robert W. Service's] poetry it made a section of the North in the pioneer days live for many people. Some have said that it is not true to the spirit of the Yukon, that there was little gun play and outlawry. However, he has limned in vivid and occasionally vulgar phrase a memorable picture of strong men, mastering passions, and a malignant climate. Some of his descriptions are memorable. He sketches with a vigorous abandon, and achieves some striking effects. However, he is more interested in men, and extracts the last atom of melodramatic possibility when dealing with them. Some of his poems are simple and sentimental, but he is at his best in poems like **"The Law of the Yukon,"** etc. His novels are either melodramatic or erotic or both, and unimportant. His later books of verse are not distinctive, although there are a few poems in *Rhymes of a Red Cross Man* which can be read with pleasure. Service, an Englishman, fascinated by a passing phase of pioneer life, and having to hand the popular anapestic, galloping verse form popularized by Kipling, added his own syncopating and barbarous alliteration. With a keen eye for the dramatic human element, and a grim sense of humor, and aiming at the man in the street, he beat out his violent lines. People were ready to be entertained, the author's popularity swept over the world, and has now disappeared. (pp. 98-9)

Lorne Pierce, "The Poets: Robert W. Service," in his An Outline of Canadian Literature: French and English, *Ryerson Press, 1927, pp. 97-9.*

V. B. RHODENIZER (essay date 1930)

[*In the following excerpt, Rhodenizer summarizes Service's place in Canadian literature, noting several flaws that have kept Service out of the front rank of Canadian poetry.*]

[Service's] work resembles that of Kipling, his avowed favourite author, in close observation of the "primal facts of life'' and in the vivid, incisive diction in which he expresses his observations. Unlike his master, except in the few early poems that artistically reflect the spirit of the North, he rarely rises to the level of poetry, and that for two reasons. To his material, often sordidly and brutally realistic, he does not apply the principle of selection, which is necessary to produce good realistic or even naturalistic prose fiction, still more so to produce good poetry. Again, because of his fatal facility in popular metres and his lack of artistic conscience, he rarely attains formal excellence. His verse, the appeal of which lies in the broad human sympathy and the sense of reality that characterize his material and in the irresistible sweep of his unpolished rhythms, records a phase of life not typically but only transiently and accidentally Canadian. The transitoriness of the kind of life that Service depicted accounts in the main for the fact that, though he had numerous imitators, of whom the most significant was Robert J. C. Stead, he has had no permanent following. To command attention, verse dealing with typical human conditions must have good form. (pp. 230-31)

> V. B. Rhodenizer, ''Other Canadian Poets to Service,'' in his A Handbook of Canadian Literature, Graphic Publishers Limited, 1930, pp. 224-31.*

ARTHUR L. PHELPS (essay date 1951)

[In the following excerpt, Phelps contends that Service's anti-intellectual stance and robust verbal technique were instrumental in creating a voice for the Canadian North and in contributing to the immense popularity of his verse.]

Service rhymes readily. He has an ear for easy rhythms; an eye for shape and colour. Apart from that, in his own mind, he has licensed himself to be rough and careless. It isn't that he deliberately set out to write down to a presumably vulgar and insensitive public. Rather, with some real talent for versifying, he never attempted to refine his expression. He made a virtue out of being himself. As a result, there is a sort of uninhibited crudity in his writing which now and then has the strength and even attraction of natural vigour. (p. 29)

[From 1907, when he paid a private publisher to print his Yukon poems, until now,] Robert W. Service has been a universally known name in Canada. No anthology of Canadian verse dare leave him out. No academic critic knows quite what to do with him. He has become an event in the writing annals of Canada on his own terms. Incidentally, his verse has made him well-off—almost wealthy. . . .

[Service] has gone on writing and he has always had his public. In nearly every book store in Canada two volumes of collected poetry can invariably be found: Kipling, of course, is the author of one; Robert W. Service is the author of the other.

Quite frankly, Service took Kipling as model. It is inevitable that he be called the Kipling of Canada. But the suggestion of subservience and pallid imitation can be misleading. Service found the Canadian Yukon. The Canadian Yukon found Service. And the colour and romance, the vigour and wildness of frontier days under the northern lights got some authentic essence of itself channelled into expression in a way that made Canadians cry out with delight. This is the story of that first printing in Toronto of the Service verse as told in a Canadian trans-Canada broadcast about ten years ago:

> In the composing room the men who set up the words got so enthusiastic that they went about reciting them like crazy schoolboys. They took

the sheets home, spouted them to their spouses, and shouted them to their neighbours over the garden fence. On trains going West, salesmen read them from the galley proofs to receptive roughnecks; while in the bars of the prairie towns, drummers declaimed them to the boys in the back room. Rarely has there been such a riot of glee over the printing of a book. And to the amazement of the publishers, before the book actually came out, many thousands of advance copies were sold.

For some there may be a kind of literary pathos in the fact that Service never advanced beyond the first volume Songs of a Sourdough and the second Ballads of a Cheechako, of 1909. Readers who purchase the Complete Poems published in 1940, may read and enjoy much of the added material, but to find Service and the original justifying delight they search out the Sourdough and the Cheechako pieces.

I think the clue to the justifying core of the Service achievement may be in his own words concerning his best-known poem The Cremation of Sam McGee. (pp. 31-3)

The story builds a grotesque gruesomeness into a folk tale of unquestioned natural vitality. The story is simple and there is imaginative gusto and comic relief as well as a fine touch of the ironic in it. (p. 33)

In this tale, by oblique inclusion, there is built up something of the mind, the imagination, the humour, the capacity for adjustment to any and all of life's exigencies and incalculable surprises, of the men and times of our Canadian North. Every Canadian feels that the great white North, and those nights when the long quivering silver and saffron fingers of the northern lights blaze and flicker and palpitate as from the source of all mystery, are his peculiar possession. Through a knack for easy taletelling and implicit involvement, Service recorded something we recognize as our own. (p. 34)

Canadians with some pretensions to literary taste are always half ashamed of Service; he is no artist, it is alleged. He lacks taste and range. He is sentimental. But to tens of thousands forty years ago he was the adequate expression of the excitement, colour and raw vigour of a romantic phase of Canada's development. Even today, he is loved and recited; a ballad maker for the folk who will not let him die.

For those outside Canada, Robert W. Service is a mirror not only of a vivid part of the Canadian scene, but of an aspect of what, in a broad use of the word, can be called Canadian culture. (p. 35)

> Arthur L. Phelps, ''Robert W. Service,'' in his Canadian Writers, McClelland and Stewart Limited, 1951, pp. 28-35.

MARTIN BUCCO (essay date 1965)

[In the following excerpt, Bucco examines the folkloric qualities of Service's poetry and how those qualities contributed to establishing a Yukon mythology.]

To millions of people Dan McGrew and Sam McGee are as familiar as Prince Hamlet and Gunga Din. At schools, colleges, camps, bars, clubs, conventions, smokers, and parties, the ''manly'' metrics of Robert W. Service are parodied and recited—perhaps more than any other North American verse. Yet fictive characters who flourish in the popular imagination do not always attract critical attention to themselves, to their contexts, or to their creators. Literary analysts who focus on complexity, nuance, and stylistic innovation dismiss Service's achievement as naive, banal, and facile. As "folk poetry," however, the early efforts of "The Bard of the Yukon" merit study. Since the folklorist customarily deals with non-aesthetic facts, he values Service's contribution for what it is, rather than for what it is not. (p. 16)

Although in British Columbia he became a bank clerk instead of a prospector, Service's sedentary occupation perpetuated his romantic outlook. He saturated himself in oral and written tales of northwestern North America. . . . The stories about exploration and danger that Service appropriated from folklore, myth, and ritual are ideal narrative material, and his own background helped integrate cultural patterns from diverse traditions. The quality of collective authorship which marks his early ballads stems from his capacity for defining in bold emotion, vivid images, dynamic meter, and fierce rhyme an unsophisticated people's feelings, attitudes, beliefs, sorrows, and aspirations. . . . His curiosity about the dwindling group of isolated muckers—Stampeders in the Gold Rush of 1898—their native intelligence, memory, and imagination, along with his own affinity for the foibles and folly of low society, down-and-outers, riffraff, and people uncontaminated by learned tradition, was highly suitable for a rich folk literature. Unlike the "folksy" Edgar A. Guest, Service saw vice as dramatically more vital than virtue. Therefore, in telling the inside story of the Yukon, he created a "Red Light Atmosphere" and tried through hard Anglo-Saxon and picturesque slang to blend realism and romanticism. Service longed to recreate a past that "otherwise would be lost forever."

The durable *Spell of the Yukon and Other Verses* . . . along with *Ballads of a Cheechako* . . . and the isolated Northland poems in his later volumes contain two strong mythic themes: Wonder and Initiation. The state of wonder or mystification results from Man's confrontation with environmental austerities and associations; the initiatory rites (*rites de passage*) involve quests and tasks. More often than not, these two "archetypal patterns"—treated tragically, comically, or tragicomically—blend in particular poems.

Some spectacular images of nature that cram Service's pages—legendary cliches that inflate the mind—are northern lights, groaning ice, burning sunsets, great stars, profound crevasses, blinding snow, bludgeoning silence, ice-locked land, rivers of blood, glacier-glutted streams, fanged mountains, fantastic sky colors, giant canyons, roaring avalanches, and the nail-driving wind. The barbaric land is alive with pine, spruce, tundra, and moss. Real and imaginary wolves, moose, deer, bears, foxes, panthers, and men prowl this land—at times an Earthly Paradise, at times a Howling Wilderness. Ostensibly, most men there seek gold. They dream, prospect, camp, hunt, fish, find, fail, drink, gamble, fornicate, lose, understand. The talk mainly is of claims, caches, grub-stakes, pay-streaks, pokes, kilters, picks, pans, bed-rock holes, sluicing-boxes. When not in log or stone settlements, the men sleep in tents and thrive on tinned tomatoes, embalmed beef, sourdough bread, rusty beans, and moldy bacon. Culture comes in the form of the Bible and the mouth organ. The initiate is either the narrator, another person, or a few men. Always preferring the ordeals of raw nature to the comforts of urban confinement, the seekers set forth on a quest involving challenge, struggle, hardship; the end—in simplest terms—is death or survival, failure or success. Those who succeed (and some who die) are real men, code heroes, a quasi-religious Brotherhood of the North.

At bottom, all religion rests on the memory of environmental mystery and holiness. Viewing the Northland ambivalently—loving its freshness and freedom, hating its famine and scurvy—the successful old prospector of "**The Spell of the Yukon**" yet is awed by it all. . . . Weary of champagne, the old prospector remembers the early struggle, and his recollection of the heroic land strengthens him. In terms of mythology, his desire to return to the Other World signifies a need to regain a lost power; in terms of psychology or religion, a rebirth. Similarly, the speaker in "**The Prospector**" who revisits the ghost-ridden Bonanza concludes that his sacred dream made the search for gold good. Reality was in the quest, not in the lucre. As such, one could readily substitute a Holy Mission, the Holy Grail, or God.

Conspicuous in many of Service's hyperbolic figures of speech is the wide-spread custom of viewing the land as an Earth Mother. Service's most complete contribution to this folk motif is the personification of a forbidding yet just Mother Earth in "**The Law of the Yukon.**" Here she is a celibate queen crushing the weak who come to rape, but embracing the strong who come to serve. Dreaming of her future blessed condition, of her good reputation, of motherhood, of fame, of bestowing riches "in the eager lap of the world," Queen Yukon clearly represents a frontier people's aspirations and enterprise. (pp. 17-19)

Besides portraying ancient and traditional frontier religious fervor, the agnostic Service also gives expression to pantheistic tendencies found in the folk. "**The Three Voices,**" for example, depicts the sea, wind, and stars imparting sentimentalities about bravery, freedom, and God. The stars singing of "the God in man" sounds like nineteenth-century romantic transcendentalism, and both the Adamic Emerson and Thoreau would agree that "a star or soul is part of the whole."

The universal belief in a god of place (*deus loci*) who confers benefits—material and spiritual—to pilgrims at his shrine makes the rich and awesome North an ideal place for dislocating "standard" values, for finding the self, and for establishing a new relationship between that self and the universe. The speaker in "**The Heart of Sourdough,**" his kit packed, is leaving, "ere another day is done," to seek things elemental and timeless. Though the mighty land will best the puny man, the wild romantic fight for survival is a blessing—one feels fully *alive*! The "Envoy" to *The Spell of the Yukon* insists that "even to win is to fail." The catalog of natural wonders in "**The Call of the Wild**" . . . beckons a man from the cradle of convention to the knowledge of self. (pp. 19-20)

Sometimes the journey is neither for God nor Self, but simply for the sake of duty or humanity. "**Clancy of the Mounted Police,**" for example, eulogizes the duteous Scarlet Riders. Talking as tall as Paul Bunyan or Mike Fink, Constable Clancy boasts that he can "cinch like a bronco the Northland, and cling to the prongs of the Pole." Into the Great White Silence moves the red-headed Mountie to rescue a starving madman on the banks of the Nordenscold. "Suffering, straining, striving, stumbling, struggling on," Clancy gets his man—and frostbite gets the heroic Constable's toes. Another frosted man—the teller of "**My Friends**"—ironically describes how two guilt-ridden criminals—a murderer and a thief—nurse him, haul him a hundred stormy miles to the nearest Mounted Police post, and then are arrested, men "wicked beyond belief."

Almost unprincipled beyond credulity is "the lady that's known as Lou" in one of Service's most famous ballads—"**The Shoot-**

ing of Dan McGrew.'' According to the balladeer's testimony, the editor of the *White Horse Star* urged him to give as his ''piece'' at the next church concert ''something about our own bit of earth.'' Tired of reciting ''Casey at the Bat,'' ''The Face on the Barroom Floor,'' or ''Gunga Din,'' Service determined to tell a story by musical suggestion. Strolling through town on a rowdy Saturday night, Service invented the opening line: 'A bunch of the boys were whooping it up in the Malamute saloon . . .'' His plot he discovered later that evening when the bank guard, thinking a thief had broken in, fired a shot at Service—but missed. Before five the next morning the tale of the celebrated shooting was on paper. Notwithstanding Service's judgment that the ballad was indecorous for recitation at the church concert, the setting, conflict, and action are felicitous as folklore. Hence, even the famous Sourdough, Klondike Mike, came to believe the rumor that he had witnessed the love triangle, the drinking, piano-playing, gambling, swearing, gunfighting, and double expiration in the frontier barrel house. Oddly enough, the demise of Dan McGrew is no more pivotal in the tale than that of the Stranger—as much a folk type as the Gambler and the Prostitute. Indeed, what might account, in part, for the ballad's wide appeal is its mystifying lack of organic centrality. Certainly, the first-person peripheral narrator sympathizes with the besotted Stranger more than he does with the undercharacterized McGrew. Further, the psychological conflict between the Stranger and Lady Lou is as desperate as the shooting between the Stranger and McGrew; and, finally, the common folk theme of true love and revenge rides tandem with that of forsaken love and greed. Contrast, repetition, heavy-handed rhythm, and climactic order carry conventional associations until the tag end. Fortunately, Lou's greed is as plausible (on second thought) as the narrator's black humor.

Besides the doomed gunfighters, Service versifies such fated humans as Dago Kid, Sailor Swede, Ole Olson, and Hard-Luck Harry, along with a host of nameless figures. In the vernacular of folk memory, Ole Olson of **''The Ballad of the Northern Lights''** spins his yarn to a stranger: the Big Stampede and the Trail of '98, when the Klondike was the center of the world and local legend ran wild. Broke after rioting in the ''siren town,'' each of the ''Unholy Trinity'' dream of a dead relative who promises the Golden Land. The folkloristic vision of fate spur their greedy kin to seek the lone moose trail along the Arctic rim. In time, the fevered men are driven mad by the fantastic Northern Lights—in Eskimo lore the capering spirits of the dead. After Dago Kid shoots himself and Sailor Swede freezes, Ole Olson staggers to the crater of a low, round mountain by the Polar rim and stakes ''the source and spring of the mystic Northern Lights.'' For ten dollars, Ole now offers to the stranger at the bar a quarter share in the crater full of radium (worth a million dollars a pound). In this tall tale about hidden treasure, a variation on the old story about selling the Brooklyn Bridge to bumpkins, Ole settles for the loan of a dollar. (pp. 20-1)

Of Service's tall tales, none surpasses **''The Cremation of Sam McGee''**—a comic version of the wide-ranging folktale of the return from the dead. Sam McGee's fiery resuscitation rates him high in the hierarchy of Northern folk heroes—higher, to be sure, than the anonymous Southwest buffalo hunter who crawled into a buffalo robe during a storm and endured emprisonment until the frozen skin was thawed out by fire. Service avers that he first heard the cremation yarn at a party in White Horse, where a miner from Dawson preambled it with the declaration that he would ''tell a story that Jack London never

got.'' Excited, Service (he states early in his autobiography that pictures of burning saints in Fox's *Book of Martyrs* gave him a ''gruesome delight'') afterwards left the party for a moonlit trail and began composing the key to his success: *''There are strange things done in the midnight sun . . .''* He claims that he finished the fourteen stanzas in six hours and spontaneously wrote it down the next day. As well as breaking the law of nature, Service's Southern prospector also disrupts the code of honor of the Brotherhood of the North—a type of inverse brag; instead of ''grinning'' about the Polar cold or ''laughing it off,'' he whines. A true code hero bent on keeping his promise to cremate the frozen body, McGee's trail companion voices the ballad's grotesque humor and irony, first when he declares that the derelict *Alice May* will serve as ''my cre-ma-tor-eum'' and later when he explains that he ''stuffed'' his friend in the glowing coal, but had to hike away from the ''sizzle.'' In short, Sam's is no Beowulfian cremation. The final sight of the grinning McGee and the sound of his peppery appeal is legion:

> ''Please close that door.
> It's fine in here, but I greatly fear you'll let in cold
>   and storm—
> Since I left Plumtree, down in Tennessee, it's the first
>   time I've been warm.''

(pp. 22-3)

In several of Service's poems, conspicuous supernatural and superstitious folk elements occur. **''The Ballad of the Black Fox Skin,''** for example, features shapeshifting, a motif common to thousands of far-flung anecdotes. In many North American Indian tales, transformation or metamorphosis facilitates homicide. The black fox pelt, according to ''squaw tales,'' comes from the unkillable devil-fox, a well-known folk creature. Scuffling over the pelt of the murdered ''man-with-no-name,'' Windy Ike hurls his mistress-accomplice, Claw-fingered Kitty, over a bluff and into the icy river; the note found beside the hole through which Ike himself later perishes reads:

> ''Here met his fate by evil luck a man who lived in sin,
> And to the one who loves me least I leave this black
>   fox skin.''

No one ever retrieves the pelt, but the narrator certifies that ''one man said he saw the tread of *hoofs* deep in the ground.''

Here and elsewhere Service, like the quizzically folk-conscious Hawthorne, employs the literary device of alternative possibility. **''The Ballad of One-Eyed Mike,''** another example, pictures the hypnotic dream of the persecuted crystal-eyed speaker. The river before him shrinks to a backdrop for wobbly flakes, wriggling snakes, and goblin eyes, reminding one of Coleridge's ''The Rime of the Ancient Mariner.'' Then Mike's dead enemy, seeking atonement, looms as an ''inky blot''; folkloristic terms for this phenomenon are floater, fireball, will-o'-the-wisp, or *ignis fatuus*. Even after his haunting dream, the appearance-reality dilemma remains, for Mike discerns ''something'' bobbing in the black water before it heads downstream. Not only hallucination, but folkish premonition—parapsychology today—informs ''Lost.'' Bathetically freezing to death in a blizzard, the ''erring'' son envisions his old parents and the old home trail; simultaneously, his mother presages his peril, hears his cry, and then sees her boy's frozen face pressed to the window pane. Old Father explains that what Mother heard was a wounded bird, and what Mother saw was snow falling from the maple tree. (pp. 24-5)

Undoubtedly, Service's humorous or pathetic grotesquerie derives, in part, from new ways of living in the raw subarctic wilderness and from the sense that the single man—no matter how communal or community-minded—is, after all, discrete. These aspects of frontier individualism impart to Service's Yukonistic *mores* the kind of unity and coherence discoverable in the local color tradition of New England's Harriet Beecher Stowe, California's Bret Harte, and Indiana's Edward Eggleston. However singular, Service's characters do share, among other things, common interests, lingo, legends, rituals, tales, beliefs, and skills. As a folk poet, Service cherished the protrusive differences between the Sourdoughs and the Outsiders. Likewise, earlier writers relied on such sub-literary ingredients as purple passages, exaggerated metaphors, and exuberant contrasts to express the folkways of stampedes to gold-ored California, Colorado, Nevada, and South Dakota.

Service's representative subjectivism frequently colors sense data, but he honestly reports that adventuring, westering, and prospecting more often bring gall and wormwood than milk and honey. His treatment of frontiering through archetypal folk patterns rather than through naturalistic social documentation does not veil his majestically unresponsive, supremely indifferent, and glaringly ruthless deterministic universe. But because the optimistic romanticism of the buoyant Adamic journey (a combination in Service of learned and unlearned traditions) overrides any pessimistic naturalism, he is fundamentally American. The European or Eastern American who seeks personal Manifest Destiny, whether he succeeds or fails, is better off for having discarded the stable and effete ways for the dynamic and manly. Folkloristically sympathetic with such economic failure as he depicts in "The Wage Slave," Service, however, reveals no contemporary concern for promoting security, equality, and prosperity for all men.

For many, Service's inspired myth of Northern glory replaced the tired myth of Outside shame. In short, indisputable Natural Law imposed order upon the interplay of mutualism and rivalry in the struggle for existence; the moral sentiment and the code of the Brotherhood of the North relied heavily on feelings of sublimity and inflated notions of poetic justice. Because the stampeders could not naturally forget their pasts—a source of dramatic contrast and psychological conflict—they gained not only experience of the New World, but also wisdom of the Old Self. For, as in seeking gold, the value in searching for some part of the Self is in the quest. In trying to define self, past, and place, Service also defined a folk, introducing them to one another, to Outsiders, and to their heirs. Like the mythic prospectors of the Glory Trail, today's Northlander—learned or unlearned—bears the burden of his past, but instead of willing vainly to "get shut of it," the modern Sourdough knows that his health, vanity, and pride need a vivid sense of tradition—Inside and Out—and that the folk poetry of Robert Service is a signal part of that tradition.... (pp. 25-6)

Martin Bucco, "Folk Poetry of Robert W. Service," in Alaska Review, Vol. II, No. 1, Fall, 1965, pp. 16-26.

STANLEY S. ATHERTON (essay date 1971)

[*In the following excerpt, Atherton discusses Service's attempts to create in his works a mythology about the Yukon. In Atherton's estimation, Service only partially succeeded at this goal because of his eclectic selection of Northern physical and climatic characteristics.*]

The Klondike Trail of 1898, symbol of the last great gold rush in history, captured the imagination of a continent. By the time Robert Service reached the Yukon in 1904 as a teller for the Canadian Bank of Commerce, public interest in the area was widespread. Well before Service himself began to record his impressions, a "Klondike literature" was already rapidly accumulating from the numerous eye-witness reports, the travellers' accounts, and the books of advice to prospective gold-seekers. For the most part, however, these works emphasized factual events and situations, and only those that were specifically connected with the Gold Rush....

Service, stimulated by the recent and contemporary events in his new surroundings, began to produce both poetry and fiction in an imaginative reconstruction of this world. What fame he has achieved continues to rest chiefly on the few volumes his eight years of residence in the Yukon yielded. These include [*Songs of a Sourdough* (also published as *The Spell of the Yukon*), *Ballads of a Cheechako*, *Rhymes of a Rolling Stone*, and the novel, *The Trail of Ninety-Eight*].... This body of work, rarely examined critically, deserves attention as one of the earliest attempts in Canadian literary history to mythologize the environment.

In his early poetry Service used the subject matter of the Gold Rush as a point of departure for his comments on man's relationship to the land. In "The Spell of the Yukon", for example, the Gold Rush is dispensed with in the first stanza. From here the poet moves to a description of the physical environment, using the Klondike as a representative northern landscape. The third stanza, and the remaining six, catalogue the varying responses and attitudes the narrator takes towards the North. (p. 67)

[In this poem] one finds a number of key concepts which recur with varying degrees of emphasis in the majority of the Klondike poems: a sense of loneliness, hints of the supernatural, hostile nature, an intense and meaningful silence, and a reminder of man's mortality.

Service is rarely content simply to describe the North. A number of his poems provide effective illustrations of the constant perils to human life in such a desolate area, perils which evoke a continual fear in man of the hostility implicit in the environment. He achieves his effects in various ways, often by utilizing the supernatural element found in indigenous Indian folklore. In "The Ballad of the Black Fox Skin", for instance, he recounts an Indian belief that a particular fox was invested with supernatural powers, and that any who attempted to do it harm would surely suffer. The sceptic who laughs at the superstition and kills the fox is later murdered, and the poem traces a trail of death marked out by all those who possess the cursed skin. By the corpse of the last possessor hoofprints are found, and the skin has mysteriously disappeared.

References such as this to specific supernatural occurrences are set against a wider background of mystery and other-worldliness which often characterizes the North for Service.... The language of death abounds in the work, often coupled with Service's characteristic sardonic humour. This pre-occupation with morbidity may account partly for his poetry's continuing appeal. In an age when the threat of violent death is more than ever man's constant companion, the macabre humour of Service takes on a contemporary relevance. Intriguing examples of this "northern gothic" can be found in many of his better-known ballads. Besides those mentioned, they include "The Cremation of Sam McGee", "The Ballad of Blasphemous Bill", and "**Clancy of the Mounted Police**". In these ballads Service creates a nether world of terror in which men are driven mad or to their deaths. (pp. 68-9)

If Service had continued to react imaginatively to the North in this fashion, he might have created a valuable mythic vision. As it was, he became a magpie, randomly picking up physical or climatic characteristics of the North and using them as they suited his fancy at the time. The result is confusion, with one poem contradicting another; and it is this inconsistency that marks his failure to create a coherent Northern myth.

The point is easily illustrated by comparing "**The Ballad of the Northern Lights**" with the well-known "**Call of the Wild**". The silent North, a "land that listens", was described by Sir Gilbert Parker as a land where the silence led man to meditate on the divine power that created the universe, and which guided man in his worldly struggles. Service treats this theme in "**The Ballad of the Northern Lights**," where in a terrifying world "purged of sound" three half-demented men hope to gain brief respite from the elemental forces harrying them by meditating on the things they "ought to think". In the world of the poem, however, the North refuses to allow such meditation; two of the men die, and the third is driven mad.

The ambivalence of Service's responses is seen clearly when the reader moves to "**The Call of the Wild**", for in this poem the silent north is revealed as the repository of truth. . . . Here Service says that only through intimate contact with the natural order can man come to a decision on the values he should use as a guide in life. The contrast with "**The Ballad of the Northern Lights**" is striking: in that poem the North is judge and executioner, resolutely condemning man to death for his weakness; here the north is teacher, benevolently aiding man to a more meaningful existence.

The conflicting attitudes toward the Canadian North which Service presents in his poetry are echoed in his novel of the Gold Rush, *The Trail of Ninety-Eight*. The novel is first of all a chronicle of a particular time and place, for, as the title indicates, it was the product of a specific historical event. Service, like Ballantyne and other writers on the North, found the subject matter for septentrional fiction in an event which had already stimulated widespread interest in the area. In one sense he was simply exploiting interest which the Gold Rush had created by producing a work of fiction to order, and one for which he could expect to find a favourable reception.

The Trail of Ninety-Eight dramatically retells the story of the struggles of men to reach the Klondike gold fields and their trials after arrival in Dawson. The hero, a romantic Scottish fortune hunter named Athol Meldrum, is introduced to the other characters on the steamer which carries him north to Skagway. Meldrum meets Berna Wilovich, the girl he eventually marries, and he comes into contact with the domineering and greedy Winklesteins, her guardians, and with Jack Locasto, the coarse brute who later intrigues with the Winklesteins to make Berna his mistress.

The terrible crossing of the mountains and the often tragic hardships of the trail from Skagway to Dawson are recounted in a series of illuminating instances which bring the trail to life in a manner reminiscent of Zola. (pp. 69-70)

Service's peculiar sensibility required a complete fidelity to fact, yet at the same time he was striving to realize his world imaginatively. But the conventions of popular fiction demanded a dramatic contrast (and conflict) between a sterling

Service at work in his cabin in the Yukon. Courtesy of the Estate of Robert W. Service.

hero and an unregenerate villain. So although Meldrum becomes thoroughly infected with the gold-fever on his arrival in Dawson, he is untouched by the easy virtue of a town where the "good old moralities don't apply". Aware of the mass appeal of exposure, Service made much of the immorality of those in positions of power. When Meldrum is cheated out of a claim he staked, for example, he makes a vehement denunciation of the official corruption which was widespread at the time. While such passages help to make *The Trail of Ninety-Eight* valuable as a social record of the Canadian North seventy years ago, the plot is all too often unduly contrived to admit them.

The intrigues of the evil Locasto with the guardians of the virtuous Berna are melodramatically portrayed in a sequence of incidents which take place while the hero is out mining. Meldrum's return to find that Berna has been forced to become Locasto's mistress, and has since been leading the life of a dance-hall girl, results in his own fall into the world of sin and debauchery about him. At length he is rescued from his self-destroying debauch, and he and Berna live together in a love-sanctified union. (p. 71)

Although it is obviously a contrived pot-boiler, *The Trail of Ninety-Eight* is nevertheless a significant contribution to literature about the Canadian North. It is one of the earliest attempts to make a myth of the north, to capture the spirit of the land and make it comprehensible. To do this, Service comes back again and again to the idea of the North as battlefield where man tests himself by contesting with the natural environment. While the idea of man and nature in conflict is conventional enough to be a cliché, Service might have used it freshly and effectively in the Northern setting. He failed to make it work, however, because he was unable to decide whether such a conflict brings out man's nobler or baser qualities. In a number of passages, of which the following evocation of the spirit of the Gold Trail is typical, the North clearly brings out the worst in man. (pp. 71-2)

Yet elsewhere, when the North is described as a new frontier, conflict with the environment calls forth nobler instincts. The challenge of untamed nature is met, the battle is joined until "overall . . . triumphed the dauntless spirit of the Pathfinder— the mighty Pioneer."

Similar contradictory reactions to the Northern landscape were noted in the poetry, and these are also evident in the novel. On the one hand, the North is repellent to man, its inhospitable nature an unwelcome reminder of his mortality. . . . On the other hand it is alluring, a compelling presence which casts its spell on the human imagination: "Who has lived in the North will ever forget the charm, the witchery of those midnight skies. . . . Surely, long after all else is forgotten, will linger the memory of those mystic nights with all their haunting spell of weird, disconsolate solitude." But here, as in the poetry, Service seems incapable of bringing the conflicting views together to create a consistent and meaningful vision of man in the north. The reader leaves his work aware of contradiction rather than ambiguity.

In the Gold Rush and the Northern setting two elements for myth-making were ready to hand. The event and the land in which it happened combined to provide the first significant opportunity for mythologizing the north. Unfortunately for Canadian literature the talents of Service were inadequate to cope with the challenge, and the opportunity was lost. (p. 72)

Stanley S. Atherton, "The Klondike Muse," in Ca-
nadian Literature, No. 47, Winter, 1971, pp. 67-72.

EDWARD HIRSCH   (essay date 1976)

[*In the following excerpt, Hirsch presents a structural analysis of Service's Yukon ballads, explaining their success as dramatic monologues. Hirsch examines the ways the ballads move through select sets of binary oppositions to present the needs, conflicts, and resolutions of conflict in the Yukon culture.*]

From the time that he published his first book of poetry in 1907, Robert W. Service's long rhyming narratives, written about the romance and hardship of the gold miner's life in the Canadian wilderness, have been extraordinarily popular. Their success was nearly instantaneous and by now many of his poetic characters have firmly lodged themselves into the popular imagination. (p. 125)

Despite their enormous popularity, Service's poems have been essentially neglected by literary scholars and critics intent on the products of elite culture. One aspect of the problem is that most scholars have confronted the poems with literary rather than sociological questions. Another is that there is some confusion concerning Service's actual intent and literary position. For though the ballads may initially appear to have been written as elite poetry, they have been most often read and transmitted as oral monologues by the people who have in fact loved them. Part of the disparity between their popularity and their literary reputation may lie in this distinction: that whereas Service's poems have been judged against other more essentially literary artifacts (and thus deemed unsuccessful), by the aesthetics of monologue composition and performance they are actually quite successful. It is important to add that Service's poems, and parodies of those poems, form an essential part of almost every monologuist's repetory. But as the few literary critics who have dealt with Service have noted, even to literary audiences the

natural oral and dramatic dualities of Service's verse almost demand, certainly invite, and perhaps even create their own performing context. (pp. 125-26)

Service himself has stated that he wanted verse instead of poetry—"something the schoolboy would spout and the fellow in the pub would quote." Insofar as that was his goal, he had indeed been successful. Therefore, by defining Service's ballads as poems which are particularly conducive to monologue performance, we at least partially account for the difference of opinion concerning Service's achievement. Moreover by viewing Service's ballads not only as poems but as texts for monologue performance, we can also account for Service's emergence as both a folk and a popular poet, two distinctions which do not always correspond. In so far as they are performed as monologues, Service's poems belong to a long tradition of oral literature (though with important differences) and hence are able to speak to specific small groups in immediate ways, even as ballads, stories, and songs do. Yet as written literature, they also have a greater circulation and are able to reach, in nearly exact form, a far wider literate audience. There can be little doubt that Service's poems have become far more widely known because they have fulfilled this dual role.

Our initial position is now clear: since Service's ballads were largely intended for public recitation and have been essentially accepted and transmitted as monologues, it is in that light which they should be studied. It is interesting to note that the very things which make Service's poems unacceptable to literary scholars also make them acceptable as monologues intended for performance. For example, Service's verse, like nursery rhymes and other forms of popular poetry, conforms closely to an ideal metrical rule . . . , thus specifically defying Ezra Pound's 1912 Imagist dictum that poetry should be composed in the sequence of the musical phrase, not to the beat of the metronome. Although this metrical regularity may be distasteful to a literati trained on stylistic nuances and metrical subtleties, Service's "clanging rhythms" serve several functions for the performer. First, they serve as a mnemonic device. Second, they allow the performer to concentrate—and to concentrate on—the drama of a story. The metrical strength not only helps to attract and to keep an audience's attention, but it also draws on the underlying metrical regularity which serves to modulate the tone and quickness of the speaking voice, hence avoiding monotony. The dramatic element of the performer's voice is in many ways necessary for the full success of Service's poems. And yet there must be something in the structure and content of the poems themselves that warrants their repeated performance. It seems likely, perhaps even requisite if they are to remain popular, that in some manner the poems articulate the needs and conflicts of the community to which they speak. (pp. 126-27)

[Since] the poems are still primarily transmitted through the written medium, and since the monologue performers are to a large extent bound by the substance of the printed text, an analysis of the material as written seems to be preliminary to other investigations. (p. 127)

By employing a structural approach we hope to reveal what is most essential to the meaning and character of the poems. Furthermore, we hope to show that the structure of the form (i.e. the metrical schema) corresponds to the structure of the content (i.e., the story the ballads tell) and that these unique analogues illuminate what is most important in the poems. Throughout this paper we will also be saying things about the nature and aesthetics of monologue performance.

We have chosen for the text of our analysis Service's Yukon ballads. . . . These ballads form a self-contained unit both in terms of the subject matter and metrical forms, and are the poems of Robert Service which are most often used, in fact almost exclusively used, by monologue performers. Though there is a great deal of diversity within the poems, it will be argued that there is at least an implicit unity in the substantive body of the material.

We begin our discussion with a lyric poem entitled **"Prelude"** which Service used as a preface to **Bar-Room Ballads,** not because it belongs to what we have depicted as the Yukon ballads, but because it illuminates several important aspects of Service's method and style. Most important of all, the poem essentially dramatizes the dichotomy between high-brow and low-brow, the Opera and the tavern, "the graceless hobo" and "the Land of Letters." The poem proceeds by a series of careful binary oppositions. . . . The rhyme scheme, a feminine-masculine alteration (ababcdcd), emphasizes this set of binary oppositions by always rhyming one of the high-brow—low-brow juxtapositions as opposed to any two like assertions or negations. Thus "unable" and "table" are rhymed, or "pity" and "ditty"; later such rhymes occur as "fetters" and "Letters" and "booze" and "Muse." The tone is both comic and serious, defensive and aggressive. Service achieves this remarkable effect by paralleling a serious word or emotion (pity) with a comic or low-brow one (ditty). In spite of the humor, however, notice that the negations are preliminary and are always rhetorically countermanded by one of the assertions. The poem ends on an aggressive, defiant note.

> A bar-room bard . . . so if a coin you're flinging,
> Pay me a pot, and let me dream and booze;
> To stars of scorn my dour defiance ringing,
> With battered banjo and a strumpet Muse.

Other oppositions, sometimes implicit, are developed as the down-and-out versus the wealthy, the graceless versus the elegant, the raucous versus the elite and self-contained, the drunken versus the sober.

"Prelude," like all of Service's poems, establishes a true democracy of language and consciously poses a colloquial diction which speaks to the masses against a sophisticated and elegant diction which speaks to the few. In Nietzschean terms the Dionysian is set against the Apollonian; in Marxist terms the working or lower class is implicitly set against the aristocratic or upper class. This is particularly crucial not only because it illuminates important aspects of Service's attitudes (which are defensive and aggressive, self-conscious and defiant) toward his high culture poetic contemporaries, but because of the values which it extolls and the community to which his verse naturally addresses itself. As they unfold, Service's poems indicate an awareness that he will be judged and misjudged by his more refined poetic peers. It can also be argued that Service's self-defined relation to those peers has analogues in the rugged Yukon miners' ambiguous relations to their safer, middle-class contemporaries who live in more domesticated territories, and thus corresponds to the binary oppositions which will be established in the Yukon ballads. It can also be stated that the verse, articulate the values and conflicts of the Yukon miners and, probably to a lesser degree, of the monologue performers and their audiences who have nothing to do with the Yukon. The final judgement about the expressive value of an art form of Service's kind must still be based on the range of its popularity. And Service's ballads are certainly popular.

What we have designated as Service's Yukon ballads depict a language of oppositions which is structured within the overall language and on which any of the single ballads may draw. These oppositions may be seen in a general schematic framework which has elements from all of the ballads, but of which elements *all* are almost never contained in any given ballad. (pp. 128-30)

The primary and omnipresent conflict of Service's Yukon ballads is the opposition between life in the Yukon and life in other places. While life in the Yukon is explicitly dramatized and individuated, life in other places is usually assumed implicitly, or conceptualized in only the most general and stereotypic terms. This pattern also corresponds to Service's dramatization of the low-brow—high-brow poetic conflict where the low-brow is assertively and dramatically revealed while the high-brow is presented only in the most general terms. Nonetheless (these ballads are, after all, ostensibly about the Yukon), if only from the most obvious juxtaposition of elements, it is possible to establish Service's defining characteristics of life outside the Yukon.

In Lévi-Strauss' terms, which are indeed relevant, Service's poems dramatize the ongoing conflict between nature and culture, the terribly raw (Dionysian man) and the elaborately cooked (Apollonian man). The terribly raw, or life in the Yukon, is associated with the hard, physical life, which in turn means life in constant confrontation with death, a natural preoccupation of the gold miners. Implicit in this is the opposition of an easy life, which is also the secure but tedious life in other places. This middle-class safety, or civilization, which we shall term death-in-life since it guarantees a secure physical life but implies a kind of spiritual death or mediocrity, defines an existence without promise (gold) or sacrifice (inherent in conditions of life in the wilderness). Its traditional virtues are warmth (both in a literal and a metaphorical sense), the security of a family, the stability of a job and a regular income. Life in the Yukon, however, which we shall term life-in-death since the barren, frozen, impoverished and dark conditions of the Yukon imitate a certain kind of physical death at the same time that they promise a high spiritual or romantic life, is of exactly the opposite order. Service's poems rationalize (often they are openly nostalgic for) the renunciation of all that life in the Yukon is not—safe, secure, and boring—while simultaneously exhibiting a longing for that familiar existence. Life in the Yukon might feasibly be equated with a physical and beastly Hell, but with the promise of Heaven (i.e., gold or extreme wealth). Dependent upon the miner's mood, be it hope or despair, the home life will take on the opposing qualities; thus it will be pictured as either Heaven or Hell, whereas when the average gold miner left it was only earth. This may, in fact, reverse (at least temporarily) what we have described as the death-in-life of middle-class life. To extend the Heaven/Hell metaphor, it is also possible to see Heaven, or the promise of gold, as the hopeful future, as opposed to Hell which is the barren present. It is only the fantastic promise of wealth that can be used to justify the risk and extreme poverty of the present. Service has localized the metaphor of Hell by making it frighteningly cold as opposed to frighteningly hot as it is usually portrayed. Finally, without the promise of gold it would be impossible to rationalize the renunciation of a secure life outside of the Yukon. Service's ballads inevitably draw on the ambiguities of that renunciation, and on the central emotional conflicts of the gold miner's existence.

One aspect of the conflict is the role that the saloon often plays in the implicit struggle between life styles. Having characteristics of both styles of life, the bar-room is something of a mediator between the two styles. Thus it can be defined as neutral territory, a social arena, a place where the conflicts can be localized. Similarly, it is both domestic and wild, a place of rest and leisure, a locale where ballads are both performed and dramatized. (pp. 130-32)

The way in which the bar-room acts as both a secondary world (a place where the art form is performed), and a primary world (a place where the dramatization takes place), and thus represents aspects of life in the Yukon and life outside the Yukon, can best be illustrated by the following chart:

Yukon	Bar-Room	Middle-Class Life
open spaces	closed space, but surrounded by the wilderness	closed space, house
extreme cold	warm, but surrounded by the cold	well-protected warmth
extremely dark	light, but surrounded by the darkness	well-lit
individual miners— alone	individual miners with other miners—social	individual miners with others—family
no women	barmaids, prostitutes, kept women, etc.	wives, daughters, mothers
sober	drunk	sober
no love	sex, cards, drink	familial love
North	North, but first stop into and out of the Yukon	South

(p. 132)

Perhaps the most perfect example of a poem in which the bar-room is a dramatic as opposed to a performing center (as in most of the Bar-Room Ballads) that mediates the essential conflict is in **"The Shooting of Dan McGrew."** This ballad primarily dramatizes love or sexual conflict. McGrew's reality (alone) and his dream of reality (a wife, a home) are mediated by the presence of the lover who betrayed him. His despair is founded on the clear juxtaposition of what he has and what he wants, and by the fact that he has lost his mediator, the lady Lou. The bar-room is the place where he expresses his feelings (by playing the piano) and indicates his poverty (by looking as if he's been in Hell). The ballad also opposes his physical wealth with his physical longing; the bar, for example, is characterized as a social arena where no one cares for each other (though they are together) and is in itself juxtaposed against a real home, even as a faithful Lou (as opposed to Lou as she really is, unfaithful), is juxtaposed against a real wife. The gunfight between Dan McGrew and the nameless miner takes place in the bar, which is the localizer of the conflict. Thus the bar serves as a kind of stage *for* the dramatization as well as an essential element *in* the dramatization. It is both backgrounded and foregrounded, the thematic center of the story of true love and revenge, forsaken love and greed. Thus the saloon is both a secondary and a primary world.

This is not to say that the bar-room is always a mediator for the oppositions of death-in-life and life-in-death. Sometimes the conflicts are set in direct dynamic tension with only the Yukon as the locale, as in **"The Cremation of Sam McGee"** where the mediation takes place in offsetting journeys. The absence of the bar, in fact, tends to heighten the juxtapositions of reality in the Yukon (Hell) and nostalgia for life outside the Yukon (which becomes Heaven). We can thus argue that the mediators change, but the overall binary oppositions remain static. Once again, the conflicts of any given poem draw from and rely upon this communal set of oppositions as established in the chart, although the chart is not identical to the conflicts in any given poem.

It is now time to proceed with a detailed analysis of a single text, **"The Cremation of Sam McGee"** both in terms of content and the metrical form used. (pp. 133-34)

We have chosen **"The Cremation of Sam McGee"** for our ballad *par excellence* because it is one of the most popularly performed monologues, it is metrically representative of all of the Yukon ballads, and at the same time it is somewhat difficult to conceptualize against the backdrop of our chart of binary oppositions, particularly since there is no bar-room to localize the conflict. The poem is ostensibly not about the conflict between middle-class life and life in the Yukon at all, and yet it will be illustrated that in terms of the underlying structure, on both the literal and symbolic levels, the poem is 'about' the juxtaposition of the life-in-death and death-in-life tension.

The metrical form of **"The Cremation of Sam McGee"** is basically an alternating anapestic and iambic heptameter, the pattern of which is consistently varied by substituting an iamb for an anapest in the last foot of each line. This creates the kind of rhythm which Mike Harding finds inherently necessary for good monologues. Once again, the language is colloquial and straightforward, immediately comprehensible. Since the form is highly conventional, both in terms of rhyme and meter, the reader can concentrate on the narrative elements of the story. (p. 135)

The first stanza and the last (the introduction and the denouement) create a frame within which the poem establishes its oppositions. The story is considered strange because it is supernatural, a tale of death and ressurection meant to astonish and perhaps frighten. However, as will be illustrated, under the exotic surface the poem expresses the normative values, feelings, and tensions of Service and the Yukon miners whom he portrays. The story also appears strange, at least to the narrator, because Sam McGee is unlike the other miners insofar as he is weak and cowardly and exceptionally obsessed by the cold. For that very reason he is an exceptional example of the ambiguous feelings which any gold miner in the Yukon would have to have. Structurally, the poem reveals and works out through "build up, attack, and pay off" many of the most crucial, literal and symbolic, binary oppositions of our chart.

After the introductory stanza, which might be viewed as a frame for the poem, the ballad begins in earnest with a series of implicit oppositions. As the first stanza progresses, the reader discovers, or might discover, that he is getting not a dramatization but a setting of oppositions already defined in our binary set. The actual dramatization, or the literal present, does not in fact focus until the third stanza. (p. 137)

What appears to be the first journey of the poem, but which, as we have seen, is in fact the second (implicit in Sam McGee's presence in the Yukon) takes place in stanza three. The next stanza fully articulates the Yukon-as-death theme (which will be played to its ultimate logical conclusion) by establishing and extending the symbolic metaphor of cold. (p. 138)

Thus we have the continuation of the journey in the Yukon . . . and Sam McGee's death. The narrator is forced to continue the journey . . . , and symbolic return both to the South and to the security of the womb. It is important that at this point in the poem (stanza eight) Sam McGee is dead, and his body is icy cold, but his journey back, which concludes with cremation and thus a final or second death, essentially culminates in resurrection. This is the second birth (''Now Sam McGee was from Tennessee'') and we have come full cycle back to the South (''Since I left Plumtree, down in Tennessee, it's the first time I've been warm.''). This of course makes for a neat closure, accentuated by the repetition of the first stanza of the poem at the end. (pp. 138-39)

In so returning, the theme of death in the Yukon (and how in this case it overwhelms spiritual life so as to make that life meaningless) is pushed to its logical extreme. As life in the Yukon becomes more and more closely identified with Hell, life in Tennessee becomes more closely identified with Heaven. . . . It is only because of Sam McGee's exceptional cowardice and fear of the cold that Tennessee becomes fully and literally associated with Heaven, and the cycle is thus completed, the theme pushed to its logical conclusion. This conclusion contains a reversal or violation of our established categories. It is in death, after all, that Sam McGee finds a second life. But what is perhaps most interesting of all is that Sam McGee's case is only exceptional in terms of its intensity, not in terms of its impulse. In fact, the essential oppositions categorized—warmth and cold, security and insecurity, or danger contemporaneous with promise—are common to all of the ballads. Because of the absolute intensity of Sam McGee's feelings, the terms are pushed to their logical extremes. At this point the tale becomes strange and supernatural, but the oppositions nonetheless remain normative. Thus, one of Service's most extraordinary ballads fits into our schema of binary oppositions. (pp. 139-40)

> Edward Hirsch, ''A Structural Analysis of Robert Service's Yukon Ballads,'' in Southern Folklore Quarterly, Vol. XL, Nos. 1 & 2, March-June, 1976, pp. 125-40.

CARL F. KLINCK (essay date 1976)

[*In the following excerpt, Klinck discusses the themes of Service's later verse.*]

Two poems, **''Dan McGrew''** and **''Sam McGee,''** had brought Robert Service fame and fortune. They had given him the freedom to pursue a career of rhyming which lasted fifty years and yielded more than two thousand pages of printed verse. Late in his life he estimated wryly that he had written thirty thousand couplets, and employed more than ten thousand rhymes. (p. 171)

[Service's **Collected Verse** and **The Complete Poems**] were succeeded by **Collected Poems**, copyrighted by the author in 1940. **The Bar-Room Ballads** . . . were made Book Six in this new collection, but the inconsequential **Twenty Bath-Tub Ballads** . . . were omitted. These facts indicate a hiatus in his writing of verse, certainly in his publication of verse, between **Ballads of a Bohemian** . . . and 1940—that is, through the ''thriller'' twenties, the possibly lazy thirties, and the war-time forties. It is difficult, however, to determine how many verses

written during the hiatus went into the first volumes of Service's post-war series of poetic books which began with **Songs of a Sun-Lover,** published in 1949. Not much, therefore, can be said to identify any poetic production of the Nice and second Hollywood periods, which ended in 1946. In that year, with the removal of Service's household to Monte Carlo, the remarkable Monaco period began.

This Monaco verse has considerable biographical and critical value, for it rounds out, on Service's own terms, the story of his life and thought. Most of it was published in separate volumes before the large collected editions were made. In the various titles, the sacred word ''poem'' is conspicuously avoided: [**Songs of a Sun-Lover, Rhymes of a Roughneck, Lyrics of a Lowbrow, Rhymes of a Rebel, Songs For My Supper, Carols of an Old Codger, Rhymes For My Rags,** and **Cosmic Carols**]. . . . (pp. 171-72)

All of these later publications show that Service was surveying his past in terms of the present in which he found himself. **Songs of a Sun-Lover** . . . seems to be related in a special way to the prose works of the 1940s, when he was turning his attention from Paris to the south of France, and, with the fresh experiences of war-time residence in North America, writing his biographies, **Ploughman of the Moon** . . . and **Harper of Heaven.** . . . Some of the songs in **A Sun-Lover** may have been ''harped'' in the early 1940s. Certainly this book is dedicated to Provence: ''O Land of Song! O golden clime!'' In a lyric for his seventy-fifth birthday on the 16th of January, 1949, he was in a mood to ''whoop it up'' and let the world know that he was still alive. Coming to terms with his destiny was going to be necessary, but chiefly as part of an on-going career in song.

Songs of a Sun-Lover gave him an opportunity to reappear as the same old poet with an even stronger assertion of his aims. His *apologia* for his early and his forthcoming verse runs through this first of the Monaco books; it is most clearly stated in **''A Verseman's Apology''**,

> Alas! I am only a rhymer,
> I don't know the meaning of Art;
> But I learned in my little school primer
> To love Eugene Field and Bret Harte.
> I hailed Hoosier Ryley with pleasure,
> To John Hay I took off my hat;
> These fellows were right to my measure,
> And I've never gone higher than that.
> . . . .
> For God-sake don't call me a poet,
> For I've never been guilty of that.
> . . . .
> And I fancy my grave-digger griping
> As he gives my last lodging a pat:
> ''That guy wrote McGrew;
> 'Twas the best he could do'' . . .
> So I'll go to my Maker with that.

In an intermediate stanza he declared that

> The Classics! Well, most of them bore me
> The Moderns I don't understand. . . .

(pp. 174-75)

There was some over-statement in this; he knew, for example, what a Pullman porter at Montreal meant when that polished servant of travellers declared that he owned all of Service's books of verse, but his taste was ''Eliot and Auden''. In **''Book-**

A photograph of Service when he was, in his own words, "crowding eighty-four." Courtesy of the Estate of Robert W. Service.

Lover'' Service gave an impressive list of great authors on his library shelves which he now no longer read. In **''My Library''** he confessed with shame that he was too old to read his thousand books, but that he ''wallowed'' in ''the Daily Press.'' It was part of his programme for living and writing in the world of the present day with plenty of time for communion with nature. In this way he hoped to stay in touch with ''simple folk.'' . . . (p. 175)

A few Yukon ballads, included in *Sun-Lover,* showed that this was indeed the McGrew and McGee storyteller that readers remembered. The comedy was in Service's coarsest vein, and he added to his Northern characterizations the first of a series of effective ballads about Montreal Maree, a dance hall girl ''as pretty as a pansy, wi' a heart o' Hunker gold.'' The tuneful lyric about **''Marie Vaux of the Painted Lips''** is a welcome addition to this book: under the title of **''The Last Supper''** it had first appeared in *The Trail of Ninety-Eight* as the work of the ''Pote'', Ollie Gaboodler. Service was now claiming it as his own. There is further sympathy for fallen women in **''Babette''**, **''No Lilies for Lisette''**, and **''White Christmas''**; these evidently belong to the Bohemian period. There are also compassionate portrayals of the various unhappy fates of an actor, a millionaire, a little Jewish orphan, an opera singer, a tippler,

a murderer, a motorcycle racer and his girl, a boxer, and the deserted sweetheart of a soldier boy. Service's portrait gallery, already packed with distinctively drawn likenesses of a host of characters, would have many more additions before he laid down his pen.

In *Sun-Lover* Service displayed a growing tendency to make explicit attacks upon war, political injustices, and oppression of the poor. The realism with which he now went to the heart of a matter was sharper than the realism of setting in the thrillers, or the realism of human activity in the earlier vignettes. But his ideas were still incorporated in the doings of men and women, often through the device of using these characters as the ostensible speakers of the lines of a poem. His favourite technique involved a brief, effective presentation of a situation followed by an expression of the consequences thereof in a rhetorical or ironic ending. He was tireless in his search for the unique word or phrase. (pp. 176-77)

In **''God's Battle-Ground''** he laid the foundations of his opinions about divinity. . . .

God is not diminished by offering to man the freedom to act in gentle kindliness or in evil ways. God being ''What is,'' the struggle is also God's: the struggle is human and divine. Thus, for Service, life was God's experiment, and it called for active realism, not for ''abstract terms,'' which appeared to set God at a distance from daily life. (p. 178)

There is a sense in which, for him, life and all his writings were religious, for he was dedicated to finding and reporting little dramas of human experience; vignettes were revelations of mingled success and failure on an individual scale. A report of life as lived was a form of identification with the universe. . . . The poet is a ''maker'': it is his business to construct an accurate verbal transcription of what he can see and know. It is his mood that counts. ''Goodness is Godness,'' and Goodness is kindliness, compassion, love, peace, tolerance, and opposition to tyranny and oppression. ''To fight that Mankind may be free . . . ,'' he said, ''There is our Immortality.'' It seemed a high calling from which a versifier of the ''common'' lot was not excluded.

It will not be possible to trace restatements of these themes through all the Monaco books, although the next one, *Rhymes of a Roughneck* . . . , shows an interesting development beyond the conclusion of **''Prayer.''** Praying was not in Service's line. . . . Yet ''when the *Cross* I see / I make the sign.'' Some of the later books have sections entitled ''Rhymes for Reverence.'' Perhaps one should not be startled when one turns to the last page of *Roughneck* where a [Roman cross] appears under the title **''Rhyme For My Tomb''.** (pp. 179-80)

The *Roughneck* book may be regarded as a supplement to *Sun-Lover,* for the Rhymes are grouped under headings appropriate to both books: ''Low-brow Lyrics,'' ''Garden Glees,'' ''Library Lays,'' ''Poems of Compassion,'' ''Ribald Rhymes,'' ''Vignettes in Verse,'' and ''Mortuary Muse.'' A fair choice from the numerous offerings in each of the categories respectively would include **''McCluskey's Nell''** (a Montreal Maree ballad); **''My Pal''** (''Brave bird, be lyric to the last. . . . And so will I, / And so will I''); **''Amateur poet''** (''To make my rhyme come right, / And find at last the phrase unique / Flash fulgent in my sight''); **''The Under-Dogs''** (''What have we done, Oh Lord, that we / Are evil starred?''); **''Include Me Out''** (''I grabbed the new *Who's Who* to see / My name— but it was not . . . / The book I held was *Who WAS Who* / Oh was I glad—and how!''); **''Humility''** (''Yet if in sheer humility / I yield this yokel place, / Will he not think it mockery / And spit into my face''); and **"The Hand"** (''How merciful a Mind / My life has planned!'').

In such verses there are few significant differences from those in *Songs of a Sun-Lover*. Yet one may sense Service's growing tendency to stress the lamentable in human existence and to moralize about it; at the same time there is no retreat from the policy of illustrating nearly everything by means of vignettes and suggestive images. The pronoun ''I'' (so often used) belongs to his *persona*, his fictional participant, but the author's heart is in that ''I'' more sympathetically than ever before. He cannot resist being part of all that he had met. Also, he gives evidence of renewed and stronger literary interests: he had been recalling and rereading his favourite authors. In **"God's Skallywags"** he asserts that he would set Villon, Baudelaire, Byron, Poe, Wilde, Francis Thompson, and Burns high above the ''merely holy'' writers. He praises Maeterlinck as ''a forgotten master,'' communes with the spirit of Thomas Hardy as one of the ''Great Rejected Poets,'' and gives ''his vote'' to Cervantes rather than to Shakespeare.

One of the novel features of **Rhymes of a Roughneck** is the appearance of travel verses. The first instalment of a series which would range through several books from ribaldry to indignation was saucily entitled ''Dago Ditties.'' As a **Tourist** he preferred ''to Mike Angelo / The slim stems of a lady tourist''; and as a **"Florentine Pilgrim"** he thought ''better than a dozen Dantes'' was ''something cute in female scanties.'' What he wrote about **The Pigeons of St. Marks** can be left to the imagination. Yet there was reverence for genius and art. The Leaning Tower of Pisa reminded him that Galileo had stood there; and the Apollo Belvedere was ''A bit o'frozen music.'' (pp. 180-81)

[*Songs For My Supper*] was the fifth of the Monaco books and stood at the end of the collection entitled **More Collected Verse**, published in 1955 while Service was still alive and writing. (p. 186)

There are several . . . unusual features in this book of *Songs*. Service here drops his Rolls Royce contentment and puts on the mask of a bard, eighty years of age, who must work for his bread because no one will buy his books. In fact he was very rich, but this device served to identify himself with the poor, the unemployed, the underprivileged, the prisoners of toil, the unwilling soldiers, and the doomed felons. He had experienced in early life all but the last two of these misfortunes. The theme is, once more, resentment on behalf of those whom systems of various kinds have caged. Service was an exponent of liberty, not of equality, not of fraternity, and not of communism. He was an individualist to the end.

In ''Domestic Ditties'' he accepts his place as Grandpa, more or less shelved by his family, while he relives in memory some childhood scenes. ''Rhymes for Irony'' is his general term for paradoxes and surprise endings concerned with miscellaneous subjects ranging here from the sex obsessions of cats and the slovenliness of Beethoven to his own anger at the *Morning Star* for printing a fleshy picture of himself as a ''tycoon.'' In ''Lyrics of the Lost'' and ''Lyrics for Reverence,'' he took up the themes and methods in which he excelled, and demonstrated ever-fresh descriptions of characters and their human problems. He scrupulously avoided repetition of settings and statements.

Very much the same applies to *Carols of an Old Codger* . . . , *Rhymes For My Rags* . . . , and the undated *Cosmic Carols,* published when he was over eighty years of age and republished

in *Later Collected Verse* after his death. In these books he maintains the pose of a poor old man whose books are not selling because his rhymes and rhythms are outmoded. There is still a substantial number of vignettes, notably two saucy Yukon ballads. . . . (pp. 186-87)

As evidence of continuing good humour, he was still indulging in ''Lyrics for Levity'' and ''Derisive Ditties,'' which were exercises in irony spreading over into ''Rhymes for Resignation'' about Clemenceau, Mistinguette, Ernie Pyle, Einstein, Tom Paine, Dylan [Thomas], Monticelli, and Benjamin Franklin.

Inevitably, however, he felt impelled to write postscripts on life and rhyme. He had often described his attitude toward religion as agnosticism, or simply ''reverence,'' in the absence of certainty. (pp. 189-90)

The ''riddle of Reality,'' which was basic to his thinking about life and religion, had also been the key to his literary practice when he wrote vignettes, which were characterized by the dramatic interplay of favourable and unfavourable forces in human lives. He was not inclined to label much that he described as wholly good or wholly evil. The riddle of life and of lives demanded ironic treatment. This attitude is confirmed in a stanza introducing the valuable ''unpublished'' selections in *Later Collected Verse:*

> I don't believe in all I write,
>   But seek to give a point of view;
> Am I unreasonable? Quite!
>   I'm ready to agree with you . . .
> Times, though opponents we deride,
>   Let's try to see the other side.
>
> (pp. 190-91)

Carl F. Klinck, in his Robert Service: A Biography, *Dodd, Mead & Company, 1976, 199 p.*

CLARE McCARTHY   (essay date 1979)

[*In the following excerpt, McCarthy reviews the* Collected Poems *of Robert Service and notes the range of experiences reflected in Service's poetry.*]

In the **Collected Poems** we have a treasure chest containing **'The Spell of the Yukon', 'Ballads of the Cheechako', 'Rhymes of a Rolling Stone', 'Rhymes of a Red Cross Man', 'Ballads of a Bohemian'** and the **'Bar Room Ballads'.** The easy style of Robert Service makes him a most readable poet. He described himself as a happy man, because his talent was in proportion to his ambition, and he was able to write the kind of verse that he liked to read. He wrote about everything he saw . . . He tells as vividly of the men and women [of the Yukon] who sort fame and fortune in its lonely wastes, where successes were few and failure usually meant death.

Many and varied were the characters who shared his Bohemian existence in Paris. Although he was by nature a solitary man, not given to making many friends, no one passed unnoticed. So that we may know who or what inspired each set of verses, during this time, they are linked by extracts from his diary, giving a complete picture of the hungry times, and the good times; and how the joy of his verses being accepted so often meant more than money to Robert Service.

With the outbreak of the 1914 war his whole world changed, but he continued to write to everyone he met, of the boys who marched gaily away to war full of Patriotic fervour, the hardened soldier who does his duty, and the women and children who love and fear for them. As an ambulance driver Robert Service served in the front line, and so we do not get the romantic death and glory view, but the full horror and futility of war. . . . His views in every aspect of life and death are presented to us to take or leave as we will. . . . (p. 276-77)

To anyone unfamiliar with the works of Service this book would be a perfect introduction. . . . (p. 277)

> *Clare McCarthy, "The Poetry of Robert Service,"*
> *in* Contemporary Review, *Vol. 234, No. 1360, May,*
> *1979, pp. 276-77.*

ADDITIONAL BIBLIOGRAPHY

Garvin, John W. "Robert Service." In his *Canadian Poets*, pp. 359-61. Toronto: McClelland, Goodchild & Stewart, 1916.
> A biographical sketch that includes several statements by Service regarding his poetry.

Kelly, Florence Finch. "The Poets Enlist under Mars." *The Bookman*, New York XLIV, No. 5 (January 1917): 510-13.*
> A favorable review of *Rhymes of a Red Cross Man.*

Rothman, Nathan L. "Poet, Dreamer." *The Saturday Review of Literature* XXVIII, No. 50 (15 December 1945): 27.
> A dispassionate review of *Ploughman of the Moon,* which is described as Service's "annals of a poor Scotch boy who dreamt of freedom and security for himself, and went about getting these things with as much realism and dispatch as possible."

Hermann Sudermann

1857-1928

German dramatist, novelist, short story writer, autobiographer, and essayist.

Sudermann was regarded as one of Germany's greatest dramatists during the late nineteenth and early twentieth centuries. The production of *Die Ehre (Honor)* in 1889 won him both critical and popular acclaim as well as recognition as Germany's foremost proponent of Ibsenian Naturalism. Despite the use of contemporary social themes and realistic dialogue, Sudermann's dramas retained conventional plotting and staging reminiscent of Alexandre Dumas *fils* and Victorien Sardou, and were eventually perceived as belonging to a middle-ground between Realism and Romanticism. In addition to his plays, Sudermann wrote a number of novels and short stories, of which the autobiographical novel *Frau Sorge (Dame Care)* is considered among his best works, sharing with the short story collection *Litauische Geschichten (The Excursion to Tilsit)* a vivid evocation of the people and environment of his native East Prussia.

Sudermann was born in Matziken, East Prussia, where German, Russian, and Lithuanian cultures intermixed. His parents sought to instill in him the Puritan Christian morality of his father's Mennonite ancestors. A brewer who worked in the village of Heydekrug, Sudermann's father was a stern disciplinarian of depressed temperament who showed his son no affection. Shy and lonely, Sudermann grew dependant upon his gentle, sympathetic mother for his emotional needs. Harassment by fellow students who found him an ideal victim intensified Sudermann's feelings of inferiority about himself and his family. An excellent student, he attended the University of Königsberg and the University of Berlin, where he majored in philology and history. Sudermann gradually grew frustrated by the conservative attitudes of his instructors and left the university, never to return to formal academic life. He worked for a while as a private tutor as well as editing and contributing articles to the liberal Berlin political journal *Deutsched Reichsblatt*. He subsidized this income by writing romances for popular magazines. From 1886 to 1889 he published two novels and two collections of short stories, but these works did not receive serious critical attention until the success of the drama *Honor* in 1889.

Honor was produced one month after the premiere of Gerhart Hauptmann's drama *Vor Sonnenaufgang (Before Dawn)*, the first work of Naturalism on the German stage. However, Sudermann's *Honor* became the first financially successful Naturalist drama in Germany. Because of similarities in outlook, style, and choice of themes, Sudermann and Hauptmann were for years mentioned in conjunction by critics. Sudermann's thematic concern with class conflict, honor, and morality also led critics to compare him to Henrik Ibsen, whose Naturalistic problem plays had been both hailed and damned internationally. The realism of *Honor* is most clearly evident in its characterizations of the peasantry, a class depicted in previous German dramas as either exemplary laborers or corrupt comic figures. In *Honor,* realistic dialogue and actions duplicated the coarse, avaricious behavior of an impoverished peasant family. The landed Junker class, for whom the peasants work, are

revealed as hypocrites concerned with the appearance rather than the substance of honor. While all moral offenders in the play are realistically unrepentant and unpunished, the play ends in a conventional and contrived manner: despite thematic insistence upon the damaging effect of wealth, a poor, honorable boy and sympathetic rich maiden find that their happiness is made possible by the acquisition of money. Sudermann sustains a realistically pessimistic tone throughout his next play, *Sodoms Ende (The Man and His Picture)*. The story of an idealistic, talented artist lured into the inner circle of Berlin's upper class by a wealthy female patron, *The Man and His Picture* scrutinizes the devastating effect of this association on the young man's ethics, talent, and finally, his life. The play was condemned as immoral and was for a time banned. Modern critics contend that while the pessimistic ending may have alienated those theatergoers used to happy endings, the play was suppressed because it attacked and therefore offended the class that made up the audience. In subsequent dramas, such as *Heimat (Magda)* and *Die Schmetterlingsschlacht (The Battle of the Butterflies)*, Sudermann continued to treat serious issues, leading to further critical comparisons with Ibsen, Hauptmann, and Émile Zola. However, while each of these writers was concerned with realism and contemporary issues, Sudermann now avoided the psychological depth and fidelity to the realistic flow of life notable in the works of his contemporaries. In

Magda, for example, the issue of the new woman is addressed as it had been in Ibsen's *A Doll's House,* providing a vehicle for some of Europe's leading actresses, including Sarah Bernhardt, Eleanora Duse, and Mrs. Patrick Campbell. In this, his most popular drama, Sudermann addressed many of the controversial pairings and situations presented in the earlier works: the staid father versus the unconventional daughter, old versus new morality, rural versus city life, traditional versus modern female roles, and independence versus filial piety. Although initially perceived as daring, the grand speeches, melodramatic climaxes, and plot coincidences were considered merely hackneyed theatrics by later critics.

While *Magda* and the other early dramas had in their time garnered overwhelming critical praise, Sudermann's later plays were more controversial. In the late 1890s, Sudermann began using mythical and biblical themes removed in time and experience from contemporary concerns, and such dramas as *Johannes (John the Baptist), Die drei Reiherfedern (The Three Heron's Feathers),* and *Johannisfeuer (St. John's Fire)* were criticized for didactically presenting moral lessons. Although he returned to his earlier themes in 1902 in *Es lebe das Leben (The Joy of Living)*—his last internationally successful drama—he had by then fallen into critical disfavor. In a changing theater, the drawing room qualities that had once distinguished Sudermann's works were now considered obsolete and predictable, with James Huneker claiming that the plays held interest "for those who don't take theater as a serious matter." Even Sudermann's characters, long considered evidence of his dramatic skill, came under attack as artificial. Among Sudermann's harshest critics was Alfred Kerr, who denounced him as a poseur who lacked sincere interest in the social issues his plays addressed. Kerr charged Sudermann with embracing popular trends while concurrently upholding a traditional moral code, thus taking no risks. Sudermann compounded the damage done by such criticism by heatedly defending himself in print. The end of his popularity as a dramatist was sealed with the production of his satire *Der Sturmgeselle Sokrates* in 1903. The political and racial issues addressed in this play, which caricatures the political idealism that inspired the liberal uprising *(Volkerfruhling)* of 1848, were considered improper material for satire by critics and the public. Sudermann failed to produce a successful drama for the remainder of his career. At the time of his death in 1928, he was best known to contemporary readers for his novels and short stories.

Sudermann had begun his career as a writer of prose fiction, his first major work being the novel *Dame Care,* published in 1887. *Dame Care* is autobiographical, and, though idealized, bears a striking resemblance to the situations recounted in the autobiography *Das Bilderbuch meiner Jugend (The Book of My Youth),* written over thirty years later. The early sections of the novel have been praised by critics for the skillful unfolding of the boy Paul's character and depiction of his intimate relationship with his mother. Despite the gloom of abject poverty, accentuated by the barren rural landscape surrounding Königsberg, *Dame Care* is perceived as a hopeful portrait of a young boy fighting for survival. Some critics have noted that while the evocation of setting in *Dame Care* and other early works such as *Der Katzensteg (Regina)* is vivid, the mass of details and objects too often subordinate or overwhelm the central story. Other prose works, such as "Der Wunsch," are marred by the author's didactic insistence upon an object lesson, construed by one critic as either Sudermann's typically German inclination toward thoroughness or his insecurity about the thematic clarity of his text. In "Der Wunsch," young Olga

grows close to her brother-in-law while the two nurse her sick sister, and Olga momentarily wishes her sister dead. When her sister does die, Olga commits suicide because of guilt. A pseudoscientific epilogue to "Der Wunsch" then seeks to explain Olga's wish in terms of a common malady. The somewhat ordinary story, though undercut by the epilogue, is elevated because of the fully developed and consistent characterization of Olga, whom some critics consider the first female in Sudermann's fiction to possess both a mind and a body—that is, the capacity for both conscience and sexual passion. The most successful fiction of Sudermann's later career includes the novels *Das hohe Lied (The Song of Songs), Der tolle Professor (The Mad Professor),* and the short-story collection *The Excursion to Tilsit.* They are considered among his best works by many modern critics, who note the economy, concision, and character consistency perfected during his years as a dramatist. In *The Excursion to Tilsit,* Sudermann wrote four stories concerning the Lithuanian peasantry and countryside. Aided by the strength of the author's personal memories and keen observations filtered through time, this collection is regarded by many critics as Sudermann's masterpiece, sustaining unity of style, tone, and characterization.

Many critics rate Sudermann's best fiction as high as or more highly than they do his most accomplished dramas, though it is as a dramatist that Sudermann is chiefly remembered today. For several years his plays dominated the German stage, and many enjoyed unprecedented international success as well. Favorably compared with Europe's most innovative dramatists during his early career, Sudermann was later charged with opportunistic insincerity and shallowness in his treatment of serious social themes. Today he is regarded as a transitional dramatist whose theatrical techniques made the harsh elements of Naturalism palatable to contemporary audiences.

(See also *Contemporary Authors,* Vol. 107.)

PRINCIPAL WORKS

Im Zwielicht   (short stories)   1886
Frau Sorge   (novel)   1887
   [*Dame Care,* 1891]
Geschwister   (short stories)   1888
Die Ehre   (drama)   1889
   [*Honor,* 1915]
Der Katzensteg   (novel)   1889
   [*Regine,* 1894; also translated as *Regina; or, The Sins of the Fathers,* 1898]
Sodoms Ende   (drama)   1890
   [*The Man and His Picture,* 1903]
Es War   (novel)   1893
   [*The Undying Past,* 1906]
Heimat   (drama)   1893
   [*Magda,* 1896]
Die Schmetterlingsschlacht   (drama)   1894
   [*The Battle of the Butterflies,* 1914]
Dies indische Lilie   (short stories)   1895-1896
   [*The Indian Lily, and Other Stories,* 1911]
Morituri   (drama)   1896
   [*Morituri,* 1910]
Johannes   (drama)   1898
   [*John,* 1902; also translated as *John the Baptist,* 1908]
Die drei Reiherfedern   (drama)   1899
   [*The Three Heron's Feathers,* 1900]

Johannisfeuer (drama) 1900
[*St. John's Fire*, 1904; also translated as *Fires of St. John*, 1904]
Es lebe das Leben! (drama) 1902
[*The Joy of Living*, 1902]
Der Sturmgeselle Sokrates (drama) 1903
Das hohe Lied (novel) 1908
[*The Song of Songs*, 1909]
Strandkinder (drama) 1909
Litauische Geschichten (short stories) 1917
[*The Excursion to Tilsit*, 1930]
Das Bilderbuch meiner Jugend (autobiography) 1922
[*The Book of My Youth*, 1923]
Dramatische Werke. 6 Vols. (dramas) 1923
Der tolle Professor (novel) 1926
[*The Mad Professor*, 1928]
Die Frau des Steffen Tromholt (novel) 1927
[*The Wife of Steffen Tromholt*, 1929]
Purzelchen (novel) 1928
[*The Dance of Youth*, 1930]

THE ATHENAEUM (essay date 1891)

[*In the following excerpt, the critic offers a favorable review of* Dame Care.]

Hermann Sudermann's **'Frau Sorge'** was well worth translation, and in spite of occasional angularities it has been Englished by Miss Overbeck so faithfully as to preserve unimpaired the simple pathos of the original. There is a freshness and romance about this tale of a German moorland which lifts it far above the ordinary level in the manner of its narrative, while the principal characters reveal themselves without any intervention on the part of the author in the way of cataloguing their qualities or any otiose description. The hero in particular—who reminds one at times of Daudet's Jack—is a finely conceived creation, whose lonely struggles after his ideal inspire the reader with a truly affectionate interest. As Herr Sudermann's name is associated with other works of a pessimistic and repellent character, it is only fair to say that **'Dame Care,'** though not without painful episodes, is essentially a pure as well as a beautiful story.

> *A review of "Frau Sorge," in* The Athenaeum, *No. 3346, December 12, 1891, p. 798.*

HJALMAR HJORTH BOYESEN (essay date 1895)

[*Boyesen was a Norwegian-born American novelist, poet, and educator who came to the attention of the distinguished critic William Dean Howells after his novel about Norwegian life,* Gunnar *(1874), was published. Howells exerted an influence over Boyesen's later career, during which he turned from his previous Romanticism to a realistic treatment of frustrated American ideals. His critical studies include* Goethe and Schiller *(1879) and* Essays on Scandinavian Literature *(1895). In the following excerpt, Boyesen, noting the psychological profundity of* Magda, *calls Sudermann a radical thinker and Germany's main disciple of Henrik Ibsen.*]

The most conspicuous disciple of Ibsen in Germany is . . . Hermann Sudermann. His magnificent play, **Die Ehre,** is to my mind the most beautiful piece of dramatic work which

Germany has produced since Lessing's *Minna von Barnhelm*. I am in no wise staggered by the fact that Schiller's *Wallenstein* and *Wilhelm Tell* belong to the interim. Not a single one of Schiller's justly famous dramas contains so delicious an intellectual problem as **Die Ehre.** Emile Augier's *Le Gendre de M. Poirier* propounds essentially the same problem—viz., the conception of honour of a superior class as contrasted with that of an inferior class; but Augier is only half-emancipated from the old conventions. He openly pleads the cause of the *bourgeois*. He apprehends, to be sure, the situation from its intellectual side, but he lacks the cool and ruthless audacity of Sudermann, and he lacks, too, the scientific equipment which enables the German to analyse the idea of honour into its last component elements. It is a marvel of marvels to me that (as far as I am aware) this triumph of dramatic art has, as yet, not been produced in English, while the farcical nonsense of Moser and Von Schönthan is eagerly watched for and promptly adapted by London and New York managers.

Die Ehre, which was Sudermann's first venture upon the boards, is, however, by no means his best. The ancient traditions were yet vaguely buzzing in his brain, and one of his characters, Count von Trast Saarberg, is none other than our old friend—the favourite of romantic playwrights—"The Uncle from America." That he comes from Java or East India makes, of course, no difference. As a *deus ex machina* who cuts the Gordian knot by choosing the plebeian hero for his partner and heir to his untold millions, he is a distinct remnant of the condition of things which Sudermann, following in Ibsen's wake, came to abolish. *Sodoms Ende* is less pleasing, but constructed far more strictly according to the naturalistic formula. It is one of the most powerful plays it has ever been my fortune to witness, and glides along with an irresistible logic and with the beautiful rhythm of life itself, without resort to the venerable tricks of the playwright's trade. Even Paris has accorded a hearing to Sudermann, whose **Heimat** is one of the most recent successes of Madame Sara Bernhardt. This is a relentless satire and an uncompromising exposure of the rottenness of the modern society, founded upon the corrupting feudal traditions which the age has outgrown. The psychology of these plays is, to my mind, profound and masterly, and betrays a fearless and radical thinker who is fully abreast of the age, if not considerably in advance of it. (p. 385)

The drama, according to Scribe and his successor, Sardou, is an ingenious mechanical contrivance, consisting of nicely adjusted wheels within wheels (as in the works of a watch), warranted to run without jar or accidents for three or four hours, as the case may be. Now it would, to my mind, be a very great mistake to assert that Ibsen and his school have emancipated themselves from all this slavery to "construction" upon which the critics discourse so learnedly. Mr. Bronson Howard once called my attention to the fact that Ibsen's plays are far more rigidly "constructed" than either Sardou's or Dumas'." . . . Never was the art of concealing art more triumphantly demonstrated than in *Ghosts, A Doll's House*, and *An Enemy of the People*. In Sudermann and Hauptmann the discarding of all rules is also more apparent than real. The scenes do not succeed each other in the haphazard fashion that they do in life. It is only the obvious stage tricks which are contemptuously rejected. The clever footman and chambermaid who have been ostensibly dusting the furniture in the opening scenes of a thousand comedies from Plautus and Molière to Scribe and Sardou, while their real business was to drop some useful indiscretions regarding the family secrets—these, of course, have been discharged and banished. The serviceable friend of the hero and the confidante of the heroine, who are likewise stock characters, could, however, not be dispensed with; not because they were stage conveniences, but because life exhibits their counterparts in many situations worth portraying.

It is in the pitch of the conversation, and what I may call the key of the action, that the chief innovation is to be observed. The dialogue has somehow acquired the note and *timbre* of the actual voice. It has been tuned down from the unnatural heroics of humour and pathos in which it was made to indulge. (p. 386)

Since seeing Ibsen, Sudermann, and Hauptmann, the old mechanical drama has become to me utterly flimsy and artificial. . . . Dumas *fils,* I admit, still gives me pleasure, in spite of his perpetual pyrotechnics of wit, which are certainly a strain upon one's credulity; for his plays are rarely without an interesting intellectual problem which is most brilliantly expounded. But for all that, they never move me as do Hauptmann's and Sudermann's intimate and unembellished studies of life itself. The glimpses they afford of the abysses of human nature seem to me more valuable and more affecting than any amount of startling cleverness in devising situations. (p. 387)

I should not have the hardihood to claim that the achievements of this school are above legitimate criticisms. They suffer from many blemishes which are easy to discover. All I assert is, that they are vital and interesting productions which may serve as guide-posts pointing the way of the probable development of the drama during the twentieth century. (p. 388)

*Hjalmar Hjorth Boyesen, "The Drama of Revolt,"
in* The Bookman, *New York, Vol. I, No. 6, July,
1895, pp. 384-88.**

KUNO FRANCKE   (essay date 1899)

[*Francke, a German-American literary historian and poet, was a pioneer of sociological and broadly cultural interpretations of literary history, the method applied in his* A History of German Literature As Determined by Social Forces *(1901). In the following excerpt from an essay originally published in* The Nation *magazine, Francke discusses* The Three Heron's Feathers, *which he considers Sudermann's greatest dramatic achievement.*]

A curious illustration of the evasiveness of genius, and of the impossibility of predicting its course from the influence of surrounding circumstances, has lately been afforded in the unexpected turn taken by the two foremost of living German dramatists. Hauptmann, after having risen in *The Sunken Bell* to sublime visions of the infinite, has allowed himself once more to be drawn into the sphere of the hopelessly earthly. Sudermann, on the other hand, the racy satirist, the impassioned orator, the rough-and-ready delineator of blunt actuality, all of a sudden reveals himself as a lyric poet in whom reëcho the most aërial sounds of mediaeval mysticism. (p. 249)

In his *Johannes* he portrayed a moral visionary who goes through the world with eyes riveted upon a fictitious ideal, and who, therefore, fails to see the needs of the life that is pressing upon him. In *Die drei Reiherfedern* he now brings before us an aesthetic visionary who chases after a magic form of womanly love and beauty that hovers before him on the distant horizon, without noticing that in his flight he tramples into the dust not only his own happiness, but also the life of the woman who has given to him her all. (pp. 250-51)

That a drama like this should in general have found little favor with the critics is not surprising. Surprising—and highly gratifying—is the fact that the verdict of the reading public seems

in this case to differ widely from that of the critics. Already, hardly three months after its first performance, the drama has reached a tenth edition. That it has its serious artistic blemishes it would be folly to deny. There is a certain forced grandeur in the heroic parts and an equally forced vulgarity in the subordinate figures. And reasonable exception might perhaps be taken to this whole genre of symbolical poetry. It certainly is true that the leading idea of his drama, embodied in characters of our own time and in actions belonging to the sphere of our own experience, would have touched the average reader of today more quickly and more surely. But may it not be that, on that very account, this work will speak more distinctly to future generations, that its very timelessness and inconcreteness will give it permanence and universal value? Even if this should not be the case, it will most assuredly live in history as a noble monument of German intellectual life at the end of the nineteenth century, as a *magna pars* of the artistic revival which has placed the German drama once more in the very front rank of European literature. For, however strange and far away at first sight its characters and its actions may seem to be, it is, after all, most closely related to our own lives; it brings before us what may be called the problem of problems of our own time,—the reconciliation of intensest activity with simple enjoyment; of restless striving with spiritual peace. (pp. 256-57)

Kuno Francke, "Sketches of Contemporary German Letters: Sudermann's 'Die drei Reiherfedern'," in *his* German Ideas of To-Day and Other Essays on German Culture, *Houghton, Mifflin and Company, 1907, pp. 249-57.*

JAMES HUNEKER   (essay date 1905)

[*Huneker, an American biographer, short story writer, novelist, and memoirist, reviewed drama, art, music, and literature for the London* Saturday Review *and* New York Sun *for many years. He studied piano in Paris under former students of Frédéric Chopin and Franz Liszt, and his biographies of Chopin and Liszt were considered the definitive works on each musician. In his criticism, Huneker illustrates the belief that psychological and biographical facts are revealed about an author through his or her works. His interest in foreign authors and musicians introduced new ideas that influenced the works of post-World War I American writers. In the following excerpt Huneker discusses Sudermann's dramas, and considers even his most unsatisfying works brilliant because of their technical power and keen observation of manners.*]

The unfailing brilliancy of expression and abundant technical power of Hermann Sudermann have so seldom failed him in the lengthy list of his plays and novels that his admirers are too often oblivious to his main defect as an artist and thinker—a dualism of style and ideas. The Prussian playwright wishes to wear three heron feathers in his cap. Cosmopolitan as he is, he would fill his dramas with the incomparable psychologic content of Ibsen; he would be a painter of manners; he would emulate Sardou in his constructive genius. To have failed, and failed more than once, in his effort to precipitate these three qualities in his surprisingly bold and delicate wit, is not strange. And to have grazed so often the edge of triumphs, not popular but genuinely artistic, warrants one in placing Sudermann high in the ranks of German dramaturgists.

In a very favourable review written by Mr. W. S. Lilly of *The Joy of Life,* he ranks Sudermann among the great painters of manners, and, after reading *Dame Care* and *The Cat's Bridge,* we are tempted to agree with the enthusiasm of the English critic. He thus sets down the qualities of a painter of manners:

''Sense and sensibility, sagacity and suppleness, openness of mind and originality of thought, depth of feeling and delicacy of touch.'' Does Sudermann's art include all these things? We think not. Rather is he as a dramatist—the expert *Techniker,* the man of the theatre, impregnated by the dominant intellectual ideas of the hour, than a poet who from a haunting necessity gazes into his heart and then writes: Sudermann is too photographic; he too often wills his characters into a mould of his own, not of their own, making; he wills his atmosphere to blend with his theses, the reverse of Hauptmann's method. He is more cerebral than emotional, more of a philosopher than a dramatic psychologist. Above all, he is literary; he has the literary touch, the formal sense, the upgushing gift of verbal expression. Add to this order of talent a real feeling for dramatic *nuance,* and Sudermann's enigmatic warring opposites of temperament and action seem remarkable.

In 1889, miraculous year of modern artistic Germany, Sudermann's dramatic début in *Honour* was more of a nine days' wonder than Hauptmann's *Before Sunrise.* The surety of touch, the easy mastery of theatric effects, the violent contrasts, and the sparkling dialogue transformed Sudermann's cometary career into a fixed star of the first magnitude. To-day this first play appears banal enough. Time has permitted us to see it in completer historic perspective. Ibsen's influence in the posing of the moral conflict is speedily recognized, just as Count Von Trast may be traced to those *raisonneurs* so dear to the younger Dumas, those human machines spouting logic and arranging the dénouement like the god behind the cloud. One inevitably recalls the relation of Björnsen to Ibsen in the present position of Sudermann and Hauptmann.

Yet it is easy to admire *Honour.* It contains, notably in the two acts of the ''hinter haus,'' real strokes of observation and profound knowledge of human nature. The elder Heinecke, rapacious rascal, is a father lost to all sense of shame, for he closes his eyes to his daughter's behaviour. This same old scamp is both true and amusing. Nor is his wife depicted with less unwavering fidelity. The motive of *Honour* is not alone the ironic contrast of real and conventional ideals of honour— it shoots a bolt toward Nietzsche's land where good and evil blend in one hazy hue. Sudermann, here and in nearly all his later pieces, challenges the moral law—Ibsen's loftiest heron feather—and if any appreciable theory of conduct is to be deduced from his works, it is that the moral law must submit to the variations of time and place, even though its infraction spells sin, even though the individual in his thirst for self-seeking smashes the slate of morality and perishes in the attempt.

This battle of good and evil Sudermann dwells upon, often to the confusion of moral values, often to the tarnishing of his art. And in his endeavour to hold the dramatic scales in strict equipoise, to intrude no personal judgments, he leaves his audiences in blank bewilderment. Better the rankest affirmations than the blandest negatives. Yes counts far more than No in the theatre, and Sudermann is happier when he is violently partisan. His contemporary, Hauptmann, shows us the shipwreck of souls in whom the spiritual stress preponderates. Sudermann, except in rare instances, sticks closer to the social scale and its problems; and when he does he is at his best, for it cannot be said that *The Three Heron Feathers,* written under the spur of *The Sunken Bell,* betrays a mastery or even a familiarity with those shadowy recesses wherein action is a *becoming,* where the soul blossoms from a shapeless mass into volitional consciousness. Sudermann's art is more external; it concerns itself with the How rather than with the Why, and one feels that storm and fury were deliberate engraftments, not the power which works from within to the outer world.

There is character drawing of an unexceptional kind in *Honour.* Robert Heinecke returns from foreign lands to find his family degraded, his sister trading on her beauty, his father and mother accepting bounty from the mansion house, the employers of the honourable son. The maze in which he is caught is constructed with infinite skill; the expository act is the best. There is not much mystery—we seem here to be in the clear atmosphere of the French dramaturgists, Augier and Dumas; while the finale is rather flat, we look for a suicide or a scandal of some sort. The author keeps himself steady in the saddle of realism. This ending is lifelike, inasmuch as the hero goes away with Graf Trast, who literally reasons him out of his dangerous mood. We feel that all the rest do not count, not the ignoble Kurt and his snobbish friends, his philistine parents; not the Heineckes with their vulgar avarice, their Zola-istic squalor. The romance is conventional. In fact, so cleverly did Sudermann mingle the new and old in the opposing currents of dramatic art that his play was instantly a success.

Accused of this ambition to drive two horses, the dramatist threw down as a gauge to criticism, *Sodom....* It was not a great play, because it lacked logic, balance, truthfulness. A distorted picture of artistic degeneracy, its satire on certain circles in Berlin caused a furore; but the piece had not the elements of sincerity. Technically it revealed the mastery of almost hopeless material, and while one's aesthetic sense and the fitness of things are hopelessly upset, the cunning hand of the prestidigitator is everywhere present. There are some episodes that stir, notably the scenes between father and son; but the grimness and sordidness are too much for the nerves. (pp. 286-90)

[*Magda*] struck a new note. Many believe it to be Sudermann at his best. Thus far he has not surpassed it in unity of atmosphere and dissection of motives. That the *morale* may be all wrong is not to the point. Again we see Ibsen's mighty shadow in the revolt of the new against the old; daughter and father posed antagonistically with the figure of the pastor, one of the German author's better creations, as a mediating principle.

One of many reasons that the *Magda* of Sudermann is a remarkable play is the critical controversy over its interpretation. Each one of us reveals his temperamental bias in the upholding of Bernhardt's or Duse's or Modjeska's respective readings. And which one of the three artists has exhausted the possibilities of Magda's many-sided character? On this point Herr Sudermann is distressingly discreet, although he has a preference for Duse, as is well known to a few of his intimates. The reason is simple. Duse presents more phases of the character, exhibits more facets of this curious dramatic gem, and by her excellences, and not her limitations, we must judge her performance. (p. 291)

Magda will probably outlive *The Joy of Life,* as it has already outlived the dramatist's *Honour.* The theme of the first is based on more fundamental facts than the others—the clash of will and affection. If all human families were loving, if father never opposed daughter or son flouted mother, then such a play as Magda never would have been written. But, alas! the newspapers prove that family life is not always celestial, indeed, that it is often bestial. But the Parson Tickletexts never acknowledge this.

There is no lesson in **Magda;** the ending is not a sermon—unless you wish it to prove that contradicting apoplectic fathers is a fatal proceeding. Magda is an individualist. She is selfish. This trait she shares with the mass of mankind. Her ''I am I'' is neither a proclamation nor a challenge to the world. It is the simple confession of a woman who knows herself, her weaknesses, her errors, who has battled and wrested from life a little, passing triumph, the stability of which she doubts.

''We must sin if we wish to grow. To become greater than our sins is worth more than all the purity you preach.'' Is this immoral? (pp. 293-94)

Poor Magda's virtue was certainly not cloistered. She ran for fame's garland in all the dust and heat of the artistic arena. She won, she lost. The bigot discerns in Magda an abandoned creature; the men and women who see life from all sides and know the fallibility of the flesh are apt to forgive her shortcomings.

''The ghost of a linen decency yet haunts us.'' She must have had a detestable disposition. Fancy what a spoilt opera singer with sore tonsils can be on a rainy day, especially when she reads the name of her dearest foe ''substituting'' on the bill. Then drop her in the sleepy old town of her nativity, where a harsh, opinionated father would worm from her every detail of her dubious past. Sudermann has done this with the result—a lifelike play, in which nothing is demonstrated except the unalterable stupidity of things in general and the naked fact that ''I am I'' is the only motto, whether secret or published, of every human crawling 'twixt earth and sky. In the pastor Sudermann attempts to paint the altruist in action. It is hardly a convincing piece of portraiture. Your true altruist is bounded by Tolstoy on the north, by Howells on the west, by Francis of Assisi on the south, and on the east by Buddha. Outside of book covers the person exists not. (pp. 294-95)

[**The Battle of the Butterflies**] is comedy of a skin-deep variety, entertaining! And here's an end to it. **Happiness in a Corner** is deeper in sentiment. It has the Ibsen touch with a pathos foreign to the Norwegian. Inspector Orb is of Ibsen, so is Pastor Weidemann, and the others—Bettina, Räcknitz, Elizabeth, and Helena—are alive and suffer and joy. There is vitality in this work. Also is there force and consummate cleverness in the three one-act plays grouped under the title **Morituri**. . . . Avowedly devoted to the theme of death they are all three illustrative of the dramatist's feeling for the right phrase, the only right situation. **Teja, Fritzchen,** and **The Eternal Masculine** show us in three widely differing modes how, as in life, we miss the happiness near at hand while longing for the ideal—a theme dealt with more broadly in **The Three Heron Feathers**. (pp. 295-96)

As a drama [**John the Baptist**] is weak, for the vacillating hero wearies us to distraction, notwithstanding the poetic charm of the prologue. If the Christ had been boldly dramatized, as was evidently the playwright's purpose, the outcome, no matter how shattering to pious nerves, would have been better artistically. But this vague dreamer, pessimistic, halting, irresolute, what can we make of him across the footlights, and for once Sudermann's technical ability failed him. (p. 296)

[**The Three Heron Feathers**] is an attempt to meet Hauptmann on equal terms. It lacks coherence, despite the occasional lift of its verse—Sudermann fancied that he had forsworn the prose of the realistic drama forever—while the lofty moral ideal, unduly insisted upon, soon becomes a thorn in the flesh. No one is alive but the trusty Lorbuss, the Prince being a theory

set in action. The next play, **St. John's Fire** . . . , we confess to having read with more pleasure than seeing it enacted. It goes up in the air soon after the curtain rises on Act III, though the story is a capital one for dramatic purposes. It would seem that Sudermann was again attacked by his doubting mania. He has contrived the atmosphere of romance, the pagan fire of St. John, the mystery of night, the passion of Georg and Marikke; but either his courage failed him, or else beset by some idea of resignation he spoilt his development and conclusion, and we leave the theatre dissatisfied, not with that spiritual dissatisfaction which Ibsen plants, a rankling sore in one's heart, but the kind that grows into resentment against the dramatist, for Marikke is a girl of whom Thomas Hardy would have been proud. And then there is a muddle of symbolism and heredity,—Sudermann endeavouring to scoop up in his too comprehensive net the floating ideas of the hour. Georg von Hartwig's sudden lapse into a selfish citizen we can never forgive.

Of the criticism of masterpieces there is no end. Take Sudermann's **The Joy of Life** as an example. (Why such an Ibsen-like title for **Es Lebe das Leben**?) Obsessed by subject and subject-matter only, many of us turn a blind side to the real qualities that make up an excellent play. (pp. 296-97)

Too great an artist to preach a moral, Sudermann nevertheless bestows the justice demanded by destiny upon the luckless Beata, Countess of Michael von Kellinghausen. **The Joy of Life** is next to **Magda** technically one of Sudermann's biggest achievements.

To present such a trite theme with new harmonies is a triumph. The tragic quality of the piece in an atmosphere bordering on the aristocratic commonplace is not the least of its excellences. We know that life is daily, that great art is rare, that the average sensual man prefers a variety show to a problem play; yet we are not abashed or downcast. The cant that clusters about cults, theatric or artistic, should not close our ears to the psychologic power and the message—if you will have the word—of this Sudermann play. If his Beata,—Ibsen has a Beata in Rosmersholm and D'Annunzio one in his La Gioconda—was a sorely beset woman, if she felt too much, thought too much,—one suspects her of poring over Nietzsche and hearing much Wagner; witness that allusion to Hans Sachs's quotation from Tristan,—yet is she not a fascinating soul? Are there to be no semitones in character? Must women be paragons and men perfect for inclusion-in a play? If this be so, then all the art of the Elizabethans is false, their magnificent freedom and their wit a beacon of warning to pure-minded playwriters. And, pray, out of what material shall the dramatist weave his pattern of good and evil?

But had Sudermann transposed his Beata to the fourteenth century, had he dowered her with mediaeval speech and the name of Beatrice, had he surrounded her with lovers in tin-plate armour, our shrinking natures might not have hied to cover. The pathos of distance would have softened the ugly truths of the modern drawing-room. **The Joy of Life** is a capital play. There is much conventionality displayed in the minor characters; only Beata and Richard are really original. And the use of the divorce debate as a symbol reveals the real weakness of the play, though structurally it has some striking virtues. The small part of Meixner, the theological student turned social-democrat, had *vraisemblance*. It suggests the character of Krogstad in *A Doll's House*. That tiresome exhorter, Count Trast, in Sudermann's **Honour,** is luckily not duplicated. And we doubt not that the absence of explicatory comment by the author is disheartening to a public which likes all the questions raised answered at the close, after the manner of a Mother Goose morality. Neither D'Annunzio nor Sudermann is a preacher. As in the ghastly illumination of a lightning flash, souls hallucinated by love, terror, pity, despair, are seen struggling in the black gulf of night. And then all becomes abysmal darkness. There are the eternal verities, the inevitable compensations in this play. The application of the moral is left to the listener. . . . (pp. 298-300)

In *Storm-Brother Socrates,* Sudermann places his scene in a small East Prussian town, possibly Matizken, where he was born in 1857. The schoolmaster, the grocer, the Jewish rabbi, the tax-collector, and the dentist are the chief characters of this satiric comedy. A lot of old cronies, men who went through the stirring times of '48, form a revolutionary guild, calling themselves "The Brotherhood of the Storm." Harmless enough, they still declaim against Bismarck—the time of action is twenty years ago—and talk of their warlike exploits. As the dramatist is preëminently a painter of manners, many of his portraits are masterly. (pp. 300-01)

The minor characters are well sketched. The waitress, Ida, is an exceedingly vital figure, as is the innkeeper. The dialogue is Sudermann almost at his best,—witty, sarcastic, ironical, tersely vigorous, and true to life. Like Daudet and Flaubert, Sudermann loves to prick the bloated German bourgeois. There is a little Hebrew, named, from sheer cruelty, Siegfried Markuse. His description of his freshman visits to a *Corps-Kneipe* at the Königsberg University is a fair example of the playwright's powers of unerring observation. (pp. 301-02)

His affinities as pointed out seem to be Parisian; at least he is Parisian in his gift of observation and style, German as is his power of reasoning. He is unmoral, following the *tendenz* of his time, but not so completely as D'Annunzio, who is satisfied with sheer shapes of beauty. With Sudermann it is, first, technical prowess, secondly, social satire, and he is always brilliant if not always satisfying. (pp. 302-03)

> *James Huneker, "Hermann Sudermann," in his*
> Iconoclasts, a Book of Dramatists: Ibsen, Strindberg,
> Becque, Hauptmann, Sudermann, Hervieu, Gorky,
> Duse and D'Annunzio, Maeterlinck and Bernard Shaw,
> *Charles Scribner's Sons, 1905, pp. 286-303.*

OTTO HELLER (essay date 1905)

[*In the following excerpt, Heller discusses Sudermann's art, comparing the reputations of Sudermann and Gerhart Hauptmann and defending Sudermann against the charge that he is a poseur who takes advantage of fashionable trends, noting that the speeches and grand scenes in his novels and dramas are not wholly Naturalistic.*]

To the great mass of the people the literature of the post-Bismarckian era seems epitomized in two names,—Gerhart Hauptmann and Hermann Sudermann, for undeniably these two have exercised the greatest formative influence on contemporaneous German letters. (p. 4)

[Their] careers show in the main features a certain external similarity, a similarity which has been strikingly emphasized through the circumstance that they have been simultaneously swept onward to the very pinnacle of fame. Yet though their great successes have very nearly tallied in point of time and measure, one can scarcely imagine two more dissimilar natures. . . . Hauptmann, high-strung, responding with nervous sensibility to the mildest stimulus, is possessed of a reproduc-

tive, feminine talent, a talent raised, to be sure, to the power of genius; whereas Sudermann is a robust masculine personality made of coarser stuff, not subtle enough to penetrate the inmost privacies of the human heart. Withal he is not the lesser artist, for to offset Hauptmann's fineness of perception he has the advantage of a stout self-confidence and broad knowledge of the inner and outer facts of life. (pp. 5-6)

Sudermann is above all things a writer with a distinct pedagogical task to which he brings a complete intellectual and moral equipment. His bold and positive utterances have awakened a ringing echo, because they have imperatively called the attention of the world to social and intellectual undercurrents of extraordinary persistency and unknown power. (pp. 6-7)

[The] most distinguished living satirist,—Hermann Sudermann,—although he has been so often called modern from top to toe, is at most a half-hearted "realist." He does not conform to the naturalist's supreme demand that the writer must not permit his personality, and above all things his philosophy, to shine through his work. On the contrary, it is not at all difficult to get a satisfying glimpse of the man Sudermann through the medium of his writings. He is a typical modern man, city bred, sagacious, and sophisticated to a degree, knowing the world so thoroughly that few things in it can baffle, puzzle, or even surprise him. Such, I think, is the first impression formed of him. Next we observe the open-mindedness of the man, the broad liberality of his sympathies. Soon we discover that his cosmopolitanism has in no way denationalized him or, as is apt to be the case, made him an utter worldling. For with his world-citizenship is coupled a strong family feeling for the German land and people and a deep religious sense. Sudermann, in these days of national self-assertion and spiritual pathseeking, is neither a scoffer nor an indifferent. His skepticism does not assail any noble human ideals, for by these he is himself deeply inspired; but he is distrustful of men's motives, and especially of the stereotyped moral notions unthinkingly accepted by one generation from the other. Morality—one may so interpret Sudermann—must be earned, not inherited; personally differentiated, not typified. How a person wins or loses his moral salvation is the problem whose fascination sets Sudermann to work, for, although a doubter by temperament, he clearly perceives in human nature latent moral forces which if set free will let it rise above the stale, warmed-over morality of workaday life. It follows naturally that a writer of this temper should be concerned with a dual purpose,—rudely to shake the decaying structure of social morality now resting largely on hollow conventions and compromises, but at the same time to stay the total collapse of society and invigorate it with his own sustaining aspirations. As his attempts toward these ends are not wholly free from theatricalities, the unthinking complaint that Sudermann is a *poseur* has passed into the stock in trade of contemporary criticism. He does not parade his personality, he is simply not quite artist enough always to hide it. To be sure, a few of his characters, notably Count Trast in *Die Ehre,* have a strong affinity with Sudermann himself. Yet they were never intended for self-portraits. In fact, not caring to admit the throng into his intimacy, he rather barricades himself defiantly behind his works. From this position he falls savagely upon that painted, slinking, day-shunning society which for him is the object of deep detestation and drags it from the privacy of its nocturnal haunts into the pitiless glare of the sunlit street. Sudermann, then, is and can be no dreamy minstrel nor yet an utterer of the "lyric cry." He is a calculating man of action, a self-conscious altruist agitated by deepest sympathy for all souls that are in distress and by implacable hatred of every form of tyranny. Fortunately this determined judge and resolute avenger is also an artist of uncommon power. His plays belong probably, his novels beyond a doubt, to the best that German literature has to show in these genres. (pp. 10-13)

Sudermann has been signally unsuccessful with his last play, the comedy *Der Sturmgeselle Sokrates*. . . . That even his stanchest adherents will have to admit. And the failure was not confined to a single feature of the play; the entire work in regard to structure, form, and substance, plot, language, and characters is past saving. Worst of all, the spirit in which it is written is to be unequivocally condemned. (p. 103)

After this outspoken condemnation of Sudermann's latest play a warning will be in place that we should not lend a serious ear to his obdurate detractors. It would simplify the study of a great writer if ethical and aesthetic development were necessarily following a straight line up or down. As a rule, however, great writers are so constituted or circumstanced that an occasional slipping back from their path of ascent or a not too frequent recrudescence into a past phase of endeavor need not be taken as a symptom of decay. We must let them take their own time and their own way to reach the summit of their art. (p. 107)

The art of Hermann Sudermann, notwithstanding the range of its capabilities, is fundamentally simple in its character. Its purpose is direct, its form clearly defined, incisive, at times lapidary. It is an art that reposes on a well-poised, full-orbed, full-veined personality. His failures refute the groundless charge that Sudermann truckles to the dominant literary taste of the hour. He fashions from a deep artist's conscience and out of the fullness of a strong outspoken temperament. Again and again he has been reviled as a mechanical imitator of the French *salon*-dramatists. It is perfectly certain and greatly to his credit that he has learned much from older and contemporary masters, both in respect to the general principles and the minor managements of dramatic art. . . . It is not true, however, that Sudermann has schooled his craftsmanship exclusively after the French pattern. The fact is, he studied in the same places as most of his competitors, but he has proved himself an apter pupil. To Ibsen and Björnson he owes probably more than to any other living writers for the technic, the subject-matter, and even the ethics of his works. Undoubtedly he has, besides, acquired constructive details from the older school of French dramatists, maybe he has also been influenced by them in giving room to some of those things which for the lack of a better word we must term with his detractors "theatricalities." . . . Yet with rare exceptions these "theatricalities" are not used as a claptrap for a gullible public, for it should be remembered that Sudermann writes for a nation to whom the drama is something far higher than a mere "show." They are in all likelihood the spontaneous outflow of a dramatic disposition. On the whole Sudermann indulges with discretion his natural propensity for the spectacular. . . . In the novels as well as in the plays there is a superfluity of speech-making and other declamation. There is also in both kinds of works a regular return of the "grand scene." But these things which fly in the face of naturalism do not constitute, as the enemies would have it, a cardinal dramaturgic vice of Sudermann. They merely prove that he aspires to no high place among the naturalists.

A play or a novel may be lifelike without being true to life. Sudermann is less concerned with external accuracy than with internal truth. The things which he depicts on the stage and in the pages of his books are not soulless copies from life, nor yet are they, on the other hand, mere inventions of the imagination. They are fragments of his own inner experience, composed and interpreted for others. Herein consists the convincing power of his art. He has had the courage from the beginning to brave the naturalistic despotism, and to hold out for the conviction that, as Amiel has it in his *Journal intime*, "the ideal, after all, is truer than the real; for the ideal is the eternal element in perishable things: it is their type, their sum, their *raison d'être*, their formula in the book of the Creator, and therefore at once the most exact and the most condensed expression of them." For this reason it is that . . . [many of Sudermann's figures] are more than ephemeral creations. They are lasting contributions to the history of contemporary morals and manners, and therefore may be fairly ranked with such imperishable products of the writer's art as Captain Dobbin, Rawdon Crawley, the Marquis of Steyne, or even the incomparable Becky Sharp herself. Though comparisons in the domain of literature are especially odious, yet one feels strongly tempted to spin out somewhat further the comparison between Sudermann and England's greatest novelist, Thackeray. The stinging lash swung by both is in appointed hands; it is wielded by righteous indignation in the name of a higher morality. And that is good additional reason why we pardon Sudermann's occasional undramatic preachments. He is not an artist for art's sake alone; he is also a vigorous reformer. Yet again like Thackeray, he is not perpetually plying the scourge of scathing sarcasm. He is also richly endowed with real benignant humor, a gift of the gods which no great writer can spare, and one which can make even an out-and-out realist almost endurable.

The art of Sudermann is simple also in that it applies itself almost invariably to a single group of problems. The keynote to the great majority of his works is the world-old conflict which is daily bred anew in the life of a progressive people: the tragic struggle between the old and the new; between the pious clinging of the soul to long-recognized creeds and the imperious claims of a nascent era.

In his attitude towards these grave questions Sudermann is consistently conservative so far as the general status of society is concerned; he is liberal, radical, nay anarchistic, in his pleas for special cases. Yet he is not stubbornly marking time on the standpoint of any one doctrine. We find, on the contrary, in his dramatic career the evidences of a growing, maturing, and refining philosophy. Roughly speaking, three phases may be distinguished. At first, the class conflict *per se* is in the foreground, the fates of the individuals are of secondary interest. The type of these dramas is *Die Ehre*. In that play the final destinies of Robert and Lenore, Alma and Kurt, are disposed of with a nonchalant wave of the hand. The most interesting part of *Die Ehre* is the perambulating social commentary of the author, here represented by the Count von Trast-Saarberg.

It is not long, however, before the major sympathies of Sudermann are transferred from the sociologic class phenomena in the abstract to the concrete, living individual. The first play of this second phase is *Magda*. The connection with the teachings of Friedrich Nietzsche is obvious. The highest duty of the exceptional type is to cultivate its true genius, regardless of the statutes and by-laws of society. (pp. 107-13)

There is a third class of plays by Sudermann representing a yet higher stage of ethical conception. A person may be at the same time sovereignly independent and sovereignly unselfish. *Teja* is an apotheosis of civic martyrdom, *Johannes* a glorification of the gospel of love. Marikke, too, and Beate in their way show their strength not so much in self-assertion as in self-abnegation.

And it may be that Sudermann as an ethicist has not yet spoken his final and decisive word. At any rate, so far as his social plays are concerned, his work up to the present time shows him only twice as the reckless satirist, in *Sodoms Ende,* where he puts profligacy into the pillory, and in *Der Sturmgeselle Sokrates,* meant as a warning either against false idealism or against want of idealism. At all other times Sudermann maintains the helpful attitude of a sober, determined reformer. He handles his chosen problems not, as so many modern writers do, for the sake of pleasing the caprice of a frivolous public, nor to gratify any morbid curiosity or idiosyncrasy of his own, but because they have come to distinct public consciousness, and because he personally is deeply stirred by them. As a novelist he has reached true greatness. In the drama he falls short of it because his strong pedagogic bent warps his plots from their natural course, not letting fate arise wholly out of the characters, and because, moreover, in his plays the horizon of the ''idea'' and the circle of action are not always coextensive.

Nevertheless, if we have outgrown that pedantic narrowness which approves or disapproves of a writer in proportion as he happens to agree or disagree with our own views of things, and if in judging him we turn from the sundry crudities and blemishes of which hardly any work of art can be wholly free, and fix our attention on his honest aims and high merits, we shall gladly acknowledge Hermann Sudermann as one of the foremost exponents of the modern novel and drama. (pp. 114-15)

> *Otto Heller, ''Hermann Sudermann,'' in his* Studies in Modern German Literature: Sudermann, Hauptmann, Women Writers of the Nineteenth Century, *1905. Reprint by Books for Libraries Press, Inc., 1967, pp. 3-115.*

WILLIAM LYON PHELPS (essay date 1910)

[*Phelps spent over forty years as a lecturer at Yale University. His early study* The Beginnings of the English Romantic Movement *(1893) is still considered an important work, and his* Essays on Russian Novelists *(1911) was one of the first influential studies of Russian realists. From 1922 until his death in 1943, Phelps wrote a regular column for* Scribner's Magazine *as well as a nationally syndicated newspaper column. During this period, his criticism became less scholarly and more journalistic, and is notable for an enthusiastic tone. In the following excerpt, Phelps discusses Sudermann's three early novels and the later novel* The Song of Songs.]

Sudermann's four novels, *Frau Sorge, Der Katzensteg, Es War,* and *Das hohe Lied,* show a steady progression in Space as well as in Time. The first is the shortest; the second is larger; the third is a long book; the fourth is a leviathan. If novelists were heard for their much speaking, the order of merit in this output would need no comment. But the first of these is almost as superior in quality as it is inferior in size. When the author prepared it for the press, he was an absolutely unknown man. Possibly he put more work on it than went into the other books, for it apparently bears the marks of careful revision. It is a great exception to the ordinary run of German novels in its complete freedom from superfluous and clogging detail. . . . Much of the huge and varied cargo of ideas, reflections, comments, and speculations carried by the regulation German freight-novel of heavy draught, has here been jettisoned. Then the

craft itself has been completely remodelled, and the final result is a thing of grace and beauty.

Frau Sorge is an admirable story in its absolute unity, in its harmonious development, and in its natural conclusion. I do not know of any other German novel that has a more attractive outline. It ought to serve as an example to its author's countrymen.

It is in a way an anatomy of melancholy. It is written throughout in the minor key, and the atmosphere of melancholy envelops it with as much natural charm as though it were a beautiful piece of music. The book is profoundly sad, without any false sentiment and without any revolting coarseness. It is as far removed from the silly sentimentality so common in Teutonic fiction, as it is from the filth of Zola or of Gorky. The deep melancholy of the story is as natural to it as a cloudy sky. The characters live and move and have their being in this grey medium, which fits them like a garment; just as in the early tales of Björnson we feel the strong sunshine and the sharp air. The early environment of the young author, the depressing landscape of his boyhood days, the daily fight with grim want in his father's house—all these elements are faithfully reflected here, and lend their colour to the narrative. And this surrounding melancholy, though it overshadows the whole book, is made to serve an artistic purpose. It contrasts favourably with Ibsen's harsh bitterness, with Gorky's maudlin dreariness, and with the hysterical outbursts of pessimism from the manikins who try to see life from the mighty shoulders of Schopenhauer. At the very heart of the work we find no sentiment of revolt against life, and no cry of despair, but true tenderness and broad sympathy. It is the clear expression of a rich, warm nature.

The story is realistic, with a veil of Romanticism. The various scenes of the tale seem almost photographically real. The daily life on the farm, the struggles with the agricultural machine, the peatbogs, the childish experiences at school, the brutality of the boys, the graphic picture of the funeral,—these would not be out of place in a genuine experimental novel. But we see everything through an imaginative medium, like the impalpable silver-grey mist on the paintings of Andrea del Sarto. The way in which the difficult conception of *Frau Sorge*—part woman, part vague abstraction—is managed, reminds one in its shadowy nature of Nathaniel Hawthorne. This might have been done clumsily, as in a crude fairy-tale, but it exhibits the most subtle art. The first description of Frau Sorge by the mother, the boy's first glimpse of the supernatural woman, his father's overcoat, the Magdalene in church, the flutter of Frau Sorge's wings,—all this gives us a realistic story, and yet takes us into the borderland between the actual and the unknown. From one point of view we have a plain narrative of fact; from another an imaginative poem, and at the end we feel that both have been marvellously blended.

The simplicity of the style gives the novel a high rank in German prose. It has that naïve quality wherein the Germans so greatly excel writers in other languages. . . . The literary style of *Frau Sorge* is naïve without ever being trivial or absurd. It is pleasant to observe, by the way, that to some extent this book is filling the place in American educational programmes of German that *L'Abbé Constantin* has for so long a time occupied in early studies of French. Both novels are masterpieces of simplicity.

But what we remember the most vividly, years after we have finished this story, is not its scenic background, nor its unearthly charm, nor the grace of its style; it is the character and temperament of the boy-hero. It is the first, and possibly the best, of Sudermann's remarkable psychological studies. The whole interest is centred in young Paul. He is not exactly the normal type of growing boy,—compare him with Tom Sawyer!—but because he is not ordinary, it does not follow that he is unnatural. To many thoroughly respectable Philistine readers, he may appear not only abnormal, but impossible; but the book was not intended for Philistines. I believe that this boy is absolutely true to life, though I do not recall at this moment any other novel where this particular kind of youth occupies the centre of the stage.

For *Frau Sorge* is a careful study and analysis of *bashfulness,* a characteristic that causes more exquisite torture to many boys and girls than is commonly recognised. Many of us, when we laugh at a boy's bashfulness, are brutal, when we mean to be merely jocular. Paul is intensely self-conscious. He is not at all like a healthy, practical, objective child, brought up in a large family, and surrounded by the noisy progeny of neighbours. His life is perforcedly largely subjective. He would give anything could he associate with schoolmates with the ease that makes a popular boy sure of his welcome. His accursed timidity makes him invariably show his most awkward and unattractive side. He is not in the least a *Weltkind.* He has none of the coarseness and none of the clever shirking of work and study so characteristic of the perfectly normal small boy. He does his duty *without any reservations,* and without understanding why. The narrative of his mental life is deeply pathetic. It is impossible to read the book without a lump in the throat. (pp. 141-46)

The next novel, *Der Katzensteg,* is more pretentious than *Frau Sorge,* but not nearly so fine a book. It abounds in dramatic scenes, and glows with fierce passion. It seems more like a melodrama than a story, and it is not surprising that its author immediately discovered—perhaps in the very composition of this romance—his genius for the stage. It is a historical novel, but the chief interest, as always in Sudermann, is psychological. The element of Contrast—so essential to true drama, and which is so strikingly employed in *Die Ehre, Sodoms Ende, Heimat,* and *Johannes*—is the mainspring of *Der Katzensteg.* We have here the irrepressible conflict between the artificial and the natural. (pp. 146-47)

The best thing about the novel is that it once more illustrates Sudermann's sympathy for the outcast and the despised. (p. 149)

The next regular novel, *Es War,* is the study of a past sin on a man's character, temperament, and conduct. . . . It is a long, depressing, but intensely interesting tale. At the very close, when it seems that wholesale tragedy is inevitable, the clouds lift, and Leo, who has found the Past stronger than he, regains something of the cheerfulness that characterises his first appearance in the narrative. Nevertheless *es war;* the Past cannot be lightly tossed aside or forgotten. It comes near wrecking the lives of every important character in the novel. Yet the idea at the end seems to be that although sin entails fearful punishment, and the scars can never be obliterated, it is possible to triumph over it and find happiness once more. The most beautiful and impressive thing in *Es War* is the friendship between the two men—so different in temperament and so passionately devoted to each other. A large group of characters is splendidly kept in hand, and each is individual and clearly drawn. One can never forget the gluttonous, wine-bibbing Parson, who comes eating and drinking, but who is a terror to publicans and sinners.

Last year appeared *Das hohe Lied,* which, although it lacks the morbid horror of much of Sudermann's work, is the most pessimistic book he has ever written. The irony of the title is the motive of the whole novel. Between the covers of this thick volume we find the entire detailed life-history of a woman. She passes through much debauchery, and we follow her into many places where we should hesitate to penetrate in real life. But the steps in her degradation are not put in, as they so often are in Guy de Maupassant, merely to lend spice to the narrative; every event has a definite influence on the heroine's character. The story, although very long, is strikingly similar to that in a recent successful American play, *The Easiest Way.* Lilly Czepanek is not naturally base or depraved. The manuscript roll of her father's musical composition, *Das hohe Lied,* which she carries with her from childhood until her final submission to circumstances, and which saves her body from suicide but not her soul from death, is emblematic of the *élan* which she has in her heart. With the best intentions in the world, with noble, romantic sentiments, with a passionate desire to be a rescuing angel to the men and women whom she meets, she gradually sinks in the mire, until, at the end, her case is hopeless. She struggles desperately, but each struggle finds her stock of resistance reduced. She always ends by taking the easiest way. Like a person in a quicksand, every effort to escape sinks the body deeper; or, like a drowning man, the more he raises his hands to heaven, the more speedy is his destruction. Much of Lilly's degradation is caused by what she believes to be an elevating altruistic impulse. And when she finally meets the only man in her whole career who respects her in his heart, who really means well by her, and whose salvation she can accomplish along with her own,—one single evening, where she begins with the best of intentions and with a sincere effort toward a higher plane, results in complete damnation. Then, like the heroine in *The Easiest Way,* she determines to commit suicide, and really means to do it. But the same weakness that has made it hitherto impossible for her to triumph over serious obstacles, prevents her from taking this last decisive step. As she hears the splash of her talisman in the cold, dark water, she realises that she is not the stuff of which heroine are made, either in life or in death. . . . And with this realisation she goes wearily back to a rich lover she had definitely forsaken, knowing that in saving her life she has now lost it for ever.

This is the last page of the story, but unfortunately it does not end here. Herr Sudermann has chosen to add one paragraph after the word "Schluss." By this we learn that in the spring of the following year the aforesaid rich lover *marries* Lilly, and takes her on a bridal trip to Italy, which all her life had been in her dreams the celestial country. She is thus saved from the awful fate of the streets, which during the whole book had loomed threatening in the distance. But this ending leaves us completely bewildered and depressed. It seems to imply that, after all, these successive steps in moral decline do not make much difference, one way or the other; for at the very beginning of her career she could not possibly have hoped for any better material fate than this. The reader not only feels cheated; he feels that the moral element in the story, which through all the scenes of vice has been made clear, is now laughed at by the author. This is why I call the book the most pessimistic of all Sudermann's writings. A novel may take us through woe and sin, and yet not produce any impression of cynicism; but one that makes a careful, serious study of subtle moral decay through over six hundred pages, and then implies at the end that the distinction between vice and virtue is, after all, a matter of no consequence, leaves an impression for which the proverbial "bad taste in the mouth" is utterly inadequate to describe. Some years ago, Professor Heller, in an admirable book on Modern German Literature, remarked, in a comparison between Hauptmann and Sudermann, that the former has no working theory of life, which the latter possessed [see excerpt above, 1905]. That Hauptmann's dramas offer no solution, merely giving sordid wretchedness; while Sudermann shows the conquest of environment by character. . . . I think this distinction in the main will justify itself to anyone who makes a thoughtful comparison of the work of these two remarkable men. Despite the depreciation of Sudermann and the idolatry of Hauptmann, an attitude so fashionable among German critics at present, I believe that the works of the former have shown a stronger grasp of life. But the final paragraph of **Das hohe Lied** is a staggering blow to those of us who have felt that Sudermann had some kind of a *Weltanschauung*. It is like Chopin's final movement in his great Sonata; mocking laughter follows the solemn tones of the Funeral March.

Up to this last bad business, **Das hohe Lied** exhibits that extraordinary power of psychological analysis that we have come to expect from Sudermann. Lilly, apart from her personal beauty, is not, after all, an interesting girl; her mind is thoroughly shallow and commonplace. Nor are the numerous adventures through which she passes particularly interesting. And yet the long book is by no means dull, and one reads it with steady attention. The reason for this becomes clear, after some reflexion. Not only are we absorbed by the contemplation of so masterly a piece of mental analysis, but what interests us most is the constant attempt of Lilly to analyse herself. We often wonder how people appear to themselves. The unspoken dialogues between Lilly and her own soul are amazingly well done. She is constantly surprised by herself, constantly bewildered by the fact that what she thought was one set of motives, turns out to be quite otherwise. All this comes to a great climax in the scene late at night when she writes first one letter, then another—each one meaning to be genuinely confessional. Each letter is to give an absolutely faithful account of her life, with a perfectly truthful depiction of her real character. Now the two letters are so different that in one she appears to be a low-lived adventuress, and in the other a noble woman, deceived through what is noblest in her. Finally she tears both up, for she realises that although each letter gives the facts, neither tells the truth. And then she sees that the truth cannot be told; that life is far too complex to be put into language. (pp. 151-57)

[There] were many critics who at the very start recognised Sudermann as primarily an artist, who chooses to paint the aspects of life that interest him. This is undoubtedly the true viewpoint. We may regret that he prefers to analyse human characters in morbid and abnormal development, but that, after all, is his affair, and we do not have to read him unless we wish to. . . . It is vain to quarrel with the direction taken by genius, however much we may deplore its course. Sudermann is one of the greatest, if not the greatest, of Germany's living writers, and every play or novel from his pen contains much material for serious thought. (pp. 157-58)

> *William Lyon Phelps, "Hermann Sudermann," in his* Essays on Modern Novelists, *1910. Reprint by The Macmillan Company, 1912, pp. 132-58.*

WILLIAM WINTER (essay date 1913)

[*Winter, an American drama critic, historian, essayist, and poet, was encouraged and influenced in his poetry by Henry Wadsworth Longfellow. During the mid-nineteenth century, he was a member of the bohemian writers group that met in the cellar of Pfaff's Broadway cafe, where he became acquainted with Walt Whitman. For years a drama critic for the* New York Tribune *and* Harper's Weekly, *Winter resigned from the* Tribune *when he could not reconcile his Romanticism with the works of such dramatists as Henrik Ibsen and Sir Arthur Wing Pinero, believing that conventional morality must always take precedence over aesthetic principles. In the following excerpt Winter discusses Sudermann's* Magda, *which he regards as an absurd, unclean work that expresses the dramatist's views through an undramatic didacticism. For further discussion of* Magda, *see the excerpt by Edward Shanks (1923).*]

The play of **Magda** pertains to the domestic order of drama and it portrays a painful conflict of will between a resolute, rebellious young woman, intolerant of social conventions, and her affectionate but arbitrary father, severe in maintenance of those conventions, at least relative to women, and dictatorially determined to direct the lives of the members of his family. It appears to have been written in a didactic spirit and with much ardor of "moral purpose." In an entirely elemental state of society the declaration that children ought to honor their parents and that parents ought not to treat their children with exasperating and tyrannical severity might possess a salutary significance: in the existing state of society it is a vapid truism, which no amount of pretentious theatrical preachment can make novel or can practically enforce. Yet that truism is the substance of Sudermann's play. (p. 373)

No woman has appeared in recent fiction who affords a more salient example than is presented by **Magda** of almost every repulsive attribute possible to a female character. She is vain, silly, perverse, obstinate, self-willed, unchaste, ugly in temper, and absolutely selfish. Such a character might be serviceable as an incident in a drama, but as the total subject of a drama it is out of all proportion, and it becomes both offensive and tedious. Persons learned in modern dramatic literature, as exemplified in some plays by Ibsen, Sudermann, and others, have kindly intimated, by way of enlightening the crass ignorance of the generality of English-speaking theatre-goers, that the true significance of such plays as **Magda** can be appreciated only by those who are thoroughly familiar with the state of society existent in the countries of Europe in which those plays have originated. That, possibly, is true. But as, being true, it renders the moral preachments of such plays inappropriate, because inapplicable, to the American community, and as, in general, they are dramatically inept, it would appear also to render the presentment of them on our Stage worse than superfluous. The benign Sudermann may have drawn **Magda** as a Frightful Example, or he may have intended her to be a model of The New Woman: in either case, to a healthful taste, she is unnecessary and obnoxious. It really is not necessary for the Stage to advise young women that they must not regulate the conduct of their lives according to the dictates of vanity and love of admiration; that they ought not to leave their homes and produce children without having been married, and that they ought not, even by a false avowal of wanton propensity or conduct, to cause their paternal progenitors to explode with fury and expire from apoplexy.

There are two classes of persons who make life miserable,—the Regulators and the Inculcators. The Regulators think that they know what is best for all their neighbors, and they are continually meddling with the affairs of others. The Inculcators are heavily freighted with Moral Lessons, and are never weary of the "damnable iteration" of moral platitudes. Hermann Sudermann appears to be a member of the tribe of Inculcators.

M A G D A
A PLAY IN FOUR ACTS

By
HERMANN SUDERMANN

Translated from the German by
CHARLES EDWARD AMORY WINSLOW

NEW YORK SAMUEL FRENCH PUBLISHERS 25 WEST 45TH STREET	LONDON SAMUEL FRENCH, LTD. 26 SOUTHAMPTON STREET STRAND

The title page of Sudermann's drama Magda. *Courtesy of Samuel French, Inc.*

He has ascertained that there are domestic troubles, and of these he makes pictures, never exercising the discriminative faculty of taste, and, the bars being thus let down, there is no end to the admitted brood of noxious subjects or to the weariness entailed by them. When Dickens was, for the first time, leaving England for the United States, a London satirist inquired whether it was not possible for him to find a sufficient supply of disagreeable persons in the Seven Dials. When the cares, trials, and perplexities of ordinary life are considered, it may well be asked whether it is necessary for the public to repair to the Theatre in order to see such vapid, morbid, repellent women as *Magda,*—and to pay for the privilege! (pp. 374-76)

> William Winter, "Helena Modjeska, 1840-1909," in his The Wallet of Time: Containing Personal, Biographical, and Critical Reminiscence of the American Theatre, Vol. 1, *Moffat, Yard and Company, 1913, pp. 359-97.*

LUDWIG LEWISOHN (essay date 1915)

[*A German-born American novelist and critic, Lewisohn was considered an authority on German literature, and his translations of Gerhart Hauptmann, Rainer Maria Rilke, and Jakob Wassermann are widely respected. In 1919 he became the drama critic*

for The Nation, serving as its associate editor until 1924, when he joined a group of expatriates in Paris. After his return to the United States in 1934, Lewisohn became a prominent sympathizer with the Zionist movement, and served as the editor of the magazine New Palestine for five years. Many of his later works reflect his humanistic concern for the plight of the Jewish people. In the following excerpt from his The Modern Drama, Lewisohn discusses Sudermann's works, the best of which he considers the occasional comedies and stories that draw upon the author's background.]

The very year (1889) in which Hauptmann inaugurated his great career with *Before Dawn,* the Lessing Theatre in Berlin achieved one of the most striking successes of the century with a play called *Die Ehre.* Its author was the East Prussian novelist, Hermann Sudermann . . . whose name, almost obscure until then, was soon to be known more widely than any German dramatist's since Kotzebue. His enemies have not spared him the withering comparison. For it is a notable fact that Sudermann whose work is often, in England and America, coupled with Hauptmann's, is almost totally discredited as a playwright in Germany and is frankly assigned, in most serious criticism, a station among the mere commercial purveyors to the popular stage. The naturalists, led by Hauptmann, have introduced into the German drama ideals of unequalled stringency. No theatrical unveracity in the dramatic treatment of life is tolerated by German criticism; no calculated concession to the mob is pardoned. The commercial theatre and the art of the drama are rigidly kept apart. Hence no voice has, for some years, been raised for Sudermann. A criticism that detects a touch of artifice in *Rose Bernd* is not likely to be lenient toward the author of *Heimat* . . . or *Es lebe das Leben.* . . .

But if the foreign critic represents a kind of contemporaneous posterity, it is possible to take a far more moderate view of Sudermann's activity as dramatist. He has undoubtedly retained, in many of his plays, the technique of Dumas *fils* and his contemporaries. His exposition is often shamelessly mechanical, his management of the fable adjusted not to the necessities of the situation but to the fancy of the audience; he uses the providential character—that French *deus ex machina*— and does not shrink from wrenching the whole nature of man for the sake of an effective curtain. On the other hand it can be said that in many of his plays these artifices are much softened. They have been a temptation to his feverishly restless temperament, but a temptation to which he has not always yielded. Nor must it be forgotten that into this discredited and rightly discredited mechanism of the stage he has almost always infused a probity of observation and a power of shaping character which are akin to the same qualities in his greater and more self-denying contemporaries. Even from amid the wretched clap-trap—the unnatural antitheses, the cheap coincidences, the sudden fortunes—of his first play arose the memorable character of Alma Heinecke, that matchless daughter of the Berlin poor who presents her case with inimitable raciness and truth. (pp. 129-30)

[Sudermann's best work] must be sought in an occasional comedy, and in many passages of those plays in which he draws sincerity and strength from his native earth—the bleak and storied shores of the Baltic Sea.

The happiest of the comedies is *Die Schmetterlingsschlacht.* . . . Beneath its lightness of mood the play is a serious and arresting study, expressed through living characters, of that Moloch of the lower middle-classes—respectability.

Sudermann's work, during the following six years, showed constant uncertainty and falseness. Only *Fritzchen in Morituri . . .*, a one-act tragedy of complete inevitableness rises above the glare and strain of his efforts. That better self of his which has never been quite blunted by haste and success reasserts itself in *Johannisfeuer. . . .* The scene of the play is once more Sudermann's homeland and one has a strong sense of the presence of the strange and ancient wildness of the Lithuanian country-side. There are coincidences, no doubt, and the dialogue is often enough pitched in a false and theatrical key—though never in a falser key than would be held quite tolerable in Lavedan or Hervieu, in Jones and Pinero. But the reality of Georg and Marikke's tragic love is profoundly brought home to us, and Vogelreuter and Haffke are of a fine and true humanity.

Berlin, the evil genius of his art, drew him once more *(Es lebe das Leben).* But in the very next year . . . appeared the East Prussian comedy, *Der Sturmgeselle Sokrates.* The discussion of burning political and racial issues has served to obscure the value of this excellent play. Nor has the truth been admitted that Sudermann stands above these issues in an attitude of kindly and philosophic humanity. The very temperate satire of the play is directed against a group of elderly men, democratic idealists of 1848, whose occupation was taken from them and whose hopes were shattered by Bismarck and the establishment of the empire. Their cause is lost. But Hartmeyer, a born fanatic, will not admit it. . . . Hartmeyer is, to be sure, won over in the end. But I detect in Sudermann's final attitude a shadow of sympathy at least for the old democratic ideals which the Prussian *régime* has subordinated to the state's welfare. The character work in the play is admirable, from the delightful rabbi to the girl at the inn which was, for so long, the meeting place of "the companions of the storm."

Since the appearance of *Der Sturmgeselle Sokrates* Sudermann has experimented variously. . . . [In *Strandkinder*], as elsewhere, Sudermann mistakes luridness for power, but there resounds through the play the crying of wild souls, the beat of icy surges, the desperate struggle of an heroic Germanic folk over whom is flung the snare of an alien civilisation. A faint, far echo of that forgotten strength of his ancestors still lives, at times, in Sudermann himself. He has never become utterly subdued to the corruptions that allure him. Although his is no free creation spirit, he has succeeded, again and again, in projecting characters or suggesting an atmosphere which, in any country but his own, would have placed him in the front rank of modern dramatists. If he has sunk to the level of Lavedan and Pinero at their worst, if he has equalled the violence of *Le Duel* and the crass bidding for popularity of *The "Mind the Paint" Girl* (1912), he has also created figures and written scenes which neither his French nor his English contemporary have equalled in reality or imaginative power. Of so much praise only an untenable severity of judgment or the personal animosity of the Berlin press can ever rob him. (pp. 130-34)

> *Ludwig Lewisohn, "The Naturalistic Drama in Germany," in his* The Modern Drama: An Essay in Interpretation, *1915. Reprint by B. W. Huebsch, Inc., 1923, pp. 103-65.**

H. L. MENCKEN (essay date 1919)

[*From the era of World War I until the early years of the Great Depression, Mencken was one of the most influential figures in American letters. His strongly individualistic, irreverent outlook on life and his vigorous, invective-charged writing style helped establish the iconoclastic spirit of the Jazz Age and significantly shaped the direction of American literature. As a social and literary critic—the roles for which he is best known—Mencken was the scourge of evangelical Christianity, public service organizations, literary censorship, boosterism, provincialism, democracy, all advocates of personal or social improvement, and every other facet of American life that he perceived as humbug. In his literary criticism, Mencken encouraged American writers to shun the anglophilic, moralistic bent of the nineteenth century and to practice realism, an artistic call-to-arms which is most fully developed in his essay "Puritanism As a Literary Force," one of the seminal essays in modern literary criticism. A man who was widely renowned or feared during his lifetime as a would-be destroyer of established American values, Mencken once wrote: "All of my work, barring a few obvious burlesques, is based upon three fundamental ideas. 1. That knowledge is better than ignorance; 2. That it is better to tell the truth than to lie; and 3. That it is better to be free than to be a slave." In the following excerpt from his* Prejudices: First Series, *Mencken discusses the faults of Sudermann's dramas and novels, finding that Sudermann's true talents lie in the writing of short fiction, noting in particular* The Indian Lily, and Other Stories.]

The fact that Sudermann is the author of the most successful play that has come out of Germany since the collapse of the romantic movement is the most eloquent of all proofs, perhaps, of his lack of force and originality as a dramatist. "Heimat," Englished, Frenched and Italianized as "Magda," gave a new and gaudy leading rôle to all the middle-aged chewers of scenery; they fell upon it as upon a new Marguerite Gautier, and with it they coaxed the tears of all nations. That was in the middle nineties. To-day the piece seems almost as old-fashioned as "The Princess Bonnie," and even in Germany it has gone under the counter. (p. 105)

Sudermann was one of the first deer flushed by Arno Holz and Johannes Schlaf, the founders of German naturalism. He had written a couple of successful novels, "Frau Sorge" and "Der Katzensteg," before the *Uberbrettl'* got on its legs, and so he was a recruit worth snaring. The initial fruit of his enlistment was "Die Ehre," a *reductio ad absurdum* of Prussian notions of honor, as incomprehensible outside of Germany as Franz Adam Beyerlein's "Zapfenstreich" or Carl Bleibtreu's "Die Edelsten der Nation." Then followed "Sodoms Ende," and after it, "Heimat." Already the emptiness of naturalism was beginning to oppress Sudermann, as it was also oppressing Hauptmann. . . . The result was this "Heimat," in which naturalism was wedded to a mellow sentimentality, caressing to audiences bred upon the drama of perfumed adultery. The whole last scene of the play, indeed, was no more than an echo of Augier's "Le Mariage d' Olympe." It is no wonder that even Sarah Bernhardt pronounced it a great work.

Since then Sudermann has wobbled, and in the novel as well as in the drama. Lacking the uncanny versatility of Hauptmann, he has been unable to conquer the two fields of romance and reality. Instead he has lost himself between them, a rat without a tail. "Das hohe Lied," his most successful novel since "Frau Sorge," is anything but a first-rate work. Its opening chapter is a superlatively fine piece of writing, but after that he grows uncertain of his way, and toward the end one begins to wonder what it is all about. No coherent idea is in it; it is simply a sentimentalization of the unpleasant; if it were not for the naughtiness of some of the scenes no one would read it. An American dramatist has made a play of it—a shocker for the same clowns who were entranced by Brieux's "Les Avariés."

The trouble with Sudermann, here and elsewhere, is that he has no sound underpinnings, and is a bit uncertain about his characters and his story. He starts off furiously, let us say, as a Zola, and then dilutes Zolaism with romance, and then pulls himself up and begins to imitate Ibsen, and then trips and falls headlong into the sugar bowl of sentimentality. Lily Czepanek, in "**Das hohe Lied**," swoons at critical moments, like the heroine of a tale for chambermaids. It is almost as if Lord Jim should get converted at a gospel mission, or Nora Helmer let down her hair. . . . But these are defects in Sudermann the novelist and dramatist, and in that Sudermann only. In the short story they conceal themselves; he is done before he begins to vacillate. In this field, indeed, all his virtues—of brisk, incisive writing, of flashing observation, of dexterous stage management, of emotional fire and address—have a chance to show themselves, and without any wearing thin. The book translated as "**The Indian Lily**" contains some of the best short stories that German—or any other language, for that matter—can offer. They are mordant, succinct and extraordinarily vivid character studies, each full of penetrating irony and sardonic pity, each with the chill wind of disillusion blowing through it, each preaching that life is a hideous farce, that good and bad are almost meaningless words, that truth is only the lie that is easiest to believe. . . .

It is hard to choose between stories so high in merit, but surely "**The Purpose**" is one of the best. Of all the latter-day Germans, only Ludwig Thoma, in "Ein bayrischer Soldat," has ever got a more brilliant reality into a crowded space. Here, in less than fifteen thousand words, Sudermann rehearses the tragedy of a whole life, and so great is the art of the thing that one gets a sense of perfect completeness, almost of exhaustiveness. . . . (pp. 105-08)

A short story of rare and excellent quality. A short story—oh, miracle!—worth reading twice. It is not so much that its motive is new—that motive, indeed, has appeared in fiction many times, though usually with the man as the protagonist—as that its workmanship is superb. Sudermann here shows that, for all his failings elsewhere, he knows superlatively how to write. His act divisions are exactly right; his *scènes à faire* are magnificently managed; he has got into the thing that rhythmic ebb and flow of emotion which makes for great drama. And in most of the other stories in this book you will find much the same skill. No other, perhaps, is quite so good as "**The Purpose**," but at least one of them, "**The Song of Death**," is not far behind. Here we have the tragedy of a woman brought up rigorously, puritanically, stupidly, who discovers, just as it is too late, that love may be a wild dance, an ecstasy, an orgy. I can imagine no more grotesquely pathetic scene than that which shows this drab preacher's wife watching by her husband's death-bed—while through the door comes the sound of amorous delirium from the next room. And then there is a strangely moving Christmas story, "**Merry Folk**"—pathos with the hard iron in it. And there are "**Autumn**" and "**The Indian Lily**," elegies to lost youth—the first of them almost a fit complement to Joseph Conrad's great paean to youth triumphant. Altogether, a collection of short stories of the very first rank. Write off "**Das hohe Lied**," "**Frau Sorge**" and all the plays: a Sudermann remains who must be put in a high and honorable place, and will be remembered. (pp. 112-13)

> *H. L. Mencken, "Hermann Sudermann," in his* Prejudices, first series, *Alfred A. Knopf, 1919, pp. 105-13.*

EDWARD SHANKS (essay date 1923)

[*An English poet, novelist, and critic, Shanks won honors for the poem* Queen of China (1919), *and reinforced his poetic reputation when* The Island of Youth *appeared in 1921. Editor of the* London Mercury *from 1919-1922, Shanks wrote notable critical essays on such authors as Bernard Shaw, Edgar Allan Poe, and Rudyard Kipling. In the following excerpt Shanks discusses* Magda *as a well constructed, skillfully developed work that falls short of genius. While the melodrama and social satire seem obvious and dated, Shanks observes that the characterizations and non-partisan point of view remain contemporary. For further discussion of* Magda, *see the excerpt by William Winter (1913).*]

[In] some lights the play **Magda** cannot avoid striking one as slightly ridiculous.

But I have noticed for some years past a curious tendency among the Higher Critics of the Higher Drama to aim a kick at Sudermann as they go by, just as there is always in any school one boy who gets kicked as a matter of routine. Sudermann's pretensions have been repeatedly exposed: indeed, I cannot think of any dramatist whose pretensions have been exposed quite so often. He an intellectual? He a successor to Ibsen? He in the forefront of the movement? No, they cry with one voice, he is not; and the unfortunate Teuton is exposed again.

This animus springs, I imagine, from the fact that solemn persons once took him more seriously than he deserved; and they are now trying to cover up the memory of their shame. But, though **Magda** is not a play of genius, it is indisputably a serviceable piece of work; and it wears well. It suffers a little so far as English audiences are concerned by the unfamiliarity of the conditions it presents. It suffers more by its change of name; and here we have an instructive example of the importance of the title. In the German original, it is called **Die Heimat**—that is to say, **Home**. Now why was the change made? Did the first great actress who attempted the piece in translation see that it was her opportunity to change Sudermann's satire into a vehicle for great emotional acting? Or was it—and this, I am inclined to believe, is the correct explanation—was it that it was felt that no satire on that sacred word would be allowed by an English audience? However that may be, it is certain that the alteration does definitely alter the tone of the play. Several times in Magda's conversation the word "home" crops up, and each time the trend of the dialogue lays on it a natural emphasis which loses half its point when it has no reference to the title. And the change is precisely from satire to a vehicle for emotional acting. As **Die Heimat** the piece has a meaning, at least a definite element of human significance. Colonel Schwartz's house is something more than that, it is also the house of Mr. Smith, the Non-conformist minister, and of M. Dupont, the grocer. Magda's tirades then express the feelings of the revolting generation, her sorrows are those of the individual soul which can never escape and make itself a completely independent individual. But as **Magda,** the piece is merely the story of a young woman who has got herself into an emotional entanglement.

So much, it may be argued, ought not to depend on a title; and perhaps that is true. To say so much involves saying only that Sudermann's social comment delivered in this play is not of the first order, that his satire is rather heavy-footed and obvious. But, I maintain, there *is* something in the play, more interesting than worked-up emotional situations, which the change of title tends to obscure. There are two strands in the play, one of social satire, the other of melodrama. And the first strand is good so far as it goes. If one is permitted to forget the melodramatic element, how is it possible not to see that the remainder is carefully and truly drawn? There *are* such homes, there *are* such fathers, there *are* such daughters—above all, such daughters, for this play is written from Magda's point of view and must be regarded as a somewhat partisan statement, honest as it is. But who has not known such persons? Who could see that picture and fail to recognise in it some relation to something he has known?

On this picture of an interior the melodramatic element is imposed. For what it is, it is not bad. The plot is well and solidly constructed, the crises are skilfully introduced; and, in the part of Magda, Sudermann let loose an engine probably more powerful than he himself ever contemplated. But take from it the element of social satire (and, as I have argued, this is what happens), and little remains but a clockwork mouse. The mouse is an admirable piece of workmanship. It functions as it was intended to, moves over the carpet without hitches, and does not wear out. It delighted our grandparents when they were children; and to-day the machinery seems to be in an unimpaired condition. If you like clockwork mice, here you will find what you like.

> Edward Shanks, *"There Was a Young Lady Named Magda,"* in The Outlook, *Vol. LI, No. 1314, April 7, 1923, p. 289.*

HENRY B. FULLER   (essay date 1923)

[*Fuller was an American novelist who wrote both romances and realistic fiction. His best-known work,* The Cliff-Dwellers *(1893), describes life in Chicago and is recognized as a pioneering contribution to the American city novel. Fuller also wrote book reviews for the Chicago* Evening Post, Poetry, *and other periodicals. In the following excerpt, he offers a generally favorable review of Sudermann's autobiographical* The Book of My Youth.]

The novelists continue to apply the skill they have gained in fiction-writing to the preparation of autobiographies—or at least to reminiscences of their early days. This is the privilege of the author who has passed the age of sixty. Thus, in this country, we have lately had Mr. Hamlin Garland's life-story, followed by the prompt award of a Pulitzer prize. In France, and elsewhere, the fourth and last of M. Anatole France's volumes dealing with his childhood and youth has come up for wide attention. . . .

Herr Sudermann's [*The Book of My Youth*] naturally resembles the offerings of Mr. Garland rather than those of M. France. A rustic origin, straightened circumstances, and a fixed determination to "write" characterize both. The sophisticated Parisian youth, with the classical tradition ever present as a sort of drop-scene, is replaced by something ruggeder, heartier, and more simply human. The young man set upon the conquest of Paris has long been a commonplace; one turns with a sense of novelty and relief to the conquest of some other European capital. (p. 475)

[Sudermann's] general family connexions are depicted with some particularity; and one sympathizes with the "inferiority-complex" which attended his first essays in "society" and which causes him to exclaim, half way through his story, that he had "always wanted so much to possess some really respectable relatives." Considering such an origin and such early surroundings, the book has much more of *Gemütlichkeit* than might be looked for: Memel and Anabaptism are less calculated to promote the flow of soul than the hills and vineyards of the Rhine or the general culture of Bavaria; while the effect of chill penury on noble rage is proverbial. Many of the pages consist of a sincere and unaffected recital of early privations: one realizes anew how, for the humbler Germans, meagre fare

is the rule, and how hard it is for youth—especially if careless, self-indulgent, susceptible and too deeply involved in student organizations—to carry through an education. (pp. 475-76)

Our author indeed "writes about himself as though he were one of his own favourite characters"—to quote the book's jacket. His easy good nature is unfailing, and his frankness seems quite perfect. His profession has made him the master of well-manipulated detail, with a multitude of varied touches involving the frivolous, the grim, the off-colour, the picaresque, and the gruesome; and yet the book as a whole seems deficient if not in flow at least in breadth. The author himself is outspokenly conscious of this. Things sift through his fingers when they might be moulded solidly into better form. Long-sustained passages are few. Yet, taken chapter by chapter and episode by episode, the volume is arresting and entertaining throughout.

Herr Sudermann's rather airy, stand-off attitude towards his own vicissitudes is paralleled in several instances by his attitude towards the vicissitudes of Germany itself. Here he is often light, incidental, casual: artistic detachment *en gros* no less than *en détail*. The English are, briefly, "our erstwhile cousins"; and a rapid flick is given to the "English island of Helgoland." When he contemplates the condition of affairs within Germany the tone deepens, though words are still few. The final debacle was "a natural result of the spirit of William II." . . . A single direct reference to France, which contrasts the triumphs of 1870 with the sufferings and motifications of to-day, concludes, curiously, thus: "Whether it be decades or centuries hence, if France again lies prostrate before us, we shall not be less generous than we were in those happier days."

These words hardly need be accepted as representative. Perhaps we have come within the aura of a kindly man who has won success against great odds and who, in the sunset hour of his middle sixties, is disposed to reflect a generous glow upon friends and enemies alike. (p. 476)

> Henry B. Fuller, *"The Youth of Sudermann,"* in The Freeman, *Vol. VII, No. 176, July 25, 1923, pp. 475-76.*

O. L. BOCKSTAHLER   (essay date 1933)

[*In the following excerpt from a lecture delivered in 1933, Bockstahler examines the degree to which Nietzsche's theory of the Superman influenced Sudermann's works. In contrast to his early characters, who do not have the courage of their convictions, Bockstahler contends that Sudermann's later protagonists are superior beings distinguished by great bodily strength, dominant personalities, and a willingness to accept the consequences of their often unconventional actions.*]

There are no traces of Nietzsche's influence, ideas or vocabulary in Sudermann's early works. While editor of the *Deutsches Reichsblatt,* Sudermann published several stories in its columns. A collection of short stories appeared in 1887 under the title of *Im Zwielicht.* The dominating characteristics of these early stories are wit and sprightliness, such as are found in the French society plays. The characters are rather indefinite, the organization is imperfect, and the purpose of these stories, which is that of entertainment, is entirely different from that expressed in the works of the next period.

In 1888 two other stories, *Die stille Mühle* and *Der Wunsch,* appeared under the title of *Geschwister.* These stories, written several years before they were published, show skill in character development. This same statement holds true for the next two stories, *Das Sterbelied* and *Die indische Lilie.*

In that same year *Frau Sorge,* an elaborate character study, also appeared. Here, in contrast to the Vollmensch of the later period, we deal with a so-called Pflichtmensch, who does not have the courage to live the life that his personality commands him to live, and so loses the triumphant joy of victory. *Frau Sorge* is pessimistic and shows the influence of Schopenhauer. It does, however, give us a faint indication of what is in Sudermann's mind, for here the concepts of "Pionier der Kultur" ["cultural pioneer"], "Nicht bereuen" ["no regrets"], and "Gutmachen" ["redress"] appear for the first time in Sudermann's works. Sudermann tells us in *Das Bilderbuch meiner Jugend* that he began to study Nietzsche in the same year that he wrote *Frau Sorge,* and the foregoing concepts are undoubtedly Nietzschean ideas working themselves out in the author's mind.

There is, however, no mistaking Nietzche's influence in Sudermann's next work, *Der Katzensteg.* . . . The author has now had two years to assimilate Nietzsche and here we find a decided change due to this new influence. Sudermann was by family tradition, nature, training, and experience prepared for a very sympathetic reception of the ideas of his fellow-countryman. Nietzsche's philosophy helped him to clarify and crystallize his own hitherto hazy and disconnected ideas. (pp. 177-78)

In [Sudermann's] *Das Hohe Lied* Dr. Salmoni speaks in terms that show that he is familiar with Nietzsche, and he gives Lilly books that deal with a discussion of Nietzsche's works. . . . The discussion in *Das Hohe Lied* also uses the expressions "Willen zur Macht," "Befreitsein," "Recht auf Ausleben," and "Individualität," all of which are terms peculiar to the Nietzschean vocabulary. (p. 178)

Purzelchen sends Fritz a whip with instructions to use it on his sweetheart because she is so haughty. The package contains a sentence quoted from Nietzsche, which says, "du gehst zu Frauen, vergiß die Peitsche nicht" ["if you take a wife, don't forget the lash."] Thea, in *Das Blumenboot,* also paraphrases Nietzsche's statement that woman finds happiness under the lash. (pp. 178-79)

One chapter in *Das Bilderbuch meiner Jugend* is entitled, "Weiblich, all' zu Weiblich." One of Sudermann's novels bears the title *Es War* (taken from *Zarathustra*). In *Rosen* Strubel says that his ideal must know Nietzsche "auswendig" ["by heart"]. Sudermann uses the term Übermensch" in quotation marks several times, thereby identifying his superior personality with that of Nietzsche's.

Thus, Sudermann tells us in his own words that in 1877 Nietzsche's thoughts were reborn in him. This statement is further supported by a definite change in his thoughts and attitudes and characters, especially by the appearance of the Vollmensch as the apex of his thinking and the incorporation of many Nietzschean words where other good German words could have been used. (p. 179)

Nearly every one of Sudermann's prominent works, at least those written between 1888 and 1910, depicts a gigantic, power-loving and yet often power-meriting character, whose ruthless will crushes all that opposes him.

Hans Lorbas in *Die drei Reiherfedern* has given the best connected description of this superior being. . . . (pp. 180-81)

Hans believes in the supremacy of Power. He is master of his own destiny and scorns all else. He laughs at the world, fate, chance. Only the aggressively dynamic shall inherit the kingdom. Moral salvation can only be attained through work of a constructive nature. Humanity has the inherent power to save itself. (p. 181)

Since what the Vollmensch wants is right, it is perfectly proper for him to employ whatever means are necessary to obtain it. In this frame of mind Hans walks into the council where uncertainty dominates and says that wherever duty, right, love, desire or law demands action, a real man does not hesitate. . . .

The only inhibitions of the Vollmensch are those of his own desiring. In other words, he lives beyond the ordinary conception of law and represents a thorough, personification of might. (p. 182)

To conform to the common standards of society is to be false to one's true self. The Vollmensch must not compromise, he must exercise his own rights. . . . The greatest enemy of the Vollmensch is the commonplace. . . . Only this Vollmensch may exercise complete freedom of choice and will; Magda, in *Die Ehre* is interested chiefly in those things which are of value to her, and only to the extent that they serve her.

This self-development has brought a consciousness of her power and the demand that her personality be recognized. . . . Magda's entire being is animated with the desire to expand life. The sole object of her existence has been the conquest of life. Scornfully disdaining the "common herd" she has concerned herself only with that which would elevate her above them, make her supreme. (pp. 182-83)

Count Trast, in *Die Ehre,* is always master of himself and his surroundings. Having cut loose from his early environment, he has disregarded all customary and generally accepted social and moral conventionalities and has become Coffee King, who makes all competitors tremble. Even though he is, in general, very broad-minded, he assumes an entirely unsympathetic and indifferent attitude towards home ties, das Hinterhaus and its conception of life, as well as toward the ideas of Kurt and his father and their conceptions of life. He has absolutely no time to waste on any one or anything that does not serve Trast and Company. He, too, must conquer and crush all opposition as he has his competitors. The Count's opinions are especially interesting since he is regarded as the spokesman for the author's ideas. (p. 183)

What has been said of Hans, Magda, and Trast can likewise be said of Regina, in *Der Katzensteg,* Teja, in *Teja,* Röcknitz, in *Glück im Winkel,* Leo, in *Es War,* and others.

The above-named characters are distinguished by great strength of body and personality. . . . These men and women know themselves, are very self-confident, and enjoy their fate. Their own will is their only law and they frequently disregard the rights of others. . . . All of them live beyond good and evil and never repent. Such individuals are always optimistic. Difficulties and disappointments are only challenges to their powers and determination. New values are sought and discovered where the ordinary individual lives complaisantly. These characters are men and women of passionate yearning, of conscious forceful volition, they are motivated by GENIUS (Sudermann's own words). Sudermann, like Nietzsche, believes that humanity can be ennobled and that it can be done chiefly by its own volition and determination. Not every one can rise to such heights, for

Sudermann insists that all men are not equal and believes in a well-defined Rangordnung. (pp. 183-84)

[It] is clear that with the help of Nietzsche's Übermensch, Sudermann worked out the idea of his ideal man, the Vollmensch, who occupies the same relative position in his Weltanschauung as the Übermensch does in Nietzsche's scheme. A comparison of the main traits of these two ideal characters shows that they have much in common.

There is, however, one striking difference. The Übermensch, according to Nietzsche, was to come to his full stature after many years of selective development. The Vollmensch comes to his full stature during his own life time. In many cases he leaves home to realize his ambition and on his return sees the weaknesses in his former environment and proceeds to point them out, or to point out new values. The product is the same, but the time and the method of development are different. (p. 184)

Nietzsche says that the notion of guilt and punishment, including the doctrine of "Grace," of "Salvation," and of "Forgiveness" are all lies through and through without a shred of psychological reality and were invented in order to destroy man's sense of causality.... The concept of sin ..., according to Nietzsche, is not only false but it is also used to perpetuate a false relationship in society. The same condition obtains regarding the popular conceptions of good and evil. Therefore, since the term sin is usually construed as meaning the transgression of a law and the superman recognizes no law but his own will, and since good and evil are only known to him as things useful or things harmful, these concepts can have no meaning in his sphere of action.

The preceding concepts also hold no value for the Vollmensch, for, since he, too, is not bound by the laws of common society, how can he sin? (pp. 184-85)

In order to attain his complete self the Vollmensch had to express himself to his fullest extent.... In this expansion the ordinary laws and conventionalities could only be considered as restrictions, which must be ignored by him. Therefore, the overstepping of these hindrances became a necessity. It is necessary to "sin" in order to obey the creative impulse within. All progress is dependent on men and women who are strong enough to do something new, to push back the frontiers of knowledge and to pioneer in the realm of the unknown. (p. 185)

Like Nietzsche, Sudermann is a writer with a constructive dynamic message of reform. In *Das Bilderbuch meiner Jugend* he tells us that he is a transformer of all moral values. This readjustment is brought about first, by destroying the false and superficial in life and second, by holding up new ideals and conceptions. Sudermann personifies these ideas and makes his "rare race" actually live its ideals in contrast to the decadent world and race of the present. So lofty is this new system that it is not made for every one. Each one of these Vollmenschen is endowed with the will to power and is the inventor of new values. Thus, the whole world is divided into classes or ranks, each having its own ideas or standards of living. (p. 186)

Sudermann summarizes his whole idea of Rangordnung, good and evil and the transvaluation of values when Der tolle Professor presents his ideas of revaluation in the form of a new system of ethics.

Every system of ethics, he says, must begin with egoism and self-interest. If a man does not want to rise above his primitive instincts, and wants in his existence nothing but pleasure and well-being and wealth, he is entitled to it and no power can make him change. He can be as uncharitable as he likes and elbow anyone out of his way. He can value his brother only in so far as he brings him advantages or amusement. That is all within one's rights. Mother Nature teaches us the same thing. The penal laws will see to it that such a man does not altogether overstep the bounds of society. This is the first and lowest stage where self-preservation is the chief force in determining values. (pp. 186-87)

In the second stage education has borne richer fruits and here reign consideration, sympathy, self-sacrifice, love of truth, love of suffering for the universal good; all the accomplishments of thousands of years of intellectual and spiritual culture. Here the approved teachers and leaders are developed. Here the bullion of human ideas is minted into currency. Here the metamorphosis which guarantees each generation its period of blossoming takes place. This is the great middle class of society that standardizes customs and usages. This is the type of men which is described by the Greek term "Aristoi."

But over and above and superior to the "Aristoi" in the Greek state were the tyrants. In this third class we have the tyrants of the human race, whose number in each generation can be counted on one's fingers.... These are the few who determine the course of society. Their thoughts, their discoveries, their inventions, their judgments eventually become the standards of the masses.

To these few we must add those who, although not exactly geniuses like the others, feel themselves strong enough to create their own standards for their actions, first in theory and then in practice. (p. 187)

It is in this manner that Sudermann wished to set up his ideals and reorganize society and then cleanse and purify it of all superficialities and misconceptions.

That Sudermann had no use for pessimism is shown by his personality and his works. He had known suffering but he had also tasted victory. Life had possibilities, and in the final analysis there was more joy than sorrow and more victory than defeat.... There is a striking resemblance between the celebration pictured in *Johannisfeuer* and the Dionysian festival described by Nietzsche. Without doubt Salome is meant to be a personification of the Dionysian spirit.

If Sudermann differs from Nietzsche in his interpretation of the Dionysian love of life it is in the application of it to the living generation. It is spiritual as well as physical with both men. It is responding to the innate impulse to live life at its best, to one's fullest extent.... It is a positive attitude towards life as opposed to a pessimistic, nihilistic one. These impulses or attitudes are the mysterious key to the ennoblement of man. If the individual feels this urge and heeds it, Nietzsche says he can become the forefather of the superman, while Sudermann says he can become the Vollmensch. (p. 188)

[It] becomes evident that by adopting the idea of the Übermensch and then making ... modifications, Sudermann reached the highest point in his Weltanschauung and his development as a writer. This idea he retained until about 1900, when his personal experiences and his inability to reconcile satisfactorily this extreme individualistic personality with society resulted in a confusion of his ideals. In fact, in his *Drei Reden* (1900) he even opposed the extreme "Ich-Kultus." The necessary submergence of all individual efforts into one great united effort during the World War further shattered this ideal. From this time until his death Sudermann's works show a decided wavering between the individualistic and the collectivistic attitude towards society. (p. 191)

O. L. Bockstahler, "Nietzsche and Sudermann," in
The German Quarterly, *Vol. VIII, No. 4, November, 1935, pp. 177-91.**

PAUL K. WHITAKER (essay date 1948)

[*In the following excerpt, Whitaker compares the novel* Dame Care *with Sudermann's autobiography* The Book of My Youth, *positing that the author's idealization of the boy Paul is an effort to compensate for his own feelings of inferiority.*]

Hermann Sudermann published, in 1922, his autobiographical *Bilderbuch meiner Jugend* and, in doing so, supplied an ideal source of material for a study of his early life and personality. This autobiography deals with his youth and early manhood until approximately his thirtieth year. . . . . The *Bilderbuch* . . . assumes great importance for the remainder of Sudermann's writing when it becomes clear to what an extent the characters and problems in his works were drawn from his character and presented the great problem of his own life—the problem of the inferiority complex.

In the *Bilderbuch meiner Jugend* Sudermann repeatedly makes reference to his feeling of inferiority. . . . He likewise describes the factors which would tend to have created or intensified his inferiority, factors such as his unfortunate experiences with certain of his companions, the nature of his home environment, and his sensitiveness to the humble social and economic status of his family. (p. 69)

[In] keeping with Sudermann's negative attitude was his use of phantasy to achieve compensation. By creating a phantasy world for himself, he was able to create an imaginary superiority for himself without any of the dangers to the "ego" which would be involved in the attempt to obtain superiority in direct competition with other individuals. (p. 72)

This attempt to escape from reality into the more satisfying world of phantasy is present in some form or other in the majority of Sudermann's works, but in his first novel, *Frau Sorge,* it takes the form of the creation of a character who is an idealized version of Sudermann himself, and of allowing this character to find a solution to the problem which he himself felt so keenly. This novel is unique among the author's fiction works, in that it is the only one in which he makes such a thorough study of an individual oppressed by the feeling of inferiority. Sudermann wrote *Frau Sorge* in 1887, at the age of thirty, and consequently anything of an autobiographical nature contained in this novel would come from the portion of his life corresponding almost exactly to that treated in the *Bilderbuch.* It is the clear-cut confessional character of this work and the fact that its full significance for Sudermann's own psychological development has never been given adequate recognition, which makes desirable . . . a rather more detailed treatment of Paul Meyhöfer, the main character in *Frau Sorge.*

Paul Meyhöfer's environment was, in its essential details, almost completely identical with that of Sudermann. His father was harsh and unjust but these characteristics are heightened as compared to the father portrayed in the *Bilderbuch;* the same understanding, sympathetic relationship between mother and son exists here as in the autobiography. Paul, like Sudermann, is pictured as having been sickly in early childhood and as having had to suffer much at the hands of two stronger school-mates. The same depressing social and economic conditions exist here as in Sudermann's own life, but are painted in even darker colors.

A sketch of Paul Meyhöfer's personality requires no comment to establish its identity with that of Sudermann. His feeling of inferiority appears even more pronounced than Sudermann's, and attention is drawn to it repeatedly. . . . (pp. 73-4)

Like Sudermann, he was sensitive regarding his clothes and regarding the inferior abilities and qualities with which he had invested himself. This sensitiveness is repeatedly expressed in a feeling of shame, which is likewise to be found in Sudermann's case but is mentioned less frequently.

The extreme apprehensiveness with which Paul Meyhöfer faced other individuals and strange situations, is scarcely more pronounced than the fear and trepidation which Sudermann attributes to himself, and it appears in both cases to grow out of the feeling of inferiority which makes them feel unequal to the situation they are called upon to face, and more than normally sensitive to ridicule. They both seek to avoid such situations, in which their inferiority feeling senses danger to the "ego", by postponing them on one pretext or another until some indefinite future time.

The same shyness and seclusiveness which Sudermann attributes to himself are also markedly present in Paul Meyhöfer's personality. . . . [He is] pictured as being pessimistic, an attitude which is not present to any extent in the Sudermann of the *Bilderbuch,* although it appears in his later life. This pessimism is, however, completely in keeping with the character of an individual suffering from an inferiority complex. On the basis of the unusually striking correspondence between the personalities of Sudermann and Meyhöfer, it seems a justifiable assumption that the author has given here a glimpse into his own personality and his own attitude toward life and its problems which might prove of great value in the study of his other works.

While Sudermann's *Frau Sorge* represents a common form of psychological release through the "confession" technique, and though the author repeatedly creates characters whose inferiority feeling is clearly a reflection of his own, there is to be discerned in his writing a deeper effect of this inferiority feeling in a gradually evolving attitude toward life and society, which appears, in the light of Sudermann's personality, as an attempt to compensate. This appears in the author's early works in the form of two separate but closely related principles, which are expressed independently at first and then later fuse, as his initial vague gropings for compensation are focused and clarified. The first of these two principles is an abnormal sensitiveness to any type of coercion, expressing itself in resentment against what Sudermann feels is the tyranny of the social order and its conventions; the second, growing out of this, is a tendency to overcompensate by an insistence upon freedom—unhampered development of the personality and free expression of the inner self.

The first of these principles is voiced in the story of **"Das römische Bad."** . . . in which he expresses his feeling against the unjust authority of social forms over the freedom of the individual. . . . In **"Sie lächelt"**, another story of the **"Im Zwielicht"** collection, Sudermann again touches upon the theme of the freedom of the personality. . . . This passive sensitiveness to the tyranny of society over the freedom of the personality is translated into an active rebellion against society in *Frau Sorge.* . . . (pp. 74-6)

In the *Katzensteg* . . . Sudermann returns to his criticism of the prejudiced, unjust nature of the "Herdenmoral" ["herd morality"] and examines critically the commonly accepted standards of good and evil, raising doubt as to the validity of the accepted moral conventions. . . .

He continues in the same vein in the drama *Die Ehre* . . . attempting to discredit the universal validity of the social authority by pointing out the inconsistencies within the framework of the system itself and challenging the right of any individual or class to force other individuals under the yoke of its own ideas of right and wrong, insisting that honor—and for this he might have substituted any other symbol of social convention— is not absolute in character, but relative, depending for its form on the requirements of the individual group which it is to serve. (p. 76)

Sudermann here directs the attention sharply to the relative nature of moral standards and demonstrates the inconsistencies of the institution which would set itself up as the arbiter of the individual's conduct.

In his next drama, *Sodoms Ende* . . . , the author shows how the artist, by compromising with society and allowing it a voice in his life, sacrifices what Sudermann clearly regards as the possession of greatest value, and essential to the creative artist—complete freedom of the personality.

Johannes.

Tragödie in fünf Akten und einem Vorspiel

von

Hermann Sudermann.

Achtzehnte Auflage.

Stuttgart 1898.
Verlag der J. G. Cotta'schen Buchhandlung
Nachfolger.

The title page of Sudermann's drama Johannes (John the Baptist).

The next drama, **Heimat,** written two years later, is a companion piece to **Sodoms Ende** but shows the reverse side of the picture. . . . Twelve years of hard work and study had enabled Magda to reach the top of her profession as a singer on the concert stage under the name Maddalena dall'Orto, and as the drama opens, she has returned to her birthplace to take part in the music festival. There immediately arises a conflict between the traditional authority of middle-class morality, as symbolized in the person of her father, and the integrity of her own personality, her proud, uncompromising insistence on inner freedom. At one time she feels herself weakening in the struggle and feels that she must escape. (pp. 77-8)

In spite of her intention to exercise patience and restraint, a dynamic spirit such as Magda's could not allow intrusion of another authority upon its own domain, and in the last act Magda has a powerful scene in which she bitterly castigates the traditional authority which cast her off and then condemned her because she jealously nurtured her freedom. . . . (p. 78)

With **Heimat** one phase of Sudermann's development was completed as he filled in the last details in his gradually evolving portrayal of the relationship between the personality and the social authority—a relationship in which the individual who would preserve the inner freedom essential to the creative personality must be uncompromising in his resistance to the tyranny of the social authority, which Sudermann pictures as full of inconsistencies and unworthy of the obedience which it attempts to exact.

During the years which followed, the philosophy voiced by Magda is echoed repeatedly—in 1898, in the Romantic dramatic ballad, **Die drei Reiherfedern,** then in 1902, in **Es lebe das Leben,** where Sudermann, through Beate's lips, pleads the case of the individual against the morality of the masses. (p. 79)

The characters of Dorrit and Wally in ["**Der gute Ruf**" and "**Die Raschhoffs**" respectively, as well as Lissa in "**Wie die Träumenden**" and Schwester Melitta in "**Notruf,**"] . . . portray women who maintain proudly their right as free personalities to determine their own actions in the face of traditional conventions and social pressure.

The theme of the free personality in conflict with the tyranny of society runs through the majority of Sudermann's works but finds its fullest expression and development just a few years prior to his death in two novels: **Der tolle Professor** . . . and **Die Frau des Steffen Tromholt.** . . . In the former, Sudermann systematizes his Weltanschauung under the title "**Die drei Stufen der Ethik**", in which he asserts the absurdity of a single standard of morality for everyone. He creates one code for those whose actions are governed by primitive instinct; another for those whom education has taught sympathy, respect for truth, philanthropy, and the like; and finally, above the masses and not subject to the morality of the herd, he creates a place for the chosen few. . . . By reserving in this select company a place for the artist, Sudermann reveals the formula by which he theoretically made himself, as an artist, free from the bonds of middle-class morality and superior to the masses. Theoretically, he had achieved compensation for his feeling of inferiority.

This freedom, however, could be realized in actuality only through the strictest avoidance of any ties or obligations which might infringe on the freedom of the personality, and in **Die Frau des Steffen Tromholt,** Sudermann shows how compromise with society robs the artist of this coveted inner freedom. This novel, even to a greater extent than **Frau Sorge,** is autobiographical and in its story of the inability of the artist to adjust himself to the marital responsibilities and restrictions, gives a faithful picture of the struggle, during the thirty years of Sudermann's own married life, between the artist nature and the bonds of middle-class morality which, symbolized in the institution of marriage, seek to fetter it. . . . Time and again throughout the novel the same theme is echoed. In its implications for Sudermann's own life and his life-long questioning of the relationship of the individual to society, this novel forms a fitting culmination to his life's work. In this novel, Sudermann admits that although he may have found the theoretical key to victory over his inferiority feeling, and may have created, in theory, a realm of freedom for himself, elevated above the masses and their morality, he never actually achieved this freedom, and experienced throughout his entire life the feeling that he was constantly being forced by social conventions into a position of servitude and inferiority. (pp. 79-81)

> Paul K. Whitaker, "The Inferiority Complex in Hermann Sudermann's Life and Works," in Monatshefte, Vol. XL, No. 1, January, 1948, pp. 69-81.

PAUL K. WHITAKER (essay date 1956)

[*In the following excerpt, Whitaker discusses the drama* The Three Heron's Feathers *as a highly autobiographical work that is based on the events of Sudermann's own marriage and its effect on his artistic life.*]

Of all the works written by Hermann Sudermann, probably none has been less understood than his enigmatic verse drama, *Die drei Reiherfedern*.

Sudermann's letters in the summer of 1896 describe the early stages of his work on this play, which was to occupy him for the next two and a half years until its Berlin premiere in January of 1899, and it is quite evident from the letters during these years that this drama had a unique personal as well as aesthetic significance for the author. One can thus readily understand Sudermann's deep disappointment when the public, and particularly the press, reacted unfavorably to the play. . . .

There can be little doubt . . . that the unreceptive attitude of the public and the unfavorable judgment of the critics stemmed in no small measure from obscurities in the drama—obscurities which result directly from the extremely personal nature of the material. (p. 78)

It is not surprising that *Die drei Reiherfedern* was so generally misunderstood, for the two works which furnish the key to this early drama were not available until some thirty years after the drama appeared. The first of these, published in 1927, is an autobiographical novel, *Die Frau des Steffen Tromholt*, giving a detailed and only thinly disguised portrayal of Sudermann's own marriage and the problems growing out of the conflict between the artist and bourgeois society. The second, *Briefe Hermann Sudermanns an seine Frau*, was published in 1932, and fully confirms the autobiographical character of the novel.

These two sources acquaint us with the artist's life from the period just prior to his marriage, through the turbulent years of adjustment following his marriage, to the death of his wife in 1924. To understand properly the fundamental character of the marriage problem in Sudermann's life, it should be pointed out that he had early developed the feeling that bourgeois society, with its insistence upon conformity and the subordination of the individual to convention, is a tyrant which stifles genius and fosters mediocrity. The serious artist finds himself en-

gaged, perforce, in a constant struggle to maintain his independence in the face of the demands of social convention. Thus a conventional marriage with its myriad restraints and demands can result only in an irreconcilable conflict between duty to Family and duty to Art. In his novel, *Die Frau des Steffen Tromholt*, Sudermann has Tromholt warn a budding artist of the fatal consequences of marriage for the artist. . . . Sudermann himself, of course, did marry but not before providing himself with safeguards intended to insure him complete freedom from any duties and responsibilities arising from the marriage. In the first place, there appears both in the letters and in the novel to have been a mutual agreement between Sudermann and Clara Lauckner and between their counterparts, Tromholt and his wife, that the marriage should be dissolved at the end of one year. . . . But even during that year, Sudermann insisted upon complete freedom within the framework of the marriage, and this his wife freely accorded him. . . . Actually, in Sudermann's case, as also in the novel, the birth of a child, along with other duties and responsibilities inescapable in any marriage, curtailed his freedom considerably. Nevertheless, mutual interests and experiences gradually bound husband and wife so firmly together that their marriage continued through not one, but through thirty-three years until Clara's death, although the bitter struggle between devotion to art and duty to wife and family brought Hermann and Clara Sudermann on more than one occasion to the brink of divorce.

Turning now to the *Drei Reiherfedern* drama, it very quickly becomes apparent that we are here dealing with the identical problem, the problem of the individual who permits marriage to interfere with the pursuit of his ideal. The result is unhappiness, bitterness, and a feeling of guilt for having permitted himself to be diverted from his mission.

The action of the play rests essentially in the hands of seven characters, and it is the failure to recognize the relationship and significance of these characters which has been primarily responsible for the obscurity of some portions of the play and for its apparently multiple motif. Since the interpretation of the various roles is a matter involving analysis of the words, actions, and attitudes of the characters through the entire drama, only the conclusions can be presented in a short treatment such as the present one. There is, however, convincing evidence that *Die drei Reiherfedern* is an allegorical presentation of the first year of Sudermann's marriage, and that, both in his own case and in Clara's, he has split up the character portrayal among three persons in the drama.

The three characters uniting to present Sudermann's own character are: Prinz Witte, who portrays the subjective aspect of his personality, his impulses and emotions, the dreamer, idealist, and artist; Hans Lorbass, his objective side, the voice of reason and sober judgment, manifesting impatience and rebellion toward actions, restraints, or authority founded on prejudice and emotion rather than upon reason and logic; and finally Unna Goldhaar, who appears to symbolize Sudermann's love.

Clara Sudermann's love appears in the role of Maria, Queen of Samland. At the Queen's side stand her chancellor, representing Clara's moral and ethical self, and Cölestin, the major domo, through whose lips Clara's reason speaks. In addition to these three main aspects of her personality which have been singled out, the subjects of the queen, *das Volk*, appear to symbolize the sum total of the less clearly defined urges, impulses, and attitudes of Clara's being, capable of acting independently, but normally subject to the rule of love, reason, and moral judgment.

The seventh main role is that of Herzog Widwolf, the tyrant, mortal enemy of Prinz Witte and Hans Lorbass, deeply feared by the Queen of Samland and her subjects. He appears to portray narrow-minded bourgeois society with its intolerance and malice, the tyranny of convention, Philistinism.

The scene of the play is the kingdom of Samland which in the drama becomes the symbol of Clara's home. In the first act, Prinz Witte has just returned from his successful quest for three magic heron feathers. The first of these, when burned, will reveal to him a vision of his ideal woman, a vision of happiness; the second will unite them in love; and the third will cause her death. Hans Lorbass tries to persuade Witte to throw away the feathers before they can bring into his life an influence which will rob him of his freedom and interfere with his pathway to the heights. Emotion, however, personified by Prinz Witte, ignores the counsel of reason and conjures up the vision of his ideal. She appears in the evening sky, misty and indistinct, and fills his whole being with restlessness and longing.

In the second act, Witte and Lorbass arrive at the court of the widowed Queen of Samland. They learn that she has yielded to the importuning of her subjects and is going to marry again. She has made a vow, however, to entrust herself and her realm only to the contender who proves himself victorious in a tournament which is being held. The tyrant Widwolf, feared by all, stands at the moment unopposed and, if no other champion appears, the Queen of Samland and her realm will find themselves subject to him. Cölestin (Clara's reason) seeks to interest Witte, but the latter replies [that he is reluctant to interrupt his search for the ideal woman]. . . . Widwolf now arrogantly confronts Witte and heaps insults upon him, but he continues firm in his determination to let nothing swerve him from his course. Finally the voice of love speaks, as the Queen appears and pleads with him to remain. Witte still appears unmoved until Widwolf breaks in, and tauntingly accuses Witte of selfish cowardice. Angered by Widwolf's insinuation, Witte turns to the Queen, asking her to forgive his previous reluctance. . . . The Queen assures him that she will do nothing to deter him in his quest, but will always stand ready to provide help and comfort if needed. . . . (pp. 79-82)

Prinz Witte engages Widwolf in combat, but Widwolf defeats him and is about to assert his claim to queen and throne, i.e., the artist and dreamer, insisting upon complete independence, which would normally imply a liaison without legal ties, finds himself for the moment powerless before Convention. A liaison would call forth social reprisals upon his partner which could not even be considered.

As Witte lies helpless, however, the populace, aroused and led by Hans Lorbass, drives the tyrant Widwolf from the realm. The chancellor, Clara's moral sense, warns that through Lorbass a pledged word has been violated. (p. 82)

Even in this very terse presentation of the second act, certain facts appear discernable: Forces within Clara, possibly physical and emotional factors, assert the need for companionship and demand that "the realm have a king." Even her reason urges the desirability of seeking a new companion and protector to fill the place of the lost husband. Clara's love (the Queen), although still feeling a strong sense of loyalty to her dead husband, nevertheless yields to the insistent demands of her nature and accepts the necessity of a "new king in the realm." The emotional side of Sudermann's nature, touched by the young widow's loveliness and her plea, agrees to become her companion and protector. He defies convention, however, by

exacting a promise that his freedom will not be impaired in any respect. Convention, naturally, can not countenance a relationship of this sort and a struggle ensues between Sudermann and convention in which the latter prevails and momentarily it appears as though bigotry and Philistinism have been triumphant. (pp. 82-3)

This entire sequence of events and considerations as presented in the symbolism of the drama coincides with the situation leading up to the marriage of Clara Lauckner and Sudermann as he himself records it.

The third act opens with Witte unhappy, critical, and unjust to those about him. . . . All about him love, loyalty, and duty impelled him to compromise, to make concessions, yet by so doing he felt he would be sinning against his true self, the artist, would be violating his sacred trust, his artistic mission. Finally, when this conflict becomes so bitter that it threatens to destroy him, Reason rebels. (p. 83)

In his despondency, Witte turns to the magic of the heron feathers. The second feather, burned in solitude, would unite him with his ideal, his happiness. As the feather flames up, the Queen appears in the doorway, and Witte bitterly assails her for nullifying the feather's magic. In the face of his bitterness she appears to feel that the gurue holds no hope for them and she offers him his freedom together with the promise of her enduring love. (p. 84)

Witte's bitterness is suddenly dissipated, the tension which had built up in his soul recedes. He is, to be sure, no freer than before, but Maria's love and generosity bring temporary relief to his soul. . . . (pp. 84-5)

The third act ends thus on a note of harmony and peace, but in the fourth act a serious problem soon compels attention. News comes that Widwolf has laid siege to the castle and threatens that the land will be spared only if Witte and Lorbass are turned over to him. At first Witte urges that they save the land through sacrificing him.

To understand the significance of the foregoing it should be pointed out that the background of much of the conflict between the Sudermanns and convention is to be found in the malicious narrow-mindedness of Königsberg society which Sudermann hated, and from which Clara suffered deeply. (p. 85)

Sudermann felt that much of what Clara suffered at the hands of Königsberg society was the direct result of her being married to him. Hence, in the play, Witte urges that the Queen rid herself of him. Similarly Sudermann, after half a year of marriage, made arrangements with his lawyer, Lobes, for a divorce. . . . The divorce, however, did not materialize, and in the play, likewise, circumstances led Witte to oppose Widwolf instead of surrendering to him. He succeeded in killing Widwolf, in removing him permanently from the scene, and there appears little doubt that this symbolizes the removal of Clara and the children from the influence of hated Königsberg eleven months after the Sudermanns' marriage, to establish a new home in Dresden. Sudermann himself now set up quarters in Berlin, feeling that by removing himself from the distractions and restrictions of domestic life, he could devote himself more effectively to his writing. So, in the play, having saved the Queen from the tyrant Widwolf, he feels that he may again seek freedom and independence. . . . [The] parting from the Queen is tender as he asks her to forgive him for his injustice to her. Maria, however, now confesses that her love had caused her to be equally unjust to him. (pp. 85-6)

Poetic necessity undoubtedly dictated this harmonious resolution of the conflict at the end of the fourth act, but in Sudermann's actual experience, the agonizing inner struggle between loyalty to Family and duty to Art continued for many years. (p. 86)

The main part of the play finishes with this parting at the end of the fourth act. Fifteen years have passed as the fifth act opens. Witte and Lorbass are again in Samland, aged and scarred; they have travelled far in quest of the ideal and have returned empty-handed, asking no longer for happiness, but only for peace and rest. By the seashore they encounter the Queen, and Witte, as he sees her, realizes that during their year together he had experienced at least a taste of the happiness for which he had searched the world in vain. . . .

Clara Sudermann was indeed his true happiness, a source of strength, aid, and encouragement for him until her death in 1924. . . . [While] the dramatic effectiveness of the play may be as open to question now as then, the biographical material now available clears away much of the former obscurity. Characters formerly appearing vaguely drawn and without clearly apparent significance, now come into clear focus and are given essential meaning. Seemingly pointless action and obscure remarks and references take on significance when referred to the now accessible autobiographical material. (p. 87)

Paul K. Whitaker, "A Key to Sudermann's 'Die Drei Reiherfedern'," in Monatshefte, *Vol. XLVIII, No. 2, February, 1956, pp. 78-87.*

WILLIAM F. MAINLAND (essay date 1963)

[*Mainland, an English educator with a recognized expertise in German language and literature, is the author of* Schiller and the Changing Past *(1957). In the following excerpt, he notes Sudermann's powers of observation in his best works, which Mainland believes were influenced by the varying languages and landscapes of the German rural provinces.*]

Problematic natures are those which are consumed by inner conflicts; they cannot cope adequately with circumstance, and so they nowhere find complete enjoyment or satisfaction. Many people—and Sudermann was probably one of them—are gratified to apply such a fine-sounding phrase to themselves. It was popularized . . . by Goethe. But it was probably Friedrich Spielhagen's revival of it as the title for one of his best novels that echoed in Sudermann's ears. He had a great admiration for this political novelist of the preceding generation, and even if there had been no brief specific reference in his own novel *Es war* (published in 1894, more than thirty years after Spielhagen's *Problematische Naturen*) we might still detect a reminiscence of the two leading characters—Oswald Stern and his old teacher, Professor Berger. In varying ways *déracinés*, these two men both embody and respond to the challenge of a time of social and political change—the time of the 1848 revolution. In Sudermann's early years a social and psychological revolution was on its way, and in one of his latest novels he cast his mind back to the Bismarck era. *Der tolle Professor* . . . is set in a scene familiar to him, the city and university of Königsberg. The leading character, a professor of very humble origin, brilliantly expounds his subversive views on society and its institutions, and as the life he leads is very closely in accord with his views, he provokes disapproval and scandal, which increase when he is induced to engage in politics. Professor Sieburth, driven to suicide, is clearly Sudermann's interpretation of the "problematic character". Through the social

conflict which is, in a sense, fought out in his mind and life, and through the story of his profound influence on his students, we catch glimpses of the Spielhagen pattern. From his early and his late works we may hazard a diagnosis of Sudermann's state of mind: we may say that with some inflation of purpose and mission, he saw himself, socially and regionally displaced, perplexed by the sign of decay and renewal around him, and compelled to find expression for it. (pp. 34-5)

[It] was in the castes and classes of Germany as a whole that Sudermann found most abundant copy. There was the wide range of the military caste, from the impertinent and indomitable subaltern to the general, either as tired roué or as citizen with a high sense of responsibility, there was the ex-criminal, there was the lion of metropolitan élite society, and the Berlin underdog, the cultured business-man and the pushing upstart, the brash "Korpsstudent" ["member of an exclusive fraternity"], the disinherited. All these had varieties of idiom and tone which had so clearly assorted and defined themselves in Sudermann's memory that passages of dialogue became the easiest thing for him to construct. . . . It is hard for us to see how this apparently automatic kind of composition was achieved. Perhaps, if we have experienced the imagined clamour of shouting voices as we have been falling asleep, Sudermann may help us to understand, when he notes that he refrained from any new stretch of composition before going to bed, lest the characters should go on talking and keep him awake! One of the most economical devices of characterization by speech is the repetition of a typical phrase or word. Sometimes Sudermann tends to overdo this in a Dickensian way, as in the repeated conversation-gambit of Wally, the generous light-o'-love in *Die Raschoffs:* "Gnädige Frau glauben doch auch an—eine Göttlichkeit der Seele?" ["Doesn't madam also believe the human soul is divine?"] But in the smooth speech of the vicar whom Leo visits in *Es war,* the word "eben" is very effectively introduced with such typical insistence that it seems in the end to dominate (and undermine) all he has to say, and Leo is hard put to it not to slip into the habit himself.

This careful technique of notation helps us to see Sudermann (of the early years at least) as a literary craftsman in tune with his time. What there was and was not of so-called Naturalism in his works has often been discussed. It is not a matter of the highest importance now, and a brief statement about it would not only be vulnerable; like much literary classification it would carry the infection of a false sense of secure knowledge. Of those writers who were for a time regarded as leading Naturalists it can be said, to their credit and their discredit, that they laid great store by differentiated dialogue. It was part of the deterministic notion of the time to insist that people's behaviour, in speech as in other matters, is patterned by their environment; if this sort of logic dominates a writer's mind, he will find it wrong to represent the speech of characters from different milieus in a homogeneous, educated paraphrase or by inaccurate convention of drawing-room and back-stairs speech; he must, he feels, be consistent in recording the little nuances of utterance. This system was followed by Sudermann in the essentially social plays, even down to *Das deutsche Schicksal* . . . when other dramatists were experimenting with terse, expressionistic techniques. His talent was not so effective when he tried to adopt a classical convention of exalted speech in plays such as *Johannes* and *Der Bettler von Syrakus*, drawn from distant periods. (pp. 36-7)

Some of Sudermann's novels which offended good taste in their time, and were immediately popular, have a manipulation of description, tender emotions and passionate episode obviously contrived to prepare and ensure a thrill. We, accustomed to a very different structure and rhythm, may accept them as patterns of a period; we greet the high-lights, the purple patches, and the lingering dalliance with a smile perhaps a little too indulgent. Such are *Der Katzensteg* and *Das Hohe Lied*. In the former there is the episode of the shooting in the night, when the hero, to protect himself, and perhaps also Regina, from the consummation of passion, fires his revolver and wounds her. We are led to expect this by the author's lavish preparations, a prying into the hero's tangled emotions, a display of the dog-like fidelity of the woman, and the contrivance of a storm to make her own bedroom uninhabitable. In *Das Hohe Lied* there is such a sequence of love-affairs, of anguished lingering and capitulations that we begin to suspect a scheme somewhat heavily imposed on reportage. Yet it is a work of serious artistic intent, over which Sudermann had thought for many years before he started the writing. It is easy to understand why the dominant note in early adverse criticism of this, in its day, immensely popular novel, should be a moral protest: to the prurient minds of his readers Sudermann offered an occasional little reward in a brief, unequivocal statement: "Im nächsten Augenblick gehörte sie ihm", ["A moment later she was his"] the rest of the line being completed by the almost inevitable succession of dashes. The immediate causes of this kind of writing in Sudermann are complex and interesting. Among them are: the urge of the '80's to tear away at least some of the veils from human behaviour; Sudermann's early reading, including the very popular *Gartenlaube;* and his own tangled temperament. (pp. 38-9)

If, in reading a novel or in watching a play, we find something that does not fit or harmonize, we suspect that the author has either taken over something from another author, or that he has introduced some raw material from his own experience. In either case he has not had due regard to the organization of his work. There are elements of both these alien intrusions in the play which first brought fame to Sudermann—*Die Ehre.* Here Count Trast plays a heavy, dominant rôle, interpreting the theme and leading the action, somewhat unexpectedly, to a happy ending. He is thus "deus ex machina" and "raisonneur". The latter function, derived from French practice (e.g. Sardou), provides a somewhat ineffective mask for Sudermann himself to parade his supposedly unbiased notions. It is cleverly done, but it is too obviously the author's own cleverness in ironical little aphorisms. And the freedom of the dramatist to dispose of his characters as he will is a fiction made less credible by the circumstances of Trast's own life. He arrives in the cramped and corrupt little world of business magnates and their employees' families as Sudermann imagines himself to arrive—a free commentator from outside. But Trast, who has flouted the conventions of his own caste by refusing to atone by suicide for an unpaid debt, is able to gain a hearing and to shape other people's lives only by virtue of his own high status. He has come back as a coffee-king, with enormous wealth. He is *not* outside the structure of his society, any more than Sudermann really was. He can be sure of a hearing, because money talks, joining in the babble of "Kulturlügen". (p. 40)

From much of [the correspondence between Sudermann and his wife Clara] we derive the picture of a man who was egocentric, opinionated, ebullient, and weak. This is not the full picture of Sudermann, yet it helps to explain many of the male characters of forceful temperament and physique whom he created, discovering in them a disturbing complexity of emotions not disciplined to withstand the attacks of prejudice and prevalent opinion, and of others, ennobled images of himself, who *were* able to overcome adverse circumstances, able, like Teja, the young king of the Ostrogoths in *Morituri* . . . to bear privation and to face certain doom with high resolve: "Tomorrow I will take my spear and my shield and go forth to seize for myself my little share of death for which like a thief I have thirsted and lain in wait since ever you chose me as leader in your lost cause."

Such a mood was easier to imagine, might have been easier to achieve on the slopes of Vesuvius in A.D. 553 than in Berlin in the 1890's, where authority and a band of critics were massed against the playwright. He could to some extent cope with authority, even when faction in the Reichstag was persecuting him, for he was not the only writers of the time threatened by official censure. But the fierce onslaught of individual critics was a more serious matter. . . . Sudermann made the mistake of counter-attacking his critics. His essay *Die Verrohung der Theaterkritik* . . . is a most useful document for the literary historian, but it did Sudermann much harm. . . . Sudermann's resentment seems to have been chiefly stirred by accusations of plagiarism. . . . It is a pity perhaps that Sudermann and his opponents could not perceive more clearly how the notion of plagiarism was giving way, in the hands of progressive literary historians, to an academic interest in influences. (pp. 41-3)

Revealing his weaknesses under provocation of the critics, Sudermann in another mood showed much estimable charity and understanding for his contemporaries. On Fontane, Max Halbe, Ricarda Huch, Gerhart Hauptmann, Ernst Wiechert he bestowed praise all the more substantial because it was acutely discriminating.

He was himself a deliberate craftsman, aware of the demands of his art, and of his own shortcomings. A gourmand in his addiction to words, he saw the need for rigorous restriction. . . . Having read with pleasure Ricarda Huch's *Ludolf Ursleu* (1898) he noted in it a congenial pattern, which, he said, would be his aim if he turned again to writing novels. Zola, on the other hand, though greatly admiring him, he criticized not only for his pessimism, but because the structure of his work was too diffuse. Such comments could help to give us the measure of Sudermann's own ideal of style. We cannot, it is true, expect to find in his narratives the conciseness achieved by some of the generation which followed. But his writing is not generally cumbersome, and there is little sign in his latest novels—*Der tolle Professor* . . . and *Die Frau des Steffen Tromholt* . . .—of that excessive elaboration which is one of the common effects of senility on syntax. There *is* elaboration in his writing, but it seems to be often the result of an almost obsessional preoccupation with certain themes, notably honour, fidelity, the wanderer's return, and sex. . . . The balance of a picture, of a piece of writing, can be destroyed by that incomplete mutation of confession to which reference has already been made. In building up the character of Johanna in *Es war* Sudermann drew perhaps a little too lavishly on his own experience. She is seventeen, and at that age Sudermann as guest in a country-house, had had a swift and passionate affair with his hostess. He had read about adultery, and now he found *himself* involved, his imagination racing ahead to the novelistic consequences— the lovers' flight, divorce proceedings, and so on. But, by the lady's decision, the chapter was closed, only to be referred to later when Sudermann had to read the memory of his own consternation into Johanna's mind, and, with nice regard for her inexperience, to try to interpret her dismay as the suspicion dawned that her admired Leo had loved another man's wife.

Because the years since the 1920's have brought a mixture of the clinical and the barbaric into the literary treatment of sex, Sudermann's mode of presenting its problems nowadays appears sluggish, sultry, and unhealthy. In the *Katzensteg* he skirmished persistently on the fringe of incest. The use of a sister to promote illicit relations either schemingly or with baffled innocence *(Blumenboot)* is unsavoury. Sudermann makes an occasional expedition into the macabre, verging on flagellation, in *Das Hohe Lied* and *Der Katzensteg.* In the short story *Sterbelied* (published in the collection *Indische Lilie*), the young wife, compelled by the cruel religious obsession of her dying husband to read gloomy hymns to him, listens in the night to the whisperings and the singing of lovers in the adjoining room in the hotel.

But there are, as we have noted, other obsessional themes in Sudermann's works. In *Die Ehre* he had made incisive comments on the relativity of notions of honour, and he found himself again and again under a compulsion to return to the theme, and the specific nature of it merges in prolonged consideration of fidelity. There is fidelity to a person, fidelity to an idea; and they are both seen to have disturbing and disruptive effects, especially when the object of reverence is found to be illusory. This is worked out with varying intensity and on different planes. The hero of the *Katzensteg,* von Schranden, opposed by a whole community, tries to prove the honour of a father whose actions are shown, by documents and the testimony of his mistress, to have been dishonourable; and the pastor's daughter, for whom he has preserved unquestioning love, is revealed by the novelist (with vicious haste) to be using him to save his rival. Tragic disclosure of deluded idealism is the theme of the one venture Sudermann made into the mode of the "Märchen-drama"—*Die Drei Reiherfedern.* Here, with elements of fantasy which may perhaps derive from a non-Germanic (Balto-slavic?) source, King Witte pursues an ideal, only to discover in the moment of her death that the love he has sought is the Queen who broke her oath in order to marry him. In *Frau Sorge,* the first of Sudermann's novels . . . , and the only one which has ever maintained a grip on the English and American school-curriculum, there is constant devotion in a cheerless life to an ideal of personal and family honour which leads the hero strangely through imprisonment into marriage with the girl who has remained faithful to him. (pp. 43-5)

There are varieties of amoral women in Sudermann's works, from the bar-maids to Beate in *Es lebe das Leben* and Regina of the *Katzensteg,* and we catch glimpses of their prototypes in the *Bilderbuch meiner Jugend.* Sometimes they represent the illusory ideals in which men have put their trust. But the woman who has drifted away from moral convention or who has been forced by circumstances and the dictates of her own nature may also entertain illusory ideals. Thus Lili Czepanek (we note how Sudermann chooses a Polish name and so detaches her from any purely German tradition) keeps the picture of the young lieutenant who was the cause of her divorce, and imagines his continued love for her. Another admirer, a businessman with considerable patience, helps to maintain the deception and makes her believe also that the money she is receiving comes from the sale of little *objets d'art* she has been making. Even the song—the score of her father's composition, which gives the symbolic title to the story—the song which she has kept hidden away, she finds obliterated when, intending to put an end to her life, she takes one last look at it: mice have gnawed it, and it bears the brown stain of blood, her own blood, shed when her demented mother had snatched up a knife to kill her. The theme of this novel . . . [had] been in Suder-

mann's mind for many years and is not, for all its faults, to be lightly dismissed. It is the story of a woman who, as her favourite teacher had told her, had "too much love in her." . . . She has histrionic and musical talent, but it is squandered on the frivolous "Bande"—the fast set with which she associates in Berlin. She is one of the countless women of Sudermann's time (for some of whom he found a place in his "comédie humaine") who, deprived of responsibility, became the toys of an affluent society. Frustrated longing for life with a meaning, which lead to the rebellion of Ibsen's Nora, is apparent in Sudermann's Lili. She leads an immoral life, and yet there is in her a naïve honesty, a kind of integrity. The symbol for this is the song—"das Hohe Lied". The score itself has been a talisman, and it is destroyed, but the song has become part of her.

One of the favourite female rôles in the high drama of social conflict at the turn of the century was Magda in Sudermann's *Heimat.* . . . If such a character provided material for some of the greatest actresses of the time, she must have embodied for that time the idea of the great artistic talent. Such characters are expected to be flamboyant, but the airs of Magda, and the paraphernalia which accompany her on her travels do more than bring the breath of the exotic into the little provincial nest; they feed our suspicion that this great emancipated woman is a little too shallow to cope with the big social problem of relative moral codes which Sudermann has thrust into her life. Sometimes he shows up the illusory nature of his characters' ideals. Here, where the courage of rebellion and hard-won success are intended to break through the tinsel of convention, the illusion seems to have possessed the author himself and so crept unawares into his play.

The title *Heimat* has a significance for the precarious union of art and life in Sudermann which is lost in the customary English translation: "*Magda*". . . . [Sudermann] had a lively and intense interest in the detail of setting, interior and out-of-doors. Sometimes there is a theatrical quality in his description, heightened when the dramatic tempo of the story quickens, as frequently in the *Katzensteg.* But mostly he has a restrained and finely differentiated pattern, in which time and place, season and atmosphere are sensitively developed by the selective massing of detail. He rarely, perhaps never, reached the heights of "fine writing"—perhaps he lacked the talent. He had not the highest skill when he tried to give purposeful symbolic meaning to a setting. . . . But because of this lack of the highest quality his descriptive passages are unobtrusive, and they are effectively adjusted to the march of episode. This is true of his descriptions of Berlin, but much more noticeable in the settings from his own region. In regional description, from *Frau Sorge,* through *Katzensteg, Es war,* to *Litauische Geschichten* there is a unison between the substance of experience and the gift and discipline of the writer's craft more nearly complete than when he looks outside East Prussia.

What is true of the landscape of these stories from the marchlands is true of the characters also. Not by a carefully studied heredity, such as that which stimulated Thomas Mann (of cosmopolitan descent) but by early environment and the inescapable memory of it, Sudermann was aware of what lay outside the vaunted heritage of the Germanic race. Sometimes he yielded to the theatrical urge, trying to pluck at the reader's heartstrings: in Regina, of the *Katzensteg* . . . there is a managed concentration of qualities some of which were perhaps derived from Kleist's *Käthchen;* but at the centre of her character, perceived directly by Sudermann is—nature. This is the sign of an undeniably romantic response, but in Sudermann, who imagined her as a child of his own region, there is the strength of direct observation. All the fidelity of which he is capable—the fidelity of the artist to his craft—is seen in some of the characterization in the *Litauische Geschichten*. It has been suggested that for these stories Sudermann had learnt a lesson from Guy de Maupassant. If it is so, the lesson was absorbed and assimilated for the treatment of a theme in which he was at home. Sudermann had many startling and some effective things to say about society life in his time; and the years of travel and of domicile in Berlin, the eager exploration of contemporary French drama and fiction trained his sense of form. He managed with skill the bright repartee of the salon, the schemings and the languishings of a brittle civilization, living in its "Märchen". This furnishes the greater bulk of his fiction and his dramas. But the man who had drifted from sectarian traditions and freed himself from the cramping environment of a German province, may well have found his own melody, "die seine Seele immer mitsingt im Wachen oder Traum", in those lives more deeply rooted in his own region. Landscape and people of that country . . . are the inspiration of his greatest work. (pp. 45-9)

> *William F. Mainland, "Hermann Sudermann," in* German Men of Letters: Twelve Literary Essays, *Vol. II, edited by Alex Natan, Oswald Wolff (Publishers) Limited, 1963, pp. 33-53.*

ADDITIONAL BIBLIOGRAPHY

Bauland, Peter. In his *The Hooded Eagle: Modern German Drama on the New York Stage.* Syracuse: Syracuse University Press, 1968, 299 p.*
>   Critical examination of English translations and dramatic interpretations of *Magda*.

Betz, Frederick. "Willy Janikow and Karl Stauffer-Bern: A Note on the Model for the Artist-Figure in Hermann Sudermann's Play *Sodoms Ende*." *Germanic Notes* 10, No. 4 (1979): 58-61.
>   Examines basis for long-held belief that Sudermann modelled the artist in *Sodoms Ende* on German artist Karl Stauffer-Bern.

Bithell, Jethro. In his *Modern German Literature: 1880-1950.* 3rd rev. ed. London: Methuen & Co., 1959, 584 p.*
>   Discussion of Sudermann's place in German literary history. Bithell calls Sudermann a "typical pseudo-naturalist" in both drama and fiction because his works use the external tendencies of Naturalism while clinging to the old tricks of conventional writing and drama.

Chandler, Frank W. "Sudermann, Theatrical Opportunist." In his *Modern Continental Playwrights*, pp. 299-318. New York: Harper & Brothers, 1931.*
>   Comparison of works by Sudermann and Hauptmann. Chandler considers the two equals as dramatists, but finds Sudermann to be the more notable novelist.

Clark, Barrett H. "Hermann Sudermann: *Magda (Home).*" In his *A Study of the Modern Drama*, rev. ed., pp. 83-7. New York: D. Appleton and Co., 1938.
>   Biographical sketch that includes a discussion of *Magda* and Sudermann's dramatic theory.

Coar, J. Firman. "Three Contemporary German Dramatists." *The Atlantic Monthly* LXXXI, No. 483 (January 1898): 71-80.*
>   Sudermann, Ernst von Wildenbruch, and Gerhart Hauptmann compared and contrasted. According to Coar, these three writers examine various aspects of individualism: Sudermann protests against formal, arbitrary morals, Wildenbruch depicts the indi-

vidual at odds with life's physical forces, and Hauptmann expresses the longing for freedom from spiritual repression.

Colby, Frank Moore. "On Certain 'Problem' Plays." In his *Imaginary Obligations*, pp. 134-44. New York: Dodd, Mead & Co., 1913.*
>   Examines *The Joy of Living.* Colby acknowledges the drama as the best of many mediocre season offerings, noting that it is both "literary" and "psychological." However, he contends that the problem around which the story is constructed holds little interest.

Florer, Warren Washburn. "Recent German Criticism: Hermann Sudermann." *Poet Lore* XVI, No. 3 (1905): 116-23.
>   Contends that Sudermann's reputation was irreparably damaged by critics who were either too ignorant or too prejudiced to appreciate his lasting influence on German literature.

Frentz-Sudermann, Hans. "Hermann Sudermann, an Appreciation." *American German Review* XXI, No. 1 (October 1949): 24-6.
>   Sudermann's son-in-law discusses the writer's works and artistic aims in later life.

Garten, H. F. "Naturalist Drama: Hermann Sudermann." In his *Modern German Drama*, rev. ed., pp. 30-4. New York: Grove Press, 1962.
>   Examines Sudermann's plays in light of his diminished reputation. Garten concludes that critic Alfred Kerr, though motivated in part by personal prejudices, did much to accurately point out the superiority of Gerhart Hauptmann's works over those of Sudermann.

Grummann, Paul H. "Hermann Sudermann." *Poet Lore* XXII, No. 3 (Summer 1911): 195-211.
>   Criticism and plot synopses. Grummann regards Sudermann's early plays and the novel *Frau Sorge* as his best works, noting a lack of development in the later, more cynical works.

Hale, Edward E., Jr. "The Renascence of the English Drama." *The Dial* XXI, No. 246 (16 September 1896): 149-50.*
>   Review of English translation of *Heimat*. Hale considers the drama a classic tragedy which portrays a wide range of human emotions.

Huneker, James. "New Plays By Hauptmann, Sudermann, and Schnitzler." In his *Ivory Apes and Peacocks*, pp. 203-21. New York: Charles Scribner's Sons, 1915.*
>   Considers Sudermann a master magician who can make even the most insignificant works attractive.

Koch, Ernst. "The Key to Sudermann." *PMLA* LI, No. 3 (September 1936): 851-62.
>   Comparison of *The Book of My Youth* and *Dame Care.* Koch examines Sudermann's autobiography and early novel, arguing that the main concerns of his fictional works echo these depictions of his own strivings and ultimate resignation.

McCarthy, Desmond. "Drama: *Magda.*" *The New Statesman* XX, No. 521 (April 1923): 773-74.
>   Observes that the otherwise old fashioned drama *Magda* still has a believable emotional effect.

Nicoll, Allardyce. "The Independent Theatre in Germany." In his *World Drama from Aeschylus to Anoulih*, pp. 564-85. New York: Harcourt, Brace and Co., 1950.*
>   Discussion of Sudermann's influence on German drama. Nicoll observes that while Sudermann's reputation has diminished over time, what has often been considered insincerity and dishonesty in his dramas was in fact responsible for making the new Naturalism palatable to general audiences. Nicoll argues that despite the commercialism of his works, Sudermann provided more than common entertainment.

Puknat, Siegfried B. "Mencken and the Sudermann Case." *Monatschefte* LI, No. 4 (April-May 1959): 183-89.
>   Discussion of critical response to Sudermann's works. H. L. Mencken and other critics who admired Sudermann's fiction before it was fashionable are compared to one another and to other contemporary critics who disliked Sudermann's works.

Shaw, Bernard. *Shaw's Dramatic Criticism (1895-98)*, edited by John F. Matthews. New York: Hill and Wang, 1959, 306 p.*

Contains several reviews of *Magda*. Shaw examines various actresses' interpretations of the title role of a drama he considers among the best of its era.

Wells, Benjamin. "Hermann Sudermann." *Forum* XXVI, No. 3 (November 1898): 374-84.
    Sudermann assessed as Hauptmann's dramatic superior.

Winter, William. In his *The Wallet of Time, Vol. 2*. New York: Moffat, Yard and Co., 1913, 680 p.*
    Considers *John the Baptist* and *The Joy of Living* disgraceful works which add nothing to the stage or to the reputations of the famous actors and actresses who star in them. Winter's disdain for foreign productions and realistic treatments of life is evident throughout the review.

Witkowski, Georg. "Hermann Sudermann." In his *The German Drama of the Nineteenth Century*, translated by L. E. Horning, pp. 152-60. New York: H. Holt and Co., 1909.*
    Discussion of Sudermann's dramas. Witkowski assesses Sudermann's works as a compromise of Naturalism and Romanticism on the stage.

Paul (Ambroise Jules) Valéry

1871-1945

French poet, critic, essayist, and dramatist.

Valéry is widely regarded as one of the most important French poets and intellectuals of the twentieth century. Many critics consider his poetry an outstanding example of late nineteenth-century Symbolist aestheticism that demonstrates that movement's concern with artistic form. Because Valéry desired to have total control over his literary creations from their conception through their composition, he directed his powers of analysis to the creative process itself. This fascination with the creative act is the impetus for much of his poetry and the subject of much of his prose. Valéry endorsed Edgar Allan Poe's dictum that a poet should create solely from his powers of concentration and intellect, rather than depending upon random inspiration. From this ideal Valéry developed a theory which holds that literary composition, like science and mathematics, is valuable only as a mirror to the workings of the creative mind.

Valéry was born to a French father and Italian mother in the Mediterranean coastal town of Cette. As a boy Valéry spent many summers vacationing in Italy, where he explored the art galleries and developed a great appreciation for the architecture and literature of that country. Some of Valéry's most descriptive and moving poems are based on these childhood reminiscences. When Valéry was fourteen, his parents moved to the nearby city of Montpellier, where he attended the lycée. Although Valéry excelled in composition, he was an indifferent student whose performance was generally unexceptional. Valéry later stated that he despised the "terroristic methods" of the lycée faculty and quietly rebelled against them by writing poetry and pursuing an interest in art.

Upon graduation from the lycée, Valéry entered law school at the University of Montpellier, hoping that such a move would provide him with some sense of direction and purpose. Although he proved an unenthusiastic law student, it was while at Montpellier that Valéry met the poet and novelist Pierre Louÿs, who introduced him to the circle of writers associated with the Symbolist poet Stéphane Mallarmé. It was Mallarmé who became the single most influential figure in shaping Valéry's aesthetic sensibility. Valéry often referred to Mallarmé as the "Master," for it was through him that he learned to appreciate the vast possibilities of intellectual effort in the writing of poetry and the emotional impact created by the skillful use of symbol and musical assonance. However, unlike Mallarmé, Valéry was more interested in the process of poetic composition than in the poem itself, which he considered necessarily imperfect due to the limitations of language and of the artist's creative powers. His skepticism about the value of poetry eventually caused Valéry to abandon art and the tutelage of Mallarmé for the study of mathematics and natural science.

After his initial appearances in French literary journals during the early 1890s, Valéry entered what many critics refer to as his "silent period," almost twenty years in which he wrote virtually no poetry and published very little prose. From approximately 1898, the year of Mallarmé's death, to 1917, Valéry lived a quiet, studious life in which he investigated math-

ematics and psychology with the intent of developing a scientifically based theory of creative activity. He recorded his insights in personal notebooks, the *Cahiers,* which eventually filled twenty-nine volumes. Valéry emerged from his silent period with the publication of one of his most highly-acclaimed poems, *La jeune parque,* a work of some five hundred lines that took nearly five years to complete. This poem firmly established Valéry's reputation as France's outstanding living poet and one of Europe's premier artists and intellectuals. In 1925, Valéry was elected to the French Academy, and from that time until his death he remained a public man of letters, serving on many committees and assuming the directorship of several academic societies. Valéry's literary work during the last twenty years of his life consisted primarily of prose, much of which was commissioned by various publishers and literary associations. Valéry, who had a strong aversion to fame, undertook these public duties somewhat reluctantly, but needed the income they provided to support his family. From 1937 until his death, Valéry served as professor of poetry at the Collège de France. He died in 1945, and was given a state funeral.

Valéry's early poetry was published in the 1920 collection *Album de vers anciens, 1890-1900.* Valéry himself considered this "an unsatisfactory collection, studies that do not exist as a harmonious whole." The poetry in *Album* clearly shows

Valéry's tendency toward imitation as a young poet, particularly his absorption of the rigorous formalism of Mallarmé's work. Valéry's most significant poetry was written during what critic Agnes Mackay has called his "second poetic period." This period began in 1917 with the appearance of *La jeune parque,* which was immediately recognized for its highly technical beauty. The theme of *La jeune parque* is essentially the awakening of consciousness in a character, the youngest Fate, who represents the universal Self. It is an extremely complex poem, the movement of which is sustained by the shifting states of the character's awareness. In it, Valéry skillfully combines the external natural world with the Fate's inner self through a series of interrelated images and precisely scored musical language. Although the poem has been criticized as rarefied and obscure, most critics acknowledge it as a work of subtle poetic genius. Valéry's other masterpiece of this period is "Le Cimetière marin" ("The Graveyard by the Sea"). This work is an introspective meditation by the poet upon the sea and the light on the Mediterranean coast, the site of Valéry's youth. "The Graveyard by the Sea" was included in Valéry's collection of poetry, *Charmes,* published in 1922. Many critics believe that the work in *Charmes* reveals Valéry at the height of his poetic powers after twenty years labor dedicated to the development of his creative theory.

Valéry's prose displays what is perhaps his most outstanding talent: the ability to apply a well-disciplined mind to a diversity of subjects, including art, politics, science, dance, architecture, and aesthetics. His most noteworthy prose includes *Introduction à la méthode de Léonard de Vinci (Introduction to the Method of Leonardo da Vinci); La soirée avec M. Teste (An Evening with Mr. Teste),* a work involving a persona that Valéry introduced in 1896 and continued to develop in assorted prose pieces throughout his career; the essays found in the five volumes of *Variété (Variety),* published from 1924 to 1944; and dialogues such as *L'idée fixe (Idée Fixe)* and *Eupalinos, ou l'architecte (Eupalinos; or, The Architect).* Whatever the ostensible themes of these individual works, there is always present a concern with form and the activity of the critical mind—an examination of the examination. Valéry's prose works are marked by precision of thought and expression while possessing a remarkable fluidity and grace that lends a poetic quality to even his densest analytic writing. Many critics have made the same charge against Valéry's prose as they have against his poetry: that it is too narcissistic and too difficult for even a diligent reader. During Valéry's lifetime, reaction against the aesthetic absorption he represented produced important changes in the world of art. The Dadaist and Surrealist movements are viewed by James R. Lawler as rebellions against Valéry and his supporters. However, Valéry never compromised his intellectual and aesthetic principals, believing that any reader who was willing to accept the challenge his writing offered would be satisfactorily rewarded for the effort.

Recently critics have begun to reassess the importance of Valéry's posthumously published *Cahiers,* in which he recorded his meditations from 1894 to 1945. The *Cahiers* substantiate the unifying characteristic of Valéry's entire literary output, which remained unaltered throughout his career: contemplation of the mind and its functioning. Judith Robinson states, "If we are really interested in discovering what Valéry thought . . . on the subject which most deeply mattered to him, we must turn to a detailed study of the *Cahiers.*" A critical trend is growing which views the rest of Valéry's writing, from such consummate works of art as `La jeune parque* to the critical essays, as extrapolations of the primary concerns stated in the

Cahiers. The significance of such a trend is that it requires that Valéry's career be considered as a single, unbroken search for the answers to the same questions, rather than a career divided into periods.

It is the entirety of Valéry's contribution to literature that has established his reputation as one of the outstanding literary personalities of this century. His commitment and achievement as a profound thinker, philosopher, and artist have earned him critical regard as one of those writers whose work may be considered among the most distinguished in twentieth-century literature. Critic and translator Jackson Mathews remarked that, "Paul Valéry stands for his age, as Voltaire and Hugo stand for theirs. As hero and symbol of the mind he is of their stature."

(See also *TCLC,* Vol. 4 and *Contemporary Authors,* Vol. 104.)

PRINCIPAL WORKS

La jeune parque (poetry) 1917
La soirée avec M. Teste (short stories) 1919
 [*An Evening with Mr. Teste,* 1925]
Album de vers anciens, 1890-1900 (poetry) 1920
Charmes (poetry) 1922
Eupalinos, ou l' architecte; precede de l'âme et la danse
 (dialogues) 1923
 [*Eupalinos; or, The Architect,* 1932; *Dance and the Soul,*
 1951]
Variété I-V (essays) 1924-44
 [*Variety,* 1927; *Variety: Second Series,* 1938]
Monsieur Teste (short stories) 1929
 [*Monsieur Teste,* 1948]
Regards sur le monde actuel (essays) 1931
 [*Reflections on the World Today,* 1948]
L'idée fixe (dialogue) 1932
 [*Idée Fixe,* 1965]
Tel quel. 2 vols. (essays and notebooks) 1941-43
Mon Faust (drama) 1946
 [*My Faust* published in *Plays,* 1960]
Cahiers. 29 vols. (notebooks) 1957-61
Plays (dramas) 1960
Poems (poetry) 1971

EDMUND WILSON (essay date 1925)

[*Wilson, considered America's foremost man of letters in the twentieth century, wrote widely on cultural, historical, and literary matters, authoring several seminal critical studies. He is often credited with bringing an international perspective to American letters through his widely read discussions of European literature. Wilson was allied to no critical school; however, several dominant concerns serve as guiding motifs throughout his work. He invariably examined the social and historical implications of a work of literature, particularly literature's significance as "an attempt to give meaning to our experience" and its value for the improvement of humanity. Although he was not a moralist, his criticism displays a deep concern with moral values. Another constant was his discussion of a work of literature as a revelation of its author's personality. In Axel's Castle (1931), a seminal study of literary symbolism, Wilson wrote: "The real elements, of course, of any work of fiction are the elements of the author's personality: his imagination embodies in the images of characters, situations and scenes the fundamental conflicts of his nature."*

Related to this is Wilson's theory, formulated in The Wound and the Bow *(1941), that artistic ability is a compensation for a psychological wound; thus, a literary work can only be fully understood if one undertakes an emotional profile of its author. Wilson utilized this approach in many essays, and it is the most-often attacked element of his thought. However, though Wilson examined the historical and psychological implications of a work of literature, he rarely did so at the expense of a discussion of its literary qualities. Perhaps Wilson's greatest contributions to American literature were his tireless promotion of writers of the 1920s, 1930s, and 1940s, and his essays introducing the best of modern literature to the general reader. In the following excerpt, Wilson discusses Valéry's poetry, favorably comparing it to that of Stéphane Mallarmé and W. B. Yeats.]*

Valéry's achievement, in *Le Cimetière Marin*, . . . has been to make a poem of one of those moments when we are visited by ideas of the void—the void of death, the void of space—but, instead of offering general reflections on this subject, he puts the emotions, the ideas, in their setting—the cemetery, the sea, the noon-day sun, the cricket's chirp, the black wreaths, the doves. He has availed himself of the inventions of the symbolists—so expert at rendering complex sensations, at making the stabilities of the external world answer to the individual's varying apprehension of them—to present the emotion merged with the idea and both bound up with the scene which provokes them in such a way that all three seem inextricably identified with one another. He is not didactic, he does not want to convince you of anything; he is not emotional, he has a rigorously objective ideal; he is not content with the poetry of sensations, the music—the music without words—of Mallarmé. As a rule, he sets a definite stage, as Mallarmé rarely does, but then puts on a drama in which it becomes difficult to tell whether the action is passing between real characters or between the ideas in the poet's head or the feelings in his heart. As M Thibaudet says [in his study *Paul Valéry*], his poetry "stands as if at the cross-roads of three poetic movements: the classic, the Parnassian and the symbolist—and combines them in one common essence." It is thus possible for him to recall Alfred de Vigny, by his moral ideas and his marmoreal effects, and Mallarmé, by his subtleties, both at the same time.

The kind of ideas which preoccupy Valéry are well illustrated by *Le Cimetière Marin.* He is fascinated, as I have suggested, by the absolute. It is not a system of thought which he is recommending, but an order of emotions which he is expressing and, in his poems, it takes many forms. As the man in **"Le Cimetière Marin"** seems only the secret change in the completeness and perfection of the noon-day sun, so in **"Le Serpent"** the universe is only a blemish in the purity of nothingness. He would suspend even satisfaction and enjoy it only in a timeless imminence: that for him is the true satisfaction. (p. 494)

[Valéry] seems to admire his mistress most when [as in **"Le Serpent"**] she appears to him in [a] timeless aspect—that is, when she is asleep: in **"Dormeuse,"** he sees her form as a pure abstraction, from which her personality has, as it were, departed, and, in **"La Fausse Morte,"** he reflects that sleep is a kind of death *"plus précieuse que la vie."* Thus other human beings, when they appear in Valéry's poems, are usually either asleep or dead—or, like the woman in **"Intérieur,"** are merely insubstantial presences which pass before the eyes of the mind like glass before the sun. . . . As a rule, he prefers marble columns or stately trees. His imaginary characters, though they have their tragedy, their humour, and their sensuous beauty, are always abstract. And like the Narcissus who is the hero of one of his finest poems, he seems interested primarily in him-

self, or rather in the mind by itself. Paul Valéry is the poet of the mind alone—the mind moved by the contradiction between the change with which life confronts it and in which it feels itself involved and the changeless abstraction to which it turns instinctively as to a native element.

Such a temperament has found a technique and a colour appropriate to it. Valéry's success with his difficult material—which does so little toward carrying the poet part way by interesting the ordinary reader on its own account—is one of the most impressive achievements in contemporary literature. His passion for durability has led him to work in a supremely accurate and compact language moulded to exacting regular forms; his poems are solid, they are constructed in a way that Mallarmé's are not. (p. 495)

Valéry's texture and colour are chiefly determined by this taste for the unstained, the absolute: his favourite adjective is *"pur."* A poet of considerable virtuosity . . . he runs by preference to effects of the crystalline, the silvery, and the translucent, in which he excels. . . . His human figures are like fine statues which have yet a vibrancy and a soft envelopment. (p. 496)

Mr. Eliot has compared Valéry to Yeats [see Additional Bibliography] by virtue of the position of importance which he occupies: he resembles Yeats, also, in the remarkable extent to which he has kept his consciousness uncluttered and untarnished at a time when it seems peculiarly difficult for the poet to strike a vein of genuine feeling and to maintain a taste sufficiently true to express it in verse of fine quality. . . .

Valéry, like Yeats, has maintained a chastity and a dignity undisturbed by the surrounding medley. But, whereas Yeats withdrew completely—and quite consciously, as it appears from his autobiographical writings—from a world spoiled for him as much by science as by democratic society, taking refuge in the more congenial, if obsolete, researches of astrology and magic; Valéry has found at least one phase of contemporary intellectual activity pure and noble enough for his taste and has nourished his appetite for abstraction with the abstractions of modern mathematics and physics. Indeed, he sometimes seems almost the poet of that part of the mind which occupies itself with these things. Is not M Teste, after all, something of a scientific hero? (p. 497)

> Edmund Wilson, "Paul Valéry," in The Dial, Vol. LXXVII, No. 6, June, 1925, pp. 491-97.

ANDRÉ GIDE (journal date 1927)

[*Many critics consider Gide among France's most influential thinkers and writers of the twentieth century. In his fiction, as well as his criticism, Gide stressed autobiographical honesty, unity of subject and style, modern experimental techniques, and the sincere confrontation of moral issues. In this excerpt from his journal, Gide expresses admiration for the musical quality of* La jeune parque, *but notes that it is not wholly original, bearing too plainly the influence of Stéphane Mallarmé. For further discussion of* La jeune parque, *see the excerpt by Wallace Fowlie (1947).*]

Reread *La Jeune Parque.* Despite some charming movements that artifice alone could not invent and in which Valéry shows himself to be truly a musician, I cannot prefer this long poem to certain other ones, more recent and shorter, of *Charmes.* Not yet sufficiently detached from Mallarmé; marking time; abuse of the return to oneself, of the meander. . . .

> André Gide, in a journal entry in 1927, in his The Journals of André Gide: 1914-1927, Vol. II, edited

and translated by Justin O'Brien, Alfred A. Knopf, 1951, p. 405.

H. A. L. FISHER　(lecture date 1927)

[*In the following excerpt, Fisher discusses Valéry's self-awareness and development as a poet, his Symbolist influences, and the impossibility of realizing his concept of pure poetry.*]

The things that interest [Valéry] are the theory of the arts and the processes of his own thinking. . . . As he conceives the business of the poet, it is not to paint the outward face of nature or the visible spectacle of human events, but to dive into the recesses of the personal consciousness and to extract whatever pearls the deep may yield. What if the pearls be sometimes cloudy, and the treasures of the sea seem dark and abstruse? It is only by the drag-nets of the mind sunk to the uttermost depths of human nature that the most precious secrets of the spirit are revealed. The French have a word *Narcissisme*. Valéry is a Narcissist, contemplating his own intellectual image in the mirror of consciousness.

Valéry then conceives himself as the poet of thought. . . . It is, in his view, the thought which makes the·man. The ordinary biography affords no indication of what a man is like. It recounts his ancestry, the outer facts of his education and activities, but the deeper part of him, the inner functioning of the intellect, the mode in which, and the passages by which, ideas flowed into his mind and stirred his will, this, which is the true index of the human character, is omitted. Valéry, on the other hand, only cares for this essential and inner kernel of history, 'the functioning of beings and the generation of works'.

Now Valéry is not the first poet who has been passionately interested in his own intellectual development. Wordsworth here finds an habitual and fruitful theme. He too endeavoured to penetrate into 'the hiding-places of man's power'. (pp. 5-6)

But whereas Wordsworth drew his poetry from

> The harvest of a quiet eye
> That broods and sleeps on his own heart,

Valéry works in singular independence of nature and no one would go to him, as we may go to Wordsworth, to enjoy 'the pliant harebell' or 'the sweetness of the common dawn' or the glories of sun and cloud upon the mountain side. Nor does he introduce into his poetry any delineation of human character. The reader must not expect to meet a leech gatherer or a rough dalesman or any French analogue of these Wordsworthian types in the rarefied atmosphere of Valerian poetry. He will not even see a woman face to face. For Valéry is a practising doctrinaire. Whatever he may be as a metaphysician, as a poet he is 'a solipsist' absorbed in the contemplation of his intellectual and emotional states. Moreover, he believes in the doctrine of *La Poésie pure*, by which he means that poetry is so fundamentally distinct from prose, that nothing which is capable of being adequately delineated in prose has its place in poetry. A sunset can be described in a guide-book, a miser can be portrayed in a novel, a statesman or a political transaction form the proper substance of a history. For this very reason no one of these phenomena has a place in pure poetry. It is only after such prosaic impurities have been drained away that we have the quintessential spirit of verbal melody. (pp. 6-7)

This doctrine which he holds in common with the symbolists is never pushed to the length of saying that the content of poetry is immaterial. The meaning in Valéry's poetry may be difficult to define with certainty and precision, but there is always some meaning, and even if there is nothing in the least resembling moral direction, there are ideas and there are symbols of ideas, shaping themselves and re-shaping themselves like a procession of clouds in the sky. (p. 7)

On all this business of what does and does not lie within the scope of his intellectual interests Valéry writes with singular candour. 'There is an abyss between an impression and an expression. I am quite capable of appreciating things which I am altogether unable to describe. I prize and revere the great art of the novelist, but I do not pretend to be at home in it. It is a mode of literature based upon a view of men which is not natural to me. I do not know how one should go about creating characters. Novelists give life and my only object is in a certain sense to eliminate life. This singular angle of vision prevents me from forming a reasonable judgement on any matter concerned with novels, theatres, politics, or even history. In brief on any kind of work which takes man as he appears to us, as a unit or element in its combinations.'

It must be admitted that the exclusions are comprehensive. A poetry which seeks in a certain sense 'to eliminate life' is a very different kind of poetry from that which the world has valued since the days of Homer. Psycho-analysis however subtle, set to music however delicate and scholarly, is not literature for the profane. It is no surprise to learn that it is very difficult literature to create; so difficult that we can well understand him again when he dismisses the idea of inspiration as part of the ordinary mythology of the mind, well understand him again when he preaches the gospel of hard work and assures us that there is no certainty about the art of versifying, that it presents at every instant insoluble problems and that a mere nothing may break a fine poem, spoil its accomplishment and destroy its charm. Nor is it surprising that the poet-mathematician who has set himself the task of trying to get as deep down into himself as possible should seek every possible assistance from nature in this arduous enterprise, and should make careful note of those natural circumstances which seem to hinder and those which on the contrary assist his arduous purpose. M. Valéry, who takes himself and his intellect with profound seriousness, does all these things. (pp. 7-8)

The admirers of Valéry have found in his work an original and inventive quality which, apart from an unusual sense for the niceties of French prosody, gives him a special place among the poets of this age. His critics admit the excellence of his technique but complain that his verse is cold, strained, and difficult, and to them M. Valéry would at once concede that neither in his choice of themes nor in his treatment of them is he concerned to stir the common heart of man. If he ever thinks of his readers, which may be gravely doubted, it is certain that he does not view them as lost souls to be saved by his verse. His gift to them is not ethical improvement but the kind of subtle and intellectual enjoyment which is excited by delicate chamber-music. Some of the audience will discover deep meanings in the music, others will simply enjoy the sounds, to others the whole performance will be unintelligible. To all critics the author's reply would be that he is giving them the deepest part of himself in the form most satisfactory to his artistic conscience, and that if they do not like it, they are under no obligation to listen. (pp. 8-9)

[Valéry] does not propose to himself to describe men and things but only the emotions which correspond with certain states of mind. The objective world is not, in itself, a fit object for contemplation. . . . Reality then must be masked. We must cultivate the state most opposed to 'mundane lucidity and inexorable clearness'. And certainly in many of M. Valéry's poems this state is cultivated to a high pitch of perfection.

It is not, however, in virtue of these affectations and obscurities but in spite of them that the lyrical poetry of this subtle and cultivated mathematical scholar will continue to attract attention. (p. 11)

The difficulty which confronts the poet . . . is that he is striving for two incompatible and incommensurable things, depth of thought and pure music, and that he is disposed, whenever obstacles arise, to sacrifice meaning to music. Nobody can read **Les Charmes** without being impressed with the care which has been taken to secure the right sequence of vowels and consonants, how every musical effect has been studied, what use is made of alliteration, and how often it would appear that the poet is started off upon a new line of thought not by any inner logical coherence but by the accident that a certain collocation of beautiful sounds has captivated his ear. (p. 12)

It requires indeed a certain violence of adjustment to attune oneself even to the simplest of M. Valéry's poems. The reader has an uneasy suspicion that the meaning which seems to him to be probable may not in fact correspond to the intention of the author, or that there may be undertones of significance only to be appreciated by the schooled ear of the initiate. The poet

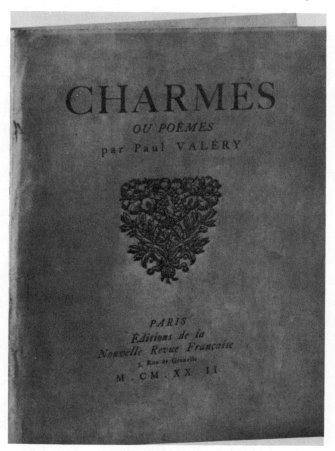

The title page of Valéry's important poetry collection Charmes. *From* Paul Valéry, *by Agathe Rouart Valéry. Gallimard, 1966. © Editions Gallimard.*

also has the perplexing habit of introducing dialogue into his Odes without any visible indication either as to who it is who is speaking or as to when his allocution begins or ends, and our perplexity is increased by the fact that in the Valerian poetry the gift of speech is not confined to human nature. In this respect M. Valéry allows himself the widest allegorical latitudes. (p. 15)

Of the two graceful prose dialogues, written in the Platonic manner, **L'Âme et la Danse** is the more original in substance, containing as it does that thought of the perpetual transmutations of life, action passing into rest, rest into action, which is central in Valéry's philosophy, and finding in the movements of Athikte, the consummate dancer, neither, as one opinion would have it, the very image of love, nor, as another contended, the bodily displacements visible to the eye, but the bare expression of that metamorphosis which runs through all nature. In **Eupalinos,** Socrates and Phaedrus discuss architecture, Phaedrus recalls to the memory of Socrates the memory of Eupalinos of Megara, the architect of the Temple of Artemis the Huntress, one of whose precepts was that in execution there was no such thing as detail, but that everyting was important. He then recalls how Eupalinos had said that his delicate temple of Hermes was the mathematical image of a girl in Corinth whom he had happily loved. Thereupon Phaedrus compares the temple to a nuptial chant, a thought pleasant to Eupalinos, who proceeds to divide buildings into three classes, those which are dumb, those which speak, and those which sing. The creative art behind the singing building is compared to an ecstasy or to the possession of the loved object in sleep. In those moments a wealth of mysterious and superabundant favours comes to the architect. Thence the dialogue wanders away to speculations as to the relations of music and architecture, and of both these arts to the basic science of geometry and afterwards we are led on to consider the difference between mechanism, life, and personality . . . , and the comparative advantages of speculation and action. Socrates says that the choice lies between being a man or a mind, and the dialogue concludes with a paean in favour of a life of action and commending the art of construction as the most complete form which human activity can take.

The idea, which is touched on in this dialogue, that there is no difference in quality between the creative impulse of the artist and the man of science was elaborated in a youthful essay on Leonardo da Vinci, and is the theme of an interesting conversation reported by M. Lefèvre. Here Valéry observes that works of art interest him less in themselves than for the reflections which they suggest as to the manner in which they are produced. 'I like', he continues, 'to try to represent to myself their embryonic state. Now in this state the distinction between the *savant* and the artist vanishes. Nothing remains but the play of excitement, of attention, of mental accidents, and conditions. True, the constructions of science are impersonal, but every act of a scientific constructor is the act of a personality. The style of a mathematician is as recognizable as the style of an artist. (pp. 16-17)

The conclusions of sound mathematical reasoning are clear. Not so, for the most part, the results of the artistic impulse applied in the Valerian manner. Why is this? The poet admits his obscurity, does not seek to defend it, but searches for an explanation, as if the obscurity of his poem were some natural phenomenon with which he was personally unconcerned. There are, he announces, three causes. The first is the difficulty of the subject-matter. States of thought and feeling can only be defined in terms of their relations and combinations, and these are unprovided with an exact and clear-cut nomenclature. The second is the number of independent conditions which the poet is expected to satisfy if he wishes to comply with the rules of classic prosody. The third cause for obscurity is a compound of the other two, the length of time which the author is compelled to take in elaborating a poetic text. It will be seen that Sheridan's 'damned easy reading, damned hard writing', is the converse of the experiences of M. Valéry's readers. The harder he writes, the more difficult he makes his writing for them. If he spends four years on the text of an Ode, his readers will probably need five years to understand it. In a word, M. Valéry does not correct and refine to clarify the meaning for his reading public, but on the contrary to deepen it or else to improve the musical effect of his verse. Neither of these operations conduces to greater intelligibility.

What else does all this mean than that M. Valéry has set himself an impossible task? His music must be flawless, his prosody classical, his theme the transmutations of human consciousness under successive stimuli from without and within. Need we wonder if, laying so great a burden on his shoulders, M. Valéry more often than not fails to win his way to clarity. The attempt to express in a lyric as musical as Schubert, as formal as Hérédia, such minute psychological changes as fill Proust's operose and interminable novels, this, if a gallant, is surely a forlorn enterprise. It is a remarkable feat of literary tact that, despite all these self-imposed and harassing conditions, M. Valéry should have published so much verse which can be read with pleasure and even with admiration. However little interest we may take in the introspective and psycho-physical content of so much of M. Valéry's verse, we cannot deny that upon occasions he can write 'pure poetry' not only in the Valerian but in the ordinary sense of the term. (pp. 18-19)

Two large questions of aesthetics are naturally raised by the technique of this fastidious and original artist. The first is the question whether the poet can hope to produce the kind of appeal which is made to the ear by the musician, and if so, whether this should be his single aim. The symbolists among whom M. Valéry served his literary apprenticeship answered both these questions in the affirmative. If romantic musicians like Berlioz and Wagner could instil into their operas some of the specific effects of literature, they saw no reason why the poets should not take their revenge. . . . Looking back upon the movement of his youth which has left so strong and enduring an imprint upon him, M. Valéry is bound to admit the failure of symbolism to establish itself. The effort to obtain pure poetry has been too arduous, the ideal has been too high, the results have been adjudged almost inhuman. The successors of the symbolists have neither endured their torment nor adopted their delicacies, and sometimes see licence in experiments which were regarded by the pioneers as a new kind of rigour.

The poets of to-day, he admits, open their eyes upon the accidents of Being where the symbolists in their effort to stand close to the essential heart of things had advisedly closed them.

In spite of this clear-sighted analysis, so much of the spirit of 'pure poetry' in the technical sense of that phrase continues to inform the verse of M. Valéry that his readers are still entitled to ask the question which was addressed to Mallarmé and his disciples. Can poetry produce the effects of music? If so, should it sacrifice clarity to sound? Now it is obvious that poetry being expressed in words cannot produce exactly the same effects as music, which is expressed in notes. Its effects may be analogous but they are not identical. . . . But the fact that poetry

cannot reproduce the exact effect of music on the nervous organism is no reason why it should not attempt to capture for itself as much of the specific musical influence as its medium admits of. Poetry, however, can never be 'pure' in the sense in which music is pure, because, do what the poet may, every word used in a poem is a complex of associations reaching out in every direction beyond the sphere of poetry. It is vain to attempt to exclude the accidents of Being from poetry. They come rushing back into the field of consciousness with every noun or adjective. Since then the specific emotional effect at the command of the musician is out of reach of the poet, is it wise for the poet to throw away the specific effect of poetry which is out of reach of the musician? By aiming at 'pure poetry' he does this, for he sacrifices articulate meaning in the hopes of reproducing an emotional state to which the instruments at his disposal are inherently unequal. (pp. 19-22)

Valéry would not now count himself among the symbolists, but he is a child of the movement, and has the better right to profess pure poetry since by the law of intellectual affinities he moves in the sphere of pure mathematics. Geometry and Poetry are old allies; and this poet, who is also a geometrician, has already given us a small body of poetical work at once so intellectual and so melodious that the jealous portals of the French Academy have been opened for his reception. His verse is confessedly difficult, but perhaps for that very reason, and because it evades the clear concrete outlines of everyday life, it has a curious power of transporting the reader into a magical world of its own in which there is nothing common and nothing definite, but only a phantasmagoria of haunting images passing before the eye to the sound of delicate unearthly music and with just so much of consistency and permanence as belong to the scent of flowers in the night breeze or to the ethereal tissues of a dream. (p. 22)

H.A.L. Fisher, in his Paul Valéry, *Oxford at the Clarendon Press, Oxford, 1927, 22 p.*

MARY M. COLUM (essay date 1939)

[*Colum, who contributed criticism regularly to such publications as* The New Republic *and* The Saturday Review of Literature, *was called "the best woman critic in America" by William Rose Benét in 1933. Others, however, have noted that Colum sometimes allowed personal prejudice to color her critical judgment. In the following excerpt, Colum draws some comparisons between Valéry and Vicomte François-René de Chateaubriand, and then focuses on the difficulty of Valéry's poetry and prose. Colum claims that Valéry's work does not attract a large audience because his thought is inaccessible to the "ordinary reader."*]

It was Chateaubriand's claim that the whole European mind and its products derived from Christianity. But the present-day French poet and philosopher, Paul Valéry, has always claimed that what is called the European spirit (in which would be included the American) results from the combined relations of Greece, Rome, and Christianity.

Valéry is himself the exact opposite of Chateaubriand: the romantic tradition wearies him, and, while paying due respect to Christianity as a cultural force, he is a skeptic, knowing nothing of a transcendental God or a revealed religion.

On the other hand he takes no stock in the popular beliefs of the rationalist-minded man of today. He has no faith, for instance, that, through leisure and material plentifulness created by the efficient use of natural energies, man can make himself more conscious, more liberated. Indeed he thinks of the modern obsession with the effective use of natural energies as dangerous to the spirit of man.

And what is this spirit?

For Valéry it is no metaphysical force or entity: it is merely the power of transformation. But this power is an activity different in kind from the known natural energies that we are making such stupendous use of. Spirit, the transforming power, triumphs by combining these natural energies or opposing them.

An easily understandable example of the functioning of spirit is in artistic creation—it is in science, too, and in the intellectual processes that lead to invention. He instances the poet or the musician—

> when they transform their affections, and even their sadness and distress, into poems, into musical compositions, into means of preserving and directly diffusing their whole emotional life by means of technical artifices.

(p. 28)

Paul Valéry's idea of the spirit, at least as it shows itself in artistic creation, corresponds to the Freudian formula; indeed, in Valéry's thought one finds correspondences with the most significant phases of contemporary thought—Freud's, Bergson's, Mussolini's.

Though posterity may recognize him as being as much a characteristic product of our time as Chateaubriand was of his, Paul Valéry is, of all well-known, significant writers, probably the one who has fewest readers. His poetry is of the most difficult; it demands not only an exercise of thought and powerful imagination but a literary initiation such as few readers of our day have got. Moreover, in much of his work there is an ironic spirit which is often extremely baffling. Like Chateaubriand, he is a man of a transition period, a transition in which is being evolved a differentiation between literature as an art and the ordinary practice of writing and a departure in philosophy from systems towards individual insights. I consider the gap between him and the ordinary reader so great that Valéry cannot exercise that influence which a real poet and a real philosopher should be able to exercise. I am all for differentiating the art of literature from the common practice of writing, which is being more and more degraded by publicity writing, by the cinema, by radio. But a poem ought not to have need of the lengthy commentaries that so much of Valéry's poetry demands.

In this collection of essays, **Variety: Second Series,** the memorable essays are not the literary ones like those on Stendhal, on Villon, or on Baudelaire—the last, indeed, is platitudinous. When he puts amongst the important bearers of Baudelairian influence Swinburne and d'Annunzio, he not only overestimates the stature of these poets but he seems to be unaware that what they have drawn from Baudelaire is only on the erotic side. On the other hand, such an essay as **"The Balance Sheet of the Intelligence"** is a contribution to the literature of education and to the mental formation of any intelligent reader. When he states that he never hesitates "to declare the diploma to be the mortal enemy of culture," he is exaggerating on the right side. . . . What is valuable about the thought shown in the best of these essays is that it is distinctively that of the modern man, the man whose mind is really contemporary with the ideas of science, of philosophy, of history as these are handled by the specialists who have imitated them. (pp. 28-9)

Mary M. Colum, in a review of "Variety: Second Series," in Forum and Century, *Vol. CI, No. 1, January, 1939, pp. 28-9.*

WALLACE FOWLIE   (essay date 1947)

[*Fowlie is among the most respected and comprehensive scholars of French literature. His work includes translations of major poets and dramatists of France (Molière, Charles Baudelaire, Arthur Rimbaud, Paul Claudel, Saint-John Perse) and critical studies of the major figures and movements of modern French letters (Stéphane Mallarmé, Marcel Proust, André Gide, the Surrealists, among many others). Broad intellectual and artistic sympathies, along with an acute sensitivity for French writing and a first hand understanding of literary creativity (he is the author of a novel and poetry collections in both French and English), are among the qualities that make Fowlie an indispensible guide for the student of French literature. In the following excerpt, Fowlie discusses the importance of Valéry's poem* La jeune parque *in his body of work. He particularly notes the conflict between the physical and intellectual natures of the poem's central figure and the way in which the image of a tear unites these disparate halves of the self. For further discussion of* La jeune parque, *see the excerpt by André Gide (1927).*]

The occasion which prompted the writing of **La Jeune Parque** illustrates a theory of poetry held by both Mallarmé and Valéry. Namely, that poems are circumstantial, that they are induced into being by events which often are quite foreign to the poems themselves. A poem is a celebration of something, a kind of "request performance." The poet is the man solicited by events, by persons, by thoughts, and perhaps especially by images. And the poem, when it is completed, is in most cases vastly different from the original shock or plan or circumstance which initiated it. (p. 318)

La Jeune Parque is a long poem occupying a central position in Valéry's poetic work, midway between **Album de Vers Anciens** and his final group of poems entitled **Charmes**. The dedication to André Gide describes the poem as an "exercise" undertaken in order to discipline the poet once again in the art of poetry which he had abandoned for so long.

Valéry had originally planned to call the work *Psyché*, but when he learned that his close friend Pierre Louys had chosen that name as title for his next novel, he withdrew it. . . . The name *Psyché* would quite obviously have served as an appropriate symbol for the soul, as a psychological symbol for the human soul seeking to see itself and to understand itself. (pp. 318-19)

Modern poets, and perhaps especially, modern dramatists ceaselessly plunder Greek mythology for well known names which stand for a given temperament or situation, and then in their contemporary re-creation quite freely universalize or alter or develop the original traits. **La Jeune Parque** is not much more than a title. The character in the poem who speaks throughout it is the feminine pronoun "I": "harmonieuse moi." The long debate in the poem, which is its principal subject, seems to take place within the conscience of a young girl who has just awakened. In three different poems Valéry uses the mythological character of Narcissus for a similar inquiry and investigation. The poet stresses the marked femaleness of the hero Narcissus whose immobility and self-exploration equate him with the adolescent girl called la jeune Parque. (p. 319)

There is no narrative to follow in **La Jeune Parque**. There are no descriptions in the traditional sense, no precise setting save the most general kind of setting which has almost to be guessed at. The movement of the poem is sustained by what Valéry states in his definition: a series of psychological states of awareness. They contain no evident order or logic. Or rather they attempt to reproduce the innate and secret order of the psyche before it is departmentalized by verbalisms and habitual responses. This innate order of the conscience takes and rejects. It discovers and loses and rediscovers. In the very linguistics of the poem, Valéry reproduces this movement of rejection and rehabilitation. He has stated that at all moments during work on the poem, when he had constant recourse to Clédat's *Dictionnaire étymologique,* he was making discoveries of purer meanings of words. Words are like palimpsests: they have layers of meanings. By new juxtapositions and new rhythms, which constitute the work of the poet, pristine meanings of words rise to the surface almost mechanically, in much the same way that any fresh concentration on self, any dialogue that is carried on with oneself, reveals unsuspected awarenesses and experiences. *La Jeune Parque* is a supreme example of the dual function of a poem: that of revealing and celebrating the original value of words and of experience. (pp. 319-20)

The theme of the tear, announced at the very beginning, seems to be one of the principal means of sustaining the poem, of giving it a semblance of structure and at least an equilibrium. In fact the major portion of the piece takes place between the forming of the tear and its course down the cheek of the young girl. The period of time which elapses between line 1 and line 324 might well be almost negligible: the poetry reproduces the rapidity and the richness of thought.

In the three opening lines la jeune Parque asks her first question on awakening. The first verb she uses is "weep." *Qui pleure là?* (Who is weeping near me?) And she immediately answers her own question, as if over-anxious to find an answer: *sinon le vent simple* (it is only the wind). As soon as she realizes it is still night and the stars are shining high above her *(avec diamants extrêmes),* she repeats the question with greater insistence and reveals that she herself is on the verge of weeping *(moi-même au moment de pleurer).* Already, in this opening question, there has been established a relationship between the girl and two worlds: the physical world of nature (wind) and the limitless cosmos of the stars.

As soon as the poem continues, the third world is announced. The girl's hand, in a mechanical or nervous reflex, rises to her cheek to brush off the tear which is about to form. But before this seemingly insignificant gesture is executed, she realizes that she is thereby obeying some deep and obscure plan *(docile à quelque fin profonde)* which may be a revelatory part or key to her destiny. The tear which is forming in the corner of her eye rises from a submerged element of her destiny, from a world underneath the purely physical world of her body. There lies the real disaster or the real grief. The tear is only an objectification of a drama to whose source she would like to have access. There are various degrees of destiny *(mes destins),* or varying levels of awareness in a human destiny. The raised hand of the girl, waiting for the tear to be formed, is thereby waiting for the purest of her destinies *(le plus pur en silence)* to illumine her broken heart *(éclaire un coeur brisé).* The word "pure" in Valéry's vocabulary is close to the meaning of "absolute." The tear will be the absolute or the real distillation of some suffering. Its creation marks a lucid point in la jeune Parque's destiny. It will be a clear sign of the secret world within her, and the poem will now unfold in an effort to relate the heart and the destiny, to discover the destiny in order to explain the broken heart and the tear.

The slowly-forming tear will be nothing in itself, unless the girl is able to descend into depths of her own being which are usually unexplored. From the outset, she senses that what she may come upon will not be noble. To know may be to know

disaster. This word "disaster," used in its full astrological sense, ends the second small section of the poem (line 17). The distant sky far above with its grape-clusters of stars *(aster—disaster)* is as unknown to la jeune Parque as her own being and the reason for the sudden shock which has awakened her, the reason for the tear which is forming outside her body and which with a gesture of her hand she is ready to efface. She wills to know, however, even if it is to know disaster *(ma soif de désastres).* Her tear is a prophetic symbol of woe, but her mind is already disengaged from her body. She is able to look at herself and begin the descent into herself.

Thus, in the first seventeen lines of *La Jeune Parque,* three distinct worlds are defined: 1. the body of the girl who rises up from sleep, to feel close kinship with the earth's body and the sound of the water and the wind; 2. the submerged consciousness of the girl which she realizes has been active during her sleep and which has created a drama sufficiently poignant and real to cause her to weep and yet still far removed from her powers of perception and memory; 3. the cosmos of the universe, the enveloping and peopled heavens which whirl above her at distances she can't comprehend. These three seemingly disparate worlds of matter, psyche and cosmos, are bound together and related by the tear. A chemical analysis of the tear would place it within the realm of matter, but the experience which caused it was not material. Her body was presumably asleep and motionless when some obscure psychological action or trauma took place. If this hidden experience, which has already transpired and which she can't remember, was not directed by her conscious self, could it be that the stars are responsible, that the great rotating movements of the planets are determining or at least recording the destiny of this girl? Is the tear, then, the result of the interplay and the interractions of the three worlds?

A change has taken place in la jeune Parque and yet she is puzzled to know exactly what change. She looks at her body as though she were separate from it *(Je me voyais me voir),* and with the naming of the serpent which she sees leaving her, after having pierced her body, she begins a song of duality, a song of the two selves who exist simultaneously in her.

La jeune Parque doesn't describe any schizophrenic complex which is growing in her character. The duplication of self, which at this point becomes the subject of the poem, is a normal and daily phenomenon transpiring in each of us. The physical self is the measurer and container and recorder of experience. It is perhaps comparable to the pages themselves of a manuscript on which the words are inscribed. The wound which la jeune Parque has felt on her body, and which she postulates as having been caused by the serpent, is the mark and the trace of an experience. The other self is the philosopher, or, quite simply, the intelligence which seeks to understand the recorded experience. The two selves are like two sisters. They are even like the two nymphs held by the faun [in Mallarme's *L'Apres-Midi d'un Faune*], the one sensuous and the other chaste. They are even jealous of one another. The physical self, which enjoys the pleasures of the senses, prefers its rôle to the contemplative self whose will to know interferes with action and physical display.

The intellectual self, or the psyche, in la jeune Parque is the stronger of the two. The wound on the body is not so deep as the knowledge of self is penetrating. . . . This girl's drama will be infinitely more intellectualized than the faun's. It is for her, as it is for anyone—but in varying degrees—a loss of the sense of unity, the failure to recognize oneself as a single individual.

With the awakening of conscience begins the drama of two beings in one, of two personalities held within one body: the one instinctive and the other reflective, the one heedless and the other attentive, the one burning with passion and the other cool with reason. This divisioning of la jeune Parque into two creatures immediately follows her awakening and her strong impression that a serpent has bitten her. She is now simultaneously a girl down whose cheek a tear is about to flow and the girl who wants to know the cause of the tear no matter what secret crime this knowledge may reveal.

The long diatribe which she addresses to the serpent (line 50-96) is the real discourse of the conscience, strong in its verbal power and intricacies, proud in its oral domination over the desires of the flesh. The conscience argues principally that the body in its weariness is a facile prey to an assault of the senses. During sleep, when the conscience cannot act, the body becomes the setting for sensuous indulgence. . . . The command, "off with you!" (*Va!*), recurs intermittently. This resurgence of the intellectual self has come at just the right moment. She is still intact. The tears she might have shed are still within her (*Toute humide des pleurs que je n'ai point versés*). She has not capitulated to the weaker self and her apostrophe to the serpent is unmistakably a chiding and a reprimand. But when the oratory is finished, the silence which follows it is disturbed by a thought which weakens the righteous sermon to the serpent and mysteriously joins the two opposing selves. . . . The pain from the wound may well be divine [as she so imagines] if it becomes a channel to self-knowledge. A renouncement of the physical self might well mean an impoverishment of the intellectual self. The mortal sister is needed by the immortal sister as the lie is needed by truth for its greater glory.

Thus, la jeune Parque concludes that her power depends, not on a rejection of a part of herself, but on a relationship between her conscience and her body, on the harmonization between her two personalities: *harmonieuse moi*. Her rôle henceforth will be the renewal rather than the sublimation of enigma. (pp. 321-25)

Immediately after the middle section of the poem, the passage where la jeune Parque refuses the thought of maternity and resolves not to give life to the vague beings within her (lines 257-267), she recites a very explicit passage on the tear (lines 280-298), which this time she calls the imminent tear desirous of melting on her face. . . . It is a passage of extreme preciosity, comparable to Crashaw's poem on *Saint Mary Magdalene, or The Weeper.* In fact, the second stanza of Crashaw's poem, with the first lines:

> Heavens thy fair eyes be;
> Heavens of ever-falling stars . . .

recalls the very opening of **La Jeune Parque** where a hypothetical relationship is established between the girl's nascent tear and the action of the stars. Whereas Crashaw compares in a descriptive fashion the tears of Mary Magdalene and the stars in the heavens, Valéry hints at a cosmological explanation for his heroine's sorrow.

The tear comes from the soul itself, from the deepest thought or agitation of her conscience, and it has moved through the labyrinth of her being, along the multiple ways, each one of which ends in death. It bears the mysteries and shadows of her being to the light of her eyes. But what gave it its initial start? The same question is asked in line 292 (*D'où nais-tu?*), which was asked in the opening of the poem. But the answer is no clearer. Her only assurance during this night of the tear's course

is the hard earth underneath her. . . . The way of the tear she has followed by means of her senses, but its origin is in a darker night than her body. (pp. 325-26)

> Wallace Fowlie, "'La jeune parque's' Imminent Tear," in Quarterly Review of Literature, Vol. III, No. 3, Spring, 1947, pp. 318-26.

T. S. ELIOT (essay date 1948)

[*Perhaps the most influential poet and critic of the first half of the twentieth century, Eliot is closely identified with many of the qualities denoted by the term Modernism: experimentation, formal complexity, artistic and intellectual eclecticism, and a classicist view of the artist working at an emotional distance from his or her creation. He introduced a number of terms and concepts that strongly affected critical thought in his lifetime, among them the idea that poets must be conscious of the living tradition of literature in order for their work to have artistic and spiritual validity. In general, Eliot upheld values of traditionalism and discipline, and in 1928 he annexed Christian theology to his overall conservative world view. Of his criticism, he stated: "It is a by-product of my private poetry-workshop: or a prolongation of the thinking that went into the formation of my verse." Eliot deeply admired Valéry's poetry, and wrote several studies of the French poet's work. In the following excerpt from the most substantial of these, originally published in 1948, Eliot examines the influence of Edgar Allan Poe's literary theories upon Valéry's career. For further discussion of Poe's influence upon Valéry, see the excerpts by Allen Tate (1970) and Henri Peyre (1980).*]

[When] we come to Valéry, it is neither the man [Poe nor Poe's] poetry, but the *theory* of poetry, that engages his attention. In a very early letter to Mallarmé, written when he was a very young man, introducing himself to the elder poet, he says: "I prize the theories of Poe, so profound and so insidiously learned; I believe in the omnipotence of rhythm, and especially in the suggestive phrase." But I base my opinion, not primarily upon this credo of a very young man, but upon Valéry's subsequent theory and practice. In the same way that Valéry's poetry, and his essays on the art of poetry, are two aspects of the same interest of his mind and complement each other, so for Valéry the poetry of Poe is inseparable from Poe's poetic theories. (p. 37)

Valéry was a poet who wrote very consciously and deliberately indeed: perhaps, at his best, not wholly under the guidance of theory; but his theorizing certainly affected the kind of poetry that he wrote. He was the most self-conscious of all poets.

To the extreme self-consciousness of Valéry must be added another trait: his extreme scepticism. It might be thought that such a man, without belief in anything which could be the subject of poetry, would find refuge in a doctrine of "art for art's sake." But Valéry was much too sceptical to believe even in art. It is significant, the number of times that he describes something he has written as an *ébauche*—a rough draft. He had ceased to believe in *ends,* and was only interested in *processes.* It often seems as if he had continued to write poetry, simply because he was interested in the introspective observation of himself engaged in writing it: one has only to read the several essays—sometimes indeed more exciting than his verse, because one suspects that he was more excited in writing them—in which he records his observations. There is a revealing remark in **Variété V,** the last of his books of collected papers: "As for myself, who am, I confess, much more concerned with the formation or the fabrication of works [of art] than with the works themselves," and, a little later in the same volume: "In my opinion the most authentic philosophy is not in the objects of reflection, so much as in the very act of thought and its manipulation."

Here we have, brought to their culmination by Valéry, two notions which can be traced back to Poe. There is first the doctrine, elicited from Poe by Baudelaire . . . : 'A poem should have nothing in view but itself'; second the notion that the composition of a poem should be as conscious and deliberate as possible, that the poet should observe himself in the act of composition—and this, in a mind as sceptical as Valéry's, leads to the conclusion, so paradoxically inconsistent with the other, that the act of composition is more interesting than the poem which results from it. (pp. 39-40)

[With] Poe and Valéry, extremes meet, the immature mind playing with ideas because it had not developed to the point of convictions, and the very adult mind playing with ideas because it was too sceptical to hold convictions. It is by this contrast, I think, that we can account for Valéry's admiration for *Eureka*—that cosmological fantasy which makes no deep impression upon most of us, because we are aware of Poe's lack of qualification in philosophy, theology or natural science, but which Valéry, after Baudelaire, esteemed highly as a "prose poem." [Then] there is the astonishing result of Poe's analysis of the composition of *The Raven*. It does not matter whether *The Philosophy of Composition* is a hoax, or a piece of self-deception, or a more or less accurate record of Poe's calculations in writing the poem; what matters is that it suggested to Valéry a method and an occupation—that of observing himself write. Of course, a greater than Poe had already studied the poetic process. In the *Biographia Literaria* Coleridge is concerned primarily, of course, with the poetry of Wordsworth; and he did not pursue his philosophical enquiries concurrently with the writing of his poetry; but he does anticipate the question which fascinated Valéry: "What am I doing when I write a poem?" Yet Poe's *Philosophy of Composition* is a *mise au point* of the question which gives it capital importance in relation to this process which ends with Valéry. For the penetration of the poetic by the introspective critical activity is carried to the limit by Valéry, the limit at which the latter begins to destroy the former. (pp. 40-1)

[It] is a tenable hypothesis that this advance of self-consciousness, the extreme awareness of and concern for language which we find in Valéry, is something which must ultimately break down, owing to an increasing strain against which the human mind and nerves will rebel; just as, it may be maintained, the indefinite elaboration of scientific discovery and invention, and of political and social machinery, may reach a point at which there will be an irresistible revulsion of humanity and a readiness to accept the most primitive hardships rather than carry any longer the burden of modern civilization. Upon that I hold no fixed opinion: I leave it to your consideration. (p. 42)

> *T. S. Eliot, "From Poe to Valéry," in his* To Criticize the Critic and Other Writings, *Farrar, Straus & Giroux, 1965, pp. 27-42.*

FRANCIS SCARFE (essay date 1954)

[*In the following excerpt, Scarfe claims that the study of Valéry's poetry, rather than his prose, should be the basis for examining his evolution as an artist.*]

[It] is becoming increasingly clear that the only complete and self-contained work by Valéry was his poetry. All the rest was "literature", either drawn haphazardly from journals kept over a period of forty or fifty years, or written or spoken in answer to some request or commission; sometimes hastily prepared or ironically intended, often repetitive, discursive, or experimental in the sense that Valéry often used his prose in order to find out what he thought or what it was possible to think, rather than to express final judgments.

But where and what is Valéry's poetry? Once we seek to isolate it the poetry is seen to be closely attached to the rest of the work by hidden strands which tug in every direction. The only solution for the critic, then, is to use the "rest of the work" to throw light on the poetry, where it is needed. Then it also becomes obvious that Valéry's poetry overflows particularly into the dialogues, the libretti, and the play *Mon Faust*. These works are complete artistic wholes, but form together a poetic Opus in which Valéry's evolution as an artist may be observed. (p. x)

Looking back on the poetic career which began with *Narcisse Parle* and ended with *Le Solitaire* it is . . . possible to see that [Valéry's] whole dramatic development . . . depended on a need to dramatise the relationship of the human mind to the body, and the various potentialities of the Self in relation to the conflicting desires of the personality.

At no stage can it be said that, as a poet, Valéry eased his task by taking the line of least resistance, for to the very end he continued to present new aspects of the human problem and to seek new methods for its presentation. It was the very nature of the *human content* of his poetry, as it may be called, that enabled him to exploit and develop semi-dramatic forms, beginning with the dramatic lyric and passing through the monologue into works for the theatre; and in doing so to create a body of poetry which fulfils some of the greater aspirations of Symbolism, while giving new life to French poetry by returning to the springs of the sixteenth and seventeenth centuries. (p. 308)

M. Picon reproaches Valéry for bolstering up Man with Intelligence, that is to say with what distinguishes man from the beasts. But surely the whole point is that Valéry did not use Intelligence as a point of departure, but was striving always towards a valuation of it. At the same time, I think it is clear that Valéry's theme is consciousness rather than intelligence. . . . What has happened in the poems is that the spiritual and intellectual *inquiétude* which is always present and always dramatised is checked and balanced by a *certainty of form*.

This is to suggest that the only certainty achieved by Valéry seems to have been an aesthetic one. The paradox of Valéry is that he who in *Monsieur Teste* struck a blow as telling as Rimbaud's against art found himself in later life incapable of giving his thought any solid and enduring form outside art. I hesitate to say what estimate of Valéry could be made on the basis of his essays and aphoristic jottings alone. It is possible to rescue a critic and a critical system even from them. . . . But there are so many Valérys to be rescued, and when that is done a heap of unclassifiable Valérys still remain. Outside his poems, dialogues and libretti he left—as Leonardo left—nothing but a clutter of magnificent fragments. Only his poetry stands unchangeable and complete. *Any final judgment on Valéry must be a judgment of his art and via his art.* (p. 309)

It is fortunate for Valéry that his poetry represents so finely and completely the same struggle towards definition as that which forms the drama of his life and his prose. It is not a poetry of decisions but of decisions being sought, a poetry of strife, an adventure into the unknown. No contemporary poet has been less comfortably ensconced in a ''point of view'' than Valéry. His achievement was to create from his chaos and scepticism a poetry which proves that there was at least one positive element in his mind—that is to say a conception of poetry, a vision of it, that was worthy of the 'Honneur des hommes, Saint Langage''. Such a vision and its pursuit are all we have the right to expect of a great poet. Whatever the uncertain future of his ''thought'' may be, Valéry's poetic work is an island in the chaos of a dying art. (p. 310)

> Francis Scarfe, in his The Art of Paul Valéry: A Study in Dramatic Monologue, *William Heinemann Ltd., 1954, 338 p.*

JACKSON MATHEWS (essay date 1955)

[*Mathews is a noted translator and critic of Valéry's work. In the following excerpt he outlines Valéry's philosophy of aesthetics, including his theory of the creative process, the distinctions he made between the various modes of artistic expression, and the central role of language in all aesthetic forms.*]

Valéry lectured at the Collège de France for eight years, from 1937 straight through the war to 1945, within a few months of his death. Only one of these lectures was ever published, the first, the **Introduction to Poïetics.** During the first two years of this Course, Valéry's aim was to construct a theory of sensibility and a theory of the creative act which together would make a complete system of dynamics of the creative process. This system was to be founded on his immediate observation of everything that belonged to his own conscious life, the life of the mind, ''la vie élaborante'' as he called it. He thought it possible to formulate a table of relations comparable to the fundamental equations of mechanics, a table that would amount to a conception of the whole mechanism of the living man. Such a system would bring together, he said, all the essential conditions of our existence. Existence itself would there find its roots. (pp. 203-04)

Very few even of those who followed Valéry's course seem to have realized what he was about. To anyone, however, with the considerable advantage of reading the verbatim record of these lectures, there can be no doubt of what he was doing: he was systematizing the findings of a lifelong exploration of his own mind at work. The first twenty-nine lectures were devoted to elaborating the dynamics of sensibility and the relation of sensibility to the various arts and intellectual disciplines. It is from these lectures that I have drawn the scheme of his aesthetic theory. Of the ideas presented here, a good many will no doubt be familiar to readers of Valéry, for they are to be found scattered through his work. Valéry repeated his principal themes over and over. But nowhere in his published work, I believe, is the *system* of his ideas, their right relation to one another, to be as clearly seen as in the Course in Poïetics. Space allows me little more than an outline of his theory, but that, after all, is the present purpose. (p. 204)

The major terms in Valéry's theory of the creative process are *sensibility* and *act.*

Sensibility is the ground of individual being. It occupies the same place in his thought as the *Cogito* does in Descartes'; it is the most general possible notion of life itself. Sensibility is *what we are;* and it becomes, or produces, *what we know.* It is the source of ourselves. At bottom it is unknown and perhaps unknowable—like consciousness, that ''pure self'' that hovers over our being. Yet sensibility may be partly known. It is the

source and object of the only self-knowledge we have. Valéry's aesthetic theory is founded on the conviction that the whole life of the mind, all its modes of knowledge—the arts, philosophy, mathematics, the sciences—are traceable to their origins in sensibility.

The second major term, act, seems to be the secret motive of Valéry's thought. An act to his mind is perhaps the only thing in the world that is really mysterious. It is that which transforms possibility into actuality, the mode and moment of creation itself. It was Valéry's notion that life's deepest function is to make. To *know* is to *do,* to *perceive* is to *produce.* The primary fact about sensibility itself is that it is not merely passive and receptive, like a photographic plate, but is by nature active, productive; it is a constant spontaneous producer. What it normally produces is a regular flow of heterogeneous responses, or as Valéry prefers to say, ''exchanges with the external world.'' (p. 205)

This normal state of production Valéry called ''the natural course of things''—a curiously unsatisfactory term but he never found a better. The ''natural course of things'' is a state in which our organism is running silently like a good engine, a state of *non-attention* in which we are unaware of its functioning, a state likewise in which the external world is held in relative stability for us. This is important, for if our senses were a thousand times keener, if they were aware (let us say) of molecular movement, we should be forced to perceive the world as being constantly destroyed and reconstructed, and this would, to say the least, complicate our physical and psychic stability.

From the mind's point of view, the ''natural course'' of sensibility is the very image of disorder, the sensibility being constantly besieged by quite heterogeneous impressions from the world of things. This gives rise to a perpetual excitation, a constant diversity of meaningless and nameless productions, by nature incoherent, instantaneous, and unstable. This disorder is basic to the mind; it furnishes at once the matter and the motive for the construction of order, which is the mind's work.

The first step towards order is sensation as it becomes distinct from general sensibility. A sensation is an *event* occurring within the ambient disorder of the natural course of things; it is an interruption of the natural course, a sudden accentuation of some element in it, an increase in normal activity, a deviation from the normal state of non-attention. Sensation is sensibility of the second degree. It plays a great rôle in the mind; sensations are ''original facts'' or ''points of origin'' for very complex developments. (pp. 205-06)

These are the basic terms of Valéry's psychology: the *natural course of sensibility* on the one hand, and on the other, *sensations.* The life of sensibility is a capricious fluctuation between these two poles. The sensibility always seems to be trying either to absorb and annul events of sensation and return to its own natural course of exchanges with the world, or on the other hand, to interrupt this equilibrium once it is established. Variability is its most important trait.

Valéry found the beginnings of the aesthetic activity in the sensibility's *peculiar economy.* It is a strange fact, he said, that we produce more sensations than we need and have more perceptions than we need simply to satisfy our organic requirements. Most of the impressions we receive through our senses play no rôle whatever in the functioning of the vital organs that keep us living. Only an extremely small portion of the vast number of sensory impulses that besiege us momently is necessary or can be utilized in our biological functions. The greater part of our sensations are actually *useless*. . . .

Out of these *useless* sensations and *arbitrary* acts man has created a special domain of activity, the arts. Creative activity consists in conferring *utility* upon useless sensations and *necessity* upon arbitrary acts. (p. 206)

A man who is an artist may feel a kind of necessity in a particular order of sensations coming to him from nature or from some art object, where another man feels nothing whatever. (p. 207)

Art organizes a system of sensible things in such a way that they have the power to arouse desire for themselves, but cannot annul the desire they arouse. A work of art always sustains the sensibility that produced it. This circular effect Valéry called "the aesthetic infinite." He did not mean the word "infinite" here to be taken literally, but rather as an indication of a continuous reciprocal action within the sensibility.

Another feature of sensibility fundamental to art is its tendency to form within itself what Valéry called "universes." This rather imposing term has no connection with what is ordinarily called the "Universe." Unlike Margaret Fuller, Valéry did not at all accept the universe; it was the constant butt of his wit and destructive analysis. The term "universe of sensibility" is a figure probably adopted from group theory in mathematics. A universe of sensibility is simply "a closed system of internal relations among sensations of the same order." The sensibility, though at bottom disorderly, has a working tendency towards order. It tends to oppose its own disorder with an order at one remove. Valéry's *Poïetics* is based on the conviction that all the functions of sensibility may be formulated, their order found. (pp. 207-08)

Valéry was almost, but not quite, willing to speak of "laws" of sensibility; for he found in the sensibility certain fundamental tendencies or modes of reaction: symmetry, contrast, periodicity, and complementarity. These features of regularity constitute intrinsic relations among sensations of the same order, thus forming closed groups or "universes." The sensibility tends quite spontaneously to create these universes within itself. The ear, for example, spontaneously separates sound from noise. Sound may be defined as those noises which the sensibility chooses to reproduce. It is this same grouping activity in the sense of hearing, carried to a further point of refinement, that has produced the scales which are the "universe" of music. The same tendency in another organ of sense, the eye, has given us the chromatic universe of the color chart, which underlies painting. These "universes" form the substance of the several arts. The arts are possible because man can master the spontaneous "universes" of his sensibility and play upon them by means of symmetries, similitudes, and contrasts, which are the essential properties of all, at least of the non-representational arts.

Valéry differed sharply from his Symbolist forebears on the question of correspondence between the senses. The various senses are not to be compared; they are really incommensurable and without communication between themselves. We cannot express color by sound. The universes of sense exist, each to itself, and yet taken together they are ourselves. (p. 208)

Among the various senses, Valéry had great partiality for the eye. This was the sense closest to the mind, the most intelligent of the senses, most like consciousness itself. In his poems and

drawings the eye *is* consciousness. . . . The eye in its ability to produce complementary colors furnishes the plainest and most convincing evidence of the sensibility's productivity. When exposed to a strong red light, the eye responds by producing green. This complementarity takes place as a gradually dying oscilliation between two colors, or between light and dark, demonstrating periodic variation in the eye's productive process. Valéry took this as an indication of the periodicity of all sensibility, which is one of the "laws" of his sensory dynamics. But complementarity is not the only internal relation among chromatic sensations. There is also the phenomenon of sensory continuity, the progression from one color to another by imperceptible gradations. These two phenomena, continuity and complementarity, together form the basis of a complex system of relations within the group of colors, which is to say they form a "chromatic universe." (pp. 208-09)

[After] the eye, the next most important order of sensation to Valéry's mind was neuro-muscular or motor sensation. For example, it is by means of our "inner muscular adaptation" that sound is translated into degrees that are measurable. When we hear a sound, our two ears necessarily receive each a slightly different impression, but by a kind of "neuro-muscular triangulation" they *produce* a single sensation corresponding to the original sound. Muscular sensation, for Valéry, was the great intermediary between the various immediate kinds of sensation on the one hand and our various psychic organizations (ideas and so forth) on the other. He believed that functions of the motor system give rise to our intellectual abstractions. (p. 209)

All the arts are special adaptations of the various universes of sensibility. In so far as the arts have recourse to sensation, they are obliged to build on the features of regularity, periodicity, and reciprocal excitation which form groups of sensations within the sensibility. The several arts are founded on the properties of these sensory groups.

The sensibility alone, however, is helpless to produce a work of art. There is a capital difference between the spontaneous products of the sensibility just described and those productions of the whole man which are works of art. In art there must be an intervention of the conscious processes of the mind, of which *attention* is the general type. The total creative act is a combination of conscious and unconscious processes terminated in motivity by an externalizing act that produces the work, after which the mental structure responsible for producing it is dissolved back into the heterogeneous activity of the natural course of sensibility: this notion of the creative process as the most complete, the most fully human act of which man is capable, Valéry calls *the cycle of the complete act*.

Works of art, or as Valéry preferred to say, "works of the mind," are those works which the mind chooses to make for itself, for its own use and benefit, works that aim to act upon the sensibility and intellect, with no practical or utilitarian purpose. A work is something undertaken by the mind *against its own nature*, and something which tends to affect the mind of another, to cause in another the creation of value. (p. 210)

Valéry thinks of the arts as in two kinds: the arts of pure sensibility and the arts of language. Among the former are music, architecture, the dance, sculpture, and painting: the arts of language are primarily poetry and philosophy, though Valéry somewhat reluctantly admits the novel, the drama, and history. (p. 211)

Valéry was responsible in the late twenties for a highly advertised debate on the notion of "pure poetry." The term has continued to be associated with his name, and somewhat mistakenly used to describe his poems. Looking back on the whole question in 1938, Valéry said: "I have never used the term 'pure' applied to poetry except in the sense given to the term in physics and chemistry—i.e., meaning a quality got by a process of separation. I merely wondered whether one could take certain poems and separate out the poetic element and then make other poems entirely out of this element. The Abbé Bremond saw something mystical in that, which was not part of my intention. From the first I have said that 'pure poetry' is *not* possible. Language is not made for that. Language is practical. I merely say that when you take as much interest in the *form* of language as in its meaning . . . , you are interested in poetry.''

For Valéry, music was theoretically the greatest of the arts. I say theoretically because he was in fact not a great music-lover; he was rather impatient with most music. His life-long devotion to Wagner was surely not unrelated to the composer's interest in theory. (p. 213)

Naturally, the arts excite other responses too, besides the perception of a total order beyond them. They stir memories, impulses of love, and so forth. Music, though non-representational, can move nearly the whole of pure sensibility. The musician works directly on the quick, the living nerve.

Another of the great pure arts for Valéry was architecture. For him a work of architecture was not immobile, since in order to be seen it requires an observer who moves around and through it, creating its forms, combinations, and perspectives as he goes. This is the movement of architecture. All its forms must be deducible one from another by a kind of modulation. (p. 214)

The most surprising and, to some including myself, a rather annoying aspect of Valéry's aesthetic is his treatment of philosophy. Here he was undoubtedly indulging in shock tactics. Valéry distinguishes between *constructive* (or creative) philosophy, by which he generally means metaphysics, and *critical* philosophy. He defines constructive philosophy as establishing a series of notions, and relations between notions, with the intention of describing the world. Critical philosophy is parasitic in the biological sense; it lives on other philosophy or on science, by analyzing them. It has become the handmaiden of science as it was the handmaiden of theology in the Middle Ages. (pp. 214-15)

Valéry compares philosophers to poets and painters, in this way: "If you look at an object too long," he says, "it loses its power of signifying, and becomes merely a spot of color—you are about to become a painter. If you say a word over and over, it loses its power of signifying, and becomes a sound—you are about to become a poet. If you ask a question over and over, turning over its terms in your mind, it loses its ordinary meaning and—you are about to become a philosopher.''

The philosopher abuses questions and answers as the poet abuses language itself. There is no limit to the question method. In mathematics, definitions are acts, or lead to acts; but in philosophy there is no act or object to limit the abuse of terms. If there were, philosophy would be stricken with sterility. A question in sensibility becomes a question in philosophy simply by the intervention of language. By translating the questioning attitude into words instead of acts, we get this curious result: we detach or mobilize the questioning attitude, set it going in the self-developing cycle of the "aesthetic infinite." This means that we have converted the questioning attitude into free play,

like practising scales on a piano; it is on the way to becoming an art. All you have to do, said Valéry, to discover for yourself the great traditional philosophic questions is to apply the five interrogative adverbs to any subject whatever. When you come to apply them to a subject not capable of precise definition, because not subject to demonstration in act, you are already in the field of philosophy.

The question reaches its final stage of development as art in its use as an element in philosophic discourse. The work of Thomas Aquinas is the classical case. Here the question has come to its perfection as form. The basic "article" of the *Summa* resembles a poem in fixed form, like a sonnet. Compared to the work of Albertus Magnus, said Valéry, the work of Aquinas shows a development that must be described as essentially aesthetic.

Valéry thus set up an "aesthetic program for philosophy." A work of philosophy can only be properly understood and praised as an aesthetic construction. Philosophy has no power of action; it can only present us "a world" as a work of art, like a poem, a symphony, a painting—a world that is not the world in the general sense of that term, but rather the world of a particular philosopher who is its creator or builder. (pp. 215-16)

In 1937, at the moment when he was formulating the general plan of his Course in Poïetics, Valéry was invited to address the Second International Congress of Aesthetics and the Science of Art, meeting in Paris. What he said on that occasion was not calculated to comfort the assembled aestheticians. Traditional philosophical aesthetics, he said, has been a failure in its own terms, in so far as it has thought it could define, measure, and formulate the principles of art. Loyalty to its own mode of discourse, to the point of making discourse an end in itself, has disqualified philosophical aesthetics from describing the creative process. What the artist makes cannot be logically deduced from what he started with; it is this fact more than anything else which assures him that he has created something.

The failure of aesthetics in its own terms, however, has been curiously fruitful for art itself. Its formulations, its reasoned conventions and rules have played an active rôle in the making of art. They help the mind to constrain the sensibility, which is the essence of the creative act. Aesthetics, said Valéry, should give up the ambition to formulate ultimate definitions and principles. Its more modest business is to describe what can actually be observed of the artistic process. To this form of aesthetics Valéry devoted the best thought of his mature years. (pp. 216-17)

*Jackson Mathews, "The Poïetics of Paul Valéry,"
in* The Romanic Review, *Vol. XLVI, No. 3 (October, 1955), pp. 203-17.*

NORTHROP FRYE   (essay date 1959)

[*Frye has exerted a tremendous influence in the field of twentieth-century literary scholarship, mainly through his study* Anatomy of Criticism *(1957). In this seminal work, Frye makes controversial claims for literature and literary critics, arguing that judgments are not inherent in the critical process and asserting that literary criticism can be "scientific" in its methods and its results without borrowing concepts from other fields of study. Literary criticism, in Frye's view, should be autonomous in the manner that physics, biology, and chemistry are autonomous disciplines. For Frye, literature is schematic because it is wholly structured by myth and symbol. The critic becomes a near-scientist, deter-*

mining how symbols and myth are ordered and function in a given work. The critic need not, in Frye's view, make judgments of value about the work; a critical study is structured by the fact that the components of literature, like those of nature, are un-changing and predictable. Frye believes that literature occupies a position of extreme importance within any culture. Literature, as he sees it, is "the place where our imaginations find the ideal that they try to pass on to belief and action, where they find the vision which is the source of both the dignity and the joy of life." The literary critic serves society by studying and "translating" the structures in which that vision is encoded. In the following excerpt, originally published in 1959, Frye discusses Valéry's interest in the poetic process and his distinctions between literary and nonliterary verbal structures. Frye largely dismisses Valéry's poetic theories by stating that his sense of tradition was limited, and that Valéry was a poet who tended to define poetry in terms of his own ever-shifting Symbolist predilections.]

There are traditionally two main centers of interest in the theory of criticism, sometimes described by the words *poesis* and *poema*. The former, or Longinian, center is primarily an interest in the psychological process of poetry and in the rhetorical relation (often arrived at by indirection) set up between poet and reader. The latter, or Aristotelian, center is primarily an interest in the aesthetic product and is based on a specific aesthetic judgment, detached by catharsis from moral anxieties and emotional perturbations. Any complete theory of criticism needs both, but in a complete theory the aesthetic judgment must take precedence, for the Longinian interest is in enthusiasm, or what "carries us away," in other words, in what uncritical feelings we may trust to afterward. (pp. 188-89)

Valéry is a Longinian critic, concerned with the poetic process. As T. S. Eliot points out [see *TCLC*, Vol. 4] . . . he has no sustained theoretical interest in any poetry except his own, not because he is egocentric, but because he is the only poet whose processes he can watch. And as he is a very good poet, the prior aesthetic judgment is taken care of. [*The Art of Poetry*] has a typically Longinian opening. Valéry begins, not like Aristotle, with what poetry is and what species it has, but with the reader in a receptive mood. There are two contexts, he tells us, to which the term *poetry* belongs. One is the context of the "poetic," a vague sense, in the mind of the reader, of the enormous significance that could be given to words and of their power, when properly handled, of expressing the reader's feelings. The other is poetry in the technical sense, as the specific supply of this general demand. The better the poem, the more precisely and inevitably it expresses the inarticulate need for articulation.

Longinian, too, is Valéry's conception of inspiration as meaning, not a state of mind that the poet is in, but a state of mind that he induces in his reader. The reader feels permeated with a sense of significance not coming from himself, so he projects this on the poet and assumes that the poet is a kind of medium for some hypothetical creative spirit. But while it is true that "poetry and the arts have sensibility as beginning and end," the process of creating it may involve any amount of purely conscious and voluntary effort, as in revision or the following out of a complex metrical form. (p. 189)

While Valéry is primarily concerned with the theoretical element in poetry, he is not, like Longinus, concerned with direct rhetoric or oratory, but with its opposite, the indirect, disinterested rhetoric of verbal elaboration. Whenever we read anything, we find our attention moving in two directions at once. One direction is outward, from the words themselves to their remembered conventional meanings. The other is inward, and

is directed toward building up a unified apprehension of the structure of words itself. (p. 190)

The distinction between inward and outward meaning, and its corollary, that verbal structures can be divided into those made for their own sake and those made to serve other purposes, is, almost certainly, the basis of all practical criticism. It is, however, a distinction between the literary and the nonliterary verbal structure. Having made the distinction, Valéry muddles it again by calling the literary structure "poetry" and the non-literary one "prose," thus confusing it with the technical distinction in rhythm between prose and verse. But while it is true that prose is, unlike verse, used for nonliterary purposes, the enormous bulk of literary prose makes nonsense of any attempt to equate prose with the extraliterary. . . . Valéry is often forced by his own confusion of terms to treat literary prose as something to be explained away. True, he does not particularly like prose, and his references even to Flaubert and Proust are somewhat disparaging. In the most systematic statement of his theory, the essay called **"Remarks on Poetry,"** he draws a distinction between the pure poetic universe and the mimesis of actual life in prose fiction that illustrates the essential affinity of prose with signal language. But his statements would apply equally well to many other genres.

The basis of Valéry's theory is in Poe: it would be difficult to get closer to Poe than Valéry does when he says: "What we call a *poem* is in practice composed of fragments of pure poetry embedded in the substance of a discourse." This means, among other things, that the difficult part of writing a poem of any length is the problem of poetic continuity. Poetic necessity, he says, can reside only in form, and "form demands a continuity of felicitous expression." But, like Poe, Valéry regards the standard narrative and didactic conventions of continuilty as nonpoetic. (p. 192)

We soon realize that by "poetry" Valéry means his own kind of poetry, that is, *symbolisme*, and what *symbolisme* is able to absorb from the poetic tradition in general. The germ of truth in this identification is the fact that the different genres of literature may (up to a point) be arranged in the order of their distance from signal meaning. Literary prose is relatively close to it; narrative and didactic verse within sight of it; but *symbolisme* stands at the greatest possible distance from it and does its best to turn its back on it. But, as with all selective traditions, even *symbolisme* breaks down, or up, into a group of conflicting heresies. The tradition of Laforge and Corbière, from which Eliot derives, is, as Eliot points out, quite different; so is the disintegrative tradition that derives from Rimbaud and Jarry. Valéry as critic is simply the disciple of Mallarmé (his relation to Poe is through Mallarmé), and it is Mallarmé's great idea of the poetic universe *(le Verbe)* that informs all his criticism. (pp. 193-94)

Poetry as close to verbal organization and as far from signal meaning as possible is what Valéry means by "pure poetry." As long as words are employed in poetry at all, of course, pure poetry cannot exist except as an ideal. But its ideal existence is very important, for it means that the creative activity of the poet is not hitched to his ego. The poet uses all the resources of skill and intelligence in the interests of an impossible demand for integrity, not in the interests of self-expression. The pure poem is really the perfect poem, and "perfection eliminates the person of the author." The minor artist impresses us as a sensitive and cultivated person; the májor artist is simply speaking with the voice of his art. (p. 194)

The sense that the background of every poem is the whole order of poetic experience is constantly present in Valéry, but is nowhere developed, partly because Valéry's sense of tradition is so limited. Consequently, the question of poetic meaning, of the poem's significance, not in terms of ordinary meaning, but as a phase of poetic experience, is left in the air.

The relation of a poem to poetry as a whole raises the question of the structural principles of poetry, and in particular the problems of convention and genre. Valéry largely ignores the problem of genre and is curiously selective in his approach to convention. Conventions of external form and of meter he accepts; conventions of narrative and of poetic concepts *(topoi)* he rejects out of hand; conventions of theme and imagery leave him with nothing to say, although he observes them in practice. He speaks of the content of the poem as its myth; *Le Cimetière Marin* and *La Jeune Parque* as clearly mythopoeic poems, and conventionally mythopoeic at that. Yet he seems to have no interest in discussing their myths or images—in short, he is not concerned to give any suggestion of what these very difficult poems are about. His attitude toward a critical explication of *Le Cimetière Marin* by someone else is one of delighted surprise that a poem of his should really have meant all that.

We naturally feel that it is not a poet's business to explain what his poems mean, even granting that "meaning" here is poetic meaning, or structural analysis. But the fact that we feel this way is significant in determining the role of the poet as critic. Valéry takes a rather sardonic view of the academic study of literature and writes with much pungency about its unreality, the pointlessness of all the "interpretations" of poets that cancel each other out. (pp. 195-96)

Yet if [*The Art of Poetry*] proves anything, it proves that all a poet can do as critic is tell us those things of which he has special knowledge, and which belong to autobiography rather than criticism. Meaning in poetry, like inspiration, is a conception that relates primarily to the reader, not the writer. In the kind of poetry that Valéry writes this means a highly trained or critical reader. For Valéry's is a post-Kantian type of poetry in which the theme or organizing form of the poem remains invisible to the poet himself, and everything in the poem is an

Valéry speaking during a debate between himself, André Chamson, and Jean Prévost. From Paul Valéry, by Agathe Rouart Valéry. Gallimard, 1966. © Editions Gallimard.

epiphany or manifestation of some aspect of it. The poet himself knows that everything he has written belongs in his poem; he does not necessarily know why. If we are to take Valéry seriously as a poet, we cannot afford to take him too seriously as a critic. (p. 196)

Northrop Frye, "Interior Monologue of M. Teste," in his Northrop Frye on Culture and Literature: A Collection of Review Essays, *edited by Robert D. Denham, The University of Chicago Press, 1968, pp. 188-96.*

SALVADOR DE MADARIAGA   (essay date 1962)

[*Madariaga is widely considered Spain's outstanding intellectual figure of the twentieth century and was a prominent diplomat in pre-Revolutionary Spain, holding several government posts, including ambassador to the United States. Trilingual, he wrote criticism, political treatises, as well as novels, poetry, and plays in Spanish, French, and English, all of which have been praised for their clarity and elegance of style. Because of their liberal and humanistic stance, Madariaga's writings have consistently aroused discussion and controversy, particularly in his native Spain. One of his most well-known works, Englishmen, Frenchmen, Spaniards (1928), is a study of the obstacles national psychologies present to international relations. A fierce opponent of the Franco regime, Madariaga entered self-imposed exile in 1936 and lived primarily in England until his death in 1978. He was the Spanish representative to the League of Nations during the 1930s, and met Valéry while serving on the Committee on Arts and Letters. In the following excerpt, Madariaga expresses admiration for Valéry's elitist intellect and aestheticism, but also states that it is responsible for the weakness in his political writings, which show a lack of understanding and tolerance for common humanity.*]

Valéry is one of the most deliberate, conscious, and conscientious artists that France has ever produced—which in this particular context means Europe as well. He will have nothing but pure gold as raw material; and he will keep it until every inch and carat of it has been wrought into a thing of beauty. That is why he seems in a way to be so present in everything he does, though his aim is to detach the work from the author and to make it free from time and space—what he calls by a word often to be found in his essays: *incorruptible*. His presence itself, however, being purely intellectual, is in a way dehumanized, and though his style is there, he personally vanishes because in fact, though the artificer has worked hard, man the has not entered into the game.

How far I feel from my Spaniards! Often, while reading him it has occurred to me that in Spain Valéry might have found a far better anti-Valéry than Pascal. Unamuno, for instance, who is everything Valéry is not. For Unamuno, the *Critique of Pure Reason* meant nothing unless it were directly referred to the man Kant. Here is Paul Valéry on the subject: "A man's true life, which is always ill-defined even for his neighbors, even for himself, cannot be utilized in an explanation of his works, except indirectly and by means of a very careful elaboration. Therefore no mistresses, no debtors, no anecdotes, no adventures! One is led to adopt a more honest method, that of disregarding such external details and of imagining a theoretical being, a psychological *model* more or less approximate, but representing in some sort one's capacity for reconstructing the work that has to be explained." This passage would have maddened Unamuno and made him overflow with contempt. As for being interested in everything from the point of view of the intellect: "The intellect? what is that?" he would have asked. And he would have answered himself: "Another mask for your passions." The parallel contrast between Unamuno and Valéry is fascinating because both could be defined as chemically pure specimens of their respective countries—I had almost said, paraphrasing a famous utterance of Unamuno himself, *alkaloids*, respectively, of France and of Spain. . . . But though in many ways so distant, Unamuno and Valéry have one feature in common: pride.

I am not sure, though, that the word fits. These words for describing tendencies of the spirit of man have a way of eluding translation. They seem to be rooted each in the soil of its own language by long, live roots so that they refuse to be transplanted. *Orgueil* comes often under the pen of Paul Valéry. For him it is the capital virtue of the writer, the force that makes him keep working hard, relentlessly, and regardless of any reward or hope of it, for the sheer sake of the dignity of his own work. And yet at times he seems to consider *orgueil* as a power that drives man away from his art, that stiffens him against any submission to the rules even of his art. (pp. xxvi-xxviii)

Anyone familiar with [Valéry's] fastidious mind could hardly be surprised if the views he expressed on political affairs did not conform to the egalitarian trends of our days. Platitudinous, multitudinous—such were bound to be the main impressions the world of our day would cast on his selective and exclusive mind. But when a closer study is attempted of the essays he devoted to these subjects, one is surprised to find another feature altogether unexpected: it would appear that political subjects did succeed at times in clouding his ruthless clarity, in "corrupting" his "incorruptible" concepts, in letting his ultrapure pen write words by no means crystal-clear as to their content.

His Preface to the *Persian Letters* is a case in point. It is as delightful a piece of creative literature as any he wrote, a building as neatly conceived and built, as glittering in its lights, as any from that wonderful intellectual architect. But the foundations? What are they but the arbitrary design of a fanciful inventor? "A society rises from brutality to order." We begin to wonder. Is this a genuine contrast? Is all brutality lacking in order, all order free from brutality? Is it a fact that societies are born in disorderly brutality? We pass on. "As barbarism is the era of *fact*, so the era of order must necessarily be the reign of *fiction*—for there is no power capable of founding order on the mere coercion of bodies by bodies. For that, fictional powers are needed."

It would be difficult to find a page richer in unwarranted assumptions and ill-defined conceptions. "Fact," "fiction," "order," "coercion of bodies by bodies," seem to me wholly unacceptable terms in this context. *Fact* is tacitly identified with *physical force; fiction* will presently reveal itself to be what is often nowadays described as "values" (the *sacred*, the *just*, the *legal*, the *decent*, the *praiseworthy*—which Valéry, with a tacit but evident pleasure, betrayed by the intellectual twist which he requires in order to achieve his performances, successively symbolizes in five institutions, beginning all with a capital T: the Temple, the Throne, the Tribunal, the Tribune, the Theater); barbarism is equated with the rule of physical force. Not one of these assumptions or implied definitions can survive a perfunctory analysis. Yet on this flimsy foundation, Valéry builds up an enchanting edifice, within which many, most, possibly all of the intellectual relationships are rigorous and correct.

This curious experience may be a pointer to the chief weakness in his political writing: his substratum of faith is not strong enough for political thinking. He is too skeptical, too contemptuous of man in general, too penetrating perhaps, too hard an observer of the weak side of man; but also too indifferent to his yearnings and longings to be able to write with any conviction on political matters, closely allied as they are to the ethical requirements of man as a social being. For some reason or other, ever since Machiavelli was praised by Bacon for showing what human relations are instead of pointing at what they should be, a certain type of scientific or positivist student of man has endeavored to eliminate ethics from the world of men in society—as if the need most human beings feel for decency in behavior were not a part of the picture in its own right as much as the rest. There is no denying the fact that Valéry is prone to take that point of view in his political writings. It leads him to strange utterances; nearly always coined with that clarity in design which is characteristic of his mint; nearly always also true and yet unsatisfactory, as either incomplete or too sweeping.

In his **"Fluctuations on Freedom,"** for instance, written in 1938, Valéry does not trouble to discriminate between majority rule and liberty; and yet he had by then recently seen the majority of the German people destroy their own liberty and that of the minority. (pp. xxxii-xxxiv)

In his essays on dictatorship one misses the compensating pages which would have completed the picture with an analysis of liberty as an essential requirement of the human spirit. This failure of so noble a mind seems to me to be due to his exclusively intellectual outlook. At no time does he seem to realize that ideas have roots in the soil of human nature, below the intellect; or if he does realize it, he will not rest until he has cut off these roots as impurities unworthy of "incorruptible" thought. This perhaps explains that when dealing with political affairs he is the more satisfactory the wider the scope and the more general the issue he is dealing with.

Yet his essays on Europe are excellent. Valéry should be considered as one of the founding fathers of a United Europe. It is a curious confirmation of what I have just said on ideas and their roots that he came to think in European terms when he felt his emotions as a European aroused under the shock of two world events which seemed to him full of European resonance: the Japanese attack on China in 1895 and the attack of the United States on Spain in 1898. These two events, as he himself relates, "shocked" him into realizing the existence of Europe. None of your "exclusively from the point of view of the intellect" here. Valéry became a European at other and deeper levels than the merely intellectual (just as if he had been a mere Pascal or Unamuno), and the result was a study of Europe which, written as it was shortly after the first World War, reveals a vigorous European spirit, rich in an awareness of the common life of our continent which, had it been more widespread then, might have spared us the second World War and our present miseries. (pp. xxxiv-xxxv)

Salvador de Madariaga, in an introduction to The Collected Works in English of Paul Valéry: History and Politics, Vol. 10 *by Paul Valéry, translated by Denise Folliot and Jackson Mathews, Bollingen Series XLV, Pantheon Books, 1962, pp. xxi-xxxvi.*

ALLEN TATE (essay date 1970)

[*Tate's criticism is closely associated with two critical movements, the Agrarians and the New Critics. The Agrarians were concerned* with political and social issues as well as literature, and were dedicated to preserving the Southern way of life and traditional Southern values. In particular, they attacked Northern industrialism as they sought to preserve the Southern farming economy. The New Critics, a group which included Cleanth Brooks and Robert Penn Warren, among others, comprised one of the most influential critical movements of the mid-twentieth century. Although the various New Critics did not subscribe to a single set of principles, all believed that a work of literature had to be examined as an object in itself through a process of close analysis of symbol, image, and metaphor. For the New Critics, a literary work was not a manifestation of ethics, sociology, or psychology, and could not be evaluated in the general terms of any nonliterary discipline. However, Tate adhered to a different vision of literature's purpose than did many of the other New Critics. A conservative thinker and convert to Catholicism, Tate attacked the tradition of Western philosophy, which he felt has alienated persons from themselves, from one another, and from nature by divorcing intellectual from natural functions in human life. For Tate, literature is the principal form of knowledge and revelation which restores human beings to a proper relationship with nature and the spiritual realm. Although this vision informs much of his work, Tate is like T. S. Eliot in that an appreciation of his criticism is not wholly dependent upon an acceptance of his spiritual convictions. His most important critical essays are on modern poetry, and on Southern traditions and the legacy of the Civil War. In the following excerpt, Tate analyzes Valéry's Symbolist apprenticeship and the influence of Edgar Allan Poe's critical thought on his poetic theories. For further discussion of Poe's influence on Valéry, see the excerpts by T. S. Eliot (1948) and Henri Peyre (1980).]

The scope of this discussion will not allow me to notice, with anything like justice to their merit, the vast number of prose works dealing with the rôle of the intellect (or of *method,* as Valéry was trying all his life to understand it) in the creative process. The typical Valerian irony of the claim to ignorance in the numerous little essays on painters—Degas, Morisot, Manet—might trap us into thinking that he was better qualified to understand the philosophical or scientific mind, since most of his prose is concerned with *ideas.* But we must not be misled; the irony I have noted is perhaps a little disingenuous intellectually; for there is no reason to believe that Valéry knew more about mathematics than about painting. It was simply that what little he knew he could *use* with greater precision than he could bring to bear upon the problem of form in painting. This is true of the twelve-year-old boy, who to the extent that he knows algebra at all, knows what he knows precisely; but the seasoned art-critic can never have knowledge more precise than the nature of the subject will allow; and this knowledge can never be as precise as one's knowledge of quadratic equations. It was not different when Valéry became interested in architecture, as he inevitably would; for here was engineering—method—an art with a specific mathematical aspect that could be abstracted from the esthetic. But his investigation of this subject is cast into a Platonic dialogue, where dialectic permits him to evade direct formulations of the relation of concrete architectural forms to their engineering, or their rationale of method conceived Platonically. Here, even with an art the most mathematical of all after music, he was not able to show that the form was "born" before the "work."

Valéry all his life, as poet, wrote like an Aristotelian; that is, he came to know the "form" (the meaning) in the completed work; but he *talked* like a Platonist whose *ideas* must always precede the *intuition.* I am inclined to believe that he might not have written the prose works (or as many as he did) had his philosophical interests developed after he had written his great poems. The early poems of **"Album des Vers Anciens"**

are the work of a minor symbolist poet who had gone to school to Hérèdia and Mallarmé (with Baudelaire and Poe in the background); these poems could not have revealed to him the deeper movements of his creative powers. Had he not got fixed in the convention of a kind of Platonic Pyrrhonism, the "play" of ideas, which began as youthful intellectual inquiry and continued into old age the vain mask of the sage, he would have learned from the great poems that the inquiry, *as he conceived it,* into form and intuition was irrelevant to his actual purpose as a poet. I take it that anybody who has any familiarity at all with **"Ébauche d'Un Serpent"** or **"Le Cimetière Marin"** would reject the idea that there is form apart from the clusters of symbol which constitute the "intuition"—this, in spite of the somewhat elaborate hocus-pocus which Valéry offers us in his long meditation on the writing of **"Le Cimetière Marin."** I call it a meditation, though **"Fragments de Mémoires d'Un Poème,"** published eighteen years after **"Le Cimetière,"** purports to be an analytical inquiry into the *method* that he had presumably adopted before he began to write the poem. Immensely more resourceful and sophisticated than Poe's "The Philosophy of Composition," "Fragments" is the direct descendant of Poe's essay and perhaps the most distinguished of its hundreds of descendants in what has become a new critical *genre.* This *genre* may be described as the rationalization of the imaginative act, in the attempt to reduce the poem to a pseudo-Cartesian criterion of "clarity" and "distinctness." The word *method* appears almost obsessively in Valéry's prose: he said many times that after poems were written he felt no interest in *what* he had said in them, but only in *how* he had been able to say it. This quasi-Platonic theory of antecedent form dominates all his writings on poetry, and form he equates with method. In this tradition of critical thought—a tradition which T. S. Eliot has described in his valuable essay, "From Poe to Valéry" [see excerpt above, 1948]—there is the progressive mechanization of the poem and the supremacy of method, until the poem itself becomes an esthetic machine. The machine produces a calculated effect upon the reader. If this is what Poe and Valéry thought they were doing, they were actually doing something smaller philosophically, and at the same time something poetically greater, than their calculations would have allowed them to do; with Valéry, at any rate, the great poems remain, and his idolatry of method cannot divert our attention from their full and mysterious wholeness. Valéry was a greater poet than his "intellect" wanted him to be; Poe's intellect, narrower than Valéry's, allowed him to see his poems, particularly "The Raven," as a greater than he could make them; there is a similar appeal in both from the poetry to omnipotent rationality.

Shortly after Valéry's death T. S. Eliot wrote a short mémoir, "Lecon de Valéry" [see Additional Bibliography], for a volume of *hommages* entitled "Valéry Vivant" (1946); Eliot said:

> He could play different rôles, but never lost himself in any. Of some great men, one's prevailing impression may be of goodness, or of inspiration, or of wisdom; I think the prevailing impression one received of Valéry was of intelligence.

Eliot's remarks would justify, I think, the addition of an adjective—an impression of *uncommitted* intelligence. (pp. 461-64)

Some ten years after [Valéry] had been acclaimed in France as the greatest living poet, he published a small book entitled **"Littérature,"** which I suppose contains more wisdom about the possibilities and limits of poetry than any other work of this century. Between the extremes of the classical and the romantic sensibility the poet of our time, cast up on Crusoe's island, and living by chance, may arrive by a sufficient cunning at an art which occupies the entire stretch between the extremes. I shall quote a long passage from "**Littérature**" because it seems to me that Valéry is talking about himself, defining what he thought he had done as poet (and perhaps in the greater poems, did):

> Since the advent of romanticism *singularity* has been imitated instead of, as in the past, *mastery*.
>
> The instinct of imitation has been the same. But to it the modern has added a contradiction.
>
> Mastery, as the word indicates, is to appear to have command over the technical resources of an art—instead of being visibly commanded by them.
>
> The acquisition of mastery then presupposes the acquired habit of always thinking, or combining, with the technical means as *point of departure*, and of never thinking of a work except in terms of its means.

The contradiction of modernism lies in the end in the impossibility of relating the singular to anything else, of combining it with another singular, since each intuition of the singular, being unique, defies the means: a method of the singular is thus a contradiction in terms. To the passage quoted above Valéry adds:

> But it sometimes happens that mastery is taken off its guard and overcome by some innovator who by *chance* [italics mine], or by gift, creates *new technical means* and seems at first to have given the world a new work. But it is never more than a question of technique.

He is not to be reproached if here, as elsewhere, he fails to solve the ultimate problem of poetry, which is the relation of the means to the subject. We are concerned only with his characteristic way of allowing for innovation or singularity. Since the classical method as starting-point cannot deal with innovation, the innovation of singularity hits upon the right means *by chance;* and he adds, *or by gift,* as a question-begging afterthought.

Singularity as an effect to be aimed at, rather than a quality of the poet's mind which suffuses the work as a secondary quality, is no doubt the hallmark of romanticism. Singularity would thus be the element of chance for the classical sensibility, but for the romantic, the means itself is hit upon by luck. The intolerable burden of the romantic sensibility cannot depend upon an objective continuity of forms and techniques. Yet it is important to remember that Valéry holds that it is only technique which counts in the end.

He seems to have conducted from youth to old age a circular argument in which means and ends chase each other round a ring, but which is the pursuer and which the pursued it is impossible to determine. Technique, or mastery of the means, would appear to be the only possible object of calculation, the focus of "clear and distinct ideas"; and I suspect that Valéry's dialectic was doomed to irresolution by his Cartesian dualism, which made a clean break between sensibility and "ideas." But in glancing at the great poems, we shall not be able to

believe of Valéry, any more than of Poe, that his techniques were as calculated as he thought, or tried to think, or tried to make us think.

If we eliminated from Valéry's poems five titles there would be little left to justify his great reputation: he would be a minor post-Symboliste poet of the school of Mallarmé. I suppose it is generally agreed that the principal poems are "**La Jeune Parque,**" "**La Pythie,**" "**Fragments du 'Narcisse,'**" "**L'Ébauche d'un Serpent,**" and "**Le Cimetière Marin.**" Since my first acquaintance with these poems I have had difficulty with them, for I can never be sure that I have got them in my ear. . . . The late Yvor Winters believed that "**L'Ebauche d'un Serpent**" is the greatest poem in any language. I wonder how he could be sure; but I am sure that it is a very great poem, though I prefer "**Le Cimetière Marin**" (which Winters acknowledges to be great); and in trying to set forth a few of the reasons why I think this I shall say all that I know enough to say about the poetics of Paul Valéry.

There is something a little haphazard about Valéry's development as a poet, in the sense that from the early nineties to his death in 1945 there is no clear line of development of either subject or methods—in spite of his obsessive preoccupation with methods—in spite of his obsessive preoccupation with method. There seems to have been a sudden burst of imaginative energy which lasted about five years, during which he wrote the "great" poems; and he then subsided. From this, it does not necessarily follow, as Winters seemed to think, that Valéry must therefore be a lesser poet than Baudelaire, though for other reasons I think he probably is. Baudelaire produced one book, and he very early set out to do so. But apart from the structure of "Les Fleurs du Mal" as a single work, we could extract eight or ten poems which for range and depth of experience and of consciousness, might surpass any similar selection from Valéry. Yet it should be difficult to find any *single poem* by Baudelaire that comes as near perfection in intellectual structure, and in implicit imagery, as the two great Valéry poems. By implicit imagery I mean a kind of unity of idea and symbol, so that most markedly in the "**Cimetière**" one never knows whether the "argument" is really there, or exists only in our sense of it. The development of the "**Serpent**" is somewhat different: the argument is formidable and paraphrasable. I shall comment on this, and in the course of doing so comment on Winters' brilliant commentary.

Winters' statement of the theme of the poem is elaborate and I think exact, and it seems to me to exhaust the rational content. But there is a good deal of the poem left over, after the paraphrase; and it is this residue which seems to me intractable and even obscure beyond any obscurity that one may find even in "**La Jeune Parque,**" a poem which Albert Thibaudet called the most obscure in French literature. I shall not quote Winters, but shall refer the interested reader to his analysis in the essay, "Problems for the Modern Critic of Literature." Winters sums up his statement of the theme as follows: "The theme is the most inclusive of tragic themes: one might describe it as the theme of tragedy."

I am inclined to doubt that this is true, in the sense that I doubt that tragedy ever quite exhibits a *theme* as such apart from tragic *action*. What Winters describes as the theme of tragedy seems to me to be merely the historic paradox of imperfection and evil existing in a world that we can imagine only if we assume that it was created by a perfect being. God compromising and limiting his perfection, in the act of creating the material universe, is the theme of the "**Serpent**"; it is an ancient theme which received its philosophical formulation by the disciples of Plotinus—Iamblichus and Porphyry—and earlier informed the various Gnostic accounts of the mystery of evil. It is a great theme, and it allowed Valéry to write a great poem. But I believe that the magnificent residue of image, the subtle interplay of thought and sub-rational perception between Eve and the Serpent, is involved in an argument which we must scrutinize on its own merits, like any other philosophical position. And this argument seems to me deeply disappointing in a man of Valéry's supposed philosophical resources. . . . [The] triumph of the poem largely consists in the poet's immense invention in this linguistic virtuosity which the French language far more than English allows.

What Winters called the tragic theme proceeds from the Gnostic theory of evil. The despair of the Serpent is his Gnosis of this evil, for it is knowledge of evil alone which constitutes evil for created beings. Hence the Serpent's despair; and hence the fact that he has only despair to offer to God. Sin seems to be a little shadowy in this scene, in spite of the magnificent imagery in which Valéry presents the Serpent's temptation of Eve. Winters points out the absence of Adam: he is not necessary to this intellectual drama, since it is not action but knowledge which dooms the Serpent, who is a surrogate of Adam. Winters' commentary is not only of great value in itself; it compels one to rethink the structure of the poem. Valéry's version of the myth seems to me a little off-center, a little "rigged," although marvelously inventive. May we ask what he might have done with the full, traditional body of the myth? We shall not at any rate get an answer. I hope that I am not invading the privacy of Paul Valéry's mind when I suggest that the Serpent is a methodologist too: that he is not interested in Eve (as Adam presumably was), that he is concerned with the method, not the action or the consequence, of temptation, and that the Gnostic philosophy of the Serpent is the inevitable projection of a mind obsessed with method.

I shall bring those observations to a close with a few cursory remarks on the **"Cimetière."** This poem has been inundated with analysis, beginning with Valéry's own. It seems to me a much greater poem than the **"Serpent,"** and its greatness was made possible because its subject did not contain the temptations to philosophical eccentricities that Valéry's private myth of Eden offered. The **"Cimetière"** has no myth. It is a meditation in the poet's own person upon a symbol which is first of all a natural phenomenon—the sea: the symbol is grounded in one of the eternal phenomenal mysteries. It has been suggested to me that the meaning of the title is: The Sea as Graveyard. We are not given a "philosophy" which we are tempted to argue with; the philosophy of **"Le Cimetière Marin"** is not reducible. If there is greater poetry in French or English in this century than the last stanza, I have not seen it. . . . (pp. 465-70)

> *Allen Tate, "A Note on Paul Valéry," in* The Virginia Quarterly Review, *Vol. 46, No. 3 (Summer, 1970), pp. 460-70.*

ROGER SHATTUCK (essay date 1970)

[*An American critic, editor, and translator, Shattuck is an authority on late nineteenth- and twentieth-century French literature. His most noted works of criticism include* The Banquet Years (1958), *a study that traces the development of French literature from the death of Victor Hugo to the end of World War I, and* Proust's Binoculars (1963), *an investigation of Proust's use of optical metaphor in* Remembrance of Things Past. *In the following excerpt, Shattuck emphasizes the importance of Valéry's prose*

writings, particularly his notebooks, as they relate to his literary theories. Shattuck notes that Valéry valued the literary process rather than its product and that his prose most clearly illustrates his creative processes at work.]

Few critics have tried to tell us anything about Valéry as a writer of French prose even though his essays appear to be as widely read as his poetry. There is a dense forest of interpretation around his writings in verse, and several intelligent critics have examined his aesthetics and his poetics. But apart from a few remarks about his occasional Italian turn of phrase and the "opacity" of his prose, one gets the impression that his style must be nondescript. It is a serious error. What characterizes his prose most is the variety, in kind and quality, of the styles Valéry can muster. (pp. xx-xxi)

Before long one notices that Valéry rarely fails to plant . . . a key sentence at intervals in every sustained prose piece. Many of them have become famous. The opening sentence of the opening essay in his first collection, **Variété,** stirred controversy for years: "We later civilizations now know that we too are mortal." The two lapidary sentences italicized in the speech to the surgeons (*Il est possible de donner la mort.* It is possible to cause death. *Tantôt je pense et tantôt je suis.* At one moment I think; at another I am) pick up the emphatic rhythm of the two I have already mentioned: *Le feu tue* (Gunfire kills). *Le doute mène à la forme.* Valéry tells us that his poem, **La Jeune Parque,** took shape around a wordless rhythm sounding in his head; he speaks elsewhere of the *vers donné* or "given line" which becomes the armature of an entire poem. I believe these italicized sentences work in a similar fashion in his prose. In the dizzy spaces of thought a distant light shines forth toward which one can sight and slowly make one's way. A single thought, a profound platitude, or a verbal formula is enough. Then the rest of the essay comes together around that spark. One could, of course, take the contrary position and argue that these startling simplicities are not what he started with as isolated markers in the wilderness, but are rather the final results of the pressure of thinking patiently applied to anything whatsoever.

But in either case we are led to a related question that particularly concerns the "occasional" writer. Did Valéry have something like a method, a sequence of mental steps to which he could submit any raw material and produce a presentable written result? Frequently he leaves precisely that impression. Gide asserted that nothing Valéry wrote could be neglected. I remember hearing one of my teachers long ago state—apropos of which author I cannot recall—that "his mind was incapable of producing anything second-rate." It could be said of Valéry except at his most dutifully formal. He never ceased searching out the central command post of all thought. By 1924—give or take a year or two—he had organized his ideas, found a method of work, and discovered that he could turn his mind to any subject without wasting his time. (pp. xxi-xxii)

Valéry's "method" had the effect of reducing the infinite variety of his subject matter to three themes: the mind, language, and everything else. His earliest metaphors for mind (a theater; a smoke ring) depict its turbulent equilibrium as circular and self-beholding. As time goes on he rejects with increasing vehemence any theory of separable mental faculties and portrays consciousness as a rhythm. His conjectures about a man hypnotized by the mere possibility of suicide relate directly to his description of Marshal Foch's dispatch in "acting on" an idea and find their full working-out in the speech to the surgeons. Valéry must have startled them with his example. If I know or think too much about what I am doing, I cannot do it. And in a beautifully turned page he asks the learned doctors: how, since you know so much about the organic functioning of the reproductive organs, can you bring yourselves to make love? He suggests that the solution lies in the existence of an alternating rhythm of being: "Now I think, now I am." We cannot be everything at once. This functional rhythm had already been described in a pithy little essay called **"The Aesthetic Infinite"**: "To justify the word *infinite* and give it a precise meaning, we need only recall that in the aesthetic order *satisfaction* revives *need, respouse* renews *demand, presence* generates *absence,* and *possession* gives rise to *desire.*"

In these most critical pronouncements about mind, Valéry falls back on the sexual metaphor, or rather on the erotic ritual with which man, more than any other animal, has sanctified the act of mere coupling. No one could miss the atmosphere saturated with erotic feelings in poems of the mind like **"Les Pas,"** **"L'Abeille,"** and above all *La Jeune Parque*. In his theoretical statements, Valéry contrasts the aesthetic realm of infinitely renewable pleasure with the practical realm, where satisfaction obeys the entropy principle and returns everything to zero.

But most important of all to Valéry and to us are two intermediate realms where pleasure and delight arise under circumstances of restraint and reticence, two realms where we come to the threshold both of ourselves and of another person. Those realms are love and language. They lead us to the most precious and fragile acts of mind and body that we can know.

Valéry's reluctance to surrender his poems for publication reveals how he acted on his conviction that a work of art is a kind of necessary and revealing by-product. The mental process that produced it is the true locus of being and value. Nothing is ever finished. The work of art constitutes both a distillate and an excretion, the part which is purged in order to allow the process to continue without poisoning itself. To my knowledge Valéry never used that figure; I insist on its aptness nevertheless. We examine feces in order to determine the health of the organism that produced them. But the byproduct may take on a value of its own. The entire Western tradition that erects the work of art into an eternal object surpassing contingencies of time, place, and personal creation, defined by intrinsic aesthetic principles and providing a substitute immortality, is now brought into question. Valéry is frequently seen as the last great representative of that classic tradition, which began with the Greeks, reappeared forcefully in the Renaissance, and reached its extreme and fetishistic stage at the end of the nineteenth century in France. (pp. xxiii-xxv)

Richard Howard pointed out in a book review how Valéry's comparison of the act of painting to a dance anticipates recent theories of action painting. But the comparison also belongs to Valéry's total aesthetic and places him further than we ever knew from art for art's sake. His personal notes for 1928 contain the following observations:

> The doing means more to me than its object. It is the doing and the making in themselves which represent the achievement, as I see it, the object. Major point. For the thing, once made, immediately becomes someone else's act. It's the perfect case of Narcissus. . . . And I come out with this paradox: Nothing is more sterile than to produce. The tree does not grow while it forms its fruit.

Valéry's poetics . . . rests its foundations on the execution of acts. It is not surprising that the controlling metaphors of that magnificent piece of thinking are economics and politics: not the creation of eternal objects but an art (and science) of action. The rest follows. A poem worthy of the name is the compressed and fragmentary record of a segment of life lived through with energy and attention. An essay pursues possibilities of thought and breaks off short of conclusions. In both style and sense the last sentence of **"A Personal View of Science"** displays Valéry's stance: "Man is an adventure. . . ." In this context one understands full well Valéry's long fascination with dance— a doing and a growing of form that does not produce anything other than what it is in the process of becoming.

Now if there is any truth in what I have been saying, one further thing becomes clear. We systematically read Valéry in improper fashion. First we probably read his poems; they are, willy-nilly, works of art belonging to special systems of language and of the fiduciary values of culture. Then we read his essays and speeches in areas that concern us. These works are admirable achievements, significant in ways I hope I have pointed out. But as *acts* they finally mean less than his letters and journals and notebooks.

In order to watch Valéry's self in action must we necessarily go to the twenty-nine monumental volumes of his notebooks and the various collections of letters? I see no alternative. In one of the texts we are likely to read last if at all, a letter written in 1917 to Pierre Louÿs, Valéry struggles with the problem of how to make proper use of those notebooks, how to publish them without systematizing, classifying, separating, uprooting, and thus killing their contents. The only answer he found was negative: "avoid discursive order" (*ne pas écrire À LA SUITE*). But he found a definition: "Literature growing wild. If you pick it, it will die." This impeccable stylist and former devotee of "pure poetry" attached increasing and probably final value to the inchoate states of his writing—the fragment, the sketch, the detached observation that has not found and may never find its place in a finished "work." This was his barbarity. (pp. xxv-xxvii)

Following a limited number of leads in literature and philosophy, devoting himself to science and language steadily enough to make most of his critics resentful, Valéry introduced a third term mediating between life and art. He sees conventional social behavior and works of art as the outermost aspects of our individual existence. Adjoining them, however, and also adjoining our innermost life, lies a neglected domain of *acts of the mind*—private writings, decisions about one's acts, preparatory stages of "creation," reflections on one's self—a domain that forms a third term and modifies the linear relationship between the original two. Valéry refers frequently to his jottings as a form of geometry, and also used the expression "algebra of acts" to refer to a painter's mode of sensibility as contrasted with both his life and his finished work. If life and art are two semi-independent variables, and not two easily related elements of biography, then Valéry's intermediate "acts of mind" suggest a form of infinitesimal calculus that seeks and reveals their relation. To that perpetually renewed relation he devotes more time and attention and attaches more human value than to either of the variables it links. Valéry's truest work, which appears on every page he wrote but more directly in his "wild" texts, is his exercise of this calculus of acts, a psycho-poetic reckoning of "changes of mental states." He liked to call it a "Geometry of Time" at the beginning of his career and (in an essay inspired by H. G. Wells' novel) developed his theory of the symbol as a "time machine" that fuses and embodies different states. Later it took the form of a fine discrimination between unconscious, subconscious, and subliminal—accompanied by a sturdy preference for the conscious mind.

Valéry is a myth, of whom and of which we remain incredibly ignorant. He did not want it thus, but the way we approach his writings has produced that effect. We tend to dismiss as irrelevant the two most important facts about him. He renounced the composition of poetry not once but twice, even though the first time he was highly esteemed by fellow poets and the second time he had earned a worldwide reputation as a poet; and secondly, he spent the greatest part of his time meditating over a morality and ontology of thought based not on art but on scientific and mathematical models. He believed profoundly in the unity of mental process in an individual; the mind is one and embodies no essential division between *l'esprit de géométrie* and *l'esprit de finesse,* between reason and imagination. With equal vehemence he rejected any external unity— any system of events or knowledge of them that could lay claim to the term *universe.* To laugh at the scientific pretensions of Valéry's thought and to admit one hundred pages of verse (out of a total production of over thirty thousand pages) as his true contribution to culture is to capitulate to our prejudices. This heir of the Symbolists was heretical to the point of sacrificing permanence to the immediate and transitory. The reader confronts not an eternal object but the scenario of an organic event. Though smiling, Valéry has weighed his words when he suggests that literature will increasingly take on the function of a sport. Not art as the supreme spiritual value or a new priesthood, nor as something purely decorative and purposeless. It is rather that art, competing with the real strengths and promise of science, will become a valuable exercise of mental acts, a process whose products are beside the point except as they improve, extend, and record the game. We can all play, and it brings great joy. Naturally, the real pros like Valéry are very rare. When they play it is worth watching, for to follow so powerful a performance is to participate. (pp. xxviii-xxx)

> *Roger Shattuck, in an introduction to* The Collected Works in English of Paul Valéry: Occasions, *Vol. 11 by Paul Valéry, translated by Roger Shattuck and Frederick Brown, Bollingen Series XLV, Princeton University Press, 1970, pp. ix-xxx.*

ENRICO GARZILLI   (essay date 1972)

[*In the following excerpt, Garzilli considers the interpretations of human consciousness presented in* Monsieur Teste.]

Monsieur Teste of Paul Valéry is an example of a man who seeks himself in the aloneness of his consciousness. While the work in which Monsieur Teste is the central character does not necessarily constitute Paul Valéry's greatest contribution to letters, the problems generated by the modus vivendi of the character of Monsieur Teste reflect a lifelong preoccupation of Valéry. The tension between the interior person and the person who recognizes outside reality is a significant theme in his writing and poetry from his early work on Leonardo da Vinci to *La Jeune Parque* and *Mon Faust. Mon Faust,* perhaps, most perfectly integrates the polarity of this tension: the tension between the internal and the external, between the body and the mind. As early as *Introduction à la méthode de Léonard de Vinci,* Paul Valéry seeks to expose the dynamics of consciousness present in the man of genius, the universal man. He finds that the problem of genius in a particular man leads inevitably

to a statement on what it means to be a person. If a man of genius, for instance, were compared to one of inferior intelligence, the structural relationship in their consciousness would show that only accidental differences exist between them. He chooses, however, to study the man of genius, because in him the act of consciousness and the act of being most perfectly coincide: "There is no act of genius which is not *inferior* to the act of being. The imbecile is grounded in a magnificent principle which also dwells within him; the most talented mind contains nothing superior to this." (p. 11)

Since it is through consciousness that man meets his most elemental self, the study of the conscious self must exclude the distraction of other people and things. Precisely because it is consciousness which all men have in common, and which identifies one with another, the study of it should reveal what it means to be a person and have a self. Valéry pursues these questions in the person of Monsieur Teste, a character distinct from Leonardo but related to him in a most fundamental way.

Monsieur Teste is an intriguing individual who has closed himself off from the exterior world. He seeks himself in his reflections on his conscious activity. The world outside is only important insofar as it sheds light on his own identity. To read *Monsieur Teste* as a temporary rejection on Valéry's part of art, poetry, and letters, is perhaps too great a simplification. While the temporary disillusionment may be true, the work itself shows an obsession with the interior man's seeking an answer to identity. The name "Teste" indicates his nature: he is "tête," the head, the pure embodiment of consciousness, who seeks to define the self in terms of consciousness; he is also "teste" meaning witness. He is a witness to things insofar as he is conscious of them, and things bear witness to his identity insofar as they act as reflectors of his consciousness. . . .

Monsieur Teste is totally turned in upon himself not for the purpose of studying himself but for reflecting upon the consciousness by which he is aware of himself. He is interested not in particularities but in the broadest possible generality. He is not interested in the contents of consciousness but in the form of consciousness itself, the structure of consciousness, the pure act of consciousness and being. Since consciousness is at the opposite pole of personality, there is no past in moments of intense consciousness. . . . (p. 13)

In his preface to *Monsieur Teste,* Paul Valéry states that Monsieur Teste is impossible. The reason for this is that Monsieur Teste is trying to capture the essence of consciousness, to perform an infinite, self-inclosed, unrestricted act of understanding. In such an act of understanding, all possible contents would be known and actualized in a presence that can only be described as eternal. This is the reason that Monsieur Teste is impossible according to Valéry in his preface:

> Why is M. Teste impossible?—This question touches the very core of Teste's being. In fact, *it changes you into* M. Teste. For he is none other than the very demon of possibility. Concern over the totality of what he can do dominates him. He observes himself; he maneuvers, he does not want anyone else to maneuver him. He knows only two categories, which are those of consciousness reduced to its activities: *the possible and the impossible.* In this curious brain where philosophy has little to commend itself and where language is always held suspect,

almost every thought is qualified by the feeling that it is provisional; scarcely anything remains but the expectation and execution of clearly defined operations.

The unrestricted act of understanding means the discovery of the relationship between the known and the unknown; in such a moment Monsieur Teste would be identical with the actual principle of consciousness, pure presence, eternal.

At these moments of intense consciousness, consciousness ceases to appear as emanating from the self; rather the self, the person, seems to be a point within a transcending field of consciousness, a field which is accessible to reflective consciousness and from which vantage point the self becomes an object of consciousness, a thing. In this moment the self becomes a you and is distinguished from the I. . . . (pp. 13-14)

Monsieur Teste's obsession is the isolation in consciousness of that which is permanent and depends upon nothing. In studying the dynamism of his consciousness, Monsieur Teste denies himself; he is no longer a person, he refuses to establish a center with a name. He identifies himself with "the pure self." . . . This pure self is identical with absolute consciousness and constitutes the ground of personality while paradoxically remaining purely impersonal. . . . Personality is distinct from the consciousness which is its ground. Consciousness is what men have in common. It is essential to man's being a man. Personality refers to what separates man, makes him unique; it is comprised of accidental qualities: "And this thing called *personality,* which we so crudely consider to be our most intimate and profound *property* and sovereign good, is merely that, a *thing,* both changeable and accidental, in stark contrast to the naked *self;* since we can think of it, calculate its interests, and even somewhat lose them from sight, personality turns out to be no more than a second-rate psychological divinity which dwells in our mirror and answers to our name."

The pure ego of which Valéry speaks, then, is universal. If the individual person is able to isolate his own consciousness and trace it back, he finds that that which he names a self is simply an object in the whole of consciousness. Consequently, the one who has liberated himself from his individuality, his personality, feels himself to be pure consciousness. . . . If an individual can transcend his personality and become identical with absolute consciousness the simultaneous existence of other individual consciousnesses becomes a problem of the one and the many.

Valéry understands that this problem of the one and the many becomes circular. It is evident that consciousness points beyond the individual person and in some way the individual can assume identity with pure consciousness and unity with the whole. (pp. 14-15)

The real meaning of the whole remains shrouded in mystery, yet in some way consciousness appears to be the vital link to this understanding of the whole. For each person, since he is a person, participates in this cosmic consciousness. Valéry pursues this point by relating matter, consciousness, and relativity physics to the problem of the person:

> We have here the strangest problem that could ever be proposed, and which others do pose to us: it consists simply in the possibility of other intelligences, in the plurality of the singular, in the coexistence of durations which are in-

dependent of one another,—tot capita, tot tempora,—a problem quite similar to the physical problem of relativity, but incomparably more difficult.

The admission of the conscious man that there are other men who also participate in consciousness is difficult because it means, as the text above suggests, the coexistence of independent psychological durations based on existence of independent individuals. Yet all of this is held together in the single continuum of the relativity schema where energy can be matter, and where matter exists at the limit of consciousness. Perhaps this finds expression in the fact that consciousness and matter are but modalities of a single force, energy itself.

Monsieur Teste is precisely an individual who wants to discover the structure of his own consciousness. He wants to be a purely transparent individual, a mirror of pure consciousness. In this way he would be both perfect receiver and the source of all reflections. To this pure state of consciousness Monsieur Teste aspires. He wishes to be "the glass man":

> My vision is so clear, my perception so pure,
> my knowledge so awkwardly complete, my
> representative power so unfettered and precise
> and my understanding so perfect that I can enter
> myself from the extremities of the earth and
> reach my silent word; and rising from the form-
> less *thing* that is the object of the search I follow
> myself along known fibers and ordered centers,
> I answer myself, I reflect and resonate myself,
> I tremble before the infinity of mirrors—I am
> made of glass.

"The glass man" finds its echoes in other writings of Paul Valéry. There are many such resonances of this same kind of self-consciousness in *La Jeune Parque,* finished in 1917. (p. 16)

In Monsieur Teste's attempt to understand his individuality he ironically transcends his personality and almost becomes an infinity of mirrors which reflect the light of consciousness. Through this prism myriad colors of the world of objects and persons are refracted. Man's center is found everywhere but nowhere. He has no name, he is simply the mysterious eye, the finite witness to an infinite act. . . .

The reflective person constantly becomes aware of the dreamlike nature of himself and of the world. For these reasons, the metaphor of *La Jeune Parque* waking from her dreamlike state at the edge of the reflecting sea is another image of the same range of possibilities. These possibilities are what constitute the identity of a person. Man realizes that he is but a single reflection of one of the infinite ranges of possibilities. When consciousness disappears, however, then he is condemned to physical death. He realizes that the self has gone full circle. . . . Monsieur Teste comes to his end when consciousness ends. He is a certain manner of being. His marks a personal, particular mode of existence. Although there may be an infinite number of dimensions of which human consciousness is but a single reflection, the totality of these possible dimensions remains eternally hidden even to the purified existence of consciousness. . . . The demon of possibility, Monsieur Teste is the dreamlike goal which seeks to obliterate everything but consciousness to study what is intrinsically personal. As consciousness ends so does Monsieur Teste and his witness to others. Ironically for Monsieur Teste, while he seeks what is uniquely his consciousness, he finds that the relationship between individuals is not distinction, but identity. He illustrates the truth that man is identified with all other men to the extent that he and they participate in and have self-consciousness. He finds that consciousness becomes a prism for his possible existences with others. The study of the structure of consciousness allows man to see how much he is like other men. Monsieur Teste thought that he could begin by finding himself, by cutting himself off from others. His wife recalls that as his witness, he spoke to her as an object, regarding her just as he did everything else outside of his consciousness. Through his experiences Monsieur Teste demonstrates that consciousness and the I cannot be completely identified. Man alone in what originally appears uniquely his, his consciousness, marks an incomplete but fundamental attempt at self-definition. (pp. 17-18)

> *Enrico Garzilli, ''Man Alone,'' in his* Circles without Center: Paths to the Discovery and Creation of Self in Modern Literature, *Cambridge, Mass.: Harvard University Press, 1972, pp. 9-27.* *

HENRI PEYRE (essay date 1980)

[*Peyre is a prolific and well-known scholar and specialist in modern French literature. His work is admired by many critics for its precision, honesty, and comprehensibility to non-specialist readers. Peyre is a staunch moralist who values literature that examines the individual's relationship to society and to a hostile or indifferent universe; he opposes structuralist criticism and experimental writing in general, endorsing Robert Penn Warren's insistence that ''experimental writing is an elite word for flop.'' Two of his major works are* The Contemporary French Novel *(1955; revised in 1967 as* French Novelists of Today) *and* Historical and Critical Essays *(1968). In the following excerpt, Peyre discusses Valéry's lifelong admiration for the work of Edgar Allan Poe, and Poe's profound impact on his art and artistic theories. For further discussion of Poe's influence upon Valéry, see the excerpts by T. S. Eliot (1948) and Allen Tate (1970).*]

The French found in E. A. Poe what they felt and thought they needed at the time, from 1850 to 1890, as a reinvigorating force in their poetry, and even more in their poetics. (p. 74)

Paradoxically, the Frenchman who was most profoundly and most lastingly impressed by Poe is the very one who should, it would seem, have pierced through what is superficial and amateurish in Poe's theories and what is sentimental and facile in his verse: Paul Valéry. That may well constitute the strangest case of a writer's influence upon another, whose favorite assertion was to deny the very possibility of influence. The supremely intellectual mind of French literature, the one who treated most romantics, and Rousseau, Pascal, Montaigne himself, (and Shakespeare) with distrust and often with disdain, acclaimed Poe in his youth, at the very time when he was composing those two masterpieces of lucid thinking and of fastidious prose: *Introduction à la Méthode de Léonard de Vinci* . . . and *La Soirée avec Monsieur Teste*. . . . (p. 78)

[Explaining] the intent of *La Jeune Parque,* [Valéry] referred to that ''poem of the consciousness of consciousness'' as being in the lineage of Poe. To another Belgian poet, André Fontainas, he characterized it, in terms reminiscent of Poe, as ''an exercise, deliberate and resumed (''repris'') and worked over: a work of will, and again of a second will whose arduous task is to mask the first.'' In 1920, in one of his greatest and most revealing texts, ''Avant-Propos à la Connaissance de la Déesse'' by Lucien Fabre, Valéry paid a glowing tribute to Poe. Repeatedly, he voiced his regret for not having written adequately and at some length on Poe. He jotted down several occasional remarks on Poe in the notebooks which he kept most of his

life. In 1921, Valéry had the courage to publish a substantial essay on Poe's most ambitious, and most controversial, cosmological poem Eureka, on which Baudelaire, Taine, Mallarmé had refused to express themselves. As late as in 1937, Valéry, world famous, august Academician, having denied that even Mallarmé could have exercised a true influence over him, went back to Poe's ideas on poetic composition in his lessons on Poetics at the Collège de France. Not a few of Valéry's admirers, in France and outside France, have naturally asked themselves the intriguing question; what could such a fastidious poet, athirst for purity and mental lucidity, an intellectual who was pitilessly severe to critics and their trade, a man who could not indulge the reading of fiction or even admit the mere possibility of the novelist's art, what could he have found in Poe, that second-rate poet, the story-teller, the dogmatic and perhaps mystifying theorist and the pretentious author of a philosophical poem in prose claiming to elucidate the origin of the universe?

Baudelaire had hailed Poe as his spiritual brother and repeated that he had, through many arduous years, translated the American author because he resembled his French devotee. There was indeed an ''imp of perversity'' in him as in Poe, an obsession with evil pitilessly plumbed to its depths (''la conscience dans le mal'') and sympathy for an ''accursèd poet'' whom a brutal society had persecuted. Valéry could at no time, even when he was struggling to eke out a modest living as a clerk in the Ministry of War, have deemed himself one of the ''maudits.'' He was a conservative in politics, distrustful even of the liberals who had rallied under the banner of the Dreyfusards in 1895-1900. At the age of forty, married in a middle-class family, a father, he could be said to be, according to the well-known French boast, ''living like a bourgeois while thinking like a demi-god.'' (pp. 79-80)

Several other features of Poe's personality, as it is reflected in his writings, might seem to be precisely the very ones which the French advocate of ''la poésie de la connaissance'' should have anathematized: the indulgence in confessional literature by the one who dreamt of writing ''My Heart Laid Bare'' and passed on the title and the attempt to live up to it, to Baudelaire. Sincerity, as aimed at by Stendhal and claimed by the poet of *les Fleurs du Mal* in some of his most moving letters as the hallmark of his verse, then advocated repeatedly by Gide, came to be the butt of Valéry's bitterest scorn. He condemned sentimentality even more brutally. His *Cahiers* reveal what was once only half apparent in his writings: that love played a large part in his life and that the Lionardo that he called himself in those jottings suffered at the hands of women and was no less ''crucified by sex'' than a Julien Green who used the phrase. But few poems bearing the same title could ever differ so completely as Poe's ''The Sleeper'' and Valéry's sonnet **''la Dormeuse.''** As to the rather facile effects of repetition, refrains, crude rhythmical devices, the use of pretentious and affected adjectives (such as Valéry deplored even in his revered master, Mallarmé), they do not mar the exquisite Racinian simplicity or the marriage of sound and sense which make Valéry the most faultless poet of his age.

Mysterious, however, is the process through which one mind impresses another. Words such as ''influence'', ''resemblance'', even ''affinities'' are out of place in these matters. At a time when he stood in reaction against much of the looseness of structure and the flabbiness of imagery and diction of some of the Symbolists through whom he had first discovered the poetry of his own generation, Valéry read Poe's essay on ''The Poetic Principle'' and a few of his Marginalia. He disregarded the lack of modesty of one who would treat a literary work like the neatly contrived clockwork of an engineer. He paid scant heed to the peremptory thesis that no long poem can be worthy of the name. After all "The Raven" itself with its eighteen stanzas of six unusually long lines each, "Ulalume", "The Bells" are, if anything, far too long, and *Eureka* is drawn out to the point of tediousness. The two poetical masterpieces of Valéry are, in the opinion of not a few of his admirers, *la Jeune Parque,* which counts over five hundred lines and *"Ebauche d'un Serpent"* which extends over three hundred and ten octosyllables. The reading of Poe's rather crude and boastful reconstruction of his creative process stimulated the French poet relentlessly to pursue his quest for calculated concentration in a work of art and to shift the emphasis in poetical composition away from whatever the poet may have experienced, or dreamt, to the effect to be produced. To arouse the reader or hearer and, in the original meaning of the verb, to "suggest" in him a poetical condition perhaps similar to the one first felt and thought by the author, was to lie at the core of Valeryan poetics.

More important still: Mallarmé excepted (and the revelation of Mallarmé came for Valéry after his encounter with Poe, and it was prepared by it), the American poet offered to his French admirer the best image of a restless mind, rejecting all intellectual quietude and ever eager to experiment anew. (pp. 80-1)

[It] was in Poe that Valéry first encountered a sentence which remained engraved in his memory. It occurs in one of the most florid and innocuous tales of the American author, amid the lush description of a garden, "The Domain of Arnheim." The hero, a certain Mr. Ellison, having come into a rich legacy, wishes to devote it to "the creation of novel forms of beauty." Poe, almost casually inserts this remark:

> I believe that the world has never seen—and that, unless through some series of accidents goading the noblest order of mind into distasteful exertion, the world will never see—that full extent of triumphant execution, in the richer domains of art, of which the human nature is absolutely capable.

Again and again, in his philosophical essays and in his Cahiers.... Valéry recurred to "that sentence by Poe which had so much influence . . . on my nineteen-year-old self. The notion of perfection took possession of me. A little later, it changed into a will to power, or to possession of power—without making use of it." . . . (p. 83)

What can a man do? . . . Monsieur Teste repeated in Valéry's admirable story of 1896. M. Teste, discarding or ignoring the modes of psychological disquisition around him, strove to alter and deepen his own mental structure as Poe's Monsieur Dupin, through fierce logic and the "consistency" dear to Poe (and to Valéry), reconstructed the working of the mind of criminals. He evinced no eagerness to manifest his power to the outside world, through publications. He preferred holding in reserve the wealth of his potentialities, choosing proud silence as Poesque Valeryans like Marcel Duchamp and the novelist and critic Maurice Blanchot were later to do. The creator of Monsieur Teste, who revered Leonardo and Descartes, went so far as to mention Poe in the same breath as the two heroes of his intellectual life (*Cahiers,* i. 1197 and 1757), confessing, in the second of those two passages, "all the influence which that old and obstinate reading had exercized upon him." Later still, in 1923, in the moving and almost sentimental reminiscences

on his early discovery of *Eureka,* Valéry recurred to some of Poe's staunchest, and most controversial, assertions: the equivalence between "perfect consistency and absolute truth" and the view that the universe is built according to a scheme, the symmetry of which is present in the innermost structure of the human mind. Valéry, by then the mature and profound thinker and the arch-doubter, cannot, in his fiftieth year, have been blind to all that is pretentiously and portentously pseudo-scientific in Poe's parading of his acquaintance with the ideas of Newton and Laplace. He could not but know that Poe's crude finalism in *Eureka* and his idle speculation on an absolute beginning amounted to little more than attempting the most perilously frail of creations, a long, verbose, cosmological poem. "In the beginning was the myth," concluded Valéry at the end of his essay.

Still to the meditations inspired in him by his youthful reading of Poe in starry-eyed wonderment can be traced Valéry's life-long ambition to reach universality as a thinker. He aimed at nothing less than at expanding to the utmost his potentialities as a thinker for whom artistic and scientific creations stemmed fundamentally from the same roots and developed according to parallel and similar methods. Once the mechanism of such creation discovered, and taken to pieces as Poe's engineer's mind had dreamt to do, boundless potentialities would lie open to the mind. Man might aspire to make himself like unto the gods. "A man who never attempted to make himself alike to the gods is less than a man," decreed Valéry in one of the aphorisms of *Choses tues.* (pp. 83-5)

> Henri Peyre, "Edgar Allan Poe and Twentieth Century French Poetry: Paul Valéry," in Laurels, *Vol. 51, No. 2, Fall, 1980, pp. 73-87.**

RENÉ WELLEK (essay date 1981)

[*Wellek's* A History of Modern Criticism *(1955-present) is a major, comprehensive study of the literary critics of the last three centuries. Wellek's critical method, as demonstrated in* A History *and outlined in his* Theory of Literature *(1949), is one of describing, analyzing, and evaluating a work solely in terms of the problems it poses for itself and how the writer solves them. For Wellek, biographical, historical, and psychological information is incidental. Although many of Wellek's critical methods are reflected in the work of the New Critics, he was not a member of that group, and rejected their more formalistic tendencies. In the following excerpt, Wellek discusses various aspects of Valéry's critical thought, particularly his preference for poetry over prose as a mode of artistic expression, his leanings toward classicism rather than romanticism, and his belief in the independence of the work of art from the artist.*]

Valéry is not a systematic philosopher or aesthetician: he propounds a number of insights which are sometimes, at least, superficially contradictory; he is, within a very limited range, a practical critic and above all a practicing poet who examines the creative process or speculates about his craft. He implicitly raises fundamental questions without often claiming or attempting to solve them within a consistent framework.

Much of the interest of Valéry's thought lies precisely in its tentativeness, in its suggestiveness, in its extremism which, however, is held only provisionally, often for the sake of a specific argument or as a contradiction to accepted opinions, in order to surprise or shock, to experiment with a thought, to see where it will lead.

Valéry, like many other theorists, sharply distinguishes between the author, the work, and the reader, but he goes further than any other writer I know in doubting the continuity and even the desirability of continuity among the three. He complains that in most aesthetics one finds ''a confusion of considerations some of which make sense only for the author, others are valid only for the work, and yet others only for the person who experiences the work. Any proposition which brings together these three entities is illusory.'' He would assert more positively that ''producer and consumer are two essentially separate systems,'' and most boldly that the ''art, as value, depends essentially on this nonidentification (of producer and consumer), this need for an intermediary between producer and consumer.'' (p. 20)

[According to Valéry] art is *not* communication, certainly not direct communication between authors and readers. ''If what has happened in the one person were communicated directly to the other, all art would collapse, all the effects of art would disappear.'' Art would become rhetoric, persuasion. Thus, ''the mutual independence of the producer and the consumer, their ignorance of each other's thoughts and needs is almost essential to the effect of a work.'' But it is hard to see how such a theory can be upheld in its extreme formulation: if the gulf between creator, work, and reader were unbridgeable, there would be no works and the works (if existent) would be completely incomprehensible. But although Valéry tries out the theory without quite seeing its consequences, he is right when he emphasizes the difficulties of these relationships: Has the work anything to do with the author? Has the reader's interpretation of a work anything to do with its supposed ''real'' meaning? He answers ''very little,'' but to my mind he can hardly answer ''nothing at all.''

If we isolate the three factors and begin with the author, we can see that Valéry has the courage of his conviction and is really not so much or not primarily interested in the product, the work of art, as in the process of production, the creative process independent of its result. As a matter of fact, if one wanted to explain the psychological or genetic origin of Valéry's theory, one would probably find that it started with his interest in the creative process and was motivated by it. Valéry is interested in this activity in itself and has thus created the somewhat monstrous self-caricature, Monsieur Teste: he has written elaborately about Leonardo da Vinci, the universal man. When, in a formal, rather empty anniversary speech, he praised Goethe in the terms he had used for Leonardo, he implicitly praised himself or rather the ideal he had set up for himself. Goethe is the potential creator, who has the genius of transformation, of metamorphosis; he is Orpheus, Proteus. Goethe's speculations on metamorphosis and evolution attract Valéry more than his poetry. He admires the combination of scientist and poet. Valéry's thought moves so much on this very general level of human creativeness that he can assimilate artistic creativeness to scientific creativeness by some general term such as *speculation.* (pp. 21-2)

If one is interested in the creative process as such, one will disparage the work of art. This is what Valéry does, both in words and in deeds. During his many years of silence, he obviously felt that he was elaborating his ideas and his personality, and that expression and especially publication were purely secondary to this inner activity. (p. 22)

It is not surprising that Valéry has given us several minute introspective accounts of the composition of his poems and that he excels in this analysis. But whatever the specific interest of these ''marvels of introspection,'' as T. S. Eliot calls them, Valéry arrives, of necessity, at very little for theory, since his introspection leads to the conclusion that there is no direct relationship between a specific state of mind of the author and the work itself. Indeed, there might be a very considerable distance between the original idea, the germ of the work, and the finished product. The organic analogy of begetting, growing, and being born is rejected: there is no continuity between the act of conception and the work produced. The germ of a work of art can be anything. . . . The poetic state is ''perfectly irregular, inconstant, involuntary, fragile . . . we lose it, as we obtain it, *by accident.*'' One could call this a theory of inspiration, but Valéry is very reluctant to admit inspiration. ''I believed and still believe that it is ignoble to write from enthusiasm alone. Enthusiasm is not a state of mind for a writer.'' Inspiration is no guarantee of the value of the product. ''The spirit blows where it listeth: one sees it blow on fools.''

If poetry or art in general is not inspiration, it is obviously not dream. In an age in which *surréalisme,* Freudianism, and symbolism asserted the kinship of poetry and dream, Valéry repudiates it emphatically, though he recognizes that ''the poetic universe bears strong analogies to the universe of dreams,'' and that as an historical fact, this confusion between poetry and dream has been understandable since the time of romanticism. But, ''the true condition of a true poet is as distinct as possible from the state of dreaming. In the former I can see nothing but voluntary efforts, suppleness of thought, a submission of the mind to exquisite constraints, and the perpetual triumph of sacrifice. . . . Whoever speaks of exactness of style invokes the opposite of dream.''

Though Valéry recognizes some initial irrational suggestion such as two rhythms insisting on being heard as he describes it in **''Mémoires d'un poèms,''** all the practical emphasis falls on the share of rational speculation after the moment of conception, on the poetic calculus, on the poet's exercise of choice among possibilities, his clairvoyant, highly conscious pursuit of a sport or game. Valéry loves to think of the art of poetry as ''a sport of people insensitive to the conventional values of common language.'' He says, in slightly different terms, that a poem is ''a game, but a solemn, regulated, significant game'' or ''a kind of calculus'' or an algebra. Thus ''every true poet is necessarily a critic of the first order,'' but, of course, this criticism by no means makes the poet a philosopher. Valéry, surprisingly enough in view of his intellectualism, sharply divorces poetry from philosophy, not as an act, but in its result. (pp. 22-4)

What Valéry demands of poetry is always something pure, something *sui generis,* and thus poetry cannot be continuous with the personality of the author; it is and must be impersonal to be perfect. . . . What Valéry admires in poetry is the effort of men such as Victor Hugo and Stéphane Mallarmé (one is surprised at this pairing) ''to form non-human ways of discourse, absolute discourse, in a sense—discourse which suggests a certain being independent of any person—a divinity of language.'' The continuity between author and work is minimized and especially the emotions of ordinary life are resented or rejected as themes of art. . . . Valéry resents the emotional effect of art: e.g., he complains that in reading Stendhal's *Lucien Leuwen* as a young man he felt the illusion so strongly that he could ''no longer distinguish clearly between my own feelings and those which the artifice of the author communicated to me. . . . *Lucien Leuwen* brought about in me the miracle of a confusion which I detest.'' We hardly need to say that Valéry has no use for confessional literature and looks very coldly at the criterion of "sincerity" or "good intention." . . . (pp. 24-5)

[He] always resented literature which tried to convert and persuade him. . . . This is the task of politics and eloquence but not of poetry and certainly not of the poetry Valéry wants to write. He wanted to go a different way and did so. He has a clear conception of a work of art constructed by the intellect, free from personal and emotional admixtures, pure, or as he sometimes says, absolute poetry.

The phrase *pure poetry*, old as such, is first used by Valéry in the Preface to Lucien Fabre's *Connaissance de la déesse* (1920) to suggest the ideal of the symbolists, which will always remain an ideal, though Valéry recognizes that it is only an abstract ideal. It is a tendency toward the utmost rigor in art, "toward a beauty ever more conscious of its genesis, ever more independent of all *subjects*, and free from the vulgar attractions of sentiment as well as from the blatant effects of eloquence." . . . Pure poetry is a "poetry which results, by a kind of *exhaustion*, from the progressive suppression of the prosaic elements of a poem. By prosaic elements we mean everything that *without damage* can be said also in prose; everything, history, legend, anecdote, morality, even philosophy, which exists by itself without the necessary co-operation of song." The purity of poetry is obviously for Valéry a standard of judgment. "A poem is worth as much as it contains of pure poetry." At times, Valéry thinks of it as a kind of admixture of pure gold among foreign matter. (pp. 26-7)

But what is this pure gold, how can it be distinguished from prose? Poetry, first of all, cannot be paraphrased, cannot be reduced to its prose content. Valéry condemns in strongest terms the heresy of paraphrase. . . . The impossibility of paraphrase logically implies the impossibility of translating poetry. "Translations of the great foreign poets are architectural blueprints which may well be admirable; only they make the edifices themselves, palaces, temples, and the rest disappear. . . ."

But why cannot poetry be reduced to prose, or to thought or theme? Valéry has several answers: one which he repeats many times is that prose language perishes when it is understood, while poetry demands repetition, demands and suggests a universe. Prose is practical, it presupposes a realm of ends. . . . But the universe of poetry is "a universe of reciprocal relations analogous to the universe of sounds within which the musical thought is born and moves. In this poetic universe, resonance triumphs over causality." (p. 27)

If poetry is words, it is, of course, not words in isolation, but words in a pattern, words formalized. One could collect from Valéry the most extreme formalist statements. He quotes Frédéric Mistral with approval: "*There is nothing but form . . . form alone preserves the works of the mind.*" He approves of Mallarmé, with whom "the material is no longer the *cause* of the 'Form': it is one of the effects." Content is "*nothing but an impure form*—that is to say a *confused* form." Valéry praises Hugo because with him "the form is always master. . . . Thought becomes with him a means and not the end of expression." And he says of himself: "I subordinate 'content' to 'form' (the nearer I am to my *best* state)—I am always inclined to sacrifice the *former* to the *latter*." (pp. 28-9)

Much more frequently Valéry thinks of poetry as a collaboration of sound and sense, a compromise between the two. He conceives of sound and sense as "two independent variables,"

between which there is absolutely no relation. Words are arbitrary signs: there is no natural relation between sound and sense. The doctrine of the *mot juste* has no justification. "Flaubert was convinced that for every idea there exists a single form. . . . This fine doctrine unfortunately makes no sense." Thus the union of sound and sense established by the poet is arbitrary but indissoluble: "The value of a poem resides in the indissolubility of sound and sense. Now this is a condition which seems to demand the impossible. There is no relation between the sound and meaning of a word. . . . Yet is the business of the poet to give us the feeling of an intimate union between the word and the mind." This union must resist dissolution. "If the sense and the sound (or the content and the form) can be easily dissociated the poem *decomposes*." This union of sound and meaning is song, but not quite song. We must remember that Valéry also said that poetry is calculus, sport, exercise, even a game. But apparently song *(chant)* in Valéry's mind is not literally song *(carmen);* it is also enchantment, incantation, charm, magic. Valéry called a collection of his poems **Charmes;** and he means it also as a suggestion of the original function of poetry. "There is a very ancient man in every true poet; he still drinks from the very springs of language." But this primitivism is reconcilable with the greatest refinement. Mallarmé, "the least primitive of poets, gave . . . the magic formula." The poet is the Orpheus who brings all nature to life, who has the animizing power of ancient man. Thus all poetry will be and must be metaphorical. "The poet who multiplies figures is only rediscovering within himself language in its *nascent state.*"

Poetry is thus figurative and incantatory and, of course, metrical. Valéry has little use for free verse. He always praises the merits of strict metrical schemes and of all poetic conventions. . . . Valéry defends stanzaic forms and is enraptured by the sonnet. He would want to encounter its inventor in the underworld. However bad his sonnets might have been, Valéry would like to tell him: "I set you in my heart above all the poets of the earth and the underworld. . . . You have invented a *form,* and the greatest have accommodated themselves to this form." The constant argument is the value of convention, of restriction, even of chains. "Restriction can be achieved only by the arbitrary." Valéry can thus revive one of the oldest doctrines of poetics, that of difficulties overcome. This "difficulty overcome" is for Valéry a criterion of value. "Every judgment which one wants to make of a work of art must first of all take into account the difficulties which the author has set up for himself to overcome." We hardly need to say that Valéry prefers classicism to romanticism: classicism is superior because of its set conventions.

All these elaborate conventions, the dance, even the dance in fetters, are there for a purpose: to achieve that ideal artwork, unified, antirelative, nontemporal, imperishable, eternal, something beyond the decay of nature and man, something absolute. The poem, Valéry says, is "a closed system of all parts in which nothing can be modified." (pp. 29-31)

This curious criterion of resistance to transformation is very central to Valéry's ideal of poetry. Racine's *Phèdre*, he discovered, resisted attempts to change it. "I learned by direct experience and immediate sensation what is perfection in a work." A lack of this resistance is what Valéry considers the main objection to the novel. . . . (pp. 31-2)

The novel is also "historical," based on truth and memory, and neither truth nor memory means anything in art for Valéry. He does not care for memories. . . . "Whereas the world of poetry is essentially closed and complete in itself, being purely a system of ornaments and accidents of language, the universe of the novel, even of the fantastic novel, is joined to the real world—just as a painted background merges imperceptibly into real objects, among which a spectator comes and goes." Valéry finds this appeal to truth puzzling.... It lends itself to an infinity of compositions of equal probability." Besides, the novel is, of course, prose in Valéry's sense. "Unlike poems, a novel can be summarized; in other words, its plot can be told. It can be shortened without materially changing the story;... it can also be translated without losing its value. It can be developed internally and prolonged indefinitely." The same is true of epic poetry, of any long poem. It "can be summarized.... A melody cannot be summarized," says Valéry, crushingly to his mind, as statement and truth are excluded *a priori* from his definition of poetry.

It is merely consistent that Valéry does not know what to do with drama although he himself wrote dramatic scenes, dialogues, and what he calls "mélodrames." ... He is frankly puzzled as to why man finds pleasure in tragedy.... Still, surprisingly, Valéry recognizes that Greek tragedy has accomplished the impossible:

> In putting on the stage the most atrocious stories in the world, they have imposed upon them all the purity and perfection of a form which insensibly communicates to the spectator of crimes and evils an indefinable feeling which makes him regard these horrible disorders with a divine eye.... [He can] always come back from the emotion to comprehension, from excess to measure, from the exceptional to the norm, and from nature overthrown to the unchangeable presence of the profound order of the world.

One cannot help reflecting that Valéry might have admitted the same transforming power of art in other cases: even in the epic or the social novel, as he himself admits that there is, "in the order of the arts, no theme and no model which execution cannot ennoble or degrade, make a cause of disgust or pretext for enthusiasm." Actually, Valéry appreciated the poetic power of Zola. But in his own practice he more and more insisted on only one theme of poetry: that of "the life of intelligence [which] constitutes an incomparable lyrical universe.... There is an immense realm of the intellectual sensibility," hitherto neglected by poetry. It was Valéry's right to insist on this discovery; every artist recommends the art he himself practices. Every artist is an apologist for his own art, and that is, in part, the interest of his criticism. But as a general theory of literature it seems an extremely narrow, exclusive, puristic view, a specialty hardly applicable beyond that unique closed system of Valéry's civilized mind.

Valéry's ideal of poetry remains absolute, almost frozen into the grandeur of a "pure form." One would imagine that such a hard structure would have to be apprehended by its audience as purely as it was conceived, as impersonally as it was created. But here Valéry's strong sense of the discontinuity of author and reader interferes. A work of art to his mind is open to many interpretations, is only in a loose relationship to its audience. A work of art is essentially ambiguous.... "My verses have the meaning which one gives to them," he says bluntly. "There is no true sense of a text. The author has no authority. Whatever he wanted to say, he has written what he has written." (pp. 32-5)

This insight into the detachment of the work from the author, into the "intentional fallacy," does not dispose of the problem of interpretation. All interpretations are not equal: there remains the problem of correctness. Valéry seems nearer the truth when he says: "There is no very fine work which is not susceptible of a great variety of equally plausible interpretations. The richness of a work is the number of senses or values which it can receive while still remaining itself. (p. 35)

In discussing Descartes he has warned us that "every system is an enterprise of the mind against itself.... If one tries to reconstruct a thinking being from an examination of the texts alone, one is led to the invention of monsters who are incapable of life in direct proportion to the strict carefulness that one has devoted to the elaboration of the study." We must not try to force unity on Valéry's thought, we must not invent a logical monster. Let us be content to have shown the main motifs of his thought on poetry. (p. 36)

René Wellek, "Paul Valéry," in his Four Critics: Croce, Valéry, Lukács, and Ingarden, *University of Washington Press, 1981, pp. 19-36.*

SUZANNE NASH (essay date 1983)

[*In the following excerpt Nash discusses the changes Valéry's poetry underwent after 1891, when the poet moved away from the consummate Symbolism of Stéphane Mallarmé toward a poetry that largely reflected the natural world.*]

The most obvious change in the poetry Valéry writes from 1891 on is the increased importance he accords the natural world through imagery, diction, and phonetic effects. This emphasis on natural forms reverses the direction of Mallarmé's imagery, which characteristically struggles to free itself of its rootedness in material existence, and reflects Valéry's acceptance of the seduction-toward-the world inherent in both thought and language. Edmund Wilson [see *TCLC* Vol. 4] was one of the first to note the tension between the sensuous and the abstract in Valéry's work, a tension which he interpreted as a sign of an irresolvable conflict that Valéry considered fundamental to the human condition.... (pp. 83-4)

The value Valéry always attached to the natural world is apparent in his earliest correspondence, the imagery of which often conflicts with the anti-naturalism of his Decadent stance.... Whereas Mallarmé's human subject is typically evoked through symbols representing its absence—bed, lute, fan, curtain, window—Valéry's subjects, in the poems from 1891 on, are frequently situated outdoors, surrounded and even touched by elements of the natural world—air, sunlight, tides, bird song, tree branch, rose. Indeed, they accede to consciousness and creative life from contact with this world.

"Narcisse parle" is a case in point. In it Valéry uses Mallarmé's own poetic vocabulary from *Hérodiade* ... in order to lament the destruction of the natural self by the reflective consciousness. The body/mind opposition is maintained in an uneasy union until the end, when the embrace of the illusory, reflected self by Narcisse causes a splitting to take place. At the moment the embracing self drowns, a new, faun-like Narcissus is liberated to pipe a seductive tune to the wood nymphs who surround him.... Valéry seems to be saying that not only does Mallarmé's poetry of pure reflection lead to the extinction of the poetic voice altogether, but for a new voice to be born, this thralldom with an illusory brother/self that pretends to perfect unity of form and meaning must be broken. It is not surprising that Mallarmé's most sensuous poem, *"L'Après-midi d'un faune,"* the poem which objectifies the mind/body polarity in the form of the two nymphs whom the Faun tries unsuccessfully to hold together, will be the intertext most insistently present in the poems of the *Album de vers anciens.*

The voyage which would eventually lead Valéry back to the writing of what Edmund Wilson called the most sensuous and the most abstract poetry in the French language, begins, however, in a highly cerebral, authority-obsessed fashion. From 1893 on, Valéry turns his back on all forms of neo-platonic idealism to dedicate himself to the "exact sciences," to rediscover the world of physical evidence (a favorite Valéryan word, and one he came to value during his twenty-odd years of scientific reading), as it is recorded and articulated by the *cogito.* (pp. 84-7)

In many of his essays on poetic process, Valéry apparently saw no contradiction in adjusting his particular brand of Cartesian, subject-centered idealism to the discoveries of the new physics. A relativistic concept of the world suited a psyche obsessed with freedom and autonomy far better than did the mystical correspondant vision of the Romantics and post-Romantics. The subject is now left adrift in space and, like a dancer, dependent upon the prodigious effort of his mind to bring a constantly transforming order to a constantly changing universe. In a sense one might say that the Valéryan subjectivity is accorded even greater primacy than that of his Romantic or Symbolist predecessors because it is no longer an extension of a higher, ideal Logos but, as in the example of Mallarmé, a solitary presence dependent only upon its unique powers of seeing and abstraction to hold back or suspend the inevitable return to formlessness which governs the natural world. Not only does the observer's ability to abstract reverse the law of entropy, according to Valéry, but the mind becomes increasingly stronger through the exercise of abstraction. . . . Whereas Baudelaire experienced enclosure within his own mind as a kind of nightmare, Valéry exults in this isolation as a source of freedom and creative energy, and in all of his meditations on the power of the creative agent seems to forget his insight into the independent power of language to which that agent is forced, at times, to submit. (pp. 90-1)

[Although] Valéry recognizes man's temporal condition and his inevitable biological need to return periodically to a state of formlessness (often figured as a sleeping woman, seductively fused with the natural world), he places priority in the wakeful, observing, synthesizing self and does not seem to grant that this wakeful self is as prey to the determining structures of language as the sleeping self is to suppressed memories from the past. Contrary to his Romantic and Symbolist predecessors, or to his Surrealist contemporaries, he sees no connection between the dream and the way our conscious mind perceives the "real" world; indeed, he never tires of stressing the unreliable nature of the dreaming or unconscious self as a source of perception, and this in the very terms ("fond," "abîme") which he uses elsewhere to describe the treachery of language. . . . (pp. 91-2)

Valéry claims that those who see the world through their deepest, most interiorized selves are prisoners of illusions . . . , whereas "godless mystics" like Berthe Morisot, who experience each instant as new, those whose seeing is not unconsciously obscured by habit, pastness, otherness of any kind, those, we must assume he means, who do not perceive through language, are those, paradoxically, most capable of the kind

of abstraction which "control" over language requires. . . . (p. 92)

Even in Valéry's two most extended meditations on the nature of language, seen as divided against itself and contaminated with impurities from past usage, *Questions de poésie* and *Poésie et pensée abstraite,* he nevertheless, as in the essays on the visual arts, proposes an artistic ideal similar to Mallarmé's of the reconciliation of form and meaning through the poet's godlike powers of invention. (p. 93)

[Dreams] like natural objects—tree, fruit, sea shell—all of which evolve according to laws of inner necessity, may serve as models for the poetic text—**"Au Platane," "Les Grenades," "L'Homme et la Coquille"**—but, for Valéry, the poem is always superior to those models because it is a conscious invention representing the inventor's powers of abstraction. It is worth noting that the terms by which he establishes the contrast between natural objects and man-made constructions are uncannily reminiscent of the ideal informing Baudelaire's "Paradis artificiels" or poems such as "Rêve parisien," where geometric regularity replaces organic growth, but these commentaries bear none of the traces of his predecessor's irony concerning the doomed nature of this ideal. . . . (pp. 93-4)

One might compare an achieved Valéry poem to an impressionist canvas or rather a series of canvasses like Monet's water lilies or the Cathedral at Rouen, where we are aware, as we look at the painting, of a perceiving consciousness composing according to the changes imposed on him by his temporal condition. In Valéry's verse we rediscover the immediate, tangible, discontinuous world of the senses. If his poetic vocabulary is generalized—sea, shore, sun, bird, tree, fruit—it nevertheless evokes the poet's origins in the Mediterranean world and the field of his empirical gaze. The poet does not use poetic language to describe what the eye records, but to provide a new structure which vivifies through figuration the disparate elements of sensuous reality in a form accessible to the intellect. In other words, the Valéryan word would not establish any direct, causal link between physical and poetic realities, but through its context within the poem acquire a relational connection to the ever-shifting perception of the thing-in-the-world.

There is probably no poet in the French language, including Mallarmé, who sought greater control over the relational possibilities of the word than Valéry. . . . Valéry's conservative interest in prosodic form can be understood as another sign of his urge to master the perversely independent nature of language. Yet the thoroughness he brought to the study of his medium produced a poetry far more striking for the complexity of the form/meaning relationship than the one described by the theoretician of "pure poetry."

Whenever Valéry speaks about the structures of language rather than about the creative process generally, he seems to modify considerably his claims for the power of the creative agent and even to recognize the control which language exerts over every one of our so-called "natural" experiences of the world. Thus, it is not surprising that the voice of the articulating agency which gives Valéry's poetry its distinctive character has an ambiguous function within his achieved verse. At the very moment it reminds us of the poet's power to create a "musicalized" poetry, free of reference, it breaks the "spell" and brings us back to the "non-poetic" world of critical commentary. Thus, one might say that the treatment of structure and figuration in Valéry's poetic work tells us more about his concept of poetry than any one of his theoretical essays. The ultimate Valéryan poem is one which not only evokes the musicalized garden in which nature and mind, form and meaning, presence and absence are reunited, but also one which introduces a third dimension which places that fragile harmony into question. The Narcissus who speaks breaks the charm of the Narcissus mirrored in the water as he comments upon the doomed beauty of the mythic couple. (pp. 95-7)

> *Suzanne Nash, in her* Paul Valéry's "Album de vers anciens:" A Past Transfigured, *Princeton University Press, 1983, 328 p.*

ADDITIONAL BIBLIOGRAPHY

Arnold, A. James. *Paul Valéry and His Critics.* Charlottesville: University Press of Virginia, 1970, 617 p.
  An annotated bibliography of criticism in French from 1890-1927 with an introduction in English.

Balakian, Anna. "The Afterglow." In her *The Symbolist Movement,* pp. 156-93. New York: Random House, 1967.*
  Examines Valéry's poem "The Graveyard by the Sea" as an example of late nineteenth-century Symbolism.

Bevan, Ernest, Jr. "Dialogue with the Self: Paul Valéry and Monsieur Teste." *Twentieth Century Literature* XXVI, No. 1 (Spring 1980): 15-26.
  Examines the Teste cycle and discusses the similarities and differences between Valéry and Teste.

Brombert, Victor. "Valéry: The Dance of Words." *Hudson Review* XXI, No. 4 (Winter 1968-69): 675-86.
  Discusses the prose texts that helped secure Valéry's literary reputation.

Burke, Kenneth. "Towards a Post-Kantian Verbal Music." *The Kenyon Review* XX, No. 4 (Autumn 1958): 529-46.
  Reviews *The Art of Poetry* and examines the musical structure of Valéry's verse.

Cruickshank, John V. "The Intellectual Response (II): Valéry and Analytical Detachment." In his *The Response to Catastrophe,* pp. 155-74. Oxford: Clarendon Press, 1982.
  Examines Valéry's political consciousness and his attitude toward World War I.

Decker, Henry. "Baudelaire and the Valéryan Concept of Pure Poetry." *Symposium* XIX, No. 2 (Summer 1965): 155-61.
  Contrasts the differing definitions of "poésie pure" proffered by Baudelaire and Valéry.

Eliot, T. S. "Dante." In his *The Sacred Wood,* pp. 159-72. London: Methuen & Co., 1920.*
  Takes issue with Valéry's statement (in *The Athenaeum,* 23 July 1920) that the role of the "modern poet" is "to produce in us a state."

——. "A Brief Introduction to the Method of Paul Valéry." In *Le Serpent,* by Paul Valéry, translated by Mark Wardle, pp. 7-15. London: The Criterion, 1924.
  A general but valuable introduction to Valéry's works and literary theory for the English-speaking reader.

Erickson, John D. "Valéry on Leonardo, Poe and Mallarmé." *L'Espirit Createur* XIII, No. 3 (1973): 252-59.
  Critiques Valéry's essays on his favorite artist and poets.

Frank, Joseph. "Paul Valéry: Masters and Friends." *Sewanee Review* LXXV, No. 3 (Summer 1967): 393-414.
  Discussion of the influences of Symbolism on Valéry's thought, his dislike of Naturalism, his disregard for the novel as an art

form, and his lifelong committment to finding a bridge between science and art.

Franklin, Ursula. "A Valéryan Trilogy: The Prose Poems 'ABC'." *Centennial Review* XX, No. 3 (Summer 1976): 244-56.
  Explains the unity and logical sequence of these prose poems.

Gibson, Robert. "Poetic Ends: Valéry." In his *Modern French Poets on Poetry,* pp. 115-25. London: Cambridge University Press, 1961.
  Explains Valéry's attitude toward poetry as a means of observing the workings of his mind.

Ince, W. N. *The Poetic Theory of Paul Valéry: Inspiration and Technique.* Leicester: Leicester University Press, 1961, 187 p.
  Outlines the six main points of Valéry's theory of inspiration.

——. "Resonance in Valéry." *Essays in French Literature* V, No. 5 (November 1968): 38-57.
  Discusses the range of meaning Valéry gives the word "resonance" in his notebooks.

Kennett, W.T.E. "Paul Valéry and the Dark Night of the Soul." *University of Toronto Quarterly* XXXIII, No. 2 (January 1964): 178-99.
  Discusses the mysticism in Valéry's poetry.

Lawler, James R. "The Meaning of Valéry's *Le Vin Perdu.*" *French Studies* XIV, No. 4 (October 1960): 340-57.
  Analysis of this poem with an examination of previous critical and scholarly commentary surrounding it.

——. "Valéry's Pureté." In his *The Language of French Symbolism,* pp. 185-217. Princeton: Princeton University Press, 1969.
  Examines Valéry's quest for a rigorous poetic language.

——, ed. Introduction to *Paul Valéry: An Anthology,* Vol. A, pp. vii-xxiii. Bollingen Series XLV. Princeton: Princeton University Press, 1977.
  Maintains that many critics falsely classify Valéry as a disciple of Mallarmé and the Symbolist movement. Lawler asserts that Valéry was intentionally creating a definition of poetry different from those of previous literary traditions.

Mackay, Agnes Ethel. *The Universal Self: A Study of Paul Valéry.* Toronto: University of Toronto Press, 1961. 263 p.
  Examines Valéry's life, his friendships, the development of his poetic theory, and the phases of his career.

[Murry, J. Middleton]. Review of *La jeune parque,* by Paul Valéry. *The Times Literary Supplement,* no. 814 (23 August 1917): 402.
  Review that introduced Valéry to the English-speaking world. Murry praises *La jeune parque* as an obscure but magnificent work.

Nadal, Octave. Introduction to *Poems in the Rough, Vol. 2.,* by Paul Valéry, translated by Hilary Corke, Bollingen Series Vol. XLV. Princeton: Princeton University Press, 1969.
  Discussion of Valéry's genius for writing prose poems, which contrasted with his longstanding refusal to acknowledge prose as an acceptable art form.

Pickering, Robert. "Energy and Integrated Poetic Experience in the Abstract Poetic Prose of Valéry's *Cahiers.*" *Australian Journal of French Studies* XVI, Part 2 (January-April 1979): 244-56.
  Discusses Valéry's notebooks in terms of their scientific expositions, with particular attention paid to Valéry's analyses of Einstein's theory of relativity and energy transference.

Quarterly Review of Literature, Special Issue: Paul Valéry III, No. 3 (Spring 1947): 92-168.
  Contains essays by such critics as T. S. Eliot, William Troy, Harold H. Watts, and Gustave Cohen. The essay by Eliot was originally titled "Leçon de Valéry" and is reprinted from the collection *Paul Valéry vivant,* published in the French in 1946.

Rice, Philip Blair. "Paul Valéry." In *Literary Opinion in America: Essays Illustrating the Status, Methods, and Problems of Criticism in the United States in the Twentieth Century, Vol. I,* edited by Morton

Dauwen Zabel, rev. ed., pp. 315-23. New York: Harper & Row Publishers, 1962.*

Discusses the universality of artistic nature, the characteristics of pure intellect, and the question of artistic purity as being of central importance to Valéry's work.

Rinsler, Norma. "The Defence of the Self: Stillness and Movement in Valéry's Poetry." *Essays in French Literature* VI, No. 6 (November 1969): 36-56.

Discusses *Monsieur Teste* as a portrayal of the artist's fear of action.

Robinson, Judith. "The Place of Literary and Artistic Creation in Valéry's Thought." *Modern Language Review* LVI, No. 4 (October 1961): 497-514.

Discusses the evidence in Valéry's works for a unified vision of the emotional and intellectual processes.

Scott, David. "Valéry and the Sonnet: A Critical Re-examination of His Theory and Practice." *Australian Journal of French Studies* XIV, No. 6 (September-December 1977): 264-277.

Analyzes Valéry's use of the sonnet form and points to the differences between his poetic theories and their practical applications.

Troy, William. "Paul Valéry and the Poetic Universe." In his *Selected Essays,* edited by Stanley Edgar Hyman, pp. 201-09. New Brunswick, N.J.: Rutgers University Press, 1967.

An analysis of Valéry's conception of a "poetic universe."

Wheelwright, Philip. Introduction to *Idée Fixe,* by Paul Valéry, translated by David Paul, pp. xiii-xxiii. New York: Pantheon Books, 1965.

Commentary on the philosophy presented in Valéry's conversational vignette.

Yale French Studies: Paul Valéry, No. 44, (1970): 3-230.

Issue devoted to the discussion of Valéry's career and writings, with essays by Judith Robinson, P. O. Walzer, Herbert S. Gershman, and many others.

Walter (Francis) White

1893-1955

American essayist, novelist, nonfiction writer, and autobiographer.

As a novelist of the Harlem Renaissance, White has been credited with expanding the thematic boundaries open to black writers in the early twentieth century. His novels *The Fire in the Flint* and *Flight* provided revolutionary depictions of middle-class black Americans and the effects of racism on their lives. A distinguished and influential civil rights activist, White gained national attention during the 1920s as an investigator of lynching for the National Association for the Advancement of Colored People (NAACP). His knowledge of mob violence in the South and his recorded interviews with witnesses and participants form the basis of his 1929 study *Rope and Faggot: A Biography of Judge Lynch,* in which White analyzed the underlying causes of lynching. White also wrote numerous essays that document the successes and failures of the American civil rights movement over a thirty-five year period, from the early 1920s through the mid-1950s. Primarily of historical significance today, White's works stirred the social conscience of America in their time.

White was one of seven children born to an Atlanta, Georgia, letter carrier and his wife, a former school teacher. The blond, blue-eyed son of light-complected black parents, White observed early that the type of reception he received from strangers often depended on whether his racial identity was known. In 1906, when he was thirteen years old, Atlanta was the scene of week-long racial violence that White later identified as the single most important influence on his decision to fight for racial justice and equality. Instigated by rumors of white women attacked by black men, roaming mobs beat, tortured, and murdered black citizens at random. White witnessed several acts of violence first hand while accompanying his father on the latter's mail route. When his family home was threatened, White and his father stood ready with firearms, but the rioters were scattered by gunfire from another house moments before they would have rampaged into the Whites' front yard.

After graduating from Atlanta Preparatory School, White went on to attend Atlanta University, and it was during his college years that he began working with the newly organized local chapter of the NAACP. In 1918 he was offered the job of assistant to the secretary by the association's national headquarters in New York. White accepted the position and was almost immediately chosen to investigate mob violence in the South, where his fair skin and youthful zeal made his impersonation of a Northern newspaper reporter believable. Most of the participants in and witnesses to mob violence whom White interviewed were eager to recount the crimes in vivid detail. Among those interviewed were public officials and community leaders who openly confessed their participation without fear of legal redress. White himself was deputized in Tulsa, Oklahoma, and told that he could kill any black person he chose. His essays on these investigations established a notoriety for White that soon made it impossible for his undercover activities to continue. However, his reputation as a champion of civil rights persisted as victims and concerned citizens from around the country sent pleas for help to the NAACP in care of White.

In 1929 White published *Rope and Faggot,* the result of two years of work in France on a Guggenheim Fellowship. This history of lynching in America was embellished with statistical tables correlating racial crimes to locale, based on population, religion, economy, and other factors. While most critics acknowledge the value of this study, many of the methods and conclusions have been questioned. Specifically, the sections that link racial violence to religious beliefs, and the chapter "Nordicism, Science and Religion," which discusses and refutes many old and previously exploded pseudoscientific theories of racial superiority and inferiority, have been charged with threatening the credibility of *Rope and Faggot* as a work of serious research. Such commentators as H. L. Mencken and Clarence Darrow, however, cite these correlations made by White as crucial to understanding and resolving the problem of mob rule. Notable in the criticism of *Rope and Faggot* are the critics' personal confessions of guilt and shame over the American people's acquiescence to lynching.

After the publication of *Rope and Faggot* and his return from France, White continued to work with the NAACP, and in 1931 he was elected to succeed James Weldon Johnson as the organization's national secretary. That same year White's father was struck by a car and later died of neglect in an Atlanta hospital, where he had been removed from the emergency room to the understaffed and poorly equipped section for black patients when it was discovered that he was not a white man. Years later White admitted that this was the one experience of his life which inspired lasting bitterness. An influential lobbyist in Washington, he stepped up efforts to secure passage of federal anti-lynching legislation, and also fought for equality in housing, education, and other areas. White's influence reached the White House, where he worked directly with presidents Franklin Roosevelt and Harry Truman to pass federal laws supporting racial equality. White was instrumental in bringing about passage of the Gavagan anti-lynching bill, and in blocking the appointment of segregationist John J. Parker to the United States Supreme Court during the 1930s. In 1939, after noted contralto Marion Anderson was denied permission to perform in the 4,000-seat Constitution Hall in Washington by the Daughters of the American Revolution, White arranged an open-air concert for her at the Lincoln Memorial, where she attracted an audience of 75,000 persons. American literature was also enriched through White's efforts on behalf of young writers, for he used his personal connections to bring the work of Nella Larsen, Countee Cullen, Langston Hughes, and others to the attention of publishers and editors.

During World War II, White travelled in Europe as a reporter for the *New York Post*. While overseas, he witnessed the officially sanctioned racism of the American armed forces as well as the European reaction to American racist myths. This prompted a series of articles on the subject that led to the collection *A Rising Wind*, essays which examine the worldwide implications of such policies. Critics generally regard the work as painfully enlightening, and consider the parallel drawn between American racism and imperialist domination throughout the third world intriguing, especially in light of White's suggestion that communism might prove an attractive alternative to the present political system for black Americans. White's work in this area, along with his struggle to bring about the deployment of black soldiers in combat areas, led to experimental integration in the armed forces. His final works, *A Man Called White* and *How Far the Promised Land?* provide a record of his work with the NAACP and the organization's overall influence on the racial policies in America during the first half of the twentieth century. Contemporary critics regarded the optimistic tone of the works, in the face of the facts they contain, a remarkable statement about White, who modestly downplayed his role in effecting the changes he recorded. Shortly before *How Far the Promised Land?* was published, White died in New York of a heart attack at the age of sixty-one.

In addition to his nonfiction, White published two novels. The first, *The Fire in the Flint*, reflects White's extensive research into lynching. The protagonist of this story, Dr. Kenneth Harper, is a Northern-educated black Atlantan who returns home to practice medicine and attempts to rise above prejudice through an optimistic faith in the power of reason. Gradually he is forced to abandon his nonconfrontational attitude and face the brutal realities of blind racism, and in the end he is lynched by a bloodthirsty mob after saving the life of a white child. The story, told from a middle-class black man's point of view, is a deliberate attempt to counter the romantic depictions of white Southerners made popular in the early decades of the twentieth century. The portrayal of culturally refined black characters was promoted by such Harlem Renaissance intellectuals as W.E.B. Du Bois, who sought to balance the American literary record with positive depictions of black people. However, such favorable stereotypes were often as unrealistic as the negative characters created by white authors. Although

the characterizations and prose style of *The Fire in the Flint* came under attack as stilted, archaic, and marred by clichés that detracted from the overall reality of the story, the novel is considered an accurate presentation of lynching and its attendant horrors. Infused with White's personal knowledge of the subject, the work nonetheless avoids dwelling on lurid details, unlike much of the socially conscious fiction written by American realists during the 1920s. Instead, graphic realism is achieved through a detailed examination of the physical, psychological, and economic effects of a racially tense environment on the people who live in it. For example, aristocratic landowners who perpetuate racial antagonism in order to maintain the status quo are contrasted with liberal, white Southerners who legitimately fear opposing the majority. The South's double-standard of justice, portrayed throughout the novel, is illustrated most effectively by the novel's pessimistic ending, in which a quotation from a newspaper report dismisses Harper as a common hoodlum slain during the commission of a crime. This marked the strongest indictment of Southern justice and morality in American fiction to that time. Most critics agree that despite the novel's heavy-handed propaganda, *The Fire in the Flint* is a compelling tragedy.

White's second novel, *Flight*, addresses the phenomenon of light-complected black people "passing" as Caucasians to escape racial barriers to equality. The story follows the life of Mimi, a New Orleans-born Creole who crosses the invisible racial boundary into mainstream white America. However, the novel breaks from the tradition of previous novels about passing, most of which depict a mulatto, envious of white society, attempting to blend in with that world. Rather, Mimi's decision to pass results from the sense of shame and disgrace she feels among black people who know about her illegitimate son. Many critics argue that White fails to achieve his major intention in the novel, which is to show the differences between black and white society. Other critics contend that White ignored an opportunity to divulge the unique psychological depths of Mimi and the other black characters in the novel. Only the early sections of the book, in which social stratification and prejudice among the black people in New Orleans and Atlanta come under scrutiny, are considered realistic and informative. Summing up the work's balance of success and failure, one critic noted that, while everything that happens to Mimi rings true, she never comes to life as a character, and that White's thesis—though based in fact—is not believably rendered.

Although his novels are little known today, White is remembered for his work as a political activist during the NAACP's most powerful years. One of the few black men in America of his time who had the ear of publishers, politicians, and world leaders, White used these associations to advance the equality of dark-skinned people in the United States and around the world.

PRINCIPAL WORKS

The Fire in the Flint (novel) 1924
Flight (novel) 1926
Rope and Faggot: A Biography of Judge Lynch
   (nonfiction) 1929
A Rising Wind: A Report of the Negro Soldier in the
   European Theater of War (nonfiction) 1945
A Man Called White (autobiography) 1948
How Far the Promised Land? (nonfiction) 1955

FREDA KIRCHWEY (essay date 1924)

[*In the following excerpt, Kirchwey praises the realism of* The Fire in the Flint, *which she finds is "warped by neither sentiment nor venom." Acknowledging weaknesses in prose style and characterization, she concludes that the novel succeeds on the strength of the "terrible truth and reality of its substance."*]

Other novels have been written about race relations in the South—novels overflowing with bitter venom and prejudice, sentimental novels, novels attempting an honest picture of a tangled, sordid scene. Novels better than [*The Fire in the Flint*] if you are looking for grace or subtlety, or depth or fire. And yet this novel is worth more than the best of the others I have read. Quite simply, in prosaic, often commonplace, phrasing, without lift or loveliness or sharp individuality, it manages to make a civilization live.

Walter F. White, Georgian and negro by birth, investigator and writer by profession, has put upon paper a problem that is in his own bone and fiber. He has taken back to a small Georgia town a young man who might have been himself, tolerant, educated, civilized and wise beyond his colored neighbors, and far beyond the majority of the white population. Kenneth Harper is a physician, and a good one. He is intelligent enough to feel superior to white intolerance, and to the growing resentment among his colored fellow-townsmen; he is intelligent enough to understand and smile and try to make life swing his way by the exercise of ability and good will.

And it does not work. To the uttermost limits of hate and blood and flame and torture, it wholly fails. Kenneth himself, almost fails. He finds himself pulled down by the horror of his sister's rape and his brother's death to a raging lust for vengeance. But he struggles up—up to a love of self-control and skill, on which he saves the life of a white girl, only to lose his own in the end at the hands of the same laughing, blood-crazy mob that killed his brother. His doctrine of amicable philosophic tolerance ends in a bewildering give and take of death.

The story is painful to a degree, and it is painful not primarily because it is tragic or bloody, but because Walter White knows so well what he is talking about. No one reading the book with any detachment could find it in him to doubt this picture of the economic and spiritual rottenness in the State of Georgia—where the negro farm worker is cheated of his poor earnings by the "land croppers" and the negro town dweller is driven to a state of sullen, dangerous resentment, and the ignorant white man through his Klan and his sheriffs and his courts, dominates the life of both races. The author does full justice to the plight of the intelligent white man, who wants to be "decent," as he does to that of the self-respecting negro who wants to be "good." Neither one is free to act; both are held by the solid mold of the life around them to helpless misery or futile opposition.

When white intolerance and ignorance and blood-lust finally come face to face with their natural offspring of black resentment and ignorance and pugnacity—what will be the end? Mr. White does not attempt to prophesy. The only reason for hope seems to lie in the steady migration northward of the more vigorous and ambitious negroes, who, like all oppressed peoples, seek a place to live and bring up their children in security and freedom. . . .

This note of hope is struck lightly. It is evident that no clear way out has shown itself to this writer. He is solidly, reasonably pessimistic. If a solution for the negro were to be found in hate and violent resistance, Kenneth's brother might have lived after avenging, so swiftly and terribly, the assault upon his sister. If friendly, self-respecting modesty on the part of the negro were to be his salvation, certainly Kenneth need not have been lynched. Both methods were tried with equal unsuccess by persons in the story, and, we may suppose they would equally fail if applied on a large and real scale. . . .

Walter White has written a book that lives and breathes by the terrible truth and reality of its substance. He has not made his way to the inner soul of his characters; he is not even their intimate friend. Nor has he painted the surface of their lives with the rich detail needed to make its straggling pattern clear before our eyes. He does not make ideas flame into drama; he achieves clarity rather than vision. But he writes from complete knowledge of a subject that is itself so full of force and feeling that it tells its own story. It hardly needs the helping hand of art or propaganda; it demands only direct and honest handling. A subject like this can properly be left to do its own exploding, work its own havoc. For the first time it has been allowed to stand out sharply, warped by neither sentiment nor venom, and declares its significance to the world.

> *Freda Kirchwey, "What Is the Solution?" in* New York Herald Tribune Books, *September 28, 1924, p. 5.*

W.E.B. DU BOIS (essay date 1924)

[*An American educator and man of letters, Du Bois is considered one of the most outstanding figures in twentieth-century American history. A founder of the National Association for the Advancement of Colored People (NAACP), Du Bois edited that organization's periodical* The Crisis *from 1910 to 1934. Considered the "dean" of the Rear Guard intellectuals whose works initiated the Harlem Renaissance in the 1920s, Du Bois deplored the movement in black literature toward exploiting sordid aspects of black American culture, and believed that the duty of the black writer was to depict exemplary characters who would counterbalance past stereotypes. In the following excerpt from a review that originally appeared in* The Crisis *in 1924, Du Bois notes that despite serious artistic problems,* The Fire in the Flint *is a good story and good propaganda. A realistic novel about the American South told from a black man's point of view,* The Fire in the Flint *is primarily important, according to Du Bois, as a landmark in American publishing.*]

Walter White has written in *The Fire in the Flint* a good, stirring story and a strong bit of propaganda against the white Klansman and the black pussyfoot. White knows his Georgia from A to Z. There is not a single incident or a single character in the book which has not its prototype in real life today. All Mr. White's white people are not villains nor are all his Negroes saints, but one gets a thrilling sense of the devilish tangle that involves good and evil in the southern South.

Perhaps most significant however is the fact that a book like this can at last be printed. For years a flood of filth about the Negro has poured out of the South while no northern firm would consider a book telling even temperately the well-known and widely proven facts concerning the Negro. Subtly and slowly the change has come and Mr. White has been among the first to sense it and to persist courageously and doggedly in having his say.

Of course one can criticise any book and particularly a first one. Perhaps on the economic side Mr. White succumbs too easily to the common mistake of piling the blame of southern wickedness on the "poor whites" and absolving the aristocrats and former slave holders. This is, of course, based on the propaganda which the sons and daughters of slave-barons have spread, but it is far from true. On the human and artistic side, with the possible exception of the younger brother, Mr. White's characters do not live and breathe and compel our sympathy. They are more like labeled figures on a chess board. But despite all this, this story goes and the reader goes with it and that is the first business of a story. (pp. 71-2)

> W.E.B. Du Bois, in a review of "The Fire in the Flint," in his Collected Published Works of W.E.B. Du Bois: Book Reviews, edited by Herbert Aptheker, KTO Press, 1977, pp. 71-2.

SURVEY   (essay date 1924)

[*In the following excerpt, The Fire in the Flint is assessed as a serious work about lynching and racism that suffers because of a contrived plot and melodramatic prose. The critic suggests that White was unable to translate the knowledge evident in his essays to fiction.*]

Walter F. White's **The Fire in the Flint** is such a serious effort by a Negro to write about Negroes that it deserves to face three questions: Did he have anything to say? Did he say it? Will anybody read it?

Did he have anything to say? He did. He had the tortuous clash of races, black on white. He had his own life as a Negro. He had stores of bitter truths learned as an investigator of race riots and lynchings. He knows what he is talking about. And to give power to all this he had the baffled emotional urge that only a Negro of culture can know in this white Nordic world. The fable for his revelations is almost too simple: an educated Negro surgeon comes back to his own little Georgia town to give his life to his profession among his fellow Negroes. Hooligan whites ravish his sister, and a younger brother who shoots a couple of them, is blood-hounded to a barn where he puts a bullet in his brain rather than surrender to lynching. The surgeon is lynched on a silly pretext, but really because he and his sweetheart are working to overthrow the Negro tenant peonage system. This sounds bloody and stark, and omits the lighter parts, but then what happens to Negroes is bloody and stark.

Did he say it? He did not. As a novel, we can praise and damn with the word "workman-like." We shall not damn it further with the apology that it is a good first novel, or a "good novel for a Negro." It is an ordinary novel; the plot a fortuitous contrivance, the characters self-conscious and talkative (save an old white judge), the style a mosaic of conventional phrases. It was learned in white schools and has no native Negro possession unless it be the underlying sense of dumb fury. What we would expect in the great Negro novel we don't know. But we cherish the hope when it comes it will have something of the Blake-like lyric symbolism of the spirituals, something of that impudence of gayety with which the race bluffs an iron cosmos.

The novel is a poor vehicle for this sort of propaganda. To make art of these matters takes almost genius—though it can be done as you'll find if you'll trouble to search out Harris Merton Lyon's little set of Graphics and read the bleak story of the Texas lynching bee. You have to deal with too strong meat; you can't be realistic enough to convince without be-

coming clinical. The agonizing details are cheapened by their veil of fiction. They demand the sombre garments of truth. Mr. White himself can tell these tragedies with noble horror—the real catharsis—as he has done in his reports for the National Association for the Advancement of Colored People. I shall remember a few sentences of his about the slitting of a pregnant Negress with a corn-knife as long as I live. But I shall forget his novel.

Will anybody read it? I hope so. Its truth is worth publishing. The sense of terror may surpass its medium. . . . It isn't a good enough novel to penetrate as literature; and as Mr. White hasn't Upton Sinclair's uncanny flair for the sensational approach, he can't win a hearing as a propagandist. However, it will penetrate some places, and by that much is helpful.

It is easily possible to make two mistakes about this book. One is to agree with a lot of critics that it is a wonderful thing for a Negro to write this book because *he knows*. Suppose he does, when did a victim write a good denunciation of his oppressor? He must be an exhibit, not an apologist. The apologists are aliens. . . . The grouch may be supremely righteous (certainly none could be more so than a Negro's claim for justice and humanity), but the fact remains that a personal grouch is not a cosmic law, and a novel based thereon never as moving as the cold-blooded detachment of a curious spectator.

The second mistake is that we unconsciously agree with the author's thesis—that the Negro wants a chance to become as much like the white man as possible. All such books are paradoxes. They must paint the whites as largely mean and brutal, yet they set up a claim that the whites' privileges (including meanness and brutality) be extended to the Negro. Reading such books I can conceive of the consuming hatred a Negro must feel against being a Negro, but I would think he would have a much more consuming hatred against being a white.

Mr. White drops two hints of a practical sort. One, perhaps not new, that the Negro's economic situation may be relieved by farmers' co-operatives conducted by and for him; and the other, that the mumbo-jumbo of the Ku Klux Klan no longer frightens him, but makes him laugh. (pp. 160-62)

> "A Novel by a Negro," in Survey, Vol. LIII, No. 3, November 1, 1924, pp. 160-62.

CARL VAN VECHTEN   (essay date 1926)

[*Van Vechten, an American critic and novelist, was one of the first established white authors after William Dean Howells to take a serious and active role in studying and promoting the works of black writers, musicians, and artists. Noted during the early 1920s for his sophisticated novels about New Yorkers, Van Vechten's most famous work is* Nigger Heaven (1926), *a novel set in Harlem. Praised by many critics as realistic and exotic, the popularity of the work helped spark interest in black culture among white Americans. The black press, however, considered the work offensive and derogatory. W.E.B. Du Bois, notable among the novel's detractors, charged Van Vechten with insinuating himself into Harlem for exploitive purposes and with presenting a one-sided picture of the community. White had introduced Van Vechten to Harlem society and had used his influence to secure advertising space for Van Vechten in initially reluctant black publications. In the following excerpt, Van Vechten commends White for presenting a believable black heroine in* Flight *and compares Mimi to the protagonists in Ellen Glasgow's works. He also notes that Mimi's decision to "pass" is a reaction to cruelty by black people rather than by white people, which places the novel outside of the propagandist school of black American literature.*]

Mr. White's first novel, **"The Fire in the Flint,"** . . . was immediately and widely hailed as a work of grim power. Dealing as it does with peonage, rape and lynching in Georgia, certain of its scenes are executed with a force sufficiently elemental to efface the memory of some amateurish writing in other passages.

It is a pleasure to be able to state that Mr. White's second novel ["**Flight**"] is much better than his first. It is written with a calm detachment of which **"The Fire in the Flint"** contains no hint. Furthermore, in Mimi Daquin, a Negro Creole girl with ivory skin and hair of reddish gold, the author has drawn a character entirely new to Afro-American fiction. Instead of the persecuted figure with which books on this general subject have made us so familiar, we are presented with a heroine who is mistress of her own fate, a woman whose ultimate acts are governed by her will. Mimi does not long permit herself to be hampered by the restrictions of Negro life and she is equally independent in her relations with the two men who play important parts in her career. She refuses to marry the father of her child; later, she leaves her white husband to return to the heart of her own race.

The subject of passing (i.e., passing for white) has infrequently been utilized by Negro authors. Charles W. Chesnutt dwelt on its tragic aspects in "The House Behind the Cedars" (1902) and James Weldon Johnson contributed a more suave study of the theme in that human document, "The Autobiography of an ex-Colored Man" (1912). . . .

This, then, is the distinguishing merit of this novel, that it focuses attention upon a Negro character who is not materially hindered in her career by white prejudice. It is the simple chronicle of a beautiful, intelligent, dignified, self-supporting Negro girl. There is, indeed, a curious resemblance between Mimi and the self-reliant heroines of Miss Ellen Glasgow. . . .

Mr. White approaches the subject from a new and sufficiently sensational point of view. Mimi Daquin does not leave the colored world because she has been insulted or humiliated by white people; she leaves it because of her momentary dissatisfaction with Negroes. . . .

The incidental Negro characters are in nowise depicted as paragons of propriety and good taste. In fact, occasionally the author deals with them even a little cruelly. The petty gossip, the small meannesses, the color snobbery of Negro society . . . are fully described, but Mr. White makes it plain that in these respects there is little to choose between the two worlds.

In short, an excellent novel which should be read with increasing wonder by those who are unfamiliar with the less sordid circles of Negro life, and which others may read simply as a story without thought of propaganda. Indeed, with this second book Mr. White takes on quite a new stature.

> Carl Van Vechten, *"A Triumphant Negro Heroine,"* in New York Herald Tribune Books, *April 11, 1926, p. 3.*

THE NEW YORK TIMES BOOK REVIEW   (essay date 1926)

[*In the following excerpt it is argued that, despite an objective thesis and a realistic plot,* Flight *fails artistically because Mimi's characterization never attains believability.*]

"Flight" is less important and persuasive than **"The Fire in the Flint."** Its conclusion seems, somehow, predetermined. The thesis of the novel has great cogency and meaning, but the novel itself, the history of Mimi, fails to achieve its first requirement—humanity. The course of her life is wholly credible; there is nothing improbable about what happens to Mimi, or about how it happens externally; but Mimi herself is inadequately humanized. There is no reason in the world why the final realization which comes to this woman, so conscious of her race and weary of the conventional life of the whites, should not be a sense of oneness and sympathy with the negroes, and an understanding that her happiness lies among them. After living as a white she comes back to the negroes as in "God of Might" Elias Tobenkin's Jew, after living with Christians, comes back to the Jews, as a thousand expatriates come back to their native land. Indeed, her return may be supremely true to type; but for that very reason it seems predestined here: because Mimi is not a living human being and must be judged from type. Mr. White, in other words, makes his thesis convincing, but not his particular example; he demonstrates a factual truth but not an artistic one.

Perhaps in the long run the thesis here is more significant than the creation of character. And Mr. White, painting pictures, driving home truths, suggesting indictments, draws that thesis with an admirable objectivity. Whatever his sense of injustice, whatever his temptation toward pathos, he lets his story speak for itself. His picture of an Atlanta riot against the negroes needs no commentary to be rousing. His indictment of our present white civilization, standardized and smug, symbolized in radios and good plumbing, is no more pointed than his indictment of the negro world which apes that civilization. That is why Mimi's realization at the end is no more predetermined than it is forceful; being predetermined, it simply becomes more acutely didactic. Only in native soil will the roots of the negro thrive and achieve florescence, Mr. White infers; and doing so he reaches a conclusion so often reached that it has the obviousness of a platitude, but the impregnability of an axiom. But in addition he suggests that many enlightened negroes must feel not only the general wisdom but also the personal necessity for doing so.

> *"Black and White," in* The New York Times Book Review, *April 11, 1926, p. 9.*

D. H. LAWRENCE   (essay date 1927)

[*An English man of letters, Lawrence was one of the first novelists to introduce themes of modern psychology into his fiction. In his lifetime he was a controversial figure, both for the explicit sexuality he portrayed in his novels and for his unconventional personal life. Much of the criticism of Lawrence's work revolves around his highly individualistic moral system, which is based on absolute freedom of expression, particularly sexual expression. In the following excerpt from a review originally published in 1927, White's novel* Flight—*which Lawrence calls another "nigger book"—is negatively critiqued. While he considers the sections on life in New Orleans and Atlanta interesting, Lawrence argues that the work is devoid of a "black soul." Therefore, he concludes, the ending of the novel is ludicrous, since Mimi is indistinguishable from bored white heroines who momentarily escape their lives only to return to the comfort and security of upper-class white America.*]

[*Nigger Heaven*, by Carl Van Vechten] is a false book by an author who lingers in nigger cabarets hoping to heaven to pick up something to write about and make a sensation—and, of course, money.

Flight is another nigger book; much more respectable, but not much more important. The author, we are told, is himself a

Negro. If we weren't told, we should never know. But there is rather a call for coloured stuff, hence we had better be informed when we're getting it.

The first part of *Flight* is interesting—the removal of Creoles, just creamy-coloured old French-Negro mixture, from the Creole quarter of New Orleans to the Negro quarter of Atlanta. This is real, as far as life goes, and external reality: except that to me, the Creole quarter of New Orleans is dead and lugubrious as a Jews' burying ground, instead of highly romantic. But the first part of *Flight* is good Negro *data.*

The culture of Mr. White's Creoles is much more acceptable than that of Mr. Van Vechten's Harlem golden-browns. If it is only skin-deep, that is quite enough, since the pigmentation of the skin seems to be the only difference between the Negro and the white man. If there be such a thing as a Negro soul, then that of the Creole is very very French-American, and that of the Harlemite is very very Yankee-American. In fact, there seems no blackness about it at all. Reading Negro books, or books about Negroes written from the Negro standpoint, it is absolutely impossible to discover that the nigger is any blacker inside than we are. He's an absolute white man, save for the colour of his skin: which, in many cases, is also just as white as a Mediterranean white man's.

It is rather disappointing. One likes to cherish illusions about the race soul, the eternal Negroid soul, black and glistening and touched with awfulness and with mystery. One is not allowed. The nigger is a white man through and through. He even sees himself as white men see him, blacker than he ought to be. And his soul is an Edison gramophone on which one puts the current records: which is what the white man's soul is, just the same, a gramophone grinding over the old records. (pp. 361-62)

Apparently there is only one feeling about the Negro, wherein he differs from the white man, according to Mr. White; and this is the feeling of warmth and humanness. But *we* don't feel even that. More mercurial, but not by any means warmer or more human, the nigger seems to be: even in nigger books. And he sees in himself a talent for life which the white man has lost. But remembering glimpses of Harlem and Louisiana, and the down-at-heel greyness of the colourless Negro *ambiente,* myself I don't feel even that.

But the one thing the Negro *knows* he can do, is sing and dance. He knows it, because the white man has pointed it out to him so often. There, again, however, disappointment! About one nigger in a thousand amounts to anything in song or dance: the rest are just as songful and limber as the rest of Americans.

Mimi, the pale-biscuit heroine of *Flight,* neither sings nor dances. She is rather cultured and makes smart dresses and passes over as white, then marries a well-to-do white American, but leaves him because he is not "live" enough, and goes back to Harlem. It is just what Nordic wives do, just how they feel about their husbands. And if they don't go to Harlem, they go somewhere else. And then they come back. As Mimi will do. Three months of Nigger Heaven will have her fed up, and back she'll be over the white line, settling again in the Washington Square region, and being "of French extraction." Nothing is more monotonous than these removals.

All these books might as well be called *Flight.* They give one the impression of swarms of grasshoppers hopping big hops, and buzzing occasionally on the wing, all from nowhere to nowhere, all over the place. What's the point of all this flight, when they start from nowhere and alight on nowhere? For the Nigger Heaven is as sure a nowhere as anywhere else. (pp. 362-63)

> *D. H. Lawrence, in a review of "Flight," in his* Phoenix: The Posthumous Papers of D. H. Lawrence, *edited by Edward D. McDonald, The Viking Press, 1936, pp. 361-63.*

CLARENCE DARROW   (essay date 1929)

[*Darrow was an American lawyer, social reformer, lecturer, and writer, who defended many unpopular causes during his legal career. His most famous case, known as the Scopes Monkey Trial, opened the door to the teaching of evolution in America's public schools. In 1925 White and the NAACP encouraged Darrow to defend the family of a black doctor who, accused of committing criminal assault, claimed self-defense against the armed attack of hostile white neighbors. The family was acquitted, and Darrow and White became friends. In the following excerpt, Darrow favorably appraises the study* Rope and Faggot, *noting in particular the chapter entitled "Science, Nordicism, and Lynching," which he contends evinces sound anthropological analysis. In an opposing view, Melville J. Herskovits (1929) cites this chapter as the book's weakest point.*]

This book [*Rope and Faggot*] is written with care and discusses every phase of lynching and burning from its inception, around the year 1830, to the present time. The facts are not taken from biased reports, but from statistics and newspaper accounts published in the vicinity of the operations. Some of the book is gruesome in the extreme, and it is impossible to understand how any people, savage or civilized, could be guilty of the atrocities depicted. The number of lynchings and burnings are taken from official figures and "credited" to the various states where they occurred. It is perfectly obvious that most of the Negroes who are the victims of these outrages were lynched and burned because they were Negroes. . . .

The reader who cares for horrors can find them galore in this book. He needs but read the details and descriptions of burnings, which seem to be enjoyed by all except the victims. . . .

Mr. White shows that in the most religious communities, where lynchings are highest, practically no minister ever raises his voice against them. Recent outbreaks he attributes to the growth of the absurd doctrine of Nordic supremacy, and to the new Ku Klux Klan, which was organized by a Methodist preacher, while many of its sub-organizers were Protestant clergymen formerly connected with the Anti-Saloon League.

Many suggestions are made as to what to do, all useful and enlightening. Mr. White seems to favor the Federal anti-lynching law. I am not so sanguine; I have seen too much of extending Federal powers to want to see any more of it, especially in a good cause. He overestimates the effect of punishment, as most people are wont to overestimate it. The truth is that even those who commit crimes often consider the penalty very little, and mobs notoriously give it no heed. . . .

To any one who cares to know about the question of race, the alleged differences between the white and colored—if there happens to be any one of this kind—I would especially commend Mr. White's chapter on Science, Nordicism and Lynching. I am convinced that he has been a good student of anthropology and knows what he is talking about. This book should be read by every citizen of the United States. It might possibly do them some good.

Clarence Darrow, "The Shame of America," in New York Herald Tribune Books, April 21, 1929, p. 3.

MELVILLE J. HERSKOVITS (essay date 1929)

[*Herskovits, an American anthropologist and scientific explorer, has written studies based on his travels in Dutch Guiana, Haiti, West Africa, Trinidad, and Brazil. The author of* The American Negro: A Study in Racial Crossing *(1928) and* The Myth of the Negro Past *(1941), Herskovits is concerned with the consequences that result from moving a culture to a new environment where another culture is already established, and with the relationship between a culture and its work, music, and art. In the following excerpt, Herskovits argues that the restrained analytical approach employed by White in* Rope and Faggot *is inappropriate to the passionate subject of the work. Although he contends that the work is "healthy, sane, and desirable," Herskovits nonetheless finds White's analysis of the relationship between lynching and sex, sadism and religion, and the chapter "Science, Nordicism, and Religion" to be poorly supported by scientific evidence and irrelevant to the general tenor of the work. For an opposing view of the chapter, see the excerpt by Clarence Darrow (1929).*]

[We] wonder if Mr. White's restrained treatment of his theme meets the purpose of his book ["**Rope and Faggot**"].

Certainly no one is more competent than Mr. White to tell of the phenomenon of lynching, especially when it has to do with Negroes. . . . In his reports and in one of his novels he has given the theme the stark treatment it deserves, making his reader blaze with indignation at the sheer barbarity he describes. But in this book there is relatively little of the passionate protest for which we hope. There is, rather, a calm, measured analysis which, while convincing, is obviously not Mr. White's forte. And the book he has produced suffers because of his academic approach. I realize that had Mr. White written with the feeling of which he is capable he would be condemned by some for not being sufficiently dispassionate. Yet Judge Lynch is a ruffian, and is not to be handled with kid gloves.

The book, therefore, must be discussed as an analytical treatment of lynching rather than as an emotional protest against it. And as such it has many excellent pages. The second chapter, which treats of the extent to which lynching occurs, is most revealing, and cites several striking cases. Taken in connection with the statistical appendix it affords a mine of factual material for those who wish to know the facts. The consideration of the relation between lynching and its economic background is a demonstration of the grasp of the subject which Mr. White possesses. The chapter entitled The Price of Lynching is another of the brilliant sections which this work contains. And the digest of what has been done to stem the tide of lynching through legal enactment is readable and useful. Nor does Mr. White end on a false note of optimism. He is, above all, a realist, and he is sufficiently tough-minded to face the situation in all its grayness of outlook.

Some of the reasoning in other chapters, I must confess, I cannot follow. I do not believe that a statement such as this can be substantiated: "It is exceedingly doubtful if lynching could possibly exist under any other religion than Christianity." If this hypothesis can be maintained it should hold true at least for all Christian sects, and not only for the Baptists and Methodists, as Mr. White claims. This statement, the thesis of an entire chapter, seems to me to be too simplistic to be acceptable, and to this extent it weakens the general argument of the book. In a similar way the chapter in which Judge Lynch

is psychoanalyzed seems to me to contain a theoretical approach which is pushed much farther than our present knowledge allows. That there is a sex element present in the sadistic performances with which those who have gone into the accounts of lynchings are familiar, must be admitted; but to make this a basic cause throws the picture out of focus.

The chapter which is entitled Science, Nordicism, and Lynching, I think is ill-advised. For one thing, too much old material is rehandled. Must one read again of Bean's study of brain-weight of Negroes and whites and Mall's refutation of it? Must the army psychological tests once more be refuted? These have been discussed so often that I do not see that they need be repeated here, where they are literally brought in by main force and where they have little to do with the main subject of the book. If Mr. White wished to discuss theories of racial inferiority and superiority, he should have found at least some of the fresh work that has recently been done. Instead, he has relied on frayed secondary sources and, as a result, gives us only these well-worn accounts.

However, Mr. White does not claim to be an expert in the fields of religious psychology, psychoanalysis, or comparative anatomy. He has fought too courageously and too intelligently against Judge Lynch for us to carp at him for these chapters in his book. There is in it much considered presentation of the highest order; there are many facts which we all should know; and there is a point of view that is healthy, sane, and desirable.

Melville J. Herskovits, "Lynching, an American Pastime," in The Nation, Vol. CXXVIII, No. 3332, May 15, 1929, p. 588.

H. L. MENCKEN (essay date 1929)

[*From the era of World War I until the early years of the Great Depression, Mencken was one of the most influential figures in American letters. His strongly individualistic, irreverent outlook on life and his vigorous invective-charged writing style helped establish the iconoclastic spirit of the Jazz Age and significantly shaped the direction of American literature. As a social and literary critic—the role for which he is best known—Mencken was the scourge of evangelical Christianity, public service organizations, literary censorship, provincialism, democracy, and every other facet of American life he perceived as humbug. In "The Sahara of the Bozart"—considered a powerful catalyst in spurring realism in Southern literature—Mencken attacked the paucity of beaux arts in Southern culture as well as the tendency in the region's literature toward romanticizing the Old South as a land of latter-day knights and fair ladies. As the editor of* The American Mercury *magazine and through his personal friendship with publisher Alfred A. Knopf, Mencken provided a forum for young black writers, whose works he critiqued with the same uncondescending standards by which he judged all literature. Black writers from James Weldon Johnson to Richard Wright have acknowledged Mencken's immense influence on the development of their personal literary standards. In correspondence with White, Mencken encouraged him to write an honest story about the South based on his own knowledge and experience, in response to* Birthright *(1922), a novel by the Tennesseean T. S. Stribling. The result of White's labors was* The Fire in the Flint, *the author's first novel. In the following excerpt, Mencken discusses White's study* Rope and Faggot, *and elaborates on the purported relationship between religious practices and racial violence in the rural South.*]

It pleases Mr. White, who is a man of somewhat bitter humor, to call himself an Aframerican; he is actually almost as albino as his name, with sandy hair and china blue eyes. . . . [The] National Association for the Advancement of Colored People has sent him into the South to investigate lynchings. . . . The result of his vast experience in the Bible country, born of this unique equipment, is that he knows more about lynching than anyone else in America. He has inquired into all sorts of communal butcheries, from the simple hanging of a village bad man to the appallingly barbarous disemboweling, torture and burning of a woman with child, and at the same time he has made shrewd examination of the social background and mental equipment of the lynchers. His book [*Rope & Faggot*], in consequence, is a mine of valuable information, set forth plausibly and without too much indignation. There are unspeakable horrors in it, but he does not dwell upon them unduly. His main business is not to describe lynching, but to describe lynchers.

It will surprise no one who knows the South, I take it, to hear from him that the incidence of lynching runs in almost direct proportion to the percentage of Methodists and Baptists in the population. The reason is not far to seek. The two great evangelical faiths, down in that country, are little more than schemes of organized hatred. Their theology has been reduced to the simple doctrine that the other fellow is a scoundrel and will go to hell. (p. 382)

Other factors, to be sure, enter into the matter: among them, density of population and wealth *per capita*. The rich and heavily populated States, such as North Carolina, tend to abandon lynching. They have relatively efficient police, and their more numerous towns give them something of the city point of view. . . .

The automobile, bringing in better roads, has also brought in a kind of civilization. Movie shows take the peasants away from the village store, and its political and theological disputations. Some of them, putting in radios, begin to defy the pastors by dancing. The revival business is not what it used to be. But in the backwaters, despite these signs of change, religion remains the chief concern of the hinds, and it is religion of a peculiarly unenlightened and degrading kind. . . . So long as it dominates the minds of the Southern poor whites they will remain barbarians, and so long as they are barbarians they will turn out ever and anon to butcher and barbecue a hapless darkey. The civilized Southerners waste their time combating, not the underlying disease, but superficial symptoms. If they would release the South from its bondage to ignorance and superstition, they must first destroy the simian theocracy that keeps it shackled. There is no other way out. (p. 383)

> *H. L. Mencken, "Sport in the Bible Country," in*
> American Mercury, *Vol. XVII, No. 67, July, 1929,*
> *pp. 382-83.*

FRANCIS HACKETT (essay date 1945)

[*Hackett was a respected Irish-American biographer, novelist, and literary critic during the first half of the twentieth century. His reviews appeared in* The New Republic, The Saturday Review of Literature, *and other prominent American periodicals. In the following excerpt from a review published in 1945, Hackett positively appraises* A Rising Wind.]

A short book on an inescapable theme is often the best, and Walter White has served his cause by being terse in *A Rising Wind.* The second half of it, partly a high and glowing account of Eboué, the Negro Frenchman who saved Chad for the United Nations, branches away from the main theme, but the first half of it probes directly and tellingly into dark places. It makes the book important, not simply because Mr. White speaks as secretary of the National Association for the Advancement of

Colored People, but because he is possessed by one of those mastering passions to which no wise American can refuse heed and no good citizen refuse sympathy. (p. 186)

Mr. White went overseas to look into the war and to see how the Negro soldier was getting on, but he could not have supposed that an English family would be providing cushions for Negro visitors, having heard from white soldiers that Negro tails were awkward. Mr. White tells of this. He also tells of a town in England that was led to believe that Negroes could bark but not talk. At first the Negro soldiers resented the legend, but their good humor got the better of them. They began by barking softly. The English caught on. They were soon barking back, and the joke was on the white men who started it.

These are gargoyles of race hatred. Mr. White found it had also been given official sanction, not at the top but through the Army. There were "off limits" rules on the basis of race. Red Cross segregation in clubs, not in hospitals, aroused Mr. White's scorn. He quotes a fantastic document telling the British about Negro infantility, issued by a Southern commanding officer. Then there were false charges of rape and specific injustices. And in Italy there were malignant circulars and posters.

It is impossible to read *A Rising Wind* without being moved to indignation. Mr. White does it by exhibiting these blind ignorances, these humiliating examples of prejudice off the limits. Much worse is it to hear of Negro combat troops willfully deprived of combat service. Knowing how white fliers felt about their Negro fellows who won proud laurels in combat, it seems atrocious that American citizens should, because of color, have "to fight for the right to fight." (pp. 186-87)

[Grimness] is not disguised; Mr. White does not hesitate to close his book with a menace, and the menace is Russia. Unless the western powers revolutionize their racial concepts and practices, he says, a World War III must be prepared for, and the colored peoples everywhere may "move into the Russian orbit as the lesser of two dangers." (p. 187)

A Rising Wind is a manifesto of this, and much that Mr. White saw of the Negro's status in World War II supports him. "World War II," he says, "has immeasurably magnified the Negro's awareness of the disparity between the American profession and practice of democracy." . . .

[One] telling though small instance of American idealism came in Devon when Mrs. Leonard Elmhirst (Dorothy Whitney) refused to comply with white officers who demanded that guests' cards be rescinded from Negro trainees invited to a dance. In specific instances, too, General Eisenhower impartially reviewed and corrected injustices. (p. 188)

A Rising Wind is based on substantial reality. In this war there are six times as many Negro officers as in the last, but there are only six thousand. The barriers to military service have only been slightly lifted. Granted that woman suffrage had to fight deep prejudice quite recently, as Mr. White knows, he still has a powerful case, and he presents it honestly and unflinchingly. Without a World War III, the pride of the Negro can be respected on American lines, but Mr. White does well to tell America that Russian race ideology is in the world to stay. Russia guarantees race status. That is a new factor. It is just as big and broad and inescapable as the Mississippi. (pp. 188-89)

Francis Hackett, "Affairs in General: Race Ideal-ogy, U.S.A.," in his On Judging Books: In General and in Particular, The John Day Company, 1947, pp. 186-89.

JOHN DESMOND (essay date 1945)

[In the following excerpt, Desmond discusses the findings of White's study A Rising Wind.]

At the last counting there were 701,678 Negroes in the United States Army. Of these, 411,368 were overseas; the rest were scattered at various stations in the United States. Only a few of the troops overseas had seen active combat duty. Those who had—like the Ninety-ninth Pursuit Squadron of the MAAF of the Ninety-second Infantry in Italy—had made combat records comparable to their white fellow-soldiers. But in the Negroes' eyes these had been few in proportion to the number of Negroes in uniform. This "discrimination" has been the subject of study by numerous observers. . . .

One such study is offered in [A Rising Wind,] Walter White's survey of the conditions of Negro troops in England, Africa and Italy. Mr. White went overseas with the consent and active cooperation of the American High Command. He had an ex-cellent opportunity to observe the relations between Negroes and whites in their billets and, in England at least, the relations between Negroes and the native white population. This book is a report on those observations. For the most part it is a pulling together and an elucidation of information that has trickled back to this country in the form of newspaper accounts and letters from soldiers.

In brief it adds up to this: that much of the racial discrimination that is an unfortunate part of American life has been exported to England and other war theaters; that many white Americans, despite the many changes that war has brought them, have not altered greatly in their racial thinking; and that, in a more hopeful vein, there has been, particularly among enlisted men, a noticeable letting down of racial bars.

In evaluating these observations Mr. White discouragingly points out that the first two represent conditions that are fairly con-stant, while the third exists chiefly in combat areas where men are drawn into close interdependence by the presence of danger. This prompted him to plead the more fervently with American military authorities to assign greater numbers of Negroes to first-line divisions. In this quest, he gratefully comments, he found many Army officers, from General Eisenhower down, sympathetic and helpful.

Mr. White concedes that it is too late in this war to change the patterns of the Army and Navy in such a way as to hasten a solution of the post-war problem. But he reminds us that Negro soldiers and sailors who have served in the uniforms of the United States in the various war theatres will not be content to return to the old way of life in the post-war era. . . .

How white America meets this challenge, Mr. White implies, may well determine the stability and durability of the peace. He points out, as have many other commentators, that the Negro problem is no longer exclusively American. In a world in which the so-called "white races" are in the minority, Mr. White reminds us, the non-whites will regard our relations among fellow-Americans as an earnest of our intentions toward the people of China, India and Africa. It is a challenge that cannot be sidestepped. Mr. White's reasoned and reserved con-tribution to it deserves to be read by all. . . .

John Desmond, "Reporting on Our Negro Troops Overseas," in The New York Times Book Review, March 4, 1945, p. 3.

ANNE L. GOODMAN (essay date 1948)

[In the following excerpt, Goodman praises A Man Called White, citing its vivid insight into the problem of American racial oppres-sion.]

[A Man Called White] is both autobiography and a study of the Negro problem in America written from a peculiar vantage point. Walter White, as he makes clear in his opening para-graph, could pass anywhere for a white man. (p. 23)

At the same time, and despite the ugly experience in his youth that first forced the fact of his race upon him, he has, it seems obvious, been spared some of the worst humiliations of the Negro—the slights from casually encountered strangers, the omnipresent fact of a black skin and the awareness of it ev-erywhere: in a store, restaurant, theatre, subway. White has moved between two worlds, consciously a member of the one but able to pass at will into the other without the constant, choking resentment of the unmistakable Negro, to whom no choice is offered.

The advantages of this have been a self-confidence, apparent in his writing, and a perspective that enables him to see the attitude of the white man to the Negro as well as the reverse, and the wider problem of prejudice. . . .

White relates his experiences in an easy and readable manner, but his facts, not his writing, give the book its force. However familiar the details of American race prejudice during the last thirty years may be, this factual, personal recapitulation of them comes with a new shock. That the struggle White de-scribes is one of the most important parts of the most important struggle in America today—the struggle to realize as well as to preserve the democracy we boast of—seems self-evi-dent. . . .

Perhaps the most shocking evidence in White's book appears in the later chapters which recount the postwar maimings and lynchings of Negro veterans. We have read of them before, but seldom in such detail and without other distracting news of the cold war and the rising cost of living, which has helped to hide their real significance.

In conclusion, White lists recent advances on behalf of the Negro, achievements which "would have seemed to most Ne-groes only a dream of the millennium even twenty-five years ago." If they seem pitifully weak when weighed against the evidence on the other side, they still cannot be overlooked . . . The NAACP's battle is far from won, but, White seems to suggest, there are signs that we approach the turning point. (p. 24)

Anne L. Goodman, "Blockade Runner," in The New Republic, Vol. 119, No. 16, October 18, 1948, pp. 23-4.

HUGH M. GLOSTER (essay date 1948)

[Gloster, an American author and critic, was contributing editor to the periodical Phylon from 1949 to 1953, and is the author of Negro Voices in American Fiction (1948). In the following excerpt from that work, he discusses White's exposé of prejudice among bourgeois black Americans in the novel Flight. The Fire in the Flint, which Gloster argues is among the best postwar propa-

gandist novels written, is praised for revealing some of the problems faced by black Southerners with professional training, and for illuminating the tactics used by upper-class white Southerners in pitting lower-class white people and black people against one another in order to preserve the social and economic status quo.]

Jessie Fauset, Walter White, and Nella Larsen present well-bred, educated, aspiring Negroes who belong mainly to the professional class of the urban North. Among these people economic security and high social standing are in evidence; and within their group, except for minor variations caused by color, they live very much like other respectable middle-class Americans. Attention is focused principally upon attractive and personable mulatto heroines who yearn to "drink life to the lees" but find it difficult to do so because of racial restrictions. When fair enough in color, these women sometimes seek happiness through escape into the white world; but, after the initial thrills of passing are over, they usually long for colored society and come to believe that Negro life, though circumscribed by prejudice and persecution, is not altogether without spiritual and cultural compensations. This point of view, by the way, stands in bold contrast to that expressed in such novels as Vara Caspary's *White Girl* (1929) and Geoffrey Barnes's *Dark Lustre* (1932), in which passing heroines, whose refinement is attributed to Nordic and whose animalism to African extraction, cross the color line because of admiration for white and abhorrence for black people but experience misery because of the "taint" of Negro blood. (p. 131)

In addition to treating the problem of passing in the urban North, Walter White's *Flight* . . . provides a study of the colored bourgeoisie of Atlanta, Georgia. (p. 139)

Flight affords a vivid commentary on Babbittry and life among Negroes of Atlanta. Through Robertson, Mimi's stepgrandparent, White satirizes Negroes who are preoccupied with the acquisition of wealth. Atlanta's social elite—placing emphasis on light pigmentation and outspoken in their dislike for Catholics, Jews, and black Negroes—are described as "victims of a system which made colour and hair texture and race a fetish." Gossip, slander, bickerings, jealousies, and sartorial competiton are listed as the chief activities of bourgeois colored women. The author finds solid worth and genuine strength, however, among poor Negroes who, though deprived and mistreated, can nevertheless sing, laugh, have faith, and find enjoyment in an industrial civilization which often makes the dominant white man unhappy, morbid, and depressed. . . . [The] power to resist and endure is attributed largely to Negroes' "rare gift of lifting themselves emotionally and spiritually far, far above their material lives and selves." (pp. 139-40)

Between 1918 and 1928 White . . . probed forty-one lynchings and eight race riots. In 1924 he produced *The Fire in the Flint,* one of the most successful exposés of lynching in American fiction; and in 1929, assisted by a Guggenheim fellowship, he wrote ***Rope and Faggot: A Biography of Judge Lynch,*** a penetrating analysis of the causes, functioning, and cures of mob violence.

The Fire in the Flint, in which White uses fiction as the medium for his attack on lynching and the Southern small town, is chiefly the story of Kenneth Harper, a young Negro physician trained in the best universities of America and France. After World War I, Harper returns to Central City, Georgia, where his family resides, to practise medicine. . . . (pp. 147-48)

White's description of Central City is an authentic portrait of a half-rural, half-urban Georgia town. The various sections of

The title page of the novel Flight, *by Walter White. Knopf, 1926. Copyright 1926 by Alfred A. Knopf, Inc. Reprinted by permission of the publisher.*

the place—the dusty trading district, the respectable residential area, the squalid and filthy Negro ghetto, and the equally dingy and unsanitary cotton mill vicinity in which tubercular and cadaverous poor whites dwell—are convincingly pictured. In this warped environment learning and culture are decadent and effete, but the noxious growth of race prejudice thrives and prospers. Selfish, hypocritical demagogues separate Negroes and poor whites by keeping alive in the latter group a confidence in their own natural superiority and a belief that their safety rests in the subjugation of black people. In every possible way Negroes are made to feel that they are predestined to a subordinate status. They have neither legal redress nor police protection. In business dealings they are the victims of thievery and chicanery. They accept dilapidated schools and underpaid teachers and tolerate the abduction of their women and the lynching of their men. To survive in this Jim-Crow environment they practise dissimulation, evasion, and secretiveness and seek an outlet for their pent-up feelings in emotional religion. Ready to terrorize and punish the black population for infractions of the Southern code, the Ku Klux Klan, having members from all classes of white society, stands dedicated to the maintenance of Nordic supremacy and the perpetuation of the *status quo.* . . . The author describes liberal and sympathetic white Southerners as men "hemmed in, oppressed, afraid to call their souls their own, creatures of the Frankenstein monster their own people had created which seemed about to rise up and destroy its creators.'' (pp. 148-49)

In training, experience, and racial philosophy Kenneth Harper is similar to his probable archetype, Dr. William Miller of Chesnutt's *The Marrow of Tradition* (1901). Both are products of the best Northern and European schools, both turn their backs on practising above the Mason-Dixon Line in order to devote their efforts to the improvement of the health of the colored people of the South, and both—in spite of all evidence and counsel to the contrary—are optimistic regarding a peaceful settlement of racial difficulties. Much like Miller's are Harper's conciliatory and accommodating views on the Negro's plight. . . . Just as Miller, after the slaying of his son in a riot, ministers to the pressing needs of a sick white boy, so Harper, after the loss of his sister and brother, comes to the rescue of a very ill white girl and thus sets the stage for his own destruction. Before his death, however, he reaches the same bitter and rebellious position which Miller finally attains.

Standing in bold contrast to his philosophical and phlegmatic brother, Bob Harper represents Negro combativeness at its zenith. Sensitive and perspicacious, he broods over prejudice and is easily stirred to resentment and anger. (pp. 149-50)

More than any other novel of the Negro Renascence, *Fire in the Flint* probes the precarious position of Negroes in a small Southern town. As a living argument against prejudice and brutality, the author presents a refined, intelligent, and prosperous family that suffers insults, injuries, and deaths because of superficial distinctions based on color and caste. The difficulties of the Negro professional man are set forth, and attention is called to his troubles with dominant whites as well as with Negroes whose slavery-conditioned minds make them reluctant to trust trained members of their own race. Also revealed is the success of the Southern ruling class in pitting poor whites against Negroes by nurturing concepts of Nordic superiority. (pp. 150-51)

> Hugh M. Gloster, ''Fiction of the Negro Renascence,'' in his Negro Voices in American Fiction, The University of North Carolina Press, 1948, pp. 116-95.*

RALPH J. BUNCHE   (essay date 1955)

[*Bunche was a distinguished American educator and diplomat who became internationally renowned for his work as the United Nations Mediator in Palestine during the late 1940s. For his role in negotiating the 1949 Arab-Israeli truce he was awarded the Spingarn medal by the NAACP and the Nobel Peace Prize. In the following excerpt from his foreword to* How Far the Promised Land? *Bunche offers high praise for White's character and for his work in the field of interracial reconciliation.*]

I was privileged over a long period to enjoy Walter White's friendship. I admired him highly and developed a deep affection for him. One so seldom meets a truly dedicated person, and when such a one is also keenly intelligent, vibrant, engaging, and warmly human—and this was Walter White—his going leaves a sorrowful void.

In this book [*How Far the Promised Land?*] are his last thoughts and written words on the progress of the Negro toward full equality in the American society. They are straightforward words which are vital and commanding for everyone who believes in democracy and freedom and the dignity of the indi-

vidual man. They are the words of a man whose life, in fuller measure than that of any I have known, was devoted to making American democracy a complete and equal reality for the black as well as the white citizen. And, characteristically, they are words of utter frankness and full integrity, and also of hope.

He gave to this book a title in the form of a question: *How Far the Promised Land?*—how far off is the day when the American citizen of Negro descent will walk beside his white fellow citizen in full equality? Thanks to Walter White's vision, his leadership, and his unflinching devotion for more than three decades, the answer today comes unmistakably clear: ''It cannot be far.'' For he brought the Negro close to the border of that land—perhaps even closer than he himself realized. Moreover, the good fight led by him will be carried on relentlessly by his surviving associates in the National Association for the Advancement of Colored People, which continues to grow in strength and prestige throughout the country, due to a steadily expanding body of sympathizers and supporters of all races and creeds who realize that democracy to be true must be color-blind. The basic element in Walter's faith in our country, in the American way of life, and in the inevitable achievement of full citizenship by the Negro was the conviction—and I believe it was soundly based—that the vast majority of Americans really believe in that democracy whose principles we profess and can therefore be arrayed against practices of racial injustice. His task it was—and he performed it well through the NAACP and the media of mass communication—to arouse the American conscience to the crude and costly injustice in the treatment of its minority-group citizens, and to mobilize sentiment behind the elimination of all undemocratic practices and attitudes. (pp. ix-x)

This is dynamic history written by a man who was one of the most dynamic figures of our times. We do not go backward, we do not stand still, he said; American democracy moves forward. There is an ever-stronger current of democracy which eventually will carry *all* Americans into the ''Promised Land.'' He left behind him the reasoned hope that Lincoln's work of emancipation, in its major aspects, can actually be completed by 1963—the centennial of Lincoln's signing of the Emancipation Proclamation. (p. xi)

> Ralph J. Bunche, in a foreword to How Far the Promised Land? by Walter White, The Viking Press, 1955, pp. ix-xii.

GERALD W. JOHNSON   (essay date 1955)

[*In the following excerpt, Johnson praises* How Far the Promised Land? *as the crowning achievement of White's career.*]

If there were no other reason this book [*How Far the Promised Land?*] would command attention as the last word of a man who was cast in the truly heroic mold. But there is another and even better reason—the book is a careful account by a close observer of one of the most remarkable achievements in human history, the rise of the American Negro. . . .

He was probably the best informed man in the country on the trend of race relations. What he says on the subject may be accepted as factually authoritative, and what he says in this book will be widely regarded as sensational. He suggests—although he does not predict—that the last legal handicap laid upon the American Negro by reason of his race may be removed by 1963, naming that particular year since it will then be exactly one hundred years since the Emancipation Proclamation went into effect. . . .

The abolition even of the legal restrictions would be an achievement of immense significance; yet a journey abroad showed White that nobody in Asia and Africa and, to tell the truth, not even the average American, has an adequate appreciation of the magnitude of the achievement. So he wrote this book to give an outline of the titanic struggle by which it came to pass. Its thesis is that whereas our enemies, especially the Communists, harp constantly on the fact that after nearly a hundred years the American Negro is still not quite free, the really remarkable thing is that in less than a hundred years former chattels have climbed almost to the rank of first-class citizens, as far as the law is concerned.

This feat is without historical parallel. So White regards the fact that the American Negro's complete success is now plainly in sight as vindication of the theory of democratic government.

The book nowhere suggests it, but the fact is that much of the credit for the feat belongs to the author. Walter White was a Negro leader not by act of God, but by his own deliberate choice. I remember my own astonishment when I first encountered him a quarter of a century ago. His eyes were blue and his skin and hair definitely lighter than my own. At any time, by moving his residence perhaps twenty miles and changing his name to Black he might have acquired all the rights and privileges appertaining to a representative of the Anglo-Saxon race. . . .

Nevertheless, White must have been aware that, although he scorned to go through it, there was always behind him an open door of escape. This raises a question as to what extent he was truly representative, psychologically, of black men for whom there is no escape. It probably accounts for the fact that among darker-skinned Negroes White's leadership, while admittedly valuable, was always regarded as a little doctrinaire, a trifle bookish. To them he stood somewhat as Woodrow Wilson stood in relation to most Democratic politicians—great, certainly, but a little apart, a shade aloof.

It is possible that his last book may be regarded in that same light by the bulk of the Negro population. Ralph Bunche, it is true, takes no such attitude in the very moving foreword he contributes to the volume, but Dr. Bunche can hardly be accepted as typical of the common man. It would be imprudent, to put it mildly, for a white reviewer to call the book representative of Negro opinion. On the other hand, it is definitely not representative of any widespread white opinion. It is, rather, an in-between opinion, and by that same token it may be closer to objective truth than the dominant habit of thought in either race.

In any event, it is an intensely American document, as regards both its subject-matter and the political axioms on which its argument is based.

> *Gerald W. Johnson, "An American Testament," in* The New York Times Book Review, *November 6, 1955, p. 46.*

ALAN PATON   (essay date 1955)

[*Paton, a South African novelist, educator, and social activist, has worked with liberal political groups fighting against South Africa's white supremacist policies. When Paton's novel,* Cry, the Beloved Country (1948) *was published, it became an international literary and commercial success. His second novel,* Too

Late the Phalarope (1953) is concerned, like the first, with the plight of black Africans in a homeland dominated by a white minority. In the following excerpt, Paton favorably summarizes How Far the Promised Land?, *and finds the most interesting part of the book to be White's analysis of black Americans' resistance to communism despite their mistreatment under a democratic system.*]

It is related in the Book of Deuteronomy that Moses the Lawgiver, leader of the Israelites, was permitted by God to climb Mount Pisgah, and to see from there the Promised Land which he himself would never enter.

To Walter White was given a like privilege before he died. He too ascended onto a high mountain and looked down on the Promised Land. This book [*How Far the Promised Land?*] is his account of it, an affirmation of his certainty that although he might not enter the land himself, others would enter it for him. Of his own leadership during the closing days of this long journey through the wilderness he says hardly a word. He has praise for the courage of others, but his own courage one must discover for oneself.

Mr. White's own estimate of the position of the Negro in America today is clear and unequivocal. There are still heights to be conquered, dangers to be overcome, sufferings to be endured; but the long journey is nearing its end.

He describes the change in American opinion that has made it possible for more and more Negroes to exercise their votes and he refutes convincingly the charge that Negroes vote as Negroes for Negroes. He describes the situation in the field of labor, and gives a balance sheet of advances and standstills (with almost no reverses). In health, travel, and all kinds of public accommodations, the direction is emphatically away from discrimination and deprivation. Mr. White is generous to the Church, even though the practices of segregation are still markedly prevalent, and he is probably right here, because the problem of the Church is no longer the persuading of one society to admit the other. It is the persuading of two separate societies to draw closer together.

It appears to me that Mr. White reserves his highest praise for the Armed Forces, and that certainly is where the highest praise belongs, even if one reflects that integration was a practical rather than a moral necessity.

It is in the field of housing that Mr. White judges the least progress to have been made. The swing away from discrimination is discernible, but the pace is too slow. He condemns utterly the National Association of Real Estate Boards as anti-Negro and advocates of segregation, and he attacks the Federal Housing Administration for the same reason. But he gives high and merited praise to the City of New York.

Mr. White writes an interesting chapter on the Negro and communism. Why did so few Negroes ever join the Communist party? Why has the party almost no Negro support today? Why did the Negro reject the Communist solution to his grievous wrongs? Mr. White rightly does not give the chief praise to American democracy and justice. He gives the chief praise to the Negro himself, to his complete rejection of any domination by man over man; it was the Negro himself who understood what American democracy should and could be and who, courageously and intelligently, used the American Constitution as the instrument of his emancipation. . . .

Mr. White describes the continuous struggle of the NAACP to have the Constitution interpreted by the Courts. It is fitting that his opening chapter should deal with the momentous decision of the United States Supreme Court on May 17, 1954, that separate educational facilities are inherently unequal, and he describes that unforgettable occasion. . . .

I am glad that he lived to hear the great decision which was the crowning of the unselfish labor of himself and his friends. But Walter White was no simpleton; he knew that the carrying out of the decision would be a long and at times painful task.

I am glad also to have the honor of recommending his account of the long journey to all those who cherish American democracy. No one did more to uphold it, maintain it, advance it, than the man who wrote this book. Happy the man who makes such use of his life.

> *Alan Paton, "A Great Negro's Story of His People's Long Journey," in* New York Herald Tribune Book Review, *December 11, 1955, p. 1.*

ROBERT A. BONE   (essay date 1965)

[*Bone, an American critic and educator, is the author of the critical histories* The Negro in America *(1958) and* Down Home: A History of Short Fiction from Its Beginnings to the End of the Harlem Renaissance *(1975). A student of Afro-American, English, and American literature, with a special interest in Shakespeare, Bone has said of himself: "A white man and critic of black literature, I try to demonstrate by the quality of my work that scholarship is not the same thing as identity." In the following excerpt from* The Negro in America, *Bone discusses White's novels and their relationship to the Harlem Renaissance literary school, which promoted the depiction of educated middle-class black characters and the psychological examination of black people who give up their cultural identity to "pass" into white America. Bone concludes that* The Fire in the Flint *and* Flight *are poor novels because White had neither the time nor the talent for creative writing.*]

The storm of controversy which greeted the Harlem School in the mid-1920's marks the beginning of a growing breach between the Negro writer and the Negro middle class. The early Negro novelist, insulated from the impact of modern literature by a culture lag, was firmly integrated into the social class which produced him. With the advent of the Harlem School, however, the Negro novelist begins to develop that sense of alienation from bourgeois society which is the mark of the modern artist. (p. 96)

A distinguishing characteristic of this school is its fondness for the novel of "passing." Walter White's *Flight* . . . , Jessie Fauset's *Plum Bun* (1928), and Nella Larsen's *Passing* (1929), all deal in a similar vein with this exotic theme. Emphasis is placed on the problems which confront the person who passes: the fear of discovery, the anxious prospect of marriage, with its fear of throwback, and so forth. The invariable outcome, in fiction if not in fact, is disillusionment with life on the other side of the line, a new appreciation of racial values, and an irresistible longing to return to the Negro community. (p. 98)

At the present time it is no longer required of a Negro author that he enter political life, nor of a Negro political leader that he write novels. There was a time, however, before the present age of specialization, when a Negro intellectual of national stature was expected to double in brass. Only a few men of rare versatility such as James Weldon Johnson were equal to the challenge. Others, like Walter White and W.E.B. DuBois, were sometimes tempted into waters beyond their depth. Able political leaders and competent writers of expository prose,

these men lacked the creative imagination which is the *sine qua non* of good fiction.

Walter White's first novel, *The Fire in the Flint* . . . , is an antilynching tract of melodramatic proportions. It was written in twelve days, according to White, and the novel itself provides no grounds for doubting his word. It is essentially a series of essays, strung on an unconvincing plot, involving the misfortunes of a colored doctor and his family in a small Southern town. White's second novel, *Flight* . . . , is an undistinguished treatment of passing, perhaps more susceptible to the influence of the Harlem School than most novels of the Rear Guard. Taken together, Walter White's novels comprise an object lesson in what Blyden Jackson has called "Faith without Works in Negro Literature." (pp. 99-100)

> *Robert A. Bone, "The Rear Guard," in his* The Negro Novel in America, *revised edition, Yale University Press, 1965, pp. 95-108.**

EDWARD E. WALDRON   (essay date 1978)

[*Waldron is an American author and critic whose articles have appeared in* CLA Journal, Phylon, Negro American Literature Forum, *and other periodicals. In the following excerpt from his critical study* Walter White and the Harlem Renaissance, *Waldron assesses* The Fire in the Flint *as a thematically interesting but artistically weak novel. In addition to his discussion of the novel's dominant theme—Kenneth Harper's awakening to the realities of racism—Waldron also discusses important secondary concerns of the novel: lynching, personal ethics, and officially sanctioned economic and political oppression. While acknowledging that* Flight *is less didactic than* Fire in the Flint, *Waldron still considers its prose weak and its characterizations sentimental. The only exceptions, Waldron notes, are in descriptive passages on movement, color, and music, which form a motif that contrasts the life-styles of black and white people.*]

In his autobiography White stated that his decision to write a novel about the true racial conditions in the South was a response to a challenge by H. L. Mencken. (p. 42)

The plot of *The Fire in the Flint* is relatively simple. Kenneth Harper, after being educated at Atlanta University and a "Northern medical school" and after serving in France during World War I, returns to his home town of Central City, Georgia, intent on becoming the best surgeon in southern Georgia; he even dreams of eventually opening a clinic "something like the Mayo Brothers up in Rochester, Minnesota." On his return he finds his younger brother Bob extremely pessimistic about the possibility of any cooperation from the whites. Kenneth believes, however, that if he leaves the white folks alone, they will leave him alone. In fact, at the beginning of the novel he voices his belief that black people have to make it on their own individual initiative. . . . *Fire,* then, becomes a study of Kenneth Harper's gradual awakening to the realities of racism and the demands imposed upon the individual by an oppressed people.

Robert Bone's analysis of the novel as "a series of essays, strung on an unconvincing plot . . ." [see excerpt dated 1965] is perhaps too severe a judgment. True, the novel is episodic and melodramatic and frequently ranges into exposition, but there is a change in the central character, however belabored, and there is occasional insight into human nature. The Reverend Mr. Wilson, a black preacher, for example, startles Kenneth when his ordinarily crude speech becomes refined in private conversation. Chuckling, the older man explains a fact of southern black life to his young and racially naive neighbor:

> There's a reason—in fact there are two reasons why I talk like that [i.e., crudely]. The first is because of my own folks. Outside of you and your folks . . . and one or two more, all of my congregation is made up of folks with little or no education. They've all got good hard common sense. . . . But they don't want a preacher that's too far above them—they'll feel that they can't come to him with their troubles if he's too highfalutin. I try to get right down to my folks, feel as they feel, suffer when they suffer, laugh with them when they laugh, and talk with them in language they can understand. . . . And then there's the other reason. . . . The white folks here are mighty suspicious of any Negro who has too much learning, according to their standards. They figure he'll be stirring up the Negroes to fight back when any trouble arises. . . .

Here, in a character many white writers would present as a Bible-banging buffoon, White gives us an insight into the workings of the mind of a man who decided to mask his true capabilities in order to serve his people. And Kenneth Harper soon learns that the Reverend Mr. Wilson's statement about the suspicions white folks have of educated Negroes is accurate. (pp. 43-4)

[His] sister is raped by a gang of white toughs, and then Bob, after he succeeds in killing two of the boys who raped his sister, is hunted down and finally kills himself to prevent being taken by the mob. . . . When [Kenneth] . . . discovers what has happened, he goes into a tirade of hate against the white world which has all but destroyed his family. . . . (p. 44)

Mrs. Ewing, a white woman whose daughter Kenneth had saved earlier, calls . . . to ask Kenneth's help. . . . His first impulse is to tell her that "if by raising one finger I could save the whole white race from destruction, and by not raising it send them all straight to hell, I'd die before I raised it!" Eventually, though, his training as a doctor and Mrs. Ewing's revelation that her husband has gone to Atlanta to warn Kenneth not to return outweigh his bitterness, and he goes to the Ewings. Meanwhile, some Klansmen (including Sheriff Parker), who have been following Harper's every move, see him enter the house. . . . When Kenneth leaves, the men grab him and, after a fierce struggle, shoot him. The next day a news dispatch headed "ANOTHER NEGRO LYNCHED IN GEORGIA" presents the "official" version of the incident. . . . Deciding to end the novel with [a] callous and obviously falsified news release was probably the most artistic stroke White accomplished in *The Fire in the Flint*. It serves as its own comment on the climactic events of the novel, and avoids the didacticism which is so characteristic of the rest of the novel.

In addition to the dominant protest against the evils of lynching, White also incorporated other minor themes of protest in *Fire*. A significant subplot is developed concerning the efforts of Kenneth Harper and some of the farmers to form a co-op from which the sharecroppers could buy their supplies at reasonable prices, instead of being gouged by the stores from which they are forced to buy. . . . Although the idea of a farmer's cooperative being used to alleviate the suffering of sharecroppers in what has been aptly termed "legalized slavery" is not new

in White's novel, the merging of the protest motif with the larger antilynching theme underscores the economic factor in racial oppression that White felt was central to the problem.

The real strength of *The Fire in the Flint* lies, finally, in what it says, not in how well it says it. There are flaws in the story and, as Bone points out, there is too much exposition for narrative fiction. White's treatment of the love story involving Kenneth Harper and Jane Phillips is incredibly naive and more fitting a sentimental novel than a novel of protest. And the characters, with a few exceptions, are flatly drawn types. The Reverend Mr. Wilson is given some depth, but only after a rather stereotyped caricature of him as a "pompous, bulbous-eyed" and vain man, "exceedingly fond of long words, especially of Latin derivation." It is almost as if White changed his mind about the good Reverend in the process of writing the story. The treatment of white characters in *Fire* is even more sparse; there are few admirable white representatives in it. Judge Stevenson is one exception, and Roy Ewing is another, although Ewing at first wants nothing to do with the "nigger doctor" who operates on his daughter. Sheriff Parker and the rest of the white townspeople are presented as ignorant, bovine creatures who mull over murder as other men debate the necessity of removing crabgrass.

But we must keep in mind that this is 1924, a time when people were still being lynched with some regularity and when most white Americans' concept of Negroes was based upon the caricatures of the minstrel shows and the beasts haunting the pages of Thomas Dixon and his compatriots. *Fire* not only presented a sympathetic examination of the trials confronting an educated black man in a society geared to grind him into submission or a grave, it also presented a look at some of the foibles of that society as seen from a black perspective. For example, at the beginning of the novel Roy Ewing comes to Kenneth Harper for treatment of a "social disease" contracted during a night of abandon in Macon. As White says: "That was Kenneth's introduction to one part of the work of a colored physician in the South. Many phases of life that he as a youth had never known about . . . he now had brought to his attention." Harper was also appalled by the whorehouses thriving in Central City, especially the ones in "Darktown": "Here were coloured women who seemed never to have to work. Here was seldom seen a coloured man. And the children around these houses were usually lighter in colour than in other parts of 'Darktown'." . . . White makes good use of his naive hero in these passages. A seasoned cynic would hardly remark the obvious discrepancies of what the whites preached about segregation and what they practiced; he would simply accept it as a matter of course. Through the eyes of the innocent Kenneth Harper, though, White can let his white reader see a world through eyes that are just as unused to the light as his own. Judging from the reactions of people who wrote White after reading the novel, this is exactly the effect the book had, at least in some quarters. (pp. 45-7)

Clearly, White was hoping his second novel would be an improvement over his first effort; he sought to overcome the propaganda label and to treat his characters more realistically. While he achieved his first goal, whether he achieved the second became the subject of some critical debate.

Flight centers on the life of Mimi Daquin (Annette Angela Daquin) as she experiences the pressures of Negro life, in the South and in the North, and the further pressures she faces when she decides to pass. (p. 83)

Walter White's style did not improve much in his second effort. In *Flight,* as in *The Fire in the Flint,* White depended heavily on melodramatic clichés in phrasing and in plot. Whenever Mimi leaves one life situation for another, inevitably she feels as if she were "opening a new book" or closing an old one. The . . . description of Jimmie Forrester after he has pined for months for Mimi is an almost classic stereotype of the rejected suitor. . . . On many occasions White's use of figurative language is awkward and, at the very least, questionable. He used this simile, for example, in describing the Atlanta gossips: "Like a great orchestra beginning *pianissimo* upon a symphony, the tongues started clacking in soft and cryptic whisperings." . . . (pp. 86-7)

There are, however, moments of some beauty or impact in *Flight,* especially centering around Jean's love of New Orleans or Mimi's fascination with Harlem. . . . In addition to the descriptions of Harlem . . . , White also offered this observation by Mimi on the Kaleidoscope of colors within the black community. Mimi is attending a dance at the Manhattan Casino when she observes

> faces of all colours, peeping from gowns of all shades. . . . There were faces of a mahogany brownness which shaded into the blackness of crisply curled hair. There were some of a blackness that shone like rich bits of velvet. There were others whose skins seemed as though made of expertly tanned leather with the creaminess of old vellum, topped by shining hair, blacker than "a thousand midnights, down in a cypress swamp." And there were those with ivory-white complexions, rare old ivory that time had mellowed with a gentle touch. To Mimi the most alluring of all were the women who were neither dark nor light, as many of them were, but those of that indefinable blend of brown and red, giving a richness that was reminiscent of the Creoles of her own New Orleans. . . .

In moments like these White is closer to the Harlem school of Hughes and McKay than to the "rear guard" of Du Bois and Fauset.

Perhaps the best description in the novel comes at the climactic scene in Carnegie Hall when Mimi is transported by the singer into a fantastic world of vision. Here White develops the impressions the spirituals create within Mimi:

> A vast impenetrable tangle of huge trees appeared, their pithy bulk rising in ebon beauty to prodigious heights. As she gazed, half afraid of the wild stillness, the trees became less and less blackly solid, shading off into ever lighter grays. Then the trees were white, then there were none at all. In their stead an immense circular clearing in which moved at first slowly, then with increasing speed, a ring of graceful, rounded, lithe women and stalward, magnificently muscled men, all with skins of midnight blackness. To music of barbaric sweetness and rhythm they danced with sinuous grace and abandon. . . .

From this vision Mimi enters another, where "weird creatures" burst upon the scene; with their "black reeds which spurted lead and flame," these invaders overpowered the dancers and took them across the ocean:

> . . . she saw a ship wallowing in the trough of immense waves. Aboard there strode up and down unshaven, deep-eyed, fierce-looking sailors who sought with oath and blow and kick to still the clamorous outcries of their black passengers. These were close packed in ill-smelling, inadequate quarters where each day stalked the specter whose visit meant one less mouth to feed. . . .

From that point the vision proceeds naturally to the plantations and fields of the new land, "a world of motion and labour . . . caught up and held immobile in the tenuous, reluctant notes" of the singer. In these passages White transcends the rather laborious prose of most of the novel and reaches a level of description that suggests both the strikingly stark work of Aaron Douglas and the rounded fullness of Hale Woodruff's paintings. Moments like these, unfortunately, are much the exception in White's novels.

As in *The Fire in the Flint,* thematic ideas are much more important in *Flight* than matters of art and style. While the themes of White's second novel are not as dramatically arresting as the dominant lynching theme of his first work, White does consider in *Flight* some essential issues facing the black community. The first of these is the idea of passing, and the forces which operate to drive one to pass out of her race into another. For Mimi the dominant forces which serve to drive her out center on pressures from within the race, specifically color consciousness, religious prejudice, and the petty jealousies of foolish gossips. In New Orleans it is Mimi's stepmother Mary who is confronted by prejudices of the "mellow old families, militantly proud of their Creole and Negro ancestry." In addition to being "an outsider," Mary has skin of "deep brown, in sharp contrast to the ivory tint of Jean and Mimi." . . . In Atlanta color is not so much a factor, at least for the Daquins, as religion. As Catholics, Jean and Mimi are totally out of step with the black community there. But it is the petty gossiping that finally drives Mimi into passing. The Fleur-de-Lis Club's gossip about Mrs. Adams's attempts to pass and the jealous "coloured person" who "turned her in" provide one sample of that gossip; the "story" Mrs. Plummer gives the Harlem gossip rag, the *Blabber,* is another, and the one which finally drives Mimi out. . . . With a great deal of sadness Mimi concludes that "her passing from the race seemed . . . persecution greater than any white people had ever visited upon her—the very intolerance of her own people had driven her from them."

In her new "white" life Mimi becomes terribly conscious of the distinctions between the two lifestyles, the white and the black. There is a quality to the latter which is completely missing in the former. . . . The contrast White draws between white folks and black folks hinges mostly on those two qualities: the lively, graceful spirit of the black community versus the somber, mechanical life of the white world.

Along with this concept of a difference between the two races goes the idea of racism, a topic which, as White himself suggested, no black writer could really ignore. In *Flight* White makes use of his own experience in the Atlanta riot of 1906 and recreates that riot in the novel, involving Jean and Mimi in some of the experiences he had faced as a young boy. In setting the stage for his fictionalized riot, White establishes the same causes he discussed in *A Man Called White* as the prime factors for the 1906 explosion: a long hot summer which frayed nerves and sharpened tempers "to razor-blade keenness''; a period of unemployment which caused ''a marked loafing of whites and Negroes followed by a long series of petty crimes''; a ''bitter political campaign, . . . its central issue the disenfranchisement of Negroes and 'Negro domination'''; a presentation of *The Clansman;* and an irresponsible, sensation-seeking press. . . . Just as Walter White and his father had been caught out in the midst of the riot, Jean and Mimi are likewise witness to several brutal scenes. (pp. 87-90)

For Mimi, as for Walter White, this riot acts as an agent for racial identity; it solidifies the racial ties. . . [After] the riot had quieted, White states: ''Mimi dated thereafter her consciousness of being coloured from September, nineteen hundred and six. For her the old order had passed, she was now definitely of a race set apart.'' . . . This sounds very close to White's comment in *A Man Called White*. . . . (pp. 90-1)

Mimi's race identity and rare pride are other important elements in the novel. Whether in Atlanta, Harlem, or white New York, Mimi constantly senses the influences that draw her to her people. When they first arrive in Atlanta, Mimi and her father listen to an unfamiliar sound in a blues exchange between a man and a woman outside their window. They strain ''to catch every note of this barbaric, melancholy wail as it [dies] in the distance, a strange thrill filling them.'' . . . Later Mimi watches a Negro convict gang at work and is fascinated by their work song. . . . While White's conception of the effect of a work song on the men working is terribly romanticized, at least he has his character in contact with the basic musical elements that make up her heritage as a black American. In fact, within a few pages White covers the work song, the spiritual, and jazz, and the effect each has on Mimi's developing race consciousness. Her reaction to the spiritual ''Were You There When They Crucified My Lord?'' in this section anticipates the effect of the Carnegie Hall concert at the end of the novel. . . . At a dance attended by Mimi and Mrs. Rodgers, Mimi marvels at the ''easy grace,'' the variety of color, and the spontaneity that mark the people of Harlem as something special. After she passes over into the white world, she becomes increasingly aware of an emptiness within her, and her trip to Harlem with Bert Bellamy and her experience at Carnegie Hall convince her that she can never be whole, can never be completely satisfied until she rejoins her people and submerges herself once more in the soothing world she left behind.

The emptiness Mimi feels during her life in the white world stems, in large part, from the mechanization of that world. The role of the machine in the (white) Western world is the last of the thematic concerns of *Flight,* and one which puts it in tune with much of the literature of White's contemporaries. . . . [We] see White playing on an important theme of early twentieth-century literature: the real possibility that man might become subordinate to his mechanical creations, and ultimately become the servant rather than the served.

Echoing another set of sentiments of the time, White offers American Negroes as a group of people who have managed to escape the trap of mechanization and who are all the better for having escaped. After listening to the black chain gang, Mimi considers with admiration the strength shown by those men in the face of terrible adversity. . . . (pp. 90-3)

Perhaps White's most noticeable improvement in *Flight* was in the area of characterization, at least in terms of fairer treatment of whites and blacks. While there are still more stereotypes than real people in the novel, there are some ''bad'' black characters and some ''good'' white ones. The almost perfect

Jean and Mimi are balanced by the gossipy Mrs. Plummer and her cohorts, and the myopic Jimmie Forrester, who spouts his disgust at blacks, Jews, ''Chinks,'' and all other people who do not share his color and beliefs, is balanced by the sympathetic Francine and Sylvia Smith.

White's greatest pride, however, was the creation of Mimi; in her, he felt, he had created what F. E. DeFrantz called ''a magnificent character.'' . . . [An] intensely personal view of his heroine made White particularly vulnerable to criticism of his character. Most of the critics found Mimi's motivation completely undeveloped. . . . As in *The Fire in the Flint,* White demonstrated in *Flight* a flair for incident, although frequently strained and contrived, but he could not create ''real'' characters or go beyond the stereotyped patterns of the sentimental novel. (pp. 93-4)

The two novels that Walter White produced were not to survive as models of excellence from the Harlem Renaissance. *The Fire in the Flint,* as we have noted, did serve as a ''trial balloon'' in the earlier years of the period, however, and it was a minor sensation for a brief time. While *Flight* did not have as big an impact as the first novel, it was an improvement in some areas of style and control, and it did precede Nella Larsen's *Passing* by three years. And in Mimi's flight from and return to her people, we are given, as White himself stated, an insight into some of the emotional and psychological problems to be confronted by those people light enough to pass for white, people like Walter White. The most important contribution White was to make to the Harlem Renaissance, however, was not his writing, but his aid to artists who were at the core of that movement: Claude McKay, Rudolph Fisher, Langston Hughes, and Countee Cullen. (p. 112)

Edward E. Waldron, in his Walter White and the Harlem Renaissance, *Kennikat Press, 1978, 185 p.*

ADDITIONAL BIBLIOGRAPHY

Broun, Heywood. ''It Seems to Heywood Broun.'' *The Nation* CXXX, No. 3385 (21 May 1930): 591.
An article written in praise of White for his role in blocking the appointment of segretationist John J. Parker to the United States Supreme Court.

Cannon, Poppy. *A Gentle Knight: My Husband, Walter White.* New York: Rinehart & Co., 1958, 309 p.
Observations of White in public and private life. White's widow discusses the people and events that shaped the American civil rights movement during the 1940s and 1950s, as well as White's national and international influence on public opinion.

Cooney, Charles F. ''Walter White and the Harlem Renaissance.'' *The Journal of Negro History* LVII, No. 3 (July 1972): 231-40.
Discussion of White's benevolent attitude toward unestablished writers. Cooney notes that despite his respect for the older generation of black writers, White aided young black writers by bringing their works to the attention of his friends in publishing, such as Frederick Lewis Allen, Alfred and Blanche Knopf, H. L. Mencken, and Carl and Irita Van Doren. Mentioned among the young writers White assisted are Claude McKay, Countee Cullen, and Rudolph Fisher.

Cournos, John. Review of *A Man Called White,* by Walter White. *Commonweal* XLIX, No. 4 (November 1948): 98-100.
Summary of and comments about the autobiography. Cournos calls the work ''a record of man's inhumanity to man and of courageous efforts to combat it.''

Du Bois, W.E.B. Review of *Rope and Faggot: A Biography of Judge Lynch,* by Walter F. White. In his *Book Reviews by W.E.B. Du Bois,* edited by Herbert Aptheker, pp. 133-34. Millwood, N.Y.: KTO Press, 1977.

　　A favorable review. Du Bois calls *Rope and Faggot* "an excellent and painstaking work. It had to be done. It ought to be read, but it is not pleasant reading."

Embree, Edwin R. "Little David." In his *13 Against the Odds,* pp. 71-95. New York: Viking Press, 1944.

　　Biographical sketch. Emphasis is placed on childhood influences and on White's work with the NAACP. In an interesting aside, there is a discussion of those who variously characterized White as either dedicated or opportunistic.

Gruening, Ernest. "Going White." *The Saturday Review of Literature* II, No. 50 (10 July 1926): 918.

　　Discussion of *Flight.* Gruening notes the artistic and thematic flaws of the work, but concludes that it presents a significant subject in a sometimes moving manner.

Kahn, E. J., Jr. "The Frontal Attack: I and II." *The New Yorker* XXIV, Nos. 28, 29 (4 September 1948; 11 September 1948): 28-38, 38-50.

　　Biographical tribute that recounts many little-known anecdotes about White's life and career.

Overstreet, H. A. "Our Sins of Commission and Omission." *The Saturday Review of Literature* XXXI, No. 40 (2 October 1948): 9-10.

　　Laudatory appraisal of *A Man Called White.* Overstreet notes the hopeful tone in a work that documents the bestial horrors and pathological perversions that are blindly accepted as a part of American life.

Ovington, Mary White. "Walter White." In her *Portraits in White,* pp. 104-17. 1927. Reprint. Freeport, N.Y.: Books for Libraries Press, 197 p.

　　Early biographical sketch by the book reviewer of the NAACP weekly *Book Chat.*

Scruggs, Charles W. "Alain Locke and Walter White: Their Struggle for Control of the Harlem Renaissance." *Black American Literature Forum* 14, No. 3 (Fall 1980): 91-9.*

　　Examines the lives of these two influential men: their work with other writers, their impact on the thought of the black intelligentsia, and the effects of ego on their personal and public relationship.

Singhn, Amrithit. In his *The Novels of the Harlem Renaissance: Twelve Black Writers, 1923-1933.* University Park: Pennsylvania State University Press, 1976, 175 p.*

　　Discusses White's works and personal impact in relationship to other Harlem Renaissance writers, to the period in general, and to various popular social and political movements of the period.

"Lynch Law." *The Times Literary Supplement,* No. 1446 (17 October 1929): 806.

　　A positive review of *Rope and Faggot,* with particular interest paid to White's discussion of lynching and religion.

Wilkins, Roy. "Walter White." In *Rising Above Color,* edited by Philip Henry Lotz, pp. 105-12. New York: Association Press, 1946.

　　Biographical sketch that focuses on White's work with the NAACP.

Mikhail (Mikhailovich) Zoshchenko

1895-1958

(Also transliterated as Mixail and Michael; also Zoščenko and Zostchenko) Russian short story writer, novelist, essayist, and autobiographer.

Zoshchenko was the most popular satirist in the Soviet Union from the early 1920s until 1946, when his works incurred official disfavor. During the two decades of his greatest renown, Zoshchenko examined both the confusion that resulted from the implementation of policies of the new Soviet state, and the ways that ignorance and greed could be masked by propaganda and government policies. To accomplish this, Zoshchenko utilized a distinctive vehicle for his trenchant satires: the *skaz,* or a first-person narrative. The *skaz* is a traditional Russian literary technique that establishes a narrator, usually a comic character, who is distinct from the author; modern writers have adopted this technique to provide a mask behind which the author may enjoy a greater freedom of expression than might otherwise be advisable. The language of Zoshchenko's *skaz* narrators—a unique blend of colloquialisms, the specialized jargon of numerous professions, half-assimilated Party slogans, and malapropisms—is one of the most notable features of his work.

Zoshchenko's father was a painter and small landowner in the Ukraine who, though not wealthy, was able to send his son to study law at the University of St. Petersburg. At the beginning of World War I, Zoshchenko abandoned his studies and joined the Imperial Army, where he became a lieutenant in the grenadiers. During the war he suffered gas poisoning, which left him in chronic ill health and which biographers believe may have caused the heart disease from which he eventually died. After the Russian Revolution Zoshchenko joined the Red Army, though he never joined the Communist Party and in fact remained politically uncommitted throughout his life. Between his two periods of military service, Zoshchenko held a number of disparate jobs, including postmaster, cobbler, poultry breeder, and border patrolman; all would work their way into the satiric situations of his later fiction. He began writing humorous sketches for newspapers primarily as a way of earning a living, in much the same way as did Anton Chekhov, to whom he is often compared. In 1921 Zoshchenko settled in Petrograd (formerly St. Petersburg; now Leningrad) and became a member of the Serapion Brothers, a loosely organized literary group formed by the novelist Yevgeny Zamyatin and including the critic Viktor Shklovsky. Although many of the Serapion Brothers belonged to the Communist Party, the group opposed political control of literature and advocated freedom of expression, stylistic experimentation, and devotion to the formal and technical aspects of art. Zoshchenko quickly became known for his humorous sketches satirizing the everyday hardships faced by the Soviet citizen. With the publication of his first volume of short stories, *Rasskazy Nazara Il'icha gospodina Sinebryukhova,* he was established as Russia's most popular humorist. During the four years from 1922 to 1926, for example, he published more than twenty collections of humorous stories that together sold millions of copies. In a typical Zoshchenko story of this period, such as "The Campaign of Economy," mass confusion results when sincere but muddled citizens attempt to implement gov-

ernment directives with no clear idea of what is expected of them. Zoshchenko also found a rich vein of humor in contrasting the ideal of life in the Soviet Union with the reality of the situation and in showing how removed some government programs were from the needs and desires of the people. In "The Woman Who Could Not Read," for example, nationwide efforts to eradicate illiteracy fail to move a woman to learn to read—until she finds a scented letter in her husband's pocket. Critics have found these works to be masterful descriptions of the vagaries and inconsistencies of human nature, as well as heartbreakingly humorous depictions of human foibles and sufferings.

Zoshchenko published similar short humorous stories for more than two decades, and had ventured into the production of longer and more serious works, including the novel *Lyudi,* which examines the ineffectual Russian intellectuals of the twentieth century, and the semiautobiographical *Pered voskhodom solntsa (Before Sunrise),* before his works came under official censure. Andrei Zhdanov, the Secretary of the Central Committee of the Soviet Communist Party and formulator of the official guidelines for Soviet media, attacked Zoshchenko in a 1946 speech, condemning him as a "vulgar Philistine" and his works as "rotten, vulgar, and empty." Zhdanov singled out the story "Adventures of a Monkey" in his denunciation of Zoshchenko's work. In this short story a monkey escapes from a zoo and, after various encounters with humans, longs for the security of her cage. Zhdanov maintained that Zoshchenko's intent was to present "the nasty, poisonous, anti-Soviet maxim . . . that it is better to live in a zoo than at liberty, and it is easier to breath in a cage than among the Soviet people." Although Zoshchenko continued to write and to publish sporadically thereafter, his career was destroyed. In place of the witty thumbnail characterizations and hastily outlined plots, compressed into a few well-chosen phrases, that had marked his earlier work, Zoshchenko's subsequent works were characterized by the conscientious application of socialist realist literary standards that celebrated the glory of the Soviet state.

Critics have often expressed surprise that Zoshchenko—who in his stories undeniably poked fun at the Soviet system—avoided censorship for so long. A primary reason for his relative freedom was that the butt of much of the humor in his stories was the petit bourgeois citizen who outwardly advocated the principles of communism but who continued to pursue private goals and to work for his own advancement rather than for the good of the community. Humor at the expense of these adherents to an outmoded social system was encouraged in the early days of the Soviet state as a method of teaching such pre-Revolutionary thinkers the errors of their ways. After twenty years, however, government officials were reluctant to allow the continued publication of stories about a class that was supposed to have disappeared under enlightened Soviet rule. Also, Zoshchenko had for years practiced in his stories a form of what V. S. Pritchett called "farcical advocacy." The correct Soviet point of view is enthusiastically espoused—but by a comic character whose absurdity shows that the author's sympathies lay elsewhere. The presence of straight Party doctrine in the stories, however facetiously employed, made it possible for the author to argue that any apparent anti-Soviet sentiment was in the mind of the reader.

Zhdanov attacked Zoshchenko's work for its implied criticism of the Soviet way of life and for its failure to introduce positive socialist ideals into his stories. He also found fault with the tendency of Zoshchenko's longer works toward introspection and self-analysis. This "bourgeois introspective individualism" was an unacceptable literary approach in the Soviet Union, where finding one's place in the group took precedence over self-expression. Zhdanov particularly criticized *Before Sunrise,* a semi-autobiographical selection of reminiscences that began appearing serially in the periodical *Oktyabr'* in 1943. The series was abruptly discontinued after the first six chapters had appeared, and the editors of *Oktyabr'* announced that they had been in "ideological error" in printing the work. *Before Sunrise* is a highly subjective work in which Zoshchenko attempts to trace the reasons for his profound habitual depression. The psychoanalytic and behaviorist theories of Sigmund Freud and Ivan Pavlov are invoked as Zoshchenko examines his past for clues to explain his melancholy. Such an introspective study would be suspect at any time in the Soviet Union, but critics applying strict Soviet standards to literature found it especially appalling that it appeared during World War II, when all literary works were expected to serve as positive propaganda glorifying the Soviet cause. Looking back at *Before Sunrise* in 1946, Zhdanov said that in his work "Zoshchenko turned his vulgar and mean little soul inside out, doing so with delight, with relish, with the desire to show everyone: look, see what a hooligan I am. . . . He spat on public opinion then, and now." The final nine chapters of *Before Sunrise* were not published in the Soviet Union until 1972.

Despite official censure, Zoshchenko's works remained popular with the reading public, and after his death Zoshchenko was officially "rehabilitated": collections of his stories, carefully edited to expunge any unorthodoxies, were republished. Zoshchenko remains best known in his own country and abroad for the brief *rasskazy* in which he exploited the humor found in the psychological confusion that often resulted when Russian citizens were suddenly expected to function by the regulations of the new Soviet system. More than any other writer, Zoshchenko has provided an accurate and intimate portrait of daily life in the Soviet Union in the mid-twentieth century.

PRINCIPAL WORKS

Rasskazy Nazara Il'icha gospodina Sinebryukhova (short stories) 1922
Svadba (drama) 1922
Nyervnyie Lyudi (short stories) 1924
Urazhayemye grazhdanye (short stories) 1926
Sentimental 'nyie povesti (short stories) 1927
Prestupleniye i nakazaniye (drama) 1932
Vozvrashchyonnaya molodost' (novel) 1933
Golubaya kniga (short stories) 1935
Russia Laughs (short stories) 1935
Rasskazy o Lenine (short stories) 1940
The Woman Who Could Not Read, and Other Tales (short stories) 1940
The Wonderful Dog, and Other Tales (short stories) 1942
*Pered voskhodom solntsa (autobiographical fragment) published in the journal *Oktyabr',* 1943
Parusinovyi portfel' (drama) 1944
Povesti i rasskazy (short stories) 1952
Rasskazy, fel'etony, povesti (short stories and novellas) 1958
Scenes from the Bathhouse, and Other Stories of Communist Russia (short stories) 1961
Nervous People, and Other Satires (short stories) 1963
*Povest 'o Razume (autobiographical fragment) published in the journal *Zvezda,* 1972

*These two works were translated and published together as *Before Sunrise* in 1974.

MIKHAIL ZOSHCHENKO (lecture date 1928)

[*In the following excerpt taken from a lecture by Zoshchenko originally published in the Soviet Union in 1928, the author notes that there is critical uncertainty as to how to classify his works and defends himself against charges that he gratuitously distorts the Russian language in his humorous stories. Zoshchenko defines himself as a proletarian writer, or rather, says that he writes parodies of what a proletarian writer would write.*]

At present some confusion has arisen among critics in regard to my literary work.

Critics don't know where exactly to moor me—to major literature or to minor literature, unworthy, perhaps, of a critic's enlightened attention.

And since the majority of my works are in a disrespected form—the journal feuilleton and short story, my fate is thus generally predetermined.

Critics generally speak of me as a humorist, a writer who causes laughter and who for the sake of this laughter is willing to do the devil knows what to his native Russian language.

Of course this is not so.

If I sometimes distort language, then I do so conventionally, since I want to create a type of character I need, a type which has almost never before figured in Russian literature.

But in regard to minor literature I don't protest. It's still unknown at present what minor literature means. (p. 403)

I don't intend to go into major literature. As it is there are enough writers in major literature.

But when the critics, and this occurs often, divide my works into two parts: on the one hand, they say, my novellas really are major literature, but on the other hand, these minor little short stories—journal humor, satire, utter rubbish; this isn't correct.

I write both novellas and minor short stories with one and the same hand. And my subdivision is not so subtle that on the one hand I can write utter rubbish but on the other a novella for posterity.

It's true, by its external form my novella comes closer to the forms of so-called major literature. I would say there are more literary traditions in it than in my humorous short story. But for me personally, their quality is identical.

But the fact is that in my novellas (**"Sentimental Novellas"**) I portray an exceptionally intelligent person. In the minor short stories I write about a simpler person. And the very task, the very theme and types dictate the form for me.

That's why it would seem harsh to divide my work into two parts.

But the critic is deceived by external signs.

And the whole trouble is that, especially these past two years, because of a certain weariness, bitter blues and obligatory weekly work, I've managed to write many bad minor works, which aren't any better than the ordinary journal short story. This confuses the critics even more, who, with great willingness and so as not to bother with me in the future, relegate me just about to the rank of reporter.

But once again I do not protest.

I only want to make one confession. Perhaps it will seem strange and unexpected. The fact is that I am a proletarian writer. Rather, I parody that imaginary, but authentic proletarian writer who would exist under today's conditions and in today's milieu. Of course, such a writer cannot exist, at least not now. But when he does exist, then his society, his milieu will advance significantly in all respects.

I only parody. I am a temporary substitute for the proletarian writer. That's why the themes of my short stories are penetrated by a naive philosophy, which is just up my readers' alley.

In my large works I am also parodying. I even parody the clumsy, cumbersome (Karamzinian) style of a contemporary red Lev Tolstoi or Rabindranath Tagore, and the sentimental theme, which is now so prevalent. I parody today's intellectual writer, who perhaps doesn't exist now, but who would have existed if he would have accurately fulfilled the social order, not of the publishing house, but of that milieu and that society which has now been pushed to the forefront. (pp. 403-04)

I write very concisely. My sentences are short. Accessible to the poor. Perhaps that's why I have many readers. (p. 405)

Mikhail Zoshchenko, "About Myself, My Critics and My Work," translated by Jacqueline Decter Cukierman, in Russian Literature Triquarterly, *No. 14, Winter, 1976, pp. 403-05.*

VICTOR SHKLOVSKY (essay date 1928)

[*A Russian critic and novelist, Shklovsky was a member of the Serapion Brothers and an early proponent of what he called "the formal method in literature" or literary Formalism. In his criticism, which has been characterized as brilliant and aggressive, if sometimes paradoxical, Shklovsky is concerned with the form and structure of a literary work and not with its content. In the following excerpt from an essay published in 1928, Shklovsky discusses Zoshchenko's use of skaz narrative technique.*]

Zoshchenko is a rather short man. He has a lusterless, presently yellowish face. Ukrainian eyes. And a cautious step. He has a very quiet voice. The manner of a man who wants to end a big scandal very politely.

Zoshchenko breathes cautiously. In World War I he got gas poisoning. His success with the reader hasn't given Zoshchenko the wherewithal to go treat his heart. To restore his blood.

That's Zoshchenko in general. He is neither a soft nor a tender man.

He moves cautiously through life.

He is not Boccaccio, for example. And not Leonov, and not even Dostoevsky. (p. 407)

Zoshchenko is read in taverns. On street cars. His stories are related on the upper berths of hard-seated carriages. His short stories are considered true events.

Zoshchenko himself probably wants to write a novel. He needs only air.

One can now write about an author in two ways. Thus, one can write about Zoshchenko, "The Problem of *Skaz*" and say that *skaz* is the illusion of oral speech. One can analyze *skaz*. Or one can discuss "The Problem of Mikhail Zoshchenko's Class Consciousness" and begin to set him straight. As if all instruments must have the shape of nails.

But this is not the point. It's not a question of method, but a question of the subject. One can't analyze the plot and style of the author separately and then determine whether Zoshchenko is a Philistine.

Zoshchenko is just what you read.

One can't separate the problem of his Philistinism from the problem of *skaz*. . . .

[*Skaz*] only motivates a second perception of the work. It's not directly stated anywhere, but comes out point-blank. . . . *Skaz* complicates the artistic work. There are two levels: 1) that which the man narrates, 2) that which as if accidentally breaks through into his story. The man lets something slip. In this respect Conan-Doyle's *The Exploits of Brigadier Gerard* is well done. The brigadier narrates miracles of bravery. They're interesting. But all these exploits are parodic, he doesn't do what's necessary. This is the second level of the work. That's why a narrow-minded person is usually chosen for *skaz*. Someone who doesn't understand the events. (p. 408)

Zoshchenko is defined as a Philistine writer, but not because the secretaries didn't get to the second level.

The reader got there.

There are possibly cases in which the second level of *skaz* work is another linguistic tradition.

Such examples can be observed in anecdotes. For example, the anecdote about the German who didn't know whether to say: "Fishes don't have toothes," "Fishs don't have tooths," or "Fish don't have tooth."

The collision of linguistic tendencies is made use of here. The appearance of different linguistic habits.

And the anecdote is funny. (pp. 408-09)

The "*skaz* speaker" doesn't cause the *skaz*, but motivates it. *Skaz* is often resorted to for the implementation of so-called "folk etymology," which in the given usage is artistic etymology. . . .

Contemporary writers make wide use of *skaz* to introduce into their works technical expressions and verbal stock phrases which are inserted out of their context. (p. 410)

"*Skaz*" must be dealt with on the same level as works about poetic language and not in connection with the role of the hero or authorial mask.

Zoshchenko's work is sometimes more complicated. His works survive repeated readings, because there are a great quantity of devices which use the material differently.

On the basic level, the plot level, Zoshchenko works to have his skaz-narrator-Philistine unmask himself while speaking.

An example is **"The Lady Aristocrat."**

Here the reader doesn't perceive the events as they are narrated to him. The skaz-narrator's fussiness and thoroughness motivate his inability to see things. At first he's involved with a water-pipe and the toilet, then with the pastry. He doesn't see himself in perspective.

The reader, in seeing this person on two levels, experiences a feeling of superiority, he sees the subject "in relief." The reader figures out, as though on his own, that one can see the subject differently. (p. 411)

Works which have a second level are usually written in a simpler form, with less deformation of the language.

A good example is the short story **"Happiness."**

There's very little happiness here. The structure of the work isn't in the description of happiness, but in the contrast of this happiness with real human happiness. Here the transparency of speech is well presented.

> While I'm drinking up my tea with sugar, I ask for fish salad, after that—ratatouille. I gobble down everything and staggering, leave the tavern. And in my hand a clean thirty rubles. If you want to—you can drink it away, if you want—spend it whichever way you want.
>
> Ach, and boy did I drink then. For two months I drank. And I did some shopping besides: I bought a silver ring and warm innersoles. I wanted to buy pants and a shirt too, but I ran out of money.

Of course, it's wrong to suggest that this is Zoshchenko's notion of happiness. Rather, Zoshchenko is portraying unhappiness.

In the purely linguistic respect, that is, in the comedy of language, Zoshchenko is ingenious.

"A dog of the poodle model" bit one of his heroes.

The comicality of this expression lies in that it is organized on the pattern," a revolver of the bulldog model."

Works structured entirely on comedy of situation are rare for Zoshchenko. (p. 413)

The high finish of Zoshchenko's works, the presence of a second level, the skillful and ingenious linguistic structure, have made Zoshchenko the most popular Russian prose writer. He's in use, not like money, but like an object. Like a train. (pp. 413-14)

> *Viktor Shklovsky, "On Zoshchenko and Major Literature," translated by Jacqueline Decter Cukierman, in* Russian Literature Triquarterly, *No. 14, Winter, 1976, pp. 407-14.**

THE CHRISTIAN SCIENCE MONITOR   (essay date 1935)

[*In the following excerpt, taken from a review of* Russia Laughs, *the anonymous reviewer expresses surprise that Zoshchenko's "little digs at Soviet manners and customs . . . are apparently tolerated by the government."*]

Contrary to general belief, laughter is permitted in Soviet Russia. Even laughter at the expense of Soviet Russia. . . . Now comes to American readers Mikhail Zostchenko with a collection of short stories, **Russia Laughs**. . . .

Zostchenko has bourgeois antecedents, and he is not a member of the Communist Party, although he has fought in the Red Army. His father was a nobleman and an artist, his mother an actress. He writes chiefly of the petty bourgeoisie. . . .

Nevertheless, Zostchenko's stories are full of little digs at Soviet manners and customs, and these are apparently tolerated by the Government.

> *L.A.S., "Humor from Russia," in* The Christian Science Monitor, *September 10, 1935, p. 14.*

JOHN COURNOS   (essay date 1935)

[*The following excerpt is taken from a review of Zoshchenko's* Russia Laughs, *the first collection of the author's short stories translated into English. Cournos disagrees with the book's dustjacket blurb hailing Zoshchenko's work as a new kind of Russian humor, comparing it instead with the work of the classic Russian satirist Nikolai Gogol.*]

"Russia Laughs." This is good news. To be sure, the laugh is as often as not a wry grimace. But what of that? The effort to laugh is commendable at any time, and what we call laughter through tears may be always interpreted as an indication of humanity asserting itself in the face of tragedy, of pathos, or of sheer tedium. Many a time and oft has the so-called bourgeois world made use of this device, which in England is associated with Dickens and in Russia with Gogol. Russia, we have been repeatedly told, is a country filled with optimism, a new kind of country which has nothing to do with old Russia, which could bring herself to laugh only in a sad way. And we began to believe it. We awaited the appearance of the new Russian humor with some expectancy. It was, of course, to be a humor full of that gayety which comes from cheerful souls confident of themselves and the future.

No, despite the blurb on the jacket, Zostchenko's stories do not come to us from Russia "like a great, swift wind sweeping aside our traditional idea of the Russian temperament and of the Russian story, and revealing the real Russian who, once bearing all stoically as the will of God, now, it seems, knows how to laugh—and laugh not only at himself but at his fate." Zostchenko's tales, indeed, reveal the same old Russian laugh, the laugh made familiar to us by Gogol. It is the traditional laugh, and has virtue, not only because the author has considerable comic gifts, but because it rings true to the Russian temperament, unchangeable in the heart of things in spite of any veneer of alien culture superimposed upon it. The encrustation may be different; the pearl in the oyster is the same. The main thing, of course, is that it is a pearl. (p. 8)

> John Cournos, "Stories by a Russian Humorist," in The New York Times Book Review, October 13, 1935, pp. 8, 26.

GLEB STRUVE (essay date 1935)

[A Russian-born educator, Struve is internationally known for his critical studies of Slavic literature. In the following excerpt from his Soviet Russian Literature, Struve finds that Zoshchenko, more than any other Russian writer, provides an accurate picture of everyday life in Soviet society. Struve also compares Zoshchenko favorably with Nikolai Gogol, Anton Chekhov, and Nikolai Leskov.]

A place apart not only among everyday life writers, but in Soviet literature in general, is occupied by Mikhail Zoshchenko. . . . He is perhaps the most widely read and popular of the present-day Russian writers, and his popularity among the Russians outside Russia is not less than in Soviet Russia itself. He has evolved a style and a manner of his own which mark him off from all the other Soviet writers and make his writings easily and instantly recognizable. This style has been evolved gradually, but one of its principal elements was present in Zoshchenko's earliest works and was in fact one of the common attributes of the dynamic prose period. It is the element of "skaz." . . . But of all the numerous writers who, in the years 1920-23, used that form of "skaz" so lavishly and unrestrainedly, Zoshchenko is the only one to have stuck to it after it fell in abeyance with the revival of the novel and of a quieter and simpler realistic manner in short stories. But in the case of Zoshchenko it has survived in a modified form and been put to a new use. (p. 69)

Even those early stories of Zoshchenko [in the collection **Rasskazy Nazara Il'icha gospodina Sinebryukhova**] revealed his unusual literary mastery. But both the subject and the language were exotic and suited to the requirements of that period. When it ended and when the "skaz" manner gradually died out in Soviet literature, Zoshchenko had to think of evolving a new manner that would suit his artistic individuality. The humorous, satirical tendency was very strong in him. To-day he is the best humorist in Russian literature. But he did not arrive at once at that manner which now makes his works so individual and so easily recognizable. He passed through an intermediate period, writing a number of short stories in which the comical effects were achieved mainly through the subject-matter, through improbable and ridiculous situations and collisions, stories told

in the ordinary, simple, "educated" language, in the name of the author himself. Then he began writing short humorous stories and anecdotes which stood on the border-line between real literature and newspaper *feuilleton*. Their subjects were usually topical, very often the so-called "small defects of mechanism" in various branches of Soviet administration, satirical pictures of Communist red-tape, corruption, inefficiency, etc.

Gradually Zoshchenko evolved a new manner, a combination of his earlier "*skaz*" stories and his purely comical anecdotes. It was the question of finding a proper "mouthpiece" for that "*skaz*", a good substitute for the author, who would no longer be exotic but would fit in with the normal course of everyday life in Soviet Russia. Such a mouthpiece has been found by Zoshchenko in the Soviet man-in-the-street, the average Soviet citizen who passively accepts the Revolution, but vaguely regrets the good old times and aspires to bourgeois philistine comfort and happiness. The happily created personage of Zoshchenko expresses himself in the peculiar jargon of a semi-educated man with a strong admixture of the specific Soviet journalese which is rapidly inundating and spoiling the Russian language.

Despite the fact that Zoshchenko's situations are often highly improbable and grotesque, to him more than to any other can be rightly applied the label of writer of everyday life. He gives the truest picture of the Soviet weekdays stripped of all heroism and romanticism, of all pretension and make-belief. Some of the orthodox Soviet critics do not really know what to make out of Zoshchenko. Now they praise him for ridiculing so cruelly the petty-bourgeois vices, the spirit of *embourgeoisement* invading large circles of the Communist society, now he is himself denounced as an essentially bourgeois writer, and identified with his own characters.

Zoshchenko is one of the most prolific writers in Soviet Russia: short stories written by him form several volumes. He is also, as I said, the most popular. It is the outward, superficial comical effects, that the large reading public appreciate in Zoshchenko. But it is their second, hidden, innermost meaning, and their technical excellence, which make them real literature of the highest order. Some of them are genuine stylistic gems. At his best he reminds one simultaneously of two of the great masters of Russian literature, so dissimilar on the whole, and yet so alike in one thing—in their keen vision of the mean vulgarity and insipidity of life; I mean Gogol and Chekhov. It is the pettiness, the vulgarity of life, the essential incomprehensibility of one man for another, that forms the psychological *leitmotiv* of a great many of Zoshchenko's stories. And in some of the best, for instance in **Wisdom,** one senses the tragedy beyond and beneath the humorous or grotesque presentation of life's vulgarity and insignificance. The most hilarious of modern Russian writers is at heart a thorough pessimist, and for an understanding reader his comical stories must inevitably leave an aftertaste of utter sadness.

To bring Zoshchenko nearer to a non-Russian reader is an almost hopeless task. His stories inevitably lose in translation the greater part of their individuality and attraction. In this respect he is rather more akin to Gogol and Leskov than to Chekhov, for his language has that individual accent and raciness which Chekhov lacked.

One of Zoshchenko's latest works, **The Restored Youth** . . . , leaves a somewhat strange impression. It is a short novel, a genre that is new to Zoshchenko—hitherto he has specialized

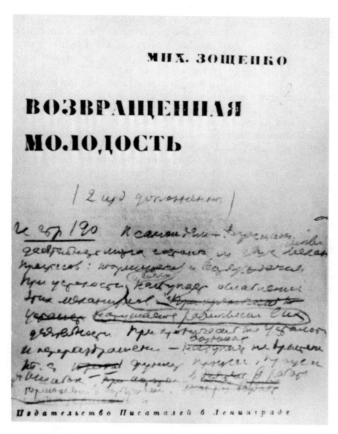

МИХ. ЗОЩЕНКО

ВОЗВРАЩЕННАЯ
МОЛОДОСТЬ

Title page, with author's notes, of Vozvrashchyonnaya Molodost' (Youth Restored). *Courtesy of Ardis Publishers.*

in very short stories. But really, both structurally and stylistically, it differs little from Zoshchenko's usual stories. It is written in the same intentionally vulgar, half-educated jargon. Its very short chapters, each containing a typically Zoshchenkian episode or anecdote, make it into a succession of short stories held together by a very simple plot. Even the fact that it falls into two parts, the first, which precedes the actual novel (the first seventeen chapters), being the author's pseudo-scientific and subtly irrelevant comments and reflections on the subject of his story (Zoshchenko himself compares it rather aptly and ingeniously to an educational film) is quite in line with Zoshchenko's typical manner and merely makes of it an extended story. It is the story of an ageing, almost decrepit Soviet professor of astronomy, vaguely hostile to the existing régime though just as vaguely in sympathy with Socialism in general, who yearns for his lost youth and finally succeeds in restoring it by an effort of will. He deserts his wife, marries a young, flighty and vulgar girl, who "at the age of nineteen has already had time to change five husbands and undergo seven or eight abortions," and goes away with her to the Crimea. She soon tires of him and begins to flirt with young men. One day the Professor . . . finds her in the arms of one of these young men. He has a stroke and one side of his body is paralysed. But in the end he is cured, and even preserves his restored youth. He returns to his wife and family, but deep in his heart never ceases to pine after his scatter-brained Tulya. In the portrayal of characters and in the picture of everyday Soviet life there is, as usual with Zoshchenko, a strong element of the grotesque. And even more acutely than usual the reader

feels all the time, beneath the story, a strong undercurrent of biting and cruel satire. The very vulgarity of Zoshchenko has an effect of great subtleness. The reader has even an unpleasant feeling that the author is laughing not only at science, at medicine, at his own ridiculous and grotesque characters, but at him, the reader, too. (pp. 70-3)

In the following passage describing the Professor's treatment at the hands of medical men there is a touch of a deliberate parody of Tolstoy:

> For six months he underwent medical treatment. He was prescribed bromide and strychnine, arsenic and phitine. He was prescribed baths and enemas. He was wrapped in wet towels and his body was pierced with electricity. He was questioned whether he had had any grave illnesses or whether he had been addicted to any excesses as a child. They talked to him about the complications of nervous ailments, heated his head with blue light and even tried to hypnotize him, in order to inspire him with bright thoughts about health. And no one told him in simple and understandable words how his illness could have originated and how to fight it apart from pills and potions.

Here is an ironical picture of a happy Soviet marriage, both husband and wife being enthusiastic Communists, and for reasons of work living apart and meeting once in five days:

> Lida, feeling a little sorry in her heart and at the same time surprised by the haste with which he had married, consented to wait a little, admitting that the search for a flat, the removal and various domestic affairs and troubles would unfavourably affect the course of his work. And he praised her for her common sense and political maturity, saying that he now realized full well that he had made no mistake in choosing her, and that, indeed, he would perhaps be unable to find at present a better wife. . . . They were happy in their own way, and in no hurry to disturb their happiness by kisses and embraces.

In the description of the Professor's pastimes after his final recuperation there is the same touch of irony. . . . (pp. 74-5)

It is therefore simply remarkable and amazing to see this new work of Zoshchenko taken quite seriously by the Soviet press as an attempt to introduce science into literature, to bring the two together. Several discussions were organized on this subject with the participation of some of the most eminent Soviet scientists . . . and nobody suggested that Zoshchenko was pulling their legs. (p. 76)

> *Gleb Struve, "Writers of Everyday Life," in his* Soviet Russian Literature, *George Routledge & Sons, Ltd., 1935, pp. 60-78.**

V. S. PRITCHETT   (essay date 1940)

[Pritchett is a highly esteemed English novelist, short story writer, and critic. He is considered one of the modern masters of the short story as well as one of the world's most respected and well-read literary critics. Pritchett writes in the conversational tone of the familiar essay, a method by which he approaches literature from the viewpoint of a lettered but not overly scholarly reader.

A twentieth-century successor to such early nineteenth-century essayist-critics as William Hazlitt and Charles Lamb, Pritchett employs much the same critical method: his own experience, judgment, and sense of literary art are emphasized, rather than a codified critical doctrine derived from a school of psychological or philosophical speculation. His criticism is often described as fair, reliable, and insightful. In the following excerpt, Pritchett discusses the intimacy and depth of Zoshchenko's portrayal of ordinary Russians, a depth he finds lacking in English short fiction of the same period. Pritchett notes that Zoshchenko escaped Soviet censorship for so long by his "farcical advocacy" of Party doctrine: in his stories it is usually a comic character who advocates—with humorous exaggeration—the ideologically correct point of view.]

The English are not a nation of good storytellers. Listen on a bus, in the train, in the pubs, cafés and sitting-rooms; it is rare to hear a story well told, neighbours vividly described, dialogue dramatically reported. . . . The English simply present their lives baldly, are half-submerged by them anyway, and think it rather immoral to present them well.

A collection of Michael Zoshchenko's short stories, ***The Woman Who Could Not Read*** . . . , shows up our short-story writing badly. We have had many writers who could turn a triviality fancifully round their pen-nibs. But they leave it still a triviality. The Russian writers—and Zoshchenko is the heir of a tradition—are realistic about their trivialities; they make them not into fanciful elaborations, but into homely illustrations of our greater cares. . . . But it is not chiefly in the detail of a story that the English short-story writer fails. He has no idea of the art of brevity. In fifteen hundred words Zoshchenko can do almost anything. The English writer of brief stories is limited over and over again either to mere whimsicality, or especially to the lyrical description of an emotional state, a piece of landscape. By this, of course, he gives voice to that meditative, ruminative romanticism of our natures. But we feel that the author, having no invention, has made the best of a bad job; he had no point of view about other people, because he had never got beyond that literary adolescence which has a point of view about itself only. Zoshchenko's stories have none of this poetical priggishness. Brief as they are, they are full of people and incident, frequently have "a plot" and they have also that suggestive quality, a hint dropped here and there, which opens up worlds for the mind to wander in a long time afterwards. And although his stories are written in conversational style, the talk is without those studied buttonholings or breezy non-intimacies of our conversational manner—what Mr. Cyril Connolly has called the "you-man" style. Zoshchenko may talk, for all one knows, as all Russians talk, and certainly as they often do in Tchekov; he talks like an ordinary man without the ordinary man's pomposity and self-consciousness; we recognize the talk, however, because it is like what we say, not indeed to each other, but to ourselves. . . .

It is easy to overrate—and also underrate—Zoshchenko's sketches. Their subjects are familiar: the farces of the housing situation in Moscow, the digs at a State which makes five-year plans but can't produce electric-light meters, the eternal Russian foolery at the expense of bureaucrats. Some readers are surprised that Zoshchenko's cynicism and satire are permitted and widely enjoyed in Russia. Miss Fen, the translator, says that the greater and better part of his work belongs to the collectivisation period, when there was more freedom for writers than there is now. To-day (she says) he is obliged to add cautions and morals to his stories. Certainly the title story, which described how a woman decided to learn to read and write—and thereby liquidate national illiteracy—because she

discovered a perfumed letter in her husband's coat, looks as if it had been tampered with and neutralised. There is no means of knowing how Zoshchenko is affected; but English short-story writers have their own difficulties, too, with the unofficial censorship of the magazines. Direct political censorship is probably less harmful to imaginative writers than the business man's indirect censorship. For censors are usually stupid or venal. They strain at gnats and swallow camels: the wise writer soon learns to give them gnats to strain at. Censorship, after its first stone-walling phase has passed, may be a stimulus. It encourages subtlety. A hint, an insinuation, the click of the tongue in the cheek, are often more effective in a story than the sullen verbosity of free protest. I assume in reading Zoshchenko's stories that the Soviet censor was wise enough to let well alone when he discovered that Zoshchenko was writing on what must be a major spiritual problem in Russia: the nostalgia for personal life. But whether the censor was indulgent, subversive, officially wily or blind, Zoshchenko is the gainer by the ever possible threat. He slips his theme across nonchalantly by pretending to be silly, a harmless, clever crank or buffoon, who always skids on the banana-skin or, by advocating with exaggeration the correct point of view:

> To have your own private flat is, no doubt, a sign of petty bourgeois mentality.

> It is better to live as one large friendly communal family than to shut yourself inside your domestic fortifications.

> You ought to live in communal flats. There everything is public. There's always someone to talk to, to ask advice from. And to have a fight with, too, if you feel inclined.

Zoshchenko gets away with anything by farcical advocacy, and by presenting himself as the idiotic enthusiast. . . .

It is easy to trace Zoshchenko's ancestry of satirical extravagance and farce in Russian literature. Every Russian writer has written something funny about teeth and preposterous about Government officials from Gogol onwards. Outside Russia, Zoshchenko seems to have affinities with the American, Wm. Saroyan, who, in the same disarming way, has picked up the man in the street and treated him naively, farcically, mystically. He and Zoshchenko are a pair of innocent hopefuls, a Laurel and Hardy, who can't stop talking. Zoshchenko, of course, is never mystical. His optimism comes in mad moments, as in the story where he goes off on a disastrous bicycle ride and is arrested. Saroyan and Zoshchenko are the two sides of the medal of writing about the people; Zoshchenko the harder, more ingenious, older lag. Saroyan urges the ordinary man into the earthly paradise with the humility of faith in man; Zoshchenko urges him on with the comic staggers of perpetual overreaching. The same zest for the future is in both.

> *V. S. Pritchett, in a review of "The Woman Who Could Not Read," in* The New Statesman & Nation, *Vol. XX, No. 510, November 30, 1940, p. 542.*

ELISAVETA FEN   (essay date 1941)

[*Fen has translated several volumes of Zoshchenko's short stories into English, including* The Woman Who Could Not Read, and Other Tales *and* The Wonderful Dog, and Other Tales. *In her foreword to* The Wonderful Dog, *written in 1941 and excerpted below, Fen characterizes Zoshchenko's humor as that of incongruity—"the discrepancy between the ideal and its realization."*]

The characteristic situation which moves Michael Zoshchenko to a display of humour is generally a situation of incongruity—admittedly the most common source of fun. These incongruities appear to be presented on a superficial plane, but are in fact related, on a deeper level, to the universal, age-long incongruity—the discrepancy between the ideal and its realization. (p. vi)

[Some of Zoshchenko's] stories stress an obvious contrast, in others it is more subtle, almost concealed. They represent a series of illustrations of a universal human fallacy, the fallacy of assuming that human beings can be transformed by didactic measures alone, by government decrees, proclamations and sermons. The fact that human beings have a way of transforming the measures imposed upon them from outside, in a most profound and subtle way, always escapes the rationalist. And Russia throughout her history had, in her immensity, provided the most tempting experimental field for adventurous rationalists, of whom Peter the Great was neither the first, nor the only one. At one time, since the establishment of Bolshevism, small groups of rationalists were given free rein. Experimentation proceeded apace: measures and reforms were introduced on paper where there were no means of carrying them into practice; people were instructed in revolutionary virtues where their past had failed to prepare them for the present; and many of the reforms were destined to remain a dead letter, with the consequent rich harvest of incongruities.

From this befogged atmosphere of ideological conflicts and practical muddles, emerges the Man-in-the-street with a grin on his face. He is the animal on whom the experiment is being performed. He is an ox, if you like, who pulls the heavy chariot of a Totalitarian State, as he had for centuries pulled the tottering vehicle of the ineffective Monarchy. He is patient and mostly good-humoured, but he is by no means dumb. The old régime had ill-used him as a beast of burden, the new régime had added a restricting harness to his load. He has become a circus ox: he has to keep to a certain, very intricate 'line' of politically orthodox behaviour. Knowing the price he will have to pay if he stumbles, he grins and picks his way with great caution. But he gets some of his own back by muttering comments on his drivers and himself.

Zoshchenko's Man-in-the-street is not a thoroughbred creature with centuries of training in his blood. In the pre-revolutionary past he had little opportunity for learning, and since then, his more sophisticated brothers had been slaughtered on the altar of the Mass god. Sometimes he finds it convenient to pretend that he is more ignorant than he really is—another device of self-protection. But frequently he is genuinely ignorant, and his vocabulary is that of a child of four. Yet, with all that, he is clearly aware of the gap existing in his environment, in his mind even, between what really is and what is desirable; he has an insatiable hankering after a 'better life', which had been promised to him so often by the visionaries and the demagogues.

Will the time ever come? In one of his stories Zoshchenko makes his Man indulge in a fantasy of a wonderful scientific invention. 'Some day, may be, they'll invent some quite incredible and fantastic apparatus, perhaps a little machine called "Three Wishes". Anyone would be able to turn a little lever, and his three wishes would come true.'

'But,' he wonders a little later, 'might it not turn out to be not an undisguised blessing, after all? Might not some people turn

Zoshchenko, circa 1923. Courtesy of Ardis Publishers.

the lever in order to grab more money, prizes, honours, and respect for themselves.'

And he shrinks away from the dangerous dream into which his unsatisfied desires have led him. 'It's best not to look too far forward,' he concludes.

One wonders, if this dream of a miraculous invention had become a reality, what would be the three secret wishes for which Zoshchenko's Man-in-the-street would turn the handle? I venture to guess that one of them, perhaps even the first, would be the one most common and natural—the wish for freedom. (pp. vii-ix)

> *Elisaveta Fen, in a preface to* The Wonderful Dog and Other Tales *by Michael Zoshchenko, translated by Elisaveta Fen, 1942. Reprint by Hyperion Press, Inc., 1973, pp. v-ix.*

ANDREI A. ZHDANOV (essay date 1946)

[*As Secretary of the Central Committee of the Soviet Communist Party from 1928 until his death in 1948, Zhdanov established guidelines to which all Russian media had to comply. Modern literary movements, such as Imagism, Symbolism, and Futurism, were all denounced as "formalism" and held to be symptomatic of decadent capitalism. Together with Joseph Stalin and novelist Maxim Gorky, Zhdanov formulated the precepts of "Socialist Realism," which called for writers to use the Realist style of nineteenth century Russian literary classics to affirm the new social order. Russian authors were to produce only works that glorified the Soviet system and demonstrated its superiority to other forms of government. For years Zoshchenko had avoided censorship by presenting any unfavorable comments about the*

Soviet system obliquely in his stories. However, in a series of pronouncements in 1946 (published in English in 1950), the Central Committee condemned Zoshchenko for the implicit criticism of the Soviet way of life in his stories, and for the personal nature of some of his more recent works. The short story that particularly aroused Zhdanov's wrath was the animal fable "Adventures of a Monkey," which has been interpreted as an allegory about the lack of freedom permitted the average Soviet citizen. As a result of Zhdanov's attack, one journal that had published Zoshchenko's stories in the past was abolished, while the editor of Zvezda, *the periodical in which "Adventures of a Monkey" had appeared, was replaced by a Central Committee member. Zoshchenko was expelled from the Union of Soviet Writers, to which all Russian writers had to belong if they hoped to be published. For further discussion of the Zhdanov attack on Zoshchenko and especially on the story "Adventures of a Monkey,"* see the excerpts by Alec Brown (1948) and Vasa D. Mihaslovich (1967).]

From the ruling of the Central Committee of the Communist Party it is clear that the grossest error of the journal *Zvezda* is the opening of its pages to the literary "creations" of Zoshchenko and Akhmatova. I think there is no need for me to cite here the "work" of Zoshchenko, **"Adventures of a Monkey."** Evidently you have all read it and know it better than I. The meaning of this "work" by Zoshchenko consists in this, that he depicts Soviet people as idlers and monsters, as silly and primitive people. Zoshchenko takes absolutely no interest in the labor of the Soviet people, their exertions and heroism, their high social and moral qualities. With him this theme is always absent. Zoshchenko, like the philistine and vulgarian that he is, chose as his permanent theme the analysis of the basest and pettiest sides of life. This digging in the trivialities of life is not accidental. It is characteristic of all vulgar philistine writers, and hence of Zoshchenko. Gorky said a lot about this in his time. You remember how at the congress of Soviet writers in 1934 Gorky branded—excuse my saying so—"men of letters" who see nothing beyond the soot in the kitchen and bathhouse.

For Zoshchenko **"Adventures of a Monkey"** does not go beyond the framework of his usual writings. This "work" has come into the focus of criticism only as the clearest reflection of the whole negative tendency that exists in the "creative genius" of Zoshchenko. It is known that since the time of his return to Leningrad from evacuation Zoshchenko has written several things characterized by the fact that he is incapable of finding in the life of the Soviet people one positive phenomenon, one positive type. As in the **"Adventures of a Monkey,"** Zoshchenko is accustomed to mock at Soviet life, Soviet ways, Soviet people, covering this mockery with a mask of vacuous diversion and pointless humor.

If you read attentively and think over the story **"Adventures of a Monkey,"** you will see that Zoshchenko casts the monkey in the role of supreme judge of our social customs and makes him read something on the order of a moral lesson to the Soviet people. The monkey is presented as some sort of rational element, whose job is to evaluate the behavior of the people. Zoshchenko needed to give a deliberately deformed, caricatured, and vulgar picture of the life of the Soviet people in order to insert in the mouth of the monkey the nasty, poisonous, anti-Soviet maxim to the effect that it is better to live in the zoo than at liberty, and that it is easier to breathe in a cage than among the Soviet people.

Is it possible to reach a lower stage of moral and political decline, and how can the people of Leningrad tolerate in the pages of their journals such filth and indecency?

If "works" of this sort are presented to Soviet readers by the journal *Zvezda*, how weak must be the vigilance of those citizens of Leningrad in the leadership of *Zvezda* for it to have been possible to publish in this journal works that are poisoned with a zoological hostility to the Soviet order. Only the dregs of literature could produce such "works" and only blind and apolitical people could put them into circulation. (pp. 15-17)

Zoshchenko, with his loathsome moral, succeeded in penetrating to the pages of a big Leningrad journal, and in settling himself there with all the conveniences. And the journal *Zvezda* is an organ whose duty it is to educate our youth. But how can a journal reckon with this task, when it gives shelter to such a vulgarian and un-Soviet writer as Zoshchenko? (p. 17)

Zoshchenko's tale, **"Before Sunrise,"** written at the height of the liberation war of the Soviet people against the German invaders, was subjected to sharp criticism in the journal *Bolshevik*. In this tale Zoshchenko turned his vulgar and mean little soul inside out, doing so with delight, with relish, with the desire to show everyone: look, see what a hooligan I am.

It would be hard to find in our literature anything more repulsive than the "moral" preached by Zoshchenko in **"Before Sunrise,"** which depicts people and himself as vile, lewd beasts without shame or conscience. And this moral he presented to Soviet readers in that period when our people were pouring out their blood in a war of unheard-of difficulty, when the life of the Soviet state hung by a hair, when the Soviet people endured countless sacrifices in the name of victory over the Germans. But Zoshchenko, having dug himself in in Alma-Ata, deep in the rear, did nothing at that time to help the Soviet people in its struggle with the German invaders. With complete justice Zoshchenko was publicly spanked in the *Bolshevik* as a libeler and vulgarian, alien to Soviet literature. He spat on public opinion then, and now, less than two years later, before the ink with which the *Bolshevik* review was written has dried, the same Zoshchenko makes his triumphal entry into Leningrad and begins strolling freely in the pages of Leningrad journals. Not only *Zvezda*, but the journal *Leningrad* also prints him eagerly. They readily present him with theatrical auditoriums. More than that, they give him the opportunity to occupy a leading position in the Leningrad division of the Writers' Union and to play an active role in the literary affairs of Leningrad. On what basis do you allow Zoshchenko to stroll in the gardens and parks of Leningrad literature? Why have the active Communist Party workers of Leningrad, its writers' organization, permitted these shameful things?

The thoroughly rotten and corrupt socio-political and literary physiognomy of Zoshchenko was not formed in the most recent period. His contemporary "works" are by no means an accident. They are only the continuation of that whole literary "heritage" of Zoshchenko which dates back to the 1920's.

Who was Zoshchenko in the past? He was one of the organizers of the literary group of the so-called "Serapion brothers." What was the socio-political physiognomy of Zoshchenko in the period of organizing the "Serapion brothers"? Permit me to turn to the journal *Literaturnye Zapiski (Literary Notes)*, No. 3 for 1922, in which the founders of this group set forth their credo. Among other revelations, Zoshchenko too has his "articles of faith" there in a piece called **"About Myself and About Something Else."** Feeling no constraint, Zoshchenko strips publicly and quite frankly expresses his political, literary "views." Listen to what he said there:

In general it is very troublesome to be a writer. Let us take ideology . . . Nowadays a writer is required to have an ideology . . . such a nuisance, really, to me. . . .

Tell me, what sort of 'exact ideology' can I have if no party attracts me as a whole?

From the point of view of party people I am an unprincipled man. All right, I myself shall speak for myself. I am not a Communist, not a Socialist-Revolutionary, not a monarchist, but simply a Russian and furthermore a politically amoral one. . . .

(pp. 17-19)

What do you say, comrades, about such an "ideology"? Twenty-five years have passed since Zoshchenko published this "confession." Has he changed since then? Not noticeably. During two and a half decades not only has he not learned anything and not only has he not changed in any way, but, on the contrary, with cynical frankness he continues to remain a preacher of ideological emptiness and vulgarity, an unprincipled and conscienceless literary hooligan. This means that now, as then, Zoshchenko does not like Soviet ways; now, as then, he is alien, and hostile to Soviet literature. If, with all this, Zoshchenko has become practically the coryphaeus of literature in Leningrad, if he is exalted in the Leningrad Parnassus, then one can only be amazed at the lack of principle, looseness, and slackness achieved by the people who paved the way for Zoshchenko and sing eulogies to him. (p. 19)

If Zoshchenko does not like Soviet ways, what is to be done: adapt oneself to Zoshchenko? It is not up to us to reconstruct our tastes. It is not up to us to reconstruct our way of life and our social order for Zoshchenko. Let him reform. And if he does not want to reform—let him get out of Soviet literature. In Soviet literature there is no place for rotten, empty, and vulgar works. (p. 20)

> Andrei A. Zhdanov, *"Literature,"* in his Essays on Literature, Philosophy, and Music, *International Publishers, 1950, pp. 7-44.**

ALEC BROWN   (essay date 1948)

[*The following excerpt demonstrates a Western reaction to the attack on Zoshchenko by Andrei Zhdanov and the Central Committee of the Communist Party (see excerpt dated 1946). For another discussion of Zhdanov's attack, see the excerpt by Vasa D. Mihaslovich (1967).*]

The latest news from Moscow concerning Zoshchenko was that at a Press Conference for foreign journalists held during some recent Moscow talks, Boris Gorbatov, a fellow novelist who enjoys an official position, stated that Zoshchenko had been suppressed because: 'for the past 25 years his work has given a distorted picture of reality, and reflected only the negative features of Soviet men and women'.

It is striking that it has taken the Communist dictatorship quarter of a century to discover how distorted were Zoshchenko's very popular pictures. But Zoshchenko himself, so Reuter's statement went on to say, 'had now realized his mistakes and was writing a book dedicated to the guerrillas of the Leningrad region'—which presumably means 'a book about the guerrillas of the Leningrad district'.

'If the book is a good one', Gorbatov is reported to have said, 'Zoshchenko will regain the trust of the people and re-enter the family of Soviet writers'.

This report that Zoshchenko is trying to cut his cloth according to the uniform specifications laid down is not at all surprising. Total suppression in a totalitarian state is a much more powerful weapon of force than suppression was under the sporadic and relatively less decided dictatorship of the tsars. (p. 215)

Zoshchenko has allegedly admitted his mistakes, and is writing a new book in which he is trying to avoid mistakes. The State suddenly asserts that for twenty-five years Zoshchenko was wrong in his opinions. Zoshchenko admits that this is so, and is trying to be right in his opinions. He is writing a book with new and 'correct' opinions. But decision as to whether Zoshchenko has or has not succeeded will no more rest with him when he finishes this new book, than it did when the State, taking twenty-five years, during which Zoshchenko was both freely and officially popular, . . . made the first decision that he was not to be allowed to write as he pleased.

In other words, however much he 'repent', Zoshchenko has clearly not undergone that revulsion of spirit which a free man may experience. It is not the change of opinion of a Tolstoy or Dostoievski who, though labouring under Tsarist tyranny, still had some freedom of expression. It is not really Zoshchenko saying: 'I see I have been wrong for twenty-five years—but here is what I now think is good writing'.

In other words, all this has been dictated to him. Less than six months since the state functionaries who control his very existence as a writer decided that the Pravda Press, Moscow, should print a popular 100,000 [copy] edition of his latest stories, these same outer forces suddenly discovered in him a sink of iniquity, and suppressed him—or what for twenty-five years had been him.

Shortly after the grandiose decrees which opened the latest mass purges were promulgated, there was a rumour in Paris that Zoshchenko the man had also been liquidated, that is to say, shot. That was crude anti-Soviet nonsense. As we now see, Zoshchenko had merely been deboned. In a few months, perhaps, in standard Soviet packing, a protein and calory balanced ration will be available in a standard canister, labelled 'Zoshchenko'. But with us, alas, will remain the corpse of another Zoshchenko. Some of us—I certainly was one—used rather to scorn that swift, bright small bird which flitted so gaily hither and thither, and seemed in his journalistic feuilleton way, to carry on the tradition of Gogol, Leskov, Chekhov. . . . Meanwhile the broad public enjoyed him; among other reasons, because he fitted so well into our unkempt English hedgerows, where the free singing of one's thought, though hampered by all manner of ginnes and springes, is still not *verboten*. (p. 216)

By a well-orchestrated medley of pronouncements and comments, the impression has been widely given that Zoshchenko is an inexpressibly vulgar writer, finally descending to the compilation of indecencies. But it has not been made *clear*. Certainly not in the sense of Descartes' *'clear and precise'*, or of the laws of evidence. Even were it true, it could not be clear to us in this country because the work on which the whole barrage of mud-slinging turns simply is not available to us. There is as yet no English translation of Zoshchenko's **Before Sunrise**, and the rare copies which were once in the library of the Society for Cultrual Relations with the Soviet Union are at best extremely difficult to obtain. Anyway they are in Russian, which still too few people read, so that most people could at best take the assertion as made in good faith and reliable.

It could not be made *clear*. Yet the impression is abroad that it has been made clear. The most favourable view of Zoshchenko now seems to be that he is a vulgar writer who, even if the treatment meted out to him is harsh, after all 'asked for it'. The whole case, instead of being enquired into, is, together with the verdict, taken over from Moscow. True judgment on it is therefore in danger of going, by default, to the accusers. (p. 217)

Wiping out the man Zoshchenko, or the writer Zoshchenko, is an easy matter. But the very popular things he has written are not so easy to dispose of. Knowing that many people must have read the 'dangerous-thoughts' novel—knowing that the germs of free thought released by Zoshchenko are everywhere in the air—they too must be wiped out. This is to be achieved by deliberate distortion of reality. The novel must be made to seem something which it never was. (p. 225)

> Alec Brown, *"The Witness Box," in* The Wind and the Rain, *Vol. IV, No. 4, Spring, 1948, pp. 215-26.*

J. A. POSIN (essay date 1951)

[Posin has contributed studies of Russian literature to several periodicals and essay collections and has translated many of Zoshchenko's short stories into English. In the following excerpt, he surveys the subject matter of the stories and discusses some of

Dust jackets of three collections of Zoshchenko's stories. Courtesy of Ardis Publishers.

the methods he used in translating Zoshchenko's colloquial Russian into comparable English.]

[In the early 1920s Zoshchenko] settled in Petrograd (later to be renamed Leningrad) and joined the Petrograd literary circle, "The Serapion Brothers." He soon found his genre: a short, satirical storiette, which he exploited for upward of two decades until his career came to an abrupt stop.

During that time he was a very popular writer—with the readers, if not always with the party-line critics (so far as is known, Zoshchenko never joined the Communist party). There were daily, weekly, and monthly publications which liberally availed themselves of his talent. There were, also, numerous editions of his stories—stories which were, as a Russian saying goes, "shorter than a sparrow's beak"—in separate volumes.

Zoshchenko consciously and deliberately wrote for the masses. He scorned conventional literary effects; he wrote in the most widely understood medium, the street talk. However, the seeming simplicity of his language is deceiving. He had to work hard to acquire it, for it was not "native" to him: he was a comparatively well-educated person. In this effort to master his literary technique, the association with such writers as Zamyatin—whose superb satire, *We,* anticipated by thirty years and far surpassed in quality the recent best seller, *1984*—with whom Zoshchenko came in contact in Petrograd, could not help benefiting Zoshchenko. He was also encouraged and helped by Maxim Gorky.

The character of the publications which served as the most frequent outlets for Zoshchenko's work makes inevitable the inference that his audience was the mass audience of the Soviet Union, not the select highbrow audience. Strictly speaking, such a highbrow audience hardly exists any longer in the Soviet Union. And even a cursory persual of Zoshchenko's stories is sufficient to convince any one that they are devoid of any "preciousness" or any special subtlety. Like *Alice In Wonderland,* they are written for anybody who can read (including children), though the more sophisticated reader will derive a great deal more from them, *as usual.*

There is no evidence to support the view that Zoshchenko's popularity diminished toward 1946, although there were some attempts on his part to change his genre and engage in writing longer, nonsatirical narratives (partly autobiographical). These attempts were not successful, either from the standpoint of merit or that of popular acceptance. They remained just isolated attempts. Anyway, as he himself once stated, there was enough material in his own genre to last him a long lifetime.

In August 1946, however, Andrei Zhdanov, at that time an all-powerful member of the Russian Politburo and a personal confidant of dictator Stalin, made a speech in which he attacked the literary periodicals *Zvezda* ("The Star") and *Leningrad* for the continuous publication of the stories of Mikhail Zoshchenko. Following this attack, all Russian periodicals stopped publishing Zoshchenko's stories, and he has completely disappeared from the literary scene. (pp. 92-3)

Thus, an epoch was closed in Russian literary life. There have been other seemingly inexplicable purges of authors in the Soviet Union before—Boris Pilnyak was one of them—but Zoshchenko had for so many years been working with the apparent approval of the authorities that his final purge could not help being a shock.

And yet, if one is to accept the initial premise of dictatorship—namely, that all the enemies of the totalitarian state should be silenced or exterminated—the severe measures taken against Zoshchenko are not without logic. For about a quarter of a century, M. Zoshchenko had poked fun at the seamy sides of Soviet life. In almost every one of his humorous sketches, the people and situations which impede the progress of socialism and collective-minded thinking are\ ridiculed. More specifically, the target of Zoshchenko's satire is the selfish, backward, not-social-minded *obyvatel,* a term difficult to translate properly, which denotes a person thoroughly devoid of social consciousness, a "hoarder" type, a person who, according to a Russian saying, proclaims: "My hut is on a side; I know nothing," or, anglicized, "I don't want to be bothered!" Another term for the same type is *meshchanin*—literally, a small-towner, but in its figurative use denoting a philistine. So far as the American reader is concerned, the important thing in Zoshchenko's writings is not the incident or the situation per se. The important thing is *byt,* i.e., the portrayal—frequently unconscious—of the Soviet way of life, in which incident and situation are important only in so far as they contribute to the portrayal. Though the situations in Zoshchenko's stories are many, the central type is always the same, the philistine. Needless to say, this philistine is practically never a Communist, certainly never a responsible Party worker. That would not be tolerated by any editor in Russia, and, if by some miracle it were once, that would be the last terrestrial deed of that particular editor. In the story called **"An Incident,"** a mother traveling with her sick child can find no one among her traveling companions to take care of the infant long enough to allow her time to get off the train at a station to eat a bowl of soup. All are afraid she might leave the child with them for good. When, finally, somebody does take the child, that person is all too willing to believe the worst when the mother is slow in returning to her car. Are the Russians so suspicious by nature? Or are the conditions of life in Russia, perhaps, such as to foster the extra-suspicious attitude?... In **"Economy Program,"** the economy-minded Soviet employees decide to stop heating the community lavatory. They save some wood but they also ruin the pipes in the building. Can one make larger deductions from this little incident?... In the story **"Pushkin,"** a peculiar problem is presented on the background of an acute housing shortage. On the ninetieth anniversary of Pushkin's death, the house where the famous poet once lived was taken over by the government—which is the huge owner of all real estate in Russia—as a shrine dedicated to the memory of the poet. Some people, including the hero of the story, lose their living quarters because they were unfortunate enough to be living in the suddenly famous house. These people are indignant at the turn of events, and perhaps there is something to say for their side of the picture. Perhaps the luxury of commemorating dead poets can wait when it means dispossessing the living human beings. In **"A Dangerous Little Play,"** the age-old Russian vice—drunkenness—is pictured in a somewhat novel situation.

The temptation is to go on citing examples, but what has already been quoted is enough to show the scope and the target of the satirist. On the whole, it can be said that the target is provided by the discrepancy between the actual and the ideal. So far, it seems, so good: surely the ruling group could find no fault with laughing at the Soviet philistine. But like a powerful poison—a substance which did no harm, and sometimes good, in small doses—Zoshchenko's satire had a lethal effect upon the Stalin dictatorship when its cumulative action over more than two decades was considered. For a legitimate query could not help arising in the minds of the readers, namely: if the average Soviet citizen, over such a long period, remains so

ridden with philistinism and petty trivialities of life, where is the *new* man, the product of the "greatest revolution in history"? Is there such a being at all?

Zoshchenko's stories have frequently been compared with the stories of Chekhov, and, indeed, there is some justification for the comparison. Like Chekhov, Zoshchenko was not an amateur in literature—that is, he did not approach it with an amateur's attitude. Chekhov started writing his brief humorous bits for the humorous weeklies of the early 'eighties with a view to earning a few rubles and helping himself through medical school. And later, when he gave up his medical career for literature, it was literature which was seeking him, not vice versa. Essentially the same attitude was displayed by Zoshchenko, who seems never to have thought in terms of glory, recognition, or the opinion of the coming generations. To him, literature was a job to be done, and, in his peculiar sphere, he did it extremely well. In their respective social strata, both Chekhov and Zoshchenko do substantially the same thing. Chekhov's chief target was the impotence, the emptiness, or the smugness of the intellectual and semi-intellectual philistine. Zoshchenko portrays the selfishness, the bewilderment before the new reality, and the subversion to his own purposes of various government measures on the part of the individual who is being addressed in the Soviet republic as "citizen" (*grazhdanin*) but who is the spiritual heir of the small-towner-philistine (*meshchanin*). As in the case of Gorky, Zoshchenko's best writing comes from personal experience or observation. He had tried a dozen or more trades—fantastically unrelated one to the other—before he settled on that of a writer. Out of his experience as a specialist in rabbit and poultry raising came his delightful story, **"The Test of Heroes,"** where the "specialist" in poultry raising is baffled by the fact that his ducks—drown, of all things. And his experience as a senior patrolman at Ligovo gave the background for that miniature classic, **"A Gay Little Episode."** His knowledge of the procedural technique of the organs of Soviet justice, and punishment, comes from his experience as an agent of the Criminal Investigation Department in Petrograd.

Like Chekhov, Zoshchenko possesses the gift of being able to grasp the essential point of a character or a situation and present it convexly with the utmost economy of words. And what words! Zoshchenko is one of the most colloquial writers; in that respect he differs from Chekhov and other humorists. This quality of extreme colloquialism makes him difficult to translate, and necessitates frequent departure from literal rendition. The substitution of *equivalent* expressions rather than literal rendition of Russian colloquialisms is frequently the only satisfactory way out. Let us take a few examples. In the story **"The Actor,"** there is an expression, *"dooy do gory"*—literally, "Blow as far as the mountain"—with which the audience tries to encourage an actor to do his utmost. Obviously, it could not be rendered literally, for it would mean nothing that way. In its place, I substituted the familiar Americanism: "Give it both barrels!"... Then there is the matter of profanity. In practically every other of Zoshchenko's stories there is an expression *"sookin syn"* which, literally, means "the son of a bitch." However, in Russian, it possesses various degrees of mildness—with or without a "smile"—or sharpness, depending on the context. In most instances, the flavor of the original is best preserved by softening the expression to "the son of a gun," and so I proceeded to soften it. On several occasions, however, the stronger form is definitely indicated—for instance, in the story **"The Mechanic"**—and in those instances I used the literal form as being also the *closest in meaning*.

While on this subject of the technique of translation, let me say that I do not regard the *improvement* of the original as a legitimate concern of a translator. The translator should be concerned with the faithful rendition—as nearly exactly as he can—of the *meaning* of the original. An ideal translation must produce the same *impression* in either language, on the same type of a reader. If one were to compare the work of a translator with that of a counterfeiter, it would be easily seen that "improvement" would make the end result worthless: from a counterfeiter's point of view, money must be made not "better than the government's," but "just as good as the government's." The translator should have a similar ambition, with allowance for the greater legitimacy and social acceptability of his profession.

The overwhelming majority of Zoshchenko's stories are extremely short—less than one thousand words, on the average—yet he makes his point clear everytime. One of the shortest of his stories is also one of the most significant—**"The Devil's Little Plaything,"** which we may call a symbolic satire. Here, a man, an average Soviet "citizen," buys in a toyshop a game for children, called *"diabolo."* It consists of two sticks tied with a cord, and a roller. The child is supposed to throw the roller up in the air and catch it on the cord when it comes down. It develops that the toy, as produced in the Soviet shop, cannot be used because the roller is made out of wood instead of rubber, as called for by foreign specifications. Instead of amusing himself, the child in the story nearly kills himself. The clerk in the store tells the indignant father who bought the toy not to let his child lay his hands on the "plaything" for fear of dire results, but to nail it up somewhere over the child's bed, and let the boy amuse himself by just *looking* at the dangerous toy. The "plaything" made on the foreign pattern obviously represents the revolution and Marxism, perverted in the process of its being applied to Russian conditions. This is one of the most telling blows against the Bolshevik dictatorship, and had the censors been more intelligent—which fortunately censors seldom are—Zoshchenko's writing career might have been stopped in the 'twenties when the sketch first appeared, instead of being allowed to develop for twenty years more.

One could cite examples of Zoshchenko's work almost ad infinitum. But there is much more satisfaction for the reader in making his own firsthand acquaintance with Zoshchenko. Apart from everything else, reading him is pure, unadulterated fun. . . . (pp. 93-9)

> *J. A. Posin, "M. Zoshchenko and His Art," in* The Pacific Spectator, *Vol. 5, No. 1, Winter, 1951, pp. 92-110.*

MARC SLONIM (essay date 1953)

[*Slonim was a Russian-born American critic who wrote extensively on Russian literature. In the following excerpt, he provides a brief history of Zoshchenko's membership in the Serapion Brothers literary group and traces some early influences on Zoshchenko's satirical writing, including the fiction of Yevgeny Zamyatin. Slonim discusses Zoshchenko's major works and characterizes him as the most important Soviet humorist of the three decades from 1920 to 1950.*]

In the winter of 1921, when political pressures were very strong and debates about proletarian hegemony rather heated, a few young men, most of them demobilized from the Red Army, gathered in Petrograd under the patronage of Gorky and Zamiatin. . . .

These young men came at last to call themselves Serapion Brethren: they were all great admirers of E.T.A. Hoffmann, the German Romantic. . . . In Hoffmann's work certain friends who gather regularly to exchange stories assume the name of the Serapion Brethren—which is also title of the book. (p. 294)

The stress on the formal and technical aspects of art, the assertion of a poet's right to dreams and fancy, the resistance to vulgar attempts at political pressure—all were present in the manifesto of the group: 'We have called ourselves the Serapion Brethren because we object to coercion and boredom, and because we object to everybody writing in the same way . . . "Each of us has his own drum," Nikitin declared at our first gathering. We think that present-day Russian literature is amazingly prim, smug, and monotonous. We are allowed to write stories, novels, and conforming dramas . . . provided they are social in content and inevitably on contemporary themes. We demand but one thing: that a work of art be organic and authentic, and that it live its own peculiar life.' (p. 295)

Despite their defense of art against political interference, all the Brethren were 'sons of the Revolution' and had colorful biographies. At the age of twenty-six Michael Zoshchenko . . . summed up his experiences in these vital statistics: 'Arrested six times; sentenced to death once; wounded three times; attempted suicide twice; beaten up three times.' He could also add that he had been an officer in the Czarist Army and a volunteer in the Red Army. Others—such as Tikhonov or Vsevolod Ivanov—had also battled against the Whites, had endured privations, had been frequently exposed to death, and had followed dozens of trades in their desperate struggle for survival . . . , while Zoshchenko was by turns a professional gambler, actor, and detective. All of them may be described as Fellow Travelers and as sympathetic to the Bolshevik regime, though none of them, at that time, was a member of the party. They all wrote about war and the Revolution—it was they, in fact, who had introduced this theme into Russian prose; but they firmly believed that young writers ought to carry on pre-Revolutionary aesthetic trends. Their opinions and attempts varied widely, and they stressed and valued this diversity. (pp. 295-96)

The Serapion Brethren were disciples of Zamiatin and had one trait in common—their interest in literary craftsmanship. Techniques and devices seemed to absorb them much more than problems of ideological orthodoxy. Their main contribution lay in stylistic inventiveness, fantasy, and the presentation of new life-material in an individual manner. Each of them occupied his own place in Soviet letters: Fedin led the revival of the novel; Vsevolod Ivanov's ornate prose initiated a regional and exotic trend; Zoshchenko became pre-eminent in the satirical vein, which stemmed directly from Zamiatin's ironical stories and attained such popularity in the 1920's. (p. 296)

[In] the effort to 'democratize' literature and bring it closer to the idiom of the masses, young writers resorted to a host of localisms and regional forms. The proletarian writers and the Fellow Travelers were responsible for a veritable eruption of dialectical turns, of slang and colloquialisms. (p. 300)

The satirical tendency that had flourished in the 1920's owing for the most part to the efforts of the Serapion Brethren eventually became incompatible with official optimism. The Fellow Travelers were intimating that the New State, the declared ambition of which was to point the way to all humanity, in reality contained millions of ignorant, coarse, and stupid people, that Soviet officials were as rigid and corrupt as their Czarist predecessors, and that the bearers of the Revolutionary flame were impeded by liars, scoundrels, and sycophants. The humorists of the period resumed the caustic and bantering tradition of Gogol and Leskov. While the latter furnished the folkloristic form and linguistic patterns, the former exerted a decisive influence on the spirit of the satirists: the blending of the comic with tragic fantasy runs throughout the work of Katayev, Kaverin, Zoshchenko, and many others. (p. 301)

The most important humorist of the period was undoubtedly Michael Zoshchenko, who had received his training in the Serapion circle. . . . He began publishing in 1921 upon joining the Serapion Brethren and in a comparatively short while attained enormous popularity.

In *The Tales by Nazar Ilyich Sinebriukhov* . . . , the book that launched Zoshchenko into fame, comic happenings continually verge on the grotesque. Corporal Sinebriukhov (Blue Belly), the narrator (Zoshchenko almost invariably employs the pattern of the *skaz,* or colloquial tale), is attracted by the aristocratic life, by titled women and refined manners—and when Communism does away with all this nonsense he becomes involved in almost unbelievable situations. He undergoes privations and humiliations in order to amass paper money, which the Revolution makes completely valueless; he has a narrow escape from bandits, and in his turn becomes a highwayman—all for the sake of Victoria, the beautiful and noble Polish lady. Eventually it becomes apparent that she is neither virtuous nor noble, and not even as pretty as the corporal had imagined her.

In this full report of his bad luck Sinebriukhov talks an absurd idiom of the half-educated and mixes popular speech with journalese or mangled bookish terms. Zoshchenko, continuing Leskov's tradition, made this language his specialty. This *skaz* style, which Zoshchenko employed throughout his work, has been tagged 'Zoshchenko language.' Essentially it is a combination of several linguistic levels (not unlike the idiom used by Damon Runyon's Broadway guys and by certain characters of Ring Lardner) and reflects mental confusion. 'It is usually maintained,' Zoshchenko has remarked in his *Letters to a Writer,* 'that I am mangling the beautiful Russian language, that I employ words not in their rightful meanings purely for comic effects, that I write in a twisted idiom with the intention of provoking belly laughs. But all that is erroneous. I hardly twist anything: I write the same language in which the man in the street thinks and talks.'

Zoshchenko's short stories, which have enjoyed great success during the last three decades, reflect the absurdities, distor-

Zoshchenko with the Serapion Brothers in the early 1920s. The members of the group are, from left to right: Konstantin Fedin, Mikhail Slonimsky, Nikolai Tikhonov, Elizaveta Polonskaya, Zoshchenko, Nikolai Nikitin, Ilya Gruzdev, and Venyamin Kaverin. Courtesy of Ardis Publishers.

tions, and psychological confusions of the Soviet era. He revealed the rut and rot of daily life, which unfolded in all their vulgarity, meanness, and stupidity behind the magnificent façade of lofty slogans and Communist aspirations. Reading his stories is like stepping from the orchestra, from which the stage appeared crowded with heroes and great events, into the wings where stagehands and spear-carriers curse and spit amid dust, rubbish, and coarse daubed canvas. Zoshchenko's hero is the philistine, the half-educated citizen, who, while using a badly digested Communist phraseology, remains avaricious, competitive, and narrow-minded. He is entangled in a web of trivial incidents to which he attaches great importance: the bus conductor has short-changed him, and the resultant squabble ends in a free-for-all; a pannikin of milk boils over in the communal kitchen, and half a dozen housewives go on the warpath; some office messengers hang about to watch a street fight, and an entire institution has to suspend work. All of Zoshchenko's absurd people—sentimental, guitar-strumming telegraph operators, 'progressive bridegrooms' who won't marry unless the bride brings a good chest of drawers into the new household, the smug clerks whose clothes are stolen at the public baths— all these are chockfull of prejudices and superstitions and other such rubbish; like funhouse mirrors, their primitive minds distort all the slogans and ideas of the times and their preposterous pidgin Russian is their best characterization.

In 1930, when the Fellow Travelers were investigated by the On Guardists, the question was raised whether Zoshchenko's satire was as innocent as it seemed. Did he not allow himself too much leeway in depicting the average Soviet citizen as a man of the past saddled with all the vices that were the exclusive attributes of the bourgeoisie? Was not his jeering actually directed against the newly risen predominant class and the new regime? After all, the Revolution was supposed to have swept away the lower middle class. Zoshchenko's defenders, however, pointed out that Russian satirists had always aimed at the same targets—inefficiency, vulgarity, ignorance, and coarseness. For some time Zoshchenko kept on with his topical stories, creating new variants of his own hero. But Soviet criticism frowned on his humor: it lacked, apparently, the required social and ideological background. The humorist understood the warning and tried to bring in new themes and to broaden the range of his satire. In *Restored Youth* . . . , a novel, he drew an old professor who became rejuvenated and married a young girl, but had so much trouble with her that he finally suffered a stroke and returned to his family. Some Soviet critics were taken in by Zoshchenko's discussion of biological problems and his psuedo-scientific digressions; they even talked of the 'union of science and fiction' which the writer had attempted, failing to see that what Zoshchenko was after was grotesque situations, a gallery of dead-end characters, and a series of episodes exposing stupidity and egotism, which were basted together by a thin thread of plot. In his next long work, *The Pale-Blue Book* . . . , he abandoned all pretense of writing a novel and simply presented a collection of historical, or, rather, pseudo-historical, anecdotes about great events, famous figures, love, money, and perfidy. It was a parody of history in the same spirit as *Restored Youth* had been a parody of science.

Like so many storytellers who are reproached with the topical and fragmentary nature of their work, Zoshchenko had always aspired to the Big Book. His last and none too successful attempt at this was an autobiography of sorts, which was serialized in 1943 under the title of *Before the Sunrise*. It provoked heated debate, which revealed that threatening clouds were gathering over the writer's head. In this new work Zosh-

chenko analyzed the reasons for his melancholy, wistfulness, and unhappiness (like so many humorists, Zoshchenko is in private life rather sad and retiring, and something of a hypochondriac). The fact that Zoshchenko published his 'confession' during the war, and that he delved into his own mannerisms, complexes, and unconscious drives while other writers were glorifying the heroic defense of the fatherland and helping to build up the morale of the people, served as the main argument for vicious attacks against him.

There were other, more specific accusations: Communist critics considered the descriptions of intimate, personal, almost pathological emotions of fear, shyness, sex, and whim 'alien to the epoch and to the people' and 'permeated with the spirit of bourgeois introspective individualism.' His attempt to explain man's conduct not in terms of social and economic conditioning but as a result of physiological factors and unconscious urges or blocks seemed to be 'socially harmful' and 'reeking of bourgeois, decadent psychology.' He was even labeled by party critics as a 'brainless and pornographic scribbler.' His lack of patriotic fervency during World War II (which, unlike so many of his confreres, he spent in the tranquillity of Alma-Ata, the capital of the Kazak Republic) hardly helped matters.

In Leningrad, after the war, Zoshchenko began to play a prominent part in the local Writers League and was, as always, popular with the reading public. Two weeks before he was publicly condemned, the party publishing house, Pravda, issued a low-priced collection of his latest stories, in a first printing of 100,000 copies. It included **'The Adventures of an Ape,'** which showed Soviet citizens as gossipy and vulgar halfwits. When Andrew Zhadanov announced in 1946 the tightening of ideological controls over literature, this was the story he singled out as a 'disgusting calumny on the Soviet people.' Was not Zoshchenko intimating that an ape often shows more intelligence and decency than the average Soviet biped?

Zoshchenko was castigated as a writer who for a long time had helped to 'disintegrate and corrupt' literature; he was expelled from the Union of Soviet Writers and was banned from the Russian press, while his name became a synonym for a ''literature vagabond.'' He made an attempt to atone for his transgressions: in September 1947, he was allowed to publish in the *New World* several short stories in which he described the German invasion and the devotion of the guerrillas to the regime. In 1950 his work appeared in other periodicals—but all his stories were pale and lifeless. His star, which had been so brilliant for three decades, was now definitely waning. (pp. 303-06)

> Marc Slonim, ''Serapion Brethren and Fellow Travelers,'' in his Modern Russian Literature: From Chekhov to the Present, *Oxford University Press, New York, 1953, pp. 294-318.**

SIDNEY MONAS (essay date 1961)

[*In the following excerpt from his introduction to* Scenes from the Bathhouse, and Other Stories of Communist Russia, *Monas provides a definition of skaz and discusses Zoshchenko's use of this technique.*]

Zoshchenko's technique is that of the *skaz*, the oral tale. The tale is supposed to have a moral, instructional point, to illustrate something; that is the excuse for telling and listening. The point gets lost on the way: the storyteller is caught up in the story itself or simply succumbs to the delight of having an audience. It is himself he expresses, and not the moral. Either he loses it completely and arrives at a conclusion as unexpected for him as it is for his audience, or he tacks it on by *force majeure*, exposing either his own clay feet or the insubstantiality of all conclusions, or both. In Russian literature it was Leskov who first developed this technique, derived from popular storytelling. The narrator is himself a character, whom we come to understand through the words and expressions he uses and misuses, his repetitions, digressions, the things he chooses to talk about, and the things we know are there between the lines but which he is clearly incapable of expressing. The difference between the *skaz* and the ordinary "point-of-view" story or novel is, first of all, its oral quality—the sound of the spoken voice—and, secondly, the untutored, "primitive" nature of the narrator, his unself-consciousness. Among American writers, Ring Lardner uses this technique in a number of places—in his baseball stories, and most successfully in the story called "Haircut." However, Lardner was much more of a moralist than either Leskov or Zoshchenko. He used the technique to condemn the narrator or to induce the reader to feel sorry for him. Leskov and Zoshchenko do this to a far lesser degree. As in Lardner, the narrator inadvertently expresses his own *poshlost*—his vulgarity, his trashiness, the cheap fake of his pretensions—but this is less important than the sheer absurdity of the tricks nature plays with him. Leskov was capable of sustaining this kind of interest over considerable length. Zoshchenko, like most moderns, is shorter-winded, but the brevity of his stories is part of their effect.

They are composed with care, with attention to details of diction, inflection, and rhythm. This is by no means obvious, and, indeed, the effect would be lost if it were. The materials are so primitive that the reader would instantly resent any kind of obvious manipulation on Zoshchenko's part as grossly unfair. The effects of spontaneity and immediacy, of the candid photograph, the sketch made hastily on the spot exactly as observed, the tape recording, are all indispensable to Zoshchenko's art.

The situations that provide the material for his stories are the most common and ordinary details of everyday Soviet reality, familiar not only to the average Soviet citizen but even to the casual tourist: the housing shortage, the scarcity of consumers' goods and the inefficiency of consumers' services, bad roads, bureaucracy and red tape, the ferocious juxtapositions of backwardness and material progress. These things are not merely the background for the stories: they determine motives, they shape or obliterate intentions, they conceal, they expose, they frustrate, they assume a shape and a character of their own, and they are felt as a natural force almost as intractable and indifferent to human concern as the desert or the sea. They may be tricked or circumvented, but they cannot be made to care; moreover, they will inevitably leave their stamp on the tricksters and circumventers. A person may resemble the desert; the desert is never like a man.

Personal problems and private griefs, fine feelings and an aesthetic sense, are reduced, against this desert, to the scale of absurdity. It isn't fidelity or infidelity in marriage that counts; it's the availability of an apartment. People will, of course, attempt to inflate their feelings in talk, but they are betrayed by the language they use. The desert is not only around them, it is in them. (pp. vii-viii)

> *Sidney Monas, in an introduction to* Scenes from the Bathhouse, and Other Stories of Communist Russia *by Mikhail Zoshchenko, edited by Marc Slonim,*

translated by Sidney Monas, The University of Michigan Press, 1961, pp. v-xvii.

VERA VON WIREN (essay date 1962)

[*In the following survey of Zoshchenko's life and career, von Wiren distinguishes between those of Zoshchenko's works that reflect his personal artistic ideals—such as* "The Campaign of Economy," "The Nervous People," *and* "The Bath"—*and those works obviously written under pressure to conform to Party literary standards—such as* "The Black Prince," "The Inglorious End," *and* Children's Tales. *In contrast, Edward J. Brown (1982) contends that Soviet censorship had little effect upon Zoshchenko's literary career.*]

Zoshchenko is read today and remembered for his humor, which belongs to the great tradition of Gogol, Leskov, and Chekhov. Yet Zoshchenko was more than a humorist. His brilliant, inquisitive mind and independent spirit eagerly searched for new ideas and new forms of artistic expression. When this search became offensive to the Party and the guardians of Soviet arts, Zoshchenko was forced to abandon it, at least on the surface, if he was to continue his existence as a writer. As evidence of his submission, he wrote about socialist construction, created "positive heroes," satirized capitalism and the capitalist countries, and extolled the achievements of the Soviet Union. But throughout this entire period of his artistic humiliation, he continued his independent experimentation. Attempting to compromise opposing forces, he produced two different, mutually antagonistic types of works: those designed to win Party approval and others testifying strongly to the torment of a dynamically independent creative spirit. For some time Zoshchenko's literary dualism succeeded, but discovery was inevitable. The Party, finally cognizant of Zoshchenko's "crime," was brutal in its vengeance. Zoshchenko was publicly denounced in 1946 and denied a voice in Soviet literature until a year and a half before his death, during the period of thaw, when a carefully selected and edited collection of his stories and tales was printed. (pp. 348-49)

In the time of the New Economic Policy (1922-1928), when his popularity reached its highest peak, Zoshchenko moved from the *povest* and *reportazh* to the humorous short story, the genre in which he was to produce his most outstanding work. The stories written during the NEP dealt with various topical issues: the program for the liquidation of illiteracy, the housing shortage, economic planning, bureaucratic red tape, etc. The heroes, usually plain citizens or government officials, appear in absurd situations. The absurdity is the result, in most cases, of a mechanical interpretation and application of the principles of the new social, economic, and political system of Communism. Determination to achieve the total transformation of society along the lines of the "new faith" frequently leads to an almost fanatically rigid adherence to the letter of the law unaccompanied by any feeling for its spirit. **"The Campaign of Economy,"** . . . a typical story of the NEP period, illustrates this well. The subject is the economy measures instituted by the Soviet government in the early post-revolutionary years. The narrator relates how the supervisor of a plant approaches the order to economize which has come "from above":

> But what should we economize, no one knows. We started to discuss the matter. Maybe we shouldn't pay the accountant's salary, or something like that, someone suggested. But the supervisor says: "If you don't pay the old devil's salary, he'll raise hell in the trade Union. That

shouldn't happen. Let's think of something else." At this point, thank goodness, our cleaning woman gave her female opinion. "Since," she says "it is such an international issue, and speaking generally a mess, why don't we, for instance, stop heating the bathroom? Why should we use up the precious logs? It ain't a living-room you know!"

Everybody agrees to this plan. When spring comes, they rejoice over the discovery that they have saved seven cubic feet of wood. The narrator then describes the outcome of the project: [the water pipe has frozen and burst]. . . . The story ends with the following statement made by the narrator:

> Well, we shall easily manage without the pipe till fall. And in the fall we will install a cheap pipe. It ain't a living-room, you know!

In their desire to carry out successfully the order "from above," the characters become blind to all the consequences of their conservation program. They can boast that they have economized, that they have succeeded in the task assigned them, but their economy is an absurdity. Zoshchenko's narrator however, does not see this absurdity. He is, as Zoshchenko claimed, an average Soviet citizen, a semi-educated petit bourgeois, the typical new semi-cultured Soviet citizen of the NEP period, who simply records indifferently, naively, what he sees around him, avoiding the expression of his own opinion. Thus the author creates the impression that the stories are free of any of his personal views, that they are simply caricatures drawn from the *byt* without satirical purpose (as Zoshchenko himself was to insist in a few articles). Yet some of the narrator's utterances suggest, by their irony, the personal intrusion of the author and cause us to question his real intention. For example, in **"The Campaign of Economy,"** the narrator declares at one point: "Such pipes [installed by the tsarist regime] should be pulled out by the roots anyway." Many such telling statements in many other stories suggest the strong possibility that the satirical element was greater than Zoshchenko could afford to admit. Perhaps this explains the vehemence of his insistence that he was a humorist, not a satirist. It may also explain his preference for the *skaz* form, apart from his natural inclination towards a genre rich in comic potential. The *skaz* narrator offered Zoshchenko (besides comical language) a more protective mask than the simple device of a pseudonym which he used in his early stories not written in the *skaz* form.

Such stories as **"The Campaign of Economy,"** **"The Nervous People,"** . . . and **"The Bath"** . . . became classics in their time and established Zoshchenko as the most popular contemporary Soviet writer. (pp. 351-53)

Zoshchenko's only departure from the humorous short stories he produced throughout the NEP period was **Sentimental Tales** . . . , an interesting work in which the gay humor we accept as characteristic of Zoshchenko's early work gives way to almost bitter irony and sarcasm. In these tales, Zoshchenko begins more or less openly to question the validity of the new social system. Even though the revolution is over, and things should begin to look brighter, the narrator of **Sentimental Tales** fails to see significant improvement. On the contrary, he sees profit-seeking and the desire for materialistic gain running rampant as a result of economic practices of the NEP, and tries to focus the reader's attention on the possible consequences of such conduct. Although the subject (*byt*) and the style (*skaz*) remain the same, the hero is no longer an average semi-cultured

citizen, but a member of the intelligentsia. Furthermore, the author himself intrudes as a social philosopher expressing his personal disillusion in the contemporary state of affairs. (pp. 353-54)

[Soviet literary critic E.] Zhubrina emphasizes that in his **Sentimental Tales** Zoshchenko demonstrates the complete downfall of the old culture and the intelligentsia. Despite some dissenting voices, other Soviet literary critics also responded favorably to Zoshchenko's works of the 1920s. If controversy developed in their ranks it was not over the writer's talent or lack of it, but his motivation. Some insisted that Zoshchenko was doing the state a favor by exposing the petty bourgeois (the *meshchanin*, the vestige of the old regime) and by ridiculing him. Others insisted that Zoshchenko was presenting the Soviet regime in a ludicrous light and exposing not the vestiges of the old regime but simply the average Soviet citizen. In 1930, the official Soviet view of humor and satire was voiced in a series of articles in *Literaturnaya gazeta*. The articles were directed primarily against "useless humor" (Zoshchenko's works were mentioned specifically) and called for "constructive" writing. As a result of this shift in literary policy, Zoshchenko changed his approach and began to participate in "Social Construction." Practically abandoning the humorous short story, Zoshchenko turned to longer works. **Youth Restored** . . . , **History of a Man Reforged** . . . , and **The Blue Book** . . . , represent Zoshchenko's major efforts of the early 1930s and differ radically from his earlier works in style and theme.

Youth Restored is the longest and perhaps the most interesting of Zoshchenko's novels. Combining his highly comical idiom with scientific jargon, Zoshchenko created a novel which demonstrates a profound sense of humor and, at the same time, a good knowledge of biology and philosophy. The work is divided into three parts: a lengthy introduction, the story proper, and a series of commentaries on the theories proposed in the book. The introduction, which is continuous with the story, consists of nineteen short sections briefly introducing the ideas to be represented. The hero of the novel, an aging professor, tries to restore his youth; he tries it by the method of "mind over matter," through the exercise of his power of will. At the end of the story, Zoshchenko included a long series of commentaries in which he explores the power of conviction, and the ability of the mind to conquer physical obstacles; much of this part is a discussion of the subconscious. This novel aroused great interest not only among general readers but also among scientists. It was the subject of numerous discussions in various organizations, including scientific institutes and doctors' clubs, and was treated more as a scientific work than fiction. Even Pavlov took an interest in it and began to invite Zoshchenko to his "Wednesdays." (pp. 354-55)

The **Blue Book** was written on the advice of Gorky, who suggested to Zoshchenko that he write a study of the history of culture. **Blue Book**, first published in *Krasnaya nov* in 1934, is actually a collection of Zoshchenko's old stories subdivided into five categories: "Money," "Love," "Treachery," "Misfortunes," and "Curious Occurrences," with a foreword to each category. The introduction contains several anti-capitalistic passages, and is rich in praise of the Soviet Union. Very much like **The Sentimental Tales, Blue Book,** shows a great concern with gross materialism and its effect on human relations. The targets of Zoshchenko's satire are universal human weaknesses, rather than specific aspects of contemporary Soviet life.

The other three stories written in the 1930s were published in periodicals and were designed to please the Party; in them Zoshchenko either glorifies the Soviet Union or adds another portrait to the gallery of positive heroes. The first story, **"The Black Prince"** . . . is a historical sketch, satirizing America, France, Germany, Italy, and especially Japan, and hailing the Soviet Union. **"Retribution"** . . . is an autobiography of a woman who becomes a "positive heroine," **"The Inglorious End"** . . . is an autobiographical sketch about Kerensky, lauding Communism. In 1939 Zoshchenko also published a book for children, a collection of some old stories and a few new ones he wrote especially for children. In response to a favorable review, Zoshchenko decided to publish another book for young readers, this time containing exclusively children's stories, and in 1940, three volumes of **Children's Tales** appeared in print (among them twelve stories about Lenin's childhood). In the same year Zoshchenko also wrote a play, **"Dangerous Connections"** for the State Academic Theatre. Here we find a perfectly "positive" hero (a party member) and a "negative" hero (a *meshchanin*). The characters are so artificial, however, that they seem to be not living people but merely "bearers" of either the "positive" or the "negative" principle. The "positive hero" of the play was enthusiastically hailed by the critics. And since Zoshchenko had abandoned his "useless" humorous short stories for "constructive" works of literature, he himself became in the eyes of the Party a "positive hero." (pp. 356-57)

In attempting to define Zoshchenko's literary development a sharp division must be made between the works he wrote in expression of his personal artistic ideals and those obviously written under Party pressure. His early career, when this pressure was minimal, was a time of great artistic endeavor, of concern with art and esthetic problems. But when he ran headlong into Party opposition Zoshchenko submitted, and published works which respected the principles of socialist realism. This was a camouflage, concealing Zoshchenko's desire to continue the psychological and philosophical investigations he began in **Youth Restored**. For a ten-year period, the dual literary existence continued, until Zoshchenko attempted to bring the first of his studies before the public in the form of **Before the Sunrise**. Two installments of the novel appeared before the Party realized what had happened. It then moved swiftly to crush the work and, with it, one of the most promising and brilliant writers of Soviet literature. (pp. 360-61)

> *Vera von Wiren, "Zoshchenko in Retrospect," in The Russian Review, Vol. 21, No. 4, October, 1962, pp. 348-61.*

HUGH McLEAN (essay date 1963)

[*In the following excerpt from McLean's introduction to* Nervous People, and Other Satires, *which contains English translations of stories from a number of early collections, McLean discusses Zoshchenko's "trademark" satirical short stories. In the unexcerpted portion of the introduction Mclean discusses several of Zoshchenko's longer works.*]

Since it extends all the way from the Revolution to 1958, Zoshchenko's literary career offers a vivid illustration of the vicissitudes of a Soviet humorist during those forty turbulent years. . . .

Doubtless the satirist's mocking, derisive, generally negative view of human beings and their pretensions was already ingrained in Zoshchenko by the time of the Revolution. It showed itself partly in the extreme restlessness which led him through

an extraordinary series of jobs and occupations during the revolutionary period, and it was probably a factor in his decision to side with the Reds in the Civil War. (p. viii)

He began writing professionally in 1921, and his first volume of collected stories appeared in 1922. It was an immediate success with the reading public—a success Zoshchenko was to repeat and maintain for many years to come, in fact for as long as he was allowed to publish. During the twenties and thirties he was, next to Gorky, the most popular living Russian writer. Huge editions of his works were reprinted again and again, and the name Zoshchenko became a household word among persons who could hardly have mentioned another contemporary writer. At the same time, this mass popularity was not purchased at the price of any loss of artistic integrity or even of the esteem of the literati; indeed, Zoshchenko is one of the few writers of modern times who have successfully bridged the gap between the elite and the average reader. The most astute and discriminating critics, like Viktor Shklovsky and Viktor Vinogradov, were as entranced by his stories as any philistine in the street.

From the very beginning of his literary career Zoshchenko showed an unusual independence and boldness of attitude—a sturdy refusal to see the world through any glasses but his own. (p. ix)

During the relatively liberal twenties and even later Zoshchenko somehow managed to get away with his irreverences. To be sure, there were warnings—rumbles, snarls, and even an occasional nip—from the regime's literary watchdogs, but as yet no all-out assault. No doubt Zoshchenko's persistence in the face of these repeated danger signals was a demonstration of his determination and courage. But that he succeeded for so long in displaying his boldness in print was one of the advantages of his peculiar artistic method—a combination of irony, ambiguity, and camouflage which for many years bewildered his censors. It was discouragingly hard to pin him down. (pp. x-xi)

[Zoshchenko's] "trade-mark" genre [was] the short-short story or sketch, only two or three pages long, which he had made peculiarly his own. These little satires, which often made their first appearance in newspapers, were largely responsible for Zoshchenko's enormous popularity. They seemed to strike a responsive chord in the hearts of Russians of every description. Seemingly innocuous anecdotes illustrating what used to be called "defects in the mechanism," that is, disparities between official mythology and the stubborn facts of everyday life, they appealed to people as an expression of their irrepressible, unofficial human needs. No matter how unabated his Communist enthusiasm, no one could deny that for most Russians life was pretty hard; and to laugh about hardship made it easier to bear. Zoshchenko had a keen eye for the comic incongruities that cropped up constantly to bedevil people's lives. (p. xvi-xvii)

The building of the Soviet Utopia required not only a complete change in the economic and social conditions of life, but also a basic transformation in the behavior patterns of its citizens. To be sure, according to the Marxist formula, "being determines consciousness"; fundamental changes in the economic and class structure of society will in time automatically produce changed human beings. But this process takes time, and in the meantime the majority of Russians had been psychologically shaped under capitalism and carried with them into the new society obnoxious "capitalist survivals in the human consciousness." Official critics friendly to Zoshchenko interpreted his satires as directed against these "capitalist survivals"; he was thus playing a historically progressive role in helping the new Soviet man to throw off these unwanted relics of the past. Zoshchenko never openly objected to this useful interpretation, but one cannot escape the impression after reading many of his stories that he hardly shared it; he did not believe that all the antisocial tendencies of Soviet citizens were attributable to capitalism. Human nature, Zoshchenko seems to be saying, is much more intractable than the Utopians think.

For instance, one of the attributes of the new socialist man was supposed to be a sense of collective responsibility. The new society was no longer the capitalist jungle where men fought one another for the necessities of life, but a co-operative enterprise where all strove together for a common goal. Zoshchenko displays his skepticism in an anecdote called **"The Bottle."** A young man accidentally drops a bottle on the sidewalk and walks away in disgust, making no effort to pick up the pieces of broken glass. Other passers-by likewise fail to take any socially responsible action against this dangerous hazard. The narrator, who is watching these events while sitting on the opposite curb, bemoans such appalling evidence of bourgeois-individualistic survivals in the popular mind. . . . The narrator, of course, accepts the "capitalist survivals" theory. But does Zoshchenko?

With his elusive, innocent manner Zoshchenko got away with themes few other writers would have dared to touch; he even skirted some of the really forbidden topics of Soviet literature, such as the Party purges. One unsettling phenomenon of Soviet life in the thirties (and also recently) was the rapid changes in the names of institutions, streets, and whole cities as the stars of leading Party personalities rose or set. In **"An Incident on the Volga"** Zoshchenko succeeded in making this ominous feature of the permanent purge petty and ridiculous. During a single excursion trip on the Volga a steamer's name is changed, much to the confusion of its passengers, from *Comrade Penkin* to *Storm* to *Korolenko*. The name *Korolenko* was likely to last, the narrator observes, ".. since Korolenko was dead. Whereas Penkin was alive. And this was his basic shortcoming, which led to his name's being replaced."

In most of these stories Zoshchenko's method might be called "reverse idealization": he debases, degrades, vulgarizes, trivializes the material. Nothing is too sacred for his mocking irony. In **"Poverty"** even Lenin's far-sighted program for the electrification of Russia, which had inspired so many poets to write hymns to planning and progress, is brought down to the setting of a petty-bourgeois bedroom, now lit up by electricity for the first time: . . .

> Over there, someone's torn slipper lying around; in another place the wallpaper is ripped off and hangs in tatters; here a bedbug races along, running away from the light; or you see some indescribable rag, a gob of spittle, a cigarette butt, and a flea capers about . . .

The reason these irreverences were tolerated as long as they were lay partly in the magic word "petty bourgeois." The petty bourgeoisie was the repository of capitalist survivals in their most squalid form. The aristocracy and big bourgeoisie had been scattered by the Revolution to the four corners of the earth, but the artisans, the petty tradespeople, the minor civil servants and clerks had mostly stayed on, adapting themselves as best they could and carrying on their vulgar and materialistic existence in the midst of Soviet cities. As a class the petty

МИХАИЛ ЗОЩЕНКО

РАССКАЗЫ
НАЗАРА ИЛЬИЧА
ГОСПОДИНА
СИНЕБРЮХОВА

Э П О Х А
ПЕТЕРБУРГ ★ БЕРЛИН

1922

Title page of an early collection of Zoshchenko's short stories. Courtesy of Ardis Publishers.

bourgeoisie was doomed by history: it would either be cast aside or else be transformed and transfigured by society's victorious march toward socialism. Therefore, if Zoshchenko's satires were aimed at the petty bourgeoisie, so much the better, ran one official interpretation. But even in the writings of official Soviet critics the term "petty bourgeois" is sometimes used as if it describes, not a concrete sociological category, but an attribute of human nature—the petty, self-seeking, vulgar, and mundane element in everyone. But of course, "we are overcoming these things," and in the future Communist society there will be no room for them. In Zoshchenko, however, belief in the universality of petty-bourgeoisdom is often quite explicit, and only slightly less so are his doubts about the possibility of overcoming "these things." (pp. xvii-xx)

Hugh McLean, in an introduction to Nervous People, and Other Satires *by Mikhail Zoshchenko, edited by Hugh McLean, translated by Maria Gordon and Hugh McLean, Pantheon Books, 1963, pp. vii-xxviii.*

F. D. REEVE   (essay date 1963-64)

[*In the following excerpt, Reeve discusses the classic nature of Zoshchenko's works.*]

Everbody ought to be reading Zoshchenko.

Zoshchenko, who died in 1958, was the greatest satirist of the first half of the twentieth century. He was clever, he was bright, he was idealistic, he was irreverent. He was a ''perfect'' satirist. He ignored the politics of the world and insisted on the vitality of appetite. He readily perceived the discrepancy between appetite and performance, and he had the literary skill to be removed enough to persuade us to see it, also. (p. 615)

Comedy has always been conspicuously successful in times when there existed a powerful literary tradition, men of literary excellence, a clear and common set of standards, and an experience of moral degeneration. All of Zoshchenko's stories depend on the dichotomy between the prevalence of old, pre-revolutionary cultural values and the effort of the newly liberated proletariat to adopt those values, in the attempt debasing both the old values and the freshly acclaimed communist ideals.

Zoshchenko is a bitter comedian, not a jokester.... Zoshchenko sits alone in despondency collating in humility and wisdom the fragments of his life, which he assumes is neither more nor less significant than any other man's. These brief episodes, going back from young manhood to early infancy, have that actuality and power which we find only in great art. Zoshchenko's modesty wins our sympathy unequivocally, and his anecdotes in pattern present the meaning of an age.... After having followed Zoshchenko's reconstruction of his life and having come to consciousness of the possible meanings and functions of a man, we are aware, with him, of the limitations our own pattern-making imposes. We follow him when he suggests that both the myth beyond philosophy and the dream beyond rationality may be entirely true. In anguish, Zoshchenko says that ''the tragedy of human reason arises not from the high level of consciousness but from its inadequacy.'' Zoshchenko wrote ''miniature'' stories, but their scope reveals all the madness of our reason, the ''matter and impertinency mix'd.'' They are the work of a great writer. (pp. 616-17)

Zoshchenko, who is five years dead now, comes to us more loudly every day; he has a high, special, subtle, personal style; his private melancholy and hypochondria are, in his fiction, overcome by his consciousness of vitality, by his compassion for the vitality of others. He comes across easily and trenchantly on this side of the ocean, as if he were one of us. (p. 617)

F. D. Reeve, ''The Autobiography of a World,'' in The Hudson Review, *Vol. XVI, No. 4, Winter, 1963-64, pp. 610-17.**

HECTOR BLAIR (essay date 1967)

[*In the following excerpt from Blair's introduction to Zoshchenko's novel* Lyudi, *the critic finds that in the character of the protagonist, Ivan Ivanovich Belokopytov, Zoshchenko satirizes two archetypes of nineteenth century Russian fiction: the ''repentant nobleman'' who attempts to atone for the suffering caused by the system under which he prospered; and the ''superfluous man'' who is too self-possessed and ineffective to deal with reality.*]

[*Lyudi*] is a story about despair and decay, about the collapse of illusions, about the struggle for existence, and about the animal in man. It is interspersed with humour, but the humour is often savage and leaves a bitter taste. The hero of *Lyudi*, Ivan Ivanovich Belokopytov, who has left Russia as a political *émigré* from tsarism, returns to his native country some time after the Revolution, brimming with idealism, goodwill, and the desire to be useful to his fellow-men and society. But little by little his illusions are shattered, he finds no place for himself in society, and comes to see life as a cruel and forlorn struggle

for existence. He becomes more and more obsessed with the animal side of his nature until in the end he is hardly recognizable as a human being.

In Belokopytov Zoshchenko parodies two of the great archetypal figures of nineteenth-century life and literature in Russia: the 'repentant nobleman' and the 'superfluous man'. The 'repentant nobleman', oppressed by a sense of social guilt, often gave away his lands and possessions to those who suffered from the iniquitous system under which he prospered. Belokopytov, 'having read a lot of liberal books', squanders his inherited fortune, but less on those in genuine need than on a host of rapacious relatives and a gang of rogues and swindlers. Unable to find a place for himself in society, Belokopytov closely resembles the nineteenth-century 'superfluous man', the well-bred intellectual, too sensitive, too cultured and too idealistic to come to terms with a brutal reality, desperately aware of the need for change, yet prevented by a morbid self-preoccupation and a paralysing lack of willpower from making any contribution to this change. Yet Belokopytov remains a figure of parody, for his attainments ('He knew Spanish, he could play the harp, and he had a slight acquaintance with electricity') are of ludicrously marginal nature and could hardly equip him to make a valuable contribution to the life of his society.

Like Zoshchenko's short stories and anecdotes, *Lyudi* is cast in the form of 'skaz'. In the shorter works, which usually run to no more than two or three pages, the narrator is typically a 'little man', an average citizen, whose colloquial and sometimes ungrammatical turns of speech and out-of-place use of official jargon and high style reveal his lack of education and his mental confusion, as well as his social and cultural pretensions. The narrator in these shorter works restricts himself to the recounting of events and the crude philosophizing which they provoke in him. In *Lyudi,* however, the narrator is himself an author and also expresses views about literature and about the writer's role in Soviet society. The use of 'skaz' frees Zoshchenko from any direct responsibility for the opinions expressed and at the same time enables him to reply obliquely to criticisms which had been levelled at his own works, notably the charge that he had failed to concern himself with social themes and positive heroes.

In truth the author-narrator in *Lyudi* is not so very far removed from the 'little man' of the short stories. He is a provincial who does not possess the 'material possibility' of living 'in the great centres or capitals of republics in which, for the most part, the historic events take place'; he is a philistine, deeply suspicious of 'educated critics, babbling in six foreign languages' or Moscow psychiatrists, writing their nonsensical reports 'no doubt under the influence of drink'; he is, in short, less travelled, less cultured, and less educated than his hero, Belokopytov. His narrative is marked by the widespread use of colloquial language, and occasional faults of syntax and grammar, and is interspersed with none-too-relevant excursions, lapses of memory and concentration, and chatty commentaries on the events of the story.

Disdaining any 'paltry and sentimental' title for his story, the narrator (and Zoshchenko himself) opted instead for the 'resounding and significant' word *Lyudi*. It would hardly be fanciful to suggest that the choice of such a title for Zoshchenko's melancholy little tale about 'people' and their struggle for existence can be regarded as evidence that it expresses something very close to Zoshchenko's own conception of the human condition. Quite apart from Belokopytov, Zoshchenko's gallery of provincials and philistines is hardly calculated to inspire confidence in humanity. There is Nina Osipovna, Belokopytov's wife, featherheaded, fussy, snobbish and materialistic, a petty-bourgeoise, dreaming only of the day when she and her husband will be able to 'open their own little co-op'. There is the fellow-lodger, Yarkin, with his 'bull-like neck', whose interest in life abroad is apparently only a cover for his desire to acquire Belokopytov's elegant foreign suitcase. There are various episodic characters, none of them, with the possible exception of Katerina Vasil'yevna, the landlady, likely to evoke much sympathy. Finally there are the onlookers and passers-by, collapsing in hilarious *Schadenfreude* ["malicious pleasure"] at the moment of Belokopytov's downfall, 'peering into other people's windows' and generally displaying a brand of crass and insolent curiosity endemic in all Zoshchenko's minor characters.

'There is a great sadness on earth.' No other work expresses Zoshchenko's belief more poignantly than *Lyudi*. (pp. 6-8)

> Hector Blair, in an introduction to Lyudi by Mikhail Zoshchenko, Cambridge at the University Press, 1967, pp. 1-8.

VASA D. MIHASLOVICH (essay date 1967)

[In the following excerpt, Mihaslovich examines the reasons behind Soviet cultural advisor Andrei Zhdanov's attack on Zoshchenko's works and particularly on the short story "Adventures of a Monkey" (see Zhdanov excerpt dated 1946). Mihaslovich theorizes that the attack was occasioned by Zhdanov's interpretation of the story as an allegory, with the monkey symbolizing the Russian people's quest for freedom from oppression. The monkey's disillusionment with life outside of its cage is equated with the Soviet people's realization that their dreams of freedom have not been fulfilled by the Revolution. For another discussion of official Soviet reaction to Zoshchenko's story, see the excerpt by Alec Brown (1948).]

When in 1946, at a meeting of Leningrad writers, Andrei Zhdanov launched his merciless attack on Mikhail Zoshchenko, it was felt among the writers loyal to the party and the regime that it was long overdue. Zoshchenko had been a thorn in the flesh of cultural officials for a long time. From several earlier skirmishes with watchdogs of "purity" and "correctness" in the Soviet literature, Zoshchenko emerged still determined to continue his own ways. (p. 84)

Zhdanov singled out two of Zoshchenko's works in attacking his "heresy"—a short story, **"Adventures of a Monkey"**. . . , and an incomplete longer tale, **"Before Sunrise"**. . . . It was the first story on which Zhdanov turned the full blast of his attack: "The meaning of this 'work' by Zoshchenko consists in his depicting Soviet people as idlers and monsters, as silly and primitive people" [see excerpt dated 1950]. Zhdanov went on to find a similar attitude in other writings of Zoshchenko, even back to his early days as a Serapion Brother. Now it became quite clear that Zoshchenko had never been a good Soviet writer; on the contrary, he had always been a "thoroughly rotten and corrupt. . .preacher of ideological emptiness and vulgarity, an unprincipled and conscienceless literary hooligan" with a "vulgar and mean little soul." In short, an unSoviet writer.

Zhdanov's attack on Zoshchenko provokes some interesting questions. Why did he assail him openly now, after so many years of tolerating his literary unorthodoxy, and only a few months after Zoshchenko received a medal "for valiant work during the Great Patriotic War of 1941-1945"? Why did Zhdanov choose to attack and to silence only Zoshchenko and Akhmatova when there are always numerous suitable targets? Finally, why did he single out **"Adventures of a Monkey"** to substantiate his accusations against Zoshchenko?

The first two questions can be answered in connection with historical and literary developments of that time. The third question, as the most intriguing of those mentioned above, deserves closer scrutiny.

"Adventures of a Monkey" was labeled by many critics, even by the Western ones, as an innocuous story meant primarily for children. Sidney Monas, in his introduction to Zoshchenko's short stories, calls **"Adventures of a Monkey"** "the curiously innocent little parable." In similar fashion, Hugh McLean, also in an introduction to Zoshchenko's stories, characterizes it as "the rather innococuous story." Rebecca Domar likes to see in the story general human traits, rather than specifically Soviet [see Additional Bibliography]. The historians of Soviet literature—Gleb Struve, Vera Alexandrova, Marc Slonim—usually mention the story only as a pretext for Zhdanov's attack. All these scholars seem to agree that **"Adventures of a Monkey,"** being basically an innocent and simple story, certainly did not warrant the severity of Zhdanov's wrath. True, the plot is a marvel of simplicity geared, most likely deliberately, to a child's level of comprehension. During a bombing raid in some southern town a monkey escapes from the zoo. A military transport driver picks the animal up but it escapes again. The surprised inhabitants of the city, seeing the loose monkey on the street, start chasing it. The monkey begins to doubt the wisdom of leaving the zoo after all. "It is easier to breathe in a cage," it concludes. A young boy catches the monkey in his yard. He has dreamed all his life of having a monkey of his own, and now he is not willing to let this opportunity slip through his hands. He bestows upon it all his affection and all the food he can muster. His grandmother, however, dislikes the animal fiercely, afraid that it may eat her candy. If it were not for her, the monkey would stay with the boy forever. Instead, it is on the road again. This time it is caught by an invalid, who immediately wants to sell it. But when he tries to wash it with soap, the terrified animal escapes for the fourth time. The young boy finds it once more. All three temporary owners lay claim to the monkey, but it is finally given to the boy, to live with him happily ever after.

As such, **"Adventures of a Monkey"** could hardly warrant Zhdanov's harsh treatment of Zoshchenko. The Soviet people are not treated as "idlers and monsters," as he asserts. The first person to be involved with the monkey, the truck driver, conscientiously does his duty. The invalid Gavrilich can be forgiven his idleness; surely he has paid his due to society. The boy Alyosha is nothing but a schoolboy—traditionally a breed of light, unpretentious toilers. His grandmother can also be excused for her idleness on account of her age. The only persons who could conceivably justify Zhdanov's insinuations are the chasers of the monkey through the city streets. This is a small town, and it is quite characteristic of small town inhabitants to snatch at any chance amusement, either to escape the deadly boredom of their isolated world or to find relief from the harshness of war.

None of the people in the story can be characterized as a "monster." The selfish natures of the invalid and the grandmother are counterbalanced by an affectionate schoolboy and a happy-go-lucky truck driver. Nor is anyone being "silly and primitive"; on the contrary, everybody acts in his own interest.

As for the charge of primitivism, Zhdanov is unjustly impugning Zoshchenko's intentions. Zoshchenko very seldom, if ever, derided or disparaged his characters. He liked to show, with light melancholy and irony, their follies and weaknesses but he has never treated them as primitive, unworthy of his concern and love. Reading Zoshchenko, one frequently gets the impression that various faces in a world created by him are only small pieces of the motley mosaic of his own complex soul. It is very questionable, to say the least, that Zoshchenko thought of himself as a silly and primitive person.

By his own explanation, Zhdanov based his accusations on Zoshchenko's alleged juxtaposition of a monkey with Soviet people or, more precisely, on the pitting of an animal, no matter how intelligent, against the good judgment of the enlightened Soviet people. (pp. 84-6)

If **"Adventures of a Monkey"** is to be understood literally, Zhdanov's accusations might have some ground. Indeed, on the first glance the monkey sometimes does act more cleverly than human beings despite Zoshchenko's repeated assurances that it "doesn't understand what's what; doesn't see the sense of" this and that. The question is, however, whether the story is what Zhdanov claims it to be. It must be kept in mind that Zoshchenko never was an innocuous writer. To maintain that he wanted nothing else but to write an innocent story for children would be to underrate him as a writer. On the other hand, to accuse him in Zhdanov's fashion would be casting him in an even more incongruous role—that of a stealthy denigrator of his own people. Indeed, even his most innocent sketches are concealed barbs at the rulers of the people through the alleged shortcomings of the people themselves. In addition, the time when the story was written—immediately after or perhaps even during the terrible war—was certainly not conducive to innocent writing. The very fact that Zhdanov found it necessary to castigate Zoshchenko in public for this story gives it a weight far exceeding the framework of a simple, humorous children's story.

There is, therefore, a distinct temptation to interpret this story as an allegory. The key figures in this allegory are the monkey and the boy Alyosha. At the outset, it is significant that Zoshchenko chose a monkey, and not some other animal, to escape from the zoo. The biological closeness of this animal to the human being, its agility and ability to adapt to the conditions of a life in captivity—all these elements illuminate Zoshchenko's choice of this highest creature in the animal kingdom to represent one of man's highest ideals—freedom. For that reason, the monkey is seen in this story as a symbol of the quest for freedom from oppression. First, it escapes from the zoo during the war. It is a well-known fact that many Russians, and especially non-Russians, considered the Second World War as a chance to attain a more tolerable form of life, if not outright freedom. . . . Even though these expectations did not materialize, "nevertheless, the portents of freedom filled the air throughout the postwar period and they alone defined its historical significance."

The monkey's quick disappointment with the newly attained freedom corresponds to the disillusionment which many Russians experienced shortly after the war as the rulers quickly sought to shut the windows that had been pried open. One of the main motives for Zhdanov's attack on Zoshchenko and Akhmatova was exactly this attempt to stem the swelling tide of hopeful expectations of more freedom and human dignity. Thus, when the monkey says, "It's easier to breathe in a cage," it is expressing a realization that nothing has come of the hopes

for freedom. Furthermore, the sudden appearance of the monkey had the effect of a bomb hitting the people; many did not recognize it as a monkey. Apparently, the world outside the cage is not yet ready for full freedom. People still live in their accustomed fashion, full of fear that changes brought by freedom would endanger the security they have bought by bowing to the rulers' whims. This is best expressed by the grandmother when she refuses to accept the monkey: "She will frighten me with her inhuman appearance. She will jump on me in the dark. She will eat my candy." She fears that the new freedom, to which she is entirely unaccustomed, leads to the only logical conclusion: "One of us two will have to be in the zoo." Freedom or comfort, that seems to be the only choice in grandmother's mind. The invalid's concern for his own comfort and well-being, though excusable, further underlines the reluctance of some people to accept freedom with all its consequences. Thus the monkey is not the only one to think that "it's easier to breathe in a cage," the cage being of a different shape but of the same essence.

The concept of freedom is an abstract one. It is more a mental attitude than a concrete set of laws. Zoshchenko repeatedly says that the monkey is not a person and it "doesn't understand what's what," as if to indicate that it is not enough for freedom to be embraced intuitively, and that it must be cherished both with one's mind and with one's heart. Furthermore, it should not be taken for granted. That is why the characters in the story, who are almost all simple, unassuming people, fail to seize the opportunity of attaining full freedom or even to recognize the opportunity.

The only person who seems to sense the true meaning of the monkey's sudden appearance is Alyosha. Being a small boy, he is far from understanding its full significance but he reacts intuitively. "All his life he dreamed of having some sort of a monkey," Zoshchenko says. Once he has it, he endeavors to keep it. Moreover, he wants to emancipate the monkey, to "Bring her up like a person," thus indicating the need of cultivating such a primitive desire as that for freedom. Zoshchenko seems to present Alyosha as a symbol of hope and the future. The fact that he is given the monkey at the end underlines the belief that the future and its premise of freedom does lie with the young. His affection for the animal, his capacity for love, his innocence and unspoiled goodness set him apart from other characters, who are either hostile, selfish, or ignorant of human needs. By the same token, the grandmother represents the old and the past. The uncertainties of old age have made her selfish and unwilling to accept any change, afraid that it may cost her security and comfort.

Other characters in the story fit, to a larger or smaller degree, into this scheme. The truck driver is a picture of a docile, servile *aparatchik* whose only concern is to perform what is asked of him. The invalid would rather cash in on sacrifices already made than make new ones for some nebulous purpose. Even the dog, which pursues the monkey most fiercely of all and gets its nose soundly pummeled in the process, could be seen as a most loyal, heartless servant of a police state.

The most difficult to interpret is the ending of the story. The monkey lives with the boy even now. Alyosha has succeeded in teaching it to wipe its nose with a handkerchief, to eat with a spoon, and not to take other people's candy. Is Zoshchenko silently and ironically laughing at man's inability to live with his ideals without training them to norms and standards? When Alyosha says of the monkey at the end, "I brought her up like a human being, and now all the children and even some adults may look to her as an example,'' one wonders whether Zoshchenko is serious about the need of taming such natural quests as that of freedom or whether he feels that they are better left unadulterated? Such questions will probably remain unanswered unless some material concerning Zoshchenko's intentions in this story is unearthed. (pp. 86-8)

Thus, the interpretation of **"Adventures of a Monkey"** as an allegory best explains the motives behind Zhdanov's wrath and the real meaning of his accusations. A loyal servant of the system and the state, he could not overlook the implications of Zoshchenko's devastating words that ''it's better to live in the zoo than at liberty.'' Not willing to admit publicly to the sting of Zoshchenko's allegory, he assailed it at its face value. Those who are acquainted with Zoshchenko's tribulations at the hands of the authorities on account of his boldness and independent spirit are inclined to see in all his works a running argument with an all-powerful, all-usurping agency—hostile to the best in himself and to the welfare of the people around him. (pp. 88-9)

Vasa D. Mihaslovich, ''Zoshchenko's 'Adventures of a Monkey' As an Allegory,'' in Satire Newsletter, *Vol. IV, No. 2, Spring, 1967, pp. 84-9.*

NADEZHDA MANDELSTAM (essay date 1972)

[*Mandelstam was the wife of Russian poet Osip Mandelstam, an early proponent of Acmeist poetry, which was condemned along with other Formalist literary movements by Andrei Zhdanov in favor of pro-Soviet literary realism. Osip Mandelstam was exiled for three years for criticizing Stalin in a line of verse, and later died in a camp for political prisoners. The following excerpt is taken from Nadezhda Mandelstam's* Hope Abandoned *(originally published in Russian in 1972), the second of two books of memoirs concerned with her husband's last four years of life and with the Russian literary scene during the 1930s. Mandelstam characterizes Zoshchenko as a political innocent who attempted in his stories to amuse even as he instructed his readers in the need for more humane treatment of others.*]

To the end of his days Zoshchenko believed in the possibility of giving ''good advice,'' and, acutely sensitive to the horror of what was going on, even when there was nothing one could do except howl like a wild animal, he still went on trying to be a restraining influence, warning us, drawing our attention in his stories to the way people behaved: a militiaman in white gloves, saluting politely, torments the life out of a much abused and harassed peasant; a woman lugs along a heavy suitcase, and passers-by, taking her for a domestic servant, are indignant at the man sauntering behind her with his hands in his pockets, but when they learn she is only his mother, they apologize— the family is sacrosanct, and you have every right to turn your mother into a beast of burden. Poor innocent Zoshchenko: people took him for a writer of funny stories and laughed themselves silly at this kind of thing. . . . (p. 187)

Poor Zoshchenko was completely unprepared for the blow [of Zhdanov's denunciation of his work.] This was clear from his conversation with some Oxford students who had come to try to help the victims [of Zhdanov's attack. In a footnote the critic writes that] This 'conversation' took place a little over a year after Stalin's death, in the first week of May 1954. The occasion was the visit to Leningrad of a group of twenty British students. . . . Akhmatova and Zoshchenko were ''produced'' for the group—who had not asked to see them—on the premises of the Leningrad branch of the Union of Writers. The meeting was presided over by Alexei Surkov, who invited the British

visitors to ask questions. Akhmatova and Zoshchenko were then asked, in all innocence, what they now thought of the ''Zhdanov Decree'' of 1946. Zoshchenko spoke first and made some critical comments on it—for which he was afterwards severely reprimanded. . . . Did those Oxford students ever realize what danger they put Zoshchenko in? He was subjected to a second wave of persecution from which he never recovered. A wonderful, pure man, he had always tried to find points of contact with the times he lived in. He believed in all the high-sounding schemes for universal happiness and thought that eventually everything would settle down—all the cruelty and savagery were only incidental, a temporary ruffling of the surface, not the essence, as we were always being told at political lectures. (In these, needless to say, there was never any actual mention of cruelty, only of things that still ''ruffled the surface.'') Many people failed to notice the transition from the popular upheaval of the Revolution, with all its spontaneous barbarity, to the carefully planned, machine-like callousness that followed. People who had tended to find excuses for the first of these phases also reconciled themselves to the second. This was true of Zoshchenko, one of the subalterns of the Revolution (in 1917 his actual rank was higher, but psychologically he belonged to this category).

Zoshchenko was a moralist by nature; his aim in his stories was to bring his contemporaries to their senses, to help them become more human, but his readers saw only the funny side and neighed like horses when they read him. Zoshchenko kept his illusions and was completely without cynicism—he always used to think everything over carefully with his head slightly on one side—and he paid a terrible price. With his artist's eye he sometimes got to the heart of things, but he could not really make sense of them because he believed implicitly in progress and all the wonderful things it would bring. During the First World War he was poisoned by gas and after it by the pseudophilosophical brew of materialism concocted for weaker spirits. Somewhere in the background there had been a pre-Revolutionary high school with its radicalism and lack of restraints— the rest followed naturally. The crisis in people's thinking went hand in hand with the crisis in their schooling. (pp. 357-59)

Nadezhda Mandelstam, ''A Honeymoon: A Tale of Two Cooks'' and ''Major Forms,'' in her Hope Abandoned, *translated by Max Hayward, Atheneum, 1974, pp. 185-200, 337-442.*

GARY KERN (essay date 1974)

[*In the following excerpt, the translator of the first English edition of the complete text of* Before Sunrise *discusses Zoshchenko's struggle against melancholia and other forms of physical and mental illness. Kern characterizes* Before Sunrise *as Zoshchenko's most important exploration of these themes—a serious study of autotherapy and the interrelationship of art and health.*]

Zoshchenko began writing about ennui, old age and the struggle against them quite early in his career. In 1923 he wrote a humoresque entitled **"A Story About How A Certain Russian Citizen Went to Europe To Get Young"** (**Rasskaz o tom, kak odin russkii grazhdanin poekhal v Evropu omolazhivat'sya**). The protagonist, grown old and weary in Russia, goes to Germany, runs out of money and pays a quack his last funds for a youth injection, which kills him. The story falls in the tradition of spoofs, initiated by Nikolai Leskov, in which uncultured Russians misunderstand the customs, gadgets and thinking of ''civilized'' countries. Other stories in this vein by Zoshchenko are the better known **"The Dictaphone,"** "The

Trap,'' and "**The Quality of Production**.'' They represent merely a fraction of the hundreds of short satires which Zoshchenko penned in the twenties and which secured his popularity with Russian readers. But at the same time Zoshchenko began to compose a different type of story, a "sentimental novella,'' in which the humor was more mellow, bittersweet, and sadness began to show through the comical situations. The first step in this direction was "**Wisdom**'' *(Mudrost')*. . . . In this story, the hero (identified in the first version as the author's "grandfather'') becomes a recluse after several years of drinking, skirt-chasing and brawling. . . . After 11 years of musty retirement, during which the flower of his youth has badly wilted, he suddenly has a change of heart. One morning he wakes up full of vim and vinegar. Surprised at himself, he spruces up, floods his dismal rooms with light, makes the rounds of his former friends and invites them to a party. In the process, he becomes younger, gay, a new man altogether. But just before the guests arrive, the revitalized and overexcited old guy has a stroke and dies. The ancient crone with whom he lives is left to explain away his demise to the famished guests. This ironic ending would seem to ridicule the hero's belated attempt to live a bright life, to preach the moral that "it's later than you think,'' but the point that a person's miseries may be self-induced and also self-treated has definitely been made. (pp. 345-46)

[Zoshchenko was a] melancholic since early manhood, he had already given up on the doctors and had begun to study the lives of great men, hoping to find there a remedy to his malaise. Perhaps at the same time he had begun to consider determination, willpower, the answer to his difficulties. (p. 347)

Zoshchenko persisted in his search for happiness through will-power. When he felt like being alone, he would force himself to visit good-natured people and mix among them. When he felt like quiet, he would seek out a noisy place. After a few years, he again told friends that he had found the answer. This answer he gave to his readers in the novella *Youth Restored* . . . , his most important work on this subject prior to *Before Sunrise*. . . . A 53-year-old professor, bored and ailing, decides "to breathe life into his broken body and to restore his youth.'' He first turns to physicians, who prescribe bromides and pills for him, give him shock treatments, hypnotise him and reduce him to a physical and emotional wreck. He decides to visit a neurologist, but here makes an important discovery. After shaving, changing his underwear, getting dressed and going out on the street, he notices to his amazement that these procedures have revived him. This caused him to ponder over his complaints and to devise his own plan to counteract them. He works out a program of moderate exercises, and his health improves. He traces his miseries back to his youth, and begins to change his habits. He links fresh feelings with romance and, abandoning his wife, begins to court the 19-year-old hussy next door, who has already run through "five husbands and seven or eight abortions.'' They marry, and the marriage works a miracle on the old boy until he finds his bride with a lover. He has a stroke, spends a month in the hospital, but does not die. Returning home, he resumes his exercises, reconciles himself with his politically-minded daughter and even listens to his wife for a long time, discovering that "she was not the ninny she had seemed to be for the last twenty years.'' His health and family life begin to flourish, but sometimes he casts a furtive glance next door and sighs over the lost hussy.

Even from this brief resume, it should be obvious that *Youth Restored* is hardly "an ordinary novella which writers write by

the score,'' as Zoshchenko characterizes it in *Before Sunrise*. For one thing, it is ambiguous in a time of simplistic messages for the proletariat—both comic and sad, serious and ironic. For another thing, it is enclosed by seventeen introductions and seventeen postscripts, or "commentaries and articles to the novella.'' But above all, it is here (in the commentaries) that the author first develops his idea of autotherapy and touches upon the interrelationship of art and health. (pp. 348-49)

Zoshchenko offers suggestions for a reasonable attitude toward one's own "body and brain,'' drawing on the lives of great men, the advice of friends and his own experience as a neurasthenic. "These medical comments of mine are not copied down from books,'' he writes. "I was the dog on which all the experiments were made.'' Zoshchenko proposes that a person learn to rest as well as to work, for, as Lenin said: "Whoever does not know how to rest also does not know how to work.'' It is good to plan a schedule in which healthful actions become habitual, for "the organism is inclined to work like a machine,'' and when pernicious habits become fixed the organism regards them as normal and even necessary. Zoshchenko cites approvingly the regularity of Kant's life, which rid Kant of his early sickness and insured him his 81 years. True, Kant did over do it, he became a "maniac'' of punctuality, and his innocence in regard to women was "tragic,'' but his experiment in controlling his own body was a "success.'' It is also healthy to have a goal, a striving toward something, and the greater the goal—the greater the life-force. (pp. 351-52)

Such, in a nutshell, are the positive pieces of advice which Zoshchenko gives the readers of *Youth Restored*. They are founded on the principles of attentiveness to one's body, moderation, reason. But they are insufficient by themselves, for many people are not in a position to follow them. Many people must first rid themselves of bad habits, physical malfunctions, nervous irritation, mental exhaustion, etc. before they can embark on a program of right living. Here Zoshchenko suggests methods founded not so much on reason as on a kind of self-hypnosis. The brain of a neurasthenic, he observes, dwells constantly on one theme, one problem, one memory, which gives it no rest, weakens the organism and prevents it from reacting directly and forcefully to its surroundings. Since it is impossible to remove this idée fixe with medicines, the only remedy is—to give it another interpretation. The sick person must tell himself that he is sick, unable to judge correctly, and then decide to rate his problem lower for a while, until he can cope with it as a healthy person. This will give him a breather and put him back on the road to health. In regard to psycho-somatic complaints, the sufferer must simply refuse to pay attention. . . . And finally, when one has minimized his problem, eliminated his complaint, found a goal and a program for life, he must forget that his neurasthenia ever existed. . . . (pp. 352-53)

In sum, Zoshchenko designs a double tactic against that ancient nemesis—mania, dementia, melancholia, neurasthenia, neurosis. First you must dismiss this nemesis as "bunk,'' and then you must live your life reasonably. This tactic, composed of so many wise maneuvers, seems in the final instance to skirt around the enemy—it leaves it unknown, untouched. Both the novella and the commentaries leave the reader with an uneasy feeling: yes, things have turned out for the best, but . . . The professor, directed down the slow road to health, glances wistfully at the fast road to hell. The author, having glorified reason and willpower, closes his work with their disappearance. He describes himself in Sestroretsk, sitting on the bed, looking out the window, at the sunshine, the clouds, dogs, children playing, a pretty woman pursued by an eager man, a little girl coming to visit his son, and he writes:

> The well-being and unshakableness of these eternal scenes for some reason rejoice and console me.

> I don't want to think anymore. And with this I break off my novella. . . .

Other commentators on Zoshchenko find this conclusion uplifting. But this reader cannot escape the impression that the daily round of life has won, the eternal scenes will be repeated and will include all the miseries of man, whatever the mind thinks.

Youth Restored is an extremely unusual, engrossing work, but one that does not admit of an easy interpretation. The ironic story and the serious commentaries do not mix, or even mock each other. . . . To confuse even further the interplay of fiction and fact, the author appears in both the novella and the commentaries, wearing two masks, first as an acquaintance of the professor and then as an apologetic layman, the experimental "dog." One suspects the author feared to call his work a scientific study, yet the fictional "novella" occupies only a small portion of the work. Certainly Zoshchenko had a master plan, he was creating a new genre out of two dissimilar ones, but the effect is bewildering. To my mind, the work makes sense if we consider the novella the more "factual" part—this is what we might expect in life (accepting all of the fictional premises). The commentaries are the more "fictional" part—the theory, the beautiful ideal which we are not yet able to attain. But we must also remember that ambiguity may have been a protective device for Zoshchenko. In Stalin's time, it was sometimes healthier to say things indirectly. The acclaim won by *Youth Restored* (probably Zoshchenko's greatest success in his lifetime) and the opprobrium won by the more direct *Before Sunrise* proved the wisdom of this tactic.

Reviewing these several precursors of *Before Sunrise,* we find that Zoshchenko, in both his fictional and factual expressions, was mulling over the same themes—lost youth, exhaustion, tragic love, recuperation, control of the body by the mind. He did not yet have a definitive answer, a coherent theory—this is why he could espouse mental control, and yet advise flight from the enemy, methods how not to think about it. So far he had not determined the cause of despair, he could not account for imaginary aches and pains, and in any event he had not yet resolved to share his researches openly with the reader. In the story **"Healing and Psychics"** . . . , according to [Vera von Wiren] . . . he creates "an impression contrary to his own convictions," seeming to ridicule psychiatry, yet on closer inspection actually ridiculing the stupid remarks of the patients. In *Youth Restored* he touches upon such subjects as inhibition, frustration, conflict, etc., but fails to discuss either Freud or Pavlov. Only by a minute analysis (sometimes of a kremlinological nature) can we determine what Zoshchenko knew and intended in these years. Nevertheless, we can make one simple generalization. In his evolution from humorist to the author of *Before Sunrise,* Zoshchenko moved constantly in the direction of self-control, reason, rationality.

Thus he aligned himself with two great figures in Russian literature: Tolstoi and Gorky. To be sure, he dismissed Tolstoi for his religion, but at the same time he admired the construction of a system which (so he supposed) answered Tolstoi's needs. More importantly, he created in *Before Sunrise* a modern parallel to Tolstoi's *Confession*. . . . (pp. 353-55)

In Gorky, Zoshchenko found a living paragon—a self-made man, a great humanist, a writer obsessed with the idea of ridding the world of suffering. . . . In Gorky's letters and writings Zoshchenko no doubt found ideas corresponding to his own. (p. 355)

Assume that Zoshchenko's conjectures on health, neurosis and conditioned reflexes are determined by science to be worthless, that nothing of use can be gleaned from his theory. What value would the book have then? In other words, what is the artistic merit of the work, apart from its message?

Our attention is drawn first to the short episodes, the recollections. In them it is possible to perceive the influence (or at least the methods) of Zoshchenko's two teachers in prose—Viktor Shklovsky and Evgeny Zamyatin. Once, in 1928, Zoshchenko paid tribute to Shklovsky for breaking up the old form of literary Russian: "He shortened the phrase. He let 'fresh air' into his articles. It became pleasant and easy to read . . . I did the same thing." No further comment appears necessary: the recollections are compressed to the final degree. As Zamyatin, Zoshchenko offers a perspective which constantly expands or contracts, slowly or abruptly, as if the author were operating a zoom lens. (pp. 357-58)

Another feature is one familiar to readers of Shklovsky, Zamyatin and the other Serapion Brothers: authorial distance. Zoshchenko describes many of the disturbing incidents in his life almost as if he were not present, or present as a non-participant. (pp. 358-59)

Are the recollections self-sufficient? I think not. It is true that Zoshchenko invented a brilliant device for reviving the form of an autobiography. Each of these recollections as "illumined with a strange light"—the author's "emotional agitation." By selecting only such "snapshots" in his memory, Zoshchenko dispensed with the descriptions, interpretations and identifications which fill most autobiographies. But if each recollection is a little jewel, why did Zoshchenko not arrange them in chronological order, tell his lifestory and be done? The reason, I submit, is that a straight line of little jewels would be tedious, and it would fail to attract attention to its individual parts. It was necessary to piece together a mosaic, with each piece sparkling.

Zoshchenko therefore arranged the recollections into three blocks and set them in reverse chronological order. This was an artistic device. No one is fooled by the repeated claim that the author mistakenly limited himself, that he was forced each time to dig deeper into his past. The same author admits that he spent eight years on this book—he could easily have put everything in chronological order. But it was necessary to create interest, even suspense. For this purpose he made use of fictional devices. A mystery is stated at the outset: "I am wretched, and know not why." Recollections are then presented as clues toward solving the mystery. Each chapter brings the reader close to the solution. At the end of chapter five, all the clues are in, but the mystery remains. It is necessary to explain a system of decoding: the theory of Pavlov in chapter six. The theory is tested on dreams in chapter seven. The solution is achieved in chapter eight. Furhter confirmation is needed: examples of other people in chapter nine, and of great men in chapter ten. The triumphal conclusion, encompassing all of human life, comes in the next three chapters. The work ends with a frame structure: an epilogue and afterword to balance the prologue and foreword. The recollections therefore cannot stand alone: they are part of a pattern, an intrigue, well deserving the name of "novella."

One more word: if the theory is discounted by science, its merit as a unifying artistic principle is not destroyed. The associatons of water-hand-beggar etc. unite the diverse materials of autobiography, biography and speculation. If science should reject this speculation, it will be welcomed by art.

But we must confront the theory. The final word, of course, will be said by the scientist, the experimental psychologist, the expert on Freud and Pavlov. As a layman, I can only offer a few observations made in the course of translation, and then close with a subjective appraisal.

Zoshchenko states his theory more directly in *Before Sunrise* than in *Youth Restored*. But he by no means loses sight of his time and place. He apologizes for the frankness of his recollections—they belong to the dead past, "this is the same thing as speaking of the dead." He plays down Freud and plays up Pavlov. He circumvents Freudian terminology: "complex combination (*slozhnaya kombinatsiya*) instead of "complex (*kompleks*), "physician" instead of "psychiatrist," etc. He justifies his personal inquiry by linking it to the war effort, the national struggle against barbarianism, base instincts. He even associates Freud with Fascism, although Freud, no less than Zoshchenko, defended the "primacy of the intellect" against blind instinct, suffering and religion (*The Future of an Illusion*, 1927). He takes care to portray his positive attitude toward the revolution (the episodes "Five O'Clock Tea," "The Roads Lead To Paris," "We Play Cards"). He claims that a discussion of death is consistent with socialist realism, for socialist realism "does not hypocritically put off decisions to questions which need to be decided." . . . (A statement which did not see the light for almost thirty years.) In short, Zoshchenko tries in every way to make his investigation acceptable to the higher powers. All these ruses need not distract us from the general theory.

Zoshchenko's ultimate defense is the assertion that the theory worked. He cured his own neurosis, "I don't know about other doors," he says, "but the keys definitely fit mine." . . . We are therefore faced with two questions: is the theory defensible in its presentation, and did it really work in Zoshchenko's case? The answer in both cases is doubtful.

Zoshchenko combines Freud's theory of trauma with Pavlov's theory of conditioned reflexes. Despair is born in infancy. An infant is traumatized by an "unfortunate experience" which establishes a false conditioned connection between the objects in the experience. The trauma is reinforced by the repetition of the conditioned stimuli or by the overly sensitive psyche of the infant. Once established, the conditioned connection does not dissipate as the infant matures, but instead is confirmed, justified, even multiplied, by its imagination. The adult finds himself beset with fears, phobias, malfunctionings which have grown out of his illogical infantine mind. Despair evaporates when he reconstructs these infantine conceptions (by dream interpretation, by imagination) and explains them away with reason.

This draws a very strange picture of human life. Because he rejects the Freudian explanation of neurosis—a conflict between the inner world and the outer, between the primitive drives of the unconscious and the civilized standards of consciousness—Zoshchenko must ascribe special power to either the one or the other. A person can become neurotic by an unfortunate "concurrence of circumstances" which establishes false conditioned connections—in other words, by a run of bad luck, mere coincidence. Or, a person can beocme neurotic because, being more imaginative than a dog, he does not allow mistaken conditioned connections to die out, but fabricates justifications for them. Either you have bad luck, or you're too smart for your own good. Or both.

A more serious problem is whether the theory is internally consistent. Is the mystery "I am wretched, and know not why" solved by the clues and their decipherment? Is the despair of chapter two dispelled by the exposition of conditioned connections? That despair, the reader will recall, was a pervasive gloom, a "pessimistic view of life," a "certain repugnance for life." Zoshchenko quotes the words of great men who experienced such despair, some of whom he later analyses. He cites the words of Tolstoi: "It seems to me that my life has been a stupid farce." The despair at this point, in fact, is a Tolstoian despair—despair at the meaninglessness of life, despair in the face of death. But as Zoshchenko proceeds in his investigation, this despair becomes identified with phobias, idiosyncracies, psychosomatic afflictions—all legitimate sources of misery and all worthy of study, but not that all-encompassing despair with which he began. He has shrunk his despair into a theory, and something has escaped.

Even if we overlook this discrepancy, we must doubt the method of the cure. This is supposedly accomplished by shedding light on the remote corners of the psyche, discovering the hidden conditioned connections and severing them one by one. It is supposedly done by logic, the scientific method, but in fact all of the gaps are filled in by untested hypotheses ("it must be that," "without a doubt," etc.) and, one could say, by imagination, by art. You must "get down on all fours," think like an animal, an infant. Zoshchenko converts his art into therapy, but his art takes revenge. In *Youth Restored* he showed the professor, returned to his wife and his reason, darting a glance at the house of his lost lover. So too, the persona of *Before Sunrise,* dedicated to reason and overflowing with happiness, lingers over the memory of Nadya V., the woman he still loves, who rejected the revolution, who cast him out of her life. Reason conquers death, suffering and old age, but, evidently, not love.

In sum, Zoshchenko's theory fails to penetrate the chief cause of despair: the need to achieve one's identity, to become a significant human being, to give and receive love, to work out a relationship to eternity. By restricting his view to conditioned connections, his science to Freud and Pavlov, the author of *Before Sunrise* reduces himself to the level of a dog, without psychic needs and without destiny. Unconsciously, through the art of his autobiography, he attempts to create his own myth, to give his life a meaningful pattern, yet consciously he theorizes himself into a thing.

But did Zoshchenko himself, the historical person, snap out of his depression and find happiness? [Russian critic, translator, and children's writer Kornei] Chukovsky reports that he did. In 1937, during the horror of the purges, Zoshchenko courageously, forcefully, defended a fellow writer. In other meetings he gave the appearance of radiant health, listed the doctors who had confirmed his cure, worked enthusiastically on his new book *The Keys to Happiness* (the first draft of *Before Sunrise*. . . . But also he had lost his sense of humor, he seemed like a man possessed. His tragic fate is well known: the publication of the first half of *Before Sunrise,* his most optimistic book, brought the furies down upon him; he worked a few more years, and then Zhdanov chose to make an example of him. Zoshchenko was thrown out of Russian literature, forced to turn to translation. (pp. 360-64)

> Gary Kern, *"After the Afterword,"* in Before Sunrise: A Novella *by Mikhail Zoshchenko, translated by Gary Kern, Ardis, 1974, pp. 345-64.*

EDWARD J. BROWN   (essay date 1982)

[*In the following excerpt from his survey of modern Soviet literature,* Russian Literature Since the Revolution, *Brown discusses the way in which Zoshchenko employed skaz narration in his stories in order to insert his own satirical comments on the Soviet way of life as direct asides to the reader. Brown is one of the few commentators to suggest that Soviet censorship and condemnation of Zoshchenko's work—including Zhdanov's attack in 1946—had little effect upon Zoshchenko's career. Vera von Wiren (1962), for example, writes that after 1946 Zoshchenko was "denied a voice in Soviet literature until a year and a half before his death."*]

[Mikhail Zoshchenko's work] does fit in a general way the concept of satire, but it is in no sense a humorous attack on a specific social organization, or on particular contemporary characters, or on a way of life. There is no evidence in his work that Zoshchenko believed in Soviet values. There is no reason to think that he held firmly to beliefs that ran counter to those values. He feels neither anger nor scorn as he observes his contemporaries, but only perverse pity and baffled amusement both at them and at himself.

For the Russian humorist Zoshchenko sadness was a way of life. His life style is an intentional caricature of the melancholy clown. The fact that both his sadness and his humor were organic to him is demonstrated by the autobiographical novel *Before Sunrise,* which is a search for the explanation of his chronic melancholy. All his life Zoshchenko had suffered, he said, from fits of depression, which at times became so acute that he could not function. He was unhappy, and he could not understand why. He concluded that in this respect he was different from other people, and therefore sought in his own life some cause or explanation of a condition peculiar to him. The novel begins with this explanation of how it happened to be written, then moves to an investigation of significant memories beginning at the age of sixteen, each one a self-contained unit of experience. In the selection of memories lies the ironic meaning of the story. Zoshchenko recalls his attempted suicide over a low mark in composition, his experience of wounds and gas poisoning during the war, a succession of ridiculously unsuitable occupations from cobbler to detective from 1917 to 1920, and incidents of his life as a literary man in Petrograd. His brief, bare account of the literary great whom he met among the Serapions is in its way appalling. The face of the poet Blok expressed only sadness and apathy; Yesenin recited his poetry dressed in a velvet blouse with lips and eyebrows made up; Gorky wearily expounded truisms on literature and culture while someone behind him carefully wrote it all down; the editor and poet Kuzmin turned down Zoshchenko's funny stories because they were "exaggerated"; his girl friend, also a writer, asked him to wait for her on the embankment while she visited another lover "for just twenty minutes" and came back feeling wonderful; Mayakovsky turned out to be a hypochondriac, excessively afraid of infection from drinking glasses, forks, and spoons. These and other memories are told in short clipped sentences which lack the rational organization imposed by syntax. They are presented as raw, untreated items of memory and while there is no explicit reflection on their meaning, the sum of all the memories covering the years from 1912 to 1926

is a picture of a lifetime of quiet desperation. But with a detached air of scientific curiosity and with his tongue in his cheek Zoshchenko asserts that he cannot find in any of this the reason for his melancholy, so he decides to carry the search farther back into his childhood. The section dealing with memories from the age of five to sixteen is entitled "A Terrifying World," and it relates memories of family and childhood, each one in some way sad. Still not satisfied that he has found the answer, he carries the search back "before sunrise," to the dawn of consciousness, the earliest years of life. But still he cannot explain his sadness. He proceeds then to study the psychologists and gives the reader a brief elementary statement of the Pavlovian theory of the conditioned reflex and of the Freudian sexual theory. He looked for the specific event which caused his unhappiness in "associations" arising from dreams and found that in them water frequently had an association with strong emotion. Certain, he said, that he was on the track of the early conditioning process that had made him an unhappy man, he promised in the sequel to tell of this, but the publication of *Before Sunrise* in the journal *October* was aborted in 1943, and the full text appeared only in 1972. It is a fascinating account of a man's effort to come to grips with his own neurosis.

Although Zoshchenko's humor arises from his observation of the general human situation it is obvious that the Soviet predicament provided the data upon which he worked. Situational

Zoshchenko in his study. Courtesy of Ardis Publishers.

and linguistic absurdities from Soviet life are the subjects of his hundreds of short tales. Zoshchenko is himself authority for the statement that he introduced the language of the street into his stories, but as Soviet linguistic scholars have pointed out, that statement is itself an absurdity. The stories are stylized both as to language and form, and only in fairy tales or narrative folk songs do characters speak with the intonation, the pauses, the retardation and repetition, and the mock-pithy asides that characterize Zoshchenko's people. No one has ever spoken the language of Zoshchenko's heroes. It is an invented speech made up of newspaper rhetoric, the pronouncements of Stalin and other heroes, misunderstood fragments of Marx or Engels, all mixed up in a weird linguistic brew and laced with the catchwords of popular prejudice. Zoshchenko's technique has been labeled as *skaz,* and his work has been compared to that of Damon Runyon and Ring Lardner, whose stories are told in the speech style of a character who represents a particular milieu. But Zoshchenko is radically different from other practitioners of *skaz.* His narrator is not the Soviet man in the street, nor is he a representative of the Soviet lower middle class or any other social group. He is not a character at all. He is the mask through which Zoshchenko himself speaks to the reader.

Each of the stories is told—one might almost say confided to the reader—by the absurd narrator, who, like the wise fools of folk stories, says much more than he seems to know. The device of the wise fool enabled Zoshchenko to comment on Soviet life without attracting fatal attention from the state. His fool is pompously loyal to the latest and most grandiose Soviet notions and full of obvious wisdom on such subjects as the decay of the intelligentsia, proper management of public baths, civilized behavior on streetcars, health, true love in Soviet conditions, the housing shortage, and correct grammar. But the items of reality that he selects as illustrations offer a ridiculous contradiction of his wise pronouncements.

The stories are frequently constructed according to a pattern which can be studied in a few examples. Following a somewhat pompous formalistic scheme, the stories may be divided into three parts: (1) exordium, (2) epic narration, (3) moral conclusion. **"Not All Is Lost"** is typical. In that story the exordium consists of general comments on "melancholics" who have no interest in this "teeming life." . . . The narrator reflects that such melancholics are "rootless intellectuals" suffering from overeducation, who would have been miserable under any regime. So you can't blame current events. The epic narration begins with the self-critical comment that perhaps one should forget all this "empty philosophy" and get down to the case in hand, one Innokenty, an intellectual who found new interest in living and stopped being a melancholic. The change in Innokenty's life occurred when the chairman of his apartment house committee announced that additional tenants would be assigned to live in his apartment, and Innokenty went off to the housing office to complain. While he was away his apartment was burglarized and some things stolen. As a result he had to visit the police station twice a day to get help and look around in the secondhand markets to see if his stuff had come up for sale. One day as he hurried about this business he fell downstairs and dislocated his arm and then had to go regularly to the doctor's office for examination and massages. So he had many things to occupy him: mornings the business of tracking down lost articles, afternoons the clinic, and evenings discussion of the day's activities with friends. And this rootless intellectual began to take an interest in things and changed radically for the better. Then comes the moral conclusions, with the fool's comment on the meaning of the story:

> Of course it's impossible to say whether he will continue to possess such spiritual boldness all his life. But maybe he will possess it all his life. It all depends on how his affairs develop. Maybe the house chairman will take him to court for nonpayment of rent. And then again maybe the Criminal Investigation Department will summon him about those goods that were stolen. And then again, maybe, as he rushes about on his affairs, Innokenty will break another arm, or dislocate his leg. And then, maybe he will die happy, in full contentment. And, dying, he will reflect on the affairs that filled his life, and on the struggle that he bore on his shoulders with honor.
>
> Not without reason did Comrade Budyonny once exclaim: "Our whole life is nothing but struggle."

Zoshchenko wore the fool's mask in almost everything he wrote—in his essays and novels as well as in his short stories. In an article published in 1922 as part of a symposium by the Serapion Brothers, he wrote:

> In general, it's kind of hard to be a writer. Just take ideology. Nowadays a writer has got to have an ideology.
>
> Here's Voronsky (a good man) who writes . . . "It is necessary that writers have a more 'exact ideology.'"
>
> But that's downright unpleasant. How can I have an "exact ideology," when not a single party among them all attracts me?
>
> I don't hate anybody—that's my "exact ideology."

The mask served him well. He was attacked from time to time, but those attacks, even Zhdanov's vicious assault, did him no permanent harm. Serious charges could hardly affect a writer who offered no serious target. (pp. 185-89)

Zoshchenko's style is a reduction to the absurd of solemn hypocrisy in whatever form. It exposes the false and trivializes the pompous. It brings to the ground all lofty sentiment loftily expressed. It reveals the vulgarity under official heroism. Through the mask of his clown-hero, Zoshchenko uttered judgments on the Soviet variant of modern life that, coming from a serious man, would have been an offense to the majesty of the state. (p. 189)

> *Edward J. Brown, "Zoshchenko and the Art of Satire," in his* Russian Literature Since the Revolution, *revised edition, Cambridge, Mass.: Harvard University Press, 1982, pp. 184-89.*

ADDITIONAL BIBLIOGRAPHY

Alexandrova, Vera. "Mikhail Zoshchenko." In her *A History of Soviet Literature,* translated by Mirra Ginsburg, pp. 97-109. Garden City, N.Y.: Doubleday & Co., 1963.

Biographical and critical study. Alexandrova characterizes Zoshchenko as being concerned from the beginning of his literary career with portraying the lives of Soviet city dwellers.

Burnett, Whit. Foreword to *Russia Laughs,* by Mikhail Zostchenko, translated by Helena Clayton, pp. v-xv. Boston: Lothrop, Lee, and Shepard, 1935.
Introduction to the first volume of Zoshchenko's stories translated into English. Burnett praises Zoshchenko's ability to produce amusing satirical works during difficult times.

Domar, Rebecca. "The Tragedy of a Soviet Satirist, or the Case of Zoshchenko." In *Through the Glass of Soviet Literature: Views of Russian Society,* edited by Ernest J. Simmons, pp. 201-243. New York: Columbia University Press, 1953.
Biographical and critical study of Zoshchenko. Domar stresses that "human foibles of all kinds," and not specifically Soviet traits, were the object of Zoshchenko's satire.

Edgerton, William. "The Serapion Brothers: An Early Soviet Controversy." *The American Slavic and East European Review* VIII, No. 1 (February 1949): 47-64.
History of the Serapion Brothers literary group, of which Zoshchenko was a member. Edgerton provides brief biographical sketches of the group's members and discusses the Serapion's ideological differences with the Communist regime, which frowned on the artistic freedom that was part of the Serapion's doctrine.

Fen, Elisaveta. Preface to *The Woman Who Could Not Read,* by Michael Zoshchenko, translated by Elisaveta Fen, pp. v-viii. 1940. Reprint. Westport, Conn.: Hyperion Press, 1973.
Characterizes Zoshchenko as a short story writer who displays the "saving grace" of self-criticism and objectivity in his short stories.

Hayward, Max. "Soviet Literature 1917-1962." In *Dissonant Voices in Russian Literature,* edited by Patricia Blake and Max Hayward, pp. vii-xlii. London: George Allen and Unwin, 1964.*
Introductory essay to a collection of previously untranslated works by Russian writers who were largely out of sympathy with the Soviet regime. Hayward's introduction provides an historical background and explains how various writers, including Zoshchenko, responded to the changing times.

Hingley, Ronald. *Russian Writers and Soviet Society, 1917-1978.* New York: Random House, 1979, 296 p.*
Historical and critical study of the relationship of Soviet writers to the Soviet state. Zoshchenko's life and career are mentioned throughout.

Kern, Gary. Review of *Neizdannyj Zoščenko,* by Mikhail Zoshchenko. *World Literature Today* 51, No. 3 (Summer 1977): 459-60.
Review of a collection of previously unpublished short works by Zoshchenko. Kern writes that with nearly all of Zoshchenko's works now available it may be time to assess his place in Russian literature. He concludes that Zoshchenko was original but not profound. Only one quarter of Zoshchenko's work, Kern suggests, was brilliant and witty—yet even that lacked the philosophical, psychological, and social depth of great literature. The remaining three-quarters of what Zoshchenko wrote "is crud."

McLean, Hugh. "Belated Sunrise: A Review Article." *The Slavic and East European Journal* 18, No. 4 (Winter 1974): 406-10.
Traces the complex publication history of *Before Sunrise,* which remained incomplete until 1972. McLean regards *Before Sunrise* as a serious exploration of the author's psychological development.

Murphy, A. B. *Mikhail Zoshchenko: A Literary Profile.* Oxford: Willem A. Meeuws, 1981, 163 p.
First book-length study of Zoshchenko in English. Murphy surveys Zoshchenko's life, career, and critical reception, providing English translations of major Russian criticism.

Review of *Russia Laughs,* by Mikhail Zoshchenko. *The Nation* CXLI, No. 3668 (23 October 1935): 489.
Brief review, noting that "censorship in the U.S.S.R. has reached a very tolerant stage" to allow the publication of Zoshchenko's satires of state programs and bureaucratic blunders.

Nicolson, Harold. "Marginal Comment." *The Spectator* 177, No. 6167 (6 September 1946): 238.
Discusses the furor aroused in the world literary community by Andrei Zhdanov's attack on the magazines *Zvesda* and *Leningrad* for publishing stories by Zoshchenko. Nicolson admits he knows nothing about Zoshchenko but deplores the politicization of Soviet literature that results in campaigns against certain authors.

Prawdin, M. "A Russian Satirist." *The Spectator* 177, No. 6169 (20 September 1946): 289-90.
Response to the article by Harold Nicolson (see Additional Bibliography). Noting that Nicolson disclaimed any knowledge of Zoshchenko, Prawdin described the Russian author as "a writer of topical short stories in which he audaciously exposes the ridiculous situations arising when planning meets with unexpected difficulties in everyday life."

Reavey, George. "*When the Sun Rises;* or, A Study in Conditional Reflexes," and "Some Examples of Present-Day Soviet Criticism: *When the Sun Rises* and Zoshchenko Is Eclipsed." In his *Soviet Literature To-Day,* pp. 101-03, 120-23. New Haven: Yale University Press, 1947.
Characterizes *Before Sunrise* as a semi-autobiographical study of the author's spiritual and physical state. The second chapter cited examines the severe Soviet censure of *Before Sunrise,* which resulted in the work's suppression for twenty-nine years.

Singer, Isaac Bashevis. "Russian Anxiety." *New York Herald Tribune Books* 40, No. 4 (25 August 1963): 6.
Review of *Nervous People, and Other Stories.* Singer praises Zoshchenko's courage in writing, against the dominant trend in Soviet literature, about the everyday tribulations of the average Soviet citizen.

Stewart, David H. "Zoshchenko." *The Michigan Quarterly Review* 1, No. 3 (Summer 1962): 208-09.
Finds that Zoshchenko can be read in either of two ways: as a sardonic humorist or as a subversive artist who was persecuted and ultimately silenced by the Soviet government.

Struve, Gleb. *Russian Literature under Lenin and Stalin.* Norman: University of Oklahoma Press, 1971, 454 p.
Insightful survey of Soviet literature. Aspects of Zoshchenko's life and career are discussed throughout the book.

Titunik, I. R. "Mixail Zoščenko and the Problem of *Skaz.*" *California Slavic Studies, Volume VI,* pp. 83-96. Berkeley and Los Angeles: University of California Press, 1971.
Discussion of the nature of *skaz* narrative technique. Titunik finds that *skaz* is intended to reproduce the "spontaneous, 'living' speech" of a fictional narrator who is distinct from the author. Numerous examples are drawn from Zoshchenko's works.

Von Wiren-Garczyński, Vera. "Zoščenko's Psychological Interests." *The Slavic and East European Journal* XI, No. 1 (Spring 1967): 3-22.
Examination of Zoshchenko's development in writing psychologically oriented works, which was informed by his studies of Pavlov and Freud but curtailed by official Soviet disapproval of psychological themes in literature.

Zavalishin, Vyacheslav. "Satirists and Humorists: Zoshchenko." In his *Early Soviet Writers,* pp. 335-42. New York: Frederick A. Praeger, 1958.
Overview of Zoshchenko's career.

Appendix

The following is a listing of all sources used in Volume 15 of *Twentieth-Century Literary Criticism*. Included in this list are all copyright and reprint rights and acknowledgments for those essays for which permission was obtained. Every effort has been made to trace copyright, but if omissions have been made, please let us know.

THE EXCERPTS IN TCLC, VOLUME 15, WERE REPRINTED FROM THE FOLLOWING PERIODICALS:

Alaska Review, v. II, Fall, 1965. Copyright 1965 Alaska Methodist University. Reprinted by permission.

The American Journal of Psychology, v. LIX, January, 1941. © 1941 by the Board of Trustees of the University of Illinois. Reprinted by permission.

American Mercury, v. IV, April, 1925 for "The Conrad Wake" by H. L. Mencken; v. XVII, July, 1929 for "Sport in the Bible Country" by H. L. Mencken. Copyright 1925, renewed 1953, 1929, renewed 1956, by American Mercury Magazine, Inc. Used by permission of The Enoch Pratt Free Library of Baltimore in accordance with the terms of the will of H. L. Mencken.

The American Political Science Review, v. VII, November, 1913.

Américas, v. 21, January, 1969. Reprinted by permission from *Américas*, a bi-monthly magazine published by the General Secretariat of the Organization of American Studies in English and Spanish.

The Annals of the American Academy of Political and Social Science, v. LXII, January, 1916. © 1916, by The American Academy of Political and Social Science. Reprinted by permission of the publisher.

The Athenaeum, n. 3325, July 18, 1891; n. 3346, December 12, 1891; n. 3359, March 12, 1892; n. 3395, November 19, 1892; n. 3507, January 12, 1895.

The Atlantic Monthly, v. 174, December, 1944 for "The Simple Art of Murder," by Raymond Chandler. Copyright © 1944 by the author. Reprinted with permission.

The Bookman, London, v. LXIV, September, 1923.

The Bookman, New York, v. I, July, 1895./ v. LIV, January, 1922. Copyright, 1922, by George H. Doran Company. Reprinted by permission.

Canadian Literature, v. 47, Winter, 1971 for "The Klondike Muse" by Stanley S. Atherton. Reprinted by permission of the author.

The Chesterton Review, v. X, May, 1984. © 1984 *The Chesterton Review*. Reprinted by permission.

The Christian Science Monitor, September 10, 1935. © 1935 The Christian Science Publishing Society. All rights reserved. Reprinted by permission from *The Christian Science Monitor*.

THE EXCERPTS IN TCLC, VOLUME 15, WERE REPRINTED FROM THE FOLLOWING BOOKS:

A. E. From "The Poetry of My Friend," in *Selected Poems*. By Oliver St. John Gogarty. Macmillan, 1933. Copyright © 1933, renewed 1961 by the Estate of George William Russell. All rights reserved. Reprinted by permission of Russell & Wolkening, Inc. as agents for the author.

Allen, Mary. From *Animals in American Literature*. University of Illinois Press, 1983. © 1983 by the Board of Trustees of the University of Illinois. Reprinted by permission of the author and the University of Illinois Press.

Asimov, Isaac. From "'Nineteen Eighty-four'," in *Asimov on Science Fiction*. Doubleday & Company, Inc., 1981. Copyright © 1980 by Field Newspaper Syndicate, Inc. Reprinted by permission of Doubleday & Co., Inc.

Ayer, A. J. From *Philosophy in the Twentieth Century*. Random House, 1982. Weidenfeld and Nicolson, 1982. Copyright © 1982 by A. J. Ayer. All rights reserved. Reprinted by permission of Random House, Inc. In Canada by Weidenfeld (Publishers) Limited.

Baldwin, James Mark. From *Fragments in Philosophy and Science*. Charles Scribner's Sons, 1902.

Barltrop, Robert. From *Jack London: The Man, the Writer, the Rebel*. Pluto Press, 1976. Copyright © Pluto Press 1976. Reprinted by permission.

Baruch, Elaine Hoffman. From "The Golden Country: Sex and Love in '1984'," in *'1984' Revisited: Totalitarianism in Our Century*. Edited by Irving Howe. Harper & Row, 1983. Copyright © 1983 by Foundation for the Study of Independent Social Ideas. All rights reserved. Reprinted by permission of Harper & Row, Publishers, Inc.

Barzun, Jacques. From *A Stroll with William James*. Harper & Row, 1983. Copyright © 1983 by Jacques Barzun. All rights reserved. Abridged selections reprinted by permission of Harper & Row, Publishers, Inc.

Basney, Lionel. From "'The Nine Tailors' and the Complexity of Innocence," in *As Her Whimsey Took Her: Critical Essays on the Work of Dorothy L. Sayers*. Edited by Margaret P. Hannay. Kent State University Press, 1979. Copyright © 1979 by The Kent State University Press, Kent, Ohio 44242. All rights reserved. Reprinted by permission.

Beard, William. From an introduction to *The Economic Basis of Politics and Related Writings*. By Charles A. Beard, edited by William Beard. Vintage Books, 1957. © 1957 by William Beard and Miriam B. Vagts. All rights reserved.

Beauchamp, Gorman. From "From Bingo to Big Brother: Orwell on Power and Sadism," in *The Future of "Nineteen Eighty-Four."* Edited by Ejner J. Jensen. University of Michigan Press, 1984. Copyright © by The University of Michigan 1984. All rights reserved. Reprinted by permission.

Belloc, Hilaire. From a letter to Guy Dawnay on July 4, 1940, in *Letters from Hilaire Belloc*. Edited by Robert Speaight. Hollis & Carter, 1958. Copyright © 1958 by Hilary Belloc. Reprinted by permission of A. D. Peters & Co. Ltd.

Bely, Andrei. From "On Vladislav Khodasevich," in *The Complection of Russian Literature: A Cento*. Edited by Andrew Field. Atheneum, 1971. Copyright © 1971 by Andrew Field. All rights reserved. Reprinted with the permission of Atheneum Publishers, New York.

Bergson, Henri. From *The Creative Mind*. Translated by Mabelle L. Andison. Philosophical Library, 1946. Copyright 1946 The Philosophical Library, Inc. Reprinted with the permission of The Philosophical Library, Inc.

Bethea, David M. From *Khodasevich: His Life and Art*. Princeton University Press, 1983. Copyright © 1983 by Princeton University Press. All rights reserved. Excerpts reprinted with permission of Princeton University Press.

Bixler, Julius Seelye. From a preface to *Religion in the Philosophy of William James*. By Julius Seelye Bixler. Marshall Jones Company, 1926. Copyright, 1926, by Marshall Jones Company. Reprinted by permission.

Black, Hugo L. From a foreword to *Charles A Beard: An Appraisal*. Edited by Howard K. Beale. University of Kentucky Press, 1954. Copyright 1954 by The University of Kentucky Press. And renewed 1982 by the Literary Estate of Howard K. Beale. Reprinted by permission of the Literary Estate of Howard K. Beale.

Blair, Hector. From an introduction to *Lyudi*. By Mikhail Zoshchenko. Cambridge at the University Press, 1967. Introduction, notes and stressed text © Cambridge University Press 1967. Reprinted by permission.

Bloom, Harold. From "'Clinamen': Towards a Theory of Fantasy," in *Bridges to Fantasy*. George E. Slusser, Eric S. Rabkin, Robert Scholes, eds. Southern Illinois University Press, 1982. Copyright © 1982 by the Board of Trustees, Southern Illinois University. All rights reserved. Reprinted by permission of the author.

Bone, Robert A. From *The Negro Novel in America*. Revised edition. Yale University Press, 1965. Revised edition © 1965 by Yale University. All rights reserved. Reprinted by permission.

Borning, Bernard D. From *The Political and Social Thought of Charles A. Beard*. University of Washington Press, 1962. Copyright © 1962 by the University of Washington Press. Reprinted by permission.

Bradley, F. H. From *Essays on Truth and Reality*. Oxford at the Clarendon Press, Oxford, 1914.

Brown, Edward J. From *Russian Literature Since the Revolution*. Revised edition. Cambridge, Mass.: Harvard University Press, 1982. Copyright © 1963, 1969, and 1982 by Edward J. Brown. All rights reserved. Excerpted by permission of the President and Fellows of Harvard College.

Bunche, Ralph J. From a foreword to *How Far the Promised Land?* By Walter White. The Viking Press, 1955. Copyright © 1955 by Poppy Cannon White. Renewed © 1983 by Jane White Viazzi. Reprinted by permission of Viking Penguin Inc.

Carens, James F. From "Gogarty and Yeats," in *Modern Irish Literature: Essays in Honor of William York Tindall*. Edited by Raymond J. Porter and James D. Brophy. Iona College Press, 1972. Copyright © 1972 by Iona College Press. Reprinted by permission.

Carens, James F. From an introduction to *The Plays of Oliver St. John Gogarty*. By Oliver St. John Gogarty, edited by James F. Carens. Proscenium Press, 1972. Reprinted by permission of the publisher and James F. Carens.

Carter, Lin. From *Tolkien: A Look Behind "The Lord of the Rings."* Ballantine Books, 1969. Copyright © 1969 by Lin Carter. All rights reserved. Reprinted by permission of Ballantine Books, a Division of Random House, Inc.

Clark, David Ridgley. From *Lyric Resonance: Glosses on Some Poems of Yeats, Frost, Crane, Cummings & Others*. Edited by Robert G. Tucker and David R. Clark. The University of Massachusetts Press, 1972. Copyright © 1972 by The University of Massachusetts Press. All rights reserved. Reprinted by permission.

Commager, Henry Steele. From *The American Mind: An Interpretation of American Thought and Character Since the 1880's*. Yale University Press, 1950. Copyright, 1950, Yale University Press. And renewed 1978 by Henry Steele Commager. All rights reserved. Reprinted by permission.

Crick, Bernard. From *George Orwell: A Life*. Atlantic-Little, Brown, 1980. Copyright © 1980 by Bernard Crick. All rights reserved. Reprinted by permission of Little, Brown and Company in association with the Atlantic Monthly Press. In Canada by Martin Secker & Warburg Ltd.

Dale, Alzina Stone. From "'The Man Born to Be King': Dorothy L. Sayers's Best Mystery Plot," in *As Her Whimsey Took Her: Critical Essays on the Work of Dorothy L. Sayers*. Edited by Margaret P. Hannay. Kent State University Press, 1979. Copyright © 1979 by The Kent State University Press, Kent, Ohio 44242. All rights reserved. Reprinted by permission.

De Camp, L. Sprague. From *Literary Swordsmen and Sorcerers: The Makers of Heroic Fantasy*. Arkham House, 1976. Copyright © 1976, by L. Sprague de Camp. Reprinted by permission of Arkham House Publishers, Inc.

Dewey, John. From *Essays in Experimental Logic*. University of Chicago Press, 1916. Copyright 1953 by Dover Publications, Inc. Reprinted by permission of The University of Chicago Press.

Dickey, James. From an introduction to *The Call of the Wild, White Fang, and Other Stories*. By Jack London, edited by Andrew Sinclair. Penguin Books, 1981. Copyright © 1981 by James Dickey. All rights reserved. Reprinted by permission of Viking Penguin Inc.

Durkin, Mary Brian, O.P. From *Dorothy L. Sayers*. Twayne, 1980. Copyright © 1980 by Twayne Publishers. All rights reserved. Reprinted with the permission of Twayne Publishers, a division of G. K. Hall & Co., Boston.

Eddison, E. R. From *The Mezentian Gate*. The Curwen Press, 1958. © Mrs. E. R. Eddison 1958.

Eliot, T. S. From "From Poe to Valery," in *To Criticize the Critic and Other Writings*. Farrar, Straus and Giroux, 1965. Copyright 1948 by Thomas Stearns Eliot. Copyright renewed © 1976 by Valerie Worth. All rights reserved. Reprinted by permission of Farrar, Straus and Giroux, Inc. In Canada by permission of Faber and Faber Ltd.

Englekirk, John Eugene. From *Edgar Allan Poe in Hispanic Literature*. Instituto de las Españas, 1934.

Esslin, Martin. From "Television and Telescreen," in *On "Nineteen Eighty-Four."* Edited by Peter Stansky. W. H. Freeman and Company, 1983. Copyright © 1983 by W. H. Freeman and Company. All rights reserved. Reprinted by permission.

MacShane, Frank. From *The Life and Work of Ford Madox Ford*. Routledge & Kegan Paul, 1965. Copyright Frank MacShane 1965. Reprinted by permission of Routledge & Kegan Paul PLC.

Madariaga, Salvador de. From an introduction to *The Collected Works in English of Paul Valéry: History and Politics, Vol. 10*. By Paul Valéry, translated by Denise Folliot and Jackson Mathews. Bollingen Series XLV, Pantheon Books, 1962. Copyright © 1962 by Princeton University Press. Excerpts reprinted with permission of Princeton University Press.

Mainland, William F. From ''Hermann Sudermann,'' *in German Men of Letters: Twelve Literary Essays, Vol. II*. Edited by Alex Natan. Wolff, 1963. © 1963 Oswald Wolff (Publishers) Limited, London. Reprinted by permission.

Mandelstam, Nadezhda. From *Hope Abandoned*. Translated by Max Hayward. Atheneum, 1974. English translation copyright © 1973, 1974 by Atheneum Publishers. All rights reserved. Reprinted with the permission of Atheneum Publishers, New York.

Matthiessen, F. O. From *The James Family* Knopf, 1948. Copyright 1947 by Alfred A. Knopf, Inc. And renewed 1975 by Ruth M. Putnam. All rights reserved. Reprinted by permission of Alfred A. Knopf, Inc.

McClintock, James I. From *White Logic: Jack London's Short Stories*. Wolf House Books, 1975. Copyright © 1975 by James I. McClintock. All rights reserved. Reprinted by permission.

McLean, Hugh. From an introduction to *Nervous People and Other Satires*. By Mikhail Zoshchenko, edited by Hugh McLean, translated by Maria Gordon and Hugh McLean. Pantheon Books, 1963. Copyright © 1963 by Pantheon Books, Inc. All rights reserved. Reprinted by permission of Pantheon Books, a Division of Random House, Inc.

Mencken, H. L. From *Prejudices, first series*. Knopf, 1919. Copyright 1919 by Alfred A. Knopf, Inc. And renewed 1947 by H. L. Mencken. Reprinted by permission of Alfred A. Knopf, Inc.

Mirsky, D. S. From *Contemporary Russian Literature: 1881-1925*. Knopf, 1926. G. Routledge & Sons, 1926. Copyright 1926 by Alfred A. Knopf, Inc. Reprinted by permission of the publisher.

Mizener, Arthur. From *The Saddest Story: A Biography of Ford Madox Ford*. The World Publishing Company, 1971. Copyright © 1971 by Arthur Mizener. All rights reserved. Reprinted by permission of Harper & Row, Publishers, Inc.

Monas, Sidney. From an introduction to *Scenes from the Bathhouse and Other Stories of Communist Russia*. By Mikhail Zoshchenko, edited by Marc Slonim, translated by Sidney Monas. University of Michigan Press, 1961. Copyright © by The University of Michigan 1961. All rights reserved. Reprinted by permission.

More, Paul Elmer. From *Shelburne Essays, seventh series*. Putnam's, 1910. Copyright 1910 by Paul Elmer More. Renewed 1938. Reprinted by permission of G. P. Putnam's Sons.

Mumford, Lewis. From a letter to Van Wyck Brooks on December 3, 1947, in *The Van Wyck Brooks-Lewis Mumford Letters: The Record of a Literary Friendship, 1921-1963*. Edited by Robert E. Spiller. Dutton, 1970. Copyright © 1970 by E. P. Dutton & Co., Inc. All rights reserved. Reprinted by permission of the publisher, E. P. Dutton, Inc.

Nabokov, Vladimir. From *Strong Opinions*. McGraw-Hill, 1973. © copyright 1973, McGraw-Hill International, Inc. With permission of McGraw-Hill Book Co.

Nash, Suzanne. From *Paul Valéry's ''Album de vers anciens'': A Past Transfigured*. Princeton University Press, 1983. Copyright © 1983 by Princeton University Press. All rights reserved. Excerpts reprinted with permission of Princeton University Press.

Nieuwenhuys, Rob. From *Mirror of the Indies: A History of Dutch Colonial Literature*. Edited by E. M. Beekman, translated by Frans van Rosevelt. The University of Massachusetts Press, 1982. Copyright © 1982 by The University of Massachusetts Press. All rights reserved. Reprinted by permission.

O'Connor, Ulick. From *The Times I've Seen: Oliver St. John Gogarty, a Biography*. Ivan Obolensky, Inc., 1963. Copyright © 1964 by Ulick O'Connor. All rights reserved. Reprinted by permission of Astor-Honor, Inc., New York, NY 10017.

Orwell, George. From a letter to F. J. Warburg on October 22, 1948 in *The Collected Essays, Journalism and Letters of George Orwell: In Front of Your Nose, 1945-1950, Vol. IV*. Edited by Sonia Orwell and Ian Angus. Harcourt Brace Jovanovich, Inc., 1968. Secker & Warburg, 1968. Copyright © 1968 by Sonia Brownell Orwell. All rights reserved. Reprinted by permission of Harcourt Brace Jovanovich, Inc. In Canada by the Estate of the late Sonia Brownell Orwell and Martin Secker & Warburg Ltd.

Orwell, George. From an extract from a letter to Francis A. Henson on June 16, 1949 in *The Collected Essays, Journalism and Letters of George Orwell: In Front of Your Nose, 1945-1950, Vol. IV*. Edited by Sonia Orwell and Ian Angus. Harcourt Brace Jovanovich, Inc., 1968. Secker & Warburg, 1968. Copyright © 1968 by Sonia Brownell Orwell. All rights reserved. Reprinted by permission of Harcourt Brace Jovanovich, Inc. In Canada by the Estate of the late Sonia Brownell Orwell and Martin Secker & Warburg Ltd.

Perry, Ralph Barton. From *In the Spirit of William James*. Yale University Press, 1938. Copyright, 1938, by Yale University Press. And renewed 1966 by Ralph Barton Perry. All rights reserved. Reprinted by permission.

Phelps, Arthur L. From *Canadian Writers*. McClelland and Stewart Limited, 1951. Copyright in Canada, 1951 McClelland and Stewart Limited, Toronto. Used by permission of The Canadian Publishers, McClelland and Stewart Limited, Toronto.

Cumulative Index to Authors

This index lists all author entries in the Gale Literary Criticism Series and includes cross-references to other Gale sources. References in the index are identified as follows:

Arnow, Harriette (Louisa Simpson)
 1908-.................CLC 2, 7, 18
 See also CA 9-12R
 See also DLB 6

Arp, Jean 1887-1966..............CLC 5
 See also CA 81-84
 See also obituary CA 25-28R

Argueta, Manlio 1936- ....CLC 31

Arquette, Lois S(teinmetz)
 See Duncan (Steinmetz Arquette), Lois
 See also SATA 1

Arrabal, Fernando 1932-..... CLC 2, 9, 18
 See also CA 9-12R

Arrick, Fran ....CLC 30

Artaud, Antonin 1896-1948 ...... TCLC 3
 See also CA 104

Arthur, Ruth M(abel)
 1905-1979....................CLC 12
 See also CANR 4
 See also CA 9-12R
 See also obituary CA 85-88
 See also SATA 7
 See also obituary SATA 26

Arundel, Honor (Morfydd)
 1919-1973....................CLC 17
 See also CAP 2
 See also CA 21-22
 See also obituary CA 41-44R
 See also SATA 4
 See also obituary SATA 24

Asch, Sholem 1880-1957......... TCLC 3
 See also CA 105

Ashbery, John (Lawrence)
 1927-..... CLC 2, 3, 4, 6, 9, 13, 15, 25
 See also CANR 9
 See also CA 5-8R
 See also DLB 5
 See also DLB-Y 81

Ashton-Warner, Sylvia (Constance)
 1908-1984....................CLC 19
 See also CA 69-72
 See also obituary CA 112

Asimov, Isaac
 1920-............. CLC 1, 3, 9, 19, 26
 See also CANR 2
 See also CA 1-4R
 See also SATA 1, 26
 See also DLB 8

Aston, James 1906-1964
 See White, T(erence) H(anbury)

Asturias, Miguel Ángel
 1899-1974...............CLC 3, 8, 13
 See also CAP 2
 See also CA 25-28
 See also obituary CA 49-52

Atheling, William, Jr. 1921-1975
 See Blish, James (Benjamin)

Atherton, Gertrude (Franklin Horn)
 1857-1948................... TCLC 2
 See also CA 104
 See also DLB 9

Atwood, Margaret (Eleanor)
 1939-........CLC 2, 3, 4, 8, 13, 15, 25
 See also CANR 3
 See also CA 49-52

Auchincloss, Louis (Stanton)
 1917-.................CLC 4, 6, 9, 18
 See also CANR 6
 See also CA 1-4R
 See also DLB 2
 See also DLB-Y 80

Auden, W(ystan) H(ugh)
 1907-1973....... CLC 1, 2, 3, 4, 6, 9,
 11, 14
 See also CANR 5
 See also CA 9-12R
 See also obituary CA 45-48
 See also DLB 10, 20

Auel, Jean M(arie) 1936-.........CLC 31
 See also CA 103

Austen, Jane 1775-1817 .... NCLC 1

Avison, Margaret 1918- .... CLC 2, 4
 See also CA 17-20R

Ayckbourn, Alan 1939-....... CLC 5, 8, 18
 See also CA 21-24R
 See also DLB 13

Aymé, Marcel (Andre)
 1902-1967....................CLC 11
 See also CA 89-92

Ayrton, Michael 1921-1975 ....CLC 7
 See also CANR 9
 See also CA 5-8R
 See also obituary CA 61-64

Azorín 1874-1967.................CLC 11
 See also Martínez Ruiz, José

Azuela, Mariano 1873-1952....... TCLC 3
 See also CA 104

"Bab" 1836-1911
 See Gilbert, (Sir) W(illiam) S(chwenck)

Babel, Isaak (Emmanuilovich)
 1894-1941................ TCLC 2, 13
 See also CA 104

Babits, Mihály 1883-1941....... TCLC 14

Bacchelli, Riccardo 1891-.........CLC 19
 See also CA 29-32R

Bach, Richard (David) 1936-.......CLC 14
 See also CA 9-12R
 See also SATA 13
 See also AITN 1

Bagnold, Enid 1889-1981..........CLC 25
 See also CANR 5
 See also CA 5-8R
 See also obituary CA 103
 See also SATA 1, 25
 See also DLB 13

Bagryana, Elisaveta 1893- ....CLC 10

Baillie, Joanna 1762-1851 .... NCLC 2

Bainbridge, Beryl
 1933-.......CLC 4, 5, 8, 10, 14, 18, 22
 See also CA 21-24R
 See also DLB 14

Baker, Elliott 1922-.................CLC 8
 See also CANR 2
 See also CA 45-48

Baker, Russell (Wayne) 1925-......CLC 31
 See also CANR 11
 See also CA 57-60

Bakshi, Ralph 1938- ....CLC 26
 See also CA 112

Baldwin, James (Arthur)
 1924-......CLC 1, 2, 3, 4, 5, 8, 13, 15,
 17
 See also CANR 3
 See also CA 1-4R
 See also SATA 9
 See also DLB 2, 7, 33

Ballard, J(ames) G(raham)
 1930-......................CLC 3, 6, 14
 See also CA 5-8R
 See also DLB 14

Balmont, Konstantin Dmitriyevich
 1867-1943................... TCLC 11
 See also CA 109

Balzac, Honoré de 1799-1850 ..... NCLC 5

Bambara, Toni Cade...............CLC 19
 See also CA 29-32R

Banks, Lynne Reid 1929-..........CLC 23
 See also Reid Banks, Lynne

Baraka, Imamu Amiri
 1934-........... CLC 1, 2, 3, 5, 10, 14
 See also Jones, (Everett) LeRoi
 See also DLB 5, 7, 16

Barbey d'Aurevilly, Jules Amédée
 1808-1889................... NCLC 1

Barbusse, Henri 1873-1935 .... TCLC 5
 See also CA 105

Barea, Arturo 1897-1957 .... TCLC 14
 See also CA 111

Barfoot, Joan 1946-...............CLC 18
 See also CA 105

Baring, Maurice 1874-1945 .... TCLC 8
 See also CA 105

Barker, George (Granville)
 1913-........................CLC 8
 See also CANR 7
 See also CA 9-12R
 See also DLB 20

Barnes, Djuna
 1892-1982........ CLC 3, 4, 8, 11, 29
 See also CA 9-12R
 See also obituary CA 107
 See also DLB 4, 9

Barnes, Peter 1931-.................CLC 5
 See also CA 65-68
 See also DLB 13

Baroja (y Nessi), Pío
 1872-1956................... TCLC 8
 See also CA 104

Barondess, Sue K(aufman) 1926-1977
 See Kaufman, Sue
 See also CANR 1
 See also CA 1-4R
 See also obituary CA 69-72

Barrett, William (Christopher)
 1913-.......................CLC 27
 See also CANR 11
 See also CA 13-16R

Barrie, (Sir) J(ames) M(atthew)
 1860-1937................... TCLC 2
 See also CA 104
 See also YABC 1
 See also DLB 10

Barry, Philip (James Quinn)
 1896-1949................... TCLC 11
 See also CA 109
 See also DLB 7

Dourado, (Waldomiro Freitas) Autran
1926-.........................CLC 23
See also CA 25-28R

Dowson, Ernest (Christopher)
1867-1900.................. TCLC 4
See also CA 105
See also DLB 19

Doyle, (Sir) Arthur Conan
1859-1930.................. TCLC 7
See also CA 104
See also SATA 24
See also DLB 18

Dr. A 1933-
See Silverstein, Alvin and Virginia
B(arbara Opshelor) Silverstein

Drabble, Margaret
1939-...........CLC 2, 3, 5, 8, 10, 22
See also CA 13-16R
See also DLB 14

Dreiser, Theodore (Herman Albert)
1871-1945.................. TCLC 10
See also CA 106
See also DLB 9, 12
See also DLB-DS 1

Drexler, Rosalyn 1926-.......... CLC 2, 6
See also CA 81-84

Dreyer, Carl Theodor
1889-1968....................CLC 16

Droste-Hülshoff, Annette Freiin von
1797-1848.................. NCLC 3

Drummond de Andrade, Carlos 1902-
See Andrade, Carlos Drummond de

Duberman, Martin 1930-...........CLC 8
See also CANR 2
See also CA 1-4R

Du Bois, W(illiam) E(dward) B(urghardt)
1868-1963..............CLC 1, 2, 13
See also CA 85-88

Dubus, Andre 1936-..............CLC 13
See also CA 21-24R

Duclos, Charles Pinot 1704-1772 ..... LC 1

Dudek, Louis 1918-........... CLC 11, 19
See also CANR 1
See also CA 45-48

Dudevant, Amandine Aurore Lucile Dupin
1804-1876
See Sand, George

Duerrenmatt, Friedrich 1921-
See also CA 17-20R

Dugan, Alan 1923-.............. CLC 2, 6
See also CA 81-84
See also DLB 5

Duhamel, Georges 1884-1966 ....CLC 8
See also CA 81-84
See also obituary CA 25-28R

Dujardin, Édouard (Émile Louis)
1861-1949................. TCLC 13
See also CA 109

Duke, Raoul 1939-
See Thompson, Hunter S(tockton)

Dumas, Henry (L.) 1934-1968.......CLC 6
See also CA 85-88

Du Maurier, Daphne 1907- ..... CLC 6, 11
See also CANR 6
See also CA 5-8R
See also SATA 27

Dunbar, Paul Laurence
1872-1906................ TCLC 2, 12
See also CA 104
See also SATA 34

Duncan (Steinmetz Arquette), Lois
1934-.......................CLC 26
See also Arquette, Lois S(teinmetz)
See also CANR 2
See also CA 1-4R
See also SATA 1, 36

Duncan, Robert
1919-.............. CLC 1, 2, 4, 7, 15
See also CA 9-12R
See also DLB 5, 16

Dunlap, William 1766-1839....... NCLC 2
See also DLB 30

Dunn, Douglas (Eaglesham)
1942-.......................CLC 6
See also CANR 2
See also CA 45-48

Dunne, John Gregory 1932-.......CLC 28
See also CA 25-28R
See also DLB-Y 80

**Dunsany, Lord (Edward John Moreton Drax
Plunkett)** 1878-1957........ TCLC 2
See also CA 104
See also DLB 10

Durang, Christopher (Ferdinand)
1949-.......................CLC 27
See also CA 105

Duras, Marguerite
1914-.................CLC 3, 6, 11, 20
See also CA 25-28R

Durrell, Lawrence (George)
1912-...........CLC 1, 4, 6, 8, 13, 27
See also CA 9-12R
See also DLB 15, 27

Dürrenmatt, Friedrich
1921-.......... CLC 1, 4, 8, 11, 15
See also Duerrenmatt, Friedrich

Dylan, Bob 1941-...........CLC 3, 4, 6, 12
See also CA 41-44R
See also DLB 16

Eastlake, William (Derry) 1917-.....CLC 8
See also CAAS 1
See also CANR 5
See also CA 5-8R
See also DLB 6

Eberhart, Richard 1904- .... CLC 3, 11, 19
See also CANR 2
See also CA 1-4R

**Echegaray (y Eizaguirre), José (María
Waldo)** 1832-1916........... TCLC 4
See also CA 104

Eckert, Allan W. 1931-............CLC 17
See also CA 13-16R
See also SATA 27, 29

Eco, Umberto 1932- ....CLC 28
See also CANR 12
See also CA 77-80

Eddison, E(ric) R(ucker)
1882-1945.................. TCLC 15
See also CA 109

Edel, (Joseph) Leon 1907- ....CLC 29
See also CANR 1
See also CA 1-4R

Edgeworth, Maria 1767-1849 ..... NCLC 1
See also SATA 21

Edmonds, Helen (Woods) 1904-1968
See Kavan, Anna
See also CA 5-8R
See also obituary CA 25-28R

Edson, Russell 1905-.............CLC 13
See also CA 33-36R

Edwards, G(erald) B(asil)
1899-1976........................CLC 25
See also obituary CA 110

Ehle, John (Marsden, Jr.)
1925-.......................CLC 27
See also CA 9-12R

Ehrenbourg, Ilya (Grigoryevich) 1891-1967
See Ehrenburg, Ilya (Grigoryevich)

Ehrenburg, Ilya (Grigoryevich)
1891-1967......................CLC 18
See also CA 102
See also obituary CA 25-28R

Eich, Guenter 1907-1971
See also CA 111
See also obituary CA 93-96

Eich, Günter 1907-1971...........CLC 15
See also Eich, Guenter

Eichendorff, Joseph Freiherr von
1788-1857......................NCLC 8

Eigner, Larry 1927- ....CLC 9
See also Eigner, Laurence (Joel)
See also DLB 5

Eigner, Laurence (Joel) 1927-
See Eigner, Larry
See also CANR 6
See also CA 9-12R

Eiseley, Loren (Corey)
1907-1977......................CLC 7
See also CANR 6
See also CA 1-4R
See also obituary CA 73-76

Ekeloef, Gunnar (Bengt) 1907-1968
See Ekelöf, Gunnar (Bengt)
See also obituary CA 25-28R

Ekelöf, Gunnar (Bengt)
1907-1968....................CLC 27
See also Ekeloef, Gunnar (Bengt)

Ekwensi, Cyprian (Odiatu Duaka)
1921-.......................CLC 4
See also CA 29-32R

Eliade, Mircea 1907-..............CLC 19
See also CA 65-68

Eliot, George 1819-1880.......... NCLC 4
See also DLB 21

Eliot, T(homas) S(tearns)
1888-1965...... CLC 1, 2, 3, 6, 9, 10,
                        13, 15, 24
See also CA 5-8R
See also obituary CA 25-28R
See also DLB 7, 10

Elkin, Stanley L(awrence)
1930-.............. CLC 4, 6, 9, 14, 27
See also CANR 8
See also CA 9-12R
See also DLB 2, 28
See also DLB-Y 80

Elliott, George P(aul)
1918-1980....................CLC 2
See also CANR 2
See also CA 1-4R
See also obituary CA 97-100

Fiedler, Leslie A(aron)
1917-.................... CLC 4, 13, 24
See also CANR 7
See also CA 9-12R
See also DLB 28

Field, Eugene 1850-1895 .... NCLC 3
See also SATA 16
See also DLB 21, 23

Fielding, Henry 1707-1754.......... LC 1

Fielding, Sarah 1710-1768 .... LC 1

Figes, Eva 1932-.................CLC 31
See also CANR 4
See also CA 53-56
See also DLB 14

Finch, Robert (Duer Claydon)
1900-....................... CLC 18
See also CANR 9
See also CA 57-60

Findley, Timothy 1930-...........CLC 27
See also CANR 12
See also CA 25-28R

Fink, Janis 1951-
See Ian, Janis

Firbank, (Arthur Annesley) Ronald
1886-1926.................. TCLC 1
See also CA 104

Firbank, Louis 1944-
See Reed, Lou

Fisher, Roy 1930- ....CLC 25
See also CA 81-84

Fisher, Rudolph 1897-1934 ...... TCLC 11
See also CA 107

Fisher, Vardis (Alvero)
1895-1968.....................CLC 7
See also CA 5-8R
See also obituary CA 25-28R
See also DLB 9

Fitzgerald, F(rancis) Scott (Key)
1896-1940.............TCLC 1, 6, 14
See also CA 110
See also DLB 4, 9
See also DLB-Y 81
See also DLB-DS 1
See also AITN 1

Fitzgerald, Penelope 1916-.........CLC 19
See also CA 85-88
See also DLB 14

FitzGerald, Robert D(avid)
1902-........................CLC 19
See also CA 17-20R

Flanagan, Thomas (James Bonner)
1923-........................CLC 25
See also CA 108
See also DLB-Y 80

Flaubert, Gustave 1821-1880...... NCLC 2

Fleming, Ian (Lancaster)
1908-1964................. CLC 3, 30
See also CA 5-8R
See also SATA 9

Follett, Ken(neth Martin)
1949-........................CLC 18
See also CANR 13
See also CA 81-84
See also DLB-Y 81

Forbes, Esther 1891-1967.........CLC 12
See also CAP 1
See also CA 13-14
See also obituary CA 25-28R
See also DLB 22
See also SATA 2

Forché, Carolyn 1950- ....CLC 25
See also CA 109
See also DLB 5

Ford, Ford Madox
1873-1939................ TCLC 1, 15
See also CA 104

Ford, John 1895-1973.............CLC 16
See also obituary CA 45-48

Forman, James D(ouglas)
1932-........................CLC 21
See also CANR 4
See also CA 9-12R
See also SATA 8, 21

Forrest, Leon 1937-................CLC 4
See also CA 89-92
See also DLB 33

Forster, E(dward) M(organ)
1879-1970...... CLC 1, 2, 3, 4, 9, 10,
                                13, 15, 22
See also CAP 1
See also CA 13-14
See also obituary CA 25-28R

Forsyth, Frederick 1938- .... CLC 2, 5
See also CA 85-88

Foscolo, Ugo 1778-1827 .... NCLC 8

Fosse, Bob 1925-.................CLC 20
See also Fosse, Robert Louis

Fosse, Robert Louis 1925-
See Bob Fosse
See also CA 110

Foucault, Michel 1926-1984........CLC 31
See also CA 105

**Fouqué, Friedrich (Heinrich Karl) de La
    Motte** 1777-1843............ NCLC 2

Fournier, Henri Alban 1886-1914
See Alain-Fournier
See also CA 104

Fournier, Pierre 1916-............CLC 11
See also CA 89-92

Fowles, John
1926-...... CLC 1, 2, 3, 4, 6, 9, 10, 15
See also CA 5-8R
See also SATA 22
See also DLB 14

Fox, Paula 1923- .... CLC 2, 8
See also CLR 1
See also CA 73-76
See also SATA 17

Fox, William Price (Jr.) 1926-......CLC 22
See also CANR 11
See also CA 17-20R
See also DLB 2
See also DLB-Y 81

Frame (Clutha), Janet (Paterson)
1924-.................CLC 2, 3, 6, 22
See also Clutha, Janet Paterson Frame

France, Anatole 1844-1924 .... TCLC 9
See also Thibault, Jacques Anatole
    Francois

Francis, Dick 1920-............ CLC 2, 22
See also CANR 9
See also CA 5-8R

Francis, Robert (Churchill)
1901-........................CLC 15
See also CANR 1
See also CA 1-4R

Franklin, (Stella Maria Sarah) Miles
1879-1954................... TCLC 9
See also CA 104

Fraser, George MacDonald
1925-........................CLC 7
See also CANR 2
See also CA 45-48

Frayn, Michael 1933-........ CLC 3, 7, 31
See also CA 5-8R
See also DLB 13, 14

Fredro, Aleksander 1793-1876 .... NCLC 8

Freeman, Douglas Southall
1886-1953................. TCLC 11
See also CA 109
See also DLB 17

Freeman, Mary (Eleanor) Wilkins
1852-1930................... TCLC 9
See also CA 106
See also DLB 12

French, Marilyn 1929- .... CLC 10, 18
See also CANR 3
See also CA 69-72

Freneau, Philip Morin
1752-1832.................. NCLC 1

Friedman, B(ernard) H(arper)
1926-........................CLC 7
See also CANR 3
See also CA 1-4R

Friedman, Bruce Jay 1930- ...... CLC 3, 5
See also CA 9-12R
See also DLB 2, 28

Friel, Brian 1929- ....CLC 5
See also CA 21-24R
See also DLB 13

Friis-Baastad, Babbis (Ellinor)
1921-1970...................CLC 12
See also CA 17-20R
See also SATA 7

Frisch, Max (Rudolf)
1911-................CLC 3, 9, 14, 18
See also CA 85-88

Frost, Robert (Lee)
1874-1963...... CLC 1, 3, 4, 9, 10, 13,
                                15, 26
See also CA 89-92
See also SATA 14

Fry, Christopher 1907-...... CLC 2, 10, 14
See also CANR 9
See also CA 17-20R
See also DLB 13

Frye, (Herman) Northrop
1912-........................CLC 24
See also CANR 8
See also CA 5-8R

Fuchs, Daniel 1909-............ CLC 8, 22
See also CA 81-84
See also DLB 9, 26, 28

Author Index

Ginsberg, Allen
    1926- .... CLC 1, 2, 3, 4, 6, 13
    See also CANR 2
    See also CA 1-4R
    See also DLB 5, 16
    See also AITN 1

Ginzburg, Natalia 1916- .... CLC 5, 11
    See also CA 85-88

Giono, Jean 1895-1970 .... CLC 4, 11
    See also CANR 2
    See also CA 45-48
    See also obituary CA 29-32R

Giovanni, Nikki 1943- .... CLC 2, 4, 19
    See also CLR 6
    See also CA 29-32R
    See also SATA 24
    See also DLB 5
    See also AITN 1

Giovene, Andrea 1904- .... CLC 7
    See also CA 85-88

Gippius, Zinaida (Nikolayevna) 1869-1945
    See also Hippius, Zinaida
    See also CA 106

Giraudoux, (Hippolyte) Jean
    1882-1944................. TCLC 2, 7
    See also CA 104

Gironella, José María 1917- .... CLC 11
    See also CA 101

Gissing, George (Robert)
    1857-1903.................. TCLC 3
    See also CA 105
    See also DLB 18

Glanville, Brian (Lester) 1931- ...... CLC 6
    See also CANR 3
    See also CA 5-8R
    See also DLB 15

Glasgow, Ellen (Anderson Gholson)
    1873?-1945................ TCLC 2, 7
    See also CA 104
    See also DLB 9, 12

Glassco, John 1909-1981 .... CLC 9
    See also CA 13-16R
    See also obituary CA 102

Glissant, Edouard 1928- .... CLC 10

Glück, Louise 1943- .... CLC 7, 22
    See also CA 33-36R
    See also DLB 5

Godard, Jean-Luc 1930- .... CLC 20
    See also CA 93-96

Godwin, Gail 1937- .... CLC 5, 8, 22, 31
    See also CA 29-32R
    See also DLB 6

Goethe, Johann Wolfgang von
    1749-1832................... NCLC 4

Gogarty, Oliver St. John
    1878-1957................. TCLC 15
    See also CA 109
    See also DLB 15, 19

Gogol, Nikolai (Vasilyevich)
    1809-1852.................. NCLC 5

Gökçeli, Yasar Kemal 1923-
    See Kemal, Yashar

Gold, Herbert 1924- .... CLC 4, 7, 14
    See also CA 9-12R
    See also DLB 2
    See also DLB-Y 81

Goldbarth, Albert 1948- .... CLC 5
    See also CANR 6
    See also CA 53-56

Golding, William (Gerald)
    1911- .... CLC 1, 2, 3, 8, 10, 17, 27
    See also CANR 13
    See also CA 5-8R
    See also DLB 15

Goldman, Emma 1869-1940 ..... TCLC 13
    See also CA 110

Goldman, William (W.) 1931- .... CLC 1
    See also CA 9-12R

Goldmann, Lucien 1913-1970 ..... CLC 24
    See also CAP 2
    See also CA 25-28

Gombrowicz, Witold
    1904-1969................ CLC 4, 7, 11
    See also CAP 2
    See also CA 19-20
    See also obituary CA 25-28R

Gómez de la Serna, Ramón
    1888-1963.................... CLC 9

Goncharov, Ivan Alexandrovich
    1812-1891.................. NCLC 1

Goncourt, Edmond (Louis Antoine Huot) de
    1822-1896
    See Goncourt, Edmond (Louis Antoine
    Huot) de and Goncourt, Jules (Alfred
    Huot) de

Goncourt, Edmond (Louis Antoine Huot) de
    1822-1896 and **Goncourt, Jules (Alfred**
    Huot) de 1830-1870 .... NCLC 7

Goncourt, Jules (Alfred Huot) de 1830-1870
    See Goncourt, Edmond (Louis Antoine
    Huot) de and Goncourt, Jules (Alfred
    Huot) de

Goncourt, Jules (Alfred Huot) de 1830-1870
    and **Goncourt, Edmond (Louis Antoine**
    Huot) de 1822-1896
    See Goncourt, Edmond (Louis Antoine
    Huot) de and Goncourt, Jules (Alfred
    Huot) de

Goodman, Paul
    1911-1972............... CLC 1, 2, 4, 7
    See also CAP 2
    See also CA 19-20
    See also obituary CA 37-40R

Gordimer, Nadine
    1923- .... CLC 3, 5, 7, 10, 18
    See also CANR 3
    See also CA 5-8R

Gordon, Caroline
    1895-1981.............. CLC 6, 13, 29
    See also CAP 1
    See also CA 11-12
    See also obituary CA 103
    See also DLB 4, 9
    See also DLB-Y 81

Gordon, Mary (Catherine)
    1949-.................... CLC 13, 22
    See also CA 102
    See also DLB 6
    See also DLB-Y 81

Gordon, Sol 1923- .... CLC 26
    See also CANR 4
    See also CA 53-56
    See also SATA 11

Gordone, Charles 1925- .... CLC 1, 4
    See also CA 93-96
    See also DLB 7

Gorenko, Anna Andreyevna 1889?-1966
    See Akhmatova, Anna

Gorky, Maxim 1868-1936 .... TCLC 8
    See also Peshkov, Alexei Maximovich

Goryan, Sirak 1908-1981
    See Saroyan, William

Gotlieb, Phyllis (Fay Bloom)
    1926-........................CLC 18
    See also CANR 7
    See also CA 13-16R

Gould, Lois 1938?- .... CLC 4, 10
    See also CA 77-80

Goyen, (Charles) William
    1915-1983.............. CLC 5, 8, 14
    See also CANR 6
    See also CA 5-8R
    See also obituary CA 110
    See also DLB 2
    See also DLB-Y 83
    See also AITN 2

Goytisolo, Juan 1931- .... CLC 5, 10, 23
    See also CA 85-88

Grabbe, Christian Dietrich
    1801-1836.................. NCLC 2

Gracq, Julien 1910-...............CLC 11

Grade, Chaim 1910-1982..........CLC 10
    See also CA 93-96
    See also obituary CA 107

Graham W(illiam) S(ydney)
    1918-.......................CLC 29
    See also CA 73-76
    See also DLB 20

Graham, Winston (Mawdsley)
    1910-.......................CLC 23
    See also CANR 2
    See also CA 49-52

Granville-Barker, Harley
    1877-1946.................. TCLC 2
    See also CA 104

Grass, Günter (Wilhelm)
    1927-........CLC 1, 2, 4, 6, 11, 15, 22
    See also CA 13-16R

Grau, Shirley Ann 1929- .... CLC 4, 9
    See also CA 89-92
    See also DLB 2
    See also AITN 2

Graves, Robert 1895- ......CLC 1, 2, 6, 11
    See also CANR 5
    See also CA 5-8R
    See also DLB 20

Gray, Amlin 1946-.................CLC 29

Gray, Francine du Plessix
    1930-........................CLC 22
    See also CANR 11
    See also CA 61-64

Gray, Simon 1936- .... CLC 9, 14
    See also CA 21-24R
    See also DLB 13
    See also AITN 1

Greeley, Andrew M(oran)
    1928-........................CLC 28
    See also CANR 7
    See also CA 5-8R

Author Index

Author Index

Author Index

Author Index

Schneider, Leonard Alfred 1925-1966
See Bruce, Lenny
See also CA 89-92

Schnitzler, Arthur 1862-1931 ..... TCLC 4
See also CA 104

Schorer, Mark 1908-1977 ....CLC 9
See also CANR 7
See also CA 5-8R
See also obituary CA 73-76

Schrader, Paul (Joseph) 1946-......CLC 26
See also CA 37-40R

Schreiner (Cronwright), Olive (Emilie
Albertina) 1855-1920 .... TCLC 9
See also CA 105
See also DLB 18

Schulberg, Budd (Wilson) 1914- .....CLC 7
See also CA 25-28R
See also DLB 6, 26, 28
See also DLB-Y 81

Schulz, Bruno 1892-1942 .... TCLC 5

Schulz, Charles M(onroe)
1922-.......................CLC 12
See also CANR 6
See also CA 9-12R
See also SATA 10

Schuyler, James (Marcus)
1923-..................... CLC 5, 23
See also CA 101
See also DLB 5

Schwartz, Delmore
1913-1966............... CLC 2, 4, 10
See also CAP 2
See also CA 17-18
See also obituary CA 25-28R
See also DLB 28

Schwartz, Lynne Sharon 1939- .....CLC 31
See also CA 103

Schwarz-Bart, André 1928- ...... CLC 2, 4
See also CA 89-92

Schwarz-Bart, Simone 1938- ....CLC 7
See also CA 97-100

Sciascia, Leonardo 1921- .... CLC 8, 9
See also CA 85-88

Scoppettone, Sandra 1936-.........CLC 26
See also CA 5-8R
See also SATA 9

Scorsese, Martin 1942- ....CLC 20
See also CA 110

Scotland, Jay 1932-
See Jakes, John (William)

Scott, Duncan Campbell
1862-1947.................. TCLC 6
See also CA 104

Scott, F(rancis) R(eginald)
1899-.......................CLC 22
See also CA 101

Scott, Paul (Mark) 1920-1978 ....CLC 9
See also CA 81-84
See also obituary CA 77-80
See also DLB 14

Seare, Nicholas 1925-
See Trevanian
See also Whitaker, Rodney

Sebestyen, Igen 1924-
See Sebestyen, Ouida

Sebestyen, Ouida 1924-............CLC 30
See also CA 107

Seelye, John 1931-.................CLC 7
See also CA 97-100

Seferiades, Giorgos Stylianou 1900-1971
See Seferis, George
See also CANR 5
See also CA 5-8R
See also obituary CA 33-36R

Seferis, George 1900-1971 ...... CLC 5, 11
See also Seferiades, Giorgos Stylianou

Segal, Erich (Wolf) 1937-....... CLC 3, 10
See also CA 25-28R

Seghers, Anna 1900-...............CLC 7
See Radvanyi, Netty

Seidel, Frederick (Lewis) 1936-.....CLC 18
See also CANR 8
See also CA 13-16R

Selby, Hubert, Jr.
1928-..................CLC 1, 2, 4, 8
See also CA 13-16R
See also DLB 2

Sender, Ramón (José)
1902-1982.....................CLC 8
See also CANR 8
See also CA 5-8R
See also obituary CA 105

Serling, (Edward) Rod(man) 1924-1975
See also CA 65-68
See also obituary CA 57-60
See also DLB 26
See also AITN 1

Service, Robert W(illiam)
1874-1958.................. TCLC 15
See also SATA 20

Seton, Cynthia Propper
1926-1982....................CLC 27
See also CANR-7
See also CA 5-8R
See also obituary CA 108

Settle, Mary Lee 1918-............CLC 19
See also CAAS 1
See also CA 89-92
See also DLB 6

Sexton, Anne (Harvey)
1928-1974....... CLC 2, 4, 6, 8, 10, 15
See also CANR 3
See also CA 1-4R
See also obituary CA 53-56
See also SATA 10
See also DLB 5

Shaara, Michael (Joseph)
1929-.......................CLC 15
See also CA 102
See also DLB-Y 83
See also AITN 1

Shaffer, Anthony 1926-............CLC 19
See also CA 110
See also DLB 13

Shaffer, Peter (Levin)
1926-................. CLC 5, 14, 18
See also CA 25-28R
See also DLB 13

Shalamov, Varlam (Tikhonovich)
1907?-1982...................CLC 18
See also obituary CA 105

Shamlu, Ahmad 1925- ....CLC 10

Shange, Ntozake 1948- .... CLC 8, 25
See also CA 85-88

Shapiro, Karl (Jay) 1913-..... CLC 4, 8, 15
See also CANR 1
See also CA 1-4R

Shaw, (George) Bernard
1856-1950................. TCLC 3, 6
See also CA 104, 109
See also DLB 10

Shaw, Irwin 1913-1984........ CLC 7, 23
See also CA 13-16R
See also obituary CA 112
See also DLB 6
See also AITN 1

Shaw, Robert 1927-1978 ....CLC 5
See also CANR 4
See also CA 1-4R
See also obituary CA 81-84
See also DLB 13, 14
See also AITN 1

Sheed, Wilfrid (John Joseph)
1930-................... CLC 2, 4, 10
See also CA 65-68
See also DLB 6

Shepard, Sam 1943- .... CLC 4, 6, 17
See also CA 69-72
See also DLB 7

Sherburne, Zoa (Morin) 1912- .....CLC 30
See also CANR 3
See also CA 1-4R
See also SATA 3

Sheridan, Richard Brinsley
1751-1816.................. NCLC 5

Sherman, Martin ....CLC 19

Sherwin, Judith Johnson
1936-..................... CLC 7, 15
See also CA 25-28R

Sherwood, Robert E(mmet)
1896-1955.................. TCLC 3
See also CA 104
See also DLB 7, 26

Shiel, M(atthew) P(hipps)
1865-1947................... TCLC 8
See also CA 106

Shimazaki, Haruki 1872-1943
See Shimazaki, Tōson
See also CA 105

Shimazaki, Tōson 1872-1943 ...... TCLC 5
See also Shimazaki, Haruki

Sholokhov, Mikhail (Aleksandrovich)
1905-1984................. CLC 7, 15
See also CA 101
See also obituary CA 112
See also SATA 36

Shreve, Susan Richards 1939-......CLC 23
See also CANR 5
See also CA 49-52

Shulman, Alix Kates 1932-...... CLC 2, 10
See also CA 29-32R
See also SATA 7

Shuster, Joe 1914-
See Siegel, Jerome and Shuster, Joe

Shute (Norway), Nevil
1899-1960...................CLC 30
See also Norway, Nevil Shute

Author Index

Author Index

Author Index

Cumulative Index to Nationalities

AMERICAN
Adams, Henry **4**
Agee, James **1**
Anderson, Maxwell **2**
Anderson, Sherwood **1, 10**
Atherton, Gertrude **2**
Barry, Philip **11**
Baum, L. Frank **7**
Beard, Charles A. **15**
Belasco, David **3**
Benchley, Robert **1**
Benét, Stephen Vincent **7**
Bierce, Ambrose **1, 7**
Bromfield, Louis **11**
Burroughs, Edgar Rice **2**
Cabell, James Branch **6**
Cable, George Washington **4**
Cather, Willa **1, 11**
Chandler, Raymond **1, 7**
Chapman, John Jay **7**
Chesnutt, Charles Waddell **5**
Chopin, Kate **5, 14**
Comstock, Anthony **13**
Crane, Hart **2, 5**
Crane, Stephen **11**
Crawford, F. Marion **10**
Cullen, Countee **4**
Davis, Rebecca Harding **6**
Dreiser, Theodore **10**
Dunbar, Paul Laurence **2, 12**
Fisher, Rudolph **11**
Fitzgerald, F. Scott **1, 6, 14**
Freeman, Douglas Southall **11**
Freeman, Mary Wilkins **9**
Gale, Zona **7**
Garland, Hamlin **3**
Gilman, Charlotte Perkins **9**
Glasgow, Ellen **2, 7**
Goldman, Emma **13**

Grey, Zane **6**
Harper, Frances Ellen Watkins **14**
Harris, Joel Chandler **2**
Harte, Bret **1**
Hearn, Lafcadio **9**
Henry, O. **1**
Hergesheimer, Joseph **11**
Howard, Robert E. **8**
Howells, William Dean **7**
James, Henry **2, 11**
James, William **15**
Jewett, Sarah Orne **1**
Johnson, James Weldon **3**
Kornbluth, C. M. **8**
Kuttner, Henry **10**
Lardner, Ring **2, 14**
Lewis, Sinclair **4, 13**
London, Jack **9, 15**
Lovecraft, H. P. **4**
Lowell, Amy **1, 8**
Marquis, Don **7**
Masters, Edgar Lee **2**
McKay, Claude **7**
Mencken, H. L. **13**
Millay, Edna St. Vincent **4**
Mitchell, Margaret **11**
Monroe, Harriet **12**
O'Neill, Eugene **1, 6**
Rawlings, Majorie Kinnan **4**
Reed, John **9**
Robinson, Edwin Arlington **5**
Rogers, Will **8**
Rourke, Constance **12**
Runyon, Damon **10**
Saltus, Edgar **8**
Sherwood, Robert E. **3**
Slesinger, Tess **10**
Stein, Gertrude **1, 6**

Stevens, Wallace **3, 12**
Tarkington, Booth **9**
Teasdale, Sara **4**
Thurman, Wallace **6**
Twain, Mark **6, 12**
Washington, Booker T. **10**
West, Nathanael **1, 14**
Wharton, Edith **3, 9**
White, Walter **15**
Wolfe, Thomas **4, 13**
Woollcott, Alexander **5**
Wylie, Elinor **8**

ARGENTINIAN
Lugones, Leopoldo **15**
Storni, Alfonsina **5**

AUSTRALIAN
Franklin, Miles **7**
Richardson, Henry Handel **4**

AUSTRIAN
Hofmannsthal, Hugo von **11**
Kafka, Franz **2, 6, 13**
Kraus, Karl **5**
Musil, Robert **12**
Schnitzler, Arthur **4**
Steiner, Rudolf **13**
Trakl, Georg **5**
Werfel, Franz **8**

BELGIAN
Maeterlinck, Maurice **3**
Verhaeren, Émile **12**

BRAZILIAN
Machado de Assis, Joaquim Maria **10**

CANADIAN
Campbell, Wilfred **9**
Carman, Bliss **7**
Garneau, Hector Saint-Denys **13**
Grove, Frederick Philip **4**
Leacock, Stephen **2**
McCrae, John **12**
Nelligan, Émile **14**
Roberts, Charles G. D. **8**
Scott, Duncan Campbell **6**
Service, Robert W. **15**

CHILEAN
Mistral, Gabriela **2**

CHINESE
Liu E **15**
Lu Hsün **3**

CZECHOSLOVAKIAN
Capek, Karel **6**
Hašek, Jaroslav **4**

DANISH
Brandes, Georg **10**

DUTCH
Couperus, Louis **15**

ENGLISH
Baring, Maurice **8**
Besant, Annie **9**
Beerbohm, Max **1**
Belloc, Hilaire **7**
Bennett, Arnold **5**
Bentley, E. C. **12**
Blackwood, Algernon **5**
Bridges, Robert **1**

573

Cumulative Index to Critics

Altrocchi, Rudolph
Gabriele D'Annunzio **6**:135

Alvarez, A.
Hart Crane **2**:118
Thomas Hardy **10**:221
D. H. Lawrence **2**:364
Wallace Stevens **3**:454
William Butler Yeats **1**:564

Alworth, E. Paul
Will Rogers **8**:336

Amann, Clarence A.
James Weldon Johnson **3**:247

Amis, Kingsley
G. K. Chesterton **1**:185
C. M. Kornbluth **8**:213
David Lindsay **15**:218
Jules Verne **6**:493

Ammons, Elizabeth
Edith Wharton **9**:552

Amoia, Alba della Fazia
Edmond Rostand **6**:381

Amon, Frank
D. H. Lawrence **9**:220

Anders, Gunther
Franz Kafka **2**:302

Anderson, David D.
Sherwood Anderson **1**:52
Louis Bromfield **11**:85, 87
Sinclair Lewis **13**:351

Anderson, Frederick
Mark Twain **12**:445

Anderson, Isaac
Raymond Chandler **7**:167
Rudolph Fisher **11**:204

Anderson, Margaret C.
Anthony Comstock **13**:90
Emma Goldman **13**:210

Anderson, Maxwell
Sherwood Anderson **10**:31
Vicente Blasco Ibáñez **12**:32
Joseph Hergesheimer **11**:261
Edna St. Vincent Millay **4**:306

Anderson, Quentin
Willa Cather **1**:163

Anderson, Sherwood
Sherwood Anderson **10**:31
Stephen Crane **11**:133
Theodore Dreiser **10**:169
Ring Lardner **14**:291
Sinclair Lewis **13**:333
Gertrude Stein **6**:407
Mark Twain **6**:459

Andreas, Osborn
Henry James **11**:330

Andrews, William L.
Charles Waddel Chesnutt **5**:136

Angenot, Marc
Jules Verne **6**:501

Angoff, Charles
Havelock Ellis **14**:116

Angus, Douglas
Franz Kafka **13**:264

Annenkov, P. V.
Leo Tolstoy **4**:444

Annensky, Innokenty
Innokenty Annensky **14**:16

Anninsky, L.
Andrei Platonov **14**:403

Anouilh, Jean
Jean Giraudoux **7**:320

Anthony, Edward
Don Marquis **7**:443

Anthony, G. F. Penn
Pierre Teilhard de Chardin **9**:501

Antoninus, Brother
Hart Crane **2**:119

Appignanesi, Lisa
Robert Musil **12**:257

Apter, T. E.
Thomas Mann **14**:359

Aptheker, Herbert
Booker T. Washington **10**:530

Aquilar, Helene J.F. de
Federico García Lorca **7**:302

Aragon, Louis
Paul Éluard **7**:249

Aratari, Anthony
Federico García Lorca **1**:316

Arce de Vazquez, Margot
Gabriela Mistral **2**:477

Archer, William
Bliss Carman **7**:135
W. S. Gilbert **3**:207
A. E. Housman **10**:239
Laurence Housman **7**:352
Henrik Ibsen **2**:224
Selma Lagerlöf **4**:229
Alice Meynell **6**:294
Duncan Campbell Scott **6**:385
Arthur Symons **11**:428
Francis Thompson **4**:434
Mark Twain **12**:427
William Butler Yeats **11**:510

Arden, Eugene
Paul Laurence Dunbar **12**:113

Arendt, Hannah
Bertolt Brecht **1**:114
Franz Kafka **2**:301

Arms, George
Kate Chopin **5**:149

Armstrong, Martin
Katherine Mansfield **2**:446

Arner, Robert D.
Kate Chopin **5**:155; **14**:63, 65

Arnold, Matthew
Leo Tolstoy **11**:458

Aron, Albert W.
Jakob Wassermann **6**:509

Arrowsmith, William
Cesare Pavese **3**:334
Dylan Thomas **1**:468

Arvin, Newton
Henry Adams **4**:12

Ashbery, John
Gertrude Stein **1**:442

Ashworth, Arthur
Miles Franklin **7**:264

Asimov, Isaac
George Orwell **15**:314

Aswell, Edward C.
Thomas Wolfe **4**:515

Atheling, William Jr.
See also **Blish, James**
Henry Kuttner **10**:266

Atherton, Gertrude
Ambrose Bierce **7**:88
May Sinclair **3**:434

Atherton, Stanley S.
Robert W. Service **15**:406

Atkins, Elizabeth
Edna St. Vincent Millay **4**:311

Atkins, John
Walter de la Mare **4**:75; **15**:352
George Orwell **6**:341; **15**:352

Atkinson, Brooks
Rudolph Fisher **11**:204
Ring Lardner **14**:293

Atlas, James
Gertrude Stein **1**:442
Thomas Wolfe **4**:538

Atlas, Marilyn Judith
Sherwood Anderson **10**:54

Attebery, Brian
L. Frank Baum **7**:25

Atterbury, Rev. Anson P.
Annie Besant **9**:13

Auchincloss, Louis
Paul Bourget **12**:72
Willa Cather **1**:164
Ellen Glasgow **2**:188
Henry James **2**:275
Sarah Orne Jewett **1**:367
Edith Wharton **3**:570

Auden, W. H.
Max Beerbohm **1**:72
Hilaire Belloc **7**:41
C. P. Cavafy **2**:90
Raymond Chandler **7**:168
G. K. Chesterton **1**:184, 186
Walter de la Mare **4**:81
Hugo von Hofmannsthal **11**:310
A. E. Housman **1**:358
Rudyard Kipling **8**:189
George MacDonald **9**:295
George Orwell **2**:512
Rainer Maria Rilke **6**:359
Frederick Rolfe **12**:268
Bernard Shaw **3**:389
Paul Valéry **4**:499
Nathanael West **1**:480
Oscar Wilde **1**:504, 507
Charles Williams **1**:516
Virginia Woolf **1**:546
William Butler Yeats **1**:562

Austin, Henry
Charlotte Gilman **9**:96

Austin, James C.
Rebecca Harding Davis **6**:151

Avseenko, V. G.
Leo Tolstoy **4**:446

Ayer, A. J.
William James **15**:186

Azorín
Ramón del Valle-Inclán **5**:479

Bab, Julius
Alfred Döblin **13**:158

Babbitt, Irving
H. L. Mencken **13**:371

Babel, Isaac
Isaac Babel **13**:17

Bacon, Leonard
Alexander Woollcott **5**:522

Bailey, Joseph W.
Arthur Schnitzler **4**:391

Bailey, Mabel Driscoll
Maxwell Anderson **2**:7

Baird, James
Wallace Stevens **3**:471

Baker, Carlos
Sherwood Anderson **1**:64
Edwin Muir **2**:483

Baker, George P.
Philip Barry **11**:45

Baker, Houston A., Jr.
Countee Cullen **4**:52
Paul Laurence Dunbar **12**:128
Booker T. Washington **10**:533

Baker, I. L.
E. C. Bentley **12**:16

Bakewell, Charles M.
William James **15**:148

Balakian, Anna
Guillaume Apollinaire **8**:19
Paul Claudel **10**:131
Paul Éluard **7**:257

Baldwin, Charles C.
Louis Bromfield **11**:71
Booth Tarkington **9**:458

Baldwin, James Mark
William James **15**:137

Baldwin, Richard E.
Charles Waddell Chesnutt **5**:135

Baldwin, Roger N.
Emma Goldman **13**:216

Ball, Robert Hamilton
David Belasco **3**:88

Balmforth, Ramsden
Laurence Housman **7**:355

Balogh, Eva S.
Emma Goldman **13**:223

Baltrušaitis, Jurgis
Émile Verhaeren **12**:467

Bander, Elaine
Dorothy L. Sayers **2**:537

Bandyopadhyay, Manik
Saratchandra Chatterji **13**:83

Bangerter, Lowell A.
Hugo von Hofmannsthal **11**:311

Banks, Nancy Huston
Charles Waddell Chesnutt **5**:130

Bannister, Winifred
James Bridie **3**:134

Barbour, Ian G.
Pierre Teilhard de Chardin **9**:488

Barbusse, Henri
Henri Barbusse **5**:14

Critic Index

Critic Index

Critic Index

Critic Index

Critic Index

Critic Index

Critic Index

Critic Index

Critic Index

Critic Index